Rick Steves'

BEST OF EUROPE 2003

Other ATP travel guidebooks by Rick Steves
Rick Steves' Europe Through the Back Door
Rick Steves' Europe 101: History and Art for the Traveler (with Gene Openshaw)
Rick Steves' Mona Winks: Self-Guided Tours of Europe's Top Museums (with Gene Openshaw)
Rick Steves' Postcards from Europe
Rick Steves' France (with Steve Smith)
Rick Steves' Germany, Austria & Switzerland
Rick Steves' Great Britain
Rick Steves' Ireland (with Pat O'Connor)
Rick Steves' Italy
Rick Steves' Scandinavia
Rick Steves' Spain & Portugal
Rick Steves' Amsterdam, Bruges & Brussels (with Gene Openshaw)
Rick Steves' Florence (with Gene Openshaw)
Rick Steves' London (with Gene Openshaw)
Rick Steves' Paris (with Steve Smith and Gene Openshaw)
Rick Steves' Rome (with Gene Openshaw)
Rick Steves' Venice (with Gene Openshaw)
Rick Steves' Phrase Books: French, German, Italian, Portuguese, Spanish, and French/Italian/German

Avalon Travel Publishing, 1400 65th Street, Suite 250, Emeryville, CA 94608

Printed in the United States of America by R.R. Donnelley
First printing January 2003

For the latest on Rick Steves' lectures, guidebooks, tours, and public television series, contact Europe Through the Back Door, Box 2009, Edmonds, WA 98020, tel. 425/771-8303, fax 425/771-0833, www.ricksteves.com, or e-mail: rick@ricksteves.com.

ISBN: 1-56691-452-3 • ISSN: 1096-7702

Europe Through the Back Door Managing Editor: Risa Laib
Europe Through the Back Door Editors: Jill Hodges, Cameron Hewitt
Avalon Travel Publishing Editor and Series Manager: Laura Mazer
Research Assistance: Ben Cameron, Colleen Cox, Carlos Galvin, Donna Gibson, Sonja Groset, Cameron Hewitt, Amy McKenna, Sarah Murdoch, Pat O'Connor, Heidi Sewell, and Steve Smith
Production & Typesetting: Kathleen Sparkes, White Hart Design
Design: Linda Braun
Cover Design: Janine Lehmann
Maps and Graphics: David C. Hoerlein, Rhonda Pelikan, Zoey Platt
Front matter color photos: p. i, Ireland, © Rick Steves; p. xiv, Koln (Cologne) Cathedral, © Andrea Johnson
Cover Photo: Il Duomo (cathedral and temple), Siena, Italy; © Leo de Wys Inc./Jacobs

Distributed to the book trade by Publishers Group West, Berkeley, California

CONTENTS

Europe's Best Destinations

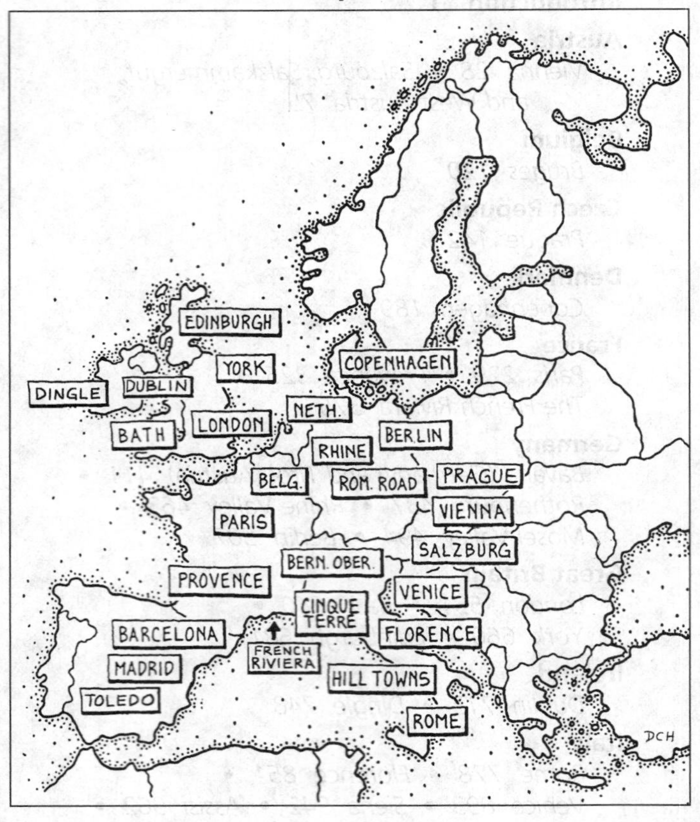

INTRODUCTION

This book breaks Europe into its top big-city, small-town, and rural destinations. It then gives you all the information and opinions necessary to wring the maximum value out of your limited time and money in each of them. If you plan to stay for two months or less in Europe, this lean and mean book is all you need.

Experiencing Europe's culture, people, and natural wonders economically and hassle-free has been my goal for more than 25 years of traveling, tour guiding, and travel writing. With this book, I pass on to you the lessons I've learned, updated for 2003.

Rick Steves' Best of Europe is the crème de la crème of places featured in my Country Guides. This book is balanced to include a comfortable mix of exciting big cities and cozy small towns: from Paris, London, and Rome to traffic-free Italian Riviera ports, alpine villages, and mom-and-pop châteaux. It covers the predictable biggies and mixes in a healthy dose of Back Door intimacy. Along with Leonardo in the Louvre, you'll enjoy Caterina in her Cantina. I've been selective. For example, rather than listing countless castles and hill towns, I recommend the best three or four of each.

The best is, of course, only my opinion. But after more than two decades of travel research, I've developed a sixth sense for what grabs the traveler's imagination.

This Information Is Accurate and Up-to-Date

This book is updated every year. Most publishers of guidebooks that cover Europe from top to bottom can afford an update only every two or three years (and even then, it's rarely researched in person). Since this book covers only my favorite places, my research partners and I are able to update it in person each year. Even with an annual update, things change. But if you're traveling with the current edition of this book, I guarantee you're using the most up-to-date information available (for the latest, visit www.ricksteves.com/update). If you're packing an old book, you'll learn the seriousness of your mistake ...in Europe. Your trip costs at least $10 per waking hour. Your time is valuable. This guidebook saves lots of time.

Planning Your Trip

This book is organized by destinations. Each destination is covered as a mini-vacation on its own, filled with exciting sights and homey, affordable places to stay. In each chapter, you'll find the following:

Planning Your Time contains a suggested schedule, with thoughts on how to best use your limited time.

Orientation includes tourist information, city transportation, and an easy-to-read map designed to make the text clear and your arrival smooth.

Sights are rated: ▲▲▲—Don't miss; ▲▲—Try hard to see; ▲—Worthwhile if you can make it; No rating—Worth knowing about.

Sleeping and Eating includes addresses and phone numbers of my favorite budget hotels and restaurants.

Transportation Connections covers how to reach nearby destinations by train or bus.

The **appendix** is a traveler's tool kit, with telephone tips, a climate chart, and a list of national tourist offices.

Browse through this book, choose your favorite destinations, and link them up. Then have a great trip! You'll travel like a temporary local, getting the most out of every mile, minute, and dollar.

You won't waste time on mediocre sights because this guidebook, unlike others, covers only the best. Since your major financial pitfalls are lousy, expensive hotels, I've worked hard to assemble good-value accommodations for each stop. And as you travel the route I know and love, I'm happy you'll be meeting some of my favorite Europeans.

Trip Costs

Five components make up your trip cost: airfare, surface transportation, room and board, sightseeing/entertainment, and shopping/miscellany.

Airfare: Don't try to sort through the mess yourself. Get and use a good travel agent. A basic round-trip U.S.A.-to-Europe flight should cost $700 to $1,000 (even cheaper in winter), depending on where you fly from and when. Always consider saving time and money in Europe by flying "open-jaw" (flying into one city and out of another, such as flying into London and out of Rome).

Surface Transportation: Your best mode depends upon the time you have and the scope of your trip. For many it's a Eurailpass . Train passes are normally available only outside of Europe. You may save money by simply buying tickets as you go (for more information, see "Transportation," below).

Drivers can figure $200 per person per week (based on 2 people splitting the cost of the car, tolls, gas, and insurance). Car rental is cheapest to arrange from the United States. Leasing, for trips over three weeks, is even cheaper.

Room and Board: You can thrive in Europe in 2003 on an overall average of $80 a day per person for room and board (less for the smaller cities). An $80 a day budget allows $10 for lunch, $5 for snacks, $15 for dinner, and $50 for lodging (based on 2 people splitting the cost of a $100 double room that includes

Exchange Rates

I've priced things in local currencies throughout this book. Most countries in this book have adopted the euro currency: Austria, Belgium, France, Germany, Ireland, Italy, Spain, and the Netherlands.

1 euro (€) = $1.

One euro is broken down into 100 cents. You'll find coins ranging from 1 cent to 2 euros, and bills from 5 euros to 500 euros.

Britain, Denmark, Switzerland, and the Czech Republic have kept their traditional currencies:

1 British pound (£) = about $1.50, and £0.70 = about $1.

1 Danish kroner (kr) = about 13 cents, and 7.5 kr = about $1.

1 Swiss franc (SF) = about 67 cents, and 1.50 SF = about $1.

1 Czech koruna (kč) = about 3 cents, and 30 kč = about $1.

To convert British prices into dollars, add 50 percent: £6 is about $9, £3 is about $4.50, and 80p is about $1.20. To roughly translate Danish prices into U.S. dollars, divide by 8 (e.g., 100 kr = about $12, actually $13.30). To convert prices from Swiss francs into dollars, subtract one-third (e.g., 60 SF = $40). To convert Czech prices into dollars, drop the last digit and divide by three (2,000 k˘c = about $65).

breakfast). That's doable. Students and tightwads will do it on $35 or $40 ($15–20 per bed, $20 for meals and snacks). But budget sleeping and eating require the skills and information covered below (or much more extensively in *Rick Steves' Europe Through the Back Door*).

Sightseeing and Entertainment: In big cities, figure $5 to $10 per major sight, $2 for minor ones, and $25 for splurge experiences (e.g., tours, concerts, gelato binges). An overall average of $15 a day works for most. Don't skimp here. After all, this category directly powers most of the experiences all the other expenses are designed to make possible.

Shopping and Miscellany: Figure $1 per postcard and $2 per coffee, beer, and ice-cream cone. Shopping can vary in cost from nearly nothing to a small fortune. Good budget travelers find that this category has little to do with assembling a trip full of lifelong and wonderful memories.

Prices, Times, and Discounts

The prices in this book, as well as the hours and telephone numbers, are accurate as of late 2002. Europe is always changing, and I know you'll understand that this, like any other guidebook, starts to yellow even before it's printed.

In Europe—and in this book—you'll be using the 24-hour clock. After 12:00 noon, keep going—13:00, 14:00, and so on. For anything over 12, subtract 12 and add p.m. (14:00 is 2 p.m.).

While discounts for sights and transportation are not listed in this book, seniors (60 and over), students (with International Student Identity Cards), and youths (under 18) may snare discounts—but only by asking. Some discounts (particularly for sights) are granted only to European residents.

When to Go

May, June, September, and October are the best travel months. Peak season (July and August) offers the sunniest weather and the most exciting slate of activities—but the worst crowds. During this busy time, it's best to reserve rooms well in advance, particularly for the big cities (see "Making Reservations," below).

Off-season, October through April, expect generally shorter hours at attractions, more lunchtime breaks, fewer activities, and fewer guided tours in English. If you're traveling off-season, be careful to confirm opening times.

As a general rule of thumb any time of year, the climate north of the Alps is mild (like Seattle), and south of the Alps it's like Arizona. For specifics, check the Climate Chart in the appendix. If you wilt in the heat, avoid the Mediterranean in summer. If you want blue skies in the Alps, Britain, and Scandinavia, travel in the height of summer. Plan your itinerary to beat the heat (for a spring trip, start in the south and work north) but also to moderate culture shock (start in mild Britain and work south and east) and minimize crowds. Touristy places in the core of Europe (Germany, the Alps, France, Italy, and Greece) suffer most from crowds.

Sightseeing Priorities

Depending on the length of your trip, here are my recommended priorities. Assuming you're traveling by train, I've taken geographical proximity into account.

5 days:	London, Paris
7 days, add:	Amsterdam, Haarlem
10 days, add:	Rhine, Rothenburg
14 days, add:	Salzburg, Swiss Alps
17 days, add:	Venice, Florence
21 days, add:	Rome, Cinque Terre

24 days, add: Siena, Bavarian sights
30 days, add: Arles (Provence), Barcelona, Madrid
36 days, add: Vienna, Prague, Berlin
40 days, add: Copenhagen, Bath

Red Tape, News, and Banking

Red Tape: You currently need a passport but no visa and no shots to travel in Europe. Crossing borders is easy. Sometimes you won't even realize it's happened. When you do change countries, however, you change phone cards, postage stamps, gas prices, ways to flush a toilet, words for "hello," figurehead monarchs, and breakfast breads. Plan ahead for these changes (use up stamps and phone cards, brush up on the new language).

Twelve European countries have adopted the euro currency, but some haven't, including Denmark, Britain, Switzerland, and the Czech Republic. If you're about to cross a border with spare coins you won't be able to use anywhere else, spend them on candy, souvenirs, gas, or a telephone call home.

News: Americans keep in touch with the *International Herald Tribune* (published almost daily via satellite throughout Europe). Every Tuesday, the European editions of *Time* and *Newsweek* hit the stands with articles of particular interest to European travelers. Sports addicts can get their fix from *USA Today*. News in English will only be sold where there's enough demand: in big cities and tourist centers. Good Web sites include www.europeantimes.com and http://news.bbc.co.uk. If you're concerned about how some event might affect your safety as an American traveling abroad, call the U.S. consulate or embassy in the nearest big city for advice (see Appendix for list).

Banking: Bring plastic (ATM, credit, or debit cards) along with a couple hundred dollars as a backup. Traveler's checks are a waste of time and money.

To withdraw cash from a bank machine, you'll need a PIN code (numbers only, no letters) and your bankcard. Before you go, verify with your bank that your card will work, then use it whenever possible (bring 2 cards in case one gets demagnetized or eaten by a machine). If you plan on getting cash advances with your regular credit card, be sure to ask the card company about fees before you leave.

Visa and MasterCard are more commonly accepted than American Express. Just like at home, credit or debit cards work easily at larger hotels, restaurants, and shops, but smaller businesses prefer payment in local currency.

Regular banks have the best rates for changing money and traveler's checks. For a large exchange, it pays to compare rates and fees. Post offices and train stations usually change money if you can't get to a bank.

You should use a money belt. Thieves target tourists. A money belt provides peace of mind (please order online at www.ricksteves.com, or call 425/771-8303 for our free newsletter/catalog). You can carry lots of cash safely in a money belt.

Don't be petty about changing money. You don't need to waste time every few days returning to a bank or tracking down a cash machine. Change a week's worth of money, get big bills, stuff it in your money belt, and travel!

VAT Refunds for Shoppers

Wrapped into the purchase price of your souvenirs is a Value-Added Tax (VAT) ranging from seven to 22 percent. If you make a purchase that meets your host country's minimum purchase requirement (an average of $100; see chart in appendix) at a store that participates in the VAT refund scheme, you're entitled to get most of that tax back. Personally, I've never felt that VAT refunds are worth the hassle, but if you do, here's the scoop.

If you're lucky, the merchant will subtract the tax when you make your purchase (this is more likely if the store ships the goods to your home). Otherwise, you'll need to:

Get the paperwork. Have the merchant completely fill out the necessary refund document, typically called a "cheque." You'll have to present your passport at the store.

Have your cheque(s) stamped at the border by the customs agent who deals with VAT refunds. If you're in a European Union country, then you get the stamp at your last stop in the European Union. Otherwise, get your cheque stamped when you leave the country.

It's best to keep your purchases in your carry-on for viewing, but if they're too large or considered too dangerous (such as knives) to carry on, then track down the proper customs agent to inspect them before you check your bag. You're not supposed to use your purchased goods before you leave. If you show up at customs wearing your new lederhosen, officials might look the other way—or deny you a refund.

To collect your refund, you'll need to return your stamped documents to the retailer or its representative. Many merchants work with a service that has offices at major airports, ports, and border crossings, such as Easy Tax-Free (www.easytaxfree.com), Global Refund (www.globalrefund.com) or Cashback (www.cashback.it). These services, which extract a four percent fee, usually can refund your money immediately in your currency of choice or credit your card (within two billing cycles). If you have to deal directly with the retailer, mail the store your stamped documents and then wait. It could take months.

Travel Smart

Your trip to Europe is like a complex play—easier to follow and really appreciate on a second viewing. While no one does the same trip twice to gain that advantage, reading this book's chapters on your intended destinations before your trip accomplishes much the same thing.

Reread this book as you travel and visit local tourist information offices. Upon arrival in a new town, lay the groundwork for a smooth departure. Buy a phone card and use it for reservations, reconfirmations, and double-checking hours. Enjoy the friendliness of the local people. Slow down and ask questions. Most locals are eager to point you in their idea of the right direction. Wear your money belt, learn the local currency, and develop a simple formula to quickly estimate rough prices in dollars. Keep a notepad in your pocket for organizing your thoughts. Those who expect to travel smart, do.

As you read this book, note the days of markets and festivals and when sights are closed. Anticipate problem days: Mondays are bad in Florence, Tuesdays are bad in Paris. Museums and sights, especially large ones, usually stop admitting people 30 to 60 minutes before closing time.

Sundays have the same pros and cons as they do for travelers in the United States. Sightseeing attractions are generally open, shops and banks are closed, and city traffic is light. Rowdy evenings are rare on Sundays. Saturdays in Europe are virtually weekdays with earlier closing hours. Hotels in tourist areas are most crowded on Fridays and Saturdays.

Plan ahead for banking, laundry, post office chores, and picnics. Mix intense and relaxed periods. Every trip (and every traveler) needs at least a few slack days. Pace yourself. Assume you will return.

Tourist Information

The tourist information office is your best first stop in any new city. Try to arrive, or at least telephone, before it closes. In this book, I'll refer to a tourist information office as a TI. Throughout Europe, you'll find TIs are usually well organized and English speaking.

As national budgets tighten, many TIs have been privatized. This means they become sales agents for big tours and hotels, and their "information" becomes unavoidably colored. While the TI has listings of all the rooms and is eager to book you one, use their room-finding service only as a last resort. Across Europe, room-finding services are charging commissions from hotels, taking fees from travelers, blacklisting establishments that buck their materialistic rules, and are unable to give hard opinions on the relative value of one place over another. The accommodations stakes are too high to go potluck through the TI. By using the listings in this book, you can avoid that kind of "help."

Tourist Offices, U.S.A. Addresses: Each country has a national tourist office in the U.S.A. (see the appendix for addresses). Before your trip, you can ask for the free general information packet and for specific information (such as city maps and schedules of upcoming festivals).

Recommended Guidebooks

You may want some supplemental information, especially if you'll be traveling beyond my recommended destinations. When you consider the improvements they'll make in your $3,000 vacation, $25 or $35 for extra maps and books is money well spent. Especially for several people traveling by car, the weight and expense are negligible.

The Lonely Planet guides to various European countries are thorough, well researched (though not updated annually), and packed with good maps and hotel recommendations for low- to moderate-budget travelers. The hip, insightful Rough Guide series (by British researchers, not updated annually) and the highly opinionated Let's Go series (annually updated by Harvard students) are great for students and vagabonds. If you're a backpacker with a train pass and interested in the youth and night scene, get Let's Go. The popular, skinny green Michelin guides (covering most southern countries and French regions) are excellent, especially if you're driving. They're known for their city and sightseeing maps, dry but concise and helpful information on all major sights, and good cultural and historical background. English editions are sold locally at tourist shops and gas stations.

Rick Steves' Books and Videos

Rick Steves' Europe Through the Back Door 2003 gives you budget travel tips on minimizing jet lag, packing light, planning your itinerary, traveling by car or train, finding budget beds without reservations, changing money, avoiding rip-offs, outsmarting thieves, using cell phones, hurdling the language barrier, staying healthy, taking great photographs, using your bidet, and much more. The book also includes chapters on my 35 favorite "Back Doors."

Rick Steves Country Guides are a series of eight guidebooks—including this one—covering Britain; Ireland; France;

Italy; Spain/Portugal; Scandinavia; and Germany/Austria /Switzerland. Most are available in bookstores in December, and the rest in January. If you wish this book covered more of any particular country, my Country Guides are for you.

My **City Guides** feature Rome, Venice, Florence, Paris, London, and—new for 2003—*Rick Steves' Amsterdam, Bruges & Brussels*. For more thorough coverage of Europe's greatest cities, complete with self-guided, illustrated tours through the grandest museums, consider these handy, easy-to-pack guidebooks (updated annually, available in December and January).

Rick Steves' Europe 101: History and Art for the Traveler (with Gene Openshaw, 2000) gives you the story of Europe's people, history, and art. Written for smart people who were sleeping in their history and art classes before they knew they were going to Europe, *101* helps Europe's sights come alive.

Rick Steves' Mona Winks (with Gene Openshaw, 2001) gives you fun, easy-to-follow self-guided tours of the major museums and historic highlights in cities covered in this book, including **Amsterdam** (Rijksmuseum and Van Gogh Museum), **London** (British Museum, British Library, National Gallery, Tate Britain, Westminster Abbey, and a Westminster Walk), **Paris** (Louvre, Orsay Museum, Rodin Museum, Notre-Dame, Sainte-Chapelle, and Versailles), **Madrid** (Prado), **Venice** (St. Mark's, Doge's Palace, and Accademia Gallery), **Florence** (Uffizi Gallery, Bargello, Michelangelo's *David*, and a Renaissance Walk), and **Rome** (Colosseum, Forum, Pantheon, National Museum of Rome, Borghese Gallery, Vatican Museum, and St. Peter's Basilica). If you're planning on touring these sights, *Mona* will be a valued friend.

Rick Steves' Phrase Books: After more than 25 years as an English-only traveler struggling with other phrase books, I've designed a series of practical, fun, and budget-oriented phrase books to help you ask the gelato man for a free little taste and the hotel receptionist for a room with no street noise. If you want to chat with your cabbie and make hotel reservations over the phone, my pocket-sized Rick Steves' Phrase Books (French, German, Italian, Portuguese, Spanish, and French/Italian/German) will come in handy.

My new public TV series, *Rick Steves' Europe*, keeps churning out shows. Many of the 82 episodes (from the new series and from *Travels in Europe with Rick Steves*) explore the destinations featured in this book. These air nationally on public television and on the Travel Channel. They're also available in information-packed home videos and seven- or eight-episode DVDs (order online at www.ricksteves.com or call us at 425/771-8303 for our free newsletter/catalog).

Rick Steves' Postcards from Europe (1999), my autobiographical book, packs 25 years of travel anecdotes and insights into the ultimate 2,000-mile European adventure. Through my guidebooks, I share my favorite European discoveries with you. *Postcards* introduces you to my favorite European friends.

All of my books are published by Avalon Travel Publishing (www.travelmatters.com).

Maps

The black-and-white maps in this book, drawn by Dave Hoerlein, are concise and simple. Dave, who is well-traveled in Europe, has designed the maps to help you locate recommended places and get to the tourist offices, where you can pick up a more in-depth map (usually free) of the city or region. The color maps at the front of the book will help you navigate from town to town and country to country.

For an overall map of Europe, consider my new Rick Steves' Europe Planning Map—geared to travelers' needs—with sightseeing destinations listed prominently (order online at www.ricksteves.com or call 425/771-8303 for our free newsletter/catalog).

European bookstores, especially in tourist areas, have good selections of maps. For drivers, I'd recommend a 1:200,000 or 1:300,000 scale map for each country. Train travelers can usually manage fine with the freebies they get with their train pass and at the local tourist offices.

Tours of Europe

Travel agents will tell you about typical tours of Europe, but they won't tell you about ours. At Europe Through the Back Door, we run 21-day tours of Europe featuring most of the highlights in this book (departures April-October, 26 people on a big roomy bus with 2 great guides). We also offer regional tours of Britain, Ireland, France, Spain/Portugal, Italy, Germany/Austria /Switzerland, Scandinavia, Turkey, and Eastern Europe (with groups of 19-26, depending on the tour). And we lead week-long indepth getaways to seven of the most magical cities in Europe: London, Paris, Rome, Florence, Venice, Prague, and Barcelona (departures March-Dec, max 20 people). For details, call us at 425/771-8303 or visit www.ricksteves.com.

Transportation in Europe

By Car or Train?

Each has pros and cons. Cars are an expensive headache in big cities but give you more control for delving deep into the countryside.

Europe by Rail: Time and Cost

This map can help you determine if a railpass is right for you. Add up the ticket prices for your route. If your total is about the same or more than the cost of a pass, buy the pass (unless you like waiting in lines at train stations).

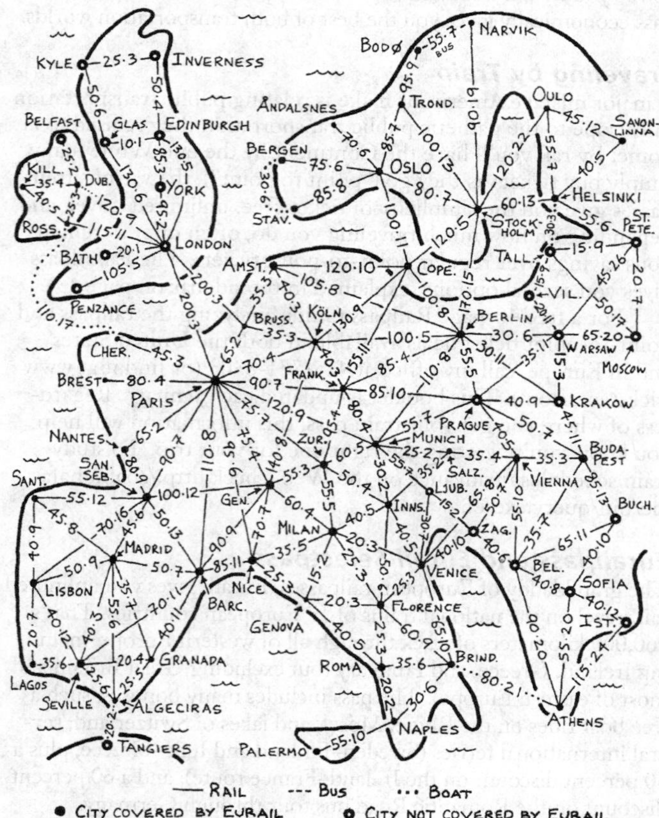

The first number between cities = approximate cost in $US for a 1-way, 2nd class ticket. The second number = number of hours the trip takes.

Important: These fares and times are based on the Eurail Tariff Guide. Actual prices may vary due to currency fluctuations and local promotions. Local competition can cut the actual price of some boat crossings (from Italy to Greece, for example) by 50% or more. For approximate 1st class rail prices, multiply the prices shown by 1.5. Travelers under age 26 can receive up to 1/3 off the 2nd class fares shown (buying at student travel agencies in Europe). Travel times are for express trains where applicable.

Groups of three or more go cheaper by car. If you're packing heavy (with kids), go by car. Trains are best for city-to-city travel and give you the convenience of doing long stretches overnight. By train, I arrive relaxed and well rested—not so by car. A rail 'n' drive pass allows you to mix train and car travel. When thoughtfully used, this pass economically gives you the best of both transportation worlds.

Traveling by Train

A major mistake Americans make is relating public transportation in Europe to the pathetic public transportation they're used to at home. By rail you'll have the Continent by the tail. While many simply buy tickets as they go ("point to point"), the various train passes give you the simplicity of ticket-free, unlimited travel, and depending on how much traveling you do, often offer a tremendous savings over regular point-to-point tickets. The Eurailpass gives you several options (explained in the sidebar on page 13).

For a free 40-page Railpass Guide analyzing the railpass and point-to-point ticket deals available in both the United States and in Europe, call my office at 425/771-8303 (or find it at www.ricksteves.com). This booklet is updated each January. Regardless of where you get your train pass, this information will help you know you're getting the right one for your trip. To study train schedules in advance on the Web, check http://bahn.hafas.de/bin/query.exe/en.

Eurailpass and Eurail Selectpass

The granddaddy of European railpasses, Eurail, gives you unlimited rail travel on the national trains of 17 European countries. That's 160,000 kilometers of track through all of western Europe, including Ireland, Greece, and Hungary (but excluding Great Britain and most of eastern Europe). The pass includes many bonuses, such as free boat rides on the Rhine, Mosel, and lakes of Switzerland; several international ferries (Sweden–Finland and Italy–Greece, plus a 50 percent discount on the Ireland–France route); and a 60 percent discount on the Romantic Road bus tour through Germany.

The Eurail Selectpass covers any three, four, or five Eurail countries connected by rail or ferry (e.g., a three-country Selectpass could cover France, Italy, and Greece). Selectpasses are fine for a focused trip, but to see the Best of Europe, you'd do best with a Eurailpass. Either pass gives a 15 percent Saverpass discount to two or more companions traveling together.

Eurail Analysis

Break-even point? For an at-a-glance break-even point, remember that a one-month Eurailpass pays for itself if your route is

Prices listed are for 2003. My free *Rick Steves' Guide to European Railpasses* has more details. To get the railpass guide, call us at 425/771-8303 or visit www.ricksteves.com/rail. Prices subject to change.

EURAILPASSES

These passes cover all 17 Eurail countries: Austria, Belgium, Denmark, Finland, France, Germany, Greece, Hungary, Ireland, Italy, Luxembourg, Netherlands, Norway, Portugal, Spain, Sweden, and Switzerland.

	1st class	1st class Saver	2nd class Youth
10 days in 2 months flexi	$694	$592	$488
15 days in 2 months flexi	914	778	642
15 consecutive days	588	498	414
21 consecutive days	762	648	534
1 month consec. days	946	804	664
2 months consec. days	1338	1138	938
3 months consec. days	1654	1408	1160

To order Rail and Drive passes, call your travel agent or Rail Europe at 800-438-7245.

FIRST CLASS EURAILDRIVE PASSES

4 first class rail days and 2 car days in a 2 month period.

Car categories	2 adults	1 adult	Extra car day	Extra rail day
Economy	$371	$419	$46	$42
Compact	384	449	59	42
Intermediate	399	469	71	42
Small Automatic	419	509	89	42

Prices are per person. Third and fourth persons sharing car get a 4-day out of 2-month railpass for approx. $329 (kids 4-11 $165). You can add rail days (max. 5) and car days (no limit). Rail travel in all 17 Eurail countries, car available in most (not Scandinavia).

FIRST CLASS SELECTPASS DRIVE

Any 3 days of rail travel + 2 days of Hertz or Avis car rental in 2 months within 3 adjoining countries.

Car Categories	2 adults	1 adult	Extra car day	Extra rail day
Economy	$272	$319	$49	$35
Compact	286	349	64	35
Intermediate	299	375	75	35
Small Automatic	319	409	95	35

Prices are per person. You can add rail days (max. 7) and car days (no limit). Rail travel and car rental in three connecting Eurail countries (no car in Scandinavia). Third and fourth adults sharing the car pay $229 (kids 4-11 $115).

SELECTPASSES

This pass covers travel in three, four, or five adjacent countries. For details, visit www.ricksteves.com/rail or see *Rick Steves' Guide to European Railpasses.*

3 Countries	**1st class Selectpass**	**1st class Saverpass**	**2nd class Youthpass**
5 days in 2 months	$356	$304	$249
6 days in 2 months	394	336	276
8 days in 2 months	470	400	329
10 days in 2 months	542	460	379

4 Countries	**1st class Selectpass**	**1st class Saverpass**	**2nd class Youthpass**
5 days in 2 months	$398	$340	$279
6 days in 2 months	436	372	306
8 days in 2 months	512	436	359
10 days in 2 months	584	496	409

5 Countries	**1st class Selectpass**	**1st class Saverpass**	**2nd class Youthpass**
5 days in 2 months	$438	$374	$307
6 days in 2 months	476	406	334
8 days in 2 months	552	470	387
10 days in 2 months	624	530	437
15 days in 2 months	794	674	556

Saverpass prices are per person for 2 or more people traveling together at all times.
Youthpasses: Under age 26 only.
Kids 4-11 pay half adult fare; under 4: free.

Eurailpass/Selectpass diagram key:

Every ***Eurailpass*** *includes travel in every country shown here. A* ***Selectpass*** *can be designed to connect a "chain" of any three, four, or five countries in this diagram linked by direct lines. (Examples that qualify: Norway-Sweden-Germany; Spain-France-Italy; Austria-Italy-Greece.) "Benelux" is considered one country.*

Amsterdam–Rome–Madrid–Paris on first class or Copenhagen–Rome–Madrid–Copenhagen on second class. A one-month Eurail Youthpass saves you money if you're traveling from Amsterdam to Rome to Madrid and back to Amsterdam. Passes pay for themselves quicker in the north, where the cost per kilometer is higher. Check the "Europe by Rail: Time and Cost" map above to see if your planned travels merit the purchase of a train pass. If it's just about even, go with the pass for the convenience of not having to wait in line to buy tickets and for the fun and freedom to travel "free."

Using one Eurailpass versus a series of country passes: While nearly every country has its own mini-version of the Eurailpass, trips covering several countries are usually cheapest with the budget whirlwind traveler's old standby, the Eurailpass, or its budget cousin, the Eurail Selectpass. This is because the more rail days included in a pass, the cheaper your per-day cost is. A group of country passes with a few rail days apiece will have a high per-day cost, while a Eurailpass with a longer life span offers a better deal overall. However, if you're traveling in a single country, an individual country railpass (such as Francerail or Germanrail) is often a better value than any of the Eurail passes.

EurailDrive Pass: The EurailDrive Pass is for those who want to combine train travel with the freedom of having a car a day here and a day there. Great areas for a day of joyriding include the Dutch countryside; Germany's Rhine, Mosel, or Bavaria; France's Provence; Italy's Tuscany and Umbria; or the Alps (for "car hiking"). When comparing prices, remember that each day of car rental comes with about $30 of extra expenses (CDW insurance, gas, parking), which you can divide among the people in your party.

Car Rental

It's cheaper to arrange European car rentals in the United States, so check rates with your travel agent or directly with the companies. Rent by the week with unlimited mileage. If you'll be renting for three weeks or more, ask your agent about leasing, which is a scheme to save on insurance and taxes. I normally rent the smallest, least expensive model. Explore your drop-off options (and costs).

For peace of mind, I spring for the Collision Damage Waiver insurance (CDW, about $10–15 per day), which has a zero- or low-deductible rather than the standard value-of-the-car "deductible." Ask your travel agent about money-saving alternatives to CDW. A few gold credit cards cover CDW insurance; quiz your credit card company on the worst-case scenario. Or consider Travel Guard, which offers CDW insurance for $6 a day (U.S. tel. 800/826-1300, www.travelguard.com); it'll cover you throughout Europe but not in Scotland, Ireland, and Italy.

Note that if you'll be driving in Italy, theft insurance (separate from CDW insurance) is mandatory. The insurance usually costs about $10 to $15 a day, payable when you pick up the car.

If you plan to drive your rental car into the Czech Republic, keep these tips in mind: State your travel plans up front to the rental company. Some won't allow any of their rental cars to enter eastern European countries due to the high theft rate. Some won't

Standard European Road Signs

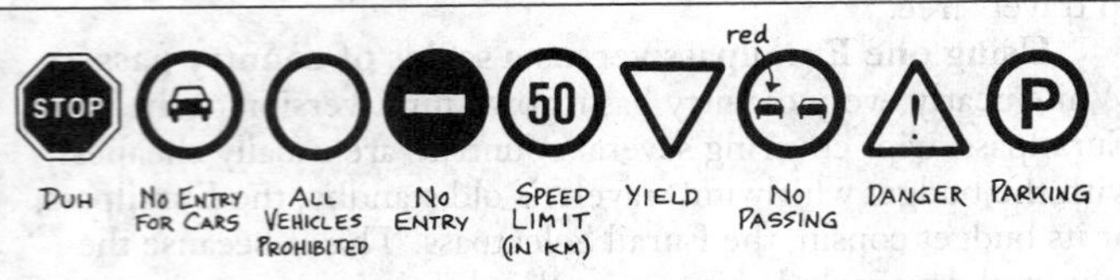

allow certain types of cars: BMWs, Mercedes, and convertibles. Ask about extra fees—some companies automatically tack on theft and collision coverage for a Czech excursion. To avoid hassles at the Czech border, ask the rental agent to mark your contract with the company's permission to cross.

Driving

For much of Europe, all you need is your valid U.S. driver's license and a car. Confirm with your rental company if an international license is required in the countries you plan to visit. Those traveling in Austria, Germany, Italy, Portugal, Spain, and eastern Europe should probably get an international driver's license (at your local AAA office—$10 plus the cost of two passport-type photos).

While gas is expensive, if you keep an eye on the big picture, paying $4 per gallon is more a psychological trauma than a financial one. I use the freeways whenever possible. They are free in the Netherlands and Germany. You'll pay a one-time road fee of about $25 as you enter Switzerland, about $7 for Austria, and about $3 for the Czech Republic. The Italian autostradas and French autoroutes are punctuated by toll booths (charging about $1 for every 10 minutes). The alternative to these superfreeways often is being marooned in rural traffic. The autostrada/autoroute usually saves enough time, gas, and nausea to justify its expense. Mix scenic country-road rambling with high-speed autobahning, but don't forget that in Europe, the shortest distance between two points is the autobahn.

Metric: Outside of Britain, get used to metric. A liter is about a quart, four to a gallon. A kilometer is six-tenths of a mile. I figure kilometers to miles by cutting them in half and adding back 10 percent of the original (120 km: 60 + 12 = 72 miles, 300 km: 150 + 30 = 180 miles).

Parking: Parking is a costly headache in big cities. You'll pay about $20 a day to park safely. Ask at your hotel for advice. I keep a pile of coins in my ashtray for parking meters, public phones, Laundromats, and wishing wells.

Telephones, Mail, and E-mail

Smart travelers learn the phone system and use it daily to reserve or reconfirm rooms, find tourist information, or phone home. Many European phone booths take insertable phone cards rather than coins.

Phone Cards: There are two kinds of phone cards: official phone cards that you insert into the phone (which can only be used in phone booths), and long-distance scratch-off PIN cards that can be used from virtually any phone (you dial a toll-free number and enter your PIN code). Both kinds of cards work only in the country where you bought them (for example, a Swiss phone card works when you're making calls in Switzerland, but is worthless in France).

You can buy insertable phone cards from post offices, newsstands, or tobacco shops. Insert the card into the phone, make your call, and the value is deducted from your card. These are a good deal for calling within Europe, but it's cheaper to make international calls with a PIN card.

PIN cards, which have a scratch-off Personal Identification Number, allow you to call home at the rate of about a dime a minute. To use a PIN card, dial the toll-free access number listed on the card; then, at the prompt, enter your Personal Identification Number (also listed on card) and dial the number you want to call. These are sold at newsstands, exchange bureaus, souvenir shops, and mini-marts. There are many different brands. Ask for a "cheap international telephone card." Make sure you get a card that allows you to make international calls (some types permit only local calls). Buy a lower denomination in case the card is a dud.

If you use **coins** to make your calls, have a bunch handy. Or look for a **metered phone** ("talk now, pay later") in the bigger post offices. Avoid using hotel-room phones for anything other than local calls and PIN card calls.

Making Calls within a European Country: You'll save money by dialing direct. You just need to learn to break the codes. About half of all European countries—including Britain—use area codes; the other half uses a direct-dial system without area codes.

In countries that use area codes (such as Austria, Britain, Germany, Ireland, and the Netherlands), you dial the local number when calling within a city, and you add the area code if calling long-distance within the country. For example, Berlin's area code is 030, and the number of one of my recommended Berlin hotels is 3150-3944. To call it from Frankfurt, dial 030/3150-3944.

To make calls within a country that uses a direct-dial system (Belgium, the Czech Republic, Denmark, France, Italy, Spain, and Switzerland), you dial the same number whether you're calling across the country or across the street.

Making International Calls: You always start with the international access code (011 if you're calling from America or Canada, or 00 from Europe), then dial the country code of the country you're calling (see chart in appendix).

What you dial next depends on the phone system of the country you're calling. If the country uses area codes, drop the initial zero of the area code, then dial the rest of the number. To call the Berlin hotel from Copenhagen, dial 00, 49 (Germany's country code), 30/3150-3944 (omitting the initial zero in the area code).

Countries that use direct-dial systems (no area codes) vary in how they're accessed internationally by phone. For instance, if you are making an international call to Denmark, Italy, or Spain, simply dial the international access code, country code, and phone number. But if you're calling Belgium, France, or Switzerland, drop the initial zero of the phone number. Example: To call a Paris hotel (tel. 01 47 05 49 15) from London, dial 00, 33 (France's country code), then 1 47 05 49 15 (phone number without the initial zero).

To call my office from Europe, I dial 00 (Europe's international access code), 1 (U.S.A.'s country code), 425 (Edmonds' area code), and 771-8303.

European time is six/nine hours ahead of the east/west coast of the U.S.A.

U.S. Calling Cards: Calling home from Europe is easy but expensive with AT&T, MCI, or Sprint calling cards. Since direct-dial rates have dropped, U.S. calling cards are no longer a good value. It's also outrageously expensive to use your calling card to make calls between European countries. It's much cheaper to make your calls using a phone card or PIN card purchased in Europe.

Cell Phones: Many travelers buy cheapie cell phones—about $70 on up—to make local and international calls. The cheapest phones work only in the country where they're sold; the pricier phones work throughout Europe (but it'll cost you about $40 per country for the necessary chip to operate in that country and for prepaid phone time). Because of their expense, cell phones are most economical for travelers staying in one country for two weeks or more.

If you're interested, stop by one of the ubiquitous phone shops or at a cell-phone counter at a department store. Confirm with the clerk whether the phone works only in the country in which it is purchased or throughout Europe. To understand all the extras, get a brand that has instructions in English. Make sure the clerk shows you how to use the phone—practice making a call to the store or, for fun, to the clerk's personal cell phone. You'll need to pick out a policy; different policies offer, say, better rates for making calls at night or for calling cell phones rather than fixed phones, etc. I get the basic fixed rate: a straight 30 cents per minute to the U.S.A. and 15 cents per minute to any fixed or cell phone in the home country at any hour. Receiving calls is generally free. When you run out of calling time, buy more time at a newsstand. Upon arrival in a different country, purchase a new chip (which comes with a new phone number). Remember, if you're on a tight budget, skip cell phones and buy PIN phone cards instead.

Mail: To arrange for mail delivery, reserve a few hotels along your route in advance and give their addresses to friends or use American Express Company's mail services (free for AmEx cardholders and available at a minimal fee for others). Allow 10 days for a letter to arrive. Federal Express makes two-day deliveries—for a price. Phoning is so easy that I've dispensed with mail stops all together.

E-mail: More and more hoteliers have e-mail addresses and Web sites (listed in this book). Note that mom-and-pop pensions, which can get deluged by e-mail, are not always able to respond immediately to an e-mail you've sent.

Internet service providers can change with alarming frequency, so if your e-mail message to a hotel bounces back, use an engine such as www.google.com to search for the hotel name to see if it has a new Web site, and if that doesn't work, fax or call the hotel.

If the extension dot-com (.com) doesn't work at the end of an URL, try .at for Austria, .be for Belgium, .co.uk for Britain, .cz for the Czech Republic, .dk for Denmark, .fr for France, .de for Germany, .ie for Ireland, .it for Italy, .nl for the Netherlands, .es for Spain, and .ch for Switzerland.

Internet cafés are available in most cities, giving you reasonably inexpensive and easy access. Look for the Internet cafés listed in this book, or ask at the local TI, computer store, or your hotel.

If you're planning to log on from your laptop in your hotel room, you'll need an Internet service provider that has local phone numbers for each country you'll visit. While an American modem cable plugs into European phone jacks, you may have to tweak your settings to make your computer recognize a pulse instead of the U.S. dial tone. Bring a phone jack tester that reverses line polarity as needed.

Sleeping

In the interest of smart use of your time, I favor hotels and restaurants handy to your sightseeing activities. Rather than list hotels scattered throughout a city, I describe my favorite two or three neighborhoods and recommend the best accommodations values in each, from $10 bunks to $150 doubles.

Sleep Code

To give maximum information in a minimum of space, I use this code to describe accommodations listed in this book. Prices listed are per room, not per person. When there is a range of prices in one category, the price will fluctuate with the season, size of room, or length of stay.

S = Single room (or price for one person in a double).

D = Double or twin. Double beds are usually big enough for non-romantic couples.

T = Triple (often a double bed with a single bed moved in).

Q = Quad (an extra child's bed is usually less).

b = Private bathroom with toilet and shower or tub.

s = Private shower or tub only (the toilet is down the hall).

CC = Accepts credit cards.

no CC = Does not accept credit cards; you'll need to pay with the local currency.

SE = Speaks English. This code is used only when it seems predictable that you'll encounter English-speaking staff.

NSE = Does not speak English. Used only when it's unlikely you'll encounter English-speaking staff.

According to this code, a couple staying at a "Db-€90, CC, SE" hotel in Spain would pay a total of 90 euros (about $90) for a double room with a private bathroom. The hotel accepts credit cards or euros in payment, and the staff speaks English.

Now that hotels are so expensive and tourist information offices' room-finding services are so greedy, it's more important than ever for budget travelers to have a good listing of rooms and call directly to make reservations. This book gives you a wide range of budget accommodations to choose from: hostels, bed-and-breakfasts, guest houses, pensions, small hotels, and splurges. I like places that are quiet, clean, small, central, traditional, friendly, and not listed in other guidebooks. Most places I list are a good value, having at least five of these seven virtues.

Rooms with private bathrooms are often bigger and renovated, while the cheaper rooms without bathrooms often will be on the top floor or not yet refurbished. Any room without a bathroom has access to a bathroom in the corridor (free unless otherwise noted). Rooms with tubs often cost more than rooms with showers. All rooms have a sink. Unless I note a difference, the cost of a room includes a continental breakfast. When breakfast is not included, the price is usually posted in your hotel room.

Before accepting a room, confirm your understanding of the complete price. The only tip my recommended hotels would like is a friendly, easygoing guest. I appreciate feedback on your hotel experiences.

Hotels

While most hotels listed in this book cluster around $70 to $100 per double, they range from $25 (very simple, toilet and shower down the hall) to about $200 (maximum plumbing and more) per double. The cost is higher in big cities and heavily touristed cities and lower off the beaten track. Three or four people can save money by requesting one big room. Traveling alone can get expensive: A single room is often only 20 percent cheaper than a double. If you'll accept a room with twin beds and you ask for a double, you may be turned away. Ask for "a room for two people" if you'll take a twin or a double.

Rooms are generally safe, but don't leave valuables lying around. More (or different) pillows and blankets are usually in the closet or available on request. Remember, in Europe towels and linen aren't always replaced every day. Drip-dry and conserve.

A very simple continental breakfast is almost always included. (Breakfasts in Europe, like towels and people, get smaller as you go south.) If you like juice and protein for breakfast, supply it yourself. I enjoy a box of juice in my hotel room and often supplement the skimpy breakfast with a piece of fruit and cheese.

Pay your bill the evening before you leave to avoid the time-wasting crowd at the reception desk in the morning.

Making Reservations

It's possible to travel at any time of year without reservations (especially if you arrive early in the day), but given the high stakes, erratic accommodations values, and the quality of the gems I've found for this book, I'd highly recommend calling for rooms at least a day or two in advance as you travel (your fluent receptionist will likely help you call your next hotel if you pay for the call). Even if a hotel clerk says the hotel is fully booked, you can try calling between 9:00 and 10:00 on the day you plan to arrive. That's when the hotel clerk knows who'll be checking out and just which rooms will be available. I've taken great pains to list telephone numbers with long-distance instructions (see "Telephones," above and the appendix). Use the telephone and the convenient phone cards. Most hotels listed are accustomed to English-only speakers. A hotel receptionist will trust you and hold a room until 16:00 (4:00 p.m.) without a deposit, though some will ask for a credit card number. Honor (or cancel by phone) your reservations. Long distance is cheap and easy from public phone booths. Don't let these people down—I promised you'd call and cancel if for some reason you won't show up. Don't needlessly confirm rooms through the tourist office; they'll take a commission.

If you know exactly which dates you need and really want a particular place, reserve a room well in advance before you leave home. To reserve from home, call, e-mail, or fax the hotel. Phone and fax costs are reasonable, e-mail is a steal, and simple English is usually fine. To fax, use the form in the appendix (or find it online at www.ricksteves.com/reservation). A two-night stay in August would be "2 nights, 16/8/03 to 18/8/03" (Europeans write the date in this order—day/month/year—and hotel jargon counts your stay from your day of arrival through your day of departure).

If you send a reservation request and receive a response with rates stating that rooms are available, this is not a confirmation. You must confirm that the rates are fine and that indeed you want the room. You'll often receive a response requesting one night's deposit. A credit card number and expiration date will usually work. If you use your credit card for the deposit, you can pay with your card or cash when you arrive; if you don't show up, you'll be billed for one night. Reconfirm your reservations several days in advance for safety.

Bed-and-Breakfasts

You can stay in private homes throughout Europe and enjoy double the cultural intimacy for about half the cost of hotels. You'll find them mainly in smaller towns and in the countryside (so they are most handy for those with a car). In Germany, look for *Zimmer* signs. For Italian *affitta camere* and French *chambre d'hôte* (CH), ask at local tourist offices. Doubles cost about $50, and you'll often share a bathroom with the family. While your European hosts will rarely speak English (except in Switzerland, the Netherlands, Belgium, and Scandinavia), they will almost always be enthusiastic, delightful hosts.

Hostels

For $10 to $20 a night, you can stay at one of Europe's 2,000 youth hostels. While most hostels admit nonmembers for an extra fee, it's best to join the club and buy a youth hostel card before you go (call Hostelling International at 202/783-6161 or order online at www.hiayh.org). Except in Bavaria (where you must be under 27 to stay in a hostel), travelers of any age are welcome as long as they don't mind dorm-style accommodations and making lots of traveling friends. Cheap meals are sometimes available, and kitchen facilities are usually provided for do-it-yourselfers. Expect crowds in the summer, snoring, and lots of youth groups giggling and making rude noises while you try to sleep. Family rooms and doubles are often available on request, but it's basically boys' dorms and girls' dorms. Many hostels are locked up from about 10:00 until 17:00, and a 23:00 curfew is often enforced. Hosteling is ideal for those traveling single: prices are per bed, not per room, and you'll have an instant circle of friends. More and more hostels are getting their business acts together, taking credit card reservations over the phone and leaving sign-in forms on the door for each available room. If you're serious about traveling cheaply, get a card, carry your own sheets, and cook in the members' kitchens.

Camping

For $5 to $10 per person per night, you can camp your way through Europe. "Camping" is an international word, and you'll see signs everywhere. All you need is a tent and a sleeping bag. Good campground guides are published, and camping information is also readily available at local tourist information offices. Europeans love to holiday camp. It's a social rather than a nature experience and a great way for traveling Americans to make local friends. Camping is ideal for families traveling by car on a tight budget.

Eating European

Europeans are masters at the art of fine living. That means eating long and eating well. Two-hour lunches, three-hour dinners, and endless hours sitting in outdoor cafés are the norm. Americans eat on their way to an evening event and complain if the check is slow in coming. For Europeans, the meal is an end in itself, and only rude waiters rush you.

Even those of us who liked dorm food will find that the local cafés, cuisine, and wines become a highlight of our European adventure. This is sightseeing for your palate, and even if the rest of you is sleeping in cheap hotels, your taste buds will want an occasional first-class splurge. You can eat well without going broke. But be careful: You're just as likely to blow a small fortune on a mediocre meal as you are to dine wonderfully for $15.

Tips on Tipping

Tipping in Europe isn't as automatic and generous as it is in the U.S., but for special service, tips are appreciated, if not expected. As in the U.S., the proper amount depends on your resources, tipping philosophy, and the circumstance, but some general guidelines apply.

Restaurants: Tipping is an issue only at restaurants that have waiters and waitresses. If you order your food at a counter, don't tip.

At restaurants with wait staff, the service charge (10-15 percent) is usually listed on the menu and included in your bill. When the service is included, there's no need to tip beyond that, but if you like to tip and you're pleased with the service, you can round up the bill (but not more than five percent).

If the service is not included, tip up to 10 percent by rounding up or leaving the change from your bill. Leave the tip on the table or hand it to your server. It's best to tip in cash even if you pay with your credit card. Otherwise the tip may never reach your waitress.

Taxis: To tip the cabbie, round up. For a typical ride, round up to the next euro on the fare (to pay a €13 fare, give €14); for a long ride, to the nearest 10 (for a €75 fare, give €80). If the cabbie hauls your bags and zips you to the airport to help you catch your flight, you might want to toss in a little more. But if you feel like you're being driven in circles or otherwise ripped off, skip the tip.

Special services: It's thoughtful to tip a couple of euros to someone who shows you a special sight and who is paid in no other way (such as the man who shows you an Etruscan tomb in his backyard). Tour guides at public sites sometimes hold out their hands for tips after they give their spiel; if I've already paid for the tour, I don't tip extra, though some tourists do give a euro or two, particularly for a job well done. I don't tip at hotels, but if you do, give the porter a euro for carrying bags and leave a couple of euros in your room at the end of your stay for the maid if the room was kept clean. In general, if someone in the service industry does a super job for you, a tip of a couple of euros is appropriate . . . but not required.

When in doubt, ask. If you're not sure whether (or how much) to tip for a service, ask your hotelier or the TI; they'll fill you in on how it's done on their turf.

Restaurants

When restaurant hunting, choose a place filled with locals, not the place with the big neon signs boasting "We Speak English and Accept Credit Cards." Look for menus posted outside; if you don't see one, move along.

For a no-stress meal in France and Italy, look for set-price menus (called the tourist menu, *menu del giorno*, *prix-fixe*, or simply *le menu*) that give you several choices of courses. At some restaurants, the *menu* is cheaper at lunch than dinner. Combination plates (*le plat* in France, *plato combinado* in Spain) provide house specialties at reasonable prices.

Galloping gourmets bring a menu translator. The *Marling Menu Master*, available in French, Italian, and German editions, is excellent.

When you're in the mood for something halfway between a restaurant and a picnic meal, look for take-out food stands, bakeries (with sandwiches and small pizzas to go), delis with stools or a table, a department store cafeteria, or simple little eateries for fast and easy sit-down restaurant food.

Picnics

So that I can afford the occasional splurge in a nice restaurant, I like to picnic. In addition to the savings, picnicking is a great way to sample local specialties. And, in the process of assembling your meal, you get to plunge into local markets like a European.

Gather supplies early. Many shops close for a lunch break. While it's fun to visit the small specialty shops, a *supermarché* gives you more efficiency with less color for less cost.

When driving, I organize a backseat pantry in a cardboard box: plastic cups, paper towels, a water bottle (the standard disposable European half liter plastic mineral water bottle works fine), a damp cloth in a Zip-loc baggie, a Swiss army knife, and a petite tablecloth. To take care of juice once and for all, stow a rack of liter boxes of orange juice in the trunk. (Look for "100%" on the label or you'll get a sickly sweet orange drink.)

Picnics (especially French ones) can be an adventure in high cuisine. Be daring: Try the smelly cheeses, midget pickles, ugly pâtés, and minuscule yogurts. Local shopkeepers sell small quantities of produce and even slice and stuff a sandwich for you.

A typical picnic for two might be fresh bread (half loaves on request), two tomatoes, three carrots, 100 grams of cheese (about a quarter-pound, called an *etto* in Italy), 100 grams of meat, two apples, a liter box of orange juice, and yogurt. Total cost for two: about $8.

Stranger in a Strange Land

We travel all the way to Europe to enjoy differences—to become temporary locals. You'll experience frustrations. Certain truths that we find "God-given" or "self-evident," like cold beer, ice in drinks, bottomless cups of coffee, hot showers, body odor smelling bad, and bigger being better, are suddenly not so true. One of the benefits of travel is the eye-opening realization that there are logical, civil, and even better alternatives. A willingness to go local ensures that you'll enjoy a full dose of local hospitality.

If there is a negative aspect to the European image of Americans, we can appear loud, aggressive, impolite, rich, and a bit naive. While Europeans look bemusedly at some of our Yankee excesses—and worriedly at others—they nearly always afford us individual travelers all the warmth we deserve.

Back Door Manners

While updating this book, I heard over and over again that my readers are considerate and fun to have as guests. Thank you for traveling as temporary locals who are sensitive to the culture. It's fun to follow you in my travels.

Send Me a Postcard, Drop Me a Line

If you enjoy a successful trip with the help of this book and would like to share your discoveries, please fill out the survey at the end of this book (or find it online at www.ricksteves.com/feedback) and send it to me at Europe Through the Back Door, Box 2009, Edmonds, WA 98020. I personally read and value all feedback.

For our latest travel information, tap into our Web site: www.ricksteves.com. To check on updates for this book, visit www.ricksteves.com/update. My e-mail address is rick @ricksteves.com. Anyone is welcome to request a free issue of our *Back Door* quarterly newsletter.

Judging from all the positive feedback I receive from travelers who have used this book, it's safe to assume you'll enjoy a great, affordable vacation—with the finesse of an experienced, independent traveler. Thanks, and happy travels!

BACK DOOR TRAVEL PHILOSOPHY

from *Rick Steves' Europe Through the Back Door*

Travel is intensified living—maximum thrills per minute and one of the last great sources of legal adventure. Travel is freedom. It's recess, and we need it.

Experiencing the real Europe requires catching it by surprise, going casual . . . "through the Back Door."

Affording travel is a matter of priorities. (Make do with the old car.) You can travel—simply, safely, and comfortably—anywhere in Europe for $80 a day plus transportation costs. In many ways, spending more money only builds a thicker wall between you and what you came to see. Europe is a cultural carnival, and, time after time, you'll find that its best acts are free and the best seats are the cheap ones.

A tight budget forces you to travel close to the ground, meeting and communicating with the people, not relying on service with a purchased smile. Never sacrifice sleep, nutrition, safety, or cleanliness in the name of budget. Simply enjoy the local-style alternatives to expensive hotels and restaurants.

Extroverts have more fun. If your trip is low on magic moments, kick yourself and make things happen. If you don't enjoy a place, maybe you don't know enough about it. Seek the truth. Recognize tourist traps. Give a culture the benefit of your open mind. See things as different but not better or worse. Any culture has much to share.

Of course, travel, like the world, is a series of hills and valleys. Be fanatically positive and militantly optimistic. If something's not to your liking, change your liking. Travel is addictive. It can make you a happier American as well as a citizen of the world. Our Earth is home to six billion equally important people. It's humbling to travel and find that people don't envy Americans. They like us, but, with all due respect, they wouldn't trade passports.

Globe-trotting destroys ethnocentricity. It helps you understand and appreciate different cultures. Travel changes people. It broadens perspectives and teaches new ways to measure quality of life. Many travelers toss aside their hometown blinders. Their prized souvenirs are the strands of different cultures they decide to knit into their own character. The world is a cultural yarn shop. And Back Door travelers are weaving the ultimate tapestry. Come on, join in!

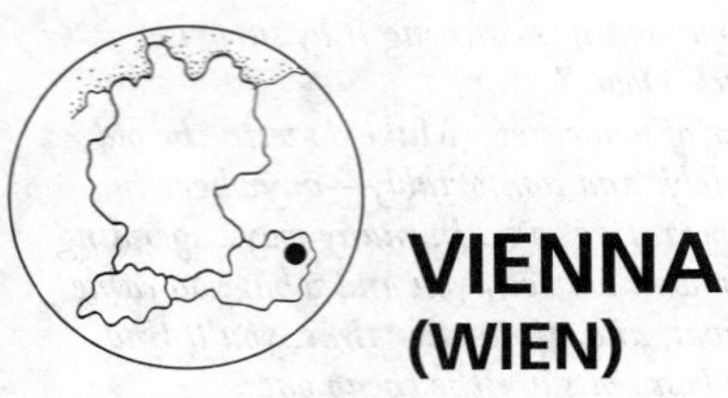

VIENNA (WIEN)

Vienna is a head without a body. For 640 years the capital of the once-grand Hapsburg empire, she started and lost World War I, and with it her far-flung holdings. Today, you'll find an elegant capital of 1.6 million people (20 percent of Austria's population) ruling a small, relatively insignificant country. Culturally, historically, and from a sightseeing point of view, this city is the sum of its illustrious past. The city of Freud, Brahms, Maria Theresa's many children, a gaggle of Strausses, and a dynasty of Holy Roman Emperors ranks right up there with Paris, London, and Rome.

Vienna has always been the easternmost city of the West. In Roman times, it was Vindobona, on the Danube facing the Germanic barbarians. In medieval times, Vienna was Europe's bastion against the Ottoman Turks (a "horde" of 300,000 was repelled in 1683). While the ancient walls held out the Turks, World War II bombs destroyed nearly a quarter of the city's buildings. In modern times, Vienna took a big bite out of the USSR's Warsaw Pact buffer zone.

The truly Viennese person is not Austrian, but a second-generation Hapsburg cocktail, with grandparents from the distant corners of the old empire—Poland, Serbia, Hungary, Romania, the Czech Republic, and Italy. Vienna is the melting-pot capital of a now-collapsed empire that, in its heyday, consisted of 60 million people—only 8 million of whom were Austrian.

In 1900, Vienna's 2.2 million inhabitants made it the world's fifth-largest city (after New York, London, Paris, and Berlin). But the average Viennese mother today has 1.3 children, and the population is down to 1.6 million. (Dogs are the preferred "child.")

Some ad agency has convinced Vienna to make Elisabeth, wife of Emperor Franz Josef, with her narcissism and difficulties with

Vienna Overview

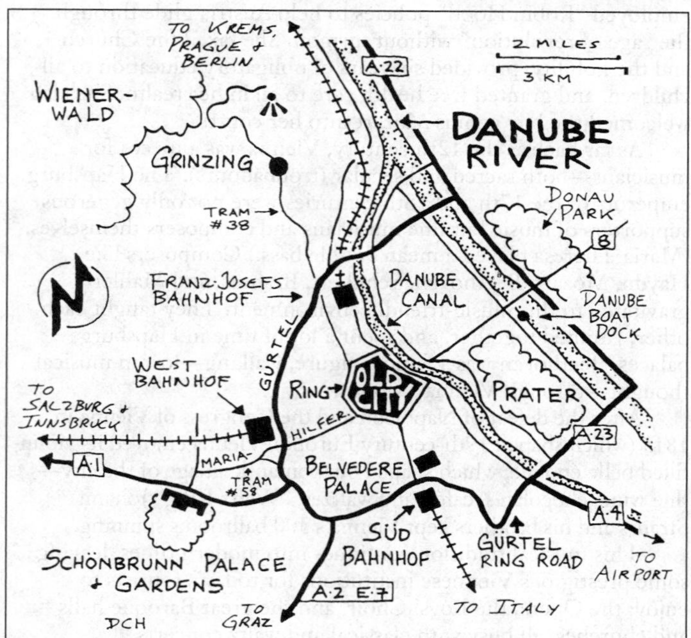

royal life, the darling of the local tourist scene. You'll see "Sissy" all over town. But stay focused on the Hapsburgs who mattered.

Of the Hapsburgs who ruled Austria from 1273 to 1918, Maria Theresa (ruled 1740–1780) and Franz Josef (ruled 1848–1916) are the most famous. People are quick to remember Maria Theresa as the mother of 16 children (12 survived). This was actually no big deal back then (one of her daughters had 18 kids, and a son fathered 16). Maria Theresa's reign followed the Austrian defeat of the Turks, when Europe recognized Austria as a great power. She was a strong and effective queen. (Her rival, the Prussian emperor, said, "When at last the Hapsburgs get a great man, it's a woman.")

Maria Theresa was a great social reformer. During her reign, she avoided wars and expanded her empire by skillfully marrying her children into the right families. After daughter Marie Antoinette's marriage into the French Bourbon family (to Louis XVI), for instance, a country that had been an enemy became an ally. (Unfortunately for Marie, she arrived in time for the Revolution, and she lost her head.)

A great reformer and in tune with her era, Maria Theresa employed "Robin Hood" policies to help Austria glide through the "age of revolution" without turmoil. She taxed the Church and the nobility, provided six years of obligatory education to all children, and granted free health care to all in her realm. She also welcomed the boy genius Mozart into her court.

As far back as the 12th century, Vienna was a mecca for musicians—both sacred and secular (troubadours). The Hapsburg emperors of the 17th and 18th centuries were not only generous supporters of music but fine musicians and composers themselves. (Maria Theresa played a mean double bass.) Composers like Haydn, Mozart, Beethoven, Schubert, Brahms, and Mahler gravitated to this music-friendly environment. They taught each other, jammed together, and spent a lot of time in Hapsburg palaces. Beethoven was a famous figure, walking—lost in musical thought—through Vienna's woods.

After the defeat of Napoleon and the Congress of Vienna in 1815 (which shaped 19th-century Europe), Vienna enjoyed its violin-filled belle époque, which shaped our romantic image of the city—fine wine, chocolates, cafés, and waltzes. "Waltz King" Johann Strauss and his brothers kept Vienna's 300 ballrooms spinning.

This musical tradition continues into modern times, leaving some prestigious Viennese institutions for today's tourists to enjoy: the Opera, the Boys' Choir, and the great Baroque halls and churches, all busy with classical and waltz concerts.

Planning Your Time

For a big city, Vienna is pleasant and laid-back. Packed with sights, it's worth two days and two nights on the speediest trip. It seems like Vienna was designed to help people just meander through a day. To be grand-tour efficient, you could sleep in and sleep out on the train (Berlin, Venice, Rome, the Swiss Alps, Paris, and the Rhine are each handy night trains away). For the best Austrian experience, I'd come in from Salzburg via Hallstatt, and spend two days this way:

Day 1: 9:00-Circle the "Ring" by tram, following the self-guided tour (see "Do-It-Yourself Bus Orientation Tour," below), 10:00-Drop by TI for any planning and ticket needs, then see the sights in Vienna's old center (described below): Monument against War and Fascism, Kaisergruft crypt, Kärntner Strasse, St. Stephan's Cathedral, and Graben, 12:00-Finger sandwiches for lunch at Buffet Trzesniewski, 13:00-Tour the Hofburg and treasury, 16:00-Time to hit one more museum or shop, or browse and people-watch, 19:30-Choose classical music (concert or opera), House of Music museum, or *Heurige* wine garden.

Day 2: 9:00-Schönbrunn Palace (drivers: this is conveniently on the way out of town toward Salzburg; horse-lovers: you'll need to rearrange—or rush the palace—to see the Lipizzaner stallions' morning practice), 12:00-Lunch at Rosenberger Markt, 13:00-Tour the Opera, 14:00-Kunsthistorisches Museum, 16:00-Your choice of the many sights left to see in Vienna, Evening-See Day 1 evening options.

Orientation (area code: 01)

Vienna—Wien in German (pron. veen)—sits between the Vienna Woods (Wienerwald) and the Danube (Donau). To the southeast is industrial sprawl. The Alps, which arc across Europe from Marseilles, end at Vienna's wooded hills. These provide a popular playground for walking and new-wine–drinking. This greenery's momentum carries on into the city. More than half of Vienna is parkland, filled with ponds, gardens, trees, and statue-maker memories of Austria's glory days.

Think of the city map as a target. The bull's-eye is the cathedral, the first circle is the Ring, and the second is the Gürtel. The old town—snuggling around towering St. Stephan's Cathedral south of the Danube—is bound tightly by the Ringstrasse. The Ring, marking what was the city wall, circles the first district (or *Bezirk*). The Gürtel, a broader ring road, contains the rest of downtown (*Bezirkes* 2–9).

Addresses start with the *Bezirk*, followed by street and building number. Any address higher than the ninth *Bezirk* is beyond the Gürtel, far from the center. The middle two digits of Vienna's postal codes show the district, or *Bezirk*. The address "7, Lindengasse 4" is in the seventh district, #4 on Linden Street. Its postal code would be 1070. Nearly all your sightseeing will be done in the core first district or along the Ringstrasse. As a tourist, concern yourself only with this compact old center. When you do, sprawling Vienna suddenly becomes manageable.

Tourist Information

Vienna has one real tourist office, a block behind the Opera House at Albertinaplatz (daily 9:00–19:00, tel. 01/2111-4222 or 01/24555, www.info.wien.at). Confirm your sightseeing plans and pick up the free and essential city map with a list of museums and hours (also available at most hotels), the monthly program of concerts (called "Programm"), and the youth guide *(Ten Good Reasons For Vienna)*. While hotel and ticket booking agencies answer questions and give out maps and brochures at the train stations and airport, I'd rely on the TI if possible.

Consider the TI's handy €3.75 *Vienna from A to Z* booklet.

Every important building sports a numbered flag banner that keys into this guidebook. A to Z numbers are keyed into the TI's city map. When lost, find one of the "famous-building flags" and match its number to your map. If you're at a "famous building," check the map to see what other key numbers are nearby, then check the A to Z book description to see if you want to go in. This system is especially helpful for those just wandering aimlessly among Vienna's historic charms.

The much-promoted €17 Vienna Card might save the busy sightseer a few euros. It gives you a 72-hour transit pass (worth €12) and discounts of 10 to 20 percent at the city's museums.

Arrival in Vienna

By Train at the West Station (Westbahnhof): Train travelers arriving from Munich, Salzburg, and Melk land at the Westbahnhof. The Reisebüro am Bahnhof books hotels (for a €4 fee), has maps, answers questions, and has a train info desk (daily 8:00–21:00). To get to the city center (and most likely, your hotel), catch the U-3 metro (buy your ticket or transit pass—described below—from a *Tabak* shop in the station or from a machine—good on all city transit). U-3 signs lead down to the metro tracks. If your hotel is along Mariahilfer Strasse, your stop is on this line (direction: Simmering; see "Sleeping," below). If you're sleeping in the center or just sightseeing, ride five stops to Stephansplatz, escalate in the exit direction Stephansplatz, and you'll hit the cathedral. The TI is a five-minute stroll down the busy Kärntner Strasse pedestrian street.

The Westbahnhof has a grocery store (daily 5:30–23:00), ATMs, Internet access, change offices, and storage facilities. Airport buses and taxis wait in front of the station.

By Train at the South Station (Südbahnhof): Those arriving from Italy and Prague land here. The Südbahnhof has all the services, left luggage, and a TI (daily 9:00–19:00). To reach Vienna's center, follow the S *(Schnellbahn)* signs to the right and down the stairs, and take any train in the direction Floridsdorf; transfer in two stops (at Landsstrasse/Wien Mitte) to the U-3 line, direction Ottakring, which goes directly to Stephansplatz and Mariahilfer Strasse hotels. Also, tram D goes to the Ring, and bus #13A goes to Mariahilfer Strasse.

By Train at Franz Josefs Station: If you're coming from Krems (in the Danube Valley), you'll arrive at Vienna's Franz Josefs station. From here, take tram D into town. Better yet, get off at Spittelau (the stop before Josefs) and use its handy U-bahn station.

By Plane: The airport (16 km/10 miles from town, tel. 01/7007-22233 for info and to connect with various airlines) is connected by €6 shuttle buses (2/hr) to either the Westbahnhof (35 min) or the City Air Terminal (3/hr, 20 min; next to Hilton and Wien-Mitte station—with easy metro connections, near river in old center). A speedy new train connecting the airport and the Südbahnhof is planned for 2003. Taxis into town cost about €35 (including €10 airport surcharge). Hotels arrange for fixed-rate car service to the airport (€30, 30-min ride).

Getting around Vienna

By Bus, Tram, and Metro: Take full advantage of Vienna's simple, cheap, and super-efficient transit system. Buses, trams, and the metro all use the same tickets. Buy your tickets from *Tabak* shops, station machines, or Vorverkauf offices in the station. You have lots of choices:

- single tickets (€1.50, €2 if bought on tram, good for 1 journey with necessary transfers)
- 24-hour pass (€5)
- 72-hour pass (€12)
- 7-day pass (€12.50, Mon–Sun)
- 8 Tage Karte: eight all-day trips for €24 (can be shared, e.g., 4 people for 2 days each). With a per-person cost of €3/day (compared to €5/day for a 24-hour pass), this can be a real saver for groups.

Take a moment to study the eye-friendly city center map on metro station walls to internalize how the metro and tram system can help you (metro routes are signed by the end-of-the-line stop). I use the tram mostly to zip along the Ring (tram #1 or #2) and take the metro to outlying sights or hotels. The free tourist map has essentially all the lines marked, making the too-big €1.50 transit map unnecessary. Numbered lines (e.g., #38) are trams, numbers followed by an "A" (e.g., #38A) are buses. Lines that begin with "U" (e.g., U-3) are subways, or *U-bahnen*. And blue lines are the speedier S-bahns *(Schnellbahnen)*.

Stamp a time on your ticket or transit pass as you enter the system or tram. Cheaters pay a stiff €44 fine if caught—and then they make you buy a ticket. Rookies miss stops because they fail to open the door. Push buttons, pull latches—do whatever it takes. Study the excellent wall-mounted street map before you exit the metro. Choosing the right exit—signposted from the moment you step off the train—saves lots of walking (for information, call 01/790-9105).

By Taxi: Vienna's comfortable, civilized, and easy-to-flag-down taxis start at €2. You'll pay about €8 to go from the Opera to the West Train Station (Westbahnhof). Consider the luxury of having your own car and driver. Johann (John)

Lichtl is a kind, honest, English-speaking cabbie who can take up to four passengers in his car (€25/1 hr, €20/hr for 2 or more hours, cellular 0676-670-6750).

By Bike: Handy as you'll find the city's transit system, you may want to rent a bike (list of rental places at the TI) and follow one of the routes recommended in the TI's biking brochure.

By Buggy: Rich romantics get around by traditional horse and buggy. You'll see the horse buggies, called *Fiakers*, clip-clopping tourists on tours lasting 20 minutes (€40—old town), 40 minutes (€65—old town and the Ring), or one hour (€95—all of the above, but more thorough). You can share the ride and cost with up to five people. Because it's a kind of guided tour, before settling on a carriage, talk to a few drivers and pick one who's fun and speaks English.

Helpful Hints

Banking: ATMs are everywhere. Banks are open weekdays roughly from 8:00 to 15:00 and until 17:30 on Tuesday and Thursday. After-hours, you can change money at train stations, the airport, post offices, or the American Express office (Mon–Fri 9:00–17:30, Sat 9:00–12:00, closed Sun, Kärntner Strasse 21-23, tel. 01/5154-0456).

Post Offices: Choose from the main post office (Postgasse in center, open 24 hrs daily, handy metered phones), West and South Train Stations (daily 6:00–23:00), or near the Opera (Mon–Fri 7:00–19:00, closed Sat–Sun, Krugerstrasse 13).

English Bookstores: Consider the **British Bookshop** (Mon–Fri 9:30–18:30, Sat 9:30–17:00, closed Sun, at corner of Weihburggasse and Seilerstätte, tel. 01/512-1945; same hours at branch at Mariahilferstrasse 4, tel. 01/522-6730) or **Shakespeare & Co.** (Mon–Sat 9:00–19:00, closed Sun, north of Höher Markt square, Sterngasse 2, tel. 01/535-5053).

Internet Access: The TI has a list of Internet cafés. BigNet is the dominant outfit, with lots of stations at Kärntner Strasse 61 and Hoher Markt 8 (€7.20/hr, daily 10:00–24:00, tel. 01/533-2939). Surfland Internet Café is near the Opera (daily 10:00–23:00, Krugerstrasse 10, tel. 01/512-7701).

City Tours

Walks—The *Walks in Vienna* brochure at the TI describes Vienna's guided walks. The basic 90-minute "Vienna First Glance" introductory walk is given daily throughout the summer (€11, 14:15 from TI, in English and German, tel. 01/894-5363, www.wienguide.at).

Local Guides—The tourist board Web site (www.info.wien.at)

has a long list of local guides with specialties and contact information. Lisa Zeiler is a good English-speaking guide (2- to 3-hour walks for €120—if she's booked, she can set you up with another guide, tel. 01/402-3688, e-mail: lisa.zeiler@gmx.at).

Bus Tours—The Yellow Cab Sightseeing company offers a one-hour, €12, quickie double-decker bus tour with a tape-recorded narration, departing at the top of each hour (10:00–17:00) from in front of the Opera (corner of Operngasse). Vienna Line offers hop-on, hop-off tours covering the 14 predictable sightseeing stops. Given Vienna's excellent public transportation and this outfit's meager one-bus-per-hour frequency, I'd take this not to hop on and off, but only to get the narrated orientation drive through town (recorded narration in 8 languages, €18, ticket good for 2 days if purchased after 15:00, or €12 if you stay on for the 60-minute circular ride). Their basic Vienna city sights tour includes a visit to the Schönbrunn Palace and a bus tour around town (€32, 2/day, 3.5 hrs; to book this or get info on other tours, call 01/7124-6830).

Do-It-Yourself Bus Orientation Tour

▲▲Ringstrasse Tram #2 Tour—In the 1860s, Emperor Franz Josef had the city's ingrown medieval wall torn down and replaced with a grand boulevard 60 meters (190 feet) wide. The road, arcing nearly five kilometers (3 miles) around the city's core, predates all the buildings that line it—so what you'll see is neoclassical, neo-Gothic, and neo-Renaissance. One of Europe's great streets, it's lined with many of the city's top sights. Trams #1 and #2 and a great bike path circle the whole route—and so should you.

This self-service tram tour gives you a fun orientation and a ridiculously quick glimpse of the major sights as you glide by (€1.50, 30-min circular tour). Tram #1 goes clockwise; tram #2, counter-clockwise. Most sights are on the outside, so use tram #2 (sit on the right, ideally in the front seat of the front car; or—for maximum view and minimum air—sit in the bubble-front seat of the second car). Start immediately across the street from the Opera House.

You can jump on and off as you go (trams come every 5 min). Read ahead and pay attention—these sights can fly by. Let's go:

☛ Immediately on the left: The city's main pedestrian drag, Kärntner Strasse, leads to the zigzag roof of **St. Stephan's Cathedral**. This tram tour makes a 360-degree circle around the cathedral, staying about this same distance from it.

☛ At first bend (before first stop): Look right toward the tall fountain and the guy on a horse. Schwartzenberg Platz shows off its **equestrian statue** of Prince Charles Schwartzenberg, who fought Napoleon. Behind that is the Russian monument (behind the fountain), which was built in 1945 as a forced thanks to the

Vienna

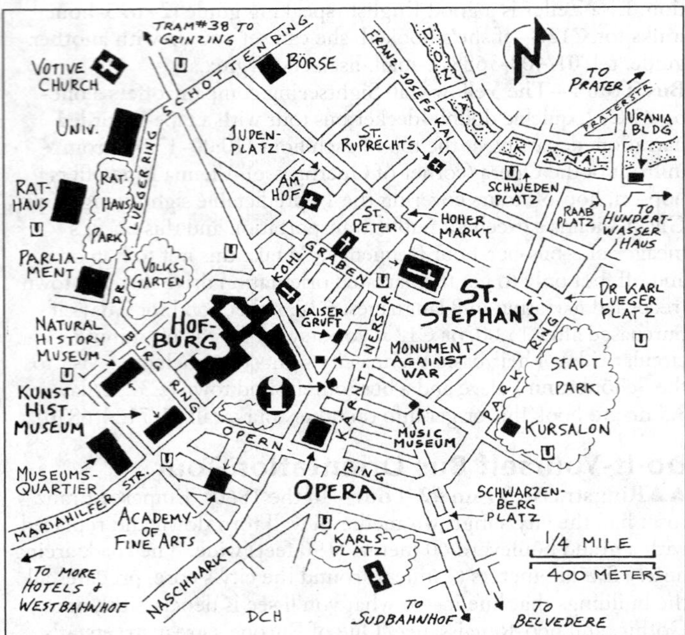

Soviets for liberating Austria from the Nazis. Formerly a sore point, now it's just ignored.

☛ Going down Schubertring, you reach the huge **Stadtpark** (city park) on the right, which honors many great Viennese musicians and composers with statues. At the beginning of the park, the gold-and-cream concert hall behind the trees is the **Kursalon**, opened in 1867 by the Strauss brothers, who directed many waltzes here. The touristy Strauss concerts are held here (see "Summer Music Scene," below).

☛ Immediately after next stop, look right: In the same park, the gilded statue of Waltz King **Johann Strauss** holds a violin as he did when he conducted his orchestra, whipping his fans into a two-stepping frenzy.

☛ At next stop at end of park: On the left, a green statue of Dr. Karl Lueger honors the popular man who was mayor of Vienna until 1910.

☛ At next bend: On the right, the quaint white building with military helmets decorating the windows was the Austrian ministry of war—back when that was a big operation. Field Marshal

Radetzky, a military big shot in the 19th century under Franz Josef, still sits on his high horse. He's pointing toward the post office, the only Art Nouveau building facing the Ring. Locals call the architecture along the Ring "historicism" because it's all neo-this and neo-that—generally fitting the purpose of the particular building (for example, farther along the Ring, we'll see a neo-Gothic city hall—recalling when medieval burghers ran the city government in Gothic days, a neoclassical parliament building—celebrating ancient Greek notions of democracy, and a neo-Renaissance opera house—venerating the high culture filling it).

☛ At next corner: The white-domed building over your right shoulder as you turn is the Urania, Franz Josef's 1910 **observatory**. Lean forward and look behind it for a peek at the huge red cars of the giant 100-year-old Ferris wheel in Vienna's Prater Park (fun for families, described in "Top People-Watching and Strolling Sights," below).

☛ Now you're rolling along the **Danube Canal**. This "Baby Danube" is one of the many small arms of the river that once made up the Danube at this location. The rest have been gathered together in a mightier modern-day Danube, farther away. This neighborhood was thoroughly bombed in World War II. The buildings across the canal are typical of postwar architecture (1960s). This was the site of the original Roman town, Vindobona. In three long blocks, on the left (opposite the BP station, be ready—it passes fast), you'll see the ivy-covered walls and round Romanesque arches of St. Ruprechts, the oldest church in Vienna (built in the 11th century on a bit of Roman ruins). Remember, medieval Vienna was defined by that long-gone wall which you're tracing on this tour. Relax for a few stops until the corner.

☛ Leaving the canal, turning left up Schottenring, at first stop: On the left, the orange-and-white, neo-Renaissance temple of money, the **Börse**, is Vienna's stock exchange.

☛ Next stop, at corner: The huge, frilly, neo-Gothic church on the right is a "votive church," built as a thanks to God when an 1853 assassination attempt on Emperor Franz Josef failed. Ahead on the right (in front of tram stop) is the Vienna University building (established in 1365, it has no real campus as the buildings are scattered around town). It faces (on the left, behind a gilded angel) a chunk of the old city wall.

☛ At next stop on right: The neo-Gothic city hall, flying the flag of Europe, towers over **Rathaus Platz**, a festive site in summer with a huge screen showing outdoor movies, opera, and concerts. Immediately across the street (on left) is the **Hofburg Theater**, Austria's national theater.

☛ At next stop on right: The neo-Greek temple of democracy

houses the **Austrian Parliament**. The lady with the golden helmet is Athena, goddess of wisdom. Across the street (on left) is the royal park called the "Volksgarten."

☛ After the next stop on the right is the **Natural History Museum**, the first of Vienna's huge twin museums. It faces the **Kunsthistorisches Museum**, containing the city's greatest collection of paintings. The **MuseumsQuartier** behind them completes the ensemble with a collection of mostly modern art museums. A hefty statue of Empress Maria Theresa sits between the museums, facing the grand gate to the **Hofburg**, the emperor's palace (on left). Of the five arches, only the center one was used by the emperor. (Your tour is essentially finished. If you want to jump out here, you're at many of Vienna's top sights.)

☛ Fifty meters (165 feet) after the next stop, on the left through a gate in the black iron fence, is the statue of Mozart. It's one of many charms in the **Burggarten**, which until 1880 was the private garden of the emperor. Vienna had more than its share of intellectual and creative geniuses. A hundred meters (330 feet) farther (on left, just out of the park), the German philosopher Goethe sits in a big, thought-provoking chair playing trivia with Schiller (across the street on your right). Behind the statue of Schiller is the Academy of Fine Arts.

☛ Hey, there's the **Opera** again. Jump off the bus and see the rest of the city.

Sights—Vienna's Old Center

▲▲▲Opera (Staatsoper)—The Opera, facing the Ring and near the TI, is a central point for any visitor. While the critical reception of the building 130 years ago led the architect to commit suicide, and though it's been rebuilt since the WWII bombings, it's still a dazzling place (€4.50, by guided 35-min tour only, daily in English, July–Aug at 11:00, 13:00, 14:00, 15:00, and often at 10:00 and 16:00; Sept–June fewer tours, afternoon only). Tours are often canceled for rehearsals and shows, so check the posted schedule or call 01/514-442-613 or 01/514-442-421.

The Vienna State Opera—with musicians provided by the Vienna Philharmonic Orchestra in the pit —is one of the world's top opera houses. There are 300 performances a year, except in July and August, when the singers rest their voices. Since there are different operas nearly nightly, you'll see big trucks out back and constant action backstage—all the sets need to be switched each day. Even though the expensive seats normally sell out long in advance, the opera is perpetually in the red and subsidized by the state.

Tickets for seats: For ticket information, call 01/513-1513 (phone answered daily 10:00–21:00, www.culturall.com or www.wiener-staatsoper.at). Last-minute tickets (for pricey seats—up to €100) are sold for €30 from 9:00 to 14:00 only the day before the show.

Standing room: Unless Pavarotti is in town, it's easy to get one of 567 *Stehplätze* (standing-room spots, €2 at the top or €3.50 downstairs). While the front doors open 60 minutes early, a side door (on the Operngasse side, the door under the portico nearest the fountain) is open 80 minutes before curtain time, giving those in the know an early grab at standing-room tickets. Just walk in straight, then head right until you see the ticket booth marked *Stehplätze* (tel. 01/5144-42419). If fewer than 567 people are in line, there's no need to line up early. You can even buy standing-room tickets after the show has started—in case you want only a little taste of opera (see "Rick's crude tip," below). Dress is casual (but do your best) at the standing-room bar. Locals save their spot along the rail by tying a scarf to it.

Rick's crude tip: For me, three hours is a lot of opera. But just to see and hear the Opera House in action for half an hour is a treat. You can buy a standing-room spot and just drop in for part of the show. Ushers don't mind letting tourists with standing-room tickets in for a short look. Ending time is posted in the lobby—you could stop by for just the finale. If you go at the start or finish, you'll see Vienna dressed up. With all the time you save, consider stopping by...

Sacher Café, home of every chocoholic's fantasy, the Sacher torte, faces the rear of the Opera. While locals complain that the cakes have gone downhill, a coffee and slice of cake here is €8 well-invested. For maximum elegance, sit inside (daily 8:00–23:30, Philharmoniker Strasse 4, tel. 01/51456). The adjacent Café Mozart is better for a meal.

The U-bahn station in front of the Opera is actually a huge underground shopping mall with fast food, newsstands, lots of pickpockets, and even an Opera Toilet Vienna experience (€0.50).

▲Albertina Museum—After years of being closed for restoration, this sumptuous collection of drawings, etchings, and prints by the great masters—including Rubens, Rembrandt, Raphael, and a huge collection of precise drawings by Albrecht Dürer—reopens in March 2003 (€9, daily 10:00–19:00, overlooking Albertinaplatz across from TI and Opera House, tel. 01/534-830). Special exhibits in 2003 include Edvard Munch (March–June), From Michelangelo to Rubens (July–Aug), and Albrecht Dürer (Sept–Nov).

▲Monument against War and Fascism—A powerful four-part statue stands behind the Opera House on Albertinaplatz. The split white monument, *The Gates of Violence*, remembers victims of the 1938–1945 Nazi rule of Austria. A montage of wartime images—

clubs and gas masks, a dying woman birthing a future soldier, slave laborers—sits on a pedestal of granite cut from the infamous quarry at Mauthausen, a nearby concentration camp. The hunched-over figure on the ground behind is a Jew forced to wash anti-Nazi graffiti off a street with a toothbrush. The statue with its head buried in the stone reminds Austrians of the consequences of not keeping their government on track. Behind that, the 1945 declaration of Austria's second republic is cut into the stone. This monument stands on the spot where several hundred people were buried alive while hiding in the cellar of a building demolished in a WWII bombing attack. Like "ground zero" in New York, this is considered a kind of sacred ground and has never been built upon.

Austria was pulled into World War II by Germany, which annexed the country in 1938, saying Austrians were wannabe Germans, anyway. But Austrians are not Germans—never were . . . never will be. They're quick to tell you that while Austria was founded in 976, Germany wasn't born until 1870. For seven years during World War II (1938–1945), there was no Austria. In 1955, after 10 years of joint occupation by the victorious Allies, Austria regained total independence.

▲▲Kaisergruft (Remains of the Hapsburgs)—The crypt for the Hapsburg royalty, a block down the street from the Monument against War and Fascism, is described in detail under "More Hofburg Sights," below.

▲Kärntner Strasse—This grand, mall-like street (traffic-free since 1974) is the people-watching delight of this in-love-with-life city. It points south in the direction of the southern Austrian state of Kärnten (for which it's named). Starting from the Opera, you'll find lots of action—shops, street music, the city casino (at #41), American Express (#21–23), and then, finally, the cathedral.

▲▲St. Stephan's Cathedral—Stephansdom is the Gothic needle around which Vienna spins. It has survived Vienna's many wars and symbolizes the city's freedom (Mon–Sat 6:00–22:00, Sun 7:00–22:00, closed daily 12:00–13:00 for Mass, entertaining English tours daily April–Oct at 15:45, information board inside entry has tour schedules).

This is the third church to stand on this spot. (In fact, an older Romanesque chapel—the Virgilkapelle—is on display in the adjacent metro station.) The last bit of the 13th-century Romanesque church—the portal, round windows of the towers, and fascinating carvings in the tympanum—can be seen on the west end (above the entry). The church survived the bombs of World War II, but, in the last days of the war, fires from the street fighting between Russian and Nazi troops leapt to the rooftop; the original timbered Gothic rooftop burned, and the cathedral's huge bell crashed to the ground. With a financial outpouring of civic pride, the roof of this symbol of Austria was rebuilt in its original splendor by 1952. The ceramic tiles are purely decorative (locals who contributed to the postwar reconstruction each "own" one for their donation).

Inside, find the Gothic sandstone **pulpit** in the middle of the nave (on left). A spiral stairway winds up to the lectern, surrounded and supported by the four Latin Church fathers: Saints Ambrose, Jerome, Gregory, and Augustine. The railing leading up swarms with symbolism: lizards (animals of light), battle toads (animals of darkness), and the "Dog of the Lord" standing at the top to be sure none of those toads pollutes the sermon. Below the toads, wheels with three parts (the Trinity) roll up, while wheels with four parts (standing for the four seasons, symbolizing mortal life) roll down. This work, by Anton Pilgram, has all the elements of flamboyant Gothic in miniature. But this was around 1500, and the Renaissance was going strong in Italy. While Gothic persisted in the north, the Renaissance spirit had already arrived. Pilgram included what's thought to be a rare self-portrait bust in his work (the guy with sculptor's tools, looking out a window under the stairs). Gothic art was done for the glory of God. Artists were anonymous. In the more humanist Renaissance, man was allowed to shine—and artists became famous.

You can ascend both towers, the north (via crowded elevator inside on the left) and the south (outside right transept, by spiral staircase). The north shows you a big **bell** (the 21-ton Pummerin, cast from the cannon captured from the Turks in 1683, supposedly the second biggest bell in the world that rings by swinging) but a mediocre view (€4, daily 9:00–18:00). The 135-meter-high (450-foot) **south tower**, called St. Stephan's Tower, offers a great view—343 tightly wound steps up the spiral staircase (€3, daily 9:00–17:30, this hike burns about 1 Sacher torte of calories). From the top, use your *Vienna from A to Z* to locate the famous sights.

The forlorn **Cathedral Museum** *(Dom Museum,* outside left transept past horses) gives a close-up look at piles of religious paintings, statues, and a treasury (€5, Tue–Sat 10:00–17:00, closed Sun–Mon, Stephansplatz 6).

▲▲Stephansplatz, Graben, and Kohlmarkt—The atmosphere of the church square, Stephansplatz, is colorful and lively. At nearby Graben Street (which was once a *Graben,* or "ditch"—originally the moat for the Roman military camp), top-notch street entertainers dance around an exotic **plague monument** (at Bräuner Strasse). In medieval times, people did not understand the causes of plagues and figured they were a punishment from God. It was common for survivors to thank God with a monument like this one from the 1600s. Find Emperor Leopold, who ruled during the plague and made this statue in gratitude. (Hint: The typical inbreeding of royal families left him with a gaping underbite.) Below Leopold, "Faith" (with the help of a disgusting little cupid) tosses old naked women—symbolizing the plague—into the abyss.

Just beyond the plague monument, you'll pass a fine set of public WCs, the recommended restaurant Julius Meinl am Graben (see "Eating," below), and the Dorotheum auction house (see "More Sights—Vienna," below). Turning left on **Kohlmarkt**, you enter Vienna's most elegant shopping street (except for "American Catalog Shopping," at #5, second floor) with the emperor's palace at the end. Strolling Kohlmarkt, daydream about the edible window displays at **Demel** (#14). These delectable displays change about weekly, reflecting current happenings in Vienna. Drool through the interior (coffee and cake-€7.50). Shops like this boast "K. u. K."—good enough for the *König und Kaiser* (king and emperor—same guy). Farther along on Kohlmarkt, at #11, you can pop into a charming little Baroque carriage courtyard, with the surviving original carriage garages.

Kohlmarkt ends at Michaelerplatz, with a scant bit of Roman Vienna exposed at its center. On the left are the fancy Laden Plankl shop, with traditional formal wear, and the stables of the Spanish Riding School. Study the grand entry facade to the Hofburg Palace—it's neo-Baroque from around 1900. The four heroic giants are Hercules wrestling with his great challenges (much like the Hapsburgs, I'm sure). Opposite the facade, notice the modern Loos House, which was built at about the same time. It was nicknamed the "house without eyebrows" for the simplicity of its windows. This anti–Art Nouveau statement was actually shocking at the time. To quell some of the outrage, the architect added flower boxes. Enter the Hofburg Palace by walking through the gate, under the dome, and into the first square (In der Burg).

Sights—Vienna's Hofburg Palace

▲▲Hofburg—The complex, confusing, and imposing Imperial Palace, with 640 years of architecture, demands your attention. This first Hapsburg residence grew with the family empire from the 13th century until 1913, when the last "new wing" opened. The winter residence of the Hapsburg rulers until 1918, it's still the home of the Spanish Riding School, the Vienna Boys' Choir, the Austrian president's office, 5,000 government workers, and several important museums.

Rather than lose yourself in its myriad halls and courtyards, focus on three sections: the Imperial Apartments, Treasury, and Neue Burg (New Palace).

Hofburg orientation from In der Burg Square: The statue is of Emperor Franz II, grandson of Maria Theresa, grandfather of Franz Josef, and father-in-law of Napoleon. Behind him is a tower with three kinds of clocks (the yellow disk shows the stage of the moon tonight). On the right, a door leads to the Imperial Apartments. Franz faces the oldest part of the palace. The colorful gate, which used to have a drawbridge, leads to the 13th-century Swiss Court (named for the Swiss mercenary guards once stationed here), the Schatzkammer (treasury), and the Hofburgkapelle (palace chapel, where the Boys' Choir sings the Mass). For the Heroes' Square and the New Palace, continue opposite the way you entered In der Burg, passing through the left-most tunnel (with a tiny but handy sandwich bar—Hofburg Stüberl, daily 7:00–18:00—your best bet if you need a bite or drink before touring the Imperial Apartments).

▲▲Imperial Apartments (Kaiserappartements)—These lavish, Versailles-type, "wish-I-were-God" royal rooms are the downtown version of the grander Schönbrunn Palace. If you're rushed and have time for only one palace, do this (€7.50, daily 9:00–17:00, last entry 16:30, from courtyard through St. Michael's Gate, just off Michaelerplatz, tel. 01/533-7570). Palace visits are a one-way romp through 20 rooms. You'll find some helpful English information within, and, with that and the following description, you won't need the €7.50 Hofburg guidebook. The €3.20 audioguide is only worthwhile for a Hapsburg history buff. Tickets include the royal silver and porcelain collection *(Silberkammer)* near the turnstile. If touring the silver and porcelain, do it first to save walking.

Get your ticket, study the big model of the palace complex, and (just after the turnstile) notice the family tree tracing the Hapsburgs from 1273 to their messy WWI demise. The first two rooms give an overview (in English) of Empress Elisabeth's fancy world—her luxury homes and fairy-tale existence. A map and mannequins from the many corners of the Hapsburg realm illustrate the multiethnicity of the empire. Throughout the tour, banners describe royal life.

Amble through the first several furnished rooms to the...

Waiting room for the audience room: Every citizen had the right to meet privately with the emperor. Three huge paintings entertained guests while they waited. They were propaganda, showing crowds of commoners enthusiastic about their Hapsburg royalty. On the right: An 1809 scene of the emperor returning to Vienna, celebrating news that Napoleon had begun his retreat. Left: The return of the emperor from the 1814 Peace of Paris, the treaty that ended the Napoleonic wars. (The 1815 Congress of Vienna that followed was the greatest assembly of diplomats in

Vienna's Hofburg Palace

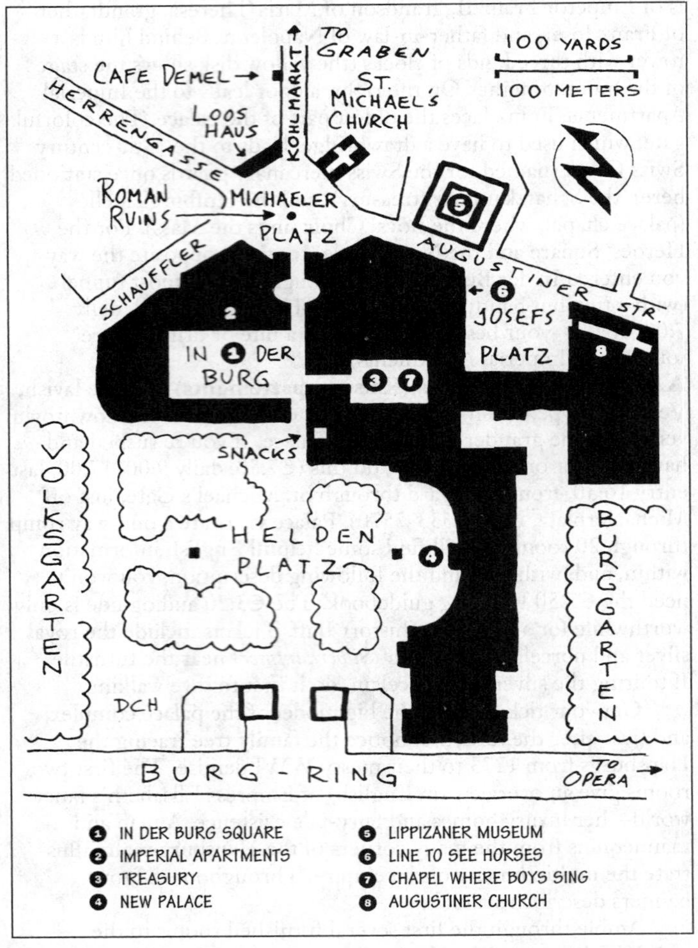

European history. Its goal: to establish peace through a "balance of power" among nations. While rulers ignored nationalism in favor of continued dynastic rule, this worked for about 100 years, until a colossal war—World War I—wiped out Europe's royal families.) Center: Less important, the emperor makes his first public appearance to adoring crowds after recovering from a life-threatening illness (1826). The chandelier—considered the best in the palace—is Baroque, made of Bohemian crystal.

Emperor Franz Josef

Franz Josef I—who ruled for 68 years (1848–1916)—was the embodiment of the Hapsburg empire as it finished its six-century-long ride. Born in 1830, Franz Josef had a stern upbringing that instilled in him a powerful sense of duty and—like so many men of power—a love of things military. His uncle, Ferdinand I, was a dimwit, and, as the revolutions of 1848 were rattling royal families throughout Europe, the Hapsburgs replaced him, putting 18-year old Franz Josef on the throne. FJ was very conservative. But worse, he figured he was a talented military tactician, leading Austria into disastrous battles against Italy (which was fighting for its unification and independence) in the 1860s. His army endured severe, avoidable casualities. It was clear: FJ was a disaster as a general. Wearing his uniform to the end, he never saw what a dinosaur his monarchy was becoming, and never thought it strange that the majority of his subjects didn't even speak German. He had no interest in democracy and pointedly never set foot in Austria's parliament building. But, like his contemporary Queen Victoria, he was the embodiment of his empire—old-fashioned but sacrosanct. His passion for low-grade paperwork earned him the nickname "Joe bureaucrat." Mired in these petty details, he missed the big picture. He helped start a world war that ultimately ended the age of monarchs. The year 1918 marked the end of Europe's big royal families: Hohenzollerns (Prussia), Romanovs (Russia), and Hapsburgs (Austria).

Audience room: Suddenly, you were face-to-face with the emp. The portrait on the easel shows Franz Josef in 1915, when he was over 80 years old. Famously energetic, he lived a spartan life dedicated to duty. He'd stand at the high table here to meet with commoners, who came to show gratitude or make a request. (Standing kept things moving.) On the table, you can read a partial list of 56 appointments he had on January 3, 1910 (family name and topic of meeting).

Conference room: The emperor presided here over the equivalent of cabinet meetings. Remember, after 1867, he ruled the Austro-Hungarian Empire, so Hungarians sat at these meetings. The paintings on the wall show the military defeat of a popular Hungarian uprising . . . subtle.

Emperor Franz Josef's study: The desk was originally

between the windows. Franz Josef could look up from his work and see his lovely, long-haired empress Elisabeth's reflection in the mirror. Notice the trompe l'oeil paintings above each door, giving the believable illusion of marble relief.

The walls between the rooms are wide enough to hide servants' corridors (the door to his valet's room is in the back left corner). The emperor lived with a personal staff of 14: three valets, four lackeys, two doormen, two manservants, and three chambermaids.

Emperor's bedroom: This features his famous spartan iron bed and portable washstand (necessary until 1880, when the palace got running water). A small painted porcelain portrait of the newlywed royal couple sits on the dresser. Franz Josef lived here after his estrangement from Sissy. An etching shows the empress—an avid hunter—riding sidesaddle while jumping a hedge. The big ornate stove in the corner was fed from behind. Through the 19th century, this was a standard form of heating.

Great salon: See the paintings of the emperor and empress in grand gala ballroom outfits from 1865.

Small salon/smoking room: This is dedicated to the memory of the assassinated Emperor Maximilian of Mexico (bearded portrait, Franz Josef's brother, killed in 1867). A smoking room was necessary in the early 19th century, when smoking was newly fashionable (but only for men—never in the presence of women).

Empress' bedroom and drawing room: This was Sissy's, refurbished neo-rococo in 1854. She lived here—the bed was rolled in and out daily—until her death in 1898.

Sissy's dressing/gymnastic room: The open bathroom door shows her huge copper tub. Servants worked two hours a day on Sissy's famous hair here. She'd exercise on the wooden structure. While she had a tough time with people, she did fine with animals. Her favorite circus horses, Flick and Flock, prance on the wall.

In 2003, a detour is planned here allowing visitors to actually wander through the servants' quarters, with walls delicately painted by Bergl in the late 1700s, plus the first linoleum ever used in Vienna (from around 1880).

Empress' great salon: The room is painted with Mediterranean escapes, the 19th-century equivalent of travel posters. The statue is of Elisa, Napoleon's oldest sister (by the neoclassical master, Canova). A few rooms later, at the end of the hall, admire the empress' hard-earned thin waist (20 inches at age 16, 21 inches at age 50 . . . after giving birth to 4 children). Turn the corner and pass through the anterooms of Alexander's apartments.

Sissy

Empress Elisabeth, Emperor Franz Josef's mysterious, narcissistic, and beautiful wife, is in vogue. She was mostly silent, worked out frantically to maintain her Barbie Doll figure, and spent hours each day tending to her ankle-length hair. Sissy's main goals in life seem to have been preserving her reputation as a beautiful empress and maintaining her fairytale hair. In spite of severe dieting and fanatic exercise, age took its toll. After turning 30, she allowed no more portraits to be painted and was generally seen in public with a delicate fan covering her face (and bad teeth). Complex and influential, she was adored by Franz Josef, whom she respected. Her personal mission and political cause was promoting Hungary's bid for nationalism. Her personal tragedy was the death of her son Rudolf, the crown prince, by suicide. Disliking Vienna and the confines of the court, she traveled more and more frequently. Over the years, the restless Sissy and her hardworking husband became estranged. In 1898, while visiting Geneva, Switzerland, she was murdered by an Italian anarchist. Sissy has been compared to Princess Diana because of her beauty, bittersweet life, and tragic death.

Red salon: The Gobelin wall hangings were a 1776 gift from Marie Antoinette and Louis XVI in Paris to their Viennese counterparts.

Dining room: It's dinnertime, and Franz Josef has called his extended family together. The settings are modest . . . just silver. Gold was saved for formal state dinners. Next to each name card was a menu with the chef responsible for each dish. (Talk about pressure.) While the Hofburg had tableware for 4,000, feeding 3,000 was a typical day. The cellar was stocked with 60,000 bottles of wine. The kitchen was huge—50 birds could be roasted on the hand-driven spits at once.

After a few more rooms and the shop, you're back on the street. Two quick lefts take you back to the palace square (In der Burg), where you can pass through the black, red, and gold gate and to the treasury.

▲▲▲Treasury (Weltliche und Geistliche Schatzkammer)—This Secular and Religious Treasure Room contains the best jewels on the Continent. Slip through the vault doors and reflect on the glitter of 21 rooms filled with scepters, swords, crowns, orbs, weighty robes, double-headed eagles, gowns, gem-studded bangles, and a 2.5-meter-tall (8 feet), 500-year-old unicorn horn (or maybe the tusk of a narwhal)—which was considered incredibly powerful in the old days, giving its owner the grace of God. These were owned by the Holy Roman Emperor—a divine monarch. The well-produced audioguide provides a wealth of information (€7, Wed–Mon 10:00–18:00, closed Tue, follow Schatzkammer signs to the Schweizerhof, tel. 01/533-6046).

Room 2: The personal crown of Rudolf II has survived since 1602 because it was considered too well-crafted to cannibalize for other crowns. This crown is a big deal because it's the adopted crown of the Austrian Empire, established in 1806 after Napoleon dissolved the Holy Roman Empire (so named because it tried to be the grand continuation of the Roman Empire). Pressured by Napoleon, the Austrian Francis II—who had been Holy Roman Emperor—became Francis I, Emperor of Austria. Francis I/II (the stern guy on the wall) ruled from 1792 to 1835. Look at the crown. Its design symbolically merges the typical medieval king's crown and a bishop's miter.

Rooms 3 and 4: These contain some of the coronation vestments and regalia needed for the new Austrian emperor.

Room 5: Ponder the Throne Cradle. Napoleon's son was born in 1811 and made king of Rome. The little eagle at the foot is symbolically not yet able to fly, but glory-bound. Glory is symbolized by the star, with dad's big "N" raised high.

Room 11: The collection's highlight is the 10th-century crown of the Holy Roman Emperor. The imperial crown swirls with symbolism "proving" that the emperor was both holy and Roman. The jeweled arch over the top is reminiscent of the parade helmet of ancient Roman emperors whose successors the HRE claimed to be. The cross on top says the HRE ruled as Christ's representative on earth. King Solomon's portrait (right of cross) is Old Testament proof that kings can be wise and good. King David (next panel) is similar proof that they can be just. The crown's eight sides represent the celestial city of Jerusalem's eight gates. The jewels on the front panel symbolize the Twelve Apostles.

The nearby 11th-century Imperial Cross preceded the emperor in ceremonies. Encrusted with jewels, it carried a substantial chunk of *the* cross and the holy lance (supposedly used to pierce the side of Jesus while on the cross; both items displayed in the same glass case). Look behind the cross to see how it was actually a box that could be clipped open and shut. You can see bits of the "true cross" anywhere, but this is a prime piece—with the actual nail hole.

The other case has jewels from the reign of Karl der Grosse (Charlemagne), the greatest ruler of medieval Europe. Notice

Charlemagne modeling the crown (which was made a hundred years after he died) in the tall painting adjacent.

Room 12: The painting shows the coronation of Josef II in 1764. He's wearing the same crown and royal garb you've just seen.

Room 16: Most tourists walk right by perhaps the most exquisite workmanship in the entire treasury, the royal vestments (15th century). Look closely—they are painted with gold and silver threads.

▲Heroes' Square and the New Palace (Heldenplatz and the Neue Burg)—This last grand addition to the palace, from just before World War I, was built for Franz Ferdinand but never used. (It was tradition for rulers not to move into their predecessor's quarters.) Its grand facade arches around Heldenplatz, or Heroes' Square. Notice statues of the two great Austrian heroes on horseback: Prince Eugene of Savoy (who beat the Turks that had earlier threatened Vienna) and Archduke Charles (first to beat Napoleon in a battle, breaking Nappy's image of invincibility and heralding the end of the Napoleonic age). The frilly spires of Vienna's neo-Gothic city hall break the horizon, and a line of horse-drawn carriages await their customers.

▲▲New Palace Museums: Armor, Music, and Ancient Greek Statues—The Neue Burg—labeled "Kunsthistorisches Museum" because it contains one wing from the main museum across the way—houses three fine museums (same ticket): an armory (with a killer collection of medieval weapons), historical musical instruments, and classical statuary from ancient Ephesus. The included radio headsets bring the exhibits to life and let you actually hear the fascinating old instruments in the collection being played. An added bonus is the chance to wander all alone among those royal Hapsburg halls, stairways, and painted ceilings (€7.50, Wed–Mon 10:00–18:00, closed Tue, almost no tourists).

More Hofburg Sights

These sights are near—and associated with—the palace.

▲Lipizzaner Museum—A must for horse-lovers, this tidy museum in the Renaissance Stallburg Palace shows (and tells in English) the 400-year history of the famous riding school. Lipizzaner fans have a warm spot in their hearts for General Patton, who, at the end of World War II—knowing that the Soviets were about to take control of Vienna—ordered a raid on the stable to save the horses and ensure the survival of their fine old bloodlines. Videos show the horses in action on TVs throughout the museum. The "dancing" originated as battle moves: *pirouette* (quick turns) and *courbette* (on hind legs to make a living shield for the knight). The 45-minute movie in the basement theater also has great horse footage (showings alternate between German and English).

A highlight for many is the opportunity to view the stable from a museum window and actually see the famous white horses just sitting there looking common. Don't bother waving... it's a one-way mirror (€5, daily 9:00–18:00, Reitschulgasse 2 between Josefsplatz and Michaelerplatz, tel. 01/533-7811).

Seeing the Lipizzaner Stallions: Seats for performances by Vienna's prestigious Spanish Riding School book up long in advance, but standing room is usually available the same day (tickets-€22–65, standing room-€18, May–June and Sept–Oct Sun at 10:45, sometimes also Fri at 18:00). Lucky for the masses, training sessions (with music) in a chandeliered Baroque hall are open to the public (€11.60 at the door, roughly Feb–June and Sept–Oct, Tue–Sat 10:00–12:00 when the horses are in town, tel. 01/533-9031, www.spanische-reitschule.com). Tourists line up early at Josefsplatz, gate 2. Save money and avoid the wait by buying the €14.50 combo-ticket that covers both the museum and the training session (and lets you avoid that ticket line). Or, better yet, simply show up late. Tourists line up for hours to get in at 10:00, but almost no one stays for the full two hours—except for the horses. As people leave, new tickets are printed continuously, so you can just waltz in with no wait at all. If you arrive at 10:45, you'll see one group of horses finish and two more perform before they quit at noon.

▲Augustinian Church—The Augustinerkirche (on Josefsplatz) is the Gothic and neo-Gothic church where the Hapsburgs latched, then buried, their hearts (weddings took place here and the royal hearts are in the vault). Don't miss the exquisite, tomb-like Canova memorial (neoclassical, 1805) to Maria Theresa's favorite daughter, Maria Christina, with its incredibly sad, white-marble procession. The church's 11:00 Sunday Mass is a hit with music-lovers—both a Mass and a concert, often with an orchestra accompanying the choir. To pay, contribute to the offering plate and buy a CD afterwards. (Programs are available at the table by the entry all week.)

▲▲Kaisergruft, the Remains of the Hapsburgs—Visiting the imperial remains is not as easy as you might imagine. These original organ donors left their bodies—about 150 in all—in the Kaisergruft (Capuchin Crypt), their hearts in the Augustinian Church (church open daily, but to see the goods you'll have to talk to a priest; Augustinerstrasse 3), and their entrails in the crypt below St. Stephan's Cathedral. Don't tripe.

Upon entering the Kaisergruft (€3.50, daily 9:30–16:00, last entry 15:40, behind Opera on Neuer Markt), see the Capuchin brother at the door and buy the €0.50 map with a Hapsburg family tree and a chart locating each coffin.

The double coffin of Maria Theresa and her husband is worth a close look for its artwork. Maria Theresa outlived her husband by 15 years—which she spent in mourning. Old and fat, she installed a special lift enabling her to get down into the crypt to be with her dead husband (even though he had been far from faithful). The couple recline—Etruscan style—atop their fancy lead coffin. At each corner are the crowns of the Hapsburgs—the Holy Roman Empire, Hungary, Bohemia, and Jerusalem. Notice the contrast between the rococo splendor of Maria Theresa's tomb and the simple box holding her more modest son, Josef II (at his parents' feet). An enlightened monarch, Josef mothballed the too-extravagant Schönbrunn, secularized the monasteries, established religious tolerance within his realm, and freed the serfs. Josef was a model of practicality (he even invented a reusable coffin)—and very unpopular with other royals.

Franz Josef (1830–1916) is nearby in an appropriately austere military tomb. Flanking Franz Josef are the tombs of his son, Rudolf II, and Empress Elizabeth. Rudolf committed suicide in 1898 and—since the Church wouldn't allow such a burial for someone who took his own life—it took considerable legal hair-splitting to win Rudolf this spot (after examining his brain, it was determined that he was physically retarded and therefore incapable of knowingly killing himself). *Kaiserin* Elisabeth (1837–1898), a.k.a. Sissy, always gets the "Most Flowers" award.

In front of those three is the most recent Hapsburg tomb. Empress Zita was buried in 1989. Her burial procession was probably the last such Old Regime event in European history. The monarchy died hard in Austria. Take a whiff. The crypt smells funny and will probably be closed sometime in the near future for restoration and freshening up.

Rather than chasing down all these body parts, remember that the magnificence of this city is the real remains of the Hapsburgs. Pan up. Watch the clouds glide by the ornate gables of Vienna.

▲Imperial Furniture Collection (Kaiserliches Hofmobiliendepot)—Bizarre, sensuous, eccentric, or precious, this is your peek at the Hapsburgs' furniture—from grandma's wheelchair to the emperor's spittoon—all thoughtfully described in English. The Hapsburgs had many palaces, but only the Hofburg was permanently furnished. The rest were furnished on the fly—set up and taken down by a gang of royal roadies called the "Depot of Court Movables" (Hofmobiliendepot). When the monarchy was dissolved in 1918, the state of Austria took possession of the Hofmobiliendepot's inventory—165,000 items. Now this royal storehouse is open to the public in a fine, new, sprawling museum. Don't go here for the Biedermeier or *Jugendstil* furnishings. The older Baroque and rococo pieces are the most impressive and tied most intimately to the royals. Combine a visit to this museum with a stroll down the lively shopping boulevard, Mariahilfer Strasse (€7, Tue–Sun 10:00–18:00, closed Mon, Mariahilfer Strasse 88, tel. 01/5243-3570).

Sights—Schönbrunn Palace

▲▲▲Schönbrunn Palace—Among Europe's palaces, only Schloss Schönbrunn rivals Versailles. Located six kilometers (4 miles) from the center, it was the Hapsburgs' summer residence. It's big—1,441 rooms—but don't worry, only 40 rooms are shown to the public. (The families of 260 civil servants actually rent simple apartments in the rest of the palace.)

While the exterior is Baroque, the interior was finished under Maria Theresa in let-them-eat-cake rococo. The chandeliers are either of hand-carved wood with gold-leaf gilding or of Bohemian crystal. Thick walls hid the servants as they ran around stoking the ceramic stoves from the back, and so on. Most of the public rooms are decorated in neo-Baroque, as they were under Franz Josef (ruled 1848–1916). When WWII bombs rained on the city and the palace grounds, the palace itself took only one direct hit. Thankfully, that bomb, which crashed through three floors—including the sumptuous central ballroom—was a dud.

Reservations and Hours: Schönbrunn suffers from crowds. To avoid the long delays in July and August (mornings are worst), make a reservation by telephone (tel. 01/8111-3239, answered daily 8:00–17:00). You'll get an appointment time and a ticket number. Check in at least 30 minutes early. Upon arrival, go to the group desk, give your number, pick up your ticket, and jump in ahead of the masses. If you show up in peak season without calling first, you deserve the frustration. Wait in line, buy your ticket, and wait until the listed time to enter (which could be tomorrow). Kill time in the gardens or coach museum (palace open April–Oct daily 8:30–17:30, July–Aug until 19:30, Nov–March daily 8:30–16:30). Crowds are worst from 9:30 to 11:30 especially on weekends and in July and August; it's least crowded from 12:00 to 14:00 and after 16:00.

Cost and Tours: The admission price is the price of the tour you select. Choose among two recorded audioguide tours: the Imperial Tour (22 rooms, €8, 50 min, Grand Palace rooms plus apartments of Franz Josef and Elisabeth) or the Grand Tour (40 rooms, €10.50, 75 min, adds apartments of Maria Theresa). The VIP Pass includes the Grand Tour, delightfully painted Bergl rooms, Gloriette viewing terrace, maze, court bakery, and theater (€15, available April–Oct, theater open only mid-June–mid-Sept). I'd go for the Grand Tour.

Getting to Palace: Take tram #58 from Westbahnhof directly to the palace, or ride U-4 to Schönbrunn and walk

400 meters (1,300 feet). The main entrance is in the left side of the palace as you face it.

Coach Museum Wagenburg—The Schönbrunn coach museum is a 19th-century traffic jam of 50 impressive royal carriages and sleighs. Highlights include silly sedan chairs, the death-black hearse carriage (used for Franz Josef in 1916, and most recently for Empress Zita in 1989), and an extravagantly gilded imperial carriage pulled by eight Cinderella horses. This was rarely used other than for the coronation of Holy Roman Emperors, when it was disassembled and taken to Frankfurt for the big event (€4.50, April–Oct daily 9:00–18:00, Nov–March daily10:00–16:00, last entry 30 min before closing time, closed Mon in winter, 200 meters, or 650 feet, from palace, walk through right arch as you face palace, tel. 01/877-3244).

Palace Gardens—After strolling through all the Hapsburgs tucked neatly into their crypts, a stroll through the emperor's garden with countless commoners is a celebration of the natural evolution of civilization from autocracy into real democracy. As a civilization, we're doing well.

The sculpted **gardens** (with a palm house, €3.50, May–Sept daily 9:30–18:00, Oct–April daily 9:30–17:00) lead past Europe's oldest **zoo** (*Tiergarten*, €9, combo-ticket for zoo plus palm house costs €10.50, May–Sept daily 9:00–18:30, less off-season, built by Maria Theresa's husband for the entertainment and education of the court in 1752, tel. 01/877-9294) up to the **Gloriette**, a purely decorative monument celebrating an obscure Austrian military victory and offering a fine city view (viewing terrace-€2.10, included in €15 VIP Pass, April–Sept daily 9:00–18:00, July–Aug until 19:00, Oct until 17:00, closed Nov–March). The park itself is free (daily sunrise to dusk, entrance on either side of the palace). A touristy choo-choo train makes the rounds all day, connecting Schönbrunn's many attractions.

More Sights—Vienna

▲▲▲Kunsthistorisches Museum—This exciting museum, across the Ring from the Hofburg Palace, showcases the great Hapsburg art collection—masterpieces by Dürer, Rubens, Titian, Raphael, and especially Brueghel. There's also a fine display of Egyptian, classical, and applied arts, including a divine golden salt bowl by Cellini. The paintings are well-hung on one glorious floor. Try the very helpful included audioguide (€7.50, higher depending on special exhibitions, Tue–Sun 10:00–18:00, Thu until 21:00, closed Mon, tel. 01/525-240).

▲Natural History Museum—In the twin building facing the art museum, you'll find moon rocks, dinosaur stuff, and the fist-sized

Venus of Willendorf—at 30,000 years old, the world's oldest sex symbol, found in the Danube Valley (€4, Wed–Mon 9:00–18:30, Wed until 21:00, closed Tue, tel. 01/521-770).

MuseumsQuartier—This sprawling collection of blocky, modernist museums is housed within the Baroque facade of the former imperial stables. The centerpiece is the **Leopold Museum**, which features modern Austrian art, including the best collection of works by Egon Schiele (1890–1918) and a few works by Kokoschka and Klimt (€9, Wed–Mon 10:00–19:00, Fri 10:00–21:00, closed Tue, behind Kunsthistorisches Museum, U-2 or U-3: Volkstheater/ Museumsplatz, Museumsplatz 1-5, tel. 01/525-700).

The new **Museum of Modern Art** (Museum Moderner Kunst Stiftung Ludwig, a.k.a. Mumok), also in the MuseumsQuartier, is Austria's leading modern art gallery. Its huge, state-of-the-art building displays revolving exhibits showing off art of the last generation—including Klee, Picasso, and Pop (€6.50, Tue–Sun 10:00–18:00, Thu until 21:00, closed Mon, tel. 01/525-001-440, www.mumok.at). Rounding out the sprawling MuseumsQuartier are an architecture museum, Transeuropa; Electronic Avenue, a children's museum; and the Kunsthalle Wien—an exhibition center for contemporary art. Various combo-tickets are available for those interested in more than just the Leopold Museum (visit www.mqw.at). Walk into the center from the Hofburg side, where the main entrance (with visitor center and info room) leads to a big courtyard with cafés, fountains, and huge lounging sponges surrounded by the quarter's various museums.

▲Academy of Fine Arts—This small but exciting collection includes works by Bosch, Botticelli, and Rubens; a Venice series by Guardi; and a self-portrait by 15-year-old Van Dyck (€3.75, Tue–Sun 10:00–16:00, closed Mon, 3 blocks from Opera at Schillerplatz 3, tel. 01/5881-6225). As you wander the halls of this academy, ponder how history might have been different if Hitler—who applied to study architecture here but was rejected—had been accepted as a student.

▲▲KunstHausWien: Hundertwasser Museum—This "make yourself at home" museum is a hit with lovers of modern art. It mixes the work and philosophy of local painter/environmentalist Hundertwasser. Stand in front of the colorful checkerboard building and consider Hundertwasser's style. He was against "window racism." Neighboring houses allow only one kind of window. $100H_2O$'s are each different—and he encouraged residents to personalize them. He recognized tree tenants as well as human tenants. His buildings are spritzed with a forest and topped with dirt and grassy little parks—close to nature, good for the soul. Floors and sidewalks are irregular—to "stimulate the brain" (although current residents complain it just causes wobbly furniture and sprained ankles). 100H_2O waged a one-man fight—during the 1950s and 1960s, when concrete and glass ruled—to save the human soul from the city. (Hundertwasser claimed that "straight lines are godless.") Inside the museum, start with his interesting biography (which ends in 2000). His fun-loving paintings are half *Jugendstil* (youth style) and half just kids' stuff. Notice the photographs from his 1950s days as part of Vienna's bohemian scene. Throughout the museum, notice the fun philosophical quotes from an artist who believed, "If man is creative, he comes nearer to his creator" (€8 for Hundertwasser Museum, €14 combo-ticket includes special exhibitions, half price on Mon, daily 10:00–19:00, extremely fragrant and colorful garden café, U-3: Landstrasse, Weissgerberstrasse 13, tel. 01/712-0491).

The KunstHausWien provides by far the best look at Hundertwasser. For an actual lived-in apartment complex by the green master, walk five minutes to the one-with-nature **Hundertwasserhaus** (free, at Löwengasse and Kegelgasse). This complex of 50 apartments, subsidized by the government to provide affordable housing, was built in the 1980s as a breath of architectural fresh air in a city of boring, blocky apartment complexes. While not open to visitors, it's worth visiting for its fun-loving and colorful patchwork exterior and the Hundertwasser festival of shops across the street. Don't miss the view from Kegelgasse to see the "tree tenants" and the internal winter garden residents enjoy.

▲Belvedere Palace—This is the elegant palace of Prince Eugene of Savoy—the still-much-appreciated conqueror of the Turks. Eugene, a Frenchman considered too short and too ugly to be in the service of Louis XIV, offered his services to the Hapsburgs. While he was short and ugly indeed, he became the greatest military genius of his age. Today, his palace houses the Austrian Gallery of 19th- and 20th-century art. Skip the lower palace and focus on the garden and the upper palace *(Oberes Belvedere)* for a winning view of the city, a fine collection of *Jugendstil* art, and Vienna's best look at the dreamy work of Gustav Klimt (€7.50, Tue–Sun 10:00–18:00, closed Mon, winter until 17:00, entrance at Prinz Eugen Strasse 27, tel. 01/7955-7134). Your ticket includes the Austrian Baroque and Gothic art in the Lower Palace.

▲▲Haus der Musik—Vienna's House of Music has a small first-floor exhibit on the Vienna Philharmonic, and upstairs you'll enjoy fine audiovisual exhibits on each of the famous hometown boys (Haydn, Mozart, Beethoven, Strauss, and Mahler). But the museum is unique for its effective use of interactive touch-screen computers and headphones to actually explore the physics of sound. You can twist, dissect, and bend sounds to make your own musical language, merging your voice with a duck's quack or a city's traffic roar. Wander through the "sonosphere" and marvel at the amazing acoustics—I could actually hear what I thought only a piano tuner could hear. Pick up a virtual baton to conduct the Vienna Philharmonic Orchestra (each time you screw up, the orchestra stops and ridicules you). Really seeing the place takes time. It's open late and makes a good evening activity (€8.50, €5 for Vienna Philharmonic museum in same building, €10 combo-ticket for both, daily 10:00–22:00, 2 blocks from Opera at Seilerstatte 30, tel. 01/51648, www.hdm.at).

▲Vienna's Auction House, the Dorotheum—For an aristocrat's flea market, drop by Austria's answer to Sotheby's, the Dorotheum. Its five floors of antique furniture and fancy knickknacks have been put up either for immediate sale or auction, often by people who inherited old things they don't have room for (Mon–Fri 10:00–18:00, Sat 9:00–17:00, closed Sun, classy little café on second floor, between Graben and Hofburg at Dorotheergasse 17, tel. 01/515-600). Fliers show schedules for actual auctions, which you are welcome to attend.

Judenplatz Memorial and Museum—Judenplatz marks the location of Vienna's 15th-century Jewish community, one of Europe's largest at the time. The square, once filled with a long-gone synagogue, is now dominated by a blocky memorial to the 65,000 Austrian Jews killed by the Nazis. The memorial—a library turned inside out—symbolizes Jews as "people of the book" and causes one to ponder the huge loss of culture, knowledge, and humanity that took place during 1938 to 1945.

The Judenplatz Museum, while sparse, has displays on medieval Jewish life and a well-done video re-creating community scenes from five centuries ago. Wander the scant remains of the medieval synagogue below street level—discovered during the construction of the Holocaust memorial. This was the scene of a medieval massacre. Since Christians weren't allowed to lend money, Jews were Europe's moneylenders. As so often happened in Europe, when Christian locals fell too deeply into debt, they found a convenient excuse to wipe out the local ghetto—and their debts at the same time. In 1421, 200 of Vienna's Jews were burned at the stake. Others who refused a forced conversion committed mass suicide in the synagogue (€3, €7 combo-ticket includes a synagogue and Jewish Museum of the City of Vienna, Sun–Thu 10:00–18:00, Fri 10:00–14:00, closed Sat, Judenplatz 8, tel. 01/535-0431).

Honorable Mention—There's much, much more. The city map lists everything. If you're into butterflies, Esperanto, undertakers, tobacco, clowns, fire fighting, Freud, or the homes of

Jugendstil

Vienna gave birth to its own curvaceous brand of Art Nouveau around the early 1900s: *Jugendstil* (youth style). The TI has a brochure laying out Vienna's 20th-century architecture. The best of Vienna's scattered *Jugendstil* sights: the Belvedere Palace collection, the clock on Hoher Markt (which does a musical act at noon), and the Karlsplatz metro stop, where you'll find the gilded-cabbage-domed Secession gallery with the movement's slogan: "To each century its art, and to art its liberty." Klimt, Wagner, and friends (who called themselves the Vienna Secession) first exhibited their "liberty-style" art here in 1897.

dead composers, you'll find them all in Vienna. Several good museums that try very hard but are submerged in the greatness of Vienna include: **Jewish Museum of the City of Vienna** (€5.10, or €7 combo-ticket includes synagogue and Judenplatz Museum—listed above, Sun–Fri 10:00–18:00, Thu 10:00–20:00, closed Sat, Dorotheergasse 11, tel. 01/535-0431, www.jmw.at), **Historical Museum of the City of Vienna** (Tue–Sun 9:00–18:00, closed Mon, Karlsplatz), **Folkloric Museum of Austria** (Tue–Sun 10:00–17:00, closed Mon, Laudongasse 15, tel. 01/406-8905), and **Museum of Military History**, one of Europe's best if you like swords and shields (Heeresgeschichtliches Museum, Sat–Thu 9:00–17:00, closed Fri, Arsenal district, Objekt 18, tel. 01/795-610). The vast **Austrian Museum of Applied Arts** (Österreichisches Museum für Angewandte Kunst, or MAK) is Vienna's answer to London's Victoria & Albert collection. The museum shows off the fancies of local aristocratic society, including a fine *Jugendstil* collection (€6.60, €2.20 without exhibition halls, free Sat, open Tue–Sun 10:00–18:00, Tue until 24:00, closed Mon, Stubenring 5, tel. 01/711-360, www.mak.at).

For a walk in the **Vienna Woods**, catch the U-4 metro to Heiligenstadt, then bus #38A to Kahlenberg, for great views and a café overlooking the city. From there, it's a peaceful 45-minute downhill hike to the *Heurigen* of Nussdorf or Grinzing to enjoy some wine (see "Vienna's Wine Gardens," below).

Top People-Watching and Strolling Sights

▲City Park—Vienna's Stadtpark is a waltzing world of gardens, memorials to local musicians, ponds, peacocks, music in bandstands, and locals escaping the city. Notice the *Jugendstil* entry at the Stadtpark metro station. The Kursalon, where Strauss was the violin-toting master of waltzing ceremonies, hosts daily touristy concerts in 3/4 time.

▲**Prater**—Vienna's sprawling amusement park tempts many visitors with its huge 65-meter-high (220-foot), famous, and lazy Ferris wheel *(Riesenrad)*, roller coaster, bumper cars, Lilliputian railroad, and endless eateries. Especially if you're traveling with kids, this is a fun, goofy place to share the evening with thousands of Viennese (daily 9:00–24:00 in summer, U-1: Praterstern). For a local-style family dinner, eat at Schweizerhaus (good food, great beer) or Wieselburger Bierinsel.

Sunbathing—Like most Europeans, the Austrians worship the sun. Their lavish swimming centers are as much for tanning as swimming. To find the scene, follow the locals to their "Danube Sea" and a 30-kilometer (20-mile), skinny, man-made beach along Danube Island. It's traffic-free concrete and grass, packed with in-line skaters and bikers, with rocky river access and a fun park (easy U-bahn access on U-1: Donauinsel).

▲**Naschmarkt**—Vienna's ye olde produce market bustles daily near the Opera along Wienzeile Street. It's likeably seedy and surrounded by sausage stands, Turkish *döner kebab* stalls, cafés, and theaters. Each Saturday, it's infested by a huge flea market where, in olden days, locals would come to hire a monkey to pick little critters out of their hair (Mon–Fri 7:00–18:00, Sat 6:00–13:00, U-4: Kettenbruckengasse). For a picnic park, walk a block down Schleifmuhlgasse.

Summer Music Scene

Vienna is Europe's music capital. It's music *con brio* from October through June, reaching a symphonic climax during the Vienna Festival each May and June. Sadly, in July and August, the Boys' Choir, the Opera, and many more music companies are—like you—on vacation. But Vienna hums year-round with live classical music. In the summer, you have these basic choices:

Touristy Mozart and Strauss Concerts—If the music comes to you, it's touristy—designed for flash-in-the-pan Mozart fans. Powdered-wig orchestra performances are given almost nightly in grand traditional settings (€25–50). Pesky wigged-and-powdered Mozarts peddle tickets in the streets with slick sales pitches about the magic of the venue and the quality of the musicians. Second-rate orchestras, clad in historic costumes, perform the greatest hits of Mozart and Strauss. While there's not a local person in the audience, the tourists generally enjoy the evening. To sort through all your options, check with the ticket office in the TI (same price as on the street but with all venues to choose from).

Strauss Concerts in the Kursalon—For years, Strauss concerts have been held in the Kursalon, where the Waltz King himself directed wildly popular concerts 100 years ago (€24–47, 4 concerts nightly April–Oct, 1 concert nightly other months, tel. 01/512-5790). Shows are a touristy mix of ballet, waltzes, and a 15-piece orchestra in wigs and old outfits. For the cheap option, enjoy a summer afternoon coffee concert (free if you buy a drink weekends and maybe also weekdays July–Aug 15:00–17:00).

Serious Concerts—These events, including the Opera, are listed in the monthly *Programm* (available at TI). Tickets run from €22 to €73 (plus a stiff 22 percent booking fee when booked in advance or through a box office like the one at the TI). If you call a concert hall directly, they can advise you on the availability of (cheaper) tickets at the door. Vienna takes care of its starving artists (and tourists) by offering cheap standing-room tickets to top-notch music and opera (1 hour before show time).

Vienna's **Summer of Music Festival** assures that even from June through September, you'll find lots of great concerts, choirs, and symphonies (special *Klang Bogen* brochure at TI; get tickets at Wien Ticket pavilion off Kärntner Strasse next to Opera House, or go directly to location of particular event; Summer of Music tel. 01/42717).

Musicals—The Wien Ticket pavilion sells tickets to contemporary American and British musicals (such as *Hair* or *Cabaret*—€10–70 with €3 standing room) and offers these tickets at half price at 14:00 the day of the show. Or you can reserve (full-price) tickets for the musicals by calling up to one day ahead (CC, call combined office of the 3 big theaters at tel. 01/58885).

Vienna Boys' Choir—The boys sing (heard but not seen, from a high balcony) at Mass in the Imperial Chapel *(Hofburgkapelle)* of the Hofburg (entrance at Schweizerhof, from Josefs Platz go through tunnel) 9:15–10:30 on Sundays, except in July and August. While seats must be reserved two months in advance (€5–28, tel. 01/533-9927, fax 011-431-533-992-775 from the U.S., or write Hofmusikkapelle, Hofburg-Schweizerhof, 1010 Wien), standing room inside is free and open to the first 60 who line up. Rather than line up early, you can simply swing by and stand in the narthex just outside, where you can hear the boys and see the Mass on a TV monitor. Boys' Choir concerts (on stage in the Konzerthaus) are also given Fridays at 15:30 in May, June, September, and October (€29–32, tel. 01/5880-4141). They're nice kids, but, for my taste, not worth all the commotion. Remember, many churches have great music during Sunday Mass. Just 200 meters (650 feet) from the Boys' Choir chapel, Augustinian Church has a glorious 11:00 service each Sunday.

Vienna's Cafés

In Vienna, the living room is down the street at the neighborhood coffeehouse. This tradition is just another example of Viennese expertise in good living. Each of Vienna's many long-established (and sometimes even legendary) coffeehouses has its individual character (and characters). They offer newspapers, pastries, sofas, elegance, smoky ambience, and "take all the time you want" charm for the price of a cup of coffee. Order it *melange* (with a little milk) or *schwarzer* (black). Rather than buy the *Herald Tribune* ahead of time, buy a cup of coffee and read it for free, Vienna-style.

My favorites are: **Café Hawelka**, with a dark, "brooding Trotsky" atmosphere, paintings by struggling artists who couldn't pay for coffee, a saloon-wood flavor, chalkboard menu, smoked velvet couches, an international selection of newspapers, and a phone that rings for regulars (Wed–Mon 8:00–2:00, Sun from 16:00, closed Tue, just off Graben, Dorotheergasse 6); **Café Central**, with *Jugendstil* decor and great *Apfelstrudel* (high prices and stiff staff, Mon–Sat 8:00–20:00, closed Sun, Herrengasse 14, tel. 01/533-376-326); the **Café Sperl**, dating from 1880 with furnishings identical to the day it opened, from the coat tree to the chairs (Mon–Sat 7:00–23:00, Sun 11:00–20:00 except closed Sun in July–Aug, just off Naschmarkt near Mariahilfer Strasse, Gumpendorfer 11, tel. 01/586-4158); and the basic, untouristy **Café Ritter** (daily 7:30–23:30, Mariahilfer Strasse 73, U-3: Neubaugasse, near several recommended hotels, tel. 01/587-8237).

Vienna's Wine Gardens

The *Heurige* is a uniquely Viennese institution celebrating the *Heurige*, or new wine. When the Hapsburgs let Vienna's vintners sell their own wine tax-free, several hundred families opened *Heurigen* (wine-garden restaurants clustered around the edge of town), and a tradition was born. Today, they do their best to maintain the old-village atmosphere, serving the homemade new wine (the last vintage until November 11, when a new vintage year begins) with light meals and strolling musicians. Most *Heurigen* are decorated with enormous antique presses from their vineyards. Wine gardens might be closed on any given day; always call ahead to confirm if you have your heart set on a particular place. (For a near-*Heurige* experience right downtown, drop by Gigerl Stadtheuriger; see "Eating," below.)

At any *Heurige*, fill your plate at a self-serve cold-cut buffet (€6–9 for dinner). Dishes to look out for: *Stelze* (grilled knuckle of pork), *Fleischlaberln* (fried ground meat patties), *Schinkenfleckerln* (pasta with cheese and ham), *Schmalz* (a spread made with pig fat), *Blunzen* (black pudding . . . sausage made from blood), *Presskopf* (jellied brains and innards), *Liptauer* (spicy cheese spread), *Kornspitz* (wholemeal bread roll), and *Kummelbraten* (crispy roast pork with caraway). Waitresses will then take your wine order (€2.20 per quarter liter, about 8 oz). Many locals claim it takes several years of practice to distinguish between *Heurige* and vinegar.

There are over 1,700 acres of vineyards within Vienna's city limits, and countless *Heurige* taverns. For a *Heurige* evening, rather than go to a particular place, take a tram to the wine-garden district of your choice and wander around, choosing the place with the best ambience.

Getting to the *Heurigen:* You have three options: trams and buses, a 15-minute taxi ride, or a goofy tourist train.

Trams make a trip to the Vienna Woods quick and affordable. The fastest way is to ride U-4 to its last stop, Heiligenstadt, where trams and buses in front of the station fan out to the various neighborhoods. Ride tram D to its end point for Nussdorf. Ride bus #38A for Grinzing and to the Kahlenberg viewpoint—#38A's end station (note that tram #38, different from bus #38A, starts at the Ring and finishes at Grinzing). To get to Neustift am Walde, ride U-6 to Nussdorfer Strasse and catch bus #35A. Connect Grinzing and Nussdorf with bus #38A and tram D (transfer at Grinzingerstrasse).

The Heuriger Express train is tacky but handy and relaxing, chugging you on a circle from Nussdorf through Grinzing and around the Vienna Woods (30 min, 2/hour, April–Oct 14:00–19:00, departs from end station of tram D in Nussdorf, tel. 01/479-2808).

Here are four good Heurige neighborhoods:

Grinzing: Of the many *Heurige* suburbs, Grinzing is the most famous, lively . . . and touristy. Many people precede their visit to Grinzing by riding bus #38A to its end (up to Kahlenberg for a grand Vienna view) and then ride 20 minutes back into the *Heurige* action. From the tram stop (Grinzing), follow Himmelgasse uphill toward the onion-top dome. You'll pass plenty of wine gardens—and tour buses—on your way up. Just past the dome, you'll find the heart of the *Heurige*.

Pfarrplatz: Between Grinzing and Nussdorf, this area features several decent spots, including the famous and touristy **Beethovenhaus** (Mon–Sat 16:00–24:00, Sun 11:00–24:00, bus #38A stop: Fernsprechamt/Heiligenstadt, walk 5 min uphill on Dübling Nestelbachgasse to Pfarrplatz 2, tel. 01/370-3361). Beethoven lived—and composed his Sixth Symphony—here in 1817. He hoped the local spa would cure his worsening deafness. **Weingut and Heuriger Werner Welser,** a block uphill from Beethoven's place, is lots of fun, with music nightly from 19:00 (daily from 15:30, Probusgasse 12, tel. 01/318-9797).

Nussdorf: A less-touristy district—characteristic and popular with locals—Nussdorf has plenty of *Heurige* ambience. Right at the end station of tram D, you'll find three long and skinny places side by side: **Heuriger Kierlinger** (daily 15:30–24:00, Kahlenbergerstrasse 20, tel. 01/370-2264), **Steinschaden** (Mon–Fri 15:00–23:30, Sat 14:30–23:30, Sun 14:30–22:00, Kahlenbergerstrasse 18, tel. 01/370-1375), and **Schübel-Auer Heuriger** (Mon–Sat 16:00–24:00, closed Sun, Kahlenbergerstrasse 22, tel. 01/370-2222). Walk through any of these and you pop out on Kahlenbergerstrasse, where a walk uphill takes you to some more eating and drinking fun: **Bamkraxler** (the tree jumper), the only beer garden amidst all these vineyards. It's a fun-loving, youthful place with fine keg beer and a regular menu, rather than the Heuriger cafeteria line (€6–10 meals, veggie options, Tue–Sun 16:00–24:00, closed Mon, Kahlenbergerstrasse 17, tel. 01/318-8800).

Neustift am Walde: This neighborhood has lots of *Heurigen*, plenty of charm, and the fewest tourists of all (U-6: Nussdorferstrasse, then bus #35A, stop: Neustift am Walde). Leave the bus at the stop. A line of big, venerable places invite you through welcoming arches that lead up terraced backyards filled with rough tables until you hit the actual vineyards. Pop into **Weingut Wolff** (daily from 11:00, Rathstrasse 50, tel. 01/440-3727) and **Fuhrgassl Huber Weingut** (music Tue–Sat 14:00–24:00, Neustift am Walde 68, tel. 01/440-1405) and take your choice. If you want to really be rural—surrounded by vineyards—hike 10 minutes from there to **Weinhof Zimmermann** (daily 15:00–24:00, Mitterwurzergasse 20, tel. 01/440-1207). Find Mitterwurzergasse—the lane behind the two places listed above—and hike to the right. Look for the sign taking you uphill into a farm. There you'll see 50 rough picnic tables between the farmhouse and the vines.

Nightlife

If old music and new wine aren't your thing, Vienna has plenty of alternatives. For an up-to-date rundown on fun after dark, get the TI's free *Ten Good Reasons for Vienna* booklet. An area known as the "Bermuda Dreieck" (Triangle), north of the cathedral between Rotenturmstrasse and Judengasse, is the hot local nightspot, with lots of classy pubs, or *Beisl* (such as Krah Krah, Salzamt, Slammer, and Bermuda Bräu), and music spots. On balmy summer evenings, the liveliest scene is at Danube Island (especially during the Summer Stage festival). If you just want a good movie, the English Cinema Haydn plays three different English-language movies nightly (Mariahilfer Strasse 57, tel. 01/587-2262).

Sleeping in Vienna

(€1 = about $1, country code: 43, area code: 01)

Sleep Code: **S** = Single, **D** = Double/Twin, **T** = Triple, **Q** = Quad, **b** = bathroom, **s** = shower only, **CC** = Credit Cards accepted, **no CC** = Credit Cards not accepted. English is spoken at each place.

To help you sort easily through these listings, I've divided the rooms into three categories based on the price for a standard double room with bath:

Higher Priced—Most rooms more than €110.
Moderately Priced—Most rooms €110 or less.
Lower Priced—Most rooms €75 or less.

Book accommodations by phone a few days in advance. Most places will hold a room without a deposit if you promise to arrive before 17:00. My recommendations stretch mainly from the center, and along the likeable Mariahilfer Strasse, to the Westbahnhof (West Station). Unless otherwise noted, prices include a continental breakfast. Postal code is 1XX0, with XX being the district. Even places with elevators often have a few stairs to climb, too.

Sleeping within the Ring, in the Old City Center

You'll pay extra to sleep in the old center. But if you can afford it, staying here gives you the best classy Vienna experience.

HIGHER PRICED

The first four places are nearest St. Stephan's Cathedral, where the elegance of Old Vienna strums happily over the cobbles. The last one is near the Opera and TI, five minutes from the cathedral.

Pension Pertschy circles an old courtyard and is bigger and more hotelesque than the others listed here. Its 50 rooms are huge, but well-worn and a bit musty. Those on the courtyard are quietest (Sb-€75, Db-€110–135 depending on size, cheaper off-season, extra bed-€30, CC, elevator, U-1 or U-3: Stephensplatz, Hapsburgergasse 5, tel. 01/534-490, fax 01/534-4949, www.pertschy.com, e-mail: pertschy@pertschy.com).

Pension Neuer Markt is a four-star place that feels family-run, with 37 quiet and comfy rooms in a perfectly central locale (Ds-€88, Db-€112, extra bed-€20, CC, elevator, Seilergasse 9, tel. 01/512-2316, fax 01/513-9105, e-mail: hotelpension.neuer.markt@aon.at, SE).

Pension Aviano is another peaceful four-star place, with 17 comfortable rooms on the fourth floor above lots of old center action (Sb-€82, Db-€122, extra bed-€30, CC, elevator, between Neuer Markt and Kärntner Strasse at Marco d'Avianogasse 1, tel. 01/512-8330, fax 01/5128-3306, e-mail: aviano@pertschy.com, SE).

Hotels and Restaurants in Central Vienna

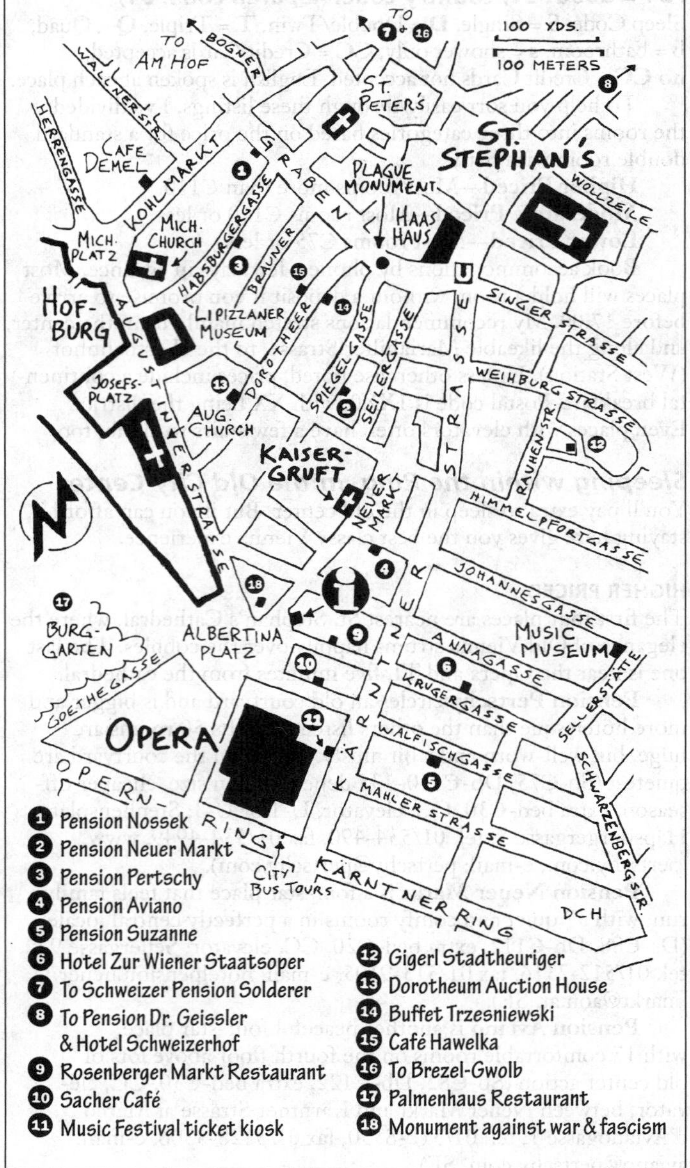

1. Pension Nossek
2. Pension Neuer Markt
3. Pension Pertschy
4. Pension Aviano
5. Pension Suzanne
6. Hotel Zur Wiener Staatsoper
7. To Schweizer Pension Solderer
8. To Pension Dr. Geissler & Hotel Schweizerhof
9. Rosenberger Markt Restaurant
10. Sacher Café
11. Music Festival ticket kiosk
12. Gigerl Stadtheuriger
13. Dorotheum Auction House
14. Buffet Trzesniewski
15. Café Hawelka
16. To Brezel-Gwolb
17. Palmenhaus Restaurant
18. Monument against war & fascism

Hotel Schweizerhof is a classy 55-room place with big rooms, three-star comforts, and a more formal ambience. It's centrally located midway between St. Stephan's Cathedral and the Danube canal, with all its rooms at least four floors above any street noise (Sb-€84–88, Db-€109–124, Tb-€131–146, low prices are for July–Aug and slow times, with cash and this book get your best price and then claim a 10 percent discount, CC, elevator, Bauernmarkt 22, tel. 01/533-1931, fax 01/533-0214, www.schweizerhof.at, e-mail: office@schweizerhof.at, SE).

Hotel zur Wiener Staatsoper (the Schweizerhof's sister hotel) is quiet and rich. Its 22 tight rooms come with high ceilings, chandeliers, and fancy carpets on parquet floors—a good value for this locale, and ideal for people whose hotel tastes are a cut above mine. The singles are tiny, with beds too short for anyone over six feet tall (Sb-€76–88, Db-€109–131, Tb-€131–146, extra bed-€22, prices depend on season, July–Aug and Dec–March are cheaper, CC, elevator, U-1, U-2, or U-4: Karlsplatz, a block from Opera at Krugerstrasse 11, 1010 Wien, tel. 01/513-1274, fax 01/513-127-415, www.zurwienerstaatsoper.at, e-mail: office@zurwienerstaatsoper.at).

MODERATELY PRICED

At **Pension Nossek,** an elevator takes you above any street noise into Frau Bernad's and Frau Gundolf's world, where the children seem to be placed among the lace and flowers by an interior designer. Right on the wonderful Graben, this is a particularly good value (26 rooms, S-€47–54, Ss-€58, Sb-€65–68, Db-€101, €20 extra for sprawling suites, extra bed-€33, no CC, elevator, U-1 or U-3: Stephensplatz, Graben 17, tel. 01/5337-0410, fax 01/535-3646, e-mail: reservation@pension-nossek.at).

Pension Suzanne, Baroque and doily as you'll find in this price range, is wonderfully located a few meters from the Opera. It's quiet and simple, but run with the class of a bigger hotel (Sb-€69, Db-€87–108 depending on size, extra bed-€30, discounts in winter, CC, 28 rooms, elevator, a block from Opera, U-1, U-2, or U-4: Karlsplatz, follow signs for the Opera exit, Walfischgasse 4, 1010 Wien, tel. 01/513-2507, fax 01/513-2500, www.pension-suzanne.at, e-mail: info@pension-suzanne.at).

Schweizer Pension Solderer, family-owned for three generations, is run by sisters Monica and Anita. They run an extremely tight ship (lots of rules), but offer 11 homey rooms, parquet floors, and lots of tourist info (S-€35–42, Ss-€51–55, Sb-€58–62, D-€55–62, Ds-€65–76, Db-€76–87, Tb-€97–100, Qb-€115–125, extra bed-€20, no CC, non-smoking, elevator, laundry-€11/load, U-2 and U-4: Schottenring,

Heinrichsgasse 2, 1010 Wien, tel. 01/533-8156, fax 01/535-6469, e-mail: schweizer.pension@chello.at).

Pension Dr. Geissler has 23 comfortable rooms on the eighth floor of a modern building about 10 blocks northeast of St. Stephan's, near the canal (S-€43, Ss-€58, Sb-€66, D-€58, Ds-€72, Db-€89, 25 percent less in winter, elevator, CC, U-1 and U-4: Schwedenplatz, Postgasse 14, 1010 Wien, tel. 01/533-2803, fax 01/533-2635, e-mail: hotelpension.dr.geissler@aon.at, SE).

Hotels and Pensions along Mariahilfer Strasse

Lively Mariahilfer Strasse connects the West Station and the city center. The U-3 metro line, starting at the Westbahnhof, goes down Mariahilfer Strasse to the cathedral. This very Viennese street is a tourist-friendly and vibrant area filled with local shops and cafés. Most hotels are within a few steps of a metro stop, just one or two stops from the West Train Station (direction from the station: Simmering).

HIGHER PRICED

Astron Suite Hotel Wien consists of two stern, passionless business hotels a few blocks apart on Mariahilfer Strasse, with a complex pricing scheme. Both rent ideal-for-families suites, each with a living room, two TVs, bathroom, desk, and kitchenette (Db suite-€90–170, cheaper Sat–Sun, apartments for 2–3 adults, kids under 12 free, CC, non-smoking rooms, elevator). One hotel is at Mariahilfer Strasse 78 (U-3: Zieglergasse, tel. 01/5245-6000, fax 01/524-560-015) and the other is at Mariahilfer Strasse 32 (U-3: Neubaugasse, tel. 01/521-720, fax 01/521-7215). The Web site for both is www.astron-hotels.de.

MODERATELY PRICED

Pension Mariahilf is a four-star place offering a clean, aristocratic air in an affordable and cozy pension package. Its 12 rooms are spacious and feel new, but with an Art Deco flair. With four stars, everything's done just right. You'll find the latest American magazines and even free Mozart balls at the reception desk (Sb-€59–66, Db-€95–102, Tb-€124, CC, elevator, U-3: Neubaugasse, Mariahilfer Strasse 49, tel. 01/586-1781, fax 01/586-178-122, e-mail: penma@atnet.at, warmly run by Frau and Herr Ender).

Pension Corvinus is bright, modern, and warmly run by Miklos, Judith, and family. Its eight comfortable rooms are spacious, with small yacht-type bathrooms (Sb-€58, Db-€91, Tb-€101, extra bed-€26, CC, portable air-con-€10, elevator, free Internet access, Mariahilfer Strasse 57-59, tel. 01/587-7239, fax 01/587-723-920, www.corvinus.at, e-mail: hotel@corvinus.at). If heading for the Corvinus, don't be pirated by the people in the Haydn Hotel (below).

In the same building, **Haydn Hotel** is a big, fancy place with 40 spacious rooms (Sb-€58–70, Db-€72–100, suites and family apartments, extra bed-€30, CC, elevator, Mariahilfer Strasse 57-59, tel. 01/587-4414, fax 01/586-1950, www.haydn-hotel.at, e-mail: info@haydn-hotel.at).

Beyond its plain lobby, **Hotel Admiral** is a huge, quiet, family-run hotel that has 80 large, comfortable rooms. Alexandra works hard to keep her guests happy, though others on the staff are less friendly (Sb-€66, Db-€91, extra bed-€23, prices promised through 2003 with this book, breakfast-€5, CC, free parking, U-2 or U-3: Volkstheater, a block off Mariahilfer Strasse at Karl Schweighofer Gasse 7, tel. 01/521-410, fax 01/521-4116, www.admiral.co.at, e-mail: hoteladmiralwien@aon.at).

LOWER PRICED

Pension Hargita rents 24 generally small, bright, and tidy rooms (mostly twins) with Hungarian decor (S-€31, Ss-€35, Sb-€52, D-€45, Ds-€52, Db-€60, Ts-€63, Tb-€71, Qb-€87, breakfast-€3, CC but not for 1-night stays, U-3: Zieglergasse, corner of Mariahilfer Strasse and Andreasgasse, Andreasgasse 1, 1070 Wien, tel. 01/526-1928, fax 01/526-0492, www.hargita.at, e-mail: pension@hargita.at, classy Amalia SE).

Two women rent rooms out of their dark and homey apartments in the same building at Lindengasse 39 (1070 Wien, classic old elevator). Each has high ceilings and Old World furnishings, with two cavernous rooms sleeping two to four and a skinny twin room, all sharing one bathroom. These places are great if you're on a tight budget and wish you had a grandmother to visit in Vienna: **Budai Ildiko** lives on the mezzanine level and speaks English (S-€29, D-€44, T-€64, Q-€82, no breakfast but free coffee, no CC, laundry, apt. #5, tel. 01/523-1058, tel. & fax 01/526-2595, e-mail: budai@hotmail.com). **Maria Pribojszki** lives on the first floor (S-€33, D-€48, D for 2 nights-€44, T-€69, Q-€88, breakfast-€4, no CC, no clothes-washing in room, smoky place, apt. #7, tel. 01/523-9006, e-mail: e.boehm@xpoint.at).

K&T Boardinghouse rents four big, comfortable rooms facing the bustling Mariahilfer Strasse above a sex shop (S-€37–44, D-€51, Db-€58, Tb-€77, Qb-€95, 2-night minimum, no breakfast, no CC, non-smoking, free Internet access, 3 flights up, no elevator, Mariahilfer Strasse 72, tel. 01/523-2989, fax 01/522-0345, www.kaled.at, e-mail: kaled@chello.at, Tina SE).

Hilde Wolf, with the help of her grandson Patrick, shares

Vienna: Hotels Outside the Ring

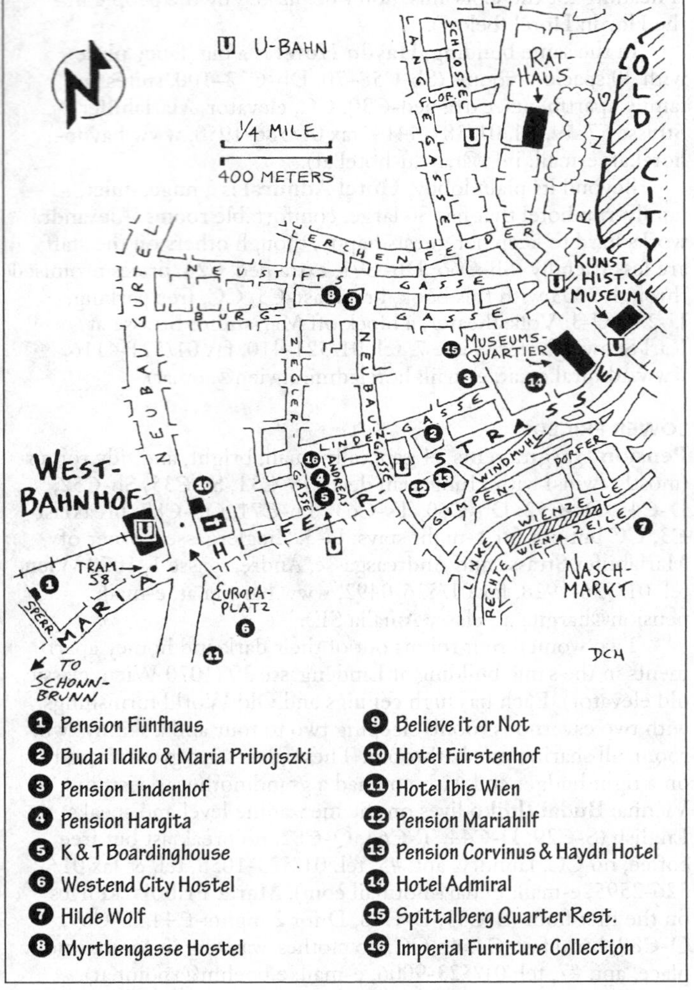

her homey apartment with travelers. Her four huge but stuffy rooms are like old libraries (S-€33, D-€48, T-€70, Q-€90, breakfast-€4, reserve with CC but pay in cash, U-2: Karlsplatz, 3 blocks below Naschmarkt at Schleifmühlgasse 7, 1040 Vienna, tel. 01/586-5103, fax 01/689-3505, www.schoolpool.at/bb, e-mail: santa.claus@aon.at).

Pension Lindenhof rents 19 worn but clean rooms and is filled with plants (S-€29, Sb-€36, D-€48,Db-€64, cheaper in winter, no CC, elevator, U-3: Neubaugasse, Lindengasse 4, 1070 Wien, tel. 01/523-0498, fax 01/523-7362, e-mail: pensionlindenhof@yahoo.com, Zara and Keram SE).

Sleeping near the Westbahnhof Train Station

MODERATELY PRICED

Hotel Ibis Wien, a modern high-rise hotel with American charm, is ideal for anyone tired of quaint old Europe. Its 340 cookie-cutter rooms are bright, comfortable, and modern and have all the conveniences (Sb-€64–69, Db-€84, Tb-€99, breakfast-€9, CC, non-smoking rooms, elevator, parking garage-€10/day, exit Westbahnhof to the right and walk 400 meters, or 1,300 feet, Mariahilfer Gürtel 22-24, A-1060 Wien, tel. 01/59998, fax 01/597-9090, e-mail: h0796@accor-hotels.com).

Hotel Fürstenhof, right across from the station, charges top euro for its 58 spacious but borderline-musty rooms. This venerable hotel has an Old World, maroon-velvet feel (S-€42, Sb-€64–88, D-€60, Db-€104, Tb-€111, Qb-€116, CC, elevator, Europlatz 4, tel. 01/523-3267, fax 01/523-326-726, www.hotel-fuerstenhof.com).

LOWER PRICED

Pension Fünfhaus is big, clean, stark, and quiet. Although the neighborhood is run-down and comes with a few ladies loitering late at night, this place is a good value (S-€29, Sb-€37, D-€44, Db-€51, T-€66, Tb-€72, apartments for 4 people-€88, prices promised through 2003 with this book, no CC, closed mid-Nov–Feb, Sperrgasse 12, 1150 Wien, tel. 01/892-3545 or 01/892-0286, fax 01/892-0460, Frau Susi Tersch). Half the rooms are in the fine main building and half are in the annex, which has good rooms but is near the train tracks and a bit scary on the street at night. From the station, ride tram #52 or #58 two stops down Mariahilfer Strasse to Kranzgasse stop, backtrack two blocks to Sperrgasse.

Cheap Dorms and Hostels near Mariahilfer Strasse

Believe It or Not is a tiny, basic place with two coed rooms for up to 10 travelers and the cheapest beds in town. Hardworking and friendly Gosha warns that this place is appropriate only for the young at heart. It's locked up from 10:00 to 12:30, has kitchen facilities, and has no curfew (bed-€12.50, €9 Nov–Easter, no CC, Myrthengasse 10, ring apt. #14, tel. 01/526-4658, e-mail: believe_it_or_not_vienna@hotmail.com, SE).

Jugendherberge Myrthengasse is a well-run youth hostel (250 beds-€15–17 each in 3- to 6-bed rooms, includes sheets and breakfast, nonmembers-€3.50 extra, CC, some private rooms for couples and families, Myrthengasse 7, 1070 Wien, tel. 01/523-6316, fax 01/523-5849, e-mail: hostel@chello.at).

Other hostels with €14 beds near Mariahilfer Strasse are **Wombats City Hostel** (Grangasse 6, tel. 01/897-2336, e-mail: wombats@chello.at) and **Hostel Ruthensteiner** (Robert-Hamerling-Gasse 24, tel. 01/893-4202, e-mail: info@hostelruthensteiner.com).

Westend City Hostel, just a block from the West Station and Mariahilfer Strasse, is new, with 180 beds in 2- to 12-bed dorms (€15–19 per bed including sheets, breakfast, and a locker, no CC, Fuegergasse 3, tel. 01/597-6729, fax 01/597-672-927, www.westendhostel.at, e-mail: westendcityhostel@aon.at, SE).

Eating in Vienna

The Viennese appreciate the fine points of life, and right up there with waltzing is eating. The city has many atmospheric restaurants. As you ponder the Slavic and eastern European specialties on menus, remember that Vienna's diverse empire may be gone, but its flavor lingers.

While cuisines are routinely named for countries, Vienna claims to be the only *city* with a cuisine of its own: Vienna soups come with fillings (semolina dumpling, liver dumpling, or pancake slices). *Gulasch* is a beef ragout of Hungarian origin (spiced with onion and paprika). Of course, Vienna Schnitzel (Wiener schnitzel) is a breaded and fried veal cutlet. Another meat specialty is boiled beef *(Tafelspitz)*. While you're sure to have *Apfelstrudel*, try the sweet cheese strudel, too (*Topfenstrudel*, wafer-thin strudel pastry filled with sweet cheese and raisins).

On nearly every corner, you can find a colorful *Beisl* (Viennese tavern) filled with poetry teachers and their students, couples loving without touching, housewives on their way home from cello lessons, and waiters who enjoy serving hearty food and good drink at an affordable price. Ask at your hotel for a good *Beisl*.

Wherever you're eating, some vocabulary will help. Try the *grüner Veltliner* (dry white wine), *Traubenmost* (a heavenly grape juice—alcohol-free but on the verge of wine), *Most* (the same thing but lightly alcoholic), and *Sturm* (stronger than *Most*, autumn only). The local red wine (called *Portugieser*) is pretty good. Since the Austrian wine is often sweet, remember the word *trocken* (dry). You can order your wine by the *Viertel* (quarter liter, 8 oz) or *Achtel* (eighth liter, 4 oz). Beer comes in a *Krügel* (half liter, 17 oz) or *Seidel* (0.3 liter, 10 oz).

Eating near St. Stephan's Cathedral

All of these places are within a five-minute walk of the cathedral.

Gigerl Stadtheuriger offers a near-*Heurige* experience (à la Grinzing, see "Vienna's Wine Gardens," above), often with accordion or live music—without leaving the city center. Just point to what looks good. Food is sold by the weight; 200 grams is about a quarter of a pound (cheese and cold meats cost about €2.50–5 per 100 grams, salads are about €2 per 100 grams; price sheet is posted on the wall to right of buffet line, 10 *dag* equals 100 grams). They also have menu entrées, along with spinach strudel, quiche, *Apfelstrudel*, and, of course, casks of new and local wines. Meals run from €7 to €11 (daily 16:00–24:00, indoor/outdoor seating, behind cathedral, a block off Kärntner Strasse, a few cobbles off Rauhensteingasse on Blumenstock, tel. 01/513-4431).

The next five places are within a block of Am Hof square (U-3: Herrengasse). **Restaurant Ofenloch** serves good, old-fashioned Viennese cuisine with friendly service, both indoors and out. This 300-year-old eatery, with great traditional ambience, is central, but not overrun with tourists (€15–22 meals, Tue–Sat 11:30–24:00, closed Sun–Mon, Kurrentgasse 8, tel. 01/533-8844). **Brezel-Gwölb**, a wonderfully atmospheric wine cellar with outdoor dining on a quiet square, serves delicious light meals, fine *Krautsuppe*, and old-fashioned local dishes. It's ideal for a romantic late-night glass of wine (daily 11:30–24:00, take Drahtgasse 20 meters, or 65 feet, off Am Hof, Ledererhof 9, tel. 01/533-8811). Around the corner, **Zum Scherer Sitz und Stehbeisl** is just as untouristy, with indoor or outdoor seating, a soothing woody atmosphere, intriguing decor, and local specialties (Mon–Sat 11:30–22:00, closed Sun, near Am Hof, Judenplatz 7, tel. 01/533-5164). Just below Am Hof, **Stadtbeisl** offers a good mix of value, local cuisine, and atmosphere (daily 10:00–24:00, Naglergasse 21, tel. 01/533-3507). Around the corner, the ancient and popular **Esterhazykeller** has traditional fare deep underground or outside on a delightful square (Mon–Fri 11:00–23:00, Sat–Sun 16:00–23:00, self-service buffet in lowest cellar or from menu, Haarhof 1, tel. 01/533-2614).

These wine cellars are fun and touristy but typical, in the old center, with reasonable prices and plenty of smoke: **Melker Stiftskeller**, less touristy, is a *Stadtheurige* in a deep and rustic cellar with hearty, inexpensive meals and new wine (Tue–Sat 17:00–24:00, closed Sun–Mon, between Am Hof and Schottentor metro stop at Schottengasse 3, tel. 01/533-5530). **Zu den Drei Hacken** is famous for its local specialties (Mon–Sat 10:00–24:00, closed Sun, indoor/outdoor seating, CC, Singerstrasse 28).

Wrenkh Vegetarian Restaurant and Bar is popular for its

high vegetarian cuisine. Chef Wrenkh offers daily lunch menus (€8–10) and dinner plates (€8–11) in a bright, mod bar or in a dark, smoke-free, fancier restaurant (daily 11:30–24:00, Bauernmarkt 10, tel. 01/533-1526).

Buffet Trzesniewski is an institution—justly famous for its elegant and cheap finger sandwiches and small beers (€0.75 each). Three different sandwiches and a *kleines Bier (Pfiff)* make a fun, light lunch. Point to whichever delights look tasty and pay for them and a drink. Take your drink tokens to the lady on the right. Sit on the bench and scoot over to a tiny table when a spot opens up (Mon–Fri 8:30–19:30, Sat 9:00–17:00, closed Sun, 50 meters, or 165 feet, off Graben, nearly across from brooding Café Hawelka, Dorotheergasse 2, tel. 01/512-3291). This is a good opportunity to try the fancy grape juices—*Most* or *Traubenmost* (see above).

Julius Meinl am Graben has been famous since 1862 as a top-end delicatessen with all the gourmet fancies (including a highly rated restaurant upstairs, shop open Mon–Sat 8:00–19:30, restaurant later, Am Graben 19, tel. 01/532-3334).

Akakiko Sushi: If you're just schnitzeled out, this small chain of Japanese restaurants with an easy sushi menu may suit you. Three locations are very convenient: Singerstrasse 4 (a block off Kärntner Strasse near the cathedral), Heidenschuss (near other recommended eateries just off Am Hof), and Mariahilfer Strasse 40 (near many recommended hotels). The Bento "box" meals are great (daily 10:00–24:00, tel. 01/533-8514).

Ice Cream! For a gelato treat or fancy dessert with a mob of happy Viennese, stop by the thriving **Zanoni & Zanoni** (daily 7:00–24:00, 2 blocks up Rotenturmstrasse from cathedral at Lugeck 7, tel. 01/512-7979).

Eating near the Opera

Cafe Restaurant Palmenhaus, overlooking the palace garden *(Burggarten)*, tucked away in a green and peaceful corner two blocks behind the Opera in the Hofburg's backyard, is a world apart. If you want to eat modern Austrian cuisine with palm trees rather than tourists, this is it. And at the edge of a huge park, it's great for families (€11 lunches, €15 dinners, daily 10:00–2:00, serious vegetarian dishes, fish, and an extensive wine list, indoors in greenhouse or outdoors, at Burggarten, tel. 01/533-1033). While nobody goes to the Palmenhaus for good prices, the **Palmenhaus BBQ**—a cool parkside outdoor pub just below that uses the same kitchen—is a wonderful value with more casual service (summer Wed–Sun from 20:00, closed Mon–Tue, informal with €8 BBQ and meals posted on chalkboard).

Rosenberger Markt Restaurant is my favorite for a fast,

light, and central lunch. Just a block toward the cathedral from the Opera, this place—while not cheap—is brilliant. Friendly and efficient, with special theme rooms for dining, it offers a fresh, smoke-free, and healthy cornucopia of food and drink (daily 10:30–23:00, lots of fruits, veggies, fresh-squeezed juices, addictive banana milk, ride the glass elevator downstairs, Maysedergasse 2, tel. 01/512-3458). You can stack a small salad or veggie plate into a tower of gobble for €2.50.

Eating in the Spittelberg Quarter

A charming cobbled grid of traffic-free lanes and Biedermeier apartments has become a favorite place for Viennese wanting a little dining charm between the MuseumsQuartier and Mariahilfer Strasse (handy to many recommended hotels; take Stiftgasse from Mariahilfer Strasse, or wander over here after you close down the Kunsthistorisches or Leopold Museum). Tables tumble down sidewalks and into breezy courtyards filled with appreciative locals enjoying dinner or a relaxing drink. Stroll Spittelberggasse, Schrankgasse, and Gutenberggasse and pick your favorite place. Check out the courtyard inside Spittelberggasse 3, and don't miss the vine-strewn wine garden inside Schrankgasse 1. I ate well and cheaply at **Plutzer Bräu** (daily 11:00–24:00, good daily specials and beer from the keg, Schrankgasse 4, tel. 01/526-1215). For traditional Viennese cuisine with tablecloths, consider the classier **Witwe Bolte** (daily 11:30–24:00, Gutenberggasse 13, tel. 01/523-1450).

Eating near Mariahilfer Strasse

Mariahilfer Strasse is filled with reasonable cafés serving all types of cuisine. **Restaurant Beim Novak** serves good local cuisine away from the modern rush (Mon–Sat 11:30–14:30 & 18:00–24:00, closed Sun, a block down Andreasgasse from Mariahilfer Strasse at Richtergasse 12, tel. 01/523-3244).

Naschmarkt is Vienna's best Old World market, with plenty of fresh produce, cheap local-style eateries, cafés, and *döner kebab* and sausage stands (Mon–Fri 7:00–18:00, Sat until 12:00, closed Sun).

Transportation Connections—Vienna

Vienna has two main train stations: the Westbahnhof (West Train Station), serving Munich, Salzburg, Melk, and Budapest; and the Südbahnhof (South Train Station), serving Italy, Budapest, and Prague. A third station, Franz Josefs, serves Krems and the Danube Valley (but Melk is served by the Westbahnhof). Metro line U-3 connects the Westbahnhof with the center, tram D takes you from the Südbahnhof and the Franz Josefs station to downtown, and tram #18 connects West and South stations. Train info: tel. 051717 (wait through long German recording for operator).

By train to: Melk (hrly, 75 min, sometimes change in St. Pölten), **Krems** (hrly, 1 hr), **Salzburg** (hrly, 3 hrs), **Innsbruck** (every 2 hrs, 5.5 hrs), **Budapest** (6/day, 3 hrs), **Prague** (4/day, 4.5 hrs), **Munich** (hrly, 5.25 hrs, change in Salzburg, a few direct trains), **Berlin** (2/day, 10 hrs, longer on night train), **Zurich** (3/day, 9 hrs), **Rome** (1/day, 13.5 hrs), **Venice** (3/day, 7.5 hrs, longer on night train), **Frankfurt** (4/day, 7.5 hrs), **Amsterdam** (1/day, 14.5 hrs).

To Eastern Europe: Vienna is the springboard for a quick trip to Prague and Budapest—three hours by train from Budapest (€27 one-way, €54 round-trip, free with Eurail) and four hours from Prague (€35 one-way, €75 round-trip, €51.60 round-trip with Eurail). Americans don't need a visa to enter the Czech Republic, but Canadians do. Purchase tickets at most travel agencies. Eurail passholders bound for Prague must pay to ride the rails in the Czech Republic; for details, see "Transportation Connections" in the Berlin chapter.

Route Tips for Drivers

Driving in and out of Vienna: Navigating in Vienna isn't bad. Study the map. As you approach from Krems, you'll cross the North Bridge and land on the Gürtel, or outer ring. You can continue along the Danube canal to the inner ring, called the Ringstrasse (clockwise traffic only). Circle around either thoroughfare until you reach the "spoke" street you need.

Vienna West to Hall in Tirol (450 km/280 miles): To leave Vienna, follow the signs past the Westbahnhof to Schloss Schönbrunn (Schönbrunn Palace), which is directly on the way to the West A-1 autobahn to Linz. Leave the palace by 15:00, beating rush hour, and follow autobahn signs to West A-1, passing Linz and Salzburg, nipping through Germany, and turning right onto Route 93 in the direction of Kufstein, Innsbruck, and Austria at the Dreieck Inntal (autobahn intersection). Crossing back into Austria, you'll follow the scenic Inn River valley until you stop eight kilometers (5 miles) east of Innsbruck at Hall in Tirol. There's an autobahn tourist information station just before Hall (in season daily 10:00–22:00, works for the town's hotels but still helpful).

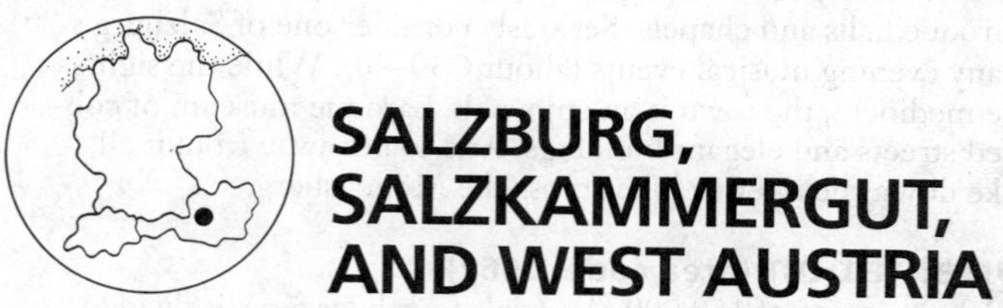

SALZBURG, SALZKAMMERGUT, AND WEST AUSTRIA

Enjoy the sights, sounds, and splendor of Mozart's hometown, Salzburg, then commune with nature in the Salzkammergut, Austria's *Sound of Music* country. Amid hills alive with the S.O.M., you'll find the tiny town of Hallstatt, pretty as a postcard (and not much bigger). Farther west, the Golden Roof of Innsbruck glitters—but you'll strike it rich in neighboring Hall, which has twice the charm and none of the tourist crowds. These are the highlights of Austria's Tirol.

SALZBURG

Salzburg is forever smiling to the tunes of Mozart and *The Sound of Music*. Thanks to its charmingly preserved old town, splendid gardens, Baroque churches, and Europe's largest intact medieval fortress, Salzburg feels made for tourism. It's a museum city with class. Vagabonds wish they had nicer clothes.

But even without Mozart and the von Trapps, Salzburg is steeped in history. In about A.D. 700, Bavaria gave Salzburg to Bishop Rupert for his promise to Christianize the area. Salzburg remained an independent state until Napoleon came (around 1800). Thanks in part to its formidable fortress, Salzburg managed to avoid the ravages of war for 1,200 years . . . until World War II. Half the town was destroyed by WWII bombs, but the historic old town survived.

Eight million tourists crawl its cobbles each year. That's a lot of Mozart balls—and all that popularity has led to a glut of businesses hoping to catch the tourist dollar. Still, Salzburg is a must.

Planning Your Time

While Vienna measures much higher on the Richter scale of sightseeing thrills, Salzburg is simply a touristy, stroller's delight.

If you're going into the nearby Salzkammergut lake country, skip the *Sound of Music* tour—if not, allow half a day for it. The *S.O.M.* tour kills a nest of sightseeing birds with one ticket (city overview, *S.O.M.* sights, and a fine drive through the lakes). You'll probably need two nights for Salzburg; nights are important for swilling beer in atmospheric local gardens and attending concerts in Baroque halls and chapels. Seriously consider one of Salzburg's many evening musical events (about €30–40). While the sights are mediocre, the town is an enjoyable Baroque museum of cobbled streets and elegant buildings. And to get away from it all, bike down the river or hike across the Mönchsberg.

Orientation (area code: 0662)

Salzburg, a city of 150,000 (Austria's fourth largest), is divided into old and new. The old town, sitting between the Salzach River and the 480-meter-high (1,600-foot) hill called Mönchsberg, holds nearly all the charm and most of the tourists.

Tourist Information: Salzburg's many TIs are helpful. There's one at the train station (April–Sept daily 8:45–19:45, Oct–March daily 8:45–19:00), on Mozartplatz in the old center (daily 9:00–19:00 in summer, closes at 18:00 off-season), on freeway exits, and at the airport (tel. 0662/889-870 or 0662/8898-7330, www.salzburginfo.or.at). At any TI, you can pick up a city map (€0.75, free at most hotels), a list of sights with current hours, and a schedule of events. Book a concert upon arrival. The TIs also book rooms (€2.25 fee for up to 2 people, or €4.40 for 3 people or more).

Salzburg Card: The TI sells a Salzburg Card, which covers all your public transportation (including elevator and funicular) and admission to all the city sights (including Hellbrunn Palace). The card is pricey (€18/24 hrs, €26/48 hrs), but if you'd like to pop into all the sights without concern for the cost, this can save money and enhance your experience.

Arrival in Salzburg

By Train: The little Salzburg station is user-friendly. The TI is at track 2A. Downstairs at street level, you'll find a place to store your luggage, buy tickets, and get train information. Bike rental is nearby (see below). The bus station is across the street (where buses #1, #5, #6, #51, and #55 go to the old center; get off at the first stop after you cross the river for most sights and city center hotels, or just before the bridge for Linzergasse hotels). Figure €6.50 for a taxi to the center. To walk downtown (15 min), leave the station ticket hall to the left and walk straight down Rainerstrasse, which leads under the tracks past Mirabellplatz, turning into Dreitaltigkeitsgasse. From here, you can turn left

Salzburg

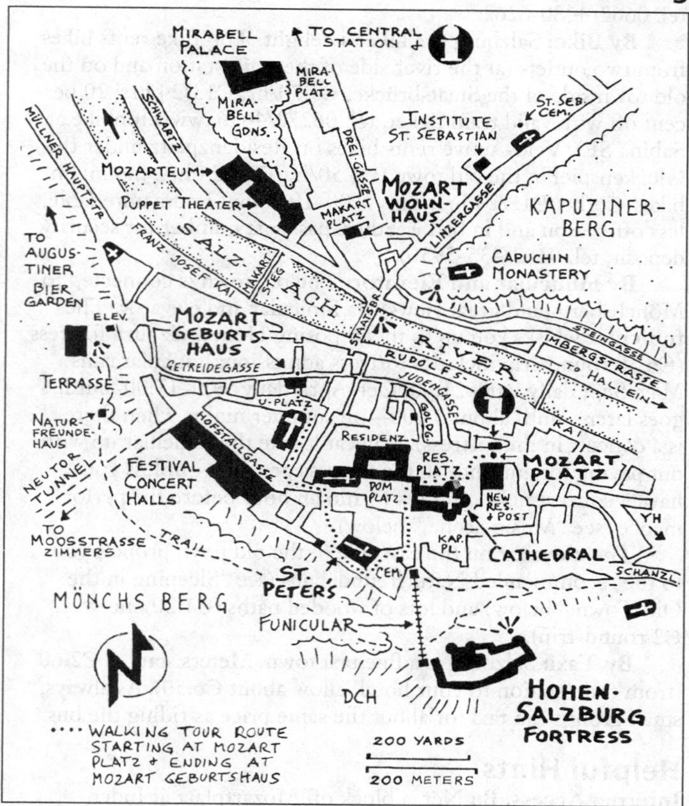

onto Linzergasse for many of the recommended hotels or cross the Staatsbrücke (bridge) for the old town (and more hotels). For a more dramatic approach, leave the station the same way but follow the tracks to the river, turn left, and walk the riverside path toward the fortress.

By Car: Follow *Zentrum* signs to the center and park short-term on the street or longer under Mirabellplatz. Ask at your hotel for suggestions.

Getting around Salzburg

By Bus: Single-ride tickets are sold on the bus for €1.70. Cheaper single tickets and €3.20 day passes called *Tageskarte* (good for 1 calendar day only) are sold at *Tabak* shops. To signal the driver you want to get off, press the buzzer on the pole. Bus info: tel. 0662/4480-6262.

By Bike: Salzburg is a biker's delight. Top Bike rents bikes from two outlets (at the river side of the train station and on the old town side of the Staatsbrücke, €3.70/hr, €13/24 hrs, 20 percent off with valid train ticket, tel. 06272/4656, www.topbike.at, Sabina SE). Velo-Active rents bikes on Residenzplatz under the Glockenspiel in the old town (€4.50/hr, €15/24 hrs, mountain bikes-€6/hr, €18/24 hrs, daily 9:00–19:00 but hours unreliable, less off-season and in bad weather, passport number for security deposit, tel. 0662/435-5950).

By Funicular and Elevator: The old town is connected to Mönchsberg (and great views) via funicular and elevator. The **funicular** whisks you up to the imposing Hohensalzburg fortress (€6.50 round-trip includes fortress admission; funicular runs May–Sept daily 9:00–21:00, Oct–April daily 9:00–17:00, but lift goes later—until about 22:00—on summer nights when there is a concert in the fortress). You can't take the funicular up without paying for entrance to the fortress grounds—unless you have a concert ticket and it's within an hour before the performance (see "Music Scene," below).

The **elevator** on the east side of the old town propels you to the recommended Naturfreundehaus (see "Sleeping in the Old Town," below) and lots of wooded paths (€1.20 one-way, €2 round-trip).

By Taxi: Salzburg is a fine taxi town. Meters start at €2.60 (from train station to your hotel, allow about €6.50). As always, small groups can taxi for about the same price as riding the bus.

Helpful Hints

Internet Access: BigNet, a block off Mozartplatz at Judengasse 5, has 33 terminals (€7.40/hr, daily 9:00–22:00). The Internet Café is on Mozartplatz next to the TI (€9/hr, daily 10:00–24:00, off-season until 23:00, 12 terminals, Mozartplatz 5, tel. 0662/844-822).

Guide Association: Salzburg's many guides can give you a good three-hour walk through town for €120 (tel. 0662/840-406). Barbel Schalber, who enjoys leaving the touristy places, offers my readers a two-hour walk packed with information and spicy opinions for €75 per family or group (tel. 0662/632-225, e-mail: baxguide@utanet.at).

American Express: AmEx has travel agency services, but doesn't sell train tickets—and it charges no commission to cash AmEx checks (Mon–Fri 9:00–17:30, closed Sat–Sun, Mozartplatz 5, A-5010 Salzburg, tel. 0662/8080).

Self-Guided Old Town Walking Tour

The tourist office offers two-language, one-hour guided walks of the old town. They are informative and worthwhile if you don't mind listening to a half hour of German (€8, daily at 12:15, not on Sun in winter, start at TI on Mozartplatz, tel. 0662/8898-7330—just show up and pay the guide). But you can easily do it on your own.

Here's a basic old-town orientation walk, worth ▲▲▲. Start on Mozartplatz in the old town.

Mozartplatz—This square features a statue of Mozart erected in 1842. Mozart spent much of his first 20 years (1756–1777) in Salzburg, the greatest Baroque city north of the Alps. But the city's much older. The Mozart statue actually sits on bits of Roman Salzburg. And the pink church of St. Michael overlooking the square is from A.D. 800. The first Salzburgers settled right around here. Surrounding you are Café Glockenspiel, the Internet Café, the American Express office, and the tourist information office with a concert box office. Just around the downhill corner is a pedestrian bridge leading over the Salzach River to the quiet, most medieval street in town, Steingasse (see "Sights—Across the River," below). Walk toward the cathedral and into the big square with the huge fountain.

Residenz Platz—Salzburg's energetic Prince-Archbishop Wolf Dietrich (who ruled from 1587–1612) was raised in Rome, counted the Medicis as his buddies, and had grandiose Italian ambitions for Salzburg. After a convenient fire destroyed the cathedral, he set about building "the Rome of the North." This square, with his new cathedral and palace, was the centerpiece of his Baroque dream city. A series of interconnecting squares—like you'll see nowhere else—lead from here through the old town.

For centuries, Salzburg's leaders were both important church officials and princes of the Holy Roman Empire, hence the title "Prince-Archbishop"—mixing sacred and secular authority. Wolf Dietrich misplayed his power and spent his last five years imprisoned in the Salzburg castle.

The fountain is as Italian as can be, with a Triton matching Bernini's famous Triton Fountain in Rome. Lying on a busy trade route to the south, Salzburg was well aware of the exciting things going on in Italy. Things Italian were respected (as in colonial America, when a bumpkin would "stick a feather in his cap and call it macaroni"). Local artists even Italianized their names in order to raise their rates.

Residenz—Dietrich's skippable palace is connected to the cathedral by a skyway. A series of ornately decorated rooms and an art gallery are open to visitors with time to kill (€7.50 includes both palace and gallery with audioguide, €4.75 for picture gallery only, daily 10:00–17:00, tel. 0662/8042-2690).

Opposite the old Residenz is the new Residenz, which has long been a government administration building. Today, it houses the central post office and the Heimatwerk, a fine shop showing off all the best local handicrafts (Mon–Fri 9:00–18:00, Sat 9:00–13:00, closed Sun). Atop the new Residenz is the famous…

Glockenspiel—This bell tower has a carillon of 35 17th-century bells (cast in Antwerp) that chimes throughout the day and plays tunes (appropriate to the month) at 7:00, 11:00, and 18:00. There was a time when Salzburg could afford to take tourists to the top of the tower to actually see the big barrel with adjustable tabs turn (like a giant music box mechanism)…pulling the right bells in the right rhythm. Notice the ornamental top: an upside-down heart in flames surrounding the solar system (symbolizing that God loves all of creation).

Look back, past Mozart's statue, to the 1,266-meter-high (4,220-foot) Gaisberg—the forested hill with the television tower. A road leads to the top for a commanding view. Its summit is a favorite destination for local nature-lovers (by city bus or bike). Walk under the Prince-Archbishop's skyway and step into Domplatz, the cathedral square.

Salzburg Cathedral—Built in the 17th century, this was one of the first Baroque buildings north of the Alps. It was built during the Thirty Years' War to emphasize Salzburg's commitment to the Roman Catholic cause and the power of the Church here. Salzburg's archbishop was technically the top papal official north of the Alps (donation requested, May–Oct Mon–Sat 9:00–18:30, Sun 13:00–18:30, Nov–April Mon–Sat 10:00–17:00, Sun 13:00–17:00). The dates on the iron gates refer to milestones in the church's history: In 774, the previous church (long since destroyed) was founded by St. Virgil, to be replaced in 1628 by the church you see today. In 1959, the reconstruction was completed after a WWII bomb blew through the dome.

Wander inside. Built in just 14 years (1614–1628), the church boasts harmonious architecture. When the pope visited in 1998, 5,000 people filled the cathedral (dimensions: 100 meters/330 feet long and 70 meters/230 feet tall). The baptismal font (dark bronze, left of the entry) is from the previous cathedral (c. 1320). Mozart was baptized here (Amadeus means "beloved by God"). Gape up. The interior—with its five independent organs—is marvelous. Concert and Mass schedules are posted at the entrance; the Sunday Masses at 10:00 and 11:30 are famous for their music. Mozart, who worked here as the organist for two years, would advise you that the acoustics are best in pews immediately under the dome.

Under the skyway, a stairway leads down to the *Domgrabungen*, an **excavation site** under the church with a few second-century Christian Roman mosaics and the foundation stones of the previous Romanesque and Gothic churches (€1.80, May–Oct Wed–Sun 9:00–17:00, closed Mon–Tue, closed Nov–April, 0662/845-295). The **Cathedral Museum** (Dom Museum) has a rich collection of church art (entry at portico).

From Cathedral Square to St. Peter's: The cathedral square is surrounded by "ecclesiastical palaces." The statue of Mary (1771) is looking away from the church, but, if you stand in the rear of the square immediately under the middle arch, you'll see how she's positioned to be crowned by the two angels on the church facade.

From the cathedral, walk toward the fortress into the next square (passing the free underground public WCs and the giant chessboard) to the pond. This was a horse bath, the 18th-century equivalent of a car wash. Notice the puzzle above it—the artist wove the date of the structure into a phrase. It says, "Leopold the Ruler Built Me," using the letters LLDVICMXVXI, which total 1732—the year it was built. A small road (back by the chessboard) leads uphill to the fortress (and fortress lift). The stage is set up for the many visiting choirs who are unable to line up a gig. They are welcome to sing here anytime at all. Leave the square through a gate on the right that reads "St. Peter." It leads to a waterfall and St. Peter's Cemetery.

The **waterfall** is part of a canal system that has brought water into Salzburg from Berchtesgaden, 25 kilometers (16 miles) away, since 1150. The stream, divided from here into smaller canals, was channeled through town to power factories (more than 100 water-mill-powered firms as late as the 19th century), provide fire protection, and flush out the streets (Sat morning was flood-the-streets day). Drop into the traditional **bakery** at the waterfall. It's hard to beat their rock-like *Roggenbrot* (sold Thu–Tue 7:00–17:30 except Sat mornings, closed Wed). Then step into the cemetery *(Katakomben)*.

St. Peter's Cemetery—This collection of lovingly tended mini-gardens is butted up against the Mönchberg's rock wall (April–Sept daily 6:30–19:00, Oct–March daily 6:30–18:00). Iron crosses were much cheaper than stone tombstones. The graves are cared for by relatives. (In Austria, grave sites are rented, not owned. Rent bills are sent out every 10 years. If no one cares enough to make the payment, you're gone.) Look up the cliff. Medieval hermit monks lived in the hillside—but "catacombs" they're not. For €1, you can climb lots of steps to see a few old caves, a chapel, and some fine views (May–Sept Tue–Sun 10:30–17:00, closed Mon, Oct–April Wed–Sun 10:30–15:30, closed Mon–Tue). While the cemetery the von Trapp family hid out in was actually in Hollywood, it was inspired by this one. Walk through the cemetery (silence is requested) and out the opposite end. Drop into St. Peter's Church, a Romanesque basilica done up beautifully Baroque. Continue through the arch opposite the church entry and through a modern courtyard (past dorms for student monks).

Toscanini Hof faces the 1925 Festival Hall. Its three halls seat 5,000. This is where the nervous Captain von Trapp waited before walking onstage to sing "Edelweiss" just before he escaped with Maria and his family to Switzerland. On the left is the city's 1,500-space, inside-the-mountain parking lot; ahead behind the Felsen Keller sign is a tunnel (generally closed) leading to the actual concert hall; and to the right is the backstage of a smaller hall where carpenters are often building stage sets (open on hot days). Walk downhill through Max Reinhardt Platz, past the church and public WC to . . .

Universitätsplatz—This square comes with a busy open-air produce market—Salzburg's liveliest (mornings Mon–Sat, best on Sat). Locals are happy to pay more here for the reliably fresh and top-quality produce (half of Austria's produce is now grown organically). The market really bustles on Saturday mornings, when the farmers are in town. Public marketplaces have fountains for washing fruit and vegetables. The fountain here (notice the little ones for smaller dogs and bigger dogs)—a part of the medieval water system—plummets down a hole and to the river. The sundial is accurate (except for the daylight savings hour), showing both the time (obvious) and the date (less obvious). Continue to the end of the square (opposite cathedral), passing several characteristic and nicely arcaded medieval tunnel passages (on right) connecting the square to Getreidegasse. At the big road (across from the giant horse troughs), take two right turns and you're at the start of . . .

Getreidegasse—This street was old Salzburg's busy, colorful main drag. (*Schmuck* means jewelry.) Famous for its old wrought-iron signs, the street still looks much as it did in Mozart's day. (The Nordsee Restaurant was even more of a scandal than the coming of McDonald's—notice the medieval golden arches street sign.) At #40, Eisgrotte serves good ice cream. Across from #40, a tunnel leads to Bosna Grill, the local choice for the very best sausage in town (see "Eating Cheap in the Old Town," page 99). Wolfgang was born on this street. Find his very gold house at #9 (follow the crowds).

Mozart's Birthplace (Geburtshaus)—Mozart was born here in 1756. It was in this building—the most popular Mozart sight in town—that he composed most of his boy-genius works. Filled with scores of scores, portraits, his first violin (picked up at age 5), the clavichord (a predecessor to the piano with simple teeter-totter keys that played very softly) on which he composed *Magic Flute* and the *Requiem*, a relaxing video concert hall, and exhibits about the life of Wolfgang on the road and Salzburg in Mozart's day, including a furnished middle-class apartment (all well-described in English), it's almost a pilgrimage site (€5.50, or €9 for combo-ticket to Mozart's *Wohnhaus*—see "Sights—Across the River," below, July–Aug daily 9:00–19:00, Sept–June daily 9:00–18:00, last entry 30 min before closing time, Getreidegasse 9, tel. 0662/844-313). Note that Mozart's *Wohnhaus* provides a more informative visit than this more-visited site.

Sights—Above the Old Town

▲Hohensalzburg Fortress—Built on a rock 120 meters (400 feet) above the Salzach River, this fortress was never really used. That's the idea. It was a good investment—so foreboding, nobody attacked the town for a thousand years. One of Europe's mightiest, it dominates Salzburg's skyline and offers incredible views. You can hike up or ride the *Festungsbahn* (funicular, €6.50 round-trip includes fortress courtyard, €5.50 one-way, pleasant to walk down). The fortress visit has two parts—a relatively dull courtyard with some fine views (€3.75 or included in €6.50 funicular fare) and the palatial interior (worth the €3.75 extra admission). Tourists are allowed inside only with an escort, so you'll go one room at a time, listening to the entire 50-minute audioguide narration (included).

The decorations are from around 1500—fantastic animals and plants inspired by tales of New World discoveries. While the interior furnishings are mostly gone—to the museums of Vienna, Paris, London, and Munich—the rooms survived as well as they did because no one wanted to live there after 1500, so it was never modernized. Your tour includes the obligatory room dedicated to the art of "intensive questioning"—filled with tools of that gruesome trade—and a sneak preview of the room used for the nightly fortress concerts. The last rooms show music, daily life in the castle, and an exhibit dedicated to the Salzburg regiment in World War I and World War II. The highlight is the commanding city view from the top of a tower. (Fortress open daily year-round; mid-March–mid-June: grounds 9:00–18:00, interior 9:30–17:30; mid-June–mid-Sept: grounds 8:30–20:00, interior 9:00–18:00; mid-Sept–mid-March: grounds 9:00–17:00, interior 9:30–17:00; last entry 30 min before closing time, tel. 0662/8424-3011). Warning: The one-room marionette exhibit in the fortress courtyard is a bad value—you'll see more for free in its lobby than by paying to go inside.

▲The Hills Are Alive Walk—For a great little hike, exit the fortress by taking the trail across Salzburg's little mountain, Mönchsberg. The trail leads through the woods high above the city (stick to the high lanes, or you'll end up back in town), taking you to the Naturfreundehaus (café, light meals, cheap beds, elevator nearby for a quick descent to Neumayr Platz in the old town) and eventually to the church that marks the rollicking Augustiner Bräustübl (described in "Eating Away from the Center," below).

In 1669, a huge Mönchsberg landslide killed more than 200 townspeople. Since then, the cliffs have been carefully checked each spring and fall. Even today, you might see crews on the cliff, monitoring its stability.

Sights—Across the River

Salzach River—Cross the river (ideally on one of two pedestrian bridges). It's called "salt river" not because it's salty, but because of its original precious trade—the salt mines of Hallein are just 15 kilometers (9 miles) upstream. Salt could be transported from here all the way to the Danube and on to Russia. The riverbanks and roads were built in 1860. Before that, the Salzach was much wider and slower moving. Houses opposite the old town fronted the river with docks and garages for boats.

▲Steingasse—This street, a block in from the river, was the only street in the Middle Ages going south to Hallein. Today, it's wonderfully tranquil and free of Salzburg's touristy crush. Wander down Steingasse (from Mozartplatz, cross the river via the Mozartsteg pedestrian bridge, cross the busy Imbergstrasse, jog left and go a block farther inland to a quiet cobbled lane, and turn left).

Stroll down this peaceful chunk of old Salzburg—once the only road on this side of the river. Just after the Maison de Plaisir at #24 (for centuries, a town brothel—open from 14:00), you'll find a magnificent fortress viewpoint. Notice the red dome marking the oldest nunnery in the German-speaking world (established in 712) under the fortress and to the left. The real Maria from *The Sound of Music* taught in this nunnery's school. In 1927, she and Herr von Trapp were married in the church you see here (not the church filmed in the movie). He was 47. She was 22. Hmmmm.

At #19, find the carvings on the old door—notices from beggars to the begging community (more numerous after the economic dislocation caused by the wars over religion following the Reformation) indicating whether the residents would give or not. The four ringers indicate four families lived at this address.

At #9, a plaque shows where Joseph Mohr, who wrote the words to *Silent Night*, was born, poor and illegitimate, in 1792. Stairs lead from near here up to the monastery.

Across the street, on the corner you just passed, the wall is gouged out. This was left even after the building was restored so locals could remember the American GI who tried to get a tank down this road during a visit to #24.

▲**St. Sebastian Cemetery**—Wander through this quiet place—so Baroque and so Italian (free, April–Oct daily 9:00–19:00, Nov–March daily 9:00–16:00, entry usually at Linzergasse 43). While Mozart is buried in Vienna, his father and most of his family are buried here (from the Linzergasse entry, take 17 paces and look left). When Prince-Archbishop Wolf Dietrich had the cemetery moved from around the cathedral and put here, across the river, people didn't like it. To help popularize it, he had his mausoleum built as its centerpiece. Continuing straight past the Mozart tomb, step into his dome. Read the legalistic epitaph (posted in English) and look at the tomb through the grate in the floor. To get to the cemetery (Friedhof St. Sebastian), take Linzergasse, the best shopping street in Salzburg.

▲▲**Mozart's Wohnhaus**—This reconstruction of Mozart's second home (his family moved here when he was 17) is the most informative Mozart sight in town. The English-language audioguide (free with admission, keep it carefully pointed at the ceiling transmitters and don't move while listening) provides a fascinating insight into Mozart's life and music, with the usual scores, old pianos, and an interesting 30-minute-long film that runs continuously, all in English (€5.50, or €9 for combo-ticket to birthplace, guidebook-€4.30, daily 9:00–18:00, July–Aug until 19:00, last tickets sold 30 min before closing, allow 1 hour for visit, across the river from the old town, Makartplatz 8, tel. 0662/8742-2740).

▲**Mirabell Gardens and Palace (Schloss)**—The bubbly gardens, laid out in 1730, are always open and free. You may recognize the statues and the arbor featured in the *S.O.M.* A brass band plays free park concerts (summers, Sun 10:30 and Wed 20:30). To properly enjoy the lavish Mirabell Palace—once the prince bishop's summer palace and now the seat of the mayor—get a ticket to a *Schlosskonzert* (my favorite venue for a classical concert). Baroque music flying around a Baroque hall is a happy bird in the right cage. Tickets (€26–31, student-€14) are rarely sold out (tel. 0662/848-586). The **Café Bazar**, a few blocks away (on Schwarzstrasse, toward Staatsbrücke) and overlooking the river, is a great place for a classy drink with an old town and castle view.

More Sights—Salzburg

▲▲**Riverside Bike Ride**—The Salzach River has smooth, flat, and scenic bike paths along each side. On a sunny day, I can think of no more shout-worthy escape from the city. The six-kilometer (3.75-mile) path to Hellbrunn Palace is easy, with a worthy destination. For a 15-kilometer (9-mile) ride, head out to Hallein

Sound of Music Debunked

Rather than visit the real-life sights from the life of Maria von Trapp and family, most tourists want to see the places where Hollywood chose to film this fanciful story. Local guides are happy not to burst any *S.O.M.* pilgrim's bubble, but keep these points in mind:

- "Edelweiss" is not a cherished Austrian folk tune or national anthem. Like all the "Austrian" music in the *S.O.M.*, it was composed for Broadway by Rodgers and Hammerstein. It was, however, the last composition that the famed team wrote together, as Hammerstein died in 1960—nine months after the musical opened.
- The movie implies that Maria was devoutly religious throughout her life, but Maria's foster parents raised her as a socialist and atheist. Maria discovered her religious calling while studying to be a teacher. After completing school, she joined the convent as a novitiate.
- Maria's position was not as governess to all the children, as portrayed in the musical, but specifically as governess and teacher for the Captain's second-oldest daughter, Maria, who was bedridden with rheumatic fever.
- The Captain didn't run a tight domestic ship. In fact, his seven children were as unruly as most. But he did use a whistle to call them—each kid was trained to respond to a certain pitch.
- Though the von Trapp family did have seven children, the show changed all their names and even their genders. Rupert, the eldest child, responded to the often-asked tourist question, "Which one are you?" with a simple, "I'm Leisl!"
- The family never escaped by hiking to Switzerland (which is a

(where you can tour a salt mine, see "Sights—Near Salzburg," below, the north or "new town" side of river is most scenic). Even a quickie ride from one end of town to the other is a great Salzburg experience. In the evening, the riverbanks are a hand-in-hand, floodlit-spires world.

▲▲*Sound of Music* Tour—I took this tour skeptically (as part of my research chores) and liked it. It includes a quick but good general city tour, hits the *S.O.M.* spots (including the stately home, gazebo, and wedding church), and shows you a lovely stretch of the Salzkammergut. This is worthwhile for *S.O.M.* fans and those who won't otherwise be going into the Salzkammergut. Warning:

5-hour drive away). Rather, they pretended to go on one of their frequent mountain hikes. With only the possessions in their backpacks, they "hiked" all the way to the train station (it was at the edge of their estate) and took a train to Italy. Hitler immediately closed the Austrian borders when he learned of this. The movie scene showing them climbing into Switzerland was actually filmed near Berchtesgaden, Germany . . . home to Hitler's Eagle's Nest, and certainly not a smart place to flee.

- The actual von Trapp family house exists . . . but it's not the one in the film. The mansion in the movie is actually two different buildings, one used for the front, the other for the back. The interiors were all filmed on Hollywood sets.
- For the film, Boris Levin designed a reproduction of Nonnberg Abbey courtyard so faithful to the original (down to its cobblestones and stained-glass windows) that many still believe the cloister scenes were really shot at the abbey. And no matter what you hear in Salzburg, the graveyard scene (in which the von Trapps hide from the Nazis) was also filmed on the Fox lot.
- In 1956, a German film producer offered Maria $10,000 for the rights to her book. She asked for royalties, too, and a share of the profits. The agent explained that German law forbids film companies from paying royalties to foreigners (Maria had by then become a U.S. citizen). She agreed to the contract and unknowingly signed away all film rights to her story. Only a few weeks later, he offered to pay immediately if she would accept $9,000 in cash. Because it was more money than the family had seen in all of their years of singing, she accepted the deal. Later, she discovered the agent had swindled them—no such law existed.

Many think rolling through the Austrian countryside with 30 Americans singing "Doe, a deer" is pretty schmaltzy. Local Austrians don't understand all the commotion. Of the many companies doing the tour, I like Bob's Special Tours (more friendly and intimate minibus) and the Panorama tours (more typical, professional big bus). Each one provides essentially the same tour (in English with a live and lively guide, 4 hrs, free hotel pick-up) for the same price. Getting a spot is simple—just call and make a reservation. Each company gives my readers who book direct a discount on any of their tours (€5 per tour for Bob's, 10 percent for Panorama). Note: If you let your hotel call, you will not get the discount I've negotiated for readers of this book. Each company also offers an extensive array of other day trips from Salzburg (Berchtesgaden Eagle's Nest, salt mines, and Salzkammergut lakes and mountains are the most popular, with similar discounts and big bus vs. minibus differences as above)—all explained in their brochures, which litter hotel lobbies all over town.

Minibus option: Bob's Special Tours charges €35 for their *S.O.M.* tour, less €5 for readers of this book (departs Mozartplatz daily at 9:00 and 14:00 year-round, Rudolfskai 38, tel. 0662/849-511, www.bobstours.com). Ninety percent of Bob's tours use a minibus and therefore have better access for old town sights, promote a more casual feel, and spend less time waiting and picking up. Nearly all of Bob's tours stop for the luge ride when the weather is dry (mountain bobsled-€4 extra).

Big-bus option: Salzburg Panorama Tours charges €33 for their 50-seater bus *S.O.M.* tour, less 10 percent for readers of this book (departs Mirabellplatz daily at 9:30 and 14:00 year-round, tel. 0662/874-029 or 0662/883-211, www.panoramatours.at). While they try to stop for a luge ride, there's generally not enough time (as shopping and coffee are a priority).

▲Hellbrunn Castle—The attractions here are a garden full of clever trick fountains and the sadistic joy the tour guide gets from soaking tourists. (Hint: when you see a wet place, cover your camera.) The Baroque garden, one of the oldest in Europe, now features *S.O.M.*'s "I am 16, going on 17" gazebo (€7.50, includes 35-min tour, daily 9:00–17:30, July–Aug tours on the hour until 22:00, April and Oct until 16:30, closed Nov–March, tel. 0662/820-372). The archbishop's mediocre 17th-century palace, in the courtyard, is open by tour only (audioguide included in admission). Hellbrunn is almost five kilometers (3 miles) south of Salzburg (bus #55 from station or downtown, 2/hr, 20 min). It's most fun on a sunny day or with kids, but, for many, it's a lot of trouble for a few water tricks.

Music Scene

▲▲Salzburg Festival—Each summer, from late July to the end of August, Salzburg hosts its famous Salzburger Festspiele, founded in 1920 to employ Vienna's musicians in the summer. This fun and festive time is crowded, but there are plenty of beds (except for a few August weekends). Tickets are normally available the day of the concert unless it's a really big show (the ticket office on Mozartplatz, in the TI, prints a daily list of concerts). You can contact the Austrian National Tourist Office in the United States for specifics on this year's festival schedule and tickets (Box 1142, New York, NY 10108-1142, 212/944-6880, fax 212/730-4568, www.austria-tourism.com, e-mail: info@oewnyc.com), but I've never planned in advance and have enjoyed great concerts with every visit.

▲▲**Musical Events outside of Festival Time**—Salzburg is busy throughout the year, with 2,000 classical performances in its palaces and churches annually. Pick up the events calendar at the TI (free, bimonthly). Whenever you visit, you'll have a number of concerts (generally small chamber groups) to choose from. There are nearly nightly concerts at the Fortress (for beginners—Mozart's greatest hits) and at the Mirabell Palace (with more sophisticated programs). Both feature small chamber groups, have open seating, and charge roughly €29 to €36 for tickets (concerts at 19:30, 20:00, or 20:30, doors open 30 min early). The *Schlosskonzerte* at the Mirabell Palace offer a fine Baroque setting for your music (tel. 0662/848-586). The fortress concerts, called *Festungskonzerte*, are held in the "prince's chamber" (tel. 0662/825-858 to reserve, you can pick up tickets at the door). This medieval-feeling room atop the fortress has windows overlooking the city, and the concert gives you a chance to enjoy the grand city view and a stroll through the castle courtyard. (The €6.50 round-trip funicular is discounted to €2.80 within an hour of the show if you have a concert ticket.)

The "5:00 Concert" next to St. Peter's is cheaper, since it features young artists (€8.75, July–Sept daily except Wed, 45 min, tel. 0662/8445-7619). While the series is formally named after the brother of Joseph Haydn, it offers music from various masters.

Salzburg's impressive **Marionette Theater** performs operas with remarkable marionettes and recorded music (€22–35, nearly nightly May–Sept except Sun, tel. 0662/872-406, www.marionetten.at).

For those who'd like some classical music but would rather not sit through a concert, Stiftskeller St. Peter offers a **Mozart Dinner Concert,** with a traditional candlelit meal and Mozart's greatest hits performed by a string quartet and singers in historic costumes gavotting among the tables. In this elegant Baroque setting, you'll enjoy three courses of food mixed with three 20-minute courses of top-quality music (€45, almost nightly at 20:00, see "Eating," below, call to reserve at 0662/828-6950).

The ***S.O.M.* dinner show** at the Sternbräu Inn (see "Eating," below) is Broadway in a dirndl with tired food. But it's a good show, and *S.O.M.* fans are mesmerized by the evening. A piano player and a hardworking quartet of singers perform an entertaining mix of *Sound of Music* hits and traditional folk songs (€43 includes a schnitzel and crisp apple strudel dinner at 19:30,

€30 for 20:30 show only, those booking direct get a 10 percent discount with this book, reserve ahead, fun for families, daily mid-May–mid-Oct, Griesgasse 23, tel. 0662/826-617, www.soundofmusicshow.com).

Sights—Near Salzburg

▲Bad Dürnberg Salzbergwerke—This salt mine tour above the town of Hallein (15 km/9 miles from Salzburg) is a fun experience. Wearing white overalls and sliding down the sleek wooden chutes, you'll cross underground from Austria into Germany while learning about the old-time salt mining process (€15.50, daily from 9:00 with last tour at 17:00, English-speaking guides, easy bus and train connections from Salzburg, tel. 06245/852-8515). A convenient "Salt Ticket" from Salzburg's train station covers admission, train, and shuttle bus tickets, all in one money-saving round-trip ticket.

▲Berchtesgaden—This alpine ski town in the region of the same name just across the German border (20 km/12 miles from Salzburg) flaunts its attractions very successfully. During peak season, you may find yourself in a traffic jam of desperate tourists trying to turn their money into fun.

The TI is next to the train station (TI: German tel. 08652/967-150, from Austria tel. 00-49-8652/967-150). From the station, buses go to the salt mines (a 20-min walk otherwise) and the idyllic Königsee (popular €11, 2-hr scenic cruises, 2/hr, with the pilot demonstrating the lake's echo with a trumpet, stopovers anywhere, German tel. 08652/963-618, from Austria tel. 00-49-8652/963-618).

At the Berchtesgaden **salt mines**, you put on traditional miners' outfits, get on funny little trains, and zip deep into the mountain. For one hour, you'll cruise subterranean lakes; slide speedily down two long, slick, wooden banisters; and learn how they mined salt so long ago. Call for crowd-avoidance advice. When the weather gets bad, this place is mobbed. You can buy a ticket early and browse through the town until your appointed tour time (€12, May–mid-Oct daily 9:00–17:00, mid-Oct–April Mon–Sat 12:30–15:30, German tel. 08652/60020, from Austria tel. 00-49-8652/60020).

Hitler's famous **Eagle's Nest**—designed as a retreat for diplomatic meetings—towers high above Obersalzberg near Berchtesgaden. The road and building were constructed in an impressive 13 months—just in time to be given to Hitler for his 50th birthday. The view will blow your cake out. The site is open to visitors (mid-May–Oct), but little remains of the alpine retreat Hitler visited only 10 times. The round-trip bus

Greater Salzburg

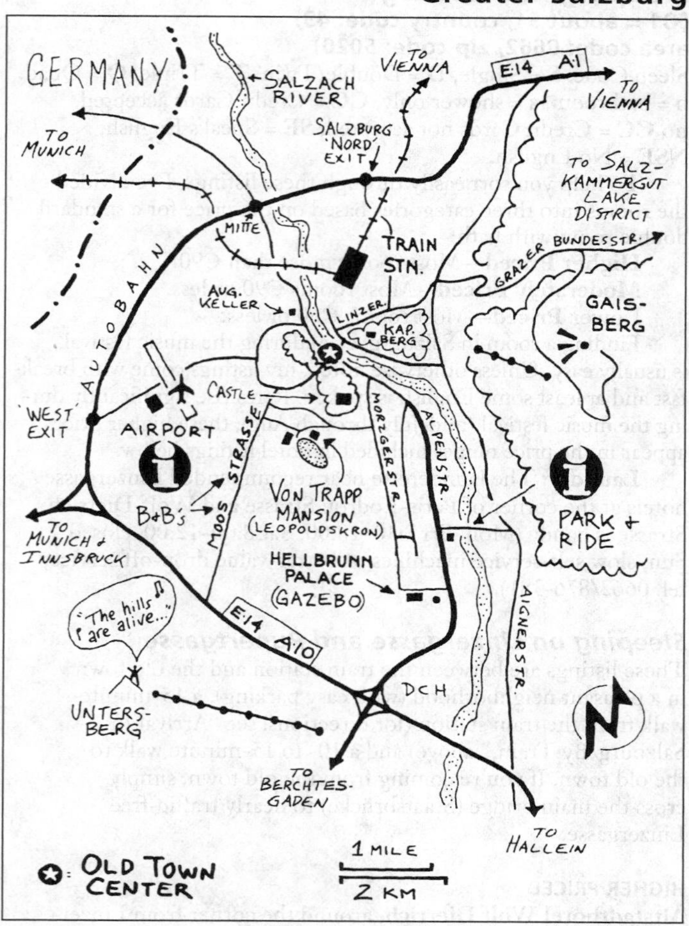

ride up the private road and the lift to the top (a 600-meter/2,000-foot altitude gain) cost €16 from the station, €12 from the parking lot. If the weather's cloudy, as it often is, you won't see a thing.

Getting from Salzburg to Berchtesgaden, the bus is more scenic and direct than the train (2/hr, 30 min, bus station across street from Salzburg's train station). Some travelers visit Berchtesgaden en route from Munich (hrly trains from Munich, 2.5 hrs, with 1 change).

Sleeping in Salzburg
(€1 = about $1, country code: 43, area code: 0662, zip code: 5020)

Sleep Code: **S** = Single, **D** = Double/Twin, **T** = Triple, **Q** = Quad, **b** = bathroom, **s** = shower only, **CC** = Credit Cards accepted, **no CC** = Credit Cards not accepted, **SE** = Speaks English, **NSE** = No English.

To help you sort easily through these listings, I've divided the rooms into three categories based on the price for a standard double room with bath:

Higher Priced—Most rooms more than €90.
Moderately Priced—Most rooms €90 or less.
Lower Priced—Most rooms €60 or less.

Finding a room in Salzburg, even during the music festival, is usually easy. Unless otherwise noted, my listings come with breakfast and at least some English is spoken. Rates rise significantly during the music festival (mid-July through Aug); these higher prices appear in the price ranges included in hotel listings below.

Laundry: The launderette near recommended Linzergasse hotels at the corner of Paris-Lodron Strasse and Wolf-Dietrich Strasse is handy (Mon–Fri 7:30–18:00, Sat 8:00–12:00, closed Sun, slow self-service machines or better-value drop-off service, tel. 0662/876-381).

Sleeping on Linzergasse and Rupertgasse

These listings are between the train station and the old town in a pleasant neighborhood (with easy parking), a 15-minute walk from the train station (for directions, see "Arrival In Salzburg/By Train," above) and a 10- to 15-minute walk to the old town. If you're coming from the old town, simply cross the main bridge (Staatsbrücke) to nearly traffic-free Linzergasse.

HIGHER PRICED

Altstadthotel Wolf Dietrich, around the corner from Linzergasse on Wolf-Dietrich Strasse, is well-located and a reasonable big-hotel option, if that's what you want (27 rooms, Db-€100–154, family deals, €20 more during festival time, complex pricing but readers of this book get a 10 percent discount on prevailing price, CC, garage, pool, sauna, Wolf-Dietrich Strasse 7, tel. 0662/871-275, fax 0662/882-320, www.salzburg-hotel.at).

Hotel Trumer Stube, a few blocks from the river just off Linzergasse, has 20 clean, cozy rooms (but avoid the low-ceilinged attic room) and a friendly, can-do owner (Sb-€56–70,

Db-€89–103, Tb-€89–125, Qb-€132–140, higher mid-July–Aug: Sb-€81–96, Db-€118–132, Tb-€140–146, Qb-€147–161, CC to reserve but pay cash, small breakfast in small breakfast room, non-smoking, elevator, Bergstrasse 6, tel. 0662/874-776, fax 0662/874-326, www.trumer-stube.at, pleasant Silvia SE).

MODERATELY PRICED

Hotel Goldene Krone, about five blocks from the river, is big, quiet, and creaky-traditional but modern, with comforts rare in this price range (S-€25, Sb-€50, Db-€80, Tb-€115, claim your 10 percent discount with this book, CC, 26 rooms, elevator, relaxing garden in backyard, Linzergasse 48, tel. 0662/872-300, fax 0662/8723-0066, www.hotel-goldenekrone.com, Claudia and Günther SE). They have a video library in the lounge with *The Sound of Music* and other Salzburg videos for guests to play when they like. In 2003, Günther plans to offer a free orientation talk on Salzburg nightly at 18:00 (starting in March), and a four-hour walking, biking, and driving tour of untouristy, romantic Salzburg (€5, Tue, Thu, and Sat at 14:00, in good weather only, reserve ahead, starting in May).

Pensions on Rupertgasse: These two hotels are about five blocks farther from the river up Paris-Lodron Strasse to Rupertgasse, a breeze for drivers but with more street noise than the places on Linzergasse. **Pension Bergland** is charming and classy, with comfortable rooms (Sb-€50, Db-€80, Tb-€90, Qb-€110, CC, elevator, Internet access, English library, bike rental, Rupertgasse 15, tel. 0662/872-318, fax 0662/872-3188, www.berglandhotel.at). The similar, boutique-like **Hotel Jedermann**, a few doors down, is also tastefully done and comfortable, with a backyard garden (Sb-€55, Db-€85, Tb-€100, Qb-€130, CC, Internet access, Rupertgasse 25, tel. 0662/873-241, fax 0662/873-2419, www.hotel-jedermann.com).

LOWER PRICED

Institute St. Sebastian—a somewhat sterile but very clean, historic building—has spacious public areas, a roof garden, and some of the best rooms and dorm beds in town for the money. The immaculate doubles come with modern baths and head-to-toe twin beds (Sb-€31, Db-€53, Tb-€68, Qb-€82, including breakfast, CC, elevator, laundry, reception open July–Sept 7:30–12:00 & 13:00–22:00, Oct–June 8:00–12:00 & 16:00–21:00, Linzergasse 41, enter through arch at #37, tel. 0662/871-386, fax 0662/8713-8685, www.st-sebastian-salzburg.at, e-mail: office@st-sebastian-salzburg.at). Students like the €17 bunks in 4- to 10-bed dorms (€2.25 less if you

Salzburg Center Hotels and Restaurants

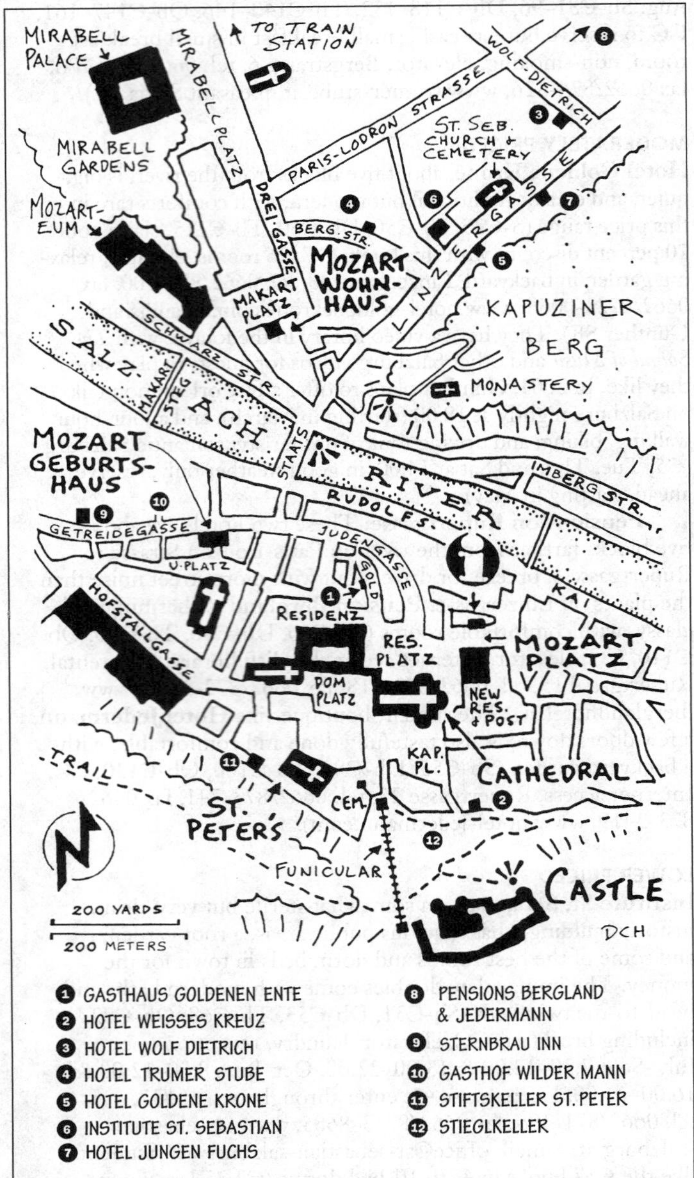

have sheets, no lockout time, lockers, free showers). You'll find self-service kitchens on each floor (fridge space is free; request a key).

Pension zum Jungen Fuchs terrifies claustrophobes and titillates troglodytes. It's plain but sleepable, wonderfully located in a funky, dumpy old building (16 rooms, S-€27, D-€38, T-€48, no breakfast, no CC, just up from Hotel Krone at Linzergasse 54, tel. 0662/875-496).

Sleeping in (or above) the Old Town

HIGHER PRICED

Hotel Weisse Taube is a big, quiet, 30-room place with more comfort than character, perfectly located about a block off Mozartplatz (Sb-€57–65, Db-€91–120, 20 percent more mid-July–Sept, CC, elevator, tel. 0662/842-404, fax 0662/841-783, Kaigasse 9, www.weissetaube.at, e-mail: hotel@weissetaube.at, SE).

MODERATELY PRICED

Gasthaus zur Goldenen Ente is in a 600-year-old building with medieval stone arches and narrow stairs. Located above a good restaurant, it's as central as you can be on a pedestrian street in old Salzburg. The 17 rooms are modern yet worn, and the service is uneven—from friendly to brusque—depending on who's on duty. For the price, it's a great value (Sb-€53, Db-€79 with this book, extra person-€29; in July, Aug, and Dec Sb-€60, Db-€93, CC, elevator, parking-€6/day, Goldgasse 10, tel. 0662/845-622, fax 0662/845-6229, www.ente.at, e-mail: hotel@ente.at, Robert and family Steinwender SE).

Hotel Restaurant Weisses Kreuz is a Tolkienesque little family-run place on a cobbled backstreet under the fortress away from the crowds with a fine restaurant, four rooms, and a peaceful roof garden (Sb-€66, Db-€90, Tb-€120, CC, garage, Bierjodlgasse 6, tel. 0662/845-641, fax 0662/845-6419, e-mail: weisses.kreuz@eunet.at).

LOWER PRICED

Naturfreundehaus, also called "Gasthaus Stadtalm," is a local version of a mountaineer's hut and a great budget alternative. In a forest guarded by singing birds, it's snuggled in the remains of a 15th-century castle wall atop the little mountain overlooking Salzburg, with magnificent town and mountain views (€10/person in 2-, 4-, and 6-bed dorms, cheap breakfasts extra, CC, €6 bike rental, open mid-April–Oct, 2 min from top of €2 round-trip Mönchsberg elevator, Mönchsberg 19, tel. & fax 0662/841-729, Peter SE).

Sleeping Away from the Center

HIGHER PRICED

Hotel am Nussdorferhof is a creatively run, 31-room place, located about halfway between the old town and the *Zimmer* on Moosstrasse (listed below). Run enthusiastically by Herbert and Ilse, the hotel has all the amenities, including a sauna, whirlpool, and Internet access. It's a 15-minute walk or short bus ride from the old town (Sb-€68, Db-€98, big Db-€115, prices in July, Aug, and Dec: Sb-€79, Db-€115, Tb-€130, 1–2 kids sleep free, claim a 10 percent discount with this book when you reserve, CC, some waterbeds, some theme rooms, elevator, free unlimited bus pass and loaner bikes, attached Italian restaurant, free shuttle to/from train station or airport—just call, Moosstrasse 36, bus stop: Nussdorferstrasse, tel. 0662/824-838, fax 0662/824-8389, www.nussdorferhof.at, e-mail: info@nussdorferhof.at).

Zimmer (Private Rooms)

LOWER-PRICED

These are generally roomy and comfortable and come with a good breakfast, easy parking, and tourist information, and do not accept credit cards unless specified. Off-season, competition softens prices. They are a bus ride from town, but, with a day pass and the frequent service, this shouldn't keep you away. In fact, most will happily pick you up at the train station if you simply telephone them and ask. Most will also do laundry for a small fee for those staying at least two nights. Unsavory *Zimmer* skimmers lurk at the station. Ignore them. I've listed prices for two nights or more. If staying only one night, expect a 10 percent surcharge.

Brigitte Lenglachner fills her big, traditional home with a warm welcome (S-€24, bunk bed D-€30, D-€40, Db-€44, T-€50, Tb-€64, Qb-€80, apartment with kitchen for up to 5, Scheibenweg 8, tel. & fax 0662/438-044). It's a 10-minute walk northeast of the station (cross pedestrian Pioneer Bridge, turn right, walk along the river to the third street—Scheibenweg—turn left, and it's halfway down on the right).

Trude Poppenberger's three pleasant rooms share a long, mountain-view balcony (S-€24, D-€37, T-€55; Wachtelgasse 9, tel. & fax 0662/430-094, e-mail: trudeshome@yline.com). Call for a pick-up or walk 30 minutes northwest of the station (cross pedestrian Pioneer Bridge, turn right, walk along river 300 meters, or 985 feet, cross canal, left on Linke Glanzeile for 3 min, right onto Wachtelgasse).

***Zimmer* on Moosstrasse:** The busy street called Moosstrasse, southwest of Mönchsberg, is lined with *Zimmer*. Those farther out are farmhouses. To get to these from the train station, take bus #1, #5, #6, #51, or #55 to Makartplatz and then change to #60, or take bus #1 and change to bus #60 at the first stop after crossing the river (Hanuschplatz). If you are coming from the old town, catch bus #60 from Hanuschplatz, just downstream of the Staatsbrücke near the *Tabak* kiosk. Buy a €1.70 *Einzelkarte-Kernzone* ticket (for 1 trip) or a €3.20 *Tageskarte* (for the entire day) from the streetside machine and punch it when you board the bus. If you're driving from the center, go through the tunnel, straight on Neutorstrasse, and take the fourth left onto Moosstrasse.

Maria Gassner rents 10 basic rooms in her modern house (Sb-€29, D-€36, Db-€44, big fancy Db with balcony-€58, Tb-€72, Qb-€86, family deals, CC, €4 coin-op laundry, Moosstrasse 126-B, bus stop: Sendelweg, tel. 0662/824-990, fax 0662/822-075, e-mail: pension-maria.gassner@utanet.at).

Frau Ballwein offers cozy, charming rooms in a 160-year-old farmhouse that feels new (S-€22, D-€40, Db-€48, Tb-€65, family deals, farm-fresh breakfasts, no CC, Moosstrasse 69, bus stop: Gsengerweg, tel. & fax 0662/824-029, e-mail: haus.ballwein@gmx.net).

Haus Reichl rents three good rooms (D/Db-€48, T/Tb-€66, Qb with balcony and view-€80, no CC, between Ballwein and Bankhammer B&Bs, 200 meters, or 650 feet, down Reiterweg to #52, bus stop: Gsengerweg, tel. & fax 0662/826-248, www.privatzimmer.at/haus-reichl, e-mail: haus.reichl@telering.at).

Helga Bankhammer rents pleasant rooms in a farmhouse, with farm animals nearby (D-€39, Db-€43, no surcharge for one-nighters, family deals, CC, laundry, Moosstrasse 77, bus stop: Marienbad, tel. & fax 0662/830-067, www.privatzimmer.at/helga.bankhammer, e-mail: helga.bankhammer@telering.at).

Gästehaus Blobergerhof is rural and comfortable (Sb-€32–46, Db-€51–55, big new Db with balcony-€75–79, extra bed-€15, family apartment, CC, 20 rooms, free loaner bikes, will pick up at the station, Hammerauerstrasse 4, bus stop: Hammerauerstrasse, tel. 0662/830-227, fax 0662/827-061, www.blobergerhof.at, e-mail: office@blobergerhof.at).

Sleeping near the Train Station

MODERATELY PRICED

Pension Adlerhof, a plain and decent old place, is two blocks in front of the train station (left off Kaiserschutzenstrasse), but a 15-minute walk from the sightseeing action. It has a quirky staff and 35 well-maintained rooms (Sb-€50, D-€52–62, Db-€72–80,

Tb-€94, Qb-€102, Internet access, elevator, Elisabethstrasse 25, tel. 0662/875-236, fax 0662/873-6636).

LOWER PRICED

International Youth Hotel, a.k.a. the "Yo-Ho," is the most lively, handy, and American of Salzburg's hostels (€14 in 6- to 8-bed dorms, D-€19/person, Q-€16/person, sheets included, breakfast cheap, CC, 6 blocks from station toward Linzergasse and 6 blocks from river at Paracelsusstrasse 9, tel. 0662/879-649, www.yoho.at). This easygoing place speaks English first; has cheap meals, 170 beds, lockers, Internet access, laundry, tour discounts, and no curfew; plays *The Sound of Music* free daily at 13:30; runs a lively bar; and welcomes anyone of any age. The noisy atmosphere and lack of a curfew can make it hard to sleep.

Eating in Salzburg

Salzburg boasts many inexpensive, fun, and atmospheric places to eat. I'm a sucker for big cellars with their smoky, Old World atmosphere, heavy medieval arches, time-darkened paintings, antlers, hearty meals, and plump patrons. These places, all centrally located in the old town, are famous with visitors but are also enjoyed by the locals.

Gasthaus zum Wilder Mann is the place if the weather's bad and you're in the mood for Hofbräu atmosphere and a hearty, cheap meal at a shared table in one small, well-antlered room (€6–8 daily specials, Mon–Sat 11:00–21:00, closed Sun, smoky, 2 min from Mozart's birthplace, enter from Getreidegasse 22 or Griesgasse 17, tel. 0662/841-787). For a quick lunch, get the *Bauernschmaus*, a mountain of dumplings, kraut, and peasant's meats (€8).

Stiftskeller St. Peter has been in business for more than 1,000 years—it was mentioned in the biography of Charlemagne. It's classy (with strolling musicians) and central as can be, serving uninspired traditional Austrian cuisine (meals €15–24, daily 11:00–24:00, CC, indoor/outdoor seating, next to St. Peter's church at foot of Mönchsberg, restaurant tel. 0662/841-268). They host the Mozart Dinner Concert described in "Music Scene," above (€45, nearly nightly at 20:00, call 0662/828-6950 to reserve).

Gasthaus zur Goldenen Ente (see "Sleeping," above) serves great food in an elegant, subdued hotel dining room or on a quiet pedestrian lane. The chef, Robert, specializes in roast duck *(Ente)* and Tirolean traditions. But he'll happily replace your kraut and dumplings with a wonderful selection of steamed green and orange vegetables for no extra charge. Their *Salzburger Nockerl*, the mountainous sweet soufflé served all over town, is big enough for four—try it (Mon–Fri 11:30–21:00, closed Sat–Sun, Goldgasse 10, tel. 0662/845-622).

Stieglkeller is a huge, atmospheric institution that has several rustic rooms and outdoor garden seating with a great rooftop view of the old town (May–Sept daily 10:00–23:00, closed Oct–April, 50 meters, or 165 feet, uphill from the lift to the fortress, Festungsgasse 10, tel. 0662/842-681).

Sternbräu Inn is a sprawling complex of popular eateries (traditional, Italian, self-serve, and vegetarian) in a cheery garden setting—explore both courtyards before choosing a seat. One fancy, air-conditioned room hosts the *Sound of Music* dinner show (see "Music Scene," above).

Resch & Lieblich Bierhaus, wedged between the cliffside and the back of the big concert hall, is a rough and characteristic place popular with locals for salads, goulash, and light meals (daily 10:00–24:00, indoor/outdoor seating in rustic little cellar or under umbrellas on square, Toscaninihof, tel. 0662/843-675).

Café Glockenspiel, on Mozartplatz 2, is the place to see and be seen. Overpriced, but—like St. Mark's Square in Venice—it's worth it if you want to linger and enjoy the spot (long hours daily, tel. 0662/841-403).

Restaurant Weisses Kreuz, nestled behind the cathedral and under the fortress, serves good Balkan cuisine in a pleasant dining room (Wed–Mon 11:30–14:45 & 17:00–22:45, closed Tue, Bierjodlgasse 6, tel. 0662/845-641).

Eating Cheap in the Old Town

Toskana Cafeteria Mensa is the students' lunch place, fast and cheap—with fine indoor seating and a great courtyard for sitting outside with students and teachers instead of tourists. They serve a daily soup and main course special for €3.50 (Mon–Thu 8:30–17:00, Fri 8:30–15:00, closed Sat–Sun, behind the Residenz, in the courtyard opposite Sigmund-Haffnergasse 16).

Sausage stands serve the local fast food. The best places (such as the one on the side of the Collegiate Church just off Universitätsplatz) use the same boiling water all day, which fills the weenies with more flavor. Key words: *Weisswurst*—boiled white sausage, *Bosna*—with onions and curry, *Käsekrainer*—with melted cheese inside, *Debreginer*—spicy Hungarian, *Frankfurter*—our weenie, *frische*—fresh ("eat before the noon bells"), and *Senf*—mustard (ask for sweet—*süss* or sharp—*scharf*). Only a tourist puts the sausage in a bun like a hot dog. Munch alternately between the meat and the bread (that's why you have 2 hands), and you'll look like a local. Generally, the darker the weenie, the spicier it is. The best spicy sausage is at **Bosna Stand** (€2.40, to go only, daily 11:00–19:00, across from Getriedegasse 40).

Picnickers will appreciate the bustling morning **produce market** (daily except Sun) on Universitätsplatz, behind Mozart's house (see "Self-Guided Old Town Walking Tour," above).

Nordsee, a popular chain, serves good, fast, and inexpensive seafood next to Mozart's House on Getriedegasse.

Eating Away from the Center

These two places are on the old-town side of the river, about a 15-minute walk along the river (river on your right) from the Staatsbrücke bridge.

Augustiner Bräustübl, a monk-run brewery, is rustic and crude. It's closed for lunch, but on busy nights, it's like a Munich beer hall with no music but the volume turned up. When it's cool, you'll enjoy a historic setting with beer-sloshed and smoke-stained halls. On balmy evenings, it's a Monet painting with beer breath under chestnut trees in the garden. Local students mix with tourists eating hearty slabs of schnitzel with their fingers or cold meals from the self-serve picnic counter, while children frolic on the playground kegs. Waiters only bring drinks. For food, go up the stairs, survey the hallway of deli counters, and assemble your meal (or, as long as you buy a drink, you can bring in your own picnic, open daily 15:00–23:00, Augustinergasse 4, tel. 0662/431-246; head up Müllner Hauptstrasse northwest along the river and ask for "Müllnerbräu," its local nickname). Don't be fooled by second-rate gardens serving the same beer nearby. Augustiner Bräustübl is a huge, 1,000-seat place within the Augustiner brewery. For your beer: Pick up a half-liter or full-liter mug ("*shank*" means self-serve price, "*bedienung*" is the price with waiter service), pay the lady, wash your mug, give Mr. Keg your receipt and empty mug, and you will be made happy.

For dessert—after a visit to the strudel kiosk—enjoy the incomparable floodlit view of old Salzburg from the nearby Müllnersteg pedestrian bridge and a riverside stroll home.

Krimplestätter employs 450 years of experience serving authentic old-Salzburger food in its authentic old-Austrian interior or its cheery garden (Tue–Sun 11:00–24:00, closed Mon all year and Sun Sept–April, Müllner Hauptstrasse 31, tel. 0662/432-274). For fine food with a wild finale, eat here and drink at the nearby Augustiner Bräustübl.

Eating on or near Linzergasse

These cheaper places are near the recommended hotels on Linzergasse. **Frauenberger** is friendly, picnic-ready, and inexpensive, with indoor or outdoor seating (Mon 8:00–14:00, Tue–Fri 8:00–

14:00 & 15:00–18:00, Sat 8:00–12:30, closed Sun, across from Linzergasse 16). **Spicy Spices** is a trippy vegetarian Indian restaurant serving tasty curry and rice take-out, samosas, organic salads, vegan soups, and fresh juices (€5 lunch specials, Mon–Sat 10:00–22:00, Sun 12:00–21:00, Wolf-Dietrich Strasse 1, tel. 0662/870-712). The very local **Biergarten Weisse** is closer to the hotels on Rupertgasse and away from the tourists (Mon–Sat 11:00–24:00, Sun 16:00–24:00, on Rupertgasse east of Bayerhamerstrasse, tel. 0662/872-246).

Transportation Connections—Salzburg

By train, Salzburg is the first stop over the German–Austrian border. Travelers using a Eurail Selectpass that does not include Austria do not have to pay extra to get to Salzburg, provided they are going no farther into Austria. So, if Salzburg is your only stop in the country, you won't have to add Austria to your pass or pay extra to get there.

By train to: Innsbruck (direct every 2 hrs, 2 hrs), **Vienna** (2/hr, 3.5 hrs), **Hallstatt** (hrly, 50 min to Attnang Puchheim, 20-min wait, then 90 min to Hallstatt), **Reutte** (every 2 hrs, 4 hrs, transfer to a bus in Innsbruck), **Munich** (2/hr, 1.5–2 hrs). Train info: tel. 051717 (wait through long German recording for operator).

By car: To leave town driving west, go under the Mönchsberg tunnel and follow blue A1 signs to Munich. It's 90 minutes from Salzburg to Innsbruck.

SALZKAMMERGUT LAKE DISTRICT AND HALLSTATT

Commune with nature in Austria's Lake District. "The hills are alive," and you're surrounded by the loveliness that has turned on everyone from Emperor Franz Josef to Julie Andrews. This is *Sound of Music* country. Idyllic and majestic, but not rugged, it's a gentle land of lakes, forested mountains, and storybook villages, rich in hiking opportunities and inexpensive lodging. Settle down in the postcard-pretty, lake-cuddling town of Hallstatt.

Planning Your Time

While there are plenty of lakes and charming villages, Hallstatt is really the only one that matters. One night and a few hours to browse are all you'll need to fall in love. To relax or take a hike in the surroundings, give it two nights and a day. It's a relaxing break between Salzburg and Vienna. My best Austrian week: the two big cities (Salzburg and Vienna), a bike ride along the Danube, and a stay in Hallstatt.

Orientation (area code: 06134)

Lovable Hallstatt is a tiny town bullied onto a ledge between a selfish mountain and a swan-ruled lake, with a waterfall ripping furiously through its middle. It can be toured on foot in about 15 minutes. The town is one of Europe's oldest, going back centuries before Christ. The symbol of Hallstatt, which you'll see all over town, is two adjacent spirals—a design based on jewelry found in Bronze Age Celtic graves high in the nearby mountains.

The charms of Hallstatt are the village and its lakeside setting. Go there to relax, nibble, wander, and paddle. While tourist crowds can trample much of Hallstatt's charm in August, the place is almost dead in the off-season. The lake is famous for its good fishing and pure water.

Tourist Information: The friendly and helpful TI, on the main drag, can explain hikes and excursions, arrange private tours of Hallstatt (€65), and find you a room (Mon–Fri 9:00–12:00 & 14:00–17:00, Wed 9:00–12:00 only, in July–Aug also Sat–Sun 10:00–14:00, less off-season, a block from Marktplatz toward the lakefront parking, above post office, Seestrasse 169, tel. 06134/8208, www.hallstatt.net). Hallstatt gives anyone spending the night a "guest card" allowing free parking and discounts to local attractions (free from your hotel, ask for it).

Arrival in Hallstatt

By Train: Hallstatt's train station is a wide spot on the tracks across the lake. *Stefanie* (a boat) meets you at the station and glides scenically across the lake into town (€1.80, meets each train until about 17:00—don't arrive after that). The last departing boat-train connection leaves Hallstatt around 17:00, and the first boat goes in the morning at 6:55 (9:00 on Sun). Walk left from the boat dock for the TI and most hotels. Since there's no train station in town, the TI can help you find schedule information, or check www.oebb.at.

By Car: The main road skirts Hallstatt via a long tunnel above the town. Parking is tight mid-June through mid-October. Hallstatt has several numbered parking areas outside the town center. Parking lot #1 is in the tunnel above the town (swing through to check for a spot, free with guest card). Otherwise, several numbered lots are just after the tunnel. If you have a hotel reservation, the guard will let you drive into town to drop your bags (ask if your hotel has any in-town parking). It's a lovely 10- to 20-minute lakeside walk to the center of town from the lots. Without a guest card, you'll pay €4.20 per day for parking. Off-season parking in town is easy and free.

Hallstatt

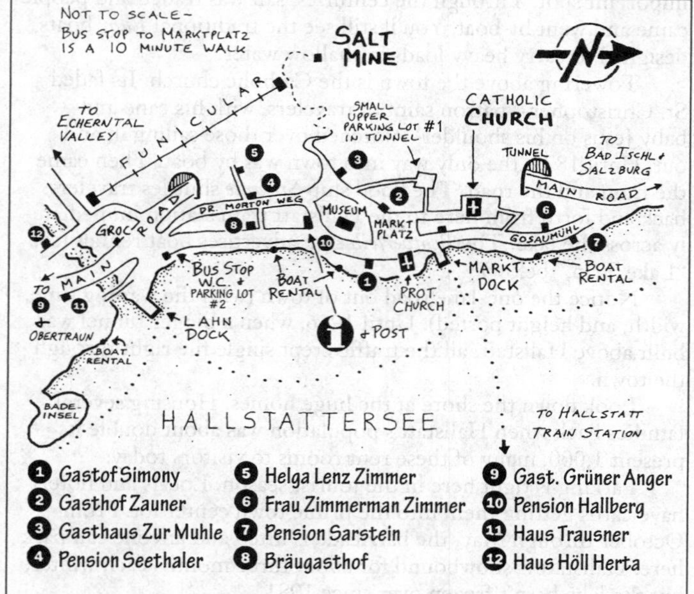

Helpful Hints

Bike Rental: Hotel Grüner Baum, facing the market square, rents bikes (€6/half day, €9/full day).

Parks and Swimming: Green and peaceful lakeside parks line the south end of Lake Hallstatt. If you walk 10 minutes south of town to Hallstatt-Lahn, you'll find a grassy public park, playground, and swimming area *(Badestrand)* with a fun man-made play island *(Bade-Insel)*.

Views: For a great view over Hallstatt, hike above Helga Lenz's *Zimmer* as far as you like (see "Sleeping," below), or climb any path leading up the hill. The 40-minute steep hike down from the salt mine tour gives the best views (see "Sights," below).

Internet: Try Hallstatt Umbrella Bar (€4/hr, summers only, daily 9:15–23:00, weather permitting, halfway between Lahn boat dock and Museum Square at Seestrasse 145).

Hallstatt Historic Town Walk

This short walk starts at the dock.

Boat Landing—There was a Hallstatt before there was a Rome. In fact, because of the importance of salt mining here, an entire epoch—the Hallstatt era, from 800 to 400 B.C.—is named for this important spot. Through the centuries, salt was traded and people came and went by boat. You'll still see the traditional *Fuhr* boats, designed to carry heavy loads in shallow water.

Towering above the town is the Catholic church. Its faded St. Christopher—patron saint of travelers, with his cane and baby Jesus on his shoulder—watched over those sailing in and out. Until 1875, the only way into town was by boat. Then came the train and the road. The good ship *Stefanie* shuttles travelers back and forth from here to the Hallstatt train station immediately across the lake. The *Bootverleih* sign advertises boat rentals (see "Lake Trip," below).

Notice the one-lane road out of town (with the waiting time, width, and height posted). Until 1966, when a bigger tunnel was built above Hallstatt, all the traffic crept single file right through the town.

Look down the shore at the huge homes. Housing several families back when Hallstatt's population was about double its present 1,000, many of these rent rooms to visitors today.

Parking is tight here in the tourist season. Locals and hotels have cards getting them into the prime town center lot. From October through May, the barricade is lifted and anyone can park here. Hallstatt is snowbound for about three months each winter, but the lake hasn't frozen over since 1981.

See any swans? They've patrolled the lake like they own it since the 1860s, when Emperor Franz Josef and Empress Sissy—the Princess Di of her day—made this region their annual holiday retreat. Sissy loved swans, so locals made sure she'd see them here. During this period, the Romantics discovered Hallstatt, many top painters worked here, and the town got its first hotel.

Tiny Hallstatt has two big churches—Protestant (step into its cemetery, which is actually a grassy lakeside playground) and Catholic up above (described below, with its fascinating bone chapel). After the Reformation, most of Hallstatt was Protestant. Then, under Hapsburg rule, it was mostly Catholic. Today, 60 percent of the town is Catholic. Walk over the town's stream, past the Protestant church, one block to the . . .

Market Square—In 1750, a fire leveled this part of town. The buildings you see now are all late 18th century and built of stone, rather than burnable wood. Take a close look at the two-dimensional, up-against-the-wall pear tree (it likes the sun-warmed wall). The statue features the Holy Trinity. Continue a block past Gasthof Simony to the pair of phone booths and step into the . . .

Museum Square—Because 20th-century Hallstatt was of no industrial importance, it was untouched by World War II. But once upon a time, its salt was worth defending. High above, peeking out of the trees, is Rudolf's Tower (Rudolfsturm). Originally a 13th-century watchtower protecting the salt mines, and later the mansion of a salt-mine boss, it's now a restaurant with a great view. A zigzag trail connects the town with Rudolfsturm and the salt mines just beyond. The big white houses by the waterfall were water-powered mills that once ground Hallstatt's grain. If you hike up a few blocks, you'll see the river raging through town. Around you are the town's TI, post office, a museum, city hall, and the Dachstein Sport shop (with a prehistoric basement, described below). The statue on the square is of the mine manager, who excavated prehistoric graves around 1850. Much of the *Schmuck* (jewelry) sold locally is inspired by the jewelry found in the area's Bronze Age tombs.

For thousands of years, people have been leaching salt out of this mountain. A brine spring sprung here, attracting Bronze Age people around 1500 B.C. Later, they dug tunnels to mine the rock, which was 70 percent salt, dissolved it into a brine, and distilled out salt—precious for preserving meat (and making French fries so tasty). For a look at early salt-mining implements, visit the museum.

Sights—Hallstatt

World Heritage Hallstatt Museum—This newly renovated museum tells the story of how little Hallstatt was once a crucial salt-mining hub of a culture that spread from France to the Balkans during the Hallstatt period (800–400 B.C.). Back then, Celtic tribes dug for precious salt, and Hallstatt was, as its name means, the "place of salt" (€6, July–Aug daily 10:00–19:00, May–June and Sept–Oct daily 10:00–18:00, Nov–April Tue–Sun 10:00–16:00, closed Mon, Seestrasse 56, adjacent to TI, tel. 06134/828-015). The Dachstein Sport shop across from the TI dug into a prehistoric site, and now its basement is another small museum (free).

▲▲Hallstatt's Catholic Church and Bone Chapel—The Catholic church overlooks the town from above. From near the boat dock, hike up the covered wooden stairway and follow signs to "*Kath. Kirche.*" The lovely church has 500-year-old altars and frescoes dedicated to St. Barbara (patron of miners) and St. Catherine (patron of foresters—lots of wood was needed to fortify the many kilometers of tunnels and boil the brine to distill out the salt). The last priest modernized parts of the church, but since Hallstatt is a UNESCO World Heritage Site, now they're changing it all back to its original state.

Behind the church, in the well-tended graveyard, is the 12th-century Chapel of St. Michael (even older than the church).

Its bone chapel—or charnel house *(Beinhaus)*—contains over 600 painted skulls. Each skull has been lovingly named, dated, and decorated (skulls with dark, thick garlands are oldest—18th century; flowers indicate more recent—19th century). Space was so limited in this cemetery that bones had only 12 peaceful, buried years here before making way for the freshly dead. Many of the dug-up bones and skulls ended up in this chapel. They stopped this practice in the 1960s, about the same time the Catholic Church began permitting cremation (€1, mid-May–Sept daily 10:00–17:00, Oct and Easter–mid-May 10:00–16:00 weather permitting, closed Nov–Easter).

▲Lake Trip—While there are full lake tours, you can ride *Stefanie* across the lake and back for €3.60. It stops at the tiny Hallstatt train station for 30 minutes, giving you time to walk to a hanging bridge and enjoy the peaceful, deep part of the lake. Longer lake tours are also available from the same dock (€7/50 min, €8.50/75 min). Those into relaxation can rent a sleepy electric motorboat to enjoy town views from the water (two rental places: Riedler, next to ferry dock or across from Bräugasthof, tel. 06134/8320, or Hemetsberger, near Gasthof Simony or past bridge before Bad Insel, tel. 06134/8228; both until 19:00; boats have 2 speeds: slow and stop; €9/hr, spend an extra €3/hr for faster 500-watt boats).

▲▲Salt Mine Tour—If you have yet to pay a visit to a salt mine, Hallstatt's—which claims to be the oldest in the world—is a good one. You'll ride a steep funicular high above the town (€7.75 round-trip, €4.75 one-way, May–Sept daily 9:00–18:00, Oct until 16:30, closed Nov–April, tel. 06132/200-2400), take a 10-minute hike, check your bag and put on old miners' clothes, hike 200 meters (650 feet) higher in your funny outfit to meet your guide, load onto the train, and ride into the mountain through a tunnel actually made by prehistoric miners. Inside, you'll listen to a great video (English headsets), slide down two banisters, and follow your guide. While the tour is mostly in German, the guide is required to speak English if you ask—so ask (€14, €19.50 combo-ticket includes entrance and round-trip cable car, can buy tickets at cable car station, May–Sept daily 9:30–16:30, Oct daily 9:30–15:00, the 16:00 funicular departure catches the last tour at 16:30, no children under age 4, rarely a long wait but arrive after 15:00 and you'll find no lines and a smaller group, tel. 06132/200-2400). The well-publicized ancient Celtic graveyard excavation sites nearby are really dead (precious little to see). If you skip the funicular, the scenic 40-minute hike back into town is (with strong knees) a joy.

At the base of the funicular, notice train tracks leading to the Erbstollen tunnel entrance. This lowest of the salt tunnels goes many kilometers into the mountain, where a shaft connects it to

Salzkammergut Lakes

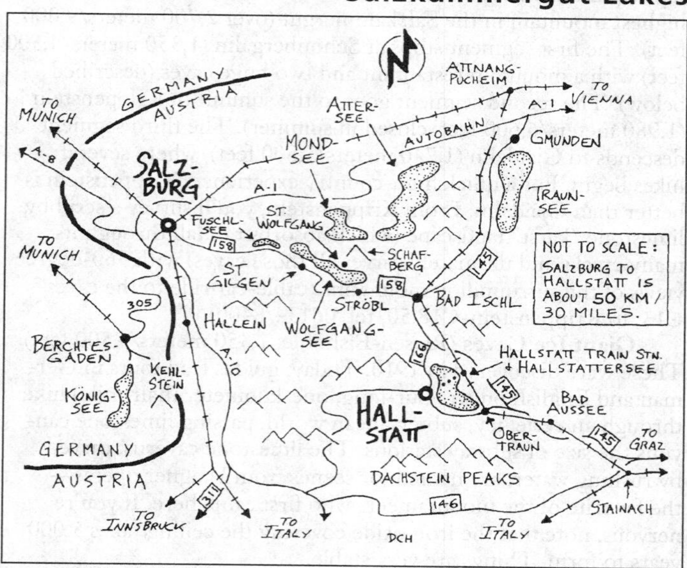

the tunnels you just explored. Today, the salty brine from these tunnels flows 40 kilometers (25 miles) through the world's oldest pipeline to the huge modern salt works (next to the highway) at Ebensee. You'll pass a stack of the original 120-year-old wooden pipes between the lift and the mine.

▲**Local Hikes**—Mountain-lovers, hikers, and spelunkers keep busy for days, using Hallstatt as their home base (ask the TI for ideas). Local hikes are well-described in the TI's *Dachstein Hiking Guide* (€5.80, English). A good, short, and easy walk is the two-hour round-trip up the Echerntal Valley to the Waldbachstrub waterfall and back. With a car, consider hiking around nearby Altaussee (flat, 3-hour hike) or along Grundlsee to Tolpitzsee. Regular buses connect Hallstatt with Gosausee for a pleasant hour-long walk around that lake. The TI can recommend a great two-day hike with an overnight in a nearby mountain hut.

Sights—Near Hallstatt

▲▲**Dachstein Mountain Cable Car and Caves**—For a refreshing activity, ride a scenic cable car up a mountain to visit huge, chilly caves.

Dachstein Cable Car: From Obertraun, five kilometers (3 miles) beyond Hallstatt, a mighty gondola goes in three stages high up the Dachstein Plateau—crowned by Dachstein, the highest mountain in the Salzkammergut (over 2,700 meters/9,000 feet). The first segment stops at Schonbergalm (1,350 meters/4,500 feet) with a mountain restaurant and two huge caves (described below). The second segment goes to the summit of Krippenstein (1,980 meters/6,600 feet, closed in summer). The third segment descends to Gjaidalm (1,740 meters/5,800 feet), where several hikes begin. For a quick high-country experience, Krippenstein is better than Gjaidalm. From Krippenstein, you'll survey a scrubby limestone "karst" landscape (which absorbs rainfall through its many cracks and ultimately carves all those caves) with 360-degree views of the surrounding mountains (cable-car ride to the caves-€13, to Krippenstein-€18.50, tel. 06134/8400).

Giant Ice Caves (Riesen-Eishohle, 1,350 meters/4,500 feet): These were discovered in 1910. Today, guides lead tours in German and English on an hour-long, one-kilometer (half-mile) hike through an eerie, icy, subterranean world, passing limestone canyons the size of subway stations. The limestone caverns, carved by rushing water, are named for scenes from Wagner operas—the favorite of the mountaineers who first came here. If you're nervous, note that the iron oxide covering the ceiling takes 5,000 years to form. Things are very stable.

At the lift station, report to the ticket window to get your cave appointment. While the temperature is just above freezing and the 600 steps help keep you warm, bring a sweater. Allow 90 minutes, including the 10-minute hike from the station (€8, or €12.30 combo-ticket with Mammoth Caves, open mid-May–mid-Oct, hour-long tours 9:00–16:00, stay in front and assert yourself for English information, tel. 06134/8400).

Drop by the little free museum near the lift station—in a local-style wood cabin designed to support 200 tons of snow—to see the huge cave system model, exhibits about its exploration, and info about life in the caves.

Mammoth Caves: While huge and well-promoted, these are much less interesting than the Ice Caves and—for most—not worth the time. Of the 48-kilometer (30-mile) limestone labyrinth excavated so far, you'll walk a kilometer (half-mile) with a German-speaking guide (€8, or €12.30 combo-ticket with Ice Caves, open mid-May–mid-Oct, hour-long tours 10:00–15:00, call a few days before to check on the schedule for an English guide, entrance a 10-min hike from lift station).

Luge Rides on the Hallstatt–Salzburg Road—If you're driving between Salzburg and Hallstatt, you'll pass two luge rides. Each is a ski lift that drags you backwards up the hill as you sit on your go-cart. At the top, you ride the cart down the winding metal course. Operating the sled is simple. Push to go, pull to stop, don't take your hands off your stick or you'll get hurt.

Each course is just off the road with easy parking. The ride up and down takes about 15 minutes. Look for *Riesen-Rutschbahn* or *Sommerrodelbahn* signs. The one near Fuschlsee (closest to Salzburg) is half as long and half the price (€3.25/ride, €23.50/10 rides, 750 meters, or 2,460 feet). The one near Wolfgangsee is a double course, more scenic with grand lake views (€5/ride, €35/10 rides, 1,300 meters, or 4,265 feet, each track is the same speed). Courses are open Easter through October from 10:00 to 18:00 (July–Aug 9:30–20:00, tel. 06235/7297). These are fun, but the concrete courses near Reutte are better.

Sleeping in Hallstatt
(€1 = about $1, country code: 43, area code: 06134, zip code: 4830)

Sleep Code: **S** = Single, **D** = Double/Twin, **T** = Triple, **Q** = Quad, **b** = bathroom, **s** = shower only, **CC** = Credit Cards accepted, **no CC** = Credit Cards not accepted, **SE** = Speaks English, **NSE** = No English.

To help you sort easily through these listings, I've divided the rooms into three categories based on the price for a standard double room with bath:

Higher Priced—Most rooms more than €75.
Moderately Priced—Most rooms €75 or less.
Lower Priced—Most rooms €50 or less.

Hallstatt's TI can almost always find you a room (either in town or at B&Bs and small hotels outside of town—which are more likely to have rooms available and come with easy parking). Mid-July and August can be tight. Early August is worst. A bed in a private home costs about €20 with breakfast. It's hard to get a one-night advance reservation. But if you drop in and they have a spot, one-nighters are welcome. Prices include breakfast, lots of stairs, and a silent night. "*Zimmer mit Aussicht*?" means "Room with view?"—worth asking for. Only a few of my listings accept plastic, which goes for most businesses here.

Laundry: A small, full-service launderette is at the campground up from the island of Bade-Insel, just off the main road (about €7/load, based on weight). In the center, Hotel Grüner Baum does laundry for non-guests (€14.50/load, facing Market Square).

HIGHER PRICED

Gasthof Zauner is a business machine offering 12 modern, pine-flavored rooms with all the comforts on the main square, and a restaurant specializing in grilled meat and fish (Db-€90,

CC, Marktplatz 51, tel. 06134/8246, fax 06134/82468, www.zauner.hallstatt.net, e-mail: zauner@hallstatt.at).

MODERATELY PRICED

Gasthof Simony, my 500-year-old favorite, is right on the square, with a lake view, balconies, creaky wood floors, slippery rag rugs, antique furniture, a lakefront garden for swimming, and a huge breakfast. Reserve in advance. For safety, reconfirm a day or two before you arrive and call again if arriving late (S-€30, Sb-€60, D-€40, Ds-€55, Db-€75, third person-€26–33, no CC, Markt 105, tel. & fax 06134/8231, e-mail: susanna.scheutz@multikom.at, Susanna Scheutz SE). Downstairs and in the lakefront garden, Frau Regina Zopf runs a traditional Austrian restaurant—try her delicious homemade desserts and meals.

Bräugasthof Hallstatt is another creaky old place—a former brewery—with eight mostly lakeview rooms near the town center (Sb-€40, Db-€73, Tb-€98, less off-season, CC, just past TI on the main drag at Seestrasse 120, tel. 06134/8221, fax 06134/82214, Lobisser family).

Gasthof Pension Grüner Anger is a practical, modern 11-room place away from the medieval town center. It's big and quiet, a block from the base of the salt mine lift, and a 10-minute walk from Market Square (Sb-€33, Db-€63, €66 in July–Aug, more for 1-night stays, third person-€15, CC, parking, Lahn 10, tel. 06134/8397, fax 06134/83974, www.hallstatt.net/gruener.anger, e-mail: anger@aon.at, Sulzbacher family).

Pension Hallberg-Tauchergasthof (Diver's Inn), across from the TI, has six big rooms and a funky mini-museum of WWII artifacts found in the lake (Sb-€40, Db-€60, Tb/Qb with kitchen-€90, CC but prefer cash, tel. 06134/8286, fax 06134/82865, e-mail: hallberg@aon.at, Gerda the "Salt Witch" and Eckbert Winkelmann).

LOWER PRICED

Helga Lenz is a five-minute climb above the Pension Seethaler (look for the green *Zimmer* sign). This big, sprawling, woodsy house has a nifty garden perch, wins the best-view award, and is ideal for those who sleep well in tree houses (S-only available April–June & Oct-€17, D-€30, Db-€36, T-€44, Tb-€51, 1-night stays-€2 per person extra, family room, no CC, closed Nov–March, Hallberg 17, tel. & fax 06134/8508, e-mail: haus-lenz@aon.at).

These two listings are 200 meters (650 feet) to the right of the ferryboat dock, with your back to the lake: the appropriately named **Frau Zimmermann** runs a three-room *Zimmer* in a

500-year-old, ramshackle house with low beams, time-polished wood, and fine lake views (S-€16, D-€32, no CC, can be musty, Gosaumühlstrasse 69, tel. 06134/86853). She speaks little English, but you'll find yourself caught up in her charm and laughing together like old friends. A block away, **Pension Sarstein** has 25 beds in basic, dusty rooms with flower-bedecked, lakeview balconies, in a charming building run by friendly Frau Fischer. You can swim from her lakeside garden (D-€29, Ds-€41, Db-€50 with this book, 1-night stays-€1.50 per person extra, no CC, Gosaumühlstrasse 83, tel. 06134/8217, NSE).

For more budget *Zimmer*, consider **Haus Höll Herta** (Db-€38, apartment-€20 per person, no CC, 3 rooms, Malerweg 45, tel. 06134/8531, fax 06134/825-533, e-mail: frank.hoell@aon.at) or **Haus Trausner** (Ds-€38, Tb-€52.50, no CC, 4 rooms, includes breakfast, Lahnstrasse 27, tel. 06134/8710, e-mail: trausner1@utanet.at, Maria Trausner SE).

Gasthaus zur Mühle Jugendherberge, below the waterfall with the best cheap beds in town, is popular for its great pizzas and cheap grub (bed in 3- to 20-bed coed dorms-€10, D-€22, sheets-€3 extra, family quads, breakfast-€3, big lockers with a €20 deposit, no CC, closed Nov, below tunnel car park, Kirchenweg 36, tel. & fax 06134/8318, e-mail: toeroe.f@magnet.at, run by Ferdinand Törö).

Pension Seethaler is a homey old lodge with 45 beds and a breakfast room mossy with antlers, perched above the lake. The staff won't win any awards for congeniality—*Zimmer* are friendlier and cheaper—but this place is a reasonable last resort (€18/person in S, D, T, or Q, €26/person in rooms with private bath, 3 nights or more-€1.50 less, no CC, coin-op showers downstairs-€1/8 min, Dr. Morton Weg 22, find the stairs to the left of Seestrasse 116, at top of stairs turn left, tel. 06134/8421, fax 06134/84214, e-mail: pension.seethaler@kronline.at).

Eating in Hallstatt

You can enjoy good food inexpensively, with delightful lakeside settings. While everyone cooks the typical Austrian fare, your best bet here is trout. *Reinanke* trout is from Lake Hallstatt. Restaurants in Hallstatt tend to have unreliable hours and close early on slow nights, so don't wait too long to get dinner.

Grab a front table at **Restaurant Simony's** lakeside garden (daily 11:00–21:00, tel. 06134/8427, under Gasthof Simony, see "Sleeping," above). **Hotel Grüner Baum's** romantic restaurant is fancier and also good (May–Oct Tue–Sun 11:30–22:00, closed Mon and Nov–April, right on Market Square, tel. 06134/8263). Or feed the swans while your trout is being cooked at **Restaurant**

Bräugasthof (May–Oct daily 10:00–21:00, closed Nov–April, fun menu, CC, tel. 06134/20012, see "Sleeping," above). While it lacks a lakeside setting, **Gasthof Zauner's** classy restaurant is well-respected for its grilled meat and fish; the interior of its dining room is covered in real ivy that grows in through the windows (daily 11:30–14:30 & 17:30–22:00, see "Sleeping," above). For the best pizza in town with a fun-loving local crowd, chow down cheap and hearty at **Gasthaus zur Mühle** (daily 11:00–14:00 & 17:00–21:00, closed Tue in Oct–May, see "Sleeping," above). Locals like the smoky **Strand Café,** a 10-minute lakeside hike away, near the town beach (April–Oct Tue–Sun 11:30–14:00 & 18:00–21:00, closed Mon and Nov–March, great garden setting on the lake, Seelande 102, tel. 06134/8234). For your late-night drink, savor the Market Square from the trendy little pub called **Ruth Zimmermann** (June–Oct daily 9:00–2:00, Nov–May daily 12:00–2:00, tel. 06134/8306).

Transportation Connections—Hallstatt

By train to: Salzburg (hrly, 90 min to Attnang Puchheim, short wait, 50 min to Salzburg), **Vienna** (hrly, 90 min to Attnang Puchheim, short wait, 2.5 hrs to Vienna). Day-trippers to Hallstatt can check bags at the Attnang Puchheim station. (Note: Connections there and back can be very fast—about 5 min; have coins ready for the lockers at track 1.)

INNSBRUCK

Innsbruck is world famous as a resort for skiers and a haven for hikers. But when compared to Salzburg and Vienna, it's stale strudel. Still, a quick look is easy and interesting.

Innsbruck was the Hapsburgs' capital of the Tirol. Its medieval center, now a glitzy, tourist-filled pedestrian zone, still gives you the feel of a provincial medieval capital. The much-ogled Golden Roof *(Goldenes Dach)* is the centerpiece. Built by Emperor Maximilian in 1494, this balcony (with 2,657 gilded copper tiles) offered an impressive spot from which to view his medieval spectacles.

From this square, you'll see the Golden Roof, the Baroque-style Helblinghaus, and the city tower (climb it for a great view, €2.50). Nearby are the palace (Hofburg), church (Hofkirche), and Folklife Museum.

Orientation (area code: 0512)

Tourist Information: Innsbruck has a TI downtown (Easter–mid-Dec daily 9:00–18:00, mid-Dec–Easter daily 8:00–18:00, on Burggraben, 3 blocks in front of Golden Roof, tel. 0512/5356, www.innsbruck-information.at) and a helpful hotel room–finding service at the train station (summer daily 9:00–21:00, winter daily 9:00–20:00, tel. 0512/562-000). The €19 24-hour Innsbruck Card pays for itself only if you take the Mountain Lift (also covers Igls Lift, as well as the buses, trams, museums, zoo, and castle). The TI offers two-hour tours—combining bus and some walking—for €13 year-round (in English and German, July–Sept at 12:00 and 14:00, Oct–June at 12:00 only). A one-hour walking tour leaves from the TI daily in the summer (in English and German, €8, July–Sept at 11:00 and 14:00, no walking tours Oct–June).

Arrival in Innsbruck: From the train station, it's a 10-minute walk to the old-town center. Leave by veering right to Brixnerstrasse. Follow it past the fountain at Boznerplatz and straight until it dead-ends into Maria-Theresa Strasse. Turn right and go 250 meters (820 feet) into the old town (you'll pass the TI on Burggraben on your right), where you'll see the Golden Roof and Hotel Weisses Kreuz. Tram #3 does the same trip in two stops (pay the driver €1.60 or buy a €3.20 all-day pass from the machine at the tram stop or at a *Tabak*).

Sights—Innsbruck

▲▲Folklife Museum (Tiroler Volkskunst Museum)—This offers the best look anywhere at traditional Tirolean lifestyles. Fascinating exhibits range from wedding dresses and gaily painted cribs and nativity scenes, to maternity clothes and babies' trousers. The upper floors show Tirolean homes through the ages (€4.35, Sept–June Mon–Sat 9:00–17:00, Sun 9:00–12:00, July–Aug Mon–Sat 9:00–17:30, Sun 9:00–12:00, hard to appreciate without the €2.50 English guidebook, tel. 0512/584-302).

Maria-Theresa Strasse—From the medieval center stretches the fine Baroque Maria-Theresa Strasse. St. Anne's Column marks the center of the old marketplace. At the far end, the Triumphal Arch is a gate Maria Theresa built to celebrate the marriage of her son, Leopold II.

▲Ski Jump View—A new ski jump has been built in the same location as the original ski jump (demolished in 2000) that was used for the 1964 and 1976 Olympics. It's an inviting side-trip with a superb view, overlooking the city just off the Brenner Pass road on the south side of town (drivers follow signs to *Bergisel* or take tram #1). For the best view, hike to the Olympic rings under the dish that held the Olympic flame, where Dorothy Hamill and a host of others who brought home the gold are honored. Near the car park is a memorial to Andreas Hofer, the hero of the Tirolean battles against Napoleon.

Mountain Lifts and Hiking—A popular mountain-sports center

Innsbruck and Hall

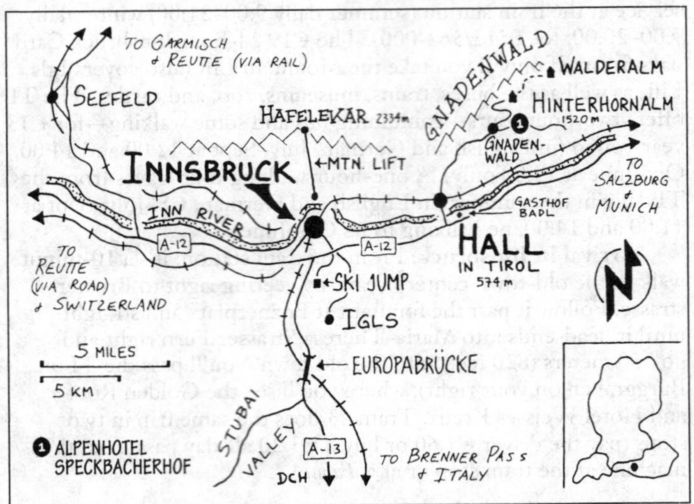

and home of the 1964 and 1976 Winter Olympics, Innsbruck is surrounded by 150 mountain lifts, 2,000 kilometers (1,250 miles) of trails, and 250 hikers' huts. If it's sunny, consider riding the lift right out of the city to the mountaintops above (€22). Ask your hotel or hostel for an Innsbruck Club card, which offers overnight guests various discounts, bike tours, and free guided hikes in summer. Hikers meet in front of Congress Innsbruck daily at 8:45; each day, it's a different hike in the surrounding mountains and valleys (bring only lunch and water; boots, rucksack, and transport are provided; confirm with TI).

Alpenzoo—This zoo is one of Innsbruck's most popular attractions (understandable when the competition is the Golden Roof). You can ride the funicular up to the zoo (free if you buy your zoo ticket before boarding) and get a look at all the animals that hide out in the Alps: wildcats, owls, elk, vultures, and more (€5.80, €7.30 combo-ticket at TI includes round-trip transit, May–Sept daily 9:00–18:00, Oct–April daily 9:00–17:00, Weiherburggasse 37, tel. 0512/292-323, www.alpenzoo.at).

▲Slap Dancing—For your Tirolean folk fun, Innsbruck hotels offer an entertaining evening of slap dancing and yodeling nearly nightly at 20:40 from April through October (€17 includes a drink with 2-hour show, tickets at TI). And every summer Thursday, the town puts on a free outdoor folk show under the Golden Roof (weather permitting).

Sights—Near Innsbruck

▲▲Alpine Side-Trip by Car to Hinterhornalm—In Gnadenwald, a village sandwiched between Hall and its Alps, pay a €4.50 toll, pick up a brochure, then corkscrew your way up the mountain. Marveling at the crazy amount of energy put into such a remote road project, you'll finally end up at the rustic Hinterhornalm Berg restaurant (often closed, cellular 0664-211-2745). Hinterhornalm is a hang-gliding springboard. On good days, it's a butterfly nest. From there, it's a level 20-minute walk to Walderalm, a cluster of three dairy farms with 70 cows that share their meadow with the clouds. The cows—cameras dangling from their thick necks—ramble along ridge-top lanes surrounded by cut-glass peaks. The ladies of the farms serve soup, sandwiches, and drinks (very fresh milk in the afternoon) on rough plank tables. Below you spreads the Inn River Valley and, in the distance, tourist-filled Innsbruck.

Sleeping in Gnadenwald: Alpenhotel Speckbacherhof is a grand rustic hotel set between a peaceful forest and a meadow with all the comforts, mini-golf, laundry, and so on (D-€44, Db-€66–90, 2 apartments as Db-€110–115 plus €12 per additional person, half board €13 extra per person, ask for 10 percent discount with this book, CC, includes breakfast, closed Nov–mid-Dec, Sankt Martin 2, A-6060 Gnadenwald/Tirol, tel. 05223/52511, fax 05223/525-1155, family Mayr). Drive 10 minutes uphill from Hall to the village of Gnadenwald. It's across the street from the Hinterhornalm toll road.

Sleeping in Innsbruck

(€1 = about $1, country code: 43, area code: 0512)

Hotel Weisses Kreuz, near the Golden Roof, has been housing visitors for 500 years. While it still feels like an old inn, its 40 rooms are newly renovated and comfortable (S-€34–39, Sb-€56–60, D-€64–67, small Db-€83–90, the big Db at €93–106 is a better value, includes breakfast, CC, non-smoking rooms, elevator, Internet access, 50 meters, or 165 feet, from Golden Roof, as central as can be in the old town at Herzog-Friedrichstrasse 31, A-6020 Innsbruck, tel. 0512/594-790, fax 0512/594-7990, www.weisseskreuz.at, e-mail: hotel@weisseskreuz.at).

Pension Stoi, which rents 10 pleasant rooms, is a very basic place hiding behind a dumpy exterior 200 meters (650 feet) from the train station (S-€32, Sb-€37, D-€52, Db-€58, T-€58, Tb-€65, Q-€65, Qb-€80, no breakfast, no CC, free parking in alleyway behind pension, Salurnerstrasse 7, 6020 Innsbruck, tel. 0512/585-434, fax 05238/87282, www.stoi.cjb.net, e-mail: info@stoi.cjb.net).

Transportation Connections—Innsbruck

To: Hall (4 buses/hr, 30 min; hrly trains, 15 min), **Salzburg** (trains every 2 hrs, 2 hrs), **Vienna** (trains every 2 hrs, 5.5 hrs), **Reutte** (trains every 2 hrs, 2.5 hrs with transfer in Garmisch and sometimes also in Mittenwald; or by bus: 4/day, 2.5 hrs), **Bregenz** (every 2 hrs, some with transfer in Feldkirch, 2.5 hrs), **Zurich** (3/day, 4 hrs), **Munich** (every 2 hrs, 2 hrs), **Paris** (2 trains/day, transfer in Munich or Salzburg, 11 hrs), **Milan** (2/day, 5.5 hrs), **Venice** (1/day, 5 hrs). Night trains run to Vienna, Milan, Venice, and Rome. Train info: tel. 051717 (wait through long German recording for operator).

HALL IN TIROL

Hall was a rich salt-mining center when Innsbruck was just a humble bridge *(Brücke)* town on the Inn River. Hall actually has a larger old town than does its sprawling neighbor, Innsbruck. Hall hosts a colorful morning scene before the daily tour buses arrive, closes down tight for its daily siesta, and sleeps on Sunday. There's a brisk farmers' market on Saturday mornings. (For drivers, Hall is a convenient overnight stop on the long drive from Vienna to Switzerland.)

Tourist Information: Hall's TI is just off the main square (June–Sept Mon–Fri 8:30–18:00, Sat 9:00–12:00, closed Sun, Oct–May Mon–Fri 8:30–12:30 & 14:00–18:00, Sat 9:00–12:00, closed Sun, Wallpachgasse 5, tel. 05223/56269, www.hall-in-tirol.at).

Bike Rental: You can rent bikes at the campground (tel. 05223/454-6475). The riverside bike path (11 km/7 miles from Hall to Volders) is a treat.

Sights—Hall

Hasegg Castle—This was the town mint. As you walk over the old pedestrian bridge from Gasthof Badl (see "Sleeping," below), it's the first old building you'll see. You can pick up a town map and a list of sights here.

Parish Church—Facing the town square, this much-appended Gothic church is decorated Baroque, with fine altars, a twisted apse, and a north wall lined with bony relics.

Salt Museum (Bergbaumuseum)—Back when salt was money, Hall was loaded. Try catching a tour at this museum, where the town has reconstructed one of its original salt mines, complete with pits, shafts, drills, tools, and a slippery but tiny wooden slide (€3, May–Sept Mon–Sat, closed Sun, by guided tour only, 45-min tours depart on the hour from 13:00–16:00 if there are at least 6 people, call ahead to check on English tours, tel. 05223/56269).

Walking Tours—The TI organizes town walks in English (€6/1 hr, €8/1.5 hrs, minimum 6 people or pay total of €36, includes admissions, by reservation only, tel. 05223/56269).

Swimming—If you want to make a splash, check out Hall's magnificent *Freischwimmbad*, a huge outdoor pool complex with four diving boards, a giant lap pool, a big slide, and a kiddies' pool, all surrounded by a lush garden, sauna, mini-golf, and lounging locals (€3, May–Aug daily 9:00–19:00, closed Sept–April, follow signs from downtown, tel. 05223/45464).

Sleeping and Eating in Hall
(€1 = about $1, country code: 43, area code: 05223)

Lovable towns that specialize in lowering the pulse of local vacationers line the Inn Valley. Hall, while the best town, has the shortest list of accommodations. Up the hill on either side of the river are towns strewn with fine farmhouse hotels and pensions. Most *Zimmer* charge about €20 per person but don't accept one-night stays.

Gasthof Badl is a big, comfortable, friendly place run by sunny Frau Steiner and her daughter, Sonja. I like its convenience, peace, big breakfast, easy telephone reservations, and warm welcome (Sb-€36, Db-€57, Tb-€81, Qb-€105, CC, 25 rooms, elevator, rental bikes for guests for fine riverside path, Innbrücke 4, A-6060 Hall in Tirol, tel. 05223/56784, fax 05223/567-843, www.hotel-badl-tirol.com, e-mail: badl@tirol.com). Hall's kitchens close early, but Gasthof Badl's restaurant serves excellent dinners until 21:30 (€7–11, closed Tue). They stock the essential TI brochures and maps of Hall and Innsbruck in English. It's easy to find: From the east, it's immediately off the Hall-Mitte freeway exit; you'll see the orange-lit Bed sign. From Innsbruck, take the Hall-Mitte exit and, rather than turning left over the big bridge into town, go straight.

For a cheaper room in a private home, **Frieda Tollinger** rents out three rooms and accepts one-nighters (€16/person with breakfast, no CC, across the river from Badl and downstream about a kilometer, or half-mile, follow Untere Lend, which becomes Schopperweg, to Schopperweg 8, tel. 05223/41366, NSE).

Transportation Connections—Hall
Innsbruck is the nearest major train station. Hall and Innsbruck are connected by train and bus. Trains do the trip faster but leave only hourly, and Hall's train station is a 10-minute walk from the town center. The white bus #4 takes a bit longer (20 min, €2.30) but leaves four times per hour and drops you in Hall at the edge of town at the wooden bridge by the Billa Supermarket or the

Kurhaus at the top of town. Buses go to and from the Innsbruck train station, a 10-minute walk from the old-town center. Drivers staying in freeway-handy Hall can side-trip into Innsbruck using bus #4. Immediately over the bridge entering Hall (on right) is a convenient parking lot (90 min free with cardboard clock under windshield, 5-min walk to old center).

Route Tips for Drivers

Into Salzburg from Munich: After crossing the border, stay on the autobahn, taking the Süd Salzburg exit in the direction of Anif. First, you'll pass Schloss Hellbrunn (and zoo), then the TI and a great park-and-ride service. Get sightseeing information and a €3.20 one-day *Tageskarte* bus pass from the TI (summer daily 9:00–19:00, off-season Mon–Sat 9:00–18:00, closed Sun, tel. 0662/8898-7360), park your car (free), and catch the shuttle bus (€1.70, included in day ticket, every 5 min, bus #51 or #95) into town. Mozart never drove in the old town, and neither should you. If you don't believe in park-and-rides, the easiest, cheapest, most central parking lot is the 1,500-car Altstadt lot in the tunnel under the Mönchsberg (€14/day; note your slot number and which of the twin lots you're in, tel. 0662/846-434). Your hotel may provide discounted parking passes.

From Salzburg to Hallstatt (80 km/50 miles): Get on the Munich–Wien autobahn (blue signs), head for Vienna, exit at Thalgau, and follow signs to Hof, Fuschl, and St. Gilgen. The Salzburg-to-Hallstatt road passes two luge rides (see "Sights—Near Hallstatt," above), St. Gilgen (pleasant but touristy), and Bad Ischl (the center of the Salzkammergut with a spa, the emperor's villa if you need a Hapsburg history fix, and a good TI—tel. 06132/277-570).

Hallstatt is basically traffic-free. To park, try parking lot #1 in the tunnel above the town (free with guest card). Otherwise, try the lakeside lots (a pleasant 10- to 20-min walk from the town center) after the tunnel on the far side of town. If you're traveling off-season and staying downtown, you can drive in and park by the boat dock. (For more on parking in Hallstatt, see "Arrival in Hallstatt," above.)

From Hall into Innsbruck and on to Switzerland: For Old Innsbruck, take the autobahn from Hall to the Innsbruck Ost exit and follow the signs to *Zentrum*, then *Kongresshaus*, and park as close as you can to the old center on the river (Hofgarden).

Just south of Innsbruck is the new ski jump (from the autobahn take the Innsbruck Süd exit and follow signs to *Bergisel*). Park at the end of the road near the Andreas Hofer Memorial, and climb to the empty, grassy stands for a picnic.

Leaving Innsbruck for Switzerland (from ski jump, go down into town along huge cemetery—thoughtfully placed just beyond the jump landing—and follow blue A12, Garmisch, Arlberg signs), head west on the autobahn (direction: Bregenz). The 13-kilometer-long (8-mile) Arlberg tunnel saves you 30 minutes, but costs you lots of scenery and €9.50 (Swiss francs and credit cards accepted). For a joyride and to save a few bucks, skip the tunnel, exit at St. Anton, and go via Stuben.

After the speedy Arlberg tunnel, you're 30 minutes from Switzerland. Bludenz, with its characteristic medieval quarter, makes a good rest stop. Pass Feldkirch (and another long tunnel) and exit the autobahn at Rankweil/Feldkirch Nord, following signs for Altstätten and Meiningen (CH). Crossing the baby Rhine River, leave Austria.

Leaving Hall or Innsbruck for Reutte, go west (as above, direction Switzerland) and leave the freeway at Telfs where signs direct you to Reutte (a 90-min drive).

Side-Trip over Brenner Pass into Italy: A short swing into Italy is fast and easy from Innsbruck or Hall (45-min drive, easy border crossing). To get to Italy, take the great Europa Bridge over Brenner Pass. It costs about €12, but in 30 minutes, you'll be at the border. (Note: Traffic can be heavy on summer weekends.)

In Italy, drive to the colorful market town of Vipiteno/Sterzing. **Reifenstein Castle** is a unique and wonderfully preserved medieval castle, just south of town on the west side of the valley, down a small road next to the autobahn. The lady who lives at the castle gives tours in German, Italian, and a little English (open Easter–Oct, entry by tour only, €3.50, tours on Mon at 14:00 and 15:00, Tue–Thu and Sat–Sun at 9:30, 10:30, 14:00, and 15:00, closed Fri and Nov–Easter, tel. from Austria 00-39-0472-765-879, in Italy: tel. 0472-765-879).

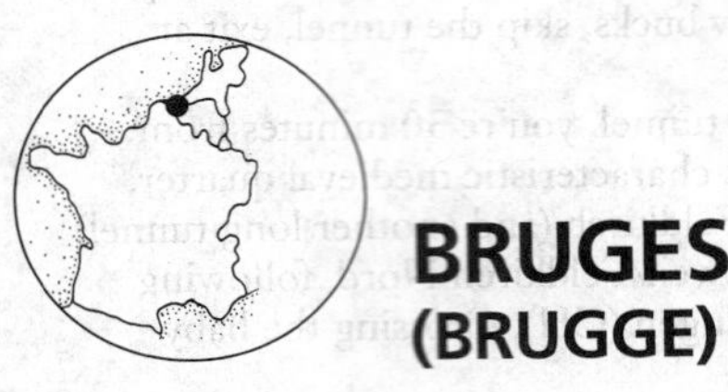

BRUGES (BRUGGE)

With Renoir canals, pointy gilded architecture, vivid time-tunnel art, and stay-awhile cafés, Bruges is a heavyweight sightseeing destination as well as a joy. Where else can you ride a bike along a canal, munch mussels, wash them down with the world's best beer, savor heavenly chocolate, and see Flemish Primitives and a Michelangelo, all within 300 meters of a bell tower that jingles every 15 minutes? And there's no language barrier.

The town is Brugge (pron. BROO-ghah) in Flemish, or Bruges (pron. broozh) in French and English. Its name comes from the Viking word for wharf. Right from the start, Bruges was a trading center. In the 11th century, the city grew wealthy on the cloth trade.

By the 14th century, Bruges' population was 40,000, as large as London's. As the middleman in sea trade between Northern and Southern Europe, it was one of the biggest cities in the world and an economic powerhouse. In addition, Bruges had become the most important cloth market in Northern Europe.

In the 15th century, while England and France were slogging it out in a 100-year-long war, Bruges was the favored residence of the powerful Dukes of Burgundy—and at peace. Commerce and the arts boomed. The artists Jan van Eyck and Hans Memling had studios here.

But by the 16th century, the harbor had silted up and the economy had collapsed. The Burgundian court left, Belgium became a minor Hapsburg possession, and Bruges' Golden Age abruptly ended. For generations, Bruges was known as a mysterious and dead city. In the 19th century, a new port, Zeebrugge, brought renewed vitality to the area. And in the 20th century, tourists discovered the town.

Today Bruges prospers because of tourism: It's a uniquely well-preserved Gothic city and a handy gateway to Europe. It's no secret, but even with the crowds, it's the kind of city where you don't mind being a tourist.

Bruges' ultimate sight is the town itself, and the best way to enjoy that is to get lost on the back streets, away from the lace shops and ice-cream stands.

Planning Your Time

Bruges needs at least two nights and a full, well-organized day. Even nonshoppers enjoy browsing here, and the Belgian love of life makes a hectic itinerary seem a little senseless. With one day (other than Monday, when all the museums are closed), the speedy visitor could do the Bruges town walk described below:

9:30 Climb the bell tower on the Market Square.
10:00 Tour the sights on the Burg Square.
11:00 Tour the Groeninge Museum.
12:00 Tour Gruuthuse Museum.
13:00 Eat lunch and buy chocolates.
14:00 Take a short canal cruise (from the discount dock—see "Tours of Bruges," below).
14:30 Visit the Church of Our Lady and see the Michelangelo Madonna.
15:00 Tour the Memling Museum.
16:00 Catch the Straffe Hendrik Brewery tour.
17:00 Calm down in the Begijnhof.
18:00 Ride a bike around the quiet back streets of town or take a horse-and-buggy tour.
20:00 Lose the tourists and find a dinner.

(If this schedule seems insane, skip the bell tower and the brewery—or stay another day.)

Orientation

The tourists' Bruges (you'll be sharing it) is contained within a one-kilometer-square canal, or moat. Nearly everything of interest and importance is within a cobbled and convenient swath between the train station and Market Square (a 15-min walk). Many of my quiet and charming recommended accommodations lie just beyond Market Square.

Tourist Information

The main office is on Burg Square (April–Sept Mon–Fri 9:30–18:30, Sat–Sun 10:00–12:00 & 14:00–18:30, Oct–March Mon–Fri 9:30–17:00, Sat–Sun 9:30–13:00 & 14:00–17:30, lockers, money-exchange desk, WC in courtyard, tel. 050-448-686,

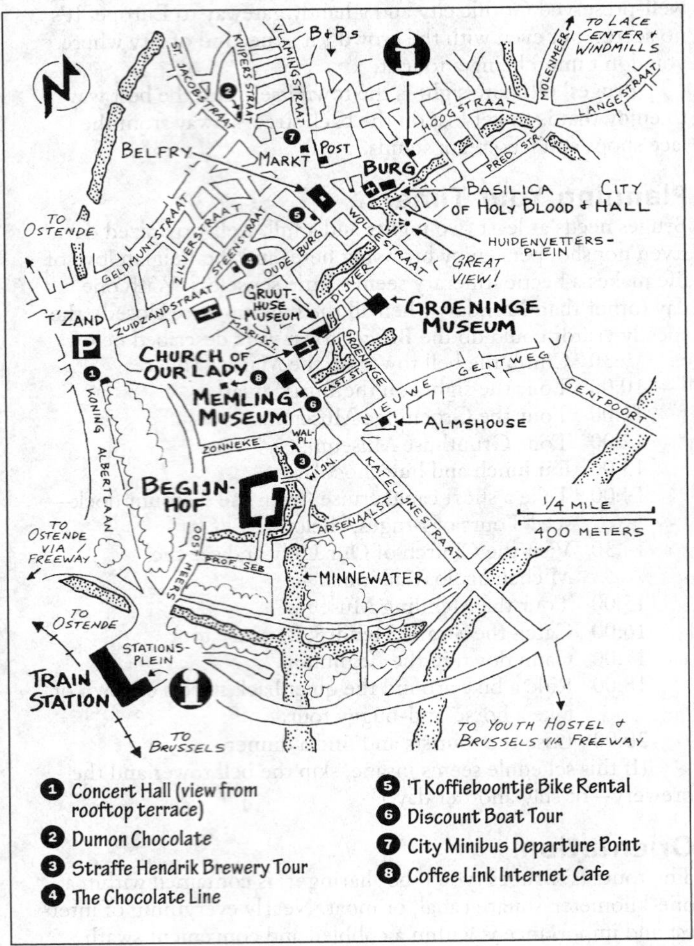

www.brugge.com). The other TI is at the train station (generally Mon-Sat 10:00-18:00, closed Sun).

The TIs sell a great €1 Bruges visitors guide with a map and listings of all of the sights and services. You can also pick up a bimonthly English-language program called *events@brugge*. The TIs have information on train schedules and on the many tours available (see "Tours" below). Bikers will want the *5X on the Bike around Bruges* map/guide (€1.25) that shows five routes through

Museum Tips

Admission prices are steep but include great audioguides—so plan on spending some time and getting into it. The information number for all museums is 050-448-711.

Combo-Ticket: The TIs and participating museums sell a museum combo-ticket (any 5 museums for €15). Since the Groeninge and Memling museums cost €8 each, anyone interested in art will save money with this pass.

Black Monday: In Bruges, nearly all sights are open Tuesday to Sunday year-round from 9:30 to 17:00 and closed on Monday. If in Bruges on a Monday, consider a tour (see "Tours," below).

the countryside. Many hotels give free maps with more detail than the map the TIs sell.

Arrival in Bruges

By Train: Coming in by train you'll see the square bell tower marking the main square. Upon arrival, stop by the station TI (has lockers) to pick up the Bruges visitors guide (map in centerfold). There are no ATMs at the station, but you can change money at ticket windows.

Your best way to get to the town center is by bus. All buses go directly to the Market Square. Simply hop on any bus, pay €1 and in four minutes you're there. The €1 tickets are good for an hour. A day pass costs €3. Buses #4 and #8 go farther, to the northeast part of town (to the windmills and recommended places on Carmersstraat).

Note that nearly all city buses go directly from the station to the Market Square and fan out from there. They then return to Market Square (bus #2 stops at post office on square; other buses stop at library on nearby Kuiperstraat) and go directly back to the station.

The **taxi** fare from the train station to most hotels is around €6 (tel. 050-334-444).

It's a 20-minute **walk** from the station to the center—no fun with your luggage. If you want to walk, cross the busy street and canal in front of the station, head up Oostmeers, and turn right on Steenstraat to reach Market Square.

You can rent a **bike** at the station for the duration of your stay, but other bike-rental shops are closer to the center (see "Helpful Hints," below).

By Car: Park at the train station for just €2.50 per day; show your parking receipt for a free bus ride into town. There are pricier (€9/day) underground parking garages at 't Zand and well-marked around town. Driving in Bruges is very complicated because of the one-way system.

Helpful Hints

Bike Rental: 'T Koffieboontje, just under the bell tower, is extremely well organized and the handiest. They swipe a credit-card imprint for a deposit and you're on your way with a nearly new bike (€3/1 hr, €6/4 hrs, or €9/24-hr day, €6/day with an ISIC student card, free city maps and child seats, daily 9:00-22:00, their €15 "bike plus any 3 museums" deal could save enough to pay for lunch, Hallestraat 4, tel. 050-338-027).

Other rental places include: **Fietsen Popelier** (50 meters from Church of Our Lady at Mariastraat 26, tel. 050-343-262), the less central **De Ketting** (cheap at €5/day, daily 9:00–20:00, Gentpoortstraat 23, tel. 050-344-196), and the **train station** (ticket window #3, daily 7:00–20:00, €9/day, €6.50/half day after 14:00, €15 deposit).

Internet Access: The relaxing Coffee Link, with mellow music and pleasant art, is centrally located across from the Church of Our Lady (€2/30 min, daily 10:00–21:30, 14 terminals, Mariastraat 38, tel. 050-349-973).

Laundry: Bruges' most convenient place to do laundry is **Mr. Wash** (€4 wash and dry self-service, daily 8:30-22:00, just off Market Square at Sint Jakobsstraat 33 in an arcade, tel. 050-335-902). A less central Laundromat is at Gentportstraat 28 (daily 7:00–22:00).

Shopping: Shops are open from 9:00 to 18:00, a little later on Friday. Grocery stores are usually closed on Sunday. The main shopping street, Steenstraat, stretches from Market Square to the square called 't Zand.

Market Days: Wednesday morning (Market Square) and Saturday morning ('t Zand) are market days. On Saturday and Sunday afternoons, a flea market hops along Dijver in front of the Groeninge Museum.

Festival of Canals: Bruges' famous festival won't be held again until 2004.

Post Office: It's on Market Square near the bell tower (Mon–Fri 9:00–19:00, Sat 9:30–12:30, closed Sun, tel. 050-331-411).

Best Town View: The bell tower overlooking the Market Square rewards those who climb it with the ultimate town view. The best view without a climb is from the rooftop terrace of Bruges' concert hall (Concertgebouw). This seven-story building, built in 2002, is the city's only modern highrise (daily 11:00-23:00, free elevator, on edge of old town on 't Zand).

Tours of Bruges

Bruges by Boat—The most relaxing and scenic (though not informative) way to see this city of canals is by boat, with the captain narrating. Boats leave from all over town (€5.50, 4/hr, 10:00–17:00, copycat 30-min rides). Boten Stael offers an €0.80 discount with this book (just over the canal from Memling Museum at Katelinjnestraat 4, tel. 050-332-771).

City Minibus Tour—City Tour Bruges gives a rolling overview of the town in an 18-seat, two-skylight minibus with dial-a-language headsets and video support (€9.50, 50 min). The tour leaves hourly from Market Square (10:00–19:00 in summer, until 18:00 in spring and fall, less in winter, tel. 050-355-024). The narration, while clear, is slow-moving and boring. But the tour is a lazy way to cruise by virtually every sight in Bruges.

Walking Tour—Local guides walk small groups through the core of town (€5, daily July-Aug, Sat-Sun only in June and Sept, depart from TI at 15:00, 2 hrs, no tours off-season). While earnest, the tours are heavy on history and in two languages, so they may be less than peppy. Still, to propel you beyond the pretty gables and canal swans of Bruges, they are good medicine. A private two-hour guided tour costs €40 (reserve at least 3 days in advance through TI, tel. 050-448-685).

Horse-and-Buggy Tour—You'll see buggies around town ready to take you for a clip-clop tour (€28/30 min, price is per carriage, not per person).

Tours from Bruges

Quasimodo Countryside Tours—This company offers those with extra time two excellent and entertaining all-day big-bus tours through the rarely visited Flemish countryside.

The "Flanders Fields" tour concentrates on World War I battlefields, trenches, memorials, and poppy-splattered fields (Sun, Tue, and Thu 9:00–16:30).

The other tour is "Triple Treat": tours of the port of Damme, a castle, monastery, brewery, and chocolate factory, as well as a sample of a waffle, chocolate, and beer (Mon, Wed, and Fri 9:00–16:30).

Hardworking Lode leads all the tours himself, in English only (€45, €38 if under 26, CC, 30-seat non-smoking bus, includes a picnic lunch, lots of walking, reserve by calling 050-370-470 or toll-free 0800-97525, www.quasimodo.be). The bus leaves from the Park Hotel on 't Zand.

Daytours in Flanders Fields Minibus Tours—This tour is like Quasimodo's (listed above) but €9 more expensive. The differences: seven travelers on a minibus rather than a big busload; hotel pick-ups (because the small bus is allowed in the town center); an included restaurant lunch rather than a picnic; and a little more serious lecturing and a stricter focus on World War I (you actually visit the Flanders Fields Museum in Ieper, called Ypres in French).

Frank, the guide, loves leading his small groups on this fascinating day trip (€59, €5 discount when booked direct with this book, Wed–Sun 9:00–17:00, no tours Mon and Tue, call 050-346-060 or toll-free 0800-99133 to book, www.visitbruges.com).

Bruges by Bike—Quasimodo Tours, an offshoot of Quasimodo Tours listed above, leads daily bike tours in and around Bruges (€16, €12 with this book, departs at 10:00, 8 km, 2 hrs) and through the nearby countryside to the port of Damme (€16, €12 with this book, departs at 13:00, 25 km, 3–4 hrs, tel. 050-330-775). Both tours include bike rental and depart from in front of the TI on Burg Square.

Bus and Boat Tour—The Sightseeing Line offers a bus trip to Damme and a boat ride back (€16.50, April–Sept daily at 16:00, 2 hrs, leaves from Market Square, tel. 050-355-024).

Sights—Bruges

These sights are listed in walking order from Market Square to Burg Square to the cluster of museums around the Church of our Lady to the Begijnhof (10-min walk from beginning to end).

▲Market Square (Markt)—Ringed by banks, the post office, lots of restaurant terraces, great old gabled buildings, and the bell tower, this is the modern heart of the city (most city buses run from here to the train station). Under the bell tower are two great Belgian French-fry stands, a quadrilingual Braille description of the old town, and a metal model of the tower. In Bruges' heyday as a trading center, a canal came right up to this square.

Geldmuntstraat, just off the square, is a delightful street with many fun and practical shops and eateries.

▲▲Bell Tower (Belfort)—Most of this bell tower has presided over Market Square since 1300. The octagonal lantern was added in 1486, making it 90 meters high—that's 290 feet and 366 steps (daily 9:30–17:00, ticket window closes 45 min early, WC in courtyard). The view is worth the climb and the €5. Just before you reach the top, peek into the carillon room. The 47 bells can be played mechanically with the giant barrel and movable tabs (as they are on each quarter hour) or with a manual keyboard (as they are during concerts). The carillon player uses his fists and feet rather than fingers. Be there on the quarter hour, when things ring. It's *bellissimo* at the top of the hour.

Atop the tower, survey the town. On the horizon you can see the towns along the North Sea coast. Back on the square, facing the bell tower, turn left (east) onto the pedestrian-only Breidelstraat and thread yourself through the lace and *wafels* to Burg Square.

▲▲Burg Square—The opulent square called Burg is Bruges' civic center, historically the birthplace of Bruges and the site of the ninth-century castle of the first Count of Flanders. Today it's the scene of outdoor concerts and home of the TI (with a €0.25 WC). It's surrounded by six centuries of architecture.

▲Basilica of the Holy Blood—Originally the Chapel of Saint Basil, the church is famous for its relic of the blood of Christ which, according to tradition, was brought to Bruges in 1150 after the Second Crusade. The lower chapel is dark and solid—a fine example of Romanesque style. The upper chapel (separate entrance, climb the stairs) is decorated Gothic (museum is next to upper chapel, €1.25, April–Sept daily 9:30–12:00 & 14:00–18:00, Oct–March Thu–Tue 10:00–12:00 & 14:00–16:00, Wed 10:00–12:00 only, tel. 050-336-792).

▲City Hall's Gothic Room—Your ticket gives you a room full of old town maps and paintings and a grand, beautifully restored "Gothic Hall" from 1400. Its painted and carved wooden ceiling features hanging arches (€2.50, includes audioguide and admission to Renaissance Hall, daily 9:30–17:00, Burg 12).

Renaissance Hall (Brugse Vrije)—This elaborately decorated room with a grand Renaissance chimney carved from oak by Bruges' Renaissance man, Lancelot Blondeel in 1531. If you're into heraldry, the symbolism (explained in the free English flier) makes this room worth a five-minute stop. If you're not, you'll wonder where the rest of the museum is (€2.50, includes audioguide and admission to City Hall's Gothic Room, Tue-Sun 9:30–12:00 & 13:30-17:00, closed Mon, entry in corner of square at Burg 11a).

▲▲▲Groeninge Museum—This museum houses a world-class collection of mostly Flemish art, from van Eyck to Memling to Magritte, including some fine Flemish works from the 1400s. Early Flemish art is less appreciated and understood today than the Italian Renaissance art produced a century later. But by focusing on a few masterpieces, you can get a sense of this subtle, technically advanced, and beautiful style (€8, Tue-Sun 9:30–17:00, closed Mon, Dijver 12, tel. 050-448-751).

▲Gruuthuse Museum—The 15th-century mansion of a wealthy Bruges merchant displays period furniture, tapestries, coins, and musical instruments. Nowhere in the city do you get such an intimate look at the materialistic revolution of Bruges' glory days. With the help of the excellent and included audioguide, just browse through rooms of secular objects that are both functional and beautiful (€6, Tue-Sun 9:30–17:00, closed Mon, Dijver 17).

▲▲**Church of Our Lady**—The church stands as a memorial to the power and wealth of Bruges in its heyday. A delicate *Madonna and Child* by Michelangelo is near the apse (to the right if you're facing the altar). It's said to be the only Michelangelo statue to leave Italy in his lifetime (thanks to the wealth generated by Bruges' cloth trade). If you like tombs and church art, pay to wander through the apse (Michelangelo free, art-filled apse €2.50, Tue-Sun 9:00-12:00 & 13:30-17:00, closed Mon, Mariastraat).

▲▲**St. Jans Hospital/Memling Museum**—The former monastery/hospital complex has two entrances—one is to a welcoming Visitors Center (free), the other to the Memling Museum. The Memling Museum, in the monastery's former church, was once a medieval hospital and now contains six much-loved paintings by the greatest of the Flemish Primitives, Hans Memling (€8 includes fine audioguide, Tue-Sun 9:30–17:00, closed Mon, across the street from the Church of Our Lady, Mariastraat 38).

▲▲**Begijnhof**—*Begijnhofs* (pron. gutturally: buh-HHHINE-hof) were built to house women of the lay order called beguines, who spent their lives in piety and service (without having to take the same vows a nun would). For military or other reasons, there were more women than men in the medieval Low Countries. The order of beguines offered women (often single or widowed) a dignified place to live and work. When the order died out, many *begijnhofs* were taken over by towns for subsidized housing, but some became homes for nuns.

Bruges' *begijnhof*—now inhabited by Benedictine nuns—almost makes you want to don a habit and fold your hands as you walk under its wispy trees and whisper past its frugal little homes. For a good slice of *Begijnhof* life, walk through the simple museum (Begijn's House, left of entry gate, €2 with English explanations, daily 10:00–12:00 & 13:45–17:30, off-season closes at 17:00).

Minnewater—Just south of the Begijnhof is Minnewater, an idyllic lake-filled park of flower boxes, canals, swans, and tour boats packed like happy egg cartons.

Almshouses—Walking from the Begijnhof back to the town center, you might detour along Nieuwe Gentweg to visit one of about 20 almshouses in the city. At #8, go through the door marked "Godshuis de Meulenaere 1613" (free) into the peaceful courtyard. This was a medieval form of housing for the poor. The rich would pay for someone's tiny room here in return for lots of prayers.

Bruges Experiences: Beer, Chocolate, Lace, and Biking

▲▲**Straffe Hendrik Brewery Tour**—Belgians are Europe's beer connoisseurs. This fun and handy tour is a great way to pay your respects. The happy gang at this working family brewery gives entertaining and informative 45-minute, three-language tours (often by friendly Inge, €4 including a beer, lots of very steep steps, great rooftop panorama, daily on the hour 11:00–16:00, 11:00 and 15:00 are your best times to avoid groups, Oct–March 11:00 and 15:00 only, 1 block past church and canal, take a right down skinny Stoofstraat to #26 on Walplein square, tel. 050-332-697).

At Straffe Hendrik ("Strong Henry"), they remind their drinkers: "The components of the beer are vitally necessary and contribute to a well-balanced life pattern. Nerves, muscles, visual sentience, and a healthy skin are stimulated by these in a positive manner. For longevity and lifelong equilibrium, drink Straffe Hendrik in moderation!"

Their bistro, where you'll be given your beer (included with the tour), serves quick and hearty lunch plates. You can eat indoors with the smell of hops or outdoors with the smell of hops. This is a great place to wait for your tour or to linger afterward.

▲**Chocolate**—Bruggians are connoisseurs of fine chocolate. You will be tempted by chocolate-filled display windows all over town. While Godiva is the best big-factory/high-price/high-quality local brand, there are plenty of smaller, family-run places in Bruges that offer exquisite handmade chocolates.

Perhaps Bruges' smoothest and creamiest chocolates are at **Dumon** (€1.60/100 grams). Madam Dumon and her children (Stefaan, Christophe, and Nathalie) make their top-notch chocolate daily and sell it fresh just off Market Square (Thu-Tue 10:00-18:00, closed Wed, Eiermarkt 6, old chocolate molds on display in basement, tel. 050-346-282, www.chocolatierdumon.com). Their Ganache, a dark creamy combo, wows chocoholics. They don't have English labels because they believe it's best to describe their chocolates in person.

Locals and tourists alike flock to **The Chocolate Line** (€3/100 grams) for their "*gastronomique*" varieties—unique concoctions such as Havana cigar (marinated in rum, cognac, and Cuban tobacco leaves—so therefore technically illegal in the United States), lemon grass, ginger (shaped like a buddha), saffron curry (a white elephant), and a spicy chili. My fave: the sheets of chocolate with crunchy roasted cocoa beans. The kitchen—busy whipping up their 80 varieties—is on display in the back (Mon-Sat 9:30–18:30, Sun from 10:30, Simon

Stevinplein 19, between Church of Our Lady and Market Square, tel. 050-341-090).

The smaller **Sweertvaegher**, near Burg Square, features top-quality chocolate (€2.50/100 grams) that's darker rather than sweeter, made with fresh ingredients and no preservatives (Tue–Sun 9:30–18:15, closed Mon, Philipstockstraat 29, tel. 050-338-367).

Lace and Windmills by the Moat—A 10-minute walk from the center to the northeast end of town brings you to four windmills strung out along a pleasant grassy setting on the "big moat" canal (between Kruispoort and Dampoort, on Bruges side of the moat). One windmill (St. Janshuismolen) is open to visitors (€2, daily 9:30–12:30 & 13:30–17:00, closed Oct–April, at the end of Carmersstraat).

To actually see lace being made, drop by the nearby **Lace Centre**, where ladies toss bobbins madly while their eyes go bad (€2 includes afternoon demonstrations and a small lace museum called Kantcentrum, as well as the adjacent Jeruzalem Church; Mon–Fri 10:00–12:00 & 14:00–18:00, until 17:00 on Sat, closed Sun, Peperstraat 3, tel. 050-330-072). The **Folklore Museum**, in the same neighborhood, is cute but forgettable (€3, daily 9:30–17:00, closed Mon, Rolweg 40, tel. 050-330-044). To find either place, ask for the Jeruzalem Church.

▲▲Biking—The Flemish word for bike is *fiets* (pron. feets). While the sights are close enough for easy walking, the town is a treat to bike through. And a bike quickly gets you into the dreamy back lanes without a hint of tourism. Take a peaceful evening ride through the back streets and around the outer canal. Consider keeping a bike for the duration of your stay. It's the way the locals get around in Bruges.

Rental shops (listed in "Helpful Hints," above) have maps and ideas. The TI sells a handy *5X on the Bike around Bruges* map/guide (€1.25) describing five different bike routes (18–30 km) through the idyllic countryside nearby. The best trip is 30 minutes along the canal out to Damme and back. The Belgium/Netherlands border is a 40-minute pedal beyond Damme.

Sights—Near Bruges

Dolfinarium—At Boudewijnpark, just outside of town, dolphins make a splash several times a day (€8 for 40-min show, Debaeckestraat 12, call for show times, tel. 050-383-838, www.boudewijnpark.be). The theme park's roller-skating rink is open in the afternoon (becomes an ice-skating rink off-season). From Bruges, catch the "Sint Michiels" bus #7 or #17 from the train station or Kuipersstraat.

Flanders Fields Museum—This World War I museum, 60 kilometers southwest of Bruges, provides a moving look at the battles fought near Ieper (Ypres in French). Use interactive computers to trace the wartime lives of individual soldiers and citizens. Powerful videos and ear-shattering audio complete the story (€7.50, April–Sept daily 10:00–18:00, Oct–March Tue–Sun 10:00–17:00, closed Mon, last entry 1 hour before closing, Grote Markt 34, Ieper, tel. 057-228-584, fax 057-228-589, www.inflandersfields.be). From Bruges, catch a train to Ieper via Kortrijk (2 hrs) or take a tour (see "Daytours in Flanders Fields" Minibus Tours, listed in "Tours from Bruges," above). Drivers follow A17 to Kortrijk, then take A19 to Ieper.

Sleeping in Bruges
(€1 = about $1, country code: 32)

Sleep Code: **S** = Single, **D** = Double/Twin, **T** = Triple, **Q** = Quad, **b** = bathroom, **s** = shower only, **CC** = Credit Cards accepted, **no CC** = Credit Cards not accepted. Everyone speaks English.

To help you easily sort through these listings, I've divided the rooms into three categories based on the price for a standard double room with bath:

Higher Priced—Most rooms €110 or more.
Moderately Priced—Most rooms less than €110.
Lower Priced—Most rooms less than €75.

Most places are located between the train station and the old center, with the most distant (and best) being a few blocks beyond Market Square to the north and east. B&Bs offer the best value (listed after "Hotels"). All include breakfast, are on quiet streets, and (with a few exceptions) keep the same prices throughout the year. Bruges is most crowded Friday and Saturday evenings Easter through October—with July and August weekends being worst.

Bruges is a great place to sleep, with Gothic spires out your window, no traffic noise, and the cheerily out of tune carillon heralding each new day at 8:00 sharp. (Thankfully, the bell tower is silent from 22:00 to 8:00.)

Hotels

HIGHER PRICED

Hansa Hotel offers 24 rooms in a completely modernized old building. It's tastefully decorated in elegant pastels and has all the amenities. It's a great splurge (standard Db-€130, superior Db-€170, deluxe Db-€210, singles take a double for nearly the same cost, extra bed-€40, suites available, CC, air-con, non-smoking, elevator, free Internet access, sauna, tanning bed, fitness

Bruges Hotels

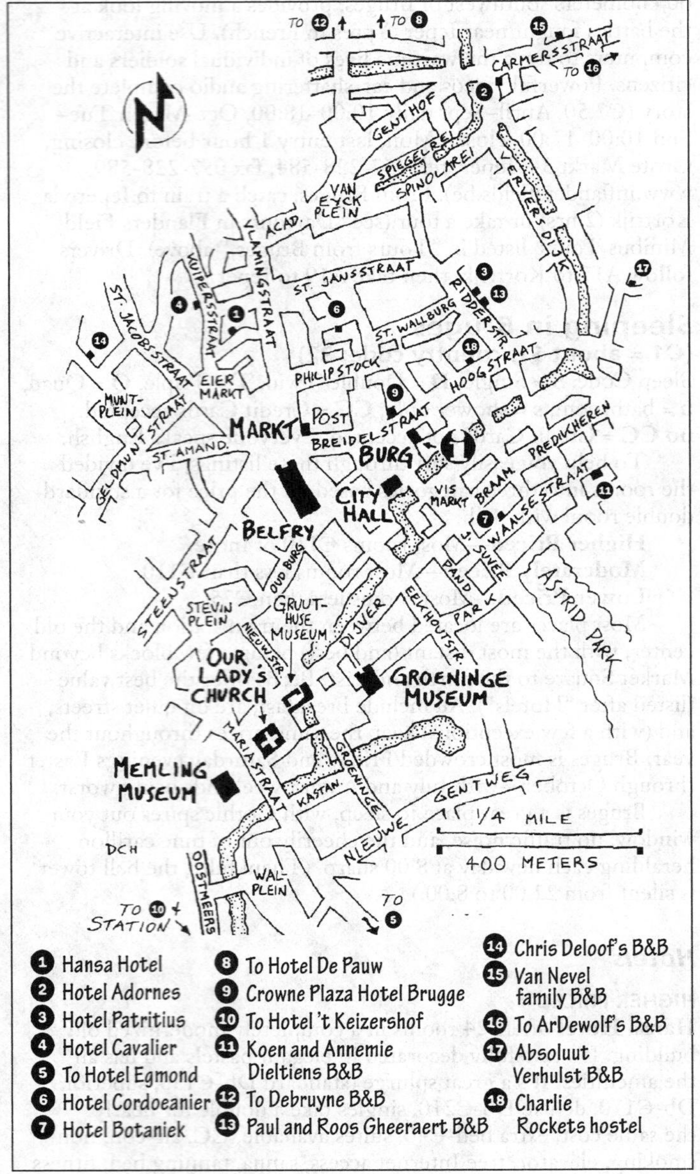

room, bike rental for €6.50/half day, €10/day, Niklaas Despars-straat 11, a block north of Market Square, tel. 050-444-444, fax 050-444-440, www.hansa.be, e-mail: information@hansa.be, run by cheery and hardworking Johan and Isabelle).

Hotel Egmond is quietly located in the middle of the melancholy Minnewater. Its eight 18th-century rooms have all the comforts (Sb-€102, Db-€120, Tb-€150, no CC, for longer stays ask about their apartments a few blocks away, free parking, Minnewater 15, tel. 050-341-445, fax 050-342-940, www.egmond.be, e-mail: info@egmond.be).

Crowne Plaza Hotel Brugge is the most modern, comfortable, and central hotel option. It's just like a fancy American hotel, with each of its 96 air-conditioned rooms equipped with a magnifying mirror and trouser press (Db-€225–240, prices drop as low as €180 on weekdays and off-season, CC, elevator, pool, Burg 10, tel. 050-446-844, fax 050-446-868, www.crowneplaza.com).

MODERATELY PRICED

Hotel Adornes is small, new, and classy—a great value. It has 20 comfy rooms with full, modern bathrooms in a 17th-century canalside house, and offers free parking, free loaner bikes, and a cellar lounge with games and videos (Db-€90–110 depending upon size, singles take a double for nearly the same cost, Tb-€125, Qb-€135, CC, elevator, near Van Nevel B&B, mentioned below, and Carmersstraat at St. Annarei 26, tel. 050-341-336, fax 050-342-085, www.adornes.be, e-mail: hotel.adornes@proximedia.be, Nathalie runs the family business, Britt provides a warm welcome).

Hotel Patritius, family-run and centrally located, is a grand circa-1830 neoclassical mansion with 16 stately rooms, and a plush lounge and breakfast room (small Db-€85, Db-€90-95, CC, free parking, Riddersstraat 11, tel. 050-338-454, fax 050-339-634, www.hotelpatritius.be, e-mail: hotel.patritius@proximedia.be, Garrett and Elvi Spaey).

Hotel Botaniek has three stars, nine small rooms, and a quiet location a block from Astrid Park (Db-€92, big Db-€96, Tb-€105, Qb-€115, 8 percent discount for 3 nights, CC, elevator, Waalsestraat 23, tel. 050-341-424, fax 050-345-939, e-mail: hotel.botaniek@pi.be).

In a jam you might try these large, well-located hotels of lesser value: **Hotel ter Reien** (26 rooms, Db-€90, Langestraat 1, tel. 050-349-100, e-mail: hotel.ter.reien@online.be) and **Hotel Sablon** (the "oldest hotel in town" with 36 rooms, Db-€110, Noordzandstraat 21, tel. 050-333-902, e-mail: info@sablon.be).

LOWER PRICED

Hotel Cavalier, which has more stairs than character, rents 10 decent rooms and serves a hearty buffet breakfast in a royal setting (Sb-€50–52, Db-€55–62, Tb-€70–75, Qb-€77–82, lofty "backpackers' doubles" on fourth floor-€41 or €46, CC, Kuipersstraat 25, tel. 050-330-207, fax 050-347-199, e-mail: hotel.cavalier@skynet.be, run by friendly Viviane De Clerck).

Hotel Cordoeanier, a family-run place, rents 22 bright, simple, modern rooms on a quiet street two blocks off Market Square (Sb-€52–62, Db-€62–70, Tb-€72–80, Qb-€85, Quint/b-€97, higher prices are for bigger rooms, small groups should ask about holiday house across the street, CC, cheap Internet access, Cordoeanierstraat 16, tel. 050-339-051, fax 050-346-111, www.cordoeanier.be, Kris, Veerle, Guy and family).

Hotel de Pauw is tall, skinny, and family-run, with straightforward rooms on a quiet street across from a church (Sb-€50, Db-€68, CC, free and easy street parking or pay garage, Sint Gilliskerkhof 8, tel. 050-337-118, fax 050-345-140, www.hoteldepauw.be, e-mail: info@hoteldepauw.be, Philippe and Hilde).

***Near the Train Station*: Hotel 't Keizershof** is a dollhouse of a hotel that lives by its motto, "Spend a night, not a fortune." It's simple and tidy, with seven small, cheery, old-time rooms split between two floors, a shower and toilet on each (S-€25, D-€36, T-€54, Q-€65, no CC, free and easy parking, laundry service-€7.50, Oostmeers 126, a block in front of station, tel. 050-338-728, e-mail: hotel.keizershof@12move.be, Stefaan and Hilde).

Bed-and-Breakfasts

These places, run by people who enjoy their work, offer a better value than hotels. Each is central and offers lots of stairs and three or four doubles you'd pay €100 for in a hotel. Parking is generally easy on the street.

MODERATELY PRICED

Absoluut Verhulst is a modern-feeling B&B in a 400-year-old building (Sb-€50, Db-€75, huge and lofty suite-€93 for 2, €115 for 3, and €125 for 4, no CC, 5-min walk east of Market Square at Verbrand Nieuwland 1, tel. & fax 050-334-515, www.b-bverhulst.com, Frieda and Benno).

LOWER PRICED

Koen and Annemie Dieltiens are a friendly couple who enjoy getting to know their guests and sharing a wealth of information on Bruges. You'll eat a hearty breakfast around a big table in their bright, comfortable, newly-renovated house (Sb-€50, Db-€55, Tb-€75, 1-night stays pay €10 extra per room, no CC, non-smoking, Waalse Straat 40, 3 blocks southeast of Burg Square, tel. 050-334-294, fax 050-335-230, http://users.skynet.be/dieltiens, e-mail: koen.dieltiens@skynet.be). The Dieltiens also rent a cozy studio and apartment for two to six people in a nearby 17th-century house (2 people pay €350 per week for studio, €400 per week for apartment, prices higher for shorter stays and more people, 20 percent cheaper off-season).

Debruyne B&B, run by Marie-Rose and her architect husband Ronny, offers artsy, original decor (check out the elephant-sized doors—Ronny's design) and genuine warmth. If the Gothic is getting medieval, this is refreshingly modern (Sb-€45, Db-€50, Tb-€65, 1-night stay-€7.50 extra per room, no CC, non-smoking, 5-min walk north of Market Square, Lange Raamstraat 18, tel. 050-347-606, fax 050-340-285, www.bedandbreakfastbruges.com).

Paul and Roos Gheeraert live on the first floor, while their guests take the second. This neoclassical mansion with big, bright, comfy rooms is another fine value (Sb-€45, Db-€50, Tb-€70, no CC, strictly no smoking; rooms have coffeemakers, TVs, and fridges; Ridderstraat 9, 4-min walk east of Market Square, tel. 050-335-627, fax 050-345-201, http://users.skynet.be/brugge-gheeraert, e-mail: gheeraert.brugge @skynet.be). They also rent three modern, fully-equipped apartments and a large loft nearby (3-night minimum).

Chris Deloof's big, homey rooms are a good bet in the old center. Check out the fun, lofty A-frame room upstairs (Sb-€50, Ds/Db-€53, pleasant breakfast room and a royal lounge, no CC, non-smoking, Geerwiynstraat 14, tel. 050-340-544, fax 050-343-721, www.sin.be/chrisdeloof, e-mail: chris.deloof@pi.be). Chris also rents a nearby apartment (Qb-€70-80) and a holiday house for a family or group of up to five (€100-150).

The **Van Nevel family** rents three attractive top-floor rooms with built-in beds in a 16th-century house (D-€45–55, Ds-€60, third person pays €17, CC but cash preferred, non-smoking, 10-min walk from Market Square, or bus #4 or #8 from train station or Market Square to Carmersbridge, Carmersstraat 13, tel. 050-346-860, fax 050-347-616, http://home.tiscali.be/rvanneve, e-mail: robert.vannevel@advalvas.be). Robert, who works at the Memling Museum, enthusiastically shares the culture and history of Bruges with his guests.

ArDewolf's B&B is a family-friendly place warmly run by Nicole and Arnold in a stately, quiet neighborhood at the edge of the old town near the windmills and moat (S-€30, D-€35–37, T-€50, Q-€60, Quint-€70, no CC, Oostproosse 9, tel. 050-338-366, www.ardewolf.be). From the train station, take bus #4 to Sasplein. Walk to the path behind the first windmill and turn left on Oostproosse.

Lower Priced Hostels

Bruges has several good hostels offering beds for around €10 to €12 in two- to eight-bed rooms (singles go for about €15). Breakfast is about €3 extra. The American-style **Charlie Rockets** bar and hostel is the liveliest and most central (56 beds, €13 per bed, 2–6 per room, no CC, Hoogstraat 19, tel. 050-330-660, fax 050-343-630, www.charlierockets.com). The dull **Snuffel Travelers Inn** (Ezelstraat 47, tel. 050-333-133) and the funky **Passage** (Dweerstraat 26, tel. 050-340-232; its hotel next door rents €40 doubles) are both small, loose, and central.

Eating in Bruges

Bruges' specialties include mussels cooked a variety of ways (one order can feed two), fish dishes, grilled meats, and french fries. Don't eat before 19:30 unless you like eating alone. Tax and service are always included.

You'll find plenty of affordable, touristy restaurants on floodlit squares and along dreamy canals. Bruges feeds 3.5 million tourists a year, and most are seduced by a high-profile location. These can be fine experiences for the magical setting and views, but the quality of food and service is low. I wouldn't blame you for eating at one of these places, but I won't recommend any. I prefer the candle-cool bistros that flicker on back streets.

Rock Fort is a chic new eight-table place with a mod, fresh coziness and a high-powered respect for good food. Two young chefs (Peter and Hermes) give their French cuisine a creative twist, and after just a few months in business had become the talk of the town (€10 Mon-Fri lunch special with coffee, €15-20 beautifully-presented dinner plates, Thu-Tue 12:00-14:30 & 18:00–23:00, closed Wed and at lunch on Sun, great pastas and salads, reservations smart for dinner, Langestraat 15, tel. 050-334-113).

Restaurant Chez Olivier—a classy, white tablecloth, 10-table place—is considered the best fancy French cuisine splurge in town. While delicate Anne serves, her French husband, Olivier, is busy cooking up whatever he found freshest that day. While you can order à la carte, it is wise to go with the recommended daily *menu* (3-course lunch €35, 4-course dinner-€50, wine adds €20, 12:00-13:30 & 19:00-21:30, closed Sun and Thu, reserve for dinner, Meestraat 9, tel. 050-333-659).

Restaurant de Koetse is a good bet for central, affordable, quality local-style food. The ambience is traditional, yet fun and

Bruges Restaurants

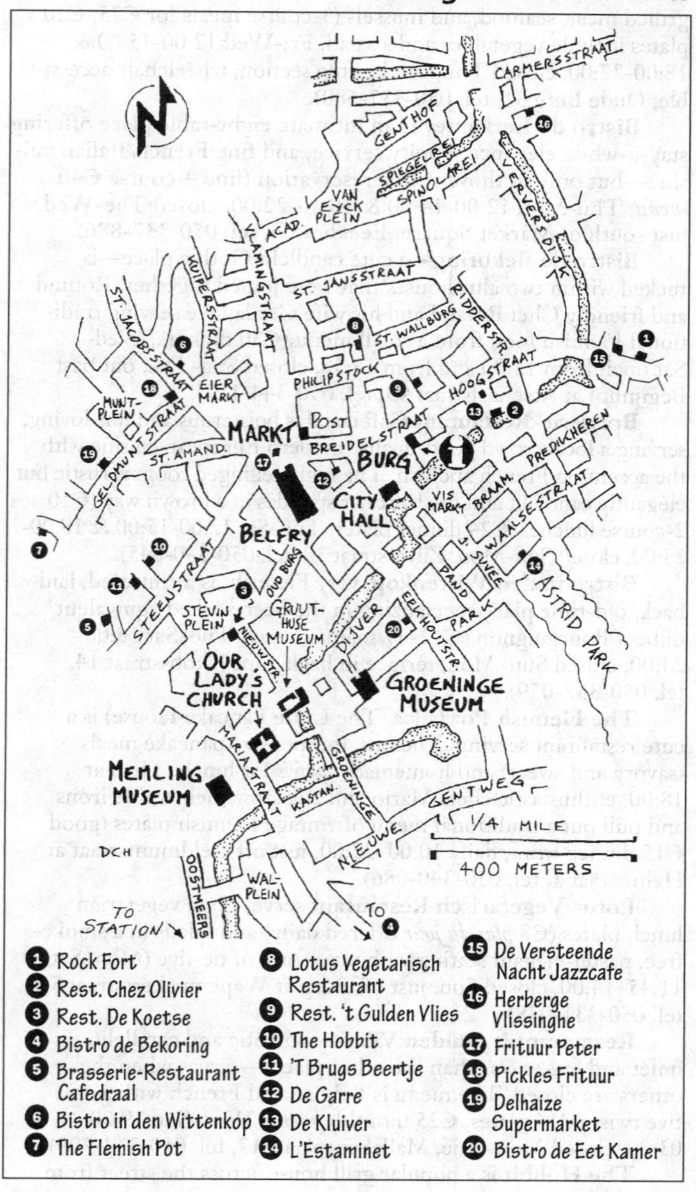

kid-friendly. The cuisine is Belgian and French with a stress on grilled meat, seafood, and mussels (3-course meals for €25, €20 plates include vegetables and a salad, Fri-Wed 12:00-15:00 & 18:00-22:00, closed Thu, smoke-free section, wheelchair accessible, Oude Burg 31, tel. 050-337-680).

Bistro de Eetkamer is an intimate eight-table place offering stay-a-while elegance, uppity service, and fine French/Italian cuisine—but only to those with a reservation (fine 4-course €40 *menu*, Thu-Mon 12:00-14:00 & 18:30-22:00, closed Tue-Wed, just south of Market Square, Eeekhout 6, tel. 050-337-886).

Bistro de Bekoring—a cute candlelit Gothic place—is tucked within two almshouses that were joined together. Rotund and friendly Chef Roland and his wife Gerda love serving traditional Flemish food from a small menu (€30 dinners, Wed–Sat open from 12:00 and from 18:30, closed Sun-Tue, out past Begijnhof at Arsenaalstraat 53, tel. 050-344-157).

Brasserie-Restaurant Cafedraal is boisterous and fun-loving, serving a local crowd good-quality modern European cuisine with the accent on French and fish. The high-ceilinged room is rustic but elegantly candlelit and the back bar sparkles in a brown way (€10 2-course lunches, €24 dinner plates, Tue–Sat 12:00-15:00 & 18:00-23:00, closed Sun-Mon, Zilverstraat 38, tel. 050-340-845).

Bistro in den Wittenkop, very Flemish, is a cluttered, laid-back, old-time place specializing in the beer-soaked equivalent of beef Bourguignon (€12–17 main courses, Tue–Sat 18:00–24:00, closed Sun–Mon, terrace in back, Sint Jakobsstraat 14, tel. 050-332-059).

The Flemish Pot (a.k.a. The Little Pancake House) is a cute restaurant serving delicious, inexpensive pancake meals (savory and sweet) and homemade *wafels* for lunch. Then at 18:00, enthusiastic chefs Mario and Rik stow their waffle irons and pull out a traditional menu of vintage Flemish plates (good €15 dinner *menu*, daily 10:00–22:00, just off Geldmuntstraat at Helmstraat 3, tel. 050-340-086).

Lotus Vegetarisch Restaurant serves good vegetarian lunch plates (€8 *plat du jour* offered daily) and salads in a smoke-free, pastel-elegant setting without a trace of tie-dye (Mon–Sat 11:45–14:00, closed Sun, just off Burg at Wapenmakersstraat 5, tel. 050-331-078).

Restaurant 't Gulden Vlies—romantic and candlelit, quiet and less *ye olde* than the other places—serves when the others are closed. The menu is Belgian and French with a creative twist (€16 plates, €25 monthly *menu*, Wed–Sun 19:00–03:00, closed Mon–Tue, Mallebergplaats 17, tel. 050-334-709).

The Hobbit is a popular grill house across the street from the recommended bar, 't Brugs Berrtje (listed below). It features an entertaining menu, including all-you-can-eat spareribs with salad for €13—nothing fancy, just good basic food in a fun traditional setting (daily 18:00–24:00, Kemelstraat 8-10, tel. 050-201-827).

Bars Offering Light Meals, Beer, and Ambience

Stop into one of the city's atmospheric bars for a light meal or a drink with great Bruges ambience. Straffe Hendrik ("Strong Henry"), a potent and refreshing local brew, is—even to a Bud Lite kind of guy—obviously great beer. Among the more unusual to try: Dentergems (with coriander and orange peel) and Trappist (a malty, usually dark, monk-made beer). Non-beer drinkers enjoy Kriek (a cherry-flavored beer) and Frambozen Bier (raspberry-flavored beer).

Any pub or restaurant carries the basic beers, but for a selection of more than 300 types, including brews to suit any season, drink at **'t Brugs Beertje.** For a light meal, consider their traditional cheese plate (Thu-Tue 16:00–24:00, closed Wed, Kemelstraat 5, tel. 050-339-616).

Another good place to gain an appreciation of the Belgian beer culture is **de Garre**. Rather than a noisy pub scene, it has a more dressy sit-down-and-focus-on-your-friend-and-the-fine-beer ambience (huge selection, off Breidelstraat, between Burg and Markt, on tiny Garre alley, daily 12:00–24:00, tel. 050-341-029).

De Kluiver is a lost-at-sea pub serving hot snacks, light €10 meals, and great sea snails in spiced bouillon (*warme wulken*) all simmered in a whispering jazz ambience (Wed–Mon 18:00–24:00, closed Tue, Hoogstraat 12, tel. 050-338-927).

L'Estaminet is a youthful, trendy, jazz-filled eatery. Away from the tourists, it's popular with local students who come for hearty €6 spaghetti (11:30–24:00, closed Mon afternoon and all day Thu, facing peaceful Astrid Park at Park 5, tel. 050-330-916). **De Versteende Nacht Jazzcafe** is another popular young hang-out serving vegetarian dishes, salads, and pastas on Langestraat 11 (€12.50 meals, Tue–Thu 19:00–24:00, Fri–Sat 18:00–24:00, closed Sun–Mon, live jazz on Wed from 21:00, tel. 050-343-293).

Herberge Vlissinghe, the oldest pub in town (1515), serves hot snacks in a great atmosphere (Wed-Sun open from 11:00 on, closed Mon–Tue, Blekersstraat 2, tel. 050-343-737).

Fries, Fast Food, and Picnics

Local french fries (*frites*) are a treat. Proud and traditional *frituurs* serve tubs of fries and various local-style shish kebabs. Belgians dip their *frites* in mayonnaise, but ketchup is there for the Yankees (along with spicier sauces). For a quick, cheap, and scenic meal, hit a *frituur* and sit on the steps or benches overlooking Market Square, about 50 meters past the post office. The best fries in town are from **Frituur Peter**—twin take-away carts on the Market Square at the base of the bell tower (daily 10:00-24:00).

Pickles Frituur, a block off Market Square, is handy for sit-down fries. Run by Marleen, its forte is greasy, fast, deep-fried Flemish corn dogs. Their "menu 2" comes with three traditional gut bombs (Mon–Sat 11:00–24:00, at the corner of Geldmuntstraat and Sint Jakobstraat, tel. 050-337-957).

Delhaize Supermarket is great for picnics (push-button produce pricer lets you buy as little as one mushroom, Mon–Sat 9:00–18:30, Fri until 19:00, closed Sun, 3 blocks off the Market Square on Geldmuntstraat). The small **Delhaize grocery** is on Market Square opposite the bell tower (Mon–Sat 9:00–12:00 & 14:00–18:00, Sun 14:00-18:00). For midnight munchies, you'll find Indian-run corner grocery stores.

Belgian Waffles

While Americans think of "Belgian" waffles for breakfast, the Belgians (who don't eat waffles or pancakes for breakfast) think of *wafels* as Liege-style (dense, sweet, eaten plain and heated up) and Brussels-style (lighter, often with powdered sugar or whipped cream and fruit, served in teahouses only in the afternoons from 14:00–18:00). You'll see waffles sold at restaurants and take-away stands.

For good €1.50 Liege-style *wafels*, stop by **Tea-Room Laurent** (Steenstraat 79) or **Restaurant Hennon** (between Market Square and Burg at Breidelstraat 16).

Transportation Connections—Bruges

From **Brussels**, an hour away by train, all of Europe is at your fingertips. Train info: tel. 050-302-424.

By train to: Brussels (2/hr, usually at :33 and :59, 1 hr, €10), **Ghent** (4/hr, 40 min), **Ostende** (3/hr, 15 min), **Köln** (6/day, 4 hrs), **Paris** (hrly via Brussels, 2.5 hrs, must pay supplement of €10.50/second class, €21/first class, even with a railpass), **Amsterdam** (hrly, 3.5 hrs, transfer in Antwerp or Brussels), **Amsterdam's Schiphol Airport** (hrly, 3.5 hrs, transfer in Antwerp or Brussels, €35).

Trains from England: Bruges is an ideal "welcome to Europe" stop after London. Take the Eurostar train from London to Brussels under the English Channel (9/day, 3 hrs), then transfer, backtracking to Bruges (2/hr, 1 hr). Or, if you'd prefer to cross the Channel by boat, catch the London-to-Dover train (2 hrs, from London's Victoria Station), then the catamaran to Ostende (2 hrs;

train station at Ostende catamaran terminal), then the Ostende-to-Bruges train (15 min). Five boats run daily from London to Bruges and vice versa (€37 one-way, 5-hrs, same price for cheap 5-day return ticket, reserve by phone with CC and pick up your ticket at the dock, tel. 059-559-955).

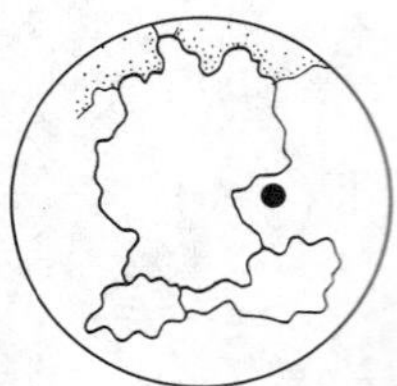

PRAGUE

It's amazing what 14 years of freedom can do. Prague has always been historic. Now it's fun, too. No place in Europe has become so popular so quickly. And for good reason: The capital of the Czech Republic—the only major city of central Europe to escape the bombs of the last century's wars—is one of Europe's best-preserved cities. It's filled with sumptuous Art Nouveau facades, offers tons of cheap Mozart and Vivaldi, and brews the best beer in Europe. But even beyond its architecture and traditional culture, it's an explosion of pent-up entrepreneurial energy jumping for joy after 40 years of Communist rule. And its low prices will make your visit enjoyable and nearly stress-free.

For a relaxing pause between the urban bustle of Vienna and Prague, visit the Czech town of Český Krumlov, the perfect big-city antidote, peaceful and happily hemmed in by its lazy river.

Planning Your Time

Two days (with 3 nights, or 2 nights and a night train) make the long train ride in and out worthwhile and give you time to get beyond the sightseeing and enjoy Prague's fun-loving ambience. Many wish they'd scheduled three days for Prague. From Munich, Berlin, and Vienna, it's about a five-hour train ride. Also from Munich, you could take a longer night train.

With two days in Prague, I'd spend a morning seeing the castle and a morning in the Jewish Quarter—the only two chunks of sightseeing that demand any brainpower. Spend your afternoons loitering around the Old Town, Charles Bridge, and the Little Quarter and your nights split between beer halls and live music. Keep in mind that Jewish sites close on Saturday.

Český Krumlov, 2.5 hours from Prague by train, could be a

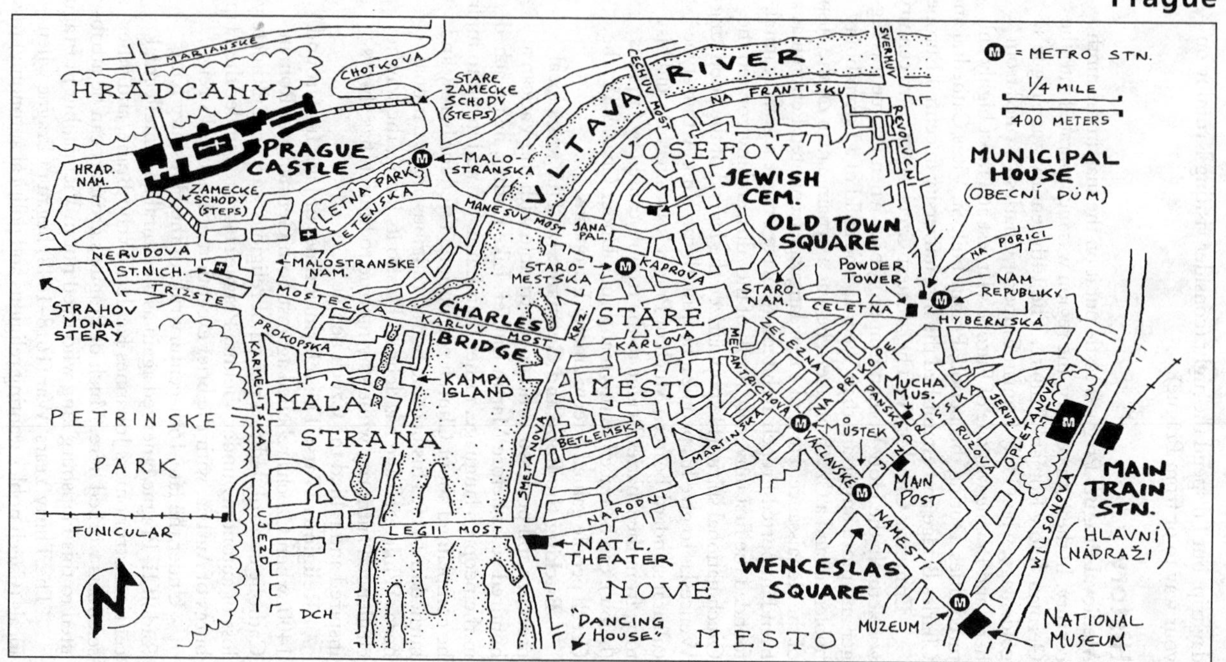
Prague
M = METRO STN.
1/4 MILE
400 METERS
HRADCANY
MARIANSKE
CHOTKOVA
STARE ZAMECKE SCHODY (STEPS)
PRAGUE CASTLE
HRAD. NAM.
ZAMECKE SCHODY (STEPS)
MALOSTRANSKA
LETNA PARK
LETENSKA
NERUDOVA
ST. NICH.
MALOSTRANSKE NAM.
TRZISTE
STRAHOV MONASTERY
MOSTECKA
PROKOPSKA
KARMELITSKA
PETRINSKE PARK
FUNICULAR
MALA STRANA
KAMPA ISLAND
CHARLES BRIDGE
KARLUV MOST
MANESUV MOST
CECHUV MOST
VLTAVA RIVER
NA FRANTISKU
SVERHUV
REVOLUCNI
JOSEFOV
JEWISH CEM.
JANA PAL.
STAROMESTSKA
KAPROVA
OLD TOWN SQUARE
STARO NAM.
STARE MESTO
KRIZ.
KARLOVA
MUNICIPAL HOUSE
(OBECNÍ DŮM)
NA PORICI
POWDER TOWER
NAM REPUBLIKY
CELETNA
HYBERNSKÁ
ZELEZNA
NA PRIKOPE
MELANTRICHOVA
MARTINSKA
BETLEMSKA
SMETANOVA
NARODNI
MUCHA MUS.
PANSKA
JINDRISSKA
JERUZ
RUZOVA
OPLETANOVA
WILSONOVA
MŮSTEK
MAIN POST
VÁCLAVSKÉ NAMESTI
MAIN TRAIN STN.
(HLAVNÍ NÁDRAŽI)
UJEZD
LEGII MOST
NAT'L. THEATER
DCH
"DANCING HOUSE"
NOVE MESTO
WENCESLAS SQUARE
MUZEUM
NATIONAL MUSEUM

day trip, but I'd spend the night (consider visiting Krumlov on your way to or from Prague).

History

Medieval Prague: Prague's castle put it on the map in the ninth century. In the 10th century, the region was incorporated into the German "Holy Roman" Empire. The 14th century was Prague's golden age, when Holy Roman Emperor Charles IV ruled from here, and Prague was one of Europe's largest and most highly cultured cities. During this period, Prague built St. Vitus Cathedral and Charles Bridge and established the first university in central Europe.

Emperor Charles IV: The greatest Czech ruler (14th century) was actually the Holy Roman Emperor, back when Prague was bigger and more important than Vienna. The child of a Luxembourg nobleman and a Czech princess, he was a dynamic man on the cusp of the Renaissance. He spoke four languages, counted Petrarch as a friend, imported French architects to make Prague a grand capital, founded the first university north of the Alps, and invigorated the Czech national spirit. (He popularized the legend of the good king Wenceslas to give his people a near mythical, King Arthur–type cultural standard-bearer.) Much of Prague's architecture and history, from the Charles Bridge to the trouble caused by Jan Hus (below), can be traced to this man's rule. Under Charles IV, the Czech people gained esteem among Europeans.

Bucking the Pope and Germany: Jan Hus was a local preacher and professor who got in trouble with the Vatican a hundred years before Martin Luther. Like Luther, he preached in the people's language, rather than Latin. To add insult to injury, he complained about Church corruption. Tried for heresy and burned in 1415, Hus became both a religious and a national hero. While each age has defined Hus to its liking, the way he challenged authority while staying true to himself has always inspired and rallied the Czech people.

Religious Wars: The reformist times of Jan Hus (around 1400, when Czechs rebelled against both German and Roman Catholic control) led to a period of religious wars, and ultimately loss of autonomy under Vienna. Prague stagnated under the Hapsburgs of Austria, with the brief exception of Rudolf II's reign.

Under the late-16th-century rule of the Hapsburg King Rudolf II, Prague emerged again as a cultural and intellectual center. Astronomers Johannes Kepler, Tycho Brahe, and other scientists worked here. Much of Prague's great art can be attributed to this Hapsburg king who lived not in Vienna, but in Prague.

The Thirty Years' War (1618–1648) began in Prague when locals (Czech nobles wanting religious and political autonomy) tossed two Catholic/Hapsburg officials out the window of the Prague Castle. Often called "the first world war" because it engulfed so many nations, this 30-year conflict was particularly tough on Prague. During this period, its population dropped from 60,000 to 25,000. The result of this war was 300 years of Hapsburg rule. Prague became a backwater of Vienna.

Czech Nationalist Revival: The 19th century was a time of nationalism for people throughout Europe, including the Czechs, as the age of divine kings and ruling families came to a fitful end. Architecture and the arts (such as the completion of the cathedral, and Smetana's operas performed in the new National Theater) stirred the national spirit. With the end of World War I, the Hapsburgs were history, and in 1918, the independent country of Czechoslovakia was proclaimed, with Prague as its capital.

Troubled 20th Century: Independence lasted only until 1939, when the Nazis swept in. Prague escaped the bombs of World War II, but went almost directly from the Nazi frying pan into the Communist fire. Almost. A local uprising freed the city from the Nazis on May 8, 1945. The Russians "liberated" them again on May 9.

For centuries, the Czechs were mostly rural folks, with German merchants running the cities. Prague's cultural make-up comes from a rich mix of Czech, German, and Jewish people—historically about evenly divided. But after World War II, only 5 percent of the Jewish population remained, and virtually all the Germans were deported.

The Communist chapter (1948–1989) was grim. The "Prague Spring" revolt—initiated by a young generation of reform-minded Communists in 1968—was crushed. The charismatic leader Alexander Dubček was exiled (and made a forest ranger in the backwoods), and the years after 1968 were particularly gray and disheartening. The Communists started construction on Prague's huge TV tower (now the city's tallest structure) in the late 1980s. The tower was planned not only to broadcast Czech TV transmission, but also to jam Western signals. The metro, built around the same time, was intended for mass transit—but first and foremost, it was designed to be a giant fallout shelter for protection against capitalist bombs.

But eventually, the Soviet empire crumbled. Czechoslovakia regained its freedom in the student- and artist-powered 1989 "Velvet Revolution" (so-called because there were no casualties). In 1993, the Czech and Slovak Republics agreed on the "Velvet Divorce" and became two separate countries.

Today, while not without its problems, the Czech Republic is enjoying a growing economy and a strong democracy. It is on track to be admitted in the European Union by 2004. Prague has emerged as one of the most popular tourist destinations in Europe.

Orientation

Locals call their town "Praha." It's big, with 1.2 million people, but focus on its small old-town core during a quick visit. I will refer to the tourist landmarks in English (with the Czech name in parentheses). Study the map and learn these key places:

Main Train Station:	*Hlavní Nádraží* (pron. hlav-nee nah-dra-shzee)
Old Town:	*Staré Město* (pron. sta-rey min-yes-toh)
Old Town Square:	*Staroměstské Náměstí* (pron. star-roh-min-yes-ststi-keh nah-min-yes-tee)
New Town:	*Nové Město* (pron. no-vay min-yes-toh)
Little Quarter:	*Malá Strana* (pron. mah-lah strah-nah)
Jewish Quarter:	*Josefov* (pron. yoo-zef-fohf)
Castle Area:	*Hradčany* (pron. hrad-chah-nee)
Charles Bridge:	*Karluv Most* (pron. kar-loov most)
Wenceslas Square:	*Václavske Náměstí* (pron. vah-slawf-skeh nah-min-yes-tee)
The River:	*Vltava* (pron. vul-tah-vah)

The Vltava River divides the west side (castle and Little Quarter) from the east side (train station, Old Town, New Town, and nearly all of the recommended hotels). Prague addresses come with a general zone. Praha 1 is in the old center on either side of the river. Praha 2 is in the new city south of Wenceslas Square. Praha 3 and higher indicate a location farther from the center.

Tourist Information

TIs are at four key locations: **main train station** (Easter–Oct Mon–Fri 9:00–19:00, Sat–Sun 9:00–16:00; Nov–Easter Mon–Fri 9:00–18:00, Sat 9:00–15:00, closed Sun), **Old Town Square** (Easter–Oct Mon–Fri 9:00–19:00, Sat–Sun 9:00–18:00; Nov–Easter Mon–Fri 9:00–18:00, Sat–Sun 9:00–17:00, tel. 224-482-018), **below Wenceslas Square** at Na Príkope 20 (Easter–Oct Mon–Fri 9:00–19:00, Sat–Sun 9:00–17:00; Nov–Easter Mon–Fri 9:00–18:00, Sat 9:00–15:00, closed Sun, tel. 224-226-088), and the castle side of **Charles Bridge** (Easter–Oct daily 10:00–18:00, closed Nov–Easter). They offer maps, phone cards, information on guided walks and bus tours, and bookings for concerts, hotel rooms, and rooms in private homes. There are several monthly events guides—all of them packed with ads—including *Prague Guide* (29 kč), *Prague This Month* (free), and *Heart of Europe* (free, summer only). The English-language *Prague Post* is handy for entertainment listings and current events.

Helpful Hints

Formalities: Travel in Prague is like travel in western Europe—15 years ago and for half the price. Americans don't need a visa,

Prague's Four Towns

Until about 1800, the city was actually four distinct towns with four town squares separated by fortified walls.

***Hradčany* (Castle Quarter):** Built regally on the hill, this was the home of the cathedral, monastery, castle, royal palace, and high nobility. Even today, you feel like clip-clopping through it in a fancy carriage. It has the high art and grand buildings, yet feels a bit sterile.

***Malá Strana* (Little Quarter):** This Baroque town of fine homes and gardens was built by the aristocracy and merchant elite at the foot of the castle. The quarter burned in the 1500s and was rebuilt with the mansions of the generally domesticated European nobility who moved in to be near the king. The tradition remains, as the successors of this power-brokering class—today's Parliament—now call this home.

***Staré Město* (Old Town):** Charles Bridge connects the Little Quarter with the Old Town. A boom town in the 14th century, this has long been the busy commercial quarter filled with merchants, guilds, and natural supporters of Jan Hus (folks who wanted a Czech stamp on their religion). Trace the walls of this town in the modern road plan (with the Powder Tower being a remnant of a wall system that completed a fortified ring half provided by the river). The marshy area closest to the bend—least inhabitable and therefore allotted to the Jewish community—became the ghetto.

***Nové Město* (New Town):** Nové Město rings the Old Town, cutting a swath from riverbank to riverbank, and is fortified with Prague's outer wall. In the 14th century, the king initiated the creation of this town, tripling the size of what would become Prague. Wenceslas Square was once the horse market of this busy working-class district. When you cross the moat (Na Príkope) that separates the Old and New Towns, you leave the tourists behind and enter the real workaday town.

but because of a recent reciprocation flap, Canadians do need a visa. Just flash your passport at the border. The U.S. Embassy in Prague is near the Little Quarter Square, or Malostranske Náměstí (Trziste 15, tel. 257-530-663). Since Eurailpasses don't cover the Czech Republic, you'll need to buy train tickets or a Prague Excursion pass for your travels to and from Prague (see "Transportation Connections—Prague," below).

Rip-offs: Prague's new freedom comes with new scams. There's no particular risk of violent crime—but green, rich tourists do get taken by con artists. Simply be on guard: traveling on trains (thieves thrive on overnight trains), changing money (tellers anywhere with bad arithmetic and inexplicable pauses while counting back your change), dealing with taxis (see "Getting around Prague," below), and in restaurants (see "Eating in Prague," below).

Anytime you pay for something, make a careful note of how much it costs, how much you're giving them, and—most importantly—how much you expect back. Don't let them get away with giving you any less. Remember how Czechs—and all Europeans—write their numbers: 1's have a long tail (which makes them look like 7's to American eyes), and 7's are crossed. Someone selling you a phone card marked 190 kč might first tell you it's 790 kč, hoping to pocket the difference. Call the bluff and they'll pretend it never happened.

Plainclothes policemen "looking for counterfeit money" are con artists. Don't show them your cash. If you are threatened with a fine by a "policeman," conductor, or other official, ask for the receipt that they are legally required to provide. Pickpockets (who can be little children or adults dressed as professionals, or even as tourists) target Western tourists. Many thieves drape jackets over their arms to disguise busy fingers. Be careful if anyone creates a commotion at the door of a metro or tram car (especially the made-for-tourists trams #22 and 23)—it's a smokescreen for theft. Car theft is also a big problem in Prague (many western European car-rental companies don't allow their rentals to cross the Czech border). Never leave anything valuable in your car—not even in broad daylight in the middle of Old Town Square.

Telephoning: Czech phones work like any in Europe. For international calls, buy a phone card at a kiosk or your hotel (various prices). If you call the United States directly (dial 00-1, the area code, and the number) from a public phone booth with the local phone card, you'll get about three minutes for $1. If you start with 0521 instead of 001, the connection won't be as good but you'll save about 30 percent (since the connection is carried over the Internet). The Czech Republic doesn't use area codes, so you'll dial the same number whether you're calling across the street or across the country. To call Prague from abroad, dial the international code (00 in Europe or 011 in the U.S.), the Czech Republic code (420), then the local number. For cheap calls to America, get a PIN card; ask for an international calling card (cards differ in cost per minute; compare rates before you buy, or ask the clerk for advice).

Money: 30 crowns (kč, *koruna* in Czech) = about U.S. $1. ATMs are everywhere and offer the best way to change money.

Don't exchange too much; Czech money is tough to change in the West.

There is no black market. Assume anyone trying to sell money on the streets is peddling obsolete (or Bulgarian) currency. Buy and sell easily at the station (5 percent fees), banks, or hotels. Change bureaus advertise no commission and decent but deceptive rates. These rates are for selling dollars. Their rates for buying your dollars are worse. Hidden fees abound; ask exactly how many crowns you'll walk away with before you agree to the transaction.

American Express: Václavske Náměstí 56, Praha 1 (foreign exchange daily 9:00–19:00, travel service Mon–Fri 9:00–18:00, Sat 9:00–12:00, closed Sun, tel. 222-211-136).

Internet Access: Internet cafés—which beg for business all along Karlova Street on the city side of the Charles Bridge—are commonplace. Consider Bohemia Bagel (see "Eating in Prague," below).

Medical Help: For English-speaking help, contact the American Medical Center (open 24 hrs, Janovskeho 48, Praha 7, tel. 220-807-756). A 24-hour pharmacy is at Palackeho 5 (Praha 1, tel. 224-946-982).

Local Help: Athos Travel books rooms (see "Sleeping," below); rents cars; has guides for hire (1–5 people-700 kč/hr, see "Tours of Prague," below); and perhaps best of all, provides stress-free taxi transfers to and from your hotel and airport (1–4 people-550 kč) or either train station (1–4 people-200 kč, see "Arrival in Prague," below; tel. 241-440-571, fax 241-441-697). Readers of this book get a discount for booking online (2 percent discount on rooms or car rental, 10 percent discount on local guide or airport and train station transfers); to get the discount, log on to www.athos.cz with Username: Rick, Password: Steves.

Magic Praha is a tiny travel service run by hardworking, English-speaking Lida Steflova. A charming jill-of-all-trades who takes her clients' needs seriously, she's particularly helpful with accommodations, private tours, side trips to historic towns, and airport or train station transfers anywhere in the Czech Republic (Národní 17, Praha 1, 5th floor, tel. 224-232-755, cellular 604-207-225, emergency home tel. & fax 235-325-170, e-mail: magicpraha@magicpraha.cz).

Best Views: Enjoy "the golden city of a hundred spires" during the early evening, when the light is warm and the colors are rich. Good viewpoints include the restaurant terrace at the Strahov Monastery (above the castle), the top of St. Vitus Cathedral at the castle, Petřín Tower (Eiffel's little brother—take funicular up from Malá Strana south of castle), the top of the east tower of Charles Bridge, the Old Town Square clock tower, and the steps of the National Museum overlooking Wenceslas Square.

Language: Czech, a Slavic language, has little resemblance to western European languages. These days, English is "modern," and you'll find the language barrier minimal. If you speak German, it's helpful. An acute accent means you linger on that vowel. The little accent above the c, s, or z makes it ch, sh, or zh.

Learn these key Czech words:

Hello/Goodbye (familiar)	*Ahoj* (pron. ah-hoi)
Good day, Hello (formal)	*Dobrý den* (pron. DOH-bree den)
Yes/No	*Ano* (pron. AH-no)/*Ne* (pron. neh)
Please	*Prosím* (pron. proh-zeem)
Thank you	*Děkuji* (pron. dyack-quee)
You're welcome	*Prosím* (pron. proh-zeem)
Where is . . . ?	*Kde je* . . . ? (pron. gday yeh)
Do you speak English?	*Mluvíte anglicky*? (pron. MLOO-vit-eh ANG-litz-key)
crown (the money)	*koruna* (pron. koh-roo-nah)

Arrival in Prague

Prague unnerves many travelers—it's relatively run-down, it's behind the former Iron Curtain, and you've heard stories of rip-offs and sky-high hotel prices. But in reality, Prague is charming, safe, and ready to show you a good time.

By Train: Most travelers coming from and going to the West use the main station (Hlavní Nádraží) or the secondary station (Nádraží Holešovice). Trains to other points within the country use Masarykovo or Smíchov stations. Trains to/from Český Krumlov usually use Prague's main station, sometimes the Smíchov station. (For information on getting to Prague, see "Transportation Connections—Prague," below.)

Upon arrival, change money. The stations have ATMs (at the main station, a cash machine is near the subway entrance). Exchange bureau rates vary—compare by asking at two windows what you'll get for $100 (but keep in mind that many of the windows are run by the same company). Count carefully. At an exchange window or the tobacco stand, buy a city map with trams and metro lines marked and tiny sketches of the sights for ease in navigating (many different brands, 40–69 kč). It's a mistake to try doing Prague without a good map—you'll refer to it constantly. Confirm your departure plans at the train information window. Consider arranging a room or tour at the TI or AVE travel agency (AVE has branches in both stations). The left-luggage counter is reportedly safer than the lockers.

At Prague's train stations, anyone arriving on an international train will be met at the tracks by room hustlers (snaring tourists for cheap rooms).

At Prague's main station, **Hlavní Nádraží**, the orange, low-ceilinged hall is a fascinating mix of travelers, kiosks, gamblers, loitering teenagers, and older riffraff. The creepy station ambience is the work of Communist architects, who took a classy building and made it just big. If you're killing time here (or for a glimpse of a more genteel age), go upstairs into the Art Nouveau hall. The station was originally named for Emperor Franz Josef, later named for President Woodrow Wilson (his promotion of self-determination led to the creation of the free state of Czechoslovakia in 1918), and then called simply the Main Station by the Communists (who weren't big fans of Wilson). Here, under an elegant dome, you can trace this history as you sip coffee, enjoy music from the 1920s, and watch new arrivals spilling into the city.

From the main station, it's a 10-minute walk to Wenceslas Square (turn left out of the station and follow Washingtonova to the huge Narodni Museum and you're there). You can also catch tram #9 (or, at night, tram #55 or #58; to find the stop, walk into park, head 2 min to right) or take the metro (inside station, look for the red M with 2 directions: Muzeum or Florenc; take Muzeum, then transfer to the green line—direction Dejvická—and get off at either Můstek or Staroměstska; these stops straddle the Old Town).

The courageous and savvy get a cabby to treat them fairly and get to their hotel fast and sweat-free for no more than 150 kč (see "Getting around Prague," below; to avoid the train station taxi stand, call AAA Taxi at 233-113-311, or ride the metro a stop and catch one on the street). The park in front of the station—nicknamed Sherwood Forest—is filled with thieves at night.

Athos Travel provides transfers from either train station to anywhere in Prague (1–4 people-200 kč, 5–8 people-350 kč, tel. 241-440-571, fax 241-441-697, www.athos.cz); to get a 10 percent discount for online booking, see "Helpful Hints," above.

The **Nádraží Holešovice** station is suburban mellow. The main hall has all the services of the main station in a compact area. Outside the first glass doors, the ATM is on the left, the metro is straight ahead (follow *Vstup*, which means "entrance"; take it 3 stops to the main station, 4 stops to the city center Muzeum stop), and taxis and trams are outside to the right (allow 200 kč for a cab to the center). Train info tel. 224-224-200.

By Plane: Prague's new, tidy, low-key **Ruzyně Airport**—a delightful contrast to the old, hulking, dreary main train station—is 20 kilometers (12 miles, or about 30 min) west of the city center. Your hotel can arrange for a shuttle minibus to take you to the airport economically. Taxis called "Airport Cars" take you into town at a fixed rate (without turning on the meter) of about 600 kč; firmly establish the price to your specific hotel before boarding. Airport info: tel. 220-113-314.

Athos Travel provides airport pick-up or drop-off (1–4 people-550 kč, 5–8 people-900 kč, tel. 241-440-571, fax 241-441-697, www.athos.cz); to get a 10 percent discount for online booking, see "Helpful Hints," above.

Getting around Prague

You can walk nearly everywhere. But the metro is slick, the trams fun, and the taxis quick and easy once you're initiated. For details, pick up the handy transit guide at the TI.

Public Transport: The trams and metro work on the same cheap tickets. Buy from machines (select ticket price, then insert coins) at kiosks or purchase at hotels. For convenience, buy all the tickets you think you'll need: 15-minute ticket—8 kč, 60-minute ticket—12 kč, 24-hour ticket—70 kč, three-day pass—200 kč. Estimate conservatively. Remember, Prague is a great walking town, so unless you're commuting from a hotel far outside the center, you will likely find that individual tickets work best. You technically have to pay an additional 6 kč to transport luggage, but the rule is rarely enforced. The metro closes at midnight, but some trams keep running all night (identified with white numbers on blue backgrounds at tram stops).

City maps show the tram/bus/metro lines. The three-line metro system is handy and simple, but doesn't serve many hotels and sights. Although it seems that all metro doors lead to the neighborhood of *Výstup*, that's simply the Czech word for "exit." Trams are also easy to use; track your route with your city map. They run every 5 to 10 minutes in the daytime (a schedule is posted at each stop). Get used to hopping on and off. Be sure to always validate your ticket on the tram/bus/metro by sticking it in the machine (which stamps a time on it). Cheaters—including those who don't stamp their tickets—are fined 800 kč, or 400 kč if the fine is paid on the spot.

Taxis: Prague's taxis—notorious for meters that spin for tourists like pinwheels—are being tamed. Still, many cabbies are no-neck mafia types who consider one sucker a good day's work. While most hotel receptionists and guidebooks advise avoiding taxis, I find Prague is a great taxi town and use them routinely. With the local rate, they're cheap (read the rates on the door: drop charge—30 kč, per-kilometer charge—22 kč, and wait time per min—5 kč). Unfortunately, the meter isn't always reliable; some crooked cabbies use "turbo boxes" to speed it up.

Prague Metro

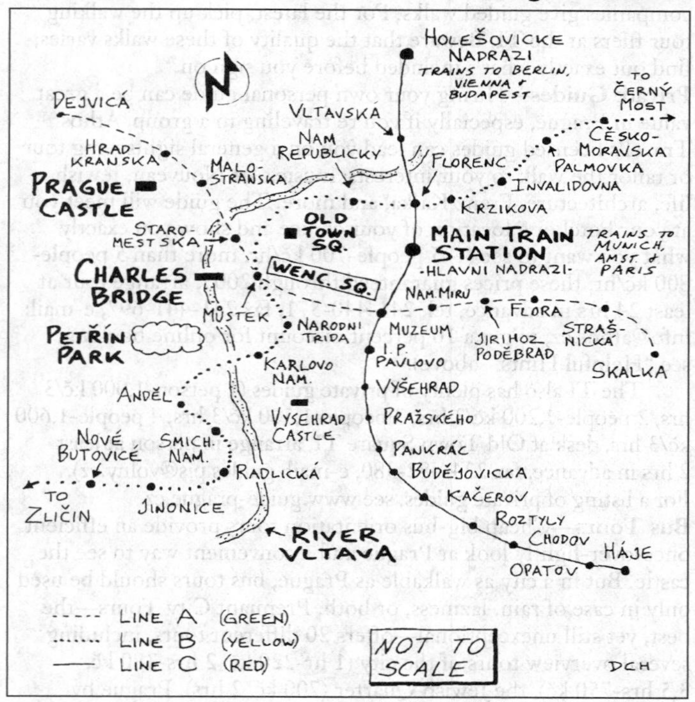

Anytime you take a cab, the first rule is to always request a price estimate up front. If the price seems unreasonable, keep looking. This way, even the tricky turbo-charged cabbies won't be able to surprise you at the end with an astronomical fare. If a cabby tries to rip you off, simply pay 200 kč for a long ride. Let him follow you into the hotel if he insists you owe him more. (He won't.) The receptionist will defend you. Don't bother with any taxi parked in a touristy zone. If you hail a cab on the street (rather than at a taxi rank), you're most likely to be treated fairly. If you have a cab called from a hotel or restaurant (try AAA Taxi, tel. 233-113-311), you're likely to get a fair meter rate (which starts only when you take off).

Tours of Prague

Walking Tours—Prague Walks offers walking tours of the Old Town, the castle, the Jewish Quarter, and more (all 300 kč, 90 min-3 hrs, tel. 261-214-603, www.praguewalks.com, e-mail: pwalks@comp.cz). Consider their clever Good Morning Walk that starts at 8:00, before the crowds hit. Several other decent companies give guided walks. For the latest, pick up the walking tour fliers at the TI. Beware that the quality of these walks varies; find out exactly what's included before you sign on.

Private Guides—Hiring your own personal guide can be a great value in Prague, especially if you're traveling in a group. Athos Travel's licensed guides can lead you on a general sightseeing tour or tailor the walk to your interests: music, Art Nouveau, Jewish life, architecture, Franz Kafka, and more. The guide will meet you at your hotel or a location of your choice and show you exactly what you want to see (1–5 people-700 kč/hr, more than 5 people-800 kč/hr, these prices guaranteed through 2003, arrange tour at least 24 hrs in advance, tel. 241-440-571, fax 241-441-697, e-mail: info@athos.cz; to get a 10 percent discount for online booking, see "Helpful Hints," above).

The TI also has plenty of private guides (1 person-1,000 kč/3 hrs, 2 people-1,200 kč/3 hrs, 3 people-1,500 kč/3 hrs, 4 people-1,600 kč/3 hrs, desk at Old Town Square TI, arrange in person at least 2 hrs in advance, fax 224-482-380, e-mail: guides.pis@volny.cz). For a listing of private guides, see www.guide-prague.cz.

Bus Tours—Cheap big-bus orientation tours provide an efficient once-over-lightly look at Prague and a convenient way to see the castle. But in a city as walkable as Prague, bus tours should be used only in case of rain, laziness, or both. Premiant City Tours—the best, yet still unexceptional—offers 20 different tours, including several overview tours of the city (1 hr-220 kč, 2 hrs-380 kč, 3.5 hrs-750 kč), the Jewish Quarter (700 kč, 2 hrs), Prague by night, Bohemian glass, Terezín Concentration Camp memorial, Karlštejn Castle, Český Krumlov (1,750 kč, 10 hrs), and a river cruise. The tours feature live guides (English and sometimes also German) and depart from near the bottom of Wenceslas Square at Na Príkope 23. Get tickets at an AVE travel agency, hotel, on the bus, or at Na Príkope 23 (tel. 224-946-922, cellular 606-600-123, www.premiant.cz).

Tram Joyride—Trams #22 and #23 (following the same route) both make a fine joyride through town. Consider it a scenic lead-up to touring the castle. Catch it at metro: Náměstí Míru, roll through a bit of new town, the old town, across the river, and hop out just above the castle (at Hotel Savoy, stop: Pohorelec, and hike down the hill into castle area).

Self-Guided Walking Tour

The King's Walk *(Královská cesta)*, the ancient way of coronation processions, is touristy but great. Pedestrian-friendly and full of playful diversions, it connects the essential Prague sites. The king would be crowned in St. Vitus Cathedral in the Prague Castle, walk through the Little Quarter to the Church of St. Nicholas, cross Charles Bridge, and finish at the Old Town Square. If he hurried, he'd be done in 20 minutes. Like the main drag in Venice between St. Mark's and the Rialto Bridge, this walk mesmerizes tourists. Use it as a spine, but venture off it—especially to eat.

While you could cover this route in the same direction as the king, he's long gone and it's a new morning in Prague. Here are Prague's essential sights in walking order, starting at Wenceslas Square, where modern independence was proclaimed, proceeding through the Old Town and across the bridge, and finishing at the castle. This walk laces together all the following recommended sights except the Jewish Quarter.

▲▲Wenceslas Square (Václavske Náměstí)—More a broad boulevard than a square (until recently, trams rattled up and down its park-like median strip), it's named for the equestrian statue of King Wenceslas that stands at the top of the boulevard.

The square is a stage for modern Czech history: The Czechoslovak state was proclaimed here in 1918. In 1968, the Soviets put down huge popular demonstrations here. Starting at the top (Metro: Muzeum), stroll down the square:

The **National Museum** (Národní Muzeum) stands grandly at the top. The only exciting thing about it is the view (80 kč, summer daily 10:00–18:00, winter daily 9:00–17:00, free first Mon of each month, closed first Tue of each month, halls of Czech fossils and animals).

The metro stop (Muzeum) is the cross point of two metro lines. From here, you could roll a ball straight down the boulevard and through the heart of Prague to Charles Bridge.

Stand behind the statue facing the museum (uphill). The light-colored patches in the columns are from the very recent repair of bullet holes from the Russian crackdown in 1968. Look left (about 10:00 on an imaginary clock) at the ugly Communist-era building—it housed the Parliament back when they voted with Moscow. A social-realism statue showing workers triumphing still stands at its base. It's now home to Radio Free Europe. After Communism fell, RFE lost its funding and could no longer afford its Munich headquarters. As gratitude for how its broadcasts kept their people in touch with real news, the current Czech government now rents the building to RFE for one crown a year.

As you wander down this great square, notice the fun mix of **architectural styles**, all post-1850: Romantic neo-Gothic, neo-Renaissance, neo-Baroque from the 19th century, Art Nouveau from 1900, ugly functionalism from the mid-20th century (the "form follows function," "ornamentation is a crime" answer to

Central Prague

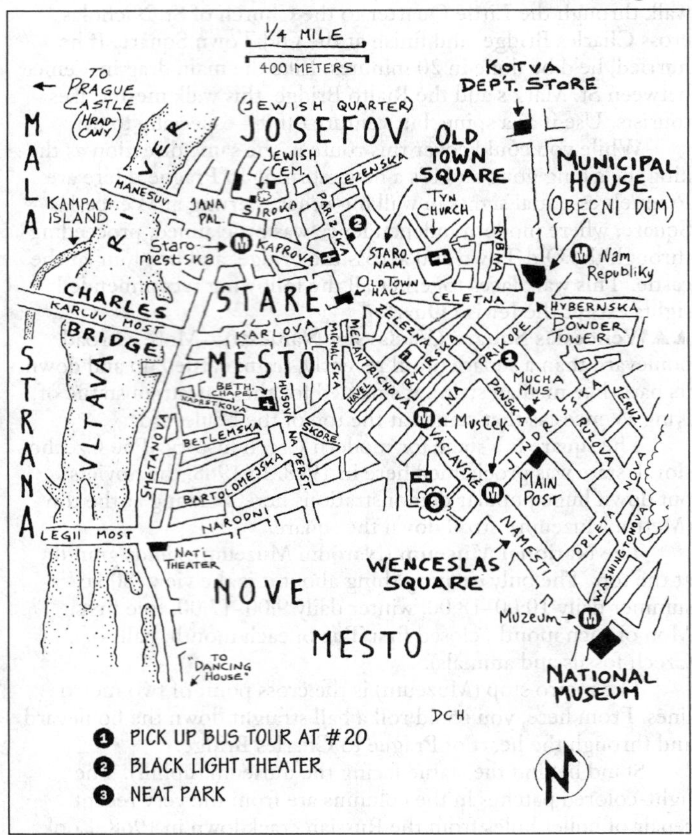

Art Nouveau), Stalin Gothic from the 1950s "Communist epoch" (a good example is the Jalta building—a block downhill on the right), and glass-and-steel buildings of the 1970s.

St. Wenceslas (Václav), commemorated by the statue, is the "good king" of Christmas-carol fame. He was never really a king, but the wise and benevolent 10th-century duke of Bohemia. A rare example of a well-educated and literate ruler, he was credited by his people for Christianizing his nation and lifting up the culture. Wenceslas astutely allied the Czechs with Saxony rather than Bavaria, giving the Czechs a vote when the Holy Roman Emperor was selected (and therefore more political importance). After being assassinated in 929, he became a symbol of Czech nationalism and statehood. Study the statue. Wenceslas is surrounded by the four other Czech patron saints. Notice the focus on books. A small nation without great military power, the Czech Republic chose national heroes who enriched the culture by thinking, rather than fighting. This statue is a popular meeting point. Locals say, "I'll see you under the horse's tail."

Thirty meters (100 feet) below the big horse is a small, round garden with a low-key **memorial** "to the victims of Communism"—such as Jan Palach. In 1969, a group of patriots decided that a self-immolation would stoke the fires of independence. They drew straws, and Jan Palach got the short one. He set himself on fire for the cause of Czech independence and died on this place. Czechs are keen on anniversaries. On the 20th anniversary of Palach's death, demonstrations stoked the popular fire which, 10 months later, led to the overthrow of the Czech Communist government.

Walk a couple of blocks downhill through the real people of Prague (not tourists) to the Grand Hotel Europa, with its hard-to-miss, dazzling, Art Nouveau exterior and plush café interior.

In November 1989, this huge square was filled with hundreds of thousands of ecstatic Czechs believing freedom was at hand. Assembled on the balcony of the Melantrich building (opposite the Grand Hotel Europa; look for the KNIHY sign) was a priest, a rock star (famous for his kick-ass-for-freedom lyrics), Alexander Dubček (hero of the 1968 revolt), and Václav Havel (the charismatic playwright, newly released from prison, and every freedom-loving Czech's Mandela). Through a sound system provided by the rock star, Havel's voice boomed over the gathered masses, announcing the resignation of the Czech politburo and saying the Republic of Czechoslovakia's freedom was imminent. Picture the cold November evening with thousands of Czechs jingling their key chains for solidarity, chanting, "It's time to go now!" (While the revolt stirred, government tanks could have given it the Tiananmen Square treatment—which spilled lots of patriotic blood in China just six months earlier. Locals figure Gorbachev must have made a phone call saying, "Let's not shed blood over this.")

Havel ended his second (and, constitutionally, last) five-year term early in 2003. He is still popular among Czechs, but his popularity took a hit when he got married for the second time—to an actress 17 years his junior. (Some say his brain dropped about one meter.)

Immediately opposite the Grand Hotel Europa is the **Lucerna Gallery** (use entry marked Divadlo Rokoko and work your way back to Lucerna). This is a classic mall from the 1920s and 1930s with shops, theaters, a ballroom in the basement, and the fine Lucerna café upstairs. Curiously, the place was built and is owned by the Havel family.

If you're ready for a coffee with a grand Wenceslas Square view (and if the building's renovation is completed), ride the elevator at the foot of Wenceslas Square (at Na Príkope 9, under cover near top of metro station) to the **Blue Terrace** restaurant (described below).

▲Na Príkope—The bottom of Wenceslas Square meets a spacious pedestrian mall lined with stylish shops. Na Príkope (meaning "the moat") follows the line of the old town wall, leading from Wenceslas Square right to a former gate in that wall, the Powder Tower (Prasná Brána, not worth touring). While the tower area is probably not worth the detour on this walk, consider these reasons to explore it later: City tour buses leave from along this street. And, next to the Powder Tower, the dazzling **Municipal House** (Obecní Dům), with a great Art Nouveau facade, contains three recommended restaurants (see "Eating in Prague," below).

Before you venture on, consider a stop at the **Museum of Communism** (turn right on Na Príkope, nestled between a McDonald's and a casino—somewhere, Stalin spins in his grave). The museum is a hodgepodge of artifacts from the Czech Republic's 40-year stint with Soviet economics. You'll find propaganda posters, busts of Communist All-Stars (Marx, Lenin, Stalin), and re-created slices of Communist life, from a bland store counter to a typical classroom (with a poem on the chalkboard extolling the virtues of the tractor). It's fun and described in English but lacks the cheeky spunk of other such museums in Eastern Europe (180 kč, daily 9:00–21:00, upstairs at Na Príkope 10, tel. 224-212-966, www.muzeumkomunismu.cz).

▲Havelská Market—Central Prague's best open-air flower and produce market scene is a block toward the Old Town Square from the bottom of Wenceslas Square. Laid out in the 13th century for the German trading community, it still keeps hungry locals and vagabonds fed cheaply. Since only those who produce their goods personally are allowed to have a stall, you'll be dealing with the actual farmer or craftsperson.

Czech Sex—The strip between the base of Wenceslas Square and the market is notorious for its sex clubs, filled mostly with Russian girls and German and Asian guys. Be warned: These routinely rip off naive tourists and can be dangerous.

▲▲▲Old Town Square (Staroměstské Náměstí)—The focal point for most visits, this has been a market square since the 11th century. It became the nucleus of a town (Staré Město) in the 13th century when its city hall was built. Today, the old-time market stalls have been replaced by cafés, touristy horse buggies, and souvenir hawkers.

The **Hus Memorial**—erected in 1915, 500 years after his

burning—marks the center of the square and symbolizes the long struggle for Czech freedom. Walk around the memorial. The Czech reformer Jan Hus stands tall between two groups of people: victorious Hussite patriots and Protestants defeated by the Hapsburgs. One of the patriots holds a cup—in the medieval Church, only priests could drink the wine at Communion. Hussites fought for the right to take both the wine and the bread. Behind Hus, a mother with her children represents the ultimate rebirth of the Czech nation. Hus was excommunicated and burned in Germany a century before the age of Martin Luther.

Do a **spin tour** in the center of the square to get a look at architectural styles: Gothic, Renaissance, Baroque, rococo, and Art Nouveau.

Spin clockwise, starting with the green domes of the Baroque Church of St. Nicholas. A Hussite church, it's a popular venue for concerts. (There's another green-domed Church of St. Nicholas across the Charles Bridge in Malá Strana.) The Jewish Quarter (Josefov) is a few blocks behind it, down the uniquely tree-lined Paris Street (Parizska)—a cancan of mostly Art Nouveau facades. On the horizon, at the end of Paris Street, a giant metronome ticks where an imposing statue of Stalin once stood. Spin to the right past the Hus Memorial and the fine golden and mosaic Art Nouveau facade of the Ministry of the Economy. Notice the Gothic Tyn Church (described below), with its fanciful spires flanking a solid gold effigy of the Virgin Mary. Lining the uphill side of the square is an interesting row of pastel houses with Gothic, Renaissance, and Baroque facades. The pointed 75-meter-tall (246-foot) spire marks the 14th-century Old Town Hall, famous for its astronomical clock (described below). In front of the city hall, 27 white inlaid crosses mark the spot where 27 Protestant nobles, merchants, and intellectuals were beheaded in 1621 after rebelling against the Catholic Hapsburgs.

Tyn Church—The towering Tyn (pronounced "teen") Church facing the Old Town Square was rebuilt fancier than the original—but enjoy it. For 200 years after Hus' death, this was Prague's leading Hussite church.

The lane leading to the church from the Old Town Square has a public WC and the most convenient box office in town (see "Entertainment," below).

▲Old Town Hall Astronomical Clock—Ignore the ridiculous human sales racks, and join the gang for the striking of the hour (daily 8:00–21:00, until 20:00 in winter) on the 15th-century town hall clock. As you wait, see if you can figure out how the clock works.

With revolving disks, celestial symbols, and sweeping hands, this clock keeps several versions of time. Two outer rings show the hour: Bohemian time (Gothic numbers, counts from sunset—find the zero, next to 23…supposedly the time of tonight's sunset) and modern time (24 Roman numerals, XII at the top being noon, XII at the bottom being midnight). Five hundred years ago, everything revolved around the earth (the fixed middle background).

To indicate the times of sunrise and sunset, arcing lines and moving spheres combine with the big hand (a sweeping golden sun) and the little hand (the moon showing various stages). Look for the orbits of the sun and moon as they rise through day (the blue zone) and night (the black zone).

If this seems complex today, it must have been a marvel 500 years ago. The circle below (added in the 19th century) shows the zodiac, scenes from the seasons of a rural peasant's life, and a ring of saints' names—one for each day of the year, with a marker showing today's special saint (out of order).

Four statues flanking the clock represent 15th-century Prague's four biggest worries: invasion (a Turkish conqueror, his hedonism symbolized by a mandolin), death (a skeleton), greed (a miserly moneylender, which used to have "Jewish" features until after World War II, when anti-Semitism became politically incorrect), and vanity (enjoying the mirror). Another interpretation: earthly pleasures brought on by vanity, greed, and hedonism are fleeting because we are all mortal.

At the top of the hour (don't blink—the show is pretty quick): (1) Death tips his hourglass and pulls the cord, ringing the bell; (2) the windows open and the Twelve Apostles parade by, acknowledging the gang of onlookers; (3) the rooster crows; and (4) the hour is rung. The hour is often off because of daylight saving time (completely senseless to 15th-century clock makers). At the top of the next hour, stand under the tower—protected by a line of banner-wielding, powdered-wigged concert salespeople—and watch the tourists.

Old Town Hall Tower, Hall, and Chapel—The main TI, left of the astronomical clock, contains a guides' desk and these sights: the tower climb (30 kč, long hike, fine view) and a tour of the town hall and Gothic chapel (40 kč, only interesting for a close-up of Twelve Apostles and clock mechanism).

Torture Museum—This gimmicky moneymaker is similar to other European torture museums, but is nevertheless interesting, showing models of gruesome medieval tortures with well-written English descriptions (100 kč, daily 10:00–22:00, on the Old Town Square at Staroměstské Náměstí 20, tel. 224-215-581).

To reach the bridge, turn your back to the fancy Tyn Church and march with the crowds.

Hus and Luther

The word *catholic* means universal. The Roman Catholic Church—in many ways the administrative ghost of the Roman Empire—is the only organization to survive from ancient times. For over a thousand years, it enforced its notion that the Vatican was the sole interpreter of God's word on earth, and the only legitimate way to be a Christian was as a Roman Catholic. Jan Hus lived and preached 100 years before Martin Luther. Both were college professors, as well as priests. Both drew huge public crowds as they preached in their university chapels. Both promoted a local religious autonomy. And both helped establish their national languages. (Hus gave the Czechs their unique accents to enable the letters to fit the sounds.) Both got in big trouble. While Hus was burned, Luther survived. Living after Gutenberg, Luther was able to spread his message more cheaply and effectively thanks to the new printing press. Since Luther was high profile and German, killing him would have caused major political complications. While Hus may have loosened Rome's grip on Christianity, Luther orchestrated the Reformation that finally broke it. Today, both are revered as national heroes as well as religious reformers.

Karlova Street—This street winds through medieval old Prague from the City Hall Square to the Charles Bridge (it zigzags... just follow the crowds). This is a commercial gauntlet, and it's here that the touristy feeding frenzy of Prague is most ugly. Street signs keep you on track, and *Karluv Most* signs point to the bridge. Obviously, you'll find great people-watching, but no good values, on this drag.

For a detour from this hyper-capitalistic orgy—every good Communist's worst nightmare—take a left on Husova to reach one of Prague's most important medieval buildings, the Bethlehem Chapel.

Bethlehem Chapel (Betlémská Kaple)—Emperor Charles IV founded the first university north of the Alps, and this was its chapel. The room is plain, with a focus on the pulpit and the message of the sermon. Around 1400, priest and professor Jan Hus preached his reformist ideas from this pulpit. While meant primarily for students and faculty, the Mass was open to the public. Soon, huge crowds were drawn by Hus' empowering Luther-like ideas: such as that people should be more involved in worship (e.g., actually drinking the wine at Communion) and have better access to the word of God through services and scriptures written in the people's language, rather than Latin. Standing-room-only crowds of more than 3,000 were the norm when Hus preached. The stimulating and controversial ideas debated at the university spread throughout the city (30 kč, April–Oct daily 9:00–18:00, Nov–March daily 9:00–17:00, cellular 602-664-079).

▲▲▲**Charles Bridge (Karluv Most)**—This much-loved bridge, commissioned by the Holy Roman Emperor Charles IV in 1357, offers one of the most pleasant and entertaining 450-meter (500-yard) strolls in Europe. Until 1850, it was the only bridge crossing the river here. Be on the bridge when the sun is low for the best light, people-watching, and photo opportunities.

Before crossing the bridge, step into the little square on the right with the statue of the Holy Roman Emperor Charles IV (Karlo Quatro). Charles ruled his vast empire from Prague in the 14th century. He's holding a contract establishing Prague's university—the first in central Europe. The women around his pedestal symbolize the university's four faculties: medicine, law, theology, and the arts. The statue was erected in 1848 to celebrate the university's 500th birthday. Enjoy the view across the river. The bridge tower—once a tollbooth—is considered one of the finest Gothic gates anywhere. Climb it for a fine view but nothing else (30 kč, daily 10:00–19:00, last entry 18:30).

Charles Bridge is famous for its statues. But most of those you see today are replicas—the originals are in city museums and out of the polluted air.

Two statues on the bridge are worth a comment: the crucifix (facing the castle, near the start on the right) is the spot where convicts would pause to pray on their way to execution on the Old Town Square. Farther on (midstream, on right) the statue of John Nepomuk—a saint of the Czech people—draws a crowd (look for the guy with the five golden stars and the shiny dog). Back in the 14th century, he was the priest to whom the queen confessed all her sins. The king wanted to know her secrets, but Father John dutifully refused to tell. He was tortured, eventually killed, and tossed off the bridge. When he hit the water, five stars appeared. The shiny spot on the base of the statue shows the heave-ho. Locals touch it to help wishes come true. The shiny dog killed the queen . . . but that's another story. From the end of the bridge (TI in tower on castle side), the street leads two blocks to the Little Quarter Square at the base of the huge St. Nicholas church.

Kampa Island and Lennon Wall—One hundred meters (330 feet) from the castle end of Charles Bridge, stairs lead down to the Kampa Island and its relaxing, pub-lined square, breezy park, new art gallery, and river access.

From the square, a lane on the right leads past a water mill (many of which once lined the canal here) to the Lennon Wall (Lennonova zed').

While the ideas of Lenin sat like a water-soaked trench coat upon the Czech people, the ideas of John Lennon gave many locals hope and a vision. When Lennon was killed in 1980, a memorial wall filled with graffiti spontaneously appeared. Night after night, the police would paint over the "all you need is love" and "imagine" graffiti. And day after day, it would reappear. Until independence came in 1989, travelers, freedom-lovers, and local hippies gathered here. Even today, while the tension and danger associated with this wall is gone, the message stays fresh.

▲▲Little Quarter (Malá Strana)—This is the most characteristic, fun-to-wander old section of town. It's one of four medieval towns (along with Hradčany, Staré Město, and Nové Město) that united in the late 1700s to make modern Prague. It centers on the Little Quarter Square (Malostranské Náměstí) with the huge St. Nicholas church standing in the middle and a plague monument facing the church entry (uphill side).

Church of St. Nicholas (Kostel Sv. Mikuláše)—When the Jesuits came, they found the perfect piece of real estate for their church and associated school—the Little Quarter Square. Imagine this square without the big church in its middle—a real square. The Church of St. Nicholas (built 1703–1760) is the best example of High Baroque in town. It's a Jesuit church, giddy with curves and illusions. The altar features a lavish gold-plated Nicholas flanked by the two top Jesuits: St. Ignatius Loyola and St. Francis Xavier. For a good look at the city and the church's 75-meter (250-foot) dome, climb the tower for 30 kč; the entrance is outside the right transept (church entry-50 kč, but free for prayer daily 8:30–9:00, open daily April–Nov 9:00–16:45, Dec–March 9:00–15:45, tower open daily 10:00–18:00, church used as a concert venue in evenings). From here, hike 10 minutes uphill to the castle.

Sights—Prague's Castle Area

▲▲Prague Castle (Prazský Hrad)—For over a thousand years, Czech rulers have ruled from the Prague Castle. It's huge (by some measures, the biggest castle on earth) and confusing—with plenty of sights not worth seeing. Rather than worry about rumors that you should spend all day here with long lists of museums to see, keep things simple. Five stops matter and are explained here: Castle Square, St. Vitus Cathedral, Old Royal Palace, Basilica of St. George, and the Golden Lane.

You can choose from three ticket routes: Route A includes the cathedral, Old Royal Palace, Basilica, Powder Tower, Golden Lane, and sometimes also temporary exhibitions for 220 kč. Route B includes the cathedral, Old Royal Palace, and the Golden Lane for 180 kč. Route C covers only the Golden Lane for 40 kč (castle hours: April–Oct daily 9:00–17:00, Nov–March 9:00–16:00, last entry 15 min before closing, tel. 224-373-368 or 224-372-434). For most people (and for the purposes of this tour), Route B is best. If you rent the worthwhile audioguide (200-kč/2 hrs or 250-kč/3 hrs), you won't be able to exit the castle area from the bottom since you need to return the audioguide where you got it.

Hour-long **tours** in English depart from main ticket office about three times a day, but cover only the cathedral and Old Royal Palace (80 kč, reserve a week in advance if you want a private guide-400 kč for up to 5 people, then 80 kč per additional person, tel. 224-373-368).

Getting to the Castle: You can ride a taxi, catch a tram, or hike. Those hiking follow the main cobbled road from Charles Bridge through Malá Strana, the Little Quarter (the nearest subway stop is Malostranska). From the big church, hike uphill along Nerudova Street. After about 10 minutes, a steep lane on the right leads to the castle. (If you continue straight, Nerudova becomes Úvoz and heads past two recommended restaurants to the Strahov Monastery and Library.)

Trams #22 and #23 go from the National Theater or Malostranska to the castle. You have two options: Get off at the stop Královský Letohrádek for the castle, or stay on farther to Pohorelec to visit the Strahov Monastery (go uphill and through the gate toward the twin spires) and then hike down to the castle.

If you get off the tram at Královský Letohrádek, you'll see the royal summer palace across the street. This love gift—a Czech Taj Mahal—from Emperor Ferdinand I, who really did love his Queen Anne, is the finest Renaissance building in town. Notice the fine reliefs, featuring classical rather than Christian stories. From here, walk through the park with fine views of the cathedral to the gate taking you over the moat and into the castle grounds. This garden—once the private grounds and residence (you'll see the building) of the Communist president—was opened to the public with the coming of freedom under Václav Havel.

Castle Square (Hradčanske Náměstí)—The big square facing the castle feels like the castle's entry, but it's actually the central square of the Castle Town. Enjoy the awesome city view and the two string quartets that play regularly at the gate (their CD is terrific; say hello to friendly, mustachioed Josef). A tranquil café (Espresso Kajetánka—see "Eating in Prague," below) hides a few

Prague's Castle Area

steps down immediately to the right as you face the castle. From here, stairs lead into the Little Quarter.

The Castle Square was a kind of Czech Pennsylvania Avenue. Look uphill from the gate. The Renaissance Schwarzenberg Palace (*Svarcenberskč palác*, on the left, with the fake big stones scratched on the wall) is now a museum of military history. The statue marked "TGM" honors Thomáš Masaryk, Czechoslovakia's George Washington. At the end of World War I, this pal of Woodrow Wilson united the Czechs and the Slovaks into one nation, and became its first president. A plague monument stands in the center (built by the city in thanks for surviving the Black Plague). On the right, find the archbishop's rococo yellow palace.

Through the portal on the left-hand side, a lane leads to the Sternberg Palace *(Sternberskč palác)*, filled with the National Gallery's skippable collection of European paintings—mostly minor works by Dürer, Rubens, Rembrandt, and El Greco (90 kč, Tue–Sun 10:00–18:00, closed Mon).

Survey the castle from this square—the tip of a 500-meter-long (1,600-foot) series of courtyards, churches, and palaces. Huge throngs of tourists make the castle grounds one sea of people during peak times; late afternoon is least crowded. The guard changes on the hour, with the most ceremony at noon. Walk under the fighting giants, under an arch, into the second courtyard. The mod green awning with the golden winged cat (just past the ticket office) marks the offices of the Czech president. You can walk through the castle and enter the cathedral without a ticket, but you'll need a ticket to see the castle properly (see ticket options above).

▲St. Vitus Cathedral (Katedrála Sv. Vita)—This Roman Catholic cathedral—containing the tombs and relics of the most important local saints and kings, including the first three Hapsburg kings— symbolizes the Czech spirit. What's up with the guys in suits carved into the facade below the big round window? They're the architects and builders who finished the church. Started in 1344, construction was stalled by wars and plagues. But, fueled by the 19th-century rise of Czech nationalism, Prague's top church was finished in 1929 for the 1,000th anniversary of the death of St. Wenceslas. It looks all Gothic, but it's two distinct halves: modern neo-Gothic and the original 14th-century Gothic. For 400 years, a temporary wall sealed off the unfinished cathedral.

Go inside and find the third stained-glass window on the left. This masterful 1931 Art Nouveau window is by Czech artist Alfons Mucha (if you like this, you'll love the Mucha museum downtown—described below under "Art Nouveau"). Notice Mucha's stirring nationalism: Methodious and Cyril top and cen-ter (leaders in Slavic-style Christianity). Cyril is baptizing the mythic, lanky, long-haired Czech man. Lower, you'll see two Czech flappers and the classic Czech patriarch in the lower right. Also notice Mucha's novel use of color: your eyes are drawn from blue (symbolizing the past) to the golden center (where the boy and the seer look into the future).

Show your ticket and circulate around the **apse** past a carved wood relief of Prague in 1630 (before Charles Bridge had any statues), lots of faded Gothic paintings, and tombs of local saints. A fancy roped-off chapel (right transept) houses the **tomb of Prince Wenceslas,** surrounded by precious 14th-century murals showing scenes of his life, and a locked door leading to the crown jewels. More kings are buried in the royal mausoleum in front of the high altar and in the crypt underneath. You can climb 287 steps up the **spire** for a fine view (included in Route A or B ticket, or pay 20 kč at the cathedral ticket window, April–Oct daily except Sunday morning, 9:00–17:00, last entry 16:15).

Leaving the cathedral, turn left (past the public WC). The **obelisk** was erected in 1919—a single piece of granite celebrating the establishment of Czechoslovakia. (It was originally much taller but broke in transit—an inauspicious start for a nation destined to last only 70 years.) Find the 14th-century mosaic of the *Last Judgment* outside on the right transept. It was built Italian-style by the modern-and-cosmopolitan-for-his-era King Charles IV. Jesus oversees the action, as some go to heaven and some go to hell. The Czech king and queen kneel directly below Jesus and the six patron saints. On coronation day, they would walk under this arch, which would remind them (and their subjects) that even those holding great power are not above God's judgment. The royal crown and national jewels are kept in a chamber (see the grilled windows) above this entryway, which was the cathedral's main entry for centuries while the church was incomplete. Twen-ty meters (65 feet) to the right, a door leads to the…

Old Royal Palace (Starý Královský Palác)—This was the seat of the Bohemian princes in the 12th century. While extensively rebuilt, the large hall is late Gothic. It was a multipurpose hall for the old nobility. It's big enough for jousts—even the staircase was designed to let a mounted soldier gallop in. It was filled with market stalls, giving nobles a chance to shop without actually going into town. In the 1400s, the nobility met here to elect their king. This tradition survives today, as the parliament crowds into this room every five years to elect the Czech president. Look up at the impressive vaulted ceiling, look down on the chapel from the end, and go out on the balcony for a fine Prague view. Is that Paris in the distance? No, it's Petřín Tower, built for an exhibition in 1891 (60 meters/200 feet tall, a quarter of the height of the Parisian big brother built in 1889). The spiral stairs on the left lead up to several rooms with painted coats of arms and no English explanations. The downstairs of the palace sometimes houses special exhibitions. Across from the palace exit is the basilica.

Basilica of St. George and Convent (Bazilika Sv. Jiří)—Step into the beautifully lit Basilica of St. George to see Prague's best-preserved Romanesque church. St. Ludmila was buried here in 973. The first Bohemian convent was established here near the palace. To visit the basilica in addition to the other castle sights described here, you'll pay an extra 40 kč for the Route A ticket—worth it if you're interested in Romanesque.

Today, the convent next door houses the National Gallery's Collection of Old Masters (best Czech paintings from Gothic, Renaissance, and Baroque periods, 50 kč, Tue–Sun 10:00–18:00, closed Mon). Continue walking downhill through the castle grounds. Turn left on the first street, which leads into a cute lane.

Golden Lane (Zlatá Ulička)—This street of old buildings, which originally housed goldsmiths, is now jammed with tourists and lined with expensive gift shops, boutiques, galleries, and cafés. The Czech writer Franz Kafka lived at #22. There's a deli/bistro at the top and a convenient public WC at the bottom (Golden Lane-40 kč for "Route C" ticket, also included in Routes A and B). Beyond that, at the end of the castle, are fortifications beefed up in anticipation of the Turkish attack—the cause for most medieval arms buildups in Europe—and steps funneling the mobs of tourists back into town. At the bottom of the castle, continue down into the Little Quarter (Malá Strana) or follow the garden along the castle back to the castle square and on to the monastery.

Strahov Monastery and Library (Strahovský Kláster a Knihovna)—Twin Baroque domes standing high above the castle (a 10-min hike uphill) mark the Strahov Monastery. If you want to visit this sight and the castle, take tram #22 or #23 (from the National Theater or Malostranska) to the Pohorelec stop, visit the monastery (go uphill and through the gate toward the twin spires), then hike down to the castle.

The monastery is a Romanesque structure decorated in textbook Baroque (look through the window inside the front door to see its interior). The adjacent library (50 kč, daily 9:00–11:45 & 13:00–16:45, last entry 15 min before closing) offers a peek at how enlightened thinkers in the 18th century impacted learning. Two rooms are filled with 17th-century books under ceilings decorated with appropriate themes. Because the Czechs were a rural people with almost no high culture at this time, there were few books in the Czech language. The theme of the first and bigger hall is philosophy, with the history of man's pursuit of knowledge painted on its ceiling. The other is theology. Notice the gilded locked case containing the "*libri prohibiti*" (prohibited books) at the end of the room. Only the abbot had the key, and you could read these books—like Copernicus, Jan Hus, even the French encyclopedia—only with the abbot's blessing. As the Age of Enlightenment took hold in Europe, monasteries still controlled the books. With the Enlightenment, the hallway connecting these two library rooms was filled with cases illustrating the new practical approach to natural sciences. Find the baby dodo bird (which went extinct in the 17th century).

Sights—Prague's Jewish Quarter

▲▲▲Jewish Quarter (Josefov)—The Jewish people were dispersed by the Romans 2,000 years ago. Over the centuries, their culture survived in enclaves throughout the Western world: "The Torah was their sanctuary which no army could destroy." Jews first came to Prague in the 10th century. The main intersection of Josefov (Maiselova and Siroka Streets) was the meeting point of two medieval trade routes.

When the pope declared that Jews and Christians should not live together, Jews had to wear yellow badges, and their quarter was walled in so that it became a ghetto. In the 16th and 17th centuries, Prague had one of the biggest ghettos in Europe, with 11,000 inhabitants. Within its six gates, Prague's Jewish Quarter was a gaggle of 200 wooden buildings. Someone wrote: "Jews nested rather than dwelled."

The "outcasts" of Christianity relied mainly on profits from moneylending (forbidden to Christians) and community solidarity to survive. While their money protected them, it was often also a curse. Throughout Europe, when times got tough and Christian debts to the Jewish community mounted, entire Jewish communities were evicted or killed.

In the 1780s, Emperor Joseph II eased much of the discrimination against Jews. In 1848, the walls were torn down and the neighborhood, named Josefov in honor of the emperor who was less anti-Semitic than the norm, was incorporated as a district of Prague.

In 1897, ramshackle Josefov was razed and replaced with a new modern town—the original 31 streets and 220 buildings became 10 streets and 83 buildings. This is what you'll see today: an attractive neighborhood of fine, mostly Art Nouveau buildings, with a few surviving historic Jewish buildings. In the 1930s, some 50,000 Jews lived in Prague. Today, only a couple of thousand remain.

As the Nazis decimated Jewish communities in the region, Prague's Jews were allowed to collect and archive their treasures in this museum. While the archivists ultimately died in concentration camps, their work survives. Seven sites scattered over a three-block area make up the tourists' Jewish Quarter. Six of the sites, called "the Museum," are treated as one admission. Your ticket comes with a map locating the sights and admission appointments: times you'll be let in if it's very crowded. (Without crowds, ignore the times.)

For all seven sights, you'll pay 500 kč (300 kč for "the Museum" and 200 kč for the Old-New Synagogue, all sites open Sun–Fri 9:00–17:30, closed Sat—the Jewish Sabbath).

Prague's Jewish Quarter

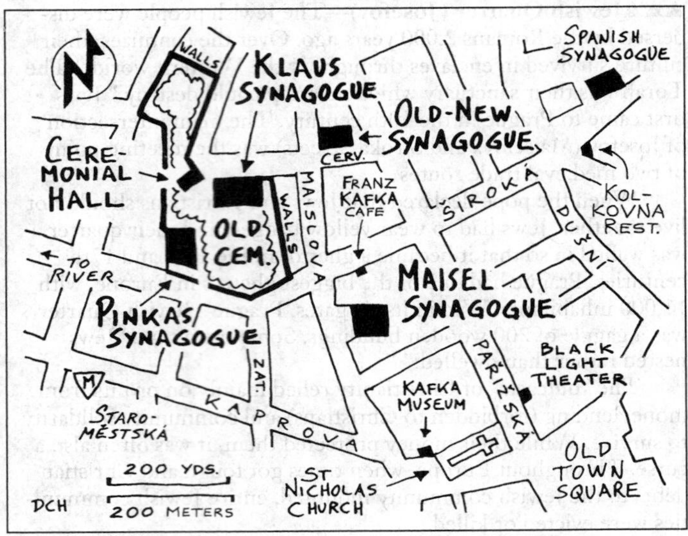

There are occasional guided walks in English (often at 14:00, 40 kč, 2.5 hrs, start at Maisel Synagogue, tel. 222-317-191). Most stops are described in English. This museum is well-presented and profoundly moving: It tells the story of the Jews of this region and is, for me, the most interesting Jewish site in Europe.

Maisel Synagogue (Maiselova Synagóga)—This shows a thousand years of Jewish history in Bohemia and Moravia. Exhibit topics include the origin of the Star of David, Jewish mysticism, discrimination, and the creation of Prague's ghetto.

Spanish Synagogue (Španělská Synagóga)—This 19th-century, ornate, Moorish-style synagogue continues the history of the Maisel Synagogue, covering the 18th, 19th, and tumultuous 20th centuries. The upstairs is particularly intriguing (with c. 1900 photos of Josefov).

Pinkas Synagogue (Pinkasova Synagóga)—A site of Jewish worship for 400 years, today this is a poignant memorial to the victims of the Nazis. Of the 120,000 Jews living in the area in 1939, only 10,000 lived to see liberation in 1945. The walls are covered with the handwritten names of 77,297 Czech Jews who were sent from here to the gas chambers of Auschwitz and other camps. Hometowns are in gold, family names are in red, followed in black by the individual's first name, birthday, and last date known to be alive. Notice that families generally perished together. Climb six steps into the women's gallery. The names in poor condition near the ceiling are from 1953. When the Communists moved in, they closed the synagogue and erased everything. With freedom, in 1989, the Pinkas Synagogue was reopened and all the names rewritten.

Upstairs is the **Terezín Children's Art Exhibit**. Terezín, near Prague, was a fortified town of 7,000 Czechs. The Nazis moved these people out and moved in 60,000 Jews, creating Theresienstadt, their model "Jewish town," a concentration camp dolled up for propaganda purposes. The town's medieval walls, originally to keep people from getting in, were used by Nazis to prevent people from getting out. Jewish culture seemed to thrive in Terezín, as "citizens" put on plays and concerts, published a magazine, and raised their families in ways impressive to Red Cross inspectors. But virtually all of the Jews ended up dying at concentration camps in the East, such as Auschwitz. The art of the children of Terezín survives as a striking testimony to the horror of the Holocaust. While the Communists kept the art away from the public, it is now well-displayed and described in English.

Terezín is a powerful day trip from Prague for those interested in touring the concentration camp memorial/museum. You can either take a public bus (6/day, 60 min, leaves from Prague's Florenc bus station) or a tour bus (see "Tours of Prague," above).

Old Jewish Cemetery (Starý Zidovsý Hřbitov)—As you wander among 12,000 evocative tombstones, remember that from 1439 until 1787, this was the only burial ground allowed for the Jews of Prague. With limited space and about 12,000 graves, tombs were piled atop each other. With its many layers, the cemetery became a small plateau. The Jewish word for cemetery means "House of Life"; like Christians, Jews believe that death is the gateway into the next world. Pebbles on the tombstones are "flowers of the desert," reminiscent of the old days when a rock was placed upon the sand gravesite to keep the body covered. Often a scrap of paper with a prayer on it is under a pebble.

Ceremonial Hall (Obradní Sín)—Leaving the cemetery, you'll find a neo-Romanesque mortuary house built in 1911 for the purification of the dead (on left). It's filled with a worthwhile exhibition, described in English, on Jewish burial traditions with historic paintings of the cemetery.

Klaus Synagogue (Klauzová Synagóga)—This 17th-century synagogue (also at the exit of the cemetery) is the final wing of this museum, devoted to Jewish religious practices. On the ground floor, exhibits explain the festive Jewish calendar. Upstairs features the ritual stages of Jewish life.

Old-New Synagogue (Staronová Synagóga)—For more than

700 years, this has been the most important synagogue and central building in Josefov. Standing like a bomb-hardened bunker, it feels like it's survived plenty of hard times. Stairs take you down to the street level of the 13th century and into the Gothic interior. Built in 1270, it's the oldest synagogue in Europe. The Shrine of the Ark in front is the focus of worship. The holiest place in the synagogue, it holds the sacred scrolls of the Torah. The old rabbi's chair to the right remains empty out of respect. Twelve is a popular number (e.g., windows) because it symbolizes the 12 tribes of Israel. The slit-like windows on the left are an 18th-century addition allowing women to view the men-only services (separate 200 kč admission, Sun–Thu 9:30–18:00, Fri 9:30–17:00, closed Sat).

Art Nouveau

Prague is the best Art Nouveau town in Europe, with fun-loving facades gracing streets all over town. The streets of Josefov, the Mucha window in the St. Vitus Cathedral, and Hotel Europa and its sisters on Wenceslas Square are just a few highlights. The top two places for Art Nouveau fans are the Mucha Museum and the Municipal House.

▲▲Mucha Museum (Muchovo Muzeum)—This is one of Europe's most enjoyable little museums. I find the art of Alfons Mucha (pron. moo-kah, 1860–1939) insistently likeable. See the crucifixion scene he painted as an eight-year-old boy. Read how this popular Czech artist's posters, filled with Czech symbols and expressing his people's ideals and aspirations, were patriotic banners arousing the national spirit. And check out the photographs of his models. With the help of this abundant supply of slinky models, Mucha was a founding father of the Art Nouveau movement. Prague isn't much on museums, but, if you're into Art Nouveau, this one is great. Run by Mucha's grandson, it's two blocks off Wenceslas Square and wonderfully displayed on one comfortable floor (120 kč, daily 10:00–18:00, Panska 7, tel. 224-233-355, www.mucha.cz). While the exhibit is well described in English, the 40-kč English brochure on the art is a good supplement. The video is also worthwhile (30 min, at least once hourly in English, ask upon entry).

Municipal House (Obecní Dům)—The Municipal House (built 1905–1911, near Powder Tower) features Prague's largest concert hall, a great Art Nouveau café, and two other restaurants. Look for the *Homage to Prague* mosaic—with a goddess-like Praha presiding over a land of peace and high culture—on the building's striking facade; it stoked cultural pride and nationalist sentiment. Then choose your place for a meal or drink (see "Eating in Prague," below).

The Dancing House (Tancici Dům)—Prague also has some delightful modern architecture. If ever a building could get your toes tapping, check out the building nicknamed Fred and Ginger. This metallic samba was designed by Frank Gehry (who designed the equally striking Guggenheim Museum in Bilbao, Spain, and Seattle's Experience Music Project). It's easy to spot (2 bridges down from Charles Bridge where Jiraskuv bridge hits Nové Město, tram #17). A pleasant riverside walk from Charles Bridge to the Dancing House takes you by a famous riverside ballroom and the grand National Theater. Across the street from the theater is the venerable haunt of Prague's intelligentsia, **Kavarna Slavia**, a Vienna-style coffeehouse fine for a meal or drink with a view of the river.

Entertainment

Prague booms with live (and inexpensive) theater, classical, jazz, and pop entertainment. Everything's listed in several monthly cultural events programs (free at TI) and in the *Prague News*.

Black Light Theater, a kind of mime/modern dance variety show, has no language barrier and is, for many, more entertaining than a classical concert. Unique to Prague, this originated in the 1960s as a playful and almost mystifying theater of the absurd.

Six or eight classical "tourist" **concerts** daily fill delightful Old Town halls and churches with music of the crowd-pleasing sort: Vivaldi, Best of Mozart, Most Famous Arias, and works by local boy Anton Dvořák. Leafleteers are everywhere announcing the evening's events. Concerts typically cost 400–1,000 kč, start anywhere from 13:00 to 21:00, and last one hour.

Common venues are in the Little Quarter Square—Malostranské Náměstí (at the St. Nicholas church and the Prague Academy of Music in Liechtenstein Palace), at the city end of Charles Bridge (St. Francis Church), and on the Old Town Square (another St. Nicholas church).

To really understand all your options (the street Mozarts are pushing only their concert), drop by the **Týnská Galerie** box office at the Tyn Church. The wall display clearly shows what's playing today and tomorrow (concerts, Black Light Theater, marionette shows, photos of each venue, and a map locating everything, daily 10:00–19:00, tel. 224-826-969).

Young locals keep countless music clubs in business. A favorite with a handy locale, **Malostranská Beseda** offers live music nightly (on the downhill side of the Little Quarter's main square). Many of the best local rock and jazz groups perform here (nightly from 20:30, generally about 100 kč cover).

Prague isn't great for a boat tour. Still, the hour-long **Vltava River cruises**, which leave from near the Malá Strana end of Charles Bridge about hourly (100 kč), are scenic and relaxing, though not informative.

Prague's top **sports** are soccer (that's football in the U.S.) and hockey (they are a world power, routinely beating even Canada). Think about it: There are over a hundred Czech players in America's NHL. Tickets are normally easy to get (soccer—usually late Sat or Sun afternoon Feb–May and Aug–Nov; hockey—weeknights Sept–April; see *Prague News*). The two big Czech hockey rivals are Sparta and Slavia. Near the top of Castle Hill is the enormous 200,000-seat Strahov Stadium. This was built during Communist times as a venue for *Spartakiade*, sort of a synchronized calisthenics encouraged by the regime. Now it's used for soccer and other sports.

Shopping

The Czech malls are the galleries built in the 1920s, mothballed through the Communist era, and once again vibrant. You'll see these arcades leading off of Wenceslas Square and from the moat (Na Príkope). The best—a classic arcade from a more elegant age—is the **Lucerna Gallery** on Wenceslas Square, immediately opposite Hotel Europa (use entry marked Divadlo Rokoko and shop your way back to Lucerna).

Sleeping in Prague

(30 kč = about $1, country code: 420)

Sleep Code: **S** = Single, **D** = Double/Twin, **T** = Triple, **Q** = Quad, **b** = bathroom, **s** = shower only, **CC** = Credit Cards accepted, **no CC** = Credit Cards not accepted.

To help you sort easily through these listings, I've divided the rooms into three categories based on the price for a standard double room with bath:

Higher Priced—Most rooms more than 4,000 kč.

Moderately Priced—Most rooms 4,000 kč or less.

Lower Priced—Most rooms 3,000 kč or less.

Finding a bed in Prague worries Western tourists. It shouldn't. You have several options. Capitalism is working as Adam Smith promised: With a huge demand, the supply is increasing and the price is going up. Peak time is May, June, September, October, Christmas, and Easter. July and August are not too bad. Expect crowds on weekends. I've listed peak-time prices. If you're traveling in July or August, you'll find slightly lower rates. Prices tend to go up even more on holidays (especially German ones). English is generally spoken. Reserve by phone or e-mail. Generally, you simply promise to come and need no deposit.

Prague's hotels, plenty professional and comfortable, are often beholden to agencies that have a lock on rooms (generally until 6 weeks in advance). Agencies get a 30 percent discount and can sell the rooms at whatever price they like between that and the "rack rate." Consequently, Prague has a reputation of being perpetually booked up. But because the agencies rarely use up their allotment, the crowds are only an illusion. You need to make reservations either long in advance, when the few rooms not reserved for agencies are still available, or a few weeks in advance, after the agencies have released their rooms.

The **launderette** nearest most recommended hotels is at Karolíny Světlé 10 (200 kč/load, Mon–Sat 7:30–19:00, closed Sun, 200 meters, or 650 feet, from Charles Bridge on old town side).

To call Prague from outside the country, dial the international access code (00 for Europe or 011 for U.S./Canada), the Czech Republic's country code (420), then the local number.

Room-Booking Services

Prague is awash with fancy rooms on the push list; private, small-time operators with rooms to rent in their apartments; and roving agents eager to book you a bed and earn a commission. You can save about 30 percent by showing up in Prague without a reservation and finding accommodations upon arrival. If driving, you'll see booking agencies as you enter town. Generally, book here and your host can come and lead you to their place.

Athos Travel, run by friendly entrepreneur Filip Antoš, will find the right room for you from among 140 properties (from hostels to five-star hotels), 90 percent of which are in the historical center. Its handy Web site allows you to search based on various criteria to find the right room (best to arrange in advance during peak season, can also help with last-minute booking off-season, tel. 241-440-571, fax 241-441-697, www.athos.cz, e-mail: info@athos.cz); to get a 2 percent discount for online booking, see "Helpful Hints," above.

AVE, at the main train station **(Hlavní Nádraží)**, is a less friendly but helpful booking service (daily 6:00–23:00, tel. 251-551-011, fax 251-555-156, www.avetravel.cz, e-mail: ave@avetravel.cz). With the tracks at your back, walk down to the orange ceiling and past the "meeting point" (don't go downstairs)—their office is in the left corner by the exit to the rip-off taxis. AVE has several other offices—at Holešovice station, the airport, Wenceslas Square, and Old Town Square. Their display board shows discounted hotels. They have a slew of hotels and small pensions available ($70 pension doubles in old center, $35 doubles a metro ride away). You can reserve by e-mail (using your credit card as a deposit) or just show up at the office and request a room. Many of AVE's rooms are not very convenient to the center; be clear on the location before you make your choice.

For a more personal touch, contact Lida at **Magic Praha**

for help with accommodations (tel. 224-232-755, e-mail: magicpraha@magicpraha.cz, see "Helpful Hints," above).

Sleeping in the Old Town

You'll pay higher prices to stay in the Old Town, but for many travelers, the convenience is worth the expense. These places are all within a 10-minute walk of the Old Town Square.

HIGHER PRICED

Hotel Central is a sentimental favorite—I stayed there in the Communist days. Now it's changing with the times, like the rest of Prague—its 69 rooms have recently been renovated, leaving it fresh and bright. The place is well-run and the location, three blocks east of the Old Town Square, is excellent (Sb-3,600 kč, Db-4,200 kč, deluxe Db-4,900 kč, Tb-4,700 kč, low season-30–40 percent less, CC, elevator, Rybná 8, Praha 1, Metro: Náměstí Republiky, tel. 224-812-041, fax 222-328-404, e-mail: central@orfea.cz).

Cloister Inn is a well-located, modern place with 75 rooms. The exterior is more concrete than charm—the building used to be shared by a convent and a secret police prison—but inside, it's newly renovated and plenty comfortable (Sb-3,000–3,600 kč, Db-3,300–4,200 kč, Tb-3,800–5,000 kč, CC, elevator, free Internet access, Konviktska 14, Praha 1, tel. 224-211-020, fax 224-210-800, www.cloister-inn.cz, e-mail: cloister@cloister-inn.cz).

MODERATELY PRICED

Betlem Club, a shiny jewel of comfort, is on a pleasant medieval square in the heart of the Old Town, across from the Bethlehem Chapel (where Jan Hus preached his troublemaking sermons). Its 22 modern and comfy rooms face a quiet inner courtyard, and breakfast is served in a Gothic cellar (Sb-2,700 kč, Db-3,900 kč, extra bed-1,000 kč, prices flex with season, CC, elevator, Internet access, airport pickup-800 kč, airport drop-off-650 kč, Betlémské Náměstí 9, Praha 1, tel. 222-221-575, fax 222-220-580, www.betlemclub.cz, e-mail: betlem.club@login.cz).

Pension Ů Medvídků has 31 comfortably renovated rooms in a big, rustic, medieval shell with dark wood furniture. Upstairs, you'll find lots of beams to run into (Sb-2,300 kč, Db-3,500 kč, Tb-4,500 kč, extra bed-500 kč, "historical" rooms 10 percent more, apartment 20 percent more, prices flex with season, CC, Internet access-70 kč/hr, Na Perštýně 7, Praha 1, tel. 224-211-916, fax 224-220-930, www.umedvidku.cz, e-mail: info@umedvidku.cz). The pension runs a popular restaurant that has live music most Fridays and Saturdays until 23:00.

Prague Hotels and Restaurants

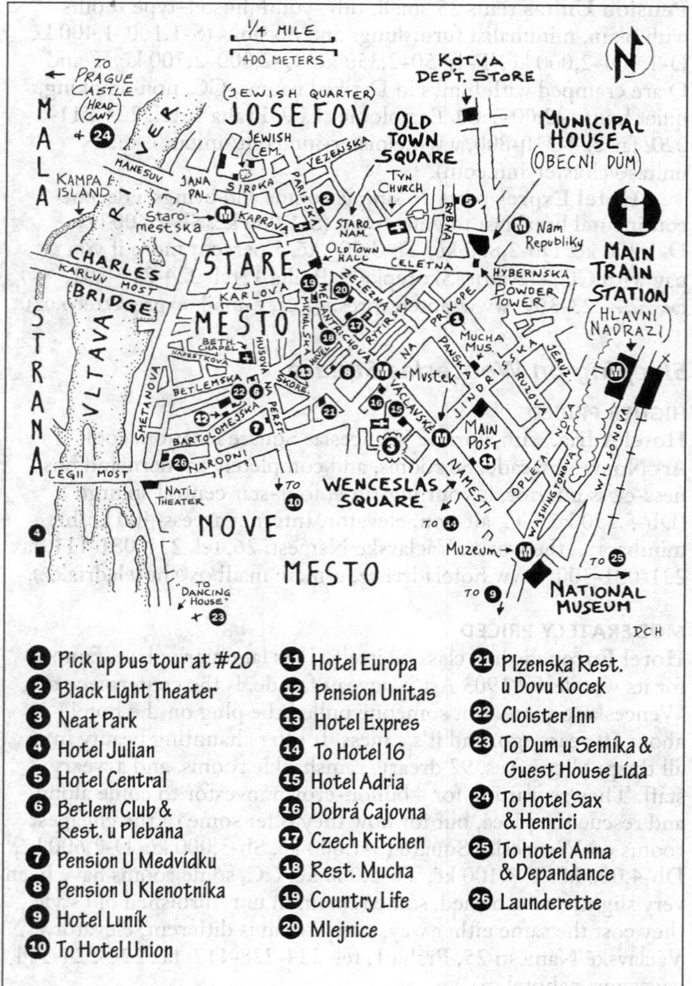

Hotel U Klenotníka, with 10 modern and comfortable rooms in a plain building, is three blocks off the Old Town Square (Sb-2,500 kč, Db-3,800 kč, Tb-4,500 kč, 10 percent off when booking direct with this book, CC, Rytiřska 3, Praha 1, tel. 224-211-699, fax 224-221-025, www.uklenotnika.cz, e-mail: info@uklenotnika.cz). They run a good restaurant.

LOWER PRICED

Pension Unitas rents 35 small, tidy, youth hostel–type rooms with plain, minimalist furnishings and no sinks (S-1,100–1,400 kč, D-1,400–2,000 kč, T-1,750–2,350 kč, Q-2,000–2,700 kč, T and Q are cramped with bunks in D-sized rooms, CC, non-smoking, quiet hours 22:00–7:00, Bartolomejská 9, Praha 1, tel. 224-211-020, fax 224-210-800, www.cloister-inn.com/unitas, e-mail: unitas@cloister-inn.com).

Hotel Expres rents 26 simple rooms and brings a decent continental breakfast to your room (S-1,000 kč, Sb-2,600 kč, D-1,200 kč, Db-2,800 kč, Tb-3,200 kč, 5 percent more if you pay with CC, elevator, Skořepka 5, Praha 1, tel. 224-211-801, fax 224-223-309, www.hotelexpres.wz.cz, e-mail: expres@zero.cz).

Sleeping on Wenceslas Square

HIGHER PRICED

Hotel Adria, with a prime Wenceslas Square location, cool Art Nouveau facade, 88 rooms, and completely modern and business-class interior, is your big-time, four-star central splurge (Db-5,250 kč, CC, air-con, elevator, Internet access-400 kč/hr, minibars . . . the works, Václavske Náměstí 26, tel. 221-081-111, fax 221-081-300, www.hoteladria.cz, e-mail: mailbox@hoteladria.cz).

MODERATELY PRICED

Hotel Europa is in a class by itself. This landmark place, famous for its wonderful 1903 Art Nouveau facade, is the centerpiece of Wenceslas Square. But someone pulled the plug on the hotel about 50 years ago, and it's a mess. It offers haunting beauty in all the public spaces, 92 dreary, ramshackle rooms, and a weary staff. They're waiting for a billion-crown investor to come along and rescue the place, but for now they offer some of the cheapest rooms on Wenceslas Square (S-1,600 kč, Sb-3,000 kč, D-2,600 kč, Db-4,000 kč, T-3,100 kč, Tb-5,000 kč, CC, some rooms have been very slightly refurbished, some remain in unrefurbished old style, they cost the same either way, every room is different, elevator, Václavské Náměstí 25, Praha 1, tel. 224-228-117, fax 224-224-544, www.europahotel.cz).

Sleeping Away from the Center

Moving just outside the Old Town saves you money—and gets you away from the tourists and into some fun residential neighborhoods. These listings (great values compared to Old Town hotels) are all within a five- to 15-minute tram or metro ride from the center.

MODERATELY PRICED

Hotel Julian—an oasis of professional, predictable decency in a quiet, untouristy neighborhood—is a five-minute taxi or tram ride from the action on the castle side of the river. Its 32 spacious, fresh, well-furnished rooms and big, homey public spaces hide behind a noble neoclassical facade. The staff is friendly and helpful (Sb-3,280 kč, Db-3,580 kč, suite Db-4,280 kč, extra bed-900 kč, family room, CC, 5 percent discount off best quoted rate with this book, velvety elevator, Internet access, parking lot, Elišky Peškové 11, Praha 5, tel. 257-311-150, reception tel. 257-311-144, fax 257-311-149, www.julian.cz, e-mail: casjul@vol.cz). Free lockers and a shower are available for those needing to check out early but stay until late (e.g., for an overnight train). Mike's Chauffeur Service, based here, is reliable and affordable (see "Transportation Connections," below).

Hotel Anna, bright, pastel, and classically charming, is in an upscale residential neighborhood (near former royal vineyards, or *Vinohrady*) 10 minutes by foot east of Wenceslas Square (Sb-2,300 kč, Db-3,100 kč, Tb-3,900 kč, cheaper off-season, CC, non-smoking rooms, elevator, Budečská 17, Praha 2, Metro: Náměstí Míru, tel. 222-513-111, fax 222-515-158, www.hotelanna.cz). The hotel runs a cheaper but similarly pleasant annex, the **Depandance**, two blocks away (Sb-1,650 kč, Db-2,300 kč, cheaper off-season, no elevator but all rooms on first floor, reception and breakfast at main hotel).

Hotel 16, a stately little place with an intriguing Art Nouveau facade, high ceilings, and a clean, sleek interior, rents 14 fine rooms (Sb-2,500–2,700 kč, Db-3,400–3,900 kč, Tb-4,600 kč, 10 percent lower off-season, CC, back/quiet rooms face the garden, front/noisier rooms face the street, air-con, elevator, a 10-min walk south of Wenceslas Square, Metro: I. P. Pavlova, Kateřinská 16, Praha 2, tel. 224-920-636, fax 224-920-626, www.hotel16.cz, e-mail: hotel16@hotel16.cz).

Hotel Union is a grand 1906 Art Nouveau building, filling its street corner with 57 rooms. It's away from the touristy center in a more laid-back neighborhood a direct 10-minute ride to Wenceslas Square on tram #24, or to Charles Bridge on tram #18 (Sb-2,815 kč, Db-3,380 kč, Db deluxe-4,050 kč, Tb-4,495 kč, extra bed-1,115 kč, all rates at least 1,000 kč cheaper Jan–Feb, rates higher during several holidays, CC, elevator, Ostrčilovo Náměstí 4, Praha 2-Nusle, tel. 261-214-812, fax 261-214-820, www.hotelunion.cz, e-mail: hotelunion@hotelunion.cz).

LOWER PRICED

Dům U Šemíka, a friendly hotel named for a heroic mythical horse, is in a residential neighborhood just below Vyšehrad castle, a 10-minute tram ride from the center (Sb-1,700 kč, Db-2,100–2,650 kč, apartment-2,800–4,850 kč depending on size, extra bed-700 kč, from the center take tram #18 to Albertov then walk 2 blocks uphill, or take tram #7 to Výtoň, go under rail bridge, and walk 3 blocks uphill to Vratislavova 36, Praha 2, tel. 224-920-736, fax 224-911-602, www.usemika.cz).

Hotel Luník, with 35 rooms, is a stately but friendly, no-nonsense place out of the medieval faux-rustic world in a normal, pleasant business district. It's two metro stops from the main station (Metro: I. P. Pavlova) or a 10-minute walk from Wenceslas Square (Sb-2,050 kč, Db-2,900 kč, Tb-3,350 kč, CC, elevator, Londýnská 50, Praha 2, tel. 224-253-974, fax 224-253-986, www.hotel-lunik.cz, e-mail: recepce@hotel-lunik.cz).

Guest House Lída, with 12 homey and spacious rooms, fills a big house in a quiet residential area a 30-minute walk or 15-minute tram ride from the center. Jan and Jiří Prouza, who run the place, are a wealth of information and know how to make people feel at home (small Db-1,350 kč, Db-1,650 kč, Tb-1,980 kč, 10 percent off Nov–March, no CC, family rooms, top-floor family suite with kitchenette, parking in garage-150 kč/day, Metro: Pražského Povstání, exit metro and turn left on Lomnicka between the metro station and big blue glass ČSOB building, follow Lomnicka for 500 meters, then turn left on Lopatecka, go uphill and ring bell at Lopatecka #26, no sign outside, Praha 4, tel. & fax 261-214-766, e-mail: lida@login.cz). The Prouza brothers also rent four apartments across the river (Db-1,500 kč, Tb-1,920 kč, Qb-2,100 kč).

Sleeping across the River, near the Castle

HIGHER PRICED

Hotel Sax, on a quiet corner a block below the Malá Strana action, will delight the artsy yuppie with its 22 rooms, fruity atrium, and modern, stylish decor (Sb-3,700 kč, Db-4,400 kč, Db suite-5,100 kč, extra bed-1,000 kč, cheaper off-season, CC, elevator, near St. Nicholas church, 1 block below Nerudova at Jánský Vršek 3, Praha 1, reserve long in advance, tel. 257-531-268, fax 257-534-101, www.sax.cz, e-mail: hotelsax@bon.cz).

Residence Domus Henrici, just above the castle square, is a quiet retreat that charges—and gets—top prices for its eight smartly appointed rooms, some of which include good views (Ds-4,650 kč, Db-5,400–5,700 kč depending on size, extra bed-810 kč, less off-season, CC, pleasant terrace, Loretánská 11, Praha 1, tel. 220-511-369, fax 220-511-502, www.domus-henrici.cz, e-mail: reception@domus-henrici.cz). This is a five-minute walk above the castle gate in a stately and quiet area.

Eating in Prague

The beauty of Prague is wandering aimlessly through the winding old quarters marveling at the architecture, watching the people, and sniffing out fun restaurants. You can eat well for very little money. What you'd pay for a basic meal in Vienna or Munich will get you an elegant meal in Prague. Choose between traditional, dark Czech beer hall–type ambience, elegant *Jugendstil*/early-20th-century atmosphere, ethnic, or hip and modern.

Watch out for scams. Many restaurants put more care into ripping off green tourists (and even locals) than in their cooking. Tourists are routinely served cheaper meals than what they ordered, given a menu with a "personalized" price list, charged extra for things they didn't get, or shortchanged. Avoid any menu without clear and explicit prices. Carefully examine your itemized bill and understand each line (a 10 percent service is sometimes added—no need to tip beyond that). Be careful of waiters padding the tab: tax is always included in the price, so it shouldn't be tacked on later. Deliberately count your change, parting with very large bills only if necessary. Never let your credit card out of your sight and check the numbers carefully. Make it a habit to get cash from an ATM to pay for your meals. Remember, there are two parallel worlds in Prague: the tourist town and the real city. Generally, if you walk two minutes away from the tourist flow, you'll find much better value, ambience, and service.

Art Nouveau Restaurants

The sumptuous Art Nouveau concert hall—**Municipal House**—has three special restaurants: a café, a French restaurant, and a beer cellar (Náměstí Republiky 5). The dressy café, **Kavarna Obecní Dům**, is drenched in chandeliered Art Nouveau elegance (light meals, 1 hot meal special daily—220 kč, daily 7:30–23:00, live piano or jazz trio 17:00–21:00, tel. 222-002-763). **Francouzska Restaurace**, the fine and formal French restaurant, is in the next wing (600–700-kč meals, daily 12:00–16:00 & 18:00–23:00, tel. 222-002-777). **Plzeňská Restaurace**, downstairs, brags it's the most beautiful Art Nouveau pub in Europe (cheap meals, great atmosphere, daily 11:30–23:00, tel. 222-002-780).

Restaurant Mucha is touristy, with decent Czech food in a formal Art Nouveau dining room (300-kč meals, daily 12:00–24:00, Melantrichova 5, tel. 224-225-045).

Uniquely Czech Places near the Old Town Square

Prices go way down when you get away from the tourist areas. At least once, eat in a restaurant with no English menu.

Plzeňská Restaurace U Dvou Koček is a typical Czech

pub with cheap, no-nonsense, hearty Czech food, great beer, and—once upon a time—a local crowd (200 kč for 3 courses and beer, serving original Pilsner Urquell with accordion music nightly until 23:00, under an arcade, facing the tiny square between Perlova and Skořepka Streets).

Restaurace Mlejnice is a fun little pub strewn with farm implements and happy eaters, tucked away just out of the tourist crush two blocks from the Old Town Square (order carefully and understand your itemized bill, daily 11:00–24:00, between Melantrichova and Zelezna at Kožná 14, reservations smart in evening, tel. 224-228-635).

Restaurant U Plebána is a quiet little place with good service, Czech cuisine, and a modern yet elegant setting (daily 12:00–24:00, live piano music nightly 19:00–23:00, Betlémské Náměstí 10, tel. 222-221-568).

Country Life Vegetarian Restaurant is a bright, easy, and smoke-free cafeteria that has a well-displayed buffet of salads and veggie hot dishes. It's midway between the Old Town Square and the bottom of Wenceslas Square. They are serious about their vegetarianism, serving only plant-based, unprocessed, and unrefined food (Mon–Thu 9:00–20:30, Fri 9:00–18:00, Sun 11:00–20:30, closed Sat, through courtyard at Melantrichova 15/Michalska 18, tel. 224-213-366).

Czech Kitchen (Ceská Kuchyně) is a blue-collar cafeteria serving steamy old Czech cuisine to a local clientele. There's no English. Just pick up your tally sheet at the door, grab a tray, and point liberally to whatever you'd like. It's extremely cheap (daily 9:00–20:00, across from Havelská Market at Havelská 23, tel. 224-235-574).

Bohemia Bagel is hardly authentic Czech—exasperated locals insist that bagels have nothing to do with Bohemia. Owned by an American, this trendy place caters mostly to youthful tourists (and advertises heavily along the tourist drag), but has good sandwiches (100–125 kč) and Internet access (1.5 kč/min) close to the Old Town Square (daily 24 hrs, locations at Újezd 16, tel. 257-310-529, and Masná 2, tel. 224-812-560, www.bohemiabagel.cz).

Eating above the Castle

Oživlé Dřevo, a stately yet traditional restaurant, feels like a country farmhouse and comes with perhaps the most commanding view terrace in all of Prague. It serves good quality traditional cuisine. Hiking up the Nerudova/Úvoz road, bypass the castle and carry on five minutes more to the Strahov Monastery (daily 11:00–23:00, Strahovske Nadvori 1, tel. 220-517-274).

Maly Buddha ("Little Buddha") serves delightful food—especially vegetarian—and takes its theme seriously. You'll step into a mellow, low-lit escape of bamboo and peace to be served by people with perfect complexions and almost no pulse. Ethnic eateries like this are trendy with young Czechs (Tue–Sun 13:00–22:30, closed Mon, smoke-free, continue on road to castle, bypassing castle turnoff about 100 meters/330 feet to Úvoz 46, tel. 220-513-894).

U Hrocha ("By the Hippo") is a very local little pub packed with beer drinkers and smoke. Just below the castle near Malá Strana's main square, it's actually the haunt of many members of Parliament—located just around the corner (daily 12:00–23:00, chalkboard lists daily meals, Thunovska 10).

Espresso Kajetánka, just off of Castle Square, is a pricey café worth considering for the view and convenience (tel. 257-533-735).

Eating near the Jewish Quarter

Kolkovna is a big, new, woody yet modern place catering to locals and serving a fun mix of Czech and international cuisine (ribs, salads, cheese plates, great beer, daily 11:00–24:00, across from Spanish Synagogue at U Kolkovna 8, tel. 224-819-701).

The **Franz Kafka Café** is pleasant for a snack or drink (daily 10:00–21:00, Siroká 12, a block from the cemetery).

Eating with a View at Wenceslas Square

The **Modra Terasa (Blue Terrace) Restaurant** may still be closed for renovation. When open, it serves good food, uniquely perched for those wanting to survey Prague's grandest square while eating without a tourist in sight (smoky interior, fun terrace on sunny days, ride elevator at Na Mustku 9—from top of metro station at the base of Wenceslas Square, tel. 224-226-288).

Czech Beer

For many, *pivo* (beer) is the top Czech tourist attraction. After all, the Czechs invented lager in nearby Pilsen. This is the famous Pilsner Urquell, a great lager on tap everywhere. Budvar is the local Budweiser, but it's not related to the American brew. Czechs are among the world's biggest beer drinkers—adults drink about 80 gallons a year. The big degree symbol on bottles and menus marks the beer's heaviness, not its alcohol content (12 degrees is darker, 10 degrees lighter). The smaller figure shows alcohol content. Order beer from the tap *(sudove pivo)* in either small (0.3 liter, or 10 oz, *male pivo*) or large (0.5 liter, or 17 oz, *pivo*).

In many restaurants, a beer hits your table like a glass of water in the United States. *Pivo* for lunch has me sightseeing for the rest of the day on Czech knees. Be sure to venture beyond the Pilsner Urquell. There are plenty of other good Czech beers.

Teahouses

Many Czech people prefer the mellow, smoke-free environs of a teahouse to the smoky, traditional beer hall. While there are teahouses all over town, one fine example in a handy locale is **Dobrá Čajovna** (Mon–Sat 10:00–23:00, Sun 14:00–23:00, near the base of Wenceslas Square at Václavske Náměstí 14). This teahouse, just a few steps off the bustle of the main square, takes you into a very peaceful world that elevates tea to an almost religious ritual. Ask for the English menu, which lovingly describes each tea (www.cajovna.com).

Transportation Connections—Prague

Getting to Prague: Those with railpasses need to purchase tickets to cover the portion of their journey from the border of the Czech Republic to Prague (buy at station before you board train for Prague). Or supplement your pass with a Prague Excursion pass, giving you passage from any Czech border station into Prague and back to any border station within seven days. Ask about this pass (and get reservations) at the EurAide offices in Munich or Berlin (first class-€50, second class-€40, youth second class-€30). EurAide's U.S. office sells these passes for a bit less (U.S. tel. 941/480-1555, fax 941/480-1522). Direct night trains leave Munich for Prague daily around 23:00 (8.5-hr trip). Tickets cost about €60 from Munich or, if you have a railpass covering Germany, €20 from the border.

For Czech train and bus schedules, see www.vlak-bus.cz.

By train to: Český Krumlov (8/day, 4 hrs, verify departing station), **Berlin** (5/day, 5 hrs), **Munich** (3/day, 5 hrs), **Frankfurt** (3/day, 6 hrs), **Vienna** (3/day, 5 hrs), **Budapest** (6/day, 9 hrs). Train info: tel. 224-224-200.

By bus to Český Krumlov (6/day, 3.5 hrs, 190 km/ 120 miles, take metro to Florenc station; an easy direct bus leaves at about 9:00).

By car, with a driver: Mike's Chauffeur Service is a reliable little company with fair and fixed rates around town and beyond. Friendly Mike's motto is, "we go the extra mile for you" (round-trip fares with waiting time included, guaranteed through 2003 with this book: **Český Krumlov**-3,500 kč, **Terezín**-1,700 kč, **Karlštejn**-1,500 kč, up to 4 people, tel. 241-768-231, cellular 602-224-893, www.mike-chauffeur.cz, e-mail: mike.chauffeur@cmail.cz). On the way to Krumlov, Mike will stop for no extra charge at Hluboka Castle or České Budějovice, where the original Bud beer is made.

ČESKÝ KRUMLOV

Český Krumlov means "Czech bend in the river." Lassoed by its river and dominated by its castle, this simple, enchanting town feels lost in a time warp. Krumlov is the Czech Republic's answer to Germany's Rothenburg, but 40 years ago. Its buildings are slowly being restored; for every tired building with peeling paint, there's one just renovated. The town is best at night—save energy for a romantic post-dinner stroll.

While popular with Czech and German tourists, Krumlov is found by few Americans. The town attracts a young, Bohemian crowd, drawn here for its simple beauty and cheap living. Hostels cost $6, comfortable pensions with private baths run $30 for a double, and a good dinner will set you back $3 to $5.

Orientation

This place is initially confusing, thanks to the snaking Vltava River, which makes a perfect S through the town. Use the pink castle tower and the soaring spire of the Church of St. Vitus to stay oriented. With only three bridges (one is a footbridge) and one square, you'll get your bearings quickly enough. Most hotels and restaurants are in the island center, within a few blocks of the main square, Náměstí Svornosti. The TI, banks, ATMs, a few hotels, and taxis are on the square. Banks close at 17:00, stores at 18:00.

Tourist Information: The eager-to-please TI is on the main square (July–Aug daily 9:00–20:00, June and Sept daily 9:00–19:00, March–May and Oct daily 9:00–18:00, Nov–Feb daily 9:00–17:00, tel. 380-711-183). Pick up the free city map. The 129-kč *City Guide* has a great 3-D map on one side, with key sights and many hotels identified; it gives you a basic but helpful English background on the city and key sights. The TI can check train, bus, and flight schedules, and change traveler's checks (fair rate). Ask about concerts, city walking tours in English, car rentals, and canoe trips on the river (400–900 kč). The TI can reserve a room, but it'll take a 10 percent deposit that will be deducted from your hotel bill. Save your host's money and go direct.

Internet Access: Try South Bohemian University, situated just off the main square (Mon–Fri 9:00–18:00, Horni 155, tel. 380-913-075).

Arrival in Český Krumlov

By Train and Bus: The train station is a 20-minute walk from town (turn right out of the station, walk downhill onto a steep cobbled path leading to an overpass into town center), while the bus station is just three blocks away from the center (from the bus station, drop down to main road and turn left, then turn right at Potraving grocery store to reach center). Taxis are cheap; don't hesitate to take one from the train station (about 140 kč).

Sights—Český Krumlov

Main Square (Náměstí Svornosti)—This square will seduce you, rather than bowl you over. Best at twilight, a colorful huddle of Renaissance and Baroque facades surrounds this simple, unpretentious square. The local economy can't support more than the two small cafés. Enjoy people-watching from the benches. The white, Venetian-looking town hall (housing the TI) seems strangely out of place.

Mansion—On the hill, that looming castle, or "Mansion" as locals call it, is Krumlov's key sight. You'll find a live bear pit below the entry and, high above, a cylindrical castle tower looking like a beer stein just begging to be climbed (30 kč, June–Aug 9:00–17:00, Sept and May 10:00–16:00, great view, 162 steps). If you want to tour the surprisingly opulent and impressive castle interior, hold off on the tower and continue uphill through the courtyard to the ticket room. Admission is by one-hour guided tour only (140 kč, daily 9:00–17:00, ask for next tour in English, then kill time at tower or in gardens). The upper castle gardens are modest but pleasant.

District Museum of Natural History—Located in the center, this small museum offers a quick look at regional costumes, tools, and traditions; ask for the simple English translation that also gives a lengthy history of Krumlov (30 kč, daily 10:00–12:30 & 13:00–18:00, across from Hotel Ruze at Horni 152).

Sleeping in Český Krumlov

(30 kč = about $1, country code: 420)

To help you sort easily through these listings, I've divided the rooms into three categories based on the price for a standard double room with bath:

Higher Priced—Most rooms more than 3,000 kč.

Moderately Priced—Most rooms 3,000 kč or less.

Lower Priced—Most rooms 1,500 kč or less.

Krumlov is filled with small, good, family-run pensions offering doubles with baths from 1,000 kč to 1,500 kč and hostel beds for 200 kč (buyer beware). Summer weekends and festivals are busiest; reserve ahead when possible. Unless otherwise noted, all prices include breakfast. Hotels speak some English and accept credit cards; pensions rarely do either.

Český Krumlov

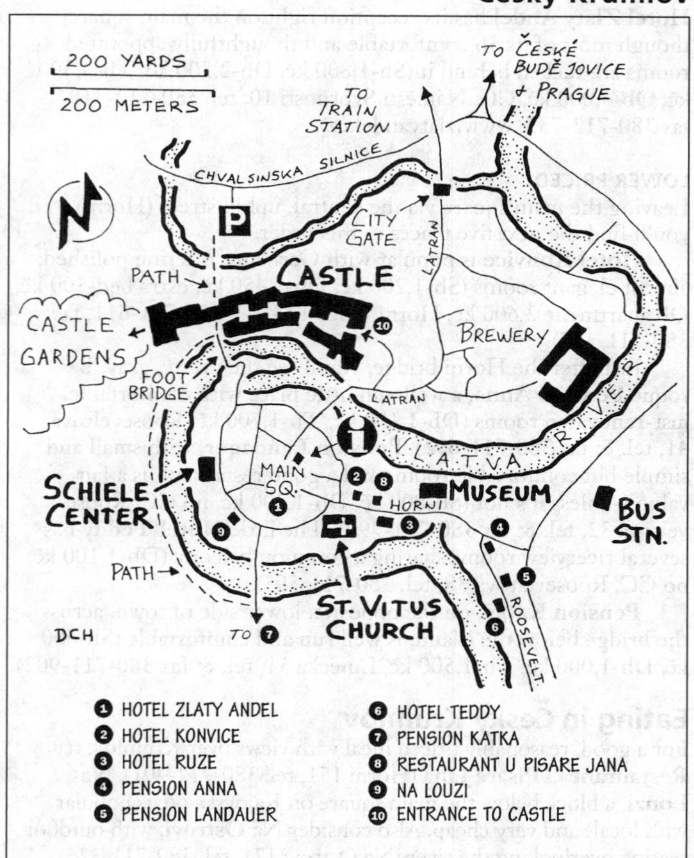

HIGHER PRICED

Hotel Ruze, from its red-carpeted halls to its elegant, wood-furnished rooms, feels like a Spanish parador. Krumlov's four-star splurge, located in a beautifully renovated historic building, has grand public spaces, a brilliant backyard terrace overlooking the river, rooms with all the comforts and then some, and the slickest kids' beds in town (Sb-2,300–4,000 kč, Db-3,200–4,900 kč, deluxe Db-3,900–5,600 kč, apartment-4,500–7,500 kč, extra bed-800–1,000 kč, higher prices are for peak season, CC, Horni 154, tel. 380-772-100, fax 380-713-146, www.hotelruze.cz, e-mail: hotelruze@ck.ipex.cz).

MODERATELY PRICED

Hotel Zlaty Andel has its reception right on the main square, though most of its 36 comfortable and thoughtfully appointed rooms are tucked behind it (Sb-1,800 kč, Db-2,500 kč, Tb-3,500 kč, Qb-4,000 kč, CC, Náměstí Svornosti 10, tel. 380-712-310, fax 380-712-735, www.zlatyandel.cz).

LOWER PRICED

Leaving the main square via the central, uphill street (Horni), you'll find the next five places in this order:

Hotel Konvice is popular with Germans, offering polished, almost elegant rooms (Sb-1,200 kč, Db-1,450 kč, extra bed-500 kč, Qb apartment-2,600 kč, Horni Ulice 144, tel. 380-711-611, fax 380-711-327).

Just after the Horni bridge, you'll see the pretty, gray, Baroque **Pension Anna**, a well-run little place with comfortable, just-renovated rooms (Db-1,100 kč, Tb-1,700 kč, Rooseveltova 41, tel. & fax 380-711-692). **Pension Landauer**, with small and simple but comfortable rooms and a good restaurant, is a fair value—unless it's hot (Sb-800 kč, Db-1,200 kč, no CC, Rooseveltova 32, tel. & fax 380-711-790). The little **Hotel Teddy** has several riverview rooms sharing a common balcony (Db-1,100 kč, no CC, Rooseveltova 38, tel. 380-711-595).

Pension Katka, on the opposite, lower side of town, across the bridge below the island, is well run and comfortable (Sb-600 kč, Db-1,000 kč, Tb-1,500 kč, Linecka 51, tel. & fax 380-711-902).

Eating in Český Krumlov

For a good, reasonably priced meal with views over Krumlov, try **Restaurant U Pisare Jana** (Horni 151, tel. 380-712-401). **Na Louzi**, a block below the main square on Kajovska 66, is popular with locals and very cheap. Also consider **Na Ostroví**, with outdoor seating overlooking the river (Na Ostroví 171, tel. 380-711-326).

Transportation Connections—Český Krumlov

By train to: Prague (7/day, 2.5 hrs), **Vienna** (4/day, 7 hrs), **Budapest** (4/day, 11 hrs). Virtually all train rides to/from Český Krumlov require a transfer in České Budějovice.

By bus to: Prague (6/day, 3.5 hrs).

COPENHAGEN

Copenhagen (København), Denmark's capital, is the gateway to Scandinavia. And now, with the bridge connecting Sweden and Denmark, Copenhagen is energized and ready to dethrone Stockholm as Scandinavia's powerhouse city. A busy day cruising the canals, wandering through the palace, and taking an old-town walk will give you your historical bearings. Then, after another day strolling the Strøget (Europe's greatest pedestrian shopping mall), biking the canals, and sampling the Danish good life, you'll feel right at home. Copenhagen is Scandinavia's cheapest and most fun-loving capital. So live it up.

Planning Your Time

A first visit deserves two days.

Day 1: Catch the 10:30 city walking tour (see "Tours of Copenhagen," below). After a Riz-Raz lunch, visit the Use It information center and catch the relaxing canal-boat tour out to *The Little Mermaid* and back. Enjoy the rest of the afternoon tracing Denmark's cultural roots in the National Museum and touring the Ny Carlsberg Glyptotek art gallery. Spend the evening strolling Strøget (follow "Heart and Soul" walk described below) or dipping into Christiania.

Day 2: At 10:00 explore the subterranean Christiansborg Castle ruins under today's palace or go neoclassical at Thorvaldsen's Museum. At 11:00 take the 50-minute guided tour of Denmark's royal Christiansborg Palace. After a *smørrebrød* lunch in a park, spend the afternoon seeing the Rosenborg Castle/crown jewels and the Nazi Resistance museum. Spend the evening at Tivoli Gardens.

With a third day, side-trip out to Roskilde and Frederiksborg.

Copenhagen Overview

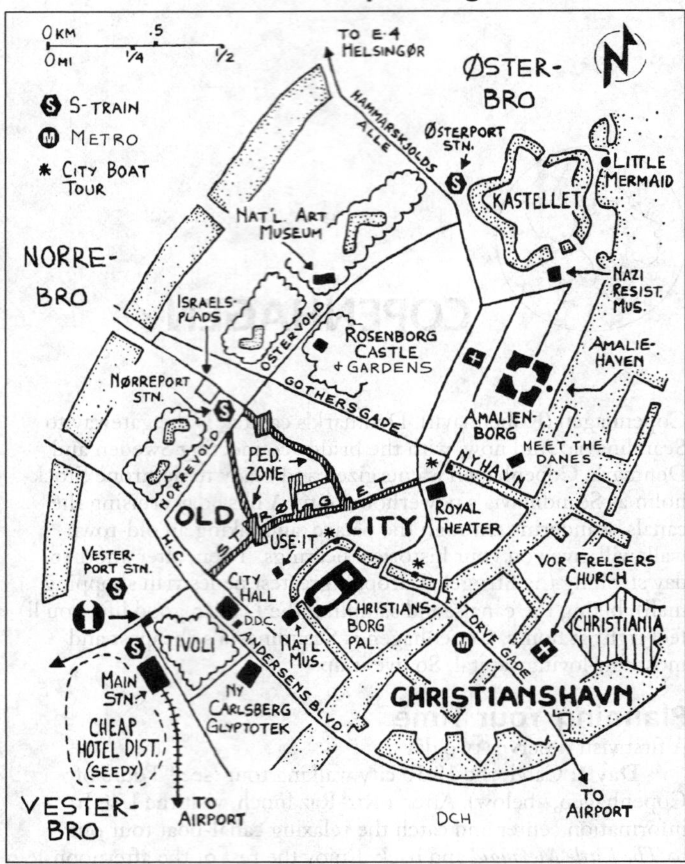

Remember the efficiency of sleeping while traveling in and out of town. Most flights from the States arrive in the morning. After you arrive, consider taking an overnight train that evening for Stockholm or an overnight boat to Oslo. Kamikaze sightseers see Copenhagen as a Scandinavian bottleneck. They sleep in and out heading north and in and out heading south, with two days and no nights in Copenhagen. Considering the joy of Oslo and Stockholm, this isn't that crazy if you have limited time. You can check your bag at the station.

If you've yet to do so, take the time to book my top recommended rooms for your entire Scandinavian tour with a phone card and a quick trip to a pay phone.

Orientation

Nearly all of your sightseeing is in Copenhagen's compact old town. By doing things by bike or on foot you'll stumble into some charming bits of Copenhagen that many miss.

Study the map to understand the city: The medieval walls are now roads that define the center: Vestervoldgade (literally, "west rampart street"), Nørrevoldgade, and Østervoldgade. The fourth side is the harbor and the island of Slotsholmen where København ("merchants' harbor") was born in 1167. The next of the city's islands is Amager, where you'll find the local "Little Amsterdam" district of Christianshavn. What was Copenhagen's moat is now a string of pleasant lakes and parks, including Tivoli Gardens. You can still make out some of the zigzag pattern of the moats in the city's greenbelt. In 1850 Copenhagen's 120,000 residents all lived within this defensive system. Building in the "no-man's-land" outside the walls was only allowed with the understanding that in the event of an attack, you'd burn your dwellings to clear the way for a good defense. Today, the buildings of historic importance lie within the *voldgade* ring. In the 17th century, King Christian IV extended the fortifications to the north, doubling the size of the city, adding a grid plan of streets and his Rosenborg Castle. This old "new town" has the Amalienborg Palace and *The Little Mermaid*.

For most visitors, the core of the town is the axis formed by the train station, Tivoli Gardens, Rådhus (City Hall) Square, and the Strøget pedestrian street. Bubbling with street life and colorful pedestrian zones, Copenhagen's great on foot. But be sure to get off the Strøget.

You need to remember one character in Copenhagen's history: Christian IV. Ruling from 1588 to 1648, he was Denmark's Renaissance king and royal party animal. The personal energy of this "Builder King" sparked a golden age when Copenhagen prospered and many of the city's grandest buildings were erected. Locals love to tell stories of everyone's favorite king, whose drinking was legendary.

Tourist Information

The tourist office is a for-profit company called "Wonderful Copenhagen." This colors the advice and information it provides. Drop by to get a city map and *Copenhagen This Week* (a free, handy, and misnamed monthly guide to the city, worth reading for its good maps, museum hours with telephone numbers, sightseeing tour ideas, shopping suggestions, and calendar of events, including free English tours and concerts; online at www.ctw.dk). Browse the TI's racks of brochures and get your questions answered (May–Sept Mon–Sat 9:00–20:00, closed Sun; July–Aug until 18:00 plus

Sun 10:00–18:00, Oct–April Tue–Sat 10:00–16:00, closed Sun–Mon, across from train station on Bernstorffsgade, tel. 70 22 24 52, www.visitcopenhagen.dk). They also book rooms for a 60-kr fee. Thinking ahead, get tourist information and ferry schedules for your entire trip in Denmark (Frederiksborg Castle, Louisiana Museum, Kronborg Castle, and Roskilde). This week's entertainment program for Tivoli is posted near the front door. The TI now also offers travelers the opportunity to dine with a Danish family (see "Eating," below).

Use It is a better information service (a 10-minute walk from the train station). Government-sponsored and student-run, it caters to Copenhagen's young but welcomes travelers of any age. It's a friendly, driven-to-help, energetic, no-nonsense source of budget travel information, offering a free budget room-finding service, free Internet access, a jazz bar, a ride-finding board, free condoms, and free luggage lockers. Their free *Playtime* publication has Back Door–style articles on Copenhagen and the Danish culture, special budget tips, and self-guided tours for bikers, walkers, and those riding scenic bus #6. They have a list of private rooms (350-kr doubles). From the station, head down Strøget, then turn right on Rådhustræde for three blocks to #13 (mid-June–mid-Sept daily 9:00–19:00; otherwise Mon–Wed 11:00–16:00, Thu 11:00–18:00, Fri 11:00–14:00, closed Sat–Sun; tel. 33 73 06 20).

Meet the Danes is the third and newest place that has all the information you'll need on Copenhagen. They're not as conveniently located (on Nyhavn), unless you're arriving on a ferry from Oslo or staying at one of the recommended private rooms near Amalienborg Palace. They offer a hotel/room-finding service (65-kr fee), the opportunity to dine with a Danish family (see "Eating," below), and a variety of bus, boat, and walking tours of Copenhagen and the surrounding area (May–Sept daily 10:00–21:00, Oct–April Mon–Fri 9:00–19:00, Sat–Sun 10:00–18:00, Nyhavn 65, tel. 33 46 46 46, fax 33 46 46 47, www.meetthedanes.dk, e-mail: info@meetthedanes.dk).

The two essential publications you need—a map and *Copenhagen This Week*—are free and available at the airport TI, the TI across from the train station, Use It, Meet the Danes, the city hall's lobby, and most hotels. For more information on events and attractions, visit the Danish Tourist Board's Web site: www.visitdenmark.com.

The **Copenhagen Card** covers the public transportation system and admissions to nearly all the sights in greater Copenhagen, which stretches from Helsingør to Roskilde. It includes virtually all the city sights, Tivoli, and the train from the airport. It's available at any TI (including the airport's): 24 hours for

215 kr; 48 hours for 375 kr; and 72 hours for 495 kr). It's hard to break even, unless you're planning to side-trip on the included (and otherwise expensive) rail service. It comes with a handy book explaining over 70 sights, such as: Christiansborg Castle ruins (20 kr), National Museum (40 kr), Ny Carlsberg Glyptotek (30 kr), Tivoli (50 kr), Frederiksborg Castle (50 kr), and Roskilde Viking Ships (60 kr), as well as discounts of 10–20 kr on several other sights, including the Danish Design Center, Christiansborg Castle royal reception rooms, canal boat tours, and Rosenborg Castle. It also includes round-trip train rides to Roskilde (100 kr) and Frederiksborg Castle (100 kr).

Arrival in Copenhagen

By Train: The main train station is called Hovedbanegården (pron. HOETH-bahn-gorn; learn that word—you'll need to recognize it). It's a temple of travel and a hive of travel-related activity, offering lockers (35 kr/day), a checkroom (*garderobe*, Mon–Sat 5:30–24:00, Sun 6:00–24:00, 40 kr/day per backpack), a post office (Mon–Fri 8:00–21:00, Sat 9:00–16:00, Sun 10:00–16:00), a grocery store (daily 8:00–24:00), a bike rental shop, and 24-hour thievery. The station has ATMs and long-hour FOREX and X-CHANGE exchange desks (both daily 8:00–21:00, 10-kr fee per traveler's check). Showers (10 kr) are available at the public rest rooms at the back of the station (and under the bus terminal opposite city hall). The Wonderful Copenhagen TI also has a hotel/room-finding office here (60 kr, Mon–Wed 10:00–20:00, Thu–Sat 9:00–20:00, closed Sun).

While you're in the station, reserve your overnight train seat or *couchette* out at the Rejse-bureau (Mon–Fri 9:00–16:00, closed Sat–Sun, tel. 33 54 55 10). International rides and all IC (fast) trains require reservations (usually 20 kr). If you have a railpass, you must make your reservations at the *Billetsalg* (Mon–Fri 8:00–19:00, Sat 9:30–16:00, Sun 12:30–19:00). The *Kviksalg* office sells tickets within Denmark (including the regional train to Malmö, Sweden). This office will also help you with reservations for international trips if the *Billetsalg* office is closed and you're departing by train within one hour or early the next day (daily 5:45–23:30).

To get to the recommended Christianshavn B&Bs from the train station, catch bus #8 (14 kr, 4/hr, in front of station on near side of Bernstorffsgade, get off at stop just after *Knippelsbro*-Knippels bridge). Note the time the bus departs, then stop by the TI (across the street) and pick up a free Copenhagen city map that shows bus routes.

By Plane: Kastrup, Copenhagen's international airport, is a traveler's dream, with a TI, bank (standard rates), post office, telephone center, shopping mall, grocery store, and bakery. You can use U.S. dollars at the airport and get change back in kroner (airport info tel. 32 47 47 47, SAS info tel. 70 10 20 00). Need to kill a night at the airport? Try the Transfer Hotel located under the Transit Hall. These fetal rest cabins, called *hvilekabiner*, are especially handy for early flights (Sb-390 kr, Db-580 kr for 8 hrs, prices vary for 2- to 16-hr periods, reception open daily 5:30–23:30, easy telephone reservations, CC, sauna and showers available, tel. 32 31 24 55, fax 32 31 31 09, e-mail: transferhotel@cph.dk).

Getting Downtown from the Airport: Taxis are fast and civil, accept credit cards, and, at about 150 kr to the town center, are a good deal for foursomes.

The Air Rail train (19.50 kr, 3/hr, 12 min) links the airport with the train station, as well as Nørreport and Østerport stations for a couple kroner more.

City bus #250s gets you downtown (City Hall Square, train station) in 30 minutes for 19.50 kr (6/hr, across the street and to the right as you exit airport).

If you're going from the airport to Christianshavn, ride #9 just past Christianshavn Torv and get off at Strandgade, the stop before crossing *Knippelsbro*-Knippels bridge.

Helpful Hints

Ferries: Book any ferries now that you plan to take later in Scandinavia. Any travel agent can help, or just call direct. For the Denmark–Norway ferry, call DFDS (Mon–Fri 8:30–18:00, Sat–Sun 9:00–17:00, tel. 33 43 30 00). For the cruise from Stockholm to Helsinki, call Silja Line's Danish office (one-way or round-trip available, Mon–Thu 9:00–16:30, Fri 9:00–16:00, closed Sat–Sun, tel. 96 20 32 00). With the new Øresund Bridge, you'll no longer need a ferry to drive to Sweden, but the toll (220 kr) is the same as the Helsingør–Helsingborg ferry, which still goes twice every hour.

Jazz Festival: The Copenhagen Jazz Festival—10 days starting the first Friday in July (July 4–13 in 2003)—puts the town in a rollicking slide-trombone mood. The Danes are Europe's jazz enthusiasts, and this music festival fills the town with happiness. The TI prints up an extensive listing of each year's festival events, or get the latest at www.jazzfestival.dk. There's also an autumn version of the festival the first week of November.

Telephones: Use the telephone liberally. Everyone speaks English, and *This Week* and this book list phone numbers for everything you'll be doing. All telephone numbers in Denmark are eight digits, and there are no area codes. Calls anywhere in Denmark are cheap; calls to Norway and Sweden cost 6 kr per minute from a booth (half that from a private home). Get a phone card (at newsstands, starting at 30 kr).

Emergencies: Dial 112 and specify fire, police, or ambulance. Speak slowly and clearly and give your phone number and address. Emergency calls from public phones are free; no coins are needed.

Pharmacy: Steno Apotek is across from the train station (open 24 hrs daily, Vesterbrogade 6c, tel. 33 14 82 66).

U.S. Embassy: Dag Hammerskjolds Alle 24, tel. 35 55 31 44.

Getting around Copenhagen

By Bus, S-tog, and Metro: It's easy to navigate Copenhagen with its fine buses, new Metro, and S-tog, a suburban train system with stops in the city (Eurail valid on S-tog, pron. S-tohg). A 14-kr two-zone ticket (pay as you board, or for the Metro, buy from station ticket offices or vending machines) gets you an hour's travel within the center. Consider the blue two-zone *klippekort* (90 kr for 10 1-hour "rides") and the 24-hour pass (85 kr, validate day pass in yellow machine on bus or at station, both sold at stations and the TI). Assume you'll be within the middle two zones. Bus drivers are patient, have change, and speak English. City maps list bus and subway routes. Locals are friendly and helpful.

Copenhagen's new Metro system consists of just one line thus far, connecting Christianshavn and Nørreport (which is 2 stops on S-tog from main train station). Eventually the Metro will run from Copenhagen to Ørestad, the industrial and business center created after the new Øresund bridge was built, linking Denmark and Sweden (for the latest, see www.m.dk/).

By Bus Tour: Open Top Tour buses do a hop-on, hop-off 60-minute circle connecting the city's top sights; for details, see "Tours of Copenhagen," below. If you're on a budget, simply ride city bus #6: From the Carlsberg Brewery, it stops at Tivoli, city hall, National Museum, Royal Palace, Nyhavn, Amalienborg Castle, Kastellet, and *The Little Mermaid* (14 kr for a stop-and-go hour). The entire tour is described in Use It's *Playtime* magazine.

By Taxi: Taxis are plentiful and easy to call or flag down (22-kr drop charge, then 10 kr per km, CC). For a short ride, four people spend about the same by taxi as by bus (e.g., 50 kr from train station to recommended Christianshavn B&Bs). Calling 35 35 35 35 will get you a taxi within minutes.

By Bike: Free! Copenhagen's radical "city bike" program is great for sightseers (though bikes can be hard to find at times). From May through November, 2,000 clunky but practical little bikes are scattered around the old-town center (basically the terrain covered in the Copenhagen map in this chapter). Simply locate one of the 150 racks, unlock a bike by popping a 20-kr coin into the handlebar, and pedal away. When you're done, plug your bike back into any other rack and your deposit coin will pop back out (if you can't find a rack, just abandon it and a bum will take it back and pocket your coin). These simple bikes come with "theft-proof" parts (unusable on regular bikes) and—they claim—computer tracer chips embedded in them so bike patrols can retrieve strays. These are funded by advertisements painted on the wheels and by a progressive electorate. Try this once and you'll find Copenhagen suddenly a lot smaller and easier.

For a serious bike tour, rent a more comfortable bike at the main train station's Cykelcenter (75 kr/day, Mon–Fri 8:00–18:00, Sat 9:00–13:00, summer Sun 9:00–13:00, tel. 33 33 85 13). Bikers see more, save time and money, and really feel like temporary locals by doing everything by bike. Consider it.

Tours of Copenhagen

▲▲▲**Walking Tours**—Once upon a time, American **Richard Karpen** visited Copenhagen and fell in love with the city (and one of its women). Today, he leads daily 90-minute tours that wander in and out of buildings, courtyards, backstreets, and unusual parts of the old town. Along the way, he gives insightful and humorous background on the history and culture of Denmark, Copenhagen, and the Danes. Richard offers four entertaining tours: three city walks (each about two kilometers/1.25 miles with breaks, covering different parts of the historic center) and a Rosenborg Castle tour (city tours depart from TI May–Sept Mon–Sat at 10:30, 75 kr, kids under 12 free; the Rosenborg Castle tour leaves from outside the castle ticket office at 13:30 Mon and Thu, 100 kr, which includes 60-kr castle admission; pick up schedule at TI, no reservations needed). Richard has an infectious love of Copenhagen. His tours, while all different, complement each other and are of equal "introduction" value.

Bus Tours—A variety of guided bus tours depart from City Hall Square in front of the Palace Hotel. **Copenhagen Excursions** runs both city tours and jaunts into the countryside, with themes such as Vikings, castles, and Hamlet. Their hop-on, hop-off **Open Top Tour** does the basic 60-minute circle of the city sights—Tivioli, Royal Palace, National Museum, *The Little Mermaid*, Rosenborg Castle, Nyhavn, and more—with a taped narration (100 kr, 2/hr, April–Oct daily 9:30–17:00; you can get off, see a sight, and catch a later bus; bus departs city hall below the *Lur Blowers* statue to the left of city hall or at many other stops throughout city, pay driver, ticket good for 48 hrs, tel. 32 54 06 06, www.cex.dk). One of their tours (offered on Thu only) goes to Sweden, giving you a chance to enjoy a trip over Europe's long Øresund Bridge from the windy open top of a double-decker bus, a brief stop in Malmö, and a few hours on

Copenhagen

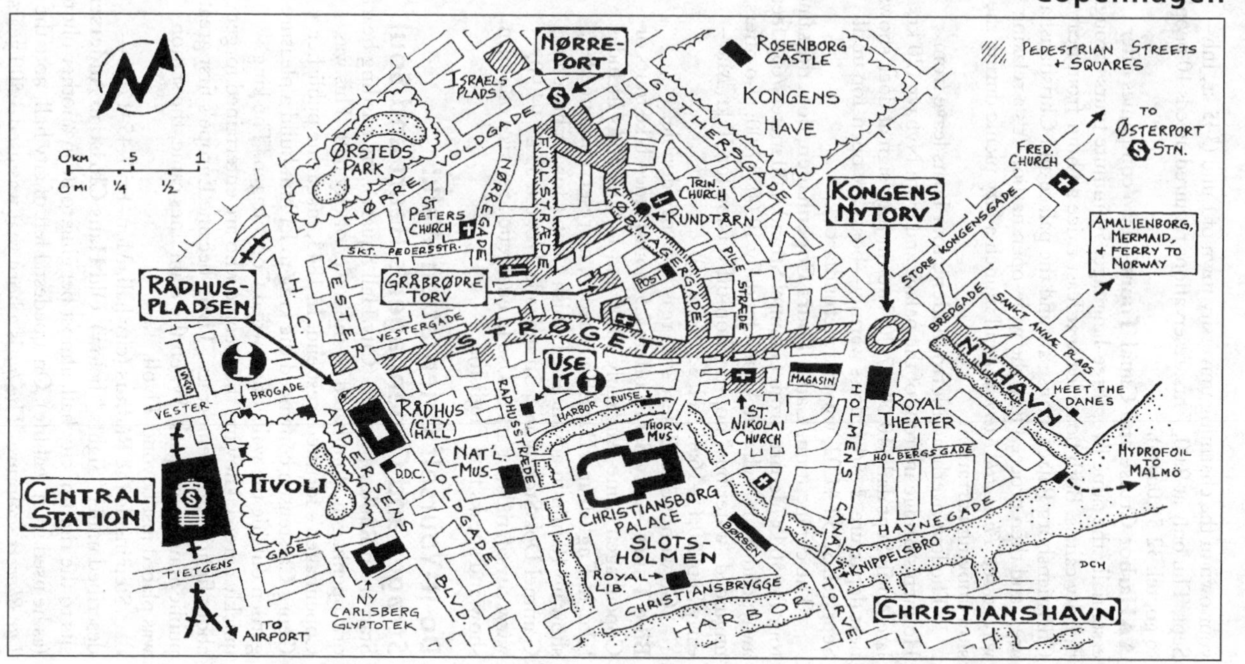
Nørreport
Rosenborg Castle
Pedestrian Streets + Squares
Israels Plads
Kongens Have
To Østerport Stn.
Ørsteds Park
Nørre Voldgade
Gothersgade
Fred. Church
0 km .5 1
0 mi 1/4 1/2
Fiolstræde
Nørregade
Trin. Church
Rundtårn
Kongens Nytorv
St Peters Church
Købmagergade
Store Kongensgade
Amalienborg, Mermaid, + Ferry to Norway
Skt. Pedersstr.
Pile Stræde
Post
Rådhuspladsen
Gråbrødre Torv
Bredgade
Sankt Annæ Plads
H. C.
Vester
Vestergade
Strøget
Nyhavn
Use It
Magasin
Meet the Danes
Brogade
Vester-
Rådhus (City Hall)
Rådhusstræde
Harbor Cruise
St. Nikolai Church
Royal Theater
Thorv. Mus.
Holmens Canal
Andersens
Nat'l. Mus.
Holbergsgade
Hydrofoil to Malmö
D.D.C.
Voldgade
Tivoli
Central Station
Christiansborg Palace
Børsen
Havnegade
Slotsholmen
Gade
Tietgens
Knippelsbro
DCH
Royal Lib.
Christiansbrygge
Ny Carlsberg Glyptotek
Blvd.
Harbor
Torve
Christianshavn
To Airport

your own in the charming university town of Lund (345 kr, July–Sept, Thu only at 9:00, 7 hrs, reservations required, needs 10 people to go, tel. 32 54 06 06).

▲▲**Harbor Cruise and Canal Tours**—Two companies offer essentially the same live, three-language, 50-minute tours through the city canals. Both boats leave at least twice an hour from near Christiansborg Palace, cruise around the palace and Christianshavn area, and then proceed into the wide-open harbor. It's a relaxing way to see *The Little Mermaid* and munch a lazy picnic during the slow-moving narration.

The low-overhead **Netto-Bådene** tour boats leave from Holmen's Bridge in front of the palace and from Nyhavn (20 kr, late April–Sept daily 10:00–17:00, later in July, sign at dock shows next departure, 2–5/hr, dress warmly—boats are open-top until Sept, tel. 32 54 41 02, www.havnerundfart.dk).

The competition, **Canal Tours Copenhagen**, does the same tour for 50 kr (departs from Gammel Strand, 200 meters/650 feet away; and from Nyhavn, April–Oct daily 10:00–17:00; also offers unguided "water bus" hop-on, hop-off version for 30 kr, May–early Sept 10:15–16:45, tel. 33 93 42 60).

Go with Netto. There's no reason to pay double.

Bike Tours—City Safari offers 2.5-hour guided bike tours of Copenhagen (June–Aug daily 10:00 and 13:00, 150 kr includes bike, in English and Danish as needed, no reservation needed, show up 10 min in advance at Danish Center for Architecture, Gammel Dok Storehouse, Strandgade 27b, tel. 33 23 94 90, www.citysafari.dk, or ask at Use It; energetic Steen is a one-man show and speaks fine English).

Do-It-Yourself Orientation Walk: Strøget and Copenhagen's Heart and Soul

Start from **Rådhuspladsen** (City Hall Square), the bustling heart of Copenhagen, dominated by the tower of city hall. This was Copenhagen's fortified west end. In 1843, magazine publisher Georg Carstensen convinced the king to let him build a pleasure garden outside the walls of crowded Copenhagen. The king quickly agreed, knowing that people who are entertained forget about fighting for democracy. **Tivoli** became Europe's first great public amusement park. When the train lines came, the station was placed just beyond Tivoli.

Step inside the **Rådhus** (city hall, Mon–Fri 7:45–17:00—described under "Sights," below). Old **Hans Christian Andersen** sits to the right of city hall, almost begging to be in another photo (as he used to in real life). On a pedestal left of city hall, note the *Lur Blowers* sculpture. The *lur* is a horn that was used 3,500 years ago. The ancient originals (which still play) are displayed in the National Museum. (City tour buses leave from below these horns.)

The **golden girls** high up on the tower (marked "Philips" in blue) opposite the Strøget's entrance tell the weather: on a bike (fair) or with an umbrella. These two have been called the only women in Copenhagen you can trust. Here in the traffic hub of this huge city you'll notice . . . not many cars. Denmark's 180 percent tax on car purchases makes the bus or bike a sweeter option.

The American trio of Burger King, 7-Eleven, and KFC marks the start of the otherwise charming **Strøget**. Copenhagen's 25-year-old experimental, tremendously successful, and most-copied pedestrian shopping mall is a string of lively (and individually named) streets and lovely squares that bunny-hop through the old town from city hall to Nyhavn, which is a 15-minute stroll (or *strøg)* away.

As you wander down this street, remember that the commercial focus of a historic street like Strøget drives up the land value, which generally trashes the charm and tears down the old buildings. Look above the street-level advertising to discover much of the 19th-century character intact. While Strøget has become hamburgerized, historic bits and charming pieces of old Copenhagen are just off this commercial cancan.

After one block (at Kattesundet), make a side-trip two blocks left into Copenhagen's colorful **university district**. Formerly the old brothel area, today this "Latin Quarter" is Soho chic. At Studiesstræde, turn right and walk two blocks to the big neoclassical Cathedral of Our Lady (with John the Baptist up where the Greek mythological gods would normally be). Enter and find statues of Christ and the 12 apostles—masterpieces by the great Danish sculptor Thorvaldsen—all looking quite Greek. By standing on the corner across the street from the church, you can see why golden-age Copenhagen (early 1800s) fancied itself a Nordic Athens. To the left is the university. And 300 meters/985 feet to your right are the Greek temple–like law courts.

Step up the middle steps of the University's big building and enter a colorful lobby starring Athena and Apollo. The frescoes celebrate high thinking and themes such as the triumph of wisdom over barbarism. Notice how harmoniously the architecture, sculpture, and painting work together.

Rejoin Strøget (down where you see the law courts) at **Gammel Torv** and **Nytorv** (Old Square and New Square). This was the old town center. The Oriental-looking kiosk was one of the city's first community telephone centers before phones were privately owned. Look at the reliefs ringing its top: an airplane with bird wings (c. 1900) and two women talking on the

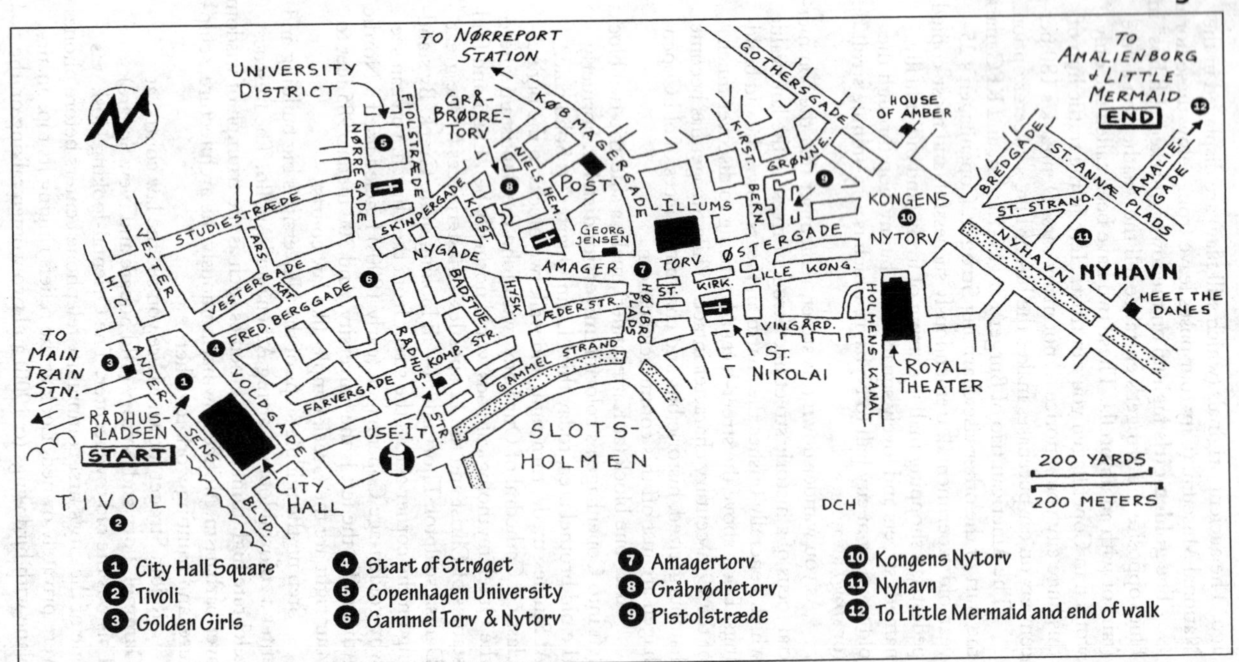
Strøget
TO NØRREPORT STATION
UNIVERSITY DISTRICT
GRÅ-BRØDRE-TORV
KØBMAGERGADE
GOTHERSGADE
TO AMALIENBORG & LITTLE MERMAID
END
12
HOUSE OF AMBER
BREDGADE
ST. ANNÆ PLADS
AMALIE-GADE
5
NØRREGADE
FIOLSTRÆDE
8
NIELS HEM.
POST
KIRST.
GRØNNE.
9
BERN.
KONGENS
10
NYTORV
ST. STRAND.
11
NYHAVN
NYHAVN
MEET THE DANES
STUDIESTRÆDE
SKINDERGADE
KLOST.
GEORG JENSEN
ILLUMS
ØSTERGADE
LARS.
VESTER
H. C.
NYGADE
AMAGER
7
TORV
LILLE KONG.
VESTERGADE
KAT.
6
BADSTUE.
HYSK.
ST.
KIRK.
HØJBRO PLADS
FRED. BERGGADE
LÆDER STR.
VINGÅRD.
HOLMENS KANAL
ROYAL THEATER
TO MAIN TRAIN STN.
3
ANDER.
4
RÅDHUS-STR.
KOMP. STR.
GAMMEL STRAND
ST. NIKOLAI
1
VOLDGADE
FARVERGADE
RÅDHUS-PLADSEN
START
SENS
USE-IT
SLOTS-HOLMEN
200 YARDS
200 METERS
TIVOLI
2
CITY HALL
BLVD.
DCH
1 City Hall Square
2 Tivoli
3 Golden Girls
4 Start of Strøget
5 Copenhagen University
6 Gammel Torv & Nytorv
7 Amagertorv
8 Gråbrødretorv
9 Pistolstræde
10 Kongens Nytorv
11 Nyhavn
12 To Little Mermaid and end of walk

newfangled phone. (It was thought business would popularize the telephone, but actually it was women.... Now, 100 years later, look at the cell phones.) The squirting woman and boy on the very old fountain in Gammel Torv were so offensive to people from the Victorian age that the pedestal was added, raising it—they hoped—out of view.

Walk down **Amagertorv** to the stately brick Holy Ghost church (note the fine spire, typical of old Danish churches). Under the step gable was a hospital run by monks. A block behind the church (walk down Valkendorfsgade and through a passage under a rust-colored building) is the leafy and caffeine-stained **Grey Friars' Square (Gråbrødretorv)**—a popular place for an outdoor meal or drink in the summer—surrounded by fine old buildings. At the end of the square, the street Niels Hemmingsens Gade returns (past the Copenhagen Jazz House, a good place for live music nightly) to Strøget. Continue down the pedestrian street to the next square with the stork fountain.

Amagertorv delights shoppers. Spin around and see Royal Copenhagen Porcelain (with demos), Holmegaard Glassware, George Jensen Jewelry and Silverware, and Illums Bolighus (modern design, Mon–Sat 10:00–18:00, Sun 12:00–17:00). Café Norden is a smoky but good place for a coffee with a view. Go to the second floor for the best vantage point. From here you can see the imposing Parliament building, Christiansborg Palace, and a horse statue of Bishop Absalon, the city's founder (canal boat tours leave nearby from Holmen's Bridge). A block toward the canal, running parallel to Strøget, starts Strædet, a second Strøget with cafés, antique shops, and no fast food. North of Amagertorv a broad pedestrian mall, Købmagergade, leads past the Museum of Erotica to Christian IV's Round Tower.

The final stretch of Strøget leads past **Pistolstræde** (a cute lane of shops in restored 18th-century buildings leading off Strøget to the right from Østergade; wander back into half-timbered section; Kransekagehuset bakery nearby, see "Eating," below); McDonald's (good view from top floor); and major department stores (Illum and Magasin—see "Shopping," below) to Kongens Nytorv.

Kongens Nytorv, the biggest square in town, is home to the Royal Theater, French Embassy, and venerable Hotel D'Angleterre. On the right, Hviids Vinstue, the town's oldest wine cellar (from 1723), is a colorful if smoky spot for an open-face sandwich and a beer (Kongens Nytorv 19). The statue in the middle celebrates Christian V who, in the 1670s, extended Copenhagen, adding this "King's New Square" (Kongens Nytorv). Across the square is the trendy harbor of Nyhavn.

Nyhavn, a recently gentrified sailors' quarter, is just opposite

Kongens Nytorv. With its trendy cafés, tattoo shops (pop into Tattoo Ole at #17—fun photos, very traditional), and jazz clubs, Nyhavn is a wonderful place to hang out. The canal is filled with glamorous old sailboats of all sizes. Any historic sloop is welcome to moor here in Copenhagen's ever-changing boat museum. Hans Christian Andersen lived and wrote his first stories here (in the red double-gabled building on the right).

Continuing north along the harborside (from end of Nyhavn canal, turn left), you'll pass a huge ship that sails to Oslo every evening (at 17:00—see "Transportation Connections," below). Follow the waterfront to the modern fountain of Amaliehave Park.

The Amalienborg Palace and Square (a block inland, behind the fountain) is a good example of orderly Baroque planning. Queen Margrethe II and her family live in the palace to your immediate left as you enter the square from the harborside. Her son and heir to the throne, Crown Prince Frederik, recently moved into the palace directly opposite his mother's. While the guards change with royal fanfare at noon only when the queen is in residence, they shower every morning.

Leave the square on Amaliegade, heading north to Kastellet (Citadel) Park and past Denmark's WWII Resistance Museum. A short stroll past the Gefion fountain (illustrating the myth of the goddess who was given one night to carve a chunk out of Sweden to make into Denmark's main island, Zealand—which you're on) and an Anglican church built of flint brings you to the overrated, overfondled, and overphotographed symbol of Copenhagen, ***Den Lille Havfrue—The Little Mermaid***.

You can get back downtown on foot, by taxi, or on bus #1, #6, or #9 from Store Kongensgade on the other side of Kastellet Park (a special bus may run from *The Little Mermaid* in summer).

Tivoli

The world's grand old amusement park—160 years old in 2003—is 20 acres, 110,000 lanterns, and countless ice-cream cones of fun. You pay one admission price and find yourself lost in a Hans Christian Andersen wonderland of rides, restaurants, games, marching bands, roulette wheels, and funny mirrors. Tivoli is wonderfully Danish. It doesn't try to be Disney.

Cost, Hours, and Location: 50 kr, April–Sept daily 11:00–23:00, Wed–Thu until 24:00, Fri–Sat until 1:00; mid-June–mid-Aug daily 11:00–24:00, Fri–Sat until 1:00. Tivoli also opens for a Christmas Market (mid-Nov–Dec daily 11:00–22:00—with ice skating on Tivoli Lake, tel. 33 15 10 01, www.tivoli.dk). Rides range in price from 10 to 50 kr (180 kr for all-day pass). All children's amusements are in full swing by 11:30; the rest of the amusements open by 14:00. Tivoli is across from the train station. If you're catching an overnight train, this is the place to spend your last Copenhagen hours.

Entertainment in Tivoli: Upon arrival (through main entry, on right in shop), pick up a map and events schedule. Take a moment to sit down and plan your entertainment for the evening. Events are spread between 15:00 and 23:00; the 19:30 concert in the concert hall can be free or max cost up to 500 kr, depending on the performer (box office tel. 33 15 10 12). If the Tivoli Symphony is playing, it's worth paying for. Concert hall tickets include your Tivoli entry, so purchase before paying park admission (to see if a fee concert is planned, you can check the events schedule at Tivoli's ticket window before paying).

Free concerts, pantomime theater, ballet, acrobats, puppets, and other shows pop up all over the park, and a well-organized visitor can enjoy an exciting evening of entertainment without spending a single kroner. The children's theater, Valmuen, plays excellent traditional fairy tales daily at 12:00, 13:00, and 14:00 (13:00 show is in English in summer). Friday evenings feature a (usually free) rock or pop show at 22:00. On Wednesday and Saturday from late April through late September, fireworks light up the sky at 23:45.

Eating at Tivoli: Generally, you'll pay amusement-park prices for amusement-park quality food inside. **Søcafeen**, by the lake, allows picnics if you buy a drink. The *pølse* (sausage) stands are cheap. **Færgekroen** is a good lakeside place for typical Danish food, beer, and an impromptu sing-along with a bunch of drunk Danes. The Croatian restaurant, **Hercegovina**, serves a 99-kr lunch buffet and a 169-kr dinner buffet. For a cake and coffee, consider the **Viften** café. **Georg**, to the left of the concert hall, has tasty 45-kr sandwiches and 150-kr dinners (dinner includes glass of wine). Indulge in some candy floss (that's cotton candy to Yankees) or ice cream (*lakrids* is black licorice–swirled ice-cream, a must in Scandinavia).

More Sights near the Train Station

▲City Hall (Rådhus)—This city landmark, between the train station/Tivoli/TI and Strøget pedestrian mall, offers private tours and trips up its 105-meter/345-foot-tall tower. It's draped, inside and out, in Danish symbolism. The city's founder, Bishop Absalon, stands over the door. The polar bears climbing on the rooftop symbolize the giant Danish protectorate of Greenland.

Step inside. The lobby has racks of tourist information (city maps and *This Week*). The building was inspired by the city hall in Siena, Italy (with the necessary addition of a glass roof). Huge functions fill this grand hall (the iron grill in the center of the floor is an elevator for bringing up 1,200 chairs) while the busts of four illustrious local boys—the fairy-tale writer Hans Christian Andersen, the sculptor Bertel Thorvaldsen, the physicist Niels Bohr, and the building's architect Martin Nyrop—look on. Underneath the floor are national archives dating back to 1275, popular with Danes researching their family roots. The city hall is free and open to the public (Mon–Fri 9:30–16:00, open on Sat only for tours—see below). You can wander throughout the building and into the peaceful garden out back.

Guided English-language **tours**, which get you into more private, official rooms, are not as entertaining as they are interesting (30 kr, 45 min, year-round Mon–Fri at 15:00, Sat at 10:00 and 11:00).

Tourists romp up the **tower**'s 300 steps for the best aerial view of Copenhagen (20 kr, Mon–Fri 10:00, 12:00, and 14:00, Sat 12:00, off-season Mon–Sat 12:00, tel. 33 66 25 82).

▲▲Christiansborg Palace—A complex of government buildings stands on the ruins of Copenhagen's original 12th-century castle: the Parliament, Supreme Court, prime minister's office, royal reception rooms, royal library, several museums, and the royal stables.

While the current palace dates only from 1928 and the royal family moved out 200 years ago, it's the sixth to stand here in 800 years and is rich with tradition. The information-packed 50-minute English-language tours of the royal reception rooms are excellent. As you slip-slide on protect-the-floor slippers through 22 rooms, you'll gain a good feel for Danish history, royalty, and politics. (For instance, the family portrait of King Christian IX shows why he's nicknamed the father-in-law of Europe—with children eventually becoming or marrying royalty in Denmark, Russia, Greece, Britain, France, Germany, and Norway.) The highlight is the dazzling set of tapestries—Danish-designed but Gobelin-made in Paris. This gift, given to the queen on her 60th birthday in 2000, celebrates 1,000 years of Danish history with wild wall-hangings from the Viking age to our chaotic age (admission by tour only, 40 kr, May–Sept daily 11:00, 13:00, and 15:00; Oct–April Tue, Thu, and Sat 11:00 and 15:00; from the equestrian statue in front, go through the wooden door, past the entrance to the Christiansborg Castle ruins, into the courtyard, and up the stairs on the right; tel. 33 92 64 92).

▲Christiansborg Castle Ruins—An exhibit in the scant remains of the first castle built by Bishop Absalon—the 12th-century founder of Copenhagen—lies under the palace. There's precious little to see, but it's old and very well-described (20 kr, daily May–Sept 9:30–15:30, closed off-season Mon, Wed, and Fri, good 1-kr guide, guided tours on Sun at 13:00 July–Aug). Early birds note that this sight opens 30 minutes before other nearby sights.

▲**Thorvaldsen's Museum**—This museum tells the story and shows the monumental work of the great Danish neoclassical sculptor Bertel Thorvaldsen (1770–1844). Considered Canova's equal among neoclassical sculptors, Thorvaldsen spent 40 years in Rome. He was lured home to Copenhagen with the promise to showcase his work in a fine museum—which opened in the revolutionary year of 1848 as Denmark's first public art gallery (20 kr, Tue–Sun 10:00–17:00, closed Mon, free Wed, well-described, located in neoclassical building with colorful walls next to Christiansborg Palace, tel. 33 32 15 32).

Royal Library—Copenhagen's "Black Diamond" library is a striking building made of shiny black granite, leaning over the harbor at the edge of the palace complex. Wander through the old and new sections, read a magazine, and enjoy a classy—and pricey—lunch (restaurant open Mon–Sat 11:00–22:30, café 10:00–17:00, closed Sun; library hours: Mon–Fri 10:00–19:00, Sat 10:00–14:00, closed Sun, tel. 33 47 47 47).

▲▲▲**National Museum**—Focus on the excellent and curiously enjoyable Danish collection, which traces this civilization from its ancient beginnings. Exhibits are laid out chronologically and described in English. Pick up the museum map. The headsets (free with deposit) describe the highlights but add nothing to the printed descriptions you'll find inside. Start with room #1 (opposite the entrance), and follow the numbers through the "prehistory" section on the ground floor—oak coffins with still-clothed and armed skeletons from 1300 B.C., ancient and still-playable *lur* horns, the 2,000-year-old Gundestrup Cauldron of art-textbook fame, lots of Viking stuff, and an excellent collection of well-translated rune stones. Then go upstairs, find room 101, and carry on to find fascinating material on the Reformation, an exhibit on everyday town life in the 16th and 17th centuries, and, in room 126, a unique "cylinder perspective" of the royal family (from 1656) and two peep shows. The next floor takes you into modern times (40 kr, free Wed, Tue–Sun 10:00–17:00, closed Mon, mandatory bag check—10 kr coin deposit, cafeteria, enter at Ny Vestergade 10, tel. 33 13 44 11).

▲**Ny Carlsberg Glyptotek**—Scandinavia's top art gallery is an impressive example of what beer money can do. Enjoy the intoxicating Egyptian, Greek, and Etruscan collections; a fine sample of Danish golden age (early-19th-century) painting; and a heady, if small, exhibit of 19th-century French paintings (in the new "French Wing," including Géricault, Delacroix, Manet, Impressionists, and Gauguin before and after Tahiti). Linger with marble gods under the palm leaves and glass dome of the very soothing winter garden. Designers, figuring Danes would be more interested in a lush garden than classical art, used this wonderful space as leafy bait to cleverly introduce locals to a few Greek and Roman statues. (It works for tourists, too.) One of the original Rodin *Thinkers* (wondering how to scale the Tivoli fence?) is in the museum's backyard. This collection is artfully displayed and thoughtfully described (30 kr, free Wed and Sun, Tue–Sun 10:00–16:00, closed Mon, 2-kr English brochure/guide, classy cafeteria under palms, behind Tivoli, Dantes Plads 7, tel. 33 41 81 41).

Danish Design Center—This center, a masterpiece in itself, shows off the best in Danish design as well as top examples from around the world, from architecture to fashion and graphic arts. A visit to this high-tech but low-key display case for sleek Scandinavian design offers an interesting glimpse into the culture (30 kr, Mon–Fri 10:00–17:00, Sat–Sun 13:00–16:00, across from Tivoli at H. C. Andersens Boulevard 27, tel. 33 69 33 69, www.ddc.dk). The boutique next to the ticket counter features three themes: travel light (chic travel accessories and gadgets), modern Danish classics, and books and posters. The café on the main level, under the atrium, serves light lunches (60–70 kr).

Hovedbanegården—Copenhagen's great train station is a fascinating mesh of Scandinavian culture and transportation efficiency. Even if you're not a train traveler, check it out (see "Arrival in Copenhagen," above).

Sights—Rosenborg Castle

▲▲Rosenborg Castle—This finely furnished Dutch Renaissance–style castle was built by Christian IV in the early 1600s as a summer castle. Today it houses the Danish crown jewels and 500 years of royal knickknacks, including some great Christian IV memorabilia, such as the shrapnel (removed from his eye and forehead after a naval battle) that he had made into earrings for his girlfriend. It would be fascinating if anything were explained in English. If you don't want to buy and read the palace guidebook or follow Richard Karpen's English-language guided tour (offered Mon and Thu, see "Tours of Copenhagen," above), here are a few highlights:

In the Long Hall, the **throne** is made of unicorn horn (actually narwhal tusk from Greenland). Unicorn horn was believed to bring protection from evil and poison. The military themes decorating the room celebrate Danish victories over archenemy Sweden. The delightful **royal porcelain** display in a side room shows off the herbs and vegetables found in the realm.

The two **treasuries** (downstairs) will dazzle you. In the upper treasury, the two diamond- and pearl-studded saddles were Christian IV's—the first for his coronation, the second for his son's wedding (constructed lavishly when the kingdom was nearly bankrupt to impress visiting dignitaries and bolster Denmark's credit rating). See if you can find the golden ring—a gift from a jealous king—with a promiscuous queen shaking hands with a penis. (Hint: It sits above a brooch showing a cupid complete with bow and arrow.) In the lower treasury, the tall, two-handed, 16th-century coronation sword was drawn by the new king, who cut crosses into the air in four directions, symbolically promising to defend the realm from all attacks. Some consider Christian IV's coronation crown (from 1596, 7 pounds of gold and precious stones) the finest Renaissance crown in Europe. It radiates symbolism. Find the symbols of justice (sword and scales); charity (a woman nursing—meaning the king will love God and his people as a mother loves her child); and fortitude (a woman on a lion with a sword). Climb the footstool to look inside. The shields of various Danish provinces remind the king that he's surrounded by his realms. The painting shows the coronation of Christian V at Frederiksburg in 1671 (60 kr, daily June–Aug 10:00–17:00, May and Sept 10:00–16:00, Oct 11:00–15:00, Nov–April Tue–Sun 11:00–14:00, closed Mon, S-tog: Nørreport, tel. 33 15 32 86).

▲**Rosenborg Gardens**—The Rosenborg Castle is surrounded by the royal pleasure gardens and, on sunny days, a minefield of sunbathing Danish beauties and picnickers. When the royal family is in residence, there's a daily changing-of-the-guard mini-parade from the Royal Guard's barracks adjoining Rosenborg Castle (at 11:30) to Amalienborg Castle (at 12:00). The Queen's Rose Garden (across the moat from the palace) is a royal place for a picnic (cheap open-face sandwiches to go at Soe's Smørrebrød, nearby at the corner of Borgergade and Dronningens Tværgade). The fine statue of Hans Christian (H. C.) Andersen in the park, actually erected in his lifetime (and approved by H. C., pron. HOH see), is meant to symbolize how his stories had a message even for adults.

National Art Museum (Statens Museum for Kunst)—This museum fills an impressive building with Danish and European paintings from the 14th century through today. Of most interest is the Danish golden age of paintings, 1800–1850 (40 kr, Tue–Sun 10:00–17:00, Wed until 20:00, closed Mon, Sølvgade 48, tel. 33 74 84 94).

Sights—Near Strøget

Museum of Erotica—This museum's focus: The love life of *Homo sapiens*. Better than the Amsterdam equivalents, it offers a chance to visit a porno shop and call it a museum. It took some digging, but they've documented a history of sex from Pompeii to present day. Visitors get a peep into the world of 19th-century Copenhagen prostitutes and a chance to read up on the sex lives of Mussolini, Queen Elizabeth, Charlie Chaplin, and Casanova. After reviewing a lifetime of *Playboy* centerfolds and realizing how dull Marilyn Monroe's dress is without her in it, visitors sit down for the arguably artistic experience of watching the "electric *tabernakel,*" a dozen silently slamming screens of porn (worth the 89 kr entry fee only if fascinated by sex, includes graphic booklet, daily May–Sept 10:00–23:00, Oct–April 11:00–20:00, a block north of Strøget at Købmagergade 24, tel. 33 12 03 11). For a look at the real thing—unsanitized but free—wander Copenhagen's dreary little red-light district along Istedgade behind the train station.

Round Tower—Built in 1642 by Christian IV, the tower connects a church, library, and observatory (the oldest functioning observatory in Europe) with a ramp that spirals up to a fine view of Copenhagen (20 kr, June–Aug Mon–Sat 10:00–20:00, Sun 12:00–20:00; Sept–May Mon–Sat 10:00–17:00, Sun 12:00–17:00; nothing to see inside but the ramp and the view, just off Strøget on Købmagergade).

Sights—Near *The Little Mermaid*

▲Denmark's Resistance Museum (Frihedsmuseet)—The fascinating story of Denmark's heroic Nazi resistance struggle (1940–1945) is well-explained in English. Stop in to gain a different perspective on World War II (30 kr, May–mid-Sept Tue–Sat 10:00–16:00, Sun 10:00–17:00, closed Mon; off-season Tue–Sat 11:00–15:00, Sun 11:00–16:00, closed Mon, free on Wed, guided tours at 14:00 Tue and Thu in the summer, on Churchillparken between Queen's Palace and *The Little Mermaid*, bus #1, #6, #19, or #29, tel. 33 13 77 14).

Amalienborg Palace Changing of the Guard—This noontime event is boring in the summer when the queen is not in residence—the guards just change places. For more information, see "Heart and Soul" walk, above.

Sights—Christianshavn

▲Our Savior's (Vor Frelsers) Church—The church's bright Baroque interior (1696), with the pipe organ supported by the royal elephants, is worth a look (free, helpful English flier, April–Aug Mon–Sat 11:00–16:30, Sun 12:00–16:30, off-season closes 1 hour earlier, bus #2a, #8, #19, Sankt Annægade 29, tel. 32 57 27 98). The unique spiral spire that you'll admire from afar can be climbed for a great city view and a good aerial view of the Christiania commune below (20 kr, 400 steps, 95 meters/ 311 feet high, closed in bad weather and Nov–March).

Lille Mølle—This tiny, intimate museum shows off a 1916 Christianshavn house (40 kr, visits by guided tour only at

13:00, 14:00, 15:00, 16:00, closed Mon, just off south end of Torvegade at Christianshavn Voldgade, tel. 33 47 38 38). A fine restaurant, Bastionen & Løven (see "Eating," below) serves light lunches, dinners, and huge weekend brunches in the museum's terrace garden.

Christiania—In 1971, the original 700 Christianians established squatters' rights in an abandoned military barracks just a 10-minute walk from the Danish parliament building. A generation later, this "free city"—an ultra-human mishmash of 1,000 idealists, anarchists, hippies, dope fiends, nonmaterialists, and people who dream only of being a Danish bicycle seat—not only survives, it thrives. This is a communal cornucopia of dogs, dirt, soft drugs, and dazed people, or a haven of peace, freedom, and no taboos, depending on your perspective. Locals will remind judgmental Americans that a society must make the choice: Allow for alternative lifestyles... or build more prisons.

For 25 years, Christiania was a political hot potato; no one in the Danish establishment wanted it—or had the nerve to mash it. These days Christiania is connecting better with the rest of society—paying its utilities and taxes, and even offering daily walking tours (see below).

Passing under the city gate you'll find yourself on Pusher Street... the main drag. This is a line of stalls selling hash, pot, pipes, and souvenirs leading to the market square and a food circus beyond. Make a point of getting past this touristy side of Christiania. You'll find a fascinating ramshackle world of moats and earthen ramparts, alternative housing, unappetizing falafel stands, carpenter shops, hippie villas, children's playgrounds, and peaceful lanes. Be careful to distinguish between real Christianians and Christiania's uninvited guests—motley low-life vagabonds from other countries who hang out here in the summer, skid row–type Greenlanders, and gawking tourists.

Soft Drugs: While hard drugs are out, pot, hash, and psychedelic mushrooms are sold openly (individual joints—40 kr, senior discounts) and smoked happily. While locals will assure you you're safe within Christiania, they'll remind you that it's risky to take pot out—Denmark is required by Uncle Sam to make a token effort to snare tourists leaving the "free city" with pot. Beefy marijuana plants stand on proud pedestals at the market square. Beyond that an open-air food circus (or the canal-view perch above it, on the earthen ramparts) creates just the right ambience to lose track of time.

Graffiti on the wall declares "a mind is a wonderful thing to waste." If you agree, buy a joint on Pusher Street, buy a drink, light up in a bar that allows smoking, and then wander. Find the **Månefiskeren** (The Moonfisher) bar (it looks like a Brueghel painting...

from 2003). Cap your evening cruising through Tivoli with an ice-cream cone and singing, "Wonderful, Wonderful Copenhagen."

Nitty-Gritty: Christiania is open all the time, and visitors are welcome (down Prinsessegade behind Vor Frelsers' spiral church spire in Christianshavn). Photography is absolutely forbidden on Pusher Street (if you value your camera, don't even sneak a photo). Otherwise, you're welcome to snap photos, but ask residents before you photograph them. Guided tours are supposed to leave from the front entrance of Christiania at 15:00 (30 kr, 90 min, up to 4/day, daily late June–Aug, Sat–Sun rest of year, in English and Danish, tel. 32 57 96 70). **Morgenstedet** is a good, cheap vegetarian café (left after Pusher Street). **Spiseloppen** is the classy, good-enough-for-Republicans restaurant (see "Eating," below).

Sights—Greater Copenhagen

Carlsberg Brewery—Denmark's beloved source of legal intoxicants, Carlsberg, welcomes you to its Visitors Center with a free half-liter of beer (Tue–Sun 10:00–16:00, closed Mon, last entry 30 min before closing, bus #6 or #18, enter at Gamle Carlsbergvej 11, around corner from brewery entrance, tel. 33 27 13 14).

Open Air Folk Museum (Frilandsmuseet)—This park is filled with traditional Danish architecture and folk culture (40 kr, free Wed, April–Sept Tue–Sun 10:00–17:00, closed Mon, shorter hours off-season, outside of town in the suburb of Lyngby, S-tog: Sorgenfri or bus #184 or #194 to Kongevejen 100, Lyngby, tel. 33 13 44 11).

Bakken—Danes gather at Copenhagen's other great amusement park, Bakken (free, April–Aug daily 12:00–24:00, S-tog: Klampenborg, then walk 10 min through the woods, tel. 39 63 73 00, www.bakken.dk).

Dragør—For a look at small-town Denmark, consider a trip a few minutes out of Copenhagen to the fishing village of **Dragør** (bus #250s or 5a from station 5 stops at Sundbyvesterplads, change to #350s).

Shopping

Copenhagen's colorful flea market is small but feisty and surprisingly cheap (summer Sat and Sun 8:00–14:00 at Israels Plads). An antique market enlivens Nybrogade (near Christiansborg Palace) every Friday and Saturday. For other street markets, ask at the TI.

Shops are generally open Monday through Friday from 10:00 to 19:00 and Saturday from 9:00 to 16:00. For a street's worth of shops selling "Scantiques," wander down Ravnsborggade from Nørrebrogade.

The city's top department stores (Illum at Østergade 52,

tel. 33 14 40 02; and Magasin at Kongens Nytorv 13, tel. 33 11 44 33) offer a good, if expensive, look at today's Denmark. Both are on Strøget and have fine cafeterias on their top floors. The department stores and the Politiken Bookstore on the Rådhus Square have a good selection of maps and English travel guides.

Shoppers who like jewelry look for amber, known as "gold of the North." Globs of this petrified sap wash up on the shores of all the Baltic countries. **House of Amber,** at Kongens Nytorv 2, has a shop and museum with fine examples of prehistoric insects trapped in the amber (remember *Jurassic Park?*).

If you buy anything substantial (over 300 kr, about $40) from a shop displaying the Danish Tax-Free Shopping emblem, you can get a refund of the Value Added Tax, roughly 20 percent of the purchase price (VAT is MOMS in Danish). If you have your purchase mailed, the tax can be deducted from your bill. For details, call 32 52 55 66 (Mon–Fri 7:00–22:00), and see "VAT Refunds for Shoppers" in the Introduction.

Nightlife in Copenhagen

For the latest on the city's hopping jazz scene, inquire at the TI or pick up the "alternative" *Playtime* magazine at Use It. The **Copenhagen Jazz House** is a good bet for live jazz (around 90 kr, Tue–Thu and Sun at 20:30, Fri–Sat at 21:30, closed Mon, Niels Hemmingsensgade 10, tel. 33 15 47 00, www.jazzhouse.dk). For blues, try the **Mojo Blues Bar** (daily 20:00–5:00, Løngangsstræde 21 C, tel. 33 11 64 53, www.mojo.dk).

If you'd rather dance, join Denmark's salsa-wave at **Sabor Latino Salsa Club**. Located one block south of the City Hall Square, it offers free salsa lessons in English. Salsa dancing is surprisingly easy to learn in this friendly environment, and you'll get a chance to know the fun-loving Danes (free on Thu, 50 kr Fri–Sat, Thu–Sat 21:00-3:00, free lesson 22:00–23:00, no reservation required, wear comfortable shoes, Vestervoldgade 85, tel. 33 11 97 66).

Sleeping in Copenhagen
(7.5 kr = about $1, country code: 45)

Sleep Code: **S** = Single, **D** = Double/Twin, **T** = Triple, **Q** = Quad, **b** = bathroom, **CC** = Credit Cards accepted, **no CC** = Credit Cards not accepted. Breakfast is generally included at hotels but not at private rooms or hostels.

To help you sort easily through these listings, I've divided the rooms into three categories based on the price for a standard double room with bath during high season:

Higher Priced—Most rooms more than 1,000 kr.

Moderately Priced—Most rooms 1,000 kr or less.

Lower Priced—Most rooms 450 kr or less.

I've listed the best budget hotels in the center, cheap rooms in private homes (my favorite choice) in great neighborhoods an easy bus ride from the station, and a few backpacker dorm options.

Hotels in Central Copenhagen

These are listed in geographical order from the train station. Prices include breakfast unless noted otherwise. All are big and modern places with elevators and smoke-free rooms upon request, and all accept credit cards.

HIGHER PRICED

Hotel Nebo, a calm refuge with a friendly welcome and comfy, spacious rooms, is half a block from the station on the edge of Copenhagen's red-light district (S-510 kr, Sb-820 kr, D-700 kr, older Db-920 kr, newly renovated Db-1,230 kr, cheaper Oct–April, extra bed-250 kr, CC, Istedgade 6, DK-1650, tel. 33 21 12 17, fax 33 23 47 74, www.nebo.dk, e-mail: nebo@email.dk).

Hotel Excelsior is similar but with a little less warmth (Sb-1,075 kr, Db-1,275 kr, CC, a block from station and a block off busy Vesterbrogade at Colbjørnsensgade 6, DK-1652 Copenhagen, tel. 33 24 50 85, fax 33 24 50 87, www.choicehotels.dk).

Webers Scandic Hotel, my classiest hotel by the train station, faces busy Vesterbrogade but has a peaceful garden courtyard (nice for breakfast). It has a modern, inviting interior (high-season rack rates: small Sb-1,095 kr, Sb-1,495 kr, Db-1,695 kr; but ask about weekend/summer rates June–Aug and Fri–Sun all year—you can save over 200 kr, 10 percent discount when you show this book, CC, sauna, exercise room, Vesterbrogade 11B, DK-1620 Copenhagen, tel. 33 31 14 32, fax 33 31 14 41, e-mail: webers@scandic-hotels.com).

Ibsens Hotel is an elegant, 118-room hotel in a charming neighborhood away from the station commotion and a short walk from the old center (Sb-925–1,025 kr, Db-1,100–1,300 kr, higher prices for bigger rooms, they deal on slow days, third person-200 kr, CC, Vendersgade 23, DK-1363 Copenhagen, bus #14, #16, or #40 from the station, or S-tog: Nørreport, tel. 33 13 19 13, fax 33 13 19 16, e-mail: hotel@ibsenshotel.dk).

Sophie Amalie Hotel is a classy and modern Danish-style hotel a block from the big cruise-ship harbor and a block from trendy Nyhavn (134 rooms, Sb-875/1,075/1,275 kr, Db-1,075/1,175/1,275 kr, prices vary with size of room from pretty tight to very spacious and include "environmental fee" of 22.50 kr,

Copenhagen Hotels

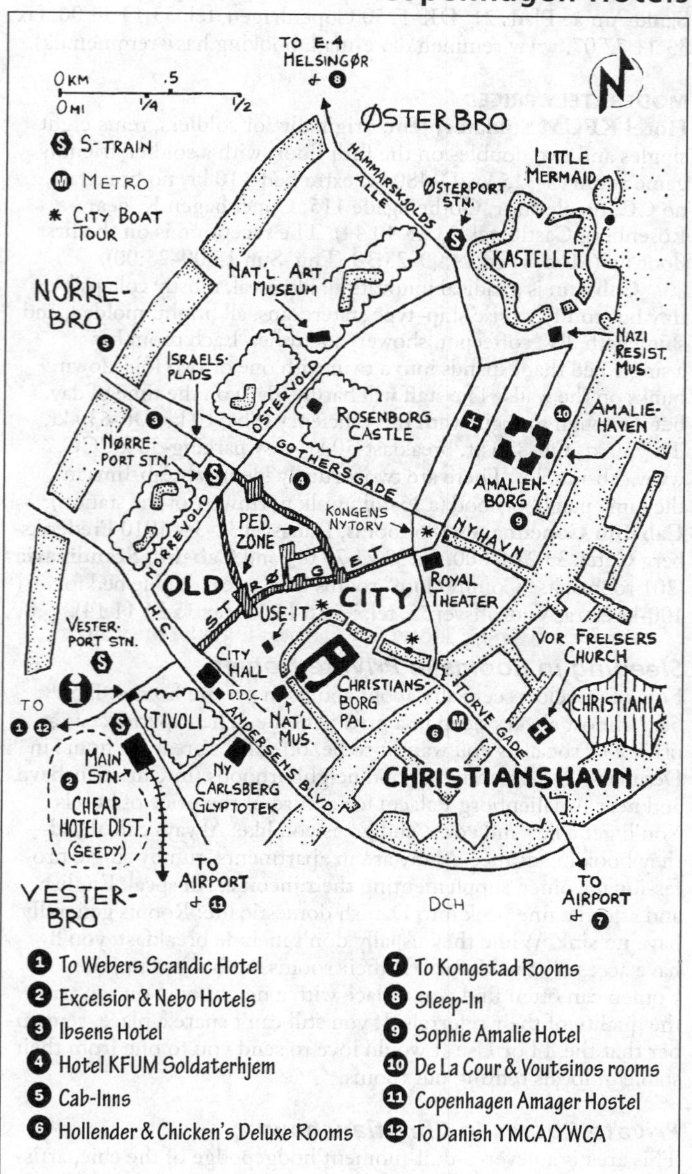

breakfast-95 kr, CC, but pay with cash and get 10 percent off, Sankt Annae Plads 21, DK-1250 Copenhagen, tel. 33 13 34 00, fax 33 11 77 07, www.remmen.dk, e-mail: booking.has@remmen.dk).

MODERATELY PRICED

Hotel KFUM Soldaterhjem, originally for soldiers, rents eight singles and two doubles on the fifth floor, with a soldier-friendly game room (S-315 kr, D-480 kr, extra bed-110 kr, no breakfast, no CC, no elevator, Gothersgade 115, Copenhagen K, near Rosenberg Castle, tel. 33 15 40 44). The reception is on the first floor up (Mon–Wed 14:00–23:30, Thu–Sun 15:00–23:00).

Cab-Inn is a radical innovation: identical, mostly collapsible, tiny but comfy, cruise ship–type staterooms, all bright, molded, and shiny with TV, coffeepot, shower, and toilet. Each room has a single bed that expands into a twin with one or two fold-down bunks on the walls. The staff will hardly give you the time of day, but it's tough to argue with this efficiency (Sb-510 kr, Db-630 kr, Tb-750 kr, Qb-870 kr, breakfast-50 kr, easy parking-50 kr, CC, www.cab-inn.dk). There are two virtually identical Cab-Inns in the same neighborhood (a 15-min walk northwest of the station): **Cab-Inn Copenhagen** (86 rooms, Danasvej 32-34, 1910 Frederiksberg C, tel. 33 21 04 00, fax 33 21 74 09) and **Cab-Inn Scandinavia** (201 rooms, its "Commodore" rooms have a real double bed for 100-kr extra, Vodroffsvej 55, tel. 35 36 11 11, fax 35 36 11 14).

Sleeping in Rooms in Private Homes

Lots of travelers seem shy about rooms in private homes. Don't be. I almost always sleep in a private home. The experience is as private or social as you want it to be, offering a great "at home in Denmark" opportunity in good neighborhoods (in Christianshavn and near Amalienborg Palace) for a third of the price of hotels. You'll get a key and come and go as you like. Always call ahead—they book in advance. Many are in apartments, run by single professional women supplementing their income. All speak English and afford a fine peek into Danish domestic life. Rooms generally have no sink. While they usually don't include breakfast, you'll have access to the kitchen. If their rooms are booked up, the women can often find you a place with a neighbor. You can trust the quality of their referrals. If you still can't snare a place, remember that the TI or Use It would love to send you to one from their stable of locals renting out rooms.

Private Rooms in Christianshavn

This area is a never-a-dull-moment hodgepodge of the chic, artistic, hippie, and hobo, with beer-drinking Greenlanders harmlessly

Christianshavn

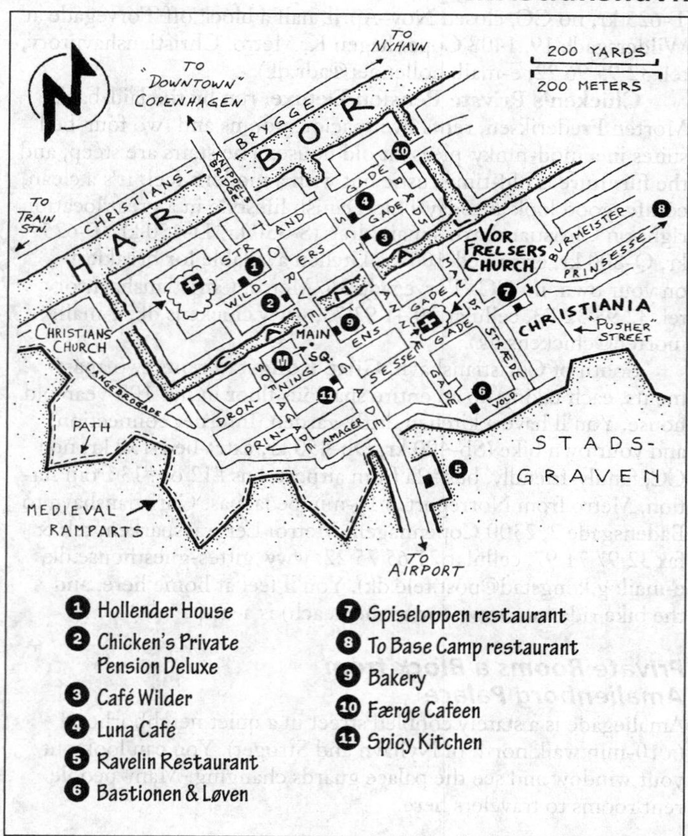

littering streets in the shadow of fancy government ministries. Colorful with lots of shops, cafés, and canals, Christianshavn is an easy 10-minute walk to the center and has good bus connections to the airport and downtown. Take bus #2a or #8 to City Hall or the Central Station and #2a to the airport. The new Metro connects Christianshavn and Nørreport (2 stops on S-tog from main train station).

LOWER PRICED

Annette and Rudy Hollender enjoy sharing their 300-year-old home with my readers. Even with a long and skinny staircase, sinkless rooms, and two rooms sharing one toilet/shower, it's a comfortable and cheery place to call home (S-350 kr, D-450 kr, T-625 kr, no CC, closed Nov–April, half a block off Torvegade at Wildersgade 19, 1408 Copenhagen K, Metro: Christianshavntorv, tel. 32 95 96 22, e-mail: hollender@adr.dk).

Chicken's Private Pension Deluxe, run by the laid-back Morten Frederiksen, rents five spacious rooms and two four-bed suites in a mod-funky-pleasant old house. The stairs are steep, and the furniture is old-time rustic but with a modern feel. It's a clean, comfy, good look at today's hip Danish lifestyle in a great location right on Christianshavn's main drag (S-350 kr, D-450 kr, T-625 kr, Q-800 kr, extra bed-100 kr, kitchen available for breakfast on your own, no CC, Torvegade 36, Metro: Christianshavntorv, tel. 32 95 32 73, cellular 20 41 92 73, www.chickens.dk, e-mail: morten@chickens.dk).

South of Christianshavn, **Gitte Kongstad** rents two apartments, each taking up an entire spacious floor in her 100-year-old house. You'll have a kitchen, little garden, Internet connection, and your own bike (Sb-400 kr, Db-450 kr, extra bed-150 kr, no CC, family-friendly, bus #2a from airport, bus #12 or #13 from station, Metro from Nørreport, a 10-min pedal past Christianshavn to Badensgade 2, 2300 Copenhagen, Metro: Lergravsparken, tel. & fax 32 97 71 97, cellular 21 65 75 22, www.gittes-guesthouse.dk, e-mail: g.kongstad@post.tele.dk). You'll feel at home here, and the bike ride into town (or to the beach) is a snap.

Private Rooms a Block from Amalienborg Palace

Amaliegade is a stately cobbled street in a quiet neighborhood (a 10-min walk north of Nyhavn and Strøget). You can look out your window and see the palace guards changing. Many people rent rooms to travelers here.

LOWER PRICED

Puk (pron. pook) and Line (LEE-nuh) are artistic and professional women who each rent out two rooms in their wonderfully mod and Danish flats: **Puk de la Cour** (S-350 kr, D-425 kr with breakfast, extra bed-150 kr, no CC, kitchen/lounge available, Amaliegade 34, fourth floor, tel. 33 12 04 68, cellular 23 72 96 45, e-mail: holgerdelacour@private.dk) and **Line Voutsinos** (May–Sept only, 2 double rooms, 1 with queen bed, 1 with 2 large single beds, D-425 kr including breakfast, extra bed-150 kr, no CC, Amaliegade 34, third floor, tel. & fax 33 14 71 42, e-mail: line.voutsinos @privat.dk). Down the street, **Mrs. Thordahl** also rents rooms (S-350 kr, D-400 kr, no breakfast, no CC, Amaliegade 26, tel. 33 12 05 78, e-mail: t.thordahl@mail.tele.dk).

Sleeping in Hostels

Copenhagen energetically accommodates the young vagabond on a shoestring. The Use It office is your best source of information. Each of these places charges about 100 kr per person for a bed and breakfast. Some don't allow sleeping bags, and if you don't have your own hostel bedsheet you'll usually have to rent one for around 30 kr. IYHF hostels normally sell non-cardholders a "guest pass" for 25 kr.

The modern **Copenhagen Amager Hostel** (IYHF) is huge (528 beds), with 300-kr doubles, 390-kr triples, 460-kr quads, and five-bed dorms at 95 kr per bed (membership required, sheets-35 kr, no curfew, excellent facilities, breakfast-45 kr, dinner-65 kr, Internet access, self-serve laundry). Unfortunately, it's on the edge of town (30 min from center by bus #250s with change to #100s, direction Svanmøllen S, Vejlands Alle 200, 2300 Copenhagen S, tel. 32 52 29 08, fax 32 52 27 08, www.danhostel.dk).

The following two big, grungy, central crash pads are open in July and August only: **Danish YMCA/YWCA** (dorm bed-85 kr, 4- to 10-bed rooms, breakfast-25 kr, sheets-15 kr, Valdemarsgade 15, DK-1665, 10-min walk from train station or bus #6, tel. 33 31 15 74) and **Sleep-In** (dorm bed-90 kr plus 20-kr deposit, sheets-30 kr plus 40-kr deposit, 4- or 6-bed cubicles in a huge 452-bed room, no curfew, breakfast-10 kr, lockers, always has room and free condoms, Blegdamsvej 132, bus #1, #6, or #14 to Triangle stop and look for sign, tel. 35 26 50 59, www.sleep-in.dk).

Sleep-in Green, the "ecological hostel," is very young, cool, and open mid-April through October (95-kr bunks, sheets-30 kr, organic breakfast-30 kr, in a quiet spot a 15-min walk from center, off Nørrebrogade at Ravnsborggade 18, tel. 35 37 77 77, www.sleep-in-green.dk).

Eating in Copenhagen

Cheap Meals

For a quick lunch, try a *smørrebrød*, a *pølse*, or a picnic. Finish it off with a pastry.

Smørrebrød

Denmark's 300-year-old tradition of open-face sandwiches survives. Find a *smørrebrød* take-out shop and choose two or three that look good (around 15 kr each). You'll get them wrapped and ready for a park bench. With a cold drink, it makes for a fine, quick, and very Danish lunch. Tradition calls for three sandwich courses: herring first, then meat, then cheese. Downtown, you'll find these handy local alternatives to Yankee fast-food chains:

Tria Cafe (Mon–Fri 8:00–14:00, closed Sat–Sun, Gothersgade 12, near Kongens Nytorv); **Café Halvvejen** for sit-down *smørrebrød* (lunch only, on Krystalgade near the Round Tower); **Sorgenfri** for a local experience in a dark, woody spot just off Strøget (Brolæggerstræde 8, Mon–Sat 11:00–21:00, Sun 12:00–21:00, tel. 33 11 58 80), and, my favorite, **Domhusets Smørrebrød** (Mon–Fri 7:00–14:30, Kattesundet 18, near Gammeltorv/Nytorv, tel. 33 15 98 98).

The Pølse

The famous Danish hot dog, sold in *pølsevogn* (sausage wagons) throughout the city, is another typically Danish institution that has resisted the onslaught of our global, Styrofoam-packaged, fast-food culture. Study the photo menu for variations. These are fast, cheap, tasty, and—like their American cousins—almost worthless nutritionally. Even so, what the locals call the "dead man's finger" is the dog kids love to bite.

There's more to getting a *pølse* than simply ordering a hot dog. Employ these handy phrases: *rød* (red, the basic weenie); *medister* (spicy, better quality); *knæk* (short, stubby, tastier than *rød); ristet* (fried); *brød* (a bun, usually smaller than the sausage); *svøb* ("swaddled" in bacon); *Fransk* (French style, buried in a long skinny hole in the bun with sauce); and *flottenheimer* (a fat one with onions and sauce). *Sennep* is mustard and *ristet løg* are crispy, fried onions. Wash everything down with a *sodavand* (soda pop).

By hanging around a *pølsevogn*, you can study this institution. Denmark's "cold feet cafés" are a form of social care: People who have difficulty finding jobs are licensed to run these wiener-mobiles. As they gain seniority, they are promoted to work at more central locations. Danes like to gather here for munchies and *pølsesnak* the local slang for empty chatter (literally "sausage talk").

Picnics

Throughout Copenhagen, small delis *(viktualiehandler)* sell fresh bread, tasty pastries, juice, milk, cheese, and yogurt (drinkable, in tall liter boxes). Two of the largest supermarket chains are **Irma** (in arcade on Vesterbrogade next to Tivoli) and **Super Brugsen**. **Netto** is a cut-rate outfit with the cheapest prices. The little grocery store in the central station is expensive but handy (daily 8:00–24:00).

Pastry

Bakeries have a golden pretzel sign hanging over the door or windows. The pastry we call a Danish is called a *wienerbrød* (Vienna bread) in Denmark. It's named for the Viennese bakers who brought the art of pastry-making to Denmark, where the Danes say they perfected it. Try these bakeries: **Nansens** (on corner of Nansensgade and Ahlefeldtsgade near Ibsens Hotel), **Kransekagehuset** (in Pilegaarden on Pilestræde, just off Strøget, near Kongens Nytorv), and **Lagekagehuset** (on Torvegade in Christianshavn).

If you want to try your hand at making Danish pastries, **KKA**, a community center offering night classes for locals, provides cooking classes in July to tourists. Learn to bake Danish pastry or make a traditional Danish lunch (300 kr, Danish pastry, Wed 14:00–17:00; Danish lunch, Mon 17:00–20:00; tel. 33 30 66 88, www.kka.dk).

Dining with Danes

For a unique experience and a great opportunity to meet locals in their homes, try dining with a Danish family. You can book these dinners through two of the city's TIs. The Wonderful Copenhagen TI offers **Dine with the Danes** for 260 kr (reserve 1 day in advance, tel. 26 85 39 61, www.dinewiththedanes.dk). **Meet the Danes** does the same thing for 425 kr for one person and 360 kr for more than one person (tel. 33 46 46 46, www.meetthedanes.dk). For information on the TIs, see "Tourist Information," above.

Restaurants

Eating in the Center

Det Lille Apotek, the "little pharmacy," is a reasonable, candle-lit place that's been popular with locals for 200 years (sandwich lunches, traditional dinners for 120–170 kr nightly from 17:30, just off Strøget, between Frue Church and Round Tower at St. Kannikestræde 15, tel. 33 12 56 06). Their specialty is "Stone Beef," a big slab of tender, raw steak plopped down in front of you on a scalding-hot lava stone. Flip it over a few times and it's cooked within minutes.

Riz-Raz has two locations in Copenhagen: around the corner from the canal boat rides at Kompagnistræde 20 (tel. 33 15 05 75) and across from Det Lille Apotek at Store Kannikestræde 19 (tel. 33 32 33 45). At both places, you'll find a healthy all-you-can-eat 49-kr Mediterranean/vegetarian buffet lunch (daily 11:30–16:00) and an even bigger 59-kr dinner buffet (until 24:00). The dinner has to be the best deal in town. And they're happy to serve free water with your meal.

Cafe Norden, smoky and very Danish with fine pastries, overlooks Amagertorv by the swan fountain. They have good light meals and salads and great people-watching from window seats on the second floor (order at the bar upstairs).

Bryggeriet Apollo, just outside the main entrance to Tivoli, offers pub atmosphere Danish-style. Beer is brewed on the premises (look for the large copper kettles downstairs) while the kitchen cranks out generous portions of meat-and-potatoes dishes for reasonable prices (1-course dinner-135 kr, 2 courses-190 kr, 3 courses-225 kr, Mon–Sat 11:30–24:00, Sun 15:00–24:00, kitchen closes from 14:30–17:30 and at 22:00, Vesterbrogade 3, reservations smart in summertime, tel. 33 12 33 13). Try their "beer of the month" in quarter-liter, half-liter, or one-liter glasses. You have to give up a shoe for a deposit on the one-liter glass so that you don't run off with it!

Gråbrødretorv is perhaps the most popular square in the old center for a meal. It's a food circus—especially in good weather. Choose from Greek, Mexican, Danish, or a meal in the old streetcar #14.

Department stores serving cheery, reasonable meals in their cafeterias include **Illum** (head to the elegant glass-domed top floor, Østergade 52) and **Magasin** (Kongens Nytorv 13), which also has a great grocery and deli in the basement.

Gammel Strand serves "Danish-inspired French cuisine" and is ideal for a dressy splurge in the old center (3-course menu-300 kr, Mon–Sat 12:00–15:00 & 17:30–22:00, closed Sun, reservations wise, across from "Canal Tours Copenhagen" tour boats at Gammel Strand 42, tel. 33 91 21 21).

Eating in Christianshavn

This neighborhood is so cool, it's worth combining an evening wander with dinner even if you're not staying here.

Færge Cafeen is a fun-loving pub with a local following serving inexpensive traditional Danish specialties indoors or along the canal (daily specials about 70 kr, daily 12:00–16:00 & 17:00–21:00, Strandgade 50, tel. 32 54 46 24).

Twin cafés serve creative and hearty dinner salads by candlelight to a trendy local clientele: **Café Wilder** serves a three-salad plate (61 kr with bread) and a budget dinner plate for around 85 kr (tel. 32 54 71 83). Across the street, **Luna Café** is also good and serves a slower-paced meal (reservations recommended, tel. 32 54 20 00). Each are open daily until 24:00 and located at the corner of Wildersgade and Skt. Annæ Gade, a block off Torvegade.

Ravelin Restaurant, on a tiny island on the big road just south of Christianshavn, serves good, traditional Danish food at reasonable prices to happy local crowds. Dine indoors or on the lovely lakeside terrace (*smørrebrød* lunches 40–100 kr, dinners 100–170 kr, Torvegade 79, tel. 32 96 20 45).

Bastionen & Løven, at the little windmill (Lille Mølle), serves Scandinavian nouveau cuisine from a small but fresh menu on a Renoir terrace or in its Rembrandt interior (85-kr lunch specials; 145–180-kr dinners, 310-kr 3-course menu; 125-kr weekend brunch; daily 10:00–24:00, brunch Sat–Sun 10:00–14:00, Voldgade 50, walk to the end of Torvegade and follow the ramparts up to the restaurant, at south end of Christianshavn, tel. 32 95 09 40).

Lagkagehuset, with a big selection of pastries and excellent freshly baked bread and sandwiches, is a great place for breakfast (take-out coffee and pastries for 15 kr, Torvegade 45). **Spicy Kitchen** serves cheap and good Indian food (Torvegade 56).

In Christiania, the wonderfully classy **Spiseloppen** (meaning "the flea eats") serves great 120-kr vegetarian meals and 150-kr meaty ones by candlelight. Christiania is the free city/squatter town, located three blocks behind the spiral spire of Vor Frelser's church (restaurant open Tue–Sun 17:00–22:00, closed Mon, on top floor of old brick warehouse, turn right just inside Christiania's gate, reservations often necessary on weekends, tel. 32 57 95 58).

Base Camp lets you eat/drink/party in a military barracks converted into a sprawling restaurant with enough seating for you and 800 travel companions. Dance under an enormous disco ball inside, or settle a lounge chair into the sand at a grill table where you choose some tapas and a slab of raw meat or fish to cook (from 150 kr). Tucked away 400 meters/1,300 feet past Christiania (go 400 meters/1,300 feet out Prinsessegade, cross the hidden canal at Trangravsvej, look right), it's a great place to mingle with young, festive Danes (dinners daily from 18:00, disco usually Fri–Sat until dawn, 90-kr brunch Sun 11:00–15:00, occasionally closes for private parties, call ahead for evening's events, tel. 70 23 23 18).

Eating near Nørreport

These places are near the recommended Ibsens Hotel. **Kost Bar** serves good-sized portions of pub fare, indoors or outdoors (50–75 kr for lunch, 75–120 kr for dinner, daily 11:00–late, Vendersgade 16, tel. 33 33 00 35). **Café Klimt,** which draws a young, hip, heavy-smoking crowd, offers great omelettes and sandwiches (50–100 kr, Frederickborggade 29, tel. 33 11 76 70). **El Porron** has good Spanish tapas (Vendersgade 10, a block from Ibsens Hotel near Nørreport).

Transportation Connections—Copenhagen

By train to: Hillerød/Frederiksborg (6/hr, 40 min), **Louisiana Museum** (take regional train—*regionaltog*—in the direction of Helsingør to Humlebæk, 3/hr, 40 min; or connect from Frederiksborg Castle—see listing below), **Roskilde** (1–3/hr, 30 min),

Odense (2/hr, 1.75 hrs), **Helsingør** (3/hr, 50 min), **Malmö** (3/hr, 35 min), **Stockholm** (11/day, 5 hrs on X2000 high-speed train, night service via Malmö 23:10–6:10, take regional train to Malmö first), **Växjö** (5/day, 2.5 hrs), **Kalmar** (5/day, 3.75 hrs), **Oslo** (3/day, 8–9 hrs, change in Göteborg or Malmö, Sweden; no night train), **Berlin** (4/day, 9 hrs, via Hamburg), **Amsterdam** (2/day, 11 hrs), and **Frankfurt/Rhine** (4/day, 8 hrs). Convenient overnight trains from Copenhagen run to Stockholm, Amsterdam, and Frankfurt, some with one connection. National train info tel. 70 13 14 15. International train info tel. 70 13 14 16. Cheaper bus trips are listed at Use It.

Overnight Cruises to Oslo

Luxurious DFDS cruise ships leave nightly from Copenhagen for Oslo, and from Oslo for Copenhagen. The 16-hour sailings leave at 17:00 and arrive at 9:00 the next day. So you can spend eight hours in Norway's capital and then return to Copenhagen, or take this cruise from Oslo and do Copenhagen as a day trip. Or just go one-way in either direction.

One-way costs: bed in standard inside quad-$136, bed in standard inside double-$157, single cabin-$212. Round-trip is simply double the cost unless you go and return on two successive nights, which is a good value: round-trip with bed in standard inside double costs $235 per person, plus $74 per person for a meal package that includes two breakfast buffets and two dinner buffets.

DFDS operates two ships on this route—the M.S. *Pearl of Scandinavia* and the M.S. *Crown of Scandinavia*. Both offer all the cruise-ship luxuries: big buffets for breakfast and dinner (at an additional cost), a kids' playroom, pool (outdoor & indoor on the *Crown*, indoor on the *Pearl)*, sauna, nightclub, and tax-free shopping (Danish office tel. 33 42 30 00, 800/533-3755 in the U.S., www.seaeurope.com).

NEAR COPENHAGEN: ROSKILDE, FREDERIKSBORG CASTLE, LOUISIANA, KRONBORG CASTLE

Copenhagen's the star, but there are several worthwhile sights nearby, and the public transportation system makes side-tripping a joy. Visit Roskilde's great Viking ships and royal cathedral. Tour Frederiksborg, Denmark's most spectacular castle, and slide along the cutting edge at Louisiana—a superb art museum with a coastal setting as striking as its art. At Helsingør, do the dungeons of Kronborg Castle before heading on to Sweden.

Planning Your Time

Roskilde's Viking ships and the Frederiksborg Castle are the area's essential sights. Each take a half day; they're both easy 30- to 40-minute commutes from Copenhagen (followed by a 15-min walk). You'll find fewer tour-bus crowds in the afternoon. While you're in Roskilde, you can also pay your respects to the tombs of the Danish royalty.

If you're choosing between castles, Frederiksborg is the beautiful showpiece, and Kronborg—darker and danker—is more typical of the way most castles really were.

By car, you can see these sights on your way into or out of Copenhagen. By train, do day trips from Copenhagen—then sleep to and from Copenhagen while traveling to Oslo (overnight cruise) or Stockholm (night train). Consider getting a Copenhagen Card (see "Orientation" at the beginning of the chapter), which covers your transportation and admission to all major sights.

ROSKILDE

Denmark's roots, both Viking and royal, are on display in Roskilde, a pleasant town 30 kilometers/18 miles west of Copenhagen. Five hundred years ago, Roskilde was Denmark's leading city. Today the town that introduced Christianity to Denmark in A.D. 980 is most famous for hosting northern Europe's biggest annual rock/jazz/folk festival (June 26–29 in 2003). Wednesday and Saturday are flower/flea/produce market days. Its TI is helpful (Mon–Fri 9:00–17:00, Sat 10:00–13:00, open 1 hour later late June–Aug, closed Sun, 3 blocks from cathedral, follow signs to *Turistbureau*, tel. 46 35 27 00, fax 46 35 14 74). Roskilde is an easy side-trip from Copenhagen by train (1–3/hr, 30 min).

Sights—Roskilde

▲▲Roskilde Cathedral—Roskilde's imposing 12th-century, twin-spired cathedral houses the tombs of 38 Danish kings and queens. It's a stately, modern-looking old church with great marble work, paintings (notice the impressive 3-D painting with Christian IV looking like a pirate, in the room behind the small pipe organ), wood carvings in and around the altar, a great 16th-century Baroque organ, and a silly little glockenspiel that plays high above the entrance at the top of every hour (15 kr, good 25-kr guidebook, April–Sept Mon–Sat 9:00–16:45, Sun 13:00–16:45; Oct–March Tue–Fri 10:00–15:45, Sat 11:30–15:45, Sun 13:00–15:45, closed Mon; occasionally closes during the day for baptisms and weddings, private tours available for 400 kr, tel. 46 35 27 00). From the cathedral, it's a pleasant walk through a park down to the harbor and Viking ships.

▲▲▲Viking Ship Museum (Vikingeskibshallen)—Roskilde is strategically located on a shallow inlet. (*Vik* means shallow inlet). Vikings are people who lived along them. Roskilde's award-winning museum displays five different Viking ships—one boat is like the one Leif Eriksson took to America 1,000 years ago; another is like those depicted in the Bayeux Tapestry. The descriptions are excellent—and in English. It's the kind of museum where you want to read everything. As you enter, buy the 15-kr guidebook and request the 22-minute English-language movie introduction. These ships were deliberately sunk 1,000 years ago to block a nearby harbor and were only recently excavated, preserved, and pieced together. The ships aren't as intact or as ornate as those in Oslo, but this museum does a better job of explaining shipbuilding (60-kr entry, less off-season, daily May–Sept 9:00–17:00, Oct–April 10:00–16:00, from station catch bus #605 toward Boserup, 2/hr, 7-min ride, tel. 46 30 02 00). Inside, you'll find an informative exhibit (offered through 2003) on the Vikings in Ireland; those busy redheads were the founders of Dublin. An archaeological workshop lets visitors observe the ongoing work on newly discovered ships (10:00–15:00), and a fun outdoor workshop gives wanna-be Vikings some hands-on fun.

FREDERIKSBORG CASTLE AND HILLERØD

The castle is located in the cute town of Hillerød. The town's traffic-free center is worth a wander (just outside the gates of the mighty Frederiksborg Castle, past the TI). Hillerød's TI can book rooms in private homes for 125 kr to 175 kr per person (Mon–Fri 10:00–18:00, Sat 10:00–15:00, closed Sun, Slangerupgade 2, tel. 48 24 26 26, www.hillerodturist.dk, e-mail: turistbureau@hillkomm.dk).

To reach the castle from Copenhagen, take the S-tog to Hillerød (6/hr, 40 min) and enjoy a pleasant 15-minute walk, or catch bus #701 or #702 (free with S-tog ticket, or Copenhagen Card) from the train station (tel. 48 26 04 39).

▲▲Frederiksborg Castle—This grandest castle in Scandinavia is often called the Danish Versailles. Frederiksborg (built 1602–1620) is the castle of Denmark's king Christian IV. Much of it was reconstructed after an 1859 fire, with the normal Victorian over-the-top flair, by the brewer J. C. Jacobsen and his Carlsberg Foundation.

A museum since 1878, it takes you on a chronological walk through the story of Denmark from 1500 until today (the third floor covers modern times). Many rooms have a handy English information sheet. The countless musty paintings are a fascinating scrapbook of Danish history.

Sights near Copenhagen

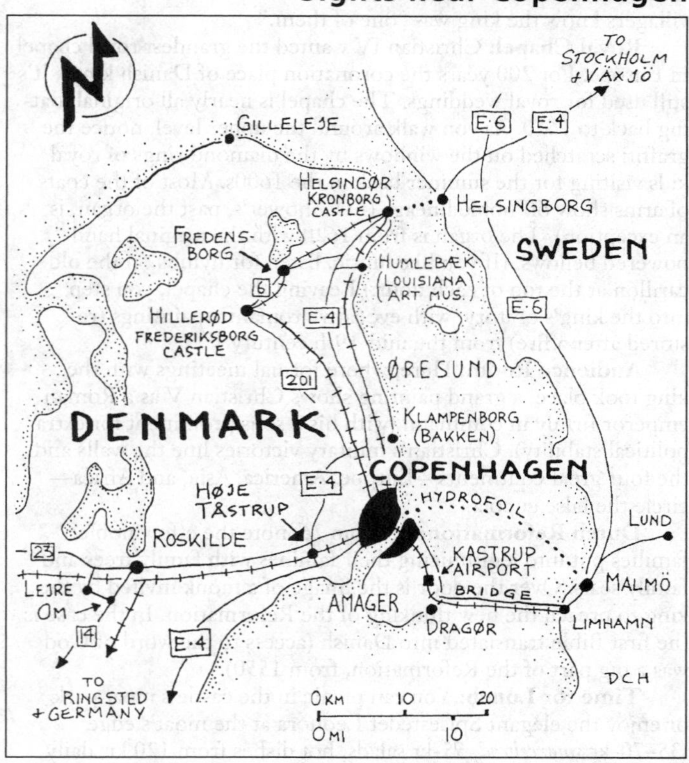

Cost and Hours: 50 kr, daily April–Oct 10:00–17:00, Nov–March 11:00–15:00. Drivers will find easy parking.

Approach: You can almost hear the crackle of royal hoofs as you walk over the moat through the first island (which housed the small businesses needed to support a royal residence), the second island (home to the government when the king was here—domestic and foreign ministries), and then down a windy (easy to defend) lane to the main palace—where the king lived.

Main Courtyard: Survey the castle exterior from the Fountain of Neptune in the main courtyard. Christian IV imported Dutch architects to create this Christian IV style, which you'll see all over Copenhagen. The brickwork and sandstone are products of the local clay and sandy soil. The building, with its horizontal lines, triangles, and squares, is generally Renaissance style. But notice how this is interrupted by a few token Gothic elements on the church's facade. This homey touch was to let the villagers know the king was "one of them."

Royal Chapel: Christian IV wanted the grandest royal chapel in Europe. For 200 years the coronation place of Danish kings, it's still used for royal weddings. The chapel is nearly all original, dating back to 1620. As you walk around the upper level, notice the graffiti scratched on the windows by the diamond rings of royal kids visiting for the summer back in the 1600s. Most of the coats of arms show off noble lineage (Eisenhower's, past the organ, is an exception). The organ is from 1620 with the original hand-powered bellows. (If you like music, listen for hymns on the old carillon at the top of each hour.) Leaving the chapel, you step into the king's oratory, with evocative romantic paintings (restored after a fire) from the mid-19th century.

Audience Room: Here, where formal meetings with the king took place, a grand painting shows Christian V as a Roman emperor firmly in command (with his 2 sons prominent for extra political stability). Christian's military victories line the walls and the four great continents—Europe, America, Asia, and Africa—circle the false cupola.

Dutch Reformation: In room 26, note the effort noble families put into legitimizing their families with family trees and family seals. Over the door is the image of a monk invited by the king to preach the new thinking of the Reformation. In the case is the first Bible translated into Danish (access to the word of God was a big part of the Reformation, from 1550).

Time for Lunch: You can picnic in the castle's moat park or enjoy the elegant Spisestedet Leonora at the moat's edge (35–70-kr *smørrebrød*, 55-kr salads, hot dishes from 120 kr, daily 10:00–17:00, slow service, tel. 48 26 75 16).

LOUISIANA

This is Scandinavia's most raved-about modern art museum. Located in the town of Humlebæk, beautifully situated on the coast 30 kilometers/18 miles north of Copenhagen, Louisiana is a holistic place that masterfully mixes its art, architecture, and landscape. Wander from famous Chagalls and Picassos to more obscure art. Poets spend days here nourishing their creative souls with new angles, ideas, and perspectives. Frequent special exhibitions allow visitors an extra treat (visit www.louisiana.dk for the latest). The views over one of the busiest passages in the nautical world (the Øresund) are nearly as inspiring as the art. The cafeteria (indoor/outdoor) is reasonable and welcomes picnickers who buy a drink (68-kr museum admission; discount with Copenhagen Card; included in a special 120-kr round-trip/tour ticket from

Copenhagen—ask at Copenhagen's TI or any train station; daily 10:00–17:00, Wed until 22:00, tel. 49 19 07 91).

Take the train from Copenhagen toward Helsingør, get off at Humlebæk (3/hr, 40 min), and follow the signs to Louisiana along a busy road about 15 minutes. Or walk 10 minutes through the woods—exit the station and immediately go left onto Hejreskor Allé, a residential street, and then along a path through the woods. If you're coming from Frederiksborg Castle, catch the "Lille Nord" train at Hillerød station toward Helsingør. Change trains at Snekkersten or Helsingør, and go south to reach Humlebæk.

KRONBORG CASTLE AND HELSINGØR

Often confused with its Swedish sister, Helsingborg, just three kilometers/1.9 miles across the channel, Helsingør is a small, pleasant Danish town with a TI (tel. 49 21 13 33), medieval center, Kronborg Castle, and lots of Swedes who come over for lower-priced alcohol.

There's a fine beachfront hostel, **Vandrerhjem Villa Moltke** (dorm bed-110 kr, S-250 kr, Sb-400 kr, D-300 kr, Db-400 kr, T-350 kr, Tb-400 kr, larger rooms available, nonmembers 30-kr extra per night, breakfast-45 kr, 1.5 km/1 mile north of castle, Nedre Strandvej 24, tel. 49 21 16 40, fax 49 21 13 99, www.helsingorhostel.dk). People who prefer small towns and small prices can day-trip to Copenhagen by train (5/hr, 50 min) with this hostel as their base.

▲▲Kronborg Castle—Helsingør's Kronborg Castle (also called Elsinore) is famous for its questionable (but profitable) ties to Shakespeare. Most of the "Hamlet" castle you'll see today, darling of every big bus tour and travelogue, was built long after Hamlet died, and Shakespeare never saw the place. But there was a castle here in Hamlet's day, and a troupe of English actors worked here in Shakespeare's time (Shakespeare may have known them). To see or not to see? It's most impressive from the outside.

If you're heading to Sweden, Kalmar Castle (see the South Sweden chapter) is a better medieval castle. But you're here, and if you like castles, see Kronborg. Duck in the creepy casements under the castle where the servants and guards lived.

The royal apartments include English explanations (40 kr, daily May–Sept 10:30–17:00, April and Oct Tue–Sun 11:00–16:00, Nov and March Tue–Sun 11:00–15:00, closed Dec–Feb, 2 tours/day, tel. 49 21 30 78 for recorded info or 49 21 80 88). Don't miss the 20-minute dungeon tours that leave on the half-hour. In the basement, notice the statue of Holger Danske, a mythical Viking hero revered by Danish children. The story goes that if the nation is ever in danger, this Danish superman will awaken and restore peace and security to the land.

The free grounds between the walls and sea are great for picnics, with a pleasant view of the strait between Denmark and Sweden.

ØRE-CITY

When the Øresund (pron. UH-ra-soond) Bridge, which connects Denmark and Sweden, opened in July 2000, it created Europe's newest and perhaps most dynamic new metropolitan area. Overnight, the link forged an economic power with the 12th-largest gross domestic product in Europe. The "Øresund region" has surpassed Stockholm as the largest metro area in Scandinavia. Now 3.5 million Danes and Swedes—a highly trained and highly technical workforce—are within an easy commute of each other.

The bridge opens up new questions of borders. Historically, southern Sweden (the area across from Copenhagen, called Skåne) has Danish blood. It was Danish for 1,000 years before Sweden took it in 1658. Notice how Copenhagen is the capital on the fringe of its realm—at one time it was in the center.

The 16-kilometer/10-mile-long link, which has a motorway for cars (220-kr toll) and a two-track train line, ties together the main islands of Denmark with Europe and Sweden. The $4 billion project consists of a four-kilometer/2.5-mile-long tunnel, an artificial island called Peberholm, and an eight-kilometer/five-mile-long bridge. With speedy connecting trains, Malmö in Sweden is now an easy half-day side-trip by train from Copenhagen (65 kr each way, 3/hr, 35 min), or by tour bus from Copenhagen (Thu only, see "Tours of Copenhagen," above).

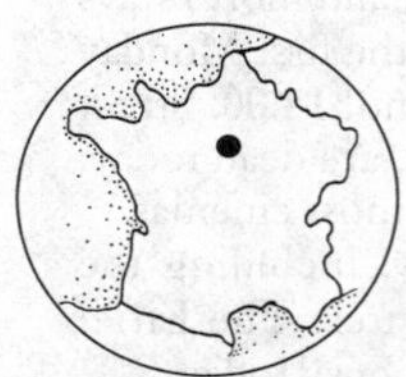

PARIS

Paris offers sweeping boulevards, sleepy parks, world-class art galleries, chatty crêpe stands, Napoleon's body, sleek shopping malls, the Eiffel Tower, and people-watching from outdoor cafés. Climb the Notre-Dame and the Eiffel Tower, cruise the Seine and the Champs-Elysées, and master the Louvre and Orsay Museums. Save some after-dark energy for one of the world's most romantic cities. Many people fall in love with Paris. Some see the essentials and flee, overwhelmed by the huge city. With the proper approach and a good orientation, you'll fall head over heels for Europe's capital.

Planning Your Time: Paris in One, Two, or Three Days

Day 1

Morning: Follow "Historic Core of Paris" Walk (see "Sights," below), featuring Ile de la Cité, Notre-Dame, Latin Quarter, and Sainte-Chapelle (consider lunch at nearby Samaritaine view café).
Afternoon: Visit the Pompidou Center (at least from the outside), then walk to the Marais neighborhood, visit the place des Vosges, and consider touring any of three museums nearby: Carnavalet Museum (city history), Jewish Art and History Museum, or Picasso Museum.
Evening: Cruise Seine River or take illuminated Paris by Night bus tour.

Day 2

Morning: Visit Arc de Triomphe, then walk down the Champs-Elysées to the Tuileries Garden.
Afternoon: Have lunch in the Tuileries (several lunch cafés in the park), then tour the Louvre.

Daily Reminder

Monday: These sights are closed today—Orsay, Rodin, Marmottan, Montmartre, Carnavalet, Catacombs, Giverny, and Versailles; the Louvre is more crowded because of this, but the Denon wing (with *Mona Lisa*, Venus de Milo, and more) stays open until 21:45. Napoleon's Tomb is closed the first Monday of the month. Some small stores don't open until 14:00. Street markets, such as rue Cler and rue Mouffetard, are dead today. Some banks are closed. It's discount night at most cinemas.
Tuesday: Many museums are closed today, including the Louvre, Picasso, Cluny, and Pompidou Center. The Eiffel Tower, Orsay, and Versailles are particularly busy today.
Wednesday: All sights are open (Louvre until 21:45). The weekly *Pariscope* magazine comes out today. School is out, so many kids' sights are busy. Some cinemas offer discounts.
Thursday: All sights are open (except the Sewer Tour). The Orsay is open until 21:45. Department stores are open late.
Friday: All sights are open (except the Sewer Tour). Afternoon trains and roads leaving Paris are crowded; TGV reservation fees are higher.
Saturday: All sights are open (except the Jewish Art and History Museum). The fountains run at Versailles (July–Sept). Department stores are busy. The Jewish Quarter is quiet.
Sunday: Some museums are two-thirds price all day and/or free the first Sunday of the month, thus more crowded (e.g., Louvre, Orsay, Rodin, Cluny, Pompidou, and Picasso). The fountains run at Versailles (early April–early Oct). Most of Paris' stores are closed, but shoppers find relief in the Marais' lively Jewish Quarter—and in Bercy Village, where many stores are open. Look for organ concerts at St. Sulpice and possibly other churches. The American Church sometimes offers a free evening concert at 18:00 (Sept–May only). Most recommended restaurants in the rue Cler neighborhood are closed for dinner.

Evening: Enjoy Trocadero scene and twilight ride up the Eiffel Tower.

Day 3

Morning: Tour the Orsay Museum.
Afternoon: Either tour the nearby Rodin Museum and Napoleon's Tomb or visit Versailles (take RER train direct from Orsay).
Evening: Visit Montmartre and Sacré-Coeur.

Orientation

Paris is split in half by the Seine River, divided into 20 *arrondissements* (proud and independent governmental jurisdictions), and circled by a ring-road freeway (the *périphérique)*. You'll find Paris easier to navigate if you know which side of the river you're on, which *arrondissement* you're in, and which subway (Métro) stop you're closest to. If you're north of the river (the top half of any city map), you're on the Right Bank *(rive droite)*. If you're south of it, you're on the Left Bank *(rive gauche)*. Most of your sightseeing will take place within five blocks of the river.

Arrondissements are numbered, starting at Notre-Dame (ground zero) and moving in a clockwise spiral out to the ring road. The last two digits in a Parisian zip code are the *arrondissement* number. The notation for the Métro stop is "Mo." In Parisian jargon, Napoleon's tomb is on *la rive gauche* (the Left Bank) in the *7ème* (7th *arrondissement*), zip code 75007, Mo: Invalides. Paris Métro stops are used as a standard aid in giving directions, even for those not using the Métro. As you're tracking down addresses, these definitions will help: *place* (square), *rue* (road), and *pont* (bridge).

Tourist Information

Avoid the Paris tourist offices, which are long on lines, short on information, and charge for maps. This book, *Pariscope* magazine (see below), and one of the free maps available at any hotel (plus the sights and Métro maps at the front of this book) are all you need. The main TI is at 127 avenue des **Champs-Elysées** (daily 9:00–20:00, tel. 08 36 92 31 12—phone tree), and the other, less crowded TIs are at **Gare de Lyon** (daily 8:00–20:00), the **Eiffel Tower** (May–Sept daily 11:00–18:42, yes, 18:42, closed off-season, tel. 01 45 51 22 15), and the **Louvre** (Wed–Mon 10:00–19:00, closed Tue). Both **airports** have handy TIs (called ADP) with long hours and short lines (see "Transportation Connections," below). For a complete list of museum hours and scheduled English-language museum tours, pick up the free *Musées, Monuments Historiques, et Expositions* booklet from any museum.

Pariscope: *Pariscope* weekly magazine (or one of its clones, €0.50 at any newsstand) lists museum hours, art exhibits, concerts, music festivals, plays, movies, and nightclubs. Smart tour guides and sightseers rely on this for all the latest (in French, www.pariscope.fr).

Web Sites: Here's a short list of sites that I find entertaining and, at times, useful: www.bonjourparis.com (a newsy site that claims to offer a virtual trip to Paris, with interactive French lessons, tips on wine and food, and news on the latest Parisian trends),

The Paris Museum Pass

In Paris, there are two classes of sightseers—those with a Paris museum pass, and those who stand in line. Serious sightseers save time and money by getting the pass.

Most of the sights listed in this chapter are covered by the Paris museum pass, except for the Eiffel Tower, Montparnasse Tower, Marmottan Museum, Garnier Opéra, Notre-Dame treasury, Jacquemart-André Museum, Jewish Art and History Museum, Grande Arche de la Défense, Jeu de Paume Exhibition Hall, Catacombs, *Paris Story* film, and the ladies of Pigalle. Outside Paris, the pass covers the châteaux of Versailles, Chantilly, and Fontainebleau.

The pass pays for itself in two admissions and gets you into most sights without lining up (1 day-€15, 3 consecutive days-€30, 5 consecutive days-€45, no youth or senior discount). It's sold at museums, main Métro stations (including Ecole Militaire and Bastille stations), and TIs (even at the airports). Try to avoid buying the pass at a major museum (such as the Louvre), where supply can be spotty and lines long.

The pass isn't activated until the first time you use it (you enter the date on the pass). Think and read ahead to make the most of your pass, since some museums are free (e.g., Carnavalet, the Petit Palais, and Victor Hugo's House), many are discounted on Sundays, and your pass must be used on consecutive days.

The pass isn't worth buying for children, as most museums are free for those under 18. Note that kids can skip the lines with their passholder parents.

The free museum and monuments directory that comes with your pass lists the latest hours, phone numbers, and specifics on

www.paris-touristoffice.com (the official site for Paris' TIs, offering practical information on hotels, special events, museums, children's activities, fashion, nightlife, and more), and www.paris-anglo.com (similar to bonjourparis.com, with informative stories about visiting Paris, plus a directory of over 2,500 English-speaking businesses).

Maps: While Paris is littered with free maps, they don't show all the streets. You may want the huge Michelin #10 map of Paris. For an extended stay, I prefer the pocket-size, street-indexed *Paris Pratique* (€6), with an easy-to-use Métro map.

Bookstores: There are many English-language bookstores in Paris where you can pick up guidebooks (for nearly double what kids pay. The cutoff age for free entry ranges from five to 18. Most major art museums let young people under 18 in for free, but anyone over age five has to pay to tour the sewers—go figure.

Included sights (and admission prices without the pass) you're likely to visit: Louvre (€7.50), Orsay (€7), Sainte-Chapelle (€5.50), Arc de Triomphe (€7), Les Invalides Museums/Napoleon's Tomb (€6), Conciergerie (€5.50), Panthéon (€5.50), Sewer Tour (€4), Cluny Museum (€7), Pompidou Center (€5.50), Notre-Dame towers (€5.50) and crypt (€3.50), Picasso Museum (€5.50), Rodin Museum (€5), and the Cité des Sciences et l'Industrie museum (€9). Outside Paris, the pass covers the Palace of Versailles (€7.50) and its Trianons (€5); Château of Fontainebleau (€5.50); and Château of Chantilly (€6).

Tally up what you want to see—and remember, an advantage of the pass is that you skip to the front of some lines, saving hours of waiting, especially in summer (though everyone must pass through the slow-moving metal-detector lines at some sights, and a few places, such as Notre-Dame's tower, can't accommodate a bypass lane). With the pass you'll pop freely into sights that you're walking by (even for a few minutes) that might otherwise not be worth the expense (e.g., Notre-Dame crypt, Conciergerie, Picasso Museum, and the Panthéon).

Museum Strategy: Arriving 20 minutes before major museums open is line-time well spent. Remember, most museums require you to check day packs and coats, and important museums have metal detectors that will slow your entry. If you're still ahead of the pack when you enter, consider hustling to the most popular works first.

their American prices). A few of the best: Shakespeare & Company (daily 12:00–24:00, some used travel books, 37 rue de la Bûcherie, across the river from Notre-Dame, tel. 01 43 26 96 50), W. H. Smith (248 rue de Rivoli, Mo: Concorde, tel. 01 44 77 88 99), and Brentanos (37 avenue de L'Opéra, Mo: Opéra, tel. 01 42 61 52 50). The friendly Red Wheelbarrow Bookstore in the Marais neighborhood sells Rick Steves' books (13 rue Charles V, Mo: St. Paul, tel. 01 42 77 42 17).

American Church: The American Church is a nerve center for the American émigré community. It distributes a free, handy, and insightful monthly English-language newspaper called the *Paris Voice* (with useful reviews of concerts, plays, and current events;

Paris Overview

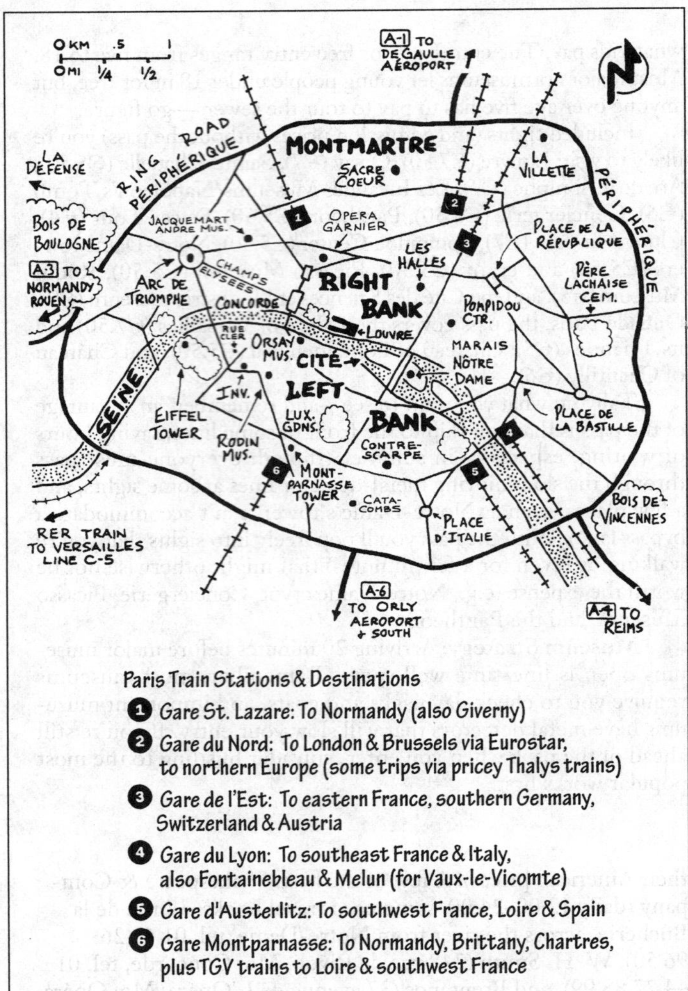

available at about 200 locations in Paris, http://parisvoice.com) and an advertisement paper called *France—U.S.A. Contacts* (full of useful information for those seeking work or long-term housing). The church faces the river between the Eiffel Tower and Orsay Museum (reception open Mon–Sat 9:30–22:30, Sun 9:00–19:30, 65 quai d'Orsay, Mo: Invalides, tel. 01 40 62 05 00).

Arrival in Paris

By Train: Paris has six train stations, all connected by Métro, bus, and taxi. All have ATMs, banks or change offices, information desks, telephones, cafés, lockers *(consigne automatique)*, newsstands, and clever pickpockets. Hop the Métro to your hotel (see "Getting around Paris," below).

By Plane: For detailed information on getting from Paris' airports to downtown Paris (and vice versa), see "Transportation Connections" at the end of this chapter.

Helpful Hints

Theft Alert: Pickpockets in Paris seem more numerous and determined than ever. Métro and RER lines that serve popular sights are infested with thieves. Be sure to wear a money belt, put your wallet in your front pocket, loop your day bag over your shoulders (consider wearing it in front), and keep a tight grip on a purse or shopping bag. If you're out late, avoid the riverfront quays if the lighting is dim and pedestrian activity is minimal.

Useful Telephone Numbers: American Hospital—01 46 41 25 25, English-speaking pharmacy—01 45 62 02 41 (Pharmacie les Champs, open 24 hrs, 84 avenue des Champs-Elysées, Mo: George V), Police—17, U.S. Embassy—01 43 12 22 22, Paris and France directory assistance—12.

Street Safety: Be careful on foot! Parisian drivers are notorious for ignoring pedestrians. Look both ways, as many streets are one-way, and be careful of seemingly quiet bus/taxi lanes. Don't assume you have the right of way, even in a crosswalk. When crossing a street, keep your pace constant and don't stop suddenly. By law, drivers must miss pedestrians by one meter/three feet (1.5 meters/5 feet in the countryside). Drivers carefully calculate your speed and won't hit you, provided you don't alter your route or pace.

Watch out for a lesser hazard: *merde*. Parisian dogs decorate the city's sidewalks with 16 tons of droppings a day. People get injured by slipping in it.

Toilets: Carry small change for pay toilets, or walk into any sidewalk café like you own the place and find the toilet in the back. The toilets in museums are free and generally the best you'll find, and if you have a museum pass, you can drop into almost any museum for the clean toilets. Modern, super-sanitary, street-booth toilets provide both relief and a memory (coins required, don't leave small children inside unattended). Keep some toilet paper or tissues with you, as some toilets are poorly supplied.

Getting around Paris

By Métro

By Métro: Europe's best subway is divided into two systems—the Métro (for puddle-jumping everywhere in Paris; see map in this book) and the RER (connects suburban destinations with a few stops in central Paris). You'll use the Métro for almost all your trips (daily from 5:30 until 00:30). Occasionally, you'll find the RER more convenient, as it makes fewer stops (like an express bus).

Tickets and Passes: In Paris, you're never more than a 10-minute walk from a Métro station. One ticket takes you anywhere in the system with unlimited transfers. Save 40 percent by buying a ***carnet*** (pron. car-nay) of 10 tickets for €10 at any Métro station (a single ticket is €1.40, kids 4–10 pay €5 for a *carnet*). Métro tickets work on city buses, though one ticket cannot be used as a transfer between subway and bus. If you're staying in Paris for a week or more, consider the ***Carte Orange*** (pron. kart oh-rahnzh), which gives you free run of the bus and Métro system for one week (about €15, ask for *Carte Orange Coupon Vert* and supply a passport-size photo) or a month (about €50, ask for *Carte Orange Coupon Orange*). These passes cover only central Paris; you can pay more for passes covering regional destinations (such as Versailles). The weekly pass begins Monday and ends Sunday, and the monthly pass is valid from the first to last day of the month, so midweek or mid-month pass purchases aren't worthwhile. All passes can be purchased at any Métro station, most of which have photo booths where you can get the photo required for the pass. While some Métro agents may hesitate to sell you *Carte Orange* passes because you're not a resident (and encourage you to buy the bad-value *Paris Visite* pass instead), *Carte Orange* passes are definitely not limited to residents; if you're refused, simply go to another station to buy your pass. The overpriced ***Paris Visite*** passes were designed for tourists, offering minor reductions at minor sights but costing more than a *carnet* of 10 tickets or a *Carte Orange* (1 day-€9, 2 days-€14, 3 days-€19, 5 days-€28).

How the Métro works: To get to your destination, determine the closest "Mo" stop and which line or lines will get you there. The lines have numbers, but they're best known by their direction or end-of-the-line stop. (For example, the La Défense/Château de Vincennes line runs between La Défense in the west and Vincennes in the east.) Once in the Métro station, you'll see blue-and-white signs directing you to the train going in your direction (e.g., *direction: La Défense*). Insert your ticket in the automatic turnstile, pass through, and reclaim and keep your ticket until you exit the system. Fare inspectors regularly check

Paris

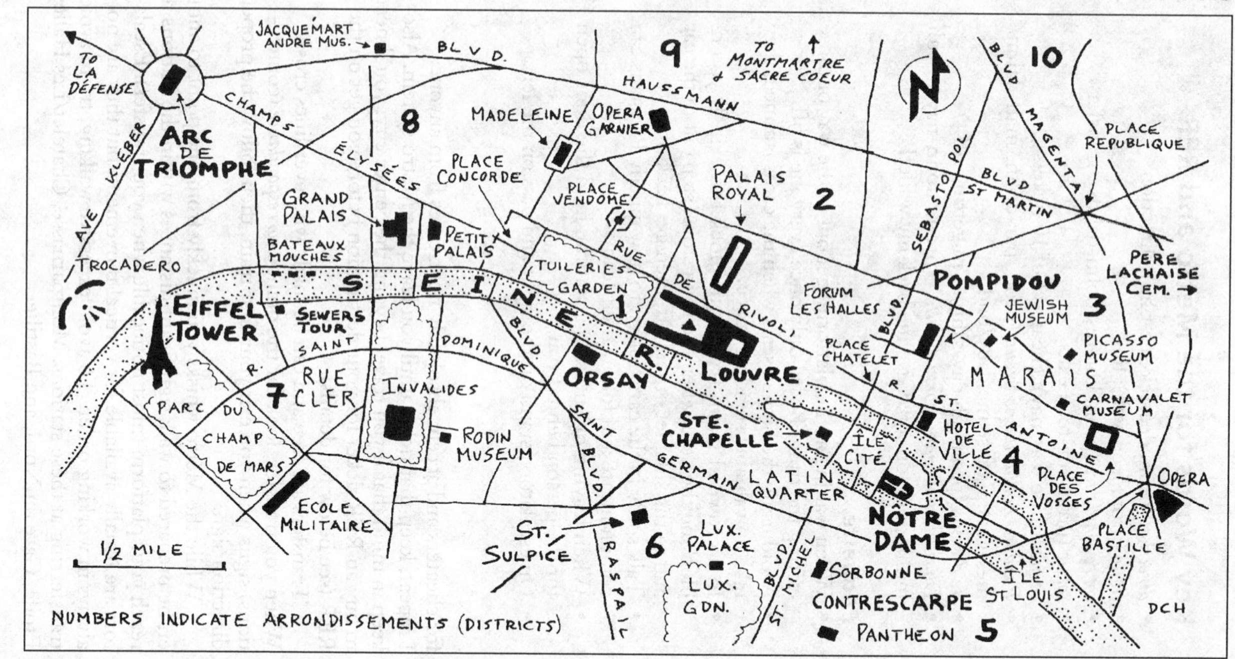
TO LA DÉFENSE
JACQUEMART ANDRE MUS.
BLVD.
9
TO MONTMARTRE & SACRE COEUR
10
HAUSSMANN
CHAMPS
8
MADELEINE
OPERA GARNIER
ARC DE TRIOMPHE
AVE KLEBER
ÉLYSÉES
PLACE CONCORDE
PLACE VENDOME
PALAIS ROYAL
2
BLVD MAGENTA
PLACE REPUBLIQUE
BLVD SEBASTOPOL
BLVD ST MARTIN
GRAND PALAIS
PETIT PALAIS
BATEAUX MOUCHES
TROCADERO
TUILERIES GARDEN
RUE DE RIVOLI
PERE LACHAISE CEM.
SEINE
1
FORUM LES HALLES
POMPIDOU
JEWISH MUSEUM
3
EIFFEL TOWER
SEWERS TOUR
R. SAINT DOMINIQUE
BLVD.
PLACE CHATELET
PICASSO MUSEUM
R. LOUVRE
ORSAY
MARAIS
RUE CLER
7
INVALIDES
R. ST. ANTOINE
CARNAVALET MUSEUM
PARC DU CHAMP DE MARS
RODIN MUSEUM
BLVD. SAINT GERMAIN
STE. CHAPELLE
ÎLE CITÉ
HOTEL DE VILLE
4
LATIN QUARTER
PLACE DES VOSGES
OPERA
ECOLE MILITAIRE
NÔTRE DAME
PLACE BASTILLE
ST. SULPICE
6
LUX. PALACE
1/2 MILE
RASPAIL
BLVD ST MICHEL
SORBONNE
ÎLE ST LOUIS
LUX. GDN.
CONTRESCARPE
DCH
NUMBERS INDICATE ARRONDISSEMENTS (DISTRICTS)
PANTHEON
5

Key Words for the Métro and RER

- *direction* (pron. dee-rek-see-ohn): direction
- *ligne* (pron. leen-yuh): line
- *correspondance* (pron. kor-res-pohn-dahns): transfer
- *sortie* (pron. sor-tee): exit
- *carnet* (pron. car-nay): cheap set of 10 tickets
- *Pardon, madame/monsieur* (pron. par-dohn, mah-dahm/mes-yur): Excuse me, lady/bud.
- *Je descend* (pron. juh day-sahn): I'm getting off.
- *Donnez-moi mon porte-feuille!* (pron. dohn-nay-mwuh mohn port-foo-ay): Give me back my wallet!

Etiquette

- When waiting at the platform, get out of the way of those exiting the train. Board only once everyone is off.
- Avoid using the hinged seats when the car is jammed; they take up valuable standing space.
- In a crowded train, try not to block the exit. If you're blocking the door when the train stops, step out of the car and to the side, let others off, then get back on.
- Talk softly in the cars. Listen to how quietly Parisians can communicate and follow their lead.
- When leaving or entering a station, hold the door open for the person behind you.
- On escalators, stand on the right and pass on the left.

for cheaters and accept absolutely no excuses from anyone. I repeat, keep that ticket until you leave the Métro system. Also keep in mind that if you travel beyond the center city, you'll need to buy an RER ticket for your destination before you get on the RER (see below for details).

Transfers are free and can be made wherever lines cross. When you transfer, look for the orange *correspondance* (connections) signs when you exit your first train, then follow the proper direction sign.

While the Métro whisks you quickly from one point to another, be prepared to walk significant distances within the stations to reach your platform (most noticeable when you transfer). Escalators are usually available for vertical movement, but they are not always in working order. To avoid excessive walking, try to avoid transferring at these stations: Montparnasse, Chatelet/Les Halles, Etoile, Gare du Nord, and Bastille.

Before you head for the *sortie* (exit), check the helpful *plan du quartier* (map of the neighborhood) to get your bearings, locate your destination, and decide which *sortie* you want. At stops with several *sorties*, you can save lots of walking by choosing the best exit.

After you exit the system, toss or tear your ticket so you don't confuse it with your unused tickets. Used and unused tickets look virtually identical.

Thieves spend their days in the Métro. Be on guard. For example, if your pocket is picked as you pass through a turnstile, you end up stuck on the wrong side while the thief strolls away. Any jostle or commotion (especially when boarding or leaving trains) is likely the sign of a thief or team of thieves in action.

Paris has a huge homeless population and higher than 11 percent unemployment, so expect a warm Métro welcome from panhandlers, musicians, and those selling magazines produced by the homeless community.

By RER: The RER (Réseau Express Régionale; pron. air-ay-air) is the suburban train system serving destinations such as Versailles, Disneyland Paris, and the airports. These routes, indicated by thick lines on your subway map, are identified by letters A, B, C, and so on. The RER works like the Métro, but can be speedier (if it serves your destination directly) because it makes only a few stops within the city. One Métro ticket is all you need for RER rides within central Paris. You can transfer between the Métro and RER systems with the same ticket. Unlike the Métro, you need to insert your ticket in a turnstile to exit the RER system, and also unlike the Métro, signage can vary between RER stations, meaning you have to pay attention and verify that you're heading the right direction (RER lines often split at the end of the line leading to different signed *destinations*—study your map or confirm with a local and you'll do fine). To travel outside the city (to Versailles or the airport, for example), you'll need to buy a separate, more expensive ticket at the station window before boarding; make sure your stop is served by checking the signs over the train platform. Not all trains serve all stops. If you see "*toutes les gares*" on the platform sign describing your train, it means the train will stop at all of the stations.

By City Bus: The trickier bus system is worth figuring out. Métro tickets are good on both bus and Métro, though you can't use the same ticket to transfer between the two systems. One ticket gets you anywhere in central Paris, but if you leave the city center (shown as zone 1 on the diagram on board the bus), you must validate a second ticket. While the Métro shuts down about 00:30, some buses continue much later. Schedules are posted at bus stops.

Handy bus-system maps *(plan des autobus)* are available in any Métro station and are provided in your *Paris Pratique* map book if you invest €6.

Big system maps, posted at each bus and Métro stop, display the routes. Individual route diagrams show the exact routes of the lines serving that stop. Major stops are painted on the side of each bus. Enter through the front doors. Punch your Métro ticket in the machine behind the driver, or pay the higher cash fare. Get off the bus using the rear door. Even if you're not certain you've figured it out, do some joyriding (outside of rush hour). Lines #24, #63, and #69 are Paris' most scenic routes and make a great introduction to the city. Bus #69 is particularly handy, running between the Eiffel Tower, rue Cler (recommended hotels), Orsay, Louvre, Marais (recommended hotels), and the Père Lachaise Cemetery. The handiest bus routes are listed for each hotel area recommended (see "Sleeping," below).

By Taxi: Parisian taxis are reasonable—especially for couples and families. The meters are tamper-proof. Fares and supplements (described in English on the back windows) are straightforward. There's a €5 minimum. A 10-minute ride costs about €8 (versus €1 to get anywhere in town on the Métro). You can try waving one down, but it's easier to ask for the nearest taxi stand (*Où est une station de taxi?*; pron. oo ay oon stah-see-ohn duh taxi). Taxi stands are indicated by a circled T on many city maps, including Michelin's #10 Paris. A typical taxi takes three people (maybe 4 if you're polite and pay €2.50 extra); groups of up to five can use a *grand taxi*, which must be booked in advance (ask your hotel to call). If a taxi is summoned by phone, the meter starts as soon as the call is received—adding €3 or €4 to the bill. Higher rates are charged at night from 19:00 to 7:00, all day Sunday, and to either airport. There's a €1 charge for each piece of baggage and for train station pick-ups. To tip, round up to the next euro (minimum €0.50). Taxis are tough to find on Friday and Saturday nights, especially after the Métro closes (around 00:30). If you need to catch a train or flight early in the morning, consider booking a taxi the night before.

Organized Tours of Paris

Bus Tours—Paris Vision offers handy bus tours of Paris, day and night (advertised in hotel lobbies); their "Paris Illumination" tour is much more interesting (see "Nightlife in Paris," below). Far better daytime bus tours are the hop-on, hop-off double-decker bus services connecting Paris' main sights while providing running commentary (ideal in good weather when you can sit on top; see also Bâtobus under "Boat Tours" below).

Two companies provide hop-on, hop-off bus service: L'Open Tours and Les Cars Rouges (pick up their brochures showing routes and stops from any TI or on their buses). **L'Open Tours**, which uses yellow buses, provides more extensive coverage and offers three different routes rolling by most of the important sights in Paris (the Paris Grand Tour offers the best introduction). Tickets are good for any route. Buy your tickets from the driver (€25/1-day ticket, €27/2-day ticket, kids 4–11 pay €12.50 for 1 or 2 days, 20 percent less if you have a *Carte Orange* Métro pass). Two or three buses depart hourly from about 10:00 to 18:00; expect to wait 10 to 20 minutes at each stop (stops can be tricky to find). You can hop off at any stop, then catch a later bus following the same circuit. You'll see these bright yellow topless double-decker buses all over town—pick one up at the first important sight you visit, or start your tour at the Eiffel Tower stop (the first street on non-river side of the tower, tel. 01 42 66 56 56). **Les Cars Rouges'** bright red buses offer largely the same service with fewer stops on a single, Grand Tour Route for less money (2-day tickets, €22-adult, €11-kids 4–12, tel. 01 53 95 39 53).

Boat Tours—Several companies offer one-hour boat cruises on the Seine (by far, best at night). The huge, mass-production **Bâteaux-Mouches** boats depart every 20 to 30 minutes from pont de l'Alma's right bank and right in front of the Eiffel Tower, and are convenient to rue Cler hotels (€7.50, €4.50 for ages 4–12, daily 10:00–22:30, useless taped explanations in 6 languages and tour groups by the dozens, tel. 01 40 76 99 99). The smaller and more intimate **Vedettes de pont Neuf** depart only once an hour from the center of pont Neuf (twice an hour after dark), but they come with a live guide giving explanations in French and English and are convenient to Marais and Contrescarpe hotels (€9.50, €5 for ages 4–12, tel. 01 46 33 98 38).

From April through October, **Bâtobus** operates hop-on, hop-off boats on the Seine, connecting eight popular stops every 15 to 25 minutes: Eiffel Tower, Champs-Elysées, Orsay/place de la Concorde, Louvre, Notre-Dame, St. Germain-des-Prés, Hôtel de Ville, and Jardin des Plantes. Pick up a schedule at any stop (or TI) and use them as a scenic alternative to the Métro. Tickets are available for one day (€10, €5.50 under 12) and two days (€12.50, €6.50 under 12); boats run from 10:00 to 19:00, and until 21:00 June through September, www.batobus.com.

Paris Canal departs twice daily for three-hour, one-way cruises between the Orsay and Parc de la Vilette. You'll cruise up the Seine then along a quiet canal through nontouristy Paris, accompanied by English explanations (€17, €9.50 for kids 4–11, €12.50 for ages 12–25, tel. 01 42 40 96 97); the one-way trips depart at 9:30 from quai Anatole France (near the Orsay), and from Parc de la Vilette (at Folie des Visites du Parc) at 14:30.

Canauxrama offers a 2.5-hour cruise on a peaceful canal without the Seine in sight, starting from place de la Bastille and ending at Bassin de la Vilette, near Métro stop Stalingrad (€14, €9 for kids, €11 for seniors and students, departs at 9:45 and 14:30 across from Bastille Opéra, just below boulevard de la Bastille, opposite #50, where the canal meets place de la Bastille, tel. 01 42 39 15 00).

Paris Walking Tours—This company offers a variety of excellent two-hour walks, led by British or American guides, nearly daily for €10 (tel. 01 48 09 21 40 for recorded schedule in English, fax 01 42 43 75 51, see www.paris-walks.com for their complete schedule). Tours focus on the Marais, Montmartre, Ile de la Cité and Ile St. Louis, and Hemingway's Paris. Ask about their family-friendly tours. Call ahead a day or two to learn their schedule and starting point. No reservations are required. These are thoughtfully prepared, relaxing, and humorous. Don't hesitate to stand close to the guide to hear.

Private Guide Service—For many, Paris merits hiring a Parisian as your personal guide. Two excellent licensed local guides who freelance for individuals and families are Arnaud Servignat, who runs Accueil-France-Paris-Guide (also does car tours of countryside around Paris, tel. 06 72 77 94 50, fax 01 42 57 00 38, e-mail: arnotour@noos.fr or franceparisguide@noos.fr), and Marianne Siegler (€150/4 hrs, €250/day, reserve in advance if possible, tel. 01 42 52 32 51).

Bike Tours—Mike's Bullfrog Bike Tours attract a younger crowd for its three- to four-hour rolls through Paris (€20, May–Nov daily at 11:00, also at 15:30 June–July, no CC, in English, no bikes or reservations needed, meet at south pillar of Eiffel Tower, cellular 06 09 98 08 60, www.mikesbiketours.com).

Excursion Tours—Many companies offer minivan and big bus tours to regional sights, including all of the day trips described in this book. **Paris Walking Tours** are the best, with informative though infrequent tours of the Impressionist artist retreats of Giverny and Auvers-sur-Oise (€47–56, includes admissions, tel. 01 48 09 21 40 for recording in English, fax 01 42 43 75 51, www.paris-walks.com).

Paris Vision offers mass-produced, full-size bus and minivan tours to several popular regional destinations, including the Loire Valley, Champagne region, D-Day beaches, and Mont St. Michel. Their minivan tours are more expensive but more personal, given in English, and offer pick up at your hotel (€130–200/person). The full-size bus tours are multilingual and cost about half the price of a minivan tour—worth it for some simply for the ease of transportation to the sights (full-size buses depart from 214 rue de Rivoli, Mo: Tuileries, tel. 01 42 60 30 01, fax 01 42 86 95 36, www.parisvision.com).

Sights—The "Historic Core of Paris" Walk

(This information is distilled from the Historic Paris Walk chapter in *Rick Steves' Mona Winks*, by Gene Openshaw and Rick Steves.)

Allow four hours for this self-guided tour, including sightseeing. Start where the city did—on the Ile de la Cité. Face Notre-Dame and follow the dotted line on the "Core of Paris" map (see page 58). To get to Notre-Dame, ride the Métro to Cité, Hôtel de Ville, or St. Michel and walk to the big square facing the . . .

▲▲Notre-Dame Cathedral—This 700-year-old cathedral is packed with history and tourists. Study its sculpture and windows, take in a Mass, eavesdrop on guides, and walk all around the outside (free, daily 8:00–18:45; treasury-€2.50, not covered by museum pass, daily 9:30–17:30; ask about free English tours, normally Wed and Thu at 12:00 and Sat at 14:30; Mo: Cité, Hôtel de Ville, or St. Michel). Climb to the top for a great view of the city; you get 400 steps for only €5.50 (daily April–Sept 9:30–19:30, until 21:00 July–Aug on Sat and Sun, Oct–March 10:00–17:30, last entry 45 min before closing, covered by museum pass though you can't bypass line, arrive early to avoid long lines). There are clean €0.50 toilets in front of the church near Charlemagne's statue.

The **cathedral facade** is worth a close look. The church is dedicated to "Our Lady" (Notre-Dame). Mary is center stage—cradling Jesus, surrounded by the halo of the rose window. Adam is on the left and Eve is on the right.

Below Mary and above the arches is a row of 28 statues known as the Kings of Judah. During the French Revolution, these biblical kings were mistaken for the hated French kings. The citizens stormed the church, crying, "Off with their heads!" All were decapitated, but have since been recapitated.

Speaking of decapitation, look at the carving above the doorway on the left. The man with his head in his hands is St. Denis. Back when there was a Roman temple on this spot, Christianity began making converts. The fourth-century bishop of Roman Paris, Denis, was beheaded. But these early Christians were hard to keep down. The man who would become St. Denis got up, tucked his head under his arm, and headed north until he found just the right place to meet his maker: Montmartre. (Although the name "Montmartre" comes from the Roman "Mount of Mars,"

Core of Paris

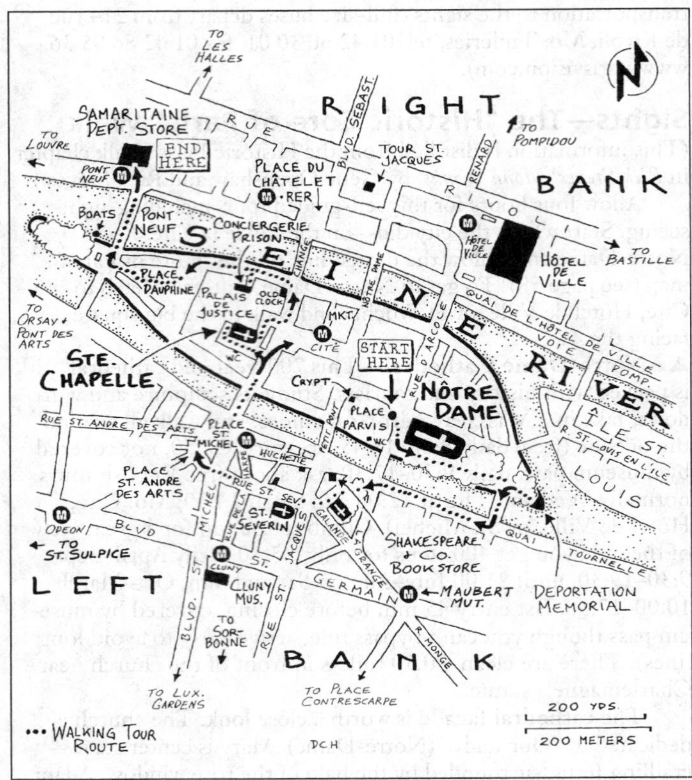

later generations—thinking of their beheaded patron St. Denis—preferred a less pagan version, "Mount of Martyrs.") The Parisians were convinced of this miracle, Christianity gained ground, and a church soon replaced the pagan temple.

Medieval art was OK if it embellished the house of God and told Bible stories. For a fine example, move to the base of the central column (at the foot of Mary, about where the head of St. Denis could spit if he was real good). Working around from the left, find God telling a barely created Eve, "Have fun, but no apples." Next, the sexiest serpent I've ever seen makes apples à la mode. Finally, Adam and Eve, now ashamed of their nakedness, are expelled by an angel. This is a tiny example in a church covered with meaning.

Now move to the right and study the carving above the **central portal**. It's the end of the world, and Christ sits on the throne of Judgment (just under the arches, holding his hands up). Below him an angel and a demon weigh souls in the balance. The "good" stand to the left, looking up to heaven. The "bad" ones to the right are chained up and led off to . . . Versailles on a Tuesday. The "ugly" ones must be the crazy sculpted demons to the right, at the base of the arch.

Wander through the interior. You'll be routed around the ambulatory, much as medieval pilgrims would have been. Don't miss the rose windows filling each of the transepts. Back outside, walk around the church through the park on the riverside for a close look at the flying buttresses.

The neo-Gothic, 90-meter/300-foot **spire** is a product of the 1860 reconstruction. Around its base are apostles and evangelists (the green men) as well as Viollet-le-Duc, the architect in charge of the work. Notice how the apostles look outward, blessing the city, while the architect (at top, seen from behind the church) looks up, admiring his spire.

The archaeological **crypt** is a worthwhile 15-minute stop with your museum pass (€3.50, Tue–Sun 10:00–18:00, closed Mon, enter 100 meters/330 feet in front of church). You'll see Roman ruins, trace the street plan of the medieval village, and see diagrams of how the earliest Paris grew and grew, all thoughtfully explained in English.

If you're hungry near Notre-Dame, the nearby Ile St. Louis has inexpensive *crêperies* and grocery stores open daily on its main drag. Plan a picnic for the quiet, bench-filled park immediately behind the church (public WC available).

Behind Notre-Dame, squeeze through the tourist buses, cross the street, and enter the iron gate into the park at the tip of the island. Look for the stairs and head down to reach . . .

▲▲Deportation Memorial (Mémorial de la Déportation)—This memorial to the 200,000 French victims of the Nazi concentration camps draws you into their experience. As you descend the steps, the city around you disappears. Surrounded by walls, you have become a prisoner. Your only freedom is your view of the sky and the tantalizing glimpse of the river below.

Enter the single-file chamber ahead. Inside, the circular plaque in the floor reads, "They descended into the mouth of the earth and they did not return." A hallway stretches in front of you, lined with 200,000 lighted crystals, one for each French citizen that died. Flickering at the far end is the eternal flame of hope. The tomb of the unknown deportee lies at your feet. Above, the inscription reads, "Dedicated to the living memory of the 200,000 French deportees sleeping in the night and the fog, exterminated in the Nazi concentration camps."

Above the exit as you leave is the message you'll find at all Nazi sights: "Forgive, but never forget." (Free, April–Sept daily 10:00–12:00 & 14:00–19:00, Oct–March daily 10:00–12:00 & 14:00–17:00, east tip of the island Ile de la Cité, behind Notre-Dame and near Ile St. Louis, Mo: Cité.)

Ile St. Louis—Look across the river to the Ile St. Louis. If the Ile de la Cité is a tug laden with the history of Paris, it's towing this classy little residential dinghy laden only with boutiques, famous sorbet shops, and restaurants (see "Eating in Paris," below). This island wasn't developed until much later (18th century). What was a swampy mess is now harmonious Parisian architecture. The pedestrian bridge, pont Saint Louis, connects the two islands, leading right to rue Saint Louis en l'Ile. This spine of the island is lined with interesting shops. A short stroll takes you to the famous Berthillon ice-cream parlor (#31). Loop back to the pedestrian bridge along the parklike quays (walk north to the river and turn left). This walk is about as peaceful and romantic as Paris gets.

Before walking to the opposite end of the Ile de la Cité, loop through the Latin Quarter (as indicated on the map). From the Deportation Memorial cross the bridge onto the Left Bank and enjoy the riverside view of the Notre-Dame and window shop among the green book stalls, browsing through used books, vintage posters, and souvenirs. At the little park and church (over the bridge from the front of Notre-Dame), venture inland a few blocks, basically arcing through the Latin Quarter and returning to the island two bridges down at place St. Michel.

▲Latin Quarter—This area, which gets its name from the language used here when it was an exclusive medieval university district, lies between Luxembourg Garden and the Seine, centering around the Sorbonne University and boulevards St. Germain and St. Michel. This is the core of the Left Bank—it's crowded with international eateries, far-out bookshops, street singers, and jazz clubs. For colorful wandering and café sitting, afternoons and evenings are best (Mo: St. Michel).

Along rue Saint-Severin, you can still see the shadow of the medieval sewer system (the street slopes into a central channel of bricks). In the days before plumbing and toilets, when people still went to the river or neighborhood wells for their water, "flushing" meant throwing it out the window. Certain times of day were flushing times. Maids on the fourth floor would holler, "*Garde de l'eau!*" ("Look out for the water!") and heave it into the streets, where it would eventually be washed down into the Seine.

Consider a visit to the Cluny Museum for its medieval art and unicorn tapestries (listed under "Sights—Southeast Paris," below).

Place St. Michel (facing the St. Michel bridge) is the traditional core of the Left Bank's artsy, liberal, hippie, bohemian district of poets, philosophers, winos, and tourists. In less-commercial times, place St. Michel was a gathering point for the city's malcontents and misfits. Here, in 1871, the citizens took the streets from the government troops, set up barricades *Les Mis*–style, and established the Paris Commune. During World War II, the locals rose up against their Nazi oppressors (read the plaques by St. Michel fountain). And in the spring of 1968, a time of social upheaval all over the world, young students—battling riot batons and tear gas—took over the square and demanded change.

From place St. Michel, look across the river and find the spire of Sainte-Chapelle church and its weathervane angel (below). Cross the river on pont St. Michel and continue along boulevard du Palais. On your left, you'll see the high-security doorway to Sainte-Chapelle. But first, continue another 30 meters/100 feet and turn right at a wide pedestrian street, the rue de Lutèce.

Cité "Métropolitain" Stop—Of the 141 original turn-of-the-19th-century subway entrances, this is one of 17 survivors preserved as national art treasures. The curvy, plantlike ironwork is a textbook example of Art Nouveau, the style that rebelled against the erector-set squareness of the Industrial Age (e.g., Mr. Eiffel's tower).

The flower market here on place Louis Lepine is a pleasant detour. On Sundays, this square chirps with a busy bird market. And across the way is the Prefecture de Police, where Inspector Clouseau of *Pink Panther* fame used to work, and where the local resistance fighters took the first building from the Nazis in August 1944, leading to the Allied liberation of Paris a week later.

Pause here to admire the view. Sainte-Chapelle is a pearl in an ugly architectural oyster, part of a complex of buildings that includes the Palace of Justice (to the right of Sainte-Chapelle, behind the fancy gates). Return to the entrance of Sainte-Chapelle. Everyone needs to pass through a metal detector to get in. Free toilets are ahead on the left. The line into the church may be long. (Museum passholders can go directly in; pick up the excellent English info sheet.) Enter the humble ground floor of…

▲▲▲Sainte-Chapelle—This triumph of Gothic church architecture is a cathedral of glass like no other. It was speedily built from 1242 to 1248 for Louis IX (the only French king who is now a saint) to house the supposed Crown of Thorns. Its architectural harmony is due to the fact that it was completed under the direction of one architect in only six years—unheard of in Gothic times. (Notre-Dame took more than 200 years to build.)

The design clearly shows an Old Regime approach to worship. The basement was for staff and other common folk. Royal

Christians worshiped upstairs. The ground-floor paint job, a 19th-century restoration, is a reasonably accurate copy of the original.

Climb the spiral staircase to the **Chapelle Haute**. Fill the place with choral music, crank up the sunshine, face the top of the altar, and really believe that the Crown of Thorns was there, and this becomes one awesome space.

"Let there be light." In the Bible, it's clear: Light is divine. Light shining through stained glass was a symbol of God's grace shining down to earth. Gothic architects used their new technology to turn dark stone buildings into lanterns of light. The glory of Gothic shines brighter here than in any other church.

There are 15 separate panels of stained glass (6,500 square feet—two-thirds of it 13th-century original), with more than 1,100 different scenes, mostly from the Bible. In medieval times, scenes like these helped teach Bible stories to the illiterate.

The altar was raised up high to better display the relic—the Crown of Thorns—around which this chapel was built. The supposed crown cost King Louis three times as much as this church. Today, it is kept in the Notre-Dame treasury and shown only on Good Friday.

Louis' little private viewing window is in the wall to the right of the altar. Louis, both saintly and shy, liked to go to church without dealing with the rigors of public royal life. Here, he could worship still dressed in his jammies.

Lay your camera on the ground and shoot the ceiling. Those ribs growing out of the slender columns are the essence of Gothic.

Books in the gift shop explain the stained glass in English. There are concerts (€16–25) almost every summer evening (€5.50, €8 combo-ticket covers Conciergerie, both covered by museum pass, daily 9:30–18:00, Mo: Cité, tel. 01 44 07 12 38 for concert information).

Palais de Justice—Back outside, as you walk around the church exterior, look down and notice how much Paris has risen in the 800 years since Sainte-Chapelle was built. You're in a huge complex of buildings that has housed the local government since ancient Roman times. It was the site of the original Gothic palace of the early kings of France. The only surviving medieval parts are the Sainte-Chapelle church and the Conciergerie prison.

Most of the site is now covered by the giant Palais de Justice, home of France's supreme court (built in 1776). "*Liberté, Egalité, Fraternité*," emblazoned over the doors, is a reminder that this was also the headquarters of the Revolutionary government.

Now pass through the big iron gate to the noisy boulevard du Palais and turn left (toward the Right Bank). On the corner is the site of the oldest public clock in the city (built in 1334). While the present clock is said to be Baroque, it somehow still manages to keep accurate time.

Turn left onto quai de l'Horologe, and walk along the river. The round medieval tower just ahead marks the entrance to the Conciergerie. Pop in to visit the courtyard and lobby (free). Step past the serious-looking guard into the courtyard.

Conciergerie—This former prison is a gloomy place. Kings used it to torture and execute failed assassins. The leaders of the Revolution put it to similar good use. The tower next to the entrance, called "the babbler," was named for the painful sounds that leaked from it.

Look at the stark lettering above the doorways. This was a no-nonsense revolutionary time. Everything, even lettering, was subjected to the test of reason. No frills, or we chop 'em off.

Step inside; the lobby, with an English-language history display, is free. Marie-Antoinette was imprisoned here. During a busy eight-month period in the Revolution, she was one of 2,600 prisoners kept here on the way to the guillotine. The interior, with its huge vaulted and pillared rooms, echoes with history but is pretty barren (€5.50, €8 combo-ticket covers Sainte-Chapelle, both covered by museum pass, daily April–Sept 9:30–18:30, Oct–March 10:00–17:00, good English descriptions). You can see Marie-Antoinette's cell, housing a collection of her mementos. In another room, a list of those made "a foot shorter at the top" by the "national razor" includes ex-King Louis XVI, Charlotte Corday (who murdered Marat in his bathtub), and the chief revolutionary who got a taste of his own medicine, Maximilien Robespierre.

Back outside, wink at the flak-proof-vested guard, and turn left. Listen for babbles and continue your walk along the river. Across the river you can see the rooftop observatory—flags flapping—of the Samaritaine department store, where this walk will end. At the first corner, veer left past France's supreme-court building and into a sleepy triangular square called place Dauphine. Marvel at how such quaintness could be lodged in the midst of such greatness as you walk through the park to the end of the island. At the equestrian statue of Henry IV, turn right onto the bridge and take refuge in one of the nooks on the Eiffel Tower side.

Pont Neuf—This "new bridge" is now Paris' oldest. Built during Henry IV's reign (around 1600), its 12 arches span the widest part of the river. The fine view includes the park on the tip of the island (note Seine tour boats), the Orsay Museum, and the Louvre. These turrets were originally for vendors and street entertainers. In the days of Henry IV, who originated the promise of "a chicken in every pot," this would have been a lively scene.

Directly over the river, the first building you'll hit on the Right Bank is the venerable old department store, Samaritaine.

▲Samaritaine Department Store Viewpoint—Enter the store and go to the rooftop. Ride the glass elevator from near the pont Neuf entrance to the ninth floor (you'll be greeted by a WC—check out the sink). Pass the 10th-floor *terrasse* (with café) for the 11th-floor panorama (€2, tight spiral staircase; watch your head). Quiz yourself. Working counterclockwise, find the Eiffel Tower, Invalides/Napoleon's Tomb, Montparnasse Tower, Henry IV statue on the tip of the island, Sorbonne University, the dome of the Panthéon, Sainte-Chapelle, Notre-Dame, Hôtel de Ville (city hall), Pompidou Center, Sacré-Coeur, Opéra, and the Louvre. The Champs-Elysées leads to the Arc de Triomphe. Shadowing that—even bigger, while two times as distant—is the Grande Arche de la Défense. You'll find light, reasonably priced, and incredibly scenic meals on the breezy 10th-floor terrace, and there's a supermarket in the basement (daily 9:30–19:00, Mo: Pont Neuf, tel. 01 40 41 20 20).

Sights—Paris Museums near the Tuileries Garden

The newly renovated Tuileries Garden was once private property of kings and queens. Paris' grandest public park links these museums.

▲▲▲Louvre—This is Europe's oldest, biggest, greatest, and maybe most crowded museum. There is no grander entry than through the pyramid, but metal detectors create a long line at times.

There are several ways to avoid the line. Museum passholders can use the group entrance in the pedestrian passageway between the pyramid and rue de Rivoli (facing the pyramid with your back to the Tuileries Garden, go to your left, which is north; under the arches, you'll find the entrance and escalator down). Otherwise, you can enter the Louvre underground directly from the Métro stop Palais Royal/Musée du Louvre (exit following signs to Musée du Louvre) or from the Carrousel shopping mall, which is connected to the museum. Enter the mall at 99 rue de Rivoli (the door with the red awning, daily 8:30–23:00). The taxi stand is across rue de Rivoli next to the Métro station.

Pick up the free "Louvre Handbook" in English at the information desk under the pyramid as you enter. Don't try to cover the entire museum. Consider taking a tour (see "Tours," below).

Self-Guided Tour: Start in the Denon wing and visit the highlights, in the following order (thanks to Gene Openshaw for his help with this).

Wander through the **ancient Greek and Roman works** to see the Parthenon frieze, Pompeii mosaics, Etruscan sarcophagi, and Roman portrait busts. You can't miss lovely Venus de Milo

Paris Museums near the Tuileries Garden

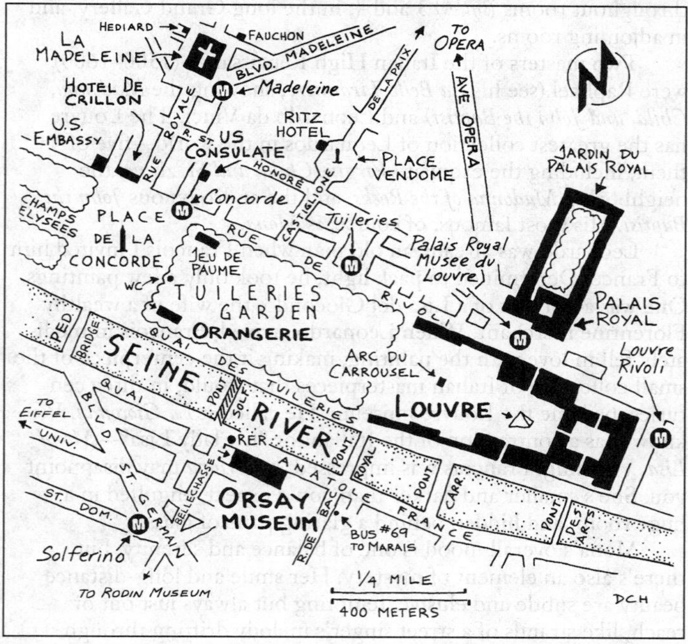

(Aphrodite). This goddess of love (c. 100 B.C., from the Greek island of Milos) created a sensation when she was discovered in 1820. Most "Greek" statues are actually later Roman copies, but Venus is a rare Greek original. She, like Golden Age Greeks, epitomizes stability, beauty, and balance. Later Greek art was Hellenistic, adding motion and drama. For a good example, see the exciting Winged Victory of Samothrace (*Victoire de Samothrace*, on the landing). This statue of a woman with wings, poised on the prow of a ship, once stood on a hilltop to commemorate a great naval victory. This is the Venus de Milo gone Hellenistic.

The **Italian collection** is on the other side of the Winged Victory. The key to Renaissance painting was realism, and for the Italians "realism" was spelled "3-D." Painters were inspired by the realism and balanced beauty of Greek sculpture. Painting a 3-D world on a 2-D surface is tough, and after a millennium of Dark Ages, artists were rusty. Living in a religious age, they painted mostly altarpieces full of saints, angels, Madonnas-and-bambinos, and crucifixes floating in an ethereal gold-leaf heaven. Gradually, though, they brought these otherworldly scenes down to earth. The Italian collection—including *Mona Lisa*—is scattered throughout rooms *(salles)* 3 and 4, in the long Grand Gallery, and in adjoining rooms.

Two masters of the Italian High Renaissance (1500–1600) were Raphael (see his *La Belle Jardinière*, showing the *Madonna, Child, and John the Baptist)* and Leonardo da Vinci. The Louvre has the greatest collection of Leonardos in the world—five of them, including the exquisite *Virgin, Child, and St. Anne*, the neighboring *Madonna of the Rocks*, and the androgynous *John the Baptist*. His most famous, of course, is *Mona*.

Leonardo was already an old man when François I invited him to France. Determined to pack light, he took only a few paintings. One was a portrait of a Lisa del Giocondo, the wife of a wealthy Florentine merchant. When Leonardo arrived, François immediately fell in love with the painting, making it the centerpiece of the small collection of Italian masterpieces that would, in three centuries, become the Louvre museum. He called it *La Gioconda*. We know it as a contraction of the Italian for "my lady Lisa"—*Mona Lisa*. Warning: François was impressed, but *Mona* may disappoint you. She's smaller and darker than you'd expect, engulfed in a huge room, and hidden behind a glaring pane of glass.

Mona's overall mood is one of balance and serenity, but there's also an element of mystery. Her smile and long-distance beauty are subtle and elusive, tempting but always just out of reach, like strands of a street singer's melody drifting through the Métro tunnel. *Mona* doesn't knock your socks off, but she winks at the patient viewer.

Now for something **neoclassical**. Notice the fine work, such as *Coronation of Napoleon* by J. L. David, near *Mona* in the Salle Daru. Neoclassicism, once the rage in France (1780–1850), usually features Greek subjects, patriotic sentiment, and a clean, simple style. After Napoleon quickly conquered most of Europe, he insisted on being made emperor (not merely king) of this "New Rome." He staged an elaborate coronation ceremony in Paris, and rather than let the pope crown him, he crowned himself. The setting is the Notre-Dame cathedral, with Greek columns and Roman arches thrown in for effect. Napoleon's mom was also added, since she couldn't make it to the ceremony. A key on the frame describes who's who in the picture.

The **Romantic** collection, in an adjacent room (Salle Mollien), has works by Géricault *(Raft of the Medusa)* and Delacroix *(Liberty at the Barricades)*. Romanticism, with an emphasis on motion and emotion, is the complete flip side of neoclassicism, though they both flourished in the early 1800s. Delacroix's *Liberty*, commemorating the stirrings of democracy in France, is also a fitting tribute to the Louvre, the first museum opened to the common rabble of humanity. The good things in life don't belong only to a small wealthy part of society, but to all. The motto of France is "*Liberté, Egalité, Fraternité*"—liberty, equality, and brotherhood.

Exit the room at the far end (past the café) and go downstairs, where you'll bump into the bum of a large, twisting male nude who looks like he's just waking up after a thousand-year nap. The two ***Slaves*** (c. 1513) by Michelangelo Buonarroti are a fitting end to this museum—works that bridge the ancient and modern worlds. Michelangelo, like his fellow Renaissance artists, learned from the Greeks. The perfect anatomy, twisting poses, and idealized faces look like they could have been done 2,000 years earlier. Michelangelo said that his purpose was to carve away the marble to reveal the figures God put inside. The *Rebellious Slave*, fighting against his bondage, shows the agony of that process and the ecstasy of the result.

Cost: €7.50, €5 after 15:00 and on Sunday, free on first Sunday of month and for those under 18, covered by museum pass. Tickets good all day. Reentry allowed. Tel. 01 40 20 51 51, recorded info tel. 01 40 20 53 17 (www.louvre.fr).

Hours: Wed–Mon 9:00–18:00, closed Tue. All wings open Wed until 21:45. On Mon, only the Denon wing is open until 21:45, but it contains the biggies: *Mona Lisa*, Venus de Milo, and more. Galleries start closing 30 minutes early. Closed Jan 1, Easter, May 1, Nov 1, and Dec 25. Crowds are worst on Sun, Mon, Wed, and mornings. Save money by visiting after 15:00.

Tours: The 90-minute English-language tours, which leave six times daily except Tuesday, when the museum is closed, and Sunday, boil this overwhelming museum down to size (normally at 11:00, 14:00, and 15:45, €3 plus your entry ticket, tour tel. 01 40 20 52 63). Clever €5 digital audioguides (after ticket booths, at top of stairs) give you a receiver and a directory of about 130 masterpieces, allowing you to dial a (rather dull) commentary on included works as you stumble upon them. Rick Steves' and Gene Openshaw's museum guidebook, *Rick Steves' Mona Winks* (buy in United States), includes a self-guided tour of the Louvre.

Louvre Complex: The newly renovated Richelieu wing and the underground shopping-mall extension add the finishing touches to Le Grand Louvre Project (which started in 1989 with the pyramid entrance). To explore this most recent extension of the Louvre, enter through the pyramid, walk toward the inverted pyramid, and uncover a post office, a handy TI and SNCF (train tickets) office, glittering boutiques and a dizzying assortment of good-value eateries (up the escalator), and the Palais-Royal Métro entrance. Stairs at the far end take you right into the Tuileries Garden, a perfect antidote to the stuffy, crowded rooms of the Louvre.

▲▲▲**Orsay Museum**—The Musée d'Orsay (pron. mew-zay dor-say) houses French art of the 1800s (specifically, art from 1848 to 1914), picking up where the Louvre leaves off. For us, that means Impressionism. The Orsay houses the best general collection anywhere of Manet, Monet, Renoir, Degas, van Gogh, Cézanne, and Gauguin.

The museum shows art that is also both old and new, conservative and revolutionary. You'll start on the ground floor with the Conservatives and the early rebels who paved the way for the Impressionists, then head upstairs to see how a few visionary young artists bucked the system and revolutionized the art world, paving the way for the 20th century.

For most visitors, the most important part of the museum is the upstairs Impressionist collection. Here, you can study many pictures you've probably seen in books, such as Manet's *Luncheon on the Grass*, Renoir's *Dance at the Moulin de la Galette*, Monet's *Gare St. Lazare*, *Whistler's Mother*, van Gogh's *Church at Auvers*, and Cezanne's *Card Players*. As you approach these beautiful, easy-to-enjoy paintings, remember that there is more to this art than meets the eye.

Impressionism 101: The camera threatened to make artists obsolete. A painter's original function was to record reality faithfully, like a journalist. Now a machine could capture a better likeness faster than you could say Etch A Sketch.

But true art is more than just painted reality. It gives us reality from the artist's point of view, putting a personal stamp on the work. It records not only a scene—a camera can do that—but the artist's impressions of that scene. Impressions are often fleeting, so the artist has to work quickly.

The Impressionist painters rejected camera-like detail for a quick style more suited to capturing the passing moment. Feeling stifled by the rigid rules and stuffy atmosphere of the Academy, the Impressionists took as their motto, "out of the studio, into the open air." They grabbed their berets and scarves and took excursions to the country, setting up their easels on riverbanks and hillsides or sketching in cafés and dance halls. Gods, goddesses, nymphs, and fantasy scenes were out; common people and rural landscapes were in.

The quick style and simple subjects were ridiculed and called childish by the "experts." Rejected by the Salon, the Impressionists staged their own exhibition in 1874. They brashly took their name from an insult thrown at them by a critic, who laughed at one of Monet's impressions of a sunrise. During the next decade, they exhibited their own work independently. The public, opposed at first, was slowly drawn in by the simplicity, color, and vibrancy of Impressionist art.

Cost: €7; €5 after 16:15, on Sun, and for ages 18 to 25; free for youth under 18 and for anyone first Sun of month; covered by museum pass. Tickets are good all day. Museum passholders can enter to the left of the main entrance (during the renovation, they can walk to the front of the line and show their passes).

Hours: June 20–Sept 20: Tue–Sun 9:00–18:00; Sept 21–June 19: Tue–Sat 10:00–18:00, Sun 9:00–18:00; Thu until 21:45 all year, always closed Mon. Last entrance is 45 minutes before closing. The Impressionist Galleries start closing at 17:15, frustrating many unwary visitors. Note that the Orsay is crowded on Tue, when the Louvre is closed.

Tours: Live English-language tours of the Orsay usually run daily (except Sun) at 11:30. The 90-minute tours cost €6 and are also available on audioguide (€5). Tours in English focusing on the Impressionists are offered Tuesdays at 14:30 and Thursdays at 18:30 (sometimes also on other days, €6).

Cafés: The museum has a cheap café on the fourth floor, and the elegant Salon de Thé du Musée is on the second floor (good salad bar).

Location: The Orsay sits above the RER-C stop called Musée d'Orsay. The nearest Métro stop is Solferino, three blocks south of the Orsay. Bus #69 from the Marais and rue Cler neighborhoods stops at the museum on the river side (Quai Anatole France).

In the summer of 2003, the main entry to the Orsay will be reopened after renovation. Until then, visitors are admitted through a temporary entry facing the river.

Jeu de Paume—Previously home to the Impressionist art collection now located in the Orsay, the Jeu de Paume now hosts rotating exhibits of top contemporary artists (€6, not covered by museum pass, Tue 12:00–21:30, Wed–Fri 12:00–19:00, Sat–Sun 10:00–19:00, closed Mon, on place de la Concorde, just inside Tuileries Garden on rue de Rivoli side, Mo: Concorde).

L'Orangerie—This excellent Impressionist museum is closed until 2004. The small, quiet, and often-overlooked museum houses Monet's water lilies, many famous Renoirs, and a scattering of other great Impressionist works. The breezy, round rooms of water lilies are two of the most enjoyable rooms in Paris (located in Tuileries Garden near place de la Concorde, Mo: Concorde).

Sights—Southwest Paris: The Eiffel Tower Neighborhood

▲▲▲Eiffel Tower (La Tour Eiffel)—It's crowded and expensive, but worth the trouble. Go early (by 8:45) or late in the day (after 20:00 in summer, otherwise 18:00) to avoid most crowds; weekends are worst. The Pilier Nord (north pillar) has the biggest

Eiffel Tower to Les Invalides

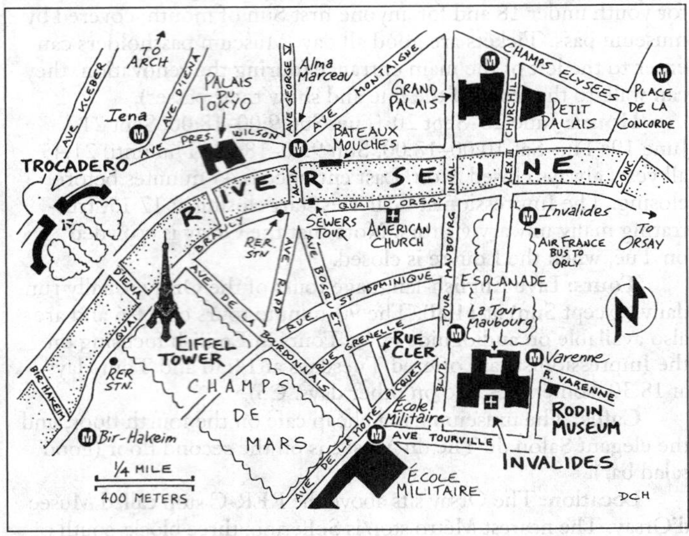

elevator and, therefore, the fastest-moving line. It takes two elevators to get to the top (transfer at level 2), which means two lines and very long waits if you don't go early or late. A TI/ticket booth is between the Pilier Nord and Pilier Est (east pillar). The stairs (yes, you can walk up partway) are next to the Jules Verne restaurant entrance. A sign in the jam-packed elevator reminds you to beware of pickpockets.

The tower is 300 meters/1,000 feet tall, 15 centimeters/6 inches taller in hot weather, covers 2.5 acres, and requires 50 tons of paint. Its 7,000 tons of metal are spread out so well at the base that it's no heavier per square inch than a linebacker on tiptoes. Visitors to Paris may find *Mona Lisa* to be less than expected, but the Eiffel Tower rarely disappoints, even in an era of skyscrapers.

Built one hundred years after the French Revolution (and in the midst of an Industrial one), the tower served no function but to impress. Bridge-builder Gustave Eiffel won the contest for the 1889 Centennial World's Fair by beating out such rival proposals as a giant guillotine. To a generation hooked on technology, the tower was the marvel of the age, a symbol of progress and of man's ingenuity. To others, it was a cloned-sheep monstrosity. The writer Guy de Maupassant routinely ate lunch in the tower just so he wouldn't have to look at it.

Delicate and graceful when seen from afar, it's massive—

even a bit scary—from close up. You don't appreciate the size until you walk toward it; like a mountain, it seems so close but takes forever to reach. There are three observation platforms at 60, 120, and 270 meters (200, 400, and 900 feet); the higher you go, the more you pay. Each requires a separate elevator (and line), so plan on at least 90 minutes if you want to go to the top and back. The view from the 120-meter-high (400 feet) second level is plenty. As you ascend through the metal beams, imagine being a worker, perched high above nothing, riveting this giant erector set together. On top, all of Paris lies before you, with a panorama guide. On a good day, you can see for 65 kilometers/40 miles.

The first level has exhibits, a post office (daily 10:00–19:00, cancellation stamp will read Eiffel Tower), snack bar, WCs, and souvenirs. Read the informative signs (in English) describing the major monuments, see the entertaining free movie on the history of the tower, and don't miss a century of fireworks including the entire millennium blast on video. Then consider a drink or a sandwich overlooking all of Paris at the snack café (outdoor tables in summer) or at the city's best view bar/restaurant, **Altitude 95** (€19–28 lunches, €46 dinners, dinner seatings at 19:00 and 21:00, reserve well ahead for a view table; before you ascend to dine, drop by the booth between the north *(nord)* and east *(est)* pillars to buy your Eiffel Tower ticket and pick up a pass that enables you to skip the line; tel. 01 45 55 20 04, fax 01 47 05 94 40).

The second level has the best views (walk up the stairway to get above the netting), a small cafeteria, WCs, and an Internet gimmick to have your photo at the Eiffel Tower sent into cyberspace (La Gallerie des Visiteurs).

It costs €4 to go to the first level, €7 to the second, and €10 to go all the way for the 270-meter/900-foot view (not covered by museum pass). On a budget? You can climb the stairs to the second level for only €3 (March–Sept daily 9:00–24:00, Oct–Feb 9:30–23:00, last entry 1 hour before closing, shorter lines at night, Mo: Trocadero, RER: Champ de Mars, tel. 01 44 11 23 23).

The best place to view the tower is from Trocadéro Square to the north (a 10-min walk across the river, and a happening scene at night). Consider arriving at the Trocadéro Métro stop, then walking toward the tower. Another great viewpoint is the long, grassy field, le Champ de Mars, to the south (after about 20:00, the gendarmes look the other way as Parisians stretch out or picnic on the grass). However impressive it may be by day, it's an awesome thing to see at twilight, when the tower becomes engorged with light, and virile Paris lies back and lets night be on top.

▲Paris Sewer Tour (Egouts)—This quick and easy visit takes you along a few hundred meters of underground water tunnel lined with interesting displays, well described in English, explaining the evolution of the world's longest sewer system. (If you straightened out Paris' sewers, they would reach beyond Istanbul.) Don't miss the slideshow, the fine WCs just beyond the gift shop, and the occasional tour in English (€4, covered by museum pass, Sat–Wed 11:00–17:00, closed Thu–Fri, where pont de l'Alma greets the Left Bank, Mo: Alma Marceau, RER: Pont de l'Alma, tel. 01 47 05 10 29).

▲▲Napoleon's Tomb and Army Museum (Les Invalides)—The emperor lies majestically dead inside several coffins under a grand dome—a goose-bumping pilgrimage for historians. Napoleon is surrounded by the tombs of other French war heroes and a fine military museum in Hôtel des Invalides. Check out the interesting World War II wing. Follow signs to the "crypt" to find Roman Empire–style reliefs listing the accomplishments of Napoleon's administration. The restored dome glitters with 26 pounds of gold (€6, students and kids 12–17-€5, under 12 free, daily April–Sept 9:00–17:45, mid-June–mid-Sept until 18:45, Oct–March 10:00–16:45; closed first Mon of month; open 30 min longer Sun, Napoleon's Tomb open 45 min longer daily June 15–Sept 15, closed Jan 1, May 1, Nov 1, and Dec 25, Mo: La Tour Maubourg or Varennes, tel. 01 44 42 37 72).

▲▲Rodin Museum (Musée Rodin)—This user-friendly museum is filled with passionate works by the greatest sculptor since Michelangelo. See *The Kiss*, *The Thinker*, *The Gates of Hell*, and many more. Don't miss the room full of work by Rodin's student and mistress, Camille Claudel (€5, €3 on Sun and for students, free for youth under 18 and for anyone first Sun of month; covered by museum pass; €1 for gardens only, which may be Paris' best deal as many works are well displayed in the beautiful gardens; April–Sept Tue–Sun 9:30–17:45, closed Mon, gardens close 18:45, Oct–March Tue–Sun 9:30–17:00, closed Mon, gardens close 16:45; near Napoleon's Tomb, 77 rue de Varennes, Mo: Varennes, tel. 01 44 18 61 10). There's a good self-serve cafeteria as well as idyllic picnic spots in the family-friendly back garden.

▲▲Marmottan Museum (Musée Marmottan)—In this private, intimate, less-visited museum, you'll find more than 100 paintings by Claude Monet (thanks to his son Michel), including the *Impressions of a Sunrise* painting that gave the movement its start—and name (€6.50, not covered by museum pass, Tue–Sun 10:00–18:00, closed Mon, 2 rue Louis Boilly, Mo: La Muette, follow museum signs 6 blocks through a delightful kid-filled park, tel. 01 44 96 50 33). Nearby is one of Paris' most pleasant shopping streets, the rue de Passy (from La Muette Métro stop).

Sights—Southeast Paris: The Latin Quarter

▲Latin Quarter (Quartier Latin)—This Left Bank neighborhood, just opposite Notre-Dame, is the Latin Quarter. (For more information and a walking tour, see the "Historic Core of Paris Walk," above.) This was a center of Roman Paris. But its touristic fame relates to the Latin Quarter's intriguing artsy, bohemian character. This was perhaps Europe's leading university district in the Middle Ages—home, since the 13th century, to the prestigious Sorbonne University. Back then, Latin was the language of higher education. And, since students here came from all over Europe, Latin served as their linguistic common denominator. Locals referred to the quarter by its language: Latin. In modern times, this was the center of Paris' café culture. The neighborhood's main boulevards (St. Michel and St. Germain) are lined with cafés—once the haunts of great poets and philosophers but now the hangout of tired tourists. While still youthful and artsy, the area has become a tourist ghetto filled with cheap North African eateries.

▲▲Cluny Museum (Musée National du Moyen Age)—This treasure trove of medieval art fills the old Roman baths, offering close-up looks at stained glass, Notre-Dame carvings, fine goldsmithing and jewelry, and rooms of tapestries—the best of which is the exquisite *Lady with the Unicorn*. In five panels, a delicate-as-medieval-can-be noble lady introduces a delighted unicorn to the senses of taste, hearing, sight, smell, and touch (€7, €5.50 on Sun, free first Sun of month, covered by museum pass, Wed–Mon 9:15–17:45, closed Tue, near corner of boulevards St. Michel and St. Germain, Mo: Cluny, tel. 01 53 73 78 00).

St. Germain-des-Prés—A church was first built on this site in A.D. 452. The church you see today was constructed in 1163. The area around the church hops at night with fire eaters, mimes, and scads of artists (Mo: St. Germain-des-Prés).

▲St. Sulpice Organ Concert—For pipe-organ enthusiasts, this is a delight. The Grand-Orgue at St. Sulpice has a rich history, with a succession of 12 world-class organists (including Widor and Dupré) going back 300 years. Widor started the tradition of opening the loft to visitors after the 10:30 service on Sundays. Daniel Roth continues to welcome guests in three languages while playing five keyboards at once. The 10:30 Sunday Mass is followed by a high-powered 25-minute recital at 11:40. Then, just after noon, the small, unmarked door is opened (left of entry as you face the rear). Visitors scamper like 16th notes up spiral stairs, past the 18th-century StairMasters that were used to fill the bellows, into a world of 7,000 pipes, where they can watch the master play during the next Mass.

Latin Quarter

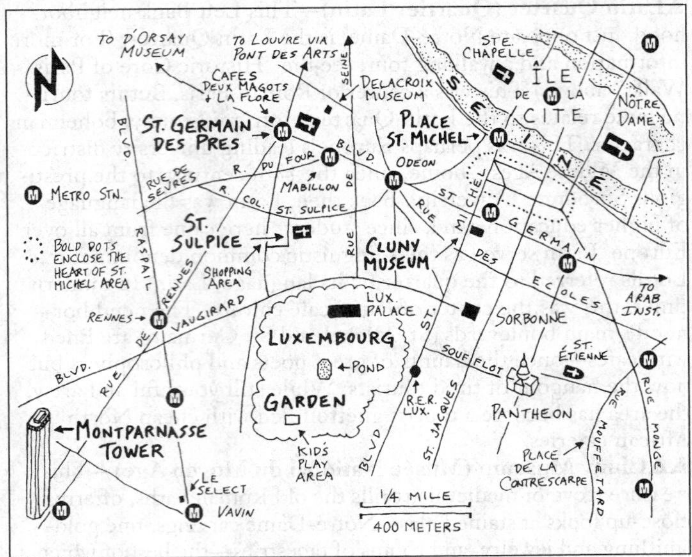

You'll generally have 30 minutes to kill (there's a plush lounge) before the organ plays; visitors can leave at any time. If late or rushed, show up around 12:30 and wait at the little door. As someone leaves, you can slip in (Mo: St. Sulpice or Mabillon). The Luxembourg Garden and St. Germain market are both nearby and open daily (the St. Germain market is between St. Sulpice and Métro stop Mabillon on rue Clément).

▲▲Luxembourg Garden (Jardin du Luxembourg)—Paris' most beautiful, interesting, and enjoyable garden/park/recreational area is a great place to watch Parisians at rest and play. These private gardens are property of the French Senate (housed in the château) and have special rules governing their use (e.g., where cards can be played, where dogs can be walked, where joggers can run, when and where music can be played). The brilliant flower beds are completely changed three times a year, and the boxed trees are brought out of the orangerie in May. Challenge the card and chess players to a game (near the tennis courts), or find a free chair near the main pond and take a breather. Notice any pigeons? The story goes that a poor Ernest Hemingway used to hand-hunt (read: strangle) them here. Paris Walking Tours offers a good tour of the park (see "Organized Tours of Paris," page 240).

The grand, neoclassical-domed Panthéon, now a mausoleum

housing the tombs of several great Frenchmen, is a block away and only worth entering if you have a museum pass. The park is open until dusk (Mo: Odéon, RER: Luxembourg).

If you enjoy the Luxembourg Garden and want to see more, visit the nearby, colorful Jardin des Plantes (Mo: Jussieu or Gare d'Austerlitz, RER: Luxembourg) and the more elegant Parc Monceau (Mo: Monceau).

Montparnasse Tower (La Tour Montparnasse)—This 59-floor superscraper is cheaper and easier to get to the top of than the Eiffel Tower, and has the added bonus of one of Paris' best views—since the Eiffel Tower is in it, and the Montparnasse Tower isn't. Buy the photo guide to the city, then go to the rooftop and orient yourself (€8, not covered by museum pass, daily in summer 9:30–23:30, off-season 10:00–22:00, disappointing after dark, entrance on rue l'Arrivé, Mo: Montparnasse). The tower is an efficient stop when combined with a day trip to Chartres, which begins at the Montparnasse train station.

▲Catacombs—These underground tunnels contain the anonymous bones of six million permanent Parisians. In 1785, the Revolutionary government of Paris decided to make its congested city more spacious and sanitary by emptying the city cemeteries (which traditionally surrounded churches) into an official ossuary. The perfect locale was the many kilometers of underground tunnels from limestone quarries, which were, at that time, just outside the city. For decades, priests led ceremonial processions of black-veiled, bone-laden carts into the quarries, where the bones were stacked into piles 1.5 meters/5 feet high and as much as 24 meters/80 feet deep behind neat walls of skull-studded tibiae. Each transfer was completed with the placement of a plaque indicating the church and district from which that stack of bones came and the date they arrived.

From the entry of the catacombs, a spiral staircase leads 18 meters/60 feet down. Then you begin a 1.5-kilometer-long (1 mile) subterranean walk. After several blocks of empty passageways, you ignore a sign announcing: "Halt, this is the empire of the dead." Along the way, plaques encourage visitors to reflect upon their destiny: "Happy is he who is forever faced with the hour of his death and prepares himself for the end every day." You emerge far from where you entered, with white, limestone-covered toes, telling anyone in the know you've been underground gawking at bones. Note to wanna-be Hamlets: An attendant checks your bag at the exit for stolen souvenirs. A flashlight is handy (€5, not covered by museum pass, 1 place Denfert-Rochereau, Mo: Denfert-Rochereau, Wed–Sun 9:00–16:00, Tue 11:00–16:00, closed Mon, tel. 01 43 22 47 63).

Sights—Northwest Paris

▲▲Place de la Concorde and the Champs-Elysées—This famous boulevard is Paris' backbone, and has the greatest concentration of traffic. All of France seems to converge on the place de la Concorde, the city's largest square. It was here that the guillotine took the lives of thousands—including King Louis XVI and Marie-Antoinette. Back then it was called the place de la Revolution.

Catherine de' Medici wanted a place to drive her carriage, so she started draining the swamp that would become the Champs-Elysées. Napoleon put on the final touches, and it's been the place to be seen ever since. The Tour de France bicycle race ends here, as do all parades (French or foe) of any significance. While the boulevard has become a bit hamburgerized, a walk here is a must. Take the Métro to the Arc de Triomphe (Mo: Etoile) and saunter down the Champs-Elysées (Métro stops every few blocks: FDR, George V, and Etoile).

▲▲▲Arc de Triomphe—Napoleon had the magnificent Arc de Triomphe commissioned to commemorate his victory at the Battle of Austerlitz. There's no triumphal arch bigger (50 meters/164 feet high, 40 meters/130 feet wide). And, with 12 converging boulevards, there's no traffic circle more thrilling to experience—either behind the wheel or on foot (take the underpass). An elevator or a spiral staircase leads to a cute museum about the arch and a grand view from the top, even after dark (€7, covered by museum pass, April–Sept daily 10:00–23:00, Oct–March daily 10:00–22:30, Mo: Etoile, use underpass to reach arch, tel. 01 55 37 73 77).

▲Old Opera House (Le Palais Garnier)—This grand palace of the belle époque was built for Napoleon III and finished in 1875. (After completing this project, the architect—Garnier—went south to do the casino in Monte Carlo.) From the grand avenue de l'Opéra, once lined with Paris' most fashionable haunts, the newly restored facade seems to say "all power to the wealthy." While huge, the actual theater seats only 2,000. The real show was before and after, when the elite of Paris—out to see and be seen—strutted their elegant stuff in the extravagant lobbies. Think of the grand marble stairway as a theater itself. As you wander the halls and gawk at the decor, imagine the place filled with the beautiful people of the day. The massive foundations straddle an underground lake (creating the mysterious world of the *Phantom of the Opera*). Tourists can peek from two boxes into the actual red velvet theater to see Marc Chagall's colorful ceiling (1964) playfully dancing around the eight-ton chandelier. Note the box seats next to the stage—the most expensive in the house, with an obstructed view of the stage but just right if you're there only to be seen. The elitism of this place prompted Mitterand to have a people's opera house built in the 1980s (symbolically, on place de la Bastille, where the French Revolution started in 1789). This left the Garnier Opéra home only to a ballet and occasional concerts (usually no performances mid-July–mid-Sept). While the library/museum is of interest to opera buffs, anyone will enjoy the second-floor grand foyer and Salon du Glacier, iced with decor typical of 1900 (€6, not covered by museum pass, daily 10:00–17:00 except when in use for performance, €10 English tours summers only, normally at 12:00 and 14:00, 90 min, includes entry, call to confirm; enter through the front off place de l'Opéra, Mo: Opéra, tel. 01 40 01 22 53). American Express and the *Paris Story* film are on the left side of the opera, and the venerable Galeries Lafayette department store is just behind.

***Paris Story* Film**—This entertaining film gives a good and painless overview of Paris' turbulent and brilliant past, covering 2,000 years in 45 fast-moving minutes. The theater's wide-screen projection and cushy chairs provide an ideal break from bad weather and sore feet and make it fun with kids (€8, kids 6–18-€5, families with 2 kids and 2 parents-€21, not covered by museum pass, claim a 20 percent discount with this book, shows are on the hour daily 9:00–19:00, next to opera at 11 rue Scribe, Mo: Opéra, tel. 01 42 66 62 06).

▲▲Jacquemart-André Museum (Musée Jacquemart-André)—This thoroughly enjoyable museum showcases the lavish home of a wealthy, art-loving, 19th-century Parisian couple. After wandering the grand boulevards, you now get inside for an intimate look at the lifestyles of the Parisian rich and fabulous. Edouard André and his wife, Nélie Jacquemart—who had no children—spent their lives and fortunes designing, building, and then decorating a sumptuous mansion. What makes this visit so rewarding is the fine audioguide tour (in English, free with admission). The place is strewn with paintings by Rembrandt, Botticelli, Uccello, Mantegna, Bellini, Boucher, and Fragonard—enough to make a painting gallery famous. Plan on spending an hour with the audioguide (€8, not covered by museum pass, daily 10:00–18:00, elegant café, 158 boulevard Haussmann, Mo: Miromesnil, tel. 01 42 89 04 91).

▲Grande Arche de la Défense—On the outskirts of Paris, the centerpiece of Paris' ambitious skyscraper complex (La Défense) is the Grande Arche. Inaugurated in 1989 on the 200th anniversary of the French Revolution, it was dedicated to human rights and brotherhood. The place is big—38 floors holding offices for 30,000 people on more than 200 acres. Notre-Dame Cathedral could fit under its arch. The complex at La Défense is an interesting study in 1960s land-use planning. More than 100,000 workers commute here daily, directing lots of business and development away from downtown and allowing central Paris to retain its more elegant feel. This makes sense to most Parisians, regardless of whatever else they feel about this controversial complex. You will enjoy city views from the Arche elevator (€7, under 18-€5.50, not covered by museum pass, daily 10:00–19:00, includes a film on its construction and art exhibits, RER or Mo: La Défense, follow signs to Grande Arche or get off 1 stop earlier at Esplanade de la Défense and walk through the interesting business complex, tel. 01 49 07 27 57).

Sights—North Paris: Montmartre

▲▲Sacré-Coeur and Montmartre—This Byzantine-looking church, while only 130 years old, is impressive (daily until 23:00). One block from the church, the place du Tertre was the haunt of Toulouse-Lautrec and the original bohemians. Today, it's mobbed with tourists and unoriginal bohemians, but it's still fun (go early in the morning to beat the crowds). Take the Métro to the Anvers stop (1 Métro ticket buys your way up the funicular and avoids the stairs) or the closer but less scenic Abbesses stop. A taxi to the top of the hill saves time and avoids sweat.

Pigalle—Paris' red-light district, the infamous "Pig Alley," is at the foot of butte Montmartre. *Ooh la la*. It's more shocking than dangerous. Walk from place Pigalle to place Blanche, teasing desperate barkers and fast-talking temptresses. In bars, a €150 bottle of cheap champagne comes with a friend. Stick to the bigger streets, hang on to your wallet, and exercise good judgment. Cancan can cost a fortune, as can con artists in topless bars. After dark, countless tour buses line the streets, reminding us that tour guides make big bucks by bringing their groups to touristy nightclubs like the famous Moulin Rouge (Mo: Pigalle or Abbesses).

Sights—Northeast Paris: Marais Neighborhood and More

The Marais neighborhood extends along the Right Bank of the Seine from the Pompidou Center to the Bastille. It contains more pre-revolutionary lanes and buildings than anywhere else in town and is more atmospheric than touristy. It's medieval Paris. This is how much of the city looked until, in the mid-1800s, Napoleon III had Baron Haussmann blast out the narrow streets to construct broad boulevards (wide enough for the guns and ranks of the army, too wide for revolutionary barricades), creating modern Paris. Originally a swamp *(marais)* during the reign of Henry IV, this area became the hometown of the French aristocracy. In the 17th century, big shots built their private mansions *(hôtels)*, close to Henry's place des Vosges. When strolling the Marais, stick to the

Marais Neighborhood

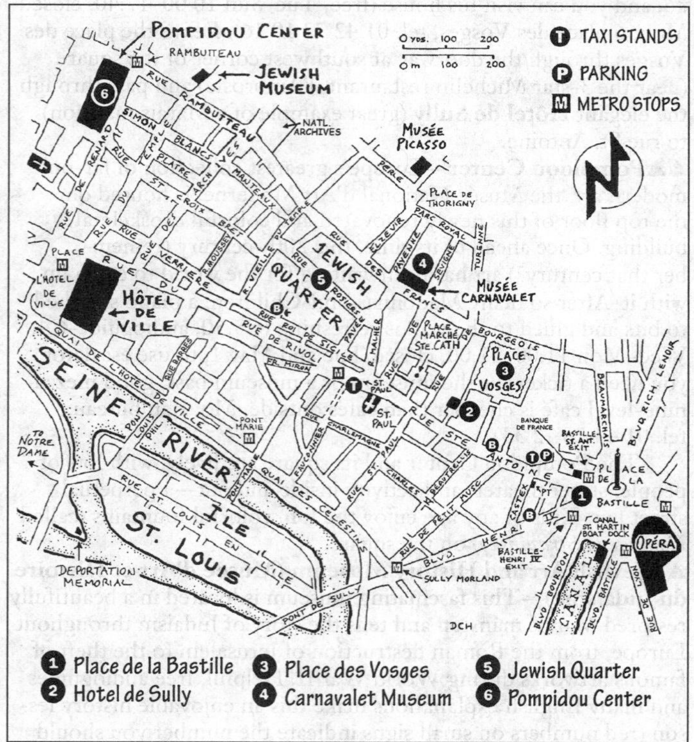

west-east axis formed by rue Sainte Croix de la Bretonnerie, rue des Rosiers (heart of Paris' Jewish community), and rue St. Antoine. On Sunday afternoons, this trendy area pulses with shoppers and café crowds.

▲Place des Vosges—Study the architecture in this grand square: nine pavilions per side. Some of the brickwork is real, some is fake. Walk to the center, where Louis XIII sits on a horse surrounded by locals enjoying their community park. Children frolic in the sandbox, lovers warm benches, and pigeons guard their fountains while trees shade this retreat from the glare of the big city. Henry IV built this centerpiece of the Marais in 1605. As hoped, this turned the Marais into Paris' most exclusive neighborhood. As the nobility flocked to Versailles in a later age, this too was a magnet for the rich and powerful of France. With the Revolution, the aristocratic elegance of this quarter became working-class, filled with gritty shops, artisans, immigrants, and Jews. **Victor Hugo** lived at #6, and you can visit his house (free, Tue–Sun 10:00–17:40, closed Mon, 6 place des Vosges, tel. 01 42 72 10 16). Leave the place des Vosges through the doorway at southwest corner of the square (near the 3-star Michelin restaurant, l'Ambrosie) and pass through the elegant **Hôtel de Sully** (great example of a Marais mansion) to rue St. Antoine.

▲▲Pompidou Center—Europe's greatest collection of far-out modern art, the Musée National d'Art Moderne, is housed on the top floor of this newly renovated and colorful exoskeletal building. Once ahead of its time, this 20th-century (remember that century?) art has been waiting for the world to catch up with it. After so many Madonnas-and-Children, a piano smashed to bits and glued to the wall is refreshing (€5.50, audioguide-€4, Wed–Mon 11:00–21:00, closed Tue and May 1, to use escalator you need a ticket for the museum or a museum pass, good mezzanine-level café is cheaper than cafés outside, Mo: Rambuteau, tel. 01 44 78 12 33).

The Pompidou Center and its square are lively, with lots of people, street theater, and activity inside and out—a perpetual street fair. Kids of any age enjoy the fun, colorful fountains (called *Homage to Stravinsky*) on the square.

▲▲Jewish Art and History Museum (Musée d'Art et Histoire du Judaïsme)—This fascinating museum is located in a beautifully restored Marais mansion and tells the story of Judaism throughout Europe, from the Roman destruction of Jerusalem to the theft of famous artworks during World War II. Helpful, free audioguides and many English explanations make this an enjoyable history lesson (red numbers on small signs indicate the number you should press on your audioguide). Move along at your own speed. The museum illustrates the cultural unity maintained by this continually dispersed population. You'll learn about the history of Jewish traditions from bar mitzvahs to menorahs, and see exquisite traditional costumes and objects around which daily life revolved. Don't miss the explanation of "the Dreyfus affair," a major event in early 1900 French politics. You'll also see photographs of and paintings by famous Jewish artists, including Chagall, Modigliani, and Soutine. A small but moving section is devoted to the deportation of Jews from Paris (€6.50, ages 18–26-€4, under 18 free, not covered by museum pass, Mon–Fri 11:00–18:00, Sun 10:00–18:00, closed Sat, 71 rue du Temple, Mo: Rambuteau or Hôtel de Ville a few blocks farther away, tel. 01 53 01 86 60).

▲Picasso Museum (Musée Picasso)—Hidden in a far corner of the Marais and worth **▲▲▲** if you're a Picasso fan, this museum contains the world's largest collection of Picasso's paintings, sculptures, sketches, and ceramics, and includes his small collection of Impressionist art. The art is well-displayed in a fine old mansion with a peaceful garden café. The room-by-room English introductions help make sense of Picasso's work—from the Lautrec-like portraits at the beginning of his career, to his gray-brown Cubist period, to his Salvador Dalí–like finish. The well-done €3 English guidebook helps Picassophiles appreciate the context of his art and learn more about his interesting life. Most will be happy reading the posted English explanations while moving at a steady pace through the museum—the ground and first floors satisfied my curiosity (€5.50, free first Sun of month, covered by museum pass, Wed–Mon 9:30–18:00, closes at 17:30 Oct–March, closed Tue, 5 rue Thorigny, Mo: St. Paul or Chemin Vert, tel. 01 42 71 25 21).

▲▲Carnavalet Museum—The tumultuous history of Paris is well-displayed in this converted Marais mansion. Unfortunately, explanations are in French only, but many displays are fairly self-explanatory. You'll see paintings of Parisian scenes, French Revolution paraphernalia, old Parisian store signs, a small guillotine, a model of 16th-century Ile de la Cité (notice the bridge houses), and rooms full of 15th-century Parisian furniture (free, Tue–Sun 10:00–18:00, closed Mon, 23 rue de Sévigné, Mo: St. Paul, tel. 01 44 59 58 58).

▲Promenade Plantée Park—This three-kilometer-long (2 miles), narrow garden walk on a viaduct was once a railroad and is now a joy. It runs from place de la Bastille (Mo: Bastille) along avenue Daumesnil to Saint-Mandé (Mo: Michel Bizot). Part of the park is elevated. At times, you'll walk along the street until you pick up the next segment. To reach the park from place de la Bastille, take avenue Daumesnil (past opera building) to the intersection with avenue Ledru Rollin; walk up the stairs and through the gate (free, opens Mon–Fri at 8:00, Sat–Sun at 9:00, closes at sunset). The shops below the viaduct's arches make for entertaining window-shopping.

▲Père Lachaise Cemetery (Cimetière Père Lachaise)—Littered with the tombstones of many of the city's most illustrious dead, this is your best one-stop look at the fascinating, romantic world of "permanent Parisians." More like a small city, the place is confusing, but maps will direct you to the graves of Chopin, Molière, Edith Piaf, Oscar Wilde, Gertrude Stein, Jim Morrison, and Héloïse and Abelard. In section 92, a series of statues memorializing World War II makes the French war experience a bit more real (helpful €1.50 maps at flower store near entry, closes at dusk, across street from Métro stop, Mo: Père Lachaise or bus #69).

Shopping Parisian-Style

Even staunch anti-shoppers may be tempted to partake of chic Paris. Wandering among the elegant and outrageous boutiques provides a break from the heavy halls of the Louvre, and, if you approach it right, a little cultural enlightenment.

Here are some tips for avoiding *faux pas* and making the most of the experience.

French Etiquette: Before you enter a Parisian store, remember the following points.

• In small stores, always greet the clerk by saying *Bonjour*, plus the appropriate title *(Madame, Mademoiselle,* or *Monsieur).* When leaving, say, *Au revoir, Madame/Mademoiselle/Monsieur.*

• The customer is not always right. In fact, figure the clerk is doing you a favor by waiting on you.

• Except for in department stores, it's not normal for the customer to handle clothing. Ask first.

• Observe French shoppers. Then imitate.

Department Stores: Like cafés, department stores were invented here (surprisingly, not in America). Parisian department stores, monuments to a more relaxed and elegant era, begin with their spectacular perfume sections. Helpful information desks are usually nearby (pick up the handy store floor plan in English). Most stores have a good selection of souvenirs and toys at fair prices and reasonable restaurants; some have great view terraces. Choose from these four great Parisian department stores: Galeries Lafayette (behind old Opéra Garnier, Mo: Opéra), Printemps (next door to Galeries Lafayette), Bon Marché (Mo: Sèvres-Babylone), and Samaritaine (near pont Neuf, Mo: Pont Neuf). Forum des Halles is a huge subterranean shopping center (Mo: Les Halles).

Boutiques: I enjoy window-shopping, pausing at cafés, and observing the rhythm of neighborhood life. While the shops are more intimate, sales clerks are more formal—mind your manners. Here are four very different areas to explore:

A stroll from Sèvres-Babylone to St. Sulpice allows you to sample smart, classic clothing boutiques while enjoying one of Paris' prettier neighborhoods—for sustenance along the way, there's La Maison du Chocolat at 19 rue de Sèvres, selling handmade chocolates in exquisitely wrapped boxes.

The ritzy streets connecting place de la Madeleine and place Vendôme form a miracle mile of gourmet food shops, jewelry stores, four-star hotels, perfumeries, and exclusive clothing boutiques. Fauchon's, on place Madeleine, is a bastion of over-the-top food products, hawking €7,000 bottles of Cognac (who buys this stuff?). Hediard's, across the square from Fauchon's, is an older, more appealing, and accessible gourmet food shop. Next door, La Maison des Truffes sells black mushrooms for about €180 a pound, and white truffles from Italy for €2,500 a pound.

For more eclectic, avant-garde stores, peruse the artsy shops between the Pompidou Center and place des Vosges in the Marais.

For a contemporary, more casual, and less frenetic shopping experience, and to see Paris' latest urban renewal project, take the Métro to Bercy Village, a once-thriving wine warehouse district that has been transformed into an outdoor shopping mall (Mo: Cour St. Emilion).

Flea Markets: Paris hosts several sprawling weekend flea markets (*marché aux puces*, pron. mar-shay oh poos; literally translated, since *puce* is French for flea). These oversized garage sales date back to the Middle Ages, when middlemen would sell old, flea-infested clothes and discarded possessions of the wealthy at bargain prices to eager peasants. Today, some travelers find them claustrophobic, crowded, monster versions of those back home, though others find their French diamonds-in-the-rough and return happy.

The Puces St. Ouen (pron. poos sahn-wahn) is the biggest and oldest of them all, with more than 2,000 vendors selling everything from flamingos to faucets (Sat 9:00–18:30, Sun–Mon 10:00–18:30, Mo: Porte de Clingancourt).

Street Markets: Several traffic-free street markets overflow with flowers, produce, fish vendors, and butchers, illustrating how most Parisians shopped before there were supermarkets and department stores. Good market streets include the rue Cler (Mo: Ecole Militaire), rue Montorgueil (Mo: Etienne Marcel), rue Mouffetard (Mo: Cardinal Lemoine or Censier-Daubenton), and rue Daguerre (Mo: Denfert-Rochereau). Browse these markets to collect a classy picnic (open daily except Sun afternoons and Mon, also closed for lunch 13:00–15:00).

Souvenir Shops: Avoid souvenir carts in front of famous monuments. Prices and selection are better in shops and department stores. The riverfront stalls near Notre-Dame sell a variety of used books, magazines, and tourist paraphernalia in the most romantic setting.

Whether you indulge in a new wardrobe, an artsy poster, or just one luscious pastry, you'll find that a shopping excursion provides a priceless slice of Parisian life.

Disappointments de Paris

Here are a few negatives to help you manage your limited time:

La Madeleine is a big, stark, neoclassical church with a postcard facade and a postbox interior. The famous aristocratic deli behind the church, Fauchon, is elegant, but so are many others handier to your hotel.

Paris' **Panthéon** (nothing like Rome's) is another stark neoclassical edifice, filled with the mortal remains of great Frenchmen who mean little to the average American tourist.

The **Bastille** is Paris' most famous non-sight. The square is there, but confused tourists look everywhere and can't find the famous prison of Revolution fame. The building's gone and the square is good only as a jumping-off point for Promenade Plantée Park (see "Sights—Northeast Paris," above).

Finally, the **Latin Quarter** is a frail shadow of its characteristic self. It's more Tunisian, Greek, and Woolworth's than old-time Paris. The café life that turned on Hemingway and endeared the "boul' Miche" and boulevard St. Germain to so many poets is also trampled by modern commercialism.

Palace of Versailles

Every king's dream, Versailles was the residence of the French king and the cultural heartbeat of Europe for about 100 years—until the Revolution of 1789 ended the notion that God deputized some people to rule for Him on Earth. Louis XIV spent half a year's income of Europe's richest country turning his dad's hunting lodge into a palace fit for a divine monarch. Louis XV and Louis XVI spent much of the 18th century gilding Louis XIV's lily. In 1837, about 50 years after the royal family was evicted, King Louis Philippe opened the palace as a museum. Europe's next-best palaces are Versailles wannabes.

Information: A helpful TI is just past Sofitel Hôtel on your walk from the station to the palace (May–Sept daily 9:00–19:00, Oct–April daily 9:00–18:00, tel. 01 39 24 88 88, www.chateauversailles.fr). You'll also find information booths inside the château (doors A, B-2, and C) and, in peak season, kiosks scattered around the courtyard. The useful brochure "Versailles Orientation Guide" explains your sightseeing options. A baggage check is available at door A.

Cost: €7.50 (main palace and both Trianons are covered by museum pass); €5.50 after 15:30, under 18 free (the palace is also theoretically free for all teachers, professors, and architecture students). Admission is payable at entrances A, C, and D. Tours cost extra (see "Touring Versailles," below). The Grand and Petit Trianons cost €5 together, €3 after 15:30 (both covered

Versailles

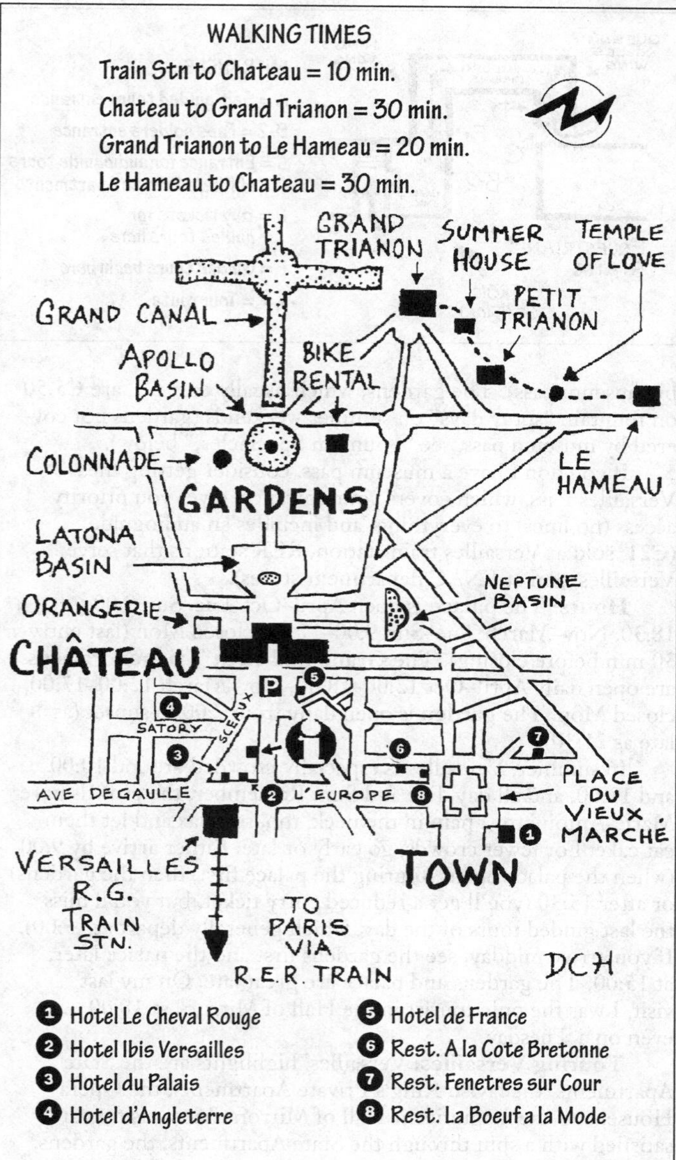
WALKING TIMES
Train Stn to Chateau = 10 min.
Chateau to Grand Trianon = 30 min.
Grand Trianon to Le Hameau = 20 min.
Le Hameau to Chateau = 30 min.
GRAND TRIANON
SUMMER HOUSE
TEMPLE OF LOVE
PETIT TRIANON
GRAND CANAL
APOLLO BASIN
BIKE RENTAL
COLONNADE
LE HAMEAU
GARDENS
LATONA BASIN
NEPTUNE BASIN
ORANGERIE
CHÂTEAU
P
SATORY
SCEAUX
AVE DEGAULLE
L'EUROPE
PLACE DU VIEUX MARCHÉ
VERSAILLES R.G. TRAIN STN.
TOWN
TO PARIS VIA R.E.R. TRAIN
DCH
1 Hotel Le Cheval Rouge
2 Hotel Ibis Versailles
3 Hotel du Palais
4 Hotel d'Angleterre
5 Hotel de France
6 Rest. A la Cote Bretonne
7 Rest. Fenetres sur Cour
8 Rest. La Boeuf a la Mode

Entrances to Versailles

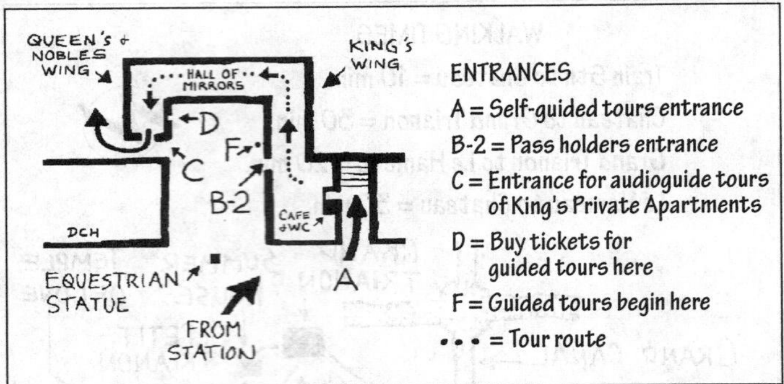

by museum pass). The gardens, which usually cost €3, are €5.50 on fountain "spray days" on summer weekends (gardens not covered by museum pass, see "Fountain Spectacles," below).

If you don't have a museum pass, consider getting the Versailles Pass, which covers your entrance, gives you priority access (no lines) to everything, and includes an audioguide (€21, sold at Versailles train station, RER stations that serve Versailles, and at FNAC department stores).

Hours: The **palace** is open April–Oct Tue–Sun 9:00–18:30, Nov–March Tue–Sun 9:00–17:30, closed Mon (last entry 30 min before closing). The **Grand and Petit Trianon Palaces** are open daily April–Oct 12:00–18:00, Nov–March 12:00–17:00, closed Mon. The **garden** is open daily from 7:00 to sunset (as late as 21:30).

In summer, Versailles is especially crowded around 10:00 and 13:00, and all day Tue and Sun. Remember, the crowds gave Marie-Antoinette a pain in the neck, too, so relax and let them eat cake. For fewer crowds, go early or late: Either arrive by 9:00 (when the palace opens, touring the palace first, then the gardens) or after 15:30 (you'll get a reduced entry ticket, but you'll miss the last guided tours of the day, which generally depart at 15:00). If you arrive midday, see the gardens first and the palace later, at 15:00. The gardens and palace are great late. On my last visit, I was the only tourist in the Hall of Mirrors at 18:00... even on a Tuesday.

Touring Versailles: Versailles' highlights are the State Apartments, the lavish King's Private Apartments, the Opera House, and the magnificent Hall of Mirrors. Most visitors are satisfied with a spin through the State Apartments, the gardens, and the Trianon Palaces. Versailles aficionados should spend the time (and money) to see the King's Private Apartments, which can be visited only with an audioguide or live guide (neither tour covered by museum pass).

Guided tours—You may select a one-hour guided tour from a variety of themes, such as the daily life of a king or the lives of such lesser-known nobles as the well-coiffed Madame de Pompadour (€4, join first English tour available). Or consider the 90-minute tour (€6) of the King's Private Apartments (Louis XV, Louis XVI, and Marie-Antoinette) and the chapel. This tour, which is the only way visitors can see the Opera House, can be long depending upon the quality of your guide.

For a live tour, make reservations at entrance D immediately upon arrival, as tours can sell out by 13:00 (first tours generally begin at 10:00, last tours depart usually at 15:00 but as late as 16:00). Guided tours begin at entrance F. The price of any tour is added to the €7.50 entry fee to Versailles (entry covered by museum pass, tours extra).

If you don't have a museum pass or Versailles Pass, and you think you might want to take a guided tour after you've seen the palace on your own, remember to keep your ticket to prove you've already paid for admission.

Audioguide tours—There are two informative but dry audioguide tours. One covers the State Apartments (€4, includes Hall of Mirrors and queen's bedchamber; start at entrance A or, if you have a museum pass, entrance B-2). The other includes more of the King's Private Apartments (Louis XIV) and a sampling of nobles' chambers (€4, entrance C). Both audioguide tours are sold until one hour before closing and are available at each entrance.

Self-guided tour—To tour the palace on your own, join the line at entrance A if you need to pay admission. Those with a museum pass are allowed in through entrance B-2 without a wait. Enter the palace and take a one-way walk through the State Apartments from the King's Wing, through the Hall of Mirrors, and out via the Queen's and Nobles' Wing.

The Hall of Mirrors was the ultimate hall of the day—75 meters/250 feet long, with 17 arched mirrors matching 17 windows with royal garden views, 24 gilded candelabra, eight busts of Roman emperors, and eight classical-style statues (7 are ancient originals). The ceiling is decorated with stories of Louis' triumphs. Imagine this place filled with silk gowns and powdered wigs, lit by thousands of candles. The mirrors—a luxurious rarity at the time—were a reflection of a time when aristocrats felt good about their looks and their fortunes. In another age altogether, this was the room in which the Treaty of Versailles was signed, ending World War I.

Before going downstairs at the end, take a stroll clockwise around the long room filled with the great battles of France murals. If you don't have *Rick Steves' Paris* or *Rick Steves' Mona Winks*, the guidebook called *The Châteaux, The Gardens, and Trianon* gives a room-by-room rundown.

Fountain Spectacles: Classical music fills the king's backyard, and the garden's fountains are in full squirt, on Sat July–Sept and on Sun early April–early Oct (schedule for both days: 11:00–12:00 & 15:30–17:00 & 17:20–17:30). On these "spray days," the gardens cost €5.50 (not covered by museum pass, ask for a map of fountains). Louis had his engineers literally reroute a river to fuel these fountains. Even by today's standards, they are impressive. Pick up the helpful brochure of the fountain show ("Les Grandes Eaux Musicales") at any information booth for a guide to the fountains. Also ask about the impressive *Les Fêtes de Nuit* nighttime spectacle (some Sat, July–mid-Sept).

Getting around the Gardens: It's a 30-minute hike from the palace, down the canal, past the two mini-palaces to the Hamlet. You can rent bikes (€6/hr). The fast-looking, slow-moving tourist train leaves from behind the château and serves the Grand Canal and the Trianon Palaces (€5, 4/hr, 4 stops, you can hop on and off as you like; nearly worthless commentary).

Palace Gardens: The gardens offer a world of royal amusements. Outside the palace is *l'orangerie*. Louis, the only person who could grow oranges in Paris, had a mobile orange grove that could be wheeled in and out of his greenhouses according to the weather. A promenade leads from the palace to the Grand Canal, an artificial lake that, in Louis' day, was a mini-sea with nine ships, including a 32-cannon warship. France's royalty used to float up and down the canal in Venetian gondolas.

While Louis cleverly used palace life at Versailles to "domesticate" his nobility, turning otherwise meddlesome nobles into groveling socialites, all this pomp and ceremony hampered the royal family as well. For an escape from the public life at Versailles, they built more intimate palaces as retreats in their garden. Before the Revolution there was plenty of space to retreat—the grounds were enclosed by a 40-kilometer-long (25 miles) fence.

The beautifully restored **Grand Trianon Palace** is as sumptuous as the main palace, but much smaller. With its pastel-pink colonnade and more human scale, this is a place you'd like to call home. The nearby **Petit Trianon**, which has a fine neoclassical exterior and a skippable interior, was Marie-Antoinette's favorite residence (€5 for both Trianons, €3 after 15:30, covered by museum pass, daily April–Oct 12:00–18:00, Nov–March 12:00–17:00, closed Mon).

You can almost see princesses bobbing gaily in the branches as you walk through the enchanting forest, past the white marble temple of love (1778) to the queen's fake-peasant **Hamlet** (*le Hameau;* interior not tourable). Palace life really got to Marie-Antoinette. Sort of a back-to-basics queen, she retreated further and further from her blue-blooded reality. Her happiest days were spent at the Hamlet, under a bonnet, tending her perfumed sheep and her manicured gardens in a thatch-happy wonderland.

Cafés: The cafeteria and WCs are next to door A. You'll find a sandwich kiosk and a decent restaurant are at the canal in the garden. For more recommendations, see "Eating in Versailles," page 129. A handy McDonald's is immediately across from the train station (WC without crowds).

Trip Length: Allow two hours for the palace and two for the gardens. Including two hours to cover your round-trip transit time, it's a six-hour day trip from Paris.

Getting There: Take the **RER-C train** (€5 round-trip, 30 min one-way) to Versailles R.G. or "Rive Gauche"—not Versailles C.H., which is farther from the palace. Trains named "Vick" leave about five times an hour for the palace from these RER stops: Gare d'Austerlitz, St. Michel, Musée d'Orsay, Invalides, Pont de l'Alma, and Champ de Mars. Any train named Vick goes to Versailles; don't board other trains. Get off at the last stop (Versailles Rive Gauche), turn right out of the station, and turn left at the first boulevard. It's a 10-minute walk to the palace.

Your Eurailpass covers this inexpensive trip, but it uses up a valuable "flexi" day. If you really want to use your railpass, consider seeing Versailles on your way in to or out of Paris. To get free passage, show your railpass at an SNCF ticket window—for example, at the Les Invalides or Musée d'Orsay RER stops—and get a *contremarque de passage*. Keep this ticket to exit the system.

When returning from Versailles, look through the windows past the turnstiles for the departure board. Any train leaving Versailles serves all downtown Paris RER line C stops (they're marked on the schedule as stopping at "*toutes les gares jusqu'à Austerlitz*," meaning "all stations until Austerlitz").

Taxis for the 30-minute ride between Versailles and Paris cost about €25.

To reach Versailles from Paris by **car**, get on the *périphérique* freeway that circles Paris and take the toll-free autoroute A-13 toward Rouen. Follow signs into Versailles, then look for Château signs and park in the huge lot in front of the palace (pay lot). The drive takes about 30 minutes one-way.

Town of Versailles (zip code: 78000): After the palace closes and the tourists go, the prosperous, wholesome town of Versailles feels a long way from Paris. The central market thrives on place du Marché on Sunday, Tuesday, and Friday until 13:00 (leaving the RER station, turn right and walk 10 min). Consider the wisdom of picking up or dropping your rental car in Versailles rather than in Paris. In Versailles, the Hertz and Avis offices are at Gare des Chantiers (Versailles C.H., served by Paris' Montparnasse station). Versailles makes a fine home base; see Versailles accommodations and recommended restaurants under "Sleeping" and "Eating," below.

More Day Trips from Paris

Chartres

Chartres and its cathedral make a ▲▲▲ day trip.

In 1194, a terrible fire destroyed the church at Chartres that housed the much-venerated veil of Mary. With almost unbelievably good fortune, the monks found the veil miraculously preserved in the ashes. Money poured in for the building of a bigger and better cathedral—decorated with 2,000 carved figures and some of France's best stained glass. The cathedral feels too large for the city because it was designed to accommodate huge crowds of pilgrims. One of those pilgrims, an impressed Napoleon, declared after a visit in 1811: "Chartres is no place for an atheist." Rodin called it the "Acropolis of France." British Francophile Malcolm Miller or his assistant gives great "Appreciation of Gothic" tours Monday through Saturday, usually at noon and 14:45 (verify times in advance, no tours off-season, tel. 02 37 28 15 58, fax 02 37 28 33 03). Each €10 tour is different; many people stay for both tours. Just show up at the church (daily 7:00–19:00).

Explore Chartres' pleasant city center and discover the picnic-friendly park behind the cathedral. The helpful TI, next to the cathedral, has a map with a self-guided tour of Chartres (Mon–Sat 9:00–19:00, Sun 9:30–17:30, tel. 02 37 18 26 26).

Getting There: Chartres is a one-hour train trip from the Gare Montparnasse (about €11.50 one-way, 10/day).

Sleeping in Chartres: To stay overnight, try the comfy **Hôtel Chatelet***** with its welcoming lobby and its spotless, spacious, well-furnished rooms (Sb-€65–75, Db-€72–83, extra person-€10, streetside rooms are cheaper, CC, 6 avenue Jehan de Beauce, tel. 02 37 21 78 00, fax 02 37 36 23 01, e-mail: hchatel@club-internet.fr). **Hôtel Jehan de Beauce**** is basic, but clean and quiet, with some tiny bathrooms (S-€31, D-€40, Ds-€43, Db-€54, Tb-€62, CC, 19 avenue Jehan de Beauce, tel. 02 37 21 01 41, fax 02 37 21 59 10). **Trois Lys** *crêperie* makes good and cheap crêpes just across the river on pont Boujou (3 rue de la Porte Guillaume, tel. 02 37 28 42 02).

Chartres

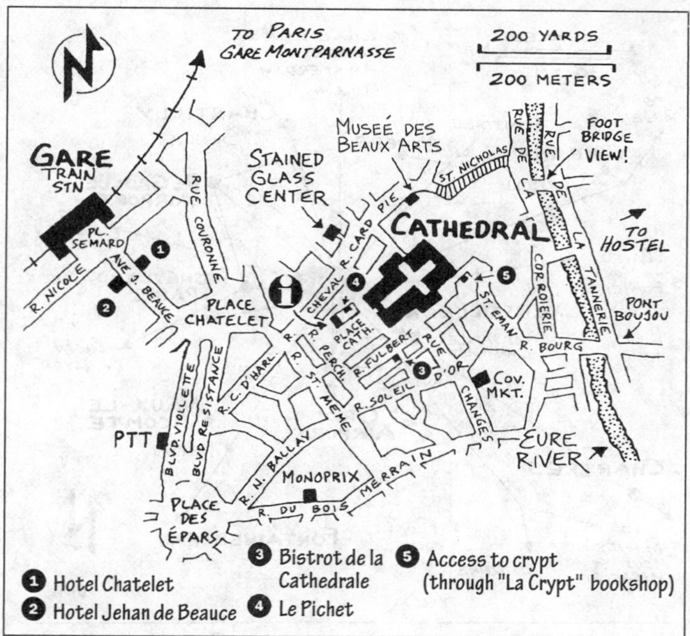

Giverny

Monet spent 43 of his most creative years here (1883–1926). His gardens and home, a ▲ sight, are unfortunately split by a busy road and are very popular with tourists. Buy your ticket, walk through the gardens, and take the underpass into the artist's famous lily pad land. The path leads you over the Japanese Bridge, under weeping willows, and past countless scenes that leave artists aching for an easel. Back on the other side, stroll through his more robust, structured garden and his mildly interesting home. The jammed gift shop at the exit is Monet's actual skylit studio.

While lines may be long and tour groups may trample the flowers, true fans still find magic in those lily pads. Minimize crowds by arriving before 10:00 (get in line) or after 16:00 (€5.50, €4 for gardens only, April–Oct Tue–Sun 10:00–18:00, closed Mon and Nov–March, tel. 02 32 51 94 65).

Take the Rouen-bound train from Paris' Gare St. Lazare station to Vernon (about €22 round-trip, long gaps in service, know schedule before you go). From the Vernon train station to Monet's garden (4 km/2.5 miles one-way), you have three good options (bus, taxi, and

Paris Day Trips

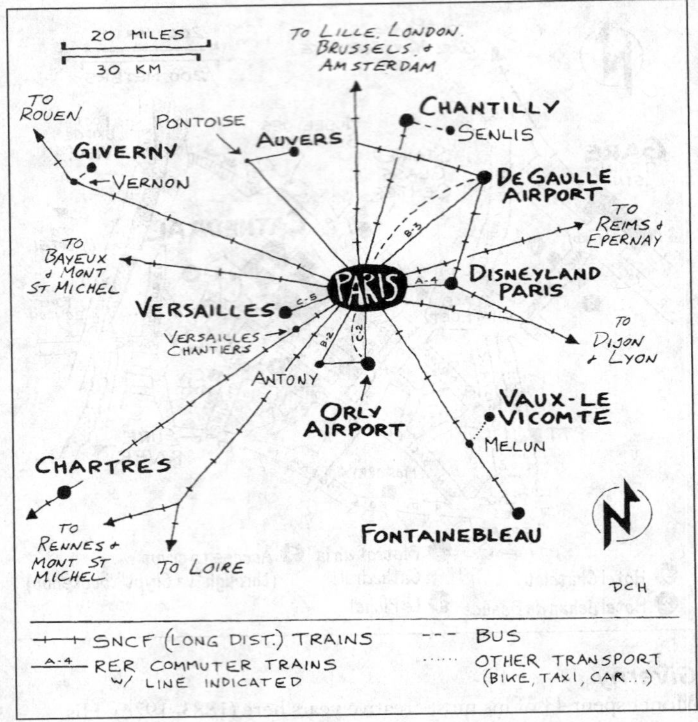

bike). The Vernon–Giverny **bus** is scheduled to meet most trains (4/day, make sure the driver knows you plan to return by bus and on which trip, otherwise he may not make the last Giverny pickup). If you miss the last bus, find others to share a **taxi** (about €11 for up to 3, €12 for 4, tel. 06 07 34 36 68, 06 76 08 50 78, or 02 32 21 31 31). The ticket office at Monet's home in Giverny has bus schedules and can call a taxi if you don't see one waiting by the bus stop (see taxi phone numbers above). The bus stop is on the main road from Vernon, just below Monet's home. You can also rent a **bike** at the bar opposite the train station (€12, tel. 02 32 21 16 01), and follow a paved bike path *(piste cyclable)* that runs along an abandoned railroad right-of-way (the bike path begins across the river from Vernon in Veronnet).

Big tour companies do a Giverny day trip from Paris for around €65. Ask at your hotel.

The **Musée de l'Art Americain** (American Art Museum,

turn left when leaving Monet's place and walk 100 meters) is devoted to American artists who followed Claude to Giverny. Giverny had a great influence on American artists of Monet's day. This bright, modern gallery—with a good little Mary Cassatt section—is well-explained in English (same price and hours as Monet's home), though its most appealing feature might be its garden café.

Sleeping in Giverny: To sleep two blocks from Monet's home, try the adorable **Hôtel La Musardiere**** (Db-€50–66, Tb-€65–75, CC, 132 rue Claude Monet, 27620 Giverny, tel. 02 32 21 03 18, fax 02 32 21 60 00). You'll find a café and sandwich stand near the entry to Monet's home, but the garden café at the overlooked American Impressionist Museum is better—peaceful, and surrounded by gardens Monet would appreciate (€9 salads, picnics possible at the far end).

Disneyland Paris

Europe's Disneyland, a ▲▲ sight, is basically a modern remake of California's, with most of the same rides and smiles. The main difference is that Mickey Mouse speaks French (and you can buy wine with your lunch). My kids went ducky. Locals love it. It's worth a day if Paris is handier than Florida or California. Crowds are a problem (tel. 01 64 74 30 00 for the latest). If possible, avoid Saturday, Sunday, Wednesday, school holidays, and July and August. After dinner, crowds are gone, and you'll walk right onto rides that had a 45-minute wait three hours earlier. The free FASTPASS system is a worthwhile timesaver for popular rides (reserve a time to go on a ride when you buy your ticket at the gate). You'll also save time by buying your tickets ahead (at airport TIs, over 100 Métro stations, or along the Champs-Elysées at the TI, Disney Store, or Virgin Megastore). Food is fun and not outrageously priced. (Still, many smuggle in a picnic.)

The hours and prices for Disneyland Paris are listed below.

Walt Disney Studios: The new zone, opened in 2002 next to the 10-year-old Disneyland Paris, has a Hollywood focus that aims at an older crowd with animation, special effects, and movie magic "rides." The Aerosmith Rock 'n' Roller Coaster is nothing special. The highlight is the Stunt Show Spectacular, filling a huge back-lot stadium five times a day for 45 minutes of car chases and thriller filming tips. An actual movie sequence is filmed with stunt drivers, audience bit players, and brash MTV-style hosts.

Cost and Hours: Disneyland Paris and Walt Disney Studios share the same hours, contact information, and prices—which you pay separately. Only the three-day passes (called "Hopper" tickets) include entry to both parks. From March 31 through Nov 5, adults pay €38 for one day (€72 for 2 days, €99 for 3-day "Hopper" ticket) and kids ages 3–11 pay €29 for one day (€56 for 2 days, €80 for 3-day "Hopper" ticket). Regular prices are about 25 percent less off-season. Kids under three are always free. On summer evenings (17:00–23:00) at the Disneyland Park only, everyone pays €19. The only budget deal (and, I think, the only way the Walt Disney Studios are worth visiting) is to pay for a full-price Walt Disney Studios ticket, which gets you into the Disneyland Park for free during the last three hours of that day when lines at rides are nearly nonexistent (April–June daily 9:00–20:00, July–Aug daily 9:00–23:00, Sept–March Mon–Fri 10:00–20:00, Sat–Sun 9:00–20:00, tel. 01 60 30 60 30, www.disneylandparis.com).

Sleeping at Disneyland Paris: Most are better off sleeping in reality (Paris), though with direct buses and freeways to both airports, Disneyland makes a convenient first- or last-night stop. Seven different Disney-owned hotels offer accommodations at or near the park in all price ranges. The cheapest is **Davy Crockett,** but you'll need a car. **Hôtel Sante Fe**** offers the best value, with shuttle service to the park every 12 minutes (Db-€214 includes breakfast and 2-day park pass, CC). The most expensive is **Disneyland Hotel******, right at the park entry (Db-€427 for the same deal, CC). To reserve any Disneyland hotel, call 01 60 30 60 30, fax 01 60 30 60 65, or check www.disneylandparis.com. The prices you'll be quoted include entry to the park.

Transportation Connections—Disneyland Paris

By train: TGV trains connect Disneyland directly with **Charles de Gaulle airport** (10 min), the **Loire Valley** (1.5 hrs, Tours-St. Pierre des Corps station, 15 min from Amboise), **Avignon** (3 hrs, TGV station), **Lyon** (2 hrs, Part Dieu station), and **Nice** (6 hrs, main station).

By RER: The slick, one-hour RER trip is the best way to Disneyland from downtown Paris. Take RER line A-4 to Marne-la-Vallee-Chessy (from Etoile, Auber/Opera, Chatelet, and Gare de Lyon stations, about €7.50 each way, hrly, drops you 1 hour later right in the park). The last train back to Paris leaves shortly after midnight. Be sure to get a ticket that is good on both the RER and Métro; returning, remember to use your RER ticket for your Métro connection in Paris.

By bus: Both airports have direct shuttle buses to Disneyland Paris (€13, daily 8:30–19:45, every 45 min).

By car: Disneyland is about 40 minutes east of Paris on the A-4 autoroute (direction Nancy/Metz, exit #14). Parking is €7 per day at the park.

Nightlife in Paris

Paris is brilliant after dark. Save energy from your day's sightseeing and get out at night. Whether it's a concert at Sainte-Chapelle, an elevator up the Arc de Triomphe, or a late-night café, experience the city of light lit. If a **Seine River cruise** appeals, see "Organized Tours of Paris," page 240.

Pariscope magazine (see "Tourist Information," above), offers a complete weekly listing of music, cinema, theater, opera, and other special events. *Paris Voice* newspaper, in English, has a monthly review of Paris entertainment (available at any English-language bookstore, French-American establishments, or the American Church, www.parisvoice.com).

Music

Jazz Clubs: With a lively mix of American, French, and international musicians, Paris has been an internationally acclaimed jazz capital since World War II. You'll pay €6–24 to enter a jazz club (a drink may be included; if not, expect to pay €5–9 per drink; beer is cheapest). See *Pariscope* magazine under "Musique" for listings; or, better yet, check out the American Church's *Paris Voice* paper for a good monthly review, or drop by the clubs to check out their calendars posted on the front door. Music starts after 21:00 in most clubs. Some offer dinner concerts from about 20:30 on. Here are several good bets:

Caveau de la Huchette, a characteristic old jazz club, fills an ancient Latin Quarter cellar with live jazz and frenzied dancing every night (€9 weekday, €12 weekend admission, €5 drinks, Tue–Sun 21:30–2:30 or later, closed Mon, 5 rue de la Huchette, Mo: St. Michel, recorded info tel. 01 43 26 65 05).

For a hotbed of late-night activity and jazz, go to the two-block-long rue des Lombards, at boulevard Sebastopol, midway between the river and Pompidou Center (Mo: Chatelet). **Au Duc des Lombards**, right at the corner, is one of the most popular and respected jazz clubs in Paris, with concerts generally at 21:00 (42 rue des Lombards, tel. 01 42 33 22 88). **Le Sunside** offers more traditional jazz—Dixieland and big band—and fewer crowds, with concerts generally at 21:00 (60 rue des Lombards, tel. 01 40 26 21 25).

At the more down-to-earth and mellow **Le Cave du Franc Pinot**, you can enjoy a glass of chardonnay at the main-floor wine bar, then drop downstairs for a cool jazz scene (good dinner-and-jazz values as well, located on Ile St. Louis where pont Marie meets the island, 1 quai de Bourbon, Mo: Pont Marie, tel. 01 46 33 60 64).

Classical Concerts: For classical music on any night, consult *Pariscope* magazine; the "Musique" section under "Concerts

Classiques" lists concerts (free and fee). Look for posters at the churches. Churches that regularly host concerts (usually March–Nov) include St. Sulpice, St. Germain-des-Prés, Basilique de Madeleine, St. Eustache, St. Julien-le-Pauvre, and Sainte-Chapelle. It's worth the €16–25 entry for the pleasure of hearing Mozart surrounded by the stained glass of the tiny Sainte-Chapelle (it's unheated—bring a sweater). Look also for daytime concerts in parks, such as the Luxembourg Garden. Even the Galeries Lafayette department store offers concerts. Many concerts are free *(entrée libre)*, such as the Sunday atelier concert sponsored by the American Church (18:00, not every week, Sept–May, 65 quai d'Orsay, Mo: Invalides, RER: Pont de l'Alma, tel. 01 40 62 05 00).

Opera: Paris is home to two well-respected opera venues. The Opéra de la Bastille is a massive, modern opera house that dominates place de la Bastille. Come here for state-of-the-art special effects and modern interpretations of classic ballets and operas. In the spirit of this everyman's opera, unsold seats go on sale at a big discount to seniors and students 15 minutes before the show (Mo: Bastille, tel. 01 43 43 96 96). The Opéra Garnier, Paris' first opera house, hosts opera and ballet performances. Come here for less expensive tickets and grand belle époque decor (Mo: Opéra, tel. 01 44 73 13 99). For tickets, call 01 44 73 13 00, go to the opera ticket offices (open 11:00–18:00), or reserve on the Web at www.opera-de-paris.org (for both operas).

Bus Tours

Paris Illumination Tours, run by Paris Vision, connect all the great illuminated sights of Paris with a 100-minute bus tour in 12 languages. Double-decker buses have huge windows, but customers continuing to the overrated Moulin Rouge get the most desirable front seats.

You'll stampede along with a United Nations of tourists, get an audioguide, and listen to a tape-recorded spiel (interesting, but occasionally hard to hear). Uninspired as it is, this tour provides an entertaining first-night overview of the city at its floodlit and scenic best (bring your city map to stay oriented as you go). Left-side seats are marginally better. Visibility is fine in the rain. You're always on the bus, except for one five-minute cigarette break at the Eiffel Tower viewpoint (adults-€23, kids under 11 ride free, departures at 20:30 nightly all year, also at 21:30 April–Oct only, departs from Paris Vision office at 214 rue de Rivoli, across the street from Mo: Tuileries).

The same company will take you on the same route for twice the price by minivan—pickup is at your hotel, the driver is a qualified guide, and there's a maximum of seven clients (adult-€46, kids ages 4–11-€23).

These trips are sold through your hotel (brochures in lobby) or at Paris Vision (214 rue de Rivoli, tel. for bus and minivans 01 42 60 30 01, fax 01 42 86 95 36, www.parisvision.com).

Sleeping in Paris

(€1 = about $1, country code: 33)

Sleep Code: **S** = Single, **D** = Double/Twin, **T** = Triple, **Q** = Quad, **b** = bathroom, **s** = shower only, **CC** = Credit Cards accepted, **no CC** = Credit Cards not accepted, * = French hotel rating system (0–4 stars).

To help you sort easily through these listings, I've divided the rooms into three categories based on the price for a standard double room with bath:

Higher Priced—Most rooms more than €140.
Moderately Priced—Most rooms €140 or less.
Lower Priced—Most rooms €100 or less.

I've focused on three safe, handy, and colorful neighborhoods: rue Cler, Marais, and Contrescarpe. For each, I list good hotels, helpful hints, and restaurants (see "Eating in Paris," below). Before reserving, read the descriptions of the three neighborhoods closely. Each offers different pros and cons, and your neighborhood is as important as your hotel for the success of your trip.

Reserve ahead for Paris, the sooner the better. Conventions clog Paris in September (worst), October, May, and June (very tough). In August, when Paris is quiet, some hotels offer lower rates to fill their rooms (if you're planning to visit Paris in the summer, the extra expense of an air-conditioned room can be money well spent). Most hotels accept telephone reservations, require prepayment with a credit-card number, and prefer a faxed follow-up to be sure everything is in order. For more information, see "Making Reservations" in this book's introduction.

French hotels are rated by stars (indicated in this chapter by a *). One star is simple, two has most of the comforts, three is generally a two-star with a minibar and fancier lobby, and four is luxurious. Hotels with two or more stars are required to have an English-speaking staff. Nearly all hotels listed here will have someone who speaks English.

Old, characteristic, budget Parisian hotels have always been cramped. Retrofitted with elevators, toilets, and private showers (as most are today), they are even more cramped. Even three-star hotel rooms are small and often not worth the extra expense in Paris. Some hotels include the hotel tax (*taxe du séjour*, about €0.50–1 per person per day), though most will add this to your bill.

Recommended hotels have an elevator unless otherwise noted. Quad rooms usually have two double beds. Because rooms with double beds and showers are cheaper than rooms with twin beds and baths, room prices vary within each hotel.

You can save as much as €20–25 by finding the increasingly rare room without a private shower, though some hotels charge for down-the-hall showers. Singles (except for the rare closet-type rooms that fit only 1 twin bed) are simply doubles used by one person. They rent for only a little less than a double.

Continental breakfasts average €6, buffet breakfasts (baked goods, cereal, yogurt, and fruit) cost €8 to €10. Café or picnic breakfasts are cheaper, but hotels usually give unlimited coffee.

Get advice from your hotel for safe parking (consider long-term parking at Orly Airport and taxi in). Meters are free in August. Garages are plentiful (€14–23/day, with special rates through some hotels). Self-serve launderettes are common; ask your hotelier for the nearest one (*Où est un laverie automatique?*; pron. ooh ay uh lah-vay-ree auto-mah-teek).

If you have any trouble finding a room using our listings, try this Web site: www.parishotel.com. You can select from various neighborhood areas (e.g., Eiffel Tower area), give the dates of your visit and preferred price range, and presto—they'll list options with rates. You'll find the hotels listed in this book to be better located and objectively reviewed, though as a last resort, this online service is handy.

Rue Cler Orientation

Rue Cler, a village-like pedestrian street, is safe and tidy, and makes me feel like I must have been a poodle in a previous life. How such coziness lodged itself between the high-powered government district and the wealthy Eiffel Tower and Invalides areas, I'll never know. This is a neighborhood of wide, tree-lined boulevards, stately apartment buildings, and lots of Americans. The American Church, American library, American University, and many of my readers call this area home.

Become a local at a rue Cler café for breakfast or join the afternoon crowd for *une bière pression* (a draft beer). On rue Cler, you can eat and browse your way through a street full of tart shops, delis, cheeseries, and colorful outdoor produce stalls. For an after-dinner cruise on the Seine, it's just a short walk to the river and the Bâteaux-Mouches (see "Organized Tours of Paris," above).

Your neighborhood **TI** is at the Eiffel Tower (May–Sept daily 11:00–18:42, no kidding, tel. 01 45 51 22 15). There's a **post office** at the end of rue Cler on avenue de la Motte Piquet, and a handy **SNCF office** at 78 rue St. Dominique (Mon–Fri

9:00–19:00, Sat 10:00–12:20 & 14:00–18:00, closed Sun). Rue St. Dominique is the area's boutique-browsing street. The Epicerie de la Tour **grocery** is open until midnight (197 rue de Grenelle). **Cyber World Café** is at 20 rue de l'Exposition (open daily, tel. 01 53 59 96 54).

The **American Church and College** is the community center for Americans living in Paris and should be one of your first stops if you're planning to stay awhile (reception open Mon–Sat 9:00–22:00, Sun 9:00–19:30, 65 quai d'Orsay, tel. 01 40 62 05 00). Pick up copies of the *Paris Voice* for a monthly review of Paris entertainment, and *France-U.S.A. Contacts* for information on housing and employment through the community of 30,000 Americans living in Paris. The interdenominational service at 11:00 on Sunday, the coffee hour after church, and the free Sunday concerts (18:00, not every week, Sept–May only) are a great way to make some friends and get a taste of émigré life in Paris. Afternoon *boules* (lawn bowling) on the esplanade des Invalides is a relaxing spectator sport. Look for the dirt area to the upper right as you face the Invalides.

Key **Métro** stops are Ecole Militaire, La Tour Maubourg, and Invalides. The **RER-C** line runs along the river, serving Versailles to the west and the Orsay Museum, Latin Quarter (St. Michel stop), and Austerlitz train station to the east (in rue Cler area, use Pont de l'Alma or Invalides RER stops). Smart travelers take advantage of these helpful **bus routes:** Line #69 runs along rue St. Dominique and serves Les Invalides, Orsay, Louvre, Marais, and Père Lachaise Cemetery. Line #63 runs along the river (the Quai d'Orsay), serving the Latin Quarter along boulevard St. Germain to the east, and the Trocadero and the Musée Marmottan to the west. Line #92 runs along avenue Bosquet north to the Champs-Elysées and Arc de Triomphe and south to the Montparnasse Tower. Line #87 runs on avenue de la Bourdonnais and serves St. Sulpice, Luxembourg Garden, and the Sèvres-Babylone shopping area. Line #28 runs on boulevard La Tour Maubourg and serves the St. Lazare station.

Sleeping in the Rue Cler Neighborhood (7th arrondissement, Mo: Ecole Militaire, zip code: 75007)

Rue Cler is the glue that holds this pleasant neighborhood together. From here, you can walk to the Eiffel Tower, Napoleon's Tomb, the Seine, and the Orsay and Rodin Museums. Hotels here are relatively spacious and a great value, considering the elegance of the neighborhood and the high prices of the more cramped hotels in the trendy Marais.

Rue Cler Hotels

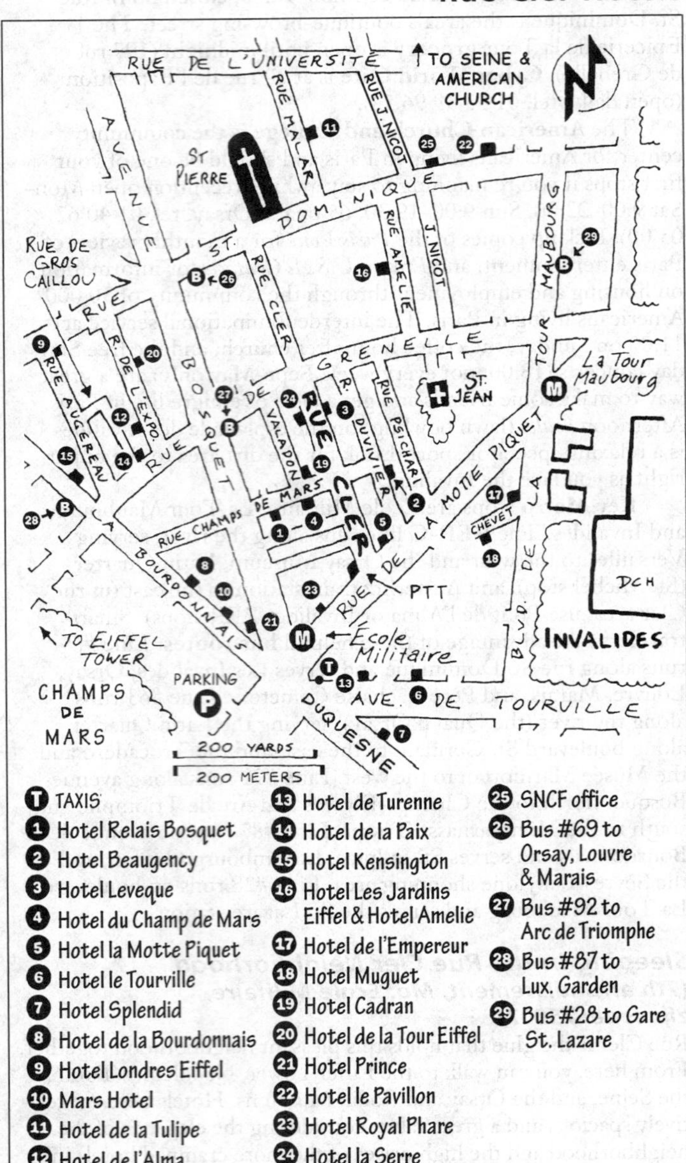
RUE DE L'UNIVERSITÉ
TO SEINE & AMERICAN CHURCH
RUE MALAR
RUE J. NICOT
AVENUE
ST PIERRE
ST. DOMINIQUE
RUE AMELIE
J. NICOT
TOUR MAUBOURG
RUE DE GROS CAILLOU
RUE CLER
GRENELLE
RUE R. DE L'EXPO.
BOSQUET
RUE AUGEREAU
RUE
DE VALADON
R. DUVIVIER
RUE PSICHARI
ST. JEAN
La Tour Maubourg
RUE CLER
DE LA MOTTE PIQUET
RUE CHAMPS DE MARS
CHEVET
LA
BLVD. DE
LA BOURDONNAIS
RUE DE
PTT
DCH
TO EIFFEL TOWER
École Militaire
INVALIDES
PARKING
CHAMPS DE MARS
AVE. DE TOURVILLE
DUQUESNE
200 YARDS
200 METERS
T TAXIS
1 Hotel Relais Bosquet
2 Hotel Beaugency
3 Hotel Leveque
4 Hotel du Champ de Mars
5 Hotel la Motte Piquet
6 Hotel le Tourville
7 Hotel Splendid
8 Hotel de la Bourdonnais
9 Hotel Londres Eiffel
10 Mars Hotel
11 Hotel de la Tulipe
12 Hotel de l'Alma
13 Hotel de Turenne
14 Hotel de la Paix
15 Hotel Kensington
16 Hotel Les Jardins Eiffel & Hotel Amelie
17 Hotel de l'Empereur
18 Hotel Muguet
19 Hotel Cadran
20 Hotel de la Tour Eiffel
21 Hotel Prince
22 Hotel le Pavillon
23 Hotel Royal Phare
24 Hotel la Serre
25 SNCF office
26 Bus #69 to Orsay, Louvre & Marais
27 Bus #92 to Arc de Triomphe
28 Bus #87 to Lux. Garden
29 Bus #28 to Gare St. Lazare

Many of my readers stay in this neighborhood. If you want to disappear into Paris, choose a hotel away from the rue Cler, or in the other neighborhoods I list. And if nightlife matters, sleep elsewhere. The first five hotels listed below are within Camembert-smelling distance of rue Cler; the others are within a five- to 10-minute stroll.

Sleeping in the Heart of Rue Cler

HIGHER PRICED

Hôtel Relais Bosquet*** is modern, spacious, and a bit upscale, with snazzy, air-conditioned rooms, electric darkness blinds, and big beds. Gerard and his staff are polite, formal, and friendly (Sb-€125–146, standard Db-€140, spacious Db-€160, extra bed-€30, CC, parking-€14, 19 rue de Champ de Mars, tel. 01 47 05 25 45, fax 01 45 55 08 24, www.relaisbosquet.com).

MODERATELY PRICED

Hôtel Beaugency***, on a quieter street a short block off rue Cler, has 30 small but comfortable rooms, a lobby you can stretch out in, and friendly Chantal in charge. When I have tour groups in Paris, this is my first choice for their home base (Sb-€104, Db-€111, Tb-€127, CC, buffet breakfast, 21 rue Duvivier, tel. 01 47 05 01 63, fax 01 45 51 04 96, www.hotel-beaugency.com).

LOWER PRICED

Warning: The first two hotels listed here—while the best value—are overrun with my readers (book long in advance . . . or avoid).

Hôtel Leveque** is ideally located, with a helpful staff (Pascale and Christophe SE), a singing maid, and a Starship Enterprise elevator. It's a classic old hotel with well-designed rooms that have all the comforts (S–€53, Db-€84–91, Tb-€114 for two adults and one child only, breakfast-€7, first breakfast free for readers of this book, CC, air-con, 29 rue Cler, tel. 01 47 05 49 15, fax 01 45 50 49 36, check room availability on Web site, www.hotel-leveque.com, e-mail: info@hotelleveque.com).

Hôtel du Champ de Mars**, with charming pastel rooms and helpful English-speaking owners Françoise and Stephane, is a homier rue Cler option. This plush little hotel has a Provence-style, small-town feel from top to bottom. Rooms are small, but comfortable and a good value. Single rooms can work as tiny doubles (Sb-€66, Db-€72–76, Tb-€92, CC, 30 meters/100 feet off rue Cler at 7 rue de Champ de Mars, tel. 01 45 51 52 30, fax 01 45 51 64 36, www.hotel-du-champ-de-mars.com, e-mail: stg@club-internet.fr).

Hôtel la Motte Piquet**, at the end of rue Cler, is reasonable and spotless and comes with a cheery welcome from Daniele. Most of its 18 cozy rooms face a busy street, but the twins are on the quieter rue Cler (Ss-€57, Sb-€60–64, Db-€73–81, CC, 30 avenue de la Motte Piquet, tel. 01 47 05 09 57, fax 01 47 05 74 36).

Sleeping near Rue Cler

The following listings are a five- to 10-minute walk from rue Cler.

HIGHER PRICED

Hôtel le Tourville**** is the most classy and expensive of my rue Cler listings. This four-star place is surprisingly intimate and friendly, from its designer lobby and vaulted breakfast area to its pretty but small pastel rooms (small standard Db-€145, superior Db-€215, Db with private terrace-€240, junior suite for 3–4 people-€310, extra bed-€17, CC, air-con, 16 avenue de Tourville, Mo: Ecole Militaire, tel. 01 47 05 62 62, fax 01 47 05 43 90, e-mail: hotel@tourville.com).

Hôtel Splendid*** is Art Deco mod, friendly, and worth your while if you land one of its suites with great Eiffel Tower views (Db-€124–146, Db suite-€205–220, CC, 29 avenue Tourville, tel. 01 45 51 24 77, fax 01 44 18 94 60, e-mail: splendid@club-internet.fr).

Hôtel de la Bourdonnais*** is a *très* Parisian place, mixing slightly faded Old World elegance with professional service and mostly spacious rooms (their smaller rooms can be cramped, confirm that room is not small, Sb-€120, Db-€150, Tb-€160, Qb-€180, 5-person suite-€210, CC, air-con, 111 avenue de la Bourdonnais, tel. 01 47 05 45 42, fax 01 45 55 75 54, www.hotellabourdonnais.fr).

MODERATELY PRICED

Hôtel Londres Eiffel*** is my closest listing to the Eiffel Tower and Champs de Mars park. It offers immaculate, warmly decorated rooms, cozy public spaces, and Internet access. The helpful staff take good care of their guests (Sb-€93–102, Db-€105–115, Tb-€137, extra bed-€17, CC, use handy bus #69 or the RER Alma stop, 1 rue Augerau, tel. 01 45 51 63 02, fax 01 47 05 28 96, www.londres-eiffel.com).

Eber-Mars Hôtel**, with helpful owner Jean-Marc, is a good midrange value with larger-than-average rooms and a beam-me-up-Jacques, coffin-sized elevator (small Db-€75, large Db-€90–110, Tb-€130, extra bed-€20, CC, 117 avenue de la Bourdonnais, tel. 01 47 05 42 30, fax 01 47 05 45 91).

Hôtel de la Tulipe*** is a unique place two blocks from

rue Cler toward the river, with a seductive wood-beamed lounge and a peaceful, leafy courtyard. Its artistically decorated rooms (each one different) come with small, stylish bathrooms (Db-€105–135, Tb-€160, CC, no elevator, 33 rue Malar, tel. 01 45 51 67 21, fax 01 47 53 96 37, www.hoteldelatulipe.com).

Hôtel de l'Alma*** is well-located on "restaurant row," with good rooms, but small bathrooms and reasonable rates (Db-€100–115, CC, 32 rue de l'Exposition, tel. 01 47 05 45 70, fax 01 45 51 84 47, e-mail: almahotel@minitel.net, Carine SE).

LOWER PRICED

Hôtel de Turenne**, with sufficiently comfortable, air-conditioned rooms, is a good value when it's hot. It also has five truly single rooms (Sb-€61, Db-€71–81, Tb-€96, extra bed-€9.50, CC, 20 avenue de Tourville, tel. 01 47 05 99 92, fax 01 45 56 06 04, e-mail: hotel.turenne.paris7@wanadoo.fr).

Hôtel de la Paix**, a smart hotel located away from the fray on a quiet little street, offers 23 plush, well-designed rooms for a good value (Sb-€61, Db-€80, big Db-€91, Tb-€11, CC, fine buffet breakfast, Internet access, 19 rue du Gros-Caillou, tel. 01 45 51 86 17, fax 01 45 55 93 28, e-mail: hotel.de.lapaix @wanadoo.fr).

Hôtel Kensington** is impersonal and has teeny rooms, but is a fair value (Sb-€53, Db-€67–82, CC, 79 avenue de la Bourdonnais, tel. 01 47 05 74 00, fax 01 47 05 25 81, www .hotel-kensington.com).

Sleeping near Métro: La Tour Maubourg

The next three listings are within two blocks of the intersection of avenue de la Motte Piquet and Les Invalides.

HIGHER PRICED

Hôtel Les Jardins Eiffel*** feels like a modern motel, but earns its three stars with professional service, a spacious lobby, an out-door patio, and 80 comfortable, air-conditioned rooms—some with private balconies (ask for a room *avec petit balcon*). Even better: Readers of this book get free buffet breakfasts (Db-€130–160, extra bed-€21 or free for a child, CC, parking-€17/day, 8 rue Amelie, tel. 01 47 05 46 21, fax 01 45 55 28 08, e-mail: eiffel@unimedia.fr, Marie SE).

LOWER PRICED

Roomy **Hôtel de l'Empereur**** lacks personality, but is a fine value. Its 38 pleasant, woody rooms come with sturdy furniture and all the comforts except air-conditioning. Streetside rooms have views but some noise; fifth-floor rooms have small balconies and Napoleonic views (Sb-€70–75, Db-€75–85, Tb-€105, Qb-€120, CC, 2 rue Chevert, tel. 01 45 55 88 02, fax 01 45 51 88 54, www.hotelempereur.com, Petra SE).

Hôtel Muguet**, a peaceful and clean hotel, gives you three-star comfort for the price of two. The remarkably spacious hotel offers 48 sharp, air-conditioned rooms and a small garden courtyard. The hands-on owner, Catherine, gives her guests a peaceful and secure home in Paris (Sb-€85, Db-€95–103, Tb-€130, CC, 11 rue Chevert, tel. 01 47 05 05 93, fax 01 45 50 25 37, www.hotelmuguet.com).

Lesser Values

Given this fine area, these are acceptable last choices.

HIGHER PRICED

Perfectly located **Hôtel Cadran***** has a shiny lobby, but no charm and tight, narrow, overpriced rooms (Db-€148–165, CC, air-con, 10 rue du Champs de Mars, tel. 01 40 62 67 00, fax 01 40 62 67 13, www.hotelducadran.com).

LOWER PRICED

Hôtel de la Tour Eiffel** is a modest little place with fair-priced rooms but cheap furnishings and foam mattresses (Sb-€65, Db-€80, Tb-€100, CC, 17 rue de l'Exposition, tel. 01 47 05 14 75, fax 01 47 53 99 46, Muriel SE). **Hôtel Prince****, just across avenue Bosquet from the Ecole Militaire Métro stop, has good-enough rooms, many overlooking a busy street (Sb-€70, Db-€82–105, CC, 66 avenue Bosquet, tel. 01 47 05 40 90, fax 01 47 53 06 62, www.hotel-paris-prince.com). **Hôtel le Pavillon**** is quiet, with basic rooms, no elevator, and cramped halls in a charming location (Sb-€72, Db-€80, Tb, Qb, or Quint/b-€105, CC, 54 rue St. Dominique, tel. 01 45 51 42 87, fax 01 45 51 32 79, e-mail: patrickpavillon@aol.com). **Hôtel Royal Phare**** is very simple (Db-€61–74, CC, facing Ecole Militaire Métro stop, 40 avenue de la Motte Piquet, tel. 01 47 05 57 30, fax 01 45 51 64 41, www.hotel-royalphare-paris.com). **Hôtel Amelie**** is another possibility (Db-€95, CC, 5 rue Amelie, tel. 01 45 51 74 75, fax 01 45 56 93 55). The basic **Hôtel La Serre*** has a good location on rue Cler, but generates readers' complaints for its rude staff and bizarre hotel practices—you can't see a room in advance or get a refund (Db-€90, CC, 24 rue Cler, across from Hôtel Leveque, Mo: Ecole Militaire, tel. 01 47 05 52 33, fax 01 40 62 95 66).

Marais Orientation

Those interested in a more Soho–Greenwich Village locale should make the Marais their Parisian home. Only 15 years ago, it was a forgotten Parisian backwater, but now the Marais is one of Paris' most popular residential, tourist, and shopping areas. This is jumbled, medieval Paris at its finest, where elegant stone mansions sit alongside trendy bars, antique shops, and fashion-conscious boutiques. The streets are a fascinating parade of artists, students, tourists, immigrants, and babies in strollers munching baguettes—and the Marais is also known as a hub of the Parisian gay and lesbian scene. This area is *sans* doubt livelier (and louder) than the rue Cler area.

In the Marais, you have these sights at your fingertips: Picasso Museum, Carnavalet Museum, Victor Hugo House, Jewish Art and History Museum, and the Pompidou Center (modern art). You're also a manageable walk from Paris' two islands (Ile St. Louis and Ile de la Cité), where you'll find Notre-Dame and Sainte-Chapelle. The Opera de la Bastille, Promenade Plantée Park, place des Vosges (Paris' oldest square), Jewish Quarter (rue des Rosiers), and nightlife-packed rue de Lappe are also nearby. Two good open markets lie nearby: the sprawling Marché Bastille on place Bastille (Thu and Sun until 12:30) and the more intimate Marché de la place d'Aligre (daily 9:00–12:00, a few blocks behind opera on place d'Aligre).

The nearest **TIs** are in the Louvre (Wed–Mon 10:00–19:00, closed Tue) and Gare de Lyon (daily 8:00–20:00, tel. 08 92 68 31 12, wait for English recording). Most banks and other services are on the main drag, rue de Rivoli/St. Antoine. For your Parisian Sears, find the **BHV** next to Hôtel de Ville. Marais **post offices** are on rue Castex and on the corner of rues Pavée and Francs Bourgeois.

Métro service is excellent to the Marais neighborhood, with direct service to the Louvre, Champs-Elysées, Arc de Triomphe, and four major train stations: Gare du Lyon, Gare du Nord, Gare de l'Est and Gare d'Austerlitz. Key Métro stops in the Marais are, from east to west: Bastille, St. Paul, and Hôtel de Ville (Sully Morland, Pont Marie, and Rambuteau stops are also handy). There are also several helpful **bus routes:** Line #69 on rue St. Antoine takes you to the Louvre, Orsay, Rodin, and Napoleon's Tomb and ends at the Eiffel Tower. Line #86 runs down boulevard Henri IV, crossing Ile St. Louis and serving the Latin Quarter along boulevard St. Germain. Line #96 runs on rues Turenne and Francois Miron and serves the Louvre and boulevard St. Germain (near Luxembourg Garden). Line #65 serves the train stations d'Austerlitz, Est, and Nord from place de la Bastille.

You'll find **taxi stands** on place Bastille, on the north side of rue St. Antoine (where it meets rue Castex), and on the south side of rue St. Antoine (in front of St. Paul Church).

Sleeping in the Marais Neighborhood
(4th arrondissement, Mo: St. Paul or Bastille, zip code: 75004)

The Marais runs from the Pompidou Center to the Bastille (a 15-min walk), with most hotels located a few blocks north of the main east-west drag, rue de Rivoli/St. Antoine (one street with two names). It's about 15 minutes on foot from any hotel in this area to Notre-Dame, Ile St. Louis, and the Latin Quarter. Strolling home (day or night) from Notre-Dame along the Ile St. Louis is marvelous.

MODERATELY PRICED

Hôtel Castex*,** on a quiet street near the Bastille, is completely renovating and upgrading to three stars in early 2003, with the addition of an elevator, air-conditioning, and brand-spanking-new rooms (estimated new prices: Sb-€100, Db-€120, Tb-€140, CC, closed until March, just off place de la Bastille and rue St. Antoine, 5 rue Castex, Mo: Bastille, tel. 01 42 72 31 52, fax 01 42 72 57 91, www.castexhotel.com, e-mail: info@castexhotel.com).

Hôtel Bastille Speria***, a short block off the Bastille, offers business-type service. The 42 plain but cheery rooms have air-conditioning, thin walls, and curiously cheap and sweaty foam mattresses. It's English-language friendly, from the *Herald Tribune*s in the lobby to the history of the Bastille posted in the elevator (Sb-€95, Db-€112–120, child's bed-€20, CC, 1 rue de la Bastille, Mo: Bastille, tel. 01 42 72 04 01, fax 01 42 72 56 38, www.hotel-bastille-speria.com).

Hôtel de la Place des Vosges** is so well-located—in a medieval building on a quiet street just off place des Vosges—that the staff can take or leave your business. Still, its customers leave happy (Sb-€84, Db-€120, CC, 16 rooms, 1 flight of stairs then elevator, 12 rue de Biraque, Mo: St. Paul, tel. 01 42 72 60 46, fax 01 42 72 02 64, e-mail: hotel.place.des.vosges@gofornet.com).

Hôtel des Chevaliers***, a little boutique hotel one block northwest of place des Vosges, offers small, pleasant rooms with modern comforts. Eight of its 24 rooms are off the street and quiet—worth requesting (Db-€110–130, prices depend on season, CC, 30 rue de Turenne, Mo: St. Paul, tel. 01 42 72 73 47, fax 01 42 72 54 10, e-mail: info@hoteldeschevaliers.com, Christele SE).

Hôtel St. Louis Marais** is a tiny place, well-situated on a quiet residential street between the river and rue St. Antoine, with

Marais Hotels

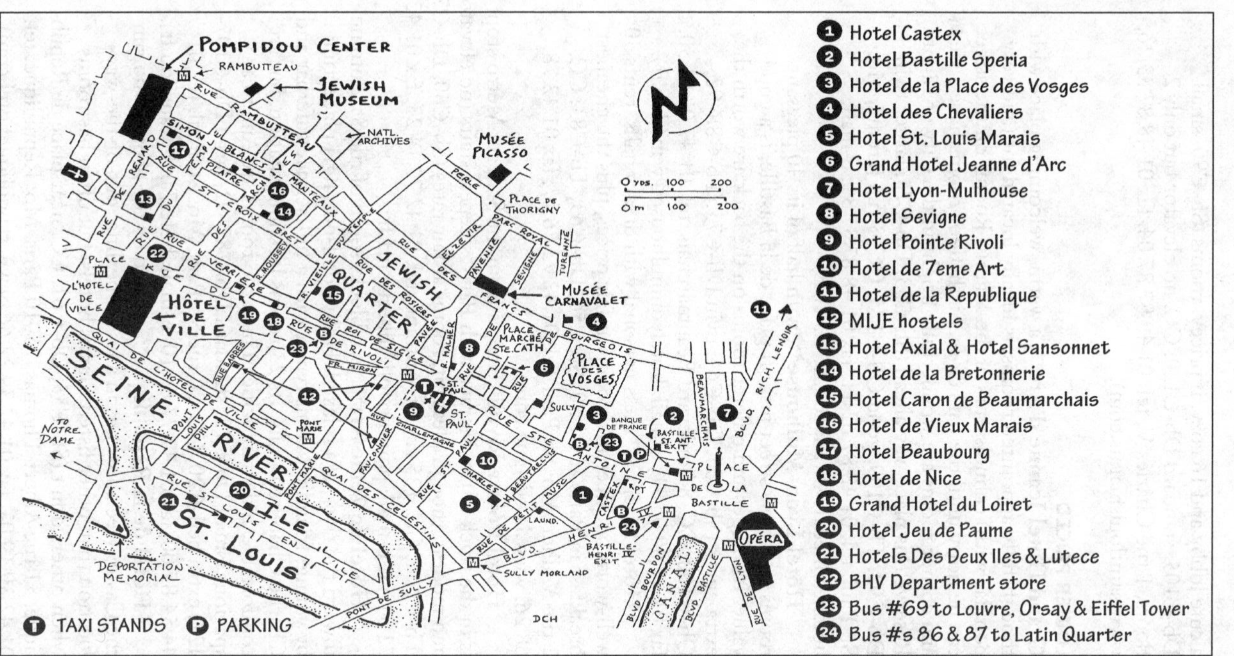

a cute lobby and 16 cozy, if pricey, rooms (Sb-€90, small Db-€105, standard Db-€120, CC, no elevator but only 2 floors, 1 rue Charles V, tel. 01 48 87 87 04, fax 01 48 87 33 26, www.saintlouismarais.com).

LOWER PRICED

Grand Hôtel Jeanne d'Arc**, a warm, welcoming place with thoughtfully appointed rooms, is ideally located for (and very popular with) connoisseurs of the Marais. Rooms on the street can be noisy until the bars close. Sixth-floor rooms have a view, and corner rooms are wonderfully bright in the City of Lights. Reserve this place way ahead (Sb-€53, Db-€73, larger twin Db-€92, Tb-€109, good Qb-€125, CC, 3 rue Jarente, Mo: St. Paul, tel. 01 48 87 62 11, fax 01 48 87 37 31, e-mail: hoteljeannedarc@wanadoo.fr, Gail SE).

Hôtel Lyon-Mulhouse**, with half of its 40 pleasant rooms on a busy street just off place de la Bastille, is a good value. Its bigger and quieter rooms on the back are worth the extra euros (Sb-€55, Db-€64, twin Db-€75, Tb-€88–92, Qb-€100, CC, 8 boulevard Beaumarchais, tel. 01 47 00 91 50, fax 01 47 00 06 31, e-mail: hotelyonmulhouse@wanadoo.fr).

Hôtel Sévigné**, less personal with dreary halls, rents 30 well-worn but sleepable rooms at fair prices, plus the cheapest breakfast in Paris at €3.50 (Sb-€56, Db-€63, Tb-€83, CC, 2 rue Malher, Mo: St. Paul, tel. 01 42 72 76 17, fax 01 42 78 68 26, www.le-sevigne.com).

Hotel Pointe Rivoli*, across from the St. Paul Métro stop, is in the thick of the Marais, with Paris' steepest stairs (no elevator) and modest, though pleasant, rooms at fair rates (Sb-€60, Db-€70, Tb-€100, CC, 125 rue St. Antoine, tel. 01 42 72 14 23, fax 01 42 72 51 11, e-mail: pointerivoli@libertysurf.fr).

Hôtel de 7ème Art**, two blocks south of rue St. Antoine toward the river, is a relaxed, Hollywood-nostalgia place, run by young, friendly Marais types, with a full-service café/bar and Charlie Chaplin murals. Its 23 rooms lack imagination, but are comfortable and a fair value. The large rooms are American-spacious (small Db-€72, standard Db-€82–92, large Db-€107–122, extra bed-€20, CC, 20 rue St. Paul, Mo: St. Paul, tel. 01 44 54 85 00, fax 01 42 77 69 10, e-mail: hotel7art@wanadoo.fr).

Hôtel de la République**, owned by the people who run the Castex (see above), is in a less appealing, out-of-the-way location than other listed Marais hotels, but often has rooms when others don't (Sb-€53, Db-€61, CC, near place de République, 31 rue Albert Thomas, 75010 Paris, Mo: République, tel. 01 42 39 19 03, fax 01 42 39 22 66, www.republiquehotel.com).

MIJE Youth Hostels: The Maison Internationale de la Jeunesse des Etudiants (MIJE) runs three classy, old residences clustered a few blocks south of rue St. Antoine. Each offers simple, clean, single-sex, one- to four-bed rooms for families and travelers under the age of 30 (exceptions are made for families). None has an elevator or double beds, each has an Internet station, and all rooms have showers. Prices are per person and favor single travelers (2 people can find a double in a simple hotel for similar rates). You can pay more to have your own room or be roomed with as many as three others (Sb-€37, Db-€27, Tb-€24, Qb-€22, no CC, includes breakfast but not towels, which you can get from a machine; required membership card-€2.50 extra/person; rooms locked 12:00–15:00 and at 1:00). The hostels are: **MIJE Fourcy** (€9 dinners available to anyone with a membership card, 6 rue de Fourcy, just south of rue Rivoli), **MIJE Fauconnier** (11 rue Fauconnier), and the best, **MIJE Maubisson** (12 rue des Barres). They all share the same contact information (tel. 01 42 74 23 45, fax 01 40 27 81 64, www.mije.com) and Métro stop (St. Paul). Reservations are accepted, though you must arrive by noon.

Sleeping near the Pompidou Center

These hotels are farther west and closer to the Pompidou Center than to place Bastille.

HIGHER PRICED

Hotel Axial Beaubourg***, a block from the Hôtel de Ville toward the Pompidou Center, has a minimalist lobby and 28 nicely decorated, plush rooms, many with wood beams (standard Db-€134–142, big Db-€165, CC, air-con, 11 rue du Temple, tel. 01 42 72 72 22, fax 02 42 72 03 53, www.axialbeaubourg.com).

MODERATELY PRICED

Hôtel de la Bretonnerie***, three blocks from Hôtel de Ville, is a fine Marais splurge. It has an on-the-ball staff, a big, welcoming lobby, elegant decor, and tastefully decorated rooms with an antique, open-beam warmth (perfectly good standard "classic" Db-€108, bigger "charming" Db-€140, Db suite-€180, Tb suite-€205, Qb suite-€230, CC, closed Aug, between rue du Vielle du Temple and rue des Archives at 22 rue Sainte Croix de la Bretonnerie, Mo: Hôtel de Ville, tel. 01 48 87 77 63, fax 01 42 77 26 78, www.bretonnerie.com).

Hôtel Caron de Beaumarchais*** feels like a dollhouse, with a lobby cluttered with bits from an elegant 18th-century Marais house and 20 sweet little rooms. Short antique collectors love this place (small back-side Db-€130, larger Db on the front–€145, CC, air-con, 12 rue Vielle du Temple, Mo: Hôtel de Ville, tel. 01 42 72 34 12, fax 01 42 72 34 63, www.carondebeaumarchais.com).

Hôtel de Vieux Marais** is tucked away on a quiet street two blocks east of the Pompidou Center. It offers bright, spacious, well-maintained rooms, simple decor, and we-try-harder owners. Marie-Helene, the in-love-with-her-work owner, gives this place its charm. Greet Leeloo, the hotel hound (Db-€125, extra bed-€23, CC, air-con, just off rue des Archives at 8 rue du Platre, Mo: Rambuteau/Hôtel de Ville, tel. 01 42 78 47 22, fax 01 42 78 34 32, www.vieuxmarais.com).

Hôtel Beaubourg*** is a good three-star value on a quiet street in the menacing shadow of the Pompidou Center. Its 28 rooms are wood-beam comfy, and the inviting lounge is warm and pleasant (Db-€93–122 depending on the size, some with balconies-€122, twins are considerably larger than doubles, includes breakfast, CC, 11 rue Simon Lefranc, Mo: Rambuteau, tel. 01 42 74 34 24, fax 01 42 78 68 11, e-mail: htlbeaubourg@hotellerie.net).

LOWER PRICED

Hôtel de Nice**, on the Marais' busy main drag, is a turquoise-and-rose "Marie-Antoinette does tie-dye" place. Its narrow halls are littered with paintings, and its 23 rooms are filled with thoughtful touches and have tight bathrooms. Twin rooms, which cost the same as doubles, are larger, but on the street side—with effective double-paned windows (Sb-€62, Db-€97, Tb-€117, Qb-€135, CC, 42 bis rue de Rivoli, Mo: Hôtel de Ville, tel. 01 42 78 55 29, fax 01 42 78 36 07).

At **Grand Hôtel du Loiret****, you get what you pay for in an inexpensive, basic, laid-back place (S-€37, Sb-€47–62, D-€42, Db-€56–72, Tb-€72–84, CC, just north of rue de Rivoli, 8 rue des Garçons Mauvais, Mo: Hôtel de Ville, tel. 01 48 87 77 00, fax 01 48 04 96 56, e-mail: hoteloiret@aol.com).

Hotel Sansonnet**, a block from the Hôtel de Ville toward the Pompidou Center, is a homey, unassuming place with no elevator but 26 comfortable, well-maintained and good value rooms (Sb-€46–55, Db-€58–78, CC, 48 rue de la Verrerie, Mo: Hôtel de Ville, tel. 01 48 87 96 14, fax 01 48 87 30 46, www.hotel-sansonnet.com, e-mail: info@hotel-sansonnet.com).

Sleeping near the Marais on Ile St. Louis

The peaceful, residential character of this river-wrapped island, its brilliant location, and homemade ice cream have drawn Americans for decades, allowing hotels to charge top euro for their rooms. There are no budget values here, but the island's coziness and proximity to the Marais, Notre-Dame, and the Latin Quarter compensate for higher rates. These hotels are on the island's main drag, the rue St. Louis en l'Ile, where I list several restaurants (see "Eating," below).

HIGHER PRICED

Hôtel Jeu de Paume**,** located in a 17th-century tennis center, is the most expensive hotel I list in Paris. When you enter its magnificent lobby, you'll understand why. Ride the glass elevator for a half-timbered-tree-house experience and marvel at the cozy lounges. The 30 quite comfortable rooms have muted tones and feel more three-plus than four-star (you're paying for the location and public spaces). Most face a small garden and all are peaceful (Sb-€152, standard Db-€210, larger Db-€220–250, Db suite-€450, CC, 54 rue St. Louis en l'Ile, tel. 01 43 26 14 18, fax 01 40 46 02 76, www.jeudepaumehotel.com).

The following two hotels are owned by the same person. For both, if you must cancel, do so a week in advance or pay fees: **Hôtel de Lutèce***** is the best value on the island, with a sit-a-while wood-paneled lobby and fireplace and appealing air-conditioned rooms. Twin rooms are larger and the same price as double rooms (Sb-€125, Db-€149, Tb-€165, CC, 65 rue St. Louis en l'Ile, tel. 01 43 26 13 35, fax 01 43 29 60 25, www.hotel-ile-saint-louis.com). **Hôtel des Deux Iles***** is a *très* similar value, with marginally smaller rooms (Sb-€125, Db-€149, CC, air-con, 59 rue St. Louis en l'Ile, tel. 01 43 26 13 35, fax 01 43 29 60 25, www.hotel-ile-saintlouis.com).

Contrescarpe Orientation

I've patched together several areas to construct this diverse hotel neighborhood, whose strength is its central location and proximity to the Luxembourg Garden. The Latin Quarter, Luxembourg Garden, boulevard St. Germain, and Jardin des Plantes are all easily reachable by foot. Hotel listings are concentrated near the monumental Panthéon and along the more colorful rue Mouffetard. Perfectly Parisian place Contrescarpe ties these distinctly different areas together.

The rue Mouffetard is the spine of this area, running south from place Contrescarpe to rue Bazelles. Two thousand years ago, it was the principal Roman road south to Italy. Today, this small, meandering street has a split personality. The lower part thrives in the daytime as a pedestrian market street. The upper part sleeps during the day but comes alive after dark, teeming with bars, restaurants, and nightlife.

The flowery Jardin des Plantes park is just east, and the sublime Luxembourg Garden is just west. Both are ideal for afternoon walks, picnics, naps, and kids. The doorway at 49 rue Monge leads to a hidden **Roman arena** (Arènes de Lutèce). Today, *boules* players occupy the stage while couples cuddle on the seats. Admire the Panthéon from the outside (it's not worth paying to enter), and peek inside the exquisitely beautiful St. Etienne-du-Mont church.

The nearest **TI** is at the Louvre Museum. The **post office** (PTT) is between rue Mouffetard and rue Monge at 10 rue de l'Epée du Bois. Place Monge hosts a good **outdoor market** on Wednesday, Friday, and Sunday mornings until 13:00. The **street market** at the bottom of rue Mouffetard bustles daily except Monday (Tue–Sat 8:00–12:00 & 15:30–19:00, Sun 8:00–12:00, 5 blocks south of place Contrescarpe). Lively cafés at place Contrescarpe hop with action from the afternoon into the wee hours. **Bus #47** runs along rue Monge north to Notre-Dame, the Pompidou Center, and Gare du Nord.

Sleeping in the Contrescarpe Neighborhood (5th arrondissement, Mo: Place Monge, zip code: 75005)

The first six hotels here are a 10- to 15-minute walk from Notre-Dame, Ile de la Cité, and Ile St. Louis, and a five- to 10-minute walk from the Luxembourg Garden, St. Sulpice, and the grand boulevards St. Germain and St. Michel. Add 10 minutes for the last five hotels to reach the same places.

Sleeping near the Seine

MODERATELY PRICED

Hôtel des Grandes Ecoles*** is simply idyllic. A short alley leads to three buildings protecting a flower-filled garden courtyard, preserving a sense of tranquillity that is rare in a city this size. Its 51 rooms are reasonably spacious and comfortable with large beds. This romantic place is deservedly popular, so call well in advance (reservations not accepted more than 4 months ahead, Db-€95–110, a few bigger rooms-€120, extra bed-€15, parking-€25, CC, 75 rue de Cardinal Lemoine, Mo: Cardinal Lemoine, tel. 01 43 26 79 23, fax 01 43 25 28 15, www.hotel-grandes-ecoles.com, mellow Marie speaks some English, Mama does not).

LOWER PRICED

Hôtel Central* defines unpretentiousness, with a charming location, smoky reception area, steep, slippery, castle-like stairway, so-so beds, and basic but cheery rooms (all with showers, though toilets are down the hall). It's a fine budget value (Ss-€29–37, Ds-€39–45, no CC, no elevator, 6 rue Descartes, Mo: Cardinal Lemoine, tel. 01 46 33 57 93, sweet Pilar NSE).

Contrescarpe Hotels and Restaurants

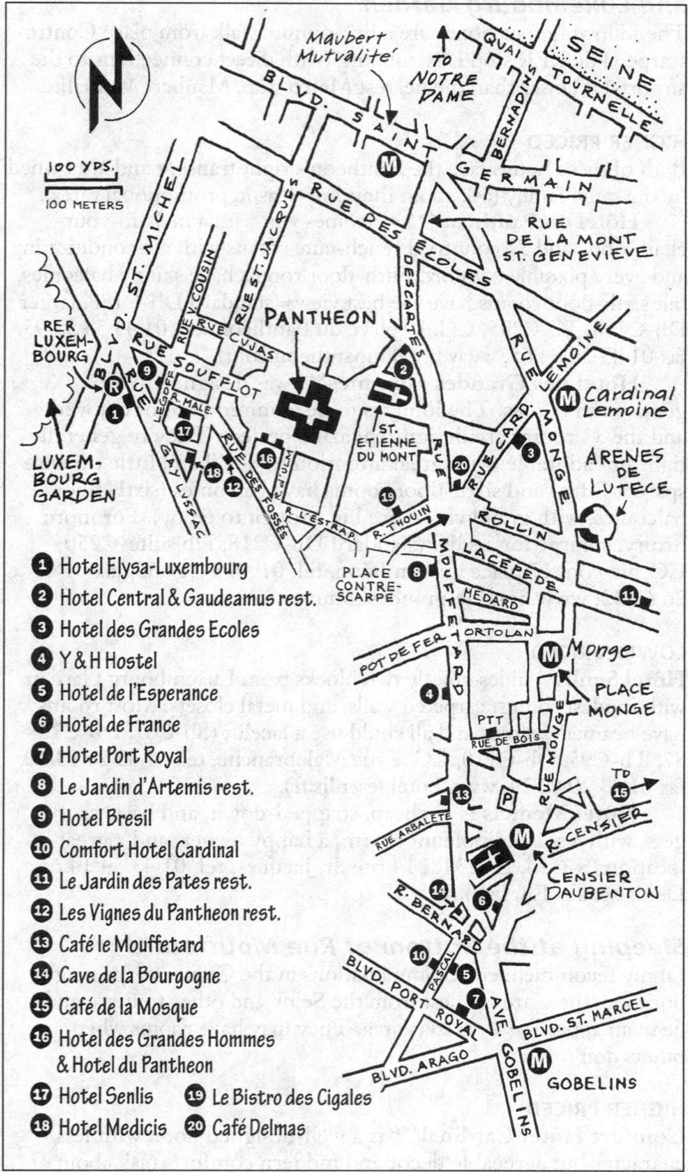

Sleeping between the Panthéon and Luxembourg Garden

The following four hotels are a five-minute walk from place Contrescarpe. The RER stop Luxembourg (with direct connections to the airports) is closer than the nearest Métro stop, Maubert Mutualité.

HIGHER PRICED

Both of these hotels face the Panthéon's right transept and are owned by the same family (ask about their low-season promotional rates).

Hôtel du Panthéon*** welcomes you with a melt-in-your-chair lobby and 32 country-French-cute rooms with air-conditioning and every possible comfort. Fifth-floor rooms have skinny balconies, but sixth-floor rooms have the best views (standard Db-€188, larger Db-€218, Tb-€235, CC, 19 place du Panthéon, tel. 01 43 54 32 95, fax 01 43 26 64 65, www.hoteldupantheon.com).

Hôtel des Grandes Hommes*** was designed to look good—and it does. The lobby is to be admired but not enjoyed, and the 31 rooms are design-magazine perfect. They're generally tight but adorable, with great attention to detail and little expense spared. Fifth- and sixth-floor rooms have balconies (sixth-floor balconies, with grand views, are big enough to enjoy). For more luxury, splurge for a suite (standard Db-€218, Db suite-€250, CC, air-con, 17 place du Panthéon, tel. 01 46 34 19 60, fax 01 43 26 67 32, www.hoteldesgrandeshommes.com).

LOWER PRICED

Hôtel Senlis** hides quietly two blocks from Luxembourg Garden, with modest rooms, carpeted walls, and metal closets. Most rooms have beamed ceilings and all could use a facelift (Sb-€67, Db-€72–87, Tb-€95, Qb-€110, CC, 7 rue Malebranche, tel. 01 43 29 93 10, fax 01 43 29 00 24, www.hoteldesenlis.fr).

Hôtel Medicis is as cheap, stripped-down, and basic as it gets, with a soiled linoleum charm, a happy owner, and a great location (S-€16, D-€31, 214 rue St. Jacques, tel. 01 43 54 14 66, Denis speaks English).

Sleeping at the Bottom of Rue Mouffetard

Of my recommended accommodations in the Contrescarpe neighborhood, these are farthest from the Seine and other tourists, and lie in an appealing workaday area. They may have rooms when others don't.

HIGHER PRICED

Comfort Hôtel Cardinal*** is a well-designed hotel with less character but agreeable decor and modern comforts (ask about off-season promotional rates, Sb-€100, standard Db-€138, large Db-€185, CC, air-con, 20 rue Pascal, tel. 01 47 07 41 92, fax 01 47 07 43 80, e-mail: hotelcardinal@aol.com).

LOWER PRICED

Don't let **Hôtel Port Royal***'s lone star fool you—this 46-room place is polished bottom to top and has been well-run by the same proud family for 66 years. You could eat off the floors of its spotless, comfy rooms. Ask for a room off the street (S-€37–48, D-€64, big hall showers-€2.50, Db-€73, deluxe Db-€84, no CC, requires cash deposit, climb stairs from rue Pascal to busy boulevard de Port Royal, 8 boulevard de Port Royal, Mo: Gobelins, tel. 01 43 31 70 06, fax 01 43 31 33 67, www.portroyal.fr.st).

Hôtel de l'Esperance** is a solid two-star value. It's quiet, pink, fluffy, and comfortable, with thoughtfully appointed rooms complete with canopy beds and a flamboyant owner (Sb-€70, Db-€73–86, small Tb-€101, CC, 15 rue Pascal, Mo: Censier-Daubenton, tel. 01 47 07 10 99, fax 01 43 37 56 19, e-mail: hotel.esperance@wanadoo.fr).

Hôtel de France** is set on a busy street, with adequately comfortable rooms, fair prices, and less welcoming owners. The best and quietest rooms are *sur le cour* (on the courtyard), though streetside rooms are OK (Sb-€64, Db-€76–80, CC, requires 1 night nonrefundable deposit, 108 rue Monge, Mo: Censier-Daubenton, tel. 01 47 07 19 04, fax 01 43 36 62 34, e-mail: hotel.de.fce@wanadoo.fr).

Y&H Hostel is easygoing and English-speaking, with Internet access, kitchen facilities, and basic but acceptable hostel conditions (beds in 4-bed rooms-€22, beds in double rooms-€25, sheets-€2.50, no CC, rooms closed 11:00–16:00 but reception stays open, 2:00 curfew, reservations require deposit, 80 rue Mouffetard, Mo: Cardinal Lemoine, tel. 01 47 07 47 07, fax 01 47 07 22 24, e-mail: smile@youngandhappy.fr).

Lesser Values

MODERATELY PRICED

Hôtel Elysa-Luxembourg*** sits on a busy street at Luxembourg Garden and charges top euro for its plush, air-conditioned rooms (Db-€138, CC, 6 rue Gay Lussac, tel. 01 43 25 31 74, fax 01 46 34 56 27, www.elysa-luxembourg.fr).

LOWER PRICED

Hôtel Brésil** lies one block from Luxembourg Garden and offers little character, some smoky rooms, and reasonable rates

(Sb-€64, Db-€68–85, CC, 10 rue le Goff, tel. 01 43 54 76 11, fax 01 46 33 45 78, e-mail: hoteldubresil@wanadoo.fr).

Sleeping near Paris, in Versailles

For a laid-back alternative to Paris within easy reach of the big city by RER train (5/hr, 30 min), Versailles, with easy, safe parking and reasonably priced hotels, can be a good overnight stop (see map on page 271). Park in the château's main lot while looking for a hotel, or leave your car there overnight (free from 19:30 to 8:00). Get a map of Versailles at your hotel or at the TI. For restaurant recommendations, see "Eating," below.

MODERATELY PRICED

Hôtel de France***, in an 18th-century town house, offers four-star value, with air-conditioned, appropriately royal rooms, a pleasant courtyard, comfy public spaces, a bar, and a restaurant (Db-€125–130, Tb-€168, CC, just off parking lot across from château, 5 rue Colbert, tel. 01 30 83 92 23, fax 01 30 83 92 24, www.hotelfrance-versailles.com).

LOWER PRICED

Hôtel Le Cheval Rouge**, built in 1676 as Louis XIV's stables, now houses tourists. It's a block behind place du Marché in a quaint corner of town on a large, quiet courtyard with free, safe parking and sufficiently comfortable rooms (Ds-€49, Db-€58–72, Tb-€86, Qb-€90, CC, 18 rue Andre Chenier, tel. 01 39 50 03 03, fax 01 39 50 61 27).

Ibis Versailles** offers fair value and modern comfort, but no air-conditioning (Db-€71, cheaper weekend rates can't be reserved ahead, CC, across from RER station, 4 avenue du General de Gaulle, tel. 01 39 53 03 30, fax 01 39 50 06 31).

Hôtel du Palais, facing the RER station, has clean, sharp rooms—the cheapest I list in this area. Ask for a quiet room off the street (Ds-€43, Db-€49, extra person-€11, CC, piles of stairs, 6 place Lyautey, tel. 01 39 50 39 29, fax 01 39 50 80 41).

Hôtel d'Angleterre**, away from the frenzy, is a tranquil old place with comfortable and spacious rooms. Park nearby in the palace lot (Db-€56–72, extra bed-€15, CC, just below palace to the right as you exit, 2 rue de Fontenay, tel. 01 39 51 43 50, fax 01 39 51 45 63).

Eating in Paris

Paris is France's wine and cuisine melting pot. While it lacks a style of its own (only French onion soup is truly Parisian), it draws from the best of France. Paris could hold a gourmet's Olympics and import nothing.

Picnic or go to bakeries for quick take-out lunches, or stop at a café for a lunch salad or *plat du jour*, but linger longer over dinner. Cafés are happy to serve a *plat du jour* (garnished plate of the day, about €11) or a chef-like salad (about €9) day or night, while restaurants expect you to enjoy a full dinner. Restaurants open for dinner around 19:00, and small local favorites get crowded after 21:00. Most of the restaurants listed below accept credit cards.

To save piles of euros, review the budget eating tips in this book's introduction and consider dinner picnics (great take-out dishes available at charcuteries). My recommendations are centered around the same three great neighborhoods I list accommodations for (above); you can come home exhausted after a busy day of sightseeing and have a good selection of restaurants right around the corner. And evening is a fine time to explore any of these delightful neighborhoods, even if you're sleeping elsewhere.

Restaurants

If you are traveling outside of Paris, save your splurges for the countryside, where you'll enjoy regional cooking for less money. Many Parisian department stores have huge supermarkets hiding in the basement and top-floor cafeterias offering affordable, low-risk, low-stress, what-you-see-is-what-you-get meals. The three neighborhoods highlighted in this book for sleeping in Paris are also pleasant areas to window-shop for just the right restaurant, as is the Ile St. Louis. Most restaurants we've listed in these areas have set-price *menus* between €15 and €30. In most cases, the few extra euros you pay for not choosing the least expensive option is money well spent as it opens up a variety of better choices. You decide.

Good Picnic Spots: For great people-watching, try the Pompidou Center (by the *Homage to Stravinsky* fountains), the elegant place des Vosges (closes at dusk), the gardens at the Rodin Museum, and Luxembourg Garden. The Palais Royal (across the street from the Louvre) is a good spot for a peaceful, royal picnic.

For a romantic picnic place, try the pedestrian bridge (pont des Arts) across from the Louvre, with its unmatched views and plentiful benches; the Champ de Mars park under the Eiffel Tower; and the western tip of Ile St. Louis, overlooking Ile de la Cité. Bring your own dinner feast and watch the riverboats or the Eiffel Tower light up the city for you.

Eating in the Rue Cler Neighborhood

The rue Cler neighborhood caters to its residents. Its eateries, while not destination places, have an intimate charm. My favorites are small mom-and-pop places with a love of serving good French food at good prices to a local clientele. You'll generally find great dinner *menus* for €15–23 and *plats du jour* for around €12. My first two recommendations are easygoing cafés, ideal if what you want is a light dinner (good dinner salads) or a more substantial but simple meal. Eat early with tourists or late with locals.

Café du Marché, with the best seats, coffee, and prices on rue Cler, serves hearty €7 salads and good €9 *plats du jour* for lunch or dinner to a trendy, smoky, mainly French crowd (Mon–Sat 11:00–23:00, closed Sun, at the corner of rue Cler and rue du Champ de Mars, tel. 01 47 05 51 27, well-run by Frank, Jack, and Bruno). Arrive before 19:30. It's packed at 21:00. A chalkboard lists the plates of the day—each a meal. You'll find the same dishes and prices with better (but smoky) indoor seating at their other restaurant, **Le Comptoir du Septième**, two blocks away at the Ecole Militaire Métro stop (39 avenue de la Motte Piquet, tel. 01 45 55 90 20).

Café le Bosquet is a vintage Parisian brasserie with dressy waiters and classic indoor or sidewalk tables on a busy street. Come here for a bowl of French onion soup, a salad, or a three-course set *menu* for €16 (closed Sun, many choices from a fun menu, the house red wine is plenty good, corner of rue du Champs de Mars and avenue Bosquet, tel. 01 45 51 38 13).

Leo le Lion, a warm, charming souvenir of old Paris, is popular with locals. Expect to spend €23 per person for fine à la carte choices (closed Sun, 23 rue Duvivier, tel. 01 45 51 41 77).

L'Ami de Jean celebrates the rustic joys of Basque living—and that includes good peasant-pleasing food. Beginners should trust the €15 *menu Basque.* And for a full red wine, try the Spanish Rioja. Stepping into the jumbled little room is like leaving Paris. Wear your beret (closed Sun, 27 rue Malar, tel. 01 47 05 86 89).

At **L'Affriole,** you'll compete with young professionals for a table. This small and trendy place is well-deserving of its rave reviews. Item selections change daily and the wine list is extensive, with some good bargains (€32 *menu*, closed Sun, 17 rue Malar, tel. 01 44 18 31 33).

Au Petit Tonneau is a purely Parisian experience. Fun-loving owner-chef Madame Boyer prepares everything herself, wearing her tall chef's hat like a crown as she rules from her family-style kitchen. The small dining room is plain and a bit smoky (allow €30/person with wine, open daily, 20 rue Surcouf, tel. 01 47 05 09 01).

Thoumieux, the neighborhood's classy, traditional Parisian brasserie, is a local institution and deservedly popular. It's big and dressy with formal but good-natured waiters (daily, €14 lunch *menu*, 3-course with wine dinner *menu* for €31, really good *crème brûlée*, 79 rue St. Dominique, tel. 01 47 05 49 75).

Le P'tit Troquet is a petite place, taking you back to Paris

Rue Cler Restaurants

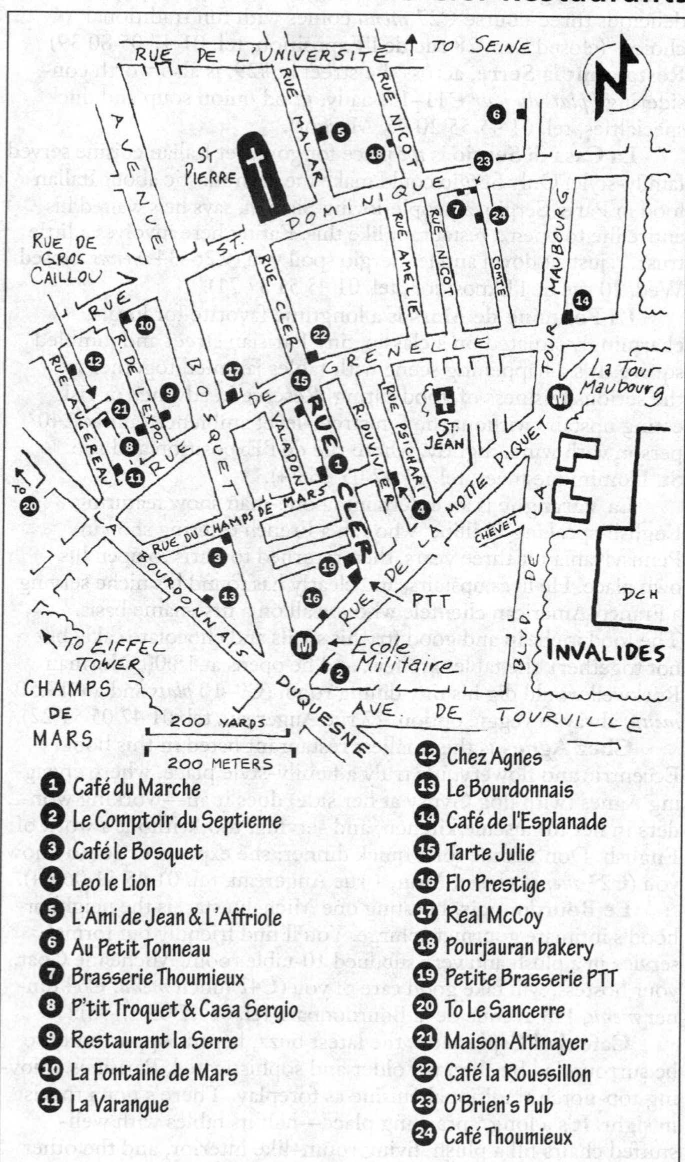

TO SEINE
RUE DE L'UNIVERSITE
RUE MALAR
RUE NICOT
AVENUE
ST PIERRE
DOMINIQUE
ST.
RUE DE GROS CAILLOU
RUE CLER
RUE AMELIE
RUE NICOT
COMTE
MAUBOURG
RUE
R. DE L'EXPO.
RUE AUGEREAU
BOSQUET
GRENELLE
DE
VALADON
RUE
R. DUVIVIER
RUE PSICHARI
ST. JEAN
La Tour Maubourg
TOUR
RUE
TO
RUE DU CHAMPS DE MARS
CLER
DE LA MOTTE PIQUET
LA
BOURDONNAIS
CHEVET
RUE DE
PTT
BLVD. DE LA
DCH
TO EIFFEL TOWER
Ecole Militaire
INVALIDES
CHAMPS DE MARS
DUQUESNE
AVE. DE TOURVILLE
200 YARDS
200 METERS
1 Café du Marche
2 Le Comptoir du Septieme
3 Café le Bosquet
4 Leo le Lion
5 L'Ami de Jean & L'Affriole
6 Au Petit Tonneau
7 Brasserie Thoumieux
8 P'tit Troquet & Casa Sergio
9 Restaurant la Serre
10 La Fontaine de Mars
11 La Varangue
12 Chez Agnes
13 Le Bourdonnais
14 Café de l'Esplanade
15 Tarte Julie
16 Flo Prestige
17 Real McCoy
18 Pourjauran bakery
19 Petite Brasserie PTT
20 To Le Sancerre
21 Maison Altmayer
22 Café la Roussillon
23 O'Brien's Pub
24 Café Thoumieux

in the 1920s, gracefully and earnestly run by Dominique. The delicious three-course €27 *menu* comes with fun traditional choices (closed Sun, 28 rue de l'Exposition, tel. 01 47 05 80 39). **Restaurant la Serre**, across the street at #29, is also worth considering (*plats du jour* €11–15, daily, good onion soup and duck specialties, tel. 01 45 55 20 96, Margot).

La Casa di Sergio is *the* place for gourmet Italian cuisine served family-style. Only Sergio could make me enthusiastic about Italian food in Paris. Sergio, a people-loving Sicilian, says he's waited his entire life to open a restaurant like this. Eating here involves a little trust... just sit down and let Sergio spoil you (€26–34 *menus*, closed Wed, 20 rue de l'Exposition, tel. 01 45 51 37 71).

La Fontaine de Mars is a longtime favorite for locals, charmingly situated on a classic, tiny Parisian street and jumbled square. It's a happening scene with tables jammed together for the serious business of good eating. Reserve in advance or risk eating upstairs without the fun street-level ambience (allow €40/person with wine, nightly, where rue de l'Exposition and rue St. Dominique meet, tel. 01 47 05 46 44).

La Varangue is an entertaining one-man show featuring English-speaking Phillipe, who ran a French catering shop in Pennsylvania for three years, then returned to Paris to open his own place. He lives upstairs, and clearly has found his niche serving a Franco-American clientele who are all on a first-name basis. The food is cheap and good (try his snails and chocolate cake, but not together), the tables are few, and he opens at 18:00. Norman Rockwell would dig his tiny dining room (€9–10 *plats* and a €13.50 *menu*, always a veggie option, 27 rue Augereau, tel. 01 47 05 51 22).

Chez Agnes is the smallest restaurant listed in this book. Eccentric and flowery, it's truly a family-style place, where engaging Agnes (with dog Gypsy at her side) does it all—working wonders in her minuscule kitchen, and serving, too, without a word of English. Don't come for a quick dinner; she expects to get to know you (€23 *menu*, closed Mon, 1 rue Augereau, tel. 01 45 51 06 04).

Le Bourdonnais, boasting one Michelin star, is the neighborhood's intimate gourmet splurge. You'll find friendly but formal service in a plush and very subdued 10-table room. Micheline Coat, your hostess, will take good care of you (€42 lunch *menu*, €64 dinner *menu*, 113 avenue de la Bourdonnais, tel. 01 47 05 47 96).

Café de l'Esplanade, the latest buzz, is your opportunity to be surrounded by chic, yet older and sophisticated, Parisians enjoying top-notch traditional cuisine as foreplay. There's not a tourist in sight. It's a long, sprawling place—half its tables with well-stuffed chairs fill a plush, living room–like interior, and the other half are lined up outside under its elegant awning facing the street, valet boys, and park. Dress competitively, as this is *the* place to be seen in the 7th *arrondissement* (€20 *plats du jour*, plan on €40 plus wine for dinner, open daily, reserve—especially if you want curb-side table, smoke-free room in the back, bordering Les Invalides at 52 rue Fabert, tel. 01 47 05 38 80).

Picnicking: The rue Cler is a moveable feast that gives "fast food" a good name. The entire street is clogged with connoisseurs of good eating. Only the health-food store goes unnoticed. A festival of food, the street is lined with people whose lives seem to be devoted to their specialty: polished produce, rotisserie chicken, crêpes, or cheese.

For a magical picnic dinner at the Eiffel Tower, assemble it in no fewer than five shops on rue Cler and lounge on the best grass in Paris (the police don't mind after dusk), with the dogs, Frisbees, a floodlit tower, and a cool breeze in the Parc du Champ de Mars.

The **crêpe stand** next to Café du Marché does a wonderful top-end dinner crêpe for €4. **Asian delis** (generically called *Traiteur Asie*) provide tasty, low-stress, low-price, take-out treats (€6 dinner plates, 2 delis have tables on the rue Cler—one across from Hôtel Leveque, and the other near the rue du Champ de Mars). For a variety of savory quiches or a tasty pear-and-chocolate tart, try **Tarte Julie** (take-out or stools, 28 rue Cler). The elegant **Flo Prestige** charcuterie is open until 23:00 and offers mouthwatering meals to go (at the Ecole Militaire Métro stop). **Real McCoy** is a little shop selling American food and sandwiches (194 rue de Grenelle). A good, small, **late-night grocery** is at 197 rue de Grenelle.

The **bakery** *(boulangerie)* on the corner of rue Cler and rue de Grenelle is the place for sandwiches, *pain au chocolat*, or almond croissants. And the **Pourjauran** bakery, offering great baguettes, hasn't changed in 70 years (20 rue Jean Nicot). The **bakery** at 112 rue St. Dominique is worth the detour, with classic decor and tables where you to enjoy your café au lait and croissant.

Cafés and Bars: If you want to linger over coffee or a drink at a sidewalk café, try **Café du Marché** (see above), **Petite Brasserie PTT** (local workers eat here, opposite 53 rue Cler), or **Café le Bosquet** (46 avenue Bosquet, tel. 01 45 51 38 13). **Le Sancerre** wine bar/café is wood-beam warm and ideal for a light lunch or dinner, or just a glass of wine after a long day of sightseeing. The owner's cheeks are the same color as his wine (open until 21:30, great omelettes, 22 avenue Rapp, tel. 01 45 51 75 91). **Maison Altmayer** is a hole-in-the-wall place good for a quiet drink (9:00–19:30, next to Hôtel Eiffel Rive Gauche, 6 rue du Gros Caillou). Cafés like this originated (and this one still functions) as a place where locals enjoyed a drink while their heating wood, coal, or gas was prepared for delivery.

Nightlife: This sleepy neighborhood is not the place for night owls, but there are a few notable exceptions. **Café du Marché** and its brother, **Le Comptoir du Septième** (both listed above), hop with a Franco-American crowd until about midnight, as does the flashier **Café la Roussillon** (at corner of rue de Grenelle and rue Cler). **O'Brien's Pub** is a relaxed, Parisian rendition of an Irish pub (77 avenue St. Dominique). **Café Thoumieux** (younger brother of the brasserie listed above) has big-screen sports and a trendy young crowd (4 rue de la Comète, Mo: La Tour Maubourg).

Eating in the Marais Neighborhood

The trendy Marais is filled with locals enjoying good food in colorful and atmospheric eateries. The scene is competitive and changes all the time. Here is an assortment of places—all handy to recommended hotels that offer good food at reasonable prices, plus a memorable experience.

Eating at place du Marché Ste. Catherine: This tiny square just off rue St. Antoine is an international food festival cloaked in extremely Parisian, leafy square ambience. On a balmy evening, this is clearly a neighborhood favorite, with five popular restaurants offering €20–25 meals. Survey the square and find two French-style bistros (**Le Marché** and **Au Bistrot de la Place**), a fun Italian place, a popular Japanese/Korean restaurant, and a Russian eatery with an easy but adventurous menu. You'll eat under the trees surrounded by a futuristic-in-1800 planned residential quarter. Just around the corner with none of the ambience is **L'Auberge de Jarente,** a reliable rainy-day budget option, where a hardworking father and son team serve good Basque food (€18 3-course *menu* with wine, closed Sun–Mon, just off the square at 7 rue de Jarente, tel. 01 42 77 49 35).

Eating at place des Vosges: This elegant square, built by King Henry IV in 1605, put the Marais on the aristocratic map. And today, the posh ambience survives, with several good places offering romantic meals under its venerable arches, overlooking one of Paris' most elegant little parks. And prices are reasonable. The mod and pastel **Nectarine** at #16 is a teahouse serving healthy salads, quiches, and inexpensive *plats du jour* both day and night. Its fun menu lets you mix and match omelettes and crêpes (tel. 01 42 77 23 78). **Café Hugo**, next door (named for the square's most famous resident), is a typical bistro serving good traditional favorites such as onion soup (€5) and crêpes (€4). **Ma Bourgogne** has the snob appeal—bigger, darker, and more traditional. You'll sit under arcades in a whirlpool of Frenchness as bow-tied and black-aproned waiters serve traditional Burgundian specialties: steak, coq au vin, lots of French fries, escargot, and great red wine.

Marais Restaurants

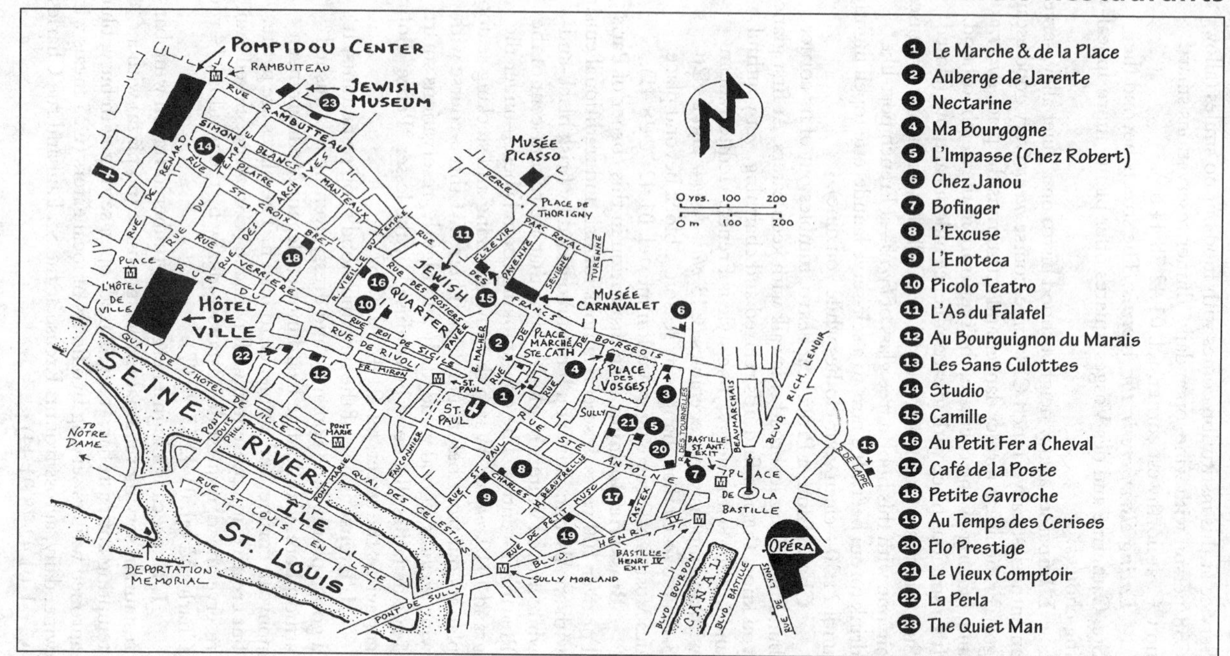
1 Le Marche & de la Place
2 Auberge de Jarente
3 Nectarine
4 Ma Bourgogne
5 L'Impasse (Chez Robert)
6 Chez Janou
7 Bofinger
8 L'Excuse
9 L'Enoteca
10 Picolo Teatro
11 L'As du Falafel
12 Au Bourguignon du Marais
13 Les Sans Culottes
14 Studio
15 Camille
16 Au Petit Fer a Cheval
17 Café de la Poste
18 Petite Gavroche
19 Au Temps des Cerises
20 Flo Prestige
21 Le Vieux Comptoir
22 La Perla
23 The Quiet Man
POMPIDOU CENTER
RAMBUTEAU
JEWISH MUSEUM
MUSÉE PICASSO
PLACE DE THORIGNY
MUSÉE CARNAVALET
JEWISH QUARTER
HÔTEL DE VILLE
PLACE L'HÔTEL DE VILLE
PLACE MARCHÉ STE. CATH
PLACE DES VOSGES
ST. PAUL
PONT MARIE
PLACE DE LA BASTILLE
BASTILLE-ST. ANT. EXIT
BASTILLE-HENRI IV EXIT
SULLY MORLAND
OPÉRA
CANAL
SEINE RIVER
ILE ST. LOUIS
TO NOTRE DAME
DEPORTATION MEMORIAL
0 YDS. 100 200
0 m 100 200

Service at this institution comes with food but no smiles (allow €38/person with wine, open daily, dinner reservations smart, no CC, at northwest corner, tel. 01 42 78 44 64).

Eating elsewhere in the Marais: The streets beyond the Ste. Catherine and des Vosges squares offer plenty more appealing choices.

L'Impasse, a cozy neighborhood bistro on a quiet alley, serves an enthusiastically French €24 three-course *menu* (very good escargot). Françoise, a former dancer and artist, runs the place *con brio* and, judging by the clientele, she's a fixture in the neighborhood. It's a spacious place with great ambience indoors and out (closed Sun, 4 impasse Guéménée, tel. 01 42 72 08 45). Françoise promises anyone with this book a free glass of *byrrh*—a French port-like drink (pron: beer). It's next to a self-serve launderette (open nightly until 21:30—clean your clothes while you dine).

Chez Janou, a Provençal bistro, tumbles out of its corner building, filling its broad sidewalk with keen eaters. At first glance, you know this is a find. It's relaxed and charming, yet youthful and busting with energy. The style is French Mediterranean with an emphasis on vegetables (€13 *plats du jour* and a €26 3-course *menu* that changes by season, a block beyond place des Vosges at 2 rue Roger-Verlomme, tel. 01 42 72 28 41).

Brasserie Bofinger is an institution in this corner of Paris. For over 100 years, it's been famous for fish and traditional cuisine with an Alsatian flair. You'll be surrounded by brisk black-and-white attired waiters in plush rooms that are reminiscent of the Roaring Twenties. The non-smoking room is best—under the grand 1919 *coupole*. Watch the boys shucking and stacking seafood platters out front before going in. Their €31 three-course with wine *menu* is a good value (daily and nightly, reservations smart, 5 rue de la Bastille, don't be confused by the lesser "Petite" Bofinger across the street, tel. 01 42 72 87 82).

L'Excuse is one of the neighborhood's top restaurants. It's a good splurge for a romantic and dressy evening in a hushed atmosphere, with lounge lizard music, elegant Mediterranean nouveau cuisine, and ambience to match. The plates are petite, but creative and presented with panache (€36 *menu*, closed Sun, reserve ahead, request downstairs—ideally by the window, 14 rue Charles V, tel. 01 42 77 98 97).

L'Enoteca is a high-energy, half-timbered Italian wine bar restaurant serving reasonable Italian cuisine (no pizza) with a tempting antipasti bar. It's a relaxed, open setting with busy, blue-aproned waiters serving two floors of local eaters (€25 meals with wine, daily, across from L'Excuse at rue St. Paul and rue Charles V, tel. 01 42 78 91 44).

Vegetarians will appreciate the excellent cuisine at the popular **Picolo Teatro** (closed Mon, near rue des Rosiers, 6 rue des Ecouffes, tel. 01 42 72 17 79) or **L'As du Falafel**, which serves the best falafel on rue des Rosiers (at #34).

Au Bourguignon du Marais, a small wine bar on the other side of rue de Rivoli, is a place that wine-lovers shouldn't miss. The excellent Burgundy wines blend well with a fine, though limited, selection of *plats du jour* (closed Sat–Sun, call by 19:00 to reserve, 52 rue Francois Miron, tel. 01 48 87 15 40).

Lively rue de Lappe is what the Latin Quarter wants to be. This street, just beyond the more stately place de la Bastille, is currently one of the wildest nightspots in Paris. You'll walk past a dizzying array of wacky eateries, bars, and dance halls. Then, sitting there like a van Gogh painting, is the popular, zinc-bar classic **Bistrot les Sans Culottes**—a time-warp bistro serving traditional French cuisine with a proper respect for fine wine (€20 3-course *menu*, 27 rue de Lappe, tel. 01 48 05 42 92). Plan on staying out past your normal bedtime. Eat here. Then join the rue de Lappe party.

Le Studio is wonderfully located close to the Pompidou Center on a 17th-century courtyard below a dance school. It's best when you can sit outside, but the salads, €12 *plats du jour*, and Tex-Mex meals are good day or night (daily, 41 rue de Temple, tel. 01 42 74 10 38).

Eating at the east end of the Marais: **Camille,** a traditional corner brasserie, is a neighborhood favorite with great indoor and sidewalk seating. White-aproned waiters serve €9 salads and very French *plats du jour* for €15 to a down-to-earth but sophisticated clientele (daily, 24 rue des Francs-Bourgeois at corner of rue Elzévir, tel. 01 42 72 29 50). **Au Petit Fer à Cheval,** named for its horseshoe-shaped bar, is an authentic gem with mirrored walls and tiled floors. The tight woody interior takes you back to the 1930s—and you'll sit on old wooden Métro seats. The sidewalk tables put you in the front row at the neighborhood's trendy and gay promenade (€10 salads, €15 *plats du jour*, explore the fun chalkboard menu, reasonable wines by the glass, daily until 24:00, 30 rue Vieille du Temple, tel. 01 42 72 47 47).

Cheap eating in the Marais: **Chinese fast food** is cheap and easy at several places along rue St. Antoine. These hardworking little places are great for a €5 meal or a quick late-night snack. **Café de la Poste** is a very tight little place serving very good €11 *plats du jour* from a small but reliable menu (closed Sun, near place de la Bastille at 13 rue Castex, tel. 01 42 72 95 35). For dirt-cheap French cooking, try €8 *plats du jour* at the charmingly basic **Petite Gavroche** (15 rue Sainte Croix de la Bretonnerie, tel. 01 48 87 74 26). **Au Temps des Cerises**, a *très* local wine bar, is relaxed and amiably run by the incredibly mustachioed Monsieur Vimard. This place is great for a colorful lunch or a very light dinner of cheese or cold meats with good wine (Mon–Fri until 20:00, closed Sat–Sun, at rue du Petit Musc and rue de la Cerisaie).

Picnicking: Picnic at the peaceful place des Vosges (closes at dusk) or on the Ile St. Louis quai (described below). Hobos stretch their euros at the supermarket in the basement of the **Monoprix** department store (near place des Vosges on rue St. Antoine). A couple of small grocery shops are open until 23:00 on rue St. Antoine (near intersection with rue Castex). For a cheap breakfast, try the tiny ***boulangerie/pâtisserie*** where the hotels buy their croissants (coffee machine-€0.70, baby quiche-€1.50, *pain au chocolat*-€1, 1 block off place de la Bastille, corner of rue St. Antoine and rue de Lesdiguières). Pick up something good to go at the elegant **Flo Prestige** charcuterie (open until 23:00, 10 rue Saint Antoine, tel. 01 53 01 91 91).

Nightlife: The best scene is the bars and dance halls of rue de Lappe (beyond the place de la Bastille, see above). Trendy cafés and bars also cluster on rue Vielle du Temple, rue des Archives, and rue Ste. Croix de la Bretonnerie (open generally until 2:00 in the morning), and are popular with gay men. **Le Vieux Comptoir** is tiny, lively, and just hip enough (just off place des Vosges at 8 rue de Biraque). **La Perla** is trendy and full of Parisian yuppies in search of the perfect margarita (26 rue François Miron). **The Quiet Man** is a traditional Irish pub with happy hour from 16:00 to 20:00 (5 rue des Haudriettes).

Eating on Ile St. Louis

The Ile St. Louis is a romantic and peaceful place to window-shop for plenty of promising dinner possibilities. Cruise the island's main street for a variety of options, from cozy *crêperies* to Italian (intimate pizzeria and upscale) to typical brasseries (several with fine outdoor seating face the bridge to Ile de la Cité). After dinner, sample Paris' best sorbet. Then stroll across to the Ile de la Cité to see an illuminated Notre-Dame. All listings below line the island's main drag, the rue St. Louis en l'Ile. Consider skipping dessert at a restaurant to enjoy a stroll licking the best ice cream in Paris. Read on.

These two little family-run places serve top-notch traditional French cuisine with white-tablecloth, candlelit elegance in small, 10-table rooms under heavy wooden beams. Their *menus* start with three courses at €26 and offer plenty of classic choices that change with the season for freshness. **Le Tastevin** at #46, run by Madame Puisieux, is a little more intimate (daily, tel. 01 43 54 17 31). **Auberge de la Reine Blanche** is a bit more touristy—but in the best sense, with friendly Françoise and her crew working hard to please in a characteristic little place with dollhouse furniture on the walls and a two-dove welcoming committee at the door (at #30 daily, tel. 01 46 33 07 87). Reservations are smart for each.

Café Med, closest to Notre-Dame at #77, is best for inexpensive salads, crêpes, and lighter *menus* in a tight but cheery setting (daily, 30 rue de St. Louis en l'Ile, tel. 01 43 29 73 17, charming Eva SE). Very limited wine list.

Two side-by-side places are famous for their rowdy medieval cellar atmosphere, serving all-you-can-eat buffets with straw baskets of raw veggies (cut whatever you like with your dagger), massive plates of pâté, a meat course, and all the wine you can stomach for €34. The food is just food; burping is encouraged. If you want to eat a lot, drink a lot of wine, and holler at your friends while receiving smart-aleck buccaneer service, these food fests can be fun. **Nos Ancêtres les Gaulois** ("Our Ancestors the Gauls," daily from 19:00, tel. 01 46 33 66 07) has bigger tables and seems made-to-order for local stag parties. If you'd rather be surrounded by drunk tourists than locals, pick **La Taverne du Sergeant Recruteur**. The "Sergeant Recruteur" used to get young Parisians drunk and stuffed here, then sign them into the army (daily from 19:00, #41, tel. 01 43 54 75 42).

Riverside picnic: On sunny lunchtimes and balmy evenings, the quai on the Left Bank side of Ile St. Louis is lined with locals—who have more class than money—spreading out tablecloths and even lighting candles for elegant picnics. The grocery store on the main drag at #67 is open daily until midnight if you'd like to join them. Otherwise, it's a great stroll.

Ice cream dessert: Half the people strolling Ile St. Louis are licking an ice cream cone because this is the home of "*les glaces Berthillon*." The original Berthillon shop, at 31 rue St. Louis en l'Ile, is marked by the line of salivating customers. It's so popular that the wealthy people who can afford to live on this fancy island complain about the congestion it causes. For a less famous but at least as tasty treat, try the homemade Italian gelato a block away at **Amorino Gelati**. It's giving Berthillon competition (no line, bigger portions, easier to see what you want, and they offer little tastes—whereas Berthillon doesn't need to, 47 rue Saint Louis en l'Ile). Having some of each is a fine option.

Eating in the Contrescarpe Neighborhood

There are a few diamonds for fine dining in this otherwise rough area. Most come here for the lively and cheap eateries that line rues Mouffetard and du Pot-de-Fer. Study the many menus, compare crowds, then dive in and have fun (see map on page 299).

Near the Panthéon, **Les Vignes du Panthéon** is a homey,

traditional place with a zinc bar and original flooring. It serves a mostly local clientele and makes you feel you're truly in Paris (allow €23 for à la carte, closed Sat–Sun, 4 rue des Fossés St. Jacques, tel. 01 43 54 80 81). **Le Bistro des Cigales,** between the Panthéon and place de la Contrescarpe, offers an escape to Provence, with deep yellow and blue decor, a purely Provençal menu, helpful staff, and air-conditioned rooms (€17–22 *menus*, daily, 12 rue Thouin, tel. 01 40 46 03 76). **Gaudeamus**, with a low-profile café on one side and a pleasant bistro on the other, has friendly owners and cheap, €15 *menus* (daily, behind the Panthéon, 47 rue de la Montagne Ste. Geneviève, tel. 01 40 46 93 40). **L'Ecurie**, almost next door, is for those who prefer ambience and setting over top cuisine, with inexpensive and acceptable meals served on small, wood tables around a zinc bar in an unpretentious setting with a few outdoor tables (daily, *menus* from €15, 58 rue de la Montagne Ste. Genevieve, tel. 01 46 33 68 49).

Right on place de la Contrescarpe, sprawling **Café Delmas** is the place to see and be seen with a broad outdoor terrace, tasty salads, and good *plats du jour* from €12 (open daily). **Le Jardin d'Artemis** is one of the better values on rue Mouffetard, at #34 (€15–23 *menus*, closed Tue). **Le Jardin des Pates** is popular with less strict vegetarians, serving pastas and salads at fair prices (daily, near Jardin des Plantes, 4 rue Lacépède, tel. 01 43 31 50 71).

Cafés: The cafés on place de la Contrescarpe are popular until late (see Café Delmas, above). Both indoors and outdoors provide good people-watching. **Café le Mouffetard** is in the thick of the street-market hustle and bustle (at corner of rue Mouffetard and rue de l'Arbalète). The outdoor tables at **Cave de la Bourgogne** are picture-perfect (at the bottom of rue Mouffetard on rue de Bazeilles). At **Café de la Mosque,** you'll feel like you've been beamed to Morocco. In this purely Arab café, order a mint tea, pour in the sugar, and enjoy the authentic interior and peaceful outdoor terrace (behind mosque, 2 rue Daubenton).

Eating on Montmartre

The Montmartre is extremely touristy, with all the mindless mobs following guides to cancan shows. But the ambience is undeniable and an evening up here overlooking Paris is a quintessential experience in the City of Lights. To avoid the crowds and enjoy a classic neighborhood corner, hike from the Sacré-Coeur church away from the tourist zone down the stairs to **L'Eté en Pente Douce,** with fine indoor and outdoor seating, €9 *plats du jour* and salads, veggie options, and good wines (23 rue Muller, tel. 01 42 64 02 67). Just off the jam-packed place du Tertre, **Restaurant Chez Plumeau** is a touristy yet cheery, reasonably priced place with great seating on a tiny characteristic square (€18 *menu*, place du Calvaire, tel. 01 46 06 26 29). Along the touristy main drag and just off, several fun piano bars serve reasonable crêpes with great people-watching.

Eating in Versailles

In the pleasant town center, around place du Marché Notre-Dame, you'll find a variety of reasonable restaurants, cafés, and a few cobbled lanes (market days Sun, Tue, and Fri until 13:00; see map on page 271). The square is a 15-minute walk from the château (veer left when you leave château). From the place du Marché, consider shortcutting to Versailles' gardens by walking 10 minutes west down rue de la Paroisse. The château will be to your left after entering; the main gardens, Trianon palaces, and Hameau are straight ahead. The quickest way to the château's front door is along avenue de St. Cloud and rue Colbert.

These places are on or near place du Marché Notre-Dame, and all are good for lunch or dinner. **La Boeuf à la Mode** is a bistro with traditional cuisine right on the square (€23 *menu*, open daily, 4 rue au Pain, tel. 01 39 50 31 99). **Fenêtres sur Cour** is the romantic's choice, where you dine in a glass gazebo surrounded by antique shops, just below the square in "the antique village," on place de la Geôle (closed all day Mon and Tue–Wed eves, tel. 01 39 51 97 77). **A la Côte Bretonne** is the place to go for crêpes in a cozy setting (daily, a few steps off the square on traffic-free rue des Deux Ponts, at #12).

Rue Satory is another pedestrian-friendly street lined with restaurants on the south side of the château near the Hôtel d'Angleterre (10-min walk, angle right out of the château). **Le Limousin** is a warm, traditional restaurant sitting at the corner nearest the château with mostly meat dishes (lamb is a specialty, allow €30 with wine, 4 rue de Satory, tel. 01 39 50 21 50).

Transportation Connections—Paris

Paris is Europe's rail hub, with six major train stations, each serving different regions: Gare de l'Est (eastbound trains), Gare du Nord (northern France and Europe), Gare St. Lazare (northwestern France), Gare d'Austerlitz (southwest France and Europe), Gare de Lyon (southeastern France and Italy), and Gare Montparnasse (northwestern France and TGV service to France's southwest). Any train station can give you schedules, make reservations, and sell tickets for any destination. Buying tickets is handier from an SNCF neighborhood office (e.g., Louvre, Invalides, Orsay, Versailles, airports) or at your neighborhood travel agency—worth their small fee (SNCF signs in window indicate they sell train tickets). For schedules, call 08 36 35 35 35 (€0.50/min, English sometimes available).

All six train stations have Métro, bus, and taxi service. All have banks or change offices, ATMs, information desks, telephones, cafés, baggage storage *(consigne automatique)*, newsstands, and clever pickpockets. Each station offers two types of rail service: long distance to other cities, called *Grandes Lignes* (major lines); and suburban service to outlying areas, called *banlieue* or RER. Both *banlieue* and RER trains serve outlying areas and the airports; the only difference is that *banlieue* lines are operated by SNCF (France's train system) and RER lines are operated by RATP (Paris' Métro and bus system). Paris train stations can be intimidating, but if you slow down, take a deep breath, and ask for help, you'll find them manageable and efficient. Bring a pad of paper for clear communication at ticket/info windows. All stations have helpful *accueil* (information) booths; the bigger stations have roving helpers, usually in red vests.

Station Overview

Here's an overview of Paris' major train stations. Métro, RER, buses, and taxis are well-signposted at every station. When arriving by Métro, follow signs for *Grandes Lignes*-SNCF to find the main tracks.

Gare du Nord: This vast station serves cities in northern France and international destinations to the north of Paris, including Copenhagen, Amsterdam (via pricey Thalys Train) and the Eurostar to London (see "The Eurostar Train to London," below) as well as two of the day trips described in this book (Auvers-sur-Oise and Chantilly). Arrive early to allow time to navigate this huge station. From the Métro, follow *Grandes Lignes* signs (main lines) and keep going up and up until you reach the tracks at street level. *Grandes Lignes* depart from tracks 3–21, suburban *(banlieue)* lines from tracks 30–36, and RER trains depart from tracks 37–44 (tracks 41–44 are 1 floor below). Glass train information booths *(accueil)* are scattered throughout the station and information staff circulate to help (all rail staff are required to speak English). Information booths for the **Thalys Train** (high-speed trains to Brussels and Amsterdam) are opposite track 8. All non-Eurostar ticket sales are opposite tracks 3–8. Passengers departing on the **Eurostar** (London via Chunnel) must buy tickets and check in on the second level, opposite track 6. (Note: Britain's time zone is 1 hour earlier than the Continent's; times listed on Eurostar tickets are local times.) A peaceful café/bar hides on the upper level past the Eurostar ticket windows. Storage lockers, baggage check, taxis, and rental cars are at the far end, just opposite track 3 and down the steps.

Key destinations served by Gare du Nord *Grandes Lignes:* **Brussels** (21/day, 1.5 hrs, via pricey Thalys Train), **Bruges** (18/day, 2 hrs, change in Brussels, 1 direct), **Amsterdam** (10/day,

4 hrs; see "Thalys Train" under "Gare du Nord," above), **Copenhagen** (1/day, 16 hrs, 2 night trains), **Koblenz** (6/day, 5 hrs, change in Köln), **London** Eurostar via Chunnel (17/day, 3 hrs, tel. 08 36 35 35 39; see "The Eurostar Train to London," below). By *Banlieue*/RER lines to: **Chantilly-Gouvieux** (hrly, fewer on weekends, 35 min), **Charles de Gaulle** airport (2/hr, 30 min, runs 5:30–23:00, track 4), **Auvers-sur-Oise** (2/hr, 1hr, transfer at Pontoise).

Gare Montparnasse: This big and modern station covers three floors, serves Lower Normandy and Brittany, and offers TGV service to the Loire Valley and southwestern France and suburban service to Chartres. At street level, you'll find a bank, *banlieue* trains (serving Chartres; you can also reach the *banlieue* trains from the second level), and ticket windows in the center, just past the escalators. Lockers *(consigne automatique)* are on the mezzanine level between levels 1 and 2. Most services are provided on the second level, where the *Grandes Lignes* arrive and depart (ticket windows to the far left with your back to glass exterior). *Banlieue* trains depart from tracks 10 through 19. The main rail information office is opposite track 15. Taxis are to the far left as you leave the tracks.

Key destinations served by Gare Montparnasse: Chartres (20/day, 1 hr, *banlieue* lines), **Pontorson-Mont St. Michel** (5/day, 4.5 hrs, via Rennes, then take bus; or take train to Pontorson via Caen, then bus from Pontorson), **Dinan** (7/day, 4 hrs, change in Rennes and Dol), **Bordeaux** (14/day, 3.5 hrs), **Sarlat** (5/day, 6 hrs, change in Bordeaux, Libourne, or Souillac), **Toulouse** (11/day, 5 hrs, most require change, usually in Bordeaux), **Albi** (7/day, 6–7.5 hrs, change in Toulouse, also night train), **Carcassonne** (8/day, 6.5 hrs, most require changes in Toulouse and Bordeaux, direct trains take 10 hrs), **Tours** (14/day, 1 hr).

Gare de Lyon: This huge station offers TGV and regular service to southeastern France, Italy, and other international destinations (for trains to Italy, see also "Gare de Bercy," below). Frequent *banlieue* trains serve Melun (near Vaux-le-Vicomte) and Fontainebleau (some depart from main *Grandes Lignes* level, more frequent departures one level down, follow RER-D signs, and ask at any *accueil* or ticket window where next departure leaves from).

Grande Ligne trains arrive and depart from one level but are divided into two areas (tracks A–N and 5–23). They are connected by the long platform along tracks A and 5, and by the hallway adjacent to track A and opposite track 9. This hallway has all the services, ticket windows, ticket information, banks, shops, and access to car rental. *banlieue* ticket windows are just inside the hall adjacent to track A *(billets Ile de France)*. *Grandes Lignes* and *banlieue* lines share the same tracks. A Paris TI (Mon–Sat 8:00–20:00, closed Sun) and a train information office are opposite track L. From the RER or Métro, follow signs for *Grandes Lignes Arrivées* and take the escalator up to reach the platforms. Train information booths *(accueil)* are opposite tracks G and 11. Taxis stands are well-marked in front of the station and one floor below.

Key destinations served by Gare de Lyon: Vaux-le-Vicomte (train to Melun, hrly, 30 min), **Fontainebleau** (nearly hrly, 45 min), **Beaune** (12/day, 2.5 hrs, most require change in Dijon), **Dijon** (15/day, 1.5 hrs), **Chamonix** (9/day, 9 hrs, change in Lyon and St. Gervais, direct night train), **Annecy** (8/day, 4–7 hrs), Lyon (16/day, 2.5 hrs), **Avignon** (9/day in 2.5 hrs, 6/day in 4 hrs with change), **Arles** (14/day, 5 hrs, most with change in Marseille, Avignon, or Nîmes), **Nice** (14/day, 5.5–7 hrs, many with change in Marseille), **Venice** (3/day, 3/night, 11–15 hrs, most require changes), **Rome** (2/day, 5/night, 15–18 hrs, most require changes), **Bern** (9/day, 5–11 hrs, most require changes, night train).

Gare de Bercy: This smaller station handles some rail service to Italy during renovation work at the Gare de Lyon, Mo: Bercy, 1 stop east of Gare de Lyon on line 14).

Gare de l'Est: This single-floor station (with underground Métro) serves eastern France and European points to the east of Paris. Train information booths are at tracks 1 and 26; ticket windows and the main exit to buses and Paris are opposite track 8; luggage storage is opposite track 12.

Key destinations served by the **Gare de l'Est: Colmar** (12/day, 5.5 hrs, change in Strasbourg, Dijon, or Mulhouse), **Strasbourg** (14/day, 4.5 hrs, many require changes), **Reims** (12/day, 1.5 hrs), **Verdun** (5/day, 3 hrs, change in Metz or Chalon), **Munich** (5/day, 9 hrs, some require changes, night train), **Vienna** (7/day, 13–18 hrs, most require changes, night train), **Zurich** (10/day, 7 hrs, most require changes, night train), **Prague** (2/day, 14 hrs, night train).

Gare St. Lazare: This relatively small station serves Upper Normandy, including Rouen and Giverny. All trains arrive and depart one floor above street level. Follow signs to *Grandes Lignes* from the Métro to reach the tracks. You'll pass a mini-mall. Ticket windows and a Thomas Cook exchange are in the first hall on the second floor. The tracks are through the small hallways (lined with storage lockers). *Grandes Lignes* (main lines) depart from tracks 17–27; *banlieue* (suburban) trains depart from 1–16. The train information office *(accueil)* is opposite track 15; the reservation office is opposite track 16.

Baggage consignment and the post office are along track 27, and WCs are opposite track 19.

Key destinations served by the **Gare St. Lazare: Giverny** (train to Vernon, 5/day, 45 min; then bus or taxi 10 min to Giverny), **Rouen** (15/day, 75 min), **Honfleur** (6/day, 3 hrs, via Lisieux, then bus), **Bayeux** (9/day, 2.5 hrs, some with change in Caen), **Caen** (12/day, 2 hrs).

Gare d'Austerlitz: This small station provides non-TGV service to the Loire Valley, southwestern France, and Spain. All tracks are at street level. The information booth is opposite track 17, and a Thomas Cook exchange and all ticket sales are in the hall opposite track 10. Baggage consignment and car rental are near Porte 27 (along the side, opposite track 21).

Key destinations served by the **Gare d'Austerlitz: Amboise** (8/day in 2 hrs, 12/day in 1.5 hrs with change in St. Pierre des Corps), **Cahors** (7/day, 5–7 hrs, most with changes), **Barcelona** (1/day, 9 hrs, change in Montpellier, night trains), **Madrid** (2 night trains only, 13–16 hrs), **Lisbon** (1/day, 24 hrs).

Buses

The main bus station is Gare Routière du Paris-Gallieni (28 avenue du General de Gaulle, in suburb of Bagnolet, Mo: Gallieni, tel. 01 49 72 51 51). Buses provide cheaper—if less comfortable and more time-consuming—transportation to major European cities. Eurolines' buses depart from here (tel. 08 36 69 52 52, www.eurolines.com). Eurolines has a couple of neighborhood offices: in the Latin Quarter (55 rue Saint-Jacques, tel. 01 43 54 11 99) and in Versailles (4 avenue de Sceaux, tel. 01 39 02 03 73).

The Eurostar Train to London

Crossing the Channel by Eurostar Train

The quickest way to London is by rail. The Eurostar train whisks you from downtown Paris to London (17/day, 3 hrs) faster and easier than flying.

You can check and book fares by phone or online:

U.S.: 800/EUROSTAR, www.raileurope.com (prices listed in dollars).

France: Tel. 08 36 35 35 39, www.voyages-sncf.com (prices listed in euros). In France, you also can buy tickets at any of the train stations, neighborhood SNCF offices, and most travel agencies (expect a booking fee).

Depending on whom you book with, you'll find different prices and discount deals on similar tickets (see below)—if you order from the United States, check out both. It can be a better deal to buy your ticket from a French company instead of a U.S. company—or vice-versa. If you buy from a U.S. company, you'll pay a FedEx charge for ticket delivery in the United States. If you order over the phone or online in Europe, you'll pick up your tickets at the train station—be sure to read the fine print to find out how long you have to pick up the tickets. You can purchase a Eurostar ticket in person at most European train stations, but passholder discounts are only available at Eurostar stations (such as Gare du Nord, Lille, and Calais in France).

Note that France's time zone is one hour later than Britain's. Times listed on tickets are local times.

Here are typical fares available in 2002. For 2003 fares, check the Eurostar and SNCF phone numbers and Web sites listed above.

Eurostar Full-Fare Tickets

Full-fare tickets are fully refundable even after the departure date. As with plane tickets, you'll pay more to have fewer restrictions. In 2002, one-way Business First (*Affaires* in French) cost €315 in France/$279 in the United States and included a meal (a dinner departure nets you more grub than breakfast). Full-fare second-class tickets (Standard Flexi or *Seconde Affaires* in French) cost €255/$199.

Cheaper Tickets

Since full-fare, no-restrictions tickets are so expensive, most travelers sacrifice flexibility for a cheaper ticket with more restrictions. Second class is plenty comfortable, making first class an unnecessary expense for most; prices listed below are for second class unless otherwise noted. Some of these tickets are available only in France, others only in the United States. They are listed roughly from most expensive to cheapest (with more restrictions as you move down the list).

Leisure Flexi (Loisir Flexi): €215 round-trip (round-trip purchase required, partially refundable before departure date, not available in U.S.).

U.S. Leisure: $139 one-way (partially refundable before departure date, not available in France).

Leisure (Loisir): €145 round-trip (round-trip purchase required, nonrefundable, not available in U.S.).

Leisure 7 (Loisir 7): €115 round-trip (round-trip purchase required, nonrefundable, purchase at least 7 days in advance, not available in U.S.).

Leisure 14 (Loisir 14): €95/$178 round-trip (round-trip purchase required, nonrefundable, purchase at least 14 days in advance, stay 2 nights or over a Sat, available in U.S. and France).

Weekend Day Return (Loisir Journée): €85 for same-day round-trip on a Saturday or Sunday (round-trip purchase required, nonrefundable, not available in U.S.). Note that this round-trip ticket is cheaper than many one-way tickets.

Eurostar Discounts

For Railpass Holders: Discounts are available in the United States or France to travelers holding railpasses that include France or Britain ($75 one-way for second class, $155 one-way for first class).

For Youth and Seniors: Discounts are available in the United States and France for children under 12 (€45/$69 one-way for second class) and youths under 26 (€75/$79 one-way for second class). Only in the United States can seniors over 60 get discounts ($189 one-way for first class).

Airports

Charles de Gaulle Airport

Paris' primary airport has three main terminals: T-1, T-2, and T-9. British Air, SAS, United, US Air, KLM, Northwest, and Lufthansa all normally use T-1. Air France dominates T-2, though you'll also find Delta, Continental, American, and Air Canada. Charter flights leave from T-9. Airlines sometimes switch terminals, so verify your terminal before flying. Terminals are connected every few minutes by a free *navette* (shuttle bus, line #1). The RER (Paris subway) stops near the T-1 and T-2 terminals, and the TGV (*train à grande vitesse;* pron. tay-zhay-vay) station is at T-2. There is no bag storage at the airport.

Those flying to or from the United States will almost certainly use T-1 or T-2. Below is information for each terminal. For flight information, call 01 48 62 22 80.

Terminal 1: This round terminal covers three floors—arrival (top floor), departure (one floor down) and shops (basement level). The ADP (quasi–tourist office) provides helpful tourist information on the arrival level at gate 36 (look for Meeting Point signs). They have museum passes and free maps and hotel information (daily 7:00–22:00). A nearby Relay store sells phone cards. A bank (with lousy rates) is near gate 16. An American Express cash machine and an ATM are near gate 32. Car-rental offices are on the arrival level from gates 10 to 24; the SNCF (train) office is at gate 22.

Shuttle buses to the RER and to terminal 2 (and the TGV station) leave from outside gate 36—take the elevator down to level *(niveau)* 2, walk outside to find the buses (line #1 serves T-2 including the TGV station, line #2 goes directly to the RER station). **Air France bus** departs outside gate 34. **Roissy Bus** leaves outside gate 30 (buy tickets inside at gate 30). **Taxis** wait outside gate 20 and the **Disneyland Express** bus departs from gate 32 (see below under "Transportation between Charles de Gaulle airport and Paris").

Those departing from terminal 1 will find restaurants, a PTT (post office), a pharmacy, boutiques, and a handy grocery store one floor below the ticketing desks (level 2 on the elevator).

Terminal 2: This long, horseshoe-shaped terminal is divided into several sub-terminals (or halls), each identified by a letter. Halls are connected with each other, the RER, the TGV station, and T-1 every five minutes with free *navettes* (shuttle buses, line #1 runs to Terminal 1). Here is where you should find these key carriers: in Hall A—Air France, Air Canada, and American Airlines; in Hall C—Delta, Continental, and more Air France. The RER and TGV stations are below the Sheraton Hotel (access by *navette* buses or on foot). Stops for *navette* buses, Air France buses, and Roissy Buses are all well signed and near each hall (see below under "Transportation between Charles de Gaulle airport and Paris"). ADP information desks are located near gate 5 in each hall. Car-rental offices, post offices, pharmacies, and ATM machines *(Point Argent)* are also well signed.

Transportation between Charles de Gaulle airport and Paris: Three efficient public-transportation routes, taxis, and airport shuttle vans link the airport's terminals with central Paris. All are marked with good signage and their stops are centrally located at all terminals. The **RER,** with stops near T-1 and at T-2 (€8), runs every 15 minutes and stops at Gare du Nord, Chatelet, St. Michel, and Luxembourg Garden in central Paris. When coming from Paris to the airport, T-1 is the first RER stop at Charles de Gaulle; T-2 is the second stop.

Roissy Buses run every 15 minutes to Paris' Opéra Garnier (€8, 40 min); the Opéra stop is on rue Scribe at the American Express office). Three **Air France bus** routes serve central Paris about every 15 minutes (Arc de Triomphe and Porte Maillot-€11, 40 min; Montparnasse Tower/train station-€12, 60 min; or the Gare de Lyon station-€12, 40 min).

Taxis with luggage will run from €40 to €55. If taking a cab to the airport, ask your hotel to call for you (the night before if you must leave early) and specify that you want a real taxi *(un taxi normal)* and not a limo service that costs €20 more.

Airport **shuttles** offer a stress-free trip between either of Paris' airports and downtown, ideal for single travelers or families of four or more (taxis are limited to three). Reserve from home and they'll meet you at the airport (€23 for 1 person, €27 for 2, €41 for 3, €55 for 4, plan on a 30-min wait if you ask them to pick you up at the airport). Choose between **Airport Connection** (tel. 01 44 18 36 02, fax 01 45 55 85 19, www.airport-connection.com) and **Paris Airport Services** (tel. 01 55 98 10 80, fax 01 55 98 10 89, www.parisairportservice.com).

Sleeping at or near Charles de Gaulle airport: Hôtel Ibis**, outside the RER Roissy rail station for T-1 (the first RER stop coming from Paris), offers standard and predictable accommodations (Db-€85, CC, near *navette* bus stop, free shuttle bus to either terminal, tel. 01 49 19 19 19, fax 01 49 19 19 21, e-mail: h1404sb@accor-hotels.com). **Novotel***** is next door and the next step up (Db-€130–145, CC, tel. 01 49 19 27 27, fax 01 49 19 27 99, e-mail: h1014@accor-hotels.com).

Drivers wanting to avoid rush-hour traffic may consider sleeping north of Paris in the pleasant, medieval town of **Senlis** (15 min north of airport) at **Hostellerie de la Porte Bellon** (Db-€70, CC, in the center at 51 rue Bellon, near rue de la République, tel. 03 44 53 03 05, fax 03 44 53 29 94).

Orly Airport

This airport feels small. Orly has two terminals: Sud and Ouest. International flights arrive at Sud. After exiting Sud's baggage claim (near gate H), you'll see signs directing you to city transportation, car rental, and so on. Turn left to enter the main terminal area, and you'll find exchange offices with bad rates, an ATM, the ADP (a quasi–tourist office that offers free city maps and basic sightseeing information, open until 23:00), and an SNCF French rail desk (closes at 18:00, sells train tickets and even Eurailpasses, next to the ADP). Downstairs are a sandwich bar, WCs, a bank (same bad rates), a newsstand (buy a phone card), and a post office (great rates for cash or American Express traveler's checks). Car-rental offices are located in the parking lot in front of the terminal. For flight info on any airline serving Orly, call 01 49 75 15 15.

Transportation between Paris and Orly airport: Several efficient public-transportation routes, taxis, and a couple of airport shuttle services link Orly and central Paris. The gate locations listed below apply to Orly Sud, but the same transportation services are available from both terminals.

Bus services to central Paris: The **Air France bus** (outside gate K) runs to Paris' Invalides Métro stop (€8, 4/hr, 30 min) and is handy for those staying in or near the rue Cler neighborhood (from Invalidesbus stop, take the Métro 2 stops to Ecole Militaire to reach recommended hotels, see also under RER access below). The **Jetbus #285** (outside gate H, €5, 4/hr) is the quickest way to the Paris subway and the best way to the Marais and Contrescarpe neighborhoods (take Jetbus to Villejuif Métro stop, buy a *carnet* of 10 Métro tickets, then take the Métro to the Sully Morland stop for the Marais area, or the Censier-Daubenton or Monge stops for the Contrescarpe area. If going to the airport, make sure your train serves Villejuif, as the route splits at the end of the line). The **Orlybus** (outside gate H, €6, 4/hr) takes you to the Denfert-Rochereau RER-B line and the Métro, offering subway access to central Paris.

These routes provide access to Paris via **RER trains:** an ADP shuttle bus takes you to RER line C, with connections to Austerlitz, St. Michel, Musée d'Orsay, Invalides, and Pont de l'Alma stations (outside gate G, 4/hr, €5.5). The **Orlyval trains** are overpriced (€9) and require a transfer at the Antony stop to reach RER line B (serving Luxembourg, Chatelet, St. Michel, and Gare du Nord stations in central Paris).

Taxis are to the far right as you leave the terminal, at gate M. Allow €26–35 for a taxi into central Paris.

Airport shuttle minivans are ideal for single travelers or families of four or more (see "Charles de Gaulle Airport," above, for the companies to contact; from Orly, figure about €18 for 1 person, €12/person for 2, less for larger groups and kids).

Sleeping near Orly Airport: Hôtel Ibis** is reasonable, basic, and close by (Db-€60, CC, tel. 01 56 70 50 60, fax 01 56 70 50 70, e-mail: h1413@accor-hotels.com). **Hôtel Mercure***** provides more comfort for a price (Db-€120–135, tel. 01 49 75 15 50, fax 01 49 75 15 51, e-mail: h1246@accor-hotels.com). Both have free shuttles to the terminal.

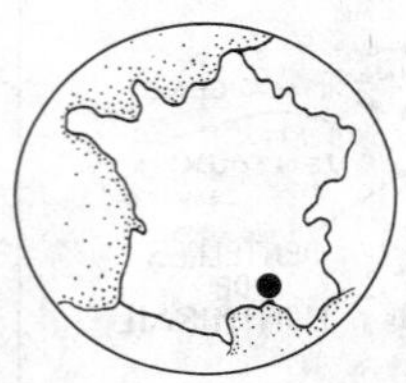

PROVENCE

This magnificent region is shaped like a giant wedge of quiche. From its sunburned crust, fanning out along the Mediterranean coast from Nîmes to Nice, it stretches north along the Rhône Valley to Orange. The Romans were here in force and left many ruins—some of the best anywhere. Seven popes; great artists, such as van Gogh, Cézanne, and Picasso; and author Peter Mayle all enjoyed their years in Provence. The region offers a splendid recipe of arid climate (except for occasional vicious winds known as the mistral), captivating cities, exciting hill towns, dramatic scenery, and oceans of vineyards.

Explore the ghost town that is ancient Les Baux and see France's greatest Roman ruin, Pont du Gard. Spend your starry, starry nights where van Gogh did, in Arles. Uncover its Roman past, then find the linger-longer squares and café corners that inspired Vincent. Youthful but classy Avignon bustles in the shadow of its brooding pope's palace. It's a short hop from Arles or Avignon into the splendid scenery and villages of the Côtes du Rhône and Luberon regions that make Provence so popular today. And if you need a Provençal beach fix, consider Cassis, barely east of Marseille.

Planning Your Time

Make Arles or Avignon your sightseeing base, particularly if you have no car. Arles has an undeniably scruffy quality and good-value hotels, while Avignon (three times larger than Arles) feels sophisticated and offers more nightlife and shopping. Italophiles prefer smaller Arles, while poodles pick urban Avignon.

To measure the pulse of Provence, spend at least one night in a smaller town. Vaison la Romaine is ideal for those heading

Provence

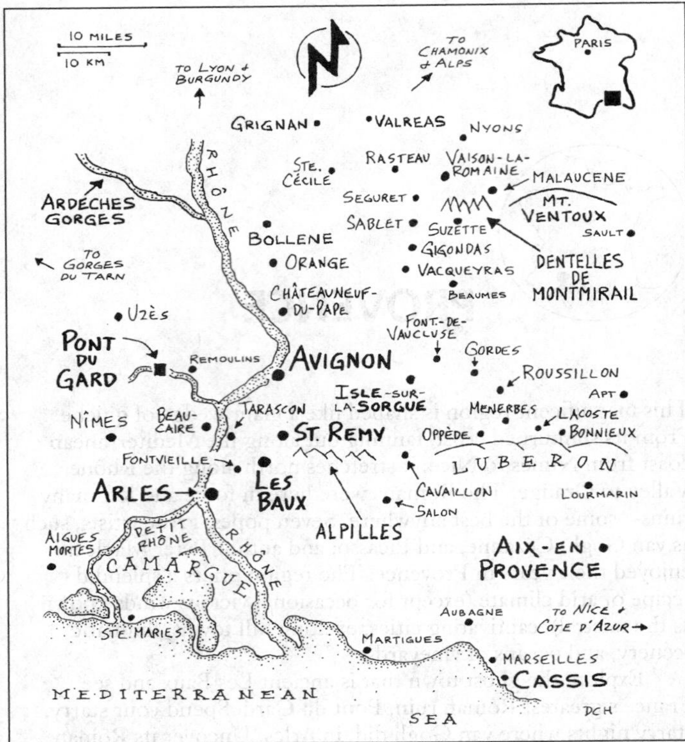

to/from the north, and Isle sur la Sorgue is centrally located between Avignon, the wine route, and the Luberon (all described below). The small port town of Cassis is a worthwhile Mediterranean meander between Provence and the Riviera (and more appealing than the resorts of the Riviera). Most destinations are accessible by public transit.

You'll want a full day for sightseeing in Arles (best on Wed or Sat, when the morning market rages), a half day for Avignon, and a day or two for the villages and sights in the countryside.

Getting around Provence

By Car: The yellow Michelin map of this region is essential for drivers. Avignon (population 100,000) is a headache for drivers; Arles (population 35,000) is easier, though it still requires go-cart driving skills. Park only in well-watched spaces and leave nothing in your car. For some of Provence's most scenic drives, follow my day trip routes (see "Villages of the Côtes du Rhône" and "The Hill Towns of Luberon," below). If you're heading north from Provence, consider a three-hour detour through the spectacular Ardèche Gorges (see Côtes du Rhône loop trip, below).

By Bus or Train: Public transit is good between cities and marginal at best to small towns. Frequent trains link Avignon, Arles, and Nîmes (about 30 min between each), and buses connect smaller towns. Les Baux is accessible by bus from Arles. Pont du Gard and St. Rémy—and to a lesser extent, Vaison la Romaine and some Côtes du Rhône villages—are accessible by bus from Avignon. While a tour of the villages of Luberon is possible only by car or bus excursion from Avignon, nearby Isle sur la Sorgue is an easy hop by train or bus from Avignon. The TIs in Arles and Avignon have information on bus excursions to regional sights that are hard to reach *sans* car (€18/half day, €30/full day). Cassis has train service via Marseille or Toulon.

Cuisine Scene—Provence

The almost extravagant use of garlic, olive oil, herbs, and tomatoes makes Provence's cuisine France's liveliest. To sample it, order anything *à la Provençale*. Among the area's spicy specialties are ratatouille (a thick mixture of vegetables in an herb-flavored tomato sauce), *brandade* (a salt cod, garlic, and cream mousse), aioli (a garlicky mayonnaise often served atop fresh vegetables), tapenade (a paste of pureed olives, capers, anchovies, herbs, and sometimes tuna), *soupe au pistou* (vegetable soup with basil, garlic, and cheese), and *soupe à l'ail* (garlic soup). Look also for *riz Camarguaise* (rice from the Camargue) and *taureau* (bull meat). Banon (wrapped in chestnut leaves) and Picodon (nutty taste) are the native cheeses. The region's sheep's milk cheese, Brousse, is creamy and fresh. Provence also produces some of France's great wines at relatively reasonable prices. Look for Gigondas, Sablet, Côtes du Rhône, and Côte de Provence. If you like rosé, try the Tavel. This is the place to splurge for a bottle of Châteauneuf-du-Pape.

Remember, restaurants serve only during lunch (11:30–14:00) and dinner (19:00–21:00, later in bigger cities); cafés serve food throughout the day.

Provence Market Days

Provençal market days offer France's most colorful and tantalizing outdoor shopping. The best markets are on Monday in Cavaillon, Tuesday in Vaison la Romaine, Wednesday in St. Rémy, Thursday in Nyons, Friday in Lourmarin, Saturday in Arles, Uzès, and Apt, and, best of all, Sunday in Isle sur la Sorgue. Crowds and parking problems abound at these popular events—arrive by 9:00, or, even better, sleep in the town the night before.

Monday: Cavaillon, Cadenet (near Vaison la Romaine)
Tuesday: Vaison la Romaine, Tarascon, and Gordes
Wednesday: St. Rémy, Arles, and Violes (near Vaison la Romaine)
Thursday: Nyons, Beaucaire, Vacqueyras, and Isle sur la Sorgue
Friday: Lourmarin (a good one), Remoulins (near Pont du Gard), Bonnieux (smaller but fun), and Châteauneuf-du-Pape
Saturday: Arles, Uzès, Valreas, and Apt (near Luberon hill towns)
Sunday: Isle sur la Sorgue, Mausanne (near Les Baux), and Beaucaire

ARLES

By helping Julius Caesar defeat Marseille, Arles (pron. arl) earned the imperial nod and was made an important port city. With the first bridge over the Rhône River, Arles was a key stop on the Roman road from Italy to Spain, the Via Domitia. After reigning as a political hot spot of the early Christian Church (the seat of an archbishopric for centuries) and thriving as a trading city on and off until the 18th century, Arles all but disappeared from the map. Van Gogh settled here a hundred years ago, but left only memories. American bombers destroyed much of Arles in World War II. Today, Arles thrives again with one of France's few communist mayors. This compact city is alive with great Roman ruins, an eclectic assortment of museums, made-for-ice-cream pedestrian zones, and squares that play hide-and-seek with visitors.

Orientation

Arles faces the Mediterranean and turns its back to Paris. Its spaghetti street plan disorients the first-time visitor. Landmarks hide in the medieval tangle of narrow, winding streets. Everything is deceptively close. While Arles sits on the Rhône, it completely ignores the river (the part of Arles most damaged by Allied bombers in World War II). The elevated riverside walk provides a direct route to the excellent Ancient History Museum, an easy return to the station, and fertile ground for poorly trained dogs. Hotels have good, free city maps, but Arles works best if you simply follow street-corner signs pointing you toward the sights and hotels of the town center. Racing cars enjoy Arles' medieval lanes, turning sidewalks into tightropes and pedestrians into leaping targets. The free "Starlette" minibus-shuttle circles the town's major sights every

15 minutes, but does not serve the Ancient History Museum, so it isn't very helpful (just wave at the driver and hop in; Mon–Sat 7:30–19:30, never on Sun). It does serve the train station, the only stop you pay for (€0.80).

Tourist Information: The main TI is on the ring road, esplanade Charles de Gaulle (April–Sept daily 9:00–18:45, Oct–March Mon–Sat 9:00–17:45, Sun 10:30–14:30, tel. 04 90 18 41 20). There's also a TI at the train station (all year, Mon–Sat 9:00–13:00, closed Sun). Both TIs can reserve a hotel room (€1 fee). Pick up the good city map and information on the Camargue wildlife area. Ask about bullfights and bus excursions to regional sights.

Arrival in Arles

By Train and Bus: Both stations are next to each other on the river and a 10-minute walk from the center. Lockers are not available. Pick up a city map at the train station TI and get the bus schedule to Les Baux at the bus station (tel. 04 90 49 38 01). To reach the old town, turn left out of the station.

By Car: Follow signs to *Centre-ville*, then follow signs toward *gare SNCF* (train station). You'll come to a huge roundabout (place Lamartine) with a Monoprix department store to the right. Park along the city wall or in nearby lots; pay attention to No Parking signs on Wednesday and Saturday until 13:00, and note that some hotels have limited parking. Leave nothing in your car as theft is a big problem. From place Lamartine, walk into the city through the two stumpy towers or take bus #1 (€0.80, 2/hr).

Helpful Hints

Launderettes: One is at 12 rue Portagnel; another is nearby at 6 rue Cavalarie, near place Voltaire (both daily 7:00–21:00, later once you're in, look for English directions for machines).

Public Pools: Arles has two public pools (one indoor and one outdoor). Ask at the TI or your hotel.

Taxis: Arles' taxis charge a minimum fee (about €10). Nothing in town is worth a taxi ride (figure €35–45 to Les Baux or St. Rémy, tel. 04 90 96 90 03).

Bike Rental: Try the Peugeot store (15 rue du Pont, tel. 04 90 96 03 77). While Vaison la Romaine and Isle sur la Sorgue make better biking bases (see below), rides to Les Baux (very steep climb) or into the Camargue work from Arles, provided you're in great shape (forget it in the wind).

Car Rental: Avis is at the train station (tel. 04 90 96 82 42), Europcar is downtown (2 bis avenue Victor Hugo, tel. 04 90 93 23 24), National is just off place Lamartine toward the station (4 avenue Paulin Talabot, tel. 04 90 93 02 17).

Local Guide: Jacqueline Neujean, an excellent guide, knows Arles like the back of her hand (€90/2 hrs, tel. 04 90 98 47 51).

Sights—Roman Arles

The worthwhile **monument pass** *(le pass monuments)* covers Arles' many sights and is valid for one week (€12, €10 under 18, sold at each sight). Otherwise, it's €3–4 per sight and €5.50 for the Ancient History Museum. While any sight is worth a few minutes, many aren't worth the individual admission. Many sights begin closing rooms 30 minutes early. Start at the Ancient History Museum for a helpful overview, then dive into the sights (ideally in the order described below).

▲▲▲Ancient History Museum (Musée de L'Arles Antique)—Begin your visit of Arles in this superb, air-conditioned museum. Models and original sculpture (with the help of the free English handout) re-create the Roman city of Arles, making workaday life and culture easier to imagine. Notice what a radical improvement the Roman buildings were over the simple mud-brick homes of the pre-Roman inhabitants. Models of Arles' arena even illustrate the moveable stadium cover, good for shade and rain. While virtually nothing is left of Arles' chariot racecourse, the model shows that it must have rivaled Rome's Circus Maximus. Jewelry, fine metal and glass artifacts, and well-crafted mosaic floors make it clear that Roman Arles was a city of art and culture. The finale is an impressive row of pagan and early Christian sarcophagi (second through fifth centuries). In the early days of the Church, Jesus was often portrayed beardless and as the good shepherd—with a lamb over his shoulder.

Built at the site of the chariot racecourse, this museum is a 20-minute walk from Arles along the river. Turn left at the river and take the riverside path to the big modern building just past the new bridge—or take bus #1 (€0.80) from boulevard des Lices and the TI (€5.50, March–Oct daily 9:00–19:00, Nov–Feb 10:00–17:00, tel. 04 90 18 88 88).

▲▲Roman Forum (Place du Forum)—After seeing the Ancient History Museum, start your explorations here, at the political and religious center of Roman Arles. Named for the Roman Forum that once stood here, this café-crammed square is always lively and best at night. The bistros on the square, while no place for a fine dinner, put together a good salad—and when you sprinkle in the ambience, that's €10 well spent.

Stand at the corner of the Hôtel Nord Pinus and find the information plaque. The illustration shows the two parts of the forum—the upper part dating from the first century B.C., where public meetings were held and temples were tended, and the lower

Arles

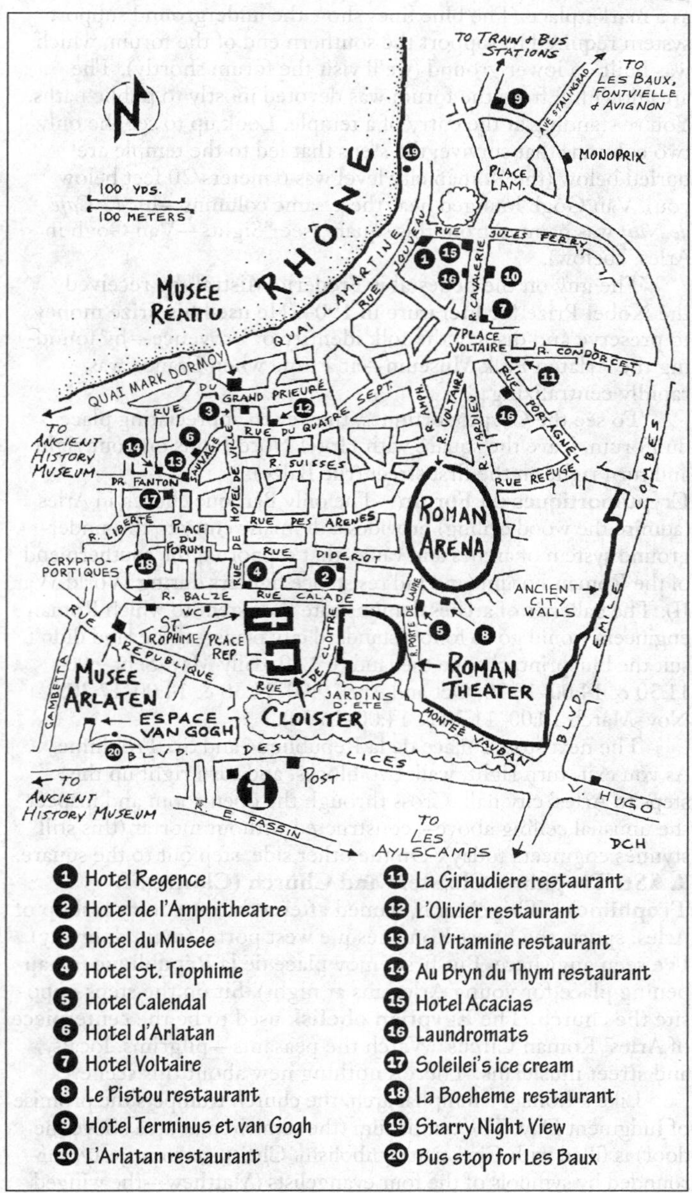
TO TRAIN & BUS STATIONS
TO LES BAUX, FONTVIELLE & AVIGNON
AVE STALINGRAD
MONOPRIX
PLACE LAM.
100 YDS.
100 METERS
RHÔNE
RUE JOUVEAU
RUE JULES FERRY
RUE LAMARTINE
R. CAVALERIE
MUSÉE RÉATTU
QUAI LAMARTINE
PLACE VOLTAIRE
R. CONDORCET
QUAI MARK DORMOY
RUE DU GRAND PRIEURÉ
RUE DU QUATRE SEPT.
R. AMPH.
R. VOLTAIRE
R. TARDIEU
RUE PORTAGNEL
TO ANCIENT HISTORY MUSEUM
RUE SAUVAGE
R. SUISSES
DR. FANTON
RUE REFUGE
COMBES
ROMAN ARENA
RUE DE HOTEL DE VILLE
RUE DES ARENES
R. LIBERTÉ
PLACE DU FORUM
RUE DIDEROT
CRYPTO-PORTIQUES
R. BALZE
RUE CALADE
ANCIENT CITY WALLS
WC
ST. TROPHIME
PLACE REP.
RUE DE CLOITRE
R. PORTE DE LAURE
RUE GAMBETTA
REPUBLIQUE
MUSÉE ARLATEN
ROMAN THEATER
BLVD. EMILE
JARDINS D'ETE
CLOISTER
ESPACE VAN GOGH
MONTEE VAUBAN
BLVD. DES LICES
POST
TO ANCIENT HISTORY MUSEUM
V. HUGO
R. E. FASSIN
TO LES AYLSCAMPS
DCH
1 Hotel Regence
2 Hotel de l'Amphitheatre
3 Hotel du Musee
4 Hotel St. Trophime
5 Hotel Calendal
6 Hotel d'Arlatan
7 Hotel Voltaire
8 Le Pistou restaurant
9 Hotel Terminus et van Gogh
10 L'Arlatan restaurant
11 La Giraudiere restaurant
12 L'Olivier restaurant
13 La Vitamine restaurant
14 Au Bryn du Thym restaurant
15 Hotel Acacias
16 Laundromats
17 Soleilei's ice cream
18 La Boeheme restaurant
19 Starry Night View
20 Bus stop for Les Baux

part dating from the fourth century A.D., which served primarily as a marketplace. The blue lines show the underground support system required to support the southern end of the forum, which was built on lower ground (we'll visit the forum shortly). The area downhill from the forum was devoted mostly to public baths. You're standing at the entry of a temple. Look up to see the only two columns that survive; the steps that led to the temple are buried below (the Roman city level was 6 meters/20 feet below you). Van Gogh lounged near these same columns—his *Le Café de Nuit* was painted from this square (see "Sights—Van Gogh in Arles," below).

The guy on the pedestal is Frédéric Mistral; he received the Nobel Prize for literature in 1904. He used his prize money to preserve and display the folk identity of Provence—by founding the Arlaten Folk Museum—at a time when France was rapidly centralizing.

To see the Cryptoportiques, the key to appreciating place du Forum, leave the square with Hôtel Nord Pinus on your right and turn right on the first street (rue Balze).

Cryptoportiques du Forum—The only Baroque church in Arles (admire the wood ceiling) provides a dramatic entry to this underground system of arches and vaults that supported the southern end of the Roman Forum (and hid resistance fighters during World War II). The galleries of arches demonstrate the extent to which Roman engineers would go to follow standard city plans—if the land didn't suit the blueprint, change the land (€3.50, daily May–Sept 9:00–11:30 & 14:00–18:30, Oct and April 9:00–11:30 & 14:00–17:30, Nov–March 10:00–11:30 & 14:00–16:30).

The next stop is place de la République and St. Trophime. As you exit, turn right, walk two blocks, and turn right up the steps to Arles' city hall. Cross through the open room and inspect the unusual ceiling above—constructed without mortar (this still stymies engineers today). On the other side, step out to the square.

▲▲St. Trophime Cloisters and Church (Cloître St. Trophime)—This church, named after a third-century bishop of Arles, sports the finest Romanesque west portal (main doorway) I've seen anywhere. But first enjoy place de la République (a happening place for young Arlesians at night). Sit on the steps opposite the church. The **Egyptian obelisk** used to be the centerpiece of Arles' Roman Circus. Watch the peasants—pilgrims, locals, and street musicians. There's nothing new about this scene.

Like a Roman triumphal arch, the church trumpets the promise of Judgment Day. The tympanum (the semicircular area above the door) is filled with Christian symbolism. Christ sits in majesty, surrounded by symbols of the four evangelists (Matthew—the winged man, Mark—the winged lion, Luke—the ox, and John—the eagle). The 12 apostles are lined up below Jesus. Move closer. This is it. Some are saved and others aren't. Notice the condemned—a chain gang on the right bunny-hopping over the fires of hell. For them, the tune trumpeted by the three angels on the very top is not a happy one. Ride the exquisite detail back to a simpler age. In an illiterate medieval world, long before the vivid images of our Technicolor time, this message was a neon billboard over the town's square. A chart just inside the church (on the right) helps explain the carvings.

On the right side of the nave, a fourth-century, early-Christian sarcophagus is used as an altar. The adjacent **cloisters** are the best in Provence (enter from square, 20 meters/65 feet to right of church). Enjoy the sculpted capitals of the rounded Romanesque columns (12th century) and the pointed Gothic columns (14th century). The second floor offers only a view of the cloisters from above (€4, daily May–Sept 9:00–18:30, Oct, March, and April 9:00–17:30, and Nov–Feb 10:00–16:30).

To get to the next stop, the Classical Theater, face the church, walk left, then take the first right on rue de la Calade.

Classical Theater (Théâtre Antique)—Precious little survives from this Roman theater, which served as a handy town quarry throughout the Middle Ages. Walk to a center aisle and pull up a stone seat. Built in the first century B.C., it was capable of seating 10,000 eager-to-be-entertained Arlesians (they preferred comedy to tragedy). To appreciate the original size of the theater, look left to the upper left side of the tower and find the protrusion that supported the highest seating level (there were 3 levels). Today, 3,000 can attend events in this still well-used, restored facility. Two lonely Corinthian columns look out from the stage over the audience. The orchestra section is defined by a semicircular pattern in the stone. Walk to the left side of the stage, step up, then look down to the narrow channel that allowed the stage curtain to disappear below. Take a stroll backstage through broken bits of Rome, and loop back to the entry behind the grass (€3, you can see much of the theater by peeking through the fence for free, daily May–Sept 9:00–11:30 & 14:00–18:30, Oct and April 9:00–11:30 & 14:00–17:30, Nov–March 10:00–11:30 & 14:00–16:30). To best understand this monument, turn left as you exit, left again on the first street (rue du Cloitre) and follow signs left again to **Jardins d'Eté**. You'll find an information plaque with an illustration of the theater and have a good view of the supporting arches.

For the next stop, the Roman Arena, return to the theater entrance, pass the theater on your right and walk uphill a block.

▲▲▲Roman Arena (Amphithéâtre)—Enter and sit somewhere

in the shade. Nearly 2,000 years ago, gladiators fought wild animals here to the delight of 20,000 screaming fans—cruel. Today, matadors fight wild bulls to the delight of local fans—still cruel. In the Roman era, games were free (sponsored by city bigwigs), and fans were seated by social class (the closer to the action you sat, the higher your standing). Notice the many exits around the arena as you scan the facility. These allowed for rapid dispersal after the games (a necessity, as fans would be whipped into a frenzy after the games, and fights would break out if they couldn't exit quickly). In the halls below your seat, gladiators and animals would prepare for battle. They fought no lions here, as revered lions were kept for Rome's Colosseum. While the top row of arches is long gone, three towers survive from medieval times, when the arena was used as a fortress. The view is exceptional from the tower you can climb. Until the early 1800s, this stadium corralled 200 humble homes and functioned as a town within a town. The exterior arches of the arena were sealed—anything for security. To see two still-sealed arches, turn right on exiting the arena and walk to Andaluz restaurant, then look back (€4, daily May–Sept 9:00–18:30, Oct, March, and April 9:00–17:30, and Nov–Feb 10:00–16:30).

Sights—Van Gogh in Arles

"The whole future of art is to be found in the south of France."
—Vincent van Gogh, 1888

Vincent was 35 years old when he arrived in Arles in 1888, and it was here he discovered the light that would forever change him. Coming from the gray skies and flatlands of Holland and Paris, he was bowled over by everything Provençal—jagged peaks, gnarled olive trees, brilliant sunflowers, and the furious wind. Van Gogh painted in a flurry in Arles, producing more paintings than at any other period of his too-brief career, over 200 in just a few months. Sadly, none of his paintings remain in Arles, though we can visit the sights from which he painted. Below are several places where the spirit of Vincent can still be found.

Espace Van Gogh (Mediathèque)—The hospital where Vincent was sent to treat his self-inflicted ear wound is today a cultural center. It surrounds a garden that the artist would have loved (free, only the courtyard is open to public, near Musée Arlaten on rue President Wilson). He was sent from here to the mental institution in nearby St. Rémy (see "Sights—St. Rémy," below) before Dr. Gachet invited him to Auvers-sur-Oise, outside of Paris.

Fondation Van Gogh—A ▲▲ sight for his fans, this small, pricey gallery features works by several well-known contemporary artists paying homage to Vincent through their thought-provoking interpretations of his art (€7, not covered by monument pass, great collection of van Gogh prints and postcards in free entry area, April–mid-Oct daily 10:00–19:00, mid-Oct–March Tue–Sun 9:30–12:00 & 14:00–17:30, closed Mon, facing Roman Arena at 24 bis Rond Point des Arènes).

Café de Nuit—Across from Hôtel Nord Pinus on place du Forum, this café was the subject of one of Vincent's first paintings in Arles. While his painting showed the café a brilliant yellow due to the glow of light when he painted it, the facade was bare limestone, just like those of the other cafés on this square. The current owners of the café had it painted neon yellow to match van Gogh's famous painting.

Starry Night—From place Lamartine, walk to the river, then look toward Arles to find where Vincent set his easel for this famous painting where stars boil above the skyline of Arles. Riverfront cafés that once stood here were destroyed by bridge-seeking bombs in World War II, as was the bridge whose remains you see on your right. As you gaze over the river, be impressed (one more time) with Roman engineering—somehow, they managed to build a bridge over this powerful river 2,000 years ago.

More Sights—Arles

▲▲Wednesday and Saturday Markets—On these days until noon, Arles' ring road erupts into an outdoor market of fish, flowers, produce, and you-name-it (boulevard Emile Combes on Wed, boulevard Lices on Sat). Join in, buy flowers, try the olives, sample some wine, and swat a pickpocket. On the first Wednesday of the month, it's a grand flea market.

Musée Arlaten—This cluttered folklore museum, given to Arles by Nobel Prize–winner Frédéric Mistral (see "Roman Forum" listing, above), overflows with interesting odds and ends of life in Provence. It's like a failed 19th-century garage sale: shoes, hats, wigs, old photos, bread cupboards, and a model of a beetle-dragon monster, all crammed too close together to really be appreciated. If you're fond of folklore, this museum is for you; if you're not, duck in just to see the southern limit of the Roman Forum in the entry courtyard (€4, pick up excellent English brochure, April–Sept daily 9:00–12:30 & 14:00–18:00, Oct–March until 17:00, 29 rue de la République, tel. 04 90 96 08 23).

Musée Réattu—Housed in a beautiful, 15th-century mansion, this mildly interesting, mostly modern art collection includes 57 Picasso drawings (some two-sided and all done in a flurry of creativity—I liked the bullfights best), a room of Henri Rousseau's Camargue watercolors, and an unfinished painting by the neoclassical artist Réattu, none with English explanations (€3, plus €1.50 for special exhibits, daily April–Sept 9:00–12:00

& 14:00–18:30, Oct and March until 17:00, Nov–Feb until 16:00, 10 rue de Grand Prieuré, tel. 04 90 96 37 68).

▲▲Bullfights (Courses Camarguaise)—Occupy the same seats fans have used for nearly 2,000 years, and take in one of Arles' most memorable experiences—a bullfight *à la Provençale* in an ancient arena. Three classes of bullfights take place here. The *course protection* is for aspiring matadors; it's a daring dodge-bull game of scraping hair off the angry bull's nose for prize money offered by local businesses (no blood). The *trophée de l'avenir* is the next class, with amateur matadors. The *trophée des as excellence* is the real thing à la Spain: outfits, swords, spikes, and the whole gory shebang (tickets €5–10; Easter–Oct Sat, Sun, and holidays; skip the "rodeo" spectacle, ask at TI). There are nearby village bullfights in small wooden bullrings nearly every weekend (TI has schedule).

The Camargue—Knocking on Arles' doorstep, this is one of the few truly "wild" areas of France, where pink flamingos, wild bulls, and the famous white horses wander freely amid rice fields, lagoons, and mosquitoes. It's a ▲▲▲ sight for nature-lovers, but boring for others. The D-37 that skirts the Etang de Vaccarès lagoon has some of the best views. The **Musée Camarguais** describes the natural features and traditions of the Camargue (some English information) and has a 3.5-kilometer/two-mile nature trail. It's 12 kilometers/7.5 miles from Arles on D-570 toward Ste. Marie de la Mer; at the *Mas du Pont de Rousty* farmhouse, look for signs (€5, May–Sept daily 9:15–17:45, Oct–March Wed–Mon 10:15–16:45, closed Tue, tel. 04 90 97 10 82). Buses serve the Camargue (and the museum) from Arles' train station (tel. 04 90 96 36 25).

Sleeping in Arles

(€1 = about $1, country code: 33, zip code: 13200)

Sleep Code: **S** = Single, **D** = Double/Twin, **T** = Triple, **Q** = Quad, **b** = bathroom, **s** = shower only, **CC** = Credit Cards accepted, **no CC** = Credit Cards not accepted, **SE** = Speaks English, **NSE** = No English, * = French hotel rating system (0–4 stars).

To help you sort easily through these listings, I've divided the rooms into three categories based on the price for a standard double room with bath:

Higher Priced—Most rooms more than €90.

Moderately Priced—Most rooms €90 or less.

Lower Priced—Most rooms €60 or less.

Hotels are a great value here; many are air-conditioned, though few have elevators.

HIGHER PRICED

Hôtel d'Arlatan***, built over the site of a Roman basilica, is classy in every sense of the word. It has sumptuous public spaces, a tranquil terrace, designer pool, and antique-filled rooms, most with high, wood-beamed ceilings and stone walls. In the lobby of this 15th-century building, a glass floor looks down into Roman ruins (Db-€90–160, Db/Qb suites-€180–250, CC, great buffet breakfast-€10, parking-€11, air-con, elevator, 26 rue du Sauvage, 1 block off place du Forum, tel. 04 90 93 56 66, fax 04 90 49 68 45, www.hotel-arlatan.fr, e-mail: hotel-arlatan@provnet.fr).

MODERATELY PRICED

These hotels are worthy of three stars; each offers exceptional value.

Hôtel de l'Amphithéâtre**, a carefully decorated, boutique hotel, is just off the Roman Arena. Public spaces are very sharp and the owners pay attention to every detail of your stay. All rooms have air-conditioning, the Belvedere room has the best view over Arles I've seen, and the suite rooms have four-star comfort (Db-€44–64, Tb-€84, CC, parking-€4, 5 rue Diderot, 1 block from arena, tel. 04 90 96 10 30, fax 04 90 93 98 69, www.hotelamphitheatre.fr, SE).

Hôtel du Musée** is a quiet, delightful, manor-home hideaway with 20 comfortable, air-conditioned rooms, a flowery two-tiered courtyard, and a snazzy art-gallery lounge. The rooms in the new section are worth the few extra euros and steps. Charming Laurence speaks some English (Sb-€41–48, Db-€48–63, Tb-€60–72, Qb-€80, CC, buffet breakfast-€7, parking-€7, 11 rue du Grande Prieuré, follow signs to Musée Réattu, tel. 04 90 93 88 88, fax 04 90 49 98 15, www.hoteldumusee.com.fr, e-mail: contact@hoteldumusee.com.fr).

Hôtel Calendal**, located between the Roman Arena and Classical Theater, has Provençal chic and a large outdoor courtyard, smartly decorated rooms, Internet access, and seductive ambience (Db facing street-€45–65, Db facing garden-€65–75, Db with balcony-€80, Tb-€85, Qb-€90, CC, lunch-€12, air-con, reserve ahead for parking-€10, 5 rue Porte de Laure, just above arena, tel. 04 90 96 11 89, fax 04 90 96 05 84, www.lecalendal.com, SE).

LOWER PRICED

The first three are closest to the train station:

Hôtel Régence** sits on the river, with immaculate and comfortable rooms, good beds, safe parking, and easy access to the train station (new owners may modify these prices, Db-€30–48, Tb-€40–57, Qb-€60, choose riverview or quiet, air-con courtyard rooms, CC, 5 rue Marius Jouveau, from place Lamartine turn right immediately after passing through towers, tel. 04 90 96 39 85, fax 04 90 96 67 64).

Hôtel Acacias**, just off place Lamartine and inside the old city walls, is a modern new hotel. It's a pastel paradise, with rooms that are a smidge too small but have all the comforts, including cable TV, hair dryers, and air-conditioning (Db-€46–51, Tb-€61–75, Qb-€78–83, CC, buffet breakfast-€5.50, elevator, 1 rue Marius Jouveau, tel. 04 90 96 37 88, fax 04 90 96 32 51, www.hotel-acacias.com, e-mail: contact@hotel-acacias.com, gentle Sylvie SE).

Hôtel Terminus et van Gogh* has bright, basic rooms in van Gogh colors, facing a busy roundabout at the gate of the old town, a long block from the train station. This building appears in the painting of van Gogh's house; the artist's house was bombed in World War II (Db-€37–44, Tb-€46, Qb-€54, CC, 5 place Lamartine, tel. & fax 04 90 96 12 32).

Hôtel St. Trophime** is another fine old mansion converted to a hotel, with a grand entry, charming courtyard, broad halls, large rooms, and (rare in Arles) an elevator, but no air-conditioning (new owners may change these prices, standard Db-€48, larger, off-street Db-€57, Tb-€65, huge Qb-€73, CC, garage-€7, 16 rue de la Calade, near place de la République, tel. 04 90 96 88 38, fax 04 90 96 92 19).

Perfect for starving artists, the clean, spartan, and friendly **Hôtel Voltaire*** rents 12 small rooms with ceiling fans and great balconies overlooking a caffeine-stained square, a block below the arena (D-€25, Ds-€28, Db-€36, third or fourth person-€8 each, CC, 1 place Voltaire, tel. 04 90 96 49 18, fax 04 90 96 45 49).

Sleeping near Arles, in Fontvieille

(See also "Sleeping in and near Les Baux," below.) Many drivers, particularly those with families, prefer staying in the peaceful countryside with good access to the area's sights. Just 10 minutes from Arles and Les Baux, and 20 minutes from Avignon, little Fontvieille slumbers in the shadows of its big-city cousins (though it has its share of restaurants and boutiques).

HIGHER PRICED

Le Peiriero*** is a pooped parent's dream come true, with a grassy garden, massive pool, table tennis, badminton, and (believe it or not) three miniature golf holes. The spacious family loft rooms, capable of sleeping up to five, have full bathrooms on both levels. This complete retreat also comes with a terrace café and restaurant (the higher prices in the doubles category are for rooms over the garden, Db-€80–100, Tb-€88, Tb loft-€140, CC, breakfast buffet-€9, air-con, free parking, 34 avenue de Les Baux, just east of

Fontvieille on road to Les Baux, tel. 04 90 54 76 10, fax 04 90 54 62 60, www.hotel-peiriero.com).

Le Domaine de la Forest is a restored farmhouse with modern apartments for five to six people (kitchen, 2 bedrooms, private terrace). Surrounded by vineyards and rice fields, this rural refuge offers a pool, swings, and a volleyball court. While most spend a full week, shorter stays are possible off-season (nightly-€92, weekly rental required in summer-€534, from Arles take D-17 toward Fontvieille and look for *Gîtes Ruraux* signs, route de L'Aqueduc Romain, just off D-82, 13990 Fontvieille, tel. 04 90 54 70 25, fax 04 90 54 60 50, www.domaine-laforest.com).

Eating in Arles

All restaurants listed have outdoor seating except L'Olivier and La Boeheme.

Eating on or near place du Forum: Great atmosphere and mediocre food at fair prices await on place du Forum; **L'Estaminet** probably does the best dinner (I like the salade Estaminet). **La Vitamine** has decent salads and pastas—show this book and enjoy a free *kir* (closed Sun, just below place du Forum on 16 rue Dr. Fanton, tel. 04 90 93 77 36). Almost next door, **Au Bryn du Thym** is popular and specializes in traditional Provençal cuisine (€18 *menu*, closed Tue, 22 rue Dr. Fanton, tel. 04 90 49 95 96). A block above the forum, **La Boeheme** is a good and friendly budget option with a €13 vegetarian *menu* and a €15 Provençal *menu* (6 rue Balze, tel. 04 90 18 58 92). A few blocks below place du Forum, near the recommended Hôtel du Musée, **L'Olivier** is my Arles splurge, offering exquisite Provençal cuisine (€28 *menu*, 1 bis rue Réattu, reserve ahead, tel. 04 90 49 64 88).

Eating near the Roman Arena: For about the same price as on place du Forum, you can enjoy reliable cuisine with a point-blank view of the arena at the welcoming **Le Pistou** (*menus* from €15, open daily, at the top of the arena, 30 rond point des Arenes). **La Giraudière,** a few blocks below the arena on place Voltaire, offers good regional cooking and air-conditioning (€20 *menu*, closed Tue, tel. 04 90 93 27 52). The friendly, unpretentious **L'Arlatan,** across from the recommended Hôtel Acacias, serves fine meals and great desserts (€16 *menu*, closed Wed, opposite launderette at 7 rue Cavalarie, tel. 04 90 96 24 85).

For the best ice cream in Arles, find **Soleilei's**; all ingredients are natural, with unusual flavors such as *fadoli*, an olive-oil ice cream (across from recommended La Vitamine restaurant at 9 rue Dr. Fanton).

Picnics: A big, handy Monoprix supermarket/department store is on place Lamartine (Mon–Sat 8:30–19:25, closed Sun).

Transportation Connections—Arles

By bus to: Les Baux (4/day, 30 min, none on Sun, fewer Nov–March, first departure 8:30, last at 14:30, ideal departure is 8:30 with a return from Les Baux about 11:20 or 12:40), **Camargue/ Ste. Marie de la Mer** (8/day Mon–Sat, less on Sun, 1 hr). There are two stops in Arles: the *Centre Ville* stop is on 16 boulevard Clemenceau (2 blocks below main TI, next to Café le Wilson); the other is at the train station (tel. 04 90 49 38 01).

By train to: Paris (17/day, 2 direct TGVs in 4 hrs, 15 with change in Avignon in 5 hrs), **Avignon** (14/day, 20 min, check for afternoon gaps), **Carcassonne** (6/day, 3 hrs, 3 with change in Narbonne), **Beaune** (10/day, 4.5 hrs, 9 with change in Nîmes or Avignon and Lyon), **Nice** (11/day, 4 hrs, 10 with change in Marseille), **Barcelona** (2/day, 6 hrs, change in Montpellier), **Italy** (3/day, change in Marseille and Nice; from Arles, it's 4.5 hrs to Ventimiglia on the border, 9.5 hrs to the Cinque Terre, 8 hrs to Milan, 11 hrs to Florence, or 13 hrs to Venice or Rome).

AVIGNON

Famous for its nursery rhyme, medieval bridge, and brooding Palace of the Popes, contemporary Avignon (pron. ah-veen-yohn) bustles and prospers behind its mighty walls. During the 68 years (1309–1377) that Avignon starred as the *Franco Vaticano*, it grew from a quiet village to the thriving city it remains. With its large student population and fashionable shops, today's Avignon is an intriguing blend of youthful spirit and urban sophistication. Street mimes play to international crowds enjoying Avignon's ubiquitous cafés and trendy boutiques. If you're here in July, be prepared for the rollicking theater festival and reserve your hotel months early. Clean, sharp, and very popular Avignon is more impressive for its outdoor ambience than its museums and monuments. See the pope's palace, then explore its thriving streets and beautiful vistas from the Parc de Rochers des Doms.

Orientation

The cours Jean Jaurés (which turns into rue de la République) runs straight from the train station to place de l'Horloge and the Palace of the Popes, splitting Avignon in two. The larger right (eastern) half is where the action is. Climb to the parc de Rochers des Doms for a fine view, enjoy the people scene on place de l'Horloge, meander the backstreets (see "Sights—Discovering Avignon's Backstreets," below), and lose yourself in a quiet square. Avignon's shopping district fills the traffic-free streets where rue de la République meets place de l'Horloge. Walk or drive across pont Daladier (bridge) for a great view of Avignon and the Rhône River.

Tourist Information: The main TI is between the train station and the old town at 41 cours Jean Jaurés (April–Oct Mon–Sat 9:00–18:00, Sun 9:00–17:00, Nov–March Mon–Fri 9:00–18:00, Sat 9:00–17:00, Sun 10:00–12:00, longer hours during July festival, tel. 04 32 74 32 74, www.avignon-tourisme.com). A branch TI is inside the city wall at the entrance to pont St. Bénezet (April–Oct only, daily 9:00–19:00). Get the better tear-off map and pick up the free, handy *Guide Pratique* (info on car and bike rental, hotels, and museums) as well as their Avignon discovery guide, which includes several good (but tricky to follow) walking tours. Make sure to get the **free "Avignon Passion" discount card** if you plan to visit more than one sight. You pay full price at first sight, get your card stamped, then get good reductions at others (e.g., €2 less at Palace of the Popes, €3 less at Petit Palais). The TI offers informative English-language **walking tours** of Avignon (€8, €5 with discount card, Tue, Thu, and Sat at 10:00, Sat only Nov–March, depart from the main TI). They also have information on bus excursions to popular regional sights (including the wine route, Luberon, and Camargue). Many of Avignon's sights are closed on Tuesdays.

Arrival in Avignon

By Train: TGV passengers take the €1 shuttle bus (*navette*, 4/hr, 10 min) from the space-age new TGV station to the central station in downtown Avignon (car rental at TGV station; nothing within walking distance). All other trains serve the central station (*gare centrale*, baggage check available). From the central station, walk through the city walls onto the cours Jean Jaurés (TI 3 blocks down at #41). The bus station *(gare routière)* is 100 meters to the right of the central train station (just beyond Ibis hotel).

By Car: Drivers enter Avignon following *Centre-ville* signs. Park close to pont St. Bénezet, either outside the wall or in the big structure just inside the walls and use that TI. Figure €1.50/hour and €8/day for pay lots. Hotels have advice for smart overnight parking. Leave nothing in your car.

Helpful Hints

Reduced Prices for Sights: Get an "Avignon Passion" discount card; see "Tourist Information," above.

Book Ahead for July: During the July theater festival, rooms are rare—reserve very early or stay in Arles or St. Rémy (see "Sleeping in Arles," above, or "Sleeping in St. Rémy," below).

Laundry: Handy to most hotels is the launderette at 66 place St. Corps, where rue Agricol Perdiguier ends (daily 7:00–20:00).

Internet Access: Webzone, on place Pie, is right behind the medieval tower (daily 14:00–midnight).

English Bookstore: Try Shakespeare Bookshop (Tue–Sat 9:30–12:30 & 14:00–18:30, closed Mon, 155 rue Carreterie, in Avignon's northeast corner, tel. 04 90 27 38 50).

Car Rental: All the agencies are at the TGV station with long hours, seven days/week.

Sights—Avignon

I've listed sights in the best order to visit, and have added a short walking tour of Avignon's backstreets to get you beyond the surface. Entries are listed at full price and with discount card. Remember to pick up your discount card at the TI—you pay full price at the first sight.

Start your tour where the Romans did, on place de l'Horloge, and find a seat on a stone bench in front of city hall (Hôtel de Ville).

Place de l'Horloge—This square was Avignon's forum during Roman rule. In those days, Avignon played second fiddle to the important city of Arles. In the Middle Ages, this square served as the main market square, and today, it is Avignon's main café square (lively ambience, high prices, low food quality). Named for a medieval clock tower that city hall now hides, this square's present popularity arrived with the trains in 1854. Walk a few steps to the center, and look down the main drag, rue de la République. When trains arrived in Avignon, proud city fathers wanted a direct, impressive way to link the new station to the heart of the city (just like in Paris)—so they plowed over homes to create the rue de République and widened the place de l'Horloge. Today's new, suburban TGV train station is no less contentious. According to locals, it benefits only rich Parisians, as Provence is now within easy weekend striking distance, allowing rural homes to be gobbled at inflated prices that locals can't afford (adding insult to injury, Avignon residents must now take a bus from the city center to the train station).

To get to the next listing, Palace Square, walk past the merry-go-round, then past the Hotel des Papes into the square.

Palace Square (Place du Palais)—Sit on a stump in front of the Conservatoire National de Danse et Musique. In the 1300s, this was ground zero for the church. When the church bought Avignon, they gave it a complete facelift, turning the city into Europe's largest construction zone and clearing out vast spaces like this. The pope's palace alone demanded three acres of building; add nearly five kilometers of protective wall and 39 towers circling the city, the need for "appropriate" cardinal housing (read: mansions), and residences for other hangers-on from Rome, and you have a bonanza of a building contract. Avignon's population grew from 6,000 to 25,000 in short order (today, 16,000 people

Avignon

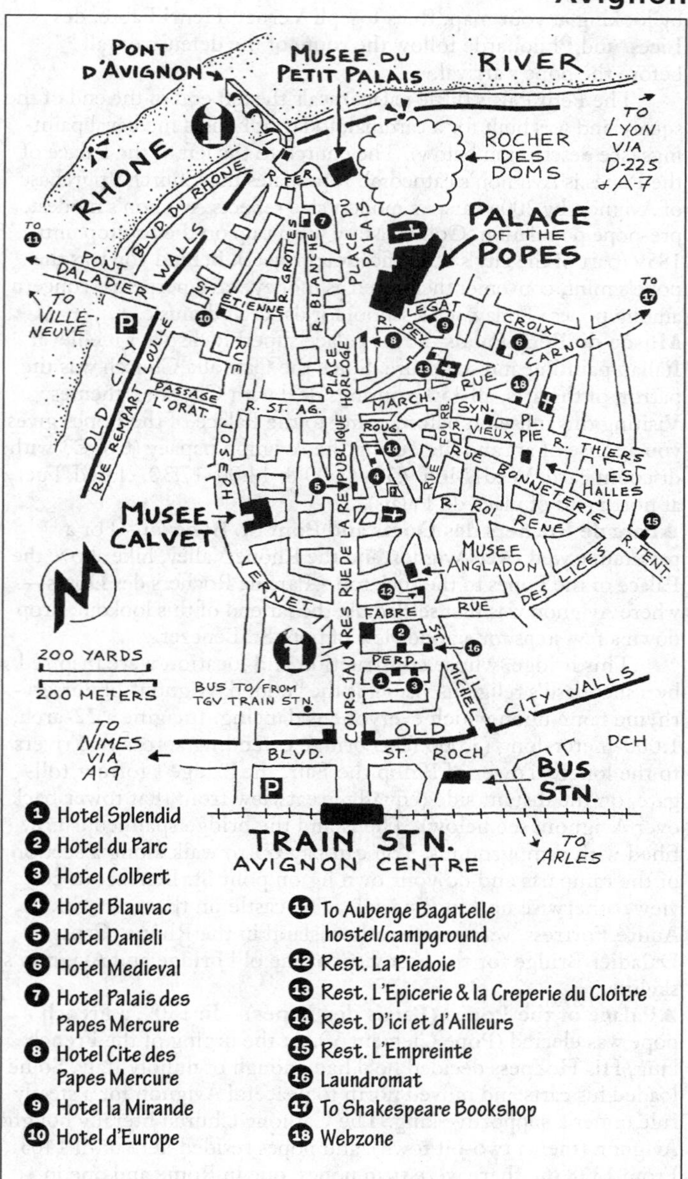
PONT D'AVIGNON
MUSEE DU PETIT PALAIS
RIVER
RHONE
TO LYON VIA D-225 & A-7
ROCHER DES DOMS
PALACE OF THE POPES
BLVD. DU RHONE
R. FER.
R. GROTTES
R. BLANCHE
PLACE DU PALAIS
TO 11
PONT DALADIER
WALLS
TO VILLE-NEUVE
ST. ETIENNE
LEGAT
CROIX
TO 17
R. PEY
CARNOT
RUE
PLACE HORLOGE
OLD CITY
RUE REMPART LOULLE
PASSAGE L'ORAT.
R. ST. AG.
MARCH.
SYN.
PL. PIE
R. VIEUX
FOURB.
ROUG.
R. THIERS
RUE BONNETERIE
LES HALLES
JOSEPH
RUE DE LA REPUBLIQUE
MUSEE CALVET
R. ROI RENE
R. TENT.
MUSEE ANGLADON
VERNET
RUE DES LICES
FABRE
COURS JAURES
ST. MICHEL
PERD.
200 YARDS
200 METERS
BUS TO/FROM TGV TRAIN STN.
CITY WALLS
OLD
TO NIMES VIA A-9
BLVD.
ST. ROCH
DCH
BUS STN.
P
TRAIN STN.
AVIGNON CENTRE
TO ARLES
1 Hotel Splendid
2 Hotel du Parc
3 Hotel Colbert
4 Hotel Blauvac
5 Hotel Danieli
6 Hotel Medieval
7 Hotel Palais des Papes Mercure
8 Hotel Cite des Papes Mercure
9 Hotel la Mirande
10 Hotel d'Europe
11 To Auberge Bagatelle hostel/campground
12 Rest. La Piedoie
13 Rest. L'Epicerie & la Creperie du Cloitre
14 Rest. D'ici et d'Ailleurs
15 Rest. L'Empreinte
16 Laundromat
17 To Shakespeare Bookshop
18 Webzone

live within the walls). You can see the limit of the pre-pope city by looking at your map. Rues Joseph Vernet, Henri Fabre, des Lices, and Philonarde follow the route of the defensive wall before the pope's arrival.

The Petit Palais (little palace) seals the left end of the end of the square and was built for a cardinal; today, it houses medieval paintings (see description below). The church to the left of the Palace of the Popes is Avignon's cathedral. It predates the Church's purchase of Avignon by 200 years; its modest size reflects Avignon's modest, pre-pope population. Golden Mary wasn't up on the rooftop until 1859 (part of the city's beautification project). Behind you was the pope's mint, conveniently located as money was a perpetual concern among popes. Today, it's a school for dance and music.

Musée du Petit Palais—This palace superbly displays medieval Italian painting and sculpture. Since the Catholic Church was the patron of the arts, all 350 paintings deal with Christian themes. Visiting this museum before going to the Palace of the Popes gives you a sense of art and life during the Avignon papacy (€6, €3 with discount card, Wed–Mon 9:30–13:00 & 14:00–17:30, closed Tue, at north end of place du Palais).

▲Parc de Rochers des Doms and Pont St. Bénezet—For a panoramic view over Avignon and the Rhône Valley, hike above the Palace of the Popes to the rock top—Parc de Rochers des Doms—where Avignon was first settled. At the far end of this lookout, drop down a few steps for a good view of pont St. Bénezet.

This bridge, whose construction and location were inspired by a shepherd's religious vision, is the "pont d'Avignon" of nursery-rhyme fame upon which everyone is dancing. Imagine a 22-arch, 1,000-meter-long (3,000 feet) bridge extending across two rivers to the lonely Tower of Philip the Fair, the bridge's former toll-gate, on the distant side (equally great view from that tower back over Avignon; see below). The island the bridge spanned is now filled with campgrounds. You can pay €3 to walk along a section of the ramparts and do your own jig on pont St. Bénezet (nice view, otherwise nothing special). The castle on the right, St. André Fortress, was once another island in the Rhône. Cross Daladier Bridge for the best view of the old bridge and Avignon's skyline.

▲Palace of the Popes (Palais des Papes)—In 1309, a French pope was elected (Pope Clement V). At the urging of the French king, His Holiness decided he'd had enough of unholy Italy. So he loaded his carts and moved north to peaceful Avignon for a steady rule under a supportive king. The Catholic Church literally bought Avignon (then a two-bit town), and popes resided here until 1403. From 1378 on, there were twin popes, one in Rome and one in

Avignon, causing a schism in the Catholic Church that wasn't fully resolved until 1417.

The pope's palace is two distinct buildings: one old and one older. Along with lots of big, barren rooms, you'll see frescoes, tapestries, and some beautiful floor tiles. The audioguide tour does a decent job of overcoming the lack of furnishings and gives a thorough history lesson while allowing you to tour this largely empty palace at your own pace. Enjoy the view and windswept café at the tower. You'll exit to the rear of the palace, where my walking tour begins (see below). To return to the palace square, make two rights after exiting (€9.50, €7.50 with discount card, daily mid-March–Oct 9:00–19:00, July–Aug until 20:00, Nov–mid-March 9:00–17:45, ticket office closes 1 hr earlier, tours in English twice daily March–Oct, tel. 04 90 27 50 74).

Discovering Avignon's Backstreets—Use the map in this chapter and the TI's barely adequate, single-sheet-of-paper city map to help navigate this easy 30-minute level walk. This tour begins in the small square behind the pope's palace, where visitors exit. (If you skipped the palace interior, walk down the Palace Square—with the palace to your left—and take the first left down a narrow cobbled lane—rue Peyrolerie; you'll pop out in a small square behind the pope's palace. Veer left and you're ready to go.)

Hôtel la Mirande, Avignon's finest hotel, faces the pope's palace and is, amazingly, a welcoming place. You're invited to explore. Find the atrium lounge and consider a coffee break amid the understated luxury (afternoon tea with all the pastries is served 15:00–18:00). Inspect the royal lounge and dining room (recommended in "Eating in Avignon," below); cooking courses are offered in the basement below. Rooms start at €300.

Turn left out of the hotel and left again on rue Peyrolerie (street of the Coppersmiths), then take your first right on rue des Oiseaux d'Or and enter the tranquillity surrounding the **Church of St. Pierre**. Admire the original chestnut doors (the interior is generally closed), then take the alley to the left under and into what was the cloister of St. Pierre's (place des Chataignes, see "Eating in Avignon" for good places to eat on both sides of the church). Leave the square with the church on your right, cross busy rue Carnot and look back to the church that now seems far larger.

Walk to the **Banque de Chaix**. The building opposite, with its beam support showing, is a rare leftover from the Middle Ages. Notice how the building widens the higher it gets. A medieval loophole based taxes on ground floor area—everything above was tax-free. Walk down the rue des Fourbisseurs (street of animal furs) and notice how the top floors almost meet. Fire was a constant danger in the Middle Ages, as flames leapt easily from one home to the next. In fact, the lookout guard's primary responsibility was alerting locals to fires, not the enemy. Virtually all of Avignon's medieval homes have been replaced by safer structures.

Turn left on the traffic-free street rue du Vieux Sextier (street of the balance, for weighing items); another left under the first arch leads to **Avignon's Synagogue**. The popes' toleration allowed the Jews a place to relocate after being kicked out of Spain. More than 500 Jewish families took advantage of this opportunity. To visit the synagogue, press the buzzer and the friendly local rabbi will be your guide (Mon–Fri 10:00–12:00 & 15:00–17:00, closed Sat–Sun).

From here, double back to rue du Vieux Sextier and turn right to return to place de l'Horloge via Avignon's shopping streets. To dive really deep into Avignon's backstreets (allow another 20 min), leave the synagogue the way you came, cross rue du Vieux Sextier and turn left on the next street, rue de la Bonneterie (street of bonnets, or hats). Follow this all the way to **rue des Tenturiers**, headquarters in Avignon for all that's hip. Earthy cafés, galleries, and a small stream (a branch of the Sorgue river) with waterwheels line this tie-dyed street that served as the cloth industry's dyeing and textile center in the 1800s. Those stylish Provençal fabrics and patterns you see for sale everywhere started here. Go as far as the second waterwheel before doubling back, then turn left on the rue des Lices (where the first medieval wall stood). This will lead you back to the rue de la République, Avignon's main drag.

More Sights—Avignon

Fondation Angladon-Dubrujeaud—This museum mixes a small but enjoyable collection of art from Post-Impressionists (including Cézanne, van Gogh, Daumier, Degas, and Picasso) with re-created art studios and furnishings from many periods. It's a quiet place with a few superb paintings (€5, €3 with discount card, Tue–Sun 13:00–18:00, closed Mon, 5 rue Laboureur).

Musée Calvet—This fine-arts museum impressively displays its good collection without a word of English explanation (€6, €3 with discount card, Wed–Mon 10:00–12:00 & 14:00–18:00, closed Tue, on quieter west half of town at 65 Joseph Vernet; its antiquities collection is a few blocks away at 27 rue de la République, same hours and ticket).

Sights near Avignon, in Villeneuve-lès-Avignon

▲Tower of Philip the Fair (Tour Phillipe-le-Bel)—Built to protect access to the pont St. Bénezet in 1307, this massive tower offers the best view over Avignon and the Rhône basin. It's best late in the day (€1.60, €0.90 with discount card, April–Sept daily 10:00–12:00 & 15:00–19:00, Oct–March Tue–Sun 10:00–12:00 & 15:00–17:30, closed Mon). To reach the tower from Avignon, it's a five-minute drive (cross pont Daladier bridge, follow signs to Villeneuve-lès-Avignon); boat ride (Bâteau-Bus departs from Mireio Embarcadere near pont Daladier); or a bus ride on #11 (2/hr, catch bus across from train station inside city wall, in front of post office, on cours President Kennedy).

Sleeping in Avignon

(€1 = about $1, country code: 33, zip code: 84000)

Hotel values are generally better in Arles, though the range of choices here is impressive. These are all solid values.

HIGHER PRICED

Cité des Papes Mercure***, a modern hotel chain within spitting distance of the Palace of the Popes, has 73 smartly designed, smallish rooms, musty halls, unbeatable views from the breakfast room, air-conditioning, elevators, and all the comforts (Db-€107, extra bed-€13, CC, many rooms have views over place de l'Horloge, 1 rue Jean Vilar, tel. 04 90 80 93 00, fax 04 90 80 93 01, e-mail: h1952@accor-hotels.com). The **Palais des Papes Mercure***** (same chain, same price) is nearby, just inside the walls, near pont St. Bénezet (87 rooms, CC, rue Ferruce, tel. 04 90 80 93 93, fax 04 90 80 93 94, e-mail: h0549@accor-hotels.com).

At **Hôtel d'Europe******, be a gypsy in the palace at Avignon's most prestigious address—if you get one of the 17 surprisingly reasonable standard rooms (standard Db-€125–155, first class-€215, deluxe Db-€298, CC, breakfast-€20, garage-€14, elevator, every comfort, 12 place Crillon, near pont Daladier, tel. 04 90 14 76 76, fax 04 90 14 76 71, www.hotel-d-europe.fr).

MODERATELY PRICED

Hôtel Blauvac** offers 16 mostly spacious, high-ceilinged rooms (most with an upstairs loft) and a sky-high atrium in a grand old manor home near the pedestrian zone (Sb-€54–61, Db-€55, Db loft-€63, Tb/Qb-€77–85, CC, 11 rue de La Bancasse, 1 block off rue de la République, tel. 04 90 86 34 11, fax 04 90 86 27 41, www.hotel-blauvac.com, friendly Nathalie SE like an American).

Hôtel Danieli** is a Hello-Dolly fluffball of a place, renting 29 generally large rooms on the main drag with air-conditioning and many tour groups (Sb-€60–65, Db-€70–85, Tb-€80–100, Qb-€92–110, CC, elevator, 17 rue de la République, tel. 04 90 86 46 82, fax 04 90 27 09 24, www.hotel-danieli-avignon.com).

Hôtel Medieval** is burrowed deep with unimaginative, big, and comfortable rooms in a massive stone mansion (Db-€50–68, extra bed-€8, kitchenettes available but require 3-day minimum stay, CC, 15 rue Petite Saunerie, 5 blocks east of place de l'Horloge, behind Eglise St. Pierre, tel. 04 90 86 11 06, fax 04 90 82 08 64, e-mail: hotel.medieval@wanadoo.fr).

LOWER PRICED

The next three listings are a 10-minute walk from the station; turn right off cours Jean Jaurés on rue Agricol Perdiguier.

At **Hôtel Splendid***, the friendly Pre-Lemoines rent 17 cheery rooms with firm beds, air-conditioning, and small bathrooms for a fair price (Sb-€39, Db-€49, CC, 17 rue Agricol Perdiguier, tel. 04 90 86 14 46, fax 04 90 85 38 55, www.avignon-et-provence.com/hotels/le-splendid/).

Hôtel du Parc*, across the street, is a similar value without air-conditioning, but with Avignon native Madame Rous in charge (D-€34, Ds-€42, Db-€46, CC, get a room over the park, tel. 04 90 82 71 55, fax 04 90 85 64 86, e-mail: hotelsurparc@aol.com).

Hôtel Colbert** is a fine midrange bet. Parisian refugees Patrice (SE) and Sylvie (NSE) are your hosts, and their care for this hotel shows in the attention to detail, from the peaceful patio to the warm room decor (Sb-€38–44, Db-€44–58, Tb-€58–79, CC, air-con, 7 rue Agricol Perdiguier, tel. 04 90 86 20 20, fax 04 90 85 97 00, e-mail: colbert.hotel@wanadoo.fr).

Auberge Bagatelle's hostel/campground offers dirt-cheap beds, a lively atmosphere, busy pool, café, grocery store, launderette, great views of Avignon, and campers for neighbors (D-€24, dorm bed-€11, CC, across pont Daladier on the Island—Ile de la—Barthelasse, bus #10 from main post office, tel. 04 90 86 30 39, fax 04 90 27 16 23).

Eating in Avignon

Skip the overpriced places on the place de l'Horloge and find a more intimate location for your dinner (many to choose from).

Eating near the Church of St. Pierre

L'Epicerie, charmingly located and popular, on a tiny square a few blocks east of place de l'Horloge, offers a good selection of à la carte items (daily, 10 place St. Pierre, tel. 04 90 82 74 22).

Crêperie du Cloitre, on the other side of the Church of St. Pierre (under the arch from L'Epicerie restaurant), has more ambience and inexpensive meals (big salad and main course crêpe for about €12, closed Sun–Mon, on place des Chataignes).

Eating Elsewhere in Avignon

At intimate **La Piedoie,** a few blocks northeast of the TI, eager-to-please owner Thierry Piedoie serves fine Provençal dishes (€27 *menu*, 26 rue des Trois Faucons, tel. 04 90 86 51 52).

D'Ici et d'Ailleurs (meaning "from here and elsewhere"), one block from place de l'Horloge, is a good budget value for discerning diners, with decor as soothing as the prices (*menu* from €14, Mon–Sat, closed Sun, 4 rue Galande, tel. 04 90 14 63 65).

L'Empreinte is good for North African cuisine in a trendy location (copious couscous for €10–15, daily, 33 rue des Tenturiers, tel. 04 32 76 36 35).

Hotel la Mirande is the perfect splurge. Reserve ahead here for understated elegance and Avignon's top cuisine (€40–50 *menus*, 4 place de la Mirande, tel. 04 90 86 93 93, fax 04 90 86 26 85, www.la-mirande.fr).

Transportation Connections—Avignon

Trains

Remember, there are two train stations in Avignon, the new suburban TGV station and the main station in the city center (€1 shuttle buses connect both stations, 4/hr, 10 min). Both have baggage checks; car rental is available at the TGV station. Some cities are served by slower local trains from the main station and by faster TGV trains from the TGV station; I've listed the most convenient stations for each trip.

By train from Avignon's main station to: Arles (12/day, 20 min), **Orange** (16/day, 20 min), **Nîmes** (14/day, 30 min), **Isle sur la Sorgue** (6/day, 30 min), **Lyon** (10/day, 2 hrs, also from TGV station—see below), **Carcassonne** (8/day, 3 hrs, 7 with change in Narbonne), **Barcelona** (2/day, 6 hrs, change in Montpellier).

By train from Avignon's TGV station to: Nice (10/day, 4 hrs, a few direct, most require transfer in Marseille), **Lyon** (12/day, 1.5 hrs), **Paris'** Gare du Lyon (14 TGVs/day, 2.5 hrs, 3 with change in Lyon), **Paris'** Charles de Gaulle airport (7/day, 3 hrs).

Buses

The bus station (*halte routière*, tel. 04 90 82 07 35) is just past and below the Ibis hotel to the right as you exit the train station (information desk open Mon–Fri 8:00–18:00, Sat 8:00–12:00, closed Sun). Nearly all buses leave from this station. The main exception is the SNCF bus service that runs from the TGV station to Arles (10/day, 30 min). The Avignon TI should have schedules. Service is reduced or nonexistent on Sunday and holidays.

By bus to: Pont du Gard (5/day in summer, 4/day off-season, 40 min, see details under "Pont du Gard," below). Consider visiting Pont du Gard, continuing on to Nîmes or Uzès (see "Sights near Pont du Gard—Uzès," below) and returning to Avignon from there (use the same Pont du Gard bus stop you arrived at to continue on to Nîmes and Uzès). Try these plans: Take the 12:05 bus from Avignon, arriving at Pont du Gard at 12:50. Then take either the 14:45 bus from there to Nîmes, where trains run hourly back to Avignon, or a 16:00 bus (Mon–Fri) on to Uzès, arriving at 16:30, with a return bus to Avignon at 18:30.

By bus to other regional destinations: St. Rémy (7/day, 45 min, handy way to visit its Wed market), **Isle sur la Sorgue** (5/day, 45 min), **Vaison la Romaine**, **Sablet**, and **Seguret** (3/day during school year, called *période scolaire*, 1/day otherwise and 1/day from TGV station, 75 min), **Gordes** (via Cavaillon, 1/day, very early, 2 hrs, spend the night or taxi back to Cavaillon), **Nyons** (2/day, 2 hrs).

More Sights in Provence

A car is a dream come true here. Below I've described key sights and two full-day excursions deep into the countryside (see "Villages of the Côtes du Rhône" and "The Hill Towns of Luberon," below), both better done as overnights. Les Baux and St. Rémy work well by car with the Luberon excursion. The town of Orange ties in tidily with a trip to the Côtes du Rhône villages. The Pont du Gard is a short hop west of Avignon and on the way to/from Languedoc for drivers. Travelers relying on public transportation will find their choices very limited. St. Rémy and Isle sur la Sorgue are the most accessible small-town experiences. However you tour this magnificent area, notice the wind buffeting rows of bamboo and cypress and how buildings are oriented south, with few or no windows facing north.

LES BAUX

Crowning the rugged Alpilles mountains, this rock-top castle and tourist village is a ▲▲▲ sight, worth visiting for the lunar landscape alone. Arrive by 9:00 or after 17:00 to avoid ugly crowds. Sunsets are sacrosanct, and nights in Les Baux are pin-drop peaceful; the castle is beautifully illuminated (though closed after dark). There's no free parking; get as close to the top as you can (€4 up top, €3 on road far below).

In the tourist-trampled live city (see definition below), you'll find the **TI** (daily April–Sept 9:00–19:00, Oct–March 9:00–18:00, in Hôtel de Ville, tel. 04 90 54 34 39), too many shops, great viewpoints, and an appealing exhibit of paintings by Yves Brayer, who spent his final years here (€3, daily 10:00–12:00 & 14:00–18:30, in Hôtel des Porcelets).

A 12th-century regional powerhouse, Les Baux was razed in 1632 by a paranoid Louis XIII, who was afraid of these trouble-making upstarts. What remains is the reconstructed "live city" of tourist shops and snack stands and, the reason you came, the "dead city" (Ville Morte or Citadelle des Baux) ruins carved into, out of, and on top of a rock 200 meters/650 feet high. Climb through the "modern village" to the sun-bleached top where la Citadelle awaits (best early in the morning or early-evening light). Find the perfect view from the highest perch and try to imagine 6,000 people living within these stone walls. Survey the small museum as you enter la Citadelle (good exhibits, pick up the English explanations) and don't miss the slide show on van Gogh, Gauguin, and Cézanne in the little chapel across from the museum (€6.50 entry to la Citadelle, includes a free and helpful audioguide, and entry to all the town's sights, daily Easter–Oct 9:00–19:00, until 20:00 July–Aug, Nov–Easter 9:30–17:00).

The best view of Les Baux day or night is one kilometer north on D-27 near **Caves de Sarragnan**, where you can sample wines in a very cool rock quarry that dates from the Middle Ages (daily April–Sept 10:00–12:00 & 14:00–19:00, Oct–March closes at 18:00, tel. 04 90 54 33 58). On the way, you'll pass **Cathédrale d'Images**, a mesmerizing sound-and-slide show that immerses visitors in regional themes by projecting 3,000 images inside a rock quarry (€7, daily 10:00–18:00, just above Les Baux on D-27).

Four daily buses serve Les Baux from the Arles bus station (30 min, see "Transportation Connections—Arles," above).

Sights between Les Baux and Arles

Abbey de Montmajour—You can't miss this brooding structure, just a few minutes from Arles toward Les Baux. A once-thriving abbey and a convenient papal retreat, it dates from 948. The vast, vacant abbey church is a massive example of Romanesque architecture, though for me, it's another big empty space (€6, April–Sept daily 9:00–19:00, Oct–March 10:00–13:00 & 14:00–17:00, tel. 04 90 54 64 17).

▲**Roman Aqueduct**—I love lost Roman ruins, and there's no better example than these 2,000-year-old crumbled arches from the principal aqueduct that served Arles (entering the city at the Roman Arena). Coming from Arles, take D-17 toward Fontvieille, then follow signs on the right to *L'Aqueduc Romain* just before Fontvieille. Follow that road for three kilometers/two miles to the romantically ruined remains (no sign, just after *Los Pozos Blancos* sign, look for stone walls on both sides of the road). Follow the dirt path to the right along the ruins for about 130 meters/425 feet where you enter the water canal, then come to a cliff over the farmland below. Now, imagine the Pont du Gard in front of you.

Sleeping in and near Les Baux
(€1 = about $1, country code: 33)

For more accommodations, see also "Sleeping near Arles," above, and "Sleeping in St. Rémy," below.

HIGHER PRICED

The appealing **Le Mas d'Aigret***** crouches just past Les Baux on the road to St. Rémy. Lie on your back and stare up at the castle walls rising beyond your swimming pool in this Provençal oasis. Many of the smartly designed rooms have private terraces and views over the valley, and the restaurant is troglodyte-chic. Some road noise is noticeable during the day (smaller Db-€100, larger Db with terrace-€130, Tb-€175–200, CC, air-con, tel. 04 90 54 20 00, fax 04 90 54 44 00, www.masdaigret.com).

LOWER PRICED

Hôtel Reine Jeanne** is 50 meters/165 feet to your right after the main entry to the live city (standard Db-€51, Db with deck-€63, great family suite-€90, CC, most air-con, ask for *chambre avec terasse*, good *menus* from €20, 13520 Les Baux, tel. 04 90 54 32 06, fax 04 90 54 32 33, www.la-reinejeanne.com).

Le Mas de L'Esparou *chambre d'hôte*, a few minutes below Les Baux, is welcoming (Jacqueline loves her job, and her lack of English only makes her more animated) and kid-friendly, with spacious rooms, a swimming pool, table tennis, and distant views of Les Baux. Monsieur Roux painted the paintings in your room and has a gallery in Les Baux (Db-€60, extra person-€16, no CC, a few kilometers north of Mausanne on D-5, look for sign, 13520 Les Baux de Provence, tel. & fax 04 90 54 41 32, NSE).

Le Mazet des Alpilles, a small home with three tidy rooms with air-conditioning just outside the unspoiled village of Paradou, five minutes below Les Baux, may have space when others don't (Db-€52, ask for her largest room, child's bed available, no CC, follow signs from the D-17, in Paradou look for route de Brunelly, 13520 Paradou, tel. 04 90 54 45 89, fax 04 90 54 44 66, e-mail: lemazet@wanadoo.fr, Annick NSE).

ST. RÉMY DE PROVENCE

This sophisticated town is famous for its Wednesday market (until 12:30), the ruins of a once-thriving Roman city (Glanum), and the mental ward where van Gogh was sent after slicing off his ear.

St. Rémy is a scenic 10-minute drive (or a 2-hour walk) over the hills and through the woods from Les Baux. Almost too close to Avignon for its own good (though very accessible by bus), St. Rémy's pleasant old city is ringed by a busy road. The small streets within the ring road are *très* strollable.

Sights—St. Rémy

▲Glanum—These crumbled stones are the foundations of a Roman market town, located at the crossroads of two ancient trade routes between Italy and Spain. A massive Roman arch and tower stand proud and lonely near the ruins' parking lot. The arch marked the entry into Glanum, and the tower is a memorial to the grandsons of Emperor Caesar Augustus. The setting is stunning, though shadeless, and the small museum at the entry sets the stage well. While the ruins are, well, ruined, they remind us of the range and prosperity of the Roman Empire. Along with other Roman monuments in Provence, they allow us to paint a more complete picture of Roman life. The English handout is helpful, but consider buying one of the two English booklets (one has better photos, the other provides much better background). Inside the ruins, signs give basic English explanations at key locations, and the view from the belvedere justifies the effort (€6, daily April–Sept 9:00–12:00 & 14:00–19:00, Oct–March 9:30–12:00 & 14:00–17:00).

Cloître St. Paul de Mausole—Just below Glanum is the still-functioning mental hospital (Clinique St. Paul) that treated Vincent van Gogh from 1889 to 1890. The €3 entry fee buys a four-minute video (English and French) and entry into the small chapel, intimate cloisters, and a re-creation of his room. You'll find limited information in English about Vincent's life. Amazingly, he painted 150 works in his 53 weeks here—none of which remain anywhere close today. The contrast between the utter simplicity of his room (and his life) and the multimillion-dollar value of his paintings today is jarring. The site is managed by VALETUDO, a center specializing in art therapy (daily April–Oct 9:30–19:00, Nov–March 10:30–13:00 & 13:30–17:00). Outside the complex, dirt paths lead to Vincent's favorite footpaths with (sometimes vandalized) copies of his paintings from where he painted them.

Sleeping in St. Rémy
(€1 = about $1, country code: 33)

HIGHER PRICED

Mas de Carassins***, a 15-minute walk from the center, is impeccably run by friendly Michel and Pierre (Paris refugees). Luxury is made affordable here, and care is given to every aspect of the hotel, from the generously sized pool and gardens to the muted room decor and the optional €25 dinner (standard Db-€92–105, deluxe Db-€115, large Tb-€145, extra bed-€13, CC, air-con, table tennis, bike rental, 1 Chemin Gaulois, look for signs 180 meters/590 feet toward Les Baux from TI, tel. 04 90 92 15 48, fax 04 90 92 63 47, e-mail: carassin@pacwan.fr).

MODERATELY PRICED

Hotel Villa Glanum**, right across from the Glanum ruins, is a modern, good midrange bet with 27 rooms and a pool (Ds-€58, Db-€76, Tb-€91, Qb-€106, CC, 46 avenue Van Gogh, 13210 Saint Rémy, tel. 04 90 92 03 59, fax 04 90 92 00 08, e-mail: villa.glanum@wanadoo.fr).

LOWER PRICED

Auberge de la Reine Jeanne** is central, cozy, and typical of many French hotels in that the rooms take a backseat to the restaurant. The 11 traditionally decorated rooms overlook a courtyard jammed with tables and umbrellas, and are clean and spacious, with big beds (Db-€59, Tb-€68, Qb-€75, CC, fine restaurant-€24 *menu*, on ring road at 12 boulevard Mirabeau, tel. 04 90 92 15 33, fax 04 90 92 49 65).

Eating in St. Rémy

The town is packed with fine restaurants. To dine well, try **Auberge de la Reine Jeanne** (see above). **Crêperie Lou Planet** is cheap and peaceful, on pleasant place Favier (open until 20:00).

PONT DU GARD

One of Europe's great ▲▲▲ treats, this perfectly preserved Roman aqueduct was built as the critical link of a 56-kilometer/35-mile canal that, by dropping one foot for every 300, supplied 44 million gallons of water daily to Nîmes, one of western Europe's largest cities. After years of work, the new **Grande Expo** does this sight justice with a phenomenal museum, a 23-minute movie, and a kid's space (called *Ludo*), all designed to improve your appreciation of this remarkable sight.

Start at the *rive gauche* (left bank of the Pont du Gard). You'll be greeted by the Grande Expo's linear new structure, housing the three exhibits. Begin with the informative but silly movie, if the English times are convenient; otherwise, skip it. Spend most of your time in the museum. The multimedia approach will draw you into daily Roman life: You'll learn about the many uses of water in Roman times; see examples of lead pipes, faucets, and siphons; marvel at the many models; walk through a rock quarry; and learn how they moved those huge rocks into place and how those massive arches were made. English video screens and information displays help make things as clear as spring water. The *Ludo* kid's space does the same for kids (English displays), giving them a scratch-and-sniff experience of various aspects of Roman life and the importance of water (€13, €43 for family of 2 adults and up to 4 kids, daily Easter–Nov 9:30–19:00, mid-June–Aug until 21:30, Dec–Easter until 18:00, tel. 04 66 37 50 99). The high-priced entry fees include all three exhibits and parking (which costs €4.60 otherwise).

The actual Pont du Gard **aqueduct** is free and open until midnight (the illumination is beautiful after dark). It's a level, 300-meter/985-foot walk to the aqueduct from the Grande Expo. Inspect the bridge closely and imagine getting those stones to the top. The entire structure relies on perfect stone placement; there's no mortar holding this together. Signs direct you to "panoramas" above the bridge on either side, but you'll get better views by walking along the riverbank below—either upstream or downstream—or, more refreshing, by floating flat on your back; bring a swimsuit and sandals for the rocks (always open and free).

Consider **renting a canoe** from the town of Collias to Pont du Gard (€27 per 2-person canoe; they pick you up at Pont du Gard—or elsewhere, if prearranged—and shuttle you to Collias, where you float down the river to nearby town of Remoulins, can be shuttled back to Pont du Gard; 2-hr trip, though you can take as long as you like, Collias Canoes, tel. 04 66 22 85 54, SE).

Transportation Connections—Pont du Gard

By car: Pont du Gard is an easy 25-minute drive due west of Avignon (follow signs to Nîmes) and 45 minutes northwest of Arles (via Tarascon). The *rive gauche* parking is off D-981 that leads from Remoulins to Uzès. (Parking is also available on the *rive droite* side but is farther away from the museum.)

By bus: Buses run to Pont du Gard *(rive gauche)* from Nîmes, Uzès, and Avignon. Combine Uzès (see below) and Pont du Gard for a good day excursion from Avignon (5/day in summer, 3/day off-season, 40 min to Pont du Gard; see info on "Transportation Connections—Avignon," above). The bus stop at Pont du Gard is in the new parking lot near the Grande Expo on the left bank *(rive gauche)*. The return stop to Avignon is to your left before crossing the traffic circle. Make sure you're waiting for the bus on the correct side of the traffic circle.

Sights near Pont du Gard

Uzès—An intriguing, less trampled town, Uzès (pron. oo-zehs) is best seen slowly on foot, with a long coffee break in its beautifully arcaded and mellow main square, the place aux Herbes (not so mellow during the colorful Wed and bigger Sat-morning market). The city is the sight; there are no important museums. Most of the center city is traffic-free and tastefully restored. (Uzès is officially in Languedoc, not Provence.)

At the **TI**, pick up the English walking tour brochure (May–Sept Mon–Fri 9:00–18:00, Sat–Sun 10:00–13:00 & 14:00–17:00; Oct–April Mon–Fri 9:00–12:00 & 13:30–18:00, Sat 10:00–13:00, closed Sun, on ring road on place Albert 1er, tel. 04 66 22 68 88). Skip the dull and overpriced palace of the Duché de Uzès (€9, French-only tour). You can enjoy the unusual Tour Fenestrelle—all that remains of a 12th-century cathedral—from the outside only.

Uzès is a short hop west (by bus) of Pont du Gard and is well-served by bus from Nîmes (9/day, 60 min) and Avignon (3/day, 60 min).

VILLAGES OF THE CÔTES DU RHÔNE: A LOOP TRIP FOR WINE-AND-VILLAGE-LOVERS

If you have a car and a fondness for wine or beautiful countryside, take this loop through Provence's Côtes du Rhône wine country (1–3 buses/day from Avignon—75 min, and Orange—30 min—follow a similar route to Vaison la Romaine). Endless vineyards, rugged mountains, and stone villages fill your windshield. While this trip is doable as a day trip by car from Arles or Avignon (allow an entire day for this 130-kilometer/80-mile round trip from Avignon), you won't regret a night or two in one of the villages listed below. Vaison la Romaine makes the best base and is ideal if you're heading to, or coming from, the north.

Here's our route: From Avignon, follow the N-7 toward Orange, then follow signs to Châteauneuf-du-Pape (short stop here). From there, track signs to Courthézon, where you'll cross the freeway and follow signs to Vaison la Romaine, then Gigondas (longer stop here). From Gigondas, follow Sablet, then Seguret (short stop), then Vaison la Romaine (longer stop). From Vaison, loop back on the other side of the Dentelles de Montmiral by driving to Malaucene, then find the D-90 turn-off to Suzette (café stop required), then follow signs to Carpentras and Beaumes de Venise, and enjoy some of Provence's most amazing scenery as you head over these hills.

This route is peppered with tasting opportunities, perfect picnic spots, and recommended lunch cafés. The Côtes du Rhône is hospitable and offers relaxed wine-tasting at its best, and most villages have a *Caveau des Vignerons* (wine-making cooperative),

Provence Wine Country

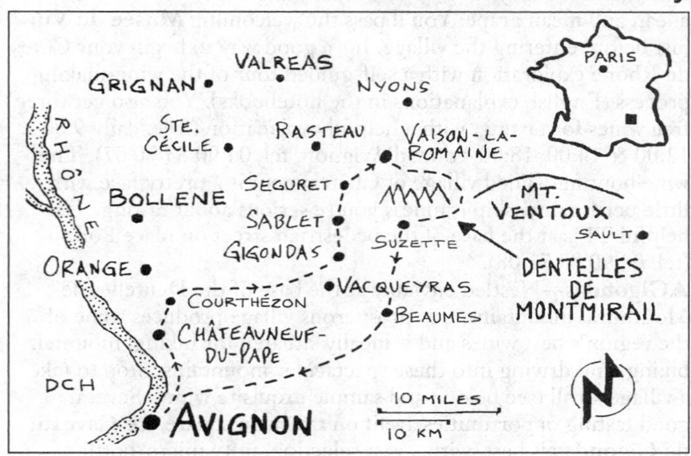

which are easy places to sample a variety of wines. I've listed places to sleep, eat, and taste throughout this route in the description below.

Those with more time should drive to the top of Mont Ventoux and visit the village of Sault, the lavender capital (this is a must if you're here anytime from late June to late July, when the lavender blooms). To add the Roman theater in Orange to this day trip, visit Orange after Châteauneuf-du-Pape.

The less traveled Dromme region just north of Vaison la Romaine is worthwhile if you're continuing to the Alps or if you're here in July when lavender blooms. It's laced with vineyards (producing less expensive yet good wines), lavender fields, and still more postcard-perfect villages. From Vaison, take the loop north to Visan, Valreas, Taulignan, and Nyons, and then back to Vaison. Pleasant Nyons is France's olive capital and hosts a dynamite Thursday-morning market. Each village is a detour waiting to happen.

Sights—The Wine Villages

Here's a review of the wine villages you'll pass on our Côtes du Rhône drive.

Châteauneuf-du-Pape—Châteauneuf-du-Pape means "new castle of the pope"; the old one was the Palace of the Popes in Avignon. This one was built as a summer retreat, and it's now a ruin capping the beautiful-to-see, little-to-do hill town. Wine-loving popes also planted the first vines here in the 1300s. Signs let you know that "here start the vineyards of Châteauneuf-du-Pape." Pull over and stroll into a vineyard with a view of the hill town. Notice the sea of stones beneath your feet. This rocky soil is perfect for making a lean and mean grape. You'll pass the welcoming **Musée du Vin** just before entering the village. It's a good way to begin your Côtes du Rhône exploration with a self-guided tour of the wine-making process (English explanations in the notebooks). You also get three free wines for tasting, with a helpful explanation (free, daily 9:00–12:00 & 14:00–18:00, route d'Avignon, tel. 04 90 83 70 07). The wine boutique–lined village of Châteauneuf is a pretty face with little personality; skip it unless you're serious about tasting. The helpful TI is at the base of the pedestrian street on place Portail (tel. 04 90 83 71 08).

▲Gigondas—Nestled enviably at the base of the Dentelles de Montmiral mountains, this prosperous village produces some of the region's best wines and is ideally situated for hiking, mountain biking, and driving into these spectacular mountains. Stop to take a village stroll (see below) and sample exquisite wines. Several good tasting opportunities await on the main square. **Le Caveau de Gigondas** is best, with a vast selection, nifty micro-bottle samples, and a donation-if-you-don't-buy system (daily 10:00–12:00 & 14:00–18:30, 2 doors down from TI).

The info-packed **TI** has a list of welcoming wineries, *chambres d'hôte*, and good hikes or drives into the mountains (closed 12:00–14:00, tel. 04 90 65 85 46). The €2.50 map *Chemins et Sentiers du Massif des Dentelles* is helpful, though not critical, since routes are well-signed. Route #1 is an ideal one-hour walk above Gigondas to great views from the Belvedere du Rocher du Midi (route #2 extends this hike into a 3-hour loop).

Drivers can bump their way into incredible scenery by following the dirt road to the Col du Cayron (drive past recommended Hôtel les Florets and park where the road turns bad, good day hikes from here).

If you're not in a hurry, seriously consider lunch on the terrace of Hôtel les Florets (listed below).

Sleeping and Eating in Gigondas: The peaceful and traditional **Hôtel les Florets****, one kilometer above the village, is a complete refuge and a good value. It's huddled at the foot of the Dentelles de Montmiral peaks (great hiking from here), with a huge terrace van Gogh would have loved, thoughtfully designed rooms, and an exceptional restaurant (Db-€85, Tb-€100, annex rooms are best, CC, *menus* from €23, 84190 Gigondas, tel. 04 90 65 85 01, fax 04 90 65 83 80).

Sablet—This perfectly circular wine village, while impressive from a distance, has little of interest except scads of *chambres d'hôte*, well-signed from the road. Sablet wines are reasonable and tasty (the TI and wine cooperative share space in the town center).

Seguret—Almost too perfect, little Seguret is etched into the side of a hill and has a smattering of shops, two cafés, made-to-stroll lanes, and a natural spring. Come here for compelling vistas and a quiet lunch.

Sitting on the road to Sablet, just below town, **La Bastide Bleue** is blue-shutter Provençal, with seven rooms at fair prices and a charming restaurant (Sb-€40, Db-€47–56, includes breakfast, *menus* from €19, CC, just below Seguret, route de Sablet, tel. & fax 04 90 46 83 43).

VAISON LA ROMAINE

With quick access to adorable villages and Mont Ventoux, and vineyards knocking at its door, this thriving little town (pop. 6,000) makes a great base for exploring the Côtes du Rhône region by car or bike. You get two villages for the price of one: Vaison's "modern" lower city is like a mini-Arles, with worthwhile Roman ruins, a lone pedestrian street, and too many cars. The medieval hill town looms above and is car-free, with meandering cobbled lanes, a dash of art galleries and cafés, and a ruined castle (good view from its base).

Orientation

The city is split in two by the Ouveze River. The newer city *(ville-basse)* lies on its right bank; the medieval city *(ville-haute)* is above on the left bank. The impressive pont Roman (Roman bridge) connects the two, and was the only bridge to survive a terrible flood that killed 30 persons in 1992.

Tourist Information: The superb TI is in the newer city, between the two Roman ruin sites, at place de Chanoine Sautel. Get English tour times for the Roman ruins, ask about festivals and bike rental, pick up the excellent *Fiches d'Itineraries* (a detailed guide to walks and bike rides from Vaison, ask for English version), and say *bonjour* to charming Valerie, who has worked here for 17 years (May–Sept Mon–Sat 9:00–12:30 & 14:00–18:45, Sun 9:00–12:00; Oct–April Mon–Sat 9:00–12:30 & 14:00–17:45, closed Sun, tel. 04 90 36 02 11, www.vaison-la-romaine.com).

Helpful Hints

The **launderette** (Laverie la Lavandiere) is on Cours Taulignan near avenue Victor Hugo (Mon–Sat 9:00–12:00 & 15:00–18:45, closed Sun). You can rent **bikes** at Lacombe on avenue Jules Ferry (tel. 04 90 36 03 29). Consider hiring the superb **local guide** Anne-Marie Melard to bring the Roman ruins to life (reserve ahead through TI).

Arrival in Vaison la Romaine

By Bus: The stop is in front of Cave la Romaine winery; walk five minutes down avenue de Gaulle to reach the TI.

By Car: Follow signs to *Centre-ville*, then *Office de Tourisme;* park free across from the TI.

Sights—Vaison la Romaine

▲Market Day—The amazing Tuesday market (until 12:30) is worth organizing your trip and parking plans around. Sleep here Monday night.

Roman Ruins—If you've seen Pompeii, this will seem like small potatoes, but the remains of Vaison's two Roman sights—La Villasse and Puymin—are well-presented and give a good picture of life during the Roman Empire. Both ancient sites, separated by a modern road, show the foundations of the same Roman town that once stood here. The worthwhile museum inside the Puymin ruins has English explanations (€7, includes both sets of ruins as well as the cloister at the cathedral Notre-Dame de Nazareth; daily June–Sept 9:30–18:00, Oct–March 10:00–12:30 & 14:00–18:00, Nov–Feb closes at 16:00; English tours of ruins available April–Sept, several days/week, usually at 11:00, check with TI; or get informative English handout and do tour on your own; even better, call ahead to the TI and reserve local guide Anne-Marie Melard, see above).

In summer, ask about night visits to the ruins. After the fall of the Roman Empire, Vaison's residents headed for the hills and established the Ville-Haute just above. It must have been strange to have peered over the walls to the onetime great civilization that La Villasse and Puymin ruins represented.

Hiking—The TI has good information on relatively easy hikes into the hills above Vaison. Hikers shouldn't leave Vaison without the free *Fiches d'Itineraries* (in English). It's about 90 minutes to the tiny hill town of Crestet, though the views begin immediately. To find this trail, drive or walk up past the *ville-haute* with the castle on your left, find the Chemin des Fontaines, and stay the course. You'll soon come to an orientation table and fine views; stay on this road to reach Crestet.

Biking—Connect these villages for a great 18-kilometer/11-mile loop ride: Vaison la Romaine, St. Romain en Viennois, Puymeras, Faucon, and St. Marcellin les Vaison (TI has details).

Wine-Tasting—Cave la Romaine, a five-minute walk up avenue General de Gaulle from the TI, offers a variety of great-value wines from nearby villages in a pleasant, well-organized tasting room (daily 8:30–13:00 & 14:00–19:00, avenue St. Quenin, tel. 04 90 36 55 90). To truly enjoy the region's bounty, drive a

Vaison la Romaine

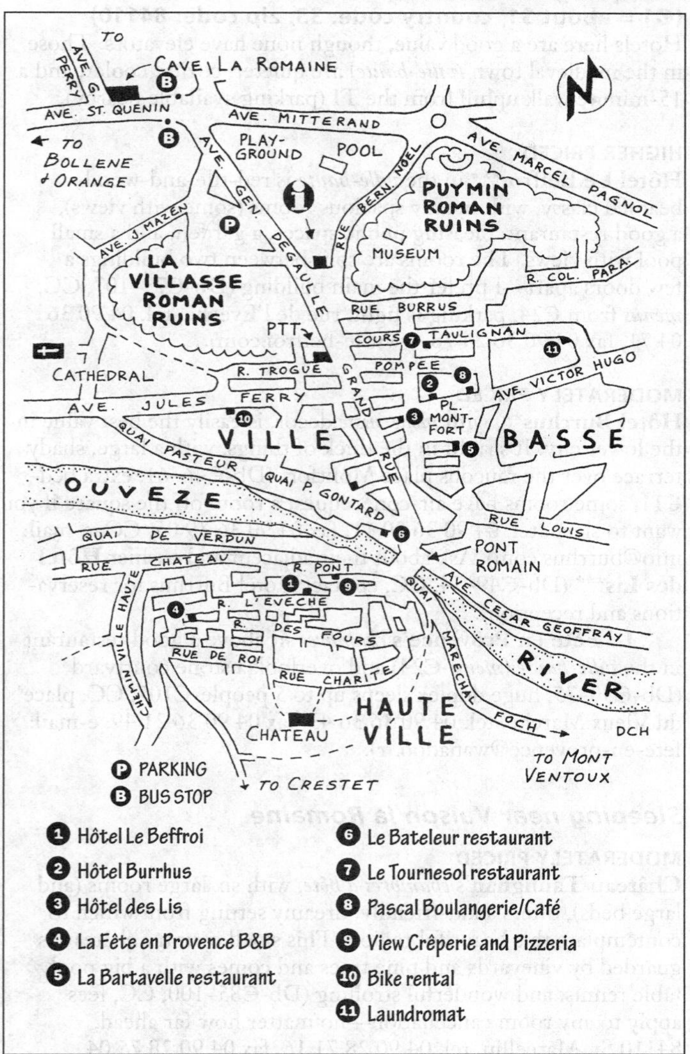

few minutes south to **Le Domaine des Girasols**, where friendly Françoise or John (SE) will take your palate on a tour of some of the area's best wine (well, that's my opinion). It's well-marked and worth a stop in Rasteau.

Sleeping in or near Vaison la Romaine
(€1 = about $1, country code: 33, zip code: 84110)

Hotels here are a good value, though none have elevators. Those in the medieval town *(ville-haute)* are quieter, cozier, cooler, and a 15-minute walk uphill from the TI (parking available nearby).

HIGHER PRICED

Hôtel Le Beffroi*** in the *ville-haute* is red-tile-and-wood-beamed classy, with mostly spacious rooms (some with views), a good restaurant, pleasing public spaces, a garden, and a small pool with views. The rooms are split between two buildings a few doors apart—I prefer the main building (Db-€73–107, CC, *menus* from €24, parking is tight, rue de l'Eveche, tel. 04 90 36 04 71, fax 04 90 36 24 78, www.le-beffroi.com).

MODERATELY PRICED

Hôtel Burrhus**, with *moderniste* decor, is easily the best value in the lower city. It's right in the thick of things, with a large, shady terrace over the raucous place Montfort (Db-€46–61, extra bed-€11, some rooms have air-con, request a room off the square if you want to sleep, tel. 04 90 36 00 11, fax 04 90 36 39 05, CC, e-mail: info@burrhus.com). Ask about their adjacent and cushier **Hôtel des Lis***** (Db-€49–74, CC, contact Hôtel Burrhus for reservations and reception).

La Fête en Provence's *chambres* sit above a good restaurant in the *ville-haute* (*menu*-€24) and overlook a stone courtyard (Db-€50–75, huge duplex sleeps up to 5 people-€107, CC, place du Vieux Marche, tel. 04 90 36 36 43, fax 04 90 36 21 49, e-mail: fete-en-provence@wanadoo.fr).

Sleeping near Vaison la Romaine

MODERATELY PRICED

Château Taulignan's *chambres d'hôte*, with six large rooms (and large beds), offers a kid-friendly, dreamy setting from which to contemplate this beautiful region. This small country château is guarded by vineyards and pine trees and comes with a big pool, table tennis, and wonderful strolling (Db-€85–100, CC, fees apply to any room cancellation—no matter how far ahead, 84110 St. Marcellin, tel. 04 90 28 71 16, fax 04 90 28 75 04, www.taulignan.com, Irish-born Helen SE). It's just five minutes from Vaison's TI; follow *Carpentras* signs and look for brown *Chambres d'hôte* signs just as you leave Vaison.

A few kilometers away, below spectacularly situated Crestet (follow Carpentras from Vaison), **l'Ermitage Chambres** is well-run by British expat Nick and native Nicole, who were born for this business. Their renovated, rustic farmhouse comes with three big, simple rooms; firm beds; and a pool with magnificent views. They also rent a two-bedroom apartment on a weekly basis (Db-€65, Tb-€80, apartment-€600/week, no CC, turn right off D-938 at Loupiotte restaurant, 84110 Crestet, tel. 04 90 28 88 29, fax 04 90 28 72 97, www.lermitage.net, e-mail: nick.jones@wanadoo.fr).

La Treille *chambres* lies on D-90 between Malaucene and Beaumes de Venise in the tiny hamlet of Suzette. Welcoming Madame Garrigou runs this perfectly situated stone home with views to live for and rooms to stretch out in. Each room comes with a private terrace and a cavernous bathroom; many have small kitchens (Db-€62–78, Tb-€73–93, Qb-€84–93, 84190 Suzette, tel. 04 90 65 03 77, cellular 06 13 89 59 00).

LOWER PRICED

L'Ecole Buissonnière *chambres* are run by another charming Anglo-French team, Monique and John, who have found complete isolation just 10 minutes from Vaison la Romaine in a tastefully restored farmhouse with three well-appointed rooms, each with very different personalities. I liked the Camargue loft room best (Db-€51, Tb-€62, Qb-€73, no CC, between Villedieu and Buisson on D-75, tel. 04 90 28 95 19, e-mail: ecole.buissonniere@wanadoo.fr).

Eating in and near Vaison la Romaine

La Bartavelle is the place to savor traditional French cuisine in the lower city (€22 *menu*, closed Mon, 12 place Sus-Auze, reserve ahead, tel. 04 90 36 02 16).

Le Bateleur is small, simply decorated, and good (€23 *menu*, closed Mon, near Roman bridge at 1 place Theodore Aubanel, tel. 04 90 36 28 04).

Le Tournesol offers the best midrange dinner value in town (€16 *menu*, 34 cours Taulignan, tel. 04 90 36 09 18).

Of the many cafés on place Montfort, **Pascal Boulangerie/Café** (at the far end) is the best value, though it's not open for dinner.

The atmospheric *ville-haute* has a view *crêperie* and a pizzeria with fair prices.

Drivers could seek out the relaxed, roadside **Restaurant Loupiote,** where the locals go (below Crestet on D-938, a 5-min drive from Vaison la Romaine, tel. 04 90 36 29 50).

Les Coquelicots café is a most scenic 20-minute drive away in adorable little Suzette and is best "in season," when you can dine outside. The food is simple and cheap, the setting is why you came (closed Tue–Wed, tel. 04 90 65 06 04). From Vaison, drive to Malaucene, then follow D-90 to Suzette.

Transportation Connections—Vaison la Romaine

The most central bus stop is at Cave Vinicole. **By bus to: Avignon** (2/day, 75 min), **Orange** (3/day, 50 min). Bus info tel. 04 90 36 09 90.

Other Highlights of the Côtes du Rhône

▲▲Orange—This most northern town in Provence is notable for its Roman arch and theater. The 18-meter-tall (60 feet) Roman Arc de Triomphe (from 25 B.C., north of city center on avenue Arc de Triomphe) honors Julius Caesar's defeat of the Gauls in 49 B.C., but is lightweight compared to the best-preserved Roman Theater *(Théâtre Antique)* in existence. Information panels in English describe many aspects of the theater. Find a seat up high to appreciate the acoustics and contemplate the idea that, 2,000 years ago, Orange residents enjoyed grand spectacles with high-tech sound and light effects, such as thunder, lightning, and rain. A huge awning could be unfurled from that awesome 40-meter-high (130 feet) stage wall to provide shade that you might appreciate now. It still seats 10,000 (€4.60, daily April–Sept 9:00–18:30, Oct–March 9:00–12:00 & 13:30–17:00). Your ticket includes entrance to the city museum across the street, which has a few interesting renderings of the theater but no English explanations.

Orange has two helpful **TIs**, one that drivers will park near, and another across from the Roman Theater (tel. 04 90 34 70 88). Drivers simply follow *Centre-ville* signs, then *Théâtre Antique* signs, and park in the big lot near the TI. Trains run hourly between Avignon and Orange (15 min). From Orange's train station, it's a 15-minute walk to the theater (follow signs to *Centre-ville*, then *Théâtre Antique*, and if you can't find it, ask a local, "*Où est la Théâtre Antique?*", pron. oo-ay lah tay-ah-truh ahn-teek).

Buses to Vaison la Romaine and other wine villages depart from the big square, place Pourtoules (turn right out of the Roman Theater and right again on rue Pourtoules).

▲Mont Ventoux and Lavender—This sight is worth **▲▲** from late June to early August, when the lavender blooms. Go only if it's clear and you can see the top of this 1,800-meter/6,000-foot, barren, wind-blown mountain; prepare for much cooler temperatures. Mont Ventoux is Provence's rooftop. You're above the tree line amid wildflowers, butterflies, and views extending from the lower Alps across what seems like all of southern France. Near the old observatory and Air Force control tower, **Le Vendran** restaurant offers jaw-dropping views. Thirty minutes east, lavender fields forever surround the village of Sault (pron. so), which produces 40 percent of France's lavender essence. To reach Mont Ventoux, go to Malaucene, then take the twisty D-974. If continuing to Sault (also worthwhile only when the lavender blooms), take D-974, then D-164. Pick up a "Les routes de la Lavande" brochure at Sault's TI for driving and walking routes in the area (TI tel. 04 90 64 01 21). Route maps can also be downloaded at www.routes-lavande.com.

▲**Ardèche Gorges**—A 45-minute drive west of Vaison la Romaine, abrupt chalky-white cliffs follow the Ardèche River through immense canyons and thick forests. From Vaison, go to Bollene then follow the villages of Pont St. Esprit to Vallon Pont d'Arc (which offers all-day canoe-kayak floats through the gorge). If continuing north, connect Privas and Aubenas, then head back to the autoroute. Adorable Balazuc, a village north of the gorges, makes a fine stop.

NOT QUITE A YEAR IN PROVENCE: THE HILL TOWNS OF LUBERON

The Luberon region, stretching 50 kilometers along a ridge of rugged hills east of Avignon, hides some of France's most appealing and popular hill towns (including Bonnieux, Lacoste, Oppède le Vieux, Roussillon, Joucas, and Gordes).

Those intrigued by Peter Mayle's *A Year in Provence* will enjoy a day joyriding through the region. Mayle's best-selling book describes the ruddy local culture from an Englishman's perspective, as he buys a stone farmhouse, fixes it up, and adopts the region as his new home. This is a great read while you're here.

The Luberon terrain in general (much of which is a French regional natural park) is as appealing as its hill towns. Gnarled vineyards and wind-sculpted trees separate tidy stone structures from abandoned buildings—little more than rock piles—that seem to challenge city slickers to fix them up.

The wind is an integral part of life here. The infamous mistral, finishing its long ride in from Siberia, hits like a hammer—hard enough, it's said, to blow the ears off a donkey. Throughout the region you'll see houses designed with windowless walls facing the mistral.

Planning Your Time

To enjoy the windblown ambience of the Luberon, plan a leisurely day trip visiting three or four of the characteristic towns (impossible *sans* car). Isle sur la Sorgue, located halfway between Avignon and the Luberon, has train service from Avignon (easy day trip) and Nice (via Marseille) and makes a good biking base.

Luberon

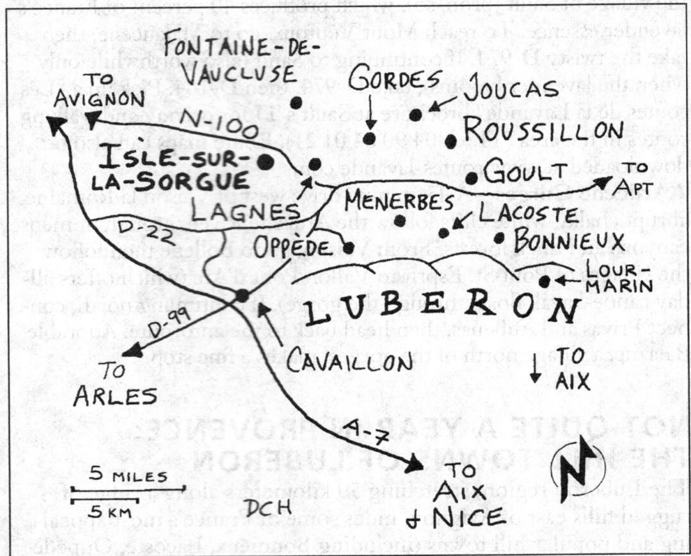

For the ultimate Luberon experience, hill-town connoisseurs with cars should bypass Isle sur la Sorgue and sleep in one of the villages described below. The famous villages are beautiful, but attract tourists like flypaper. For a quieter overnight, sleep in Oppède le Vieux, Joucas, or Lacoste. You'll pass *Chambres d'hôte* everywhere (TIs have long lists)—many are pricey and lovingly restored by foreigners.

Getting around the Luberon

By Bus: To reach the hill towns such as Roussillon, go to Cavaillon or Apt, then taxi (1 bus/day from Avignon to Gordes, 2 buses/day from Cavaillon to Gordes, bus tel. 04 90 71 03 00).

By Train: Trains get you as far as Isle sur la Sorgue from Avignon (6/day, 30 min) or from Nice (4/day, 4 hrs, transfer in Marseille). Isle sur la Sorgue's train station is called L'Isle Fontaine de Vaucluse.

By Car: Town-hop for a day, side-tripping from your home base, or visit these villages as a detour en route to the French Riviera. Of course, tumbling in for an hour from the parking lot, you'll be just another flash-in-the-pan, camera-toting Provence fan. Spend a night, and you'll feel more a part of the scene. You need Michelin #246 to follow this scenic loop: Take the N-100 east of Avignon toward Apt and find little Lagnes just after Isle sur la Sorgue. Go through Lagnes, then Cabrieres d'Avignon, Gordes, Goult, and Roussillon. From Roussillon, follow Bonnieux and cross the Roman pont Julien, then find Lacoste, Menerbes, and, to complete the loop, Oppède le Vieux. I've listed places to sleep and eat in several of these villages (see below).

ISLE SUR LA SORGUE

This sturdy market town, literally, "Island on the Sorgue River," sits within a split in its crisp, happy little river and makes a good base for exploring the Luberon and Avignon. Do not confuse it with the nearby plain town of Sorgue. And don't underestimate the importance of this river to the region's economy. The fresh spring water of the many branches of the Sorgue (that divide in Isle sur la Sorgue) have for a long time provided nourishment for crops and power for key industries. While Isle sur la Sorgue is renowned for its market days, it is otherwise a pleasantly average town with no important sights and a steady trickle of tourism. It's calm at night and downright dead on Mondays.

Isle sur la Sorgue has crystal-clear water babbling under pedestrian bridges lined with flower boxes, and its old-time carousel is always spinning. The town erupts into a market frenzy each Sunday and Thursday, with hardy crafts and local produce (Sun market is astounding and famous for its antiques; Thu market is more intimate).

Navigate the town by its mossy waterwheels, which, while still turning, power only memories of the town's wool and silk industries. The 12th-century church with a festive Baroque interior seems too big for the town.

Tourist Information: The **TI**, next door to the church, has a line on rooms in private homes, all of which are outside the town (Tue–Sat 9:00–12:30 & 14:00–18:00, Sun 9:00–12:30, closed Mon, tel. 04 90 38 04 78). Ask where you can rent a bike. These places make good biking destinations: Velleron (8 km/5 miles away, flat, a tiny version of Isle sur la Sorgue, with waterwheels, fountains, and an evening farmer's market held Mon–Sat 18:00–20:00), Lagnes (5 km away, mostly flat, a pretty, well-restored hill town with views from its ruined château), and Fontaine de Vaucluse (11 km away, uphill, see "More Luberon Towns," below). A launderette is on l'Impasse de la République (open 8:00–20:00).

Sleeping in and near Isle sur la Sorgue

(€1 = about $1, country code: 33, zip code: 84800)

Arrive the night before market day to best experience the town.

MODERATELY PRICED

Hôtel les Nevons**, two blocks from the center (behind the PTT—post office), is motel-modern outside. Inside, however, it seems to do everything right, with comfortable, air-conditioned rooms (a few family suites), small rooftop pool, Internet access, and eager-to-please owners, Mireille and Jean-Philipe (Db-€60, exrta person-€16, includes breakfast, CC, easy and secure parking-€7.75, 205 Chemin des Nevons, tel. 04 90 20 72 00, fax 04 90 20 56 20, www.hotel-les-nevons.com).

Loy Soloy Restaurant/Hôtel is the prow of the ship at the split of the river, with the best view rooms in town (rooms 1, 2, 3, and 7 have the views, reasonable comfort, and road noise, Db-€63, CC, 2 avenue Charles de Gaulle, tel. & fax 04 90 38 03 16).

LOWER PRICED

The bargain beds in town are sufficiently clean and almost quiet, above a local bar at **Hôtel Le Cours de l'Eau** (D-€21, Db-€33, CC, on ring road opposite Café de la Sorgue at place Gambetta, tel. 04 90 38 01 18, no fax, NSE).

Eating in and near Isle sur la Sorgue

Begin your dinner with a glass of wine at the cozy **Le Caveau de la Tour de l'Isle** (part wine bar, part wine shop, open until about 20:00, 12 rue de la République). **L'Oustau de l'Isle** is well-suited for a fine dinner (*menus* from €21, closed Wed–Thu off-season, 21 avenue des 4 Otages, near post office, tel. 04 90 38 54 83). The riverfront cafés, **Café de la Sorgue** and the better **Café de Bellevue**, offer credible cuisine with riverside ambience. The **Fromenterie** bakery next to the PTT sells really rich quiches.

ROUSSILLON

With all the trendy charm of Santa Fe on a hilltop, this town will cost you at least a roll of film (and €2 for parking). Climb a few minutes from either parking lot, past the picture-perfect square and under the church to the summit of the town (follow signs to *Castum*), where a dramatic view, complete with a howling mistral and a helpful *table d'orientation*, awaits. Then, back under the church, see how local (or artsy) you can look in what must be the most scenic village square in the Luberon. On the south end of town, beyond the upper parking lot, a brilliant ochre canyon—formerly a quarry—is busy with walkers and explains the color of this village (€1.50). You could paint the entire town without ever leaving the red and orange corner of your palette. Many do. While Roussillon receives its share of day-trippers, evenings are romantically peaceful. Thursday is Roussillon's market day. Every day is Christmas for thieves—take everything out of your car.

Sleeping in Roussillon
(€1 = about $1, country code: 33, zip code: 84220)

The **TI**, across from the David restaurant, posts a list of hotels and *chambres d'hôte* (April–Oct Mon–Sat 9:30–12:00 & 13:30–18:30, Sun 14:00–18:30, Nov–March Mon–Sat 13:30–17:30, closed Sun, tel. 04 90 05 60 25). For additional hotel and restaurant listings, see "More Luberon Towns," below.

MODERATELY PRICED

Hôtel Reves d'Ocres**, the only hotel in the town center, is run by charming Sandrine and laid-back Web, with reasonably comfortable, spacious rooms—the best have view terraces (Db-€61, Tb-€76, balcony room about €8 extra, CC, air-con turned on at the desk, route de Gordes, tel. 04 90 05 60 50, fax 04 90 05 79 74).

LOWER PRICED

Madame Cherel rents simple but clean rooms with firm mattresses and a common view terrace (D-€32–35, no CC, 3 blocks from upper parking lot, between gas station and school, La Burlière, tel. 04 90 05 68 47). Cherel speaks English, is a wealth of regional travel tips, and rents mountain bikes to guests only (€15/day).

Sleeping near Roussillon

For drivers only, the next three listings are most easily found by turning north off N-100 at the Roussillon/Les Huguets sign:

MODERATELY PRICED

Les Puches *chambre d'hôte* offers smart rooms with terraces and a pool that glissades over the edge (Db-€61–69, no CC, 2 km/1.25 miles below Roussillon toward Bonnieux on D-104, just past Hôtel Les Sables d'Ocre, tel. & fax 04 90 05 66 02).

LOWER PRICED

Les Passiflores *chambre d'hôte*, on D-108 between Roussillon and Bonnieux in Les Huguets, is everything a *chambre d'hôte* should be: rustic, charming, comfortable, and owned by the delightful Chantal (Db-€46–50, includes breakfast, ask if she'll cook you dinner-€18 for the works, no CC, tel. & fax 04 90 05 69 61, NSE).

Hôtel Les Sables d'Ocre** is modern and kid-friendly, with good rooms, a big pool, lots of grass, and fair rates (Db-€53, Db with garden balcony-€60–69, extra bed-€10, CC, 1 km after leaving Roussillon toward Apt at intersection of D-108 and D-104, tel. 04 90 05 55 55, fax 04 90 05 55 50, e-mail: sablesdocre@free.fr).

Eating in Roussillon

Le Piquebaure hangs on a cliff and is the best bet in town for a fine meal (€20 *menus*, €12 garnished *plats du jour*, below Hôtel Reves d'Ocres, route du Gordes, closed Mon off-season, tel. 04 90 05 79 65).

Inside the village, **Le Bistrot de Roussillon** is center-stage on the square with view tables in the rear (€23 *menu*, closed Thu, tel. 04 90 05 74 45). **Aux Agapes,** just off the main square, does a good wood-fired pizza for €8 (if you like peppers, try their *salade Agapes*).

More Luberon Towns

Fontaine de Vaucluse—You'll read and hear a lot about this sublimely located village at the source of the river Sorgue, where the medieval Italian poet Petrarch mourned for his love, Laura. This beautiful river seems to magically appear from nowhere (the actual source is a murky green water hole) and flows through Fontaine de Vaucluse, past a lineup of cafés, souvenir shops, and enough tourists to make Disney envious. Arrive by 9:00 or after 19:00, or skip it.

Gordes—This is the most touristy and trendy town in the Luberon. Parisian big shots love it. Once a virtual ghost town of derelict buildings, it's now completely fixed up and filled by people who live in a world without calluses. The view as you approach is incredible and merits a detour, though the village has little of interest. The nearby and still-functioning 12th-century **Abbey de Senanque** can be crowded but is splendidly situated and worth a visit. When the lavender blooms (late June–July) this is a ▲▲▲ sight (€4.60, Mon–Sat 10:00–12:00 & 14:00–18:00, Sun 14:00–18:00, arrive early to beat crowds).

Joucas—This village is everything Gordes is not: understated, quiet, and overlooked. Tiny cobbled lanes and well-restored homes play host to artists and a smattering of locals.

At **La Maison de Mistral**, gregarious Marie-Lucie Mistral (they named the wind after her) has five oh-so-cozy rooms in her *chambre d'hôte*, with a breakfast terrace to linger over and access to a nearby pool (Db-€53, extra person-€15.25, includes breakfast, no CC, rue de l'Eglise, tel. 04 90 05 74 01, cellular 06 62 08 15 03, fax 04 90 05 67 04, e-mail: pmistral@free.fr).

Lacoste—Slumbering under its ruined castle, tiny, steep, and quiet-at-night Lacoste has great views of the picturesque town of Bonnieux (listed below). Tuesday is market day here.

Café de Sade is spotless, with six rooms above a little restaurant (D-€32, Db-€46, family room-€61, dorm beds-€11.50, no CC, for dorm only, bring your own sheet or pay €3.80 to rent one, tel. 04 90 75 82 29, fax 04 90 75 95 68). For a country-elegant dinner, **Le Relais du Procureur** is worth the detour (€20 *menu*, closed Tue, tel. 04 90 75 84 78).

Bonnieux—Spectacular from a distance, this town disappoints up close. It lacks a pedestrian center, though the Friday morning market briefly creates one.

Oppède le Vieux—This is a windy barnacle of a town, with a few boutiques and a dusty main square at the base of a short, ankle-twisting climb to a ruined church and castle. The Luberon views justify the effort. This way-off-the-beaten-path fixer-upper of a village must be how Gordes looked before it became chic. It's ideal for those looking to perish in Provence.

Goult—Bigger than its sister hill towns, this surprisingly quiet town seems content away from the tourist path. Wander up the hill to the panorama and windmill, and review its restaurants, where you won't compete with tourists for a table.

CASSIS

Cowering in the shadow of impossibly high cliffs, Cassis (pron. kah-see) is an unpretentious beach town offering travelers a sunny time-out from their busy vacation. Two hours away from the fray of the Côtes d'Azur, Cassis is a poor man's St. Tropez. Outdoor cafés line the small port on three sides, where boaters chat up café clients while cleaning their boats. Cassis is popular with the French and close enough to Marseille to be busy on weekends and all summer. Come to Cassis for true bouillabaisse, to swim in crystal-clear water, and to scour its fjord-like *calanques*. Cassis is too far from Nice for day-tripping.

Orientation

The Massif du Puget encloses Cassis on three of its four sides. The Cap Canaille cliff with the castle (property of the Michelin family) rises from the southeast. All roads spill into the port, and drivers should park at one of the well-signed pay lots above the port to avoid parking purgatory. The train station is three kilometers/two miles from Cassis, buses connect with most trains, and taxis cost about €9 with bags.

Tourist Information: The **TI** is on the port and can answer your every question from scuba diving to kayak rental, and help you find a room (May–Sept daily 9:00–18:00, Oct–April Mon–Sat 9:00–12:30 & 13:30–17:30, Sun 10:00–12:30, quai des Moulins, tel. 04 42 01 71 17, www.cassis.enprovence.com).

Helpful Hints

The **shops** drop in price the farther you get from the port.

A terrific **launderette/Internet café** is up rue Victor Hugo at 9 rue Authemann (daily 9:00–21:00). Here, you can do your laundry (or they'll do it for you while you sightsee), check your e-mail, and buy phone cards.

Sights—Cassis

Beaches—Cassis' beaches are a sand/pebble mix. You can walk 15 minutes to plage du Bestouan and rent cushy mats, or find a sandy spot at the beach just south of the port.

▲▲*Calanques*—Cassis is all about *les Calanques* (pron. luh cah-lahnk). That's why most come here—but until you see them, it's hard to understand what all the excitement is about. The splintered, pasty-white rocks create fjord-like inlets, with translucent blue water and intimate beaches. Most *calanques* are prickly extensions of cliffs that border the shore, but some rise directly out of the Mediterranean. You can cruise by boat, kayak, or hike to several *calanques*.

Boats will take you to any combination of 10 *calanques*, providing a water-based perspective (3 *calanques*-€10.50, 2/hr, 45 min; 5 *calanques*-€12.50, 2/day, 65 min; 10 *calanques*-€20, 1/day, 2 hrs). The three-*calanques* tour seems best. Buy tickets at the small booth on the south side of the port where boats depart.

Trails allow hiking/riding to three of the *calanques*. If you plan to spend time at a *calanque*, do so at Calanque d'En Vau; a boat provides direct round-trip service (2/hr, €11.50, one-way tickets available). Boats can drop you on a cliff if the sea is calm (short jump), but it's a steep, treacherous hike down to the beach for inexperienced climbers, and an even more difficult hike back up (you'll pay a surcharge to get off unless you buy a one-way ticket, and boats are often reluctant to let you off, so make sure they understand you want to get off at Calanque d'En Vau before buying your ticket). Hiking from Cassis to Calanque d'En Vau is a safer option, though you must get a map from the TI to follow the correct route. Avoid the shoreline route that requires rappelling skills; take the inland route and you'll do fine (some enjoy taking the boat there and hiking back). The TI has complete information on hiking and boating to the *calanques*. Bring water, sunscreen, and everything you need for the day, as there are no shops.

▲La Route des Cretes—Those with cars or a willingness to hire a taxi (€25 for a good 45-min trip, 4 people per taxi) can consider this amazing drive, straight up to the top of Cap Canaille to the industrial town of La Ciotat. Acrophobics should skip this narrow, twisty road that provides numbingly high views over Cassis and the

Cassis

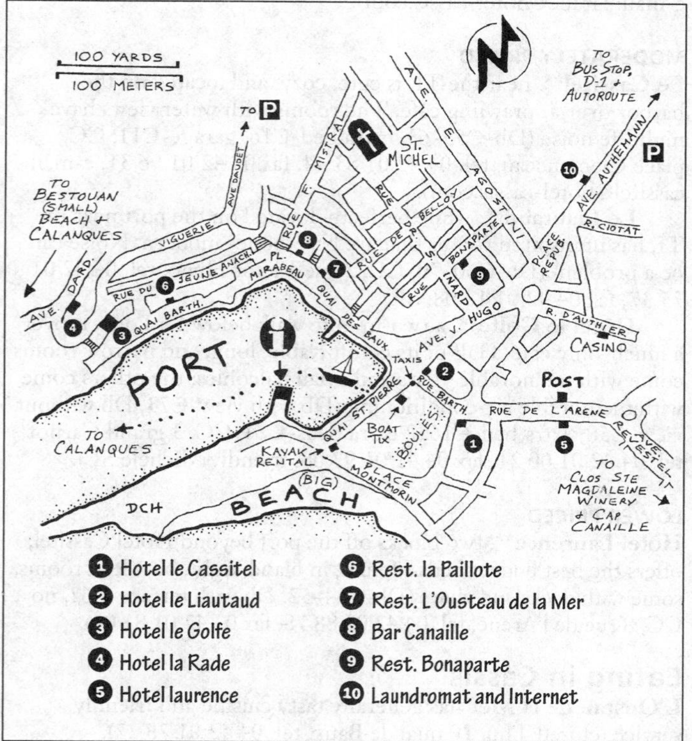

Mediterranean at every turn. From Cassis, follow signs to La Ciotat/Toulon, then *la Route des Cretes*. Drive as far as you like; it's about 45 minutes all the way to La Ciotat.

Sleeping in Cassis

(€1 = about $1, country code: 33, zip code: 13260)

Hotels are a bargain compared with those on the Côte d'Azur. Note that many close from November to March, and most come with late-night noise on weekends and in summer.

HIGHER PRICED

La Rade***, on the quieter northwest corner of the port, has great views from its teak poolside chairs. It offers small but adequate rooms with air-conditioning and a busy road below (Db-€105–115, apartments-€160–170, CC, route des Calanques, tel. 04 42 01 02 97, fax 04 42 01 01 32, www.hotel-cassis.com, e-mail: larade@hotel-cassis.com).

MODERATELY PRICED

Le Cassitel**, near the TI, is cute, cozy, and located on the harbor over a sprawling café. The rooms with water views have nightlife noise (Db-€53–63, extra bed-€16, garage-€11, CC, place Clemenceau, tel. 04 42 01 83 44, fax 04 42 01 96 31, e-mail: cassitel@hotel-cassis.com).

Le Liautaud**, while perfectly located on the port near the TI, has uninspired rooms that are bare-bones modern. Noise can be a problem (Db-€60–70, CC, 2 rue Victor Hugo, tel. 04 42 01 75 37, fax 04 42 01 12 08, SE).

Hôtel le Golfe**, a two-minute walk below La Rade, is over a lunch-only café. Half of its comfortable, long, and narrow rooms come with memorable views and small balconies; the others come with memorable air-conditioning (Db with view-€73, Db without view-€58, extra bed-€16, 2 extra beds-€24, CC, 3 grand Carnot, tel. 04 42 01 00 21, fax 04 42 01 92 08, friendly Michele SE).

LOWER PRICED

Hôtel Laurence**, two blocks off the port beyond Hôtel Cassitel, offers the best budget beds I found, in bland, tight, but clean rooms, some with decks and views (Db-€34–52, Db with terrace-€62, no CC, 8 rue de l'Arene, tel. 04 42 01 88 78, fax 04 42 01 81 04).

Eating in Cassis

L'Oustau de la Mer has generally tasty cuisine and friendly service (closed Thu, 20 quai de Baux, tel. 04 42 01 78 22).

La Paillote sits on the harbor, with fair prices given its location and generally good food (stick to seafood dishes, closed Sun–Mon, quai J-J Barthelemy, tel. 04 42 01 72 14).

Bar Canaille is a casual, lunch-only place that has fabulously fresh seafood. It's tucked away in the corner of the port; look for the bright yellow awning (22 quai des Baux, tel. 04 42 01 72 36).

Bonaparte is off the harbor and cheaper (14 rue du General Bonaparte, closed Sun–Mon, tel. 04 42 01 80 84).

Transportation Connections—Cassis

While the station is three kilometers/two miles from the port, shuttle buses meet most trains, and taxis are reasonable.

By train to: Arles (7/day, 2 hrs, change in Marseille), **Avignon** (7/day, 2 hrs, change in Marseille), **Nice** (7/day, 3 hrs, change in Toulon or Marseille), **Paris** (7/day, 4 hrs, change in Marseille).

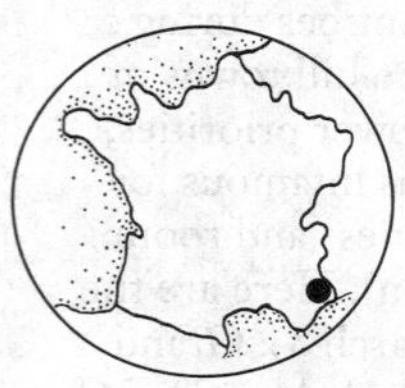

THE FRENCH RIVIERA

A hundred years ago, celebrities from London to Moscow flocked here to socialize, gamble, and escape the dreary weather at home. The belle époque is today's tourist craze, as this most sought-after, fun-in-the-sun destination now caters to budget travelers as well. Some of the Continent's most stunning scenery and intriguing museums lie along this strip of land—as do millions of heat-seeking tourists. Nice has world-class museums, a grand beachfront promenade, a seductive old town, and all the drawbacks of a major city (traffic, crime, pollution, etc.). But the day trips possible from Nice are easy and brilliant: Monte Carlo welcomes everyone with cash registers open, Antibes has a romantic port and silky-sandy beaches, and the hill towns present a breezy and photogenic alternative to the beach scene. Evenings on the Riviera, a.k.a. the Côte d'Azur, were made for a promenade and outdoor dining.

Choose a Home Base

I've focused my accommodations listings on three different places: Nice, Antibes, and Villefranche-sur-Mer. **Nice** is the region's capital and France's fifth-largest city. With excellent public transportation to most regional sights, this is the Riviera's most practical base for train travelers. Urban Nice also has a full palette of museums and rock-hard beaches, the best selection of hotels in all price ranges, and a thriving nightlife. A car is a headache in Nice. Nearby **Antibes** is smaller, with fewer hotels but fine sandy beaches, good hiking, and the Picasso Museum. It has frequent train service to Nice and Monaco, and is easier for drivers. **Villefranche-sur-Mer** is the romantic's choice, with a serene setting and small-town warmth. It has finely ground pebble beaches, good public transportation (particularly to Nice and Monaco), and easy parking. Its few hotels leap from simple to sublime, letting Nice handle the middle ground.

Planning Your Time

Most should plan a full day for Nice and at least a half day each for Monaco and Antibes. Monaco is best at night (sights are closed but crowds are few; consider dinner here), and Antibes during the day (good beaches and Picasso Museum). The hill towns of St. Paul-de-Vence, Vence, and Eze Village are lower priorities, particularly if you don't have a car. The Riviera is infamous for staging major events—it's best to avoid the craziness and room shortage if you can (unless, of course, you're a fan). Here are the three biggies in 2003: Nice Carnival (Feb 21–March 5); Grand Prix of Monaco (May 23–26); Cannes Film Festival (May 21–26).

Getting around the Riviera

Getting around the Côte d'Azur by train or bus is easy (park your car and leave the driving to others). Drivers who want to see some of the Riviera's best scenery should follow the coast road between Cannes and Fréjus (when arriving in or leaving the Côte d'Azur), take the short drive along *Moyenne Corniche* from Nice to Eze Village, and take my recommended hill-town drive to the Gorges du Loup.

Nice is perfectly located for exploring the region. Monaco, Eze Village, Villefranche, Antibes, St. Paul, and Cannes are all a 15- to 60-minute bus or train ride apart from each other. The TI (and probably your hotel) has information on minivan excursions from Nice (half day-about €60, full day-€76–107; Tour Azur is one of many, tel. 04 93 44 88 77, www.tourazur.com).

Bus service can be cheaper and more frequent than rail service, depending on the destination. At Nice's efficient bus station *(gare routière)* on boulevard J. Jaures (see map of Nice on page 382), you'll find a baggage check (called *messagerie*, available Mon–Sat 7:30–18:00), clean WCs for €0.50, and several bus companies offering free return trips to some destinations (keep your ticket). Get schedules and prices from the helpful English-speaking clerk at the information desk in the bus station (tel. 04 93 85 61 61). Buy tickets in the station or on the bus.

Here's an overview of public transport options to key Riviera destinations from Nice (rt = round-trip, ow = one-way):

Destination	Bus	Train
Monaco	4/hr, 40 min, €3.80, r/t	2/hr, 20 min, €3.40, o/w
Villefranche	4/hr, 15 min, €1.70, r/t	2/hr, 10 min, €1.50, o/w
Antibes	3/hr, 50 min, €4.20, o/w	2/hr, 25 min, €3.80, o/w

The French Riviera

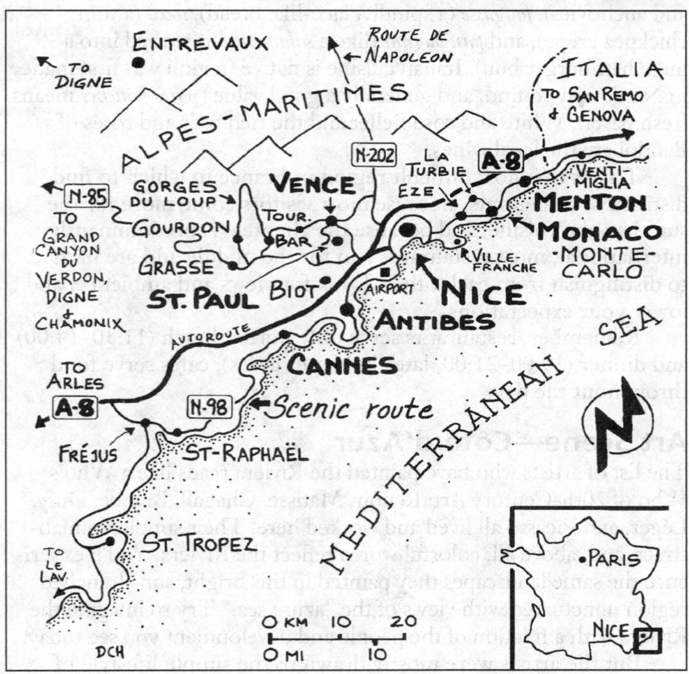

Destination	Bus	Train
Cannes	way too long	2/hr, 30 min, €4.90, o/w
St. Paul	2/hr, 45 min, €3, o/w	none
Vence	2/hr, 45 min, €4.60, o/w	none
Eze Village	every 2 hrs, 25 min, €2.50, r/t	none
La Turbie	5/day, 45 min, €2.90, r/t	none

Two bus companies, RCA and Cars Broch, provide service on the same route between Nice, Villefranche, and Monaco; RCA's buses run more frequently.

Cuisine Scene—Côte d'Azur

The Côte d'Azur (technically a part of Provence) gives Provence's cuisine a Mediterranean flair. Local specialties are bouillabaisse (the spicy seafood stew-soup that seems worth the cost only for those with a seafood fetish), *bourride* (a creamy fish soup thickened with aioli, a garlic sauce), and *salade niçoise* (pron. nee-swaz; a tomato, potato, olive, anchovy, and tuna salad). You'll also find these tasty bread treats: *pissaladière* (bread dough topped with onions, olives, and anchovies), *fougasse* (a spindly, lace-like bread), *socca* (a thin chickpea crêpe), and *pan bagnat* (like a *salade niçoise* stuffed into a huge hamburger bun). Italian cuisine is native (ravioli was first made in Nice), easy to find, and generally a good value (*pâtes fraîches* means fresh pasta). White and rosé Bellet and the rich reds and rosés of Bandol are the local wines.

This is the most difficult region in France in which to find distinctive restaurants. Because most visitors come more for the sun than the cuisine, and because the clientele is predominantly international, most restaurants aim for the middle and are hard to distinguish from each other. Look for views and ambience, and lower your expectations.

Remember, restaurants serve only during lunch (11:30–14:00) and dinner (19:00–21:00, later in bigger cities); cafés serve food throughout the day.

Art Scene—Côte d'Azur

The list of artists who have painted the Riviera reads like a Who's Who of 20th-Century Art: Renoir, Matisse, Chagall, Braque, Dufy, Léger, and Picasso all lived and worked here. Their simple, semiabstract, and, above all, colorful works reflect the Riviera. You'll experience the same landscapes they painted in this bright, sun-drenched region punctuated with views of the "azure sea." Try to imagine the Riviera with a fraction of the people and development you see today.

But the artists were mostly drawn to the simple lifestyle of fishermen and farmers that has reigned here since time began. These *très* serious artists, as they grew older, retired in the sun and turned their backs on modern art's "isms", instead painting with the wide-eyed wonder of children, using bright primary colors, simple outlines, and simple subjects.

A terrific concentration of well-organized contemporary art museums (many described below) litter the Riviera, allowing art-lovers to appreciate these artists' works while immersed in the same sun and culture that inspired them. Many of the museums were designed to blend the art with surrounding views, gardens, and fountains, highlighting that modern art is not only stimulating, but sometimes simply beautiful.

NICE

Nice (pron. neece) is the ultimate tourist melting pot. You'll share its international beaches with the chicest of the chic, the cheapest of the cheap, and everyone else in this scramble to be where the mountains meet the water. Nice's spectacular Alps-to-Mediterranean surroundings, eternally entertaining seafront promenade, and fine museums make settling into this big city relatively painless. And in Nice's traffic-free old city, Italian and French flavors mix to create a spicy Mediterranean dressing. Nice may be nice, but it's hot and jammed in July and August (reserve ahead). Get a room with air-conditioning *(une chambre avec climatization)*. Everything you'll want in Nice is walkable or a short bus ride away.

Orientation

Most sights and hotels recommended in this book are located near the avenue Jean Médecin, between the train station and the beach. It's a 20-minute walk from the train station to the beach (or a €9 taxi ride), and a 20-minute walk along the promenade from the fancy Hôtel Negresco to the heart of Old Nice.

Tourist Information: Nice has four helpful TIs: at terminal 1 at the airport (Mon–Sat 8:00–22:00, Sun 8:00–20:00); next to the train station (Mon–Sat 8:00–20:00, Sun 9:00–18:00); on RN-7 after the airport on the right (summers only, 8:00–20:00); and across from the beach at 5 promenade des Anglais (Mon–Sat 8:00–20:00, Sun 9:00–18:00). All can book rooms for a small fee, tel. 08 92 70 74 07, www.nicetourisme.com). Pick up the excellent, free Nice map (which lists all the sights and hours), the extensive *Practical Guide to Nice*, information on regional day trips (such as maps to Antibes), and the museums booklet.

Consider buying the **museum pass**. The regional *Carte Musées* is a great value for those planning to visit more than one museum in a day or several museums over a few days (€8/1 day, €15/3 consecutive days, €24/7 consecutive days, valid at all museums described in this chapter except Foundation Maeght, sold at any TI or participating museum).

Arrival in Nice

By Train: Nice has one main station (*Nice-Ville*, lockers available) where all trains stop and you get off. Avoid the suburban stations, and never leave your bags unattended. The TI is next door to the left as you exit the train station; car rental and taxis are to the right. To reach most of my recommended hotels, turn left out of the station, then right on avenue Jean Médecin. To get to the beach and the promenade des Anglais from the station, continue on foot for 20 minutes down avenue Jean Médecin or take bus #12 (stop on Jean Médecin). To get to the old city and the bus station *(gare routière)*, catch bus #5 from avenue Jean Médecin.

By Car: Follow Nice Centre/Promenade des Anglais whether arriving from east, west, or north and try to avoid arriving at rush hour, when the promenade des Anglais grinds to a halt (Mon–Fri 17:00–19:30). Ask your hotel for advice on where to park (allow €9–14/day). The parking garage at the Nice Etoile shopping center on avenue Jean Médecin is handy to many of my hotel listings (ticket booth on third floor, about €14/day, €8 20:00–8:00). All on-street parking is metered.

By Plane: Nice's mellow, user-friendly airport is on the Mediterranean, about 20 minutes west of the city center. The TI and international flights use terminal 1; domestic flights use terminal 2 (airport tel. 04 93 21 30 30). At terminal 1, you'll find the TI, banks (so-so rates), ATM, and car rental just outside customs. Taxis wait immediately outside the terminal (allow €25–30 to Nice hotels, €45 to Villefranche). Turn left after passing customs and exit the doors at the far end to find the bus information office (taxi vouchers to Villefranche and other non-Nice destinations sold here). Three bus lines run from the airport to Nice: #99 runs nonstop to the main train station (stall #1, €3.50, 2/hr until 21:00, 20 min, drops you within a 10-min walk of many of my hotel listings), local bus #23 (stall #6, €1.40, 4/hr, 40 min, direction: St. Maurice, serves stops between the airport and SNCF station), and the yellow "NICE" bus to the bus station (*gare routière*, stall #1, €3.50, 3/hr, 25 min). Buy tickets in the office or from the driver. To get to Villefranche from the airport, take the yellow "NICE" bus to the bus station *(gare routière)* and transfer to the Villefranche bus (€1.40, 4/hr). Buses also run from the airport to Antibes (1/hr, 20 min, €7), and to Monaco (1/hr, 50 min, €14).

Helpful Hints

Theft Alert: Nice is notorious for pickpockets. Have nothing important on or around your waist, unless it's in a money belt tucked out of sight (no fanny packs, please); don't leave anything visible in your car; be wary of scooters when standing at intersections; don't leave things unattended on the beach while swimming; and stick to main streets in Old Nice after dark.

Museums: Most Nice museums are closed Tuesdays, and free the first Sunday of the month. For information on the museum pass, see "Tourist Information," above.

U.S. Consulate: If you lose your passport, this is the place to go (7 avenue Gustave V, tel. 04 93 88 89 55, fax 04 93 87 07 38).

Medical Help: Riviera Medical Services has a list of English-speaking physicians. They can help you make an appointment or call an ambulance (tel. 04 93 26 12 70).

Rocky Beaches: To make life tolerable on the rocks, swimmers should buy a pair of the cheap plastic beach shoes (flip-flops fall off in the water) sold at many shops.

American Express: AmEx faces the beach at 11 promenade des Anglais (tel. 04 93 16 53 53).

English Bookstore: Try **The Cat's Whiskers** (closed Sun, 26 rue Lamartine, near Hôtel Star).

Laundry: Self-serve launderettes abound in Nice; ask your hotelier for suggestions and guard your load.

Internet Access: It's easy in Nice. Ask your hotelier for the nearest Internet café.

English Radio: Tune into Riviera-Radio at FM 106.5 for English radio.

Getting around Nice

Bus fare is €1.40 and an all-day pass is €4, though walking gets you to most places.

Taxis allow four passengers in Nice and are handy to Chagall and Matisse museums. They normally only pick up at taxi stands *(tête de station)* or by a telephoned request. You'll pay €1 per bag and supplements for service on Sunday and after 19:00 any day (tel. 04 93 13 78 78).

Sights—Nice

▲▲Promenade des Anglais—Welcome to the Riviera. There's something for everyone along this seven-kilometer-long (4 miles) seafront circus. Watch the Europeans at play, admire the azure Mediterranean, anchor yourself in a blue chair, and prop your feet up on the made-to-order guardrail. Join the evening parade of tans along the promenade. Start at the pink-domed Hôtel Negresco and, like the belle époque (late-19th-century) English aristocrats for whom the promenade was built, stroll to the old town and Castle Hill (20-min walk).

Hôtel Negresco, Nice's finest hotel and a historic monument, offers the city's most costly beds and a free "museum" interior (reasonable attire is necessary to enter). March straight through the lobby into the exquisite Salon Royal. The czar's chandelier hangs from an Eiffel-built dome. Read the explanation, check out the room photos, and stroll the circle. On your way out, pop into the Salon Louis XIV (more explanations).

The next block to your left as you exit has a lush park and the Masséna Museum (closed until 2004). The TI is beyond that. Cross over to the seaside promenade.

Pull up a chair and admire the scene. *La Baie des Anges* (Bay of Angels) is named for the arrival of Nice's patron saint, Réparate, who supposedly was escorted into this bay by angels in the fourth century. To your right is the airport, built on a landfill, and, on that tip of land way out there, Cap d'Antibes. Until 1860, Antibes and Nice were in different countries; the Italians (of Savoy-Piedmont) gave Nice to the French as thanks for their

Nice

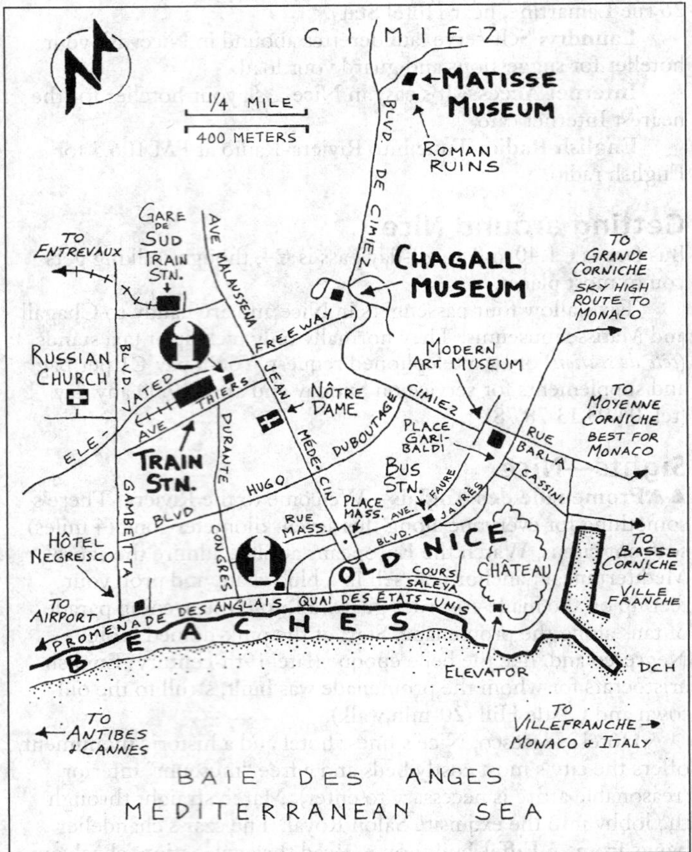

help during the reunification of Italy in 1860. To the far left lies Villefranche-sur-Mer (beyond that tower at land's end), Monaco, then Italy. Behind you are the pre-Alps (les Alpes Maritimes), which gather threatening clouds and leave the Côte d'Azur to enjoy the sunshine more than 300 days a year. The broad sidewalks of the promenade des Anglais (literally, Walkway of the English) were financed by wealthy English tourists who wanted a "safe" place to stroll and admire the view. By 1787, there was already sufficient tourism in Nice to justify its first casino (a leisure activity imported from Venice). In fact, an elegant casino stood on pilings in the sea until the Germans destroyed it during World War II.

Turn around. To the right of Hôtel Negresco sit two other belle époque establishments: the West End and Westminster hotels. These hotels represent Nice's arrival as a tourist mecca 100 years ago, when the combination of leisure time and a stable economy allowed tourists to find the sun even in winter. Tourism as we know it today took off after World War II (blame planes, trains, and automobiles), allowing even budget travelers to appreciate this once-exclusive resort. Now get down to that beach.

Beaches—Nice is where the jet set relax *à la plage*. After settling into the smooth pebbles, you can play beach volleyball, table tennis, or *boules;* rent paddleboats, personal watercraft, or windsurfing equipment; explore ways to use your zoom lens as a telescope; or snooze on comfy beach beds with end tables (mattress-€9, mattress and chaise lounge-€11, umbrella-€4.60). Have lunch in your bathing suit (€9 salads and pizzas). Before heading off in search of sandy beaches, try it on the rocks. As you stroll the promenade, look for the *Plage Publique* signs explaining the 15 beach no-nos (translated in English).

Nice in the Buff: A Walk through Old Nice (Vieux Nice)

This walk, worth ▲▲, is best done early in the morning. Allow an hour, with a stop for coffee and *socca* (chickpea crêpe), and use the free city map, focusing on the enlargement of Vieux Nice. We'll begin our tour on place Massena, at the end of avenue Jean Médecin nearest the sea.

1. Place Massena: Walk to the fountains and face them. You're standing on Nice's most important river, the Paillon (it was covered in the 1800s). Turn around. You can track the river's route under the green parkway as it makes its way to the sea at the Meridien hotel. For centuries, this river was Nice's border, and natural defense. A fortified wall ran along its length to the sea. It wasn't until the arrival of tourism in the 1800s that Nice expanded over and beyond the river. The rich red coloring of the buildings around you was the preference of Nice's Italian rulers.

Cross the square and drop into old Nice by following the steps that lead to rue de l'Opera between the curved buildings. Turn left on rue St. François de Paule.

2. Rue St. François de Paule: You've entered old Nice. Peer into the Alziari olive oil shop at #14. Dating from 1868, it produces what many claim is the world's best olive oil. Wander in and fill your own container from the vats. A block down on the left (#7), Patisserie Auer's belle époque storefront has changed little since the pastry shop opened in 1820. The writing on the window says "For over 170 years from father to son." Ask about the tastings and demonstrations in the *degustatión* room. Behind you is Nice's just-renovated grand opera house, from the same era.

Sift your way through souvenirs to the cours Saleya (pron. sah-lay-yuh).

3. Cours Saleya: Named for its broad exposure to the sun (*soleil*, pron. soh-lay), this cacophony of color, sights, smells, and people is the belly of old Nice and has been its main market square since the Middle Ages. Today, it collects people, produce, and flowers as if it's a trough between city and sea (produce market held daily except Mon until 13:00, an antique market takes over the square on Mon). Amazingly, cars could be parked here until 1980, when the mayor of Nice had an underground parking garage built and returned this square to walkers and shoppers. Thread the needle through the center. The first section is devoted to freshly cut flowers that seem to grow effortlessly and everywhere in this ideal climate. Continue to the first produce stand (Le Grand Bleu restaurant should be on your right). Facing you is Thérèse (pron. tear-ehz), self-proclaimed Queen of the Market. Listen for her sing-song sales pitch, buy some berries, and say, "*Bonjour, Madame la Reine du Marché.*"

You can climb the steps past trash sacks above the Grand Bleu restaurant for a good market view, or position yourself in front of the steps. From your perch, look up to the hill that dominates to the east. The city of Nice was first settled there by Greeks in about 500 B.C. In the Middle Ages, a massive castle stood up there, with turrets, high walls, and soldiers at the ready. With the river guarding one side and the sea the other, this mountain fortress was invincible—at least until Louis XIV leveled it in 1706. Nice's medieval seawall ran along the lineup of two-story buildings you're standing along. Now, look across cours Saleya to the large "palace." This was the Ducal Palace (called La Prefecture today), where the kings of Savoy-Piedmont (Nice's Italian rulers in the 1700s and 1800s) would reside when in Nice. Resume your stroll down the center of cours Saleya and stop when you see La Cambuse restaurant on your left. Hovering over the black barrel with the paella-like pan on top is another Theresa. She's cooking *socca*, Nice's chickpea crêpe specialty. Spring for a paper wad of *socca* (careful, it's hot, but good).

Continue down cours Saleya. That fine golden building at the end of the cours is where Henri Matisse lived for 17 years (on the second floor). Turn left at the Civette du Cours café, and find rue de la Poissonerie.

4. Rue de la Poissonerie: Stop at #4. Look up. Adam and Eve are squaring off, each holding a zucchini-like gourd. This scene represents the annual rapprochement in Nice to make up for the sins of a too-much-fun Carnival (Mardi Gras). Nice residents have partied hard during Carnival for over 700 years. The iron grill above the door allows cooling air to enter the building, but keeps out uninvited guests. You'll see lots of these open grills in old Nice. They were part of an ingenious system of sucking cool air in from the sea up, through the homes and out roof vents. Across the street, check out the small church dedicated to St. Rita, the patron saint of desperate causes. She holds a special place in locals' hearts, and this church is Nice's most popular. Baroque was the fashion (thank the Italians).

Turn right on the next street, then left on "Right" Street (rue Droite).

5. Rue Droite: In the Middle Ages, this straight, skinny street provided the most direct route from wall to wall, or river to sea, and today makes me feel like I've been beamed to Naples. Stop at Esipuno's bakery (#38). Thirty years ago, this baker was voted the best in France, and his son now runs the place. Notice the firewood stacked by the oven. Farther along at #28, the *socca*-seller's husband makes the *socca* in the wood-fired oven, then carts it to her barrel on cours Saleya. The balconies of the mansion in the next block announce the Palais Lascaris (1647), a rare souvenir from one of Nice's most prestigious families (not worth touring, but you can admire the entry).

Turn left on the rue des Loges, then left again on rue Centrale to reach our next stop, on place Rossetti.

6. Place Rossetti: The most Italian of Nice's piazzas, place Rossetti feels more like Rome than Nice. This square comes alive after dark. Don't miss the gelato at Fennochio's, but skip the lousy restaurants. Walk to the fountain and stare back at the church. This is Nice's cathedral of St. Réparate, an unassuming building for a major city's cathedral. The cathedral was relocated here in the 1500s, when Castle Hill (see below) was temporarily converted to a military-only function. The name comes from Nice's patron saint, a teenage virgin named Réparate whose martyred body was floated to Nice in the fourth century, accompanied by angels. Enter and you'll find a Baroque bonanza as wide as it is deep. Back outside the cathedral, the steps leading up rue Rossetti are the most direct path from here to Castle Hill (15 min straight up, consider the elevator on quai des Etats Unis).

7. Castle Hill (Colline du Château)—Climb or, better yet, take the elevator up this saddle horn in the otherwise flat city center for the view (elevator is next to Hôtel Suisse where bayfront road curves right, €0.70 one-way, €1 round-trip). The views over Nice, the port (to the east), the Alps foothills, and the Mediterranean make a good reward, better if you took the elevator, best at sunset or whenever it is really clear (park closes at 20:00 in summer, earlier off-season). Until the 1100s, the city of Nice was crammed on this hilltop, as it was too risky to live in the flatlands below. Today, you'll find a waterfall, a playground, two cafés (fair prices), and a cemetery, but no castle on Castle Hill. To walk down to the old town, follow signs from just below the upper café to *Vielle Ville* (not *le Port*), and turn right at the cemetery, then look for the walkway down on your left.

Museums—Nice

▲▲Musée National Marc Chagall—Even if you're suspicious of modern art, this museum—with the largest collection of Chagall's work anywhere—might appeal to you. After World War II, Chagall returned from the United States to settle in nearby Vence. Between 1954 and 1967, he painted a cycle of 17 large murals designed for, and donated to, this museum. These paintings, inspired by the books of Genesis, Exodus, and the Song of Songs, make up the "nave," or core, of what Chagall called the "House of Brotherhood."

Each painting is a lighter-than-air collage of images drawing from Chagall's Russian-folk-village youth, his Jewish heritage, biblical themes, and his feeling that he existed somewhere between heaven and earth. He felt the Bible was a synonym for nature, and color and biblical themes were key ingredients for understanding God's love for his creation. Chagall's brilliant blues and reds celebrate nature, as do his spiritual and folk themes. Notice the focus on couples. To Chagall, humans loving each other mirrored God's love of creation.

Don't miss the stained-glass windows of the auditorium (enter through the garden), early family photos of the artist, and a room full of Chagall lithographs. The small €3 guidebook begins with an introduction by Chagall (€5.50, Wed–Mon 10:00–17:00, until 18:00 July–Aug, closed Tue, ask about English tours, tel. 04 93 53 87 31). An idyllic café awaits in the garden.

Getting to Chagall and Matisse Museums: The Chagall Museum is a confusing but manageable 15-minute walk from the top of avenue Jean Médecin and the train station; the Matisse Museum (described below) is a 30-minute uphill walk from the Chagall Museum, though free bus service between the two is provided on line #15 (buses stop a block from Chagall on boulevard de Cimiez heading uphill). Buses #15 and #17 serve Chagall and Matisse from the eastern, Italy side of avenue Jean Médecin (both run 6/hr, €1.40). Consider walking to Chagall and taking the free bus to Matisse.

To walk to the Chagall Museum, go to the train-station end of avenue Jean Médecin and turn right onto rue Raimbaldi along the overpasses, then turn left under the overpasses onto avenue Comboul. Once under the overpass, angle to the right up rue

Olivetto to the alley with the big wall on your right. A pedestrian path soon emerges, leading up and up to signs for Chagall and Matisse. The bus to Matisse is on avenue Cimiez, two blocks up from Chagall.

▲**Musée Matisse** (▲▲▲ for his fans)—The art is beautifully displayed in this elegant (but unfortunately not air-conditioned) orange mansion and represents the single largest collection of Matisse paintings. While many don't get Matisse, this museum offers a painless introduction to this influential artist whose style was shaped by the southern light and by fellow Côte d'Azur artists, Picasso and Renoir. Watch as his style becomes simpler with time. A room on the top floor has models of his famous Chapelle du Rosaire in nearby Vence and illustrates the beauty of his simple design (€3.80, April–Sept Wed–Mon 10:00–18:00, Oct–March 10:00–17:00, closed Tue, ask about English tours, take bus #15 or #17 to Arènes stop, see directions under Chagall Museum listing above, tel. 04 93 81 08 08).

Modern Art Museum (Musée d'Art Moderne et d'Art Contemporain)—This ultramodern museum features an enjoyable collection of art from the 1960s and 1970s, including works by Andy Warhol and Roy Lichtenstein, and offers frequent special exhibits (€3.80, Wed–Mon 10:00–18:00, closed Tue, on promenade des Arts near bus station, tel. 04 93 62 61 62).

Other Nice Museums—These museums offer decent rainy-day options (generally open Tue–Sun 10:00–12:00 & 14:00–18:00, closed Mon). The **Fine Arts Museum** (Musée des Beaux Arts), with 6,000 works from the 17th to 20th centuries, will satisfy your need for a fine-arts fix (€3.80, 3 avenue des Baumettes, in western end of Nice, tel. 04 92 15 28 28). The **Naval Museum** (Musée de la Marine) is interesting and relevant (closed Mon–Tue, €2.50, in Tour Bellanda, halfway up Castle Hill, tel. 04 93 80 47 61). Nice's city museum, **Museum Masséna** (Musée Masséna), is closed until 2004. The **Archaeological Museum** (Musée Archeologique) displays Roman ruins and various objects from the Romans' occupation of this region (€3.80, near Matisse Museum at 160 avenue des Arenes, tel. 04 93 81 59 57).

▲**Russian Cathedral (Cathedrale Russe)**—Even if you've been to Russia, this Russian Orthodox church—which claims to be the finest outside Russia—is interesting. Its one-room interior is filled with icons and candles. In 1912, Czar Nicholas II gave this church to his aristocratic country folk, who wintered on the Riviera. (A few years later, Russian comrades who didn't winter on the Riviera shot him.) Here in the land of olives and anchovies, these proud onion domes seem odd. But, I imagine, so did those old Russians (€1.85, daily 9:00–12:00 & 14:30–18:00, services Sat at 18:00,

Sun at 10:00, no shorts, 10-min walk behind station at 17 boulevard du Tsarevitch, tel. 04 93 96 88 02).

Nightlife

Nice's bars play host to the Riviera's most happening late-night scene, full of jazz and rock 'n' roll. Most activity focuses on old Nice, near place Rossetti. Plan on a cover charge or expensive drinks. If you're out very late, avoid walking alone.

Between Nice and Monaco

▲▲▲The Three Cornices—Nice and Monaco are linked with three coast-hugging routes, all offering sensational views and a different perspective on this billion-dollar slice of real estate. The *Basse Corniche* (the Lower Cornice, often called *Corniche Inférieure*) strings ports, beaches, and villages together for a traffic-filled ground-floor view. The *Moyenne Corniche* (Middle Cornice) is higher, quieter, and far more impressive. It runs through Eze Village and provides great views over the Mediterranean with several scenic pullouts (the pullout above Villefranche-sur-Mer is best). Napoleon's crowning road-construction achievement, the *Grande Corniche* (Great Cornice), caps the cliffs with staggering views from almost 480 meters/1,600 feet above the sea. For the best of all worlds, take the *Moyenne Corniche* from Nice to Eze Village, find the *Grande Corniche/La Turbie* from there, and drop down to Monaco after La Turbie (see "Sights near Villefranche-sur-Mer," below). Buses travel each route; the higher the cornice, the less frequent the buses (get details at Nice's bus station).

Sleeping in Nice

(€1 = about $1, country code: 33, zip code: 06000)

Sleep Code: **S** = Single, **D** = Double/Twin, **T** = Triple, **Q** = Quad, **b** = bathroom, **s** = shower only, **CC** = Credit Cards accepted, **no CC** = Credit Cards not accepted, **SE** = Speaks English, **NSE** = No English, * = French hotel rating (0–4 stars). Hotels have elevators unless otherwise noted.

To help you sort easily through these listings, I've divided the rooms into three categories based on the price for a standard double room with bath:

Higher Priced—Most rooms more than €100.
Moderately Priced—Most rooms €100 or less.
Lower Priced—Most rooms €65 or less.

Don't look for charm in Nice. Go for modern and clean with a central location and, in summer, air-conditioning. Reserve early for summer visits. Prices generally drop €5–10 from October to April (the rates listed are for May–Sept) and increase during

Nice Hotels and Restaurants

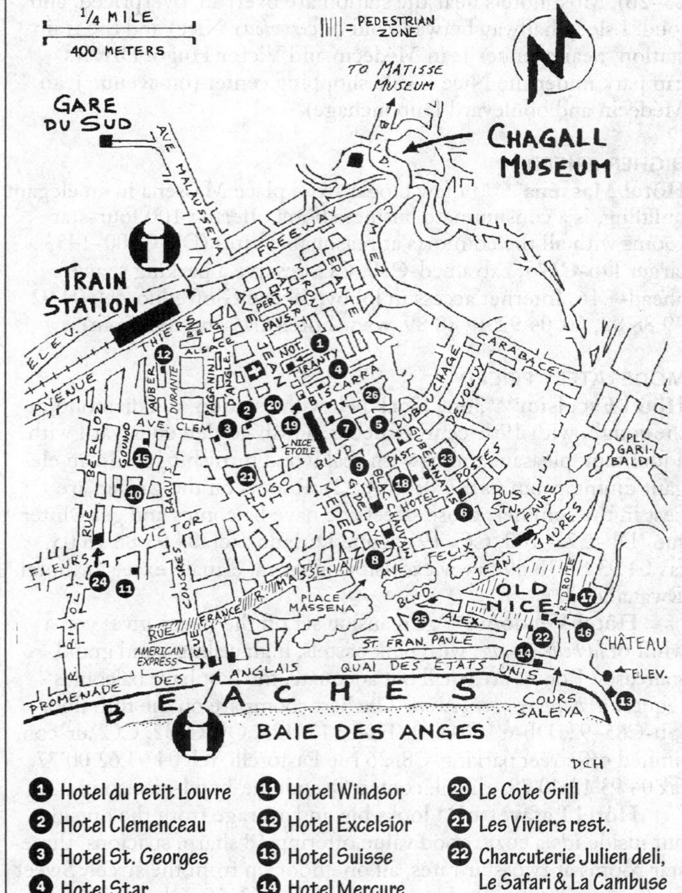

1. Hotel du Petit Louvre
2. Hotel Clemenceau
3. Hotel St. Georges
4. Hotel Star
5. Hotel Vendome
6. Hotel Lorrain
7. Hotel les Camelias
8. Hotel Massena
9. Hotel Lafayette
10. Hotel Oasis
11. Hotel Windsor
12. Hotel Excelsior
13. Hotel Suisse
14. Hotel Mercure
15. Hotel Trianon
16. Nissa Socca café
17. Acchiardo's rest.
18. Lulu's Cantine
19. L'Authentic, Le Vin sur Vin, & Le Cenac rest.
20. Le Cote Grill
21. Les Viviers rest.
22. Charcuterie Julien deli, Le Safari & La Cambuse restaurants
23. La Part des Anges rest.
24. Hotels Splendid & Gounod
25. L'Únivers restaurant
26. Lou Mourleco Rest.

Carnival (Feb 21–March 5) and the Monaco Grand Prix (May 23–26). Most hotels near the station are overrun, overpriced, and loud. I sleep halfway between old Nice (*vieux* Nice) and the train station, near avenues Jean Médecin and Victor Hugo. Drivers can park under the Nice Etoile shopping center (on avenue Jean Médecin and boulevard Dubouchage).

HIGHER PRICED

Hôtel Masséna****, a few blocks from place Masséna in an elegant building, is a consummate business hotel offering 100 four-star rooms with all the comforts at reasonable rates (Db-€100–145, larger Db-€175, extra bed-€30, CC, reserve a parking space ahead-€16, Internet access in lobby, 58 rue Giofreddo, tel. 04 92 49 88 88, fax 04 92 49 88 89, www.hotel-massena-nice.com).

MODERATELY PRICED

Hôtel Excelsior***, one block below the station, is a diamond in the rough, with 19th-century decor, a lush garden courtyard with a fountain, pleasant rooms with real wood furnishings, and an elegant dining room (*menus* from €22). Rooms on the garden are best in the summer; those streetside have balconies and get winter sun (Db-€72–100, CC, 19 avenue Durante, tel. 04 93 88 18 05, fax 04 93 88 38 69, www.excelsiornice.com, e-mail: excelsior.hotel@wanadoo.fr).

Hôtel Vendome***, a mansion set off the street, gives you a whiff of *la belle époque*, with pink pastels, high ceilings, and grand staircases. Rooms are small but adequate; the best have balconies—request a *chambre avec balcon*. The best rooms are on the fifth floor (Sb-€85–92, Db-€100–110, Tb-€113–122, Qb-€132, CC, air-con, limited off-street parking-€8, 26 rue Pastorelli, tel. 04 93 62 00 77, fax 04 93 13 40 78, e-mail: contact@vendome-hotel-nice.com).

Hôtel Lafayette*** looks big and average from the outside, but inside it's a cozy, good value offering 18 sharp, spacious, three-star rooms at two-star rates, all one floor up from the street. Sweet Sandrine will take good care of you (Sb-€62–79, Db standard-€70–79, Db spacious-€84–98, extra bed-€18, CC, no elevator, meek air-con, 32 rue de l'Hôtel des Postes, tel. 04 93 85 17 84, fax 04 93 80 47 56, e-mail: lafayette@nouvel-hotel.com).

Hôtel Mercure***, on the water behind cours Saleya, offers predictable, modern rooms at good rates, considering the location (Sb-€84, Db-€94, CC, air-con, some balconies and views, 91 quai des Etats Unis, tel. 04 93 85 74 19, fax 04 93 13 90 94, e-mail: h0962@accor-hotels.com).

Hôtel Suisse*** has Nice's best ocean views for the money, with many balconied rooms. Rooms are comfortable, with air-conditioning and modern conveniences, and are surprisingly quiet given the busy street below (skip Db without view-€74, take Db with great view-€95–115, extra bed-€20, CC, 15 quai Rauba-Capeu, tel. 04 92 17 39 00, fax 04 93 85 30 70, e-mail: hotelsuisse.nice@wanadoo.fr).

LOWER PRICED

Hôtel Trianon,** with formal owners, is a small, big-city refuge with good rates and bright, spotless rooms, half of which overlook a small park (Db-€45–60, CC, 15 avenue Auber, tel. 04 93 88 30 69, fax 04 93 88 11 35).

Hôtel du Petit Louvre* is basic, but a solid budget bet, with playful owners (the Vilas), art-festooned walls, and adequate rooms (Ds-€37, Db-€41, Tb-€43–50, CC, payment due on arrival, 10 rue Emma Tiranty, tel. 04 93 80 15 54, fax 04 93 62 45 08, e-mail: petilouvr@aol.com).

Hôtel Clemenceau** is a good value with a homey, family feel and mostly spacious, traditional, and well-cared-for rooms, some with balconies, some without closets, all air-conditioned (S-€31, Sb-€43, D-€43, Db-€46, Tb-€69, Qb-€84, kitchenette-€8 extra and for long stays only, CC, no elevator, 3 avenue Clemenceau, 1 block west of avenue Jean Médecin, tel. 04 93 88 61 19, fax 04 93 16 88 96, e-mail: hotel-clemenceau@wanadoo.fr, Marianne SE).

Hôtel St. Georges**, a block away, is big and bright, with air-conditioning, a backyard garden, reasonably clean and comfortable rooms, and happy Jacques at the reception (Sb-€55, Db-€65, 3-bed Tb-€82, extra bed-€16, CC, 7 avenue Clemenceau, tel. 04 93 88 79 21, fax 04 93 16 22 85, e-mail: nicefrance.hotelstgeorges@wanadoo.fr).

Hôtel Star**, a few blocks east of avenue Jean Médecin, is immaculate, air-conditioned, comfortable, and a truly great value. It's run by intense Françoise, who expects you to respect her high standards (Sb-€35–45, Db-€45–60, Tb-€60–75, CC, fine beds, beach towels, no elevator, 14 rue Biscarra, reserve by fax or e-mail rather than by phone, tel. 04 93 85 19 03, fax 04 93 13 04 23, www.hotel-star.com, e-mail: star-hotel@wanadoo.fr).

Hôtel les Camelias** reminds me of the Old World places I stayed in as a kid traveling with my parents. A well-located, dark, creaky, and floral place burrowed behind a small parking lot and garden, it has linoleum halls, simple rooms, lumpy beds, and a loyal clientele who give the TV lounge a retirement-home-after-dinner feeling. Some rooms have balconies—request a *chambre avec balcon* (Ss-€41, Ds-€48, Db-€63, includes breakfast, parking-€5, CC, 3 rue Spitaleri, tel. 04 93 62 15 54, fax 04 93 80 42 96, formal Madame Vimont and her son Jean Claude SE). The €11 four-course dinner is simple, hearty, and stress-free.

Hôtel Lorrain** offers kitchenettes in all of its modern, linoleum-floored, and spacious rooms and is conveniently located one block from the bus station and old Nice (Db-€42–46, Tb-€68–78, Qb-€78–111, CC, 6 rue Gubernatis, push top buzzer to release door, tel. 04 93 85 42 90, fax 04 93 85 55 54, e-mail: hotellorrain@aol.com).

Hotels near Boulevard Victor Hugo

The next four hotels are on or very near this tree-lined boulevard, several blocks west of avenue Jean Médecin and about five blocks from the beach.

HIGHER PRICED

Hôtel Windsor***, a snazzy, airy, garden retreat with contemporary rooms designed by modern artists, has a swimming pool, free gym, and €10 sauna (Db-€100–130, extra bed-€20, rooms over garden worth the higher price, CC, 11 rue Dalpozzo, 10 blocks west of Jean Médecin and 5 blocks from sea, tel. 04 93 88 59 35, fax 04 93 88 94 57, www.hotelwindsornice.com).

Hôtel Splendid**** is a worthwhile splurge if you miss your Hilton. The rooftop pool, Jacuzzi, and panoramic breakfast room alone almost justify the cost—throw in luxurious rooms, a free gym, Internet access, and air-conditioning, and you're as good as home (Db-€195, deluxe Db with terrace-€240, suites-€320, limited parking-€16, CC, 50 boulevard Victor Hugo, tel. 04 93 16 41 00, fax 04 93 16 42 70, www.splendid-nice.com).

Hôtel Gounod***, behind Hôtel Splendid, shares the same owners, allowing its clients free access to Hôtel Splendid's pool, Jacuzzi, and other amenities. Don't let the lackluster lobby fool you. Its fine rooms are spacious, air-conditioned, and richly decorated, with high ceilings (Db-€90–130, palatial 4-person suites-€190, parking €11–16, CC, 3 rue Gounod, tel. 04 93 16 42 00, fax 04 93 88 23 84, www.gounod-nice.com).

MODERATELY PRICED

Hôtel l'Oasis*** is just that, a surprising oasis of calm, set back from the street surrounding a large courtyard. Rooms are also calming, with air-conditioning, earth tones, pleasing fabrics, sharp bathrooms, and reasonable rates. Madame Le Cam and her dog, Fever, manage this well-run hotel with style (Sb-€64, Db-€74–86, Tb-€86–106, CC, 23 rue Gounod, tel. 04 93 88 12 29, fax 04 93 16 14 40, www.hotel-oasis-nice.com.fr).

Eating in Nice

My recommended restaurants are concentrated in the same neighborhoods as my recommended hotels. The promenade des Anglais is ideal for picnic dinners on warm, languid evenings, and the old town is perfect for restaurant-shopping. Wherever you dine, save room for gelati at Fenocchio's on place Rossetti in old Nice (86 flavors from tomato to lavender), and don't miss the evening parade along the Mediterranean (best view at night is from the east end of the quai des Etats Unis on the tip below Castle Hill).

Nice's dinner scene focuses on cours Saleya, which is as entertaining as the food is average. It's a fun, festive place to compare tans and mussels. Comparison-shopping is half the fun. **La Cambuse** is the lone exception, offering a more refined setting and fine cuisine for a bit more (allow €40, 5 cours Saleya, tel. 04 93 80 82 40), though **Le Safari** is the best of the rest and less (at the Castle Hill end, 1 cours Saleya, tel. 04 93 80 18 44).

Charcuterie Julien is a good deli that sells an impressive array of dishes by weight. Buy 200 grams of your choice, plopped into a plastic carton to go (*pour emporter*, pron. poor ahn-por-tay) or eat there (Thu–Tue 11:00–19:30, closed Wed, on cours Saleya at rue de la Poissonnerie).

Nissa Socca offers good, cheap Italian cuisine a few blocks from cours Saleya in a lively atmosphere (opens at 19:00, closed Sun, arrive early, a block off place Rossetti on rue Ste. Répararte, tel. 04 93 80 18 35).

Deeper in the old city, **Acchiardo's** is a budget traveler's best friend, with simple, hearty food at bargain prices and no fluff (closed Sat–Sun, 38 rue Droite, tel. 04 93 85 51 16).

The simple wood benches of **Lou Pilha Leva** offer a fun, *très* cheap dinner option with Niçoise specialties; order your food on one side and drinks from the other (located where rue des Loges and Centrale meet in old Nice).

The extreme opposite, **L'Univers** is the proud owner of a Michelin star. This Riviera-elegant place is as relaxed as a "top" restaurant can be, from its casual decor to the tasteful dinnerware (*menus* from €35, 53 boulevard Jean Juares, tel. 04 93 62 32 22, e-mail: plumailunivers@aol.com).

These restaurants lie closer to most of the recommended hotels. For the most authentic Niçoise cuisine in this book, reserve a table at the *charmant* and well-run **Bistrot Les Viviers** (allow €35 for dinner, closed Sun, 22 rue Alphonse Karr, 5-min walk west of avenue Jean Médecin, tel. 04 93 16 00 48, make sure to reserve for the *bistrot*, not their classier restaurant next door). **Lulu's Cantine** is a fine value, wonderfully small, charming, and

Czech-owned, with homemade recipes from Nice to Prague (26 rue Alberti, tel. 04 93 62 15 33). Wine-lovers will swoon for a table at **La Part des Anges**, a wine shop with a few tables in the rear serving a limited, mouthwatering menu with a large selection of wines (open daily for lunch, Fri–Sat only for dinner, reserve ahead, 17 rue Gubernatis, tel. 04 93 62 69 80).

Several relaxed cafés line the broad sidewalk on rue Biscarra, just east of avenue Jean Médecin behind Nice Etoile. **L'Authentic**, **Le Vin sur Vin**, and **Le Cenac** are all reasonable, though L'Authentic is best. One block away, friendly **Lou Mourleco** insists on serving only what's fresh, so the menu changes constantly at this more traditional Niçoise establishment (15 rue Biscarra, tel. 04 93 80 80 11). On the other side of avenue Jean Médecin, **Le Côte Grill** is bright, cool, and easy, with a salad bar, air-conditioned rooms, a large selection at reasonable prices, and a friendly staff (1 avenue Georges Clemenceau, tel. 04 93 82 45 53).

Transportation Connections—Nice

By train to: Arles (11/day, 3.5 hrs, 10 with change in Marseille), **Paris'** Gare de Lyon (14/day, 5.5–7 hrs, 6 with change in Marseille), **Venice** (3/day, 3/night, 11–15 hrs, 5 require changes), **Chamonix** (4/day, 11 hrs, 2–3 changes), **Beaune** (7/day, 7 hrs, change in Lyon), **Digne/Grenoble** (consider the scenic little trains that run from Nice to Digne, then on to Grenoble), **Munich** (2/day, 12 hrs with 2 changes, 1 night train with a change in Verona), **Interlaken** (1/day, 12 hrs), **Florence** (4/day, 7 hrs, changes in Pisa and/or Genoa, night train), **Milan** (4/day, 5–6 hrs, 3 with changes), **Venice** (4/day, 8 hrs, 2 changes required or a direct night train), **Barcelona** (3/day, 11 hrs, long change in Montpellier, or a direct night train).

By plane to: Paris (hrly, 1 hr, about same price as train ticket).

VILLEFRANCHE-SUR-MER

Come here for upscale, small-town Mediterranean atmosphere. Villefranche (between Nice and Monte Carlo, with frequent 15-min buses and trains to both) is quieter and more exotic than Nice. Narrow cobbled streets stumble into the mellow waterfront, a scenic walkway below the castle leads to the hidden port, and luxury yachts glisten in the harbor. Almost-sandy beaches, a handful of interesting sights, and quick access to Cap Ferrat keep visitors just busy enough.

The **TI** is in the park François Binon, just below the main bus stop (July–Aug daily 9:00–19:00, Sept–June Mon–Sat 9:00–12:00 & 14:00–18:30, closed Sun, a 20-min walk or €8 taxi from train station, tel. 04 93 01 73 68). Pick up the brochure detailing a self-guided walking tour of Villefranche and information on boat

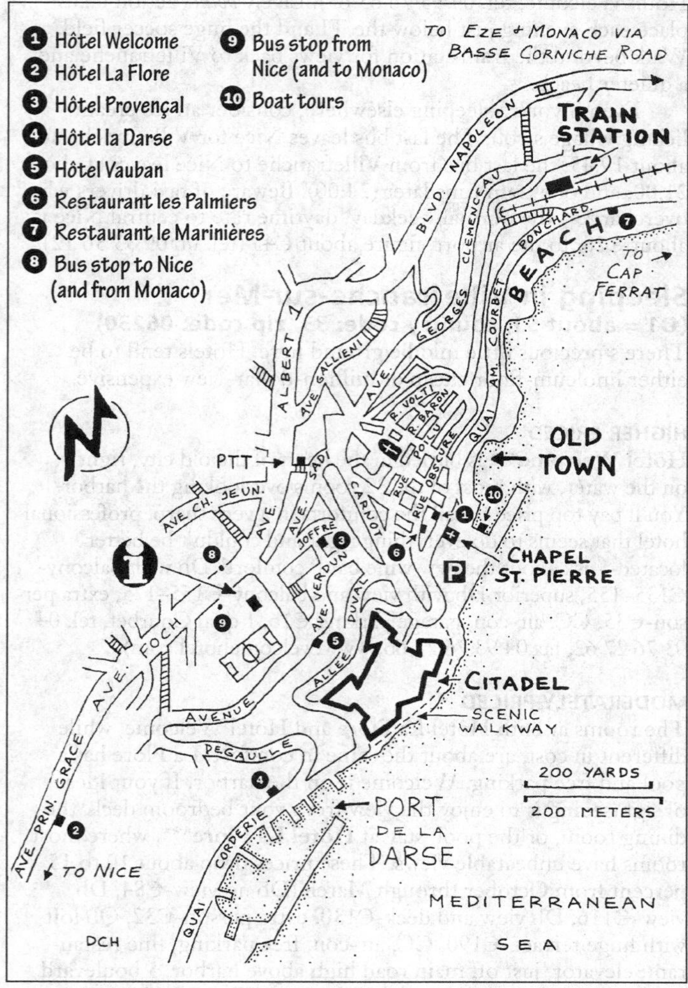

rides and the Rothschild Villa Ephrussi's gardens (see "Sights near Villefranche-sur-Mer," below).

The dramatic interior of **Chapel of St. Pierre**, decorated by Jean Cocteau, is the town's cultural highlight, but at €2 it's not worth it for many (daily 10:00–12:00 & 15:00–19:00, below Hôtel Welcome). **Boat rides** *(promenades en mer)* are offered several days a week (June–mid-Sept, €12, 2 hrs, across from Hôtel Welcome, tel. 04 93 76 65 65). Lively *boules* action takes place each evening just below the TI and the huge soccer field. Walk beyond the train station for views back to Villefranche and a quieter beach.

Even if you're sleeping elsewhere, consider an ice cream–licking village stroll. The last bus leaves Nice for Villefranche at about 19:45; the last bus from Villefranche to Nice leaves at about 21:00; and one train runs later (24:00). Beware of taxi drivers who overcharge—the normal weekday, daytime rate to central Nice is about €28; to the airport, figure about €45 (tel. 06 09 33 36 12).

Sleeping in Villefranche-sur-Mer

(€1 = about $1, country code: 33, zip code: 06230)

There's precious little middle ground here. Hotels tend to be either linoleum-floor cheap or million-dollar-view expensive.

HIGHER PRICED

Hôtel Welcome*** is buried in the heart of the old city, right on the water, with most of the 32 rooms overlooking the harbor. You'll pay top price for all the comforts in a very sharp, professional hotel that seems to do everything right and couldn't be better located—ask about the new wine bar ("comfort" Db with balcony-€135–155, superior Db with view and balcony-€155–175, extra person-€35, CC, air-con, garage parking €16, 1 quai Courbet, tel. 04 93 76 27 62, fax 04 93 76 27 66, www.welcomehotel.com).

MODERATELY PRICED

The rooms at both Hôtel La Flore and Hôtel Welcome, while different in cost, are about the same in comfort. La Flore has a pool and free parking, Welcome is on the harbor. If your idea of sightseeing is to enjoy the view from your bedroom deck, the dining room, or the pool, stay at **Hôtel La Flore*****, where most rooms have unbeatable views. These prices drop about 10 to 15 percent from October through March (Db no view-€84, Db view-€116, Db view and deck-€130, extra person-€32, Qb loft with huge terrace-€190, CC, air-con, free parking, fine restaurant, elevator, just off main road high above harbor, 5 boulevard Princess Grace de Monaco, 2 blocks from TI toward Nice, tel. 04 93 76 30 30, fax 04 93 76 99 99, www.hotel-la-flore.fr, e-mail: hotel-la-flore@wanadoo.fr, SE).

Hôtel Provençal** needs a facelift, but offers air-conditioning, fine views, and nifty balconies from well-worn rooms with awful furniture (Db-€63–92, Tb-€73–85, extra bed-€9, 10 percent off with this book and a 2-night stay, CC, skip cheaper no-view rooms, a block from TI at 4 avenue Maréchal Joffre, tel. 04 93 76 53 53, fax 04 93 76 96 00, e-mail: provencal@riviera.fr).

LOWER PRICED

Hôtel la Darse**, an appealing and unassuming little hotel sitting in the shadow of its highbrow brothers, offers a low-key alternative right on the water in Villefranche's old port. The rooms are quiet and simple, though the owners have big plans to renovate the hotel and add an elevator. Rooms facing the sea have great view balconies (Db-€47–55, Db view-€58–68, extra person-€10, CC, from TI walk or drive down avenue General de Gaulle to the old Port de la Darse, tel. 04 93 01 72 54, fax 04 93 01 84 37, e-mail: hoteldeladarse@wanadoo.fr, friendly Paola SE).

Hôtel Vauban*, two blocks down from the TI, is a curious and basic place with homey, red-velvet decor, and a few cheery, simple rooms (Db-€45, Db with view-€65, no CC, 11 avenue General De Gaulle, tel. 04 93 76 62 18, no fax, e-what?, NSE).

Eating in Villefranche-sur-Mer

Pickings are slim in this land of high rollers. The places lining the port are expensive and vary in quality; less expensive places are off the port. For a relaxed dinner (pizza, crêpes, and salads), try **Les Palmiers**, just above Hôtel Welcome. To eat well, spring for dinner at **Hôtel La Flore** (allow €28–46, see "Sleeping in Villefranche-sur-Mer," above). For a cool view and good-enough food at reasonable prices, consider **Restaurant les Marinières,** on the beach below the train station (salads and à la carte, open daily, tel. 04 93 01 76 06).

Sights near Villefranche-sur-Mer

Cap Ferrat—This is the peninsula you're staring at across the bay from Villefranche. An exclusive, largely residential community, it's just off the Nice–Monaco route and receives less traffic than other towns. Drive, bus, or walk here from Villefranche to visit the extravagant gardens of **Rothschild Villa Ephrussi**, offering stunning views east to Villefranche and west toward Monaco. You will see seven lush, varied gardens and several lavishly decorated rooms (€8, €2.50 for English tours generally between 11:00 and 14:00, Feb–Oct daily 10:00–18:00, until 19:00 in July–Aug, Nov–Jan Mon–Fri 14:00–18:00, Sat–Sun 10:00–18:00, tel. 04 93 01 45 90). From Villefranche, it's a scenic 50-minute walk around the bay past the train station or 10 minutes by bus #111. A few kilometers beyond sits the sophisticated port-village of St. Jean Cap Ferrat, offering more yachts, boardwalks, views, and boutiques in a less frenzied atmosphere.

▲**Eze Village**—Floating high above the sea, flowery Eze Village (don't confuse it with the seafront town of Eze Bord de la Mer) mixes perfume outlets, upscale boutiques, steep cobbled lanes, and magnificent views. About 15 minutes east of Villefranche on the *Moyenne Corniche* (6 buses/day from Nice, 25 min), this medieval hill town makes a handy stop between Nice and Monaco. Drop in on the Fragonard or Gallimard perfume outlets to learn about the interesting fabrication process and shop the fragrant collections (both daily 8:30–18:00, Gallimard breaks for lunch 12:00–14:00). Pull up a pew in Eze's charming church (Eglise Paroissial), but skip the Jardins Exotiques (exotic gardens). For a panoramic view and ideal picnic perch (they say on a clear day, you can see Corsica), walk up to the hill town from the parking lot, take a left at the top of the first hill, following the sign to Eze Bord de la Mer, and walk 30 steps down a dirt path. Come for sunset and stay for dinner to enjoy a more peaceful Eze. You'll dine well at the stone-cozy **Le Troubador** (€30 *menu*, closed Sun–Mon, 4 rue de Brec, tel. 04 93 41 19 03), and for less at the more basic **Nid de L'Aigle** (Eagle's Nest, tel. 04 93 41 19 08), which offers better views.

▲**La Turbie**—High above Monaco lies one of this region's most dramatic panoramas. Take a bus from Nice or Monaco, or drive the *Grande Corniche* to La Turbie (10 min east above Eze Village). Turn right at La Regence Café in La Turbie to find the viewpoint. It costs €4 to enter the grounds and climb *La Trophée des Alpes*, the massive Roman monument erected to guard the Roman road and commemorate Caesar Augustus' conquering of the Alps. It's not worth the effort nor the money for most to enter the sight, since the free viewpoint at the parking turnaround is virtually as good. (If you do enter the sight, follow signs to Panorama for the best views and picnic-perfect benches.) The village of La Turbie is worth a wander and has plenty of cafés and restaurants. The view over Monaco is even greater after dark.

ANTIBES

Antibes may be busier than Villefranche, but it's infinitely more manageable than Nice. The old town's cluster of red-tiled roofs and twin medieval lookout towers rising above the blue Mediterranean is postcard-perfect. Come here for yachts, sandy beaches, an enjoyable old town, excellent hiking, and a great Picasso collection. Twenty-five minutes west of Nice by train (skip the 50-min bus), Antibes' glamorous port anchors Europe's most sumptuous yachts—boat-lovers are welcome to browse. The festive old town is charming in a sandy-sophisticated way and sits atop the ruins of the fourth-century B.C. Greek city of Antipolis. Unfortunately, hotels aren't a very good value here, so I prefer Antibes as a day trip.

Orientation

The old town lies between the port and boulevards Albert 1er and Robert Soleau. Place Nationale is the hub of activity in the old town. Lively rue Auberon connects the port and the old town. Stroll along the sea between the Picasso Museum and place Albert 1er (where boulevard Albert 1er meets the sea); the best beaches lie just beyond place Albert 1er, and the path is beautiful. Good play areas for children are on place des Martyrs de la Resistance (close to recommended Hôtel Relais du Postillon). Near the port in the old town, you'll find **Heidi's English Bookshop** (great selection, daily 10:00–19:00, 24 rue Auberon) and a **launderette** (14 rue Thuret).

Tourist Information: There are two TIs. The most convenient is located in the old town, just inside the walls from the port at 21 boulevard D'Aguilllons (Sept–May Mon–Fri only 10:00–18:00, June–Aug daily 8:30–21:00, tel. 04 93 34 65 65). The main *Maison de Tourisme* is in the newer city (July–Aug Mon–Sat 9:00–19:00, Sun 9:00–13:00, Sept–June Mon–Sat 9:00–12:30 & 14:00–18:30, closed Sun, located just east of the old town where boulevard Albert 1er and rue de République meet at 11 place de Gaulle, tel. 04 92 90 53 00). At either TI, pick up the excellent city map, the interesting walking tour of old Antibes brochure (in English), and get details on the hikes described below. The Nice TI has Antibes maps; plan ahead.

Arrival in Antibes

By Train: To get to the port (5-min walk), cross the street right in front of the station and follow avenue de la Liberatión downhill. To reach the main TI in the modern city (15-min walk), exit right from the station on avenue Soleau; follow *Maison du Tourisme* signs to place de Gaulle. A free minibus *(Minibus Gratuit)* circulates around Antibes from the train station and serves place Albert 1er, the old town, and the port (4/hr), or you can call a taxi (tel. 04 93 67 67 67).

By Bus: The bus station is on the edge of the old town on place Guynemer, a block below the TI.

By Car: Follow *Centre-ville, Vieux Port* signs and park near the old town walls, as close to the beach as you can (first half-hour is free, €3.70/3 hrs, or about €8/day). Enter the old town through the last arch on the right.

Sights—Antibes

Market Hall (Marché Provençal)—The daily market bustles under a 19th-century canopy and features flowers, produce, Provençal products, and beach accessories (in old town behind

Picasso Museum on cours Masséna, daily until 13:00, closed Mon off-season). You'll also find antique/flea markets on place Nationale and place Audiberti (next to the port) on Thursdays and Saturdays (7:00–18:00).

▲▲Musée Picasso (Château Grimaldi)—Sitting serenely where the old town meets the sea, this museum offers a remarkable collection of Picasso's work: paintings, sketches, and ceramics. Picasso, who lived and worked here in 1946, said if you want to see work from his Antibes period, you'll have to do it in Antibes. You'll understand why Picasso liked working here. Several photos of the artist make this already intimate museum more so. In his famous *Joie de Vivre* (the museum's highlight), there's a new love in Picasso's life, and he's feelin' groovy (€4.60, June–Sept Tue–Sun 10:00–18:00, July–Aug until 20:00 on Wed and Fri; Oct–May 10:00–12:00 & 14:00–18:00, closed Mon, tel. 04 92 90 54 20).

Musée d'Histoire et d'Archéologie—Featuring Greek, Roman, and Etruscan odds and ends, this is the only place to get a sense of this city's ancient roots. I liked the 2,000-year-old lead anchors (€3, no English explanations, June–Sept 10:00–18:00, Oct–May 10:00–12:00 & 14:00–18:00, closed Mon, on the water between Picasso Museum and place Albert 1er).

Fort Carré—This impressively situated citadel dates from 1487 and was the coast's last fortification before Italy. More importantly, it protected Antibes from its two key rivals, Nice and Corsica, until the late 1800s. You can tour the unusual four-pointed fort that at its height held 200 soldiers. There's precious little to see inside the fort, though the views from the top walkways are sensational, and for me, justify the time. Tours in English and French depart every 30 minutes (€3 entry, includes tour, daily June–Sept 10:15–17:30, Oct–May closes at 16:00). Scenic footpaths link the fort to the port along the sea. It's a 35-minute portside walk from the old town to the fort (consider taking a taxi there and walking back). By foot or car, follow avenue 11 Novembre around the port, stay on the main road (walkers can follow path by sports fields), then park on the beach just after the soccer field. A signed dirt path leads to Le Fort Carré. Keep following green-lettered signs to *Le Fort/Sens de la Visite*.

Beaches (Plages)—The best beaches stretch between Antibes' port and Cap d'Antibes, and the very best (plages Salis and Ponteil) are just south of Place Albert 1er. All are golden and sandy. Plage Salis is busy in summer, but it's manageable, with snack stands every 100 meters/330 feet and views to the old town. The closest beach to the old town is at the port (plage de la Gravette) and remains relatively calm in any season.

Antibes

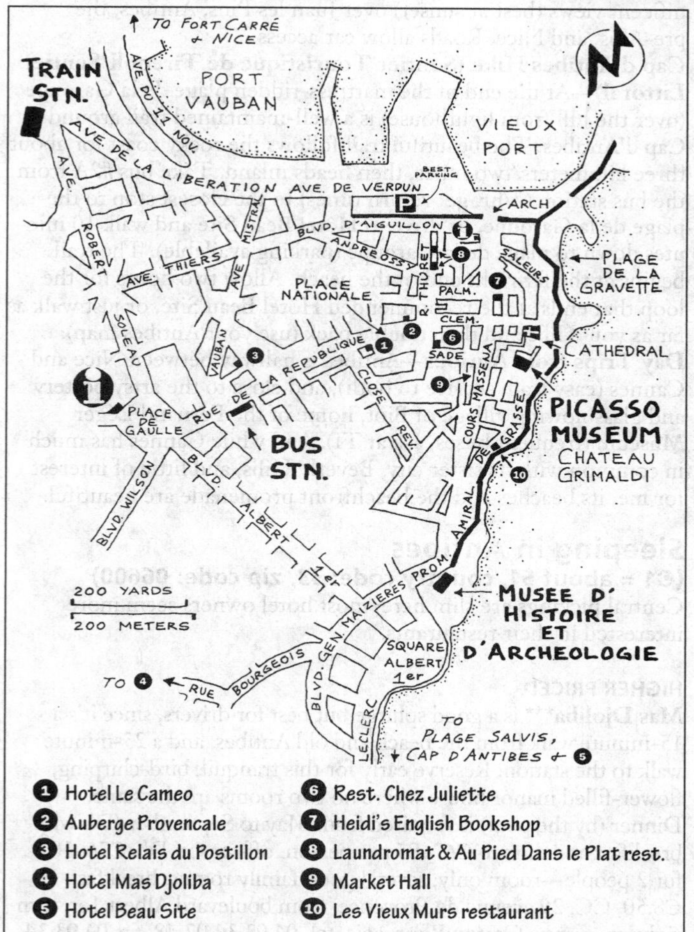

Hikes and Day Trips from Antibes

From place Albert 1er (where boulevard Albert 1er meets the beach), there's a great view of plage Salis and Cap d'Antibes. That tower on the hill is your destination for the first walk described below. The longer hike along Cap d'Antibes begins on the next beach, just over that hill (see below).

▲**Chapelle et Phare de la Garoupe**—The chapel and lighthouse, a 20-minute uphill climb from the far end of plage Salis (follow Chemin du Calvaire up to lighthouse tower), offer magnificent views (best at sunset) over Juan les Pins, Antibes, the pre-Alps, and Nice. Roads allow car access.

Cap d'Antibes Hike (Sentier Touristique de Tirepoll/Sentier Littoral)—At the end of the mattress-ridden plage de la Garoupe (over the hill from lighthouse) is a well-maintained trail around Cap d'Antibes. The beautiful trail follows the rocky coast for about three kilometers/two miles, then heads inland. Take bus #2A from the bus station (2/hr, get return times) to the closest stop to the plage de la Garoupe, or drive to Hôtel Beau Site and walk 10 minutes down to plage de la Garoupe (parking available). The trail begins at the far right end of the beach. Allow two hours for the loop that ends at the recommended Hôtel Beau Site, or just walk as far as you'd like and then double back (use your Antibes map).

Day Trips from Antibes—Antibes is halfway between Nice and Cannes (easy train service to both), and close to the artsy pottery and glassblowing village of Biot, home of the Fernand Léger Museum (frequent buses, ask at TI). And while Cannes has much in common with its sister city, Beverly Hills, and little of interest for me, its beaches and the beachfront promenade are beautiful.

Sleeping in Antibes

(€1 = about $1, country code: 33, zip code: 06600)

Central pickings are slim here; most hotel owners seem more interested in their restaurants.

HIGHER PRICED

Mas Djoliba*** is a good splurge but best for drivers, since it's a 15-minute walk from the beach and old Antibes, and a 25-minute walk to the station. Reserve early for this tranquil, bird-chirping, flower-filled manor house where no two rooms are the same. Dinner (by the pool) is required from May to September (Db with breakfast and dinner-€67–85 per person, off-season Db-€76–107 for 2 people—room only; several good family rooms, breakfast-€8.50, CC, 29 avenue de Provence, from boulevard Albert 1er, turn right up avenue Gaston Bourgeois, tel. 04 93 34 02 48, fax 04 93 34 05 81, www.hotel-djoliba.com, e-mail: hotel.djoliba@wanadoo.fr).

MODERATELY PRICED

Auberge Provençale*, on charming place Nationale, has a popular restaurant and seven reasonably nice rooms (those on the square get all the noise, day and night), but nonexistent, couldn't-care-less management (Db-€63–85, Tb-€72–94, Qb-€108, CC, reception in restaurant, 61 place Nationale, tel. 04 93 34 13 24, fax 04 93 34 89 88). Their huge loft room, named "Celine," faces the back, comes with a royal canopy bed and a dramatic open-timbered ceiling, and costs no more than the other rooms.

Hôtel Relais du Postillon**, on a thriving square, offers 15 small, tastefully designed rooms, accordion bathrooms, and helpful owners who take more pride in their well-respected restaurant (Db-€44–82, CC, *menus* from €32, 8 rue Championnet, tel. 04 93 34 20 77, fax 04 93 34 61 24, www.relais-postillon.com, SE).

Hôtel Beau Site***, my only listing on Cap d'Antibes and a 10-minute drive from the old town, is a good value if you want to get away, but not *too* far away. The friendly owners, nice pool, outdoor terrace, easy parking, and 30 pleasant rooms make it worthwhile (Db-€52–107, CC, 141 boulevard Kennedy, tel. 04 93 61 53 43, fax 04 93 67 78 16, www.hotelbeausite.net). From the hotel, it's a 10-minute walk down to the crowded plage de la Garoupe and a nearby hiking trail.

LOWER PRICED

Hôtel Le Cameo** is a rambling, refreshingly unaggressive old place above a bustling bar (what reception there is, you'll find in the bar). The public areas are dark, but its nine, very simple, linoleum-lined rooms are almost huggable. All open onto the charming place Nationale, which means you don't sleep until the restaurants close (Ds-€47, Db-€58, Ts-€55, Tb-€66, CC, 5 place Nationale, tel. 04 93 34 24 17, fax 04 93 34 35 80, NSE).

Eating in Antibes

Les Vieux Murs is the place to sample regional specialties (€40 *menu*, along ramparts beyond Picasso Museum at 25 promenade Admiral de Grasse, tel. 04 93 34 66 73).

Au Pied dans le Plat serves reliably good meals at fair prices in a pleasant setting (*menus* from €23, closed Mon, 6 rue Thuret, tel. 04 93 34 37 23).

The recommended hotels **Relais du Postillon** and **Auberge Provençale** offer well-respected cuisine (listed above).

Lively place Nationale is filled with tables and tourists (great ambience), while locals seem to prefer the restaurants along the market hall. Just off place Nationale, **Chez Juliette** offers budget meals (*menus* from €14, rue Sade).

Romantics and those on a budget should buy a picnic dinner and head for the beach.

MONACO

Still impressive despite overdevelopment, high prices, and wall-to-wall daytime tourists, Monaco will disappoint anyone looking for something below the surface. This glittering, two-square-kilometer (.7 square miles) country is a tax haven for its minuscule full-time population (30,000, 83 percent foreigners), who pay no income tax, and is the kind of place you visit once and probably don't need to see again. France surrounds Monaco on all sides but the Mediterranean and provides Monaco's telephones (French phone cards work here), electricity, and water. About the only thing you'll use that's made locally is a stamp. Try to come at night, when the real Monaco steps out.

Orientation

Monaco (the principality) is best understood when separated into its three tourist areas: Monaco-Ville, Monte Carlo, and La Condamine (a fourth area, Fontvieille, is of no interest to tourists). Monaco-Ville, dangling on the rock high above, is the oldest section and houses Prince Rainier's palace and all sights except the casino; Monte Carlo is the area around the casino; and La Condamine (the port) divides the two. A bus ride on routes #1 or #2 links all areas (10/hr, €1.40, or €3.50 for 4 tickets). It's a 15-minute uphill walk from the port (and train station) to Prince Rainier's palace, 20 minutes to the casino, and a 40-minute down-and-up walk between the palace and the casino.

Tourist Information: There are several TIs. The main TI is near the casino (2 boulevard des Moulins), but the handiest one for most is in the train station; pick up a city map (daily 9:00–19:00, tel. 00-377/92 16 61 66). From June to September, you'll find information kiosks in the Monaco-Ville parking garage and on the port.

Telephone Tip: To call Monaco from France, dial 00, then 377 (Monaco's country code), and the eight-digit number. Within Monaco, simply dial the eight-digit number.

Arrival in Monaco

By Bus from Nice and Villefranche: Keep your receipt for the return ride (RCA buses run twice as often as Cars Broch). There are three stops in Monaco, in order from Nice: in front of a tunnel at the base of Monaco-Ville (place d'Armes), on the port, and below the casino (on avenue d'Ostende). The first stop is the best starting point. From there, you can walk up to Monaco-Ville and the palace (10 min straight up), or catch a local bus (lines #1 or #2); cross the street right in front of the tunnel and walk with the rock on your right—the bus stop and steps up to Monaco-Ville are 70 meters/230 feet away. The bus stop back to Nice is across the major road from your arrival point at the light. The last bus leaves Monaco for Nice at about 19:00 (the last train leaves about 23:30).

By Train from Nice: A dazzling but confusing new train station provides central access to Monaco. The TI, baggage check, and ticket windows are up the escalator at the end of the tracks.

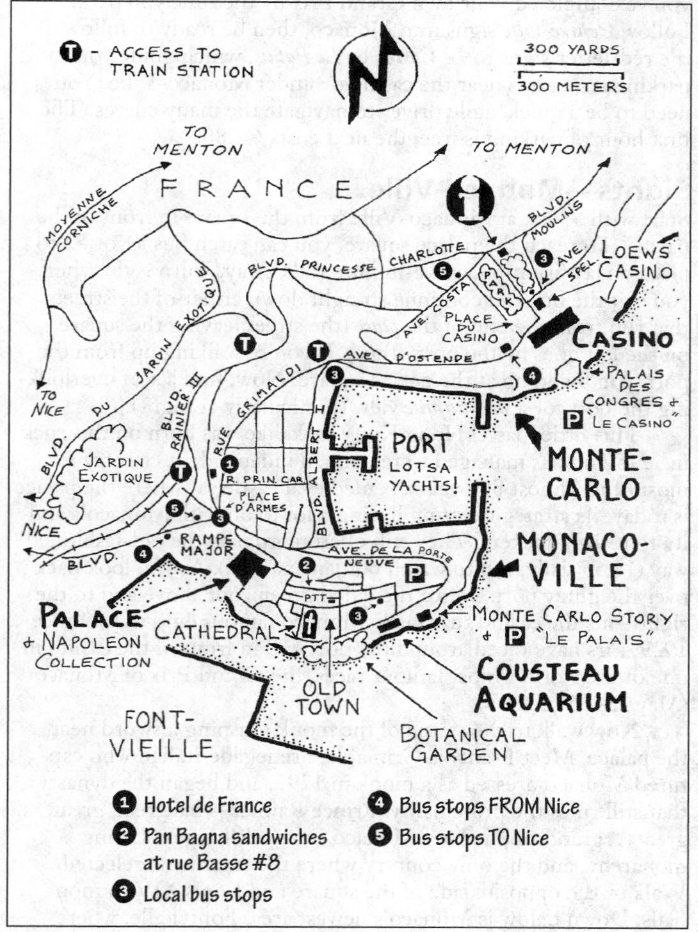

To reach Monaco-Ville, walk along the platform toward Nice following *Sortie la Condamine*, then *Access Port* signs. The stop for local buses is in front of the station exit. The port is a few blocks downhill, the casino is uphill along the left side of the port, and Monaco-Ville is uphill to the right of the port. The most direct route to the casino from the station is up the escalator from the platform, left past the TI, and up the elevator. Exit the station and turn left on boulevard Princesse Charlotte.

By Car: Driving here actually works, though you'll feel like you've completed your own Grand Prix by the time you park. Follow *Centre-ville* signs into Monaco, then be ready to follow the red-letter signs to *Le Casino* or *Le Palais*, which guide you to parking structures near the casino or under Monaco-Ville. You need to be a quick, agile driver to navigate the many curves. The first hour of parking is free; the next costs €2.80.

Sights—Monaco-Ville

Start with a look at Monaco-Ville from the square in front of the palace. To reach the palace square, you can catch bus #1 or #2 to place de la Visitatión, a five-minute walk away. Turn right when you exit the bus and continue straight down either of the streets that run from the end of the *place* (the street leaving the square on the left goes by the post office). If you're walking up from the port, you'll end up at the palace square. Now, find a seat overlooking the port for a *magnifique* view (particularly at night).

This little, pastel Hong Kong lookalike was born on this rock in 1215 and has managed to remain an independent country for most of its almost 800 years. A medieval castle sat where the palace is today, its strategic setting having a lot to do with Monaco's ability to resist attackers. They still **change guards** the old-fashioned way (11:55 daily, fun to watch but jam-packed). As you look back over the glitzy port, notice the faded green roof above and to the right—it's the casino that made Monaco famous (and rich). Since 1929, cars have raced around the port and in front of the casino in one of the world's most famous races, the Grand Prix of Monaco (May 23–26 in 2003).

Now walk to the statue of the monk grasping a sword near the palace. Meet François Grimaldi, a renegade Italian who captured Monaco dressed as a monk in 1297, and began the dynasty that still rules the principality. Prince Rainier is his great, great, great... grandson, making Monaco Europe's longest-lasting monarchy, and the only country where the ruler is not elected. Walk to the opposite side of the square and Louis XIV cannonballs. Down below is Monaco's newest area, Fontvieille, where much of its post–WWII growth has been. Prince Rainier has continued (some say, been obsessed with) Monaco's economic growth, creating landfills (such as Fontvieille), flashy ports, new beaches, and the new rail station. Today, thanks to Prince Rainier's efforts, tiny Monaco is a member of the United Nations. The current buzz is about how soon he'll hand over the reigns of the principality to his son, Albert.

Hungry? You'll find good *pan bagnat* and other sandwiches at 8 rue Basse, on the street leaving the square to the left. You can buy stamps (mail from here!) at the PTT, located a few blocks down rue Comte F. Gastaldi.

Palace—Automated and uninspired tours (in English) take you through part of the prince's lavish palace in 30 merciful minutes and yet still manage to describe every painting. The rooms are well-furnished and impressive, but interesting only if you haven't seen a château lately (€6 June–Sept daily 9:30–18:20, Oct 10:00–17:00, closed off-season).

Napoleon Collection—Napoleon occupied Monaco after the French Revolution. This is the prince's private collection of what Napoleon left behind: military medals, swords, guns, letters, and, most interesting, his hat. I found this collection more appealing than the palace (€4, June–Sept daily 9:30–18:30, Oct–May 10:00–17:00, next to palace entry).

Cathédrale de Monaco—This somber cathedral, built in 1878, is where Princess Grace is buried (near the left transept).

Jardins Botanique—Take in sensational views as you meander back to the bus stop through these immaculately maintained gardens (or pick up a *pan bagnat* sandwich in the old town and picnic here).

Cousteau Aquarium (Musée de l'Océanographique)—Inaugurated in 1910, this monumental building overhangs the Mediterranean. Its hugeness testifies to the oceanographic zeal of Prince Albert I. It can be jammed and sometimes disappoints, though kids love it (€11, ages 6–18-€5.35, April–Sept daily 9:00–19:00, until 20:00 July–Aug, March and Oct 9:30–19:00, Nov–Feb 10:00–18:00, CC, at opposite end of Monaco-Ville from palace, down the steps from Monaco-Ville bus stop).

Monte Carlo Story—This informative 35-minute film gives a helpful account (English headphones) of Monaco's history and offers a comfortable soft-chair break from all that walking (€6, usually on the hour 11:00–17:00 March–Oct, until 18:00 July–Aug, 14:00–17:00 only Nov–Feb, frequent extra showings for groups that you can join; from the Monte Carlo side of the aquarium, take the escalator into the parking garage, then take the elevator down and follow the signs, it's just past the café).

Leave Monaco-Ville and ride the shuttle bus (the stop is up the steps across from the aquarium) or stroll down through the pedestrian-pleasant port and up to Monte Carlo.

Sights—Monte Carlo

▲Casino—Stand in the park, above the traffic circle in front of the casino (opens at noon). In the mid-1800s, Prince Charles began an aggressive economic development plan to bail out Europe's poorest country. He built spas and a casino to lure a growing aristocratic class with leisure time. It worked. Today, Monaco has the world's highest per-capita income. The name Monte Carlo means "Charles' Hill" in Spanish (the Spanish were traditional protectors of Monaco and have 200 guards present today). The casino is designed to make the wealthy feel comfortable while losing money. Architect? Charles Garnier agreed to design this Casino/Opera House in 1878, in part to thank the prince for his financial help in completing the Paris Opéra, which he also designed. The central doors provide access to slot machines, private gaming rooms, and the Opera House. The private gaming rooms take up much of the left wing of the building.

Count the counts and Rolls-Royces in front of Hôtel de Paris (built at the same time), then strut inside past the slots and find the sumptuous atrium. This is the lobby for the Opera House; doors open only during performances. There's a model of the opera at the end of the room and marble WCs on the right. Anyone over 21 (even in shorts, if before 20:00) can get as far as the one-armed bandits (open at 12:00, push the button on the slot machines to claim your winnings), though you'll need decent attire to go any farther; and after 20:00, shorts are off-limits anywhere.

Cost and Hours: The first rooms, Salons Européens, open at 12:00 and cost €10 to enter. The glamorous private game rooms where you can rub elbows with high rollers open at 16:00, others not until 21:00, and cost an additional €10.

A tie and jacket are not necessary until evening, and can be rented at the bag check for €30 plus a €40 deposit. Dress standards for women are far more relaxed (only tennis shoes are a definite no-no). The scene is great at night and downright James Bond–like in the private rooms. The park behind the casino offers a peaceful café and a good view of the casino's rear facade and of Monaco-Ville. Entrance is free to all games in the new, plebeian, American-style Loews Casino, adjacent to the old casino.

The return bus stop to Nice is at the top of the park above the casino on avenue de la Costa. To return to the train station from the casino, walk up the parkway in front of the casino, turn left on boulevard des Moulins, right on impasse de la Fontaine, climb the steps, and turn left on boulevard Princesse Charlotte (the entrance to the train station is next to Parking de la Gare).

Near Monte Carlo: Menton

Grand, beautiful, and overlooked Menton is a peaceful and relaxing spa/beach town with a fine beachfront promenade and a sandy-cobbled old town (TI tel. 04 93 57 57 00). It's just a few minutes by train (8/day) from Monte Carlo or 40 minutes from Nice.

Sleeping and Eating in Monaco
(€1 = about $1, country code: 377)

Since Monaco is by far best after dark, consider sleeping here. The perfectly pleasant **Hôtel de France**** is reasonable (Sb-€67, Db-€85, includes breakfast, CC, 6 rue de la Turbie, near west exit from train station, tel. 00-377/93 30 24 64, fax 00-377/92 16 13 34, e-mail: hotel-france@monte-carlo.mc). Several cafés serve basic fare at reasonable prices (day and night) on the port, along the traffic-free rue Princesse Caroline.

INLAND HILL TOWNS OF THE RIVIERA

Some of France's most dramatic hill towns are ignored in this region more famous for its beaches and casinos. A short ride away from the Mediterranean reaps huge rewards: lush forests, spectacular canyons, and of course, hilltop villages to lose yourself in.

▲Hill-Town Drive to the Gorges du Loup—To lose the maddening crowds, connect these lost treasures: Start in Vence (if you're really early, you could try St. Paul-de-Vence), then drive to Tourrettes sur Loup, Pont du Loup, then follow signs leading into Gorges du Loup. Drive as far into the Gorges as you like, ideally all the way to the pont de Bramafen, then loop back on the other side via the sky-high village of Gourdon, then on to adorable Le Bar sur Loup before returning to Nice. Allow all day for this loop with time to wander the villages. The round-trip drive from Nice without stops would take about two hours. Buses serve Vence and St. Paul-de-Vence from Nice, and Tourrettes sur Loup from Vence.

St. Paul (-de-Vence)—This most famous of Riviera hill towns has lost its appeal and is now an overrun and over-restored artist-shopping-mall. Wall-to-wall upscale galleries and ice cream shops compete for the attention of the hordes of day-trippers. Avoid visiting between 11:00 and 18:00 (I avoid it completely). If you must go, meander deep into St. Paul's quieter streets and wander far to enjoy the panoramic views (TI tel. 04 93 32 86 95).

The best reason by far to visit St. Paul is for the nearby, prestigious, and far-out Fondation Maeght's modern art collection. It's a steep (uphill) 15-minute walk from St. Paul (ask the bus driver for best stop). This engaging museum provides a good introduction to modern art. Its world-class contemporary art collection (with works by Léger, Miró, Calder, and Braque, among others) is beautifully arranged between pleasant gardens and well-lit rooms. Don't miss the chapel, designed by Georges Braque, or the frequent special exhibits (€8.50, daily July–Sept 10:00–19:00, Oct–June 10:00–12:30 & 14:30–18:00, tel. 04 93 32 81 63).

Vence—Vence disperses St. Paul's crowds over a larger and more engaging city. The mountains are close and the breeze is fresh in this town that bubbles with work-a-day life and tourist activity (no boutique shortage here). Stroll the narrow lanes of the old town *(Cité Historique)*, look for informative wall plaques in English, enjoy a drink on a quiet square, and find the small cathedral with its Chagall mosaic. Outdoor markets thrive in the old town on Tuesdays and Fridays until 12:30, and daily on the massive place du Grand Jardin. Vence's **TI** is at 8 place du Grand Jardin (Mon–Sat 9:00–12:30 & 14:00–18:00, closed Sun, July–Aug Mon–Sat 9:00–19:00, Sun 9:00–13:00, tel. 04 93 58 06 38). The bus stop for Nice and St. Paul is next to the TI (schedules are posted in the window). If arriving by car, follow *Cité Historique* signs and park on place de Grand Jardin.

Matisse's much-raved-about **Chapelle du Rosaire** may disappoint all but his fans, for whom this is a rich and rewarding pilgrimage (an easy 20-min walk from Vence TI, turn right out of TI and walk down avenue Henri Isnare, then right on avenue de Provence, following signs to St. Jeannet). The yellow, blue, and green-filtered sunlight does a cheery dance across the simple tile sketches (€2.50, Tue and Thu 10:00–11:30 & 14:00–17:30, Mon and Wed 14:00–17:30; Mass is Sun at 10:00 followed by tour of chapel, closed Nov, tel. 04 93 58 03 26).

Sleeping and Eating in Vence (zip code: 06140): If Vence tempts you to stay, consider the little **Auberge des Seigneurs****, a short walk from the bus stop and TI (turn left out of TI then left again after a block); it's filled with character (spacious Db-€60–67, CC, no elevator, place du Frene, tel. 04 93 58 04 24, fax 04 93 24 08 01). **Hôtel la Villa Roseraie*****, an oasis with a pool, lovely garden, and carefully decorated rooms, is on the fringe of the city on the road to Col de Vence (Db-€67–133, CC, parking, easy walk to Matisse's chapel and a 15-min walk to TI, 128 avenue Henri Giraud, tel. 04 93 58 02 20, fax 04 93 58 99 31, e-mail: rvilla5536@aol.fr). **La Pecheur de Soleil Pizzeria** offers inexpensive meals on a quiet square (1 place Godeau, tel. 04 93 58 32 56). **Auberge des Seigneurs** is a cozy place for a good dinner (*menus* from €27, recommended above, closed Mon).

Tourrettes sur Loup—This impressively situated hill town is hemmed in by forests and looks ready to slide down its steep hill. Here, you'll find more arts and crafts, but fewer tourists. Known as the "Village Violette," Tourrettes produces more violets than anywhere else in France. You'll find g reat views of Tourrettes as you drive to Pont du Loup.

Le Bar sur Loup—The most peaceful and least invaded of these inland hill towns, medieval Bar huddles around its castle and Gothic church. Here, you can relax and truly smell the flowers.

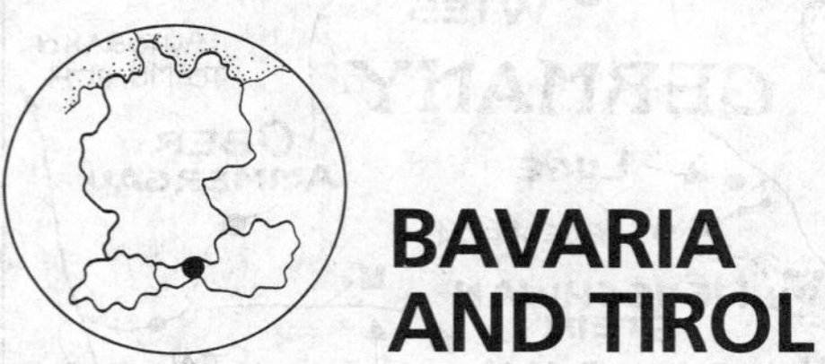

BAVARIA AND TIROL

Two hours south of Munich, between Germany's Bavaria and Austria's Tirol, is a timeless land of fairy-tale castles, painted buildings shared by cows and farmers, and locals who still yodel when they're happy.

In Germany's Bavaria, tour "Mad" King Ludwig's ornate Neuschwanstein Castle, Europe's most spectacular. Stop by the Wieskirche, a textbook example of Bavarian rococo bursting with curly curlicues, and browse through Oberammergau, Germany's wood-carving capital and home of the famous Passion Play.

In Austria's Tirol, hike to the ruined Ehrenberg castle, scream down a ski slope on an oversized skateboard, and then catch your breath for an evening of yodeling and slap dancing.

In this chapter, I'll cover Bavaria first, then Tirol. Austria's Tirol is easier and cheaper than touristy Bavaria. My favorite home base for exploring Bavaria's castles is actually in Austria, in the town of Reutte. Füssen, in Germany, is a handier home base for train travelers.

Planning Your Time

While locals come here for a week or two, the typical speedy American traveler will find two days' worth of sightseeing. With a car and more time, you could enjoy three or four days, but the basic visit ranges anywhere from a long day trip from Munich to a three-night, two-day visit. If the weather's good and you're not going to Switzerland, be sure to ride a lift to an alpine peak.

A good schedule for a one-day circular drive from Reutte is: 7:30-Breakfast, 8:00-Depart hotel, 8:30-Arrive at Neuschwanstein to pick up tickets for two castles (which you reserved by telephone several days earlier), 9:00-tour Hohenschwangau, 11:00-tour

Highlights of Bavaria and Triol

Neuschwanstein, 13:00-Drive to the Wieskirche (20-min stop) and on to Linderhof, 14:30-Tour Linderhof, 16:30-Drive along scenic Plansee back into Austria, 17:30-Back at hotel, 19:00-Dinner at hotel and perhaps a folk evening (or the Ludwig II Musical). In peak season, you might arrive later at Linderhof to avoid the crowds. The next morning, you could stroll through Reutte, hike to the Ehrenberg ruins, and ride the luge on your way to Innsbruck, Munich, Venice, Switzerland, or wherever.

Train travelers can base in Füssen and bus or bike the five-kilometer (3-mile) distance to Neuschwanstein. Reutte is connected by bus with Füssen (except on Sun). If you base in Reutte, you can bike to the Ehrenberg ruins (just outside Reutte) and to Neuschwanstein Castle/Tegelberg luge (90 min), or hike through the woods to Neuschwanstein from the recommended Gutshof zum Schluxen hotel (60 min).

Getting around Bavaria and Tirol

By Car: This region is ideal by car. All the sights are within an easy 100-kilometer (60-mile) loop from Reutte or Füssen.

By Train and Bus: It can be frustrating by public transportation. Local bus service in the region is spotty for sightseeing. If you're rushed and without wheels, Reutte, the Wieskirche, Linderhof, and the luge rides are probably not worth the trouble (but the Tegelberg luge near Neuschwanstein is within walking distance of the castle).

Füssen (with a 2-hr train ride to/from Munich every hour, some with a transfer in Buchloe) is five kilometers (3 miles) from Neuschwanstein Castle with easy bus and bike connections (see "Getting to the Castles from Füssen or Reutte," page 418). Reutte is a 30-minute bus ride from Füssen (Mon–Fri 5/day, Sat 3/day, none Sun; taxis from Reutte are €21 one-way).

To visit Oberammergau, catch one of the buses going from Füssen to Garmisch (6–10/day, less off-season, 1.75 hr, some with transfer in Echelsbacherbrücke, confirm with driver that bus will stop in Oberammergau, 4–6 buses/day return from Oberammergau to Füssen). From Munich, Oberammergau is easier to visit directly by train (hrly, 1.75 hrs, change in Murnau) than going to Füssen to catch the bus.

Füssen to Linderhof is a hassle but doable without a car in the summer. The first bus to Oberammergau (direction: Garmisch) has hourly bus connections to Linderhof from June to mid-October (mid-Oct–May only 2 buses/day). Bus trips to Garmisch and Linderhof are cheaper if you buy a *Tagesticket*, a round-trip special fare—even if you're only going one way.

Confirm all bus schedules in Füssen by checking the big board at the bus stop across from the train station, getting a bus timetable (€0.25) at the TI or train station, or calling 08362/939-0505.

By Rental Car: You can rent a car in Füssen for €50 per day (see below; or in Reutte, if you're a guest at the Hotel Maximilian).

By Tour: If you're interested only in Bavarian castles, consider an all-day organized bus tour of the Bavarian biggies as a side trip from Munich.

By Bike: This is great biking country. Shops in or near train stations rent bikes for €8 to €11 per day. The ride from Reutte to Neuschwanstein and the Tegelberg luge (90 min) is great for those with the time and energy.

By Thumb: Hitchhiking, always risky, is a slow-but-possible way to connect the public transportation gaps.

FÜSSEN

Füssen has been a strategic stop since ancient times. Its main street sits on the Via Claudia Augusta, which crossed the Alps (over

Brenner Pass) in Roman times. The town was the southern terminus of a medieval trade route now known among modern tourists as the "Romantic Road." Dramatically situated under a renovated castle on the lively Lech River, Füssen just celebrated its 700th birthday.

Unfortunately, Füssen is overrun by tourists in the summer. Traffic can be exasperating. Apart from Füssen's cobbled and arcaded town center, there's little real sightseeing here. The striking-from-a-distance castle houses a boring picture gallery. The mediocre city museum in the monastery below the castle exhibits lifestyles of 200 years ago and the story of the monastery, and offers displays on the development of the violin, for which Füssen is famous (€5, April–Oct Tue–Sun 10:00–17:00, closed Mon, shorter hours off-season, English descriptions, tel. 08362/903-145). Halfway between Füssen and the border (as you drive, or a woodsy walk from the town) is the Lechfall, a thunderous waterfall (with a handy WC).

Orientation (area code: 08362)

Füssen's train station is a few blocks from the TI, the town center (a cobbled shopping mall), and all my hotel listings (see "Sleeping," below). The TI has a room-finding service (June–mid-Sept Mon–Sat 8:30–18:30, Sun 10:00–12:00, less off-season, 3 blocks down Bahnhofstrasse from station, tel. 08362/93850, fax 08362/938-520, www.fuessen.de). After-hours, the little self-service info pavilion (7:00–24:30) near the front of the TI features an automated room-finding service.

Arrival in Füssen: Exit left as you leave the train station (lockers available) and walk a few straight blocks to the center of town and the TI. To go to Neuschwanstein or Reutte, catch a bus from in front of the station.

Bike Rental: Rent from friendly Christian at Preisschranke at the edge of the train station (€8/24 hrs, June–Aug Mon–Sat 9:00–20:00, Sept–May Mon–Sat 9:00–19:00, closed Sun, tel. 08362/921-544), or, for a bigger selection and a less convenient location, check out Rad Zacherl (€8/24 hrs, mountain bikes-€15/24 hrs, passport number for deposit, May–Sept Mon–Fri 9:00–18:00, Sat 9:00–13:00, closed Sun, less off-season, 2 km, or 1.25 miles, out of town at Kemptenerstrasse 119, tel. 08362/3292, www.rad-zacherl.de).

Car Rental: Peter Schlichtling (€50/24 hrs, includes insurance, Kemptenerstrasse 26, tel. 08362/922-122, www.schlichtling.de) is cheaper and more central than Hertz (Füssenerstrasse 112, tel. 08362/986-580).

Laundry: Pfronter Reinigung Wäscherei does full-service wash and dry in three hours (€11/load, Mon–Fri 9:00–12:00 &

14:00–18:00, closed Wed afternoon and Sat–Sun, in parking lot of huge Hotel Hirsch, 2 blocks past TI on the way out of town, Sebastianstrasse 3, tel. 08362/4529).

Sights—Neuschwanstein Castle Area, Bavaria

The most popular tourist destination in Bavaria are the "King's Castles" *(Königsschlösser)*. With fairy-tale turrets in a fairy-tale alpine setting built by a fairy-tale king, they are understandably popular. The well-organized visitor can have a great four-hour visit. Others will just stand in line and perhaps not even see the castles. The key: Phone ahead for a reservation (details below) or arrive by 8:00 (you'll have time to see both castles, consider fun options nearby—mountain lift, luge course, Füssen town—and get out by early afternoon).

Ludwig II (a.k.a. "Mad" King Ludwig), a tragic figure, ruled Bavaria for 23 years until his death in 1886 at the age of 41. Politically, his reality was to "rule" either as a pawn of Prussia or a pawn of Austria. Rather than deal with politics in Bavaria's capital, Munich, Ludwig frittered away most of his time at his family's hunting palace, Hohenschwangau. He spent much of his adult life constructing his fanciful Neuschwanstein Castle—like a kid builds a tree house—on a neighboring hill upon the scant ruins of a medieval castle. Although Ludwig spent 17 years building Neuschwanstein, he lived in it only 172 days. Ludwig was a true Romantic living in a Romantic age. His best friends were artists, poets, and composers such as Richard Wagner. His palaces are wallpapered with misty medieval themes—especially those from Wagnerian operas. Eventually, he was declared mentally unfit to rule Bavaria and taken away from Neuschwanstein. Two days after this eviction, Ludwig was found dead in a lake. To this day, people debate whether the king was murdered or committed suicide.

▲▲▲Neuschwanstein Castle—Imagine King Ludwig as a boy, climbing the hills above his dad's castle, Hohenschwangau (listed below), dreaming up the ultimate fairy-tale castle. He had the power to make his dream concrete and stucco. Neuschwanstein was designed by a painter first . . . then an architect. It looks medieval, but it's only about as old as the Eiffel Tower. It feels like something you'd see at a home show for 19th-century royalty. Built from 1869 to 1886, it's a textbook example of the Romanticism popular in 19th-century Europe. Construction stopped with Ludwig's death (only a third of the interior was finished), and within six weeks, tourists were paying to go through it.

Today, guides herd groups of 60 through the castle, giving an interesting—if rushed—30-minute tour. You'll go up and down

Neuschwanstein

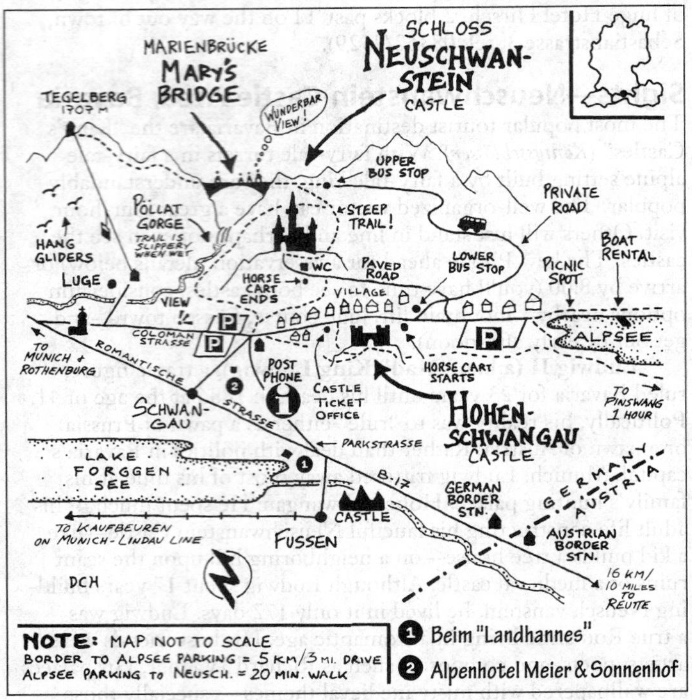

more than 300 steps, through lavish Wagnerian dream rooms, a royal state-of-the-19th-century-art kitchen, the king's gilded-lily bedroom, and his extravagant throne room. You'll visit 15 rooms with their original furnishings and fanciful wall paintings. After the tour, you'll see a room lined with fascinating drawings (described in English) of the castle plans, construction, and drawings from 1883 of Falkenstein—a whimsical, over-the-top, never-built castle that makes Neuschwanstein look stubby. Falkenstein occupied Ludwig's fantasies the year he died. Following the tour, a 20-minute slide show (alternating German and English) plays continuously. If English is on, pop in. If not, it's not worth waiting for.

▲▲Hohenschwangau Castle—Standing quietly below Neuschwanstein, the big yellow Hohenschwangau Castle was Ludwig's boyhood home. Originally built in the 12th century, it was ruined by Napoleon. Ludwig's father Maximilian rebuilt it, and you'll see it as it looked in 1836. It's more lived-in and historic, and excellent 30-minute tours actually give a better glimpse of Ludwig's life than the more visited and famous Neuschwanstein Castle tour.

Getting Tickets for the Castles: Every tour bus in Bavaria converges on Neuschwanstein, and tourists flush in each morning from Munich. A handy reservation system (see below) sorts out the chaos for smart travelers. Tickets come with admission times. (Miss this time and you don't get in.) To tour both castles, you must do Hohenschwangau first (logical, since this gives a better introduction to Ludwig's short life). You'll get two tour times: Hohenschwangau and then, two hours later, Neuschwanstein.

If you arrive late and without a reservation, you'll spend two hours in the ticket line and may find all tours for the day booked. A ticket center for both Neuschwanstein and Hohenschwangau Castles is located at street level between the two castles, a few blocks from the TI toward the Alpsee (April–Sept daily 7:30–18:00, Oct–March daily 8:30–16:00). First tours start around 9:00. Arrive by 8:00 and you'll likely be touring by 9:00. Warning: During the summer, tickets for English tours can run out by 16:00.

It's best to reserve ahead in peak season (July–Sept—especially in August). You can make reservations a minimum of 24 hours in advance by contacting the ticket office by phone (tel. 08362/930-8322 or 08362/930-830) or e-mail (info@ticket-center-hohenschwangau.de; www.ticket-center-hohenschwangau.de). Tickets reserved in advance cost €1.50 extra, and ticket holders must be at the ticket office well before the appointed entry time (30 min for Hohenschwangau, 60 min for Neuschwanstein, allowing time to make your way up to the castle). Remember that many of the businesses are owned by the old royal family, so they encourage you to space the two tours longer than necessary in hopes that you'll spend a little more money. Insist on the tightest schedule—with no lunchtime—if you don't want too much down time.

Cost and Hours: Each castle costs €7, a *Königsticket* for both castles costs €13, and children under 18 are free (April–Sept daily from 9:00 with last tour departing at 18:00, Thu last tour at 20:00, Oct–March daily from 10:00 with last tour at 16:00).

Getting to the Castles: From the ticket booth, Hohenschwangau is an easy five-minute climb. Neuschwanstein is a steep 30-minute hike. To minimize hiking to Neuschwanstein, you can take a shuttle bus (from in front of Hotel Lisl, just above ticket office and to the left) or horse carriage (from in front of Hotel Müller, just above ticket office and to the right), but neither gets you to the castle doorstep. The frequent shuttle buses drop you off at Mary's Bridge, leaving you a steep 10-minute downhill walk from the castle—be sure to see the view from Mary's Bridge before hiking down to the castle (€1.80 up; €2.60 round-trip not worth it since you have to hike up to bus stop for return trip). Horse carriages (€5 up, €2.50 down) are slower than walking and they stop below Neuschwanstein, leaving you a five-minute uphill hike. Note: If it's less than an hour until your Neuschwanstein tour time, you'll need to hike—even at a brisk pace, it still takes at least 20 minutes. For a lazy, varied, and economical plan, ride the bus to Mary's Bridge for the view, hike down to the castle, and then catch the horse from there back down.

Mary's Bridge (Marienbrücke): Before or after the tour, climb up to Mary's Bridge to marvel at Ludwig's castle, just as Ludwig did. This bridge was quite an engineering accomplishment 100 years ago. From the bridge, the frisky can hike even higher to the "Beware—Danger of Death" signs and an even more glorious castle view. For the most interesting descent (15 min longer and extremely slippery when wet), follow signs to the Pöllat Gorge.

Castle Village: The "village" at the foot of Europe's "Disney" castle feeds off the droves of hungry, shop-happy tourists. The Bräustüberl serves the cheapest grub (cafeteria line, often with live folk music). The Alpsee lake is ideal for a picnic, but there are no grocery shops in the area. Your best bet is getting food to go for a lazy lunch at the lakeside park or in one of the old-fashioned rowboats (rented by the hour in summer). Between the ticket office and TI, you'll find plenty of bratwurst stands. The bus stop, telephones, ATM, and helpful TI cluster around the main intersection (TI open April–June daily 9:00–17:00, July–Sept daily 9:00–18:00, Oct–March daily 9:00–16:00, tel. 08362/819-840, www.neuschwansteinland.com).

Getting to the Castles from Füssen or Reutte: Road signs in the region refer to the sight as *Königsschlösser* (king's castles), not "Neuschwanstein." There's plenty of parking (all lots-€4). Get there early, and you'll park where you like. Lot E—past the ticket booth and next to the lake—is my favorite. Those without cars can catch the roughly hourly bus from Füssen (€1.65 one-way, €3 round-trip, note times carefully on the meager schedule, 10 min, 5 km, or 3 miles, catch bus at train station), take a taxi (€10 one-way), or ride a rental bike. From Reutte, take the bus to Füssen (Mon–Fri 5/day, Sat 3/day, none Sun, 30 min), then hop a city bus to the castle.

For a romantic twist, hike or mountain bike from the trailhead at the recommended hotel Gutshof zum Schluxen in Pinswang (see "Sleeping near Reutte," below). When the dirt road forks at the top of the hill, go right (downhill), cross the Austria–Germany border (marked by a sign and deserted hut), and follow the narrow paved road to the castles. It's a 60- to 90-minute hike or a great circular bike trip (allow 90 min from Reutte or 30 min from Gutshof zum Schluxen; cyclists can return to Schluxen from the castles on a different 30-min bike route via Füssen).

▲Tegelberg Gondola—Just north of Neuschwanstein is a fun play zone around the mighty Tegelberg gondola. Hang gliders circle like vultures. Their pilots jump from the top of the Tegelberg Gondola. For €14 you can ride the lift to the 1,690-meter (5,500-foot) summit and back down (May–Oct daily 9:00–17:00, Dec–April daily 9:00–16:30, closed Nov, last lift goes up 10 min before closing time, in bad weather call first to confirm, tel. 08362/98360). On a clear day, you get great views of the Alps and Bavaria and the vicarious thrill of watching hang gliders and parasailors leap into airborne ecstasy. Weather permitting, scores of German thrill-seekers line up and leap from the launch ramp at the top of the lift. With one leaving every two or three minutes, it's great spectating. Thrill seekers with exceptional social skills may talk themselves into a tandem ride with a parasailor. From the top of Tegelberg, it's a steep 2.5-hour hike down to Ludwig's castle. Avoid the treacherous trail directly below the gondola. At the base of the gondola, you'll find a playground, cheery eatery, and a very good luge ride.

▲Tegelberg Luge—Next to the lift is a luge course. A luge is like a bobsled on wheels (for more details, see "Sights—Tirol, Near Reutte," below). This track, made of stainless steel and heated, is often dry and open when drizzly weather shuts down the concrete luges. It's not as scenic as Bichlbach and Biberwier (see below), but it's handy (€2.50/ride, 6-ride sharable card-€10, July–Sept daily 9:00–18:00, otherwise same hours as gondola, in winter sometimes opens later due to wet track, in bad weather call first to confirm, tel. 08362/98360). A funky cable system pulls riders (in their sleds) to the top without a ski lift.

▲Ludwig II Musical—A spectacular opera/musical based on the Romantic life and troubled times of Ludwig plays in a grand lakeside theater. While billed as a musical, *Ludwig II: Longing for Paradise* felt like opera to me—with an orchestra in the pit, creative stage sets, fine singing, wonderful acoustics, and an easy-to-follow story line about Ludwig abandoning the normal, guy-thing rush of political power to pal around with his muses (3 vampy women dressed in purple). It's Bismarck the realistic politician on one side versus Wagner the Romantic composer on the other, as "art triumphs" (and Ludwig disappears into the lake).

The music is wonderful, and the show's a hit with Germans. It's clearly top classical quality, but the superscripts in English are tough to read and tickets are pricey. The state-of-the-art theater is romantically set on a lake (Forgensee) with a view of floodlit Neuschwanstein in the distance (€50–105 per seat, nightly all year

Tue–Sun 19:30 plus a matinee Sat–Sun at 14:30, no shows Mon, 3 hrs including intermission, plenty of chances to eat a good light meal, parking-€3, about 1.5 km/1 mile north of Füssen—follow signs for "musical," book in advance, for tickets, call 01805/583-944, www.ludwigmusical.com). It's possible to book directly at the TI in Füssen. If you're staying in Füssen, catch the shuttle bus that conveniently runs to and from the play.

More Sights—Bavaria

These are listed in driving order from Füssen:

▲▲Wies Church (Wieskirche)—This pilgrimage church is built around the much-venerated statue of a scourged (or beaten) Christ, which supposedly wept in 1738. The carving—too graphic to be accepted by that generation's church—was the focus of worship in a peasant's barn. Miraculously, it wept—empathizing with all those who suffer. Pilgrims came from all around. A tiny and humble chapel was built to house the statue in 1739. (You can see it where the lane to the church leaves the parking lot.) Bigger and bigger crowds came. Two of Bavaria's top rococo architects, the Zimmermann brothers, were commissioned to build the Wieskirche that stands here today (donation requested, summer daily 8:00–19:00, winter daily 8:00–17:00, parking-€1, tel. 08862/932-930).

Germany's greatest rococo-style church, Wieskirche ("the church in the meadow") is newly restored and looking as brilliant as the day it floated down from heaven. Overripe with decoration but bright and bursting with beauty, this church is a divine droplet, a curly curlicue, the final flowering of the Baroque movement.

Follow the theological sweep from the altar to the ceiling: Jesus whipped, chained, and then killed (notice the pelican above the altar—recalling a pre-Christian story of a bird that opened its breast to feed its young with its own blood); the painting of a baby Jesus posed as if on the cross; the sacrificial lamb; and finally, high on the ceiling, the resurrected Christ before the Last Judgment. This is the most positive depiction of the Last Judgment around. Jesus, rather than sitting on the throne to judge, rides high on a rainbow—a symbol of forgiveness—giving any sinner the feeling that there is still time to repent, and there's plenty of mercy on hand. In the back, above the pipe organ, notice the empty throne—waiting for Judgment Day—and the closed door to paradise.

Above the entry to both side aisles are murky glass cases with 18th-century handkerchiefs. People wept, came here, were healed, and no longer needed their hankies. Walk up either aisle flanking the high altar to see votives—requests and thanks to God (for happy, healthy babies, and so on). Notice how the kneelers are positioned so that worshipers can meditate on scenes of biblical miracles painted high on the ceiling and visible through the ornate tunnel frames. A priest here once told me that faith, architecture, light, and music all combine to create the harmony of the Wieskirche.

Two paintings flank the door at the rear of the church. One shows the ceremonial parade in 1749 when the white-clad monks of Steingaden carried the carved statue of Christ from the tiny church to its new big one. The second painting, from 1757, is a votive from one of the Zimmermann brothers, the artists and architects who built this church. He is giving thanks for the successful construction of the new church.

The Wieskirche is 30 minutes north of Neuschwanstein. The northbound Romantic Road bus tour stops here for 15 minutes. You can take a bus from Füssen to the Wieskirche, but you'll spend more time waiting for the bus back than you will seeing the church. By car, head north from Füssen, turn right at Steingaden, and follow the signs. Take a commune-with-nature-and-smell-the-farm detour back through the meadow to the car park.

If you can't visit Wieskirche, visit one of the other churches that came out of the same heavenly spray can: Oberammergau's church, Munich's Asam Church, Würzburg's Residenz Chapel, the splendid Ettal Monastery (free and near Oberammergau), and, on a lesser scale, Füssen's cathedral.

If you're driving from Wieskirche to Oberammergau, you'll cross the Echelsbacher Bridge, which arches 70 meters (230 feet) over the Pöllat Gorge. Thoughtful drivers let their passengers walk across (for the views) and meet them at the other side. Any kayakers? Notice the painting of the traditional village woodcarver (who used to walk from town to town with his art on his back) on the first big house on the Oberammergau side, a shop called Almdorf Ammertal. It has a huge selection of overpriced carvings and commission-hungry tour guides.

▲**Oberammergau**—The Shirley Temple of Bavarian villages, exploited to the hilt by the tourist trade, Oberammergau wears way too much makeup. If you're passing through anyway, it's worth a wander among the half-timbered *Lüftlmalerei* houses frescoed (in a style popular throughout the town in the 18th century) with Bible scenes and famous fairy-tale characters. Browse through wood-carvers' shops—small art galleries filled with very expensive whittled works. The beautifully frescoed Pilat's House on Ludwig Thomastrasse is a living workshop full of wood-carvers and painters in action (free, May–Oct, Dec, and Feb Mon–Fri 13:00–18:00; closed Nov, Jan, and March–April). Or see folk art at the town's Heimatmuseum (Tue–Sun 14:00–18:00, closed Mon;

TI Mon–Fri 8:30–18:00, less on weekends and off-season, tel. 08822/92310, www.oberammergau.de). For accommodations, see "Sleeping in Oberammergau," below.

Oberammergau Church: Visit the church, a poor cousin of the one at Wies. This church looks richer than it is. Put your hand on the "marble" columns. If they warm up, they're fakes—"stucco marble." Wander through the graveyard. Ponder the deaths that two wars dealt Germany. Behind the church are the photos of three Schneller brothers, all killed within two years in World War II.

Passion Play: Still making good on a deal the townspeople struck with God when they were spared devastation by the Black Plague several centuries ago, once each decade Oberammergau presents the Passion Play. For 100 summer days in a row, the town performs an all-day dramatic story of Christ's crucifixion (in 2000, 5,000 people attended per day). Until the next performance in 2010, you'll have to settle for reading the Book, seeing Nicodemus tool around town in his VW, or browsing through the theater's exhibition hall (€2.50, German tours daily 9:30–17:00, tel. 08822/94588, ext. 33, or 08822/32278). English speakers get little respect here, with only two theater tours a day scheduled (often at 11:00 and 14:00). They may do others if you pay the €25 or gather 10 needy English speakers.

Sleeping in Oberammergau (zip code: 82487): **Hotel Bayerische Löwe** is central, with a good restaurant and 18 comfortable rooms (Db-€56, no CC, Dedlerstrasse 2, tel. 08822/1365, e-mail: gasthof.loewe@freenet.de, family Reinhofer). **Gasthof Zur Rose** is a big, central, family-run place with 20 rooms (Sb-€33, Db-€56, Tb-€71, Qb-€82, CC, Dedlerstrasse 9, tel. 08822/4706, fax 08822/6753, e-mail: gasthof-rose@t-online.de, SE). The last three are lower-priced: **Frau Maderspacher** rents three cozy, old-time rooms in her very characteristic 160-year-old home (D-€32, a block past Gasthof Zur Rose at Daisenbergerstrasse 11, tel. 08822/3978, NSE). **Frau Magold's** three bright and spacious rooms are twice as nice as the cheap hotel rooms for much less money (Db-€37–42, immediately behind Gasthof Zur Rose at Kleppergasse 1, tel. 08822/4340, NSE). Oberammergau's modern **youth hostel** is on the river a short walk from the center (€12 beds, no CC, open year-round, tel. 08822/4114, fax 08822/1695).

Getting to Oberammergau: From Füssen to Oberammergau, four to six buses run daily (fewer in winter, 1.75 hrs). Trains run from Munich to Oberammergau (hrly, 1.75 hrs, change in Murnau). Drivers entering the town from the north should cross the bridge, take the second right, and park in the free lot a block beyond the TI. Leaving town, head out past the church and turn toward Ettal on Road 23. You're 30 kilometers (20 miles) from

Reutte via the scenic Plansee. If heading to Munich, Road 23 takes you to the autobahn, which gets you there in less than an hour.

▲▲Linderhof Castle—This homiest of "Mad" King Ludwig's castles is small and comfortably exquisite—good enough for a minor god. Set in the woods 15 minutes from Oberammergau by car or bus (hrly bus, June–mid-Oct, only 2/day off-season) and surrounded by fountains and sculpted, Italian-style gardens, it's the only palace I've toured that actually had me feeling envious. Don't miss the grotto—15-minute tours are included with the palace ticket (€6, April–Sept daily 9:00–18:00, Thu until 20:00, Oct–March daily 10:00–16:00, parking-€2, fountains often erupt on the hour, English tours when 15 gather—easy in summer but sparse off-season, tel. 08822/92030). Plan for lots of walking and a two-hour stop to fully enjoy this royal park. Pay at the entry and get an admission time. Visit outlying sights in the garden to pass any wait time.

▲▲Zugspitze—The tallest point in Germany is a border crossing. Lifts from Austria and Germany travel to the 3,075-meter (10,000-foot) summit of the Zugspitze. You can straddle the border between two great nations while enjoying an incredible view. Restaurants, shops, and telescopes await you at the summit.

On the German side, the 75-minute trip from Garmisch costs €42 round-trip; family discounts are available (buy a combo-ticket for cogwheel train to Eibsee and cable-car ride to summit, drivers can park for free at cable-car station at Eibsee, tel. 08821/7970). Allow plenty of time for afternoon descents: If bad weather hits in the late afternoon, cable cars can be delayed at the summit, causing tourists to miss their train from Eibsee back to Garmisch. Hikers enjoy the easy 10-kilometer (6-mile) walk around the lovely Eibsee (German side, 5 min downhill from cable car "Seilbahn").

On the Austrian side, from the less-crowded Talstation Obermoos above the village of Erwald, the tram zips you to the top in 10 minutes (€31 round-trip, cash only, late May–Oct daily 8:40–16:40, tel. in Austria 05673/2309).

The German ascent is easier for those without a car, but buses do connect the Erwald train station and the Austrian lift almost every hour.

Sleeping in Füssen

(€1 = about $1, country code: 49, area code: 08362, zip code: 87629)

Sleep Code: **S** = Single, **D** = Double/Twin, **T** = Triple, **Q** = Quad, **b** = bathroom, **s** = shower only, **CC** = Credit Cards accepted, **no CC** = Credit Cards not accepted, **SE** = Speaks English, **NSE** = No English.

To help you sort easily through these listings, I've divided the rooms into three categories based on the price for a standard double room with bath:

Higher Priced—Most rooms more than €80.

Moderately Priced—Most rooms €80 or less.

Lower Priced—Most rooms €50 or less.

Unless otherwise noted, breakfast is included, hall showers are free, and English is spoken. Prices listed are for one-night stays. Most places give about 10 percent off for two-night stays—always request this discount. Competition is fierce, and off-season prices are soft. High season is mid-June through September. Rooms are generally about 12 percent less in shoulder season and much cheaper in off-season.

While I prefer sleeping in Reutte (see below), convenient Füssen is just five kilometers (3 miles) from Ludwig's castles and offers a cobbled, riverside retreat. While it's very touristy (notice *das* sushi bar), it seems to have plenty of rooms. All recommended places are within a few blocks of the train station and the town center. Parking is easy at the station.

HIGHER PRICED

Hotel Hirsch is a big, romantic, old tour-class hotel with 53 rooms on the main street in the center of town (Db-€100–140 depending on room size and decor, CC, elevator, family rooms, free parking, Kaiser-Maximilian Platz 7, tel. 08362/93980, fax 08362/939-877, www.hotelhirsch.de, e-mail: info@hotelhirsch.de, SE).

Hotel Kurcafé is deluxe, with 30 spacious rooms and all of the amenities, including a very tempting bakery (Sb-€82, Db-€99–113, Tb-€123, Qb-€139, €10 more for weekends and holidays, CC, non-smoking rooms, elevator, on tiny traffic circle a block in front of station at Bahnhofstrasse 4, tel. 08362/6369, fax 08362/39424, www.kurcafe.com). The attached restaurant has good and reasonable weekly specials (open daily, choose between a traditional room and a pastel "winter garden").

Hotel Sonne, in the heart of town, rents 32 mod, institutional, yet comfy rooms (Sb-€85, Db-€105, Tb-€92–129, CC, free parking, kitty-corner from TI at Reichenstrasse 37, tel. 08362/9080, fax 08362/908-100, www.hotel-sonne.de).

MODERATELY PRICED

Altstadthotel zum Hechten offers all the modern comforts in a friendly, traditional shell right under Füssen Castle in the old-town pedestrian zone (S-€30, Sb-€45, D-€55, Db-€75–79, Tb-€100, Qb-€112, free parking, cheaper off-season and for longer stays, CC, fun mini-bowling alley in basement, nearby church bells ring hourly at night; from TI, walk down pedestrian street, take the

Füssen

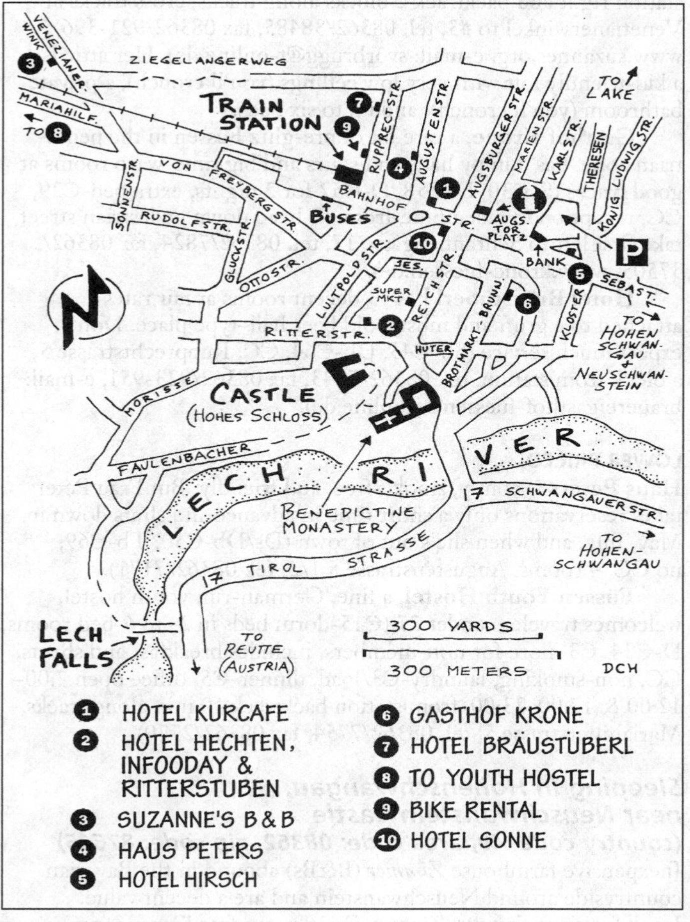

second right to Ritterstrasse 6, tel. 08362/91600, fax 08362/916-099, www.hotel-hechten.com).

Suzanne's B&B is a tidy, delightful place run by a plain-spoken, no-nonsense American woman who strikes some travelers as curt and brusque and others as warm and fun. Suzanne runs a tight ship, offering lots of local travel advice; backyard-fresh eggs; local cheese; a children's yard; laundry (€20/load); bright, woody, and spacious rooms; and feel-good balconies (Db-€75, Tb-€105, Qb-€125, attic special: €68 for 2, €95 for 3, €113 for 4; another room holds up to 6—ask for details, no CC, non-smoking, exit station right and backtrack 2 blocks along tracks, cross tracks at Venetianerwinkel to #3, tel. 08362/38485, fax 08362/921-396, www.suzannes.org, e-mail: svorbrugg@t-online.de). Her attic is a kid-friendly loft with very low ceilings (you'll crouch), a private bathroom (you'll crouch), and up to six beds.

Gasthof Krone, a rare bit of pre-glitz Füssen in the pedestrian zone, has dumpy halls and stairs and big time-warp rooms at good prices (S-€30, D-€58, D-€52 for 2 nights, extra bed-€29, CC, reception in restaurant, from TI head down pedestrian street, take first left to Schrannengasse 17, tel. 08362/7824, fax 08362/37505, www.krone-fuessen.de).

Hotel Bräustüberl has 13 decent rooms at fair rates attached to a gruff and musty, old beer hall–type place. Don't expect much service (Sb-€45, Db-€64, CC, Rupprechtstrasse 5, a block from station, tel. 08362/7843, fax 08362/923-951, e-mail: brauereigasthof-fuessen@t-online.de).

LOWER PRICED

Haus Peters is comfy, smoke-free, and friendly. But Frau Peters takes reservations only a short time in advance and shuts down in May, July, and when she's out of town (Ds/Db-€50, Tb-€69, no CC, 4 rooms, Augustenstrasse 5 1/2, tel. 08362/7171).

Füssen Youth Hostel, a fine, German-run youth hostel, welcomes travelers under 27 (€15-dorm beds in 2- to 6-bed rooms, D-€34, €3 more for non-members, includes breakfast and sheets, CC, non-smoking, laundry-€3/load, dinner-€5, office open 7:00–12:00 & 17:00–23:00, from station backtrack 10 min along tracks, Mariahilferstrasse 5, tel. 08362/7754, fax 08362/2770).

Sleeping in Hohenschwangau, near Neuschwanstein Castle
(country code: 49, area code: 08362, zip code: 87645)

Inexpensive farmhouse *Zimmer* (B&Bs) abound in the Bavarian countryside around Neuschwanstein and are a decent value. Look for signs that say *Zimmer Frei* ("room free," or vacancy). The going rate is about €50 to €65 for a double, including breakfast. The following places are a step up in quality.

MODERATELY PRICED

Beim "Landhannes" is a hundred-year-old working dairy farm run by Johann and Traudl Mayr. They rent six creaky, well-antlered rooms and keep flowers on the balconies, big bells in the halls, and cows in the yard (Sb-€30, Ds-€50, Db-€60, 10 percent discount for 2 nights, no CC, poorly signed in the village of Horn on the Füssen side of Schwangau, look for the farm 100 meters/330 feet in front of Hotel Kleiner König, Am Lechrain 22, 87645 Schwangau-Horn, tel. 08362/8349, fax 08362/819-646, www.landhannes.de, e-mail: mayr@landhannes.de).

Sonnenhof is a big, woody, old house with four spacious, traditionally decorated rooms and a cheery garden. It's a short walk through the fields to the castles (D-€44, Db-€54, no CC, cheaper for 2 nights; at Pension Schwansee on the Füssen–Neuschwanstein road, follow the small lane 100 meters/330 feet, to Sonnenweg 11, tel. 08362/8420, Frau Görlich SE).

Alpenhotel Meier is a small, family-run hotel with 15 rooms in a bucolic setting within walking distance of the castles, just beyond the lower parking lot (Sb-€46, Db-€77, plus €1.20 tourist tax per person, 5 percent discount with cash and this book, 2-night discounts, CC, all rooms have porches or balconies, family rooms, sauna, easy parking, just before tennis courts at Schwangauerstrasse 37, tel. 08362/81152, fax 08362/987-028, www.alpenhotel-allgaeu.de, e-mail: alpenhotelmeier@firemail.de, Frau Meier SE).

Eating in Füssen

Füssen's old town and main pedestrian drag are lined with a variety of eateries. Three good places cluster on Ritterstrasse, just under the castle, off the top of the main street:

Ritterstuben offers reasonable and delicious fish, salads, veggie plates, and a fun kids' menu (Tue–Sun 11:30–14:30 & 17:30–23:00, closed Mon, Ritterstrasse 4, tel. 08362/7759). Demure, English-speaking Gabi serves while her husband cooks.

Zum Hechten Restaurant serves hearty, traditional Bavarian fare and specializes in pike *(Hecht)* pulled from the Lech River (€8–12 meals, Thu–Tue 11:30–14:30 & 17:30–21:00, closed Wed, Ritterstrasse 6).

Infooday is a clever and modern self-service eatery that sells its hot meals and salad bar by weight and offers English newspapers (filling salad-€3, meals-€5, Mon–Fri 10:30–18:30, Sat 10:30–14:30, closed Sun, Ritterstrasse 6).

Transportation Connections—Füssen

To: Neuschwanstein (hrly buses, 10 min, €1.65 one-way, €3 round-trip; taxis cost €10 one-way), **Reutte** (Mon–Fri 6 buses/day, Sat 4/day, none Sun, 30 min; taxis cost €21 one-way), **Munich** (hrly trains, 2 hrs, some change in Buchloe). Train info: tel. 01805/996-633.

Romantic Road Buses: The northbound Romantic Road bus departs Füssen at 8:00; the southbound bus arrives at Füssen at 20:15 (bus stops at train station). Railpasses get you a 60 percent discount on the Romantic Road bus (and the ride does not use up a day of a Flexipass). For more information, see the Rothenburg chapter.

REUTTE, AUSTRIA

(€1 = about $1)

Reutte (pron. ROY-teh, rolled "r"), a relaxed town of 5,700, is located 20 minutes across the border from Füssen. It's far from the international tourist crowd, but popular with Germans and Austrians for its climate. Doctors recommend its "grade-1" air. Reutte's one claim to fame with Americans: As Nazi Germany was falling in 1945, Hitler's top rocket scientist, Werner von Braun, joined the Americans (rather than the Russians) in Reutte. You could say the American space program began here.

Reutte isn't featured in any other American guidebook. While its generous sidewalks are filled with smart boutiques and lazy coffeehouses, its charms are subtle. It was never rich or important. Its castle is ruined, its buildings have painted-on "carvings," its churches are full, its men yodel for each other on birthdays, and lately, its energy is spent soaking its Austrian and German guests in *Gemütlichkeit*. Most guests stay for a week, so the town's attractions are more time-consuming than thrilling. If the weather's good, hike to the mysterious Ehrenberg ruins, ride the luge, or rent a bike. For a slap-dancing bang, enjoy a Tirolean folk evening. For accommodations, see "Sleeping," page 433.

Orientation (area code: 05672)

Tourist Information: Reutte's TI is a block in front of the train station (Mon–Fri 8:00–12:00 & 14:00–17:00, Sat 8:30–12:00, closed Sun, tel. 05672/62336 or, from Germany, 00-43-5672/62336, Herr Ammann). Go over your sightseeing plans, ask about a folk evening, pick up city and biking maps, and ask about discounts with the hotel guest cards. They play their German-language town intro video (20 min) free upon request. Their "Information" booklet has a good self-guided town walk.

Bike Rental: In the center, the Heinz Glätzle shop rents out good bikes (city and mountain bikes-€15/day, kids' bikes-€7.50/day, inside toy store at Obermarkt 61, Mon–Sat 8:00–18:00, closed Sun, tel. 05672/62752). Several recommended hotels loan or rent bikes to guests. Most of the sights described in this chapter make good biking destinations. Ask about the bike path *(Radwanderweg)* along the Lech River.

Laundry: Don't ask the TI about a launderette. Unless you can infiltrate the local campground, Hotel Maximilian, or Gutshof zum Schluxen (see "Sleeping," below), the town has none.

Sights—Reutte

▲▲**Ehrenberg Ruins**—The brooding ruins of Ehrenberg Castle are 1.5 kilometers (1 mile) outside of Reutte on the road to Lermoos and Innsbruck. This is a pleasant walk or a short bike ride from Reutte; bikers can use the trail—*Radwanderweg*—along the Lech River (the TI has a good map).

Ehrenberg, a 13th-century rock pile, provides a great contrast to King Ludwig's "modern" castles and a super opportunity to let your imagination off its leash.

At the parking lot at the base of the ruin-topped hill, you'll find the café/guest house Gasthof Klaus (closed Wed), which offers a German-language flier about the castle and has a wall painting of the intact castle.

The parking lot lies on the ancient Roman road, Via Claudia, and the medieval salt road. The **fortification** at the parking lot was a castle built over the road to control traffic and levy tolls on all that passed this strategic valley. (This will open as a museum of European castle ruins in about 2004.)

Hike up 20 minutes from the parking lot for a great view from your own private ruins. Facing the hill from the parking lot, find the gravelly road at the Klaus sign. Follow the road to the saddle between the two hills. From the saddle, notice how the castle stands high on the horizon. This is Ehrenberg (which means "mountain of honor"), built in 1290. Thirteenth-century castles were designed to stand boastfully tall. With the advent of gunpowder, castles dug in. Notice the **ramparts** around you. They are from the 18th century. Approaching Ehrenberg castle, look for the small door to the left. It's the night entrance (tight and awkward, therefore safer in a surprise invasion).

While hiking up the hill, you go through two doors. Castles allowed step-by-step retreat, giving defenders time to regroup and fight back against invading forces.

Before making the final and steepest ascent, follow the path around to the right to a big, grassy courtyard with commanding views and a fat, newly restored **turret**. This stored gunpowder and held a big cannon that enjoyed a clear view of the valley below. In medieval times, all the trees approaching the castle were cleared to keep an unobstructed view.

Look out over the valley. The pointy spire marks **Breitenwang**, which was a stop on the ancient Via Claudia. In A.D. 46, there was a Roman camp there. In 1489, after the Reutte bridge crossed the Lech River, Reutte (marked by the onion-domed church) was made a market town and eclipsed Breitenwang in importance. Any gliders circling? They launch from just over the river in Höfen (see "Flying and Gliding," below).

Reutte

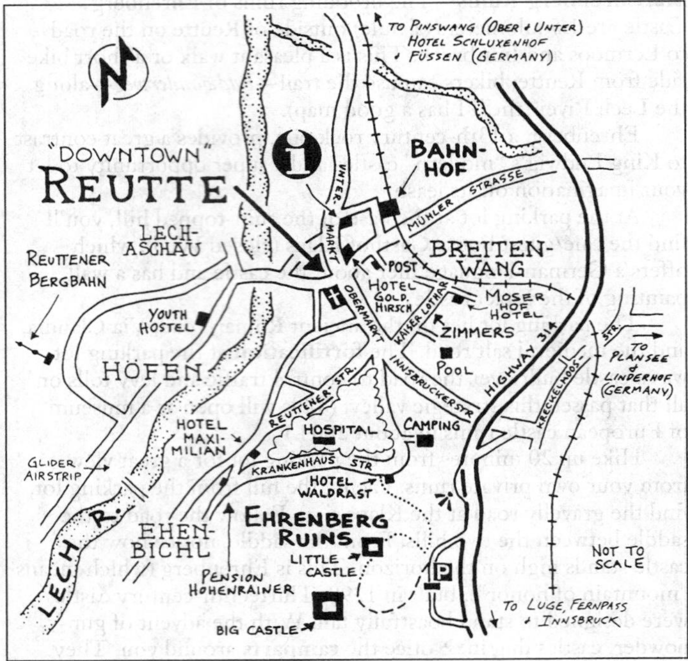

For centuries, this castle was the seat of government—ruling an area called the "judgment of Ehrenberg" (roughly the same as today's "district of Reutte"). When the emperor came by, he stayed here. In 1604, the ruler moved downtown into more comfortable quarters, and the castle was no longer a palace.

Climb the steep hill to the top of the castle. Take the high ground. There was no water supply here, just kegs of wine, beer, and a cistern to collect rain.

Ehrenberg repelled 16,000 Swedish soldiers in the defense of Catholicism in 1632. Ehrenberg saw three or four other battles, but its end was not glorious. In the 1780s, a local businessman bought the castle in order to sell off its parts. Later, when vagabonds moved in, the roof was removed to make squatting miserable. With the roof gone, deterioration quickened, leaving this evocative shell and a whiff of history.

The Ehrenberg ruins were once part of an "ensemble" of four castles (the *Schlossensemble*) that made up the largest fort in Tirol, established to defend Tirol against Bavaria. The toll fort on the valley floor is flanked by Ehrenberg and a sister castle (out of sight) on the opposite side. After locals rained cannonballs on Ehrenberg from the bluff above it, a much bigger castle was built atop that hill. In 2001, the castle was completely overgrown with trees—you couldn't see it from Reutte. Today, the trees are shaved away, and the castle has been excavated. This is part of a huge project to make a European Castle Museum, showing off 500 years of military architecture in one swoop. The museum should be ready for castle-lovers in 2004. The European Union is helping fund the project because it promotes the heritage of a region (Tirol), rather than a nation. The EU's vision is for a zone of regions, instead of nations.

Folk Museum—Reutte's Heimatmuseum, offering a quick look at the local folk culture and the story of the castle, is more cute than impressive. Ask to borrow the packet of information in English (€2, May–Oct Tue–Sun 10:00–12:00 & 14:00–17:00, closed Mon and Nov–April, in the bright green building on Untermarkt, around corner from Hotel Goldener Hirsch).

▲▲Tirolean Folk Evening—Ask the TI or your hotel if there's a Tirolean folk evening scheduled. Usually on Wednesdays in the summer (July–Sept), Reutte or a nearby town puts on an evening of yodeling, slap dancing, and Tirolean frolic worth the €6 to €9 and short drive. Off-season, you'll have to do your own yodeling. There are also weekly folk concerts in the park (summer only, ask at TI).

Swimming—Plunge into Reutte's Olympic-size "Alpenbad" swimming pool to cool off after your castle hikes (€5.25, June–Aug daily 10:00–21:00, Sept–May Tue–Sun 14:00–21:00, closed Mon; indoor/outdoor pools, big water slide, mini-golf, playground on-site, 5 min on foot from Reutte center, head out Obermarkt and turn left on Kaiser Lothar Strasse, tel. 05672/62666).

Reuttener Bergbahn—This mountain lift swoops you high above the tree line to a starting point for several hikes and an alpine flower park with special paths leading you past countless local varieties (flowers best in late July, lift usually May–Oct daily 9:00–17:00, tel. 05672/62420).

Flying and Gliding—For a major thrill on a sunny day, drop by the tiny airport in Höfen across the river, and fly. A small single-prop plane can buzz the Zugspitze and Ludwig's castles and give you a bird's-eye peek at Reutte's Ehrenberg ruins (2 people for 30 min-€110, 1 hr-€220, tel. 05672/62827, phone rarely answered, and then not in English, so your best bet is to show up at Höfen airport on good-weather afternoons). Or, for something more angelic, how about *Segelfliegen*? For €37, you get 30 minutes in a glider for two (you and the pilot). Just watching the towrope launch the graceful glider like a giant, slow-motion rubber-band gun is thrilling (late May–Oct 11:00–19:00, in good but breezy weather only, find someone in the know at the Thermic Ranch, tel. 05672/71550 or 05672/64010).

Sights—Tirol, Near Reutte

▲▲The Luge *(Sommerrodelbahn)*—Near Lermoos, on the road from Reutte to Innsbruck, you'll find two exciting luge courses, or *Sommerrodelbahn*. To try one of Europe's great €6 thrills, take the lift up, grab a sled-like go-cart, and luge down. The concrete course banks on the corners, and even a novice can go very, very fast. Most are cautious on their first run, speed demons on their second (and bruised and bloody on their third). A woman once showed me her journal illustrated with her husband's dried five-inch-long luge scab. He disobeyed the only essential rule of luging: Keep both hands on your stick. To avoid getting into a bumper-to-bumper traffic jam, let the person in front of you get way ahead before you start. No one emerges from the course without a windblown hairdo and a smile-creased face. Both places charge the same price (€6 per run, 5- and 10-trip discount cards) and shut down at the least hint of rain (call ahead to make sure they're open; you're more likely to get luge info in English if you call the TIs, see below). If you're without a car, these are not worth the trouble (consider the luge near Neuschwanstein instead—see "Tegelberg Luge," above).

The short and steep luge: Bichlbach, the first course (100-meter/330-foot drop over 800-meter/2,600-foot course), is six kilometers (less than 4 miles) beyond Reutte's castle ruins. Look for a chairlift on the right, and exit on the tiny road at the Almkopfbahn Rosthof sign (June–Sept daily 10:00–17:00, sometimes opens in spring and fall—especially weekends—depending on weather, call first, tel. 05674/5350, or contact the local TI at tel. 05674/5354).

The longest luge: The Biberwier *Sommerrodelbahn* is a better luge and, at 1,300 meters (4,250 feet), the longest in Austria (15 min farther from Reutte than Bichlbach, just past Lermoos in Biberwier—the first exit after a long tunnel). The only drawbacks are its short season and hours (open mid-May–June Sat–Sun 9:00–16:30 only, closed Mon–Fri, July–Sept daily 9:00–16:30, call first, tel. 05673/2111 or 05673/2323, TI tel. 05673/2922).

▲Fallerschein—Easy for drivers and a special treat for those who may have been Kit Carson in a previous life, this extremely remote log-cabin village is a 1,230-meter-high (4,000-foot), flower-speckled world of serene slopes and cowbells. Thunderstorms roll down the valley like it's God's bowling alley, but the pint-size church on the high ground, blissfully simple in a land of Baroque, seems to promise that this huddle of houses will survive, and the river and breeze will just keep flowing. The couples sitting on benches are mostly Austrian vacationers who've rented cabins here. Many of them, appreciating the remoteness of Fallerschein, are having affairs. Fallerschein, at the end of the two-kilometer (1.25-mile) Berwang Road, is near Namlos and about 45 minutes southwest of Reutte. You'll find a parking lot at the "end of the road," leaving you with a three-kilometer (2-mile) walk down a drivable but technically closed one-lane road. The town has a mountain hut with cheap beds (details from any regional TI).

Sleeping in and near Reutte

(€1 = about $1, country code: 43, area code: 05672, zip code: 6600)

To help you sort easily through these listings, I've divided the rooms into three categories based on the price for a standard double room with bath:

Higher Priced—Most rooms more than €80.
Moderately Priced—Most rooms €80 or less.
Lower Priced—Most rooms €50 or less.

Reutte is a mellow Füssen with fewer crowds and easygoing locals with a contagious love of life. Come here for a good dose of Austrian ambience and lower prices. Those with a car should home-base here; those without should consider it. (To call Reutte from Germany, dial 00-43-5672, then the local number.) You'll drive across the border without stopping. Reutte is popular with Austrians and Germans, who come here year after year for one- or two-week vacations. The hotels are big, elegant, and full of comfy, carved furnishings and creative ways to spend lots of time in one spot. They take great pride in their restaurants, and the owners send their children away to hotel management schools. All include a great breakfast, but few accept credit cards. Most places give about a 5 percent discount for stays of two nights or longer.

Sleeping in Reutte

HIGHER PRICED

Moserhof Hotel is a plush Tirolean splurge with polished service and facilities, including an elegant dining room (Sb-€52, Db-€84, extra bed-€35, 10 percent discount with this book, no CC, all rooms have balconies, parking garage, elevator, Internet access; from downtown Reutte, follow signs to village Breitenwang, it's just after church at Planseestrasse 44, tel. 05672/62020, fax 05672/620-2040, www.hotel-moserhof.at, Hosp family).

MODERATELY PRICED

Hotel Goldener Hirsch, located in the center of Reutte just two blocks from the station, is a grand old hotel renovated with Tirolean *Jugendstil* flair. It includes minibars, cable TV, and one lonely set of antlers (Sb-€52, Db-€76, Tb-€106, Qb-€124–131, 2-night discounts, CC, a few family rooms, elevator, quality food in their restaurant, 6600 Reutte-Tirol, tel. 05672/62508, fax 05672/625-087, www.goldener-hirsch.at, Monika, Helmut, and daughter Vanessa).

LOWER PRICED

The homey hostel **Jugendgästehaus Graben** has two to six beds per room and includes breakfast and sheets. Frau Reyman and her son Rudy keep the place traditional, clean, and friendly, and serve a great €6.60 dinner for guests only. This is a super value. If you've never hosteled and are curious (and have a car or don't mind a bus ride), try it. They accept non-members of any age (dorm bed-€18, Db-€44, no CC, non-smoking rooms, Internet access, laundry service, no curfew, bus connection to Neuschwanstein via Reutte; about 3 km, less than 2 miles, from Reutte, from downtown Reutte, cross bridge and follow main road left along river, or take the bus—1 bus/hr until 19:30, ask for Graben stop; Graben 1, A-6600 Reutte-Höfen, tel. 05672/626-440, fax 05672/626-444, www.hoefen.at, e-mail: jgh-hoefen@tirol.com).

Sleeping in Ehenbichl, near Reutte

The next two listings are a few kilometers upriver from Reutte in the village of Ehenbichl, under the Ehrenberg ruins. From central Reutte, go south on Obermarkt and turn right on Reuttenerstrasse, following signs to Ehenbichl.

MODERATELY PRICED

Hotel Maximilian is a fine splurge. It includes free bicycles, table tennis, a children's playroom, and the friendly service of the Koch family. Daughter Gabi speaks flawless English. The Kochs host many special events, and their hotel has lots of wonderful extras such as a sauna, a masseuse, and a beauty salon (Sb-€35–38, Db-€70–80, family deals, CC, fast Internet access, laundry service-€7/load even for non-guests, good restaurant, A-6600 Ehenbichl-Reutte, tel. 05672/62585, fax 05672/625-8554, www.maxihotel.com, e-mail: maxhotel@netway.at). They rent cars to guests only (1 VW Golf, 1 VW van, book in advance).

Gasthof-Pension Waldrast, separating a forest and a meadow, is run by the farming Huter family and their huge, friendly dog, Bari. The place feels hauntingly quiet and has no restaurant, but it does offer 10 nice rooms with sitting areas and castle-view balconies (Sb-€30, Db-€51–55, Tb-€66, Qb-€88, 10 percent discount with this book and 2 nights, no CC, non-smoking, 1.5 km/less than 1 mile from Reutte, just off main drag toward Innsbruck, past campground and under castle ruins on Ehrenbergstrasse, 6600 Reutte-Ehenbichl, tel. & fax 05672/62443, www.waldrast.com, e-mail: waldrast@aon.at).

LOWER PRICED

Pension Hohenrainer is a big, no-frills alternative to Hotel Maximilian—a quiet, good value with 12 modern rooms and some castle-view balconies (Sb-€23–29, Db-€41–50, CC, free Internet access, follow signs up the road behind Hotel Maximilian into village of Ehenbichl, tel. 05672/62544 and 63262, fax 05672/62052, www.hohenrainer.at).

Sleeping in Pinswang

MODERATELY PRICED

Closer to Füssen but still in Austria, **Gutshof zum Schluxen**, run by helpful Hermann, gets the "remote-old-hotel-in-an-idyllic-setting" award. This family-friendly working farm offers modern rustic elegance draped in goose down and pastels, and a chance to pet a rabbit and feed the deer. Its picturesque meadow setting will turn you into a dandelion picker, and its proximity to Neuschwanstein will turn you into a hiker. King Ludwig II himself is said to have slept here (Sb-€41, Db-€82, extra person-€22, 10 percent discount for 4 nights or more, CC, Internet access, self-service laundry, free pickup from Reutte and Füssen, good restaurant, fun bar, mountain bike rental, between Reutte and Füssen in village of Pinswang, A-6600 Pinswang-Reutte, tel. 05677/8903, fax 05677/890-323, www.schluxen.com, e-mail: welcome@schluxen.com).

Private Homes in Breitenwang, near Reutte

The Reutte TI has a list of 50 private homes *(Zimmer)* that rent out generally good rooms with facilities down the hall, pleasant communal living rooms, and breakfast. Most charge €15 per person per night and speak little or no English. Reservations are nearly impossible for one- or two-night stays, but short stops are welcome if you just drop in and fill available gaps. Most *Zimmer* charge €1.25–1.50 extra for heat in the winter (worth it). The TI can always find you a room when you arrive.

Right next door to Reutte is the older and quieter village of Breitenwang. It has all the best *Zimmer*, the recommended Moserhof Hotel (above), and a bakery (a 20-min walk from

Reutte train station—at post office roundabout, follow Planseestrasse past onion dome to pointy straight dome; unmarked Kaiser Lothar Strasse is first right past this church).

LOWER PRICED

The following three *Zimmer* are comfortable, quiet, have few stairs, and are within two blocks of the Breitenwang church steeple: **Helene Haissl** (the best of the bunch, D-€30, 2-night discounts, no CC, children's loft room available, beautiful troll-filled garden, free bikes, laundry service, across from big Alpenhotel Ernberg at Planseestrasse 63, tel. 05672/67913); **Inge Hosp** (S-€16, D-€30, no CC, an old-fashioned place, includes antlers over breakfast table, Kaiser Lothar Strasse 36, tel. 05672/62401); and **Walter and Emilie Hosp** (Inge's more formal in-laws, rent 3 rooms in a modern house across the street, D-€40, D-€36 for 2 nights, extra person-€15, no CC, Kaiser Lothar Strasse 29, tel. 05672/65377).

Eating in Reutte

Hotels here take great pleasure in earning their guests' loyalty by serving local cuisine at reasonable prices. Rather than go to a cheap restaurant, eat at your hotel. Most serve €8 to €14 dinners from 18:00 to 21:00 and are closed one night a week. Reutte itself has plenty of inviting eateries—traditional, ethnic, fast food, grocery stores, and delis. **Alina Restaurant** serves good Italian in Breitenwang village (closed Mon, Bachweg 7, tel. 05672/65008).

Transportation Connections—Reutte

By train to: Innsbruck (7/day, 2.5 hrs, change in Garmisch and sometimes also in Mittenwald), **Munich** (hrly, 2.5–3 hrs, change in Garmisch, Pfronten-Steinach, or Kempten).

By bus to: Füssen (Mon–Fri 6 buses/day, Sat 4/day, none Sun, 30 min, buses depart from in front of the train station, pay driver). Taxis cost €21 one-way.

By car into Reutte from Germany: Skip the north *(Nord)* exit and take the south *(Süd)* exit into town. While Austria requires a toll sticker for driving on its highways (€8/10 days, buy at the border, gas stations, car rental agencies, or *Tabak* shops), those just dipping into Tirol from Bavaria do not need one.

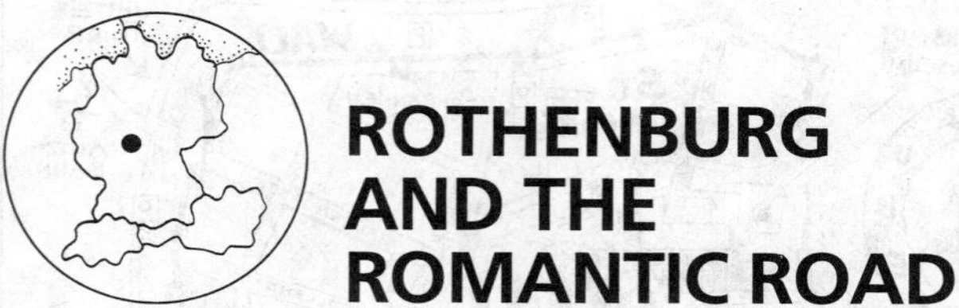

ROTHENBURG AND THE ROMANTIC ROAD

From Munich or Füssen to Frankfurt, the Romantic Road takes you through Bavaria's medieval heartland, a route strewn with picturesque villages, farmhouses, onion-domed churches, Baroque palaces, and walled cities.

Linger in Rothenburg (pron. ROE-ten-burg), Germany's best-preserved walled town. Countless travelers have searched for the elusive "untouristy Rothenburg." There are many contenders (such as Michelstadt, Miltenberg, Bamberg, Bad Windsheim, and Dinkelsbühl), but none holds a candle to the king of medieval German cuteness. Even with crowds, overpriced souvenirs, Japanese-speaking night watchmen, and, yes, even *Schneebälle*, Rothenburg is best. Save time and mileage and be satisfied with the winner.

Planning Your Time

The best one-day drive through the heartland of Germany is the Romantic Road. The road is clearly marked for drivers, and well-described in the free brochure available at any TI. Those without wheels can take the bus tour; see the end of this chapter for details (railpass holders get a 60 percent discount, so the entire Frankfurt-to-Munich trip costs €29). Apart from Würzburg, with its Prince Bishop's Residenz, the only stop worth more than a few minutes is Rothenburg. Twenty-four hours is ideal for this town. With two nights and a day, you'll be able to see the essentials and actually relax a little.

ROTHENBURG

In the Middle Ages, when Frankfurt and Munich were just wide spots on the road, Rothenburg-ob-der-Tauber was Germany's second-largest free imperial city, with a whopping population of

Rothenburg

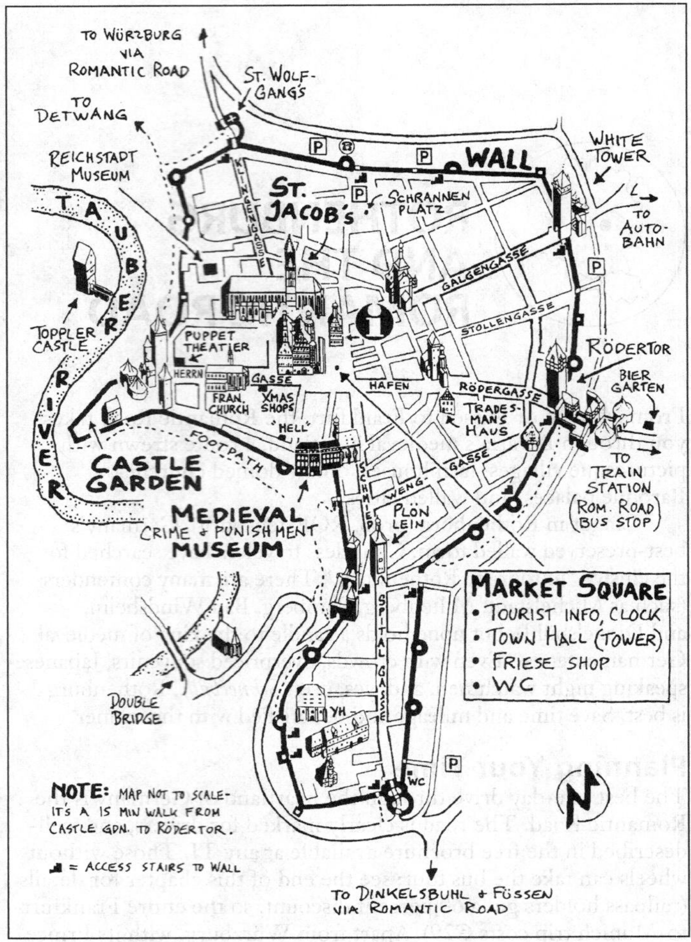

6,000. Today, it's her best-preserved medieval walled town, enjoying tremendous tourist popularity without losing its charm. Get medievaled in Rothenburg.

During Rothenburg's heyday, from 1150 to 1400, it was the crossing point of two major trade routes: Tashkent–Paris and Hamburg–Venice. Today, the great trade is tourism; two-thirds of the townspeople are employed to serve you. Too often, Rothenburg brings out the shopper in visitors before they've had a chance to see the historic city. True, this is a great place to do your German shopping, but appreciate the town's great history and sights first. While 2.5 million people visit each year, a mere 500,000 spend the night. Rothenburg is most enjoyable early and late, when the tour groups are gone. Rothenburg is very busy through the summer and in the Christmas Market month of December. Spring and fall are great, but it's pretty bleak from January through March—when most locals are hibernating or on vacation.

Rothenburg in a day is easy, with five essential experiences: the Medieval Crime and Punishment Museum, the Riemenschneider wood carving in St. Jakob's Church, the city walking tour, a walk along the wall, and the entertaining Night Watchman's Tour. With more time, there are several mediocre but entertaining museums, walking and biking in the nearby countryside, and lots of cafés and shops. Make a point to spend at least one night. The town is yours after dark, when the groups vacate and the town's floodlit cobbles wring some romance out of any travel partner.

Orientation (area code: 09861)

To orient yourself in Rothenburg, think of the town map as a human head. Its nose—the castle garden—sticks out to the left, and the neck is the skinny lower part, with the hostel and some of the best hotels in the Adam's apple. The town is a joy on foot. No sight or hotel is more than a 15-minute walk from the train station or each other.

Most of the buildings you'll see were built by 1400. The city was born around its long-gone castle—built in 1142, destroyed in 1356—which was located on the present-day site of the castle garden. You can see the shadow of the first town wall, which defines the oldest part of Rothenburg, in its contemporary street plan. A few gates from this wall still survive. The richest and biggest houses were in this central part. The commoners built higgledy-piggledy (read: picturesquely) farther from the center near the present walls.

Tourist Information: The TI is on Market Square (April–Oct Mon–Fri 9:00–12:00 & 13:00–18:00, Sat 10:00–15:00, closed Sun, shorter hours off-season, tel. 09861/40492, www.rothenburg.de). If there's a long line, just raid the rack where they keep all the free pamphlets. The "map and guide" comes with a virtual walking guide to the town. The "Information" monthly lists all the events and entertainment. Ask about the daily 14:00 walking tour (May–Oct). There's free Internet access in the TI lobby (1 terminal). A handy map with all hotels—highlighting which ones still have rooms available, with a free direct phone connection to them—is just outside the door for late arrivals. The best town map is available free at the Friese shop, two doors from the TI (toward St. Jakob's Church; see "Shopping," below).

Arrival in Rothenburg

By Train: It's a 10-minute walk from the station to Rothenburg's Market Square (following the brown *Altstadt* signs, exit left from station, turn right on Ansbacher Strasse, and head straight into the Middle Ages). Day-trippers can leave luggage in station lockers (€2, on platform) or at the Friese shop on Market Square. Arrange train and *couchette*/sleeper reservations at the travel agency in the station (no charge for quick questions, Mon–Fri 9:00–18:00, Sat 9:00–13:00, closed Sun, tel. 09861/4611). The nearest WCs are at the snack bar next door to the station. Taxis wait at the station (€5 to any hotel).

By Car: Parking lots line the town walls, ranging from free (the P5 parking lot just outside Klingentor) to €4 per day. Park outside of town and walk five minutes to the center. Only those with a hotel reservation can park within the walls after hours (but not during festivals; easiest entry often via Spittaltor).

Helpful Hints

Laundry: A handy launderette is near the station off Ansbacher Strasse (€5.50/load, includes soap, English instructions, Mon–Fri 8:00–18:00, Sat 8:00–12:00, closed Sun, Johannitergasse 8, tel. 09861/2775).

Swimming: Rothenburg has a fine modern recreation center with an indoor/outdoor pool and sauna. It's just a few minutes' walk down the Dinkelsbühl Road (Hallenbad, adult-€3, child-€1.50, swimsuit and towel rental-€1.50 each, Fri–Wed 9:00–20:00, Thu 10:00–20:00, Nordlingerstrasse 20, tel. 09861/4565).

Festivals

Rothenburgers dress up in medieval costumes and beer gardens spill out into the street to celebrate Mayor Nusch's Meistertrunk victory (Whitsun weekend, June 7–9 in 2003, see story below under "Rothenburg Town Walk—Meistertrunk Show") and 700 years of history in the Imperial City Festival (Sept 5–7 in 2003, with fireworks).

Christmas Market: Rothenburg is dead in November, January, and February, but December is its busiest month—the entire town cranks up the medieval cuteness with concerts and costumes, shops with schnapps, stalls filling squares, hot spiced wine, giddy nutcrackers, and mobs of earmuffed Germans. Christmas markets are big all over Germany, and Rothenburg's is considered one of the best. The festival takes place each year the four weeks before the last Sunday before Christmas (Nov 28–Dec 21 in 2003). Try to avoid Saturdays and Sundays, when big-city day-trippers really clog the grog.

Tours of Rothenburg

Night Watchman's Tour—This tour is flat-out the most entertaining hour of medieval wonder anywhere in Europe. The Night Watchman (a.k.a. Hans Georg Baumgartner) lights his lamp and takes tourists on his one-hour rounds, telling slice-of-gritty-life tales of medieval Rothenburg (€4, April–Dec nightly at 20:00, in English, meet at Market Square, www.nightwatchman.de). This is the best evening activity in town.

Old Town Historic Walk—The TI on Market Square offers 90-minute guided walking tours in English (€4, May–Oct daily at 14:00 from Market Square). Take this for the serious history of Rothenburg and to make sense of its architecture. Alternatively, you can hire your own **private guide**—a local historian can really bring the ramparts alive. Gisela Vogl (tel. 09861/4957, e-mail: werner.vogl@t-online.de, €50/90 min, €70/2 hr) and Anita Weinzierl (tel. 09868/7993) are both good.

Horse-and-Buggy Rides—These give you a relaxing 30-minute clip-clop through the old town, starting from Market Square or Schrannenplatz (private buggy for €30, or wait for one to fill up for €5.10 per person).

Rothenburg Town Walk

This one-hour walk weaves together Rothenburg's top sights. Start the walk on Market Square.

Market Square Spin Tour—Stand at the bottom of Market Square (3 meters/10 feet below the wooden post on the corner) and—ignoring the little white arrow—spin 360 degrees clockwise, starting with the city hall tower. Now do it again slower, following these notes:

Town Hall and Tower—The city's tallest spire is the **town hall tower.** At 62 meters (200 feet), it stands atop the old city hall, a white, Gothic, 13th-century building. Notice the tourists enjoying the best view in town from the black top of the tower (€1 and a rigorous but interesting climb, 214 steps, April–Oct daily 9:30–12:30 & 13:30–17:00, Nov–March Sat–Sun 12:00–15:00 only, enter on Market Square through middle arch of new town hall). After a fire burned down part of the original building, a **new town hall** was built alongside what survived of the old one (fronting the square). This is in Renaissance style from 1570.

Meistertrunk Show—At the top of Market Square stands the proud **Councillors' Tavern** (clock tower, from 1466). In its day, the city council drank here. Today, it's the TI and the focus of all the attention when the little doors on either side of the clock flip open and the wooden figures (from 1910) do their thing. Be on Market Square at 11:00, 12:00, 13:00, 14:00, 15:00, 20:00, 21:00, or 22:00 for the ritual gathering of the tourists to see the less-than-breathtaking reenactment of the Meistertrunk story. In 1631, the Catholic army took the Protestant town and was about to do its rape, pillage, and plunder thing when, as the story goes, the mayor said, "Hey, if I can drink this entire three-liter tankard of wine in one gulp, will you leave us alone?" The invading commander, sensing he was dealing with an unbalanced person, said, "Sure." Mayor Nusch drank the whole thing, the town was saved, and he slept for three days.

While this is a nice story, it was dreamed up in the late 1800s for a theatrical play designed to promote a romantic image of the town. In actuality, Rothenburg was occupied and ransacked several times in the Thirty Years' War, and it never recovered—which is why it's such a well-preserved time capsule today. Hint: For the best show, don't watch the clock; watch the open-mouthed tourists gasp as the old windows flip open. At the late shows, the square flickers with camera flashes.

Bottom of Market Square—On the bottom end of the square, the cream-colored building is a fine **print shop** (upstairs—see "Shopping," below). Adjoining that is the **Baumeister's House**, a touristy restaurant with a fine courtyard (see "Eating," below), with a famous Renaissance facade featuring statues of the seven virtues and the seven vices—the former supporting the latter. The green house below that is the former house of Mayor Toppler (now the recommended Greifen Guesthouse); next to it is a famous Scottish restaurant (with arches). Keep circling to the big 17th-century **St. George's fountain**. The long metal gutters slid, routing the water into the villagers' buckets. Rothenburg's many fountains had practical functions beyond providing drinking water. The water was used for fighting fires, and some fountains were stocked with fish during times of siege. Two fine buildings behind the fountain show the old-time lofts with warehouse doors and pulleys on top for hoisting. All over town, lofts were filled with grain and corn. A year's supply was required by the city so they could survive any siege. The building behind the fountain is an art gallery (free, daily 14:00–18:00) showing off the work of Rothenburg's top artists. To the right is an old-time pharmacy mixing old and new in typical Rothenburg style.

The broad street running under the town hall tower is **Herrngasse**. The town originated with its castle (built in 1142 but now long gone; only the castle garden remains). Herrngasse connected the castle to Market Square. The last leg of this circular walking tour will take you from the castle garden up Herrngasse to where you now stand. For now, walk a few steps down Herrngasse to the arch under the town hall tower (between the new and old town halls). On the left wall are the town's measuring rods—a reminder that medieval Germany was made of 300 independent little countries, each with its own weights and measures. Merchants and shoppers knew that these were the local standards: the rod (3.93 meters), the *Schuh* (or shoe, roughly a foot), and the ell (from elbow to fingertip—4 inches longer than mine . . . try it). Notice the protruding cornerstone. These are all over town—originally to protect buildings from reckless horse carts (and vice versa). Under the arch, you'll find the . . .

▲**Historical Town Hall Vaults**—This museum gives a waxy but good look at Rothenburg during the Catholics-vs.-Protestants Thirty Years' War. With fine English descriptions, it offers a look at "the fateful year 1631," a replica of the famous Meistertrunk tankard, and a dungeon complete with three dank cells and some torture lore (€2, April–Oct daily 9:30–17:30, less off-season).

From the museum, walk a couple of blocks to St. Jakob's Church (just northwest of Market Square). Outside the church, you'll see a statue of Jesus praying at Gethsemane, a common feature of Gothic churches. Downhill, notice the nub of a sandstone statue—a rare original, looking pretty bad after 500 years of weather and, more recently, pollution. Original statues are now in the city museum. Better-preserved statues you see in the church are copies. If it's your wedding day, take the first entrance. Otherwise, use the second door to enter . . .

▲▲**St. Jakob's Church**—Built in the 14th century, it's been Lutheran since 1544. Take a close look at the Twelve Apostles altar in front (from 1546, left permanently in its open festival-day position). Below Christ are statues of six saints. St. James (Jakob in German, pron. YAY-kohp) is the one with the shell. He's the saint of pilgrims, and this church was a stop on the medieval pilgrimage route to Santiago ("St. James" in Spanish) de Compostela in Spain. Study the painted panels—ever see Peter with spectacles? Around the back of the altarpiece (upper left) is a great painting of Rothenburg's Market Square in the 15th century—looking like it does today. Before leaving the front of the church, notice the old medallions above the carved choir stalls featuring the coats of arms of Rothenburg's leading families and portraits of city and church leaders.

Stairs in the back of the church, behind the pipe organ, lead to the artistic highlight of Rothenburg and perhaps the most wonderful wood carving in all of Germany: the glorious 500-year-old, 10-meter-high (33-foot) *Altar of the Holy Blood*. Tilman Riemenschneider, the Michelangelo of German wood-carvers, carved this from 1499 to 1504 to hold a precious rock crystal capsule, set in a cross that contains a scrap of tablecloth miraculously stained in the shape of a cross by a drop of communion wine. Below, in the scene of the Last Supper, Jesus gives Judas a piece of bread, marking him as the traitor, while John lays his head on Christ's lap. Everything is portrayed exactly as described in the Bible. On the left: Jesus enters Jerusalem. On the right: Jesus prays in the Garden of Gethsemane. Notice how Judas, with his big bag of cash, could be removed from the scene—illustrated by photos on the wall nearby—as was the tradition for the four days leading up to Easter (€1.50, April–Oct Mon–Sat 9:00–17:30, Sun 10:45–17:30, Nov–March daily 10:00–12:00 & 14:00–16:00, free helpful English info sheet).

From St. Jakob's Church, walk under the chapel two blocks down **Klingengasse** to Klosterhof street. (I've marked your spot with a small circular plaque in the road). Looking down Klingengasse, you see the Klingentor ("cliff tower"). This tower was Rothenburg's water cistern. From 1595 until 1910, a copper cistern high in the tower provided clean spring drinking water to the privileged. To the right of Klingentor is a good stretch of wall rampart to walk. To the left, the wall is low and simple, lacking a rampart because it guards only a cliff. The recommended Louvre Restaurant is a block down the street (see "Eating," page 454). Find the shell decorating a building on the street corner. That's the symbol of St. James (pilgrims commemorated their visit to Santiago de Compostela with a shell), indicating that this building is associated with the church. Walk under the shell, down Klosterhof (passing the colorful Altfränkische Weinstube; see "Eating," page 454) to the city history museum, housed in the former Dominican convent. Cloistered nuns used the lazy Susan embedded in the wall (to the right of museum door) to give food to the poor without being seen. Give it a wiggle.

▲▲Museum of the Imperial City (Reichsstadt Museum)—You'll get a scholarly sweep through Rothenburg's history here. Highlights include *The Rothenburg Passion*, a 12-panel series of paintings from 1492 showing scenes leading up to Christ's crucifixion; an exhibit of Jewish culture through the ages in Rothenburg; a 14th-century convent kitchen; romantic paintings of the town; and the fine Baumann collection of weapons and armor. Follow the *Rundgang Tour* signs (€3, April–Oct daily 9:30–17:30, Nov–March daily 13:00–16:00, English info sheet and descriptions, no photos, tel. 09861/939-043).

Leaving the museum, go around to the right and into the

convent garden (free)—a peaceful place to work on your tan... or mix a poison potion. Angle left through the nun's garden (site of the now-gone Dominican church), eventually leaving via an arch at the far end. But enjoy the herb garden first. Monks and nuns, who were responsible for concocting herbal cures in the olden days, often tended herb gardens. Smell (but don't pick) the *Pfefferminze*, *Juniper* (gin), *Chamomilla* (disinfectant), and *Origanum*. Don't smell the plants in the poison corner (potency indicated by the number of crosses... like spiciness stars in a Chinese restaurant).

Exiting opposite where you entered, you see the back end of an original barn (behind a mansion fronting Herrngasse). Go downhill to the town wall (view through bars). This part of the wall takes advantage of the natural fortification provided by the cliff and is therefore much smaller than the ramparts. Angle left along the wall to Herrngasse and then right under the tower (Burgtor). Notice the tiny "eye of the needle" door cut into the big door. If trying to get into town after curfew, you could bribe the guard to let you through this door (which was small enough to keep out any fully armed attackers).

Step through the gate and outside the wall. Look around and imagine being locked out in the year 1400. This was a wooden drawbridge (see the chain slits above). Notice the "pitch nose" mask—designed to pour boiling Nutella on anyone attacking. High above is the town coat of arms: a red castle *(roten Burg)*.

Castle Garden—The garden before you was once that red castle (destroyed in the 14th century). Today, it's a picnic-friendly park with a viewpoint at the far end (considered the "best place to kiss" by romantic local teenagers). But the views of the lush Tauber River Valley below (a.k.a. Tauber Riviera) are just as good from either side of the tower on this near end of the park. To the right, a path leads down to the village of Detwang (you can see the church spire below)—a town even older than Rothenburg. To the left is a fine view of the fortified Rothenburg. Return to the tower, cross carefully under the pitch nose, and hike back up Herrngasse to your starting point.

Herrngasse—Many towns have a Herrngasse—where the richest patricians and merchants (the *Herren*) lived. Predictably, it's your best chance to see the town's finest old mansions. Strolling back to Market Square, you'll pass the old-time puppet theater (German only, on left), the Franciscan Church (from 1285, oldest in town, on right) and the Eisenhut Hotel (Rothenburg's fanciest, worth a peek inside). The shop next door at #11 retains the original old courtyard. The Käthe Wohlfahrt Christmas shop (at Herrngasse 1, see "Shopping," below) is your last, and perhaps greatest, temptation before reaching your starting—and ending—point: Market Square.

Museums within a Block of Market Square

▲▲Medieval Crime and Punishment Museum—It's the best of its kind, full of fascinating old legal bits and *Kriminal* pieces, instruments of punishment and torture—even a special cage complete with a metal gag for nags. As a bonus, you get exhibits on marriage traditions and witches. Follow the yellow arrows. Exhibits are tenderly described in English (€3.20, April-Oct daily 9:30-18:00, Nov and Jan-Feb daily 14:00-16:00, Dec and March daily 10:00–16:00, fun cards and posters, tel. 09861/5359, www.kriminalmuseum.rothenburg.de).

▲Dolls and Toy Museum—Two floors of historic *Kinder* cuteness are a hit with many. Pick up the free English binder for an extensive description of the exhibits (€4, family ticket-€10, daily 9:30–18:00, just off Market Square, downhill from the fountain at Hofbronneng 13).

▲German Christmas Museum—Herr Wohlfahrt's passion is collecting and sharing historic Christmas decorations. This excellent museum, upstairs in the giant Käthe Wohlfahrt Christmas shop, features a unique and thoughtfully described collection of Christmas-tree stands, mini-trees sent in boxes to WWI soldiers at the front, early Advent calendars, old-time Christmas cards, 450 clever ways to crack a nut, and a look at tree decorations through the ages—including the Nazi era and when you were a kid (€4, April–Dec daily 10:00–18:00, Jan–March only Sat–Sun 10:00–18:00, Herrngasse 1).

More Sights in Rothenburg

▲▲Walk the Wall—Just over 2.5 kilometers (1.5 miles) around, providing great views and a good orientation, this walk can be done by those under six feet tall and without a camera in less than an hour. The hike requires no special sense of balance. Photographers go through lots of film, especially before breakfast or at sunset, when the lighting is best and the crowds are fewest. The best fortifications are in the Spitaltor (south end). Walk from there counterclockwise to the "forehead." Climb the Rödertor en route. The names you see along the way are people who donated money to rebuild the wall after World War II and those who've recently donated €1,000 per meter for the maintenance of Rothenburg's heritage.

▲Rödertor—The wall tower nearest the train station is the only one you can climb. It's worth the 135 steps for the view and a fascinating rundown on the bombing of Rothenburg in the last weeks of World War II, when the east part of the city was destroyed (€1, April–Oct daily 9:30–12:30 & 13:30–17:00, closed Nov–March, photos of WWII damage with English translations). If you climb this, you can skip the city hall tower.

Sightseeing Lowlights—St. Wolfgang's Church is a fortified Gothic church built into the medieval wall at Klingentor. Its dungeon-like passages and shepherd's dance exhibit are pretty lame (€1.50, April–Oct daily 11:00–13:00 & 14:00–17:00, closed Nov–March). The cute-looking Bäuerliches Museum (farming museum) next door is even worse. The Rothenburger Handwerkerhaus (tradesman's house, 700 years old) shows the everyday life of a Rothenburger in the town's heyday (€4, daily 9:00–18:00, closed Nov and Jan–March, Alter Stadtgraben 26, near Markus Tower).

Excursions

▲A Walk in the Countryside—Just below the *Burggarten* (castle garden) in Tauber Valley is the cute, skinny, 600-year-old castle/summer home of Mayor Toppler. The **Topplerschlösschen**—the size and shape of a fortified treehouse—is in a farmer's garden and can be open whenever he's around and willing to let you in (€1.50, Fri–Sun 13:00–16:00, closed Mon–Thu, 1.5 km/1 mile from town center). People say the mayor had this valley floor escape to get people to relax about leaving the fortified town (or to hide a mistress).

Walk on past the covered bridge and huge trout to the peaceful village of Detwang. Detwang is actually older than Rothenburg (from 968, the second-oldest village in Franconia). It also has a Riemenschneider altarpiece in its church. For a scenic return, loop back to Rothenburg through the valley along the river, just past the double-arcaded bridge following the footpath back to town.

Franconian Bike Ride—For a fun, breezy look at the countryside around Rothenburg, rent a bike from Rad & Tat (€2.50/hr, €10/day, Mon–Fri 9:00–18:00, Sat 9:00–14:00, closed Sun, Bensenstrasse 17, outside of town near corner of Bensenstrasse and Erlbacherstrasse, passport number required, free Taubertal bike route maps, tel. 09861/87984). For a pleasant half-day pedal, bike along Topplerweg to Spittaltor and down into the Tauber Riviera, over the double-arcaded bridge, and along the small riverside road to Detwang, passing the cute Topplerschlösschen (described above). From Detwang, follow *Liebliches Taubertal* bike path signs as far up the Tauber River (direction Bettwar) as you like. The easiest return from there is to retrace your path.

Franconian Open-Air Museum—A 20-minute drive from Rothenburg in the undiscovered "Rothenburgy" town of Bad Windsheim is an open-air folk museum that, compared with others in Europe, isn't much. But it tries very hard and gives you the best look around at traditional rural Franconia (€4.50, daily 9:00–18:00, closed Nov–Feb and Mon off-season, tel. 09841/66800, www.freilandmuseum.de).

Shopping

Be warned . . . Rothenburg is one of Germany's best shopping towns. Do it here and be done with it. Lovely prints, carvings, wineglasses, Christmas-tree ornaments, and beer steins are popular.

The Käthe Wohlfahrt Christmas trinkets phenomenon is spreading across the half-timbered reaches of Europe. In Rothenburg, tourists flock to two **Käthe Wohlfahrt Christmas Villages** (on either side of Herrngasse, just off Market Square). This Christmas wonderland is filled with enough twinkling lights to require a special electric hookup, instant Christmas mood music (best appreciated on a hot day in July), and American and Japanese tourists hungrily filling little woven shopping baskets with €5–8 goodies to hang on their trees. Let the spinning flocked tree whisk you in, but pause at the wall of Steiffs, jerking uncontrollably and mesmerizing little kids. (OK, I admit it, my Christmas tree sports a few KW ornaments.) Note: Prices have tour-guide incentives built into them (Mon–Fri 9:00–18:00, Sat 9:00–16:00, Sun 10:00–18:00, tel. 09861/4090, www.wohlfahrt.de). The new **Christmas Museum** upstairs (see "Museums within a Block of Market Square," above) is very good but dumps you back in the store, compelled now by the fascinating history to buy even more. Factor this likely extra expense into the museum's already steep €4 admission fee.

The **Friese shop** offers a charming contrast (just off Market Square, west of TI, on corner across from public WC). Cuckoo with friendliness, it gives shoppers with this book tremendous service: a 10 percent discount, 16 percent tax deducted if you have your purchases mailed, and a free map. Anneliese, who runs the place with her sons Frankie and Berni and grandson Rene (who plays American football), charges only her cost for shipping and money exchange, and lets tired travelers leave their bags in her back room for free. For fewer crowds and better service, visit after 14:00 (Mon–Sat 8:00–17:00, Sun 9:30–17:00, tel. & fax 09861/7166).

The Ernst Geissendörfer **print shop** sells fine prints, etchings, and paintings. Show this book for 10 percent off marked prices on all cash purchases (or minimum €50 credit-card purchases) and a free shot of German brandy to sip while you browse (Mon–Sat 10:00–18:00, Sun 10:00–17:00, late Dec–April closed Sun, enter through bear shop on corner where Market Square hits Schmiedgasse, go up 1 floor, tel. 09861/2005).

For characteristic wineglasses, oenology gear, and local wine from the town's oldest wine-makers, drop by the **Weinladen am Plönlein** (daily 8:30–18:00, Plönlein 27—see "Evening Fun," below, for info on wine-tasting).

Shoppers who mail their goodies home can get handy €1.50

boxes at the **post office** in the shopping center across from the train station (Mon–Fri 9:00–17:30, Sat 9:00–12:00).

Those who prefer to eat their souvenirs shop the *Bäckereien* (bakeries). Their succulent pastries, pies, and cakes are pleasantly distracting ...but skip the bad-tasting Rothenburger *Schneebälle*.

Sleeping in Rothenburg

(€1 = about $1, country code: 49, area code: 09861, zip code: 91541)

Sleep Code: **S** = Single, **D** = Double/Twin, **T** = Triple, **Q** = Quad, **b** = bathroom, **s** = shower only, **CC** = Credit Cards accepted, **no CC** = Credit Cards not accepted, **SE** = Speaks English, **NSE** = No English. Room prices include breakfast.

To help you sort easily through these listings, I've divided the rooms into three categories based on the price for a standard double room with bath:

Higher Priced—Most rooms more than €65.
Moderately Priced—Most rooms €65 or less.
Lower Priced—Most rooms €40 or less.

Rothenburg is crowded with visitors, but most are day-trippers. Except for the rare Saturday night and festivals (see "Festivals," page 440), finding a room is easy throughout the year. Unless otherwise noted, enough English is spoken.

Many hotels and guest houses will pick up tired, heavy packers at the station. You may be greeted at the station by *Zimmer* skimmers who have rooms to rent. If you have reservations, resist them and honor your reservation. But if you haven't booked ahead, try talking yourself into one of these more desperate bed-and-breakfast rooms for a youth-hostel price. Be warned: These people are notorious for taking you to distant hotels and then charging you for the ride back if you decline a room.

If you're driving and unable to find your accommodations, stop and give the place a call. They will likely come to rescue you.

Sleeping in the Old Town

HIGHER PRICED

Gasthof Greifen, once the home of Mayor Toppler, is a big, traditional, 600-year-old place with large rooms and all the comforts. It's run by a fine family staff and creaks with rustic splendor (small Sb-€38, Sb-€48, Db-€60–77, Tb-€97, Qb-€117, 10 percent off for 3-night stay, CC, self- or full-service laundry, free and easy parking, half a block downhill from Market Square at Obere Schmiedgasse 5, tel. 09861/2281, fax 09861/86374, www.gasthof-greifen.rothenburg.de, e-mail: info@gasthof-greifen.rothenburg.de, Brigitte and Klingler family).

Hotel Gerberhaus, a classy new hotel in an old building, is warmly run by Inge and Kurt, who mix modern comforts into bright and airy rooms while maintaining a sense of half-timbered elegance. Enjoy the pleasant garden in back (Sb-€44–56, Db-€56–79 depending on size, Tb-€90, Qb-€100, €3 less per room for 2 or more nights, CC or pay cash for 5 percent off and a free *Schneebälle*, non-smoking rooms, free Internet access, laundry-€3.60/load, Spitalgasse 25, tel. 09861/94900, fax 09861/86555, www.gerberhaus.rothenburg.de, e-mail: gerberhaus@t-online.de). The downstairs café serves good soups, salads, and light lunches.

Hotel Kloster-Stüble, deep in the old town near the castle garden, is my classiest listing. Jutta greets the guests while her husband Rudolf does the cooking, and Erika is the fun and energetic first mate (Sb-€50, Db-€85–90, Tb-€110, family rooms-€110–155, luxurious apartment with kitchen and balcony-€105 for 2 or up to €200 for 6, €3 extra on weekends, family deals, CC, Heringsbronnengasse 5, tel. 09861/6774, fax 09861/6474, www.klosterstueble.de, e-mail: hotel@klosterstueble.de).

MODERATELY PRICED

Gasthof Zur Goldenen Rose is a classic family-run place—simple, traditional, comfortable, and a great value—where scurrying Karin serves breakfast and stately Henni keeps everything in good order. The hotel has one shower per floor, but the rooms are clean, and you're surrounded by cobbles, flowers, and red-tiled roofs (S-€21, D-€36, Ds-€46, Db-€49, some triples, spacious family apartment in modern annex: for 4-€107, for 5-€128, CC, kid-friendly, streetside rooms can be noisy, closed Jan–Feb, Spitalgasse 28, tel. 09861/4638, fax 09861/86417, www.thegoldenrose.de, e-mail: info@thegoldenrose.de, Henni SE). The Favetta family also serves good, reasonably priced meals (restaurant closed Wed). Keep your key to get in after hours (side gate in alley).

Hotel Altfränkische Weinstube am Klosterhof is the place for well-heeled bohemians. Mario and lovely Hanne rent six cozy rooms above their dark and smoky pub in a 600-year-old building. It's an upscale Monty Python atmosphere, with TVs, modern showers, open-beam ceilings, and *Himmel* beds—canopied four-poster "heaven" beds (Sb-€40–45, Db-€50–60, Db suite-€70, Tb-€70, CC, kid-friendly, off Klingengasse at Klosterhof 7, tel. 09861/6404, fax 09861/6410, www.altfraenkische.de). Their pub is a candlelit classic, serving hot food until 22:30 and closing at 1:00. Drop by on Wednesday evening (19:30–24:00) for the English Conversation Club (see "Meet the Locals," below).

Rothenburg Hotels

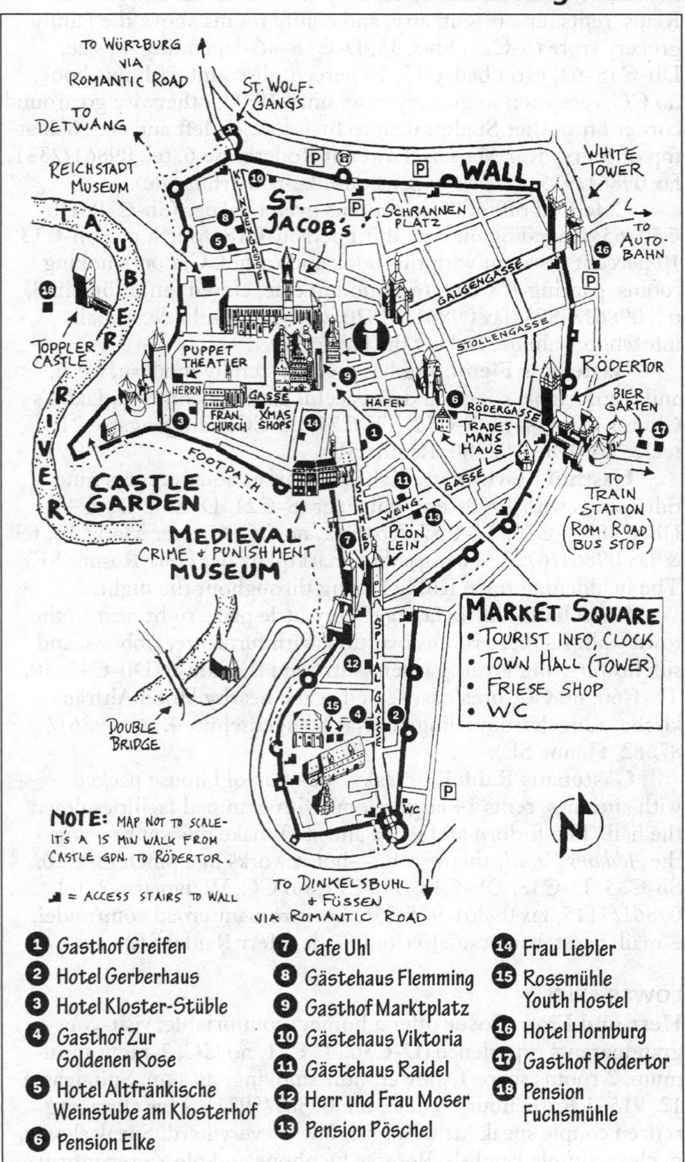
TO WÜRZBURG VIA ROMANTIC ROAD
TO DETWANG
ST. WOLF-GANG'S
REICHSTADT MUSEUM
WALL
WHITE TOWER
TO AUTO-BAHN
KLINGENGASSE
ST. JACOB'S
SCHRANNEN PLATZ
TAUBER RIVER
GALGENGASSE
STOLLENGASSE
TOPPLER CASTLE
PUPPET THEATER
HERRN GASSE
FRAN. CHURCH
XMAS SHOPS
HAFEN
RÖDERTOR
BIER GARTEN
RÖDERGASSE
TRADES-MANS HAUS
FOOTPATH
GASSE
TO TRAIN STATION
(ROM. ROAD BUS STOP)
CASTLE GARDEN
MEDIEVAL CRIME + PUNISHMENT MUSEUM
SCHMIED
WENG.
PLÖN LEIN
MARKET SQUARE
• TOURIST INFO, CLOCK
• TOWN HALL (TOWER)
• FRIESE SHOP
• WC
SPITAL GASSE
DOUBLE BRIDGE
WC
NOTE: MAP NOT TO SCALE-IT'S A 15 MIN WALK FROM CASTLE GDN. TO RÖDERTOR.
= ACCESS STAIRS TO WALL
TO DINKELSBUHL + FÜSSEN VIA ROMANTIC ROAD
1 Gasthof Greifen
2 Hotel Gerberhaus
3 Hotel Kloster-Stüble
4 Gasthof Zur Goldenen Rose
5 Hotel Altfränkische Weinstube am Klosterhof
6 Pension Elke
7 Cafe Uhl
8 Gästehaus Flemming
9 Gasthof Marktplatz
10 Gästehaus Viktoria
11 Gästehaus Raidel
12 Herr und Frau Moser
13 Pension Pöschel
14 Frau Liebler
15 Rossmühle Youth Hostel
16 Hotel Hornburg
17 Gasthof Rödertor
18 Pension Fuchsmühle

Pension Elke, run by the spry Erich Endress and his son Klaus, rents nine bright, airy, and comfy rooms above the family grocery store (S-€25, Sb-€35, D-€38–46 depending on size, Db-€58–62, extra bed-€15, 10 percent discount with this book, no CC, reception in grocery store until 19:00, otherwise go around corner onto Alter Stadtgraben to first door on left and ring bell at top of stairs, near Markus Tower at Rodergasse 6, tel. 09861/2331, fax 09861/935-355, www.pension-elke-rotherburg.de).

Cafe Uhl offers 10 fine rooms over a bakery (Sb-€30, Db-€50–65 depending on size, third person-€18, fourth person-€13, 10 percent discount with this book and cash, CC, non-smoking rooms, parking-€3/day, reception in café, closed Jan, Plönlein 8, tel. 09861/4895, fax 09861/92820, www.hotel-uhl.de, e-mail: info@hotel-uhl.de, Robert the baker SE).

Gästehaus Flemming has seven tastefully modern, fresh, and comfortable rooms and a peaceful garden behind St. Jakob's Church (Sb-€45, Db-€55, Tb-€75, no CC, Klingengasse 21, tel. & fax 09861/92380, Regina SE).

Gasthof Marktplatz, right on Market Square, rents nine tidy rooms with 1970s-era wallpaper (S-€21, D-€38, Ds-€43, Db-€48, T-€50, Ts-€57, Tb-€62, no CC, Grüner Markt 10, tel. & fax 09861/6722, www.gasthof-marktplatz.de, Herr Rosner SE). The maddening town hall bells ring throughout the night.

Gästehaus Viktoria is a cheery little place right next to the town wall. Its three rooms overflow with furniture, ribbons, and silk flowers, and lovely gardens surround the house (Db-€45–50, Tb-€60, no CC, breakfast served at the nearby Hotel Altfränkische, a block from Klingentor at Klingenschütt 4, tel. 09861/87682, Hanne SE).

Gästehaus Raidel, a creaky 500-year-old house packed with antiques, rents 14 large rooms with cramped facilities down the hall. The forlorn ambience and staff make me want to sing the *Addams Family* theme song—but it works in a pinch (S-€20, Sb-€35, D-€38, Db-€48, Tb-€71, no CC, Wenggasse 3, tel. 09861/3115, fax 09861/935-255, www.romanticroad.com/raidel, e-mail: gaestehaus-raidel@t-online.de, Herr Raidel SE).

LOWER PRICED

Herr und Frau Moser offer a homey, comfortable, visit-your-grandparents experience (D-€36, T-€51, no CC, 2-night minimum, 2 rooms share 1 shower, non-smoking, no sign, Spitalgasse 12, 91541 Rothenburg o.d.T., tel. 09861/5971). This charming retired couple speak little English but try very hard. Speak slowly, in clear, simple English. Reserve by phone and please reconfirm by phone one day before arrival.

Pension Pöschel is friendly, with seven bearskin-cozy rooms in a concrete but pleasant building with an inviting garden out back (S-€20, D-€35, T-€45, small kids free, no CC, Wenggasse 22, tel. 09861/3430, e-mail: pension.poeschel@t-online.de, Bettina SE).

Frau Liebler rents two large, modern, ground-floor rooms with kitchenettes and hardwood floors (Db-€40, no CC, breakfast in room, off Market Square behind Christmas shop, Pfaffleinsgasschen 10, tel. 09861/709-215, fax 09861/709-216, SE).

Hostel: Here in Bavaria, hosteling is limited to those under 27, except for families traveling with children under 18. The fine **Rossmühle Youth Hostel** has 184 beds in two buildings. The droopy-eyed building (the old town horse mill, used when the town was under siege and the river-powered mill was inaccessible) houses groups and the office. The adjacent hostel is mostly for families and individuals (dorm beds-€15, Db-€36, includes breakfast and sheets, dinner-€5.10, self-serve laundry-€4, Muhlacker 1, tel. 09861/94160, fax 09861/941-620, www.djh.de, e-mail: jhrothenburg@djh-bayern.de, SE). Reserve long in advance.

Sleeping outside the Wall

The first two places are a hundred meters (330 feet) outside the wall on the train-station side of town (less than a 10-min walk from the center) and are among the nicest rooms I recommend in town. The third is a rustic adventure below the town in what feels like a wilderness.

HIGHER PRICED

Hotel Hornburg, a grand hundred-year-old mansion with groomed grounds and 10 spacious, tastefully decorated rooms a two-minute walk outside the wall, is a super value (Sb-€49–67, Db-€69–95, Tb-€90–110, CC, ground-floor rooms, nonsmoking rooms, family-friendly, avoid if you're allergic to dogs, parking-€2/day, bikes for guests-€10/day, exit station and go straight on Ludwig-Siebert Strasse, turn left on Mann Strasse until you're 100 meters, or 330 feet, from town wall, Hornburgweg 28, tel. 09861/8480, fax 09861/5570, www.hotel-hornburg.de, e-mail: hotelhornburg@t-online.de, friendly Gabriele and Martin SE).

Gasthof Rödertor offers 15 decent rooms in a quiet setting one block outside the Rödertor tower. The guest house has an inviting breakfast room with farmhouse flair, a popular beer garden, and a restaurant dedicated to the potato (see "Evening Fun and Beer Drinking," below). Guest rooms in an annex inside the wall are slightly cheaper (Db-€65–80, Tb-€105, Qb-€125, kids sleep free, CC but 10 percent discount with this book and cash, Ansbacher Strasse 7, tel. 09861/2022, fax 09861/86324, www.roedertor.com, e-mail: hotel@roedertor.com, Frau Teutscher and her daughter Katie SE).

MODERATELY PRICED

Pension Fuchsmühle is a B&B in a renovated old mill on the river below the castle end of Rothenburg. The place is a work-in-progress, with kids and a linoleum-floor feel, but if you want a rustic, countryside experience, it's great. Alex and Heidi Molitor rent six rooms and take good care of their guests (Db-€45–55 depending on length of stay, healthy farm-fresh breakfasts, piano, free pickup at the station, free bikes for guests, non-smoking, across the street from Toppler's little castle at Taubertalweg 103, tel. 09861/92633, www.fuchsmuehle.de, e-mail: fuchsmuehle @t-online.de). It's a steep but pleasant 15-minute hike from the Fuchsmühle to Market Square. The Molitors provide flashlights for your return after dark.

Eating in Rothenburg

Most restaurants serve meals only from 11:30 to 13:30 and 18:00 to 20:00. All places listed are within a five-minute walk of Market Square. While all survive on tourism, many still feel like local hangouts. Your choices are typical Franconian, a fancy international splurge, or ethnic.

Traditional Franconian Restaurants

Restaurant Glocke, a *Weinstube* (wine bar) popular with locals, is run by Rothenburg's oldest winemakers, the Thürauf family. Their seasonal menu is complemented by their family wine, served under an atmospheric, big-beamed ceiling. The menu is in German only because the friendly staff wants to explain your options in person. Don't miss their €4 deal to sample five Franconian wines (€10–15, Mon–Sat 10:30–23:00, Sun 10:30–14:00, vegetarian options, Plönlein 1, tel. 09861/958-990).

At **Zur Goldenen Rose**, Reno cooks up traditional German fare at good prices, as Henne stokes your appetite (Tue 11:30–14:00, Thu–Mon 11:30–14:00 & 17:30–20:30, closed Wed, Spitalgasse 28; the leafy garden terrace out back is open in sunny weather).

Extremely picturesque and touristy, **Baumeister Haus**, tucked deep behind a streetside pastry counter and antlered dining room, fills an inviting courtyard with people who don't understand a German menu (€8–15, daily 8:00–23:00, a few doors below Market Square, Obere Schmiedgasse 3, tel. 09861/94700).

Rothenburg Restaurants

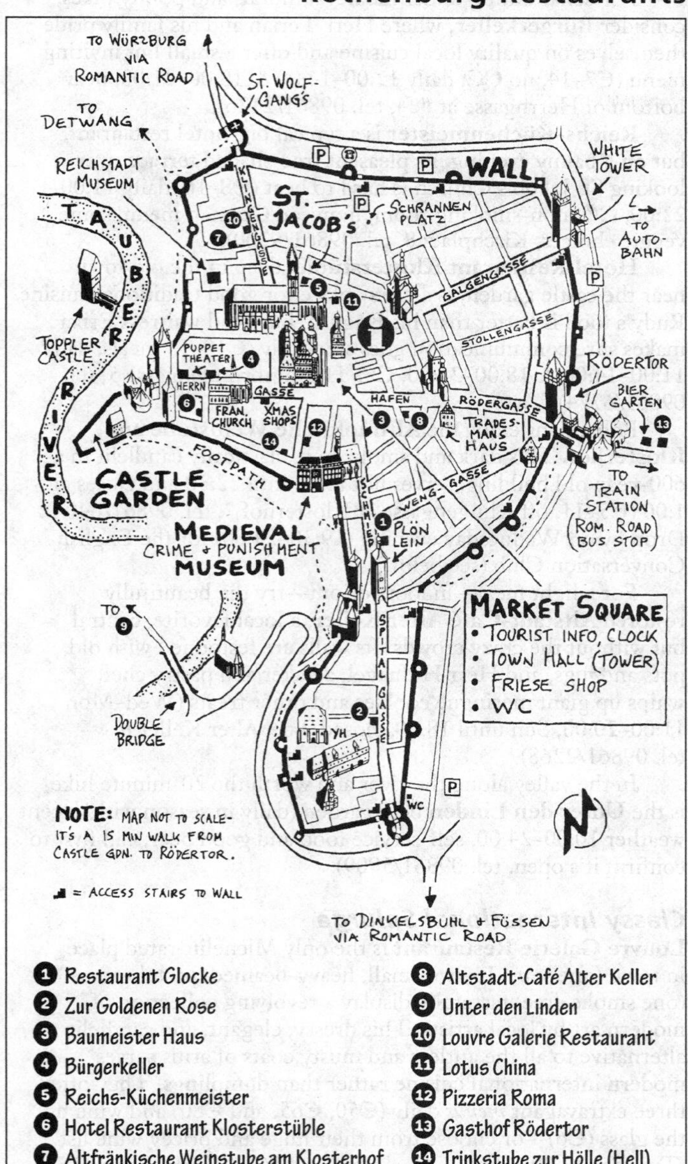
TO WÜRZBURG VIA ROMANTIC ROAD
TO DETWANG
ST. WOLF-GANG'S
REICHSTADT MUSEUM
WALL
WHITE TOWER
TO AUTO-BAHN
ST. JACOB'S
SCHRANNEN PLATZ
KLINGENGASSE
TAUBER RIVER
GALGENGASSE
STOLLENGASSE
TOPPLER CASTLE
PUPPET THEATER
HERRN GASSE
FRAN. CHURCH
XMAS SHOPS
HAFEN
RÖDERGASSE
RÖDERTOR
BIER GARTEN
TRADES-MANS HAUS
FOOTPATH
CASTLE GARDEN
WENG-GASSE
TO TRAIN STATION (ROM. ROAD BUS STOP)
MEDIEVAL CRIME + PUNISHMENT MUSEUM
SCHMIED
PLÖNLEIN
MARKET SQUARE
• TOURIST INFO, CLOCK
• TOWN HALL (TOWER)
• FRIESE SHOP
• WC
TO 9
SPITALGASSE
DOUBLE BRIDGE
YH
WC
NOTE: MAP NOT TO SCALE-IT'S A 15 MIN WALK FROM CASTLE GDN. TO RÖDERTOR.
= ACCESS STAIRS TO WALL
TO DINKELSBUHL + FÜSSEN VIA ROMANTIC ROAD
1 Restaurant Glocke
2 Zur Goldenen Rose
3 Baumeister Haus
4 Bürgerkeller
5 Reichs-Küchenmeister
6 Hotel Restaurant Klosterstüble
7 Altfränkische Weinstube am Klosterhof
8 Altstadt-Café Alter Keller
9 Unter den Linden
10 Louvre Galerie Restaurant
11 Lotus China
12 Pizzeria Roma
13 Gasthof Rödertor
14 Trinkstube zur Hölle (Hell)

For cellar dining under medieval murals and pointy pikes, consider **Bürgerkeller,** where Herr Terian and his family pride themselves on quality local cuisine and offer a small but inviting menu (€7–14, no CC, daily 12:00–14:00 & 18:00–21:00, near bottom of Herrngasse at #24, tel. 09861/2126).

Reichs-Küchenmeister is a typical big-hotel restaurant, but on a balmy evening, its pleasant tree-shaded terrace overlooking St. Jakob's Church is hard to beat (€8–16, daily 11:00–22:00, CC, non-smoking room, nouveau German menu, some veggie choices, Kirchplatz 8, tel. 09861/9700).

Hotel Restaurant Klosterstüble, deep in the old town near the castle garden, is a classy place for good traditional cuisine. Rudy's food is better than his English, but head waitress Erika makes sure communication goes smoothly (€10–15 meals, daily 11:00–14:00 & 18:00–21:00, CC, Heringsbronnengasse 5, tel. 09861/6774).

Bohemians enjoy the **Altfränkische Weinstube am Klosterhof.** This dark and smoky pub, classically candlelit in a 600-year-old building, serves hot food until 22:30 and closes at 1:00 (€5–11, off Klingengasse at Klosterhof 7, tel. 09861/6404). Drop by on Wednesday evening (19:30–24:00) for the English Conversation Club (see below).

For a light meal—indoors or out—try the beautifully restored **Altstadt-Café Alter Keller**, a local favorite, central but without the crazy crowds. Its walls are festooned with old pots and jugs, and Herr Hufnagel, a baker and pastry chef, whips up giant meringue cookies and other treats (Wed–Mon 11:00–20:00, Sun until 18:00, closed Tue, Alter Keller 8, tel. 09861/2268).

In the valley along the river and worth the 20-minute hike is the **Unter den Linden** beer garden (daily in season with decent weather 10:00–24:00, self-service food and good beer, call first to confirm it's open, tel. 09861/5909).

Classy International Splurge

Louvre Galerie Restaurant is the only Michelin-rated place in town (one star). Its two small, heavy-beamed, pastel rooms (one smoke-free) tastefully display a revolving collection of modern art by local artists. This dressy, elegant, and candlelit alternative to all the antlers and musty coats of arms serves modern international cuisine rather than dumplings. They offer three extravagant *menus* daily (€50, €65, and €80) and wine by the glass (€6)—or choose from their huge and pricey wine list (Tue–Sat 18:00–23:00, CC, closed Sun–Mon, Klingengasse 15, tel. 09861/87809, reservations smart).

Ethnic Breaks from Pork and Potatoes

Lotus China is a peaceful world apart, serving good Chinese food (€8 plates, CC, daily 11:30–14:30 & 17:30–23:00, 2 blocks behind TI near church, Eckele 2, tel. 09861/86886).

Pizzeria Roma is smoky because it's the locals' favorite for €6.50 pizza, pastas, and Italian wine. Service can be slow (Thu–Tue 11:30–24:00, closed Wed, also has schnitzel fare, Galgengasse 19, tel. 09861/4540).

You'll find a **Turkish** place on Schrannengasse and a **Greek** restaurant just outside the wall opposite Spitaltor.

Two **supermarkets** are near the wall at Rödertor. The one outside the wall is cheaper (Mon–Fri 8:00–20:00, Sat 8:00–16:00, on left as you exit wall); the one inside is nicer (Mon–Fri 8:00–19:00, Sat 8:00–16:00). Both are closed Sunday.

Evening Fun and Beer Drinking

Beer Gardens and Discos at Rothenburg's "Bermuda Dreieck": For beer-garden fun on a balmy summer evening (for dinner or beer), Rothenburgers pick **Gasthof Rödertor**, just outside the wall at the Rödertor (May–Sept daily 17:00–24:00, wood gate, near discos, see below). The Gasthof Rödertor's *Kartoffeln Stube* inside is dedicated to the potato (€6–10, daily 11:30–14:00 & 17:30–23:00, tel. 09861/2022). Two popular **discos** are just down the street (**Black Out** at Ansbacher 15, in alley next to Sparkasse bank, open Wed, Fri–Sat 22:00–3:00; and **Club 23**, around corner from bank on Adam Hörber Strasse, open Thu–Sat from 22:00).

Wine Drinking in the Old Center: Trinkstube zur Hölle (Hell) is dark and foreboding, but they offer thick wine-drinking atmosphere until late (Jan–March closed on Wed, a block past Criminal Museum on Burggasse, with devil hanging out front, tel. 09861/4229). Mario's **Altfränkische Weinstube** (see "Meet the Locals," below) is similarly atmospheric. Wine-lovers enjoy **Restaurant Glocke**'s *Weinstube* (recommended above); for €4, you can sample five of their Franconian wines—choose dry or half-dry (Mon–Sat 10:30–23:00, Sun 10:30–14:00, Plönlein 1, tel. 09861/958-990). You're welcome to enjoy just the wine without eating.

Meet the Locals

For a rare chance to mix it up with locals who aren't selling anything, bring your favorite slang and tongue twisters to the **English Conversation Club** at Mario's Altfränkische Weinstube (Wed 19:30–24:00, Anneliese from Friese shop is a regular). This dark and smoky pub is an atmospheric hangout any night (€5–11 entrées, Klosterhof 7, off Klingengasse, behind St. Jakob's Church, tel. 09861/6404).

Transportation Connections—Rothenburg ob der Tauber (o.d.T.)

By bus: The Romantic Road bus tour takes you in and out of Rothenburg each afternoon (April–Oct), heading to Munich, Frankfurt, or Füssen. See the Romantic Road bus schedule on page 460 (or check www.euraide.de/ricksteves).

By train: A tiny train line connects Rothenburg to the outside world via **Steinach** (almost hrly, 15 min). If you plan to arrive in Rothenburg by train, note that the last train to Rothenburg departs nightly from Steinach at 20:30 (if you arrive in Steinach after 20:30, call one of the **taxi** services for a €22 ride to Rothenburg; ideally order the taxi at least an hour in advance: tel. 09861/2000, 09861/7227, or 09861/95100). For those leaving Rothenburg by train, the first train to Steinach departs at 6:00, the last train to Steinach at 20:00.

Steinach by train to: Rothenburg (almost hrly, 15 min, last train at 20:30), **Würzburg** (hrly, 1 hr), **Munich** (hrly, 3 hrs, 2 changes), **Frankfurt** (hrly, 2.5 hrs, change in Würzburg). Train connections in Steinach are usually within a few minutes (to Rothenburg generally from track 5). Train info: tel. 01805/996-633.

Route Tips for Drivers

The autobahn serves Würzburg, Rothenburg, and Dinkelsbühl very efficiently, making the drive from Frankfurt to Munich with these stops very fast. But if you have the time and inclination to meander, the Romantic Road—the small (carefully signposted) road tracing the medieval trade route between the Rhine and the Roman road that went over the Alps south of Munich—is worth the effort.

Arriving from the north via the Romantic Road, you'll hit Rothenburg at Klingentor. The P5 parking lot just outside the gate is free and easy for anyone sleeping in that end of town. Arriving from the autobahn, turn left at the blue gas station to get to Spitaltor. While much of the town is closed to traffic, anyone with a hotel reservation can drive in and through pedestrian zones to get to their hotel. The easiest way to enter and leave is generally via Spittalgasse (and the Spitaltor, south end).

Heading south from Rothenburg, get an early start to enjoy the quaint hills and rolling villages of what was Germany's major medieval trade route. The views of Rothenburg from the west, across the Tauber Valley, are magnificent.

After a quick stop in the center of Dinkelsbühl, cross the baby Danube River (Donau) and continue south along the Romantic Road to Füssen. Drive by Neuschwanstein

Castle just to sweeten your dreams before crossing into Austria to get set up at Reutte.

If detouring past Oberammergau, you can drive through Garmisch, past Germany's highest mountain (Zugspitze), into Austria via Lermoos, and on to Reutte. Or you can take the small scenic shortcut to Reutte past Ludwig's Linderhof and along the windsurfer-strewn Plansee.

ROMANTIC ROAD

The Romantic Road *(Romantische Strasse)* winds you past the most beautiful towns and scenery of Germany's medieval heartland. Once Germany's medieval trade route, now it's the best way to connect the dots between Füssen, Munich, and Frankfurt (www.romantischestrasse.de).

Wander through quaint hills and rolling villages, and stop wherever the cows look friendly or a town fountain beckons. My favorite sections are from Füssen to Landsberg and Rothenburg to Weikersheim. (If you're driving with limited time, connect Rothenburg and Munich by autobahn.) Caution: The similarly promoted "Castle Road," which runs between Rothenburg and Mannheim, sounds intriguing but is nowhere near as interesting.

Throughout Bavaria, you'll see colorfully ornamented maypoles decorating town squares. Many are painted in Bavaria's colors, blue and white. The decorations that line each side of the pole symbolize the crafts or businesses of that community. Each May Day, they are festively replaced. Traditionally, rival communities try to steal each other's maypole. Locals will guard their new pole night and day as May Day approaches. Stolen poles are ransomed only with lots of beer for the clever thieves.

Getting around the Romantic Road

By Bus: The Deutsche Touring bus company runs buses daily between Frankfurt and Füssen in each direction (April–Oct, tel. 069/790-350, www.deutsche-touring.com). A second route goes daily between Munich and Rothenburg (you can transfer at Rothenburg to the other route). Buses usually leave from train stations (in towns large enough to have one). The ride (€70 and 11 hrs if you go all the way) is offered at a 60 percent discount (pay on the bus; add €1.50 per bag) to travelers who have a German railpass, Eurailpass, or a Eurail Selectpass (if Germany is one of the selected countries). Buses stop in Rothenburg (about 2 hrs) and Dinkelsbühl (about 1 hr) and too briefly at a few other attractions. The grim drivers

Romantic Road Bus Schedule (Daily, April–October)

Frankfurt	8:00	—
Würzburg	10:00	—
Arrive Rothenburg	12:45	—
Depart Rothenburg	14:30	14:30
Arrive Dinkelsbühl	15:25	15:25
Depart Dinkelsbühl	15:30	16:15
Munich	—	19:50
Füssen	20:15	—
Füssen	8:00	—
Arrive Wieskirche	8:42	—
Depart Wieskirche	8:55	—
Munich	—	9:00
Arrive Dinkelsbühl	12:45	12:45
Depart Dinkelsbühl	14:00	14:00
Arrive Rothenburg	14:50	14:50
Depart Rothenburg	16:00	—
Depart Würzburg	18:20	—
Frankfurt	20:00	

Note: These times are based on the 2002 schedule. Check www.euraide.de/ricksteves for any changes.

usually hand out maps and brochures and play a tape-recorded narration of the journey highlights in English. Bus reservations are almost never necessary. But they are free and easy, and, technically, without one you can lose your seat to someone who has one (call 069/790-350 to reserve). You can start, stop, and switch over where you like. There is no quicker or easier way to travel across Germany and get such a hearty dose of its countryside.

By Car: Follow the brown *Romantische Strasse* signs and the free tourist brochure (available all over the place) that describes the journey.

The Romantic Road

Sights along the Romantic Road

These sights are listed from north to south.

Frankfurt—The northern terminus of the Romantic Road is in this country's Manhattan: Frankfurt.

▲▲Würzburg—This historic city, though freshly rebuilt since World War II, is worth a stop for its impressive Prince Bishop's Residenz, the bubbly Baroque chapel (Hofkirche) next door, and the palace's sculpted gardens. The helpful TI is on the Marktplatz (Mon–Fri 10:00–18:00, Sat 10:00–14:00, summer Sun 10:00–14:00, tel. 0931/372-398, www.wuerzburg.de). The Residenz is a Franconian Versailles, with grand rooms, 3-D art, and a tennis-court-sized fresco by Tiepolo (EUR4, April–Oct daily 9:00–18:00, summer Thu until 20:00, Nov–March daily 10:00–16:00, last entry 30 min before closing, no photos, tel. 0931/355-170). English tours are offered daily at 11:00 and 15:00 (May–Sept, confirm at TI or call ahead). The elaborate Hofkirche chapel is next door (as you exit the palace, go left) and the entrance to the picnic-worthy garden is just beyond. Easy parking is available. Don't confuse the Residenz (a 15-min walk from the train station) with the fortress on the hilltop.

Weikersheim—This untouristy town has a palace with fine Baroque gardens (luxurious picnic spot), a folk museum, and a picturesque town square.

▲Herrgottskapelle—This peaceful church, graced with Tilman Riemenschneider's greatest carved altarpiece (Easter–Oct daily 9:15–17:30, less off-season, tel. 07933/508), is 1.5 kilometers (1 mile) south of Creglingen (TI tel. 07933/631) and across the street from the Fingerhut thimble museum (€1.50, April–Oct daily 9:00–18:00, less off-season, tel. 07933/370). The south-bound Romantic Road bus stops here for 15 minutes, long enough to see one or the other.

▲▲▲Rothenburg—See this chapter for information on Germany's best medieval town.

▲Dinkelsbühl—Rothenburg's little sister is cute enough to merit a short stop. A moat, towers, gates, and a beautifully preserved medieval wall surround this town. Dinkelsbühl's history museum is meager and without a word of English. The Kinderzeche children's festival turns Dinkelsbühl wonderfully on end in July (July 18–27 in 2003). The helpful TI on the main street sells maps with a short walking tour and can help find rooms (Mon–Fri 9:00–18:00, Sat 10:00–13:00 & 14:00–16:00, Sun 10:00–13:00, shorter hours off-season, tel. 09851/90240, www.dinkelsbuehl.de).

Rottenbuch—This is a nondescript village with an impressive church in a lovely setting.

▲▲Wieskirche—This is Germany's most glorious Baroque-rococo church. Heavenly! This beautifully restored church is in a sweet meadow. Northbound Romantic Road buses stop here for 15 minutes. (See the Bavaria and Tirol chapter.)

Füssen—This town, the southern terminus of the Romantic Road, is five kilometers (3 miles) from the stunning Neuschwanstein Castle, worth a stop on any sightseeing agenda. (See the Bavaria and Tirol chapter for description and accommodations.)

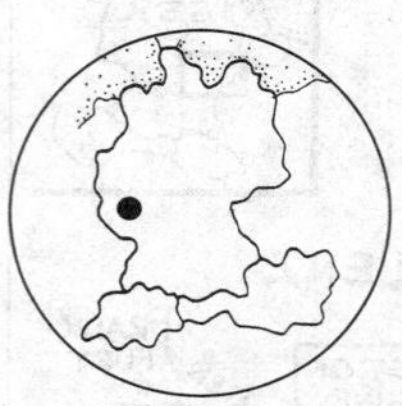

RHINE VALLEY

The Rhine Valley is storybook Germany, a fairy-tale world of legends and robber-baron castles. Cruise the most castle-studded stretch of the romantic Rhine as you listen for the song of the treacherous Loreley. For hands-on castle thrills, climb through the Rhineland's greatest castle, Rheinfels, above the town of St. Goar. Castle connoisseurs will enjoy the fine interior of Marksburg Castle. Spend your nights in a castle-crowned village, either Bacharach or St. Goar. With more time, mosey through the neighboring Mosel Valley (see next chapter).

Planning Your Time

The Rhineland does not take much time to see. The blitziest tour is an hour looking at the castles from your train window. For a better look, however, cruise in, tour a castle or two, sleep in a genuine medieval town, and take the train out. If you have limited time, cruise less and explore Rheinfels Castle.

Ideally, spend two nights here, sleep in Bacharach, cruise the best hour of the river (from Bacharach to St. Goar), and tour the Rheinfels Castle. Those with more time can ride the riverside bike path. With two days and a car, visit the Rhine and the Mosel. With two days by train, you can actually relax on the Rhine.

THE RHINE

Ever since Roman times, when this was the Empire's northern boundary, the Rhine has been one of the world's busiest shipping rivers. You'll see a steady flow of barges with 1,000- to 2,000-ton loads. Tourist-packed buses, hot train tracks, and highways line both banks.

Many of the castles were "robber-baron" castles, put there

Rhine Overview

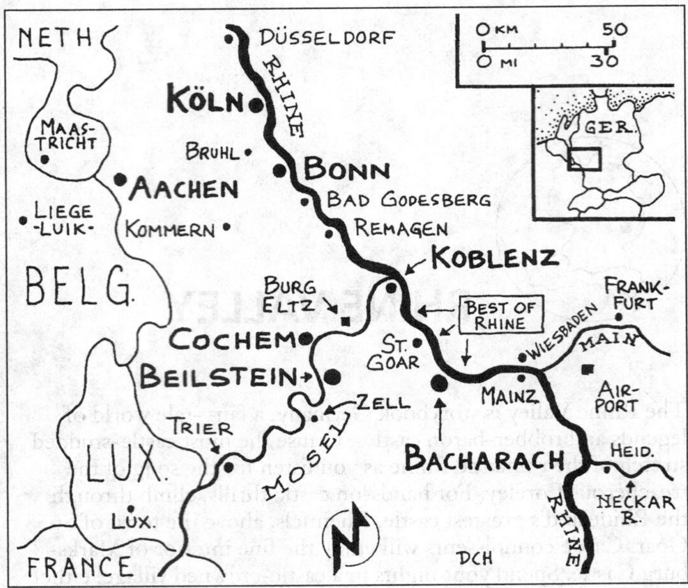

by petty rulers (there were 300 independent little countries in medieval Germany) to levy tolls on passing river traffic. A robber baron would put his castle on, or even in, the river. Then, often with the help of chains and a tower on the opposite bank, he'd stop each ship and get his toll. There were 10 customs stops in the 100-kilometer (60-mile) stretch between Mainz and Koblenz alone (no wonder merchants were early proponents of the creation of larger nation-states).

Some castles were built to control and protect settlements, and others were the residences of kings. As times changed, so did the lifestyles of the rich and feudal. Many castles were abandoned for more comfortable mansions in the towns.

Most Rhine castles date from the 11th, 12th, and 13th centuries. When the pope successfully asserted his power over the German emperor in 1076, local princes ran wild over the rule of their emperor. The castles saw military action in the 1300s and 1400s, as emperors began reasserting their control over Germany's many silly kingdoms.

The castles were also involved in the Reformation wars, in which Europe's Catholic and "protesting" dynasties fought it out using a fragmented Germany as their battleground. The Thirty

Years' War (1618–1648) devastated Germany. The outcome: Each ruler got the freedom to decide if his people would be Catholic or Protestant, and one-third of Germany was dead. Production of Gummi bears ceased entirely.

The French—who feared a strong Germany and felt the Rhine was the logical border between them and Germany—destroyed most of the castles prophylactically (Louis XIV in the 1680s, the revolutionary army in the 1790s, and Napoleon in 1806). They were often rebuilt in neo-Gothic style in the Romantic age—the late 1800s—and today are enjoyed as restaurants, hotels, hostels, and museums.

For more information on the Rhine, visit www.loreleytal.com (heavy on hotels but has maps, photos, and a little history).

Getting around the Rhine

While the Rhine flows north from Switzerland to Holland, the scenic stretch from Mainz to Koblenz hoards all the touristic charm. Studded with the crenellated cream of Germany's castles, it bustles with boats, trains, and highway traffic. Have fun exploring with a mix of big steamers, tiny ferries *(Fähre)*, trains, and bikes (see "More Rhine Sights," below).

By Boat: While many travelers do the whole trip by boat, the most scenic hour is from St. Goar to Bacharach. Sit on the top deck with your handy Rhine map-guide (or the kilometer-keyed tour in this chapter) and enjoy the parade of castles, towns, boats, and vineyards.

There are several boat companies, but most travelers sail on the bigger, more expensive, and romantic Köln-Düsseldorfer (K-D) line (free with a consecutive-day Eurailpass or with dated Eurail Flexipass, Europass, Eurail Selectpass, or German railpass—but it uses up a day of any Flexipass; otherwise about €8.40 for the first hour, then progressively cheaper per hour; the recommended Bacharach–St. Goar trip costs €8.40 one-way, €10.20 round-trip; half-price days: Tue for bicylists, Mon and Fri for seniors over 60, tel. 06741/1634 in St. Goar, tel. 06743/1322 in Bacharach, www.k-d.com). Boats run daily in both directions from April through October, with no boats off-season. Complete, up-to-date schedules are posted in any station, Rhineland hotel, TI, bank, current Thomas Cook Timetable, or at www.euraide.de/ricksteves. Purchase tickets at the dock up to five minutes before departure. (Confirm times at your hotel the night before.) The boat is rarely full. Romantics will plan to catch the *Goethe*, which sails each direction once a day (see "Rhine Cruise Schedule" in this chapter; confirm time locally).

The smaller Bingen-Rüdesheimer line is about 10 percent

cheaper than K-D (railpasses not valid, buy tickets on boat, tel. 06721/14140, www.bingen-ruedesheimer.com), with three two-hour round-trip St. Goar-to-Bacharach trips daily in summer (about €6.50 one-way, €9 round-trip; departing St. Goar at 11:00, 14:10, and 16:10, departing Bacharach at 10:10, 12:00, and 15:00).

Drivers have these options: (1) skip the boat; (2) take a round-trip cruise from St. Goar or Bacharach; (3) draw pretzels and let the loser drive, prepare the picnic, and meet the boat; (4) rent a bike, bring it on the boat for free, and bike back; or (5) take the boat one-way and return by train. When exploring by car, don't hesitate to pop onto one of the many little ferries that shuttle across the bridgeless-around-here river (see below).

By Ferry: While there are no bridges between Koblenz and Mainz, you'll see car-and-passenger ferries (usually family-run for generations) about every five kilometers (3 miles). Ferries near St. Goar and Bacharach cross the river every 10 minutes daily in the summer from about 6:00 to 20:00, connecting Bingen–Rüdesheim, Lorch–Niederheimbach, Engelsburg–Kaub, and St. Goar–St.Goarshausen (adult-€1, car and driver-€2.80, pay on the boat).

By Train: Hourly milk-run trains down the Rhine hit every town: St. Goar–Bacharach, 12 min; Bacharach–Mainz, 60 min; Mainz–Frankfurt, 45 min. Some train schedules list St. Goar but not Bacharach as a stop, but any schedule listing St. Goar also stops at Bacharach. Tiny stations are unmanned—buy tickets at the platform machines or on the train. Prices are cheap (e.g., €2.60 between St. Goar and Bacharach).

Sights—The Romantic Rhine

These sights are listed from north to south, Koblenz to Bingen.

▲▲▲Der Romantische Rhein Blitz Zug Fahrt—One of Europe's great train thrills is zipping along the Rhine in this fast train tour. Here's a quick and easy, from-the-train-window tour (also works for car, bike, or best by boat; you can cut in anywhere) that skips the syrupy myths filling normal Rhine guides. For more information than necessary, buy the handy *Rhine Guide from Mainz to Cologne* (€3.60 book with foldout map, at most shops or TIs).

Sit on the left (river) side of the train or boat going south from Koblenz. While nearly all the castles listed are viewed from this side, clear a path to the right window for the times I yell, "Crossover!"

You'll notice large black-and-white kilometer markers along the riverbank. I erected these years ago to make this tour easier to follow. They tell the distance from the Rhinefalls, where the Rhine leaves Switzerland and becomes navigable. Now the river-barge

Best of the Rhine

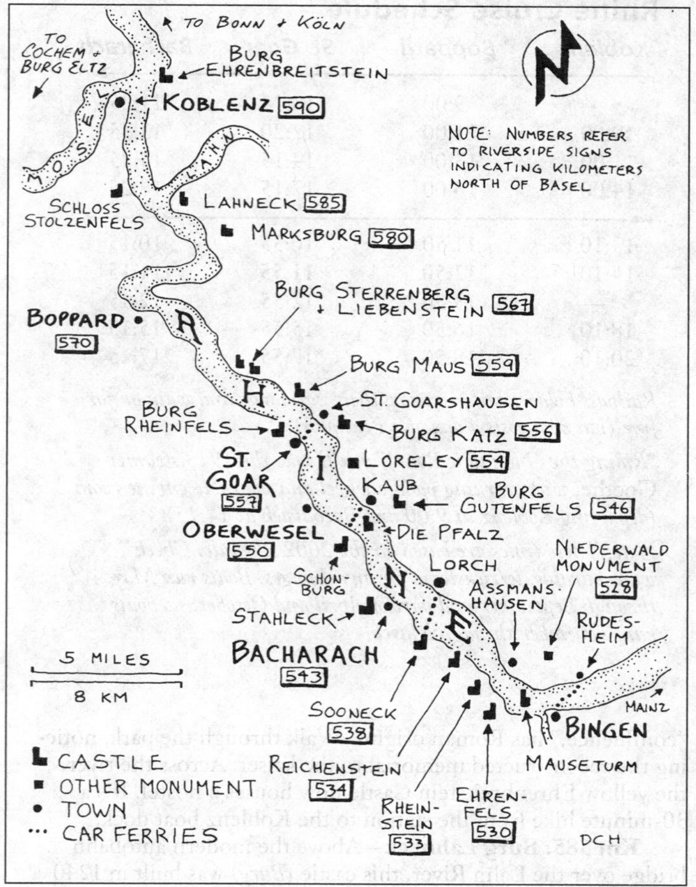

pilots have accepted these as navigational aids as well. We're tackling just 58 kilometers (36 miles) of the 1,320-kilometer-long (820-mile) Rhine. Your Blitz Rhine Tour starts at Koblenz and heads upstream to Bingen. If you're going the other direction, it still works. Just hold the book upside down.

Km 590: Koblenz—This Rhine blitz starts with Romantic Rhine thrills—at Koblenz. Koblenz is not a nice city (it was really hit hard in World War II), but its place as the historic *Deutsche Eck* (German corner)—the tip of land where the Mosel joins the Rhine—gives it a certain historic charm. Koblenz, Latin for

Rhine Cruise Schedule

Koblenz	Boppard	St. Goar	Bacharach
→			
—	9:00	10:15	11:25
*9:00	*11:00	*12:20	*13:35
11:00	13:00	14:15	15:25
14:00	16:00	17:15	18:25
←			
13:10	11:50	10:55	10:15
14:10	12:50	11:55	11:15
—	13:50	12:55	12:15
18:10	16:50	15:55	15:15
*20:10	*18:50	*17:55	*17:15

Railpass holders can just show their valid pass and walk on for free (but boat costs a day of a Flexipass).

**Riding the "Nostalgic Route," you'll take the 1913 steamer* Goethe, *with working paddle wheel and viewable engine room (departing Koblenz at 9:00 and Bacharach at 17:15).*

Note: These times are based on the 2002 schedule. Check www.euraide.de/ricksteves for any changes. Boats run May through September and part of April and October; no boats run November through March.

"confluence," has Roman origins. Walk through the park, noticing the reconstructed memorial to the kaiser. Across the river, the yellow Ehrenbreitstein Castle now houses a hostel. It's a 30-minute hike from the station to the Koblenz boat dock.

Km 585: Burg Lahneck—Above the modern autobahn bridge over the Lahn River, this castle *(Burg)* was built in 1240 to defend local silver mines; the castle was ruined by the French in 1688 and rebuilt in the 1850s in neo-Gothic style. Burg Lahneck faces another Romantic rebuild, the yellow Schloss Stolzenfels (out of view above the train, a 10-min climb from tiny car park, open for touring, closed Mon).

Km 580: Marksburg—This castle (black and white with the 3 modern chimneys behind it, just after town of Spay) is the best-looking of all the Rhine castles and the only surviving medieval castle on the Rhine. Because of its commanding position, it was never attacked. It's now open as a museum with a medieval interior second only to the Mosel's Burg Eltz (for self-guided tour and all the details, see Mosel Valley chapter). The three modern smokestacks vent Europe's biggest car battery recycling plant just up the valley.

Km 570: Boppard—Once a Roman town, Boppard has some impressive remains of fourth-century walls. Notice the Roman towers and the substantial chunk of Roman wall near the train station, just above the main square.

If you visit Boppard, head to the fascinating church below the main square. Find the carved Romanesque crazies at the doorway. Inside, to the right of the entrance, you'll see Christian symbols from Roman times. Also notice the painted arches and vaults. Originally most Romanesque churches were painted this way. Down by the river, look for the high water *(Hochwasser)* marks on the arches from various flood years. (You'll find these flood marks throughout the Rhine and Mosel Valleys.)

Km 567: Burg Sterrenberg and Burg Liebenstein—These are the "Hostile Brothers" castles across from Bad Salzig. Take the wall between the castles (actually designed to improve the defenses of both castles), add two greedy and jealous brothers and a fair maiden, and create your own legend. Burg Liebenstein is now a fun, friendly, and affordable family-run hotel (Db-€90, suite-€110, giant king-and-the-family room-€180, CC, 9 rooms, easy parking, tel. 06773/308, www.castle-liebenstein.com, e-mail: hotel-burg-liebenstein@rhinecastles.com, Nickenig family).

Km 560: While you can see nothing from here, a 19th-century lead mine functioned on both sides of the river with a shaft actually tunneling completely under it.

Km 559: Burg Maus—The Maus ("Mouse") got its name because the next castle was owned by the Katzenelnbogen family. ("Katz" means "cat.") In the 1300s, it was considered a state-of-the-art fortification . . . until Napoleon had it blown up in 1806 with state-of-the-art explosives. It was rebuilt true to its original plans around 1900. Today, the castle hosts a falconry show (€6.50, daily 11:00 and 14:30).

Km 557: St. Goar and Rheinfels Castle—Cross to the other side of the train. The pleasant town of St. Goar was named for a sixth-century hometown monk. It originated in Celtic times (really old) as a place where sailors would stop, catch their breath, send home a postcard, and give thanks after surviving the seductive and treacherous Loreley crossing. St. Goar is worth a stop to explore its mighty Rheinfels Castle. (For information, a guided castle tour, and accommodations, see below.)

Km 556: Burg Katz—Burg Katz (Katzenelnbogen) faces St. Goar from across the river. Together, Burg Katz (built in 1371) and Rheinfels Castle had a clear view up and down the river and effectively controlled traffic. There was absolutely no duty-free shopping on the medieval Rhine. Katz got Napoleoned in 1806 and rebuilt around 1900. Today, it's under rich and mysterious Japanese ownership. It's technically a hotel—Germany wouldn't allow its foreign purchase for private use—but it's so expensive, nobody's ever stayed there. Below the castle, notice the derelict grape terraces—worked since the eighth century, but abandoned only in the last generation. The Rhine wine is particularly good because the slate in which the grapes grow absorbs the heat of the sun and stays warm all night, resulting in sweeter grapes. Wine from the flat fields above the Rhine gorge is cheaper and good only as "table wine." The wine from the steep side of the Rhine gorge—harder to grow and harvest—is tastier and more expensive.

About Km 555: A statue of the Loreley, the beautiful but deadly nymph (see next listing for legend), combs her hair at the end of a long spit—built to give barges protection from vicious icebergs that occasionally rage down the river in the winter. The actual Loreley, a cliff, is just ahead.

Km 554: The Loreley—Steep a big slate rock in centuries of legend and it becomes a tourist attraction, the ultimate Rhinestone. The Loreley (flags on top, name painted near shoreline), rising 135 meters (450 feet) over the narrowest and deepest point of the Rhine, has long been important. It was a holy site in pre-Roman days. The fine echoes here—thought to be ghostly voices—fertilized the legendary soil.

Because of the reefs just upstream (at kilometer 552), many ships never made it to St. Goar. Sailors (after days on the river) blamed their misfortune on a *wunderbares Fräulein* whose long blonde hair almost covered her body. Heinrich Heine's *Song of Loreley* (the Cliffs Notes version is on local postcards) tells the story of a count who sent his men to kill or capture this siren after she distracted his horny son, causing him to drown. When the soldiers cornered the nymph in her cave, she called her father (Father Rhine) for help. Huge waves, the likes of which you'll never see today, rose from the river and carried Loreley to safety. And she has never been seen since.

But alas, when the moon shines brightly and the tour buses are parked, a soft, playful Rhine whine can still be heard from the Loreley. As you pass, listen carefully ("Sailors . . . sailors . . . over my bounding mane").

Km 552: Killer reefs, marked by red-and-green buoys, are called the "Seven Maidens." Okay, one goofy legend: The prince of Schönburg Castle (Ober Oberwesel) had seven spoiled daughters who always dumped men because of their shortcomings. Fed up, he invited seven of his knights up to the castle and demanded

Rhine River Trade and Barge-Watching

The Rhine is great for barge-watching. There's a constant parade of action, and each boat is different. Since ancient times, this has been a highway for trade. Today, the world's biggest port (Rotterdam) waits at the mouth of the river.

Barge workers are almost a subculture. Many own their own ships. The captain (and family) live in the stern. Workers live in the bow. The family car often decorates the bow like a shiny hood ornament. In the Rhine town of Kaub, there was a boarding school for the children of the Rhine merchant marine—but today it's closed, since most captains are Dutch, Belgian, or Swiss. The flag of the boat's home country flies in the stern (German; Swiss; Dutch—horizontal red, white, and blue; or French—vertical red, white, and blue). Logically, imports go upstream (Japanese cars, coal, and oil) and exports go downstream (German cars, chemicals, and pharmaceuticals). A clever captain manages to ship goods in each direction.

Tugs can push a floating train of up to five barges at once. Upstream it gets steeper and they can push only one at a time. Before modern shipping, horses dragged boats upstream (the faint remains of towpaths survive at points along the river). From 1873 to 1900, they laid a chain from Bonn to Bingen, and boats with cogwheels and steam engines hoisted themselves upstream. Today, 265 million tons travel year along the 850 kilometers from Basel on the Swiss border to Rotterdam on the Atlantic.

Riverside navigational aids are of vital interest to captains who don't wish to meet the Loreley. Boats pass on the right unless they clearly signal otherwise with a large blue sign. Since downstream ships can't stop or maneuver as freely, upstream boats are expected to do the tricky do-si-do work. Cameras monitor traffic all along and relay warnings of oncoming ships via large triangular signals posted before narrow and troublesome bends in the river. There may be two or three triangles per signpost, depending upon how many "sectors," or segments, of the river are covered. The lowest triangle indicates the nearest stretch of river. Each triangle tells if there's a ship in that sector. When the bottom side of a triangle is lit, that sector is empty. When the left side is lit, an oncoming ship is in that sector.

The **Signal and Riverpilots Museum,** located at the signal triangles at the upstream edge of St. Goar, explains how barges are safer, cleaner, and more fuel-efficient than trains or trucks (Wed and Sat 14:00–17:00, outdoor exhibits always open).

that his daughters each choose one to marry. But they complained that each man had too big a nose, was too fat, too stupid, and so on. The rude and teasing girls escaped into a riverboat. Just downstream, God turned them into the seven rocks that form this reef. While this story probably isn't entirely true, there's a lesson in it for medieval children: Don't be hard-hearted.

Km 550: Oberwesel—Cross to the other side of the train. Oberwesel was a Celtic town in 400 B.C., then a Roman military station. It now boasts some of the best Roman wall and medieval tower remains on the Rhine and the commanding Schönburg Castle. Notice how many of the train tunnels have entrances designed like medieval turrets—they were actually built in the Romantic 19th century. OK, back to the riverside.

Km 546: Burg Gutenfels and Pfalz Castle: The Classic Rhine View—Burg Gutenfels (see white painted "Hotel" sign) and the shipshape Pfalz Castle (built in the river in the 1300s) worked very effectively to tax medieval river traffic. The town of Kaub grew rich, as Pfalz raised its chains when boats came and lowered them only when the merchants had paid their duty. Those who didn't pay spent time touring its prison, on a raft at the bottom of its well. In 1504, a pope called for the destruction of Pfalz, but a six-week siege failed. Notice the overhanging outhouse (tiny white room with faded medieval stains between two wooden ones). Pfalz is tourable but bare and dull (€1.50 ferry from Kaub, €2 entry, Tue–Sun 10:00–13:00 & 14:00–18:00, closed Mon, tel. 06774/570 or 0172/262-2800).

In Kaub, a green statue honors the German general Blücher. He was Napoleon's nemesis. In 1813, as Napoleon fought his way back to Paris after his disastrous Russian campaign, he stopped at Mainz—hoping to fend off the Germans and Russians pursuing him by controlling that strategic bridge. Blücher tricked Napoleon. By building the first major pontoon bridge of its kind here at the Pfalz Castle, he crossed the Rhine and outflanked the French. Two years later, Blücher and Wellington teamed up to defeat Napoleon once and for all at Waterloo.

Km 544: The "Raft Busters"—Immediately before Bacharach, at the top of the island, buoys mark a gang of rocks notorious for busting up rafts. The Black Forest is upstream. It was poor, and wood was its best export. Black Foresters would ride log booms down the Rhine to the Ruhr (where their timber fortified coal-mine shafts) or to Holland (where logs were sold to shipbuilders). If they could navigate the sweeping bend just before Bacharach and then survive these "raft busters," they'd come home reckless and romantic, the German folkloric equivalent of American cowboys after payday.

Km 543: Bacharach and Burg Stahleck—Cross to the other side of the train. Bacharach is a great stop (see details and accommodations info below). Some of the Rhine's best wine is from this town, whose name means "altar to Bacchus." Local vintners brag that the medieval Pope Pius II ordered it by the cartload. Perched above the town, the 13th-century Burg Stahleck is now a hostel.

Km 540: Lorch—This pathetic stub of a castle is barely visible from the road. Notice the small car ferry (3/hr, 10 min), one of several between Mainz and Koblenz, where there are no bridges.

Km 538: Castle Sooneck—Cross back to the other side of the train. Built in the 11th century, this castle was twice destroyed by people sick and tired of robber barons.

Km 534: Burg Reichenstein, and **Km 533: Burg Rheinstein**—Stay on the other side of the train to see two of the first castles to be rebuilt in the Romantic era. Both are privately owned, tourable, and connected by a pleasant trail.

Km 530: Ehrenfels Castle—Opposite Bingerbrück and the Bingen station, you'll see the ghostly Ehrenfels Castle (clobbered by the Swedes in 1636 and by the French in 1689). Since it had no view of the river traffic to the north, the owner built the cute little *Mäuseturm* (Mouse Tower) on an island (the yellow tower you'll see near the train station today). Rebuilt in the 1800s in neo-Gothic style, it's now used as a Rhine navigation signal station.

Km 528: Niederwald Monument—Across from the Bingen station on a hilltop is the 36-meter-high (120-foot) Niederwald monument, a memorial built with 32 tons of bronze in 1877 to commemorate "the reestablishment of the German Empire." A lift takes tourists to this statue from the famous and extremely touristy wine town of Rüdesheim.

From here, the Romantic Rhine becomes the Industrial Rhine, and our tour is over.

More Rhine Sights

▲▲Marksburg Castle—Thanks to this castle's formidable defenses, invaders decided to give Marksburg a miss. This best-preserved castle on the Rhine can be toured only with a guide, and tours are generally in German only (4/hr in summer, 1/hr in winter). Still, it's an awesome castle, and the following walking tour fits the 50-minute German-language tour (€4.50, daily 10:00–18:00, last tour departs at 17:00, call ahead to see if a rare English tour is scheduled, tel. 02627/206, www.marksburg.de). Marksburg caps a hill above the Rhine town of Braubach (a short hike or shuttle train from the boat dock). Our tour starts inside the castle's first gate.

1. Inside the First Gate: While the dramatic castles lining the Rhine are generally Romantic rebuilds, Marksburg is the real McCoy—nearly all original construction. It's littered with bits of its medieval past, like the big stone ball that was swung on a rope to be used as a battering ram. Ahead, notice how the inner gate—originally tall enough for knights on horseback to gallop through—was made smaller, therefore safer from enemies on horseback. Climb the "Knights' Stairway," carved out of slate rock, and pass under the murder hole—handy for pouring boiling pitch on invaders. (Germans still say someone with bad luck "has pitch on his head.")

2. Coats of Arms: Colorful coats of arms line the wall just inside the gate. These are from the noble families who have owned the castle since 1283. In 1283, financial troubles drove the first family to sell to the powerful and wealthy Katzenelnbogen family (who made the castle into what you see today). When Napoleon took this region in 1803, an Austrian family who sided with the French got the keys. When Prussia took the region in 1866, control passed to a friend of the Prussians who had a passion for medieval things—typical of this Romantic period. Then it was sold to the German Castles Association in 1900. Its offices are in the main palace at the top of the stairs.

3. Romanesque Palace: White outlines mark where the larger original windows were located, before they were replaced by easier-to-defend smaller ones. On the far right, a bit of the original plaster survives. Slate, which is soft and vulnerable to the elements, needs to be covered—in this case, by plaster. Because this is a protected historic building, restorers can use only the traditional plaster methods... but no one knows how to make plaster work as well as the 800-year-old surviving bits.

4. Cannons: The oldest cannon here—from 1500—was back-loaded. This was good because many cartridges could be preloaded. But since the seal was leaky, it wasn't very powerful. The bigger, more modern cannons—from 1640—were one piece and therefore airtight, but had to be front-loaded. They could easily hit targets across the river from here. Stone balls were rough and therefore let the explosive force leak out. The best cannonballs were stones covered in smooth lead—airtight and therefore more powerful and more accurate.

5. Gothic Garden: Walking along an outer wall, you'll see 160 plants from the Middle Ages—used for cooking, medicine, and witchcraft. The *Schierling* (in the first corner, "hemlock" in English) is the same poison that killed Socrates.

6. Inland Rampart: This most vulnerable part of the castle had a triangular construction to better deflect attacks. Notice the factory in the valley. In the 14th century, this was a lead, copper, and silver mine. Today's factory—Europe's largest car battery recycling plant—uses the old mine shafts as a vent (see the three modern smokestacks).

7. Wine Cellar: Since Roman times, wine has been the traditional Rhineland drink. Because castle water was impure, wine—less alcoholic than today's beer—was the way knights got their fluids. The pitchers on the wall were their daily allotment. The bellows were part of the barrel's filtering system. Stairs lead to the . . .

8. Gothic Hall: This hall is set up as a kitchen, with an oven designed to roast an ox whole. The arms holding the pots have notches to control the heat. To this day, when Germans want someone to hurry up, they say, "give it one tooth more." Medieval windows were thin alabaster or skins. A nearby wall is peeled away to show the wattle-and-daub construction (sticks, straw, clay, mud, then plaster) of a castle's inner walls. The iron plate to the left of the next door enabled servants to stoke the heater without being seen by the noble family.

9. Bedroom: This was the only heated room in the castle. The canopy kept in heat and kept out critters. In medieval times, it was impolite for a lady to argue with her lord in public. She would wait for him in bed to give him what Germans still call "a curtain lecture." The deep window seat caught maximum light for handwork and reading. Women would sit here and chat (or "spin a yarn") while working the spinning wheel.

10. Hall of the Knights: This was the dining hall. The long table is an unattached plank. After each course, servants could replace it with another pre-set plank. Even today, when a meal is over and Germans are ready for the action to begin, they say, "Let's lift up the table." The action back then was traveling minstrels who sang and told of news gleaned from their travels.

The toilet locked from the outside because any invader knew that the toilet—which simply hung over thin air—was a weak point in the castle's defenses.

11. Chapel: This chapel is still painted in Gothic style with the castle's namesake, St. Mark, and his lion. Even the chapel was designed with defense in mind. The small doorway kept out heavily armed attackers. The staircase spirals clockwise, favoring the sword-wielding defender (assuming he was right-handed).

12. Linen Room: Around 1800, the castle—with diminished military value—housed disabled soldiers. They'd earn a little extra money working raw flax into linen.

13. Two Thousand Years of Armor: Follow the evolution of armor since Celtic times. Since helmets covered the entire head, soldiers identified themselves as friendly by tipping their visor up with their right hand. This evolved into the military salute that is still used around the world today. Armor and the close-range weapons along the back were made obsolete by the invention of the rifle. Armor was replaced with breastplates—pointed (like the castle itself) to deflect enemy fire. This design was used as late as the start of World War I. A medieval lady's armor hangs over the door. While popular fiction has men locking their women up before heading off to battle, chastity belts were actually used by women as protection against rape when traveling.

14. The Keep: This served as an observation tower, a dungeon (with a 2-square-meter/22-square-foot cell in the bottom), and a place of last refuge. When all was nearly lost, the defenders would bundle into the keep and burn the wooden bridge, hoping to outwait their enemies.

15. Horse Stable: The stable shows off bits of medieval crime and punishment. Cheaters were attached to stones or pillories. Shame masks punished gossipmongers. A mask with a heavy ball had its victim crawling around with his nose in the mud. The handcuffs with a neck hole were for the transport of prisoners. The pictures on the wall show various medieval capital punishments. Often the accused was simply taken into a torture dungeon to see all these tools and, guilty or not, confessions spilled out of him. On that cheery note, your tour is over.

The Myth of the Loreley Visitors' Center—This lightweight exhibition, built for Expo 2000, reflects on Loreley, traces her myth, and explores the landscape, culture, and people of the Rhine Valley. Displays in English tell the history well, but the highlights for any kid at heart are the echo megaphones in the little theater that (with English headphones) tell the legend of the siren (€1, April–Oct daily 10:00–18:00, Nov–March daily 11:00–17:00, tel. 06771/9100). From the exhibit, a five-minute walk (marked as 30 minutes) takes you to the impressive viewpoint overlooking the Rhine Valley from atop the famous rock. From there, it's a steep 15-minute hike down to the riverbank.

Biking the Rhine—In Bacharach, you can rent bikes at Hotel Hillen (€7/half-day, €10/day, cheaper for guests, 20 bikes) or Pension im Malerwinkel (€6/day), or get a free loaner bike if you're staying at Pension Winzerhaus. In St. Goar, Hotel am Markt loans bikes to its guests.

You can bike on either side of the Rhine, but for a designated bike path, stay on the west side, where a 60-kilometer (35-mile) path runs between Koblenz and Bingen. While the stretch between Bacharach and Bingen hugs the riverside, I'd join the in-line skaters along the fine and more interesting roadside bike lane connecting Bacharach and St. Goar (10 km/6 miles).

Consider taking a bike on the Rhine boats (free with ticket) and then biking back or designing a circular trip using the fun and frequent shuttle ferries. A good target might be Kaub (where a tiny boat shuttles sightseers to the better-from-a-distance castle on the island).

Hiking the Rhine—For a good two-hour hike from St. Goar to the Loreley viewpoint, catch the ferry across to St. Goarshausen (€1.30 round-trip, 4/hr), follow green *Burg Katz* (Katz Castle) signs up Burgstrasse under the train tracks to find steps on right *(Loreley über Burg Katz)* leading to the Katz Castle (now a private hotel for Japanese elite) and beyond. Traverse the hillside, always bearing right toward the river. You'll pass through a residential area, hike down a 50-meter (165-foot) path through trees, then cross a wheat field until you reach an amphitheater adjacent to the Loreley Visitors' Center (shops and restaurants, see above) and rock-capping viewpoint. From here, it's a steep 15-minute hike down to the river, where a riverfront trail takes you back to St. Goarshausen and the St. Goar ferry.

BACHARACH

Once prosperous from the wine and wood trade, Bacharach (pron. BAHKH-ah-rahkh, with a guttural kh sound) is now just a pleasant half-timbered village of a thousand people working hard to keep its tourists happy.

Tourist Information: The TI is on the main street in the Posthof courtyard next to the church (Mon–Fri 9:00–17:00, Sat 10:00–16:00, closed Sun, shorter hours off-season, Internet access-€6/hr, Oberstrasse 45, from train station turn right and walk 5 blocks down main street with castle high on your left, tel. 06743/919-303, Herr Kuhn). The TI stores bags for day-trippers, provides ferry schedules, and sells the handy *Rhine Guide from Mainz to Cologne* (€3.60).

Shopping: The Jost beer-stein stores carry most everything a shopper could want. One shop is across from the church in the main square, the other—which offers more deals—is a block away, next to the post office at Rosenstrasse 16 (post office closed 12:30–14:00; Jost store hours: Mon–Fri 8:30–18:00, Sat 8:30–17:00, Sun 10:00–17:00, Rosenstrasse shop closed Sun, ships overseas, 10 percent discount with this book, CC, tel. 06743/1224, www.phil-jost-germany.com). The Josts offer sightseeing advice, send faxes, and reserve German hotels for travelers (reasonable charge for phone and fax fees). Woodburn House, which engraves woody signs and knickknacks, lets travelers store bags while they look for a room and gives readers with this book a 10 percent discount (across from Altes Haus, Oberstrasse 60, Frances Geuss SE).

Tour Guide: Get acquainted with Bacharach by taking a walking tour. Charming Herr Rolf Jung, retired headmaster of the Bacharach school, is a superb English-speaking guide (€30, 90 min, call him to reserve a tour, tel. 06743/1519). The TI has a list of other English-speaking guides, or take the self-guided walk, described below. For accommodations, see "Sleeping on the Rhine," below.

Introductory Bacharach Walk

Start at the Köln-Düsseldorfer ferry dock (next to a fine picnic park). View the town from the parking lot—a modern landfill. The Rhine used to lap against Bacharach's town wall, just over the present-day highway. Every few years, the river floods, covering the highway with several meters of water. The **castle** on the hill is a youth hostel. Two of its original 16 towers are visible from here (up to 5 if you look real hard). The huge roadside wine keg declares this town was built on the wine trade.

Reefs up the river forced boats to unload upriver and reload here. Consequently, Bacharach became the biggest wine trader on the Rhine. A riverfront crane hoisted huge kegs of prestigious "Bacharach" wine (which in practice was from anywhere in the region). The tour buses next to the dock and the flags of the biggest spenders along the highway remind you today's economy is basically tourism.

At the big town map and public WC (€0.50), take the underpass, ascend on the right, make a U-turn, then—if you are less than 2.3 meters (7.5 feet) tall—walk under the train tracks through the medieval gate (1 out of an original 15 14th-century gates) and to the two-tone Protestant **church**, which marks the town center.

From this intersection, Bacharach's main street (Oberstrasse) goes right to the half-timbered, red-and-white Altes Haus (from 1368, the oldest house in town) and left way down to the train station. To the left (or south) of the church, a golden horn hangs over the old **Posthof** (TI, free WC upstairs in courtyard). The post horn symbolizes the postal service throughout Europe. In olden days, when the postman blew this, traffic stopped and the mail sped through. This post station dates from 1724, when stagecoaches ran from Köln to Frankfurt.

Step into the courtyard—once a carriage house and inn that accommodated Bacharach's first VIP visitors. Notice the fascist eagle (from 1936, on the left as you enter) and the fine view of the church and a ruined chapel above. The Posthof is the home of the **Rhineland Museum**, which hopes to open in 2003 with a cultural landscape exhibit on the Rhine Valley, well-described in English. Manager Bintz's vision even includes wine-tasting (www.mittelrheintal.de).

Two hundred years ago, Bacharach's main drag was the

Bacharach

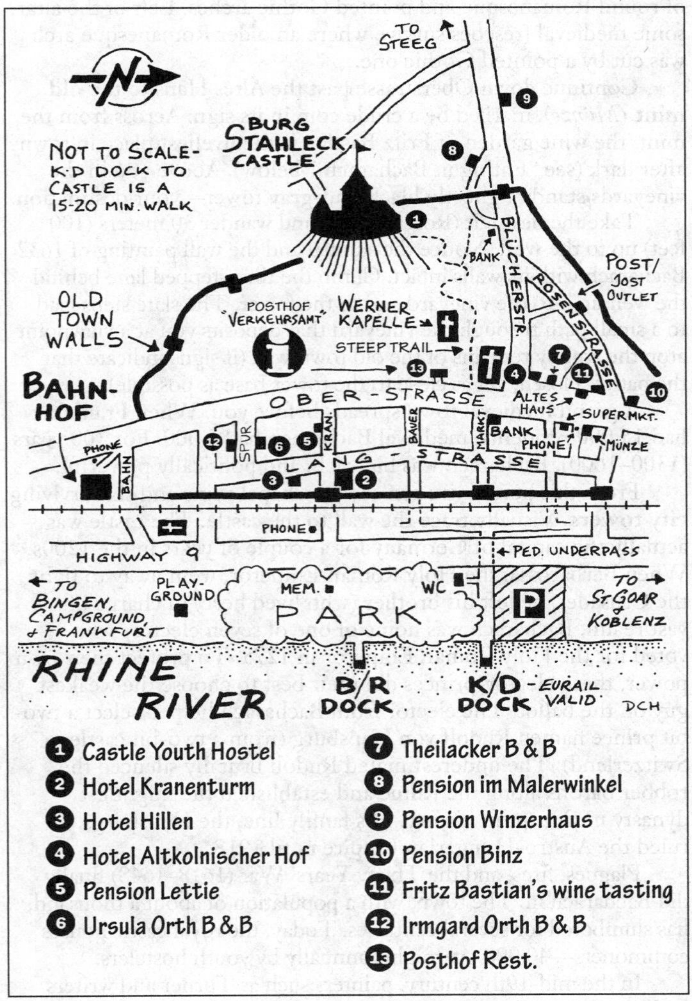

only road along the Rhine. Napoleon widened it to fit his cannon wagons. The steps alongside the church lead to the castle. Return to the church, passing the **Italian Ice Cream** café, where friendly Mimo serves his special invention: Riesling wine–flavored gelato (quite tasty, €0.60 per scoop, opposite Posthof at Oberstrasse 48).

Inside the church (English info on table near door), you'll find grotesque capitals, brightly painted in medieval style, and a mix of round Romanesque and pointed Gothic arches. Left of the altar, some medieval frescoes survive where an older Romanesque arch was cut by a pointed Gothic one.

Continue down Oberstrasse past the Altes Haus to the **old mint** *(Münze)*, marked by a crude coin in its sign. Across from the mint, the wine garden of Fritz Bastian is the liveliest place in town after dark (see "Eating in Bacharach," below). Above you in the vineyards stands a ghostly black-and-gray tower—your destination.

Take the next left (Rosenstrasse) and wander 30 meters (100 feet) up to the **well**. Notice the sundial and the wall painting of 1632 Bacharach with its walls intact. Climb the tiny-stepped lane behind the well up into the vineyard and to the tower. The slate steps lead to a small path through the vineyard that deposits you at a viewpoint atop the stubby remains of the old town wall (if signs indicate that the path is closed, get as close to the tower base as possible).

A grand medieval town spreads before you. When Frankfurt had 15,000 residents, medieval Bacharach had 4,000. For 300 years (1300–1600), Bacharach was big, rich, and politically powerful.

From this perch, you can see the chapel ruins and six surviving **city towers**. Visually trace the wall to the castle. The castle was actually the capital of Germany for a couple of years in the 1200s. When Barbarossa, the Holy Roman Emperor, went away to fight the Crusades, he left his brother (who lived here) in charge of his vast realm. Bacharach was home of one of seven electors who voted for the Holy Roman Emperor in 1275. To protect their own power, these elector-princes did their best to choose the weakest guy on the ballot. The elector from Bacharach helped select a two-bit prince named Rudolf von Hapsburg (from a two-bit castle in Switzerland). The underestimated Rudolf brutally silenced the robber barons along the Rhine and established the mightiest dynasty in European history. His family line, the Hapsburgs, ruled the Austro-Hungarian Empire until 1918.

Plagues, fires, and the Thirty Years' War (1618–1648) finally did Bacharach in. The town, with a population of about a thousand, has slumbered for several centuries. Today, the royal castle houses commoners—40,000 overnights annually by youth hostelers.

In the mid-19th century, painters such as Turner and writers such as Victor Hugo were charmed by the Rhineland's romantic mix of past glory, present poverty, and rich legend. They put this part of the Rhine on the old "grand tour" map as the "Romantic Rhine." Victor Hugo pondered the ruined 15th-century chapel, which you can see under the castle. In his 1842 travel book, *Rhein Reise (Rhine Travels)*, he wrote, "No doors, no roof or windows, a magnificent skeleton puts its silhouette against the sky. Above it, the ivy-covered castle ruins provide a fitting crown. This is Bacharach, land of fairy tales, covered with legends and sagas." If you're enjoying the Romantic Rhine, thank Victor Hugo and company.

To get back into town, take the level path that leads along the wall up the valley past the next tower. Then cross the street into the parking lot. Pass Pension Malerwinkel on your right, being careful not to damage the old arch with your head. Follow the creek past a delightful little series of half-timbered homes and cheery gardens known as Painters' Corner *(Malerwinkel)*. Resist looking into some pervert's peep show (on the right) and continue downhill back to the village center. Nice work.

ST. GOAR

St. Goar is a classic Rhine town—its hulk of a castle overlooking a half-timbered shopping street and leafy riverside park busy with sightseeing ships and contented strollers. From the boat dock, the main drag—a pedestrian mall without history—cuts through town before winding up to the castle. Rheinfels Castle, once the mightiest on the Rhine, is the single best Rhineland ruin to explore.

The St. Goar **TI**, which books rooms and offers a free left-luggage service, is on the pedestrian street, three blocks from the K-D boat dock and train station (May–Oct Mon–Fri 8:00–12:30 & 14:00–17:00, Sat 10:00–12:00, closed Sun and earlier in winter, sells *Rhine Guide from Mainz to Cologne;* from train station, go downhill around church and turn left on Heer Strasse; tel. 06741/383).

St. Goar's waterfront park is hungry for a picnic. The small Edeka **supermarket** on the main street is great for picnic fixings (Mon–Fri 8:00–18:30, Sat 8:00–13:00, closed Sun).

The friendly and helpful Montag family runs the Hotel Montag (Michael) and three shops (steins—Misha, Steiffs—Maria, and cuckoo clocks—Marion), all at the base of the castle hill road. The stein shop under the hotel has Rhine guidebooks (Koblenz–Mainz, €4), fine steins, and copies of this year's *Rick Steves' Germany, Austria & Switzerland* guidebook. All three shops offer 10 percent off any of their souvenirs (including Hummels) for travelers with this book (€5 minimum purchase). On-the-spot VAT refunds cover about half your shipping costs. The hotel offers expensive Internet access (€8/hr, coin-op).

St. Goar's Rheinfels Castle

▲▲▲Self-Guided Tour—Sitting like a dead pit bull above St. Goar, this mightiest of Rhine castles rumbles with ghosts from its hard-fought past. Burg Rheinfels (built in 1245) withstood a siege of 28,000 French troops in 1692. But in 1797, the French Revolutionary army destroyed it.

St. Goar

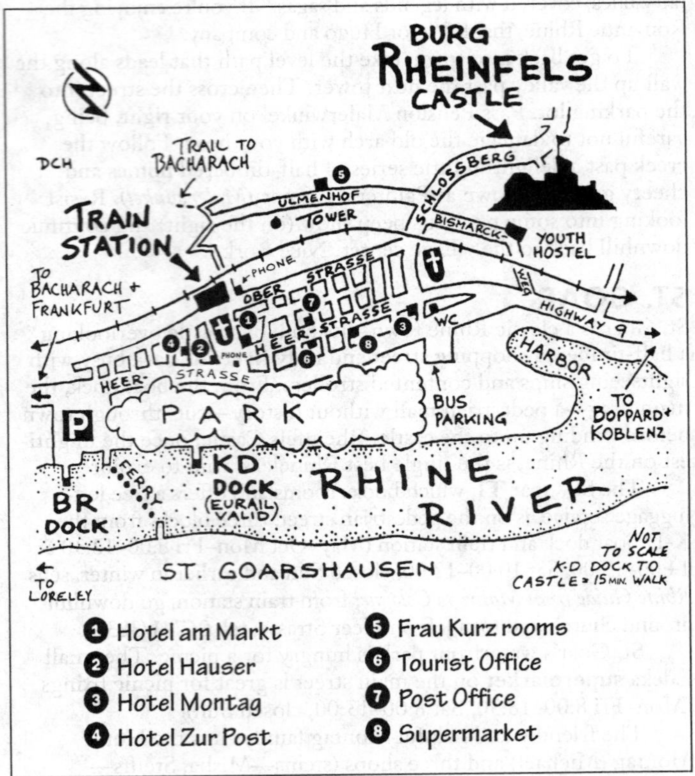

Rheinfels *was* huge. Once the biggest castle on the Rhine, it was used for ages as a quarry, and today—while still mighty—it's only a small fraction of its original size. This hollow but interesting shell offers your single best hands-on ruined-castle experience on the river (€4, mid-March–Oct daily 9:00–18:00, last entry at 17:00, Nov–mid-March only Sat–Sun 11:00–17:00, call in advance or gather 10 English-speaking tourists and beg to get an English tour—perhaps from Günther, the "last knight of Rheinfels"—free luggage check service at ticket office, tel. 06741/7753). The castle map is mediocre; the English booklet is better, with history and illustrations (€1.80). If planning to explore the mine tunnels, bring a flashlight, buy a tiny one for €2.60 at the entry, or do it by candlelight (museum sells candles with matches, €0.50). If it's damp, be careful of slippery stones. To get to the castle from St. Goar's boat dock or train station, take a steep 15-minute hike, a €5 taxi ride (€6 for a minibus, tel. 06741/7011), or the kitschy "tschu-tschu" tourist train (€3, 7-min trip, 3/hr, daily 10:00–17:00, runs from square between station and dock, also stops at Hotel Montag, complete with lusty music). A handy WC is in the castle courtyard under the stairs to the restaurant entry.

Rather than wander aimlessly, visit the castle by following this tour: From the ticket gate, walk straight. Pass *Grosser Keller* on the left (where we'll end this tour), walk through an internal gate past the *zu den gedeckten Wehrgängen* sign on the right (where we'll pass later) uphill to the museum (daily 9:30–12:00 & 13:00–17:30) in the only finished room of the castle.

1. Museum and Castle Model: The two-meter-tall (7-foot) carved stone *(Keltische Säule von Pfalzfeld)* immediately inside the door—a tombstone from a nearby Celtic grave—is from 400 years before Christ. There were people here long before the Romans... and this castle. The chair next to the door is an old library chair. If you smile sweetly, the man behind the desk may demonstrate—pull the back forward and it becomes stairs for getting to the highest shelves.

The sweeping castle history exhibit in the center of the room is well-described in English. The massive fortification was the only Rhineland castle to withstand Louis XIV's assault during the 17th century. At the far end of the room is a model reconstruction of the castle showing how much bigger it was before French revolutionary troops destroyed it in the 18th century. Study this. Find where you are (hint: look for the tall tower). This was the living quarters of the original castle, which was only the smallest ring of buildings around the tiny central courtyard (13th century). The ramparts were added in the 14th century. By 1650, the fortress was largely complete. Ever since its destruction by the French in the late 18th century, it's had no military value. While no WWII bombs were wasted on this ruin, it served St. Goar as a quarry for generations. The basement of the museum shows the castle pharmacy and an exhibit on Rhine region odds and ends, including tools and an 1830 loom. Don't miss the photos of ice breaking on the Rhine—which, thanks to global warming, hasn't been necessary since 1963.

Exit the museum and walk 30 meters (100 feet) directly out, slightly uphill into the castle courtyard.

2. Medieval Castle Courtyard: Five hundred years ago, the entire castle circled this courtyard. The place was self-sufficient and ready for a siege, with a bakery, pharmacy, herb garden, animals, brewery, well (top of yard), and livestock. During peacetime, 300 to 600 people lived here; during a siege, there would

St. Goar's Rheinfels Castle

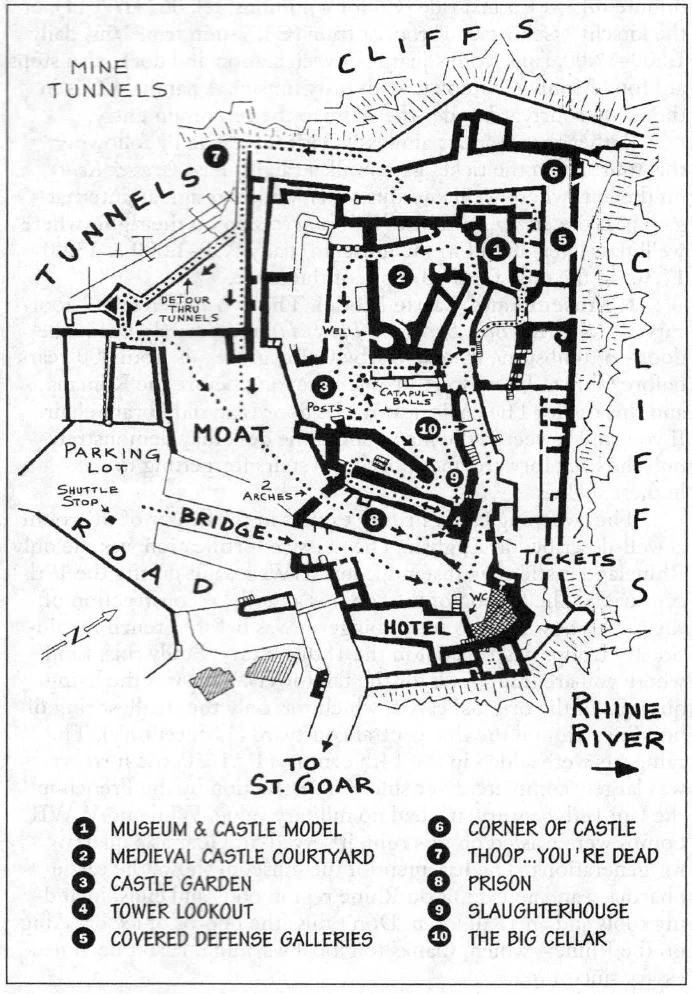

be as many as 4,500. The walls were plastered and painted white. Bits of the original 13th-century plaster survive.

Continue through the courtyard, out *Erste Schildmauer*, turn left into the next courtyard, and walk to the two old, black, upright posts. Find the pyramid of stone catapult balls.

3. Castle Garden: Catapult balls like these were too expensive not to recycle. If ever used, they'd be retrieved after the battle. Across from the balls is a well—essential for any castle during the age of siegeing. Look in. The old posts are for the ceremonial baptizing of new members of the local trading league. While this guild goes back centuries, it's now a social club that fills this court with a huge wine party the third weekend of each September.

If weary, skip to #5; otherwise, climb the cobbled path up to the castle's best viewpoint—up where the German flag waves.

4. Highest Castle Tower Lookout: Enjoy a great view of the river, castle, and the forest that were once all part of this castle. Remember, the fortress used to cover five times the land it does today. Notice how the other castles (across the river) don't poke above the top of the Rhine canyon. That would make them easy for invading armies to see.

Return to the catapult balls, walk down the road, go through the tunnel, veer left through the arch marked *zu den gedeckten Wehrgängen*, go down two flights of stairs, and turn left into the dark covered passageway. We now begin a rectangular walk taking us completely around the perimeter of the castle.

5. Covered Defense Galleries: Soldiers—the castle's "minutemen"—had a short commute: defensive positions on the outside, home in the holes below on the left. Even though these living quarters were padded with straw, life was unpleasant. A peasant was lucky to live beyond age 45.

Continue straight through the gallery and to the corner of the castle, where you'll see a white painted arrow at eye level.

6. Corner of Castle: Look up. A three-story, half-timbered building originally rose beyond the highest stone fortification. The two stone tongues near the top just around the corner supported the toilet. (Insert your own joke here.) Turn around. The crossbow slits below the white arrow were once steeper. The bigger hole on the riverside was for hot pitch.

Follow that white arrow along the outside to the next corner. Midway you'll pass stairs on the right leading down *zu den Minengängen* (sign on upper left). Adventurers with flashlights can detour here (see "Into the Mine Tunnels," below). You may come out around the next corner. Otherwise, stay with me, walking level to the corner. At the corner, turn left.

7. Thoop... You're Dead. Look ahead at the smartly placed crossbow arrow slit. While you're lying there, notice the stonework. The little round holes were for scaffolds used as they built up. They indicate this stonework is original. Notice also the fine stonework on the chutes. More boiling oil... now you're toast, too. Continue along the castle wall around the corner. At the railing, look up the valley and uphill where the sprawling fort stretched.

Below, just outside the wall, is land where attackers would gather. The mine tunnels are under there, waiting to blow up any attackers (read below).

Continue along the perimeter, jog left, go down five steps and into an open field, and walk toward the wooden bridge. You may detour here into the passageway (on right) marked *13 Hals Graben*. The old wooden bridge is actually modern. Angle left through two arches (before the bridge) and through the rough entry to *Verliess* (prison) on the left.

8. Prison: This is one of six dungeons. You walked through a door prisoners only dreamed of 400 years ago. They came and went through the little square hole in the ceiling. The holes in the walls supported timbers that thoughtfully gave as many as 15 residents something to sit on to keep them out of the filthy slop that gathered on the floor. Twice a day, they were given bread and water. Some prisoners actually survived longer than two years in here. The town could torture and execute; the castle had permission only to imprison criminals in these dungeons. Consider this: According to town records, the two men who spent the most time down here—2.5 years each—died within three weeks of regaining their freedom. Perhaps after a diet of bread and water, feasting on meat and wine was simply too much.

Continue through the next arch, under the white arrow, and turn left and walk 30 meters (100 feet) to the *Schlachthaus*.

9. Slaughterhouse: Any proper castle was prepared to survive a six-month siege. With 4,000 people, that's a lot of provisions. The cattle that lived within the walls were slaughtered in this room. The castle's mortar was congealed here (by packing all the organic waste from the kitchen into kegs and sealing it). Notice the drainage gutters. "Running water" came through from drains built into the walls (to keep the mortar dry and therefore strong... and less smelly).

Back outside, climb the modern stairs to the left. A skinny passage leads you into the...

10. Big Cellar: This *Grosser Keller* was a big pantry. When the castle was smaller, this was the original moat—you can see the rough lower parts of the wall. The original floor was four meters (13 feet) deeper. The drawbridge rested upon the stone nubs on the left. When the castle expanded, the moat became this cellar. Above the entry, holes mark spots where timbers made a storage loft, perhaps filled with grain. In the back, an arch leads to the wine cellar where finer wine was kept. Part of a soldier's pay was wine... table wine. This wine was kept in a single 180,000-liter (47,550-gallon) stone barrel, which generally lasted about 18 months.

The count owned the surrounding farmland. Farmers got

to keep 20 percent of their production. Later, in more liberal feudal times, the nobility let them keep 40 percent. Today, the German government leaves the workers with 60 percent...and provides a few more services.

You're free. Climb out, turn right, and leave. For coffee on a great view terrace, visit the Rheinfels Castle Hotel, opposite the entrance (WC at base of steps).

Into the Mine Tunnels—To protect their castle around 1600, the Rheinfellers cleverly booby-trapped the land just outside their walls by building tunnels topped with thin slate roofs and packed with explosives. By detonating the explosives when under attack, they could kill hundreds of invaders. In 1626, a handful of underground Protestant Germans blew 300 Catholic Spaniards to—they figured—hell. You're welcome to wander through a set of never-blown-up tunnels. But be warned: it's 180 meters (590 feet) long, assuming you make no wrong turns; it's completely dark, muddy, and claustrophobic, with confusing dead-ends; and you'll never get higher than a deep crouch. It cannot be done without a light (flashlights available at entry—see above). At stop #6 of the above tour, follow the stairs on the right leading down *zu den Minengängen* (sign on upper left).

The *Fuchsloch* sign welcomes you to the foxhole. Walk level (take no stairs) past the first steel railing (where you hope to emerge later) to the second steel railing. Climb down. The "highway" in this foxhole is one meter (3 feet) high. The ceiling may be painted with a white line indicating the correct path. Don't venture into the more narrow side aisles. These were once filled with the gunpowder. After a small decline, take the second right. At the T-intersection, go right (uphill). After about three meters (10 feet), go left. Take the next right and look for a light at the end of the tunnel. Head up a rocky incline under the narrowest part of the tunnel and you'll emerge at that first steel railing. The stairs on the right lead to freedom. Cross the field uphill and find the big courtyard to rejoin the tour at stop #8.

Sleeping on the Rhine

(€1 = about $1)

Sleep Code: **S** = Single, **D** = Double/Twin, **T** = Triple, **Q** = Quad, **b** = bathroom, **s** = shower only, **CC** = Credit Cards accepted, **no CC** = Credit Cards not accepted, **SE** = Speaks English, **NSE** = No English. All hotels speak some English. Breakfast is included unless otherwise noted.

To help you sort easily through these listings, I've divided the rooms into three categories based on the price for a standard double room with bath:

Higher Priced—Most rooms more than €70.
Moderately Priced—Most rooms €70 or less.
Lower Priced—Most rooms €50 or less.

The Rhine is an easy place for cheap sleeps. *Zimmer* and *Gasthäuser* with €20 beds abound (and *Zimmer* normally discount their prices for longer stays). Rhine-area hostels offer €14 beds to travelers of any age. Each town's TI is eager to set you up, and finding a room should be easy any time of year (except for winefest weekends in September and October). Bacharach and St. Goar, the best towns for an overnight stop, are 16 kilometers (10 miles) apart, connected by milk-run trains, riverboats, and a riverside bike path. Bacharach is a much more interesting town, but St. Goar has the famous castle (see "St. Goar," above). Parking in Bacharach is simple along the highway next to the tracks (3-hr daytime limit is generally not enforced) or in the boat parking lot. Parking in St. Goar is tighter; ask at your hotel.

Sleeping in Bacharach

(country code: 49, area code: 06743, zip code: 55422)

See map on page 479 for locations. Ignore guest houses and restaurants posting "Recommended by Rick Steves" signs. If they're not listed in the current edition of this book, I do not recommend them. At the **launderette** a block downhill from the church and just inside the town gate, Anja Ohm offers full-service, same-day wash-and-dry for €12.50 per load (Mon–Fri 8:00–18:00, Sat 8:00–14:00, closed Sun, this special price with this book; she may pick up and drop at your hotel; Marktstrasse 3, cellular 0160-646-4980).

MODERATELY PRICED

Hotel Kranenturm offers castle ambience without the climb—a good combination of hotel comfort with *Zimmer* coziness, a central location, and a medieval atmosphere. Run by hardworking Kurt Engel, his intense but friendly wife, Fatima, and attentive Schumi the waiter, this hotel is actually part of the medieval fortification. Its former *Kran* (crane) towers are now round rooms. When the riverbank was higher, cranes on this tower loaded barrels of wine onto Rhine boats. Hotel Kranenturm is five meters (16 feet) from the train tracks, but a combination of medieval sturdiness, triple-paned windows, and included earplugs makes the riverside rooms sleepable (Sb-€40–43, Db-€54–60, Tb-€74–80, Qb-€94–98, lower price is for off-season or stays of at least 3 nights in high season, family deals, CC but prefer cash, Rhine views come with ripping train noise, back rooms are quieter, kid-friendly, Langstrasse 30, tel. 06743/1308, fax 06743/1021, e-mail: hotel-kranenturm@t-online.de). Kurt, a good cook, serves

€6 to €18 dinners; try his ice-cream special for dessert. Trade travel stories on the terrace with new friends over dinner, letting screaming trains punctuate your conversation. Drivers park along the highway at the Kranenturm tower. Eurailers walk down Oberstrasse, then turn right on Kranenstrasse.

Hotel Hillen, a block south of the Hotel Kranenturm, has less charm and similar train noise, with friendly owners, great food, and lots of rental bikes. To minimize train noise, ask for *ruhige Seite*, the quiet side (S-€28, Sb-€36, D-€42, Ds-€52, Db-€57, Tb-€75, 10 percent less for 3 nights, CC, closed Nov–March, Langstrasse 18, tel. 06743/1287, fax 06743/1037, e-mail: hotel-hillen@web.de, Iris speaks some English).

Hotel Altkölnischer Hof, a grand old building near the church, rents 20 rooms with modern furnishings and bathrooms, some with balconies over an Old World restaurant. Public rooms are old-time elegant (Sb-€48–55, small or dark Db-€62, bright new Db-€72, new Db with terrace-€86, CC, elevator, closed Nov–March, tel. 06743/1339 or 06743/2186, fax 06743/2793, www.hotel-bacharach-rhein.de, e-mail: altkoelnischer-hof@t-online.de).

Pension im Malerwinkel sits like a grand gingerbread house just outside the wall at the top end of town in a little neighborhood so charming it's called the Painters' Corner *(Malerwinkel)*. The Vollmer family's 20-room place is super-quiet and comes with a sunny garden on a brook and easy parking (Sb-€32, Db-€55, €48 for 2 nights, €45 for 3 nights, cash only, bike rental-€6/day, from town center, go uphill and up the valley 5 min until you pass the old town gate and look left to Blücherstrasse 41, tel. 06743/1239, fax 06743/93407, www.im-malerwinkel.de, e-mail: pension@im-malerwinkel.de, SE).

Pension Binz offers four large, bright rooms and a plain apartment in a serene location (Sb-€33, Db-€51, third person-€18, apartment for 2-night minimum-€61, CC, fine breakfast, Koblenzer Strasse 1, tel. 06743/1604, e-mail: pension.binz@freenet.de, cheery Karla speaks a little English).

LOWER PRICED

At **Pension Lettie**, effervescent and eager-to-please Lettie offers four bright rooms. Lettie speaks good English (worked for the U.S. Army before they withdrew) and does laundry—€10.50 per load (Sb-€34, Db-€45, Tb-€61, family room for 4-€75, for 5-€95, for 6-€105, prices valid with this book, discount for 2-night stays, no CC, strictly non-smoking, no train noise, a few doors inland from Hotel Kranenturm, Kranenstrasse 6, tel. & fax 06743/2115, e-mail: pension.lettie@t-online.de).

Pension Winzerhaus, a 10-room place run by friendly

Herr and Frau Petrescu, is 200 meters (650 feet) up the valley from the town gate, so the location is less charming, but it has no train noise and easy parking. Rooms are simple, clean, and modern (Sb-€26, Db-€45, Tb/Qb-€60, 10 percent off with this book, no CC, free bikes for guests, non-smoking rooms, Blücherstrasse 60, tel. 06743/1294, fax 06743/937-779, e-mail: winzerhaus@compuserve.de, SE).

Just off the main street, the cozy home of **Herr und Frau Theilacker** is a German-feeling *Zimmer* offering four comfortable rooms, vine-covered trellises, and a pleasant stay. It's likely to have a room when others don't (S-€15, D-€31, no CC, in town center behind Altkölnischer Hof, take short lane between Altkölnischer Hof and Altes Haus straight ahead to Oberstrasse 57, no outside sign, tel. 06743/1248, NSE).

Delightful sisters-in-law run two fine little B&Bs across the lane from each other (from station walk down Oberstrasse, turn right on Spurgasse, look for *Orth* sign). **Ursula Orth** rents five stale-smelling but decent rooms (Sb-€18, D-€31, Db-€34, Tb-€45, no CC, rooms 4 and 5 on ground floor, Spurgasse 3, tel. 06743/1557, minimal English spoken). **Irmgard Orth** rents two fresh rooms. She speaks no English but is exuberantly cheery and serves homemade honey with breakfast (Sb-€20, Db-€33, Spurgasse 2, tel. 06743/1553).

Bacharach's hostel, **Jugendherberge Stahleck**, is a 12th-century castle on the hilltop—500 steps above Bacharach—with a royal Rhine view. Open to travelers of any age, this is a newly redone gem with eight beds and a private modern shower and WC in most rooms. A steep 15-minute climb on the trail from the town church, the hostel is warmly run by Evelyn and Bernhard Falke (pron. FALL-kay), who serve hearty, €5.40, all-you-can-eat buffet dinners. The hostel pub serves cheap local wine until midnight (€15.10 dorm beds with breakfast and sheets, €3 extra without a card or in a double, couples can share one of five €37 Db, groups pay €21 per bed with breakfast and dinner, no smoking in rooms, open all day but 22:00 curfew, washing machine, beds normally available but call and leave your name, they'll hold a bed until 18:00, tel. 06743/1266, fax 06743/2684, e-mail: jh-bacharach@djh-info.de, SE). If driving, don't go in the driveway; park on the street and walk 200 meters (650 feet).

Eating in Bacharach

You can easily find inexpensive (€10–15), atmospheric restaurants offering indoor and outdoor dining. The first three places are neighbors.

Altes Haus, the oldest building in town, serves reliably good food with Bacharach's most romantic atmosphere (€8–15, Thu–Tue 12:00–15:30 & 18:00–21:30, closed Wed and Dec–Easter, dead center by the church). Find the cozy little dining room with photos of the opera singer who sang about Bacharach, adding to its fame.

Kurpfälzische Münze is a popular standby for its sunny terrace and classy candlelit interior (€7–21, daily 10:00–22:00, in the old mint, a half block down from Altes Haus).

Posthof Restaurant is a historic carriage house—a stopping place for centuries of guests—newly opened as a restaurant. The menu is trendier, with free German tapas (ask), seasonal specials, and local, "as organic as possible" produce. You'll sit in a half-timbered cobbled courtyard (€5–15, good salads and veggie dishes, fun kids' play area, daily 11:00 until late, Oberstrasse 45, tel. 06743/599-663).

Hotel Kranenturm is another good value with hearty meals and good main course salads (restaurant closed Jan–Feb, see hotel listing above).

Wine-Tasting: Drop in on entertaining Fritz Bastian's **Weingut zum Grüner Baum** wine bar (also offers soup and cold cuts, good ambience indoors and out, just past Altes Haus, eves only, closed Thu, tel. 06743/1208). Fritz is on a mission to give travelers an understanding of the subtle differences among the Rhine wines. Groups of two to six people pay €13.50 for a "carousel" of 15 glasses of 14 different white wines, one lonely red, and a basket of bread. Your mission: Team up with others with this book to rendezvous here after dinner. Spin the lazy Susan, share a common cup, and discuss the taste. Fritz insists, "After each wine, you must talk to each other."

For a fun, family-run wine shop and *Stube* in the town center, visit **Weingut Karl Heidrich** (on Oberstrasse, directly in front of Hotel Kranenturm), where Suzanna and Markus proudly share their family's wine.

Sleeping in St. Goar

(country code: 49, area code: 06741, zip code: 56329)

See map on page 482 for locations.

HIGHER PRICED

Hotel Montag is on the castle end of town, just across the street from the world's largest free-hanging cuckoo clock. Manfred and Maria Montag and their son Mike speak New Yorkish. Even though the hotel gets a lot of bus tours, it's friendly, laid-back, and comfortable (Sb-€41, Db-€77, Tb-€87, price can drop if things are slow, CC, Internet access-€8/hr, Heer Strasse 128, tel. 06741/1629, fax 06741/2086, e-mail: hotelmontag@01019freenet.de). Check out their adjacent crafts shop (heavy on beer steins).

Rheinfels Castle Hotel is the town splurge. Actually part of the castle but an entirely new building, this luxury 57-room place is good for those with money and a car (Db-€130–154 depending on river views and balconies, extra bed €34, CC, elevator, free parking, indoor pool and sauna, dress-up restaurant, Schlossberg 47, tel. 06741/8020, fax 06741/802-802, www.schlosshotel-rheinfels.de, e-mail: info@burgrheinfels.de).

MODERATELY PRICED

Hotel am Markt, well-run by Herr and Frau Velich, is rustic with all the modern comforts. It features a hint of antler with a pastel flair, 18 bright rooms, and a good restaurant. It's a good value and a stone's throw from the boat dock and train station (S-€35, Sb-€43, Db-€59, Tb-€82, Qb-€88, 20 percent cheaper off-season, closed Dec–Feb, CC, Am Markt 1, tel. 06741/1689, fax 06741/1721, www.hotelammarkt1.de, e-mail: hotel.am.markt@gmx.de). The Velichs offer their guests with this book free loaner bikes.

Hotel Hauser, facing the boat dock, is another good deal, warmly run by another Frau Velich. Its 12 rooms sit over a fine restaurant (S-€21.50, D-€45, Db-€50, great Db with Rhine-view balconies-€56, show this book and pay cash to get these prices, Db cheaper off-season, costs more with CC, small bathrooms, Heer Strasse 77, tel. 06741/333, fax 06741/1464, SE).

Hotel zur Post, with creaky parquet floors and 12 forgettable, well-worn rooms, is a reasonable value a block off the riverfront (Db-€62, a block from the station at Bahnhofstrasse 3, tel. 06741/339, fax 06741/2708, e-mail: zurposthotel@gmx.de, family Bergweiler).

LOWER PRICED

St. Goar's best *Zimmer* deal is the home of **Frau Kurz**, which comes with a breakfast terrace, garden, fine view, and homemade marmalade (S-€21, D-€38, Db-€43, showers-€2.60, 1-night stays cost extra, no CC, free and easy parking, confirm prices, honor your reservation or call to cancel, Ulmenhof 11, tel. & fax 06741/459, some English spoken). It's a steep five-minute hike from the train station (exit left from station, take immediate left at the yellow phone booth, pass under tracks to paved path, go up stairs and follow zigzag path to Ulmenhof, *Zimmer* is just past tower).

The German-run **St. Goar Hostel**, the big beige building under the castle (on road to castle, veer right just after railroad bridge) has a 22:00 curfew (but you can borrow the key) and hearty €6 dinners (S-€14.60, dorm beds-€12, up to 12 beds per room, includes breakfast, no CC, open all day, check-in preferred 17:00–18:00 & 19:00–20:00, Bismarckweg 17, tel. 06741/388, fax 06741/2689, e-mail: jh-st-goar@djh-info.de, SE).

Eating in St. Goar

Hotel Am Markt serves good traditional meals (with plenty of game and fish) at fair prices (€5–16) with good atmosphere and service. For your Rhine splurge, walk, taxi, or drive up to **Rheinfels Castle Hotel** for its incredible view terrace in an elegant setting (€8–15 dinners, daily 18:30–21:15, reserve a table by the window, see hotel listing above).

Transportation Connections—Rhine

Milk-run trains stop at all Rhine towns each hour starting as early as around 6:00. Koblenz, Boppard, St. Goar, Bacharach, Bingen, and Mainz are each about 15 minutes apart. From Koblenz to Mainz takes 75 minutes. To get a faster big train, go to Mainz (for points east and south) or Koblenz (for points north, west, and along Mosel). Train info: tel. 01805/996-633.

From Mainz to: Bacharach/St. Goar (hrly, 1 hr), **Cochem** (hrly, 2.5 hrs, change in Koblenz), **Köln** (3/hr, 90 min, change in Koblenz), **Baden-Baden** (hrly, 1.5 hrs), **Munich** (hrly, 4 hrs), **Frankfurt** (3/hr, 45 min), **Frankfurt Airport** (4/hr, 25 min).

From Koblenz to: Köln (4/hr, 1 hr), **Berlin** (2/hr, 5.5 hrs, up to 2 changes), **Frankfurt** (3/hr, 1.5 hrs, 1 change), **Cochem** (2/hr, 50 min), **Trier** (2/hr, 2 hrs), **Brussels** (12/day, 4 hrs, change in Köln), **Amsterdam** (12/day, 4.5 hrs, up to 5 changes).

From Frankfurt to: Bacharach (hrly, 1.5 hrs, change in Mainz; first train to Bacharach departs at 6:00, last train at 20:45), **Koblenz** (hrly, 90 min, changes in Mannheim or Wiesbaden), **Rothenburg** (hrly, 3 hrs, transfers in Würzburg and Steinach), **Würzburg** (hrly, 2 hrs), **Munich** (hrly, 4 hrs, 1 change), **Amsterdam** (8/day, 5 hrs, up to 3 changes), **Paris** (9/day, 6.5 hrs, up to 3 changes).

From Bacharach to: Frankfurt Airport (hrly, 1.5 hrs, change in Mainz, first train to Frankfurt airport departs about 5:40, last train 21:30).

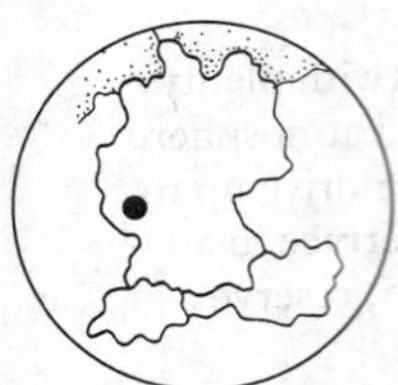

MOSEL VALLEY

The misty Mosel is what some visitors hoped the Rhine would be—peaceful, sleepy, romantic villages slipped between the steep vineyards and the river; fine wine; a sprinkling of castles (Burg Eltz is tops); and lots of friendly *Zimmer*. Boat, train, and car traffic here is a trickle compared to the roaring Rhine.

While the swan-speckled Mosel moseys 500 kilometers (300 miles) from France's Vosges Mountains to Koblenz, where it dumps into the Rhine, the most scenic piece of the valley lies between the towns of Bernkastel-Kues and Cochem. I'd savor only this section. Cochem is the handiest home base unless you want the peace of Beilstein.

Throughout the region on summer weekends and during the fall harvest, wine festivals with oompah bands, dancing, and colorful costumes are powered by good food and wine. You'll find a wine festival in some nearby villages any weekend, June through September. The tourist season lasts from April through October. Things close down tight through the winter.

Getting around the Mosel Valley

By Train and Bus: The train zips you to Cochem, Bullay, or Trier in a snap. Bullay has bus connections with Zell (nearly hrly, 10 min) and with Beilstein (4/day). Cochem has more frequent bus connections with Beilstein (hrly, 20 min, last bus departs Beilstein about 18:50). A one-way taxi from Cochem to Beilstein costs about €15. Pick up bus schedules at train stations or TIs.

By Boat: Daily departures on the Undine-Kolb Line allow you to cruise the most scenic stretch between Cochem, Beilstein, and Zell: between Cochem and Zell (1–2/day, May–Oct, but none on Fri and Mon May–June, 3 hrs, €14 one-way, €20 round-trip),

Mosel Valley

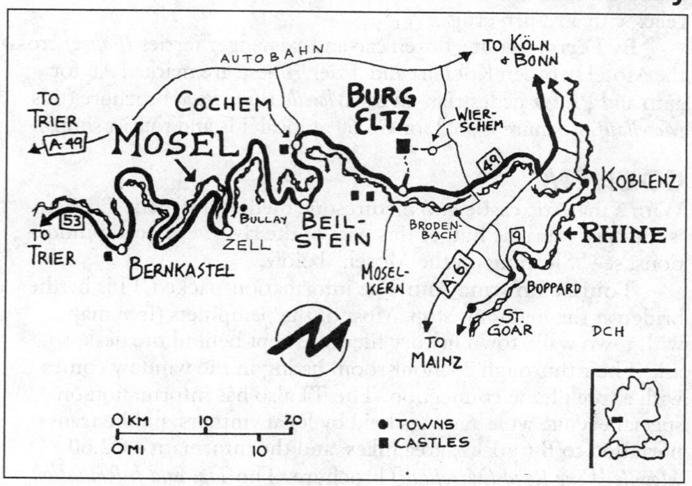

between Cochem and Beilstein (5/day, 1 hr, €8 one-way, €11 round-trip), and between Zell and Beilstein (1–2/day May–Oct, but none on Fri and Mon May–June, 2 hrs, €11 one-way, €15 round-trip, tel. 02673/1515).

The K-D (Köln-Düsseldorfer) line sails once a day in each direction, but only between Cochem and Koblenz (mid-June–Sept daily, May–mid-June and most of Oct Fri–Mon only, none in winter, Koblenz to Cochem 9:45–15:00, or Cochem to Koblenz 15:40–20:00, free with consecutive-day Eurailpass or a dated Eurail Flexipass, Europass, Eurail Selectpass, or German railpass, uses up a day of a Flexipass, tel. 02671/980-023). In early to mid-June, the locks close for 10 days of annual maintenance, and no boats run between Cochem, Koblenz, Beilstein, and Zell. With all the locks, Mosel cruises can be pretty slow.

By Car: The easygoing Mosel Wine Route turns anyone into a relaxed Sunday driver. Pick up a local map at a TI or service station. Koblenz and Trier are linked by two-lane roads that run along both riverbanks. While riverside roads are a delight, the river is very windy and shortcuts overland can save serious time—especially between Burg Eltz and Beilstein (described below) and from the Mosel to the Rhine (note the Brodenback–Boppard shortcut). Koblenz, Cochem, and Trier have car-rental agencies.

By Bike: Biking along the Mosel is the rage among Germans. You can rent bikes in most Mosel towns (see village listings below). A fine bike path follows the river (with some bits still sharing the road with cars) from Koblenz to Zell. Many pedal one way and relax with a return cruise.

By Ferry: About a dozen car-and-passenger ferries *(Fähre)* cross the Mosel between Koblenz and Trier. These are marked AF for auto and PF for pedestrian on the *Moselle Wine Road* brochure (this *Mosellauf* brochure is sold for €2.60 at local TIs and tourist shops).

COCHEM

With a majestic castle and picturesque medieval streets, Cochem is the very touristic hub of this part of the river. For accommodations, see "Sleeping on the Mosel," below.

Tourist Information: The information-packed TI is by the bridge at the main bus stop. Most of the pamphlets (free map with town walk, town history flier) are kept behind the desk, so ask. Their thorough 24-hour room listing in the window comes with a free phone connection. The TI also has information on special events, wine-tastings held by local vintners, public transportation to Burg Eltz, area hikes, and the informative €2.60 *Moselle Wine Road (Mosellauf)* brochure. The *Tips and Information from A to Z* brochure lists everything from car rental agencies to saunas and babysitters (May–Oct Mon–Sat 9:00–17:00, also Sun 10:00–12:00 in July–Oct, off-season closed weekends and at lunch, tel. 02671/60040, www.cochem.de).

Arrival in Cochem: Make a hard right out of the station (lockers available, €2/day, no WC) and walk about 10 minutes to the town center and TI (just past the bus lanes under the bridge). Drivers can park near the bridge. To get to the main square *(Markt)* and colorful medieval town center, continue under the bridge, then angle right and follow Bernstrasse.

Helpful Hints: The Edeka **supermarket** is on Ravenestrasse, a five-minute walk from the TI toward the train station. For **Internet access**, try COCbit-Kommunikation (€5/hr, Mon–Fri 10:00–18:00, Sat 10:00–13:00, closed Sun, on street facing river across from boat ticket booths, Moselpromenade 7, tel. 02671/211). Cochem's biggest **wine festival** is held the last weekend in August.

Sights—Cochem

Cochem Castle—This pointy castle is the work of overly imaginative 19th-century restorers (€4, mid-March–Oct daily 9:00–17:00, Nov–Dec only Sat–Sun 11:00–15:00, closed Jan–mid-March, 20-min walk from Cochem, follow one of the frequent 40-min German-language tours while reading English explanation sheets, or gather 12 English speakers and call a day ahead to schedule an English tour, tel. 02671/255, www.reichsburg-cochem.de). A bus shuttles castle-seekers between the bridge near the TI and the road below the castle (€2 one-way, 2/hr, walk last 10 min uphill to castle).

Town and River Activities—Stroll pleasant paths along the idyllic riverbank, play "life-size chess," or just grab a bench and watch Germany at play. Ride the *Sesselbahn* (chairlift) or hike up to the *Aussichtspunkt* (the cross—"Pinnerkreuz"—on the hill opposite the castle) for a great view. A little yellow train does a sightseeing loop (recorded spiel, €2, 2/hour, 30 min). Rent **bikes** from the K-D boat kiosk at the dock (€4/4 hrs, €7/day, May–Oct only) or from Kreutz behind the pumps at the Shell station at Ravenestrasse 42 (Mon–Fri 9:00–18:00, Sat 9:00–13:00, open year-round, closed Sun, €4/4 hrs, €7/day, includes helmet, CC, no deposit required, just your passport number, tel. 02671/91131). Consider taking a bike on the boat and riding back. The "Tanz Party mit Live Musik" **cruise** is popular with German vacationers (€13, 20:15–22:30, nightly July and Aug, Tue and Sat in spring and fall, 2-man schmaltzy band, tel. 02671/7387). For Mosel cruises, see "Getting around the Mosel Valley," above.

Transportation Connections—Cochem

By train to: Koblenz (hrly, 60 min), **Bullay** (near Zell, hrly, 10 min), and **Trier** (hrly, 60 min). Train info: tel. 01805/996-633, Cochem train info: tel. 02671/240. Bus info: tel. 02671/8976.

Sights—Mosel Valley

▲▲▲Burg Eltz—My favorite castle in all of Europe lurks in a mysterious forest. It's been left intact for 700 years and is furnished throughout as it was 500 years ago. Thanks to smart diplomacy and clever marriages, Burg Eltz was never destroyed. (It survived one 5-year siege.) It's been in the Eltz family for 820 years. The only way to see the castle is with a 45-minute tour (included in admission ticket). German tours go constantly (with helpful English fact sheets, €0.50). Guides speak English and thoughtfully collect English speakers into their own tours—well worth waiting for (never more than 20 minutes). It doesn't hurt to call ahead to see if an English tour is scheduled. Or organize your own by corralling 20 English speakers in the inner courtyard, then push the red button on the white porch and politely beg for an English guide (€5, April–Nov daily from 9:30 with the last tour departing at 17:30, closed Dec–March, tel. 02672/950-500, www.burg-eltz.de).

Eltz means stream. The first *Burg* on the *Eltz* (or castle on the stream) appeared in the 12th century to protect a trade route. By 1472, the castle looked like it does today, with the homes of three big landlord families gathered around a tiny courtyard within one formidable fortification. Today, the excellent 45-minute tour

Burg Eltz Area

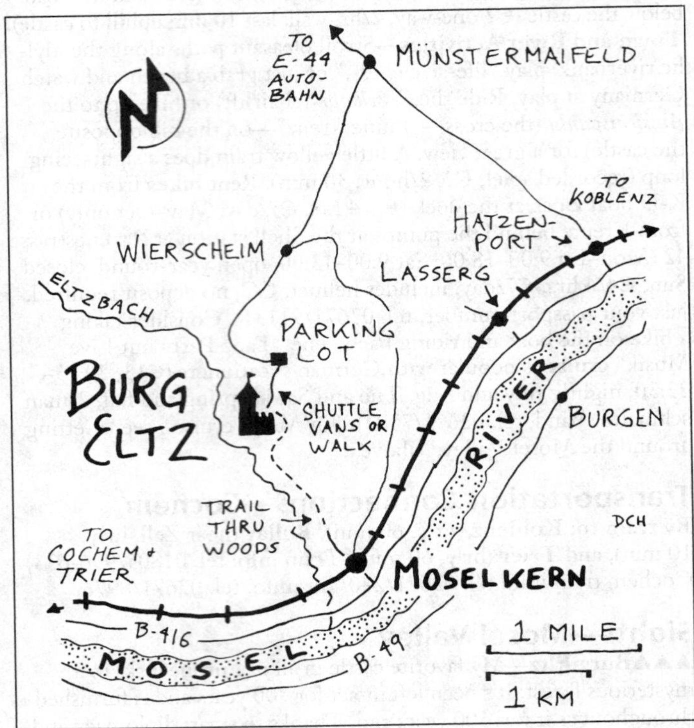

winds you through two of those homes, while the third remains the fortified quarters of the Eltz family. The elderly countess of Eltz—whose family goes back 33 generations here (you'll see a photo of her family)—enjoys flowers. Each week for 40 years, she's had grand arrangements adorn the public castle rooms.

It was a comfortable castle for its day: 80 rooms made cozy by 40 fireplaces and wall-hanging tapestries. Its 20 toilets were automatically flushed by a rain drain. The delightful chapel is on a lower floor. Even though "no one should live above God," this chapel's placement was acceptable because it fills a bay window, which floods the delicate Gothic space with light. The three families met—working out common problems as if sharing a condo—in the large "conference room." A carved jester and a rose look down on the big table, reminding those who gathered that they were free to discuss anything ("fool's freedom"—jesters could say anything to the king), but nothing discussed could leave the room (the "rose of silence"). In the bedroom, have fun with the suggestive decor: the jousting relief carved into the canopy, and the fertile and phallic figures hiding in the lusty green wall paintings.

Near the exit, the €2 treasury fills the four higgledy-piggledy floors of a cellar with the precious, eccentric, and historic mementos of this family that once helped elect the Holy Roman Emperor, and later owned a sizable chunk of Croatia (Hapsburg favors).

Arrival by Train: Get off at the Moselkern station midway between Cochem and Koblenz (hrly trains, no lockers at station, but, if you ask politely, clerk will store luggage in office—ring at the window if necessary). Leaving the station, exit right and follow "Burg Eltz" signs for about 20 minutes up, down, and inland along a residential street (signs are sparse but have faith and stay on the main road). Then take the marked trail (slippery when wet, slightly steep near end). It's a pleasant 60-minute hike between the station and castle through a pine forest where sparrows carry crossbows, and maidens, disguised as falling leaves, whisper "watch out."

Alternatively, you can taxi from Cochem (30 min, €36 one-way for up to 4 people, tel. 02671/8080) and then enjoy the hike downhill back to the train station.

Arrival by Car: From Koblenz, leave the river at Hatzenport following the white "Burg Eltz" signs through the towns of Münstermaifeld and Wierscheim. From Cochem, following the Münstermaifeld signs from Moselkern saves about 10 minutes. (Note that the Eltz signs at Moselkern lead to a trailhead for the hour-long hike to the castle. To drive directly to the castle, ignore the Eltz signs until you reach Münstermaifeld.) The castle parking lot (€1.50/day, daily 9:00–18:00) is two kilometers (1.25 miles) past Wierscheim. From the lot, hike 10 minutes downhill to the castle or wait (maximum 10 min) for the red castle shuttle bus (€1.50 one-way). There are three "Burg Eltz" parking lots; only this lot (2 km, or 1.25 miles, south of Wierscheim) is close enough for an easy walk. Another option is to park at the Moselkern station (free) and follow the "park and walk" signs (see "Arrival by Train," above). If driving between Burg Eltz and Beilstein or Zell, you'll save 30 minutes with this shortcut: from Eltz, cross the river at Karden, go through town, and bear right at the swimming pool (direction Bruttig-Fankel). This overland route deposits you in Bruttig, a scenic riverside 5-kilometer (3-mile) drive from Beilstein (34 km/21 miles from Zell).

BEILSTEIN

Upstream from Cochem is the quaintest of all Mosel towns. Beilstein is Cinderella-land—extremely peaceful except for its territorial swans. Its 180 residents run 30 or so hotels and eateries.

A shop rents bikes for pleasant riverside rides (ring bell at Bachstrasse 47, €6/day). Parking is free in any space along the riverside road you can find. For accommodations, see "Sleeping on the Mosel," below.

Beilstein (pron. BILE-shtine) has no real tourist office, but several cafés advertise that they have town info. Buses go about hourly from Beilstein to Cochem.

Introductory Beilstein Walk

Explore the narrow lanes, ancient wine cellar, resident swans, and ruined castle by following this short walk.

1. Beilstein's riverfront: Stand where the village hits the river. In 1963, the big road and the Mosel locks were built, making the river so peaceful today. Before then, access was limited to a tiny one-way lane and the small ferry. The cables that tether the ferry once allowed the motorless craft to go back and forth powered only by the current and an angled rudder. Today, it shuttles people (€1), bikes, and cars constantly from 9:00 to 18:00. The campground across the river is typical of German campgrounds—80 percent of its customers set up their trailers and tents at Easter and use them as summer homes until October, when the regular floods chase them away for the winter. If you stood where you are now through the winter, you'd have cold water up to your crotch five times. Look inland. The Earl of Beilstein—who ruled from his castle above town—built the Altes Zollhaus in 1634 to levy tolls from river traffic. Today, the castle is a ruin, the once mighty monastery (see the big church high on the left) is down to one monk, and the town's economy is based only on wine and tourists.

Beilstein's tranquillity is due to Germany's WWI loss. This war cost Germany the region of Alsace (now part of France). Before World War I, the Koblenz–Trier train line—which connects Alsace to Germany—was the busiest in Germany. It tunnels through the grape-laden hill across the river in what was the longest train tunnel in Germany. The construction of a supplemental line destined to follow the riverbank (like the lines that crank up the volume on the Rhine) was stopped in 1914 and, since Alsace went to France in 1918, the plans were scuttled.

Follow Bachstrasse into town. You'll notice blue plaques on the left marking the high-water *(Hochwasser)* points of historic floods.

At the first corner, Furst-Metternich Strasse leads left to the monastery (climb the *Klostertreppe* stairs). While its population is down to one Carmelite, Rome maintains an oversized-for-this-little-town church that runs a view restaurant.

Bachstrasse—literally, "creek street"—continues straight

through Beilstein, covering up the brook that once flowed through town providing a handy disposal service 24/7. Today, Bachstrasse is lined by wine cellars. The only way for a small local vintner to make any decent money these days is to sell his wine directly to customers in inviting little places like these. Your first right leads to the . . .

2. Market Square: For centuries, neighboring farmers sold their goods on Marktplatz. The Zehnthaus ("tithe house") was the village IRS, where locals would pay one-tenth *(zehnte)* of their produce to their landlord (either the church or the earl). Pop into the Zehnthauskeller. Packed with peasants' offerings four hundred years ago, it's now packed with vaulted medieval ambience. It's fun at night for candlelit wine-tasting, soup and cold cuts, and schmaltzy music (live Fri and Sat). The Bürgerhaus (above the fountain) had nothing to do with medieval fast food. First the village church, then the *Bürger*'s (like a mayor) residence, today it's *the* place for a town party or wedding. Haus Lipmann (on the riverside, now a recommended hotel and restaurant—see "Sleeping in Beilstein," below) dates from 1727. It was built by the earl's family as a residence after the French destroyed his castle. Haus Lipmann's main dining hall was once the knight's hall. The stepped lane leads uphill (past the Zehnthaus) to . . .

3. Beilstein's Castle: Beilstein once rivaled Cochem as the most powerful town on this part of the Mosel. Its castle (Burg Metternich) is a sorry ruin today, but those who hike up are rewarded with a postcard Mosel view and a chance to hike even higher to the top of its lone surviving tower (€2, daily 9:00–18:00, view café/restaurant).

For more exercise and an even better view, continue up behind the castle and follow the road that leads uphill and around back into the village. A hundred meters (330 feet) above the castle (take the left fork), you'll find the ultimate "castle–river bend–vineyards" photo stop. The derelict roadside vineyard is a sign of recent times—the younger generation is abandoning the family plots, opting out of all that hard winemaking work. A surprising sight—the most evocative Jewish cemetery this side of Prague *(Judenfriedhof)*—is 200 meters (650 feet) farther up the road.

During the 700 years leading up to 1942, Beilstein hosted a Jewish community. As in the rest of Europe, wealthy Jews could buy citizenship and enjoy all the protections afforded to residents. These *Schutzjuden*, or "protected Jews," were shielded from the often crude and brutal "justice" of the Middle Ages. In 1840, 25 percent of Beilstein's 300 inhabitants were Jewish. But no payment could shield this community from Hitler, so currently, there are no Jews in Beilstein. (A small Jewish community in Koblenz maintains this lovely cemetery.)

From here, the road leads downhill, where a path on the left leads back into town.

ZELL

Peaceful, with a fine riverside promenade, a pedestrian bridge over the water, and plenty of *Zimmer*, Zell makes a good overnight stop. Zell has a long pedestrian zone filled with colorful shops, restaurants, and *Weinstuben* (wine bars). A fun oompah folk band plays on weekend evenings on the main square, making evenings here a delight.

The **TI** is on the pedestrian street, four blocks downriver from the pedestrian bridge (Mon–Fri 8:00–12:30 & 13:30–17:00, Sat 10:00–13:00, closed Sun, off-season also closed Sat, tel. 06542/4031, www.zell-mosel.de). The little Wein und Heimatmuseum features Mosel history (same building as TI, Wed and Sat 15:00–17:00). Walk up to the medieval wall's gatehouse and through the cemetery to the old munitions tower for a village view. Frau Klaus rents **bikes** (€6/day, 2 km/1.25 miles out of town, downstream at Hauptstrasse 5, tel. 06542/2589). Berliner Kaffe-Kännchen offers **Internet access** (2 terminals, €6.80/hr, Thu–Tue 7:00–18:30, closed Wed, across pedestrian bridge opposite bus stop at Baldninen Strasse 107, tel. 06542/5450).

Locals know Zell for its Schwarze Katze (Black Cat) wine. Peter Weis runs the F. J. Weis winery and gives an entertaining and free tour of his 40,000-bottle-per-year **wine cellar**. The clever 20-minute tour starts at 17:00 (call ahead to reserve, open daily April–Nov 10:30–19:00, closed Dec–March, tel. 06542/41398, SE); buy a bottle or two to keep this fine tour going. A flag marks his *Weinkeller* south of town, 200 meters (650 feet) past the bridge toward Bernkastel, riverside at Notenau 30.

Sleeping on the Mosel
(€1 = about $1)

Sleep Code: **S** = Single, **D** = Double/Twin, **T** = Triple, **Q** = Quad, **b** = bathroom, **s** = shower only, **CC** = Credit Cards accepted, **no CC** = Credit Cards not accepted, **SE** = Speaks English, **NSE** = No English.

To help you sort easily through these listings, I've divided the rooms into three categories based on the price for a standard double room with bath:

Higher Priced—Most rooms more than €70.
Moderately Priced—Most rooms €70 or less.
Lower Priced—Most rooms €50 or less.

Sleeping in Cochem

(country code: 49, area code: 02671, zip code: 56812)

All rooms come with breakfast. August is very tight, with various festivals and generally inflated prices. The only **launderette** in town is across the bridge in a little mall near the youth hostel.

HIGHER PRICED

The rustic **Hotel Lohspeicher**, just off the main square on a street with tiny steps, is for those who want a real hotel—with much higher prices—in the thick of things. Its nine high-ceilinged rooms have modern comforts (Sb-€39, Db-€78, about 10 percent higher mid-July–mid-Nov, CC, elevator, breakfast in a fine stone-and-timber room, restaurant, parking-€4.50/day, closed Feb, Obergasse 1, tel. 02671/3976, fax 02671/1772, www.lohspeicher.de, e-mail: service@lohspeicher.de, Ingo SE).

For a view of Cochem, cross the bridge to the balconied rooms at **Hotel Am Hafen** (Db-€100–130, CC, air-con, Uferstrasse 3, tel. 02671/97720, fax 02671/977-227, e-mail: hotel-am-hafen@t-online.de).

MODERATELY PRICED

Gasthaus Ravene, a last resort, rents six well-worn rooms above a colorful little *Weinstube* two blocks from the train station. The place is funky, a bit dark, and a bad value, with difficult communication (Db-€50–70, CC, Ravenestrasse 43, tel. 02671/980-177, fax 02671/91119).

LOWER PRICED

Weingut Rademacher rents six beautiful ground-floor rooms. Wedged between vineyards and train tracks, with a pleasant garden and a big common kitchen, it's a great value. Charming hostess Andrea and her husband, Hermann, (both SE) give tours of their wine cellar when time permits (earlier is better); guests enter for free. If there's no tour, visitors are welcome to taste the wine (Sb-€25.50, Db on train side-€41, Db on vineyard side-€47, less for 3 nights, family deals, CC, no smoking, free parking, go right from station on Ravenestrasse, turn right under the tracks on Pinner-strasse, curve right to Pinnerstrasse 10, tel. 02671/4164, fax 02671/91341).

Haus Andreas has 10 clean, modern rooms at fair prices (Sb-€23, Db-€36–40, Tb-€54, no CC, Schlosstrasse 9, tel. 02671/1370 or 02671/5155, fax 02671/1370, Frau Pellny speaks a little English). From the main square, take Herrenstrasse; after a block, angle right up the steep hill on Schlosstrasse.

The brand-new, members-only **hostel**, opening in April 2003, is across the bridge and to the left (bed–€17, 4 Db–€44, half- and full-board options available at extra cost, Klottenenstrasse 9, tel. 02671/8633, fax 02671/8568, e-mail: jh-cochem @djh-info.de).

Sleeping in Beilstein

(country code: 49, area code: 02673, zip code: 56814)

Located between Cochem and Zell, cozier Beilstein is very small and quiet (no train; hourly buses to nearby Cochem, fewer buses on weekends, 15 min; taxi to Cochem-€15). Breakfast is included. Many hotels shut down from mid-November through March.

HIGHER PRICED

Hotel Haus Lipmann is your chance to live in a medieval mansion with hot showers and TVs. A prizewinner for atmosphere, it's been in the Lipmann family for 200 years. The creaky wooden staircase and the elegant dining hall, with long wooden tables surrounded by antlers, chandeliers, and feudal weapons, will get you in the mood for your castle sightseeing, but the riverside terrace may mace your momentum (Sb-€75, Db-€85, no CC, 5 rooms, closed Nov–April, tel. 02673/1573, fax 02673/1521, www.hotel-haus-lipmann.com, e-mail: hotel.haus.lipmann @t-online.de, SE). The entire Lipmann family—Marian and Jonas, their hardworking son David, and his wife Anja (all SE)—hustles for hotel guests.

Jonas' brother Joachim Lipmann (SE) runs two hotels of his own: The half-timbered, riverfront **Altes Zollhaus Gästezimmer** packs all the comforts into eight tight, bright, and modern rooms (Sb-€45, Db-€60, deluxe Db-€77, no CC, closed Nov–March, tel. 02673/1850, fax 02673/1287, www.hotel-lipmann.de, e-mail: lipmann@t-online.de, SE). **Hotel Am Klosterberg** is a big modern place at the extremely quiet top of town (up the main street 185 meters/600 feet inland) with 16 comfortable rooms (Db-€75, Auf dem Teich 8, same contact info as Altes Zollhaus, SE).

MODERATELY PRICED

Hotel Gute Quelle offers half-timbers, 13 comfortable rooms (plus 7 in an annex across the street), and a good restaurant (Sb-€35, D-€52, Db-€56–60, CC, closed Dec–March, Marktplatz 34, tel. 02673/1437, fax 02673/1399, www.hotel-gute-quelle.de, helpful Susan SE).

LOWER PRICED

Gasthaus Winzerschenke an der Klostertreppe is comfortable and a great value, right in the tiny heart of town (Db-€42, bigger Db-€52, no CC, discount for 2-night stays, 5 rooms, closed Nov–

Easter, tel. 02673/1354, fax 02673/962-371, www.winzerschenke-beilstein.de, Frau Sausen NSE, her son Christian SE).

Eating in Beilstein

You'll have no problem finding a characteristic dining room or a relaxing riverview terrace. **Restaurant Haus Lipmann** serves good fresh food with daily specials on a glorious, leafy, riverside terrace (daily 10:00–23:00). The **Zehnthauskeller** on the Marktplatz is *the* place for wine-tasting with soup, cold plates, and lively *Schlager* (kitschy German folk-pop), while old locals on holiday sit under a dark medieval vault.

Sleeping in Zell

(country code: 49, area code: 06542, zip code: 56856)

Zell's hotels are a disappointment, but its private homes are a fine value. The owners speak almost no English and discount their rates if you stay more than one night. They don't take reservations long in advance for one-night stays; just call a day ahead. Breakfast is included.

Trains go hourly from Cochem or Trier to Bullay, where the bus takes you to little Zell (€1.50, 2/hr, 10 min; bus stop is across street from Bullay train station, check yellow MB schedule for times, last bus at about 19:00). The central Zell stop is called Lindenplatz.

HIGHER PRICED

If you're looking for room service, a sauna, a pool, and an elevator, sleep at **Hotel zum Grünen Kranz** (Sb-€45–60, Db-€86, CC, 32 rooms, non-smoking rooms, Balduinstrasse 13, tel. 06542/98610, fax 06542/986-180, www.zum-gruenen-kranz.de). In the annex across the street, they rent 10 immense apartments (for families of up to 5) for the same €86 rate.

MODERATELY PRICED

Hotel Ratskeller, just off the main square on a pedestrian street, rents 14 sharp rooms with tile flooring and fair rates (Sb-€40, Db-€70, cheaper Nov–June, CC, above a pizzeria, Balduinstrasse 36, tel. 06542/98620, fax 06542/986-244, e-mail: ratskeller-zellmosel@web.de, Gardi SE).

Weinhaus Mayer, a stressed-out old pension, is perfectly central, with Mosel-view rooms (12 rooms, Db-€70–72, no CC, Balduinstrasse 15, tel. 06542/4530, fax 06542/61160, NSE). They have newly renovated rooms with top comforts, many with river-view balconies, at their *Neues Gästehaus* (Db-€82, no CC, tel. 06542/61169, fax same as above).

Peter Weis Apartments, of the F. J. Weis winery (recommended above), rents two luxurious apartments (Db-€55, less for 2 or more nights, extra person-€7, breakfast-€6, CC, 200 meters, or 650 feet, beyond bridge on Bernkastel road, riverside at Notenau 30, tel. 06542/41398, fax 06542/961-178, e-mail: f.j.weis@t-online.de, SE).

LOWER PRICED

Gasthaus Gertrud Thiesen is classy, with a TV-living-breakfast room and a river view. The Thiesen house has four big, bright rooms and is on the town's first corner overlooking the Mosel from a great terrace (D-€41, no CC, closed Nov–Feb, Balduinstrasse 1, tel. 06542/4453, SE).

Weinhaus zum Fröhlichen Weinberg offers four cheap, basic rooms (D-€36, €32 for 2 or more nights, no CC, family *Zimmer*, Mittelstrasse 6, tel. & fax 06542/4308) above a *Weinstube* disco (noisy on Fri and Sat nights, jolly Jürgen SE).

Homey **Gästehaus am Römerbad**, near the church, rents six cheap and sleepable rooms (Sb-€21, Db-€41, no CC, Am Römerbad 5, tel. 06542/41602, Elizabeth Münster).

Gästezimmer Rosa Mesenich is a little place facing the river (Db-€40, no CC, Brandenburg 48, tel. 06542/4297, NSE). Nearby, the vine-strewn doorway of **Gastehaus Eberhard** leads to gregarious owners, cushy rooms, and potential wine-tastings (Db-€38, no CC, Brandenburg 42, tel. 06542/41216, NSE).

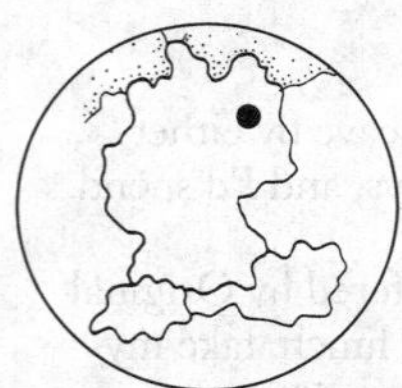

BERLIN

No tour of Germany is complete without a look at its historic and reunited capital, a construction zone called Berlin. Stand over ripped-up tracks and under a canopy of cranes and watch the rebirth of a European capital. Enjoy the thrill of walking over what was the Wall and through Brandenburg Gate.

Berlin has had a tumultuous recent history. After the city was devastated in World War II, it was divided by the Allied powers: The American, British, and French sectors became West Berlin, and the Russian sector, East Berlin. The division was set in stone when the East built the Berlin Wall in 1961. The Berlin Wall lasted 28 years. In 1990, less than a year after the Wall fell, Germany was formally reunited. When the dust settled, Berliners from both sides of the once-divided city faced the monumental challenge of reunification.

The last decade has taken Berlin through a frenzy of rebuilding. And while there's still plenty of work to be done, a new Berlin is emerging. Berliners joke they don't need to go anywhere, because the city's always changing. Spin a postcard rack to see what's new. A five-year-old guidebook on Berlin covers a different city.

Unification has had its negative side, and locals are fond of saying "the Wall survives in the minds of some people." Some "Ossies" (impolite slang for Easterners) miss their security. Some "Wessies" miss their easy ride (military deferrals, subsidized rent, and tax breaks). For free spirits, walled-in West Berlin was a citadel of freedom within the East.

The city government has been eager to charge forward with little nostalgia for anything that was "Eastern." Big corporations and the national government have moved in, and the dreary swath of land that was the Wall has been transformed. City planners are boldly taking Berlin's reunification and the return of the national government as a good opportunity to make Berlin a great capital once again.

During the grind of World War II, Hitler enjoyed rolling out the lofty plans for a postwar Berlin as capital of a Europe united under his rule. As Europe unites, dominated by a muscular Germany with its shiny new capital in the works, Hitler's dream of a grand postwar Berlin seems about to come true . . . .

Planning Your Time

Because of the city's location, try to enter and/or leave by either night train or plane. Berlin is worth a busy two days, and I'd spend them this way:

Day 1: 10:00-Take a guided walking tour (offered by Original Berlin Walks, see "Tours of Berlin," below). After lunch, take my Do-It-Yourself Orientation Tour (described on page 513), stopping midway to scale the new dome of the Reichstag building, then finishing with a walk through eastern Berlin. End your day among Greek treasures at the Pergamon Museum.

Day 2: Spend the morning lost in the painted art of the Gemäldegalerie. After lunch, hike or taxi via Potsdamer Platz to the Topography of Terror exhibit and along the surviving Zimmerstrasse stretch of Wall to the thought-provoking Museum of the Wall at Checkpoint Charlie. With extra time, consider visiting the Jewish Museum.

If you are maximizing your sightseeing, you could squeeze a hop-off, hop-on bus tour into Day 1 and start Day 2 with a visit to the Egyptian and Picasso museums at Charlottenburg. Remember that the Museum of the Wall is open late and most museums are closed on Monday.

Orientation (area code: 030)

Berlin is huge, with nearly four million people. But the tourist's Berlin can be broken into four digestible chunks:

1. The area around Bahnhof Zoo and the grand Kurfürstendamm Boulevard, nicknamed Ku'damm (transportation, tours, information, hotel, shopping hub).
2. Former downtown East Berlin (Brandenburg Gate, Unter den Linden Boulevard, Pergamon Museum, and the area around Oranienburger Strasse).
3. The new city center: Kulturforum museums, Potsdamer Platz, the Jewish Museum, and Wall-related sights.
4. Charlottenburg Palace and museums, on the outskirts of the city.

Tourist Information

Berlin's TIs are run by a for-profit agency working for the city's big hotels, which colors the information they provide. The main TI is

Berlin Sightseeing Modules

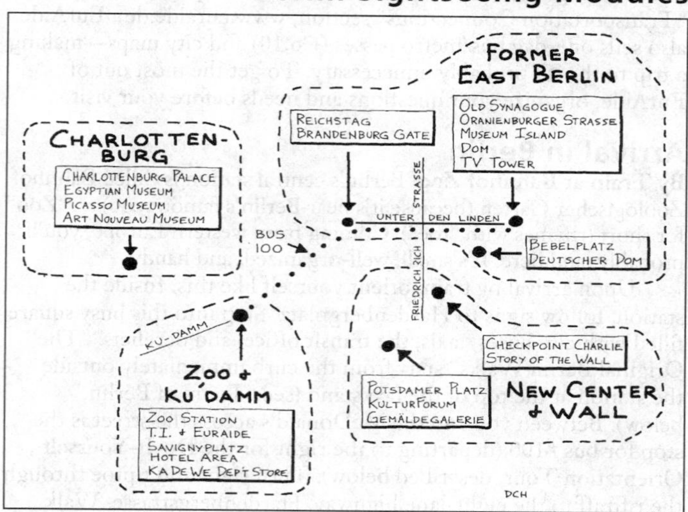

five minutes from the Bahnhof Zoo train station, in the Europa Center (with Mercedes symbol on top, enter outside to left on Budapester Strasse, Mon–Sat 8:30–20:30, Sun 10:00–18:00; calling toll tel. 0190-016-316 costs €1/min; tel. from U.S.: 011-49-180-575-4040, www.berlin-tourism.de). Smaller TIs are in the Brandenburg Gate (daily 9:30–18:00) and at the bottom of the TV Tower at Alexanderplatz (May–Oct daily 9:00–20:00, Nov–April daily 10:00–18:00). The TIs sell a good city map (€0.50—get it), the *Berlin Programm* (€1.60 comprehensive German-language monthly listing upcoming events and museum hours, www.berlin-programm .de), the Museumspass (€10, 3-day pass to several museums, including many of the biggies, see "Helpful Hints," below), and the German-English bimonthly *Berlin Calendar* magazine (€1.20, with timely features on Berlin and a partial calendar of events). The TIs also offer a €3 room-finding service (but only to hotels that give them kickbacks—many don't). Most hotels have free city maps.

EurAide's information office, in the Bahnhof Zoo, provides great service. They have answers to all your questions about Berlin or train travel around Europe. It's staffed by Americans (so communication is simple), and they have a knack for predicting your needs, then publishing free fliers to serve them (Mon–Fri 8:30–12:30 & 13:30–16:30, Sat 8:30–12:00, closed Sun, closed Sat–Sun Oct–May, closed Dec–Jan, at the back of station near lockers, great opportunity to get future *couchette* reservations nailed down ahead of time, Prague Excursion passes available—see page 550 in the "Transportation Connections" section, www.euraide.de). EurAide also sells one-day bus/metro passes (€6.10) and city maps—making a trip to the TI probably unnecessary. To get the most out of EurAide, organize your questions and needs before your visit.

Arrival in Berlin

By Train at Bahnhof Zoo: Berlin's central station is called Bahnhof Zoologischer Garten (because it's near Berlin's famous zoo)... "Zoo" for short (rhymes with "toe"). Coming from western Europe, you'll probably land here. It's small, well-organized, and handy.

Upon arrival by train, orient yourself like this: Inside the station, follow signs to Hardenbergplatz. Step into this busy square filled with city buses, taxis, the transit office, and derelicts. "The Original Berlin Walks" start from the curb immediately outside the station at the top of the taxi stand (see "Tours of Berlin," below). Between you and the McDonald's across the street is the stop for bus #100 (departing to the right for the Do-It-Yourself Orientation Tour, described below). Turn right and tiptoe through the riffraff to the eight-lane highway, Hardenbergstrasse. Walk to the median strip and stand with your back to the tracks. Ahead you'll see the black, bombed-out hulk of the Kaiser Wilhelm Memorial Church and the Europa Center (Mercedes symbol spinning on roof), which houses the main TI. Just ahead on the left, amid the traffic, is the BVG transport information kiosk (buy a €6.10 day pass covering the subway and buses, and pick up a free subway map). If you're facing the church, my recommended hotels are behind you to your right.

If you arrive at Berlin's other train stations (trains from most of eastern Europe arrive at Ostbahnhof), no problem: Ride another train (fastest option) or the S-bahn or U-bahn (runs every few min) to Bahnhof Zoo and pretend you arrived here.

By Plane: See "Transportation Connections," page 549.

Getting around Berlin

Berlin's sights spread far and wide. Right from the start, commit yourself to the fine public transit system.

By Subway and Bus: The U-bahn, S-bahn, and all buses are consolidated into one "BVG" system that uses the same tickets. Here are your options:

• Basic ticket *(Einzel Fahrschein)* for two hours of travel on buses or subways (€2.10; *Erwachsener* means adult—anyone 14 or older).

• A day pass *(Tages Karte)* covering zones A and B—the city proper—€6.10, good until 3:00 the morning after. To get out to Potsdam, you need a ticket covering zone C (€6.30).

• A cheap short-ride ticket *(Kurzstrecke Erwachsener)* for a single short ride of six bus stops or three subway stations, with one transfer (€1.30).

• Berlin/Potsdam **WelcomeCard** gives you three days of transportation in zones A, B, and C and three days of minor discounts on lots of minor and a few major museums (including Checkpoint Charlie), sightseeing tours (including the recommended Berlin Walks), and music and theater events (€18, valid for an adult and up to 3 kids). The WelcomeCard is a good deal for a three-day trip (since three one-day transit cards alone cost more than the WelcomeCard) and worth considering for a two-day trip.

Buy your tickets or cards from machines at U- or S-bahn stations or at the BVG pavilion in front of Bahnhof Zoo. To use the machine, first select the type of ticket you want, then load in the coins or paper. Punch your ticket in a red or yellow clock machine to validate it (or risk a €30 fine). The double-decker buses are a joy (can buy ticket on bus), and the subway is a snap. The S-bahn (but not U-bahn) is free with a validated Eurailpass (but it uses a Flexipass day).

By Taxi: Taxis are easy to flag down, and taxi stands are common. A typical ride within town costs €5–8. A local law designed to help people get safely and affordably home from their subway station late at night is handy for tourists any time of day: A short ride of no more than two kilometers (1.25 miles) is a flat €3. (Ask for "*Kurzstrecke, drei euro, bitte.*") To get this cheap price, you must hail a cabbie on the street rather than go to a taxi stand. Cabbies aren't crazy about the law, so insist on the price and be sure to keep the ride short.

By Bike: In western Berlin, you can rent bikes at the Bahnhof Zoo left-luggage counter (€10/day, daily 6:15–22:00); in the east, go to Fahhradstation at Hackesche Höfe (€15/day, Mon–Fri 8:00–20:00, Sat–Sun 10:00–16:00, Rosenthaler Strasse 40, tel. 030/2045-4500). Be careful: In Berlin, motorists don't brake for bikers (and bikers don't brake for pedestrians). Fortunately, some roads have special bike lanes.

Helpful Hints

Monday Activities: Most museums are closed on Monday. Save Monday for Berlin Wall sights, the Reichstag building, the Do-It-Yourself Orientation Tour (see below), walking/bus tours, the Jewish Museum, churches, the zoo, or shopping along Kurfürstendamm (Ku'damm) Boulevard or at the Kaufhaus des Westens (KaDeWe) department store. (When Monday is a holiday—as it is several times a year—museums are open then and closed Tuesday.)

Museums: All **state museums**, including the Pergamon

Museum and Gemäldegalerie (plus others as noted in "Sights," below), are free on the first Sunday of each month. There are two different types of discount passes for Berlin's museums. The state museums are covered by a one-day **day ticket** (€6, not valid for special exhibitions, purchase at participating museums, not sold at TI). Entry at most of these museums costs €6, so admission to one essentially includes all of the others on the same day. For longer stays, consider the three-day **Museumspass**, which covers most of the state museums as well as several others (including the Jewish Museum). Only €4 more than the day ticket, it's valid for three times as long and is an excellent value if you'll be doing more than two days of museum-hopping (€10, not valid for special exhibitions, purchase at TI or at participating museums). Note that if a museum is closed on one of the days of your Museumspass, you have access to that museum on the fourth day to make up for lost time.

Addresses: Many Berlin streets are numbered with odd and even numbers on the same side of the street, often with no connection to the other side (i.e., Ku'damm #212 can be across the street from #14). To save steps, check the white street signs on curb corners; many list the street numbers covered on that side of the block.

Travel Agency: Last Minute Flugböerse can help you find a flight in a hurry (next to TI in Europa Center, tel. 030/2655-1050, www.lastminuteflugboerse.de).

Internet Access: You'll find cheap and fast Internet access at easyEverything (daily 24 hrs, Ku'damm 224, 10-min walk from Bahnhof Zoo and near recommended hotels).

Tours of Berlin

▲▲▲City Walking Tours—"The Original Berlin Walks" offers a variety of worthwhile tours led by enthusiastic guides who are native English speakers. The company, run by Englishman Nick Gay, offers a three-hour **Discover Berlin** introductory walk daily year-round at 10:00 and also at 14:30 from April through October for €10 (€7.50 if you're under 26 or with WelcomeCard). Just show up at the taxi rank in front of Zoo Station (or 20 min later in eastern Berlin, at the Kilkenny Irish Pub entrance inside Hackescher Markt S-bahn station). Their high-quality, high-energy guides also offer tours of **Infamous Third Reich Sites** (at 10:00 May–Sept daily except Mon and Fri; March–April and Oct Sat–Sun only), **Jewish Life in Berlin** (at 10:00 May–Sept Mon and Fri), and **Potsdam** (see "Sights—Near Berlin," below). Many of the Third Reich and Jewish history sites are difficult to pin down without these excellent walks. Also consider their six-hour trip to the **Sachsenhausen** Concentration Camp, intended "to challenge preconceptions," according to Nick (€15, €11.25

with WelcomeCard, at 11:30 May–Sept Tue–Sun; March–April and Oct Tue and Sat; requires transit day ticket with zone C or buy from guide, call office for tour specifics). Confirm tour schedules at EurAide or by phone with Nick or his wife and partner, Serena (private tours also available, tel. 030/301-9194, www.berlinwalks.com, e-mail: berlinwalks@berlin.de).

For a more exhaustive (or, for some, exhausting) walking tour of Berlin, consider **Brewer's Berlin Tours**, run by Terry, a former British embassy worker in East Berlin, and his well-trained staff. These daily tours—especially the lengthy, in-depth "Total" version—are best for those with a long attention span and a serious interest in Berlin (€10 for either tour, all-day "Total Berlin" starts at 10:30 and can last 5–8 hrs, 4-hr "Classic Berlin" starts at 12:30, both meet at New Synagogue at Oranienburger Strasse 28/30, U-bahn: Oranienburger Tor, tour tel. 030/9700-2906, www.brewersberlin.com).

▲City Bus Tours—For bus tours, you have two choices:

1. Full-blown, three-hour bus tours. Contact **Severin & Kühn** (€22, daily 10:00 and 14:00, live guides in 2 languages, from Ku'damm 216, tel. 030/880-4190) or take BVG buses from Ku'damm 18 (€20, 2.5 hrs, leaves every 30–60 min daily 10:00–17:00, tel. 030/885-9880).

2. Hop-on, hop-off circle tours. Several companies make a circuit of the city ("City-Circle Sightseeing" is good, offered by Severin & Kühn). The TI has all the brochures. The tour offers unlimited hop-on, hop-off privileges for its 14-stop route with a good English narration (€18, 10:00–18:00, 2–4/hr, 2-hr loop, taped guides). Just hop on where you like and pay the driver. On a sunny day when some double-decker buses go topless, these are a photographer's delight, cruising slowly by just about every top sight in town.

Do-It-Yourself Orientation Tour

Here's an easy ▲▲▲ introduction to Berlin. Half the tour is by bus, the other half is on foot. Berlin's bus #100 (direction Mollstrasse and Prenzlauer Allee) is a sightseer's dream, stopping at Bahnhof Zoo, Europa Center/Hotel Palace, Siegessäule, Reichstag, Brandenburg Gate, Unter den Linden, Pergamon Museum, and ending at Alexanderplatz. If you have the €18 and two hours for a hop-on, hop-off bus tour (described above), take that instead. But this short €2.10 tour is a fine city introduction. Buses leave from Hardenbergplatz in front of the Zoo Station (and nearly next door to the Europa Center TI, in front of Hotel Palace). Buses come every 10 minutes, and single tickets are good for two hours—so take advantage of hop-on-and-off privileges. Climb aboard, stamp your ticket (giving it a time), and grab a seat on top. You could ride the bus all the way, but I'd get out at the Reichstag and walk to Alexanderplatz.

Part 1: By Bus #100 from Bahnhof Zoo to the Reichstag

(This is about a 10-min ride. Note: The next stop lights up on the reader board inside the bus.)

☛ On your left and then straight ahead, before descending into the tunnel, you'll see: the bombed-out hulk of the **Kaiser Wilhelm Memorial Church**, with its postwar sister church (described below) and the **Europa Center**. This is the west-end shopping district, a bustling people zone with big department stores nearby. When the Wall came down, East Berliners flocked to this area's department stores (especially KaDeWe, described below). Soon after, the biggest, swankiest new stores were built in the East. Now the West is trying to win those shoppers back by building even bigger and better shopping centers around Europaplatz.

Across from the Zoo station, the under-construction "Zoofenster" tower will be taller than all the buildings you see here.

Emerging from the tunnel, on your immediate right you'll see the Berlin tourist information office.

☛ At the stop in front of Hotel Palace: on the left, the elephant gates mark the entrance to the **Berlin Zoo** and its aquarium (described below).

☛ Driving down Kurfürstenstrasse, you'll pass several Asian restaurants—a reminder that, for most, the best food in Berlin is not German. Turning left, with the huge Tiergarten park in the distance ahead, you'll cross a canal and see the famous **Bauhaus Archive** (an off-white, blocky building) on the right. Built in the 1920s, this revolutionary building ushered in a new age of modern architecture that emphasized function over beauty, giving rise to the blocky steel-and-glass skyscrapers in big cities around the world. On the left is Berlin's new embassy row. The big turquoise wall marks the communal home of all five Nordic embassies.

☛ The bus enters a 400-acre park called the **Tiergarten**, packed with cycle paths, joggers, and nude sunbathers. The Victory Column (Siegessäule, with the gilded angel, described below) towers above this vast city park that was once a royal hunting grounds, now nicknamed the "green lungs of Berlin."

☛ On the left, a block after leaving the Siegessäule: The 18th-century, late-rococo **Bellevue Palace** is the German "White House." Formerly a Nazi VIP guest house, it's now the residence of the federal president (whose "power" is mostly ceremonial). If the flag's out, he's in.

Berlin

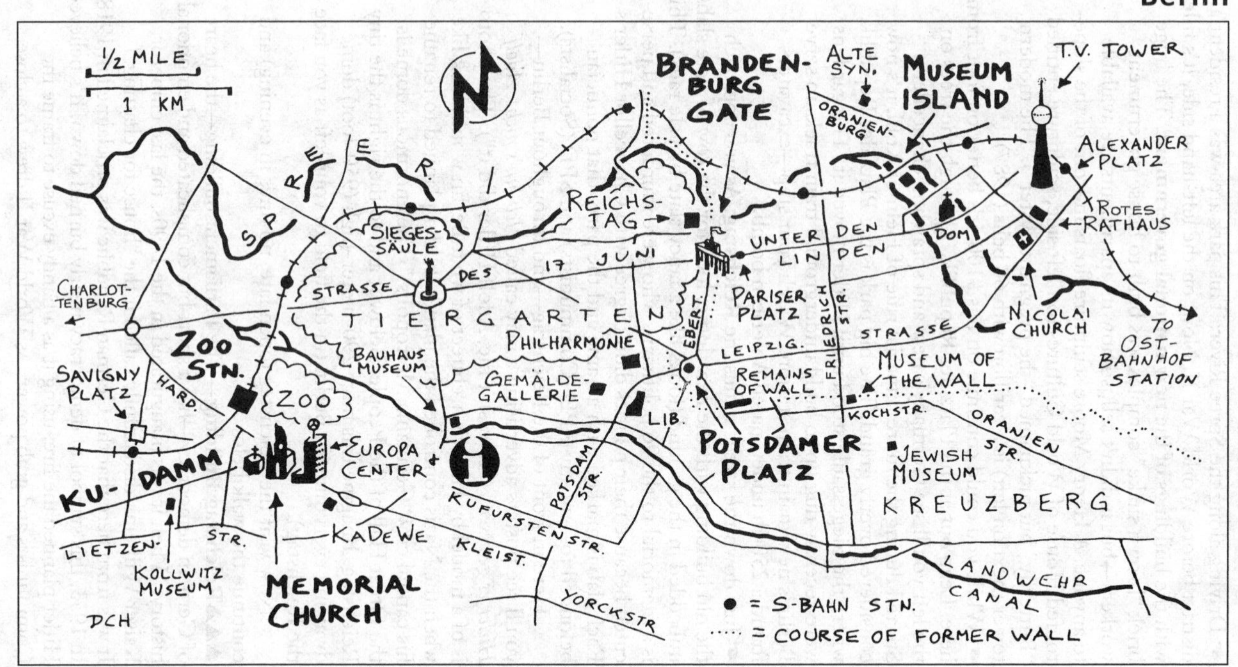
1/2 MILE
1 KM
SPREE R.
BRANDEN-BURG GATE
ALTE SYN.
ORANIEN-BURG
MUSEUM ISLAND
T.V. TOWER
ALEXANDER PLATZ
ROTES RATHAUS
REICHS-TAG
SIEGES-SÄULE
DES 17 JUNI
STRASSE
UNTER DEN LINDEN
DOM
CHARLOT-TENBURG
TIERGARTEN
PARISER PLATZ
EBERT.
FRIEDRICH STR.
NICOLAI CHURCH
STRASSE
TO OST-BAHNHOF STATION
ZOO STN.
PHILHARMONIE
LEIPZIG.
MUSEUM OF THE WALL
SAVIGNY PLATZ
HARD.
BAUHAUS MUSEUM
GEMÄLDE-GALLERIE
REMAINS OF WALL
ZOO
LIB.
KOCHSTR.
ORANIEN STR.
EUROPA CENTER
POTSDAMER PLATZ
JEWISH MUSEUM
KU-DAMM
POTSDAM STR.
KREUZBERG
KUFURSTEN STR.
LIETZEN- STR.
KADEWE
KLEIST.
KOLLWITZ MUSEUM
MEMORIAL CHURCH
LANDWEHR CANAL
YORCKSTR
● = S-BAHN STN.
..... = COURSE OF FORMER WALL
DCH

☛ Driving along the Spree River: This park area was a residential district before World War II. Now, on the left-hand side, it's filled with the buildings of the **new national government**. The huge brick "brown snake" complex was built to house government workers—but it didn't sell, so now its apartments are available to anyone. A Henry Moore sculpture floats in front of the slope-roofed House of World Cultures (on left side, sculpture entitled "Butterfly" but nicknamed "the pregnant oyster"). The modern tower (next on left) is a carillon with 68 bells (1987).

☛ While you could continue on bus #100, it's better on foot from here. Leap out at the Platz der Republik. Through the trees on the left you'll see Germany's new and sprawling chancellery. Started during the more imperial rule of Helmut Kohl, it's now considered overly grand. The big park is the Platz der Republik, where the Siegessäule stood until Hitler moved it. The gardens were recently dug up to build underground train tracks to serve Berlin's new main train station. Watch your step—excavators found a 250-lb undetonated American bomb.

☛ Just down the street stands the **Reichstag**. As you approach the old building with the new dome, look for the row of slate slabs imbedded in the ground (looks like a fancy slate bicycle rack). This is a memorial to the 96 politicians who were murdered and persecuted because their politics didn't agree with Chancellor Hitler's. Each slab is marked with a name and the party that politician belonged to—mostly KPD (Communists) and SPD (Socialists).

Here in front of the Reichstag—and throughout Berlin—you'll see posters advertising a play called "*Ich bin's nicht, Adolf Hitler es gewesen*" ("It wasn't me, Adolf Hitler did it"). The photo is of a model by Hitler's architect of what Berlin would look like when the Nazis controlled the planet. Hitler planned to rename his capital city "Germania Metropolis." The enormous dome is the Great Hall of the People. Below it and to the right is the tiny Reichstag. Imagine this huge 290-meter-high (950-foot) dome dwarfing everything in Berlin (in the field to your left as you face the Reichstag).

Now visit the Reichstag (open late, no lines in evening) and continue the walk below.

▲▲▲Reichstag Building—The Parliament building—the heart of German democracy—has a short but complicated and emotional history. When it was inaugurated in the 1890s, the last emperor, Kaiser Wilhelm, disdainfully called it the "house for chatting." It was from here that the German Republic was proclaimed in 1918. In 1933, this symbol of democracy nearly burned down. It's believed Hitler planned the fire, using it as a handy excuse to frame the Communists and grab power. As World War II drew to a close,

Stalin ordered his troops to take the Reichstag from the Nazis by May 1 (the workers' holiday). More than 1,500 Nazis made their last stand here—extending World War II by two days. On April 30, 1945, it fell to the Allies. It was hardly used from 1933 to 1999. For its 101st birthday, in 1995, the Bulgarian-American artist Christo wrapped it in silvery-gold cloth. It was then wrapped again in scaffolding, rebuilt by British architect Lord Norman Foster, and turned into the new parliamentary home of the Bundestag (Germany's lower house). To many Germans, the proud resurrection of the Reichstag—which no longer has a hint of Hitler—symbolizes the end of a terrible chapter in German history.

The **glass cupola** rises 48 meters (155 feet) above the ground, and a double staircase winds 230 meters (755 feet) to the top for a grand view. Inside the dome, a cone of 360 mirrors reflects natural light into the legislative chamber below. Lit from inside at night, this gives Berlin a memorable night-light. The environmentally friendly cone also helps with air circulation, drawing hot air out of the legislative chamber and pulling in cool air from below.

Hours: Free, daily 8:00–24:00, last entry 22:00, most crowded 10:00–16:00 (wait in line to go up—good street musicians, some hour-long English tours, tel. 030/2273-2152).

Self-Guided Tour: As you approach the building, look above the door, surrounded by stone patches from WWII bomb damage, to see the motto and promise: *Dem Deutschen Volke* (to the German people). The open and airy lobby towers 30 meters (100 feet) high with 20-meter-tall (66-foot) colors of the German flag. Glass doors show the **central legislative chamber**. The message: There will be no secrets in government. Look inside. The seats are "Reichstag blue," a lilac-blue color designed by the architect to brighten the otherwise gray interior. The German eagle (a.k.a. the "fat hen") spreads his wings behind the podium. Notice the doors marked "yes," "no," or "abstain"... the Bundestag's traditional "sheep jump" way of counting votes (for critical and close votes, all 669 members leave and vote by walking through the door of their choice).

Ride the elevator to the base of the glass **dome**. Take time to study the photos and read the circle of captions—an excellent exhibition telling the Reichstag story. Then study the surrounding architecture: a broken collage of old on new, like Germany's history. Notice the dome's giant and unobtrusive sunscreen that moves as necessary with the sun. Peer down through the skylight to look over the shoulders of the elected representatives at work. For Germans, the best view is down—keeping a close eye on their government.

Start at the ramp nearest the elevator and wind up to the top of the **double ramp**. Take a 360-degree survey of the city as you hike: First, the big park is the **Tiergarten**, the "green lungs" of Berlin. Beyond that is the **Teufelsberg,** or Devil's Hill (built of rubble from the bombed city in the late 1940s and famous during the Cold War as a powerful ear of the West—notice the telecommunications tower on top). Given the violent and tragic history of Berlin, a city blown apart by bombs and covered over by bulldozers, locals say, "You have to be suspicious when you see the nice green park." Find the **Seigessäule**, the Victory Column (moved by Hitler in the 1930s from in front of the Reichstag to its present position in the Tiergarten). Next, scenes of the new Berlin spiral into your view—**Potsdamer Platz** marked with the conical glass tower that houses Sony's European headquarters. The yellow building to the right is the Berlin Philharmonic Concert Hall. Continue circling left, and find the green chariot atop the **Brandenburg Gate**. A monument to the Gypsy Holocaust will be built between the Reichstag and Brandenburg Gate. (Gypsies, as disdained by the Nazis as the Jews, lost the same percentage of their population to Hitler.) Another Holocaust memorial will be built just south of Brandenburg Gate. Next, you'll see **former East Berlin** and the city's next huge construction zone, with a forest of 100-meter-tall (330-foot) skyscrapers in the works. Notice the TV tower (with the Pope's Revenge—explained below), the Berlin Cathedral's massive dome, the red tower of the city hall, the golden dome of the New Synagogue, and the Reichstag's **roof garden restaurant** (Dachgarten, €15–26 entrées with a view, daily 9:00–16:30, tel. 030/2262-9933). Follow the train tracks in the distance to the left toward a huge construction zone marking the future central Berlin train station, Lehrter Bahnhof. Just in front of it, alone in a field, is the Swiss Embassy. This used to be surrounded by buildings, but now it's the only one left. Complete your spin tour with the blocky **Chancellery**, nicknamed by locals "the washing machine." It may look like a pharaoh's tomb, but it's the office and home of Germany's most powerful person, the Chancellor, and his team.

Let's continue our walk as we cross what was the Berlin Wall. Leaving the Reichstag, turn left around the building. You'll see the Brandenburg Gate ahead on your right.

Part 2: Walking Tour from Brandenburg Gate up Unter den Linden to Alexanderplatz

Allow a comfortable hour for this walk through eastern Berlin, including time for dawdling but not museum stops.

▲▲Brandenburg Gate—The historic Brandenburg Gate (1791, the last survivor of 14 gates in Berlin's old city wall—which led to the city of Brandenburg), crowned by a majestic four-horse chariot with the Goddess of Peace at the reins, was the symbol of Berlin and then the symbol of divided Berlin. Napoleon took the statue to the Louvre in Paris in 1806. When the Prussians got it back, she was renamed the Goddess of Victory. The gate sat unused, part of a sad circle dance called the Wall, for more than 25 years. Now postcards all over town show the ecstatic day—November 9, 1989—when the world enjoyed the sight of happy Berliners jamming the gate like flowers on a parade float. Pause a minute and think about struggles for freedom—past and present. (There's actually a "quiet room" built into the gate for this purpose.) The TI within the gate is open daily 9:30–18:00.

▲**Pariser Platz**—From Brandenburg Gate, face Pariser Platz (toward the east). Unter den Linden leads to the TV tower in the distance (the end of this walk). The space used to be filled with important government buildings—all bombed to smithereens. Today, Pariser Platz is unrecognizable from the deserted no-man's-land it became under the Communist regime. Sparkling new banks, embassies (the French Embassy rebuilt where it was before World War II), and a swanky hotel have filled in the void.

Crossing through the gate, look to your right to a construction site—formerly the "death strip." The **U.S. Embassy** once stood here, and a new one will stand in the same spot (due to be completed in 2006). This new embassy has been controversial; for safety's sake, Uncle Sam wanted it away from other buildings, but the Germans preferred it in its original location. A compromise was reached, building the embassy by the gate—but rerouting several major roads to reduce the security risk. The new **Holocaust memorial**, consisting of over 2,500 gravestone-like pillars, will be completed in 2004 and will stand behind the new embassy.

The **DZ Bank building**, next to the old-new site of the U.S. Embassy, is by Frank Gehry, the unconventional American architect famous for Bilbao's golden Guggenheim. Gehry fans might be surprised at DZ Bank building's low profile. Structures on Pariser Platz are expected to be bland so as not to draw attention away from the Brandenburg Gate. (The glassy facade of the Academy of Arts, next to Gehry's building, is controversial for that very reason.) For your fix of the good old Gehry, step into the lobby and check out its undulating interior.

Brandenburg Gate, the center of old Berlin, sits on a major boulevard, running east–west through Berlin. The western segment, called Strasse des 17 Juni, stretches for six kilometers (4 miles) from the Siegessäule (past the flea market—see below) to the Olympic Stadium. For our walk, we'll follow this city axis in the opposite direction, east, up what is known as Unter den Linden, into the core of old imperial Berlin and past what was

Unter den Linden

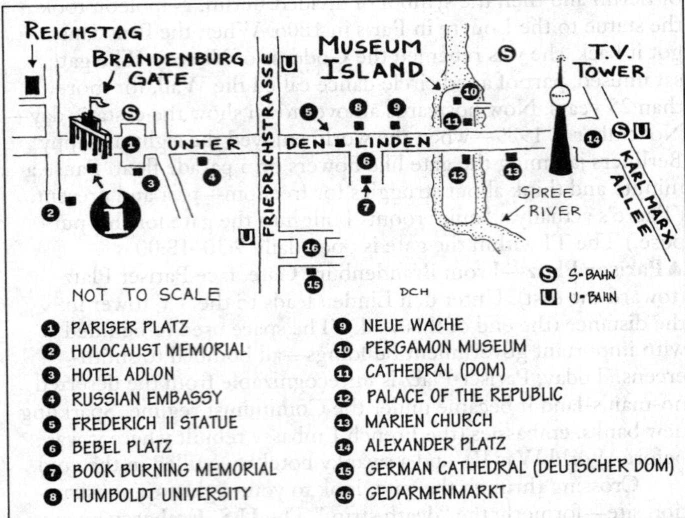

once the palace of the Hohenzollern family, who ruled Prussia and then Germany. The palace—the reason for just about all you'll see—is a phantom sight, long gone (though some Berliners hope to rebuild it).

▲▲Unter den Linden—This is the heart of former East Berlin. In Berlin's good old days, Unter den Linden was one of Europe's grand boulevards. In the 15th century, this carriageway led from the palace to the hunting grounds (today's big park). In the 17th century, Hohenzollern princes and princesses moved in and built their palaces here so they could be near the Prussian emperor.

Named centuries ago for its thousand linden trees, this was the most elegant street of Prussian Berlin before Hitler's time and the main drag of East Berlin after his reign. Hitler replaced the venerable trees—many 250 years old—with Nazi flags. Popular discontent actually drove him to replant linden trees. Today, Unter den Linden is no longer a depressing Cold War cul-de-sac, and its pre-Hitler strolling café ambience is returning.

As you walk toward the giant TV tower, the big building you see jutting out into the street on your right is the **Hotel Adlon**. It hosted such notables as Charlie Chaplin, Albert Einstein, and Greta Garbo. (This was where Garbo said, "I want to be alone," during the filming of *Grand Hotel*.) Destroyed in World War II, the grand Adlon was rebuilt in 1996. See how far you can get inside.

The Unter den Linden S-bahn station ahead of you is one of Berlin's former **ghost subway stations**. During the Cold War, most underground train tunnels were simply blocked at the border. But a few Western lines looped through the East. To make a little hard Western cash, the Eastern government rented the use of these tracks to the West, but the stations (which happened to be in East Berlin) were strictly off-limits. For 28 years, the stations were unused, as Western trains slowly passed through seeing only eerie DDR (East German) guards and lots of cobwebs. Literally within days of the fall of the Wall, these stations were reopened, and today they are a time warp, with the dreary old green tiles and the original traditional signs. Walk along the track and exit, following signs to *Russische Botschaft*... the Russian Embassy.

The **Russian Embassy** was the first big postwar building project in East Berlin. It's built in the powerful, simplified, neoclassical style Stalin liked. While not as important now as it was a few years ago, it's immense as ever. It flies the Russian white, red, and blue. Find the hammer-and-sickle motif decorating the window frames. Continuing past the Aeroflot Airline offices, look across the street to the right to see the back of the **Komische Oper** (comic opera; program and view of ornate interior posted in window). While the exterior is ugly, the fine old theater interior, amazingly missed by WWII bombs, survives. The shop ahead on your right is an amusing mix of antiques, local guidebooks, knickknacks, and East Berlin nostalgia souvenirs.

The West lost no time in consuming the East; consequently, some are feeling a wave of nostalgia—*Ost*-algia—for the old days of East Berlin. In recent local elections, nearly half of East Berlin's voters—and 6 percent of West Berliners—voted for the former Communist Party. One symbol of that era has been given a reprieve. At Friedrichstrasse, look at the DDR–style pedestrian lights, and you'll realize that someone had a sense of humor back then. The perky red and green men—*Ampelmännchen*—were under threat of replacement by the far less jaunty Western signs. Fortunately, the DDR signals will be kept after all.

At **Friedrichstrasse**, look right. Before the war, the Unter den Linden/Friedrichstrasse intersection was the heart of Berlin. In the '20s, Berlin was famous for its anything-goes love of life. This was the cabaret drag, a springboard to stardom for young and vampy entertainers like Marlene Dietrich. (Born in 1901, Dietrich starred in the first German "talkie" and then headed straight to Hollywood.) Today, this boulevard, lined with super department stores (such as Galeries Lafayette, with its cool marble and glass waste-of-space interior; belly up to its amazing ground floor viewpoint) and big-time hotels (such as the Hilton and Four Seasons), has slowly begun to replace Ku'damm as the grand commerce and café boulevard of Berlin—though the West is retaliating with some new stores of its own. American Express is across from Galeries Lafayette (handy for any train ticket needs, Mon–Sat 9:00–19:00, closed Sun, tel. 030/201-7400).

You'll notice big, colorful water pipes throughout Berlin. As long as the city remains a big construction zone, it will be laced with these drainage pipes—key to any building project. Berlin's high water table means any new basement comes with lots of pumping out.

Continue down Unter den Linden a few more blocks, past the large equestrian statue of **Frederick II** ("the Great"), and turn right into the square (Bebelplatz). Stand on the glass window in the center. (Construction of an underground parking lot might prevent you from reaching the glass plate.)

Frederick the Great, who ruled from 1740 to 1786, established Prussia as a military power. This square was the center of the "new Rome" Frederick envisioned. Much of Frederick's palace actually survived World War II but was torn down by the Communists since it symbolized the imperialist past. Now some Berliners want to rebuild the palace, from scratch, exactly as it once was. Other Berliners insist that what's done is done.

Bebelplatz is bounded by great buildings. The German State Opera was bombed in 1941, rebuilt to bolster morale and to celebrate its centennial in 1943, and bombed again in 1945. The former state library is where Lenin studied much of his exile away (climb to the second floor of the library to see a stained glass window depicting his life's work with almost biblical reverence; there's a good café with light food, Tim's Canadian Deli, downstairs). The round Catholic St. Hedwig's Church—nicknamed the "upside-down teacup"—was built to placate the subjects of Catholic lands Frederick added to his empire. (Step inside to see the cheesy DDR government renovation.)

Humboldt University, across Unter den Linden, was one of Europe's greatest. Marx and Lenin (not the brothers or the sisters) studied here along with Grimm (both brothers) and more than two dozen Nobel Prize winners. Einstein—who was Jewish—taught here until taking a spot at Princeton in 1932 (smart guy).

Look down through the glass you're standing on: The room of empty bookshelves is a memorial to the notorious Nazi **book burning**. It was on this square in 1933 that staff and students from the university threw 20,000 newly forbidden books (like Einstein's) into a huge bonfire on the orders of the Nazi propaganda minister Joseph Goebbels.

At the far end of Babelplatz, next to the green dome of St.

Hedwig's Church, is the **City Planning** office. The ground floor houses a free exhibit on the past, present, and future of Berlin. Inside and to the right is a scale model of Berlin as it was a century ago. Some buildings, like the Berliner Dom, you'll recognize. Others, such as the Royal Palace, are long gone. Inside the door and straight ahead is a model of what Berlin will look like in 2010 (free, daily 9:00–19:30, Ivalidenstrasse 44, tel. 030/2008-3234).

Continue down Unter den Linden. The next square on your right holds the Opernpalais' restaurants (see "Eating," below). On the university side of Unter den Linden, the Greek temple–like building is the **Neue Wache** (the emperor's New Guardhouse, from 1816). When the Wall fell, this memorial to the victims of fascism was transformed into a new national memorial. Look inside, where a replica of the Käthe Kollwitz statue, *Mother with Her Dead Son*, is surrounded by thought-provoking silence. This marks the tombs of Germany's unknown soldier and the unknown concentration camp victim. The inscription in front reads, "To the victims of war and tyranny." Read the entire statement in English (on wall, right of entry).

After the Neue Wache, detour down Hinter dem Giesshaus to see the new I. M. Pei–designed annex with a spiraling glass staircase—used to house special exhibitions—of the **German History Museum** (Tue–Sun 10:00–18:00, closed Mon).

Just before the bridge, wander left along the canal through a tiny but colorful flea market (weekends only). Canal tour boats leave from here.

Go back out to the main road and cross the bridge to **Museum Island**, home of Germany's first museums and today famous for its Pergamon Museum (described below). Eventually, all of the museums on this island will be connected by underground tunnels and consolidate the art collections of East and West Berlin—creating a massive complex intended to rival the Louvre. Today, the museum complex starts with an imposing red neoclassical facade on the left (a musty museum of antiquities; Pergamon is behind it). For 300 years, the square (Lustgarten) has flip-flopped between military parade ground and people-friendly park—depending upon the political tenor of the time. In 1999, it was made into a park again (read the history posted in the corner opposite the church).

The towering church is the 100-year-old **Berlin Cathedral**, or Dom (€4, €5 includes access to dome, Mon–Sat 9:00–20:00, Sun 11:30–18:00, organ concerts offered most Wed, Thu, and Fri at 15:00, free with regular admission). Inside, the great reformers (Luther, Calvin, and company) stand around the brilliantly restored dome like stern saints guarding their theology. Frederick I rests in an ornate tomb (right transept, near entry to dome). The crypt downstairs is not worth a look.

Across the street is the decrepit **Palace of the Republic** (with the copper-tinted windows). A symbol of the Communist days, it was East Berlin's parliament building and futuristic entertainment complex. Although it officially has a date with the wrecking ball, many Easterners want it saved, and its future is still uncertain.

Before crossing the next bridge (and leaving Museum Island), look right. The pointy twin spires of the 13th-century Nikolai Church mark the center of medieval Berlin. This *Nikolai-Viertel* (district) was restored by the DDR and was trendy in the last years of socialism. Today, it's dull and, with limited time, not worth a visit. As you cross the bridge, look left in the distance to see the gilded **New Synagogue**, rebuilt after WWII bombing (described below). Across the river to the left of the bridge is the construction site of a new shopping center with a huge aquarium in the center. The elevator will go right through the middle of an undersea world.

Walk toward **Marien Church** (from 1270, interesting but very faded old *Dance of Death* mural inside door) at the base of the TV tower. The big, red-brick building past the trees on the right is the city hall, built after the revolution of 1848 and arguably the first democratic building in the city. In the park are grandfatherly statues of Marx and Engels (nicknamed by locals "the old pensioners"). Surrounding them are stainless steel monoliths depicting the struggles of the workers of the world.

The **Fernsehturm (TV Tower),** at 368 meters (1,200 feet) tall, offers a fine view from 182 meters (597 feet; €6, March–Oct daily 9:00–1:00, Nov–Feb daily 10:00–24:00, tel. 030/242-3333). Consider a kitschy trip to the top for the view and lunch in its revolving restaurant. Built (with Swedish know-how) in 1969, the tower was meant to show the power of the atheistic state at a time when DDR leaders were having the crosses removed from church domes and spires. But when the sun shined on their tower, the greatest spire in East Berlin, a huge cross reflected on the mirrored ball. Cynics called it "The Pope's Revenge." East Berliners dubbed the tower "The Big Asparagus." They joked that if it fell over, they'd have an elevator to the West.

Farther east, pass under the train tracks into **Alexanderplatz**. This area—especially the Kaufhof—was the commercial pride and joy of East Berlin. Today, it's still a landmark, with a major U-bahn and S-bahn station.

For a ride through work-a-day eastern Berlin, with its Lego-hell apartments (dreary even with their new face-lifts), hop back on bus #100 from here. It loops five minutes to the end of the line and then, after a couple minutes' break, heads on back. (This bus retraces your route, finishing at Bahnhof Zoo.) Consider extending this foray into eastern Berlin to Karl Marx Allee (described below).

Sights—Western Berlin

Western travelers still think of Berlin's "West End" as the heart of the city. While it's no longer that, the West End still has the best infrastructure to support your visit and works well as a home base. Here are a few sights within an easy walk of your hotel and the Zoo station.

▲Kurfürstendamm—In the 1850s, when Berlin became a wealthy and important capital, her new rich chose Kurfürstendamm as their street. Bismarck made it Berlin's Champs-Elysées. In the 1920s, it became a chic and fashionable drag of cafés and boutiques. During the Third Reich, as home to an international community of diplomats and journalists, it enjoyed more freedom than the rest of Berlin. Throughout the Cold War, economic subsidies from the West made sure that capitalism thrived on Ku'damm, as western Berlin's main drag is popularly called. And today, while much of the old charm has been hamburgerized, Ku'damm is still a fine place to feel the pulse of the city and enjoy the elegant shops (around Fasanenstrasse), department stores, and people-watching. Ku'damm, starting at Kaiser Wilhelm Memorial Church, does its commercial cancan for three kilometers (2 miles).

▲Kaiser Wilhelm Memorial Church (Gedächtniskirche)—The church was originally a memorial to the first emperor of Germany, who died in 1888. Its bombed-out ruins have been left standing as a memorial to the destruction of Berlin in World War II. Under a fine mosaic ceiling, a small exhibit features interesting photos about the bombing (free, Mon–Sat 10:00–16:00, closed Sun). Next to it, a new church (1961) offers a world of 11,000 little blue windows (free, daily 9:00–19:00). The blue glass was given to the church by the French as a reconciliation gift. The lively square between this and the Europa Center (a shiny high-rise shopping center built as a showcase of Western capitalism during the Cold War) usually attracts street musicians.

▲Käthe Kollwitz Museum—This local artist (1867–1945), who experienced much of Berlin's stormiest century, conveys some powerful and mostly sad feelings about motherhood, war, and suffering through the black-and-white faces of her art (€5, Wed–Mon 11:00–18:00, closed Tue, a block off Ku'damm at Fasanenstrasse 24, tel. 030/882-5210).

▲Kaufhaus des Westens (KaDeWe)—The "department store of the West," with a staff of 2,100 to help you sort through its vast selection of 380,000 items, claims to be the biggest department store on the Continent. You can get everything from a haircut

Western Berlin

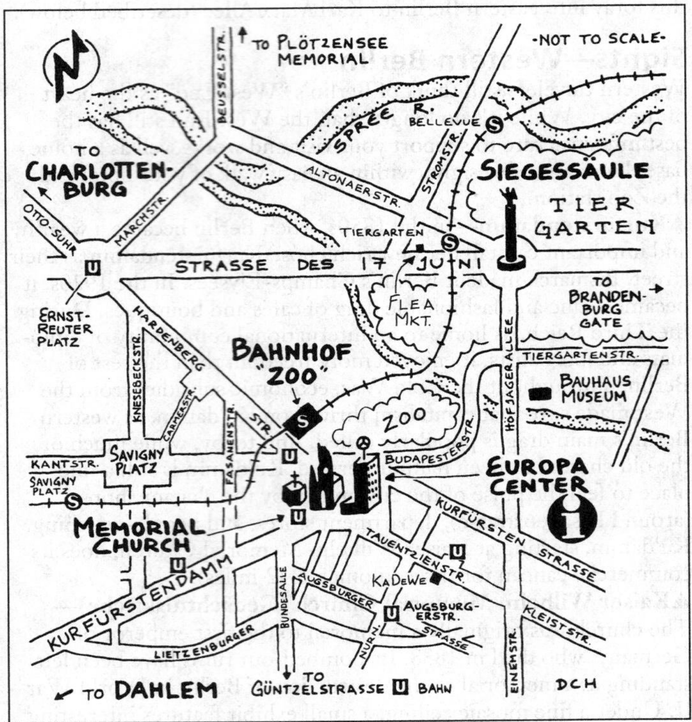

and train ticket to souvenirs (third floor). A cyber-bar is on the fourth floor. The theater and concert box office on the sixth floor charges an 18 percent booking fee, but they know all your options. The sixth floor is also a world of gourmet taste treats. The biggest selection of deli and exotic food in Germany offers plenty of classy opportunities to sit down and eat. Ride the glass elevator to the seventh floor's glass-domed Winter Garden self-service cafeteria—fun but pricey (Mon–Fri 9:30–20:00, Sat 9:00–16:00, closed Sun, tel. 030/21210, U-bahn: Wittenbergplatz). The Wittenbergplatz U-bahn station (in front of KaDeWe) is a unique opportunity to see an old-time station in Berlin. Enjoy its interior.

Berlin Zoo—More than 1,400 different kinds of animals call Berlin's famous zoo home—or so the zookeepers like to think. Germans enjoy seeing the pandas at play (straight in from the entry). I enjoy seeing the Germans at play (€8 for zoo or world-class aquarium, €13 for both, children half price, daily 9:00–18:30, in winter until 17:30, aquarium closes at 18:00, feeding times—*Fütterungszeiten*—posted on map just inside entry, enter near Europa Center in front of Hotel Palace, Budapester Strasse 32, tel. 030/254-010).

Erotic Art Museum—This offers three floors of graphic (mostly 18th-century) Oriental art, a tiny theater showing erotic silent movies from the early 1900s, and a special exhibit on the queen of German pornography, the late Beate Uhse. This amazing woman, a former test pilot for the Third Reich and groundbreaking purveyor of condoms and sex ed in the 1950s, was the female Hugh Hefner of Germany and CEO of a huge chain of porn shops. If you're traveling far and are sightseeing selectively, the sex museums in Amsterdam or Copenhagen are much better. This one, while well-described in English, is little more than prints and posters (€5, daily 9:00–24:00, last entry 23:00, hard-to-beat gift shop, at corner of Kantstrasse and Joachimstalerstrasse, a block from Bahnhof Zoo, tel. 030/886-0666). If you just want to see sex, you'll see much more for half the price in a private video booth next door.

Sights—Central Berlin

Hitler and the Third Reich—While many come to Berlin to see Hitler sights, these are essentially invisible. The German Resistance Museum (described below) is in German only and difficult for the tourist to appreciate. The Topography of Terror (SS and Gestapo headquarters) is a fascinating exhibit but—again—only in German, and all that remains of the building is its foundation. (Both museums have helpful audioguides in English.) "Hitler's Bunker" is completely gone (near the balloon site at Potsdamer Platz). Your best bet for "Hitler sights" is to take the "Infamous Third Reich Sites" walking tour offered by Berlin Walks (see "Tours of Berlin," above). EurAide has a good flier listing and explaining sights related to the Third Reich.

Tiergarten/Siegessäule—Berlin's "Central Park" stretches three kilometers (2 miles) from Bahnhof Zoo to Brandenburg Gate. Its centerpiece, the Siegessäule (Victory Column), was built to commemorate the Prussian defeat of France in 1870. The pointy-helmeted Germans rubbed it in, decorating the tower with French cannons and paying for it all with francs received as war reparations. The three lower rings commemorate Bismarck's victories. I imagine the statues of Moltke and other German military greats—which lurk in the trees nearby—goose-stepping around the floodlit angel at night. Originally standing at the Reichstag, the immense tower was actually moved to this position by Hitler in 1938 to complement his anticipated victory parades. At the first level, notice how WWII bullets chipped the fine marble columns. Climbing its 285 steps earns you a breathtaking Berlin-wide view and a close-up look at the gilded angel made famous in the U2 video (€1.20, April–Sept Mon–Thu 9:30–18:30, Fri–Sun 9:30–19:00, Oct–March daily 9:30–17:30, bus #100). From the tower, the grand Strasse des 17 Juni (named for a workers' uprising against the DDR government in the 1950s) leads east to the Brandenburg Gate.

Flea Market—A colorful flea market with great antiques, more than 200 stalls, collector-savvy merchants, and fun German fast-food stands thrives weekends beyond Siegessäule on Strasse des 17 Juni (S-bahn: Tiergarten).

German Resistance Memorial (Gedenkstätte Deutscher Widerstand)—This memorial and museum tells the story of the German resistance to Hitler. The Benderblock was a military headquarters where an ill-fated attempt to assassinate Hitler was plotted (the actual attempt occurred in Rastenburg, eastern Prussia). Stauffenberg and his co-conspirators were shot here in the courtyard. While explanations are in German only, the spirit that haunts the place is multilingual (free, Mon–Fri 9:00–18:00, Thu until 20:00, Sat–Sun 10:00–18:00, free English audioguide, €3 printed English translation, just south of Tiergarten at Stauffenbergstrasse 13, bus #129, tel. 030/2699-5000).

▲Potsdamer Platz—The Times Square of Berlin, and possibly the busiest square in Europe before World War II, Potsdamer Platz was cut in two by the Wall and left a deserted no-man's-land for 40 years. This immense commercial/residential/entertainment center (with the European corporate headquarters of Sony and others), sitting on a futuristic transportation hub, was a vision begun in 1991 when it was announced that Berlin would resume its position as capital of Germany. Sony, Daimler-Chrysler, and other huge corporations have turned it once again into a center of Berlin. While most of the complex just feels big (the arcade is like any huge, modern, American mall), the entrance to the complex and Sony Center Platz are worth a visit.

For an overview of the new construction, and a scenic route to Sony Center Platz, go to the east end of Potsdamer Strasse, facing the skyscrapers (the opposite end from Kulturforum, at main intersection of Potsdamer Strasse/Leipziger Strasse and Ebert Strasse/Stressemanstrasse, U-bahn: Potsdamer Platz). Find the green hexagonal clock tower with the traffic lights on top. This is a replica of the first automatic traffic light in Europe, which once stood at the six-street intersection of Potsdamer Platz. On either side of Potsdamer Strasse, you'll see huge cubical entrances to the brand new underground Potsdamer Platz train station (due to open in 2005). Near these entrances, notice the glass cylinders sticking out of the ground. The mirrors on the tops of the tubes move with the sun to collect the light and send it underground. Now go in one of the train station entrances and follow underground signs to "Sony Center." (While you're down there, look for the other ends of the big glass tubes.)

As you come up the escalator into Sony Center, look at the canopy above you. At night, multicolored floodlights play on the underside of this tent. Office workers and tourists eat here by the fountain, enjoying the parade of people. The modern Bavarian Lindenbrau beer hall—the Sony boss wanted a *Bräuhall*—serves good traditional food (big salads, meter-long taster boards of 8 different beers, daily 11:00–24:00, tel. 030/2575-1280). The adjacent Josty Bar is built around a surviving bit of a venerable hotel that was a meeting place for Berlin's rich and famous before the bombs. You can browse the futuristic Sony Style Store, visit the Filmhaus (a museum with an exhibit on Marlene Dietrich), and do some surfing at Web Free TV (on the street). Across Leipziger Strasse, the public is welcome to ride an elevator to a skyscraping rooftop terrace.

Sights—Kulturforum, in Central Berlin

Just west of Potsdamer Platz, with several top museums and Berlin's concert hall, is the city's cultural heart (admission to all sights covered by €6 day card or by Museumspass, free on first Sun of month). Of its sprawling museums, only the Gemäldegalerie is a must. The tourist info telephone number for all Kulturforum museums is 030/266-2951. To reach the Kulturforum, take the S- or U-bahn to Potsdamer Platz, then walk along Potsdamer Platz and Potsdamer Strasse. From the Zoo station, you can also take bus #200 to Philharmonie.

▲▲▲Gemäldegalerie—Germany's top collection of 13th- through 18th-century European paintings (over 1,400 canvases) is beautifully displayed in a building that is a work of art in itself. Follow the excellent free audioguide. The North Wing starts with German paintings of the 13th to 16th centuries—including eight by Dürer. Then come the Dutch and Flemish—Jan Van Eyck, Brueghel, Rubens, Van Dyck, Hals, and Vermeer. The wing finishes with German, English, and French 18th-century art—Gainsborough and Watteau. An octagonal hall at the end features a fine stash of Rembrandts. The South Wing is saved for the Italians—Giotto, Botticelli, Titian, Raphael, and Caravaggio (€6, covered by Museumspass, Tue–Sun 10:00–18:00, Thu until 22:00, closed Mon, clever little loaner stools, great salad bar in cafeteria upstairs, Matthäikirchplatz 4).

New National Gallery (Neue Nationalgalerie)—This features

20th-century art (€6, covered by Museumspass, Tue–Fri 10:00–18:00, Thu until 22:00, Sat–Sun 11:00–18:00, closed Mon).

Museum of Arts and Crafts (Kunstgewerbemuseum)—Wander through a thousand years of applied arts—porcelain, fine *Jugendstil* furniture, Art Deco, and reliquaries. There are no crowds and no English descriptions (€3, covered by Museumspass, Tue–Fri 10:00–18:00, Sat–Sun 11:00–18:00, closed Mon). The huge National Library is across the courtyard (free English periodicals).

▲Music Instruments Museum—This impressive hall is filled with 600 exhibits from the 16th century to modern times. Wander among old keyboard instruments and funny-looking tubas. There's no English, aside from a €0.10 info sheet, but it's fascinating if you're into pianos (€3, Tue–Fri 9:00–17:00, Sat–Sun 10:00–17:00, closed Mon, the low-profile white building east of the big, yellow Philharmonic Concert Hall, tel. 030/254-810). Poke into the lobby of Berlin's Philharmonic Concert Hall and see if there are tickets available for your stay (ticket office open Mon–Fri 15:00–18:00, Sat–Sun 11:00–14:00, must purchase tickets in person, box office tel. 030/2548-8132).

Sights—Eastern Berlin

▲▲Pergamon Museum—Of the museums on Museumsinsel (Museum Island), just off Unter den Linden, only the Pergamon Museum is essential. Its highlight is the fantastic Pergamon Altar. From a second-century B.C. Greek temple, it shows the Greeks under Zeus and Athena beating the giants in a dramatic pig pile of mythological mayhem. Check out the action spilling onto the stairs. The Babylonian Ishtar Gate (glazed blue tiles from sixth century B.C.) and many ancient Greek and Mesopotamian treasures are also impressive (€6, covered by Museumspass, Tue–Sun 10:00–18:00, Thu until 22:00, closed Mon, free on first Sun of month, café, behind Museum Island's red stone museum of antiquities, tel. for all sights on Museum Island: 030/2090-5577 or 030/209-050). The excellent audioguide (free with admission) covers the museum's highlights.

Old National Gallery—Also on Museum Island, this gallery shows 19th-century German Romantic art: man against nature, Greek ruins dwarfed in enchanted forests, medieval churches, and powerful mountains (€6, covered by Museumspass, Tue–Sun 10:00–18:00, Thu until 22:00, closed Mon, free on first Sun of month).

▲▲The Berlin Wall—The 160-kilometer (100-mile) "Anti-Fascist Protective Rampart," as it was called by the East German government, was erected almost overnight in 1961 to stop the outward flow of people (3 million leaked out between 1949

Eastern Berlin

and 1961). The Wall, which was four meters (13 feet) high, had a five-meter (16-foot) tank ditch, a no-man's-land that was 9 to 50 meters (30 to 160 feet) wide, and 300 sentry towers. During its 28 years, there were 1,693 cases when border guards fired, 3,221 arrests, and 5,043 documented successful escapes (565 of these were East German guards). The carnival atmosphere of those first years after the Wall fell is gone, but hawkers still sell "authentic" pieces of the Wall, DDR (East German) flags, and military paraphernalia to gawking tourists. Pick up the free brochure *Berlin: The Wall*, available at EurAide or the TI, which traces the history of the Wall and helps you find the remaining chunks and other Wall-related sights in Berlin.

▲▲▲**Haus am Checkpoint Charlie Museum**—While the famous border checkpoint between the American and Soviet sectors is long gone, its memory is preserved by one of Europe's most interesting museums: The House at Checkpoint Charlie. During the Cold War, it stood defiantly—spitting distance from the border guards—showing off all the clever escapes over, under, and through the Wall.

Today, while the drama is over and hunks of the Wall stand like victory scalps at its door, the museum still tells a gripping history of the Wall, recounts the many ingenious escape attempts (early years with a cruder wall saw more escapes), and includes plenty of video and film coverage of those heady days when people-power tore down the Wall (€7, assemble 10 tourists and get in for €4 each, daily 9:00–22:00, U-bahn: Kochstrasse, Friedrichstrasse 43-45, tel. 030/253-7250). If you're pressed for time, this is a good after-dinner sight.

Americans—the Cold War victors—have the biggest appetite for Wall-related sights. Where the gate once stood, notice the thought-provoking post with larger-than-life posters of a young American soldier facing east and a young Russian soldier facing west. Around you are reconstructions of the old checkpoint (named not after any guy, but "number three," as in alpha, bravo, charlie). Charlie was the most famous because this was the only place through which foreigners could pass. A few meters away (on Zimmerstrasse), a glass panel describes the former checkpoint. From there, a double row of cobbles in Zimmerstrasse marks where the Wall once stood (these innocuous cobbles run throughout the city, tracing the former Wall's path). Follow it one very long block to Wilhelmstrasse and a surviving stretch of Wall.

When it fell, the Wall was literally carried away by the euphoria. What did manage to survive has been nearly devoured by a decade of persistent "Wall peckers." The park behind the Zimmerstrasse/Wilhelmstrasse bit of Wall marks the site of the command center of Hitler's Gestapo and SS (explained by English plaques throughout). It's been left undeveloped as a memorial to the tyranny once headquartered here. In the park is . . .

The Topography of Terror—Because of the horrible things planned here, rubble of the Gestapo and SS buildings will always be left as rubble. The SS, Hitler's personal bodyguards, grew to become a state-within-a-state, with its talons in every corner of German society. Along an excavated foundation of the building, an exhibit tells the story of National Socialism and its victims in Berlin (free, info booth open May–Sept daily 10:00–20:00, Oct–April daily 10:00–18:00 or until dark, free English audioguide with passport as a deposit, written English translations-€1, tel. 030/2548-6703).

Across the street (facing the Wall) is the German Finance Ministry. Formerly the Nazi headquarters of the air force, this is the only major Hitler-era government building that survived the war's bombs. The Communists used it to house their—no joke—"Ministry of Ministries." Walk down Wilhelmstrasse to see an entry gate that looks much like it did when Germany occupied nearly all of Europe. At the far end of the building (farther down Wilhelmstrasse, at corner of Wilhelmstrasse and Leipziger Strasse) is a wonderful example of Communist art. The mural (from the 1950s) is classic "Social Realism"—showing the entire society . . . industrial laborers, farmworkers, women, and children all happily singing the same patriotic song. This was the Communist ideal. For the reality, look at the ground in the courtyard in front of the mural to see a blown-up photograph from a 1953 uprising against the Communists—quite a contrast.

▲▲Jewish Museum Berlin—This new museum is one of Europe's best Jewish sights. The highly conceptual building is a sight in itself, and the museum inside—an overview of the rich culture and history of Europe's Jewish community—is excellent. The Holocaust is appropriately remembered, but it doesn't overwhelm this celebration of Jewish life.

Designed by the American architect Daniel Libeskind, the zinc-walled building's zigzag shape is pierced by voids symbolic of the irreplaceable cultural loss caused by the Holocaust. Enter the museum through the 18th-century Baroque building next door, then go through an underground tunnel to reach the main exhibit. While underground, you can follow the "Axis of Exile" to a disorienting slanted garden with 49 pillars, or the "Axis of Holocaust" to an eerily empty tower shut off from the outside world.

When you emerge from underground, climb the stairs to the engaging, thought-provoking, and accessible museum. There are many interactive exhibits (spell your name in Hebrew) and pieces of artwork (the "Fallen Leaves" sculpture in the building's largest void is especially powerful), and it's all very kid-friendly (peel the giant garlic and climb through a pomegranate tree). English explanations interpret both the exhibits and the design of the very symbolic building. The museum is in a nondescript residential neighborhood a 10-minute walk from the Checkpoint Charlie museum, but it's well worth the trip (€5, daily 10:00–20:00, Mon until 22:00, U-bahn: Hallesches Tor, take exit marked "Jüdisches Museum," exit straight ahead, then turn right on Franz-Klühs-Strasse, the museum is 5 min ahead on your left at Lindenstrasse 9, tel. 030/2599-3300).

East Side Gallery—The biggest remaining stretch of the Wall is now "the world's longest outdoor art gallery." It stretches for over a kilometer (0.75 mile) and is covered with murals painted by artists from around the world. The murals are routinely whitewashed, so new ones can be painted. This length of the Wall makes a poignant walk. For a quick look, just go to Ostbahnhof station and look around (the freshest and most colorful art is at this end). The gallery only survives until a land ownership dispute can be solved, when it will likely be developed like the rest of the city. (Given the recent history, imagine the complexity of finding rightful owners of all this suddenly very valuable land.) If you walk the entire length, you'll find a small Wall souvenir shop at the end (they'll stamp your passport with the former East German stamp) and a bridge crossing the river to a subway station at Schlesisches Tor (in Kreuzberg).

Kreuzberg—This district—once butted against the dreary Wall and inhabited largely by poor Turkish guest laborers and their families—is still run-down, with graffiti-riddled buildings and plenty of student and Turkish street life. It offers a gritty look at melting-pot Berlin in a city where original Berliners are as rare as old buildings. Berlin is the fourth-largest Turkish city in the world, and Kreuzberg is its "downtown." But to call it a "little Istanbul" insults the big one. You'll see *döner kebab* stands, shops decorated with spray paint, and mothers wearing scarves. For a dose of Kreuzberg without getting your fingers dirty, joyride on bus #129. For a colorful stroll, take U-bahn to Kottbusser Tor and wander—ideally on Tuesday and Friday between 12:00 and 18:00, when the Turkish Market sprawls along the bank of the Maybachufer Canal.

▲▲Gendarmenmarkt—This delightful and historic square is bounded by twin churches, a tasty chocolate shop, and the concert hall (designed by Schinkel, the man who put the neoclassical stamp on Berlin and Dresden) for the Berlin symphony. The name of the square—part French and part German—reminds us that in the 17th century, a fifth of all Berliners were French émigrés, Protestant Huguenots fleeing Catholic France. Back then, tolerant Berlin was a magnet for the persecuted. The émigrés vitalized the city with new ideas and know-how.

The Deutscher Dom (German Cathedral, described below) has a history exhibit worthwhile for history buffs. The Französischer Dom (French Cathedral) offers a humble museum on the Huguenots (€1.50, Tue–Sun 12:00–17:00, closed Mon) and a chance to climb 254 steps to the top for a grand city view (€1.50, daily 9:00–19:00).

Fassbender & Rausch, on the corner near the Deutscher Dom, is Europe's biggest **chocolate store**. After 150 years of chocolate-making, this family-owned business proudly displays its sweet delights—250 different kinds—on a 17-meter-long (56-foot) buffet. Truffles are sold for about €0.50 each. The shop's evangelical Herr Ostwald (a.k.a. Benny) would love you to try his best-seller: tiramisu (Mon–Fri 10:00–20:00, Sat 10:00–16:00, closed Sun, corner of Mohrenstrasse at Charlottenstrasse 60, tel. 030/2045-8440).

German Cathedral—The Deutscher Dom houses the thought-provoking "Milestones, Setbacks, Sidetracks" (Wege, Irrwege, Umwege) exhibit, which traces the history of the German parliamentary system. The exhibit is well done and more interesting than it sounds. There are no English descriptions, but you can follow a fine and free 90-minute-long audioguide (passport required for deposit; to start, follow the blue arrows downstairs) or buy the €10 guidebook (free, June–Aug Tue–Sun 10:00–19:00, Tue until 22:00, closed Mon, Sept–May Tue–Sun 10:00–18:00, Tue until 22:00, closed Mon, on Gendarmenmarkt just off Friedrichstrasse, tel. 030/2273-0431).

▲▲New Synagogue—A shiny gilded dome marks the New Synagogue, now a museum and cultural center on Oranienburger Strasse. Only the dome and facade have been restored, and a window overlooks a vacant field marking what used to be the synagogue. The largest and finest synagogue in Berlin before World War II, it was desecrated by Nazis on "Crystal Night" in 1938, bombed in 1943, and partially rebuilt in 1990. Inside, past tight security, there's a small but moving exhibit on the Berlin Jewish community through the centuries with some good English descriptions (ground floor and first floor). On its facade, the *Vergesst es nie* message—added by East Berlin Jews in 1966—means "Never forget." East Berlin had only a few hundred Jews, but now that the city is united, the Jewish community numbers about 12,000 (€3, Sun–Thu 10:00–18:00, Fri 10:00–14:00, closed Sat, U-bahn: Oranienburger Tor, Oranienburger Strasse 28/30, tel. 030/8802-8316).

Oren, a popular near-kosher café, is next to the synagogue (see "Eating in Eastern Berlin," below). If you're heading for the Pergamon Museum next, take a shortcut by turning left after leaving the synagogue, then right on Monbijoustrasse. Cross the canal and turn left to the museum.

A block from the synagogue, walk 50 meters (160 feet) down Grosse Hamburger Strasse to a little park. This street was known for 200 years as the "street of tolerance" because the Jewish community donated land to Protestants so that they could build a church. Hitler turned it into the street of death *(Todes Strasse)*, bulldozing 12,000 graves of the city's oldest Jewish cemetery and turning a Jewish old-folks home into a deportation center. Note the two memorials—one erected by the former East Berlin government and one built later by the city's unified government. Somewhere nearby, a plain-clothes police officer keeps watch on this park.

▲Oranienburger Strasse—Berlin is developing so fast, it's impossible to predict what will be "in" next year. The area around Oranienburger Strasse is definitely trendy (but is being challenged by hip Friedrichshain, farther east).

While the area immediately around the synagogue is dull, 100 meters (300 feet) away things get colorful. The streets behind Grosse Hamburger Strasse flicker with atmospheric cafés, *Kneipen* (pubs), and art galleries.

At night, "techno-prostitutes" line Oranienburger Strasse. Prostitution is legal here, but there's a big debate about taxation. Since they don't get unemployment insurance, why should they pay taxes?

A block in front of the Hackescher Markt S-bahn station is Hackesche Höfe—with eight courtyards bunny-hopping through a wonderfully restored 1907 *Jugendstil* building. It's full of trendy restaurants, theaters, and cinema (playing movies in their original languages). This is a fine example of how to make huge city blocks livable—Berlin's apartments are organized around courtyard after courtyard off the main roads.

Karl Marx Allee—The buildings along Karl Marx Allee in eastern Berlin (just beyond Alexanderplatz) were completely leveled by the Soviets in 1945. When Stalin decided this main drag should be a showcase street, he had it rebuilt with lavish Soviet aid and named it Stalin Allee. Today, this street, done in the bold Stalin Gothic style so common in Moscow back in the 1950s, has been restored (and named after Karl Marx), providing a rare look at Berlin's Communist days. Cruise down Karl Marx Allee by taxi or ride the U-bahn to Strausberger Platz and walk to Schillingstrasse. There are some fine Social Realism reliefs on the buildings, and the lampposts incorporate the wings of a phoenix (rising from the ashes) in their design.

Natural History Museum (Museum für Naturkunde)—This place is worth a visit just to see the largest dinosaur skeleton ever assembled. While you're there, meet "Bobby" the stuffed ape (€4, Tue–Fri 9:30–17:00, Sat–Sun 10:00–18:00, closed Mon, U-6: Zinnowitzer Strasse, Invalidenstrasse 43, tel. 030/2093-8591).

Sights—Around Charlottenburg Palace

The Charlottenburg District—with a cluster of fine museums across the street from a grand palace—makes a good side-trip from downtown. Ride U-2 to Sophie-Charlotte Platz and walk 10 minutes up the tree-lined boulevard (following signs to *Schloss*), or—much faster—catch bus #145 (direction: Spandau) direct from Bahnhof Zoo.

For a Charlottenburg lunch, the **Luisen Bräu** is a comfortable brew-pub restaurant with a copper and woody atmosphere, good

Charlottenburg Palace Area

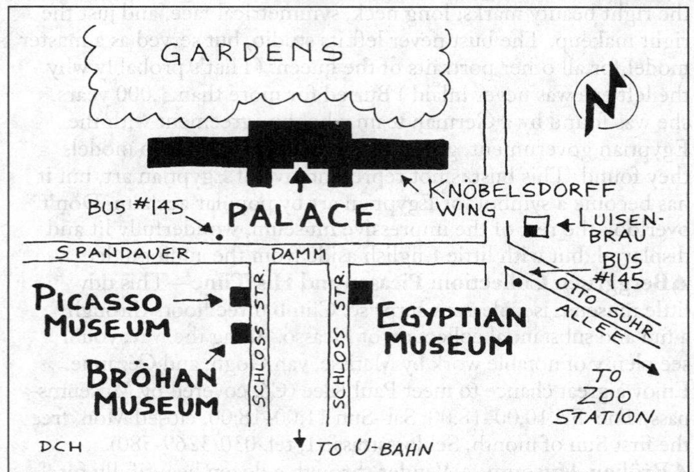

local "microbeers" (*dunkles:* dark, *helles:* light), and traditional German grub (€5–8 meals, daily 9:00–24:00, fun for groups, across from palace at Luisenplatz 1, tel. 030/341-9388).

▲Charlottenburg Palace (Schloss)—If you've seen the great palaces of Europe, this Baroque Hohenzollern palace comes in at about number 10 (behind Potsdam, too). It's even more disappointing since the main rooms can be toured only with a German guide (€7 includes 45-min tour, €2 to see just upper floors without tour, €7 to see palace grounds excluding tour areas, last tour 1 hour before closing, Tue–Sun 10:00–17:00, closed Mon, tel. 030/320-911).

The **Knöbelsdorff Wing** features a few royal apartments. Go upstairs and take a substantial hike through restored-since-the-war, gold-crusted, white rooms (€5 depending on special exhibitions, free English audioguide, Tue–Fri 10:00–18:00, Sat–Sun 11:00–18:00, closed Mon, last entry 30 min before closing, when facing the palace walk toward the right wing, tel. 030/3209-1202).

▲▲Egyptian Museum—Across the street from the palace, the Egyptian Museum offers one of the great thrills in art appreciation—gazing into the still-young and beautiful face of 3,000-year-old Queen Nefertiti, the wife of King Akhenaton (€6, covered by Museumspass, Tue–Sun 10:00–18:00, closed Mon, free on first Sun of month, free English audioguide, Schlossstrasse 70, tel. 030/343-5730).

This bust of Queen Nefertiti, from 1340 B.C., is perhaps the most famous piece of Egyptian art in Europe. Discovered in 1912, it shows the Marilyn Monroe of the early 20th century, with all the right beauty marks: long neck, symmetrical face, and just the right makeup. The bust never left its studio, but served as a master model for all other portraits of the queen. (That's probably why the left eye was never inlaid.) Buried for more than 3,000 years, she was found by a German team who, by agreement with the Egyptian government, got to take home any workshop models they found. This bust is not representative of Egyptian art, but it has become a symbol for Egyptian art by popular acclaim. Don't overlook the rest of the impressive museum, wonderfully lit and displayed, but with little English aside from the audioguide.

▲Berggruen Collection: Picasso and His Time—This tidy little museum is a pleasant surprise. Climb three floors through a fun and substantial collection of Picasso. Along the way, you'll see plenty of notable work by Matisse, van Gogh, and Cézanne. Enjoy a great chance to meet Paul Klee (€6, covered by Museumspass, Tue–Fri 10:00–18:00, Sat–Sun 11:00–18:00, closed Mon, free the first Sun of month, Schlossstrasse 1, tel. 030/3269-580).

▲Bröhan Museum—Wander through a dozen beautifully furnished Art Nouveau *(Jugendstil)* and Art Deco living rooms, a curvy organic world of lamps, glass, silver, and posters. While you're there, go to the second floor to see a fine collection of Impressionist paintings by Karl Hagemeister (€4, Tue–Sun 10:00–18:00, closed Mon, Schlossstrasse 1A, tel. 030/3269-0600).

Sights—Near Berlin

▲Sanssouci Palace, New Palace, and Park, Potsdam—With a lush park strewn with the extravagant whimsies of Frederick the Great, the sleepy town of Potsdam has long been Berlin's holiday retreat. Frederick's super-rococo Sanssouci Palace is one of Germany's most dazzling. His equally extravagant New Palace (Neues Palais), built to disprove rumors that Prussia was running out of money after the costly Seven Years' War, is on the other side of the park (it's a 30-min walk between palaces).

Your best bet for seeing Sanssouci Palace is to take the Potsdam TI's walking tour (see below). Otherwise, to make sense of all the ticket and tour options for the two palaces, stop by the palaces' TI (TI is across the street from windmill near Sanssouci entrance, helpful English-speaking staff, tel. 0331/969-4202).

Sanssouci Palace: Even though *Sanssouci* means "without a care," it can be a challenge for an English speaker to have an enjoyable visit. The palaces of Vienna, Munich, and even Würzburg offer equal sightseeing thrills with far fewer headaches. While the grounds are impressive, the interior of Sanssouci Palace can be visited only by a one-hour tour in German (with a borrowed

Greater Berlin

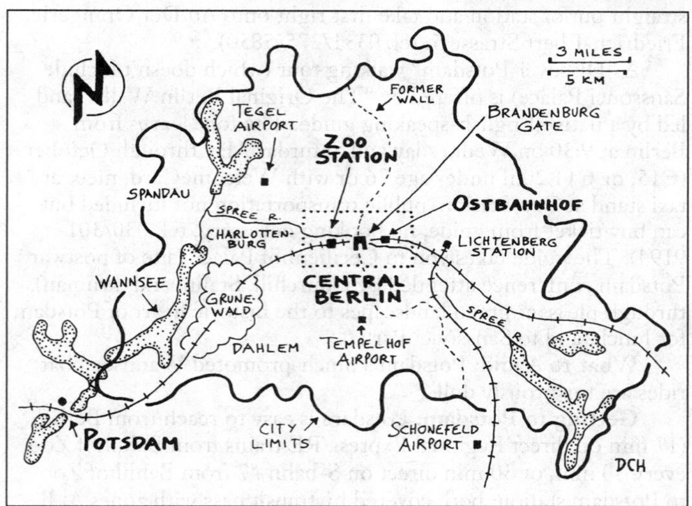

English text), and these tours get booked up quickly. The only English option is the Potsdam TI's tour (see below).

If you take a German tour of Sanssouci, you must be at the palace in person to get your ticket and the appointment time for your tour. In the summer, if you arrive by 9:00, you'll get right in. If you arrive after 10:00, plan on a wait. If you arrive after 12:00, you may not get in at all (€8, April–Oct Tue–Sun 9:00–17:00, closed Mon, Nov–March Tue–Sun 9:00–16:00, closed Mon, tel. 0331/969-4190).

New Palace: Use the free audioguide to tour Frederick's New Palace (€5, plus €1 for optional live tour in German, April–Oct Sat–Thu 9:00–17:00, closed Fri, Nov–March Sat–Thu 9:00–16:00, closed Fri). If you also want to see the king's apartments, you must take a required 45-minute tour in German (€5, offered April–Oct daily at 11:00 and 14:00). Off-season (Nov–March) you can visit the New Palace only on a German tour (€5); it can take up to an hour for enough people to gather.

Walking Tours: The Potsdam TI's handy walking tour includes Sanssouci Palace, offering the only way to get into the palace with an English-speaking guide (€25 covers walking tour, palace, and park, 11:00 daily except Mon, 3.5 hrs, departs from Film Museum across from TI, reserve by phone, in summer reserve at least 2 days in advance, tel. 0331/275-5850, Potsdam TI hours: April–Oct Mon–Fri 9:00–19:00, Sat–Sun 10:00–16:00, less off-season, 5-min walk from Potsdam S-bahn station, walk straight out of station and take first right onto An Der Orangerie, Friedrich-Ebert Strasse 5, tel. 0331/275-5850).

A "Discover Potsdam" walking tour (which doesn't include Sanssouci Palace) is offered by "The Original Berlin Walks" and led by a native English-speaking guide. The tour leaves from Berlin at 9:30 on Wednesday and Saturday May through October (€15, or €11.20 if under age 26 or with WelcomeCard, meet at taxi stand at Zoo Station, public transportation not included but can buy ticket from guide, no booking necessary, tel. 030/301-9194). The guide takes you to Cecilienhof Palace (site of postwar Potsdam conference attended by Churchill, Stalin, and Truman), through pleasant green landscapes to the historic heart of Potsdam for lunch, and to Sanssouci Park.

What to Avoid: Potsdam's much-promoted Wannsee boat rides are torturously dull.

Getting to Potsdam: Potsdam is easy to reach from Berlin (17 min on direct Regional Express/RE trains from Bahnhof Zoo every 30 min, or 30 min direct on S-bahn #7 from Bahnhof Zoo to Potsdam station; both covered by transit pass with zones A, B, and C). If you're taking the Potsdam TI's tour, walk to the TI from the Potsdam S-bahn stop (see "Walking Tours," above, for directions). If not taking the TI tour, catch bus #695 from the Potsdam station to the palaces (3/hr, 20 min). Use the same bus #695 to shuttle between the sights in the park. For a more scenic approach, take tram #96 or #X98 from the Potsdam station to Luisenplatz, then walk 15 minutes through the park and enjoy a classic view of Sanssouci Palace.

Other Day Trips—EurAide has researched and printed a *Get Me Outta Here* flier describing good day trips to small towns and another on the nearby Sachsenhausen Concentration Camp (which many think is as interesting as Dachau; a Sachsenhausen day trip is also offered by "The Original Berlin Walks," see "City Walking Tours," above).

Nightlife in Berlin

For the young and determined sophisticate, *Zitty* and *Tip* are the top guides to alternative culture (in German, sold at kiosks). Also pick up the free schedules *Flyer* and *030* in bars and clubs. *Berlin Programm* lists a nonstop parade of concerts, plays, exhibits, and cultural events (in German, sold at kiosks and TIs, www.berlin-programm.de).

Oranienburger Strasse's trendy scene (described above) is already being eclipsed by the action at Friedrichshain and Kollwitzplatz farther east. Tourists stroll the Ku'damm after dark.

Visit KaDeWe's ticket office for your music and theater options (sixth floor, 18 percent fee but access to all tickets). Ask about "competitive improvisation" and variety shows.

For jazz (blues and boogie, too) near the recommended Savignyplatz hotels (see below), consider **A Trane Jazz Club** (daily, 21:00–2:00, Bleibtreustrasse 1, tel. 030/313-2550) and **Quasimodo Live** (Kantstrasse 12a, under Delphi Cinema, tel. 030/312-8086). For quality blues and New Orleans–style jazz, stop by **Ewige Lampe** (from 21:00, Niebuhrstrasse 11a).

Bar Jeder Vernunft offers modern-day cabaret a short walk from the recommended hotels. This variety show under a classic old tent perched atop a modern parking lot is a hit with German speakers, but probably not worthwhile for non-German speakers. Tickets are generally around €15, and shows change regularly (shows start at 20:30, closed Sun, Schaperstrasse 24, tel. 030/883-1582).

To spend an evening enjoying Europe's largest revue theater, consider **Revue Berlin** at the Friedrichstadt Palast. The show basically depicts the history of Berlin, and is choreographed in a funny and musical way that's popular with the Lawrence Welk–type German crowd. It's even entertaining for your entire English-speaking family (€13–51, Tue–Sat 20:00, also Sat–Sun at 16:00, U-bahn: Oranienburger Tor, tel. 030/284-8830, www.friedrichstadtpalast.de).

Sleeping in Berlin
(€1 = about $1, country code: 49, area code: 030)

Sleep Code: **S** = Single, **D** = Double/Twin, **T** = Triple, **Q** = Quad, **b** = bathroom, **s** = shower only, **CC** = Credit Cards accepted, **no CC** = Credit Cards not accepted, **SE** = Speaks English, **NSE** = No English. Unless otherwise noted, a buffet breakfast is included.

To help you sort easily through these listings, I've divided the rooms into three categories based on the price for a standard double room with bath:

Higher Priced—Most rooms more than €100.

Moderately Priced—Most rooms €100 or less.

Lower Priced—Most rooms €80 or less.

I have concentrated my hotel recommendations around Savignyplatz. While Bahnhof Zoo and Ku'damm are no longer the center of Berlin, the trains, TI, and walking tours are all still handy to Zoo. And the streets around the tree-lined Savignyplatz (a 7-min walk behind the station) have a neighborhood charm. While towering new hotels are being built in the new center, simple, small, and friendly good-value places abound only here. My listings are generally located a couple of flights up in big, run-down buildings. Inside, they are clean, quiet, and spacious enough so that their well-worn character is actually charming. Rooms in back are on quiet courtyards.

The city is packed and hotel prices go up on holidays, including Green Week in mid-January, Easter weekend, first weekend in May, Ascension weekend in May, the Love Parade (a huge techno-Woodstock, second weekend in July), Germany's national holiday (Oct 2–4), Christmas, and New Year's.

During slow times, the best values are actually business-class rooms on the push list booked through the TI. But as the world learns what a great place Berlin is to visit, a rising tide of tourists will cause these deals to fade away.

Sleeping near Savignyplatz and Bahnhof Zoo

(zip code: 10623, unless otherwise noted)

These hotels and pensions are a 5- to 15-minute walk from Bahnhof Zoo (or take S-bahn to Savignyplatz). Hotels on Kantstrasse have street noise. Ask for a quieter room in back. The area has an artsy charm going back to the cabaret days in the 1920s, when it was the center of Berlin's gay scene. Wasch Salon is a handy **launderette** (daily 6:00–23:00, €5–8 wash and dry, Leibnizstrasse 72, near intersection with Kantstrasse).

Of the accommodations listed in this area, Pension Peters offers the best value for budget travelers.

HIGHER PRICED

Hotel Astoria is a friendly, three-star, business-class hotel with 32 comfortably furnished rooms and affordable summer and weekend rates (high season Db-€117–128; prices drop to Sb-€86–97, Db-€94–118 during low season of July–Aug, Nov–Feb, any 2 weekend nights, or if slow; rooms with showers are cheaper than rooms with baths, CC, elevator, free Internet access, parking-€10/day, around corner from Bahnhof Zoo at Fasanenstrasse 2, tel. 030/312-4067, fax 030/312-5027, www.hotelastoria.de, e-mail: info@hotelastoria.de).

Hecker's Hotel is an ultramodern, four-star business hotel with 69 rooms and all the sterile Euro-comforts (Sb-€125, Db-€150, breakfast-€15, weekends breakfast included, all rooms-€200 during conferences, CC, non-smoking rooms, elevator, parking-€8/day, between Savignyplatz and Ku'damm at Grolmanstrasse 35, tel. 030/88900, fax 030/889-0260, www.heckers-hotel.com).

Pension Savoy rents 16 rooms with all the amenities. You'll love the cheery old pastel breakfast room (Ss-€62, Sb-€73, Db-€102–109, CC, elevator, Meinekestrasse 4, 10719 Berlin, tel. 030/881-3700, fax 030/882-3746, www.hotel-pension-savoy.de).

Hotel Askanischerhof is the oldest *Zimmer* in Berlin. Posh

Berlin's Savignyplatz Neighborhood

as can be, it offers porters, valet parking, and 16 sprawling antique-furnished rooms. Photos on the walls brag of famous movie-star guests. Frau Glinicke offers Old World service and classic Berlin atmosphere (Sb-€100–107, Db-€128–143, CC, some smoke-free rooms, elevator, Ku'damm 53, tel. 030/881-8033, fax 030/881-7206, www.askanischer-hof.de, e-mail: info@askanischer-hof.de).

Hotel-Pension Funk, the former home of a 1920s silent-movie star, is delightfully quirky. It offers 14 elegant, richly furnished old rooms (S-€34–57, Ss-€41–72, Sb-€52–82, D-€52–82, Ds-€72–93, Db-€82–113, extra person-€23, CC but prefer cash, Fasanenstrasse 69, a long block south of Ku'damm, tel. 030/882-7193, fax 030/883-3329, www.hotel-pensionfunk.de, e-mail: berlin@hotel-pensionfunk.de).

MODERATELY PRICED

Hotel Carmer 16, with 30 bright, airy rooms, feels like a big, professional hotel with all the comfy extras (Sb-€72, Db-€92, these prices guaranteed through 2003 with this book, CC, elevator and a few stairs, beauty parlor and mini-spa upstairs, Carmerstrasse 16, tel. 030/3110-0500, fax 030/3110-0510, e-mail: carmer16@t-online.de).

Hotel Atlanta has 30 rooms in an older building half a block south of Ku'damm. It's next to Gucci, on an elegant shopping street, with big leather couches (Ss-€40–70, Sb-€57–90, Db-€72–100, Tb-€77–108, Qb-€82–118, CC, non-smoking rooms, Fasanenstrasse 74, 10719 Berlin, tel. 030/881-8049, fax 030/881-9872, www.hotelatlanta.de, e-mail: hatlanta68266759@aol.com).

Hotel Bogota has 125 big and comfortable rooms in a sprawling, drab old building that once housed the Nazi Chamber of Culture. (After the war, German theater stars were "denazified" here before they could go back to work.) Pieces of the owner's modern art collection lurk around every corner. Take a peek at the bizarre collage in the atrium, with mannequins suspended from the ceiling (S-€44, Ss-€51–57, Sb-€66–72, D-€66–69, Ds-€74–77, Db-€94–98, extra bed-€20, children under 15 free, CC, smoke-free rooms, elevator, bus #109 from Bahnhof Zoo to Schlüterstrasse 45, tel. 030/881-5001, fax 030/883-5887, www.hotelbogota.de, e-mail: hotel.bogota@t-online.de).

Hotel-Pension Imperator fills a sprawling floor of a grand building with 11 big, quiet, and Old World–elegant rooms (S-€42, Sb-€58, D-€78, Ds-€88–93, Db-€98, breakfast is classy but an extra €7–11, no CC, elevator, Meinekestrasse 5, tel. 030/881-4181, fax 030/885-1919).

With uninspired staff and 25 well-worn rooms in a boring building, all that **Hotel Pension Eden am Zoo** has going for it is its good location (S-€35–40, Ss-€45–50, Sb-€55–60, D-€55–65, Ds-€65–75, Db-€75–90, no CC, Uhlandstrasse 184, tel. 030/881-5900, fax 030/881-5732, www.rheingold-hotel.de).

LOWER PRICED

Pension Peters, run by a German-Swedish couple, is sunny and central, with a cheery breakfast room. Decorated sleek Scandinavian, with every room renovated, it's a winner (S-€36, Ss-€46, Sb-€58, D-€51, Ds-€67, Db-€66–77, extra bed-€8, kids under 12 free, family room, 3 percent charge if you pay with CC, Internet access, 10 meters, or 33 feet, off Savignyplatz at Kantstrasse 146, tel. 030/3150-3944, fax 030/312-3519, www.pension-peters-berlin.de, e-mail: penspeters@aol.com, Annika and Christoph SE). The same family also runs a larger hotel just outside of Berlin (see Hotel Pankow under "More Berlin Hotels," below) and rents apartments (ideal for small groups and longer stays).

Hotel Crystal Garni is professional and offers small, well-worn, comfortable rooms and a *vollkorn* breakfast room (S-€36, Sb-€41, D-€47, Ds-€57, Db-€66–77, CC, elevator, a block past Savigny-platz at Kantstrasse 144, tel. 030/312-9047, fax 030/312-6465, run by John and Dorothy Schwarzrock and Herr Vasco Flascher).

Pension Alexis is a classic old-European four-room pension in a stately 19th-century apartment run by Frau and Herr Schwarzer. The shower and toilet facilities are older and cramped, but this, more than any other Berlin listing, has you feeling at home with a faraway aunt (S-€42, D-€65, T-€97, Q-€146, no CC, big rooms, handheld showers, Carmerstrasse 15, tel. 030/312-5144, enough English spoken).

Pension Silva, a lesser value, is a basic place just off Savignyplatz with 15 spacious, well-worn rooms (S-€36, Ss-€46, Sb-€51, D-€56, Ds-€62, Db-€67, Ts-€84, Tb-€92, Qs-€112, Qb-€122, €5 less without breakfast, no CC, Knesebeckstrasse 29, tel. 030/881-2129, fax 030/885-0435).

Jugendgastehaus am Zoo is a bare-bones, cash-only youth hostel that takes no reservations and hardly has a reception desk. It's far less comfortable and only marginally cheaper than simple hotels (85 beds, dorm beds-€18, S-€25, D-€44, includes sheets, no breakfast, no CC, Hardenbergstrasse 9a, tel. 030/312-9410, fax 030/312-5430).

Sleeping South of Ku'damm (zip code: 10707)

Several small hotels are nearby in a charming, café-studded neighborhood 300 meters (985 feet) south of Ku'damm, near the intersection of Sächsische Strasse and Pariser Strasse (bus #109 from Bahnhof Zoo, direction: Airport Tegel). They are less convenient from the station than most of the Savignyplatz listings above.

MODERATELY PRICED

Hotel Austriana, with 25 modern and bright rooms, is warmly and energetically run by Thomas (S-€33–43, Ss-€41–48, Sb-€57–67, Ds-€62–69, Db-€78–89, Ts-€78–96, Qs-€96–104, prices higher for holidays and conferences, CC, elevator, Pariser Strasse 39, tel. 030/885-7000, fax 030/8857-0088, www.austriana.de, e-mail: austriana@t-online.de). **Insel Rügen Hotel**, in the same building as the Austriana, has 31 rooms and ornate, eastern decor (S-€28, Ss-€39, D-€51, Ds-€61–66, Db-€77–82, CC, elevator, Pariser Strasse 39, tel. 030/884-3940, fax 030/8843-9437, www.insel-ruegen-hotel.de, e-mail: ir-hotel@t-online.de).

LOWER PRICED

Hotel-Pension-Curtis, in the same building as the Austriana and Insel Rügen (recommended above), has 10 hip, piney, basic rooms (S-€32–37, Ss-40–45, Ds-€60–70, Ts-€75–83, Qs-€90–100, no CC, elevator, Pariser Strasse 39, tel. 030/883-4931, fax 030/885-0438, www.berlin-pension-curtis.de).

Hotel-Pension Bella, a clean, simple, masculine-feeling place with high ceilings and a cheery, attentive management, rents nine big, comfortable rooms (S-€35, Ss/Sb-€45–50, D-€50, Ds-€60–70, Db-€72–80, Ts-€85, Qs-€95, apartment also available, CC, elevator, bus #249 from Zoo, Ludwigkirchstrasse 10a, tel. 030/881-6704, fax 030/8867-9074, www.pension-bella.de, e-mail: pension.bella@t-online.de).

More Berlin Hotels

Away from the Center: **Hotel Pankow** is a new, fresh, colorful 43-room place run by friendly Annika and Christoph (from the Pension Peters, above). It's a 30-minute commute north of downtown, but a good value (S-€29, Sb-€44, D-€36, Db-€59, T-€39, Tb-€69, Q-€48, Qb-€75, family rooms, children under 16 free in room with parents, CC, elevator, Internet access, free parking in lot or €3/day in garage, tram station in front of hotel takes you to the center in 30 min, Pasewalker Strasse 14-15, tel. 030/486-2600, fax 030/4862-6060, www.hotel-pankow-berlin.de, e-mail: hotel-pankow@aol.com).

Near Augsburgerstrasse U-bahn Stop: Consider the **Hotel-Pension Nürnberger Eck** (S-€45, Sb-€60, D-€70, Db-€92, CC, Nürnberger Strasse 24a, tel. 030/235-1780, fax 030/2351-7899) or **Hotel Arco** (Sb-€64–75, Db-€82–92, CC, Geisbergerstrasse 30, tel. 030/235-1480, fax 030/2147-5178, www.arco-hotel.de).

Near Güntzelstrasse U-bahn Stop: Choose between **Pension Güntzel** (Ds-€59, Db-€69–79, single rooms €16 less, CC, Güntzelstrasse 62, tel. 030/857-9020, fax 030/853-1108, www.pension-guentzel.de), **Pension Finck** (Ss-€45, Ds-€59, no CC, Güntzelstrasse 54, tel. 030/861-2940, fax 030/861-8158), or **Hotel Pension München** (S-€40, Sb-€55, Db-€75, CC, also Güntzelstrasse 62, tel. 030/857-9120, fax 030/8579-1222, www.hotel-pension-muenchen-in-berlin.de).

In Eastern Berlin: The **Hotel Unter den Linden** is ideal for those nostalgic for the days of Soviet rule, although nowadays at least, the management tries to be efficient and helpful. Formerly one of the best hotels in the DDR, this huge, blocky place, right on Unter den Linden in the heart of what was East Berlin, is reasonably comfortable and reasonably priced. Built in 1966, with prison-like corridors, it has 331 modern, plain, and comfy rooms (Sb-€77, Db-€123, CC, non-smoking rooms, at intersection of Friedrichstrasse, Unter den Linden 14, 10117 Berlin, tel. 030/238-110, fax 030/2381-1100, www.hotel-unter-den-linden.de, e-mail: reservation@hotel-unter-den-linden.de).

Hostels in Eastern Berlin

There are plenty of great hostels. Here are four good bets (all prices listed per person): **Studentenhotel Meininger 10** (D-€46, €21-per-bed quads, includes sheets and breakfast, no CC, no curfew, elevator, free parking, near city hall on JFK Platz, Meiningerstrasse 10, U-bahn: Rathaus Schoneberg, tel. 030/7871-7414, fax 030/7871-7412, www.studentenhotel.de, e-mail: info@studentenhotel.de), **Mitte's Backpacker Hostel** (€12–15 dorm beds, D-€23, T-€20, Q-€18, sheets-€2.50, no breakfast, no CC, could be cleaner, no curfew, Internet access-€6/hr, laundry, bike rental-€6, English newspapers, U-bahn: Zinnowitzerstrasse, Chauseestrasse 102, tel. 030/2839-0965, fax 030/2839-0935, www.backpacker.de, e-mail: info@backpacker.de), **Circus** (dorm bed-€13–14, S-€20–30, D-€21–23, T-€18–20, Q-€16–17, apartments-€65–70, breakfast-€4, sheets-€2, CC, no curfew, Internet access, 2 locations, U-bahn: Alexanderplatz, Rosa-Luxemburg Strasse 39, or U-bahn: Rosenthaler Platz, Weinbergsweg 1a, both tel. 030/2839-1433, fax 030/2839-1484, www.circus-berlin.de, e-mail: info@circus-berlin.de), or **Clubhouse** (dorm bed-€14, bed in 5- to 7-bed room-€17, S-€32, D-€23, T-€20, breakfast-€4, sheets-€2, no CC, Internet access, on second floor, nightclub below, in hip Oranienburger Strasse area, S- or U-bahn: Friedrichstrasse, Kalkscheunenstrasse 4-5, tel. 030/2809-7979, fax 030/2809-7977, www.clubhouse-berlin.de, e-mail: info@clubhouse-berlin.de).

Eating in Berlin

Don't be too determined to eat "Berlin-style." The city is known only for its mildly spicy sausage. Still, there is a world of restaurants to choose from in this ever-changing city. Your best approach may be to choose a neighborhood, rather than a particular restaurant.

For quick and easy meals, colorful pubs—called *Kneipen*—offer light meals and the fizzy local beer, Berliner Weiss. Ask for it *mit Schuss* for a shot of fruity syrup in your suds. If the kraut is getting wurst, try one of the many Turkish, Italian, or Balkan restaurants. Eat cheap at *Imbiss* snack stands, bakeries (sandwiches), and falafel/kebab places. Bahnhof Zoo has several bright and modern fruit-and-sandwich bars and a grocery (daily 6:00–24:00).

Eating in Western Berlin

Near Savignyplatz

Several good places are on or within 100 meters (300 feet) of Savignyplatz. Take a walk and survey these: **Dicke Wirtin** is a smoky old pub with good *Kneipe* atmosphere, famously cheap *Gulaschsuppe*, and salads (daily 12:00–4:00, just off Savignyplatz at Carmerstrasse 9, tel. 030/312-4952). **Die Zwölf Apostel** restaurant is trendy for leafy candlelit ambience and Italian food. A dressy local crowd packs the place for €10 pizzas and €15 to €30 meals. Late-night partygoers appreciate Apostel's great breakfast (daily, 24 hrs, no CC, immediately across from Savigny S-bahn entrance, Bleibtreustrasse 49, tel. 030/312-1433). **Ristorante San Marino**, on the square, is another good Italian place, serving cheaper pasta and pizza (daily 10:00–24:00, Savignyplatz 12, tel. 030/313-6086). **Zillemarkt Restaurant,** which feels like an old-time Berlin beer garden, serves traditional Berlin specialties in the garden or in the rustic candlelit interior (€10 meals, daily 10:00–24:00, near the S-bahn tracks at Bleibtreustrasse 48a, tel. 030/881-7040).

Schell Restaurant is a dressy place (named for a gas station that once stood here) serving high Italian cuisine to a completely German crowd that seems "in the know" (€20 dinner plates, daily 9:00–24:00, packed with locals on Wed, a block off Savignyplatz at Knesebackstrasse 22, reservations smart, tel. 030/312-8310).

Weyers Café Restaurant, serving quality international and German cuisine, is a great value and worth a short walk. It's sharp, with white tablecloths, but not stuffy (€10 dinner plates, CC, daily 8:00–1:00, seating indoors or outside on the leafy square, Pariser Strasse 16, reservations smart after 20:00, tel. 030/881-9378).

Ullrich Supermarkt is the neighborhood grocery store (Mon–Fri 9:00–20:00, Sat 9:00–16:00, closed Sun, Kantstrasse 7, under the tracks near Bahnhof Zoo). There's plenty of fast food near Bahnhof Zoo and on Ku'damm.

Near Bahnhof Zoo

Self-Service Cafeterias: The top floor of the famous department store, **KaDeWe**, holds the Winter Garden Buffet view cafeteria, and its sixth-floor deli/food department is a picnicker's nirvana. Its arterials are clogged with more than 1,000 kinds of sausage and 1,500 types of cheese (Mon–Fri 9:30–20:00, Sat 9:00–16:00, closed Sun, U-bahn: Wittenbergplatz). The **Wertheim** department store, a half block from the Memorial Church, has cheap food counters in the basement and a city view from its fine self-service cafeteria, Le Buffet, located up six banks of escalators (Mon–Fri 9:30–20:00, Sat 9:00–16:00, closed Sun, U-bahn: Ku'damm). The **Marche**, a chain that's popped up in big cities all over Germany, is another inexpensive, self-service cafeteria within a half block of the Kaiser Wilhelm church (daily 8:00–24:00, CC, plenty of salads, fruit, made-to-order omelettes, Ku'damm 14, tel. 030/882-7578).

At Bahnhof Zoo: Terrassen am Zoo is a good restaurant right in the station, offering peaceful decency amidst a whirlwind of travel activity (daily 6:00–22:00, upstairs, next to track 1, tel. 030/315-9140).

Eating in Eastern Berlin

Along Unter den Linden near Pergamon Museum

The Opernpalais, preening with fancy prewar elegance, hosts a number of pricey restaurants. Its **Operncafé** has the best desserts and the longest dessert bar in Europe (daily 8:00–24:00, across from university and war memorial at Unter den Linden 5, tel. 030/202-683); sit down and enjoy perhaps the classiest coffee stop in Berlin. The shady beer and tea garden in front has a cheap food counter (from 10:00, depending on weather). More students and fewer tourists eat in the student facilities at Humboldt University across the street (go through courtyard, enter building through main door, follow signs to the cafeteria on right or the cheaper, government-subsidized *mensa* on left, both closed weekends).

Oren Restaurant and Café is a trendy, stylish, near-kosher/vegetarian place next to the New Synagogue. The food is pricey but good, and the ambience is happening (daily 12:00–24:00, north of Museum Island about 5 blocks away at Oranienburger Strasse 28, tel. 030/282-8228).

Near Checkpoint Charlie

Lekkerbek, a busy little bakery and cafeteria, sells inexpensive and tasty salads, soups, pastas, and sandwiches (Mon–Fri 5:30–18:00, Sat 5:30–13:00, closed Sun, a block from Checkpoint Charlie museum at Kochstrasse subway stop, Friedrichstrasse 211, tel. 030/251-7208). For a classier sit-down meal, try **Café Adler,** across the street from the museum (Mon–Sat 10:00–24:00, Sun 10:00–19:00, Friedrichstrasse 20b, tel. 030/251-8965).

Transportation Connections—Berlin

Berlin has three train stations (with more on the way). Bahnhof Zoo was the West Berlin train station and still serves western Europe: Frankfurt, Munich, Hamburg, Paris, and Amsterdam. The Ostbahnhof (former East Berlin's main station) still faces east, serving Prague, Warsaw, Vienna, and Dresden. The Lichtenberg Bahnhof (eastern Berlin's top U- and S-bahn hub) also handles a few eastbound trains. Expect exceptions. All stations are conveniently connected by subway and even faster by train. Train info: tel. 01805/996-633.

By train to: Frankfurt (14/day, 5 hrs), **Munich** (14/day, 7 hrs, 10 hrs overnight), **Köln** (hrly, 6.5 hrs), **Amsterdam** (4/day, 7 hrs), **Budapest** (2/day, 13 hrs; 1 goes via Czech Republic and Slovakia, so Eurail is not valid), **Copenhagen** (4/day, 8 hrs, change in Hamburg), **London** (4/day, 15 hrs), **Paris** (6/day, 13 hrs, change in Köln, 1 direct night train), **Zurich** (12/day, 10 hrs, 1 direct night train), **Prague** (4/day, 5 hrs, no overnight trains), **Warsaw** (4/day, 8 hrs, 1 night train from Lichtenberg Stn; reservations required on all Warsaw-bound trains), **Kraków** (2/day, 10 hrs), **Vienna** (2/day, 12 hrs via Czech Republic; for second-class ticket, Eurailers pay an extra €23 if under age 26 or €31 if age 26 or above; otherwise, take the Berlin–Vienna via Passau train—nightly at 20:00).

Eurailpasses don't cover the Czech Republic. The **Prague Excursion pass** picks up where Eurail leaves off, getting you from any border into Prague and then back out to Eurail country again within seven days (first class-€50, second class-€40, youth second class-€30, buy at EurAide in Berlin at the Bahnhof Zoo and get reservations for €3 at the same time).

There are **night trains** from Berlin to Amsterdam, Munich, Köln, Brussels, Paris, Vienna, Budapest, Warsaw, Stuttgart, Basel, and Zurich, but there are no night trains from Berlin to anywhere in Italy or Spain. A *Liegeplatz*, or berth (€15–21), is a great deal; inquire at EurAide at Bahnhof Zoo for details. Beds cost the same whether you have a first- or second-class ticket or railpass. Trains are often full, so get your bed reserved a few days in advance from any travel agency or major train station in Europe. Note: Since the Paris–Berlin night train goes through Belgium, railpass holders cannot use a Europass or Eurail Selectpass to cover this ride unless they've added or selected Belgium.

Berlin's Three Airports

Allow €20 for a taxi ride to or from any of Berlin's airports. **Tegel Airport** handles most flights from the United States and western Europe (6 km from center, catch the faster bus #X9 to Bahnhof Zoo, or bus #109 to Ku'damm and Bahnhof Zoo for €2; bus TXL goes to Alexanderplatz in East Berlin). Flights from the east and on Buzz Airlines usually arrive at **Schönefeld Airport** (20 km from center, short walk to S-bahn, catch S-9 to Zoo Station). **Templehof Airport**'s future is uncertain (in Berlin, bus #119 to Ku'damm or U-bahn 6 or 7). The central telephone number for all three airports is 01805/000-186. Call British Air at 01805/266-522, Delta at 01803/337-880, SAS at 01803/234-023, or Lufthansa at 01803/803-803.

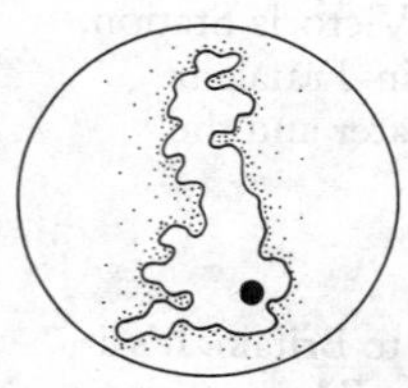

LONDON

London is more than 600 square miles of urban jungle. With nine million struggling people—many of whom speak English—it's a world in itself and a barrage on all the senses. On my first visit I felt very, very small. London is much more than its museums and famous landmarks. It's a living, breathing, thriving organism.

London has changed dramatically in recent years, and many visitors are surprised to find how "un-English" it is. Whites are now a minority in major parts of the city that once symbolized white imperialism. Arabs have nearly bought out the area north of Hyde Park. Chinese take-outs outnumber fish-and-chips shops. Many hotels are run by people with foreign accents (who hire English chambermaids), while outlying suburbs are home to huge communities of Indians and Pakistanis. London is learning—sometimes fitfully—to live as a microcosm of its formerly vast empire. Many see the English Channel Tunnel as another foreign threat to the Britishness of Britain.

With just a few days here, you'll get no more than a quick splash in this teeming human tidal pool. But, with a quick orientation, you'll get a good look at its top sights, history, and cultural entertainment, as well as its ever-changing human face.

Have fun in London. Blow through the city on the open deck of a double-decker orientation tour bus, and take a pinch-me-I'm-in-Britain walk through downtown. Ogle the crown jewels at the Tower of London, hear the chimes of Big Ben, and see the Houses of Parliament in action. Hobnob with the tombstones in Westminster Abbey, duck WWII bombs in Churchill's underground Cabinet War Rooms, and brave the earthshaking Imperial War Museum. Overfeed the pigeons at Trafalgar Square. Visit with Leonardo, Botticelli, and Rembrandt in the National Gallery.

Whisper across the dome of St. Paul's Cathedral and rummage through our civilization's attic at the British Museum. Cruise down the Thames River. At the National Portrait Gallery, watch the parade of British greats who created history—from Kings and Queens to the artists in between. You'll enjoy some of Europe's best people-watching at Covent Garden and snap to at Buckingham Palace's Changing of the Guard. Just sit in Victoria Station, at a major Tube station, at Piccadilly Circus, or in Trafalgar Square, and observe. Spend one evening at a theater and the others catching your breath.

Planning Your Time

The sights of London alone could easily fill a trip to Britain. It's a great one-week getaway. On a short tour of Britain I'd give it three busy days. If you're flying in, consider starting your trip in Bath and making London your British finale. Especially if you hope to enjoy a play or concert, a night or two of jet lag is bad news.

Here's a suggested schedule:

Day 1: 9:00–Tower of London (Beefeater tour, crown jewels), 12:00–Munch a sandwich on the Thames while cruising from the Tower to Westminster Bridge, 13:00–Follow the self-guided Westminster Walk (see below) with a quick visit to the Cabinet War Rooms, 15:30–Trafalgar Square and National Gallery, 17:30–Visit the Britain Visitors Centre near Piccadilly, planning ahead for your trip, 18:30–Dinner in Soho. Take in a play or 19:30 concert at St. Martin-in-the-Fields.

Day 2: 9:00–Take the Round London bus tour (consider hopping off near the end for the 11:30 Changing of the Guard at Buckingham Palace), 12:30–Covent Gardens for lunch and people-watching, 14:00–Tour the British Museum. Have a pub dinner before a play, concert, or evening walking tour.

Days 3 and 4: Choose among these remaining London highlights: Tour Westminster Abbey (tour, evensong), British Library, Imperial War Museum, the two Tates (Tate Modern on the south bank for modern art, Tate Britain on the north bank for British art), St. Paul's Cathedral (tour, dome climb, evensong), or the Museum of London; take a spin on the London Eye Ferris Wheel (reserve in advance) or a cruise to Kew or Greenwich; do some serious shopping at one of London's elegant department stores or open-air markets; or take another historic walking tour.

After considering nearly all of London's tourist sights, I have pruned them down to just the most important (or fun) for a first visit of up to seven days. You won't be able to see all of these, so don't try. You'll keep coming back to London. After 25 visits myself, I still enjoy a healthy list of excuses to return.

Orientation (area code: 020)

To grasp London comfortably, see it as the old town without the modern, congested sprawl. Most of the visitor's London lies between the Tower of London and Hyde Park—about a three-mile walk. Mentally—maybe even physically, using scissors—trim down your map to include only the area between the Tower of London, King's Cross Station, Paddington Station, the Victoria and Albert Museum, and Victoria Station. With this focus and a good orientation, you'll find London manageable and even fun.

Tourist Information

The **Britain Visitors Centre** is the best tourist information service in town (Mon–Fri 9:00–18:30, Sat–Sun 10:00–16:00, phone not answered after 17:00 Mon–Fri and not at all Sat–Sun, booking service, just off Piccadilly Circus at 1 Lower Regent Street, tel. 020/8846-9000, www.visitbritain.com). It's great for London information; buy your city map here. Bensons Mapguide for £2.25 is the best (also sold at newsstands), although bargain-hunters may prefer the LondonSmart Saver Street Map, which gets you a 20 percent discount at many attractions, including Tower Bridge and the Cabinet Rooms.

If you're traveling beyond London, take advantage of the center's well-equipped London/England desk, Wales desk (tel. 020/7808-3838), Ireland desk (tel. 020/7808-3841), and Scotland desk. At the center's extensive bookshop, gather whatever guidebooks, hostel directories, maps, and information you'll need. For trips through Britain, consider the *Michelin Green Guide to Britain* (£9.25; Green Guide just for London also available), the Britain road atlas (£10), and Ordnance Survey maps for areas you'll be exploring by car. The Visitors Centre has a travel agency upstairs, plus computers displaying only its Web site: www.visitbritain.com.

Nearby you'll find the **Scottish Tourist Centre** (mid-June–mid-Sept Mon–Fri 9:00–18:00, Sat 10:00–17:00, off-season Mon–Fri 9:30–17:30, Sat 12:00–16:00, Cockspur Street, tel. 0131/472-2035, www.visitscotland.com) and the slick **French National Tourist Office** (Mon–Fri 10:00–18:00, Sat until 17:00, closed Sun, 178 Piccadilly Street, toll tel. 090-6824-4123).

Unfortunately, **London's Tourist Information Centres** (TIs) are now owned by the big hotels' exchange bureaus and are simply businesses selling advertising space to companies with fliers to distribute. They are reasonably helpful but biased. Locations include Heathrow Airport's Tube station, which serves Terminals 1, 2, and 3 (daily 8:00–18:00, most convenient and least crowded); Victoria Station (daily 8:00–20:00, crowded and commercial); and Waterloo International Terminal Arrivals Hall (daily 8:30–22:30, serving trains from Paris; if you arrive by train when the TI is mobbed, skip it, buy city map at newsstand upstairs in station lobby, then return downstairs to catch the Tube or a taxi to your hotel).

At any of the TIs, bring your itinerary and a checklist of questions. Pick up these publications: *London Planner* (a great free monthly that lists all the sights, events, and hours), walking-tour schedule fliers, a theater guide, Central London Bus Guide, and the Thames River Services brochure.

TIs sell BT phone cards, long-distance bus tickets and passes, British Heritage Passes, and tickets to plays (20 percent booking fee). They also book rooms (avoid their £5 booking fee by calling hotels direct).

The **London Pass** gives free entrance to most of the city's sights, but since many museums are free and a pass can add cluttery decisions to your trip (should I go here, there, or everywhere . . . ?), it's worthwhile only for torrid sightseers (£22/1 day, £39/2 days, £49/3 days, £69/6 days, includes 128-page guidebook, buy at any London Transport Info Centre including Heathrow, Victoria, and Paddington, www.londonpass.com). London does have many mildly interesting sights worth a quick look but not their steep £6 admission fee. With this pass, you can just go crazy.

TIs also sell **Fast Track tickets** to some of London's attractions (at no extra cost), allowing you to skip the queue at the sights. They're worthwhile for places notorious for long ticket lines, such as the Tower of London, London Eye Ferris Wheel, and Madame Tussaud's Wax Museum.

Helpful Hints

U.S. Embassy: 24 Grosvenor Square (for passport concerns, open Mon–Fri 8:30–11:30 plus Mon, Wed, and Fri 14:00–16:00, Tube: Bond Street, tel. 020/7499-9000).

Theft Alert: The Artful Dodger is alive and well in London. Be on guard, particularly on public transportation and in places crowded with tourists. Tourists, considered naive and rich, are targeted. Over 7,500 handbags are stolen annually at Covent Garden alone. Thieves paw you so you don't feel the pickpocketing.

Changing Money: ATMs are the way to go. For changing traveler's checks, standard transaction fees at banks are £2 to £4. American Express offices offer a fair rate and change any brand of traveler's checks for no fee. Handy AmEx offices are at Heathrow's Terminal 4 Tube station (daily 7:00–19:00) and near Piccadilly (June–Sept Mon–Fri 9:00–18:00, Sat 9:00–18:30, Sun 10:00–17:00; Oct–May Mon–Sat 9:00–17:30, Sun 10:00–17:00; 30 Haymarket, tel. 020/7484-9600; refund office 24-hr tel. 0800-521-313). Marks & Spencer department stores also give good rates with no fees.

Avoid changing money at exchange bureaus. Their latest scam: They advertise very good rates with a same-as-the-banks fee of 2 percent. But the fine print explains that the fee of 2 percent is for buying pounds. The fee for *selling* pounds is 9.5 percent. Ouch!

What's Up: For the best listing of what's happening (plays, movies, restaurants, concerts, exhibitions, protests, walking tours, shopping, and children's activities) and a look at the trendy London scene, pick up a current copy of *Time Out* (£2, www.timeout.co.uk) or *What's On* at any newsstand. The TI's free, monthly *London Planner* lists sights, plays, and events at least as well. For a chatty, *People Magazine*–type Web site on London's entertainment, theater, restaurants, and news, visit www.thisislondon.com. For plays, go to www.officiallondontheatre.co.uk.

Sights: Free museums include the British Museum, British Library, National Gallery, National Portrait Gallery, Tate Britain (British art), Tate Modern (modern art), Imperial War Museum, Natural History Museum, Victoria and Albert Museum, and the Royal Air Force Museum Hendon. There may be a fee for special exhibitions.

Telephoning sights first to check hours and confirm plans, especially off-season, when hours can shrink, is always smart.

Internet Access: The astonishing easyEverything offers up to 500 computers per store, 24 hours daily. Depending on the time of day, a mere £2 ticket buys anywhere from 80 minutes to six hours of computer time. The ticket is valid for four weeks and multiple visits at any of their five branches: Victoria Station (across from front of station, near taxis and buses, long lines), Trafalgar Square (456 Strand), Tottenham Court Road (9–16 Tottenham Court Road), Oxford Street (358 Oxford Street, opposite Bond Street Tube station), and Kensington High Street (160–166 Kensington High Street). EasyEverything also sells 24-hour, seven-day, and 30-day passes (www.easyeverything.com).

Travel Bookstores: Stanfords Travel Bookstore is good and stocks current editions of my books at Covent Garden (Mon–Fri 9:00–19:30, Sat 10:00–19:00, Sun 12:00–18:00, 12 Long Acre, tel. 020/7836-1321) and 156 Regent Street (tel. 020/7434-4744). There are two impressive Waterstone's bookstores: the biggest in Europe on Piccadilly (Mon–Sat 10:00–23:00, Sun 12:00–18:00, 203 Piccadilly, tel. 020/7851-2400) and one on the corner of Trafalgar Square (Mon–Sat 9:30–21:00, Sun 12:00–18:00, next to Coffee Republic café, tel. 020/7839-4411).

Beatles: Fans of the still-Fabulous Four can take one of the Beatles walks (5/week, offered by Original London Walks, see "Tours of London," below), visit the Beatles Shop (231 Baker Street, next to Sherlock Holmes Museum, Tube: Baker Street), or go to Abbey Road and walk the famous crosswalk (at intersection with Grove End, Tube: St. John's Wood).

Left Luggage: As security concerns heighten, London's train stations have replaced their lockers with a left luggage counter. Each bag must go through a scanner (just like the airport), so lines can be long. Expect up to a 20-minute wait to pick up your bags, too (each item-£5/24 hrs, daily 7:00–24:00). You can also check bags at the airports (£3.50/day). If leaving London and returning later, you may be able to leave a box or bag at your hotel for free—assuming you'll be staying there again.

Arrival in London

By Train: London has eight train stations, all connected by the Tube (subway) and all with exchange offices and luggage storage (see above). From any station, ride the Tube or taxi to your hotel.

By Bus: The bus station is one block southwest of Victoria Station, which has a TI and Tube entrance.

By Plane: For detailed information on getting from London's airports to downtown London, see "Transportation Connections" later in this chapter.

Getting around London

London's taxis, buses, and subway system make a private car unnecessary. To travel smart in a city this size, you must get comfortable with public transportation. For Tube and bus information 24 hours a day, call 020/7222-1234 (www.transportforlondon.gov.uk).

By Taxi: London is the best taxi town in Europe. Big, black, carefully regulated cabs are everywhere. I never met a crabby cabbie in London. They love to talk, and they know every nook and cranny in town. I ride in one each day just to get my London questions answered. Rides start at £1.50 and cost about £1.50 per Tube stop. Connecting downtown sights is quick and easy and will cost you about £4 (e.g., St. Paul's to the Tower of London). For a short ride, three people in a cab travel at Tube prices. Groups of four or five should taxi everywhere. If a cab's top light is on, just wave it down. (Drivers flash lights when they see you.) They have a tiny turning radius, so you can wave at cabs going in either direction. If waving doesn't work, ask someone where you can find a taxi stand. While telephoning a cab gets one in minutes, it's generally not necessary and adds to the cost. London is such a great wave-'em-down taxi-town that most cabs don't even have a radio phone. Don't worry about meter cheating. British cab meters come with a sealed computer chip and clock that ensures you'll get the regular tariff #1 most of the time, tariff #2 during "unsociable hours" (18:00–6:00 and Sat–Sun), and tariff #3 only on holidays. All extra

London

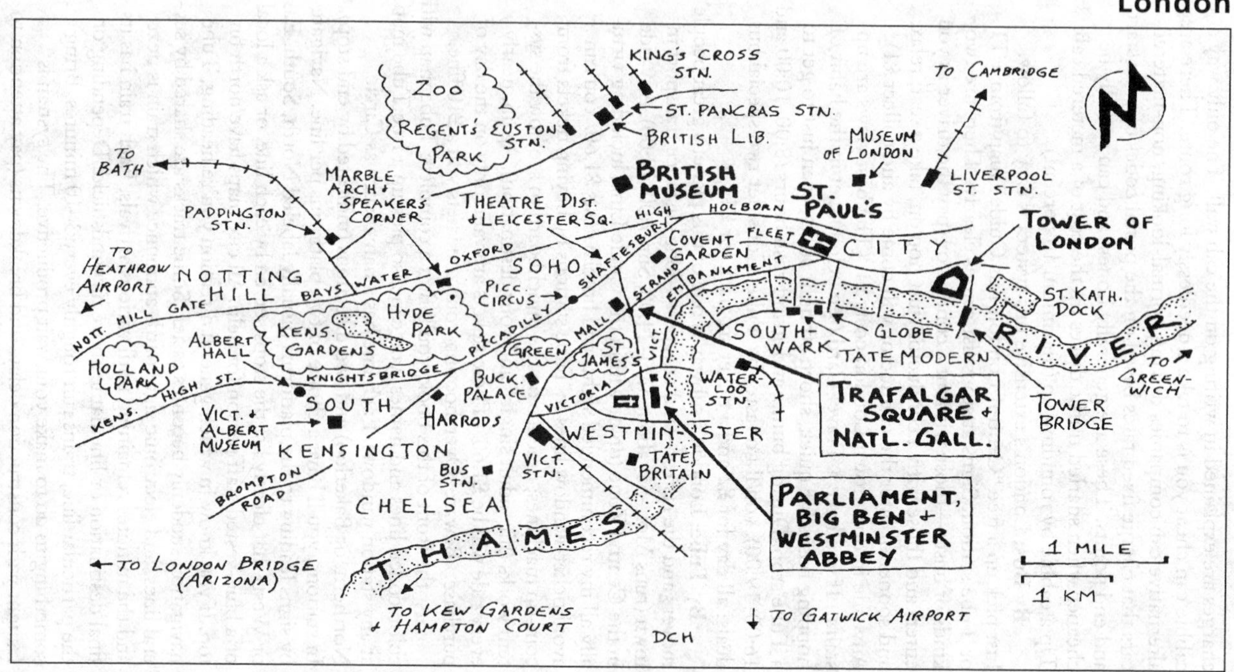
Zoo
Regent's Park
Euston Stn.
King's Cross Stn.
St. Pancras Stn.
British Lib.
To Cambridge
Museum of London
Liverpool St. Stn.
To Bath
Marble Arch + Speaker's Corner
Paddington Stn.
Theatre Dist. + Leicester Sq.
British Museum
High Holborn
St. Paul's
Fleet
City
Tower of London
To Heathrow Airport
Notting Hill
Oxford
Soho
Shaftesbury
Covent Garden
Embankment
Strand
Bayswater
Picc. Circus
Nott. Hill Gate
Hyde Park
Kens. Gardens
Piccadilly
Mall
Green
St James's
Vict.
Southwark
Globe
Tate Modern
St. Kath. Dock
River
To Greenwich
Albert Hall
Holland Park
Kens. High St.
Knightsbridge
Buck. Palace
Victoria
Waterloo Stn.
Trafalgar Square + Nat'l. Gall.
Tower Bridge
South Kensington
Vict. + Albert Museum
Harrods
Westminster
Vict. Stn.
Bus Stn.
Tate Britain
Brompton Road
Chelsea
Parliament, Big Ben + Westminster Abbey
Thames
1 Mile
1 KM
To London Bridge (Arizona)
To Kew Gardens + Hampton Court
To Gatwick Airport
DCH

charges are explained in writing on the cab wall. The only way a cabbie can cheat you is to take a needlessly long route. There are alternative cab companies driving normal-looking, non-metered cars that charge fixed rates based on the postal codes of your start and end points. These are generally honest and can actually be cheaper when snarled traffic drives up the cost of a metered cab. Tip a cabbie by rounding up (maximum 10 percent).

By Bus: London's extensive bus system is easy to follow. Just pick up a free "Central London Bus Guide" map from a TI or Tube station. Signs at stops list routes clearly. There are two kinds of buses—those without a conductor (pay the driver as you enter) and those with a conductor (just hop on, take a seat, relax, and sooner or later the conductor will come by and collect £1). Any ride in downtown London costs £1. (The best views are upstairs.) If you have a Travel Card (see below), get in the habit of hopping buses for quick, short, straight shots, even just to get to a Tube stop. During bump-and-grind rush hours (8:00–10:00 and 16:00–19:00), you'll go faster by Tube. Consider two special bus deals: all day for £2 and a ticket six-pack for £4.

By Tube: London's subway is one of this planet's great people movers and the fastest—and cheapest—long-distance transport in town (runs Mon–Sat about 5:00–24:00, Sun 7:00–23:00). Any ride in the Central Zone (on or within the Circle Line, including virtually all my recommended sights and hotels) costs £1.60. You can avoid ticket-window lines in Tube stations by buying tickets from coin-op machines; practice on the punchboard to see how the system works (hit "adult single" and your destination). Again, nearly every ride will be £1.60. (These tickets are valid only on the day of purchase.) Beware: Overshooting your zone nets you a £10 fine.

At the front of this book, you'll find a complete Tube map with color-coded lines and names (you can also pick up a free Tube map at any station window). Each line has a name (such as Circle, Northern, or Bakerloo) and two directions (indicated by end stop). In stations, you'll have a choice of two platforms per line. Navigate by signs leading to the platforms (usually labeled North, South, East, or West) that clearly list the stops served by each line, or ask a local or a blue-vested staff person for help. All city maps have north on top. If you know in which general direction you're heading, Tube navigation suddenly becomes easier. Some tracks are shared by several lines, and electronic signboards announce which train is next and the minutes remaining until various arrivals. Each train has its final destination or line name above its windshield. Depending on the particular line, trains run roughly every 3–10 minutes. Bring something to do to make your wait productive. The system is fraught with construction delays and breakdowns (pay attention to signs and announcements explaining necessary detours, etc). The Circle Line is notorious for problems. And always... mind the gap.

You can't leave the system without feeding your ticket to the turnstile. Save time by choosing the best street exit (look at the maps on the walls or ask any station personnel). "Subway" means pedestrian underpass in "English."

London Tube and Bus Passes: Consider using these passes, valid on both the Tube and buses (all passes are available for more zones and are purchased as easily as a normal ticket at any station):

One-Day pass: If you figure you'll take three rides in a day, a day pass is a good deal. The "One Day Travel Card," covering Zones 1 and 2, gives you unlimited travel for a day, starting after 9:30 on weekdays and anytime on weekends (£4.10). The all-zone version of this card costs £5 (and includes Heathrow Airport). The "One Day LT Card," covering six zones (including Heathrow) with no time restriction, costs £7.90. Families save with the "One Day Family Travel Card" (price varies depending on number in family). For details, including a handy journey planner, see www.thetube.com.

Weekend pass: The "Weekend Travel Card," covering Saturday, Sunday, and Zones 1 and 2 for £6.10, costs 25 percent less than two one-day cards.

Seven-Day pass: The "7-Day Travel Card" costs £19.30, covers Zones 1 and 2, and requires a passport-type photo (cut one out of any snapshot and bring it from home). If you have no photo, the TI at Heathrow Airport sells a similar "Visitors' Card" for about the same price without requiring a photo.

Ten rides: If you want to travel a little each day or if you're part of a group, an £11.50 *carnet* is a great deal: you get 10 separate tickets for Tube travel in Zone 1 (£1.15 per ride rather than £1.60). Wait for the machine to lay all 10 tickets.

Group deals: Groups of 10 or more can travel all day on the Tube for £3 each (not on buses).

Tours of London

▲▲▲Hop-on, Hop-off Double-Decker Bus Tours—Two competitive companies ("Original" and "Big Bus") offer essentially the same tours with buses that have live (English-only) guides, as well as some marked buses with a tape-recorded, dial-a-language narration. This two-hour, once-over-lightly bus tour drives by all the famous sights, providing a stressless way to get your bearings and at least see the biggies. You can sit back and enjoy the entire two-hour orientation tour (a good idea if you like the guide and the weather) or "hop-on and hop-off" at any of the nearly 30 stops and catch a later bus. Buses run about every 10 to 15 minutes in summer, every 20 minutes in winter. It's an inexpensive form of transport as well as an informative tour. Grab one of the maps from a TI and study it. Buses run daily (from about 9:00 until early evening in summer, until late afternoon in winter) and stop at Victoria Street (1 block north of Victoria Station), Marble Arch, Piccadilly Circus, Trafalgar Square, and elsewhere.

Each company offers a core two-hour overview tour, two other routes, and a narrated Thames boat tour covered by the same ticket (buy ticket from driver, CC accepted at major stops such as Victoria Station, ticket good for 24 hrs, bring a sweater and extra film). Note: If you start at Victoria Station at 9:00, you'll finish near Buckingham Palace in time to see the Changing of the Guard (at 11:30); ask your driver for the best place to hop off. Sunday morning—when the traffic is light and many museums are closed—is a fine time for a tour. The last full loop leaves Victoria at 18:00. Both companies have entertaining and boring guides. The narration is important. If you don't like your guide, jump off and find another. If you like your guide, settle in for the entire loop. If it rains, ask if they have a free rain poncho.

Original London Sightseeing Bus Tour: Live guided buses have a Union Jack flag and a yellow triangle on the front of the bus. If the front has many flags or a green or red triangle, it's a tape-recorded multilingual tour—avoid it, unless you have kids who'd enjoy the entertaining recorded kids' tour (£15, £2.50 discount with this book, limit 2 discounts per book, they'll rip off the corner of this page—raise bloody hell if they don't honor this discount, ticket good for 24 hrs, CC, tel. 020/8877-1722, www.theoriginaltour.com). Your ticket includes a 50-minute-long round-trip boat tour from the London Eye (departs hourly, tape-recorded narration).

Big Bus Hop-on, Hop-off London Tours: These are also good. For £16, you get the same basic tour plus coupons for four different one-hour London walks and the scenic and usually entertainingly guided Thames boat ride (normally £5) between Westminster Pier and the Tower of London. The pass and extras are valid for 24 hours. Buses with live guides are marked in front with a picture of a blue bus; buses with tape-recorded spiels display a picture of a yellow bus and headphones. While the price is steeper, Big Bus guides seem more dynamic than the Original guides (daily 8:30–18:00, July–Aug until 19:00, winter until 16:30, office a block from Victoria Station at 48 Buckingham Palace Road, tel. 020/7233-9533, www.bigbus.co.uk).

At Night: The London by Night Sightseeing Tour runs basically the same circuit as the other companies, but after hours. While the narration is pretty lame (the driver does little more than call out the names of famous places as you roll by), the views at twilight are grand (£9.50, pay driver or buy tickets at Victoria Station or Paddington Station TI, April–Oct only, 2-hr tour with live guide, can hop on and off, departs at 19:00, 20:00, and 21:00 from Victoria Station, Taxi Road, at front of station near end of Wilton Road, tel. 020/8646-1747, www.londongeneral.co.uk).

▲▲**Walking Tours**—Many times a day, top-notch local guides lead (often big) groups through specific slices of London's past. Schedule fliers litter the desks of TIs, hotels, and pubs. *Time Out* lists many, but not all, scheduled walks. Simply show up at the announced location, pay £5, and enjoy two chatty hours of Dickens, the Plague, Shakespeare, Legal London, the Beatles, Jack the Ripper, or whatever is on the agenda. Original London Walks, the dominant company, lists its extensive daily schedule in a beefy, plain black-and-white *The Original London Walks* brochure. They also run **Explorer day trips**, a good option for those with limited time and transportation (different trip daily: Stonehenge/Salisbury, Oxford/Cotswolds, York, Bath, and so on; walks offered year-round—even Christmas, get schedule at hotel or TI, private tours for £90, tel. 020/7624-3978, recorded information 020/7624-9255, www.walks.com).

Standard rates for London's registered **guides** are £85 for four hours, £136 for eight hours (tel. 020/7403-2962, www.touristguides.org.uk). Robina Brown leads tours with small groups in her Toyota Previa (£185/3 hrs, £270–400/day, tel. 020/7228-2238, www.driverguidetours.com, e-mail: robina@driverguidetours.com). Brit Lonsdale, an energetic mother of twins, is another registered London guide (£89/half day, £142/full day, tel. 020/7386-9907).

▲▲**Cruises**—Boat tours with entertaining commentaries sail regularly from **Westminster Pier** (at the base of Westminster Bridge under Big Ben). For pleasure and efficiency, consider combining a one-way cruise (to Kew, Greenwich, wherever) with a Tube ride back.

From Westminster Pier, you can sail to the **Tower of London** (£5.20 one-way, £6.30 round-trip, one-way included with Big Bus London tour; covered by £8.50 "River Red Rover" ticket that includes Greenwich—see next paragraph; 3/hr during June–Aug daily 9:40–20:40, 2/hr and shorter hours rest of year, 30 min, City Cruises).

To get from Westminster Pier to **Greenwich,** you can choose between two companies: City Cruises (£6.50 one-way, £8 round-trip; or get their £8.50 all-day, hop-on, hop-off "River Red Rover" ticket to have option of getting off at London Eye and Tower of London; June–Aug daily 9:40–18:00, less off-season, every 40 min, 70 min to Greenwich, usually narrated only downstream—to Greenwich, tel. 020/7930-9033, www.citycruises.com) and Thames River Services (£6.30 one-way,

Daily Reminder

Sunday: Some sights don't open until noon (Museum of London). The Tower of London is especially crowded today. Hyde Park Speakers' Corner rants from early afternoon until early evening. These are closed: Banqueting House, Sir John Soane's Museum, and legal sights (Houses of Parliament, Old Bailey, The City is dead). Evensong is at 15:00 at Westminster Abbey (with an organ recital at 17:45 for a fee). St. Paul's Cathedral offers an evensong service at 15:15 and a free organ recital at 17:00. Both churches are open during the day for services but are closed to sightseers (except during the organ recitals). Many stores and theaters are closed. Street markets flourish: Camden Lock, Spitalfields, Greenwich, and Petticoat Lane.

Monday: Most sights are open except Apsley House, Theatre Museum, and Sir John Soane's Museum). The St. Martin-in-the-Fields church offers a free 13:05 concert. Courtauld Gallery is free until 14:00. Vinopolis is open until 21:00.

Tuesday: All sights are open; the British Library is open until 20:00. St. Martin-in-the-Fields has a free 13:05 concert.

Wednesday: All sights are open, plus evening hours at Westminster Abbey (until 19:45), the National Gallery (until 21:00) and Victoria and Albert Museum (until 22:00).

Thursday: All sights are open. British Museum is open until 20:30 (selected galleries only), National Portrait Gallery until 21:00. St. Martin-in-the-Fields hosts a concert at 19:30 (fee).

Friday: All sights are open, British Museum until 20:30 (selected galleries only), National Portrait Gallery until 21:00, Tate Modern until 22:00. Best street market: Spitalfields. St. Martin-in-the-Fields offers two concerts (13:05—free, 19:30—fee).

Saturday: Most sights are open except legal ones (Old Bailey; Houses of Parliament—open summer Sat for tours only; skip The City). Vinopolis is open until 20:00, Tate Modern until 22:00. Best street markets: Portobello, Camden Lock, Greenwich. Evensong is at 15:00 at Westminster Abbey, 17:00 at St. Paul's. St. Martin-in-the-Fields hosts a concert at 19:30 (fee).

Notes: Evensong occurs daily at St. Paul's (Mon–Sat at 17:00 and Sun at 15:15) and daily except Wednesday at Westminster Abbey (Mon–Tue and Thu–Fri at 17:00, Sat–Sun at 15:00). London by Night Sightseeing Tour buses depart Victoria Station every evening at 20:00, 21:00, and 22:00. The London Eye Ferris Wheel spins nightly until 22:00 in summer, until 20:00 in winter (closed Jan).

£7.80 round-trip, April–Oct daily 10:00–16:00, July–Aug until 17:00, 2/hr, 50 min, has shorter hours and runs every 40 min rest of year, usually narrated only to Greenwich, tel. 020/7930-4097, www.royalriverthames.com).

Boats sail daily from Westminster Pier to **Kew Gardens** (£9 one-way, £15 round-trip, 4/day, generally departing 10:00–14:00, 90 min, narrated for 30 min, Westminster Passenger Services Association, tel. 020/7930-2062, www.wpsa.co.uk). Some boats continue on to **Hampton Court Palace** for an additional £3.

Westminster isn't the only pier in town. Fifty-minute **round-trip cruises** of the Thames leave hourly from the Waterloo Pier at the base of the London Eye (£7.50, included with Original London Bus Tour—listed above, tape-recorded narration, Catamaran Circular Cruises, tel. 020/7839-3572).

From the Embankment Pier (at Charing Cross Station), you can catch a boat to the Tower of London and Greenwich; or if you're at the Tower of London pier, you can hop a boat heading west to Westminster Pier or going east to Greenwich.

Consider exploring London's canals by taking a cruise on historic **Regent's Canal** in north London. Jenny Wren offers round-trips from Walker's Quay in Camden Town to Little Venice, including 90-minute canal boat cruises (£6, March–Oct daily 12:30, 14:30, Sat–Sun also 10:30, 16:30) and three-hour *My Fair Lady* cruises featuring gourmet spreads (£19 for Sun lunch at 13:00 year-round, £33 for 3-course dinner at 20:00—book in advance, CC, Walker's Quay, 250 Camden High Street, Tube: Camden Town, tel. 020/7485-4433 or 020/7485-6210, www.walkersquay.com). While in Camden Town, stop by the popular Camden Lock Market to browse through trendy arts and crafts (daily 10:00–18:00, busiest on weekends, a block from Walker's Quay, tel. 020/7284-2084, www.camdenlock.net).

Frog Tours—A bright-yellow amphibious vehicle takes you streetside past some famous sights (Big Ben, Buckingham Palace, Piccadilly Circus), then splashes into the Thames for a 30-minute cruise (£15, daily 10:00–18:00, 70 min, live commentary, these book up in advance, departs from Belvedere Road behind County Hall near London Eye Ferris Wheel, Tube: Waterloo or Westminster, tel. 020/7928-3132, www.frogtours.com, e-mail: enquiries@frogtours.com).

Sights—From Westminster Abbey to Trafalgar Square

▲▲**Westminster Walk**—Just about every visitor to London strolls the historic Whitehall boulevard from Big Ben to Trafalgar Square. Beneath London's modern traffic and big-city bustle lies

2,000 fascinating years of history. This three-quarter-mile, self-guided orientation walk (see map on next page) gives you a whirlwind tour and connects the sights listed in this section.

Start halfway across **Westminster Bridge** (#1 on map) for that "Wow, I'm really in London!" feeling. Get a close-up view of the **Houses of Parliament** and **Big Ben** (floodlit at night). Downstream you'll see the **London Eye Ferris Wheel**. Down the stairs to Westminster Pier are boats to the Tower of London and Greenwich.

En route to Parliament Square, you'll pass a statue of **Boadicea** (#2), the Celtic queen defeated by Roman invaders in A.D. 60.

To thrill your loved ones (or bug the envious), call home from a pay phone near Big Ben at about three minutes before the hour. You'll find a phone on Great George Street, across from Parliament Square. As Big Ben chimes, stick the receiver outside the booth and prove you're in London: Ding dong ding dong . . . dong ding ding dong.

Wave hello to Churchill in Parliament Square (#3). To his right is **Westminster Abbey** with its two stubby, elegant towers.

Walk north up Parliament Street (which turns into Whitehall) toward Trafalgar Square. You'll see the thought-provoking **Cenotaph** (#5) in the middle of the street, reminding passersby of Britain's many war dead. To visit the Cabinet War Rooms (see below) take a left before the Cenotaph, on King Charles Street (#4).

Continuing on Whitehall, stop at the barricaded and guarded little **10 Downing Street** to see the British "White House" (#6), home of the prime minister. Break the bobby's boredom and ask him a question.

Nearing Trafalgar Square, look for the **Horse Guards** behind the gated fence (11:00 inspection Mon–Sat, 10:00 on Sun; dismounting ceremony daily at 16:00) and the 17th-century **Banqueting House** across the street (#7; see below).

The column topped by Lord Nelson marks **Trafalgar Square** (#8). The stately domed building on the far side of the square is the **National Gallery** (free), which has a classy café (upstairs in the Sainsbury wing). To the right of the National Gallery is **St. Martin-in-the-Fields Church** and its Café in the Crypt.

To get to Piccadilly from Trafalgar Square, walk up Cockspur Street to Haymarket, then take a short left on Coventry Street to colorful **Piccadilly Circus**.

Near Piccadilly you'll find the **Britain Visitors Centre** and piles of theaters. **Leicester Square** (with its half-price ticket booth for plays) thrives just a few blocks away. Walk through seedy **Soho** (north of Shaftesbury Avenue) for its fun pubs (see

Westminster Walk

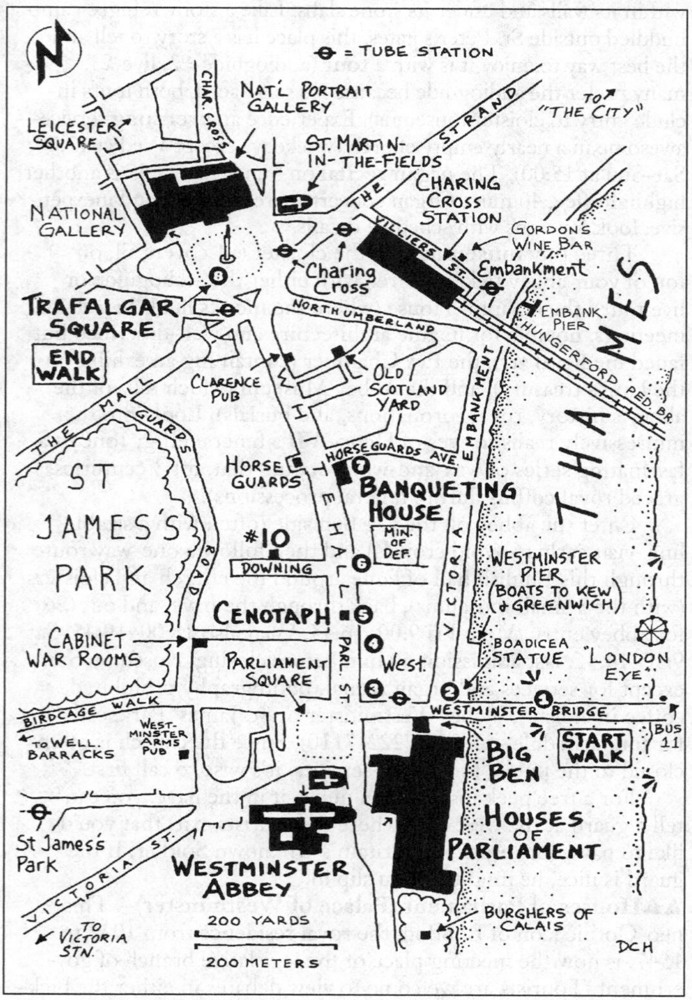

"Eating," below, for Food is Fun Dinner Crawl). From Piccadilly or Oxford Circus, you can taxi, bus, or Tube home.

▲▲▲**Westminster Abbey**—As the greatest church in the English-speaking world, Westminster Abbey has been the place where England's kings and queens have been crowned and buried since 1066. A thousand years of English history—3,000 tombs, the remains of 29 kings and queens, and hundreds of memorials—lie within its walls and under its stone slabs. Like a stony refugee camp huddled outside St. Peter's gates, this place has a story to tell and the best way to enjoy it is with a **tour** (audioguide-£2, live-£3; many prefer the audioguide because it's self-paced, both tours include entry to cloister museums). Experience an **evensong** service—awesome in a nearly empty church (weekdays except Wed at 17:00, Sat–Sun at 15:00). The **organ recital** on Sunday at 17:45 is another highlight (fee, 40 min). Organ concerts here are great and inexpensive; look for signs with schedule details.

Three tiny **museums** ring the cloister (£1 covers all, on top of your abbey ticket; or free with either the audioguide or live tour): the Chapter House (where the monks held their daily meetings, notable for its fine architecture and well-described but faded medieval art), the Pyx Chamber (containing an exhibit on the king's treasury), and the Abbey Museum (which tells of the abbey's history, royal coronations, and burials). Look into the impressively realistic eyes of Henry VII's funeral effigy (one of a fascinating series of wax-and-wood statues that, for 3 centuries, graced royal coffins during funeral processions).

Enter the abbey on the Big Ben side (often with a sizable line, visit early to avoid crowds) and then follow a one-way route through this English hall of fame around the church and cloisters (with the 3 small museums), back through the nave, and out (£6 for abbey entry, Mon–Fri 9:00–16:45, Wed also 18:00–19:45, Sat 9:30–14:45, last admission 60 min before closing, closed on Sun except for services and organ recital, photography prohibited, coffee in cloister, Tube: Westminster or St. James' Park, call for tour schedule, tel. 020/7222-7110). Since the church is often closed to the public for special services, it's wise to call first.

For a free peek inside and a quiet sit in the nave, you can tell a guard at the west end (where the tourists exit) that you'd like to pay your respects to Britain's Unknown Soldier. If the guard is nice, he might let you slip in.

▲▲Houses of Parliament (Palace of Westminster)—This neo-Gothic icon of London, the royal residence from 1042 to 1547, is now the meeting place of the legislative branch of government. Tourists are welcome to view debates in either the bickering House of Commons or the genteel House of Lords (when in session—indicated by a flag flying atop the Victoria Tower). While the actual debates are generally extremely dull, it is a thrill to be inside and see the British government inaction (House of Commons: Mon–Wed 14:30–22:30, Thu 11:30–19:30, Fri 9:30–15:00, generally less action and no lines after 18:00, use St. Stephen's entrance, Tube: Westminster, tel. 020/7219-4272 for schedule, www.parliament.uk). The House of Lords has more pageantry, shorter lines, and less interesting debates (Mon–Wed 15:00 until they finish, Thu from 15:00 on, sometimes Fri from 11:00 on, tel. 020/7219-3107 for schedule). If there's only one line outside, it's for the House of Commons. Go to the gate and tell the guard you want the Lords. You may pop right in—that is, after you've cleared the security gauntlet. Once you've seen the Lords (hide your HOL flier), you can often slip directly over to the House of Commons and join the gang waiting in the lobby. Inside the lobby, you'll find an announcement board with the day's lineup for both houses.

Just past security to the left, study the big dark **Westminster Hall**, which survived the 1834 fire. The hall is 11th century, and its famous self-supporting hammer-beam roof was added in 1397. The Houses of Parliament are located in what was once the Palace of Westminster, long the palace of England's medieval kings, until it was largely destroyed by fire in 1834. The palace was rebuilt in Victorian Gothic style (a move away from neoclassicism back to England's Christian and medieval heritage, true to the Romantic Age). It was completed in 1860.

Houses of Parliament tours are offered in August and September (£7; 75 min, Mon, Tue, Fri, and Sat 9:15–16:30; Wed and Thu 13:15–16:30; to avoid waits, book in advance through First Call, tel. 0870/906-3773, www.firstcalltickets.com, no booking fee). Meet your Blue Badge guide (at the Sovereign's Entrance—far south end) for a behind-the-scenes peek at the royal chambers and both Houses.

The **Jewel Tower,** along with Westminster Hall, is all that survives of the old Palace of Westminster. It contains a fine little exhibit on Parliament (first floor—history, second floor—Parliament today) with a 25-minute video and lonely, picnic-friendly benches (£1.60, daily April–Sept 10:00–18:00, Oct 10:00–17:00, Nov–March 10:00–16:00, closed Dec 24–26 and Jan 1, across street from St. Stephen's Gate, tel. 020/7222-2219).

Big Ben, the clock tower (315 feet high), is named for its 13-ton bell, Ben. The light above the clock is lit when the House of Commons is sitting. The face of the clock is huge—you can actually see the minute hand moving. For a great view, walk halfway over Westminster Bridge.

▲▲Cabinet War Rooms—This is a fascinating walk through the underground headquarters of the British government's fight against the Nazis in the darkest days of the Battle for Britain. The 21-room nerve center of the British war effort was used from 1939 to 1945. Churchill's room, the map room, and other rooms are just as they were in 1945. For all the blood, sweat, toil, and tears details, pick up an audioguide at the entry and follow the included and excellent 45-minute tour; be patient—it's worth it (£5.80, daily April–Oct 9:30–18:00, Nov–March 10:00–18:00, last entry 45 min before closing, on King Charles Street 200 yards off Whitehall, follow the signs, Tube: Westminster, tel. 020/7930-6961, www.iwm.org.uk). For a nearby pub lunch, try the Westminster Arms (food served downstairs, on Storey's Gate, a couple of blocks south of War Rooms).

Horse Guards—The Horse Guards change daily at 11:00 (10:00 on Sun), and there's a colorful dismounting ceremony daily at 16:00. The rest of the day, they just stand there—terrible for camcorders (on Whitehall, between Trafalgar Square and #10 Downing Street, Tube: Westminster). While Buckingham Palace pageantry is canceled when it rains, the horse guards change regardless of the weather.

▲Banqueting House—England's first Renaissance building was designed by Inigo Jones around 1620. It's one of the few London landmarks spared by the 1666 fire and the only surviving part of the original Palace of Whitehall. Don't miss its Rubens ceiling, which, at Charles I's request, drove home the doctrine of the legitimacy of the divine right of kings. In 1649—divine right ignored—Charles I was beheaded on the balcony of this building by a Cromwellian parliament. Admission includes a restful 20-minute audiovisual history, which shows the place in banqueting action; a 30-minute tape-recorded tour—interesting only to history buffs; and a look at the exquisite banqueting hall (£4, Mon–Sat 10:00–17:00, closed Sun, last entry at 16:30, subject to closure for government functions, aristocratic WC, immediately across Whitehall from the Horse Guards, Tube: Westminster, tel. 020/7930-4179). Just up the street is Trafalgar Square.

Sights—Trafalgar Square

▲▲Trafalgar Square—London's central square is a thrilling place to simply hang out. Lord Nelson stands atop his 185-foot-tall fluted granite column, gazing out to Trafalgar, where he lost his life but defeated the French fleet. Part of this 1842 memorial is made from his victims' melted-down cannons. He's surrounded by giant lions, hordes of people, and—until recently—even more pigeons. London's new mayor, nicknamed "Red Ken" for his passion for an activist government, decided that London's "flying rats" were a public nuisance and evicted the venerable seed salesmen. This high-profile square is the climax of most marches and demonstrations (Tube: Charing Cross).

▲▲▲National Gallery—Displaying Britain's top collection of European paintings from 1250 to 1900 (works by Leonardo,

Botticelli, Velázquez, Rembrandt, Turner, van Gogh, and the Impressionists), this is one of Europe's great galleries. While the collection is huge, following the 28-stop route suggested on the map on page 570–71 will give you my best quick visit. The audioguide tours are the best I've used in Europe (voluntary £4 donation requested). Don't miss the Micro Gallery, a computer room even your dad could have fun in (closes 30 min earlier than museum); you can study any artist, style, or topic in the museum and even print out a tailor-made tour map (free, daily 10:00–18:00, Wed until 21:00, free 1-hour overview tours daily at 11:30 and 14:30 plus Wed at 18:30, closed Dec 24–26, Jan 1, and Good Friday, photography prohibited, on Trafalgar Square, Tube: Charing Cross or Leicester Square, tel. 020/7747-2885, www.nationalgallery.org).

▲▲National Portrait Gallery—Put off by halls of 19th-century characters who meant nothing to me, I used to call this "as interesting as someone else's yearbook." But a selective walk through this 500-year-long Who's Who of British history is quick and free and puts faces on the story of England. A bonus is the chance to admire some great art by painters such as Holbein, Van Dyck, Hogarth, Reynolds, and Gainsborough. The collection is well described, not huge, and in historical sequence, from the 16th century on the second floor to today's royal family on the ground floor.

Some highlights: Henry VIII and wives; several fascinating portraits of the "Virgin Queen" Elizabeth I, Sir Francis Drake, and Sir Walter Raleigh; the only real-life portrait of William Shakespeare; Oliver Cromwell and Charles I with his head on; self-portraits and other portraits by Gainsborough and Reynolds; the Romantics (Blake, Byron, Wordsworth, and company); Queen Victoria and her era; and the present royal family, including the late Princess Diana.

The excellent audioguide tours (£3 donation requested) describe each room (or era in British history) and more than 300 paintings. You'll learn more about British history than art and actually hear interviews with 20th-century subjects as you stare at their faces (free, daily 10:00–18:00, Thu–Fri until 21:00, entry 100 yards off Trafalgar Square, around corner from National Gallery, opposite Church of St. Martin-in-the-Fields, tel. 020/7306-0055, recorded info tel. 020/7312-2463, www.npg.org.uk). The elegant Portrait Restaurant on the top floor comes with views and high prices (cheaper Portrait Café in basement).

▲St. Martin-in-the-Fields—This church, built in the 1720s with a Gothic spire atop a Greek-type temple, is an oasis of peace on the wild and noisy Trafalgar Square (free, donations welcome, open

National Gallery

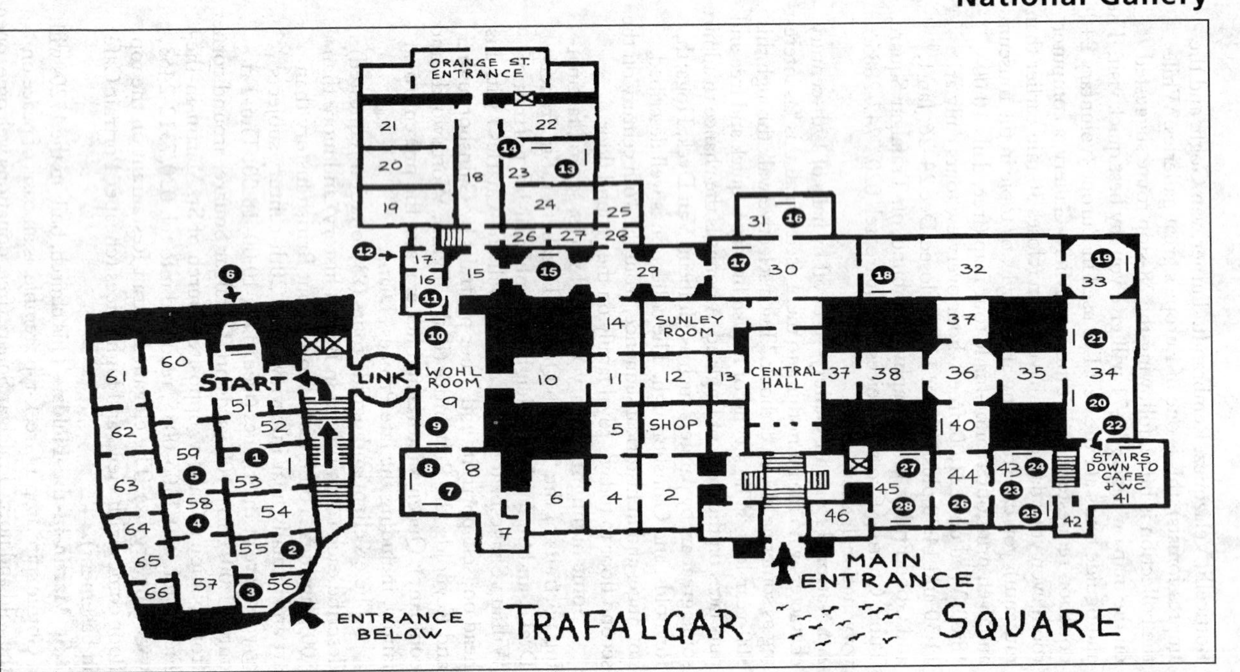

MEDIEVAL & EARLY RENAISSANCE

1 Wilton Diptych
2 UCCELLO Battle of San Romano
3 VAN EYCK Arnolfini Marriage
4 CRIVELLI Annunciation with St. Emidius
5 BOTTICELLI Venus and Mars

HIGH RENAISSANCE

6 LEONARDO DA VINCI Virgin and Child (painting and cartoon)

NATIONAL GALLERY MAIN BUILDING - HIGH RENAISSANCE

7 MICHELANGELO Entombment
8 RAPHAEL Pope Julius II

VENETIAN RENAISSANCE

9 TITIAN Bacchus and Ariadne
10 TINTORETTO Origin of the Milky Way

NORTHERN PROTESTANT ART

11 VERMEER Young Woman
12 "A PEEPSHOW"
13 REMBRANDT Belshazzar's Feast
14 REMBRANDT Self-Portrait

BAROQUE & ROCOCO

15 RUBENS The Judgment of Paris
16 VAN DYCK Charles I on Horseback
17 VELAZQUEZ The Rokeby Venus
18 CARAVAGGIO Supper at Emmaus
19 BOUCHER Pan and Syrinx

BRITISH

20 CONSTABLE The Hay Wain
21 TURNER The Fighting Temeraire
22 DELAROCHE The Execution of Lady Jane Grey

IMPRESSIONISM & BEYOND

23 MONET Gare St. Lazare
24 MONET The Water Lily Pond
25 MANET The Waitress (La Servante de Bocks)
26 SEURAT Bathers at Asnieres
27 VAN GOGH Sunflowers
28 CEZANNE Bathers

daily, www.stmartin-in-the-fields.org). St. Martin cared for the poor. "In the fields" was where the first church stood on this spot (in the 13th century), between Westminster and The City. Stepping inside, you still feel a compassion for the needs of the people in this community. A free flier provides a brief yet worthwhile self-guided tour. The church is famous for its concerts. Consider a free lunchtime concert (Mon, Tue, and Fri at 13:05) or an evening concert (£6–16, Thu–Sat at 19:30, CC, box office tel. 020/7839-8362, church tel. 020/7766-1100). Downstairs, you'll find a ticket office for concerts, a gift shop, a brass-rubbing center, and a fine support-the-church cafeteria (see "Eating," below).

More Top Squares: Piccadilly, Soho, and Covent Garden

▲▲Piccadilly Circus—London's most touristy square got its name from the fancy ruffled shirts—*picadils*—made in the neighborhood long ago. Today the square is surrounded by fascinating streets swimming with youth on the rampage. For overstimulation, drop by the extremely trashy **Pepsi Trocadero Center**'s "theme park of the future" for its Segaworld virtual-reality games, nine-screen cinema, and thundering IMAX theater (admission to Trocadero is free; individual attractions cost £2–8; before paying full price for IMAX, look for a discount ticket at brochure racks at TI or hotels; between Coventry and Shaftesbury, just off Piccadilly). Chinatown, to the east, has swollen since Hong Kong lost its independence. Nearby Shaftesbury Avenue and Leicester Square teem with fun seekers, theaters, Chinese restaurants, and street singers.

Soho—North of Piccadilly, seedy Soho is becoming trendy and is well worth a gawk. Soho is London's red-light district, where "friendly models" wait in tiny rooms up dreary stairways and voluptuous con artists sell strip shows. While venturing up a stairway to check out a model is interesting, anyone who goes into any one of the shows will be ripped off. Every time. Even a £5 show in a "licensed bar" comes with a £100 cover or minimum (as it's printed on the drink menu) and a "security man." You may accidentally buy a £200 bottle of bubbly. And suddenly, the door has no handle. By the way, telephone sex is hard to avoid these days in London. Phone booths are littered with racy fliers of busty ladies "new in town." Some travelers gather six or eight phone booths' worth of fliers and take them home for kinky wallpaper.

▲▲Covent Garden—This boutique-ish shopping district is a people-watcher's delight, with cigarette eaters, Punch-and-Judy acts, food that's good for you (but not your wallet),

London's Top Squares

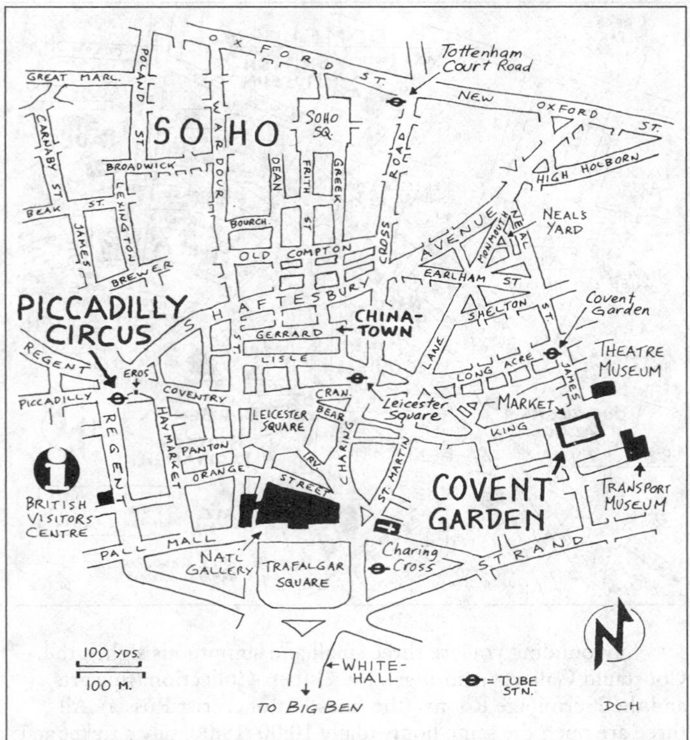

trendy crafts, sweet whiffs of marijuana, two-tone hair (neither natural), and faces that could set off a metal detector (Tube: Covent Garden). For better Covent Garden lunch deals, walk a block or two away from the eye of this touristic hurricane (check out the places north of the Tube station along Endell and Neal Streets).

Museums near Covent Garden

▲▲Somerset House—This grand 18th-century civic palace offers a marvelous public space, three fine art collections, and a riverside terrace (between the Strand and the Thames). The palace once housed the national registry that records Britain's births, marriages, and deaths ("where they hatched 'em, latched 'em, and dispatched 'em"). Step into the courtyard to enjoy the fountain. Go ahead... walk through it. The 55 jets get playful twice an hour.

Central London

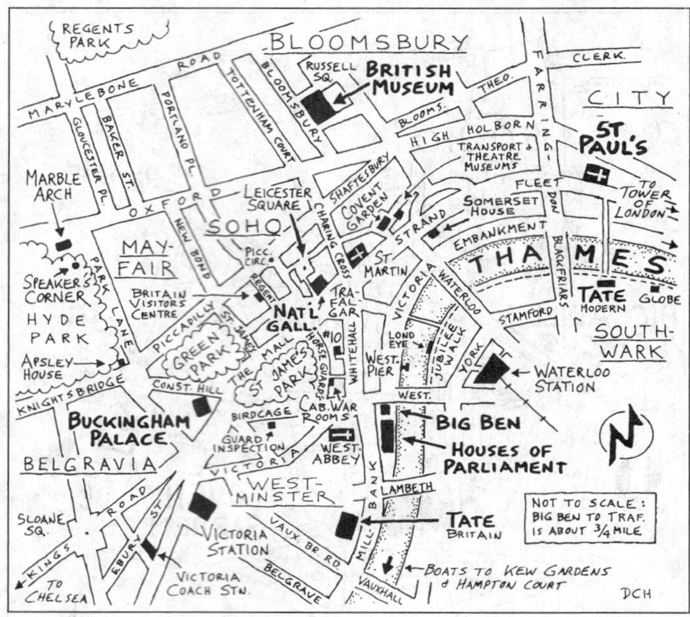

Surrounding you are three small and sumptuous sights: the Courtauld Gallery (paintings), the Gilbert Collection (fine arts), and the Hermitage Rooms (the finest art of czarist Russia). All three are open the same hours (daily 10:00–18:00, buy a ticket at 1 gallery and get a £1 discount off admission to either or both of the other 2 on the same day, easy bus #6, #9, #11, #13, #15, or #23 from Trafalgar Square, Tube: Temple or Covent Garden, tel. 020/7848-2526 or 020/7845-4600, www.somerset-house.org.uk). The Web site lists a busy schedule of tours, kids' events, and concerts. The riverside terrace is picnic-friendly (deli inside lobby).

The **Courtauld Gallery**, while less impressive than the National Gallery, is a joy. The gallery is part of the Courtauld Institute of Art, and the thoughtful descriptions of each painting in this wonderful collection remind visitors that the gallery is still used for teaching. You'll see medieval European paintings and works by Rubens, the Impressionists (Manet, Monet, Degas, Seurat), Post-Impressionists (such as Cézanne), and more (£5, free Mon until 14:00, last admission 17:15, downstairs cafeteria, cloakroom, lockers, and WC).

The **Hermitage Rooms** offer a taste of Romanov imperial

splendor. As Russia struggles and tourists are staying away, someone had the bright idea of sending the best of its art to London to raise some hard cash. These five rooms host a different collection every six months, with a standard intro to the czar's winter palace in St. Petersburg (£6, includes unmissable live video of the square, last admission 17:00, tel. 020/7420-9410). The excellent audioguide offered for some collections costs £3 . . . consider it charity for Russia.

The **Gilbert Collection** displays 800 pieces of the finest in European decorative arts, from diamond-studded gold snuff-boxes to intricate Italian mosaics. Maybe you've seen Raphael paintings and Botticelli frescoes . . . but this lush collection is refreshingly different (£5, includes free audioguide with a highlights tour and a kid-friendly tour, free after 16:30, last admission 17:30).

▲London Transport Museum—This wonderful museum is a delight for kids. Whether you're cursing or marveling at the buses and Tube, the growth of Europe's biggest city has been made possible by its public transit system. Watch the growth of the Tube, then sit in the simulator to "drive" a train (£6, kids under 16 free, Sat–Thu 10:00–18:00, Fri 11:00–18:00, 30 yards southeast of Covent Garden's marketplace, tel. 020/7379-6344).

Theatre Museum—This earnest museum, worthwhile for theater buffs, traces the development of British theater from Shakespeare to today (free, Tue–Sun 10:00–18:00, closed Mon, free guided tours at 11:00, 12:00, and 16:00, a block east of Covent Garden's marketplace down Russell Street, tel. 020/7943-4700, www.theatremuseum.org).

Sights—North London

▲▲▲British Museum, Great Court, and Reading Room—Simply put, this is the greatest chronicle of civilization . . . anywhere. A visit here is like taking a long hike through Encyclopedia Britannica National Park. Entering on Great Russell Street, you'll step into the Great Court, the glass-domed hub of a two-acre cultural complex, containing restaurants, shops, and lecture halls plus the Round Reading Room.

The most popular sections of the museum fill the ground floor: Egyptian, Mesopotamian, and ancient Greek—with the famous Elgin Marbles from the Athenian Parthenon. Huge winged lions (which guarded Assyrian palaces 800 years before Christ) guard these great ancient galleries. For a brief tour, connect these ancient dots:

Start with the **Egyptian**. Wander from the Rosetta Stone past the many statues. At the end of the hall, climb the stairs to mummy land.

British Museum

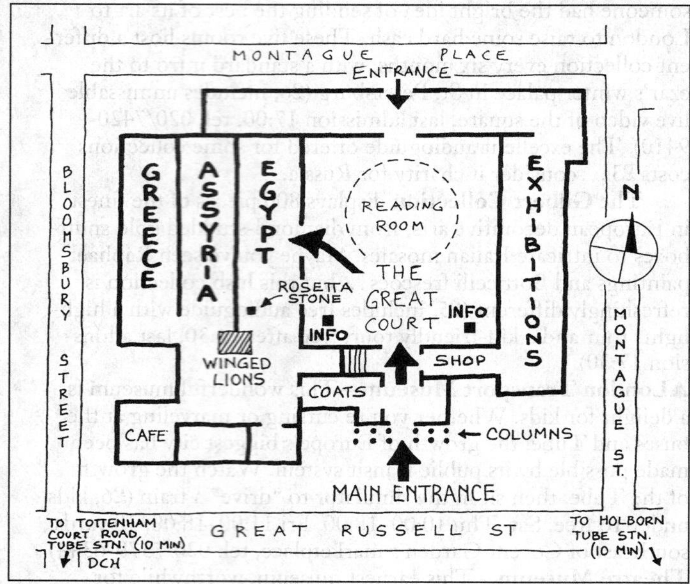

Back at the winged lions, wander through the dark, violent, and mysterious **Assyrian** rooms. The Nimrud Gallery is lined with royal propaganda reliefs and wounded lions.

The most modern of the ancient art fills the **Greek** section. Find room 11 behind the winged lions and start your walk through Greek art history with the simple and primitive Cycladic fertility figures. Later, painted vases show a culture really into partying. The finale is the Elgin Marbles. The much-wrangled-over bits of the Athenian Parthenon (from 450 B.C.) are even more impressive than they look. To best appreciate these ancient carvings, take the audioguide tour (available in this gallery).

Be sure to venture upstairs to see artifacts from **Roman Britain** (Room 50) that surpass anything you'll see at Hadrian's Wall or elsewhere in Britain. Nearby, the Dark Age Britain exhibits offer a worthwhile peek at that bleak era; look for the Sutton Hoo Ship Burial artifacts from a seventh-century royal burial on the east coast of England (Room 41). A rare Michelangelo cartoon is in Room 90.

The British Museum is revving up for its 250th birthday in 2003. The immense yet empty King's Library (once the home of the treasures of the British Library—now housed elsewhere) lines the east side of the Great Court. The plan: restore it to its Regency splendor (1827), restock the shelves with the leather-bound volumes from the House of Commons Library, and fill the hall with a special exhibit featuring museums of the Enlightenment.

The **Queen Elizabeth II Great Court** is Europe's largest covered square—bigger than a football field. This people-friendly court—delightfully out of the London rain—was for 150 years one of London's great lost spaces . . . closed off and gathering dust. While the vast British Museum wraps around the court, its centerpiece is the stately **Reading Room**—famous as the place Karl Marx hung out while formulating his ideas on communism and writing *Das Kapital*. The Reading Room—one of the fine cast-iron buildings of the 19th century—is free to wander, but there's little to see that you can't see from the doorway.

Hours and Location: The British Museum and the Reading Room are both free (£2 donation requested, daily 10:00–17:30, Thu–Fri until 20:30—only selected galleries and Reading Room are open after 17:30, least crowded weekday late afternoons, closed on Good Friday, Dec 24–26, and Jan 1, Great Russell Street, Tube: Tottenham Court Road, tel. 020/7323-8000 or 020/7388-2227, www.thebritishmuseum.ac.uk). The Great Court has longer opening hours than the museum (daily 9:00–18:00, Thu–Sat until 23:00). The Reading Room, located within the Great Court, is free and open to the quiet public (daily 12:30–17:30, Thu–Fri until 20:30, may change opening to 10:30 in 2003, Reading Room viewing area opens at 10:00). Computer terminals within the Reading Room offer COMPASS, a database of information about selected museum items.

Tours: The museum offers three **guided tours** of its immense collection: Highlights (£8, children under 11 and students with ID £5, 3/day, 90 min), Focus (£5, 1/day, 60 min), and Eye Openers (free, nearly hrly, 50 min). For tour times, call ahead or check schedule and brochures at entry. There are three kinds of **audioguide tours**: Top 50 highlights (90 min, pick up at Great Court information desks), the Parthenon Sculptures (60 min, pick up at desk outside Parthenon Galleries) and the family tour, with themes such as "bodies, board games, and beasts" (length varies, pick up at Great Court information desks); to rent an audioguide, pay £3.50 and leave a photo ID and £10 for a deposit. On the first Tuesday of the month, the museum offers evening tours, lectures, and music (£5, 18:00–21:00).

▲▲▲British Library—The British Empire built its greatest monuments out of paper. And it's in literature that England made her lasting contribution to civilization and the arts. Britain's national archives has more than 12 million books, 180 miles of shelving, and the deepest basement in London. But everything

British Library

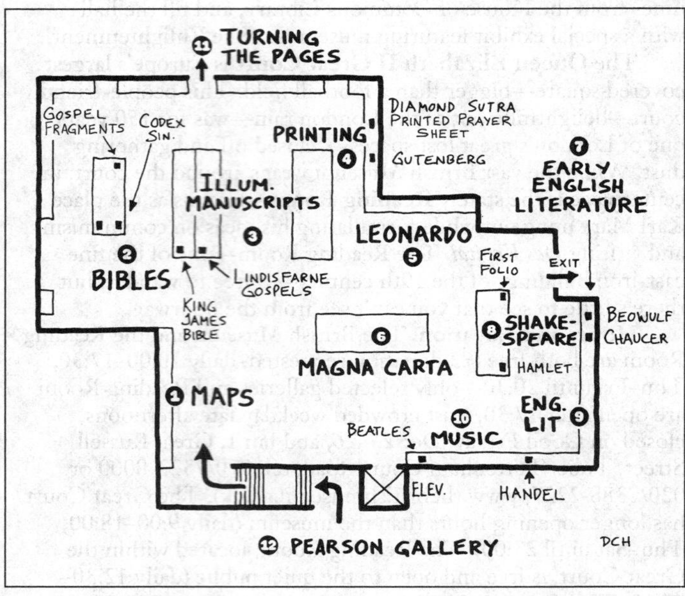

that matters for your visit is in one delightful room labeled "The Treasures." This room is filled with literary and historical documents that changed the course of history. You'll trace the evolution of European maps over 800 years. Follow the course of the Bible—from the earliest known gospels (written on scraps of papyrus) to the first complete Bible to the original King James version and the Gutenberg Bible. You'll see Leonardo's doodles, the Magna Carta, Shakespeare's First Folio, the original *Alice in Wonderland* in Lewis Carroll's handwriting, and manuscripts by Beethoven, Mozart, Lennon, and McCartney. Finish in the fascinating *Turning the Pages* exhibit, which lets you actually browse through virtual manuscripts of a few of these treasures on a computer (free, Mon–Fri 9:30–18:00, Tue until 20:00, Sat until 17:00, Sun 11:00–17:00; 1-hour tours for £5 usually offered Mon, Wed, and Fri–Sun at 15:00, also Tue 18:30, Sat 10:30, and Sun 11:30; £3.50 audioguide; £1 lockers, tel. 020/7412-7332 to confirm schedule and reserve, Tube: King's Cross, turn right out of station and walk a block to 96 Euston Road, library tel. 020/7412-7000, www.bl.uk). The ground-floor café is next to a vast and fun pull-out stamp collection, and the cafeteria upstairs serves good hot meals.

▲**Madame Tussaud's Wax Museum**—This is expensive, but

dang good. The original Madame Tussaud did wax casts of heads lopped off during the French Revolution (e.g., Marie Antoinette). She took her show on the road and ended up in London. And now it's much easier to be featured. The gallery is one big Who's Who photo-op—a huge hit with the kind of travelers who skip the British Museum. Don't miss the "make a model" exhibit (showing Jerry Hall getting waxed) or the gallery of has-been heads that no longer merit a body (such as Sammy Davis Jr. and Nikita Khruschev). After looking a hundred famous people in their glassy eyes and surviving a silly hall of horror, you'll board a Disney-type ride and cruise through a kid-pleasing "Spirit of London" time trip (£14.95, children-£10.50, under 5 free, tickets include entrance to the London Planetarium, Jan–Sept daily 9:00–17:30, Oct–Dec Mon–Fri 10:00–17:30, Sat–Sun 9:30–17:30, last entry 30 min before closing, Marylebone Road, Tube: Baker Street). The waxworks are popular. Avoid a wait by either booking ahead to get a ticket with an entry time (tel. 0870-400-3000, online at www.madame-tussauds.com for a £2 fee, or at any TI in London at no extra cost) or arriving late in the day—90 minutes is plenty of time for the exhibit.

Sir John Soane's Museum—Architects and fans of eclectic knickknacks love this quirky place (free, Tue–Sat 10:00–17:00, first Tue of the month also 18:00–21:00, closed Sun–Mon, £3 guided tours Sat at 14:30, 5 blocks east of British Museum, Tube: Holborn, 13 Lincoln's Inn Fields, tel. 020/7405-2107).

Sights—Buckingham Palace

▲Buckingham Palace—This lavish home has been Britain's royal residence since 1837. When the queen's at home, the royal standard flies; otherwise the Union Jack flaps in the wind (£11.50 for state apartments and throne room, open early Aug–Sept only, daily 9:00–17:00, only 8,000 visitors a day—to get an entry time, come early or for £1 extra book ahead by phone or online, Tube: Victoria, tel. 020/7321-2233, www.the-royal-collection.com, e-mail: buckinghampalace@royalcollection.org.uk).

Royal Mews—Actually the queen's working stables, the "mews" are open to visitors to wander, talk to the horse-keeper, and see the well-groomed horses. Marvel at the gilded coaches paraded during royal festivals, see fancy horse gear—all well-described—and learn how skeptical the attendants were when the royals first parked a car in the stables (£5, April–Oct 11:00–16:00, closed Nov–March, Buckingham Palace Road, book ahead by phone or online-£1 extra, tel.020/7321-2233, www.the-royal-collection.com, e-mail: buckinghampalace@royalcollection.org.uk).

▲▲Changing of the Guard at Buckingham Palace—The guards

change with much fanfare at 11:30 daily April through August and generally every even-numbered day September through March (no band when wet; worth a 50p phone call any day to confirm that they'll change, tel. 020/7321-2233). Join the mob behind the palace (the front faces a huge and extremely private park). You'll need to be early or tall to see much of the actual Changing of the Guard, but for the pageantry in the street you can pop by at 11:30. Stake out the high ground on the circular Victoria Monument for the best overall view. The marching troops and bands are colorful and even stirring, but the actual Changing of the Guard is a non-event. It is interesting, however, to see nearly every tourist in London gathered in one place at the same time. Hop into a big black taxi and say, "Buck House, please." The show lasts about 30 minutes: Three troops parade by, the guard changes with much shouting, the band plays a happy little concert, and then they march out. On a balmy day, it's a fun happening.

For all the pomp with none of the crowds, see the colorful **Inspection of the Guard** ceremony at 11:00 in front of the **Wellington Barracks**, 500 yards east of the palace on Birdcage Walk. Afterward, stroll through nearby St. James' Park (Tube: Victoria, St. James' Park, or Green Park).

Sights—West London

▲Hyde Park and Speakers' Corner—London's "Central Park," originally Henry VIII's hunting grounds, has more than 600 acres of lush greenery, a huge man-made lake, the royal Kensington Palace (not worth touring), and the ornate neo-Gothic Albert Memorial across from the Royal Albert Hall. Early afternoons on Sunday (until early evening), Speakers' Corner offers soapbox oratory at its best (Tube: Marble Arch). "The grass roots of democracy" is actually a holdover from when the gallows stood here, and the criminal was allowed to say just about anything he wanted to before he swung. I dare you to raise your voice and gather a crowd—it's easy to do.

▲Apsley House (Wellington Museum)—Having beaten Napoleon at Waterloo, the Duke of Wellington was once the most famous man in Europe. He was given London's ultimate address, #1 London. His newly refurbished mansion offers one of London's best palace experiences. An 11-foot-tall marble statue (by Canova) of Napoleon, clad only in a fig leaf, greets you. Downstairs is a small gallery of Wellington memorabilia (including a pair of Wellington boots). The lavish upstairs shows off the duke's fine collection of paintings, including works by Velázquez and Steen (£4.50, Tue–Sun 11:00–17:00, closed Mon, well-described by included audioguide, 20 yards from Hyde Park Corner Tube station, tel. 020/7499-5676,

West London

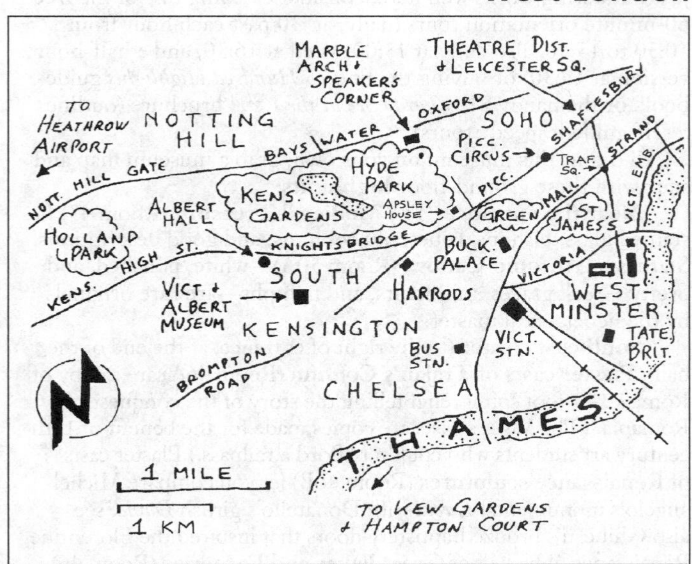

www.apsleyhouse.org.uk). Hyde Park's pleasant and picnic-wonderful rose garden is nearby.

▲▲Victoria and Albert Museum—The world's top collection of decorative arts (vases, stained glass, fine furniture, clothing, jewelry, carpets, and more) is a surprisingly interesting assortment of crafts from the West as well as Asian and Islamic cultures.

The V&A, which grew out of the Great Exhibition of 1851—that ultimate festival celebrating the Industrial Revolution and the greatness of Britain—was originally for manufactured art, but fine art sculptures (and copies) were soon added. After much support from Queen Victoria and Prince Albert, it was renamed after the royal couple, and its present building was opened in 1909. The idealistic Victorian notion that anyone can be continually improved by education and example remains the driving force behind this museum.

Cost, Hours, and Location: Free, possible fee for special exhibits, daily 10:00–17:45, open every Wed and last Fri of month until 22:00 except mid-Dec–mid-Jan (Tube: South Kensington, a long tunnel leads directly from the Tube station to the museum, tel. 020/7942-2000, www.vam.ac.uk).

Museum Overview and Tours: The museum is large and gangly, with 150 rooms and over 12 miles of corridors. While just wandering works well here, consider catching one of the free 60-minute orientation tours (daily, at :30 past each hour from 10:30 to 15:30, also daily at 13:00, Wed at 16:30, and a half-hour version at 19:30) or buying the fine £5 *Hundred Highlights* guidebook, or the handy £1 *What to See at the V&A* brochure (outlines 5 self-guided, speedy tours).

To tour this museum on your own, grab a museum map and start with these ground-floor **highlights**:

Near the entrance: The **Medieval Treasury** (Room 43) has stained glass, bishops' robes, old columns, and good descriptions. Statues by **Antonio Canova** (Room 50A)—white, polished, and pretty Greek graces, minotaurs, and nymphs—are rare originals by the neoclassical master.

Southeast corner (to the right of entrance, at the end of the hall): **Plaster casts** of **Trajan's Column** (Room 46A) are a copy of Rome's 140-foot spiral relief telling the story of the conquest of Romania. (The V&A's casts are copies made for the benefit of 19th-century art students who couldn't afford a railpass.) Plaster casts of **Renaissance sculptures** (Room 46B) let you compare Michelangelo's monumental *David* with Donatello's girlish *David;* see also Ghiberti's bronze Baptistery doors that inspired the Florentine Renaissance. The hall of **Great Fakes and Forgeries** (Room 46) chronicles concocted art and historical objects passed off as originals.

Southwest corner (left of entrance, end of hall): **Raphael's "cartoons"** (room 48A) are seven huge watercolor designs by the Renaissance master for tapestries meant for the Sistine Chapel. The cartoons were sent to Brussels, cut into strips (see the lines), and placed on the looms. Notice that the scenes, the Acts of Peter and Paul, are the reverse of the final product (lots of left-handed saints). The **Dress Gallery** (in Room 40) has 400 years of English fashion corseted into 40 display cases. The **Musical Instruments** section displays lutes, harpsichords, early flutes, big violins, and strange, curly horns—some recognizable, some obsolete (room 40A, up the staircase in the center of the Dress Gallery).

The rest of the ground floor: Room 41 has the finest collection of **Indian** decorative art outside India. There's **medieval stained glass** in room 28 (and much more upstairs).

To make a thorough, **chronological trip** through European arts from medieval to modern, start at the entrance: Medieval Treasury (Room 43), exiting to Europe 1100–1450 (Room 23), then turn left and loop counterclockwise (through Rooms 22, 21, then downstairs to Rooms 2–7), ending up back at the entrance.

Upstairs you can walk through the newly renovated **British Galleries** for centuries of British furniture, clothing, glass, jewelry, and sculpture.

▲Natural History Museum—Across the street from the Victoria and Albert Museum, this mammoth museum is housed in a giant and wonderful Victorian, neo-Romanesque building. Built in the 1870s specifically to house the huge collection (50 million specimens), it presents itself in two halves: the Life Galleries (creepy-crawlies, human biology, the origin of species, "our place in evolution," and awesome dinosaurs) and the Earth Galleries (meteors, volcanoes, earthquakes, and so on). Exhibits are wonderfully explained, with lots of creative interactive displays. Pop in, if only for the wild collection of dinosaurs and the roaring *T. Rex.* Free 45-minute tours occur daily about every hour from 11:00 to 16:00 (free, possible fee for special exhibits, Mon–Sat 10:00–17:50, Sun 11:00–17:50, last entrance 15:30, a long tunnel leads directly from South Kensington Tube station to museum, tel. 020/7942-5000, exhibit info and reservations tel. 020/7942-5011, www.nhm.ac.uk).

Sights—East London: The City

▲▲The City of London—When Londoners say The City, they mean the one-square-mile business, banking, and journalism center that 2,000 years ago was Roman Londinium. The outline of the Roman city walls can still be seen in the arc of roads from Blackfriars Bridge to Tower Bridge. Within The City are 24 churches designed by Christopher Wren, mostly just ornamentation around St. Paul's Cathedral. Today, while home to only 5,000 residents, The City thrives with over 500,000 office workers coming and going daily. It's a fascinating district to wander on weekdays, but since almost nobody actually lives there, it's dull in the evenings and on Saturday and Sunday.

▲Old Bailey—To view the British legal system in action—lawyers in little blond wigs speaking legalese with a British accent—spend a few minutes in the visitors' gallery at "Old Bailey" (free, no kids under 14, Mon–Fri 10:00–13:00 & 14:00–17:00 most weeks, reduced hours in Aug; no bags, cell phones, or cameras, but small purses OK; you can check your bag at the SPAR grocery across the street for £1, or try a travel agency or bagel shop; Tube: St. Paul's, 2 blocks northwest of St. Paul's on Old Bailey Street, follow signs to public entrance, tel. 020/7248-3277).

▲▲▲St. Paul's Cathedral—Wren's most famous church is the great St. Paul's, its elaborate interior capped by a 365-foot dome. The crypt (included with admission) is a world of historic bones and memorials, including Admiral Nelson's tomb and interesting cathedral models. The great West Door is opened only for great occasions, such as the wedding of Prince Charles and the late Princess Diana in 1981. Stand in the back of the church and imagine how Diana felt before making the hike to the altar with the

East London: The City

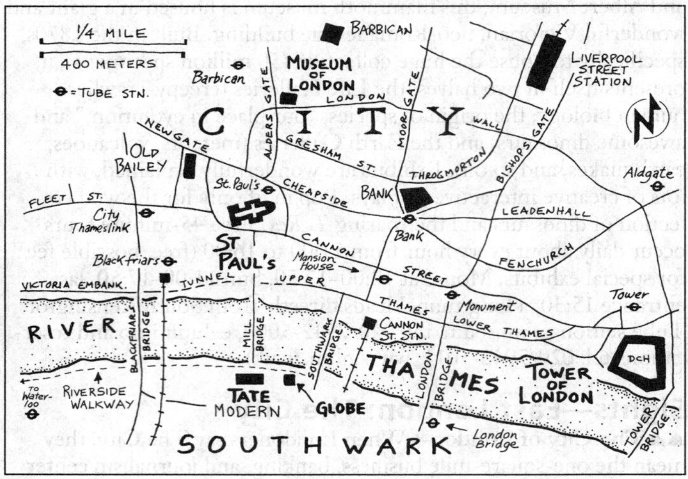

world watching. Sit under the second-largest dome in the world and eavesdrop on guided tours.

Since World War II, St. Paul's has been Britain's symbol of resistance. Despite 57 nights of bombing, the Nazis failed to destroy the cathedral, thanks to the St. Paul's volunteer fire watch, who stayed on the dome. Climb the dome for a great city view and some fun in the Whispering Gallery—where the precisely designed barrel of the dome lets sweet nothings circle audibly around to the opposite side (£6 entry, Mon–Sat 8:30–16:30, last entry 16:00, closed Sun except for worship and organ recital; allow 1 hour to climb up and down dome—closed Sun; no photography allowed within church; £2.50 for guided 90-min "super tours" of cathedral and crypt Mon–Sat at 11:00, 11:30, 13:30, and 14:00; £3.50 for an audioguide tour available Mon–Sat 8:45–15:00, CC, Tube: St. Paul's, tel. 020/7236-4128). Sunday services are at 8:00, 10:15, 11:30 (sung Eucharist), 15:15 (evensong), and 18:00, with a free organ recital at 17:00. The **evensong** services are free, but nonpaying visitors are not allowed to linger afterward (Mon–Sat at 17:00, Sun at 15:15, 40 min). You'll find an inexpensive and cheery café in the crypt.

▲**Museum of London**—London, a 2,000-year-old city, is so littered with Roman ruins that when a London builder finds Roman antiquities, he doesn't stop work. He simply documents the finds, moves the artifacts to a museum, and builds on. If you're asking, "Why did the Romans build their cities underground?" a trip to the creative and entertaining London Museum is a must. Stroll through London history from pre-Roman times through the Blitz up to today. This regular stop for the local schoolkids gives the best overview of London history in town (free, Mon–Sat 10:00–18:00, Sun 12:00–18:00, Tube: Barbican or St. Paul's, tel. 020/7600-3699).

Geffrye Decorative Arts Museum—Walk through English front rooms from 1600 to 1990 (free, Tue–Sat 10:00–17:00, Sun 12:00–17:00, closed Mon, Tube: Liverpool Street, then bus #149 or #242 north, tel. 020/7739-9893).

▲▲▲Tower of London—The tower has served as a castle in wartime, a king's residence in peace, and, most notoriously, as the prison and execution site of rebels. This historic fortress is host to more than three million visitors a year. Enjoy the free and entertaining 50-minute Beefeater tour (leaves regularly from inside the gate, last one is usually at 15:30, 14:30 off-season). The crown jewels, dating from the Restoration, are the best on Earth—and come with hour-long lines for most of the day. To avoid the crowds, arrive at 9:00 and go straight for the jewels, doing the Beefeater tour and White Tower later—or do the jewels after 16:30 (£11.50, family-£34, 1-day combo-ticket with Hampton Court Palace-£19, March–Oct Mon–Sat 9:00–18:00, Sun 10:00–18:00, Nov–Feb Tue–Sat 9:00–17:00, Sun–Mon 10:00–17:00, last entry 60 min before closing, closed Dec 24–26 and Jan 1, the long but fast-moving ticket line is worst on Sun, no photography allowed of jewels or in chapels, skip the £3 audioguide, Tube: Tower Hill, tel. 020/7709-0765, recorded info tel. 020/7680-9004, booking tel. 0870-756-7070). You can avoid the long lines by picking up your ticket at any London TI or the Tower Hill Tube station ticket office.

Ceremony of the Keys: Every night at 21:30, with pageantry-filled ceremony, the Tower of London is locked up (as it has been for the last 700 years). To attend this free 30-minute event, you need to request an invitation at least two to three months before your visit. Write to: Ceremony of the Keys, H.M. Tower of London, London EC3N 4AB. Include your name; the addresses, names, and ages of all people attending (up to 7 people, nontransferable, no kids under 8 allowed); requested date; alternative dates; and an international reply coupon (buy at U.S. post office—if your post office doesn't have the $1.75 coupons in stock, they can order them; the turnaround time is a few days). If you don't manage to score an invite ahead of time, inquire with a Yeoman about last-minute cancellations—there might be a spot available.

Sights next to the Tower—The best remaining bit of London's **Roman Wall** is just north of the tower (at Tower Hill Tube station). Freshly painted and restored, **Tower Bridge Experience**—the neo-Gothic maritime gateway to London—has an 1894-to-1994 history exhibit (£4.50, family-£14 and up, daily 9:30–18:30, last entry at 17:00, good view, poor value, tel. 020/7403-3761). The chic **St. Katherine Yacht Harbor**, just east of the Tower Bridge, has mod shops and the classic old Dickens Inn, fun for a drink or pub lunch. Across the bridge is the South Bank, with the upscale Butlers Wharf area, museums, and promenade.

Sights—South London, on the South Bank

The South Bank is a thriving arts and cultural center tied together by a riverside path. This trendy, pub-crawling walk—called the Jubilee Promenade—stretches from the Tower Bridge past Westminster Bridge, where it offers grand views of the Houses of Parliament. (The promenade hugs the river except just east of London Bridge, where it cuts inland for a couple of blocks.)

▲▲▲London Eye Ferris Wheel—Built by British Airways, the wheel towers above London opposite Big Ben. This is the world's highest observational wheel, giving you a chance to fly British Airways without leaving London. Designed like a giant bicycle wheel, it's a pan-European undertaking: British steel and Dutch engineering, with Czech, German, French, and Italian mechanical parts. It's also very "green," running extremely efficiently and virtually silently. Twenty-five people ride in each of its 32 air-conditioned capsules for the 30-minute rotation (each capsule has a bench, but most people stand). From the top of this 450-foot-high wheel—the highest public viewpoint in the city—Big Ben looks small. You only go around once; save a shot on top for the glass capsule of people next to yours.

A big hit with Londoners and tourists alike, the ride gets booked up fast, especially on weekends. To save time and guarantee a spot, reserve a time slot a day ahead—at a London TI, in person at the office near the base of the wheel, at the Big Bus Information Centre (daily 8:30–17:30, 48 Buckingham Palace Road, a block from Victoria Station), possibly through your hotel (ask), or online at www.ba-londoneye.com. You can also book by phone, but allow at least five days before your ticket is available (pick up ticket at wheel office, 50p charge, automated booking tel. 0870-500-0600). Whether you book ahead or just stand in line, you'll be assigned—or you can request—a half-hour time slot. You must arrive at the wheel during this time (earlier is better) to ensure getting on. Advance booking, which costs little or nothing extra, allows you to skip the queue to buy tickets. But you'll still have to stand in the second queue, the ticket-holders' line, to get on the wheel (line starts forming 10 min before your half-hour time slot begins; listen for announcement). Freewheeling types who don't care for lines or prebooking can usually avoid the line by riding early (before 11:00) or at night. It's open until 22:00 in peak season (last boarding 21:30). If you're lucky, you can waltz right on (£10.50, daily 9:30–22:00, mid-Sept–March 9:30–20:00, closed Jan for maintenance, shop with binoculars for rent at County Hall, Tube: Waterloo or Westminster, www.ba-londoneye.com). Skip the £30 Fast Track ticket sold here; it gets you on the wheel without a wait, but you pay triple the price.

Dalí Universe—Cleverly located next to the hugely popular London Eye Ferris Wheel, this exhibit features 500 works of mind-bending art by Salvador Dalí. While pricey, it's entertaining if you like surrealism and want to learn about Dalí (£7, daily 10:00–17:30, generally summer eves until 20:00, tel. 020/7620-2720).

▲▲Imperial War Museum—This impressive museum covers the wars of the last century, from heavy weaponry to love notes and Varga Girls, from Monty's Africa campaign tank to Schwarzkopf's Desert Storm uniform. You can trace the development of the machine gun, watch footage of the first tank battles, see one of over a thousand V2 rockets Hitler rained on Britain in 1944 (each with over a ton of explosives), hold your breath through the gruesome WWI trench experience, and buy WWII–era toys in the fun museum shop. The "Secret War" section gives a fascinating peek into the intrigues of espionage in World War I and World War II. The section on the Holocaust is one of the best on the subject anywhere. Rather than glorify war, the museum does its best to shine a light on the powerful human side of one of mankind's most persistent traits (free, daily 10:00–18:00, 90 min is enough time for most visitors, Tube: Lambeth North or bus #12 from Westminster, tel. 020/7416-5000).

The museum is housed in what was the Royal Bethlam Hospital. Also known as "the Bedlam asylum," the place was so wild it gave the world a new word for chaos: "bedlam." Back in Victorian times, locals—without trash-talk shows and cable TV—came here for their entertainment. The asylum actually opened the place to the paying public on weekends.

Bramah Tea and Coffee Museum—Aficionados of tea or coffee will find this small museum fascinating. It tells the story of each drink almost passionately. The owner, Mr. Bramah, comes from a big tea family and wants the world to know how the advent of commercial television, with breaks not long enough to brew a proper pot of tea, required a faster hot drink. In came the horrible English instant coffee. Tea countered with finely chopped leaves in tea bags, and it's gone downhill ever since (£4, daily 10:00–18:00, closed only Dec 25–26, 40 Southwark Street, 2 blocks south of Jubilee pedestrian bridge, Tube: London Bridge plus 3-min walk, tel. 020/7403-5650, www.bramahmuseum.org). Its café, which serves more kinds of coffees and teas than cakes, is open to the public (same hours as museum).

▲▲Shakespeare's Globe—The original Globe Theatre has been rebuilt—half-timbered and thatched—exactly as it was in Shakespeare's time. (This is the first thatch in London since they were outlawed after the great fire of 1666.) The Globe originally accommodated 2,000 seated and another 1,000 standing. (Today, leaving space for reasonable aisles, the theater holds 900 seated and 600 groundlings.) Its promoters brag that the theater forges "the three A's": actors, audience, and architecture, with each contributing to the play. Open as a museum and working theater, it hosts authentic old-time performances of Shakespeare's plays. The theater can be toured when there are no plays. The Globe's exhibition on Shakespeare is the world's largest, with interactive displays and film presentations, a sound lab, a script factory, and costumes (£8, mid-May–Sept Mon–Sat 9:30–12:00, Sun 9:30–11:30, free 30-min tour offered on the half hour; also open daily 12:30–16:00 but for disappointing virtual tours only; Oct–mid-May daily 10:30–17:00, free 30-min tour offered on the half hour; on South Bank directly across the Thames over Southwark Bridge from St. Paul's, Tube: London Bridge plus 10-min walk, tel. 020/7902-1500, www.shakespeares-globe.org, for details on seeing a play see "Entertainment and Theater in London," below). The Globe Café is open daily (10:00–18:00, tel. 020/7902-1433).

▲▲Tate Modern—Dedicated in the spring of 2000, this striking museum across the river from St. Paul's Cathedral opened the new century with art from the old one (remember the 20th century?). Its powerhouse collection of Monet, Matisse, Dalí, Picasso, Warhol, and much more is displayed in a converted power house (museum free, fee for special exhibitions, daily 10:00–18:00, Fri–Sat until 22:00—a good time to visit, various audioguide tours-£1, free guided tours, call for schedule, view café on top floor, walk the Millennium Bridge from St. Paul's, or get off at Southwark or Blackfriars Tube stop plus 7-min walk from either stop, tel. 020/7887-8008, www.tate.org.uk).

▲Millennium Bridge—This pedestrian bridge links St. Paul's Cathedral and Tate Modern across the Thames. This is London's first new bridge in a century. When it first opened, the $25 million bridge wiggled when people walked on it, so it promptly closed for a $7 million stabilization; now it's stable and back open (free). Nicknamed "a blade of light" for its sleek minimalist design—it's 370 yards long, four yards wide, and made of stainless steel with teak planks—it includes clever aerodynamic handrails to deflect wind over the heads of pedestrians.

Jubilee Bridge—When it's completed, this pedestrian bridge (2 bridges east of the Millennium Bridge) will provide another

Crossing the Thames on Foot

You can cross the Thames on any of the bridges that carry car traffic, but pedestrian bridges are more fun. The handy **Millennium Bridge**, connecting the sedate St. Paul's Cathedral and the great Tate Modern, is now open, apparently for good. The **Jubilee Bridge**, two bridges east of the Millennium Bridge, may be built in 2003; it was supposed to open last year to commemorate the Queen's Jubilee Year, but funding didn't materialize in time. The new **Hungerford Bridge** (consisting of two walkways that flank a railway trestle) just opened, connecting bustling Trafalgar Square on the North Bank with the London Eye Ferris Wheel and Waterloo Station on the South Bank. Replacing an old, run-down bridge, the Hungerford Bridge—well lit with a sleek, futuristic look—makes this popular route safer and more popular.

feet-friendly way to connect the North and South Banks. It may be finished late in 2003 and will be attached to the Cannon Street Railway Bridge.

▲▲Old Operating Theatre Museum and Herb Garret—Climb a tight and creaky wooden spiral staircase to a church attic where you'll find a garret used to dry medicinal herbs, a fascinating exhibit on Victorian surgery, cases of well-described 19th-century medical paraphernalia, and a special look at "anesthesia, the defeat of pain." Then you stumble upon Britain's oldest operating theater, where limbs were sawed off way back in 1821 (£3.75, daily 10:30–17:00, Tube: London Bridge, 9a St. Thomas Street, tel. 020/8806-4325, www.thegarret.org.uk).

▲▲Vinopolis: City of Wine—While it seems illogical to have a huge wine museum in London, Vinopolis makes a good case. Built over a Roman wine store and filling the massive vaults of an old wine warehouse, the museum offers an excellent audioguide with a light yet earnest history of wine. Sipping various reds and whites, ports, and champagnes—immersed in your headset as you stroll—you learn about vino from its Georgian origins to Chile to a Vespa ride through Chianti country in Tuscany. Allow some time, the audioguide takes 90 minutes—the sipping can slow things down wonderfully (£11.50 with 5 tastes, £14 with 10, don't worry . . . for £2.50 you can buy 5 more tastes inside, daily 11:00–18:00, Mon until 21:00, Sat until 20:00, last entry 2 hours before closing, Tube: London Bridge, between the Globe and

Southwark Cathedral at 1 Bank End, tel. 0870-241-4040 or 020/7940-8301, www.vinopolis.co.uk).

More South Bank Sights, in Southwark

These sights are mediocre but worth knowing about. The area stretching from Tate Modern to London Bridge, known as Southwark (pron. SUTH-uck), was for centuries the place Londoners would go to escape the rules and decency of the city and let their hair down. Bear-baiting, brothels, rollicking pubs and theater—you name it, your dreams could be fulfilled just across the Thames. Through most of the last century a run-down warehouse district, in the last 10 years it's been gentrified with classy restaurants, office parks, pedestrian promenades, major sights (such as the Tate Modern and the Globe Theatre), and this colorful collection of lesser sights. The area is easy on foot and a scenic—though circuitous—way to connect St. Paul's Cathedral and the Tower of London.

Southwark Cathedral—While made a cathedral only in 1905, this has been the neighborhood church since the 13th century and comes with some interesting history (Mon–Sat 10:00–18:00, Sun 11:00–17:00, last admission 30 min before closing, evensong services weekdays at 17:30, Sun at 15:00, audioguide-£2.50, tel. 020/7367-6711). The adjacent church-run **Long View of London Exhibition** tells the story of Southwark (£3, same hours as church).

The Clink Prison—Proudly the "original clink," this was where law-abiding citizens threw Southwark troublemakers until 1780. Today, it's a low-tech torture museum filling grotty old rooms with papier-mâché gore. Unfortunately, there's little to seriously deal with the fascinating problem of law and order in Southwark, where 18th-century Londoners went for a good time (overpriced at £4, daily 10:00–18:00, 1 Clink Street, tel. 020 /7378-1558, www.clink.co.uk).

Rose Theatre—This slight sight may be closed or open only by appointment in 2003; call ahead if you're interested (tel. 020/7593-0026). In the basement of an 11-story office building are the scant remains of the 16th-century theater that once stood here. The Rose Theatre was built in 1587, 12 years before the original Globe, and excavated in 1989. In this barren site, you view a 25-minute video on the history of theater in the days of Shakespeare (£4).

***Golden Hinde* Replica**—This is a full-size replica of the 16th-century warship in which Sir Francis Drake circumnavigated the globe from 1577 to 1580. Commanding this boat, Drake earned the reputation as history's most successful pirate. The original is long gone, but this boat has logged over 100,000 miles, including its own voyage around the world. While the ship is fun to see, its interior is not worth touring (£2.50, daily 9:30–17:30, may be

The South Bank

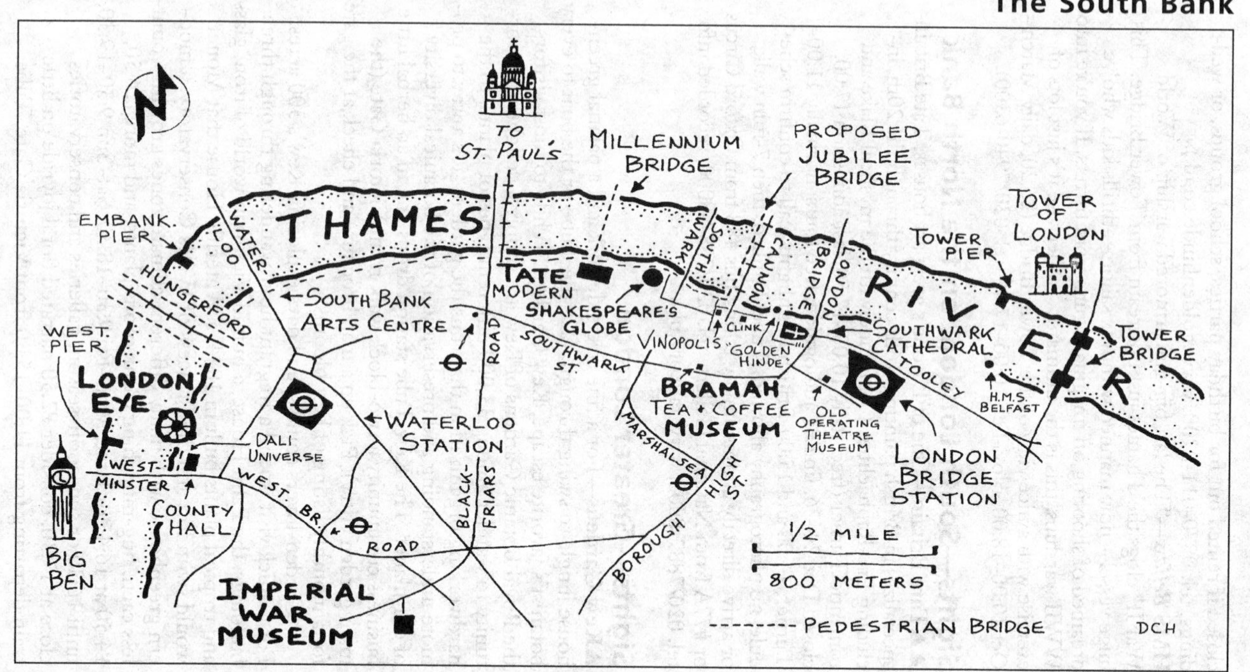

closed if rented out for birthday parties, school groups, or weddings, tel. 0870-011-8700, www.goldenhinde.co.uk).

HMS *Belfast*—"The last big-gun armored warship of World War II" clogs the Thames just upstream from Tower Bridge. This huge vessel—now manned with wax sailors—thrills kids who've dreamed of shooting off imaginary guns from turrets. If you're into WWII warships, this is the ultimate . . . otherwise it's just lots of exercise with a nice view of the Tower Bridge (£6.20, daily March–Oct 10:00–18:00, Nov–Feb 10:00–17:00, tel. 020/7940-6300).

Sights—South London, on the North Bank

▲▲Tate Britain—One of Europe's great art houses, Tate Britain specializes in British painting: 16th century through the 20th, including Pre-Raphaelites. Commune with the mystical Blake and romantic Turner (free, daily 10:00–17:50, last admission 17:00, closed Dec 24–26, fine £3 audioguide, free tours: normally 11:00-Turner, 14:00 and 15:00-British Highlights, call to confirm schedule, no photography allowed, Tube: Pimlico, then 7-min walk, or arrive directly at museum by taking bus #88 from Oxford Circus or #77A from National Gallery, tel. 020/7887-8000, recorded info tel. 020/7887-8008, www.tate.org.uk).

Sights—Greater London

▲Kew Gardens—For a fine riverside park and a palatial greenhouse jungle to swing through, take the Tube or the boat to every botanist's favorite escape, Kew Gardens. While to most visitors the Royal Botanic Gardens of Kew are simply a delightful opportunity to wander among 33,000 different types of plants, to the hardworking organization that runs the gardens, it's a way to promote understanding and preservation of the botanical diversity of our planet. The Kew Tube station drops you in an herbal little business community a two-block walk from Victoria Gate (the main garden entry). Pick up a map brochure and check at the gate for a monthly listing of best blooms.

Garden-lovers could spend days exploring Kew's 300 acres. For a quick visit, spend a fragrant hour wandering through three buildings: the Palm House, a humid Victorian world of iron, glass, and tropical plants built in 1844; a Waterlily House that Monet would swim for; and the Princess of Wales Conservatory, a modern greenhouse with many different climate zones growing countless cacti, bug-munching carnivorous plants, and more (£6.50, £4.50 at 16:45 or later, Mon–Fri 9:30–18:30, Sat–Sun 9:30–19:30, until 16:30 or sunset off-season, galleries and conservatories close at 17:30, consider £2.50 narrated floral joyride on little train departing from 11:00–15:30 from Victoria Gate, Tube:

Greater London

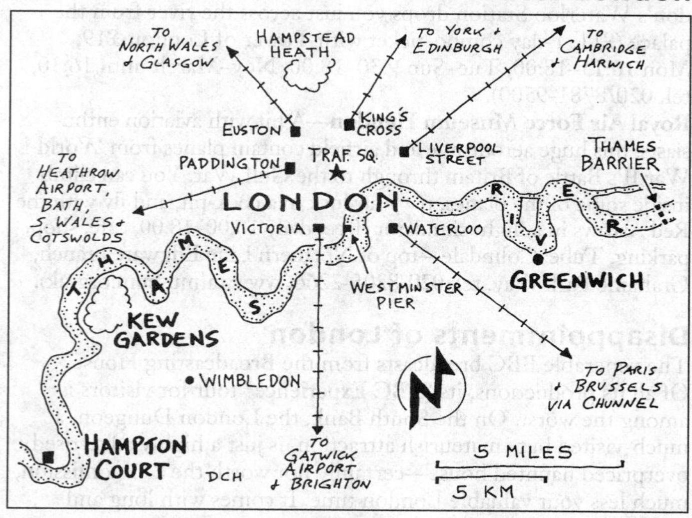

Kew Gardens, tel. 020/8332-5000). For a sun-dappled lunch, walk 10 minutes from the Palm House to the Orangery (£6 hot meals, daily 10:00–17:30).

▲Hampton Court Palace—Fifteen miles up the Thames from downtown (£15 taxi ride from Kew Gardens) is the 500-year-old palace of Henry VIII. Actually, it was the palace of his minister, Cardinal Wolsey. When Wolsey, a clever man, realized Henry VIII was experiencing a little palace envy, he gave the mansion to his king. The Tudor palace was also home to Elizabeth I and Charles I. Sections were updated by Christopher Wren for William and Mary. The palace stands stately overlooking the Thames and includes some impressive Tudor rooms, including a Great Hall, with its magnificent hammer-beam ceiling. The industrial-strength Tudor kitchen was capable of keeping 600 schmoozing courtesans thoroughly—if not well—fed. The sculpted garden features a rare Tudor tennis court and a popular maze.

The palace, fully restored after a 1986 fire, tries hard to please, but it doesn't quite sparkle. From the information center in the main courtyard, visitors book times for tours with tired costumed guides or pick up audioguides for self-guided tours of various wings of the palace (all free). The Tudor Kitchens, Henry VIII's Apartments, and the King's Apartments are most interesting. The Georgian Rooms are pretty dull. The maze in the nearby garden is a curiosity some find fun (maze free with palace ticket, otherwise £3). The train (2/hr, 30 min) from London's Waterloo Station drops you just across the river from the palace (£11, 1-day combo-ticket with Tower of London-£19, Mon 10:15–18:00, Tue–Sun 9:30–18:00, Nov–March until 16:30, tel. 020/8781-9500).

Royal Air Force Museum Hendon—A hit with aviation enthusiasts, this huge aerodrome and airfield contain planes from World War II's Battle of Britain through to the Gulf War. You can climb inside some of the planes, try your luck in a cock-pit, and fly with the Red Arrows in a flight simulator (free, daily 10:00–18:00, café, shop, parking, Tube: Colindale—top of Northern Line Edgware branch, Grahame Park Way, tel. 020/8205-2266, www.rafmuseum.org.uk).

Disappointments of London

The venerable BBC broadcasts from the Broadcasting House. Of all its productions, its "BBC Experience" tour for visitors is among the worst. On the South Bank, the London Dungeon, a much-visited but amateurish attraction, is just a highly advertised, overpriced haunted house—certainly not worth the £11 admission, much less your valuable London time. It comes with long and rude lines. Wait for Halloween and see one in your hometown to support a better cause. "Winston Churchill's Britain at War Experience" (next to the London Dungeon) wastes your time. The Kensington Palace State Apartments are lifeless and not worth a visit.

Shopping in London

Harrods—Filled with wonderful displays, Harrods is London's most famous and touristy department store. Big yet classy, Harrods has everything from elephants to toothbrushes. The food halls (ground floor) are sights to savor. If nothing else, ride the ornate Egyptian escalator (Mon–Sat 10:00–19:00, closed Sun, mandatory storage for big backpacks-£2.50, on Brompton Road, Tube: Knightsbridge, tel. 020/7730-1234). Many readers report that Harrods is overpriced (its £1 toilets are the most expensive in Europe), snooty, and teeming with American and Japanese tourists. Still, it's the palace of department stores. The nearby Beauchamp Place is lined with classy and fascinating shops.

Harvey Nichols—Once Princess Diana's favorite, "Harvey Nick's" remains the department store du jour (Mon, Tue, Sat 10:00–19:00, Wed–Fri until 20:00, Sun 12:00–18:00, near Harrods, Tube: Knightsbridge, 109 Knightsbridge, www.harveynichols.com). Want to pick up a little £20 scarf for the wife? You won't do it here, where they're more like £200. The store's fifth floor is a veritable food fest, with a gourmet grocery store, a fancy (smoky) restaurant, a Yo! Sushi bar, and a lively café. Consider a take-away tray of sushi to eat on a bench in the Hyde Park rose garden two blocks away. On Friday nights, the café hosts a popular "Film on Five" event: A three-course dinner followed by recently released films shown on big-screen televisions (£35, 20:00–24:00, for reservations call 020/7201-8562).

Toys—The biggest toy store in Britain is **Hamleys**, with seven floors buzzing with 28,000 toys managed by a staff of 200. At the "Bear Factory," kids can get a made-to-order teddy bear by picking out a "bear skin" and watch while it's stuffed and sewn (Mon–Sat 10:00–20:00, Sun 12:00–18:00, 188 Regent Street, tel. 020/8752-2277, www.hamleys.co.uk).

Street Markets—Antique buffs, people-watchers, and folks who brake for garage sales love to haggle at London's street markets. There's good early-morning market activity somewhere any day of the week. The best are **Portobello Road** (roughly Mon–Sat 9:00–17:00, go on Sat for antiques--plus the regular junk, clothes, and produce; Tube: Notting Hill Gate, tel. 020/7229-8354) and **Camden Lock Market** (daily 10:00–18:00, arts and crafts, Tube: Camden Town, tel. 020/7284-2084, www.camdenlock.net). The TI has a complete, up-to-date list. Warning: Markets attract two kinds of people—tourists and pickpockets.

Famous Auctions—London's famous auctioneers welcome the curious public for viewing and bidding. For schedules, call **Sotheby's** (Mon–Fri 9:00–16:30, closed Sat–Sun, 34-35 New Bond Street, Tube: Oxford Circus, tel. 020/7293-5000, www.sothebys.com) or **Christie's** (Mon–Fri 9:00–16:30, Tue until 20:00, closed Sat–Sun, 8 King Street, Tube: Green Park, tel. 020/7839-9060, www.christies.com).

Entertainment and Theater in London

London bubbles with top-notch entertainment seven days a week. Everything's listed in the weekly entertainment magazines (e.g., *Time Out)*, available at newsstands. Choose from classical, jazz, rock, and far-out music, Gilbert and Sullivan, dance, comedy, Baha'i meetings, poetry readings, spectator sports, film, and theater. In Leicester Square, you'll find movies that have yet to be released in the States; if Hugh Grant is attending an opening-night premiere in London, it will likely be at one of the big movie houses here.

London's theater rivals Broadway's in quality and beats it in price. Choose from the Royal Shakespeare Company, top musicals, comedy, thrillers, sex farces, and more. Performances are nightly except Sunday, usually with one matinee a week. Matinees, usually held on Wednesday, Thursday, or Saturday, are cheaper and rarely sell out. Tickets range from about £8 to £40.

What's On in the West End

Here are some of the perennial favorites that you're likely to find among the West End's evening offerings. Generally, you can book tickets for free in person at the box office or for a £1–2.50 fee by telephone or online:

Musicals

Blood Brothers—Liverpudlian twins are separated at birth and cross paths again after living different lives (£15–38, Mon–Sat 19:45, matinees Thu 15:00 and Sat 16:00, Phoenix Theatre, Charing Cross Road, Tube: Tottenham Court Road or Leicester Square, box office tel. 020/7369-1733).

Chicago—A chorus-girl-gone-bad forms a nightclub act with another murderess to bring in the bucks (£11–38, Mon–Thu and Sat 20:00, Fri 20:30, matinees Fri 17:00 and Sat 15:00, Adelphi Theatre, Strand, Tube: Covent Garden or Charing Cross, booking tel. 020/7344-0055, www.chicagothemusical.com).

Lion King—In this Disney extravaganza featuring music by Elton John, Simba the lion learns about the delicately balanced circle of life on the savanna (£18–43, Tue–Sat 19:30, matinees Wed and Sat 14:00 and Sun 15:00, Lyceum Theatre, Wellington Street, Tube: Charing Cross or Covent Garden, booking tel. 0870-243-9000 or tel. 0161/228-1953, theater info tel. 020/7420-8112, www.disney.co.uk/MusicalTheatre/TheLionKing/).

Mamma Mia—A bride-to-be reminisces to the strains of ABBA (£19–40, Mon–Thu and Sat 19:30, Fri 20:30, matinees Fri 17:00 and Sat 15:00, Prince Edward Theatre, Old Compton Street, Tube: Leicester Square, booking tel. 020/7447-5400).

Les Miserables—Claude-Michel Schönberg's musical adaptation of Victor Hugo's epic follows the life of Jean Valjean as he struggles with the social and political realities of 19th-century France (£9–40, Mon–Sat 19:30, matinees Thu and Sat 14:30, Palace Theatre,

Most theaters, marked on tourist maps, are in the Piccadilly/Trafalgar area. Box offices, hotels, and TIs offer a handy "Theater Guide." To book a seat, simply call the theater box office directly, ask about seats and available dates, and for a £1 fee, buy a ticket with your credit card. (To avoid the fee, buy the ticket in person at the box office.) You can call from the United States as easily as from England; check www.officiallondontheatre.co.uk, the American magazine *Variety*, or photocopy your hometown library's

Cambridge Circus, Tube: Leicester Square, box office tel. 020/7434-0909, www.lesmis.com).

Phantom of the Opera—A mysterious masked man falls in love with a singer in this haunting Andrew Lloyd Webber musical about life beneath the stage of the Paris opera (£10–40, Mon–Sat 19:45, matinees Wed and Sat 15:00, Her Majesty's Theatre, Haymarket, Tube: Piccadilly Circus, booking tel. 0870-890-1106 or tel. 020/7494-5400, www.thephantomoftheopera.com).

Comedies

Complete History of America—The Reduced Shakespeare Company brings you the complete history of America in two humorous hours (£8–30, Tue 20:00, Criterion Theatre, Piccadilly Circus, Tube: Piccadilly Circus, box office tel. 020/7413-1437, www.reduced-shakespeare.co.uk).

Complete Works of William Shakespeare—Get your Cliffs Notes here: the bard's best all packed into one sitting (£8–30; Wed–Sat 20:00; matinees Thu 15:00, Sat 17:00, and Sun 16:00; Criterion Theatre, Piccadilly Circus, Tube: Piccadilly Circus, box office tel. 020/7413-1437, www.reduced-shakespeare.co.uk).

Thrillers

The Mousetrap—Agatha Christie's whodunit about a murder in a country house continues to stump audiences after 50 years (£11.50–30, Mon–Sat 20:00, matinees Tue 14:45 and Sat 17:00, St. Martin's Theatre, West Street, Tube: Leicester Square, box office tel. 020/7836-1443).

The Woman in Black—The chilling tale of a solicitor who is haunted by what he learns when he closes a reclusive woman's affairs (£10–30, Mon–Sat 20:00, matinees Tue 15:00 and Sat 16:00, Fortune Theatre, Russell Street, Tube: Covent Garden, box office tel. 020/7836-2238, www.thewomaninblack.com).

London newspaper theater section. Pick up your ticket 15 minutes before the show.

For a booking fee (£1–2.50), you can reserve seats online (www.ticketmaster.co.uk or www.firstcalltickets.com) or call Global Tickets (U.S. tel. 800/223-6108). While booking through an agency is quick and easy, prices are sometimes inflated by 25 percent. Ticket agencies—whether in the United States, at London's TIs, or scattered throughout the city—are scalpers with an address. If you're buying from an agency, look at the ticket carefully; your price should be no more than 30 percent over the printed face value (the 15 percent VAT tax is already included in the face value). Understand where you're sitting according to the floor plan (if your view is restricted, it will state this on the ticket; for floor plans of the various theaters, see www.theatremonkey.com). Agencies are worthwhile only if a show you've got to see is sold out at the box office. They scarf up hot tickets, planning to make a killing after the show is sold out. U.S. booking agencies get their tickets from another agency, adding even more to your expense by involving yet another middleman. Many tickets sold on the streets are forgeries. With cheap international phone calls and credit cards, it's usually best to book directly with the box office when possible. Note that some theaters hire booking agencies to handle advance ticket sales, so in this case—if you want to book ahead—dealing with a booking agency may be unavoidable.

Theater lingo: stalls (ground floor), dress circle (1st balcony), upper circle (2nd balcony), balcony (sky-high 3rd balcony).

Cheap theater tricks: Most theaters offer returned-ticket, standing-room, matinee, and senior or student standby deals. These "concessions" are indicated with a "conc" or "s" in the listings. Picking up a late return can get you a great seat at a cheap-seat price. If a show is "sold out," there's usually a way to get a seat. Call the theater box office and ask how. I buy the second-cheapest tickets directly from the theater box office.

The famous half-price booth at Leicester (pron. LES-ter) Square sells discounted tickets for top-price seats to shows on the push list the day of the show only (Mon–Sat 10:00–19:00, Sun 12:00–15:00, matinee tickets from noon, cash only, lines often form early). Here are some sample prices: A top-notch seat to long-running *Les Miserables* (which rarely sells out) costs £40 bought directly from the theater, but only £22.50 at Leicester Square. The cheapest balcony seat (bought from the theater) is £15.

Half-price tickets can be a good deal, unless you want the cheapest seats or the hottest shows. But check the board; occasionally they sell cheap tickets to good shows. The real half-price booth is a freestanding kiosk at the edge of the garden in Leicester Square. Several dishonest outfits advertise "official half-price tickets" at agencies closer to the Tube station. Avoid these.

Many theaters are so small that there's hardly a bad seat. After the lights go down, scooting up is less than a capital offense. Shakespeare did it.

Royal Shakespeare Company—If you'll ever enjoy Shakespeare, it'll be in Britain. The RSC performs at London's Barbican Centre from December through May and in Stratford year-round. To get a schedule, contact the RSC (Royal Shakespeare Theatre, Stratford-upon-Avon, CV37 6BB Warwickshire, tel. 01789/403-403, www.rsc.org.uk).

Tickets range in price from £10 to £30 (discounts for young and old). Book directly by telephone and credit card and pick up your ticket at the door at the Barbican Centre (office open daily 9:00–20:00, box office tel. 020/7638-8891 or 020/7628-2326, recorded information tel. 020/7628-9760, Silk Street, Tube: Barbican, book online at www.barbican.org.uk).

Shakespeare's Globe—To see Shakespeare in a replica of the theater for which he wrote his plays, attend a play at the Globe. This thatch-roofed, open-air round theater presents the plays much as Shakespeare intended (with no amplification, although the lighting is now electric instead of the original light source—ropes soaked in tar).

The play's the thing from mid-May through September (usually Tue–Sat 14:00 and 19:30, Sun at either 13:00 and 18:30 or 16:00 only, no plays on Mon, tickets can be sold out months in advance).

You'll pay £5 to stand and £12 to £27 to sit (usually on a backless bench; only a few rows and the pricier Gentlemen's Rooms have seats with backs). The £5 "groundling" tickets—while the only ones open to rain—are most fun. Scurry in early to stake out a spot on the leaning rail at the stage's edge, where the most interaction with the actors occurs. You're a crude peasant. You can lean your elbows on the stage, munch a picnic dinner, or walk around. I've never enjoyed Shakespeare as much as here, performed just as it was meant to be in the "wooden O." Plays can be long. Many groundlings leave before the end. If you like, hang out an hour before the finish and beg or buy a ticket from someone leaving early (groundlings are allowed to come and go).

The theater is on the South Bank directly across the Thames over the Millennium Bridge from St. Paul's Cathedral (Tube: London Bridge plus 10-min walk, tel. 020/7902-1500, box office tel. 020/7401-9919, www.shakespeares-globe.org).

The Globe is inconvenient for public transport, but the courtesy phone in the lobby gets a minicab in minutes. (These have set fees—e.g., £8 to South Kensington—but generally cost less than a metered cab and provide fine and honest service.)

West End Theaters—The commercial, nonsubsidized theaters cluster around Soho (especially along Shaftesbury Avenue) and Covent Garden. With a centuries-old tradition of pleasing the masses, with grand-scale productions of *Les Miserables* and

Phantom of the Opera, these present London theater at its glitziest. See the "What's On in the West End" sidebar.

Fringe Theatre—London's rougher evening-entertainment scene is thriving, filling pages in *Time Out*. Choose from a wide range of fringe theater and comedy acts (generally £5).

Music—For easy, cheap, or free concerts in historic churches, check the TIs' listings for lunch concerts (especially Wren's St. Bride's Church; St. James at Piccadilly—free lunch concerts on Mon, Wed, and Fri at 13:00, info tel. 020/7381-0441; and St. Martin-in-the-Fields—free lunch concerts on Mon, Tue, and Fri at 13:05, church tel. 020/7766-1100). St. Martin-in-the-Fields also hosts fine evening concerts by candlelight (£6–16, Thu–Sat at 19:30, CC, box office tel. 020/7839-8362).

For a fun classical event (mid-July–early Sept), attend a "Prom Concert" during the annual festival at the Royal Albert Hall. Nightly concerts are offered at give-a-peasant-some-culture prices (£4 standing-room spots sold at the door, £7 restricted-view seats, most £22, depending on performance, CC, Tube: South Kensington, tel. 020/7589-8212, www.royalalberthall.com).

Some of the world's best opera is belted out at the prestigious Royal Opera House, near Covent Garden (box office tel. 020/7304-4000, www.royalopera.org), and at the less-formal Sadler's Wells Theatre (Rosebery Avenue, Islington, Tube: Angel, box office tel. 020/7863-8000, www.sadlers-wells.com).

Walks, Bus Tour, and Cruises—See "Tours of London" above for information on walking tours (some are held in the evening), the London by Night bus tour, and Regent's Canal cruise.

Of the several companies that run Thames River evening cruises with four-course meals and dancing, London Showboat offers the best value (£51, April–Oct Wed–Sun, departs 19:00 from Westminster Pier, Thu–Sat evening cruises through the winter, 3.5 hrs, tel. 020/7237-5134, www.citycruises.com). For more on cruising, get the Thames River Services brochure from a London TI.

Day Trips from London

Greenwich, Windsor, and Cambridge are three good day trip possibilities near London (covered under "Near London," below).

You could fill a book with the many easy and exciting day trips from London (Earl Steinbicker did: *Daytrips London: 50 One-Day Adventures by Rail or Car, in and around London and Southern England)*. **Original London Walks** offers a variety of Explorer day trips using the train for about £10 plus transportation costs (see their walking-tour brochure, tel. 020/7624-3978, www.walks.com).

The British rail system uses London as a hub and normally offers round-trip fares (after 9:30) that cost virtually the same as

Day Trips from London

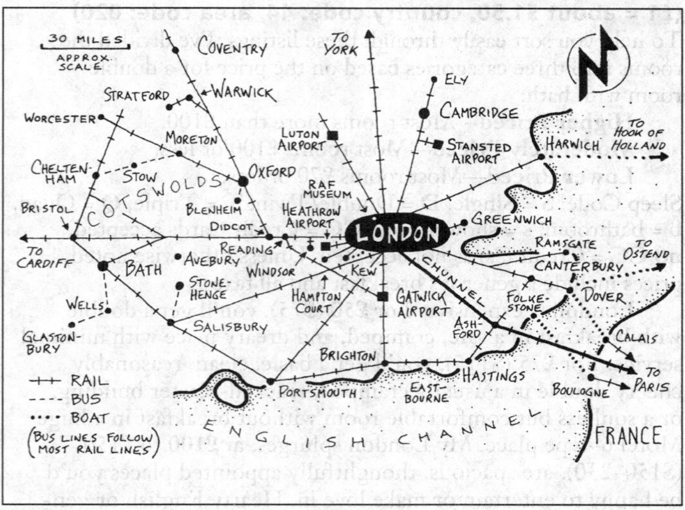

one-way fares. For day trips, "day return" tickets are best (and cheapest). You can save a little money if you purchase Super Advance tickets before 18:00 on the day before your trip. But given the high cost of big-city living and the charm of small-town England, rather than side-tripping, I'd see London and get out.

To Bath via Stonehenge: Several bus-tour companies take London-based travelers out and back every day. If you're going to Bath and want to stay overnight, consider taking a day tour to Bath and skipping the trip back to London. Depending on the type and availability of tour, you'll pay about £52, which also includes a visit to Stonehenge (compare to a £31 one-way second-class train ticket from London to Bath). Evan Evans' tour leaves from the Victoria Coach Station daily every morning at 9:00 (you can stow your bag under the bus), stops in Stonehenge (45 min), and then stops in Bath for lunch and a city tour before returning to London (£52, offered year-round, fully guided, admissions included). You can book the tour at the Victoria Coach Station, the Evan Evans' office (258 Vauxhall Bridge Road, near Victoria Coach Station, tel. 020/7950-1777, www.evanevans.co.uk), or the Green Line Travel Office (4a Fountain Square, across from Victoria Coach Station, tel. 020/7950-1777). Golden Tours also runs a fully guided Stonehenge–Bath tour for a similar price (departs from Fountain Square, located across from Victoria Coach Station, tel. 020/7233-6668, U.S. tel. 800/456-6303, www.goldentours.co.uk).

Sleeping in London

(£1 = about $1.50, country code: 44, area code: 020)

To help you sort easily through these listings, I've divided the rooms into three categories based on the price for a double room with bath:

Higher Priced—Most rooms more than £100.
Moderately Priced—Most rooms £100 or less.
Lower Priced—Most rooms £70 or less.

Sleep Code: **S** = Single, **D** = Double/Twin, **T** = Triple, **Q** = Quad, **b** = bathroom, **s** = shower only, **CC** = Credit Cards accepted, **no CC** = Credit Cards not accepted. Unless otherwise noted, prices include a generous breakfast and all taxes.

London is expensive. For £50 ($75), you'll get a double with breakfast in a safe, cramped, and dreary place with minimal service. For £75 ($115), you'll get a basic, clean, reasonably cheery double in a usually cramped, cracked-plaster building, or a soulless but comfortable room without breakfast in a huge Motel 6–type place. My London splurges, at £100 to £150 ($150–230), are spacious, thoughtfully appointed places you'd be happy to entertain or make love in. Hearty English or generous buffet breakfasts are included unless otherwise noted, and TVs are standard in rooms.

Reserve your London room with a phone call or e-mail as soon as you can commit to a date. To call a London hotel from the United States or Canada, dial 011-44-20 (London's area code without the initial zero), then the local eight-digit number. A few places will hold a room with no deposit if you promise to arrive by midday. Most take your credit-card number as security. Many inexpensive places don't take credit cards and require a cash deposit (generally a personal check if 6 weeks in advance, otherwise a bank draft in pounds). The pricier ones have expensive cancellation policies (such as no refund if you cancel with less than 2 weeks' notice). Some fancy £120 rooms rent for a third off if you arrive late on a slow day and ask for a deal.

Sleeping in Victoria Station Neighborhood, Belgravia

The streets behind Victoria Station teem with budget B&Bs. It's a safe, surprisingly tidy, and decent area without a hint of the trashy, touristy glitz of the streets in front of the station. Here in Belgravia, your neighbors include Andrew Lloyd Webber and Margaret Thatcher (her policeman stands outside 73 Chester Square). Decent eateries abound (see "Eating," below). Cheaper rooms are relatively dumpy. Don't expect £90 cheeriness in a £50 room. Off-season, it's possible to save money by arriving late without a reservation and looking around. Fierce competition softens prices, especially for multinight stays. Particularly on hot summer nights, request a quiet back room. All are within a five-minute walk of the Victoria Tube, bus, and train stations. There's a £15-per-day (with a hotel voucher) garage, a nearby **launderette** (daily 8:00–20:30, do self-service and avoid unpredictable full service, past Warwick Square at 3 Westmoreland Terrace, tel. 020/7821-8692), and an easygoing little dance club (Club D'Jan, £5 includes drink, Wed–Sat, 63 Wilton Road).

HIGHER PRICED

Lime Tree Hotel, enthusiastically run by David and Marilyn Davies, comes with spacious and thoughtfully decorated rooms and a fun-loving breakfast room. While priced a bit steep, the place has character, and there are plans in the works for more improvements (Sb-£80, Db-£110–120, Tb-£150, family room-£160, CC, possible discount with cash, all rooms non-smoking, David deals in slow times and is creative at helping travelers in a bind, 135 Ebury Street, London SW1W 9RA, tel. 020/7730-8191, fax 020/7730-7865, www.limetreehotel.co.uk).

Quality Hotel Eccleston is big, modern (but with tired carpets), well-located, and a fine value for no-nonsense comfort (Db-£125, on slow days drop-ins can ask for "saver prices"—33 percent off on first night, breakfast extra, CC, non-smoking floor, elevator, 82 Eccleston Square, London SW1V 1PS, tel. 020/7834-8042, fax 020/7630-8942, www.qualityinn.com/hotel/gb614, e-mail: admin@gb614.u-net.com).

MODERATELY PRICED

Winchester Hotel is family-run and perhaps the best value, with 18 fine rooms, no claustrophobia, and a wise and caring management (Db-£85, Tb-£110, Qb-£140, no CC, no groups, no infants, 17 Belgrave Road, London SW1V 1RB, tel. 020/7828-2972, fax 020/7828-5191, www.winchester-hotel.net, e-mail: winchesterhotel17@hotmail.com, run by Jimmy). The Winchester also recently began renting well-appointed, spacious apartments—most with kitchens and sitting rooms—around the corner from the hotel on Warwick Way (£125–230).

James House and **Cartref House** are two nearly identical, well-run, smoke-free, 10-room places on either side of Ebury Street (S-£55, Sb-£65, D-£74, Db-£90, T-£100, Tb-£115, family bunk bed quad-£130, CC, 5 percent discount with cash, all rooms with fans, James House at 108 Ebury Street, London SW1W 9QD, tel. 020/7730-2511; Cartref House at 129 Ebury

London, Victoria Station Neighborhood

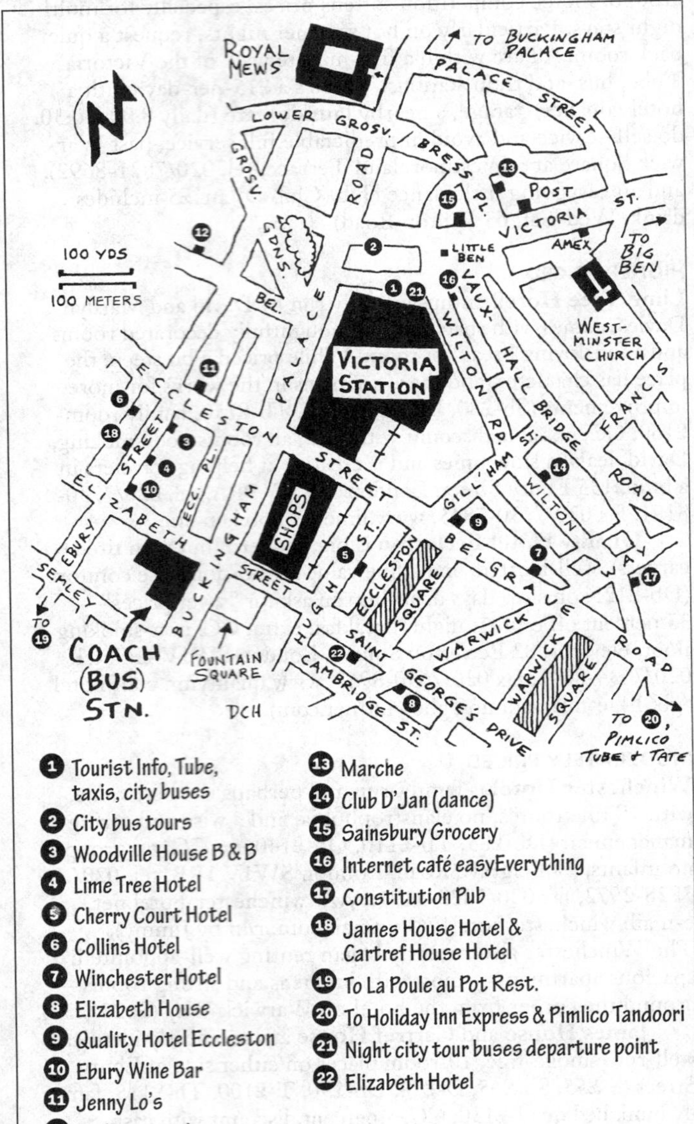

ROYAL MEWS
TO BUCKINGHAM PALACE
PALACE STREET
LOWER GROSV.
GROSV. ROAD
BRESS PL.
GROSV. GDNS.
POST
VICTORIA ST.
TO BIG BEN
AMEX
LITTLE BEN
100 YDS
100 METERS
BEL.
PALACE
VAUX. HALL BRIDGE ROAD
WILTON RD.
WEST-MINSTER CHURCH
FRANCIS ROAD
VICTORIA STATION
ECCLESTON STREET
ECC. PL.
ELIZABETH STREET
EBURY
SEMLEY
TO 19
COACH (BUS) STN.
BUCKINGHAM STREET
SHOPS
HUGH ST.
FOUNTAIN SQUARE
DCH
GILL'HAM ST.
WILTON
BELGRAVE ROAD
WAY
ECCLESTON SQUARE
WARWICK
WARWICK SQUARE
SAINT GEORGE'S DRIVE
CAMBRIDGE ST.
TO 20, PIMLICO TUBE + TATE
1 Tourist Info, Tube, taxis, city buses
2 City bus tours
3 Woodville House B & B
4 Lime Tree Hotel
5 Cherry Court Hotel
6 Collins Hotel
7 Winchester Hotel
8 Elizabeth House
9 Quality Hotel Eccleston
10 Ebury Wine Bar
11 Jenny Lo's
12 La Campagnola
13 Marche
14 Club D'Jan (dance)
15 Sainsbury Grocery
16 Internet café easyEverything
17 Constitution Pub
18 James House Hotel & Cartref House Hotel
19 To La Poule au Pot Rest.
20 To Holiday Inn Express & Pimlico Tandoori
21 Night city tour buses departure point
22 Elizabeth Hotel

Street, London SW1W 9QU, tel. 020/7730-6176, fax for both: 020/7730-7338, www.jamesandcartref.co.uk, e-mail: jandchouse@aol.com).

Elizabeth Hotel is a stately old place overlooking Eccleston Square, with fine public spaces and 38 spacious and decent rooms that could use a minor facelift (D-£68, small Db-£83, big Db-£95, Tb-£108, Qb-£120, Quint/b-£125, CC, 37 Eccleston Square, London SW1V 1PB, tel. 020/7828-6812, fax 020/7828-6814, www.elizabeth-hotel.com, e-mail: info@elizabethhotel.com). Be careful not to confuse this hotel with the nearby Elizabeth House (listed below). This one is big and comfy, the other small and dumpy.

Holiday Inn Express fills an old building with 52 fresh, modern, and efficient rooms (Db-£97, Tb-£107, CC, family rooms-prices vary, up to 2 kids free, some discounts on Web site, non-smoking floor, elevator, Tube: Pimlico, 106 Belgrave Road, London SW1V 2BJ, tel. 020/7630-8888 or 0800-897-121, fax 020/7828-0441, www.hiexpress.com, e-mail: info@hiexpressvictoria.co.uk).

Collin House Hotel, clean, simple, and efficiently run, offers 12 basic rooms in a mid-Victorian style town house (Sb-£55, D-£68, Db-£82, T-£95, non-smoking rooms, 104 Ebury St, London SWIW 9QD, tel. & fax 020/7730-8031, www.collinhouse.co.uk).

LOWER PRICED

In **Woodville House,** the quarters are dollhouse tight and showers are down the hall. This well-run, well-worn place is a good value, with lots of travel tips and friendly chat—especially about the local rich and famous—from Rachel Joplin (S-£46, D-£68, bunky family deals-£85–115 for 3–5 people, CC, 107 Ebury Street, London SW1W 9QU, tel. 020/7730-1048, fax 020/7730-2574, www.woodvillehouse.co.uk, e-mail: woodville.house@cwcom.net).

Georgian House Hotel has 50 small rooms and a cheaper annex that works well for backpackers (tiny D on fourth floor-£44, Db-£68, annex Db-£59, Tb-£86, Qb-£94, CC, Internet access, 35 St. George's Drive, London SW1V 4DG, tel. 020/7834-1438, fax 020/7976-6085, www.georgianhousehotel.co.uk, e-mail: reception@georgianhousehotel.co.uk).

Enrico Hotel, with 26 simple rooms, is basic, well-worn, and affordable (S-£50, D-£60, Ds-£65, CC, non-smoking, 77 Warwick Way, London SW1V 1QP, tel. 020/7834-9538, fax 020/7233-9995, e-mail: enricohotel@hotmail.com).

Cherry Court Hotel, run by the friendly and industrious Patel family, offers small, basic rooms for good value in a central location (Sb-£42, Db-£48, Tb-£70, Qb-£90, Quint/b-£100, prices promised with this book through 2003, CC for 5 percent extra, fruit-basket breakfast in room, non-smoking, free Internet access, peaceful garden patio, 23 Hugh Street, London SW1V 1QJ, tel. 020/7828-2840, fax 020/7828-0393, www.cherrycourthotel.co.uk, e-mail: info@cherrycourthotel.co.uk).

Elizabeth House is a last resort. It feels institutional and bland—as you might expect from a former YMCA—but it's run-down and none too clean. Only the price is right (S-£30, D-£40, Db-£50, T-£60, Q-£70, plus extra £10/room for D or Db in July–Aug, CC, 118 Warwick Way, London SW1 4JB, tel. 020/7630-0741, fax 020/7630-0740, e-mail: elizabethhouse@ehlondon.fsnet.co.uk).

Big, Cheap, Modern Hotels

These places—popular with budget tour groups—are well-run and offer elevators and all the modern comforts in a no-frills, practical package. The doubles for £65 to £94 are a great value for London. Midweek prices are generally higher than weekend rates.

MODERATELY PRICED

Jurys Inn rents 200 mod, compact, and comfy rooms near King's Cross station (Db/Tb-£94, 2 adults and 2 kids—under age 12—can share 1 room, breakfast extra, CC, non-smoking floors, 60 Pentonville Road, London N1 9LA, Tube: Angel, tel. 020/7282-5500, fax 020/7282-5511, www.jurysdoyle.com).

London County Hall Travel Inn, literally down the hall from a $400-a-night Marriott Hotel, fills one end of London's massive former County Hall building. This place is wonderfully located near the base of the London Eye Ferris Wheel and across the Thames from Big Ben. Its 300 slick and no-frills rooms come with all the necessary comforts (Db-£77 for 2 adults and up to 2 kids under age 15, couples can request a bigger family room—same price, CC, breakfast extra, book in advance, no-show rooms are released at 16:00, elevator, some smoke-free and easy-access rooms, 500 yards from Westminster Tube stop and Waterloo Station where the Chunnel train leaves for Paris, Belvedere Road, London SE1 7PB, you can call central reservations at 0870-242-8000 or 0870-238-3300 but you'll be put on hold, you can fax at 020/7902-1619 but you might not get a response; it's easiest to book online at www.travelinn.co.uk).

LOWER PRICED

Travel Inns charging about £70 per room include **London Euston** (a big, blue Lego-type building on a handy but noisy street packed with Benny Hill families on vacation, 141 Euston Road,

London NW1 2AU, Tube: Euston, tel. 0870-238-3301), **Tower Bridge** (Tower Bridge Road, London SE1, Tube: London Bridge, tel. 0870-238-3303), and **London Putney Bridge** (farther out, 3 Putney Bridge Approach, London SW6 3JD, Tube: Putney Bridge, tel. 0870-238-3302). For any of these, call 0870-242-8000, fax 0870-241-9000, or best, book online at www.travelinn.co.uk.

Hotel Ibis London Euston, which feels classier than a Travel Inn, is located on a quiet street a block behind Euston Station (380 rooms, Db-£70, breakfast-£5, CC, no family rooms, breakfast extra, non-smoking floor, 3 Cardington Street, London NW1 2LW, tel. 020/7388-7777, fax 020/7388-0001, e-mail: h0921@accor-hotels.com).

Premier Lodge is near Shakespeare's Globe on the South Bank (55 rooms, Db for up to 2 adults and 2 kids-£70, Bankside, 34 Park Street, London SE1, tel. 0870-700-1456, www.premierlodge.co.uk).

"South Kensington," She Said, Loosening His Cummerbund

To live on a quiet street so classy it doesn't allow hotel signs, surrounded by trendy shops and colorful restaurants, call "South Ken" your London home. Shoppers like being a short walk from Harrods and the designer shops of King's Road and Chelsea. When I splurge, I splurge here. Sumner Place is just off Old Brompton Road, 200 yards from the handy South Kensington Tube station (on Circle Line, 2 stops from Victoria Station, direct Heathrow connection). There's a taxi rank in the median strip at the end of Harrington Road. The handy "Wash & Dry" **launderette** is on the corner of Queensberry Place and Harrington Road (daily 8:00–21:00, bring 20p and £1 coins).

HIGHER PRICED

Aster House, run by friendly and accommodating Simon and Leona Tan, has a sumptuous lobby, lounge, and breakfast room. Its newly renovated rooms are comfy and quiet, with TV, phone, and air-conditioning. Enjoy breakfast or just lounging in the whisper-elegant Orangery, a Victorian greenhouse (Sb-£75–99, Db-£135, bigger Db-£150, deluxe 4-poster Db-£180, CC, entirely non-smoking, 3 Sumner Place, London SW7 3EE, tel. 020/7581-5888, fax 020/7584-4925, www.asterhouse.com, e-mail: asterhouse@btinternet.com).

Five Sumner Place Hotel has received several "best small hotel in London" awards. The rooms in this 150-year-old building are tastefully decorated, and the breakfast room is a Victorian-style conservatory/greenhouse (13 rooms, Sb-£100,

London, South Kensington Neighborhood

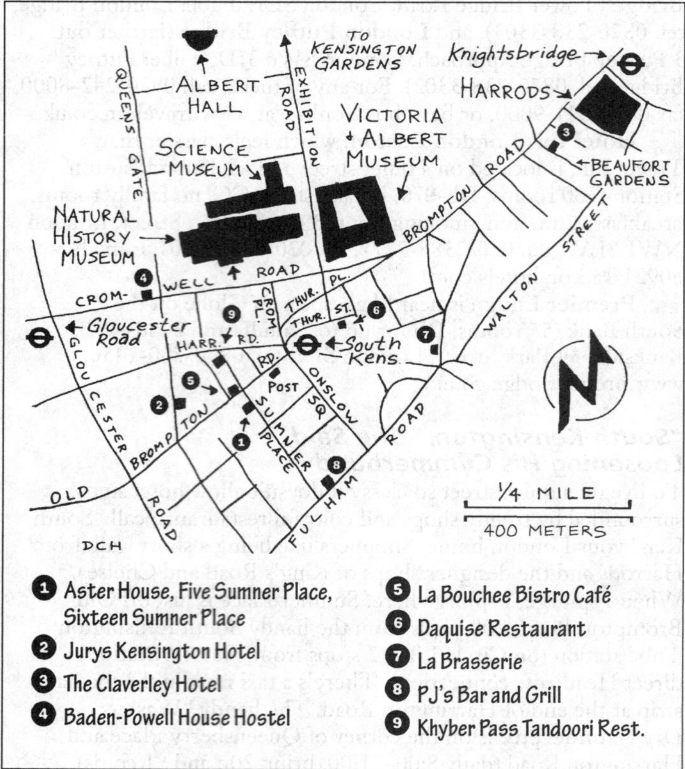

Db-£153, third bed-£22, CC, TV, phones, and fridge in rooms by request, non-smoking rooms, elevator, 5 Sumner Place, London SW7 3EE, tel. 020/7584-7586, fax 020/7823-9962, www.sumnerplace.com, e-mail: reservations@sumnerplace.com, run by Tom).

Sixteen Sumner Place, a lesser value for classier travelers, has over-the-top formality and class packed into its 39 unnumbered but pretentiously named rooms, plush lounges, and quiet garden (Db-£170, CC, breakfast in your room, elevator, 16 Sumner Place, London SW7 3EG, tel. 020/7589-5232, fax 020/7584-8615, U.S. tel. 800/533-6674, www.numbersixteenhotel.co.uk, e-mail: reservations@numbersixteenhotel.co.uk).

Jurys Kensington Hotel is big, stately, and impersonal, with a greedy pricing scheme (Sb/Db/Tb-£100–220 depending upon "availability," ask for a deal, breakfast extra, CC, piano lounge, non-smoking floor, elevator, Queen's Gate, London SW7 5LR, tel. 020/7589-6300, fax 020/7581-1492, www.jurysdoyle.com, e-mail: kensington@jurysdoyle.com).

The Claverley, two blocks from Harrods, is on a quiet street similar to Sumner Place. The 30 dark-wood-and-marble rooms come with all the comforts (S-£70, Sb-£85–120, Db-£120–190, sofa bed Tb-£190–215, prices may be flexible Dec–March, CC, plush lounge, non-smoking rooms, elevator, uneven service, 13-14 Beaufort Gardens, London SW3 1PS, Tube: Knightsbridge, tel. 020/7589-8541, fax 020/7584-3410, U.S. tel. 800/747-0398).

MODERATELY PRICED

Baden-Powell House Hostel—open to anyone—is a huge, modern, institutional place built to inexpensively house Boy and Girl Scouts and their families in central London. Those with a relative in a scouting organization get about a 30 percent discount. It's a big, bright, smoke-free place that feels safe and is well-run (180 single beds, Sb-£65, Scout rate Sb-£46, Db-£94, Scout rate Db-£70, Tb-£120, Scout rate Tb-£96, extra bed-£12, dorm beds-£29, Scout rate dorm beds-£22, CC, air-con, cheap meals served, rooms are spacious with yacht-type bathrooms, receive discount with a letter from your Boy or Girl Scout troop saying you're "family," across from Natural History Museum on corner of Cromwell Road and Queen's Gate at 65 Queen's Gate, London SW7 5JS, Tube: South Kensington, tel. 020/7584-7031, fax 020/7590-6902 and 020/7590-6900, www.scoutbase.org.uk, e-mail: bph.hostel@scout.org.uk).

Sleeping in Notting Hill Gate Neighborhood

Residential Notting Hill Gate has quick bus and Tube access to downtown, is on the A2 Airbus line from Heathrow, and, for London, is very "homely." It has a self-serve launderette, an artsy theater, a late-hours supermarket, and lots of fun budget eateries (see "Eating," below).

HIGHER PRICED

Westland Hotel is comfortable, convenient, and hotelesque, with a fine lounge and spacious rooms (Sb-£80–90, Db-£95–105, cavernous deluxe Db-£110–125, sprawling Tb-£120–140, gargantuan Qb-£135–160, Quint/b-£150–170, CC, elevator, free garage with 7 spaces, between Notting Hill Gate and Queensway Tube stations, 154 Bayswater Road, London W2 4HP, tel. 020/7229-9191, fax 020/7727-1054, www.westlandhotel.co.uk, e-mail: reservations@westlandhotel.co.uk).

London, Notting Hill Gate Neighborhood

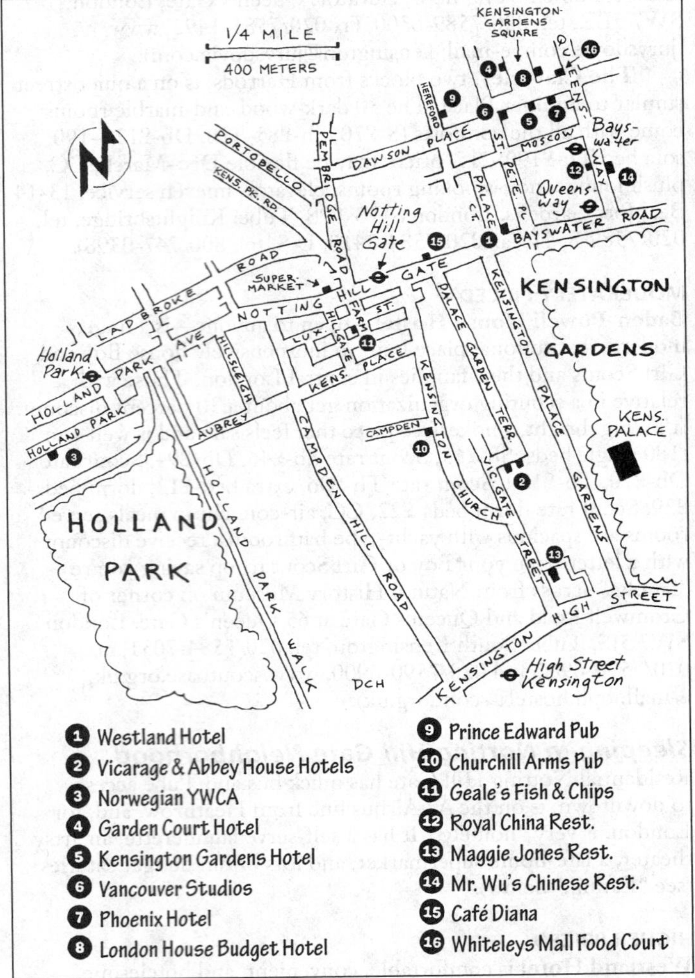

MODERATELY PRICED

Vicarage Private Hotel, understandably popular, is family-run and elegantly British in a quiet, classy neighborhood. It has 18 rooms furnished with taste and quality, a TV lounge, and facilities on each floor. Mandy, Richard, and Tere maintain a homey and caring atmosphere (S-£45, D-£74, Db-£98, T-£90, Q-£98, no

CC, 6-min walk from the Notting Hill Gate and High Street Kensington Tube stations, near Kensington Palace at 10 Vicarage Gate, London W8 4AG, tel. 020/7229-4030, fax 020/7792-5989, www.londonvicaragehotel.com, e-mail: reception@londonvicaragehotel.com).

Abbey House Hotel, next door, is similar but has a tearoom (16 rooms, S-£45, D-£74, T-£90, Q-£100, Quint-£110, no CC, 11 Vicarage Gate, London W8 4AG, tel. 020/7727-2594, fax 020/7727-1873, www.abbeyhousekensington.com, Rodrigo).

LOWER PRICED

Norwegian YWCA (Norsk K.F.U.K.) is for women under 30 only (and men with Norwegian passports). Located on a quiet, stately street, it offers non-smoking rooms, a study, TV room, piano lounge, and an open-face Norwegian ambience. They have mostly quads, so those willing to share with strangers are most likely to get a place (July–Aug: Ss-£29, shared double-£27.50/bed, shared triple-£23/bed, shared quad-£20/bed, with breakfast; Sept–June: same prices include dinner; CC, 52 Holland Park, London W11 3RS, tel. 020/7727-9897, fax 020/7727-8718, www.kfuk.dial.pipex.com, e-mail: kfuk.hjemmet@kfuk-kfum.no). With each visit, I wonder which is easier to get—a sex change or a Norwegian passport?

Sleeping on Kensington Gardens

Several big old hotels line the quiet Victorian Kensington Gardens, a block off the bustling Queensway shopping street near the Bayswater Tube station. Popular with young international travelers, Queensway is a multicultural festival of commerce and eateries (such as Mr. Wu's Chinese buffet and the Whiteleys Mall Food Court—see "Eating," below). These hotels come with the least traffic noise of all my downtown recommendations. One of several launderettes in the neighborhood is **Brookford Wash & Dry,** at Queensway and Bishop's Bridge Road (daily 7:00–19:30, service from 9:00–17:30, computerized pay point takes all coins).

HIGHER PRICED

Phoenix Hotel, a Best Western modernization of a 125-room hotel, offers American business-class comforts; spacious, plush public spaces; and big, fresh, modern-feeling rooms (Sb-£94, Db-£120, Tb-£165, Qb-£185, flaky "negotiable" pricing list, CC, elevator, 1-8 Kensington Gardens Square, London W2 4BH, tel. 020/7229-2494, fax 020/7727-1419, U.S. tel. 800/528-1234, www.phoenixhotel.co.uk).

MODERATELY PRICED

Garden Court rents 34 comfortable rooms, has a garden, and is a fine value (S-£39, Sb-£58, D-£58, Db-£88, T-£72, Tb-£99, Q-£82, Qb-£120, 5 percent discount with this book, CC, some small rooms, no elevator, 30 Kensington Gardens Square, London W2 4BG, tel. 020/7229-2553, fax 020/7727-2749, www.gardencourthotel.co.uk, e-mail: info@gardencourthotel.co.uk, Edward Connolly).

Kensington Gardens Hotel laces 16 decent but worn rooms together in a tall, skinny place with peeling wallpaper, lots of stairs, and no lift (Ss-£55, Sb-£62, Db-£85, Tb-£105, CC, 9 Kensington Gardens Square, London W2 4BH, tel. 020/7221-7790, fax 020/7792-8612, www.kensingtongardenshotel.co.uk, e-mail: info@kensingtongardenshotel.co.uk).

Vancouver Studios offers 45 modern rooms with all the amenities, and gives you a fully equipped kitchenette (utensils, stove, microwave, and fridge) rather than breakfast (small Sb-£55, big Sb-£75, small Db-£95, big Db-£110, Tb-£130, extra bed-£10, 10 percent discount with week or more stay, CC, welcoming staff, homey lounge and private garden, 30 Prince's Square, London W2 4NJ, tel. 020/7243-1270, fax 020/7221-8678, www.vienna-group.co.uk, e-mail: vancouverstudios@vienna-group.co.uk, managed by Fiona).

LOWER PRICED

London House Budget Hotel is a threadbare, nose-ringed slumber mill renting 240 beds in 93 stark rooms (S-£40, Sb-£45, twin-£54, Db-£68, dorm bed-£15, includes continental breakfast, CC, lots of school groups, 81 Kensington Gardens Square, London W2 4DJ, tel. 020/7243-1810, fax 020/7243-1723, e-mail: londonhousehotel@yahoo.co.uk).

Sleeping in Other Neighborhoods

HIGHER PRICED

Covent Garden: Fielding House Hotel, located on a charming, quiet, pedestrian street just two blocks from Covent Gardens, offers 24 clean, no-nonsense rooms, bright orange hallways, and lots of stairs (Db-£100–115, Db with sitting room-£130, CC, non-smoking, no kids under 13, 134 Broad Court, Bow Street, London WC2B 5QZ, tel. 020/7497-8305, fax 020/7497-0064, www.the-fielding-hotel.co.uk).

Paddington Station: The Royal Norfolk Hotel is a 60-room place on a busy corner just one short block from the Paddington Station terminus of the Heathrow Express train (Sb-£99, Db-£109, superior Db-£120, Tb-£139, 25 percent discount for 3-night stay, CC, elevator, 25 London Street, London W2 1HH, tel. 020/7723-3386, fax 020/7724-8442, www.royalnorfolk.co.uk, e-mail: reservations@royalnorfolkhotel.co.uk).

Downtown near Baker Street: For a less hotelesque alternative in the center, consider renting one of the 18 stark, hardwood, comfortable rooms in **22 York Street B&B** (Db-£100, Tb-£141, CC, strictly smoke-free, inviting lounge, social breakfast, from Baker Street Tube station walk 2 blocks down Baker Street and take a right, 22 York Street, London W1U 6PX, tel. 020/7224-3990, fax 020/7224-1990, www.myrtle-cottage.co.uk/callis.htm, energetically run by Liz and Michael).

MODERATELY PRICED

Near Buckingham Palace: Vandon House Hotel, formerly run by the Salvation Army, is now run by the Central University of Iowa. While filled with students most of the year, the 33 rooms are rented to travelers from late May through August at great prices. The rooms, while institutional, are comfy, and the location is excellent (S-£42, D-£66, Db-£82, Tb-£119, Qb-£149, prices promised with this book through 2003, CC, only single beds, non-smoking, elevator, on a tiny road 2 blocks west of St. James Park Tube station, near east end of Petty France Street at 1 Vandon Street, London SW1H OAH, tel. 020/7799-6780, fax 020/7799-1464, www.vandonhouse.com, e-mail: info@vandonhouse.com).

Euston Station: The **Methodist International Centre,** a modern, youthful, Christian residence, fills its lower floors with international students and its top floor with travelers. Rooms are modern and simple yet comfortable, with fine bathrooms, phones, and desks. The atmosphere is friendly, safe, clean, and controlled; also has a spacious lounge and game room (Sb-£48, Db-£71, 2-course buffet dinner-£8, CC, non-smoking rooms, elevator, on quiet street a block west of Euston Station—out Melton Street exit, 81-103 Euston Street, not Euston Road, London W1 2EZ, Tube: Euston Station, tel. 020/7380-0001, fax 020/7387-5300, www.micentre.com, e-mail: sales@micentre.com). In June, July, and August, when the students are gone, they rent simple £38 singles.

LOWER PRICED

Euston Station: Cottage Hotel is tucked away a block off the west exit of Euston Station. Established in 1950—a bit tired, cramped, and smoky—it feels like 1950. But it's cheap and quiet (40 rooms, D-£55, Db-£65, T-£70, Tb-£80, Qb-£90, CC, 10 percent discount for 2-night cash-only stays, 67 Euston Street, London NW1 2ET, tel. 020/7387-6785, fax 020/7383-0859, managed by Ali).

Near St. Paul's: The **City of London Youth Hostel** is clean, modern, friendly, and well-run. You'll pay about £25 for a bed in their three- to eight-bed rooms, £28 for a single room (hostel membership required, 193 beds, CC, cheap meals, open 24 hrs, Tube: St. Paul's, 36 Carter Lane, London EC4V 5AD, tel. 020/7236-4965, fax 020/7236-7681, www.yha.org.uk, e-mail: city@yha.org.uk).

Sleeping near Gatwick and Heathrow Airports

LOWER PRICED

Near Gatwick Airport: The **London Gatwick Airport Travel Inn** rents cheap rooms at the airport (Db-£50, CC, tel. 0870-238-3305, www.travelinn.co.uk). The **Gatwick Travelodge,** also a budget hotel, is two miles from the airport (Db-£50, CC, breakfast extra, free shuttle from south terminal, Church Road, Lowfield Heath, Crawley, tel. 0870-905-6343, www.travelodge.co.uk).

Barn Cottage, a converted 17th-century barn, sits in the peaceful countryside, with a tennis court, small swimming pool, and a good pub within walking distance. It has two wood-beamed rooms, antique furniture, and a large garden that makes you forget Gatwick is 10 minutes away (S-£40–45, D-£55, no CC, can drive you to airport or train station for £6, Leigh, Reigate, Surrey, RH2 8RF, tel. 01306/611-347, warmly run by Pat and Mike Comer).

Wayside Manor Farm is another rural alternative to a bland airport hotel. This four-bedroom countryside place is a 10-minute drive from Gatwick (Db-£60, Norwood Hill, near Charlwood, tel. 01293/862-692, www.wayside-manor.com, e-mail: info@wayside-manor.com).

Kind David Lees, his dog Ben, and two cats preside over **Latchetts Cottage**, with three rooms overlooking pastures and a peaceful garden just 10 minutes from the airport (S-£25, D-£45, includes hearty breakfast, courtesy airport transport 7:00–19:00, long-term parking £2/day, Ricketts Wood Road, Norwood Hill, Horley, Surrey RH6 0ET, tel. 01293/862-831, cellular 07774-860-413, fax 01293/862-832, e-mail: davidlees@tinyworld.co.uk).

Near Heathrow Airport: It's so easy to get to Heathrow from central London, I see no reason to sleep there. But for budget beds near the airport, consider **Heathrow Ibis** (Db-£65, Db-£40–45 on Fri–Sun nights, breakfast extra, CC, £2.50 shuttle bus to/from terminals except T-4, 112 Bath Road, tel. 020/8759-4888, fax 020/8564-7894, www.ibishotel.com, e-mail: h0794@accor-hotels.com).

Eating in London

If you want to dine (as opposed to eat), check out the extensive listings in the weekly entertainment guides sold at London newsstands (or catch a train for Paris). The thought of a £30 meal in Britain generally ruins my appetite, so my London dining is limited mostly to easygoing, fun, but inexpensive alternatives. I've listed places by neighborhood—handy to your sightseeing or hotel.

Your £7 budget choices are pub grub, a café, fish and chips, pizza, ethnic, or picnic. Pub grub is the most atmospheric budget option. Many of London's 7,000 pubs serve fresh, tasty buffets under ancient timbers, with hearty lunches and dinners priced from £6 to £8. (While pubs are going strong, the new phenomenon is coffee shops: Starbucks and its competitors have sprouted up all over town, providing cushy and social watering holes with comfy chairs, easy WCs, £2 lattes, and a nice break between sights.)

Ethnic restaurants—especially Indian and Chinese—are popular, plentiful, and cheap. Most large museums (and many churches) have inexpensive, cheery cafeterias. Of course, picnicking is the fastest and cheapest way to go. Good grocery stores and sandwich shops, fine park benches, and polite pigeons abound in Britain's most expensive city.

Eating near Trafalgar Square

To locate restaurants, see map on page 617.

For a tasty meal on a monk's budget, sitting on somebody's tomb in an ancient crypt, descend into the **St. Martin-in-the-Fields Café in the Crypt** (£5–7 cafeteria plates, cheaper sandwich bar, Mon–Sat 10:00–20:00, Sun 12:00–20:30, profits go to the church, no CC, underneath St. Martin-in-the-Fields on Trafalgar Square, tel. 020/7839-4342).

Chandos Bar's Opera Room floats amazingly apart from the tacky crush of tourism around Trafalgar Square. Enter the pub (opposite National Portrait Gallery, corner of William Street and St. Martin's Lane) and climb the stairs to the Opera Room for £6–7 pub lunches and dinners (served daily 11:00–19:00, tel. 020/7836-1401). This is a fine Trafalgar rendezvous point—smoky, but wonderfully local. Order and pay at the bar.

Gordon's Wine Bar is ripe with atmosphere. A simple, steep staircase leads into a 14th-century cellar filled with dusty old wine bottles, faded British memorabilia, local nine-to-fivers, and candlelight (hot meals only for lunch, fine plate of cheeses or various cold cuts with salad buffet all day until 21:00—1 plate of each feeds 2 for £7). While it's crowded, you can normally corral two chairs and grab the corner of a table (arrive before 18:00 to get a seat, Mon–Sat 11:00–23:00, Sun 12:00–22:00, 2 blocks from

Trafalgar Square, bottom of Villiars Street at #47, Tube: Embankment, tel. 020/7930-1408).

Down Whitehall, a block south of Trafalgar Square toward Big Ben, you'll find the touristy but atmospheric **Clarence Pub** (lunch only, decent grub) and several cheaper cafeterias and pizza joints.

For a classy lunch in the National Gallery, treat your palate to the moderately priced light Mediterranean cuisine at **Crivelli's Garden** (daily 10:00–17:00, first floor of Sainsbury Wing).

Simpson's on the Strand serves a stuffy, aristocratic, old-time carvery dinner—where the chef slices your favorite red meat from a fancy trolley at your table—in its elegant, smoky old dining room (£20, Mon–Sat 12:15–14:30 & 17:30–22:45, no tennis shoes or T-shirts, at 100 Strand, tel. 020/7836-9112).

Eating near Piccadilly

Hungry and broke in the theater district? Head for Panton Street (off Haymarket, 2 blocks southeast of Piccadilly Circus) for cheap Thai, Chinese, and two famous London eateries. **Stockpot** is a mushy-peas kind of place, famous and rightly popular for its edible, cheap meals (daily 7:00–22:00, 38 Panton Street). The **West End Kitchen** (across the street at #5, same hours and menu) is a direct competitor that's just as good. Vegetarians prefer the **Woodland South Indian Vegetarian Restaurant**, across from the West End Kitchen.

The palatial **Criterion Brasserie** serves a special £15 two-course "Anglo-French" menu (or £18 for 3 courses) under gilded tiles and chandeliers in a dreamy Byzantine church setting from 1880. It's right on Piccadilly Circus but a world away from the punk junk. The house wine is great and so is the food (specials available Mon–Sat 12:00–14:30 & 17:30–18:30, dinner served until 23:00, closed Sun lunch, CC, tel. 020/7930-0488). Anyone can drop in for coffee or a drink.

The "Food Is Fun" Dinner Crawl: From Covent Garden to Soho

London has a trendy generation-X scene that most Beefeater-seekers miss entirely. For a multicultural movable feast and a chance to sample some of London's most popular eateries, consider exploring these. Start around 18:00 to avoid lines, get in on early specials, and find waiters willing to let you split a meal. Prices, while reasonable by London standards, add up. Servings are large enough to share. All are open nightly.

Suggested nibbler's dinner crawl for two: Arrive before 18:00 at **Belgo Centraal** and split the early-bird dinner special: a kilo of mussels, fries, and dark Belgian beer. At **Yo! Sushi**,

From Covent Garden to Soho, "Food is Fun"

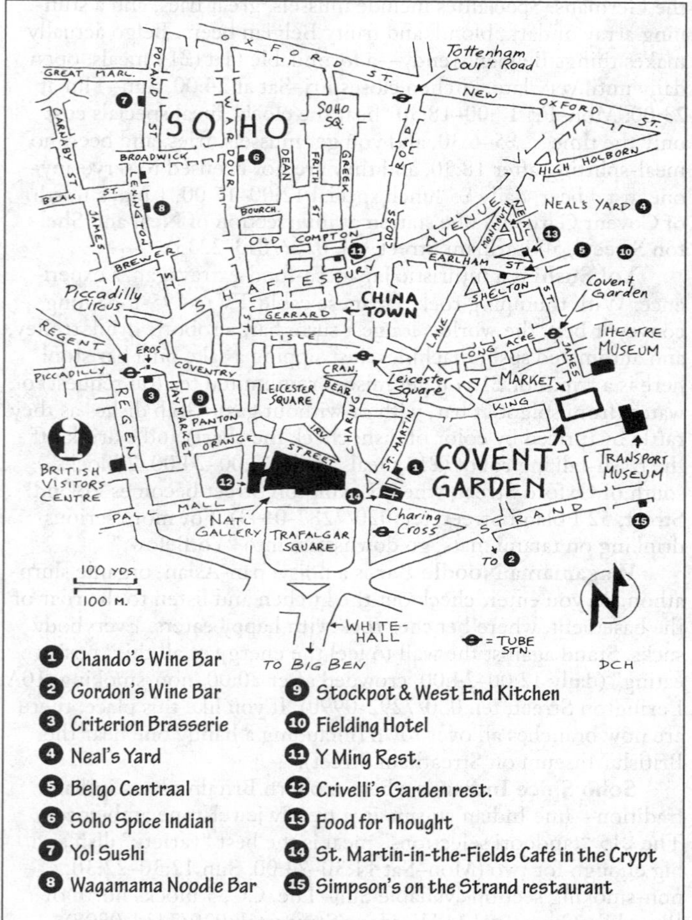

have beer or sake and a few dishes. Slurp your last course at **Wagamama Noodle Bar**. Then, for dessert, people-watch at Leicester Square, where the serf's always up.

Belgo Centraal is a space-station world overrun with Trappist monks serving hearty Belgian specialties. The classy restaurant section requires reservations, but just grabbing a bench in the boisterous beer hall (no reservations possible) is more fun. The same menu and specials work on both sides.

Belgians claim they eat as well as the French and as heartily as the Germans. Specialties include mussels, great fries, and a stunning array of dark, blond, and fruity Belgian beers. Belgo actually makes things Belgian trendy—a formidable feat (£14 meals; open daily until very late, kitchen closes Fri–Sat at 24:00, Sun–Thu at 23:00; Mon–Fri 17:00–18:30 "beat the clock" meal specials cost only the time . . . £5–6.30, and you get mussels, fries, and beer; no meal-splitting after 18:30, and they are not licensed to serve anyone just a beer; daily £5 lunch special 12:00–17:00; 1 block north of Covent Garden Tube station at intersection of Neal and Shelton Streets, 50 Earlham Street, tel. 020/7813-2233).

Yo! Sushi is a futuristic Japanese-food-extravaganza experience. With thumping rock, Japanese cable TV, a 195-foot-long conveyor belt, the world's longest sushi bar, a robotic drink trolley, and automated sushi machines, just sipping a sake on a bar stool here is a trip. For £1 you get miso, or unlimited tea (on request) or water (from spigot at bar, with or without gas). Grab dishes as they rattle by (priced by color of dish; check the chart) and a drink off the trash-talking robot (£12 meals, daily 12:00–24:00, 2 blocks south of Oxford Street, where Lexington Street becomes Poland Street, 52 Poland Street, tel. 020/7287-0443). For more serious drinking on tatami mats, go downstairs into "Yo Below."

Wagamama Noodle Bar is a noisy, pan-Asian, organic slurpathon. As you enter, check out the kitchen and listen to the roar of the basement, where benches rock with happy eaters. Everybody sucks. Stand against the wall to feel the energy of all this "positive eating" (daily 12:00–24:00, crowded after 20:00, non-smoking, 10A Lexington Street, tel. 020/7292-0990). If you like this place, there are now branches all over town (including a handy one near the British Museum on Streatham Street).

Soho Spice Indian is where modern Britain meets Indian tradition—fine Indian cuisine in a trendy jewel-tone ambience. The £15 "tandoori selections" meal is the best "variety" dish and big enough for two (Mon–Sat 11:30–24:00, Sun 12:30–22:30, non-smoking section available Sun–Tue, CC, 5 blocks north of Piccadilly Circus at 124 Wardour Street, tel. 020/7434-0808).

Y Ming Chinese Restaurant, across Shaftesbury Avenue from the ornate gates, clatter, and dim sum of Chinatown, has clean European decor, serious but helpful service, and authentic Northern Chinese cooking (good £10 meal deal offered 12:00–18:00; Mon–Sat 12:00–23:30, last order at 23:00, closed Sun, CC, 35 Greek Street, tel. 020/7734-2721).

Andrew Edmunds Restaurant is a tiny, candlelit place where you'll want to hide your camera and guidebook and act as local as possible. The modern European cooking is worth the splurge

(3 courses for £25, daily 12:30–15:00 & 18:00–22:45, reservations are generally necessary, 46 Lexington Street in Soho, tel. 020/7437-5708).

For cheap, hip, and healthy near Covent Garden, the area around Neal's Yard is busy with fun, hippie-type cafés. One of the best is **Food for Thought**, packed with local health nuts (good £5 vegetarian meals, Mon–Sat 12:00–20:30, Sun 12:00–17:00, non-smoking, 2 blocks north of Covent Garden Tube station, 31 Neal Street, tel. 020/7836-0239). **Neal's Yard** itself is a food circus of trendy, healthy eateries.

Eating near Recommended Victoria Station Accommodations

Here are places a couple of blocks southwest of Victoria Station where I've enjoyed eating (see map on page 604).

The small but classy **La Campagnola** is Belgravia's favorite budget Italian restaurant (£12–16 plus 10 percent service charge, Mon–Sat 12:00–15:00 & 18:00–23:30, closed Sun, CC, 10 Lower Belgrave Street, tel. 020/7730-2057).

The **Ebury Wine Bar**, filled with young professionals, provides a classy atmosphere and pricey but delicious meals (£15–18, Mon–Fri 11:00–23:00, Sat 12:00–23:00, Sun 18:00–23:00, CC, 139 Ebury Street, at intersection with Elizabeth Street, near bus station, tel. 020/7730-5447). Several cheap places are around the corner on Elizabeth Street (#23 for take-out or eat-in, super-absorbent fish and chips).

The **Duke of Wellington** pub is a good, if somewhat smoky, neighborhood place for dinner (£6 meals, Mon–Sat 11:00–23:00, Sun 12:00–22:30, 63 Eaton Terrace, at intersection with Chester Row, tel. 020/7730-1782).

At **Constitution Pub**, a friendly local hangout, owner Lee and his family offer a warm welcome and traditional pub grub (£4–7, Mon–Sat 11:00–22:00, Sun 12:00–22:00, 42 Churton Street, tel. 020/7834-3651).

Jenny Lo's Tea House is a simple, budget place serving up £5–7 eclectic Chinese-style meals to locals in the know (Mon–Fri 11:30–15:00 & 18:00–22:00, Sat 12:00–15:00 & 18:00–22:00, closed Sun, no CC, 14 Eccleston Street, tel. 020/7259-0399 or 020/7823-6331).

La Poule au Pot, ideal for a romantic splurge, offers a classy, candlelit ambience with well-dressed patrons and expensive but fine Mediterranean and Provençal-style French food (£20–25 dinners, daily 12:30–14:30 & 18:45–23:00, Sun until 22:00, leafy patio dining, reservations smart, CC, end of Ebury at intersection with Pimlico, 231 Ebury Street, tel. 020/7730-7763).

Pimlico Restaurant serves quality Indian cuisine (daily 12:00–14:30 & 18:00–21:30, CC, 38 Moreton Street, just off of Belgrave Street, tel. 020/7976-6331).

The **Marche** is an easy, moderately priced cafeteria a couple of blocks north of Victoria Station at Bressenden Place (Mon–Sat 7:30–23:00, Sun 11:00–21:00, CC, tel. 020/7630-1733). If you miss America, there's a mall-type food circus at Victoria Place, upstairs in Victoria Station; **Café Rouge** offers the best food here (£8–11 dinners, daily 9:30–22:30).

Groceries: The late-hours **Whistle Stop** at the station has decent sandwiches, fresh fruit, snacks, and beverages (daily, 24 hrs). A larger grocery, **Sainsbury Local**, is on Victoria Street in front of the station, just past the buses (Mon–Fri 7:00–22:00, Sat 7:00–21:00, Sun 10:00–16:00).

Eating near Recommended Notting Hill Gate B&Bs and Bayswater Hotels

Queensway is lined with lively and inexpensive eateries. See map on page 610.

The exuberantly rustic and very English **Maggie Jones** serves my favorite £20 London dinner. You'll get solid English cuisine, including huge plates of crunchy vegetables—by candlelight (daily 12:30–14:30 & 18:30–23:00, much less expensive lunch menu, reservations recommended—request upstairs for noisy but less-cramped section, CC, friendly staff, 6 Old Court Place, just east of Kensington Church Street, near High Street Kensington Tube stop, tel. 020/7937-6462). If you eat well once in London, eat here (and do it quick, before it burns down).

The **Churchill Arms** pub is a local hangout, with good beer and old English ambience in front and hearty £6 Thai plates in an enclosed patio in the back. You can bring the Thai food into the smoky but wonderfully atmospheric pub section. Arrive by 18:00 to avoid a line (Mon–Sat 12:00–14:30 & 18:00–21:30, Sun 12:00–14:30, 119 Kensington Church Street, tel. 020/7792-1246).

Prince Edward Pub serves good pub grub in a quintessential pub setting (£8 meals, Mon–Sat 12:00–15:00 & 18:00–22:00, Sun 12:00–18:00, indoor/outdoor seating, CC, 2 blocks north of Bayswater Road at the corner of Dawson Place and Hereford Road, 73 Prince's Square, tel. 020/7727-2221).

Café Diana is a healthy little eatery serving sandwiches and Middle Eastern food. It's decorated with photos of Princess Diana because she used to drop by for pita sandwiches (daily 8:00–22:30, 5 Wellington Terrace, on Bayswater Road, opposite Kensington Palace Garden Gates—where Diana once lived, tel. 020/7792-9606).

The Royal China Restaurant is filled with London's Chinese, who consider this one of the city's best eateries. It's black, white, chrome, and candles with brisk waiters and fine food (£7–9 dishes, dim sum until 17:00, Mon–Thu 12:00–23:00, Fri–Sat 12:00–23:30, Sun 11:00–22:00, CC, 13 Queensway, tel. 020/7221-2535).

Mr. Wu serves a 10-course Chinese buffet in a bright and cheery little place. Just grab a plate and help yourself (£4.50, daily 12:00–23:30, check quality of buffet—right inside entrance—before committing, pickings can get slim, across from Bayswater Tube station, 54 Queensway, tel. 020/7243-1017).

Whiteleys Mall Food Court offers a fun selection of ethnic and fast-food eateries in a delightful mall (good salads at Café Rouge, second floor, corner of Porchester Gardens and Queensway).

Supermarket: Europa is a half block from the Notting Hill Gate Tube stop (Mon–Fri 8:00–23:00, Sun 12:00–18:00, 112 Notting Hill Gate, near intersection with Pembridge Road).

Eating near Recommended Accommodations in South Kensington

Popular eateries line Old Brompton Road and Thurloe Street (Tube: South Kensington). See map on page 608.

La Bouchee Bistro Café is a classy, hole-in-the-wall touch of France serving early-bird, three-course £11 meals before 19:00 and *plats du jour* for £8 all *jour* (daily 12:00–23:00, Sun until 22:00, CC, 56 Old Brompton Road, tel. 020/7589-1929).

Daquise, an authentic-feeling Polish place, is ideal if you're in the mood for kielbasa and kraut. It's fast, cheap, family-run, and a part of the neighborhood (£10 meals, daily 11:00–23:00, non-smoking, CC, 20 Thurloe Street, tel. 020/7589-6117).

The **Khyber Pass Tandoori Restaurant** is a nondescript but handy place serving great Punjabi-style Indian cuisine. Locals in the know travel to eat here (£10 dinners, daily 12:00–14:30 & 18:00–23:30, CC, 21 Bute Street, tel. 020/7589-7311).

La Brasserie fills a big, plain room painted "nicotine yellow" with ceiling fans, a Parisian ambience, and good, traditional French cooking at reasonable prices (2-course £16 "regional menu," £13 bottle of house wine, nightly until 23:00, CC, 272 Brompton Road, tel. 020/7581-3089).

PJ's Bar and Grill is lively with the yuppie Chelsea crowd for a good reason. Traditional "New York Brasserie"–style yet trendy, it has dressy tables surrounding a centerpiece bar. It serves pricey, cosmopolitan cuisine from a menu that changes with the seasons (£20 meals, nightly until 24:00, CC, 52 Fulham Road, at intersection with Sydney Street, tel. 020/7581-0025).

Eating Elsewhere in London

Near St. Paul's, in The City: The **Counting House**, formerly an elegant old bank, offers great £7 meals, nice homemade meat pies, fish, and fresh vegetables (Mon–Fri 12:00–20:00, closed Sat–Sun, gets really busy with the buttoned-down 9-to-5 crowd after 12:15, near Mansion House in the City, 50 Cornhill, tel. 020/7283-7123).

Near the British Library: Drummond Street (running just west of Euston Station) is famous in London for very cheap and good Indian and vegetarian food. Consider **Chutneys** and **Ravi Shankar** for a good *thali*.

Transportation Connections—London

Flying into London's Heathrow Airport

Heathrow is the world's fourth busiest airport. Think about it: 60 million passengers a year on 425,000 flights from 200 destinations riding 90 airlines . . . some kind of global maypole dance. While many complain about it, I like it. It's user-friendly. Read signs, ask questions. For Heathrow's airport, flight, and transfers information, call the switchboard at 0870/000-0123. It has four terminals: T-1 (mostly domestic flights, with some European), T-2 (mainly European flights), T-3 (mostly flights from the United States), and T-4 (British Air transatlantic flights and BA flights to Paris, Amsterdam, and Athens). Taxis know which terminal you'll need.

Each terminal has an airport information desk, car-rental agencies, exchange bureaus, ATMs, a pharmacy, a VAT refund desk (VAT info tel. 020/8910-3682; you must present the VAT claim form from the retailer here to get your 15 percent tax rebate on items purchased in Britain, see page 8 for details), and a £3.50/day baggage-check desk (open 5:30–23:00). There are post offices in T-2 and T-4. Each terminal has cheap eateries (such as the cheery Food Village self-service cafeteria in T-3). The American Express desk, in the Tube station at Terminal 4 (daily 7:00–19:00), has rates similar to the exchange bureaus upstairs, but they don't charge a commission (typically 1.5 percent) for cashing any type of traveler's check.

Heathrow's small TI gives you all the help that London's Victoria Station does, but with none of the crowds (daily 8:30–18:00, 5-min walk from Terminal 3 in the Tube station, follow signs to "underground"; bypass the queue for transit info to reach the window for London questions). If you're riding the Airbus into London, have your partner stay with the bags at the terminal while you pop over to TI, get a free simple map and brochures, and, if you're taking the Tube into London, buy a one-day Travel Card day pass to cover the ride (see below). Heathrow's "Internet Exchange" provides Internet access 24 hours a day (T-3).

Transportation to London from Heathrow Airport

By Tube (Subway): For £3.60, the Tube takes you 14 miles to downtown London in 50 minutes (6/hr, depending on your destination, may require a change). Even better, buy a £5 one-day Travel Card that covers your trip into London and all your Tube travel for the day (starting at 9:30). Buy it at the ticket window at the Tube. You can hop on the Tube at any terminal.

By Airport Bus: The Airbus, running between the airport and London's King's Cross station, serves the Notting Hill Gate and Bayswater neighborhoods (£8, £12-round-trip, 2/hr, 60 min, runs 5:00–21:15, departs from each terminal, buy ticket from driver, tel. 0875-757-747). The Tube works fine, but with baggage I prefer the Airbus (assuming it serves my hotel neighborhood) because there are no connections underground and there's a lovely view from the top of the double-decker bus. Ask the driver to remind you when to get off. For people heading to the airport, exact pickup times are clearly posted at each bus stop.

If you're staying in London's Victoria Station neighborhood, consider the National Express bus that runs between Heathrow's central bus station and the Victoria Coach Station, which is one block from Victoria Station (£7, kids go free, 2/hr, 45 min, 5:40–21:45 from Heathrow, 7:45–24:00 from Victoria, tel. 08705-808-080).

By Taxi: Taxis from the airport cost about £40. For four people traveling together, this can be a deal. Hotels can often line up a cab back to the airport for £30. For the cheapest taxi to the airport, don't order one from your hotel. Simply flag down a few and ask them for their best "off-meter" rate. Another good option is Hotelink, a door-to-door airport shuttle (Heathrow-£15 per person, Gatwick-£22 per person, book the day before departure, tel. 01293/532-244, www.hotelink.co.uk, e-mail: reservations@hotelink.co.uk).

By Heathrow Express Train: This slick train service zips you between Heathrow Airport and London's Paddington Station. At Paddington Station, you're in the thick of the Tube system, with easy access to any of my recommended neighborhoods—Notting Hill Gate is just two stops away. It's only 15 minutes to downtown from Terminals 1, 2, and 3, and 20 minutes from Terminal 4 (at the airport, you can use the Express as a free transfer between terminals). Buy your ticket to London before you board or pay a £2 surcharge to buy it on the train (£12, but ask about discount promos at Heathrow ticket desk, kids under 16 ride free if you buy your ticket before boarding, CC, covered by BritRail pass, 4/hr, daily 5:10–23:30, tel. 0845/600-1515, www.heathrowexpress.co.uk). A "Go Further" ticket (£13.50) includes one Tube ride from Paddington to get you to your hotel (valid only on same day and in Zone 1, saves time). For one person on a budget, combining the Heathrow Express with either a Tube or taxi ride (between your hotel and Paddington) is nearly as fast and half the cost of taking a cab directly to (or from) the airport.

Buses from Heathrow to Destinations beyond London

The **National Express Central Bus Station** offers direct bus connections to **Gatwick Airport** (4/hr, 70 min), departing just outside arrivals at all terminals; there are two services: Speedlink for £17 and Jetlink for £14. To **Bath**, direct buses run daily from Heathrow (11/day, 2.5 hrs, £13, tel. 08705-757-747). BritRail passholders may prefer the 2.5-hour Heathrow–Bath bus/train connection via Reading (£9 for bus, rail portion free with pass, otherwise £29.20 total, payable at desk in terminal, CC); first catch the twice-hourly RailAir Link shuttle bus to Reading (pron. RED-ding), then hop on the hourly express train to Bath. Most Heathrow buses depart from the common area serving terminals 1, 2, and 3 (a 5-min walk from any of these terminals), although some depart from T-4 (bus tel. 08705-747-777).

Flying into London's Gatwick Airport

More and more flights, especially charters, land at Gatwick Airport, halfway between London and the southern coast (recorded airport info tel. 0870-000-2468). Express trains—clearly the best way into London from here—shuttle conveniently between Gatwick and London's Victoria Station (£11, £21 round-trip, children under 5 free, 4/hr during day, 1–2/hr at night, 30 min, runs 24 hrs daily, can purchase tickets on train at no extra charge, tel. 08705-301-530, www.gatwickexpress.co.uk). Or you can save a few pounds by taking South Central rail line's slower and less-frequent shuttle between Victoria Station and Gatwick (£8.20, 3/hr, 1/hr from midnight–4:00, 45 min, tel. 08457-484-950, www.southcentraltrains.co.uk).

To get to Bath from Gatwick, catch a bus to Heathrow and the bus to Bath from there.

To make a flight connection between Heathrow and Gatwick (see "Buses," above), allow three hours between your arrival at one airport and departure at the other.

London's Other Airports

If you're flying into or out of **Stansted** (airport tel. 0870-0000-303), you can take the Airbus between the airport and downtown London's

Victoria Coach Station (£8, 2/hr, 1.5 hrs, runs 4:00–24:00, picks up and stops throughout London, tel. 08705-747-777) or take the Stansted Airport Rail Link (£13, departs London's Liverpool Station, 40 min, 2–4/hr, 5:00–23:00, tel. 08705-301-530, www.stanstedexpress.com).

For **Luton** (airport tel. 01582/405-100, www.london-luton.com), take Green Line's bus #757, which runs between the airport and London's Victoria Station at Buckingham Palace Road—stop 6 (£8.50, £7.50 for easyJet passengers, 2/hr, 1–1.25 hrs depending on time of day, runs 4:30–24:00, tel. 0870-608-7261, www.greenline.co.uk).

Discounted Flights from London

Discount airlines can be cheaper than the train. Although bmi british midland has been around the longest, the others generally offer cheaper flights.

With **bmi british midland,** you can fly inexpensively to Edinburgh (8/day, 75 min, as little as £30 one-way or £60 round-trip); to Dublin, Ireland (8/day, 75 min, starting at £52 one-way, £104 round-trip); to Paris (from £36 one-way, £72 round-trip); to Brussels (from £45/£90), to Amsterdam (from £34/£68), and more. For the latest, call British tel. 0870-607-0555 or U.S. tel. 800/788-0555 (check www.flybmi.com and their subsidiary, bmi baby, at www.bmibaby.com). You can book right up until the flight departs, but the cheap seats will have sold out long before, leaving the most expensive seats for latecomers.

Ryanair is a creative Irish airline that prides itself on offering the lowest fares. It flies from London (mostly Stansted Airport) to often obscure airports in Dublin, Glasgow, Frankfurt, Stockholm, Oslo, Venice, Turin, and many others. Sample fares: London–Dublin—£78 round-trip (sometimes as low as £25), London–Frankfurt—£67 round-trip (Irish tel. 01/609-7881, British tel. 0870-333-1231, www.ryanair.com). Because they offer promotional deals any time of year, it's not essential that you book long in advance to get the best deals.

Virgin Express is a British-owned company with good rates (book by phone and pick up ticket at airport an hour before your flight, tel. 020/7744-0004, www.virgin-express.com). Virgin Express flies from London Heathrow and Brussels. From its hub in Brussels, you can connect cheaply to Barcelona, Madrid, Nice, Malaga, Copenhagen, Rome, or Milan (round-trip from Brussels to Rome for as little as £105). Their prices stay the same whether or not you book in advance.

EasyJet, with no frills and cheap fares, flies mostly from Luton and Gatwick. Prices are based on demand, so the least popular routes make for the cheapest fares, especially if you book early (tel. 0870-600-0000, www.easyjet.com).

Trains and Buses

London, Britain's major transportation hub, has a different train station for each region. Waterloo handles the Eurostar to Paris. King's Cross covers northeast England and Scotland (tel. 08457-225-225). Paddington covers west and southwest England (Bath) and South Wales (tel. 08457/000-125). For the others, call 08457-484-950. Note that due to security reasons, stations offer a left luggage service (£5/day) rather than lockers.

National Express' excellent bus service is considerably cheaper than trains. (For a busy signal, call 08705-808-080, or visit www.nationalexpress.co.uk or the bus station a block southwest of Victoria Station.)

To Bath: Trains leave London's Paddington Station every hour between 7:00 and 19:00 (at a quarter after) for the 75-minute ride to Bath (costs £32 if you leave after 9:30). To get to Bath via Stonehenge, consider taking a guided bus tour from London to Stonehenge and Bath and abandoning the tour in Bath (see page 601 for details).

To points north: Trains run hourly from London's King's Cross Station, stopping in York (2 hrs), Durham (3 hrs), and Edinburgh (5 hrs).

To Dublin, Ireland: The boat/rail journey takes between 10 and 11 hours and goes all day or all night (£24–35, 7/day, tel. 08705/143-219, www.eurolines.co.uk). Consider a cheap 70-minute Ryanair flight instead (see above).

Crossing the English Channel

Crossing the Channel by Eurostar Train

The fastest and most convenient way to get from Big Ben to the Eiffel Tower is by rail. In London, advertisements claim "more businessmen travel from London to Paris on the Eurostar than on all airlines combined."

Eurostar is the speedy passenger train that zips you (and up to 800 others in 18 sleek cars) from downtown London to downtown Paris (15/day, last departure 19:23, 3 hrs) or Brussels (9/day, 3 hrs) faster and easier than flying. The train goes 80 mph in England and 190 mph on the Continent. (When the English segment gets up to speed, the journey time will shrink to 2 hours.) The actual tunnel crossing is a 20-minute, black, silent, 100-mile-per-hour nonevent. Your ears won't even pop. You can go direct to Disneyland Paris (1/day, more frequent with transfer at Lille) or change at Lille to catch a TGV to Paris' Charles de Gaulle Airport.

Channel fares (essentially the same to Paris or Brussels) are reasonable but complicated. As with airfares, the most expensive and flexible option is a full-fare ticket with no restrictions on refundability. Cheaper tickets come with more restrictions—and sell out more quickly.

Prices vary depending on when you travel; whether you can live with restrictions; and whether you're eligible for any discounts (youth, seniors, and railpass holders all qualify). The various second-class Leisure Tickets are a good deal, but many require a round-trip purchase. Compare one-way fares with cheap round-trip fares (you can forget to return).

You can check and book fares by phone or online in the United States (U.S. tel. 800/EUROSTAR, www.eurostar.com or www.raileurope.com, prices listed in dollars) or in Britain (British tel. 08705-186-186, www.eurostar.co.uk, prices listed in pounds). These are two different companies, often with different prices and discount deals on similar tickets (see below)—if you order from the United States, check out both. (If you buy from the U.S. company, you'll pay a FedEx charge for ticket delivery in the U.S.; if you book with the British company, you'll pick up your ticket at Waterloo Station.) In Europe, you can get your Eurostar ticket at any major train station in any country or at any travel agency that handles train tickets (expect a booking fee).

Note that Britain's time zone is one hour earlier than the Continent's. Times listed on tickets are local times.

Here are typical fares available in 2002. For 2003 fares, check the Eurostar phone numbers and Web sites listed above. Notice that sometimes it's a better deal to buy your ticket in Britain instead of the United States—or vice-versa.

Eurostar Full-Fare Tickets

Full-fare tickets are fully refundable even after the departure date. As with plane tickets, you'll pay more to have fewer restrictions. In 2002, one-way "Business First" cost £210 in Britain/$279 in the United States and included a meal (a dinner departure nets you more grub than breakfast). Full-fare second-class tickets ("Standard Flexi") cost £170/$199.

Cheaper Tickets

Since full-fare, no-restrictions tickets are so expensive, most travelers sacrifice flexibility for a cheaper ticket with more restrictions. Second class is plenty comfortable, making first class an unnecessary expense for most; prices listed below are for second class unless otherwise noted. Some of these tickets are available only in Britain, others only in the United States. They are listed roughly from most expensive to cheapest (with more restrictions as you move down the list).

Leisure Flexi: £160 round-trip (round-trip purchase required, partially refundable before departure date, not available in U.S.).

U.S. Leisure: $139 one-way (partially refundable before departure date, not available in Britain).

Leisure: £120 round-trip (round-trip purchase required, nonrefundable, not available in U.S.).

Leisure Apex 7: £95 round-trip (round-trip purchase required, nonrefundable, purchase at least 7 days in advance, not available in U.S.).

Leisure Apex 14: £79/$178 round-trip (round-trip purchase required, nonrefundable, purchase at least 14 days in advance, stay 2 nights or over a Sat, available in U.S. and Britain).

Weekend Day Return: £60 for same-day round-trip on a Saturday or Sunday (round-trip purchase required, nonrefundable, not available in U.S.). Note that this round-trip ticket is cheaper than many one-way tickets.

Eurostar Discounts

For Railpass Holders: Discounts are available in the United States or Britain to travelers holding railpasses that include France, Belgium, or Britain (£50/$75 one-way for second class, £100/$155 one-way for first). In Britain, passholder tickets can be issued only at the Eurostar office in Waterloo Station or the American Express office in Victoria Station—not at any other stations. You can also order them by phone, then pick them up at Waterloo Station.

For Youth and Seniors: Discounts are available in the United States and Britain for children under 12 (£30/$69 one-way for second class) and youths under 26 (£50/$79 one-way for second class). Only in the United States can seniors over 60 get discounts ($189 one-way for first class).

Crossing the Channel without Eurostar

By Bus and Boat or Train and Boat: The old-fashioned way of crossing the Channel is cheaper than crossing via Eurostar. It's also twice as romantic, complicated, and time-consuming. You'll get better prices arranging your trip in London than you would in the United States. Taking the bus is cheapest, and round-trips are a bargain.

By Bus: To Paris, Brussels, or Amsterdam from Victoria Coach Station (via boat or Chunnel), £32 one-way, £52 round-trip; 7 hrs to Paris—7/day; 7 hrs to Brussels—10/day; 11.25 hrs to Amsterdam—6/day; day or overnight, on Eurolines (tel. 08705-143-219, www.eurolines.co.uk).

The **Hoverspeed ferry** runs between Dover, England, and Calais, France (tel. 08705-240-241 or 0870-240-8070, www.hoverspeed.com). Hoverspeed sells rail and ferry packages from London–Paris: £39 one-way; £49 round-trip with five-day return; and £58 round-trip over more than five days. You can buy this package deal in person at Waterloo or Charing Cross stations. If you book by phone (number listed above), you must book at least two weeks in advance, and the ticket will be mailed to you (no ticket pickup at station for bookings by phone).

By **P&O Stena Line ferry** from Dover to Calais: £26 one-way; £48 round-trip with five-day return; £52 round-trip over more than five days (tel. 0870-600-0613, www.posl.com). Prices are for the ferry only; you need to book your own train tickets—see P&O's Web site for details.

By Plane: Typical fares are £110 regular, less for student standby. Check with the budget airlines for cheap round-trip fares to Paris (see "Discounted Flights from London," above).

NEAR LONDON: WINDSOR, GREENWICH, AND CAMBRIDGE

WINDSOR

The pleasant pedestrians-only shopping zone of Windsor litters the approach to its famous palace with fun temptations. You'll find the **TI** on 24 High Street (April–Sept daily 10:00–17:00, Oct–March daily 10:00–16:00, tel. 01753/743-900, www.windsor.gov.uk).

▲▲Windsor Castle—Windsor Castle, the official home of England's royal family for 900 years, claims to be the largest and oldest occupied castle in the world. The queen considers this sprawling and fortified palace her primary residence. Thankfully, touring it is simple: you'll see immense grounds, lavish staterooms, a crowd-pleasing dollhouse, an art gallery, and the chapel.

Immediately upon entering, you pass through a simple modern building housing a historical overview of the castle. This excellent intro is worth a close look, since you're basically on your own after this. Inside you'll find the motte (artificial mound) and bailey (fortified stockade around it) of William the Conqueror's castle still visible. Dating from 1080, this was his first castle in England.

Follow the signs to the staterooms/gallery/dollhouse.

Queen Mary's Dollhouse—a palace in miniature (1/12 scale from 1923) and "the most famous dollhouse in the world"—comes with the longest wait. You can skip that line and go immediately into the lavish staterooms. Strewn with history and the art of a long line of kings and queens, it's the best royal display I've seen in Britain—and well restored after the devastating 1992 fire. The adjacent gallery is a changing exhibit featuring the royal art collection (and some big names, such as Michelangelo and Leonardo). Signs direct you (downhill) to St. George's Chapel. Housing 10 royal tombs, it's a fine example of Perpendicular Gothic, with classic fan vaulting spreading out from each pillar (about 1500). Next door is the sumptuous 13th-century Albert Memorial Chapel, redecorated after the death of Queen Victoria's beloved Prince Albert in 1861 and dedicated to his memory. (Admission: £11.50, £29/family, £3 audioguide is better than official guidebook for help throughout, March–Oct daily 9:45–17:15, last entry 16:00, Nov–Feb closes at 16:15, changing of the guard most days at 11:00, evensong in the chapel at 17:15, recorded info tel. 01753/831-118, live info tel. 020/7321-2233, www.royal.gov.uk).

Legoland Windsor—This huge kid-pleasing park next to Windsor Palace has dozens of tame but fun rides (often with very long lines) scattered throughout its 150 acres. An impressive Mini-Land has 28 million Lego pieces glued together to create 800 tiny buildings and a virtual mini-tour of Europe. The place is fun for Legomaniacs under 12 (£19, children-£16, under 3 free, £10 if you enter during last 2 hrs, CC, April–Oct daily 10:00–17:00, 18:00, or 19:00 depending upon season and day, closed most Tue–Wed in Sept–Oct, closed Nov–March except Dec 21–Jan 5, £2.50 round-trip shuttle bus runs from Windsor's Parish Church, 2/hr, clearly signposted, easy free parking, next to Windsor Castle, tel. 08705-040-404, www.legoland.co.uk).

Transportation Connections—Windsor

By Train: Windsor has two train stations: Windsor Central (5-min walk to palace and TI) and Windsor & Eton Riverside (10-min walk to palace and TI). Thames Trains run between London's Paddington Station and Windsor Central (2/hr, 40 min, change at Slough, www.thamestrains.co.uk). South West Trains run between London's Waterloo Station and the Windsor & Eton Riverside station (2/hr, 50 min, www.swtrains.co.uk).

By Bus: Green Line buses #700 and #702 run hourly between London's Victoria Colonnade (between the Victoria train and coach stations) and Windsor, where the bus stops in front of Legoland and near the castle—the stop is "Parish Church" (1.5 hrs). Bus info tel. 0870/608-7261.

By Car: Windsor, 20 miles from London and just off Heathrow Airport's landing path, is well signposted from the M4 motorway. It's a convenient stop for anyone arriving at Heathrow, picking up a car, and not going into London.

GREENWICH

The palace at Greenwich was favored by the Tudor kings. Henry VIII was born here. Later kings commissioned Inigo Jones and Chris Wren to beautify the town and palace. In spite of Greenwich's architectural and royal treats, this is England's maritime capital, and visitors go for things salty. Greenwich hosts historic ships, nautical shops, and hordes of tourists.

Planning Your Time

See the two ships—*Cutty Sark* and *Gipsy Moth IV*—upon arrival. Then walk the shoreline promenade, with a possible lunch or drink in the venerable Trafalgar Tavern, before heading up to the National Maritime Museum and the Royal Observatory Greenwich.

The town throbs with day-trippers on weekends because of its arts-and-crafts and antique markets. To avoid crowds, visit on a weekday.

Tourist Information

The TI, facing the riverside square a few paces from the *Cutty Sark*, has a café, WC, fast Internet connections (£1/20 min) and displays that provide a brief history of the town (daily 10:00–17:00, 2 Cutty Sark Gardens, Pepys House, tel. 0870/608-2000, www.greenwich.gov.uk). Guided walks cover the big sights (£4, daily 12:15 and 14:15). A shuttle bus runs from Greenwich Pier to the observatory on top of the hill (£1.50, ticket good all day, daily 11:00–17:00, every 15 min, erratic in winter).

Sights—Greenwich

▲▲*Cutty Sark*—The Scottish-built *Cutty Sark* was the last of the great China tea clippers. Handsomely restored, she was the queen of the seas when first launched in 1869. With 32,000 square feet of sail, she could blow with the wind 300 miles in a day. Below deck, you'll see the best collection of merchant-ship figureheads in Britain and exhibits giving a vivid peek into the lives of Victorian sailors back when Britain ruled the waves. Stand at the big wheel and look up at the still-rigged main mast towering 150 feet above. You may meet costumed storytellers spinning yarns of the high seas and local old salts giving knot-tying demonstrations (£3.90, daily 10:00–17:00, tel. 020/8858-3445, www.cuttysark.org.uk).

▲***Gipsy Moth IV***—Tiny next to the *Cutty Sark*, the 54-foot *Gipsy Moth IV* is the boat Sir Francis Chichester used for the first solo circumnavigation of the world in 1966 and 1967. Upon Chichester's return, Queen Elizabeth II knighted him in Greenwich, using the same sword Elizabeth I had used to knight Francis Drake in 1581 (free, viewable anytime, but interior not open to public).

Stroll the Thames to Trafalgar Tavern—From the *Cutty Sark* and *Gipsy Moth*, pass the pier and wander east along the Thames on Five Foot Walk (the width of the path) for grand views in front of the Old Royal Naval College (see below). Founded by William III as a naval hospital and designed by Wren, the college was split in two because Queen Mary didn't want the view from Queen's House blocked. The riverside view is good, too, with the twin-domed towers of the college (one giving the time, the other the direction of the wind) framing Queen's House and the Royal Observatory Greenwich crowning the hill beyond.

Continuing downstream, just past the college, you'll see the Trafalgar Tavern. Dickens knew the pub well and even used it as the setting for the wedding breakfast in *Our Mutual Friend*. Built in 1837 in the Regency style to attract Londoners downriver, the tavern is still popular with Londoners (and tourists) for its fine lunches. The upstairs Nelson Room is still used for weddings. Its formal moldings and elegant windows with balconies over the Thames are a step back in time (Mon–Sat 12:00–23:00, Sun from 12:00, lunch 12:00–15:00, £6–10 dinners Tue–Sat 17:00–22:00, no dinner Sun–Mon, CC, Park Row, tel. 020/8858-2437). From the pub, enjoy views of the white-elephant Millennium Dome a mile downstream.

From the Trafalgar Tavern, you can walk the two long blocks up Park Row and turn right onto the park leading up to the Royal Observatory Greenwich.

Old Royal Naval College—Now that the Royal Navy has moved out, the public is invited in to see the elaborate Painted Hall and Chapel, grandly designed by Wren and completed by other architects in the 1700s (free, Mon–Sat 10:00–17:00, Sun 12:30–17:00, in the 2 college buildings farthest from river, choral service Sun at 11:00 in chapel—all are welcome).

Queen's House—This building, the first Palladian-style villa in Britain, was designed in 1616 by Inigo Jones for James I's wife, Anne of Denmark. All traces of the queen are now gone, and the Great Hall and Royal Apartments serve as an art gallery for rotating exhibits (free, daily 10:00–17:00, June–Aug daily 10:00–18:00, tel. 020/8858-4422).

▲▲**National Maritime Museum**—Great for anyone remotely

Greenwich

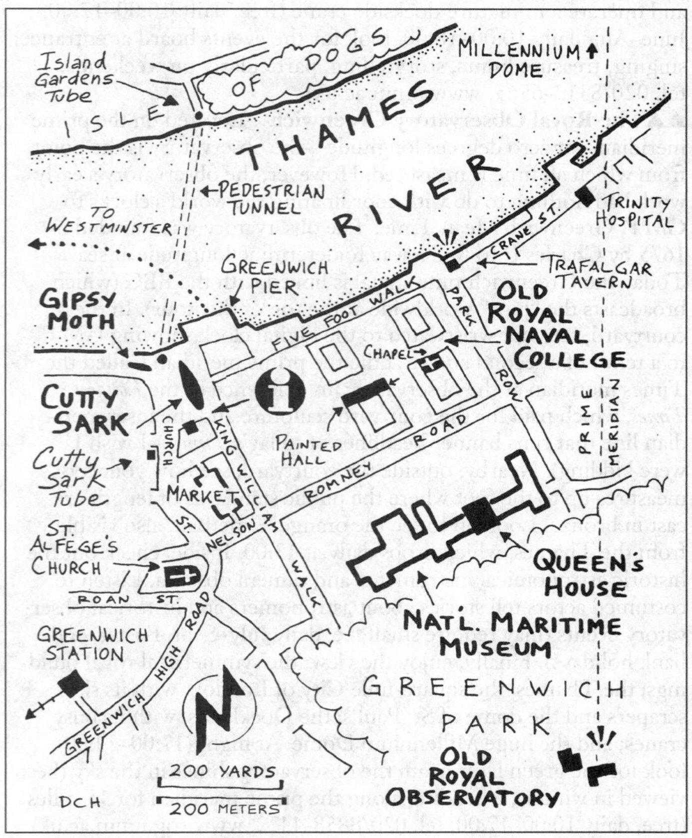

interested in the sea, this museum holds everything from *Titanic* tickets to Captain Scott's reindeer-hide sleeping bag (from his 1910 Antarctic expedition) to the uniform Admiral Nelson wore when he was killed at Trafalgar. Under a big glass roof to the sound of creaking wooden ships and crashing waves, slick, modern displays depict lighthouse technology, a whaling cannon, and a Greenpeace "survival pod." The Nelson Gallery, while taking up just a fraction of the floor space, deserves at least half your time here. It offers an intimate look at Nelson's life, the Napoleonic threat, Nelson's rise to power, and his victory and death at Trafalgar. Don't miss Turner's *Battle of Trafalgar*—his largest painting and only royal commission. Kids love the All Hands

Gallery, where they can send secret messages by Morse code and operate a miniature dockside crane (free, daily 10:00–17:00, June–Aug daily 10:00–18:00, look for the events board at entrance: singing, treasure hunts, storytelling, particularly on weekends, tel. 020/8312-6565, www.nmm.ac.uk).

▲▲**The Royal Observatory Greenwich**—Located on the prime meridian—at zero degrees longitude—the observatory is the point from which all time is measured. However, the observatory's early work had nothing to do with coordinating the world's clocks to GMT, Greenwich Mean Time. The observatory was founded in 1675 by Charles II to find a way to determine longitude at sea. Today the Greenwich time signal is linked with the BBC (which broadcasts the "pips" worldwide at the top of the hour). In the courtyard, set your wristwatch to the digital clock showing GMT to a tenth of a second and straddle the prime meridian (called the Times meridian at the observatory, in deference to the *London Times*, which paid for the courtyard sculpture and the inset meridian line that runs banner headlines of today's *Times*—I wish I were kidding). Nearby, outside the courtyard, see how your foot measures up to the foot where the public standards of length are cast in bronze. Look up to see the orange Time Ball, also visible from the Thames, which drops daily at 13:00. Inside, check out the historic astronomical instruments and camera obscura. Listen to costumed actors tell stories about astronomers and historical observatory events (may require small fee, daily July–Sept, Easter, and bank holidays). Finally, enjoy the view: the symmetrical royal buildings; the Thames; the square-mile City of London, with its skyscrapers and the dome of St. Paul's; the Docklands, with its busy cranes; and the huge Millennium Dome. At night (17:00–24:00), look for the green laser beam the observatory shines in the sky (best viewed in winter), extending along the prime meridian for 15 miles (free, daily 10:00–17:00, tel. 020/8858-4422, www.rog.nmm.ac.uk). Planetarium shows twinkle on weekdays at 14:30 and 15:30 and on Saturday and Sunday at 13:30, 14:30, and 15:30 (£4; buy tickets at observatory, a 2-min walk from planetarium).

Greenwich Town—Save time to browse the town. Covered markets and outdoor stalls make weekends lively. The arts-and-crafts market is an entertaining mini-Covent Garden between College Approach and Nelson Road (Thu–Sun 10:00–17:00, biggest on Sun), and the antique market sells old ends and odds at high prices on Greenwich High Road near the post office. Wander beyond the touristy Church Street and Greenwich High Road to where flower stands spill into the side streets and antique shops sell brass nautical knickknacks. King William Walk, College Approach, Nelson Road, and Turnpin Lane are all worth a look.

Transportation Connections—Greenwich

Getting to the town of Greenwich is a joy by boat or a snap by Tube. From London, you can cruise down the Thames from central London's piers at Westminster, Embankment, or Tower of London; or take the Tube to *Cutty Sark* in Zone 2 (free with Tube pass). Trains also go from London's Charing Cross, Waterloo East, and London Bridge stations several times each hour.

CAMBRIDGE

Cambridge, 60 miles north of London, is world-famous for its prestigious university. Wordsworth, Isaac Newton, Tennyson, Darwin, and Prince Charles are a few of its illustrious alumni. This historic town of 100,000 people is more pleasant than its rival, Oxford. Cambridge is the epitome of a university town, with busy bikers, stately residence halls, plenty of bookshops, and proud locals who can point out where electrons and DNA were discovered and where the first atom was split.

In medieval Europe, higher education was the domain of the Church and was limited to ecclesiastical schools. Scholars lived in "halls" on campus. This scholarly community of residential halls, chapels, and lecture halls connected by peaceful garden courtyards survives today in the colleges that make the universities at Cambridge and Oxford. By 1350 (Oxford is roughly 100 years older), Cambridge had eight colleges, each with a monastic-type courtyard and lodgings. Today, Cambridge has 31 colleges. While a student's life revolves around his or her independent college, the university organizes lectures, presents degrees, and promotes research.

The university dominates—and owns—most of Cambridge. The approximate term schedule is late January to late March (called Lent term), mid-April to mid-June (Easter term), and early October to early December (Michaelmas term). The colleges are closed to visitors during exams, from mid-April until late June, but King's College Chapel and the Trinity Library stay open, and the town is never sleepy.

Planning Your Time

Cambridge is worth most of a day but not an overnight. The cheap day-return train plan makes Cambridge easy and economical as a side trip from London (from London's King's Cross Station, £15.20 round-trip, 2/hr, 50 min, fast trains depart at :15 and :45 past each hr each way; the budget ticket requires a departure after 9:30 except Sat–Sun). You can arrive in time for the 11:30 walking tour—an essential part of any visit—and spend the afternoon touring King's College and Fitzwilliam Museum (closed Mon) and simply enjoying the ambience of this stately old college town.

Orientation (area code: 01223)

Cambridge is small but congested. There are two main streets, separated from the river by the most interesting colleges. The town center, brimming with tearooms, has a TI and a colorful open-air market (daily 9:30–16:00, on Market Hill Square; arts and crafts Sun 10:30–16:30, clothes and produce rest of week). Also on the main square is a Marks & Spencer grocery (Mon–Sat 8:30–20:00, Sun 11:00–17:00). A J. Sainsbury supermarket, with longer hours and a better deli, is three blocks north on Sidney Street. A good picnic spot is Laundress Green, a grassy park on the river, at the end of Mill Lane near the Silver Street punts. Everything is within a pleasant walk.

Tourist Information: At the station, a City Sightseeing/ Guide Friday office dispenses free city maps and sells fancier ones. The official TI is well signed and just off Market Hill Square (40p maps, Mon–Fri 10:00–17:30, Sat 10:00–17:00, Sun 11:00–16:00, closed Sun Nov–Easter, books rooms, tel. 01223/322-640).

Arrival in Cambridge: To get to downtown Cambridge from the train station, take a 20-minute walk (the Guide Friday map is fine for this), a £4 taxi ride, or bus #C1 or #C3 (£1, every 5 min). Drivers can follow signs to any of the handy and central Short Stay Parking Lots.

Tours of Cambridge

▲▲Walking Tour of the Colleges—A walking tour is the best way to understand Cambridge's mix of "town and gown." Walks give a good rundown on the historic and scenic highlights of the university as well as some fun local gossip. Walks are run by and leave from the TI. From mid-June through August, tours start at 10:30, 11:30, 13:30, and 14:30. In September they start at 10:30, 11:30, and 13:30. The rest of the year they often leave at 11:30 and always at 13:30. Tours cost £7.25 and include admission to King's College Chapel. Drop by the TI one hour early to snare a spot. Particularly if you're coming from London, call the TI (tel. 01223/322-640) at least to confirm that a tour is scheduled and not full. Private guides are also available (tel. 01223/457-574).

Bus Tours—Hop-on, hop-off bus tours run by City Sightseeing/ Guide Friday are informative and cover the outskirts, including the American Cemetery (£8.50, departing every 15 min, can use CC to buy tickets in their office in the train station). Walking tours go where the buses can't—right into the center.

Sights—Cambridge

▲▲King's College Chapel—Built from 1446 to 1515 by Henrys VI through VIII, England's best example of Perpendicular Gothic is the single most impressive building in town. Stand inside, look up, and marvel, as Christopher Wren did, at what was the largest single span of vaulted roof anywhere—2,000 tons of incredible fan vaulting. Wander through the Old Testament via the 25 16th-century stained-glass windows (the most Renaissance stained glass anywhere in one spot; it was taken out for safety during World War II then painstakingly replaced). Walk to the altar and admire Rubens' masterful *Adoration of the Magi* (£3.50, erratic hours depending on school and events, but usually daily 10:00–17:00). During term, you're welcome to enjoy an evensong service (Mon–Sat at 17:30, Sun at 15:30, tel. 01223/331-447).

▲▲**Trinity College**—Half of Cambridge's 63 Nobel Prize winners came from this richest and biggest of the town's colleges, founded in 1546 by Henry VIII. Don't miss the Wren-designed library, with its wonderful carving and fascinating original manuscripts (£2, 10p leaflet, Mon–Fri 12:00–14:00, also Sat 10:30–12:30 during term, always closed Sun; or visit the library for free during the same hours from the riverside entrance by the Garret Hostel Bridge). Just outside the library entrance, Sir Isaac Newton, who spent 30 years at Trinity, clapped his hands and timed the echo to measure the speed of sound as it raced down the side of the cloister and back. In the library's display cases (covered with brown cloth that you flip back), you'll see handwritten works by Newton, Milton, Byron, Tennyson, and Housman, alongside Milne's original *Winnie the Pooh* (the real Christopher Robin attended Trinity College).

▲▲**Fitzwilliam Museum**—Britain's best museum of antiquities and art outside of London is the Fitzwilliam. Enjoy its wonderful paintings (Old Masters and a fine English section featuring Gainsborough, Reynolds, Hogarth, and others, plus works by all the famous Impressionists), old manuscripts, and Greek, Egyptian, and Mesopotamian collections (free, £3 guided tour at 14:30 on Sun only, Tue–Sat 10:00–17:00, Sun 14:15–17:00, closed Mon, tel. 01223/332-900, www.fitzmuseum.cam.ac.uk).

Museum of Classical Archaeology—While this museum contains no originals, it offers a unique chance to see accurate copies (19th-century casts) of virtually every famous ancient Greek and Roman statue. More than 450 statues are on display (free, Mon–Fri 10:00–17:00, sometimes also Sat 10:00–13:00 during term, always closed Sun, Sidgwick Avenue, tel. 01223/335-153). The museum is a five-minute walk west of Silver Street Bridge; after crossing the bridge, continue straight until you reach a sign reading "Sidgwick Site" (museum is on your right; the entrance is away from the street).

▲**Punting on the Cam**—For a little levity and probably more exercise than you really want, try hiring one of the traditional

Cambridge

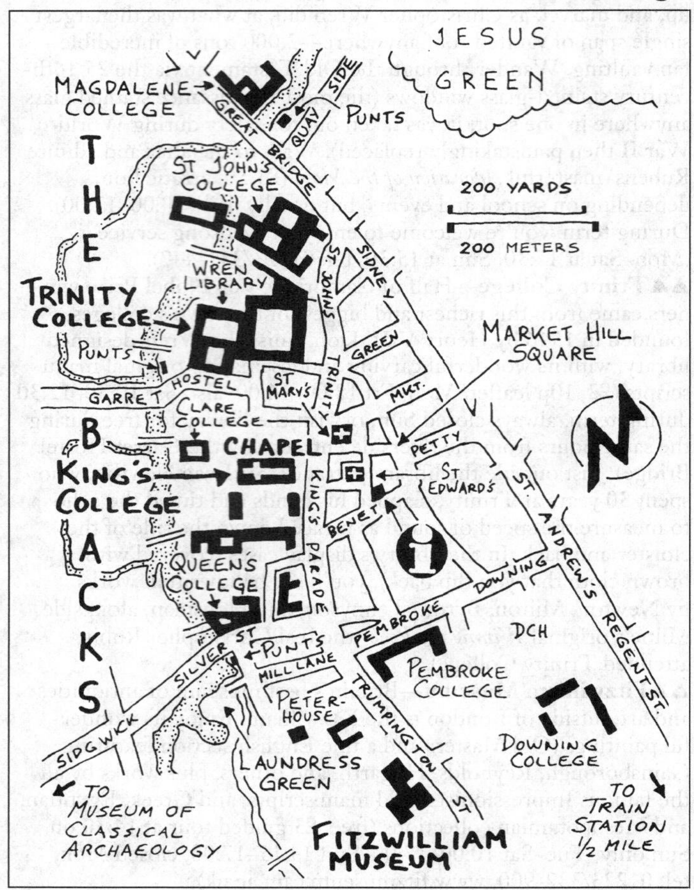

(and inexpensive) flat-bottom punts at the river and pole yourself up and down (around and around, more likely) the lazy Cam. Once you get the hang of it, it's a fine way to enjoy the scenic side of Cambridge. After 17:00 it's less crowded and less embarrassing. Three places, one at each bridge, rent punts (£60 deposit required, can use CC) and offer £10 50-minute punt tours. Trinity Punt, at Garrett Hostel Bridge near Trinity College, has the best prices (£10/hr rental, ask for free short lesson). Scudamore's runs two other locations: the central Silver Street (£12/hr rentals) and the less-convenient Quayside at Great Bridge, at the north end of town (£12/hr, tel. 01223/359-750, www.scudamores.com). Depending on the weather, punting season runs daily March through October, with Silver Street open weekends year-round.

Transportation Connections—Cambridge

By Train: To London's **King's Cross Station** (fast train departures at :15 and :45 past each hr, 50 min, one-way £15.10, cheap day-return for £15.20), **York** (1/hr, 2.5 hrs, transfer in Peterborough), **Heathrow** (1 bus/hr, 2.5 hrs). Train info tel. 08457-484-950. Bus info tel. 08705-757-747.

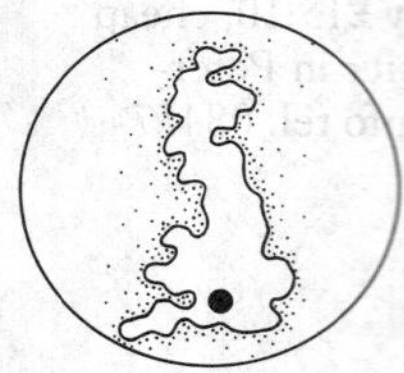

BATH

The best city to visit within easy striking distance of London is Bath—just a 75-minute train ride away. Two hundred years ago, this city of 80,000 was the trendsetting Hollywood of Britain. If ever a city enjoyed looking in the mirror, Bath's the one. It has more "government-listed" or protected historic buildings per capita than any other town in England. The entire city, built of the creamy warm-tone limestone called "Bath stone," beams in its cover-girl complexion. An architectural chorus line, it's a triumph of the Georgian style. Proud locals remind visitors that the town is routinely banned from the "Britain in Bloom" contest to give other towns a chance to win. Bath's narcissism is justified. Even with its mobs of tourists (2 million per year), it's a joy to visit.

Long before the Romans arrived in the first century, Bath was known for its hot springs. What became the Roman spa town of Aquae Sulis has always been fueled by the healing allure of its 116-degree mineral hot springs. The town's importance carried through Saxon times, when it had a huge church on the site of the present-day Abbey and was considered the religious capital of Britain. Its influence peaked in 973 with King Edgar's sumptuous coronation in the Abbey. Bath prospered as a wool town.

Bath then declined until the mid-1600s, when it was just a huddle of huts around the Abbey and some hot springs, with 3,000 residents oblivious to the Roman ruins 18 feet below their dirt floors. Then, in 1687, Queen Mary, fighting infertility, bathed here. Within 10 months she gave birth to a son . . . and a new age of popularity for Bath.

The town boomed as a spa resort. Ninety percent of the buildings you'll see today are from the 18th century. Local architect John Wood was inspired by the Italian architect Palladio to build a "new Rome." The town bloomed in the neoclassical style, and streets were lined not with scrawny sidewalks but with wide "parades," upon which the women in their stylishly wide dresses could spread their fashionable tails.

Beau Nash (1673–1762) was Bath's "master of ceremonies." He organized both the daily regimen of the aristocratic visitors and the city, lighting and improving street security, banning swords, and opening the Pump Room. Under his fashionable baton, Bath became a city of balls, gaming, and concerts and the place to see and be seen in England. This most civilized place became even more so with the great neoclassical building spree that followed.

With a new spa tapping Bath's soothing hot springs, the town will once again attract visitors in need of a cure or a soak.

Planning Your Time

Bath needs two nights even on a quick trip. There's plenty to do, and it's a joy to do it.

Here's how I'd spend the day in Bath: 9:00–Tour the Roman Baths, 10:30–Catch the free city walking tour, 12:30–Picnic on the open deck of a City Sightseeing/Guide Friday tour bus, 14:30–Free time in the shopping center of old Bath, 15:30–Tour the Costume Museum.

Evening: After a pub or classy dinner, consider a Bizarre Bath Walking Tour (see "Nightlife in Bath" on page 648).

Orientation (area code: 01225)

Bath's town square, three blocks in front of the bus and train station, is a bouquet of tourist landmarks, including the Abbey, Roman and medieval baths, and the royal Pump Room.

Tourist Information: The TI is in the Abbey churchyard (Mon–Sat 9:30–18:00, Sun 10:00–16:00, Oct–April Mon–Sat until 17:00, tel. 01225/477-101, www.visitbath.co.uk, e-mail: tourism@bathnes.gov.uk). Pick up the 50p Bath mini-guide (includes a map) and the free, info-packed *This Month in Bath*. Browse through scads of fliers, books, and maps. Skip their room-finding service (£5) and book direct. The TI sells a **Bath Pass**, giving you free entry to all the sights in town, but you have to work pretty hard to make it pay (£19/1 day, £29/2 days, £39/3 days). If you have a cell phone and are traveling with kids, ask the TI about "Texting Trails," a fun text-message scavenger hunt through Bath. An American Express office is tucked into the TI (decent rates, no commission on any checks, open same hrs as TI).

Arrival in Bath: The Bath train station is a pleasure (small-town charm, an international tickets desk, and a Guide Friday office masquerading as a TI). The bus station is immediately in front of the train station. To get to the TI, walk two blocks up Manvers Street from either station and turn left at the triangular "square," following the small TI arrow on a signpost. My recommended B&Bs are all within a 10- or 15-minute walk or a £3.50 taxi ride from the station.

Helpful Hints

Festivals: The International Music Festival bursts into song from May 16 to June 1 in 2003 (classical, folk, jazz, contemporary; tel. 01225/462-231), overlapped by the eclectic Fringe Festival from late May to mid-June (theater, walks, talks, bus trips; tel. 01225/480-079, www.bathfringe.co.uk, e-mail: admin@bathfringe.co.uk). Bath's box office sells tickets for most every event and can tell you exactly what's on tonight (2 Church Street, tel. 01225/463-362, www.bathfestivals.org.uk). Bath's local paper has a "What's On" event listing (www.thisisbath.com).

Internet Access: The Click Café is across from the train station on Manvers Street (£3/hr, daily 10:00–22:00, tel. 01225/481-008, www.click-cafe.com). Other places offering Internet access are the Itchy Feet Café & Travel Store (4 Bartlett Street, near Costume Museum) and the Bath Backpackers Hostel (13 Pierrepont Street; coming from train station, you pass hostel on way to TI).

Farmers' Market: It's at Green Park Station on the first and third Saturday of the month (9:00–15:00), with extra days for food stalls in the summer (Wed–Sat 9:00–17:00).

Car Rental: Avis (behind the station and over the river at Unit 4B Riverside Business Park, Lower Bristol Road, tel. 01225/446-680), Enterprise (Lower Bristol Road, tel. 01225/443-311), and Hertz (just outside train station, tel. 01225/442-911) are all trying harder. Sample prices: £39/day, £78/weekend, and £200/week. Most offices are a 10-minute walk from most recommended accommodations. Consider hotel delivery (usually £5, free with Enterprise). Most offices close Saturday afternoon and all day Sunday, complicating weekend pickups. Ideally, pick up your car only on the way out and into the countryside. Take the train or bus from London to Bath and rent a car as you leave Bath rather than in London.

Tours of Bath

▲▲City Bus Tours—The City Sightseeing/Guide Friday open-top tour bus makes a 70-minute figure-eight circuit of Bath's main sights with an exhaustingly informative running commentary. For one £8.50 ticket (buy from driver), tourists can stop and go at will for a whole day. The buses cover the city center and the surrounding hills (17 signposted pick-up points, 3/hr spring and fall—runs 9:30–17:00, 6/hr in summer—9:15–18:15, 1/hr in winter—9:30–15:30, tel. 01225/444-102). This is great in sunny weather and a feast for photographers. You can munch a sandwich, work on a tan, and sightsee at the same time. Several competing hop-on, hop-off tour-bus companies offer basically the same tour, but in 45 minutes and without the swing through the countryside, for a couple pounds less. Generally, the City Sightseeing/Guide Friday guides are better. (These tour buses are technically "public service vehicles"—a loophole they use to be able to run the same routes as transit buses. Consequently, tour buses are required to take passengers across town for the normal £1 fare. Nervy tourists have the right to hop on, ask for a "single fare," and pay £1.) Note that ticket stubs for any of the bus tours usually get you discounts at some sights. Pick up the various brochures at the TI and see what sights are currently discounted; if you want to see these sights, take the bus tour first.

▲▲▲**Walking Tours**—These free two-hour tours, offered by "The Mayor's Corps of Honorary Guides"—volunteers who want to share their love of Bath with its many visitors—are a chatty, historical, gossip-filled joy, essential for your understanding of this town's amazing Georgian social scene. How else will you learn that the old "chair ho" call for your sedan chair evolved into today's "cheerio" farewell? Tours leave from in front of the Pump Room (year-round daily at 10:30 plus Sun–Fri at 14:00; evening walks offered May–Sept at 19:00 on Tue, Fri, and Sat). For Ghost Walks and Bizarre Bath Comedy Walks, see "Nightlife," below. For a private walking tour, call the local guides' bureau (£46/2 hrs, tel. 01225/337-111).

Sights—Bath

▲▲▲**Roman and Medieval Baths**—In ancient Roman times, high society enjoyed the mineral springs at Bath. From Londinium, Romans traveled so often to Aquae Sulis, as the city was called, to "take a bath" that finally it became known simply as Bath. Today a fine museum surrounds the ancient bath. It's a one-way system leading you past well-documented displays, Roman artifacts, mosaics, a temple pediment, and the actual mouth of the spring, piled high with Roman pennies. Enjoy some quality time looking into the eyes of Minerva, goddess of the hot springs. The included self-guided tour audioguide makes the visit easy and plenty informative. For those with a big appetite for Roman history, in-depth 40-minute tours leave from the end of the museum at the edge of the actual bath (included, on the hour, a poolside clock is set for the next departure time). You can revisit the museum after the tour (£8.50, £11.50 combo-ticket includes Costume Museum at a good savings, family combo-£28, combo-tickets good for 1 week; April–Sept daily 9:00–18:00, July–Aug until 22:00—last entry at 21:00, Oct–March until 17:00, tel. 01225/477-784, www.romanbath.co.uk). After visiting the Roman Baths, drop by the attached Pump Room for a spot of tea.

▲**Pump Room**—For centuries, Bath was forgotten as a spa. Then, in 1687, the previously barren Queen Mary bathed here, became pregnant, and bore a male heir to the throne. Word of its wonder waters spread, and Bath was back on the aristocratic map. High society soon turned the place into one big pleasure palace. The Pump Room, an elegant Georgian hall just above the Roman baths, offers the visitor's best chance to raise a pinky in this Chippendale elegance. Drop by to sip coffee or tea or enjoy a light meal (9:30–12:00 morning coffee, 12:00–14:30 lunch—£12 2-course menu, 14:30–17:30 traditional High Tea—£8, 17:30–20:30 dinner, £7 tea/coffee and pastry available anytime except during lunch, string trio or live pianist plays sporadically between 10:00 and 17:00, tel. 01225/444-477). Above the newspaper table and sedan chairs, a statue of Beau Nash himself sniffles down at you. Now's your chance to have a famous (but forgettable) "Bath bun" and split (and spit) a 50p drink of the awfully curative water. Convenient public WCs are in the entry hallway that connects the Pump Room with the baths.

Thermae Bath Spa—Bath's natural thermal springs are once again being used for bathing and treatments, in a complex combining restored old buildings and a new, state-of-the-art leisure spa. Opened in early 2003, this is the only natural thermal spa in the United Kingdom. This hedonistic marvel includes an open-air rooftop thermal pool and all the "pamper thyself" extras—Jacuzzi, steam room, massage room, solarium, and lots of healing-type treatments and classes. Swimwear is obligatory, but you can buy suits and footwear at the spa (£17/2 hrs, £23/4 hrs, £35/full day, these prices do not include treatments, massage, or solarium, reservations recommended for these extra services, 100 meters from Roman and medieval baths on Beau Street, tel. 01225/780-308, fax 01225/780-294, www.thermaebathspa.com).

▲**Abbey**—Bath town wasn't much in the Middle Ages, but an important church has stood on this spot since Anglo-Saxon times. In 973, Edgar was crowned here. Dominating the town center, the present church—the last great medieval church of England—is 500 years old and a fine example of Late Perpendicular Gothic, with breezy fan vaulting and enough stained glass to earn it the nickname "Lantern of the West" (worth the £2 donation, Mon–Sat 9:00–18:00, Sun usually 13:00–14:30 & 15:30–17:30, closes at 16:30 in winter, handy flier narrates a self-guided 19-stop tour). The schedule for concerts, services, and **evensong** (Sun at 15:30

Bath

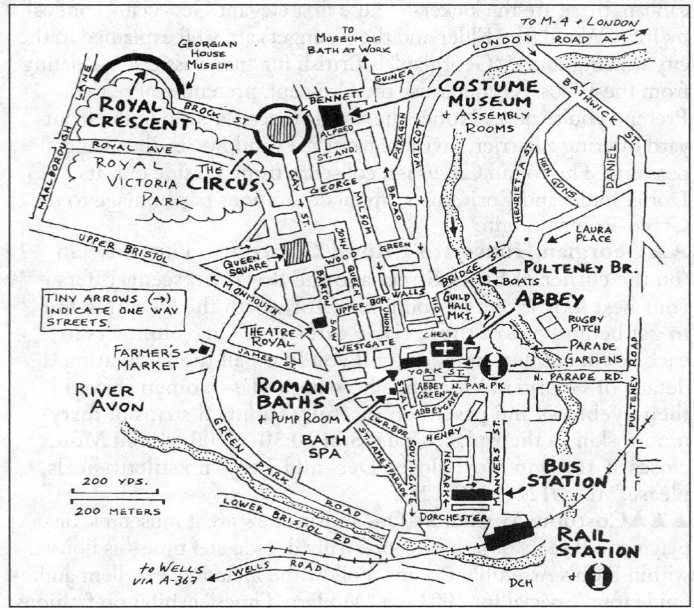

year-round, plus most Sat in Aug at 17:00) is posted on the door. Take a moment to really appreciate the Abbey's architecture from the Abbey Green square.

The Abbey's **Heritage Vaults**, a small but interesting exhibit, tell the story of Christianity in Bath since Roman times (£2, Mon–Sat 10:00–16:00, last entry 15:30, closed Sun, entrance just outside church, south side).

▲Pulteney Bridge, Parade Gardens, and Cruises—Bath is inclined to compare its shop-lined Pulteney Bridge to Florence's Ponte Vecchio. That's pushing it. To best enjoy a sunny day, pay £1.20 to enter the Parade Gardens below the bridge (daily 10:00–19:00, until 20:00 June–Aug, free after 20:00, includes deck chairs, ask about concerts held some Sun at 15:00 in summer).

Across the bridge at Pulteney Weir, tour boats run cruises from under the bridge (£5, up to 7/day if the weather's good, 50 min to Bathampton and back, WCs on board). Just take whatever boat is running. Avon Cruisers stop in Bathampton if you'd like to walk back; Pulteney Cruisers come with a sundeck ideal for picnics.

▲▲Royal Crescent and the Circus—If Bath is an architectural cancan, these are the kickers. These first elegant Georgian "condos" by John Wood (the Elder and the Younger) are well explained in the city walking tours. "Georgian" is British for "neoclassical," or dating from the 1770s. As you cruise the Crescent, pretend you're rich. Pretend you're poor. Notice the "ha ha fence," a drop in the front yard offering a barrier, invisible from the windows, to sheep and peasants. The round Circus is a coliseum turned inside out. Its Doric, Ionic, and Corinthian capital decorations pay homage to its Greco-Roman origin.

▲▲Georgian House at #1 Royal Crescent—This museum (on the corner of Brock Street and the Royal Crescent) offers your best look into a period house. It's worth the £4 admission to get behind one of those classy exteriors. The volunteers in each room are determined to fill you in on all the fascinating details of Georgian life . . . like how high-class women shaved their eyebrows and pasted on carefully trimmed strips of furry mouse skin in their place (Tue–Sun 10:30–17:00, closed Mon, closes at 16:00 in Nov, closed Dec–mid-Feb, "no stiletto heels, please," tel. 01225/428-126).

▲▲▲Costume Museum—One of Europe's great museums, displaying 400 years of fashion—one frilly decade at a time—is housed within Bath's Assembly Rooms. Follow the included, excellent audioguide tour. Special for 2003 is a "Modern Times" exhibit on fashions of the 1920s (£5.50, a £11.50 combo-ticket covers Roman Baths, family combo-£28, daily 10:00–17:00, tel. 01225/477-789). The Assembly Rooms, which you'll see en route to the museum, are big, elegant, empty rooms where card games, concerts, tea, and dances were held in the 18th century, before the advent of fancy hotels with grand public spaces made them obsolete.

▲▲▲Museum of Bath at Work—This is the official title for Mr. Bowler's Business, a 1900s engineer's shop, brass foundry, and fizzy-drink factory with a Dickensian office. It's just a pile of meaningless old gadgets until a volunteer guide lovingly resurrects Mr. Bowler's creative genius. Fascinating hour-long tours go regularly; just join the one in session upon arrival (£3.50, April–Oct daily 10:00–17:00, last entry at 16:00, weekends only in winter, 2 blocks up Russell Street from Assembly Rooms, call to be sure a volunteer is available to give a tour, café upstairs, tel. 01225/318-348).

Jane Austen Centre—This exhibition focuses on Jane Austen's five years in Bath (around 1800) and the influence Bath had on her writing. While the exhibit is thoughtfully done and a hit with "Jane-ites," there is little of historic substance here. You'll walk through a Georgian town house that she didn't live in and see mostly enlarged reproductions of things associated with her writing. After a live intro explaining how this romantic but down-to-earth girl dealt with the silly, shallow, and arrogant aristocrat's world where "the doing of nothings all day prevents one from doing anything," you see a 13-minute video and wander through the rest of the exhibit (£4.50, Mon–Sat 10:00–17:30, Sun 10:30–17:30, 40 Gay Street between Queen's Square and the Circus, tel. 01225/443-000, www.janeausten.co.uk).

The Building of Bath Museum—This offers a fascinating look behind the scenes at how the Georgian city was actually built. It's just one large room of exhibits, but those interested in construction find it worth the £4 (Tue–Sun 10:30–17:00, closed Mon, near the Circus on a street called "the Paragon," tel. 01225/333-895).

Views—For the best views of Bath, try Alexander Park (south of city, 10-min walk from train station), Camden Crescent (10- to 15-min walk north), or Becksford Tower (steep 20-min walk north up Lansdown Road, www.bath-preservation-trust.org.uk).

▲American Museum—I know, you need this in Bath like you need a Big Mac. But this museum offers a fascinating look at colonial and early-American lifestyles. Each of 18 completely furnished rooms (from the 1600s to the 1800s) is hosted by an eager guide waiting to fill you in on the candles, maps, bedpans, and various religious sects that make domestic Yankee history surprisingly interesting. One room is a quilter's nirvana (£6, April–Oct Tue–Sun 14:00–17:00, closed Mon and Nov–March, at Claverton Manor, tel. 01225/460-503). The museum is outside of town and a headache to reach if you don't have a car (15-min walk from the nearest City Sightseeing/Guide Friday stop or a 10-min walk from bus #18).

Activities in Bath

Walking—The Bath Skyline Walk is a six-mile wander around the hills surrounding Bath (70p leaflet at TI). Plenty of other scenic paths are described in the TI's literature. For more options, get *Country Walks around Bath*, by Tim Mowls (£4.50 at TI).

To Bathampton by Foot, Cruise, or Bike—Consider the idyllic **walk** up the canal path to Bathampton: from downtown, walk over Pulteney Bridge, through Sydney Gardens, turn left at the canal, and in 30 minutes you'll hit Bathampton, with its much-loved Old George Pub.

Sailors enjoy the river **cruise** up to Bathampton; hikers like walking back (see "Pulteney Bridge and Cruises," above). From Bathampton it's two hours farther along the canal to the fine old town of Bradford-on-Avon, from which you can train back to Bath.

You can **bike** this route. Avon Valley Cyclery rents bikes behind the train station (£9/4 hrs, £14/8 hrs, £18/24 hrs, no helmets, tel. 01225/442-442).

Boating—The Bath Boating Station, in an old Victorian boathouse, rents boats and punts (£5/first hour per person, then £1.50/hr, April–Sept 10:00–18:00, Forester Road, a mile northeast of center, tel. 01225/466-407).

Swimming—The Bath Sports and Leisure Centre has a swimming pool—great for laps—and lots of slides and gadgets for kids (£2.75, towels rentable for £1.50 and £5 deposit, daily 8:00–22:00, just across North Parade Bridge, call for open swim times, tel. 01225/462-565).

Shopping—There's great browsing between the Abbey and the Assembly Rooms (Costume Museum). Shops close at 17:30, later on Thursday, and many are open on Sunday (11:00–17:00). Explore the antique shops lining Bartlett Street just below the Assembly Rooms. You'll find the most stalls open on Wednesday. Pick up the local paper (usually out on Fri) and shop with the dealers at estate sales and auctions listed in "What's On."

Nightlife in Bath

This Month in Bath (free, available at TI) lists events.

Plays—The Theatre Royal, newly restored and one of England's loveliest, offers a busy schedule of London West End–type plays, including many "pre-London" dress-rehearsal runs (£11–25, cheaper matinees as low as £5, tel. 01225/448-844, www.theatreroyal.org.uk). Forty standby tickets per evening show go on sale starting at 12:00 on the day of the performance (either pay cash at box office or call and book with CC, 2 tickets maximum). Or you can buy a £10 last-minute seat 30 minutes before "curtain up."

Evening Walks—Take your choice: comedy, ghost, or history. For an immensely entertaining walking comedy act "with absolutely no history or culture," follow J. J. or Noel Britten on their creative and entertaining **Bizarre Bath** walk. This 90-minute tour, which plays off local passersby as well as tour members, is a belly laugh a minute (£5, April–Sept nightly at 20:00, smaller groups Mon–Thu, heavy on magic, careful to insult all minorities and sensitivities, just racy enough but still good family fun; leave from Huntsman pub near the Abbey, confirm at TI or call 01225/335-124, www.bizarrebath.co.uk). **Ghost Walks** are another way to pass the after-dark hours (£5, 20:00, 2 hrs, unreliably Mon–Sat April–Oct; in winter Fri only; leave from Garrick's Head pub near Theatre Royal, tel. 01225/463-618, www.ghostwalksofbath.co.uk). The TI offers **free evening walks** in summer (May–Sept at 19:00 on Tue, Fri, and Sat, 2 hrs, leave from Pump Room, confirm at TI); for more information, see "Tours of Bath," above.

Sleeping in Bath

(£1 = about $1.50, country code: 44, area code: 01225)

To help you sort easily through these listings, I've divided the rooms into three categories based on the price for a standard double room with bath:

Higher Priced—Most rooms more than £90.
Moderately Priced—Most rooms £90 or less.
Lower Priced—Most rooms £60 or less.

Sleep Code: S = Single, **D** = Double/Twin, **T** = Triple, **Q** = Quad, **b** = bathroom, **s** = shower only, **CC** = Credit Cards accepted, **no CC** = Credit Cards not accepted.

Bath is a busy tourist town. To get a good B&B, make a telephone reservation in advance. Competition is stiff, and it's worth asking any of these places for a weekday, three-nights-in-a-row, or off-season deal. Friday and Saturday nights are tightest, especially if you're staying only one night, since B&Bs favor those staying longer. If staying only Saturday night, you're very bad news. At B&Bs (and cheaper hotels), expect lots of stairs and no lifts.

Launderettes: The Spruce Goose Launderette is around the corner from Brock's Guest House on the pedestrian lane called Margaret's Buildings (self-service or full-service on same day if dropped off at 8:00, Sun–Fri 8:00–20:00, Sat 8:00–21:00, tel. 01225/483-309). Anywhere in town, "Speedy Wash" can pick up your laundry for same-day service (£9/bag, most hotels work with them, tel. 01225/427-616). East of Pulteney Bridge, the humble Lovely Wash is on Daniel Street (daily 9:00–21:00, self-service only).

Sleeping in B&Bs near the Royal Crescent

These listings are all a 15-minute uphill walk or an easy £3.50 taxi ride from the train station. Or take the City Sightseeing/Guide Friday bus tour from the station and get off at the stop nearest your B&B (for Brock's: Assembly Rooms; for Marlborough listings: Royal Avenue; confirm with driver), check in, then finish the tour later in the day. All of these B&Bs are non-smoking.

MODERATELY PRICED

Brock's Guest House will put bubbles in your Bath experience. Marion and Geoffrey Dodd have redone their Georgian town house (built by John Wood in 1765) in a way that would make the famous architect proud. It's located between the prestigious Royal Crescent and the elegant Circus (Db-£65–75, 1 deluxe Db-£75–82, Tb-£85–90, Qb-£99–110, CC, reserve with CC number far in advance, little library on top floor, 32 Brock Street, Bath BA1 2LN, tel. 01225/338-374, fax 01225/334-245, www.brocksguesthouse.co.uk, e-mail: marion@brocksguesthouse.co.uk).

Elgin Villa, also thoughtfully run and a fine value, has five comfy, well-maintained rooms (Ss-£32, Sb-£45, Ds-£45, Db-£65, Tb-£85, Qb-£105, CC, more expensive for 1 night, discounted for 3 nights, continental breakfast served in room, parking, 6 Marlborough Lane, Bath BA1 2NQ, tel. & fax 01225/424-557, www.elginvilla.co.uk, e-mail: stay@elginvilla.co.uk, Alwyn and Carol Landman).

Marlborough House Hotel is both Victorian and vegetarian, with seven comfortable rooms—well-furnished with antiques—and optional £15 organic-veggie dinners (Sb-£45–75, Db-£65–85, Tb-£75–95, price depending on season, CC, varied breakfast menu, room service, 1 Marlborough Lane, Bath BA1 2NQ, tel. 01225/318-175, fax 01225/466-127, www.marlborough-house.net, Americans Laura and Charles).

LOWER PRICED

The **Woodville House** is run by Anne and Tom Toalster. This grandmotherly little house has three tidy, charming rooms, one shared shower/WC, an extra WC, and a TV lounge. Breakfast is served at a big, family-style table (D-£40, minimum 2 nights, no CC, strictly non-smoking, some parking, below the Royal Crescent at 4 Marlborough Lane, Bath BA1 2NQ, tel. & fax 01225/319-335, e-mail: toalster@compuserve.com).

Prior House B&B, with four well-kept rooms, friendly German shepherd Toby, and thoughtful touches such as robes for guests who use the bathroom down the hall, is run by helpful Lynn and Keith Shearn (D-£54, Db-£50, CC, 3 Marlborough Lane, Bath BA1 2NQ, tel. 01225/313-587, fax 01225/443-543, www.greatplaces.co.uk/priorhouse, e-mail: priorhouse@greatplaces.co.uk).

Parkside Guest House has four Edwardian rooms and a spacious back garden (Db-£67, CC, small breakfast, 11 Marlborough Lane, BA1 2NQ, tel. & fax 01225/429-444, e-mail: parkside@lynall.freeserve.co.uk, Erica and Inge Lynall).

Sleeping in B&Bs East of the River

These listings are about a 10-minute walk from the city center.

HIGHER PRICED

The Ayrlington, next door to a lawn-bowling green, has attractive rooms that hint of a more genteel time. Though this well-maintained hotel fronts a busy street, it feels tranquil inside, with double-paned windows. Rooms in the back have pleasant views of sports greens and Bath beyond. For the best value, request a standard double with a view of Bath (standard Db-£90–110, superior

Db-£100–125, deluxe Db with Jacuzzi-£110–145, high prices on Fri, Sat, and Sun, no Sat night only, CC, access to garden in back, easy parking, 24/25 Pulteney Road, Bath BA2 4EZ, tel. 01225/425-495, fax 01225/469-029, Simon and Mee-Ling).

MODERATELY PRICED

In Sydney Gardens: The **Sydney Gardens Hotel** is a classy Casablanca-type place with six tastefully decorated rooms, an elegant breakfast room, garden views, and an entrance to Sydney Gardens park (Db-£75, Tb-£100, CC, request garden view, easy parking, located on busy road between park and canal, Sydney Road, Bath BA2 6NT, tel. 01225/464-818, fax 01225/484-347, www.sydneygardens.co.uk, Rory).

LOWER PRICED

Near North Parade Road: The **Holly Villa Guest House**, with a cheery garden, six bright rooms, and a cozy TV lounge, is enthusiastically and thoughtfully run by Jill and Keith McGarrigle (Ds-£45, Db-£50–55, Tb-£75–80, no CC, strictly non-smoking, easy parking, 8-min walk from station and city center: walk over North Parade Bridge, take the first right, and then take the second left, 14 Pulteney Gardens, Bath BA2 4HG, tel. 01225/310-331, e-mail: hollyvilla.bb@ukgateway.net).

Near Pulteney Road: Muriel Guy's B&B is another good value, mixing Georgian elegance with homey warmth and artistic taste (5 rooms, S-£25, Db-£55, Tb-£60, no CC, serves mostly organic foods, go over bridge on North Parade Road, left on Pulteney Road, cross to church, Raby Place is first row of houses on hill, 14 Raby Place, Bath BA2 4EH, tel. 01225/465-120, fax 01225/465-283, e-mail: no way).

Roman City Guest House, down the street from Muriel Guy's B&B, is a recently restored 1810 home with large bright rooms, some with views, and a welcoming lounge (Db-from £50, parking available, 18 Raby Place, Bath BA2 4EH, tel. & fax 01225/463-668, www.romancityguesthouse.co.uk, e-mail: romancityguesthse@amserve.net).

Sleeping East of Pulteney Bridge

These are just a few minutes' walk from the city center.

HIGHER PRICED

Kennard Hotel is comfortable, with 14 charming Georgian rooms and a dazzling breakfast room. Richard Ambler runs this place warmly, giving careful attention to guests (S-£48, Db-£88–118 depending upon size, CC, no kids under 12, just

Bath Hotels

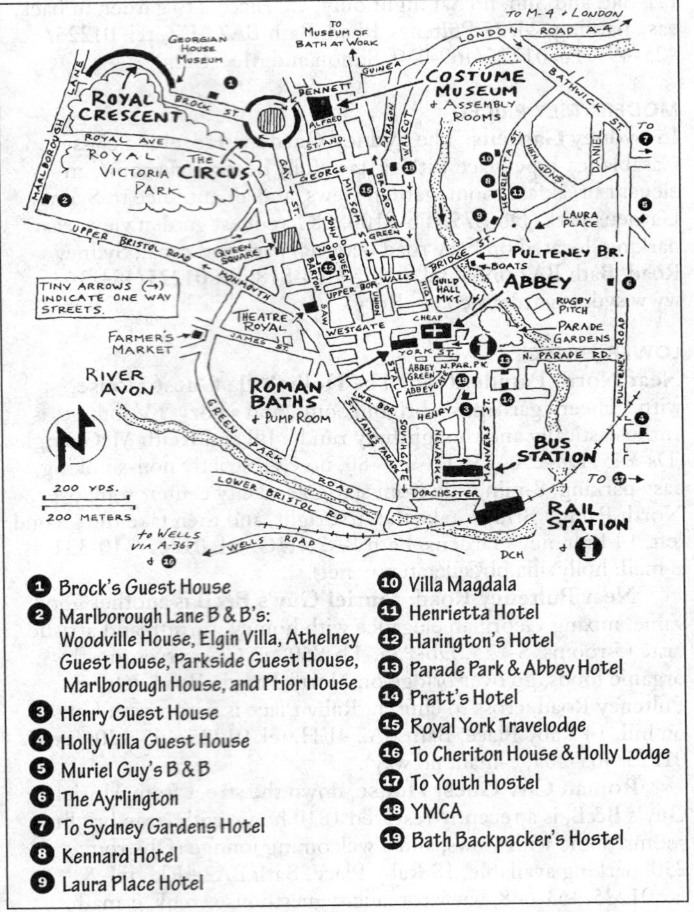

over Pulteney Bridge, turn left at Henrietta, 11 Henrietta Street, Bath BA2 6LL, tel. 01225/310-472, fax 01225/460-054, www.kennard.co.uk, e-mail: reception@kennard.co.uk).

Laura Place Hotel is another elegant Georgian place (8 rooms, 2 on the ground floor, rooftop D-£62, Db-£70–95 from small and high up to huge and palatial, CC, 2-night minimum stay, family suite, easy parking, just over Pulteney Bridge, 3 Laura Place, Great Pulteney Street, Bath BA2 4BH, tel. 01225/463-815, fax 01225/310-222, Patricia Bull).

Villa Magdala, with 18 rooms in a freestanding Victorian town house opposite a park, is formal and hotelesque (Db-£85–105, depending on size, type of bed, and plumbing; no CC, non-smoking, in quiet residential area, inviting lounge, parking, Henrietta Road, Bath BA2 6LX, tel. 01225/466-329, fax 01225/483-207, www.villamagdala.co.uk, e-mail: office@villamagdala.co.uk).

MODERATELY PRICED

Henrietta Hotel, with simple basic rooms and lots of stairs, gives you a budget-hotel option in this elegant neighborhood (10 rooms, Db-£50–75, discount with 3-night stay Sun–Thu, CC, 32 Henrietta Street, Bath BA2 6LR, tel. 01225/447-779, fax 01225/444-150, Jill).

Sleeping in the City Center

HIGHER PRICED

Harington's of Bath Hotel, with 13 newly renovated rooms on a quiet street in the town center, is run by Susan and Desmond Pow (Db-£88–118, Tb-£118–138, prices decrease midweek and increase Fri–Sat, 10 percent discount with this book for 2-night minimum stays Sun–Thu except on public holidays, CC, non-smoking, lots of stairs, attached restaurant/bar serves simple meals and pastries all day, extremely central at 10 Queen Street, Bath BA1 1HE, tel. 01225/461-728, fax 01225/444-804, www.haringtonshotel.co.uk).

Pratt's Hotel is as proper and old English as you'll find in Bath. Its creaks and frays are aristocratic. Its public places make you want to sip a brandy, and its 46 rooms are bright, spacious, and come with all the comforts (Sb-£80, Db-£110, advance reservations get highest rate, drop-ins after 16:00 often enjoy substantial discount, dogs-£4.95 but children free, breakfast extra, CC, attached restaurant/bar, elevator, 2 blocks immediately in front of the station on South Parade, Bath BA2 4AB, tel. 01225/460-441, fax 01225/448-807, www.forestdale.com, e-mail: pratts@forestdale.com).

Best Western–style **Abbey Hotel** has 60 decent rooms, some on the ground floor, a super location, and a rare elevator (standard Db-£125, deluxe Db-£140, CC, attached restaurant, non-smoking rooms, North Parade, Bath BA1 1LF, tel. 01225/461-603, fax 01225/447-758, e-mail: ahres@compasshotels.co.uk).

MODERATELY PRICED

Parade Park Hotel, in a Georgian building, has a central location, helpful owners, and comfortable basic rooms decorated in a modern style (35 rooms, S-£35, D-£50, Db-£60–80, Tb-£90,

Qb-£120, CC, non-smoking, beaucoup stairs, 10 North Parade, Bath BA2 4AL, tel. 01225/463-384, fax 01225/442-322, www.paradepark.co.uk, e-mail: info@paradepark.co.uk).

LOWER PRICED

The **Royal York Travelodge** offers American-style, characterless, comfortable rooms—worrying B&Bs and hotels alike with its reasonable prices (Db-£60, £70 on Fri–Sun, breakfast extra, CC, non-smoking rooms available, 1 York Bldg, George Street, Bath BA1 3EB, tel. 0870-191-1718, central reservation tel. 08700-850-950, www.travelodge.co.uk).

Henry Guest House is a plain, simple, old, vertical, eight-room, family-run place two blocks in front of the train station on a quiet side street. Nothing matches—not the curtains, wallpaper, carpeting, throw rugs, or bedspreads—but it is the cheapest hotel in the center (S-£25, D-£50, T-£65, no CC, lots of narrow stairs, 3 showers and 2 WCs for all, 6 Henry Street, Bath BA1 1JT, tel. 01225/424-052, fax 01225/316-669, www.thehenry.com, e-mail: enquiries@thehenry.co.uk, Sue and Derek).

Sleeping in B&Bs South of the Train Station

Up a hill a 15-minute walk south of the train station are a string of classy B&Bs in a car-friendly residential neighborhood. Here are two good ones:

Cheriton House has 11 well-furnished rooms (Sb-£50, Db-£66–90, higher rate for weekends, coach house suite-£120, 10 percent discount for 2-night stays by showing this book, CC, non-smoking, garden, 9 Upper Oldfield Park, BA2 3JX, tel. 01225/429-862, fax 01225/428-403, e-mail: cheriton@which.net, Iris and John Chiles). **Holly Lodge** has seven frilly Victorian-style rooms and a gazebo in the garden (Sb-£48–55, Db-£79–97, CC, non-smoking, phones in rooms, tel. 01225/339-187, fax 01225/481-138, www.hollylodge.co.uk, e-mail: stay@hollylodge.co.uk, Mr. George Hall).

Sleeping Outside of Town

MODERATELY PRICED

The recently opened **Holiday Inn Express** is one mile west of downtown Bath (126 rooms, Db for up to 2 adults and 2 children-£65, Qb-£85, CC, includes continental breakfast, parking, Lower Bristol Road, Brougham Hayes, Bath BA2 3QU, tel. 0870-444-2792 or 0800-405-060, fax 0870-444-2793, www.sixcontinentshotels.com/hiexpress, e-mail: managerbath@expressholidayinn28.fsnet.co.uk).

Sleeping in Lower-Priced Dorms

The **YMCA**, central on a leafy square down a tiny alley off Broad Street, has 208 beds in industrial-strength rooms with tired carpeting (S-£18, D-£32, T-£48, Q-£64, beds in big dorms-£12, includes meager continental breakfast, CC, families offered a day nursery for kids under 5, cheap dinners, no lockers, dorms closed from 10:00–16:00, Broad Street Place, Bath BA1 5LH, tel. 01225/460-471, fax 01225/462-065, e-mail: reservation@ymcabath.co.uk).

White Hart Hostel is a simple, new place offering adults and families good cheap beds in two- to six-bed dorms (£12.50/bed, Db-£40–50, family rooms, breakfast-£2.50, CC, smoke-free, kitchen, small café/bar, 5-min walk behind train station at Widcombe—where Widcombe Hill hits Claverton Street, Bath BA2 6AA, tel. 01225/313-985, www.whitehartbath.co.uk, e-mail: sue@whitehartinn.freeserve.co.uk, run by Mike and Sue).

Bath Backpackers Hostel bills itself as a totally fun-packed, mad place to stay. This youthfully run dive/hostel rents bunk beds in 6- to 10-bed rooms (£12/bed, 2 D-£30, T-£45 lockers, Internet access for non-guests as well, bar, kitchen, a couple of blocks toward city center from train station, 13 Pierrepont Street, Bath BA1 1LA, tel. 01225/446-787, e-mail: bath@hostels.co.uk).

Eating in Bath

While not a great pub-grub town, Bath is bursting with quaint and stylish eateries. There's something for every appetite and budget—just stroll around the center of town. A picnic dinner of deli food or take-out fish 'n' chips in the Royal Crescent Park is ideal for aristocratic hobos.

Eating between the Abbey and the Station

Three fine and popular places share North Parade Passage, a block south of the Abbey: **Tilley's Bistro**, popular with locals, serves healthy French, English, and vegetarian meals with candle-lit ambience. Their fun menu lets you build your meal, choosing from an interesting array of £6 starters (Mon–Sat 12:00–14:30 & 18:30–23:00, closed Sun, CC, reservations smart, non-smoking, North Parade Passage, tel. 01225/484-200). **Sally Lunn's House** is a cutesy, quasi-historic place for expensive doily meals, tea, pink pillows, and lots of lace (£15–20, nightly, CC, smoke-free, 4 North Parade Passage, tel. 01225/461-634). It's fine for tea and buns (£7–10, served until 18:00), and customers get a free peek at the basement Kitchen Museum (otherwise 30p). **Demuth's Vegetarian Restaurant** serves good £16 meals (daily 10:00–22:00, CC, vegan options available, reservations wise, tel. 01225/446-059).

Bath Restaurants

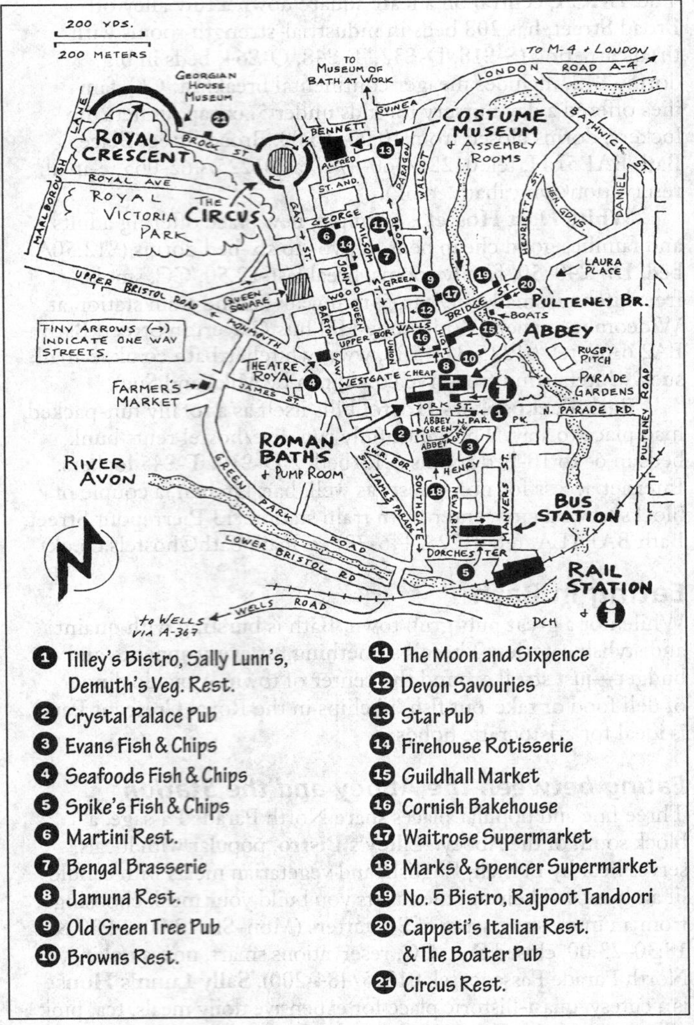

Crystal Palace Pub, with typical pub grub under rustic timbers or in the sunny courtyard, is a handy standby (£6 meals, Mon–Fri 11:30–20:00, Sat 11:00–16:00, Sun 12:00–15:30, children welcome on patio but not indoors, 11 Abbey Green, tel. 01225/482-666).

Evans is decent for fish 'n' chips (Mon–Fri 11:30–15:00, Sat 11:30–17:00, closed Sun, on Abbeygate, near Marks & Spencer). Also greasy is **Seafoods** (daily 12:00–23:00, last seating 22:30, last take-out 23:00; try the mushy peas, cup of tea, and fish and chips special for £4; 27 Kingsmeads Street, just off Kingsmead Square). For more cheap meals, try **Spike's Fish and Chips** (open very late) and the neighboring café just behind the bus station.

Eating between the Abbey and the Circus

George Street is lined with cheery eateries: Thai, Italian, wine bars, and so on. The hopping **Martini Restaurant** is purely Italian with class and jovial waiters (£12 entrées, £7 pizzas, daily 12:00–14:30 & 18:00–22:30, CC, reservations smart, smoke-free section, 9 George Street, tel. 01225/460-818, Nunzio, Franco, and Luigi).

Bengal Brasserie, a Bangladeshi place specializing in tandoori and curries, is unpretentious with good food at good prices (12:00–14:00 & 18:00–23:00, 32 Milsom Street, tel. 01225/447-906).

Jamuna makes a mean curry (daily 12:00–14:30 & 18:00–24:00, 10 percent discount for take-out, Abbey views, 9-10 High Street, tel. 01225/464-631).

The **Old Green Tree Pub** on Green Street is a rare pub with good grub, locally brewed real ales, and a non-smoking room (lunch only, served 12:00–14:30, no children, live jazz Sun–Mon 20:30 until closing, tel. 01225/448-259).

Browns, a popular, modern chain, offers affordable—though not great—English food throughout the day (Sun–Fri 12:00–23:30, Sat 10:00–23:00, CC, kid-friendly, half block east of the Abbey, Orange Grove, tel. 01225/461-199).

The Moon and Sixpence, prized by locals, offers "modern English fusion" cuisine, giving British cooking a needed international flair and flavor (£7 2-course lunch, £21 3-course dinner menu, daily 12:00–14:30 & 17:30–22:30, CC, indoor/outdoor seating, 6a Broad Street, tel. 01225/460-962).

Devon Savouries serves greasy-but-delicious take-out pasties, sausage rolls, and vegetable pies (Mon–Sat 9:00–17:30, hours vary on Sun, cheaper if you get it to go, on Burton Street, the main walkway between New Bond Street and Upper Borough Walls).

If you're missing California, try the popular **Firehouse Rotisserie** (Mon–Sat 12:00–14:30 & 18:00–23:00, closed Sun, make reservations, near Queen Square on John Street, tel. 01225/482-070).

Guildhall Market, across from Pulteney Bridge, is fun or browsing and picnic shopping, with an inexpensive Market Café if you'd like to sip tea surrounded by stacks of used books, bananas on the push list, and honest-to-goodness old-time locals (Mon–Sat 9:00–17:00, closed Sun, a block north of the Abbey, main entrance on High Street).

The **Cornish Bakehouse**, near the Guildhall Market, has good take-away pasties (open until 17:30, 11a The Corridor, off High Street, tel. 01225/426-635).

Supermarkets: **Waitrose**, at the Podium shopping center, is great for groceries (Mon–Fri 8:30–20:00, Sat 8:30–19:00, Sun 11:00–17:00, salad bar, just west of Pulteney Bridge and across from post office on High Street). **Marks & Spencer**, near the train station, has a good grocery at the back of its department store (Mon–Sat 9:00–17:30, Sun 11:00–17:00, Stall Street).

Eating East of Pulteney Bridge

For a stylish, intimate setting and "new English" cuisine worth the splurge, dine at **No. 5 Bistro** (£13–16 main courses with vegetables, Mon–Sat 18:30–22:00, closed Sun, Mon–Tue are "bring your own bottle of wine" nights—no corkage fee, smart to reserve, CC, just over Pulteney Bridge at 5 Argyle Street, tel. 01225/444-499). **Rajpoot Tandoori**, next door to No. 5, serves good Indian food. You'll hike down deep into a cellar where the classy Indian atmosphere and award-winning cooking makes paying the extra pounds OK (12:00–14:00 & 18:00–23:00, 4 Argyle Street, tel. 01225/466-833). **Cappeti's Italian Restaurant** is a checkered-tablecloth place in another deep cellar serving good Italian (Tue–Sat 12:00–14:00 & 18:30–22:30, closed Sun–Mon, CC, 12 Argyle Street, tel. 01225/442-299). Two doors down, the popular **Boater Pub** offers a good selection of ales and pub grub and a pleasant beer garden overlooking the river (Mon–Sat 11:00–23:00, Sun 12:00–20:30, 9 Argyle Street, tel. 01225/464-211).

Eating near the Circus and Brock's Guest House

Circus Restaurant is intimate and a good value, with Mozartian ambience and candlelit prices: £17 for a three-course dinner special including great vegetables and a selection of fine desserts (daily 12:00–14:00 & 18:30–22:00, reservations smart, CC, 34 Brock Street, tel. 01225/318-918, run by Felix Rosenow).

For real ale (but no food), try the **Star Pub** (at the top of Paragon Street).

Transportation Connections—Bath

Bath's train station is called Bath Spa. The National Express bus office (Mon–Sat 8:00–17:30, closed Sun) is one block in front of the train station.

To London: By train to Paddington Station (2/hr, 75 min, £32 one-way after 9:30), or cheaper by National Express bus to Victoria Station (nearly 1/hr, a little over 3 hrs, £13 one-way, £21 round-trip, www.gobycoach.com). To get from London to Bath and see Stonehenge to boot, consider an all-day organized bus tour from London (see page 601 in the London chapter). Train info: tel. 08457-484-950.

To London's Airports: By National Express bus to **Heathrow** and continuing on to London (10/day, 2.5 hrs, £13, tel. 08705-808-080) and to **Gatwick** (approx 2/hr, 4.5 hrs, £20). Trains are faster but more expensive (1/hr, 2.5 hrs, £29.20).

To the Cotswolds: By train to **Moreton-in-Marsh** (1/hr, 2 hrs, transfer in Oxford). By National Express bus to **Cheltenham** or **Gloucester** (1 direct bus/day, 2.5 hrs, more buses with transfer), **Stratford** (1/day, 4 hrs, transfer in Bristol or Birmingham), and **Oxford** (1 direct/day, 2 hrs, more buses with transfer). Bus info: tel. 08705-808-080.

By Train: To **Oxford** (1/hr, 1 hr), **Heathrow** (1/hr, transfer at Reading to bus), **Gatwick** (1/hr, 3 hrs, most transfer in Reading or Clapham Junction), **Birmingham** (1/hr, 2.5 hrs, transfer in Bristol), and **points north** (from Birmingham, a major transportation hub, trains depart for Blackpool, York, Durham, Scotland, and North Wales; use a train/bus combination to reach Ironbridge Gorge and the Lake District).

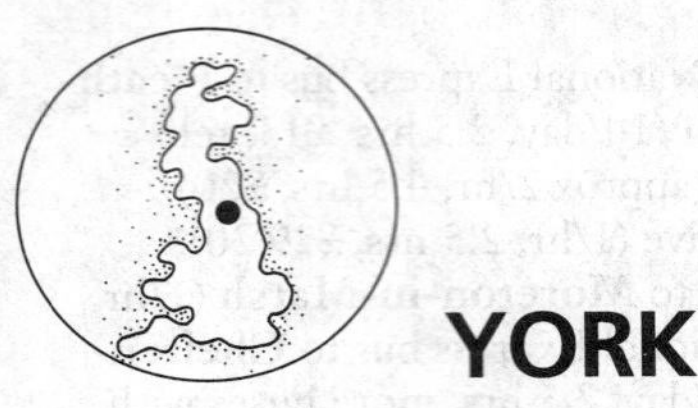

YORK

Historic York is loaded with world-class sights. Marvel at the York Minster, England's finest Gothic church. Ramble through the Shambles, York's wonderfully preserved medieval quarter. Enjoy a walking tour led by an old Yorker. Hop a train at Europe's greatest Railway Museum, travel to the 1800s in York Castle Museum, and head back a thousand years to Viking York at the Jorvik exhibit.

York has a rich history. In A.D. 71 it was Eboracum, a Roman provincial capital. Constantine was actually proclaimed emperor here in A.D. 306. In the fifth century, as Rome was toppling, a Roman emperor sent a letter telling England it was on its own, and York became Eoforwic, the capital of the Anglo-Saxon kingdom of Northumbria. A church was built here in 627, and the town became an early Christian center of learning. The Vikings later took the town, and from about 860 to 950 it was a Danish trading center called Jorvik. The invading and conquering Normans destroyed then rebuilt the city, giving it a castle and the walls you see today. Medieval York, with 9,000 inhabitants, grew rich on the wool trade and became England's second city. Henry VIII spared the city's fine minster in order to use York as his Anglican Church's northern capital. The Archbishop of York is second only to the Archbishop of Canterbury in the Anglican Church. In the Industrial Age, York was the railway hub of North England. When it was built, York's train station was the world's largest. Today, York's leading industry is tourism. Its leading drug? Starbucks and Costa are doing their best to turn high tea into high coffee.

Planning Your Time

York rivals Edinburgh as the best sightseeing city in Britain after London. On even a short trip through Britain, it deserves two nights and a day. For the best 36 hours, follow this plan: Catch the 19:00 city walking tour on the evening of your arrival. The next morning, be at the Castle Museum at 9:30 when it opens—it's worth a good two hours. Then browse and sightsee through the day. Train buffs love the National Railway Museum, and scholars give the Yorkshire Museum three stars. Tour the minster at 16:00 before catching the 17:00 evensong service (at 16:00 Sat–Sun). Finish your day with an early evening stroll along the wall and perhaps through the abbey gardens. This schedule assumes you're there in the summer (evening orientation walk) and that there's an evensong on. Confirm your plans with the TI.

Orientation (area code: 01904)

The sightseer's York is small. Virtually everything is within a few minutes' walk: the sights, train station, TI, and B&Bs. The longest walk a visitor might take (from a B&B across the old town to the Castle Museum) is 15 minutes.

Bootham Bar, a gate in the medieval town wall, is the hub of your York visit. At Bootham Bar (and on Exhibition Square facing it) you'll find the TI, the starting points for most walking tours and bus tours, handy access to the medieval town wall, and Bootham Street, which leads to the recommended B&Bs. (In York, a "bar" is a gate and a "gate" is a street. Go ahead, blame the Vikings.) When finding your way, navigate by sighting the tower of the minster or the strategically placed green signposts pointing out all places of interest to tourists.

Tourist Information: The TI at Bootham Bar sells an 85p *York Map and Guide*. Ask for the free monthly *What's On* guide and the *York MiniGuide*, which includes a map and some discounts (April–Oct Mon–Sat 9:00–18:00, Sun 10:00–16:00, sometimes longer in summer, always shorter in winter but no one really knows, WCs next door, tel. 01904/621-756). The TI books rooms for a £4 fee. The train-station TI is smaller but provides all the same information and services (April–Sept Mon–Sat 9:00–18:00, Sun 9:00–17:00, likely 10:00–16:00 off-season).

Arrival in York: The train station, which stores luggage for day-trippers (£3, Mon–Sat 8:00–20:30, Sun 9:00–20:30, platform 1), is a five-minute walk from town; turn left down Station Road and follow the crowd toward the Gothic towers of the minster. After the bridge, a block before the minster, signs to the TI send you left on St. Leonard's Place. Recommended B&Bs are a five-minute walk from there. (For a shortcut to B&B area from station, walk 1 block toward the minster, cut through parks to riverside, cross railway bridge/pedestrian walkway, cross parking lot for B&Bs on St. Mary's Street, or duck through pedestrian walkway under tracks to B&Bs

York

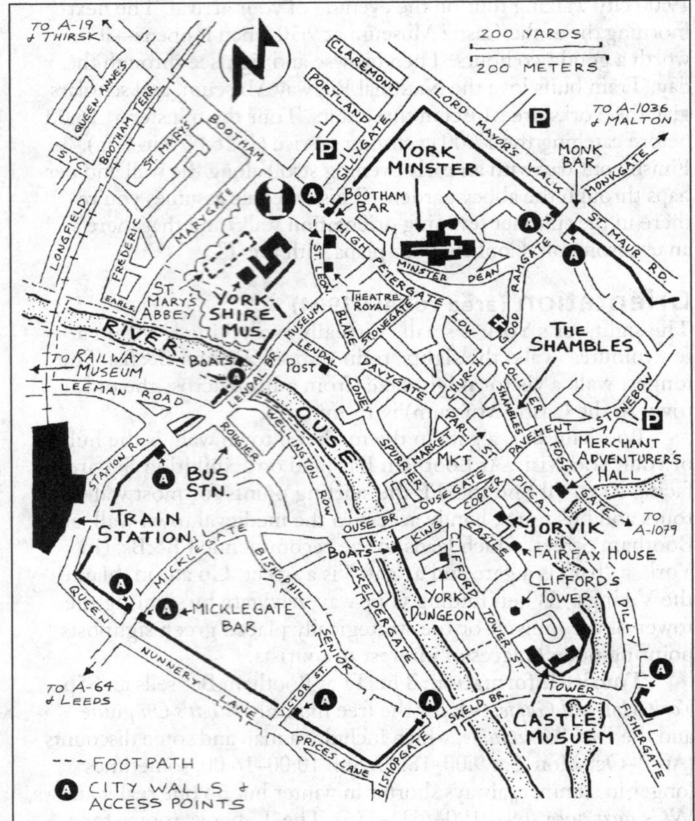

on Sycamore and Queen Anne's Road.) **Taxis** zip new arrivals to their B&B for £3.

Helpful Hints

Study Ahead: York has a great Web site: www.visityork.org.

Internet Access: Get online at Internet Exchange (Mon–Sat 9:00–21:00, Sun 11:00–18:00, 13 Stonegate, tel. 01904/638-808) or Gateway (Mon–Sat 10:00–20:00, closed Sun, 26 Swinegate, tel. 01904/646-446).

Festivals: The Viking Festival in late February is fun, with lur-blowing, warrior drills, and re-created battles. The Early Music Festival zings its strings in mid-July. The York Festival of Food and Drink takes a 10-day bite out of the middle of September. Book a room well in advance during festival times and weekends any time of year.

Bike Rental: Trotters, just outside Monk Bar, has free cycling maps. The riverside path is pleasant (£8/day, helmets-£2, Mon–Sat 9:00–17:30, Sun 10:00–16:00, tel. 01904/622-868). Europcar at the train station also rents bikes (£10/day, platform 1, tel. 01904/656-161).

Car Rental: If you're nearing the end of your trip, consider dropping your car upon arrival in York. The money saved by turning it in early nearly pays for the train ticket that whisks you effortlessly to Edinburgh or London. Here are some car-rental agencies in York: Avis (Mon–Sat, closed Sun, 3 Layerthorpe, tel. 01904/610-460), Hertz (April–Sept daily 9:00–13:00, at train station, tel. 01904/612-586), Kenning Car & Van Rental (Mon–Sat, closed Sun, inconveniently 3 miles out of town at Clifton Moor Industrial Estate, tel. 01904/479-715), Budget (daily 9:00–11:00, 1 mile past recommended B&Bs at Clifton 82, tel. 01904/644-919), and Europcar (Mon–Fri 8:00–18:00, Sat–Sun 8:00–12:00, train station platform 1, tel. 01904/656-161). Beware, car-rental agencies close Saturday afternoon and some close all day Sunday—when drop-offs are OK, but picking up is impossible.

Tours of York

▲▲▲Walking Tours—Charming local volunteer guides give energetic, entertaining, and free two-hour walks through York (daily 10:15 all year, plus 14:15 April–Oct, plus 19:00 June–Aug, from Exhibition Square across from TI). There are many other commercial York walking tours. YorkWalk Tours, for example, has reliable guides and many themes from which to choose, such as Roman York, City Walls, or Snickleways—small alleys (£5, tel. 01904/622-303, TI has schedule). The ghost tours, all offered after nightfall, are more fun than informative. Haunted Walk relies a bit more on storytelling and history than on masks and surprises (£3, April–Nov nightly at 20:00, 90 min, just show up, depart from Exhibition Square, across street from TI, end in the Shambles, tel. 01904/621-003).

▲Hop-on, Hop-off Bus Tours—York's City Sightseeing/Guide Friday bus tour offers tour guides who can talk enthusiastically to three sleeping tourists in a gale on a topless double-decker bus for an hour without stopping. Buses make the 60-minute circuit, covering secondary York sights that the city walking tours skip—the work-a-day perimeter of town (£7.50, pay driver cash, can also buy from TI with CC, departures every 15 min from 9:15 until around 17:00, tel. 01904/640-896). While you can hop on and off all day, the York route is of no value from a transportation-to-the-sights point of view. I'd catch it at the Bootham Bar TI and ride it for an orientation all the way around or get off at the Railway Museum, skipping the last five minutes. The other bus tour competitors give you a little less for a little less.

Boat Cruise—Even though York turns its back on its river, the York Boat does a lazy 60-minute lap along the River Ouse (£6, Feb–Nov daily from 10:30 on, narrated cruise, leaves from Lendal Bridge and King's Staith landing) and also offers themed evening cruises—ghost, dinner, floodlit, and so on (boat rentals possible, tel. 01904/628-324, www.yorkboat.co.uk).

Sights—York Minster

▲▲▲Minster—The pride of York, this largest Gothic church north of the Alps (540 feet long, 200 feet tall) brilliantly shows that the High Middle Ages were far from dark. The word "minster" means a place from which people go out to minister or spread the word of God.

Your first impression might be the spaciousness and brightness of the nave (built 1280–1350). The nave—from the middle period of Gothic, called "Decorated Gothic"—is one of the widest Gothic naves in Europe. Notice the Great West Window (1338) above the entry. The heart in the tracery is called "the heart of Yorkshire."

Look down the nave. The mysterious gold-and-red dragon's head (in the middle of the nave, sticking out of the side) was probably used as a crane to lift a font cover.

The north and south transepts are the oldest parts of today's church (1220–1270). The oldest complete window in the minster is the entire wall of glass in the north transept (1260). Known as the Five Sisters Window, these 50-foot-high panels were made of modern-looking grisaille (gray-silver) glass.

The fanciful choir and the east end (high altar) is from the last stage of Gothic, Perpendicular (1360–1470). The Great East Window (1405), the largest medieval glass window in existence, shows the beginning and the end of the world, with scenes from Genesis and the book of Revelation. A chart (on the right, with a tiny, more helpful chart within) highlights the core Old Testament scenes in this hard-to-read masterpiece. Enjoy the art close up on the chart and then step back and find the real thing.

There are three more extra visits to consider. The **Chapter House**, an elaborately decorated 13th-century Gothic dome—the largest in England without a central supporting pillar—features playful details carved in the stonework (pointed out in the flier at the north transept entrance). You can scale the 275-step **tower** for £3 and enjoy a great view (south transept). The **Undercroft,** also in the south transept, consists of the crypt, treasury, and foundations (£3). The crypt is an actual bit of the Romanesque church, featuring 12th-century Romanesque art, excavated in modern times. The foundations give you a chance to climb down—archaeologically and physically—through the centuries to see the roots of the much smaller, but still huge, Norman church (Romanesque, 1100) that stood on this spot and, below that, the Roman excavations. Constantine was proclaimed Roman emperor here in A.D. 306. Peek also at the modern concrete save-the-church foundations.

Hours and Tours: The cathedral opens daily at 9:00. The closing time flexes with the season (roughly July–Aug at 20:30, May–June and Sept at 19:30, Oct–April at 18:00; £2 to use your camera; tel. 01904/557-216). The Chapter House, tower, and Undercroft have shorter hours (usually April–Oct 9:30–17:30, Nov–March 10:00–16:00). The minster is open for sightseeing from 12:30 on Sundays.

While a donation of £3.50 to visit the church is reasonably requested, I skip that and pay for admission to all the little over-priced extra spots inside—eventually giving more than the £3.50.

When you enter go directly to the welcome desk, pick up the worthwhile "Welcome to the York Minster" flier, and ask when the next free guided tour departs (tours go frequently, even with just 1 or 2 people; you can join one in progress). The helpful blue-armbanded minster guides are happy to answer your questions.

Evensong and Church Bells: To experience the cathedral in musical and spiritual action, attend an evensong (Mon–Fri 17:00, Sat–Sun 16:00, 45 min). When the choir is off on school break (mid-July–Aug), visiting choirs usually fill in. Arrive 10 minutes early and wait just outside the choir in the center of the church, from where you'll be ushered in and can sit in one of the big wooden stalls. If you're a fan of church bells, Sunday morning (around 10:00) and the Tuesday-evening practice (19:30–21:30) are heavenly.

Sights—York

▲City Walls—The historic walls of York provide a fine two-mile walk. Walk from Bootham Bar (gate) to Monk Bar for outstanding cathedral views. They're free and open from dawn until dusk (barring attacks).

▲The Shambles—This is the most colorful old York street in the half-timbered, traffic-free core of town. Ye olde downtown York, while very touristy, is made for window-shopping, street musicians, and people-watching. Don't miss the more frumpy Newgate Market or the old-time Hamilton's candy store just opposite the bottom end of the Shambles. For a cheap lunch, consider the cute, tiny **St. Crux Parish Hall**. This medieval church is now used by a medley of charities selling tea, homemade cakes, and light meals. They each book the church for a day, often a year in advance. Chat up the volunteers (Mon–Sat 10:00–16:00, closed Sun, at bottom end of the Shambles, at intersection with Pavement).

▲▲▲**Castle Museum**—Truly one of Europe's top museums, this is a Victorian home show, the closest thing to a time-tunnel experience England has to offer. It includes the 19th-century Kirkgate (a collection of old shops well stocked exactly as they were 150 years ago), a "From Cradle to Grave" clothing exhibit, and a fine costume collection. The one-way plan allows you to see everything: a working water mill (April–Oct), prison cells, WWII fashions, and old toys. Bring 10p coins to jolt a mechanical Al Jolson into song. The museum's £2.50 guidebook isn't necessary but makes a fine souvenir (£6, April–Oct daily 9:30–17:00, Nov–March until 16:30, gift shop, parking, cafeteria midway through museum, CC, tel. 01904/653-611).

Clifford's Tower, across from Castle Museum, is all that's left of York's 13th-century castle, the site of a 1190 massacre of local Jews (read about this at base of hill). If you do climb inside, there are fine city views from the top of the ramparts (not worth the £2.10, April–Sept daily 10:00–18:00, Oct–March until 16:00).

▲**Jorvik**—Sail the "Pirates of the Caribbean" north and back 800 years and you get Jorvik—more a ride than a museum. Innovative 10 years ago, the commercial success of Jorvik (pron. YOR-vik) inspired copycat ride/museums all over England. You'll ride a little Disney-type train car for 13 minutes through the re-created Viking street of Coppergate. It's the year 975, and you're in the village of Jorvik. Next, your little train takes you through the actual excavation site that inspired this. Finally you'll browse through a small gallery of Viking shoes, combs, locks, and other intimate glimpses of that redheaded culture (£7, April–Oct opens at 9:00 with last entry at 17:30, Nov–March opens at 10:00, closing varies from 15:30 to 16:30, tel. 01904/643-211, www.vikingjorvik.com).

Midday lines can be an hour long. Avoid the line by going very early or very late in the day or by prebooking (call 01904/543-403, you're given a time slot, £1 booking fee, CC). Some love this "ride"; others call it a gimmicky rip-off. If you're looking for a grown-up museum, the Viking exhibit at the Yorkshire Museum is far better.If you're thinking Disneyland with a splash of history, Jorvik's fun. To me, Jorvik is a commercial venture designed for kids with nearly as much square footage devoted to its shop as to the museum.

▲▲**National Railway Museum**—If you like model railways, this is train-car heaven. The thunderous museum shows 150 fascinating years of British railroad history. Fanning out from a grand roundhouse is an array of historic cars and engines, including Queen Victoria's lavish royal car and the very first "stagecoaches on rails." There's much more, including exhibits on dining cars, post cars, sleeping cars, train posters, and videos. At the "Works" section you can see live train switchboards. And don't miss the English Channel Tunnel video (showing the first handshake at breakthrough). Red-shirted "explainers" are everywhere, eager to talk trains. This biggest and best railroad museum anywhere is interesting even to people who think "Pullman" means "don't push" (free, daily 10:00–18:00, tel. 01904/621-261).

Cute little "street trains" shuttle you between the minster and the Railway Museum (£1.50 each way, runs Easter–Oct, leaves Railway Museum every 30 min from 12:00 to 17:30 at the top and bottom of the hour; leaves minster—from Duncombe Place—every 30 min, :15 and :45 min after the hour, no trains Nov–Easter).

▲▲**Yorkshire Museum**—Located in a lush, picnic-perfect park next to the stately ruins of St. Mary's Abbey, Yorkshire Museum is the city's forgotten, serious "archaeology of York" museum. While the hordes line up at Jorvik, the best Viking artifacts are here—with no crowds and a better historical context. A stroll around this museum takes you through Roman (wonderfully described battle-bashed skull in first case), Saxon (great Anglo-Saxon helmet from A.D. 750), Viking, Norman, and Gothic York. Its prize piece is the delicately etched 15th-century pendant called the Middleham Jewel—for which the museum raised $4 million to buy. The 20-minute video about the creation of the abbey is worth a look (£4, various exhibitions can increase price, daily 10:00–17:00, tel. 01904/551-800).

Theatre Royal—A full variety of dramas, comedies, and works by Shakespeare is put on to entertain the locals (£10–16, 19:30 almost nightly, tickets easy to get, closes several weeks during the summer, CC, on St. Leonard's Place next to TI and a 5-min walk from recommended B&Bs, recorded info tel. 01904/610-041, booking tel. 01904/623-568, www.theatre-royal-york.co.uk).

Honorable Mention

York has a number of other sights and activities (described in TI material) that, while interesting, pale in comparison to the biggies. **Fairfax House** is perfectly Georgian inside, with docents happy to talk with you (£4.50, Mon–Thu and Sat 11:00–17:00, Sun 13:30–17:00, Fri by tour only at 11:00 and 14:00, a tour helps bring this well-furnished building to life, on Castlegate, near

Jorvik, tel. 01904/655-543). The **Hall of the Merchant Adventurers** claims to be the finest medieval guildhall in Europe (from 1361). It's basically a vast half-timbered building with marvelous exposed beams and 15 minutes worth of interesting displays about life and commerce back in the days when York was England's second city (£2, reopens in May 2003 after renovation, Mon–Sat 9:00–17:00, Sun 12:00–16:00, early Nov–mid-March until 15:30, below the Shambles off Piccadilly, tel. 01904/654-818). The **Richard III Museum** is interesting only for Richard III enthusiasts (£2, daily 9:00–17:00, Nov–Feb 9:30–16:00, Monk Bar). **The York Dungeon** is gimmicky but, if you insist on papier-mâché gore, is better than the London Dungeon (£7.50, daily 10:00–17:00, less off-season, 12 Clifford Street).

Visitors are welcome at the **lawn bowling green** on Sycamore Place (near recommended B&Bs, tell them which B&B you're staying at); you can buy a pint of beer and watch the action (best in the evenings). Another green is in front of the Coach House Hotel Pub on Marygate.

York—with its medieval lanes lined with classy as well as tacky little shops—is a hit with shoppers. I find the **antique malls** interesting. Three places within a few blocks of each other are filled with stalls and cases owned by antique dealers from the countryside. The malls sell the dealers' bygones on commission. Serious shoppers do better heading for the countryside, but York's shops are a fun browse: Stonegate Antiques Centre (daily 9:00–18:00, 41 Stonegate, tel. 01904/613-888), the antique mall at 2 Lendal (Mon–Sat 10:00–17:00, closed Sun), and the Red House Antiques Centre (daily 9:30–17:30, as late as 20:00 in summer, a block from the minster at Duncombe Place, tel. 01904/637-000).

Sights—Near York

Eden Camp—Once an internment camp for German and Italian POWs during World War II, this is now a theme museum on Britain's war experience. Various barracks detail the rise of Hitler and the fury of the Blitz (with the sound of bombs, the acrid smell of burning, and quotes such as "Hitler will send no warning—so always carry your gas mask.") This award-winning museum energetically conveys the spirit of a country Hitler couldn't conquer. Don't miss hut #10, which details the actual purpose of the camp—as a prison for captured Nazis during World War II. Consider the relative delight of being in the care of the gentlemanly English rather than in a Nazi camp. It's no wonder the Germans settled right in (£4, daily 10:00–17:00, closed late-Dec–mid-Jan, mess-kitchen cafeteria, in Malton, 18 miles northeast of York, tel. 01653/697-777, www.edencamp.co.uk). To get to the camp from

York, catch the Coastliner bus at the York Railway Station (leaves from front of station, on station side of road). Buses are marked with the destination "Whitby" or "Pickering" and are numbered #840, #842, or #X40, depending on the time of day (£4 round-trip, Mon–Sat 11/day, fewer on Sun, 50 min). From York, drivers take A169 toward Scarborough, then follow signs to the camp.

Sleeping in York

(£1 = about $1.50, country code: 44, area code: 01904)

Sleep Code: **S** = Single, **D** = Double/Twin, **T** = Triple, **Q** = Quad, **b** = bathroom, **s** = shower only, **CC** = Credit Cards accepted, **No CC** = Credit Cards not accepted.

To help you sort easily through these listings, I've divided the rooms into three categories based on the price for a standard double room with bath (during high season):

Higher Priced—Most rooms £100 or more.
Moderately Priced—Most rooms more than £60.
Lower Priced—Most rooms £60 or less.

I've listed peak-season, book-direct prices. Don't use the TI. Outside of July and August, some prices go soft. B&Bs will sometimes turn away one-night bookings, particularly for peak-season Saturdays. (York is worth 2 nights anyway.) Remember to book ahead during festival times (late Feb, mid-July, middle of Sept) and weekends year-round.

Sleeping in B&Bs near Bootham

These recommendations are in the handiest B&B neighborhood, a quiet residential area just outside the old-town wall's Bootham gate, along the road called Bootham. All are within a five-minute walk of the minster and TI and a 10-minute walk or taxi ride (£3) from the station. If driving, head for the cathedral and follow the medieval wall to the gate called Bootham Bar. Bootham "street" leads away from Bootham Bar.

These B&Bs are all small, non-smoking, and family run. They come with plenty of steep stairs but no traffic noise. For a good selection, call well in advance. B&B owners will generally hold a room with a phone call and work hard to help their guests sightsee and eat smartly. Most have permits for street parking. And most don't take credit cards.

Laundry: Regency Dry Cleaning does small loads for £8 (Mon–Fri 8:30–18:00, Sat 9:00–17:00, closed Sun, drop off by 9:30 for same-day service, 75 Bootham, at intersection with Queen Anne's, tel. 01904/613-311). The next-nearest place is a long 15-minute walk away (Washeteria Launderette, 124 Haxby Road, tel. 01904/623-379).

HIGHER PRICED

The Hazelwood, my most hotelesque listing in this neighborhood, is plush, though it lacks the intimacy of a B&B. This spacious house has 13 beautifully decorated rooms with modern furnishings and lots of thoughtful touches (Db-£80/90/100 depending on room size, CC, 2 ground-floor rooms, classy breakfast, quiet for being so central, laundry service-£5; a fridge, ice, and great travel library in the pleasant basement lounge; 24 Portland Street, York YO31 7EH, tel. 01904/626-548, fax 01904/628-032, www.thehazelwoodyork.com, e-mail: reservations@thehazelwoodyork.com).

MODERATELY PRICED

23 St. Mary's is extravagantly decorated. Chris and Julie Simpson have done everything super-correctly and offer nine comfy rooms, a classy lounge, and all the doily touches (Sb-£34–40, Db-£64–80 depending on season and size, CC, 23 St. Mary's, York YO30 7DD, tel. 01904/622-738, fax 01904/628-802, www.23stmarys.co.uk).

Crook Lodge B&B, with seven charming, tight rooms, is elegant for a B&B (Db-£60–70, CC, parking, quiet, 26 St. Mary's, York Y030 7DD, tel. & fax 01904/655-614, www.crooklodge.co.uk, e-mail: crooklodge@hotmail.com, Brian and Louise Aiken).

The Coach House Hotel is a labyrinthine, funky old place—a little musty, but well-located facing a bowling green and the abbey walls. It offers 12 comfortable old-time rooms and a crackerjack lounge (Sb-£32.50, D-£60.50, Db-£64.50, CC, free parking, 20 Marygate, Bootham, tel. 01904/652-780, fax 01904/679-943, www.coachhousehotel-york.com, e-mail: info@coachhousehotel-york.com).

LOWER PRICED

Airden House, the most central of my Bootham-area listings, has eight spacious rooms, a grandfather clock–cozy TV lounge, and brightness and warmth throughout. Susan and Keith Burrows, a great source of local travel tips, keep their place tastefully simple, clean, comfortable, and friendly (D-£40–44, Db-£50–54, no CC, 1 St. Mary's, York Y030 7DD, tel. 01904/638-915, www.airdenhouse.co.uk, e-mail: info@airdenhouse.co.uk).

The Sycamore is a fine value, with seven homey rooms strewn with silk flowers and personal touches. It's at the end of a dead end opposite a fun-to-watch bowling green (D-£40, Db-£50, family room-£60, no CC, 19 Sycamore Place off Bootham Terrace, York YO30 7DW, tel. & fax 01904/624-712, www.thesycamore.co.uk, run by Elizabeth).

Abbeyfields Guest House has nine cozy, bright rooms and a quiet lounge. This doily-free place, which lacks the usual clutter, has been designed with care (Sb-£36, Db-£58, no CC, 19 Bootham Terrace, York YO30 7DH, tel. & fax 01904/636-471, www.abbeyfields.co.uk, Richard and Gwen Martin).

Queen Anne's Guest House has seven clean, cheery rooms (May–Sept D-£34, Db-£36, Oct–April D-£30, Db-£34, prices good through 2003 with this book, CC, 1 family room, lounge, 24 Queen Anne's Road, York Y030 7AA, tel. 01904/629-389, fax 01904/619-529, e-mail: info@queenannes.fsnet.co.uk, Judy and David).

Alcuin Lodge has five flowery rooms and solid-wood furnishings (Db-£45–55, 1 small top-floor D-£40, no kids, CC, 15 Sycamore Place, York Y030 7DW, tel. 01904/632-222, fax 01904/626-630, e-mail: alcuinlodg@aol.com, Susan Taylor and her husband, General Patton).

Arnot House, run by a hardworking daughter-and-mother team, is homey and lushly decorated with early-1900s memorabilia. The four well-furnished rooms have little libraries (Db-£54–58, CC, minimum 2-night stay, 17 Grosvenor Terrace, York Y030 7AG, tel. & fax 01904/641-966, www.arnothouseyork.co.uk, e-mail: kim.robbins@virgin.net, Kim and Ann Robbins).

Sleeping in B&Bs along the Riverside

Three fine smoke-free places front the River Ouse midway between the train station and the minster. Each faces a pedestrian path and comes with a delightful front garden and absolutely no traffic noise. Front rooms overlook the river; back rooms watch a sprawling car park.

MODERATELY PRICED

Water's Edge B&B, a pastel place with five comfy rooms a teddy bear would like, is well-run by Julie Mett (Db-£55, 4-poster riverview Db-£55–65, CC for 3.5 percent extra, 5 Earlsborough Terrace, York, Y030 7BQ, tel. 01904/644-625, fax 01904/731-516, www.watersedgeyork.co.uk, e-mail: julie@watersedgeyork.co.uk).

LOWER PRICED

Abbey Guest House has seven basic rooms (S-£25, Sb-£32, D-£47, Db-£57, Qb-£70, CC for 2.5 percent extra, free parking, Internet access, 14 Earlsborough Terrace, York Y030 7BQ, tel. 01904/627-782, fax 01904/671-743, www.bedandbreakfastyork.co.uk, e-mail: abbey@rsummers.cix.co.uk, Hilary Summers).

Riverside Walk B&B has 12 small rooms, steep stairs, and

York Hotels and Restaurants

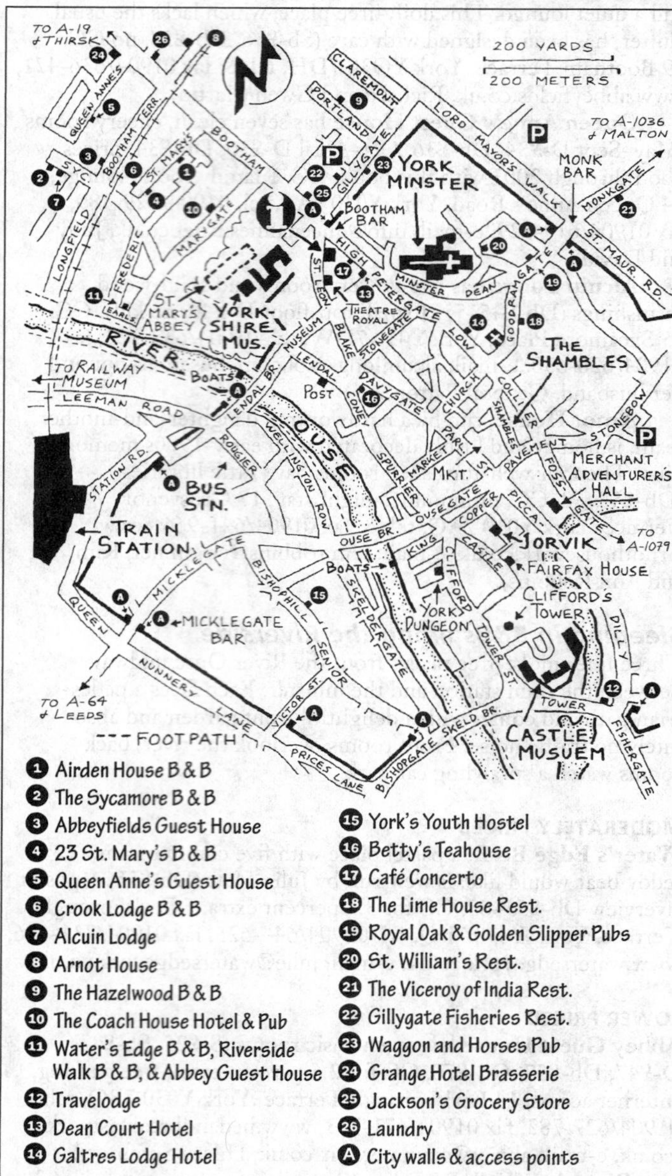

narrow hallways (Db-£52–60, CC for 2.5 percent extra, free parking, 8 Earlsborough Terrace, York Y030 7BQ, tel. 01904/620-769, fax 01904/671-743, www.bedandbreakfastyork.co.uk, Mr. Summers).

Sleeping in Hotels in the Center

HIGHER PRICED

Dean Court Hotel, facing the minster, is a big, stately Best Western hotel with classy lounges and 40 comfortable rooms (small Db-£105, standard Db-£135, superior Db-£150, spacious deluxe Db-£165, CC, some non-smoking rooms, tearoom, restaurant, elevator to most rooms, Duncombe Place, York YO1 7EF, tel. 01904/625-082, fax 01904/620-305, www.deancourt-york.co.uk).

MODERATELY PRICED

Travelodge offers 90 identical, affordable rooms near the Castle Museum (Db-£60, Oct–June Db discounted to £53, kids' bed free, CC, some smoke-free rooms, 90 Piccadilly, central reservations tel. 0870/085-0950, www.travelodge.co.uk).

Galtres Lodge Hotel, a block from the minster, offers comfy, recently refurbished rooms above a restaurant in the old-town center (S-£30–35, Sb-£35–45, Db-£70–80, CC, non-smoking, Internet access, 54 Low Petergate, York Y01 7HZ, tel. 01904/622-478, fax 01904/627-804).

LOWER PRICED

York's Youth Hostel is well run, with a kitchen, launderette, game room, and 120 beds (S-£20, bunk bed D-£30, £13 beds in 4- to 6-bed dorms, £10 beds in larger dorms, CC, less for multi-night stays, same-sex or coed possible, no breakfast, 10-min walk from station at 11 Bishophill Senior Road, York YO1 1EF, tel. 01904/625-904, fax 01904/612-494, www.yorkyouthhotel.com).

Eating in York

Traditional Tea

York is famous for its elegant teahouses. Drop into one around 16:00 for tea and cakes. Ladies love **Betty's Teahouse** where you pay £5.50 for a cream tea (tea and scones) or £10 for a full traditional English afternoon tea (tea, elegant sandwich, scones, and sweets). Your table is so full of doily niceties that the food is served on a little three-tray tower. While Betty's food is nothing special, the ambience and people-watching are hard to beat (daily 9:00–21:00, piano music nightly 18:00–21:00,

CC, mostly non-smoking, St. Helen's Square; fine view of street scene from a window seat on the main floor, downstairs near WC is a mirror signed by WWII bomber pilots—read the story). If there's a line, it moves quickly. I'd wait for a seat by the windows on the ground level rather than sit in the much bigger basement.

Eating near the Minster

Of these listings, the first listing faces the minster, the last two are behind the minster, and the rest are on Goodramgate near the minster.

Café Concerto, a French-style bistro with a fun menu, has an understandably loyal following. Their food is the best I've had in York (great £8 lunches, £15 dinners, daily 10:00–22:00, serves meals all day, CC, smoke-free, smart to reserve for dinner, facing the minster, High Petergate 21, tel. 01904/610-478).

The **Lime House Restaurant** is a small, modern, candlelit place enthusiastically run by chef Adam Fisher. His menu features European dishes revolving with the seasons and always includes a good vegetarian plate. Adam offers a free glass of house wine to anyone with this book (£12 plates, 10 percent off on orders before 19:00, Wed–Sat 12:00–14:00 & 18:00–21:30, closed Sun–Tue, lunch specials, CC, 55 Goodramgate, tel. 01904/632-734).

For **Italian**, you'll find three popular places virtually side by side along Goodramgate.

There's a pub serving grub on every block. Eat where you see lots of food. The **Royal Oak** offers £5 pub grub throughout the day, a small non-smoking room, and hand-pulled ale (daily 11:00–20:00, heavy meat dishes, fat fries, but don't look in their kitchen, CC, Goodramgate, a block from Monk Bar, a block east of the minster, tel. 01904/653-856). The **Golden Slipper**, next door, is also a classic for basic pub grub and darts.

St. Williams Restaurant, just behind the great east window of the minster in a wonderful half-timbered, 15th-century building (read the history), serves quick and tasty lunches and elegant candlelit dinners (£15 plates, daily 10:00–17:00 & 18:00–22:00, Oct–March closed Sun–Mon nights, traditional and Mediterranean, CC, College Street, tel. 01904/634-830).

The Viceroy of India—just outside Monk Bar and therefore outside the tourist zone—serves great Indian food at good prices to mostly locals. If you've yet to eat Indian on your trip, do it here (£8 plates, Sun–Thu 18:00–24:00, Fri–Sat 12:00–24:00, friendly staff, CC, continue straight through Monk Bar—pass the big old "nightly bile beans keep you healthy, bright-eyed, and slim" sign on your left—to 26 Monkgate, tel. 01904/622-370).

Eating near Bootham Bar and Your B&B

Gillygate Fisheries is a wonderfully traditional little fish-and-chips joint where tattooed people eat in and housebound mothers take out (Mel serves £4–5 meals, "eat your mushy peas," Mon 17:00–23:30, Tue–Fri 11:30–13:30 & 17:00–23:30, Sat 11:30–23:30, closed Sun, smoke-free seating, 2 blocks from the TI at 59 Gillygate).

The **Waggon and Horses** pub has local color and serves cheap "pub food with attitude" in a cozy smoke-free room or with the smoking beer drinkers (Mon–Sat 12:00–20:00, Sun 12:00–15:00, fresh vegetables, across from Wackers at 48 Gillygate, tel. 01904/654-103).

The well-worn **Coach House** serves good-quality food with fresh vegetables but can be smoky (£8–11, nightly 18:30–21:00, CC, 20 Marygate, tel. 01904/652-780).

The **Grange Hotel Brasserie**, a couple of blocks from the B&Bs, is classier than a pub and serves a smattering of traditional European dishes. Go downstairs—avoid the pricey main-floor restaurant (£9 meals, Mon–Sat 12:00–14:00 & 18:00–22:00, Sun 19:00–22:00, CC, 1 Clifton, tel. 01904/644-744).

Jackson's grocery store is open every day 7:00–23:00 (near B&Bs, outside Bootham Bar, on Bootham). For an atmospheric **picnic spot,** try the Museum Gardens (near Bootham Bar) at the evocative 12th-century ruins of St. Mary's Abbey.

Transportation Connections—York

By Train: To **Durham** (1/hr, 45 min), **Edinburgh** (2/hr, 2.5 hrs), **London** (2/hr, 2 hrs), **Bath** (1/hr, 5 hrs, change in Bristol), **Cambridge** (nearly hrly, 2 hrs, change in Peterborough), **Birmingham** (2/hr, 2.5 hrs), **Keswick** (with transfers to Penrith then bus, 4.5 hrs). **Train info**: tel. 08457/484-950.

Connections with London's Airports: **Heathrow** (1/hr, allow 2.5–3 hrs, take Heathrow Express train to London's Paddington Station, tube to King's Cross, train to York—2/hr, 2 hrs), **Gatwick** (from Gatwick catch low-profile Thameslink train to King's Cross-Thameslink station in London; from there, walk 100 yards to King's Cross station, train to York—2/hr, 2 hrs).

The **York Bus Information Centre** is at 20 Hudson Street, near the train station (Mon–Fri 8:30–17:00, tel. 01904/551-400, phone answered Mon–Sat 8:00–20:00, Sun 8:00–14:00).

Route Tips for Drivers

As you near York (and your B&B), you'll hit the A1237 ring road. Follow this to the A19/Thirsk roundabout (next to river on north-east side of town). From roundabout, follow signs for York City, traveling through Clifton into Bootham. All recommended B&Bs are four or five blocks before you hit the medieval city gate (see neighborhood map, page 269). If you're approaching York from the south, take M1 until it ends. Then follow A64 for 10 miles until you reach York's ring road (A1237), which allows you to avoid driving through the city center.

NORTH YORK MOORS

In the lonesome North York Moors, you can wander through the stark beauty of its time-passed villages, bored sheep, and powerful landscapes.

If you're driving, get a map. Without wheels, you have several choices: Take a bus/steam-train combination (below); choose one of several guided bus tours from York (focusing on Herriot or Brontë country, moors, Lake District, or Holy Island, different tour every day, offered by various companies for roughly £10/half day or £16 /full day); or hire a private guide.

John Smith, a licensed guide and driver, can take up to three people on one of his Yorkshire Tours—such as Herriot Country, a Castle Howard/steam train/Whitby combination, or a tour tailored to your interests (£15/hr, admissions extra, tel. 01904/636-653, cellular 07850/260-511).

▲The Moors—Car hike across the moors on any small road. You'll come upon tidy villages, old Roman roads, and maybe even a fox hunt. The Moors Visitors Centre provides the best orientation for exploring the moors. It's a grand old lodge offering exhibits, shows, nature walks, an information desk with plenty of books and maps, brass rubbing, a cheery cafeteria, and brochures on several good walks that start right there (free but £1.50 parking fee, April–Oct daily 10:00–17:00, Nov–Dec and March daily 11:00–16:00, Jan–Feb weekends only 11:00–16:00, a half mile from train station, tel. 01287/660-654, www.northyorkmoors-npa.gov.uk).

▲North Yorkshire Moors Railway—This 18-mile, one-hour steam-engine ride between Pickering and Grosmont (pron. GROW-mont) goes through some of the best parts of the moors almost hourly. Even with the windows small and dirty (wipe off the outside of yours before you roll) and the track mostly in a scenic gully, it's a good ride. You can stop along the way for a moors walk and catch the next train (£10 round-trip, March–Oct, first train departs Pickering about 10:20, last train departs Grosmont about 16:50, allow 3.5 hrs round-trip due to scheduling, CC, tel. 01751/472-508, talking timetable tel. 01751/473-535). It's not possible to leave luggage at any stop on the steam-train line—pack lightly if you decide to hike.

Pickering—With its rural-life museum, castle, and Monday market

North York Moors

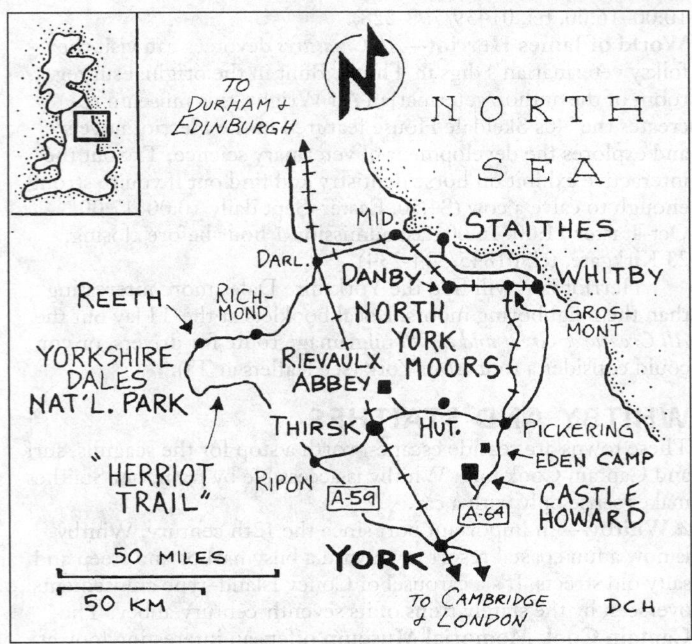

(produce, knickknacks), this town is worth a stop. You could catch an early York–Pickering bus (Mon–Sat 1/hr, only 1 on Sun, 65 min, leaves from train station), see Pickering, and carry on to Grosmont on the North Yorkshire Moors Railway (above). Grosmont is on a regular train line with limited connections to Whitby (see below) and points north and south (TI tel. 01751/473-791).

▲Hutton-le-Hole—This postcard-pretty town is home of the fine Ryedale Folk Museum, which illustrates "farm life in the moors" through reconstructed and furnished 18th-century local buildings (£3.25, mid-March–Oct daily 10:00–17:30, last entry at 16:30, tel. 01751/417-367).

Castle Howard—Especially popular since the filming of *Brideshead Revisited*, this fine, palatial 300-year-old home is about half as interesting as Blenheim Palace in the Cotswolds (£8.50, daily 11:00–17:00, closed early Nov–mid-March, 1 bus/day from York, 40 min, tel. 01653/648-333).

Rievaulx Abbey—Rievaulx (pron. ree-VOH) is a highlight of the North York Moors and beautifully situated, but if you've seen other fine old abbeys, this is a rerun (£3.60, daily April–July and

Sept 10:00–18:00, Aug 9:30–18:00, Oct 10:00–17:00, Nov–March 10:00–16:00, tel. 01439/798-228).

World of James Herriot—*All Creatures* devotees can visit the folksy veterinarian's digs in Thirsk. Built in the original surgery room of the author/veterinarian Alf Wright, this museum re-creates the '40s Skeldale House featured in the Herriot novels and explores the development of veterinary science. Try out the interactive exhibit on horse dentistry and find out if you're strong enough to calve a cow (£4.50, Easter–Sept daily 10:00–17:00, Oct–Easter 11:00–16:00, last admission 1 hour before closing, 23 Kirkgate, tel. 01845/524-234).

Herriot fans will find the Yorkshire Dales more interesting than the neighboring moors. Local booklets at the TI lay out the *All Creatures Great and Small* pilgrimage route for drivers, or you could consider a tour from York (see leaflets at TI).

WHITBY AND STAITHES

These towns are seaside escapes worth a stop for the seagulls, surf, and Captain Cook lore. Whitby is accessible by train, but Staithes makes sense only with a car.

▲**Whitby**—An important port since the 12th century, Whitby is now a fun coastal resort town with a busy harbor and steep and salty old streets. It's a carousel of Coney Island–type amusements overseen by the stately ruins of its seventh-century abbey. The **Captain Cook Memorial Museum** offers an interesting look at the famous hometown sailor and his exotic voyages (£2.80, daily 9:45–17:00, closed Nov–March, down Grape Lane in the old town just over the bridge). Two of Captain Cook's boats *(Resolution* and *Endeavour)* were built in the Whitby shipyards. The **TI** is on the harbor next to the train and bus stations (May–Sept daily 9:30–18:00, Oct–April daily 10:00–16:30, tel. 01947/602-674).

If driving, upon arrival park across from the TI at the pay-and-display supermarket lot near the train and bus station. Wander along the harbor out along Pier Road and Fish Quay past all the Coney Island–type amusements. The **Magpie Restaurant** is famous for its fish and chips (generally a line of hungry pilgrims waiting to get in). The small Dracula exhibit is a reminder that some of that story was set here. As you return to your car, cross the bridge where you'll find a warren of touristy lanes filled with hard candy, knickknack shops, and the small Captain Cook Memorial Museum.

Sleeping in Whitby: Whitby has plenty of rooms. August is the only tight month. The **Crescent House** rents six good rooms just south of the harbor with some sea views (Db-£46, family deals, no CC, non-smoking, on the bluff at the top of Khyber Pass at

6 East Crescent, Whitby YO21 3HD, tel. & fax 01947/600-091, e-mail: janet@whitby.fsbusiness.co.uk, Janet and Mike Paget). **Dolphin Hotel**, in the old-town center at the bridge overlooking the harbor, is a colorful old pub with five salty rooms upstairs (Db-£55, CC, pub closes at 23:30, 3 blocks from train station, Bridge Street, Whitby Y022 4BG, tel. 01947/602-197). The **hostel** is next to the abbey above the town (£11/bed, 58 beds in 8 rooms, CC, office closed 10:00–17:00, tel. 01947/602-878).

Connections: Buses connect Whitby and York (4–6/day depending on season, 2 hrs, tel. 01653/692-556). Trains connect Durham with Middlesbrough (5/day, 50 min, more frequent with transfer in Darlington); the Middlesbrough–Whitby train (4/day, 90 min) stops at Grosmont (where you can catch the Moors steam train) and Danby (a half mile from the Moors info center).

▲Staithes—A ragamuffin village where the boy who became Captain James Cook got his first taste of the sea, Staithes (just north of Whitby) is a salty tumble of cottages bunny-hopping down a ravine into a tiny harbor. While tranquil today, in 1816 it was home to 70 boats and the busiest fishing station in north England. Ten years ago the town supported 20 fishing boats—today, only three. But fishermen (who pronounce their town "steers") still outnumber tourists in undiscovered Staithes. The town has changed little since Captain Cook's days. Little is done to woo tourism here. Lots of flies and seagulls seem to have picked the barren cliffs raw. There's nothing to do but drop by the lifeboat house (a big deal in England; page through the history book, read the not-quite-stirring accounts of the boats being called to duty; drop a coin in the box), stroll the beach, and nurse a harborside beer or ice cream. Just an easy drive north of Whitby, Staithes is worthwhile by car—probably not by bus (hourly Whitby–Staithes buses, 30 min; 10-min walk from bus stop into town).

Sleeping in Staithes: There are no fancy rooms. It's a cash-only town with no ATMs. Parking is tough—generally you can drive in only to unload. Service trucks clog the windy main (and only) lane much of the day. There's a pay-and-display lot at the top of the town (when paying the night before, time spills over past 9:00 the next morning). Each of these three- or four-bedroom places is cramped, with tangled floor plans that make you feel like a stowaway. **Greystones B&B** provides the best beds in town (Db-£50, family deals, no CC, non-smoking, Internet access, High Street, tel. 01947/841-694, www.staithes-uk.co.uk, e-mail: tonyrd@lineone.net, Tony and Eve). The **Endeavour Restaurant B&B** is a tidy little place and the only one in town offering parking (Db-£55–60, CC, serves great food—see below, 1 High Street, tel. 01947/840-825, www.endeavour-restaurant.co.uk, Brian Kay & Charlotte Willoughby). **Harborside Guest House** is the roughest place, but the only place actually on the harbor. It provides rumpled old beds, three seaview rooms, breakfast on linoleum, and the sound of waves to lull you to sleep (D-£40, no CC, tel. 01947/841-296, James and Sue).

Eating in Staithes: The oddly classy-for-this-town **Endeavour Restaurant** offers excellent £25 dinners (Tue–Sat 18:45–21:30, closed Sun–Mon, seafood, vegetarian, reservations wise, tel. 01947/840-825). Three pubs serve dinner (generally 19:00–21:00): the **Black Lion**, the **Royal George**, and the **Cod and Lobster**. The Cod and Lobster overlooks the harbor, with outdoor benches and a cozy living room warmed by a coal fire. Drop in to see its old-time Staithes photos. For fish and chips or a coffee on the harbor, try the friendly **Sea Drift Sweet Shop** or **Harborside Guest House**.

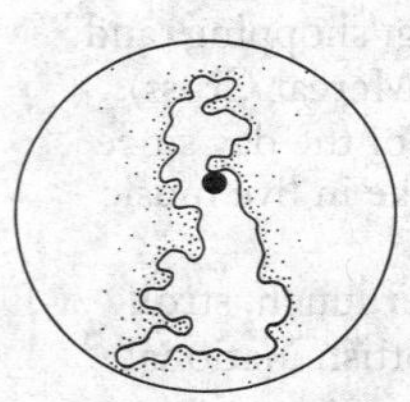

EDINBURGH

Edinburgh, the colorful city of Robert Louis Stevenson, Sir Walter Scott, and Robert Burns, is Scotland's showpiece and one of Europe's most entertaining cities. Historical, monumental, fun, and well organized, it's a tourist's delight.

Promenade down the Royal Mile through Old Town. Historic buildings pack the Royal Mile between the castle (on the top) and Holyrood Palace (on the bottom). Medieval skyscrapers stand shoulder to shoulder, hiding peaceful courtyards connected to High Street by narrow lanes or even tunnels. This colorful jumble is the tourist's Edinburgh.

Edinburgh (pron. ED'n-burah) was once the most crowded city in Europe—famed for its skyscrapers and filth. The rich and poor lived atop one another. In the Age of Enlightenment, a magnificent Georgian city, today's New Town, was laid out to the north, giving the town's upper class a respectable place to promenade. Georgian Edinburgh, like the city of Bath, shines with broad boulevards, straight streets, square squares, circular circuses, and elegant mansions decked out in colonnades, pediments, and sphinxes in the proud, neoclassical style of 200 years ago.

While the Georgian city celebrated the union of Scotland and England (with streets and squares named after English kings and emblems), "devolution" is the latest trend. In a 1998 election, the Scots voted to gain more autonomy and bring their parliament home. Though Edinburgh has been the historic capital of Scotland for centuries, parliament had not met in Scotland since 1707. In 2000, although London still calls the strategic shots, Edinburgh resumed its position as home to the Scottish Parliament. A strikingly modern new parliament building, opening in 2003, will be one more jewel in Edinburgh's crown.

Planning Your Time

While the major sights can be seen in a day, I'd linger longer and give Edinburgh two days and three nights.

Day 1: Tour the castle. Then consider catching one of the city bus tours (from a block below the castle at Tolbooth church) for a 60-minute loop, returning to the castle. Explore the Royal Mile, going downhill—lunching, museum-going, shopping, and taking a walking tour (one leaves at 14:00 from Mercat Cross). If you tour Holyrood Palace, do it near the end of the day since it's at the bottom of the Mile. In the evening, take in live music at a pub, a literary pub crawl, or a haunted walk.

Day 2: Tour the Museum of Scotland. After lunch, stroll through the Princes Street Gardens and the Scottish National Gallery. Then tour the good ship *Britannia*.

Orientation (area code: 0131)

The center of Edinburgh holds the Princes Street Gardens park and Waverley Bridge, where you'll find the TI, Princes Mall, train station, bus info office (starting point for most city bus tours), National Gallery, and a covered dance-and-music pavilion. Weather blows in and out—bring your sweater.

Tourist Information: The crowded TI is as central as can be atop the Princes Mall and train station (May–June and Sept Mon–Sat 9:00–19:00, Sun 10:00–19:00; July–Aug daily 9:00–20:00; April and Oct daily 9:00–18:00; Nov–March daily until 17:00; ATM outside entrance, tel. 0131/473-3800). Unfortunately, all their information—their assessment of museums and even which car-rental companies "exist"—is skewed by tourism payola. Buy a map (£1 if in stock, or the excellent £4 Collins Illustrated Edinburgh map, which comes with opinionated commentary and locates virtually every major shop and sight), and ask for the free monthly entertainment *Gig Guide* if you're interested in late-night music. The *Essential Guide to Edinburgh* (£1), while not essential, lists additional sights and services. Book your room direct without the TI's help (B&Bs charge more for rooms booked through the TI, and you pay the TI a £3 finder's fee). Browse the racks (tucked away in hallway at back of TI) for brochures on the various Scottish folk shows, walking tours, and regional bus tours. Connect @edinburgh, a small Internet café, is beyond the brochure racks (see "Helpful Hints," below). The best monthly entertainment listing, *The List*, sells for £2.20 at newsstands.

Arrival in Edinburgh: Arriving by train at Waverley Station puts you in the city center and below the TI (go up the many stairs until you surface at street level, TI to your left) and the city bus to my recommended B&Bs (see "Sleeping" later in this chapter,

Edinburgh

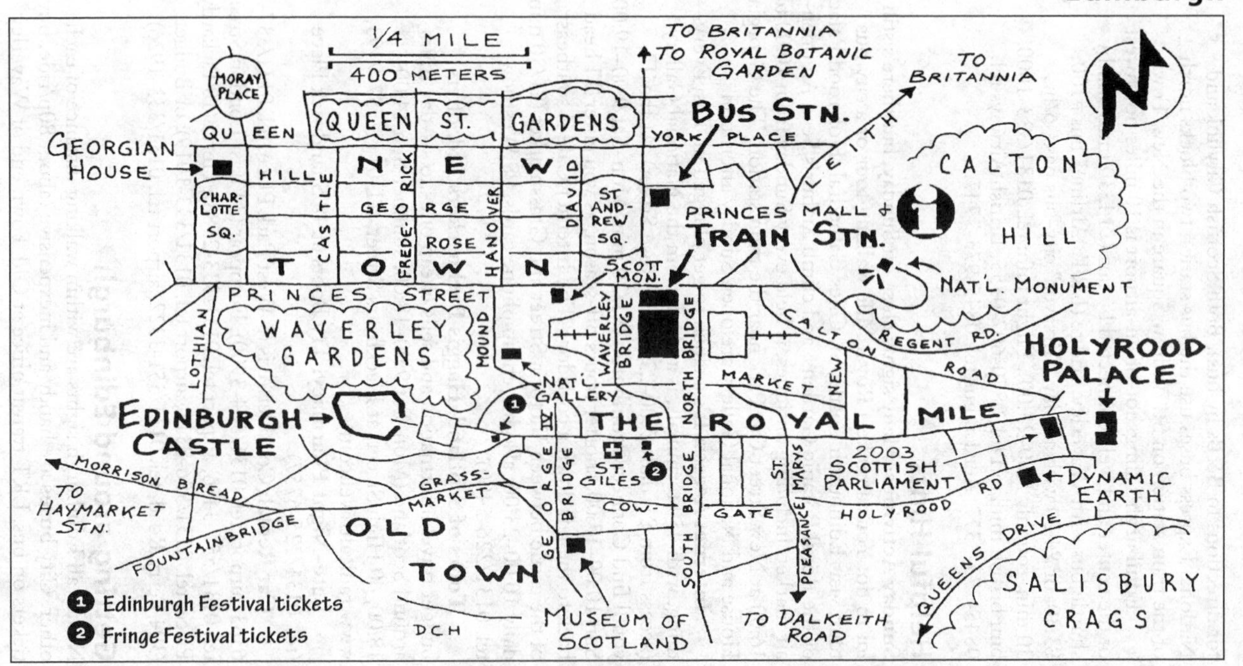
1/4 MILE
400 METERS
TO BRITANNIA
TO ROYAL BOTANIC GARDEN
TO BRITANNIA
MORAY PLACE
QUEEN ST. GARDENS
QUEEN
GEORGIAN HOUSE
HILL
CHARLOTTE SQ.
CASTLE
GEORGE
FREDERICK
ROSE
HANOVER
DAVID
ST ANDREW SQ.
NEW TOWN
BUS STN.
YORK PLACE
LEITH
CALTON HILL
PRINCES MALL & TRAIN STN.
SCOTT MON.
NAT'L. MONUMENT
PRINCES STREET
WAVERLEY GARDENS
LOTHIAN
MOUND
WAVERLEY BRIDGE
NORTH BRIDGE
CALTON
REGENT RD.
ROAD
HOLYROOD PALACE
NAT'L. GALLERY
MARKET
NEW
EDINBURGH CASTLE
THE ROYAL MILE
GEORGE IV BRIDGE
ST. GILES
2003 SCOTTISH PARLIAMENT
DYNAMIC EARTH
MORRISON
BREAD
TO HAYMARKET STN.
GRASSMARKET
COWGATE
SOUTH BRIDGE
ST. MARYS
PLEASANCE
HOLYROOD RD
FOUNTAINBRIDGE
OLD TOWN
QUEENS DRIVE
SALISBURY CRAGS
DCH
MUSEUM OF SCOTLAND
TO DALKEITH ROAD
1 Edinburgh Festival tickets
2 Fringe Festival tickets

for directions to B&Bs by bus). Both Scottish Citylink and National Express buses use the bus station two blocks north of the train station on St. Andrew Square in the New Town.

Edinburgh's slingshot-of-an-airport is 10 miles northwest of the center and well-connected by taxi (£14, 30 min) and by shuttle bus with Waverley Bridge (LRT "Airline" bus #100, £3.30, or £4.20 with all-day "Airsaver" city-bus pass, 6/hr, 30 min, roughly 5:00–23:00). Flight info: tel. 0131/333-1000, bmi british midland tel. 0870-607-0555, British Airways tel. 0845-773-3377, Aer Lingus tel. 0845-973-7747.

Helpful Hints

Sunday Activities: Many sights close on Sunday, but there's still a lot to do: You can take a Royal Mile walking tour or a city bus tour; visit Edinburgh Castle, St. Giles Cathedral, Holyrood Palace, or the Royal Botanic Gardens; and climb Arthur's Seat. An open-air market, including antiques, is held every Sunday from 10:00 to 16:00 at New Street Car Park near the train station. The Georgian House and National Gallery are open Sunday afternoon.

Internet Access: It's a cinch to get plugged in. EasyEverything, with 450 terminals, is a block from the National Gallery (access from £1, daily 7:00–23:00, 58 Rose Street). At the TI, you'll find Connect@edinburgh (£1/20 min, Mon–Sat 9:00–19:00, Sun 10:00–17:00, shorter hours off-season, as you enter TI head back to the left down a corridor). The Internet Café is southeast of the castle between Victoria Street and Grassmarket (£1/30 min, daily 10:00–23:00, also has cheap phone cards, 98 Westbow, tel. 0131/226-5400).

Tours of Scotland: **Haggis Backpackers Ltd.** offers budget travel information and sells cheap one- to six-day tours around Scotland (Mon–Sat 9:00–18:00, summer Sun 14:00–18:00, 60 High Street, at Blackfriars Street, tel. 0131/557-9393, www.radicaltravel.com).

Late-Night Pharmacy: Try Boots at 48 Shandwick Place (tel. 0131/225-6757).

Car Rental: Consider Avis (5 West Park Place, tel. 0131/337-6363, airport tel. 0131/344-3900); Europcar (24 East London Street, tel. 0131/557-3456, airport tel. 0131/333-2588); Hertz (10 Pickardy Place, tel. 0131/556-8311, airport tel. 0131/333-1019); or Budget (394 Ferry Road, tel. 0131/551-3322, airport tel. 0131/333-1926).

Getting around Edinburgh

Nearly all Edinburgh sights are within walking distance of each other. City **buses** are handy and inexpensive (about 80p/ride, buy tickets on bus, LRT transit office at Old Town end of Waverley

Bridge has schedules and route maps, tel. 0131/555-6363). Tell the driver where you're going, have change handy (most buses require exact change; you lose any excess), take your ticket as you board, push the stop button as you near your stop (so your stop isn't skipped), and exit from the middle door. Two companies handle the city routes: LRT (or Lothian) does most of it and First does the rest (e.g., to get from the city center to the recommended B&Bs on Dalkeith Road, you can catch LRT buses #14, #21, and #33 or First bus #86). Day passes sold by each company are valid only on their buses (£2.20, or £1.50 after 9:30 weekdays and all day weekends, buy from driver). Buses run from about 6:00 to 23:00. **Taxis** are reasonable and easy to flag down (average ride between downtown and B&B district-£5).

Bus Tours of Edinburgh

▲Hop-on, Hop-off City Bus Tours—Three companies offer 60-minute bus tours that circle the town center stopping at the biggies—Waverley Bridge, the castle, Royal Mile, Georgian New Town, and Princes Street—with an informative narration and pickups about every 10 to 15 minutes. You can hop on and off with one ticket all day. Hop on at any stop or go to Waverley Bridge to comparison shop between your bus-tour options.

The City Sightseeing/Guide Friday company has a live guide (£8.50, £11 combo-ticket includes round-trip transportation to *Britannia*—which normally costs £3.50, ticket gives 10 percent discount off castle admission, tel. 0131/556-2244). LRT's "Edinburgh Classic Tour," which runs a little more frequently, uses headphones with a recorded narration (£7.50, tel. 0131/555-6363). Mac Tours' "Edinburgh by Vintage Bus" has a live guide, fewer buses, and a shorter route (£7.50, 3/hr, 1 hour, ticket bought after 17:00 also valid the next day, tel. 0131/220-0770).

On sunny days they go topless (the buses), but they also suffer from traffic noise and congestion. Buses run year-round. First and last buses leave Waverley Bridge around 9:15 and continue until 19:00 mid-June through early September (last buses leave earlier off-season).

Sights—Edinburgh

▲▲▲Edinburgh Castle—The fortified birthplace of the city 1,300 years ago, this imposing symbol of Edinburgh sits proudly on a rock high above the city. While the castle has been both a fort and a royal residence since the 11th century, most of the buildings today are from its more recent use as a military garrison. This fascinating and multifaceted sight deserves several hours of your time (£8, daily April–Oct 9:30–18:00, Nov–March

9:30–17:00, CC, cafeteria, tel. 0131/225-9846; consider avoiding the long uphill walk from the nearest city bus stop by taking a cab to the castle gate).

Entry Gate: Start with the wonderfully droll 30-minute guided introduction tour (free with admission, departs 2–4 times/hr from entry, see clock for next departure; few tours run off-season). The audioguide is excellent, with four hours of quick digital dial descriptions (£3, pay at ticket office, pick up at entry gate before meeting the live guide). The clean WC at the entry annually wins "British Loo of the Year" awards (marvel at the plaques near men's room), but they use a one-way mirror showing the sink area in the women's room (women: pop your head into office near men's room to complain or make sure mirror is curtained).

In the castle there are five essential stops: Crown Jewels, Royal Palace, Scottish National War Memorial, St. Margaret's Chapel with city view, and the excellent National War Museum of Scotland. The first four are at the highest and most secure point—on or near the castle square, where your introductory guided tour ends. The War Museum is 50 yards below by the cafeteria and big shop.

1. Crown Jewels: The line of tourists leads from the square directly to the jewels. Skip this line and enter the building around to the left (next to WC), where you'll get to the jewels via a wonderful *Honors of Scotland* exhibition about the crown jewels and how they survived the harrowing centuries.

Scotland's **Crown Jewels** are older than England's. While Cromwell destroyed England's, the Scots hid theirs successfully. Longtime symbols of Scottish nationalism, they were made in Edinburgh—of Scottish gold, diamonds, and gems—in 1540 for a 1543 coronation. They were last used to crown Charles II in 1651. When the Act of Union, which dissolved Scotland's parliament into England's to create the United Kingdom in 1707, was forced upon the Scots, part of the deal was that they could keep their jewels locked up in Edinburgh. They remained hidden for more than 100 years. In 1818 Walter Scott and a royal commission rediscovered the jewels intact.

The **Stone of Scone** sits plain and strong next to the jewels. This big gray chunk of rock is the coronation stone of Scotland's ancient kings (ninth century). Swiped by the English, it sat under the coronation chair at Westminster Abbey from 1296 until 1996. With major fanfare, Scotland's treasured Stone of Scone returned to Edinburgh on Saint Andrew's Day, November 30, 1996. Talk to the guard for more details.

2. The Royal Palace (facing castle square under the flagpole) has two historic yet unimpressive rooms (through door reading

1566) and the Great Hall (separate entrance from the same castle square). Remember, Scottish royalty only lived here when safety or protocol required. They preferred the **Holyrood Palace** at the bottom of the Royal Mile. Enter the **Mary Queen of Scots room**, where in 1566 the queen gave birth to James VI of Scotland, who later became King James I of England. The **Presence Chamber** leads into **Laich Hall** (Lower Hall), the dining room of the royal family.

The **Great Hall** was the castle's ceremonial meeting place in the 16th and 17th centuries. In modern times it was a barracks and a hospital. While most of what you see is Victorian, two medieval elements survive: the fine hammer-beam roof and the big iron-barred peephole (above fireplace on right). This allowed the king to spy on his partying subjects.

3. The Scottish National War Memorial commemorates the 149,000 Scottish soldiers lost in World War I, the 58,000 lost in World War II, and the 750 lost in British battles since. Each bay is dedicated to a particular Scottish regiment. The main shrine, featuring a green Italian-marble memorial containing the original WWI rolls of honor, actually sits upon an exposed chunk of the castle rock. Above you, the archangel Michael is busy slaying the dragon. The bronze frieze accurately shows the attire of various wings of Scotland's military. The stained glass starts with Cain and Abel on the left and finishes with a celebration of peace on the right. If the importance of this place is hard to understand, consider that one out of every three adult Scottish men died in World War I.

4. St. Margaret's Chapel, the oldest building in Edinburgh, is dedicated to Queen Margaret, who died here in 1093 and was sainted in 1250. Built in 1130 in the Romanesque style of the Norman invaders, it is wonderfully simple, with classic Norman zigzags decorating the round arch that separates the tiny nave from the sacristy. Used as a powder magazine for 400 years, very little survives. You'll see an 11th-century gospel book of St. Margaret's and small windows featuring St. Margaret, St. Columba (who brought Christianity to Scotland via Iona), and William Wallace (the brave defender of Scotland). The place is popular for weddings and, since it seats only 20, particularly popular with brides' fathers.

Mons Meg—a huge and once-upon-a-time frightening 15th-century siege cannon that fired 330-pound stones nearly two miles—stands in front of the church.

Belly up to the banister (outside the chapel below the cannon) to enjoy the great view. Below you are the guns—which fire the one o'clock salute—and a sweet little line of doggie tombstones, the soldiers' pet cemetery. Beyond stretches the Georgian New Town (read the informative plaque).

5. The National War Museum of Scotland thoughtfully covers four centuries of Scottish military history. Instead of the usual musty, dusty displays of endless armor, this museum has an interesting mix of short films, uniforms, weapons, medals, mementos, and eloquent excerpts from soldiers' letters. A pleasant surprise just when you thought your castle visit was about over, this rivals any military museum you'll see in Europe.

When leaving the castle, turn around and look back at the gate. There stand King Robert the Bruce (on the left, 1274–1329) and Sir William Wallace (Braveheart—on the right, 1270–1305). Wallace (recently famous, thanks to Mel Gibson) fought long and hard against English domination before being executed in London—his body cut to pieces and paraded through the far corners of jolly olde England. Bruce beat the English at Bannockburn in 1314. Bruce and Wallace still defend the spirit of Scotland. The Latin inscription above the gate between them reads (basically) "What you do to us . . . we will do to you."

Sights—Along the Royal Mile

These are listed in walking order, from top to bottom. (Bus #35 runs along the Mile, handy for going up after you've hit bottom.)

▲▲▲Royal Mile—This is one of Europe's most interesting historic walks. Start at the top and amble down to the palace. The Royal Mile, which consists of a series of four different streets—Castlehill, Lawnmarket, High Street, and Canongate (each with its own set of street numbers)—is actually 200 yards longer than a mile. And every inch is packed with shops, cafés, and lanes leading to tiny squares. As you walk, remember that originally, there were two settlements here, divided by a wall: Edinburgh lined the ridge from the castle at the top. The lower end, Canongate, was outside the wall until 1856. By poking down the many side alleys, you'll find a few rough edges of a town well on its way to becoming a touristic mall. See it now. In a few years tourists will be slaloming through the postcard racks on bagpipe skateboards.

Royal Mile Terminology: A "close" is a tiny alley between two buildings (originally with a door that closed it at night). A close usually leads to a "court" or courtyard. A "land" is a tenement block of apartments. A "pend" is an arched gateway. A "wynd" is a narrow winding lane. And "gate" is from an old Scandinavian word for street.

Royal Mile Walking Tours: Mercat Tours offers 90-minute guided walks of the Mile—more entertaining than historic (£6, daily at 10:30, from Mercat Cross on the Royal Mile, tel. 0131/557-6464). The guides, who enjoy making a short story long, ignore the big sights, taking you behind the scenes with

Royal Mile

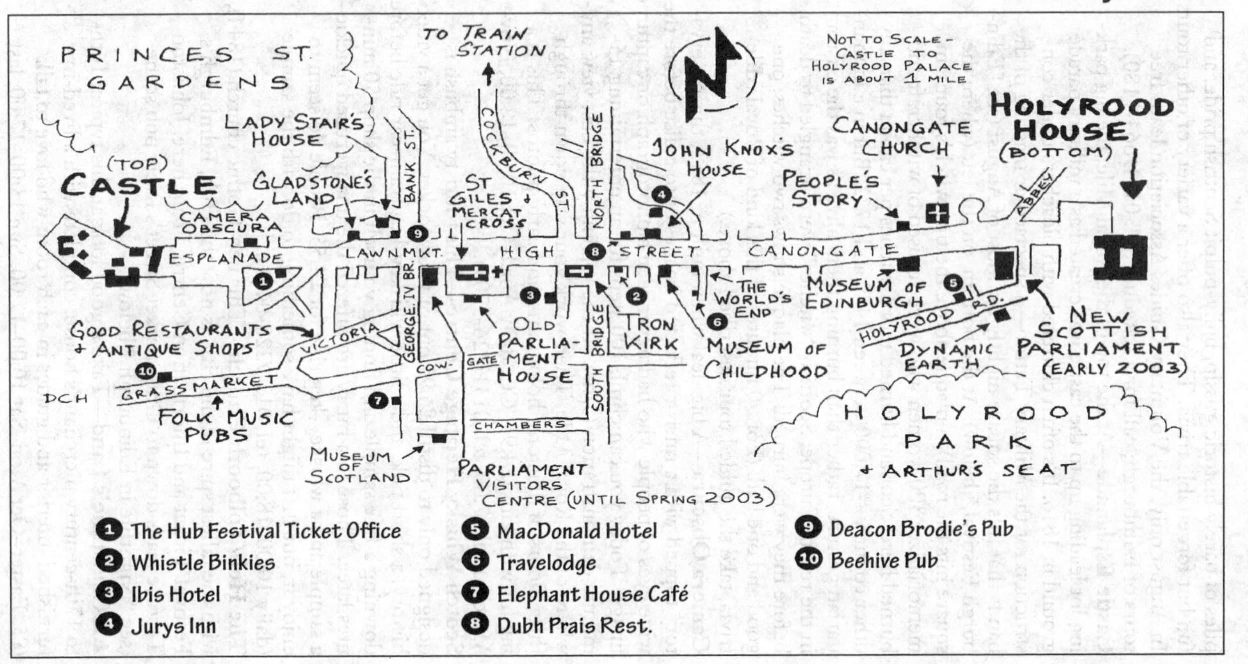
PRINCES ST GARDENS
TO TRAIN STATION
NOT TO SCALE - CASTLE TO HOLYROOD PALACE IS ABOUT 1 MILE
HOLYROOD HOUSE (BOTTOM)
LADY STAIR'S HOUSE
(TOP) CASTLE
GLADSTONE'S LAND
BANK ST.
COCKBURN ST.
NORTH BRIDGE
JOHN KNOX'S HOUSE
CANONGATE CHURCH
PEOPLE'S STORY
ABBEY
ST GILES + MERCAT CROSS
CAMERA OBSCURA
ESPLANADE
LAWNMKT.
HIGH
STREET
CANONGATE
THE WORLD'S END
MUSEUM OF EDINBURGH
HOLYROOD RD.
GOOD RESTAURANTS + ANTIQUE SHOPS
VICTORIA
GEORGE IV BR.
OLD PARLIA-MENT HOUSE
TRON KIRK
MUSEUM OF CHILDHOOD
DYNAMIC EARTH
NEW SCOTTISH PARLIAMENT (EARLY 2003)
COW-GATE
SOUTH BRIDGE
GRASSMARKET
DCH
FOLK MUSIC PUBS
CHAMBERS
HOLYROOD PARK
+ ARTHUR'S SEAT
MUSEUM OF SCOTLAND
PARLIAMENT VISITORS CENTRE (UNTIL SPRING 2003)
1 The Hub Festival Ticket Office
2 Whistle Binkies
3 Ibis Hotel
4 Jurys Inn
5 MacDonald Hotel
6 Travelodge
7 Elephant House Café
8 Dubh Prais Rest.
9 Deacon Brodie's Pub
10 Beehive Pub

piles of barely historic gossip, bully-pulpit Scottish pride, and fun but forgettable trivia. They also offer a variety of other tours. In August only, the Voluntary Guides Association leads free tours of Edinburgh; call for a schedule (tel. 0131/664-7180).

Castle Esplanade—At the top of the Royal Mile, the big parking lot leading up to the castle was created as a military parade ground in 1816. It's often cluttered with bleachers under construction for the Military Tattoo—a spectacular massing of the bands that fills the square nightly for most of August (see "Edinburgh Festival," below). At the bottom, on the left (where the square hits the road), a plaque above the tiny witch's fountain memorializes 300 women who were accused of witchcraft and burned here. Scotland burned more witches per capita than any other country—17,000 between 1479 and 1722. But in a humanitarian gesture, rather than burning them alive as was the custom in the rest of Europe, Scottish "witches" were strangled to death before they were burned. The plaque shows two witches: one good and one bad. (For 90 minutes of this kind of Royal Mile trivia, take the guided tour described above.)

Camera Obscura—A big deal when built in 1853, this observatory topped with a mirror reflected images onto a disc before the wide eyes of people who had never seen a photograph or captured image. Today you can climb 100 steps for an entertaining 15-minute demonstration (3/hr). At the top enjoy the best view anywhere of the Royal Mile. Then work your way down through three floors of illusions, holograms, and early photos. This is a big hit with kids (£4.95, CC, daily April–Oct 10:00–18:00, Nov–March until 17:00, tel. 0131/226-3709).

Scotch Whisky Heritage Centre—This touristy ambush is designed only to distill £6.95 out of your pocket. You get a video history, a short talk, and a little whiskey-keg train-car ride before downing a free sample and finding yourself in the shop 50 minutes later. Those in a hurry are offered the unadvertised quickie—a sample and a whiskey-keg ride for £4.55. People do seem to enjoy it, but that might have something to do with the sample (daily 10:00–18:00, tel. 0131/220-0441).

The Hub/Tolbooth Church—This neo-Gothic church (1844), with the tallest spire in the city, is now the Hub, Edinburgh's Festival Ticket and Information Centre. From here, Johnston Terrace leads down to Grassmarket Street's lively pub scene (see "Nightlife in Edinburgh," below).

▲▲Gladstone's Land—Take a good look at this typical 16th- to 17th-century merchant's house, complete with a lived-in furnished interior and guides in each room who love to talk (£5, Easter–Oct Mon–Sat 10:00–17:00, Sun 13:00–17:00, last entry at 16:30, closed Nov–Easter). For a good Royal Mile photo, lean out the upper-floor window (or simply climb the curved stairway outside the museum to the left of the entrance). Notice the snoozing pig outside the front door. Just like every house has a vacuum cleaner today, in the 14th century a snorting rubbish collector was a standard feature of any well-equipped house.

▲Writers' Museum at Lady Stair's House—This interesting house, built in 1622, is filled with well-described manuscripts and knickknacks of Scotland's three greatest literary figures: Robert Burns, Sir Walter Scott, and Robert Louis Stevenson. It's worth a few minutes for anyone and is fascinating for fans (free, Mon–Sat 10:00–17:00, closed Sun). Wander around the courtyard here. Edinburgh was a wonder in the 17th and 18th centuries. Tourists came here to see its skyscrapers, which towered 10 stories and higher. No city in Europe was so densely populated as "Auld Reekie."

Deacon Brodie's Pub—This is a decent place for a light meal (see "Eating in Edinburgh," page 319). Read the story of its notorious namesake on the wall facing Bank Street. Then check out both sides of the hanging signpost.

Visitors Centre of the Scottish Parliament—Until the new Scottish Parliament building opens in spring of 2003 (near Holyrood Palace), this center will show models of the new building and explain how the Scottish Parliament works (free, Mon–Fri 10:00–17:00, closed Sat–Sun, kitty-corner to Deacon Brodie's on George IV Bridge). You can sign up at the Visitors Centre to witness the Scottish Parliament's debates in their temporary quarters, a few steps north of the Royal Mile, tucked away in Mylnes Court, across from the Hub (debates Wed 14:30–17:30, Thu 9:30–12:30 & 14:30–17:30, tel. 0131/348-5411). When the new Parliament building opens, this Visitors Centre will close.

Heart of Midlothian—Near the street in front of the cathedral, find the outline of a heart in the brickwork. This marks the spot of a gallows and a prison now long gone. Traditionally, locals stand on the rim of the heart and spit into it. Hitting the middle brings good luck. Go ahead . . . do as the locals do.

▲▲St. Giles Cathedral—Wander through Scotland's most important church. Stepping inside, find John Knox's statue. Look into his eyes for 10 seconds from 10 inches away. Knox, the great reformer and founder of austere Scottish Presbyterianism, first preached here in 1559. His insistence that every person should be able to read the word of God gave Scotland an educational system 300 years ahead of the rest of Europe. For this reason it was Scottish minds that led the way in math, science, medicine,

Scottish Words

aye	yes	**inch, innis**	island
ben	mountain	**inver**	river, mouth
bonnie	beautiful	**kyle**	strait
carn	heap of stones	**loch**	lake
cellotape	Scotch tape	**neeps**	turnips
creag	rock, cliff	**tattie**	potato

haggis rich assortment of oats and sheep organs stuffed into a chunk of sheep intestine, liberally seasoned, boiled, and eaten mostly by tourists. Usually served with "neeps and tatties." Tastier than it sounds.

engineering, and so on. Voltaire called Scotland "the intellectual capital of Europe."

Knox preached Calvinism. Consider that the Dutch and the Scots were about the only nations to embrace this creed of hard work, thrift, and strict ethics. This helps explain why the English and the Scottish are so different (and why the Dutch and the Scots—both famous for their thriftiness and industriousness—are so much alike).

Speaking of intellects, look up at the modern window filling the West Wall celebrating Scotland's favorite poet, Robert Burns. It was made in 1985 by an Icelandic artist (Leifur Breidfjord).

The oldest parts of the cathedral—the four massive central pillars—date from 1120. After the English burnt the cathedral in 1385, it was rebuilt bigger and better than ever, and in 1495 its famous crown spire was completed. During the Reformation—when Knox preached here (1559–72)—the place was simplified and whitewashed. Before this, with the emphasis on holy services provided by priests, there were lots of little niches. With the new focus on sermons rather than rituals, the floor plan was opened up and the grand pulpit took center stage. The organ (1992, Austrian-built) is one of the best in Europe and comes with a glass panel in the back for peeking into the mechanism.

The neo-Gothic **Chapel of the Knights of the Thistle** (in the far right corner, from 1911), with its intricate wood carving, was built in two years entirely with Scottish material and labor. Find the angel tooting the bagpipes (from inside chapel, above the door to the right). The Scottish crown steeple from 1495 is a proud part of Edinburgh's skyline (Mon–Sat 9:00–17:00, May–Sept until 19:00, Sun 13:00–17:00 year-round; ask about concerts—some are free, usually Thu at 13:10; café and WC downstairs; see "Eating," below, tel. 0131/225-9442).

John Knox is buried out back—austerely, under the parking lot, at spot 44. The statue among the cars shows King Charles II riding to a toga party back in 1685.

Parliament House—Stop in to see the grand hall with its fine 1639 hammer-beam ceiling and stained glass. This hall housed the Scottish Parliament until the Act of Union in 1707 (explained in history exhibition under the big stained-glass depiction of the initiation of the first Scottish High Court in 1532). It now holds the law courts and is busy with wigged and robed lawyers hard at work in the old library (peek through the door) or pacing the hall deep in discussion. The friendly doorman is helpful (free, public welcome Mon–Fri 9:00–16:30, best action midmornings Tue–Fri, open-to-the-public trials 10:00–16:00--doorman has day's docket, entry behind St. Giles Cathedral near parking spot 21).

Mercat Cross—This chunky pedestal, on the downhill side of St. Giles, holds a slender column topped with a white unicorn. Royal proclamations have been read from here since the 14th century. The tradition survives. In 1952, three days (traditionally the time it took for a horse to speed here from London) after the actual event, a town crier heralded the news that England had a new queen. Today Mercat Cross is the meeting point of various walking tours—both historic and ghostly. Pop into the police information center, a few doors downhill, for a little local law-and-order history (free, May–Aug daily 10:00–21:30, less off-season).

Tron Kirk—This fine old building, used as a sales base for a local walking-tour company, sits over an old excavation site and houses a free Old Town history display.

Cockburn Street—Across from Tron Kirk, this street was cut through High Street's dense wall of medieval skyscrapers in the 1860s to give easy access to the new Georgian town and the train station. Notice how the sliced buildings were thoughtfully capped with facades in a faux 16th-century Scottish baronial style. In medieval times, only tiny lanes (like the Fleshmarket Lane just uphill from Cockburn Street) interrupted the long line of Royal Mile buildings. Continue downhill to the old half-timbered building jutting out (John Knox House). Across the street is the . . .

▲Museum of Childhood—This five-story playground of historical toys and games—called the noisiest museum in the world because of its delighted tiny visitors—is rich in nostalgia and history (free, Mon–Sat 10:00–17:00, closed Sun). Just downhill is a fragrant fudge shop offering free samples.

▲John Knox House—Fascinating for Reformation buffs, this fine 16th-century house offers a well-explained look at the life of the great reformer (£2.25, Mon–Sat 10:00–17:00, closed Sun, 43 High Street, tel. 0131/556-9579). While Knox never actually lived here, preservationists called it "his house" to save it from the wrecking ball in 1850. Parts of the museum will be closed for construction periodically during 2003.

The World's End—For centuries, a wall halfway down the Royal Mile marked the end of Edinburgh and the beginning of Canongate, a community associated with the Holyrood Abbey. Today, where the mile hits St. Mary's and Jeffrey Streets, High Street becomes Canongate. Just below John Knox House (at #43) notice the hanging sign showing the old gate. At the intersection, find the brass bricks tracing the gate (demolished in 1764). Look down St. Mary's Street to see a surviving bit of that old wall. Then, entering Canongate, you leave what was Edinburgh . . .

▲People's Story—This interesting exhibition traces the lot of the working class through the 18th, 19th, and 20th centuries (free, Mon–Sat 10:00–17:00, closed Sun). Curiously, while this museum is dedicated to the proletariat, immediately around the back is the tomb of Adam Smith—the author of *Wealth of Nations* and the father of modern capitalism (1723–1790).

▲Museum of Edinburgh—Another old house full of old stuff, this one is worth a look for its early Edinburgh history and handy ground-floor WC. Don't miss the original copy of the National Covenant (written in 1638 on an animal skin), sketches of pre-Georgian Edinburgh (which show a lake, later filled in to become Princes Street Gardens when New Town was built), and early golf balls (free, Mon–Sat 10:00–17:00, closed Sun).

White Horse Close—Step into this 17th-century courtyard (bottom of Canongate, on the left, a block before Holyrood Palace). It was from here that the Edinburgh stagecoach left for London. Eight days later, the horse-drawn carriage pulled into its destination: Scotland Yard. Across the street is the new Parliament building.

▲Scottish Parliament Building—Scotland's parliament originated in 1293, was dissolved by England in 1707, and returned in 1999. Their extravagant, and therefore controversial, new digs at the base of the Royal Mile next to Holyrood Palace are slated to open in spring 2003. For a conversation-starter, ask a local what he or she thinks about the building's architect, expense, design, and so on.

You can sign up to witness the Scottish Parliament's debating and creating Scottish history in their temporary quarters off the Royal Mile in Mylnes Court across from the Hub (free, see "Visitors Centre," page 691), and eventually, in their new building after it opens.

▲**Holyrood Palace**—A palace since the 14th century, this marks the end of the Royal Mile. The queen spends a week in Scotland each summer, during which this is her official residence and office. The abbey—part of a 12th-century Augustinian monastery—stood here first. It was named for a piece of the cross brought here as a relic by queen-then-saint Margaret. Scotland's royalty preferred living here to the blustery castle on the rock, and, gradually, the palace grew. The building is rich in history and decor. But without information or a guided tour ("There's none of either," snickered the guy who sells the boring £3.70 museum guidebooks), you're just another peasant in the dark. Docents in each room are happy to give you the answer if you know the question.

The new **Queen's Gallery** is the highlight, featuring rotating exhibits of drawings from the royal collection. Scheduled for the first part of 2003 is "Leonardo da Vinci: The Divine and the Grotesque," a collection of 75 drawings.

The rest of the palace consists of elegantly furnished rooms and a few dark older rooms filled with glass cases of historic bits and Scottish pieces that Scots find fascinating. After exiting, you're free to stroll through the ruined abbey and the queen's gardens (£6.50, daily 9:30–18:00, Nov–April until 16:30; while no tours are offered during peak season, guided tours are mandatory off-season—2/hr; last admission 45 min before closing, CC; closed when the queen's home and whenever a prince drops in, tel. 0131/556-7371). Hikers: Note that the palace is near the trail up Arthur's Seat.

Dynamic Earth—This immense exhibit, filling several underground floors under a vast Gore-Tex tent appropriately pitched at the base of the Salisbury Crags, tells the story of our planet. It's designed for younger kids and does the same thing an American science exhibit would do—but with a charming Scottish accent. Standing in a time tunnel, you watch time rewind from Churchill to dinosaurs to that first big poof. After several short films on stars, tectonic plates, and ice caps, you're free to wander past salty pools, a re-created rain forest, and various TV screens, ending your visit with a 12-minute video finale (£8, family deals, CC, April–Oct daily 10:00–18:00, Nov–March Wed–Sun 10:00–17:00, last ticket sold 70 min before closing, on Holyrood Road, between the palace and mountain, tel. 0131/550-7800).

▲▲▲**Museum of Scotland**—This huge museum has amassed more historic artifacts than everything I've seen in Scotland combined. It's all wonderfully displayed with fine descriptions offering a best-anywhere hike through the history of Scotland: prehistoric, Roman, Viking, the "birth of Scotland," all the way to life in the 20th century. Free audioguides offer a pleasant (if slow) description of various rooms and exhibits and even provide mood music for your wanderings (free, Mon–Sat 10:00–17:00, Tue until 20:00, Sun 12:00–17:00, free 1-hr orientation tours daily at 14:00, 2 long blocks south of Royal Mile from St. Giles Church, Chambers Street, off George IV Bridge, tel. 0131/247-4422, www.nms.ac.uk).

The **Royal Museum**, next door, fills a fine iron-and-glass Industrial Age building (built to house the museum in 1851) with all the natural sciences as it "presents the world to Scotland." It's great for schoolkids, but of no special interest to foreign visitors (free, same hours as Museum of Scotland). The famous statue of Greyfriars Bobby (Edinburgh's favorite dog—a terrier immortalized by Disney—who stood by his master's grave for 14 years) is across the street. Every business nearby is named for the pooch that put the fidelity into Fido.

More Bonnie Wee Sights

▲Georgian New Town—Cross Waverley Bridge and walk through Georgian Edinburgh. According to the 1776 plan, it was three streets (Princes, George, and Queen) flanked by two squares (St. Andrew and Charlotte), woven together by alleys (Thistle and Rose). George Street—20 feet wider than the others (so a 4-horse carriage could make a U-turn)—was the main drag. And, while Princes Street has gone down market, George Street still maintains its old elegance. The entire elegantly planned New Town—laid out when George was king—celebrated the hard-to-sell notion that Scotland was an integral part of the United Kingdom. The streets and squares are named after the British royalty (Hanover was the royal family surname). Even Thistle and Rose Streets are emblems of the two happily paired nations. Rose Street, mostly pedestrian-only, is famous for its rowdy pubs. Where it hits St. Andrew's Square, Rose Street is flanked by the venerable Jenners department store and a Sainsbury supermarket. Sprinkled with popular restaurants and bars, stately New Town is turning trendy.

▲▲Georgian House—This refurbished Georgian house, set on Edinburgh's finest Georgian square, is a trip back to 1796. A volunteer guide in each of the five rooms is trained in the force-feeding of stories and trivia. Start your visit with two interesting videos (£5, daily 10:00–18:00, Nov–Jan until 16:00, videos total 30 min and cover architecture and Georgian lifestyles, shown in the basement, 7 Charlotte Square, tel. 0131/225-2160). A walk down George Street after your visit here can be fun for the imagination.

▲▲National Gallery—This elegant neoclassical building has a delightfully small but impressive collection of European masterpieces, from Raphael, Titian, and Rubens to Gainsborough, Monet, and van Gogh. And it offers the best look you'll get at Scottish paintings. The gallery's free, but investing £2 in the fine audioguide makes the museum's highlights yours as well (Mon–Sat 10:00–17:00, Sun 12:00–17:00, tel. 0131/624-6200). After your visit, if the sun's out, enjoy a wander through Princes Street Gardens.

Royal Scottish Academy—Next to the National Gallery, this new museum is scheduled to open in August 2003 with a major Monet exhibit (tel. 0131/332-2266, www.nationalgalleries.org).

Princes Street Gardens—This grassy park, a former lake bed, separates Edinburgh's New and Old Towns and offers a wonderful escape from the city. Once the private domain of the local wealthy, it was opened to the public in about 1870, not as a democratic gesture, but because it was thought that allowing the public into the park would increase sales for the Princes Street department stores. There are plenty of free concerts and country dances in the summer and the oldest floral clock in the world. Join the local office workers for a picnic lunch break.

▲Walter Scott Monument—Built in 1840, this elaborate, neo-Gothic monument honors the great author, one of Edinburgh's many illustrious sons. Scott, who died in 1832, is considered the father of the romantic historical novel. The 200-foot monument shelters a marble statue of Scott and his dog Maida, surrounded by busts of 16 great Scottish poets and 64 characters from his books. Scott was a great dog lover. Of the 30 dogs he had in his lifetime, his favorite was a deerhound named Maida. Climb 287 steps for a fine view of the city (£2.50, March–Oct Mon–Sat 9:00–18:00, Sun 10:00–16:00, Nov–Feb daily until 16:00, tel. 0131/529-4068).

Royal Botanic Garden—Britain's second-oldest botanical garden, established in 1670 for medicinal herbs, is now one of Europe's best (free, March and Sept 9:30–18:00, April–Aug 9:30–19:00, Nov–Jan 9:30–16:00, Feb and Oct 9:30–17:00, 90-min "rain forest to desert" tours April–Sept daily at 11:00 and 14:00 for £2, 1 mile north of center at Inverleith Row, tel. 0131/552-7171).

Sights—Near Edinburgh

▲*Britannia*—This much-revered vessel, which carted around Britain's royal family for over 40 years and 900 voyages before being retired in 1997, is permanently moored at Edinburgh's Port of Leith. It's open to the public and worth the 15-minute bus or taxi ride from the center. After watching a video about the ship, wander through the museum filled with fascinating royal-family-afloat history. Then, armed with your included audioguide, hike the stairs to the ship's top deck and begin working your way down. You'll tour the bridge, dining room, and living quarters, following in the historic footsteps of such notables as Churchill, Gandhi, and Reagan. It's easy to see how the royals must have loved the privacy this floating retreat offered (£8, April–Sept daily 9:30–18:00, Oct–March daily 10:00–17:00, last ticket sold 1.5 hrs before closing; to get to ship from Edinburgh, catch Lothian bus #22, #34, #35, or #49 at Waverley Bridge—£3 round-trip, or take the City Sightseeing/Guide Friday bus—£3.50 round-trip—covered by their £11 combo city-tour ticket; cheap café on site, tel. 0131/555-5566, www.royalyachtbritannia.co.uk).

Edinburgh Crystal—Blowing, molding, cutting, polishing, and engraving, the Edinburgh Crystal Company glassworks tour smashes anything you'll see in Venice (£3, daily 10:00–16:30). There is a shop full of "bargain" second-quality pieces, a video show, and a cafeteria. A free minibus shuttle departs from Waverley Bridge (every 90 min from 9:45 to 15:45), or you can drive 10 miles south of town on A701 to Penicuik. You can schedule a more expensive VIP tour (£10) where you actually blow and cut glass (reserve a day in advance, tel. 01968/675-128).

Activities in Edinburgh

▲▲Arthur's Seat Hike—A 45-minute hike up the 822-foot volcanic mountain (surrounded by a fine park overlooking Edinburgh), starting from the Holyrood Palace, rewards you with a commanding view. You can drive up most of the way from behind (follow the one-way street from the palace, park by the little lake) or run up like they did in *Chariots of Fire*. Hikers: From the parking lot (immediately south of Holyrood Palace), you'll see two trails going up. For an easier grade, take the wide path to the left and skip the steeper path that begins with steps and skirts the base of the cliffs. You can also hike up to the seat from the Dalkeith B&B neighborhood. Take the road (Holyrood Park Road) that borders the Commonwealth pool, turn right (on Queen's Drive), and continue to a small car park. From here, it's a 20-minute hike.

Brush Skiing—If you'd rather be skiing, the Midlothian Ski Centre in Hillend has a hill on the edge of town with a chairlift, two slopes, a jump slope, and rentable skis, boots, and poles. While you're actually skiing over what seems like a million toothbrushes, it feels like snow skiing on a slushy day. Beware: Local doctors are used to treating an ailment called "Hillend Thumb"—thumbs dislocated when people fall here and get tangled in the brush (£6.60/first hr, then £2.70/hr, includes gear, Mon–Fri 9:30–21:00, Sat–Sun 9:30–17:00, closed last 2 weeks of June, probably closed if it snows, LRT bus #4 from Princes Street—garden side, tel. 0131/445-4433).

▲Royal Commonwealth Games Swimming Pool—This immense pool is open to the public, with a well-equipped fitness center (£6, includes swim), sauna (£6.90 extra, BYO suit), and a cafeteria overlooking the pool (£3.10 for pool admission only, Mon–Fri 6:00–21:30, Sat 6:00–7:45 & 10:00–16:30, Sun 10:00–16:30, closed 9:00–10:00 every Wed, no towels or suit rentals, tel. 0131/667-7211).

More Hikes—You can hike along the river (called Water of Leith) through Edinburgh. Locals favor the stretch between Roseburn and Dean Village, but the 1.5-mile walk from Dean Village to the Royal Botanic Garden is also good. This and other hikes are described in the TI's *Walks in and around Edinburgh* (ask for the free 1-page flier, not their £2 guide to walks).

Shopping—The streets to browse are Princes Street (the elegant old Jenners department store is nearby on Rose Street, at St. Andrew's Square), Victoria Street (antiques galore), Nicolson Street (south of the Royal Mile for a line of interesting second-hand stores), and the Royal Mile (touristy but competitively priced). Shops are usually open from 9:00 to 17:30 (later on Thu, some closed Sun).

Bus Tours to Countryside—Many companies offer day trips to regional sights (such as Loch Ness). Comparison-shop at the TI's brochure rack. Haggis Backpackers (see "Helpful Hints," above) runs cheap day trips (£21, choose between distillery visit and northern Highlands or Loch Lomond and southern Highlands) and overnight trips for young backpackers, but welcomes travelers of any age who want a quick look at the bonnie countryside. Their three-day trips (£80, overnights in hostels on Isle of Skye and Loch Ness) and six-day trips (£140, overnights in hostels in Oban, Isle of Skye, a Highlands castle, and Loch Ness) include a tour guide and transport on a 22-seat bus, but hostels cost extra.

Edinburgh Festival

One of Europe's great cultural events, Edinburgh's annual festival turns the city into a carnival of culture. There are enough music, dance, art, drama, and multicultural events to make even the most jaded traveler drool with excitement. Every day is jammed with formal and spontaneous fun. A number of festivals—official, fringe, book, film, and jazz and blues—rage simultaneously for about three weeks each August, with the Military Tattoo starting a week earlier (the best overall Web site is www.edinburghfestivals.co.uk). Many city sights run on extended hours, and those that normally close on Sunday (Writers' Museum, Museum of Edinburgh, People's Story, and Museum of Childhood) open in the afternoon. It's a glorious time to be in Edinburgh.

The official festival (Aug 10–30 in 2003) is the original, more formal, and most likely to get booked up first. Major events sell out well in advance. The ticket office is at the Hub, located in a former church (with café, ATM, and WC) near the top of the Royal Mile (tickets-£4–55, CC, booking from mid-April on, office open Mon–Sat 10:00–17:00 or longer, in Aug until 20:00 plus Sun 10:00–17:00, tel. 0131/473-2000, fax 0131/473-2003). You can also book online at www.eif.co.uk.

The less-formal **Fringe Festival** features "on the edge" comedy and theater (CC, Aug 3–25 in 2003, ticket/info office just below St. Giles Cathedral on the Royal Mile, 180 High Street, tel. 0131/226-0001, bookings tel. 0131/226-0026, can book online from mid-June on, www.edfringe.com). Tickets are usually available at the door, but popular shows can sell out.

Other festivals in August: jazz and blues (tel. 0131/467-5200, www.jazzmusic.co.uk), film (tel. 0131/229-2550, www.edfilmfest.org.uk), and book (tel. 0131/228-5444, www.edbookfest.co.uk).

The **Military Tattoo** is a massing of the bands, drums, and bagpipes with groups from all over what was the British Empire. Displaying military finesse with a stirring lone-piper finale, this grand spectacle fills the castle esplanade nightly except Sunday, normally from a week before the festival starts until a week before it finishes (Aug 1–23 in 2003). Shows occur Monday through Friday at 21:00 and on Saturdays at 19:30 and 22:30 (£10–28, CC, booking starts in Dec, Fri–Sat shows sell out first; office open Mon–Fri 10:00–16:30, during Tattoo open until show time and Sat 10:00–19:30 and Sun 12:00–17:00; 33 Market Street, behind—and south of—Waverley train station, tel. 0131/225-1188, www.edinburgh-tattoo.co.uk). If nothing else, it is a really big show.

If you do manage to hit Edinburgh during the festival, book a room far in advance and extend your stay by a day or two. While Fringe tickets and most Tattoo tickets are available the day of the show, you may want to book a couple of official events in advance. Do it directly by telephone, leaving your credit-card number. Pick up your ticket at the office the day of the show. Several publications—including the festival's official schedule, the *Edinburgh Festivals Guide Daily*, *The List*, the *Fringe Program*, and the *Daily Diary*—list and evaluate festival events.

Nightlife in Edinburgh

▲Ghost Walks—These walks are an entertaining and cheap night out (offered nightly, usually 19:00 and 21:00, easy socializing for solo travelers). The theatrical and creatively staged **Witchery Tours**, the most established of the ghost tours, offer two different walks: "Ghosts and Gore" and "Murder and Mystery" (£7, 90 min, reservations required, leave from the top of the Royal Mile near castle esplanade, tel. 0131/225-6745).

▲▲Literary Pub Tour—This two-hour walk is interesting

even if you think Walter Scott was an arctic explorer. You'll follow the witty dialogue of two actors as they debate whether the great literature of Scotland was the creative recreation of fun-loving louts fueled by a love of whiskey or high art. You'll wander from the Grassmarket, over Old Town to New Town, with stops in three pubs as your guides share their takes on Scotland's literary greats. The tour meets at the Beehive Pub on Grassmarket (£7, nightly in summer at 19:30, most nights off-season; call 0131/226-6665 to confirm).

▲**Scottish Folk Evenings**—These £35 to £40 dinner shows, generally for tour groups intent on photographing old cultural clichés, are held in huge halls of expensive hotels. (Prices are bloated to include 20 percent commissions.) Your "traditional" meal is followed by a full slate of swirling kilts, blaring bagpipes, and Scottish folk dancing with an "old-time music hall"–type emcee. If you like Lawrence Welk, you're in for a treat. You can sometimes see the show without dinner for about two-thirds the price. The TI has fliers on all the latest venues. **Prestonfield House** offers its Scottish folk evening with or without dinner Sunday to Friday (£21 for show only from 20:00–22:00, £33 includes 4-course meal at 19:00, CC, Priestfield Road, a 7-min walk from Dalkeith Road B&Bs, tel. 0131/668-3346, www.prestonfieldhouse.com).

▲▲**Folk Music in Pubs**—Edinburgh used to be a good place for folk music, but in the last few years, pub owners—out of economic necessity—are catering to twenty-somethings more interested in beer drinking than traditional music. Pubs that were regular venues for folk music have gone popular. Especially on weekends, you're unlikely to find much live folk music. The monthly *Gig Guide* (free at TI and various pubs, www.gigguide.co.uk) lists most of the live-music action. **Whistle Binkies** still offers nightly ad-lib traditional music, which can start as early as 19:30 or as late as 24:00 and goes until the wee hours (just off the Royal Mile on South Bridge, another entrance on Niddry Street, tel. 0131/557-5114).

Grassmarket (below the castle) is sloppy with live music and rowdy people spilling out of the pubs and into what was once upon a time a busy market square. It's fun to just wander through Grassmarket late at night. **Finnigan's Wake** has live music—often Irish rock—nightly (starts at 22:00, a block off Grassmarket at 9 Victoria Street, tel. 0131/226-3816). The **Fiddlers Arms**, **Biddy Mulligan**, and **White Hart Inn**, among others, all feature live music. By the noise and crowds you'll know where to go and where not to. Have a beer and follow your ear.

Theater—Even outside of festival time, Edinburgh is a fine place for lively and affordable theater. Pick up *The List* for a complete rundown of what's on (£2.20 at newsstands).

Sleeping in Edinburgh

(£1 = about $1.50, country code: 44, area code: 0131)

Sleep Code: **S** = Single, **D** = Double/Twin, **T** = Triple, **Q** = Quad, **b** = bathroom, **s** = shower only, **CC** = Credit Cards accepted, **no CC** = Credit Cards not accepted.

To help you sort easily through these listings, I've divided the rooms into three categories based on the price for a standard double room with bath (during high season):

Higher Priced—Most rooms £80 or more.
Moderately Priced—Most rooms less than £80.
Lower Priced—Most rooms £50 or less.

The advent of big, cheap hotels has made life tough for B&Bs. Still, book ahead, especially in August when the annual festival fills Edinburgh. Conventions, school holidays, and weekends can make finding a room tough at almost any time of year. For the best prices, book directly rather than through the TI, which charges a higher room fee and levies a £3 booking fee. "Standard" rooms, with toilets and showers a tissue-toss away, save you £10 a night.

Room prices in this section are usually listed as a range, from low season (winter) to high season (July–Sept). I have not listed the higher "festival prices"—which are limited to August. Prices get soft off-season, for longer visits, and sometimes for midweek stays outside of summer.

Sleeping off Dalkeith Road

These recommendations are south of town near the Royal Commonwealth Pool, just off Dalkeith Road. This comfortable and safe neighborhood is a 20-minute walk or 10-minute bus ride from the Royal Mile. All listings are non-smoking, on quiet streets, a two-minute walk from a bus stop, and well-served by city buses. B&Bs are unlikely to accept bookings for one-night stays in August.

Near the B&Bs you'll find plenty of eateries (see "Eating in Edinburgh," page 707), easy free parking, and **launderettes**—one at 208 Dalkeith Road (Mon–Sat 8:30–17:00, closed Sun, £4-self-service, tel. 0131/667-0825) and another at 13 South Clerk Street (Mon–Fri 8:00–19:00, Sat 9:00–17:00, Sun 10:00–16:00, last wash 75 min before closing, opposite Queens Hall).

To reach the hotel neighborhood from the train station, TI, or Scott Monument, cross Princes Street and wait at the **bus stop** under the small C&A sign on the department store (80p; LRT buses #14, #21, and #33, or First bus #86; tell driver your destination is "Dalkeith Road;" red bus: exact change or pay more; green bus: makes change; ride 10 min to first or second stop—depending on B&B—after the pool, push the button, exit middle door). These buses also stop at the corner of North Bridge and High Street on the Royal

Mile. Buses run from 6:00 to 23:00, and after 9:00 on Sunday morning. **Taxi** fare between the station or Royal Mile and the B&Bs is about £5.

B&Bs off Dalkeith Road

MODERATELY PRICED

Dunedin Guest House (pron. dun-EE-din)—bright, plush, and elegantly Scottish, with seven huge rooms—is a fine value (S-£20–35, Db-£40–70, CC, family rooms for up to 5, power showers, 8 Priestfield Road, Edinburgh EH16 5HH, tel. 0131/668-1949, fax 0131/668-3636, Marsella Bowen).

Turret Guest House is teddy-on-the-beddy cozy, with a great bay-windowed family room and a vast breakfast menu that includes haggis and vegetarian options (8 rooms, S-£23–27, Sb-£28–35, D-£46–54, Db-£56–72, £2/person discount with this book and cash, CC, 8 Kilmaurs Terrace, Edinburgh EH16 5DR, tel. 0131/667-6704, fax 0131/668-1368, www.turret.clara.net, e-mail: contact@turretguesthouse.co.uk, Jimmy & Fiona Mackie).

Amar Agua Guest House, next door to Turret, is an inviting Victorian home away from home (7 rooms, S-£18–27, Db-£36–58, 3 percent more with CC, 10 Kilmaurs Terrace, Edinburgh EH16 5DR, tel. 0131/667-6775, fax 0131/667-7687, e-mail: amaragua@cableinet.co.uk, run by energetic young couple Dawn-Ann and Tony Costa).

Ard-Na-Said B&B is an elegant 1875 Victorian house with a comfy lounge and five classy rooms (1 S-£22–28, Db-£44–56, family deals, 2 percent more with CC, 5 Priestfield Road, Edinburgh EH16 5HH, tel. 0131/667-8754, fax 0131/667-7815, www.ardnasaid.freeserve.co.uk, e-mail: jimandolive@ardnasaid.freeserve.co.uk, enthusiastically run by Jim and Olive Lyons).

Dorstan Private Hotel is more formal, professional, and hotelesque, with all the comforts. Several of its 14 thoughtfully decorated rooms are on the ground floor (2 Ds-£60, Db-£66, family rooms, CC, no clothes washing in room except for "smalls," 7 Priestfield Road, Edinburgh EH16 5HJ, tel. 0131/667-6721, fax 0131/668-4644, www.dorstan-hotel.demon.co.uk, e-mail: reservations@dorstan-hotel.demon.co.uk, Mairae Campbell).

Kenvie Guest House, well run by Dorothy Vidler, comes with six pleasant rooms and lots of personal touches (1 small twin-£42, D-£44, Db-£52, family deals, 3 percent more with CC, 16 Kilmaurs Road, Edinburgh EH16 5DA, tel. 0131/668-1964, fax 0131/668-1926, www.kenvie.co.uk, e-mail: dorothy@kenvie.co.uk).

Airdenair Guest House, offering views, homemade scones,

Edinburgh, Our Neighborhood

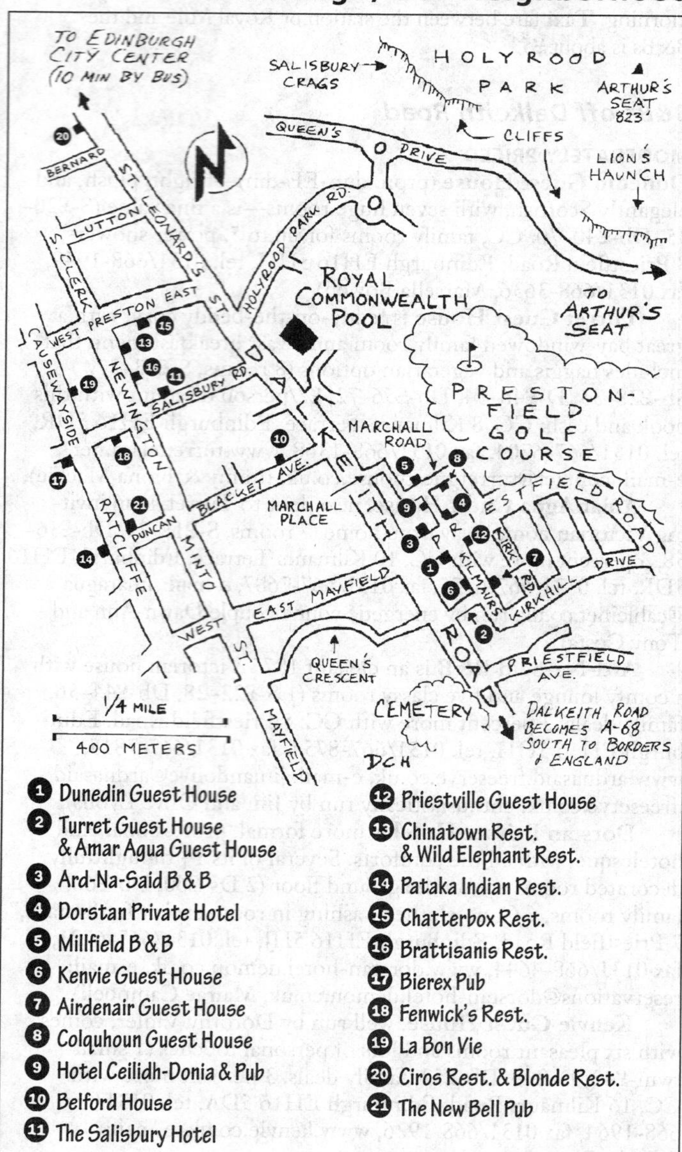

and other delicious sweets (made by the owner's mom), has five attractive rooms with a lofty above-it-all feeling (Sb-£25–35, Db-£40–60, Tb-£60–90, 2 percent more with CC, 29 Kilmaurs Road, Edinburgh EH16 5DB, tel. 0131/668-2336, www.airdenair.com, e-mail: jill@airdenair.com, Jill & Doug McLennan).

Hotel Ceilidh-Donia is recently refurbished with 14 cheery rooms and a fun pub (Sb-£25–40, Db-£45–65, CC, 14 Marchhall Crescent, Edinburgh EH16 5HL, tel. 0131/667-2743, www.hotelceilidh-donia.co.uk, e-mail: reservations@hotelceilidh-donia.co.uk, Max & Annette).

Belford House is a tidy, homey place offering seven good rooms and a warm welcome (D-£40–44, Db-£50–54, family deals, CC, 5 percent off with cash, 13 Blacket Avenue, Edinburgh EH9 1RR, tel. 0131/667-2422, fax 0131/667-7508, www.belfordguesthouse.com, e-mail: tom@belfordguesthouse.com, Isa and Tom Borthwick).

The Salisbury, more like a hotel than its neighbors, fills a classy old Georgian building with eight rooms, a large lounge, and a dumbwaiter in the breakfast room (Sb-£30–35, D-£44–52, Db-£50–60, 5 percent off with cash and this book, CC, free parking, 45 Salisbury Road, Edinburgh EH16 5AA, tel. & fax 0131/667-1264, www.salisbury-guest-house.co.uk, e-mail: Brenda.Wright@btinternet.com, Brenda Wright).

Priestville Guest House has all the comforts of home, from VCRs and a video library to Internet access in the lobby (D-£40–54, Db-£44–60, 3 percent more with CC, family rooms available, 10 Priestfield Road, Edinburgh EH16 6HJ, tel. & fax 0131/667-2435, www.priestville.com, e-mail: bookings@priestville.com, Trina and Colin Warwick).

LOWER PRICED

Millfield B&B, run graciously by Liz Broomfield, is thoughtfully furnished with antique class, a rare sit-and-chat ambience, and a comfy TV lounge. Since the showers are down the hall, you'll get spacious rooms and great prices (S-£21–23, D-£38–40, T-£48–52, no CC, reconfirm reservation by phone, 12 Marchhall Road, Edinburgh EH16 5HR, tel. & fax 0131/667-4428). Decipher the breakfast prayer by Robert Burns. Then try the "Taste of Scotland" breakfast option. See how many stone (14 pounds) you weigh in the elegant throne room.

Colquhoun Guest House, in an elegant building, has seven fine rooms, several on the ground floor (S-£22–25, D-£40, Db-£50, family room, no CC, 5 Marchhall Road, Edinburgh EH16 5HR, tel. & fax 0131/667-8481, e-mail: grace@colquhounhouse.freeserve.co.uk, run by amazing Grace McAinsh).

Big, Modern Hotels

Four of these listings are cheap as hotels go and offer more comfort than character. The first one's a splurge. In each case I'd skip the institutional breakfast and eat out.

HIGHER PRICED

MacDonald Hotel, my only fancy listing, is an opulent four-star splurge down the street from the new parliament building. With its classy marble-and-wood decor, fitness center, and pool, it's hard to leave. On a gray winter day in Edinburgh, this could be worth it. Prices can vary wildly (157 rooms, Db-£150, CC, near bottom of Mile, across from Dynamic Earth, Holyrood Road, Edinburgh EH8 6AE, tel. 0131/550-4500, fax 0131/550-4545, www.macdonaldhotels.co.uk).

Jurys Inn, a cookie-cutter place with 186 dependably comfortable rooms, is capably run and well-located a short walk from the station (Sb, Db, Tb all £90 Fri–Sat, £70 Sun–Thu, much cheaper in off-season, CC, breakfast-£8, 2 kids sleep free, non-smoking rooms, some views, pub/restaurant, on quiet street just off Royal Mile, 43 Jeffrey Street, Edinburgh EH1 1DG, tel. 0131/200-3300, fax 0131/200-0400, www.jurys.com).

MODERATELY PRICED

Ibis Hotel, mid–Royal Mile behind Tron Kirk, is well-run and perfectly located. It has 98 soulless but clean and comfy rooms drenched in prefab American charm (Sb-£54–70, Db-£60–70, top price July–Aug, discounted in off-season, lousy continental breakfast-£5, CC, non-smoking rooms, elevator, 6 Hunter Square, Edinburgh EH1 1QW, tel. 0131/240-7000, fax 0131/240-7007, e-mail: h2039@accor-hotels.com).

LOWER PRICED

Travelodge, the cheapest hotel in the center, has 193 no-nonsense, central rooms all decorated in dark blue. All rooms are the same and suitable for two adults with two kids or three adults. While sleepable, it has a cheap feel with a quickly revolving staff (Sb, Db, Tb all £50 except £70 Fri–Sun June–Sept, breakfast-£8, CC, 33 St. Mary's Street, a block off the Royal Mile, tel. 08700-850-950, www.travelodge.co.uk).

Away from the center: The characterless **Travel Inn**, the biggest hotel in Edinburgh, has a mediocre location a mile west of the Royal Mile, but has a great price. Each of its 280 rooms is modern and comfortable, with a sofa that folds out for two kids if necessary (Db-£50 for 2 adults and up to 2 kids under 15, breakfast-£6, CC, elevators, non-smoking rooms, weekends booked long in advance, near Haymarket station west of the castle at 1 Morrison Link, Edinburgh EH3 8DN, tel. 0131/228-9819, fax 0131/228-9836, www.travelinn.co.uk).

Hostels

Edinburgh's hostels are well-run and open to all, but are scruffy and don't include breakfast. They do offer Internet access, laundry facilities, and £12 bunk beds in 8- to 16-bed single-sex dorms (about a £9–12 savings over B&Bs).

Castle Rock Hostel is hip and easygoing, offering cheap beds, plenty of friends, and a great central location just below the castle and above the pubs with all the folk music (15 Johnston Terrace, tel. 0131/225-9666). Their sister hostels are nearly across the street from each other: **High Street Hostel** (laundry-£2.50, kitchen, 8 Blackfriars Street, just off High Street/Royal Mile, tel. 0131/557-3984) and **Royal Mile Backpackers** (105 High Street, tel. 0131/557-6120).

For more regulations and less color, try the IYH hostels: **Bruntsfield Hostel** (6–12 beds/room, near golf course, 7 Bruntsfield Crescent, buses #11, #15, #16, and #17 from Princes Street, tel. 0131/447-2994) and **Edinburgh Hostel** (4–10 beds/room, 5-min walk from Haymarket station, 18 Eglinton Crescent, tel. 0131/337-1120).

Eating in Edinburgh

Eating along the Royal Mile

Historic pubs and doily cafés with reasonable, unremarkable meals abound. Here are some handy, affordable places for a good bite to eat (listed in downhill order).

Deacon Brodie's Tavern serves soup, sandwiches, and snacks on the ground floor and good £8 meals upstairs in the restaurant. As in all Edinburgh pubs, kids are allowed only in the restaurant section (daily 12:00–22:00, CC, tel. 0131/225-6531). Or munch prayerfully in the **Lower Aisle** restaurant under St. Giles Cathedral (Mon–Fri 9:00–16:30, Sun 10:00–13:30, closed Sat except in Aug).

The **Filling Station**, a big noisy bar decorated with car parts, has an American-type menu, serves good burgers, and rocks at night (daily 12:00–23:30, 235 High Street, near North Bridge, tel. 0131/226-2488).

Bann UK, a vegetarian café, serves healthy cuisine that goes way beyond tofu and granola (daily 11:00–23:00, CC, just off South Bridge behind Tron Kirk at 5 Hunter Square, tel. 0131/226-1112).

Dubh Prais Scottish Restaurant—the only serious restaurant on this list—is a dressy little place filling a cellar 10 steps and a world away from the High Street bustle. The owner/chef promises to serve Scottish fayre at its very best. The only thing not Scottish here is the wine list and some of the guests (£10 lunches Tue–Fri 12:00–14:00, £25 dinners Tue–Sat 18:30–22:30, closed Sun–Mon, CC, reservations smart at night, opposite Crowne Plaza at 123b High Street, tel. 0131/557-5732).

Food Plantation has good, inexpensive, fresh sandwiches to eat in or take out (Mon–Fri 9:00–16:00, Sat 10:00–16:00, closed Sun, 274 Canongate).

The **Tea Room** serves light lunches, scones, and fine tea in yellow elegance (Thu–Tue 10:30–16:30, closed Wed, next to Museum of Edinburgh at 158 Canongate).

Clarinda's Tea Room, near the bottom of the Royal Mile, is a charming and tasty place to relax after touring the Mile or palace (Mon–Sat 9:00–16:45, Sun 10:00–16:45, 69 Canongate, tel. 0131/557-1888).

For a break from the touristic grind just off the top end of the Royal Mile, consider the **Elephant House**, where locals browse newspapers in the stay-awhile back room, listen to classic rock, and sip coffee or munch a light meal (Mon–Fri 8:00–23:00, Sat–Sun 9:00–23:00, 2 blocks south of Royal Mile near Museum of Scotland at 21 George IV Bridge, tel. 0131/220-5355).

Grassmarket Street, below the castle, is lined with lots of eateries and noisy pubs. This is the place for live music and absorbent food.

Eating in the New Town

Princes Mall Food Court, below the TI and above the station, is a circus of sticky fast-food joints littered with paper plates and shoppers (Mon–Sat 8:30–18:00, Thu until 19:00, Sun 11:00–17:00). If you'd prefer pubs, browse nearby Rose Street.

The Dome Restaurant serves decent meals around a classy bar under the elegant 19th-century skylight dome of what was a fancy bank. With soft jazz and dressy, white-tablecloth ambience, it feels a world apart (£10 lunches until 17:00, £16 dinners until 24:00, daily 12:00–24:00, modern cuisine, borderline smoky, open for a drink anytime under the dome or in the adjacent Art Deco bar, 14 George Street, tel. 0131/624-8624). Notice the facade of this former bank building—the various ways to make money fill the pediment with all the nobility of classical gods.

The **Undercroft**, in the basement of St. Andrew's church, is the cheapest place in town for lunch (£1 sandwich or soup and

Edinburgh's New Town

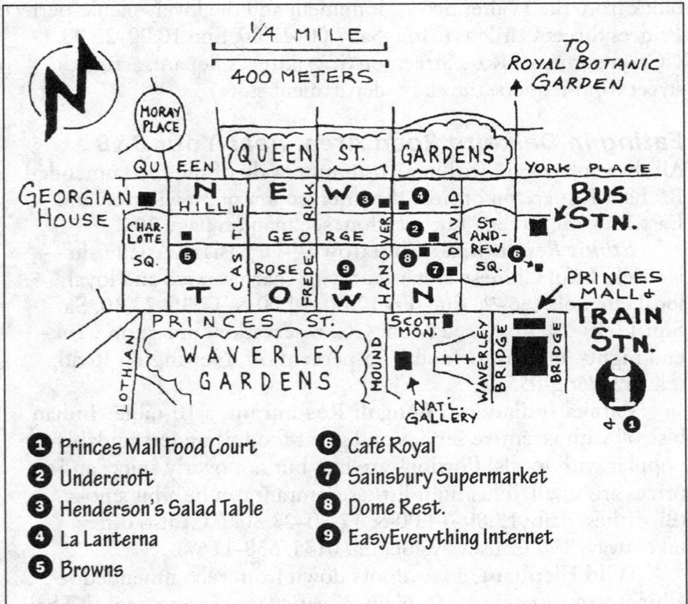

roll, Mon–Fri 12:00–14:00, closed Sat–Sun, on George Street, just off St. Andrew's Square).

Café Royal is a movie producer's dream pub—the perfect fin de siècle setting for a coffee, beer, or light meal (parts of *Chariots of Fire* were filmed in here). Drop in, if only to admire the 1880 tiles featuring famous inventors (2 blocks from Princes Mall on West Register Street, tel. 0131/556-1884).

A generation of New Town vegetarians have munched hearty cuisine and salads at **Henderson's Salad Table and Wine Bar** (£5–6, Mon–Sat 8:00–22:45, closed Sun, CC, non-smoking section, strictly vegetarian, pleasant live jazz nightly in Wine Bar, between Queen and George Streets at 94 Hanover Street, tel. 0131/225-2131). Henderson's has two different seating areas, but both use the same self-serve cafeteria line. They also run **Henderson's Bistro** upstairs with table service.

Local office workers pile into the friendly and family-run **La Lanterna** for good Italian food (Mon–Sat 12:00–14:00 & 17:15–22:00, closed Sun, CC, dinner reservations wise, 2 blocks off Princes Street, 83 Hanover Street, tel. 0131/226-3090).

Supermarket: The glorious **Sainsbury** supermarket, with a tasty assortment of take-away food and specialty coffees, is just one block from the Walter Scott Monument and the lovely picnic-perfect Princes Street Gardens (Mon–Sat 7:00–22:00, Sun 10:00–20:00, CC, on corner of Rose Street, on St. Andrew's Square, across the street from Jenners, the classy department store).

Eating in Dalkeith Road Area, near Your B&B

All these places are within a 10-minute walk of the recommended B&Bs. Most are on or near the intersection of Newington and East Preston Streets. For location, see map on page 704.

Ethnic Restaurants: **Chinatown**—an oasis of Asian calm—is a delightful Chinese restaurant with sharp service and loyal local clientele (£6–9, Tue–Fri 12:00–14:00 & 17:30–23:30, Sat–Sun 17:30–23:30, closed Mon, CC, reservations smart on weekend nights, take-away food is 25 percent off, Newington Road, tel. 0131/662-0555).

Pataka Indian and Bengali Restaurant, a 10-table "Indian bistro" with attentive service and great food, is understandably popular with locals. Portions are big, but not overly spicy, and prices are small. This tight little restaurant can be a bit smoky (£7 dishes, daily 12:00–14:00 & 17:30–23:30, CC, also offers take-away, 190 Causewayside, tel. 0131/668-1167).

Wild Elephant, a few doors down from recommended Chinatown restaurant, is a plain, cheap place serving decent Thai food to locals (£4–7, Wed–Mon 16:30–23:00, closed Tue, they don't serve wine but you can BYO wine for £1 corkage fee, CC, also does take-away, 21 Newington Road, tel. 0131/662-8822).

Scottish/French Restaurants: Several classy little eight-table places feature "Auld Alliance" cuisine—Scottish cooking with a French flair (seasoned with a joint historic disdain for England). They offer small menus with three or four items per course for two- or three-course meals (about £10 for a 2-course lunch, £20 for a 3-course dinner). These popular places take credit cards, and reservations are smart on weekend evenings. Many offer less-expensive meals outside of weekends.

Fenwicks is cozy and reliable, with tasty food and no French fries (Wed–Sat 12:00–14:00, dinner 18:00–late, Sun 12:00–15:00, CC, 15 Salisbury Place, tel. 0131/667-4265).

Ciros Restaurant is a hardworking, well-established family affair (£10 2-course lunches, £24 3-course dinners, £15 dinner Tue–Thu; open Tue–Fri 12:00–14:00 & 18:30–21:45, closed Sat–Mon; CC, 93 St. Leonard's Street, tel. 0131/668-4207, run by Christine, Jean, and Stuart Stevenson).

La Bon Vie Restaurant is candlelit chic with perhaps the most enticing menu (3-course dinners-£19, two-for-one

18:00–19:30; daily 12:00–14:00 & 18:00–22:00, 49 Causewayside, tel. 0131/667-1110).

Blonde Restaurant, with a more eclectic and European menu, is less expensive and bigger than the others with no set-price dinners (about £14 for 2 courses, Tue–Sun 12:00–14:30 & 18:00–22:00, closed Mon, 75 St. Leonard's Street, tel. 0131/668-2917).

Pubs: **Hotel Ceilidh-Donia's pub** serves good grub with live folk music most nights and offers free Internet access to diners (£6–7, Mon–Fri eves plus Sun lunch 12:00–14:30, CC, within a block of most recommended B&Bs at 14 Marchhall Crescent, tel. 0131/667-2743, Max).

Bierex, a youthful pub, is the neighborhood favorite for modern dishes and camaraderie (£6 plates, daily 10:00–24:00, food served 10:00–20:00, CC, 132 Causewayside, tel. 0131/667-2335).

The **New Bell** serves up filling classics, from steak and salmon to haggis, in a tidy pub setting (£13 plates, Tue–Sun 17:30–22:30; 2-course £10 special 17:30–18:45; closed Mon, 233 Causewayside, tel. 0131/668-2868).

Cheaper Choices: **Chatterbox**, a grandmotherly little place, is fine for a light meal with tea (£4 meals, Thu–Tue, open only until 17:30, closed Wed, around corner from Chinatown on East Preston Street).

Brattisanis is your basic fish-and-chips joint serving lousy milk shakes and great haggis. Add a cheap touch of class by bringing in a beer or half bottle of wine from next door (daily 9:30–23:00, 87 Newington Road).

On Dalkeith Road, the huge Commonwealth Pool's noisy **cafeteria** is for hungry swimmers and budget travelers alike (Mon–Fri 10:00–20:00, Sat–Sun 10:00–17:00, pass the entry without paying).

Supermarket: The nearest supermarket, **Tesco**, is located between the Royal Mile and the Dalkeith B&B neighborhood (Mon–Sat 7:00–22:00, Sun 9:00–19:00, 5 long blocks south of the Royal Mile, on Nicolson, just south of intersection with West Richmond Street).

Transportation Connections—Edinburgh

By Train: To **Inverness** (7/day, 4 hrs), **Oban** (3/day, change in Glasgow, 4.5 hrs), **York** (1/hr, 2.5 hrs), **London** (1/hr, 5 hrs), **Durham** (1/hr, 2 hrs, less frequent in winter), **Newcastle** (1/hr, 1.5 hrs), **Keswick**, the Lake District (south past Carlisle to Penrith, then catch bus to Keswick, 1/hr except Sun 6/day, 40 min), **Birmingham** (6/day, 4.5 hrs), **Crewe** (6/day, 3.5 hrs), **Bristol**, near Bath (1/hr, 6–7 hrs). Train info: tel. 08457-484-950, www.gner.co.uk.

By Bus: To **Oban** (1/day, 9:15 departure, 4 hrs, not on Sun), **Fort William** (1/day, 4 hrs), **Inverness** (1/hr, 4 hrs), **Blackpool** (requires change in Glasgow, 5 hrs), **York** (1/day at 9:45, 5 hrs). For bus info, call Scottish Citylink (tel. 08705-505-050, www.citylink.co.uk) or National Express (tel. 08705-808-080). You can get info and tickets at the bus desk inside the Princes Mall TI.

Route Tips for Drivers

Arriving in Edinburgh from the north: Rather than drive through downtown Edinburgh to the recommended B&Bs, circle the city on the A720 City Bypass road. Approaching Edinburgh on the M9, take the M8 (direction: Glasgow) and quickly get onto the A720 City Bypass (direction: Edinburgh South). After four miles you'll hit a roundabout. Ignore signs directing you into Edinburgh North and stay on A720 for 10 more miles to the next and last roundabout, named Sheriffhall. Exit the roundabout on the first left (A7 Edinburgh). From here it's four miles to the B&B neighborhood (see "Arriving from the south," below, and B&B neighborhood map, on page 704).

Arriving from the south: Coming into town on A68 from the south, take the "A7 Edinburgh" exit off the roundabout. A7 becomes Dalkeith Road. If you see the huge swimming pool, you've gone a couple of blocks too far (avoid this by referring to B&B neighborhood map on page 704).

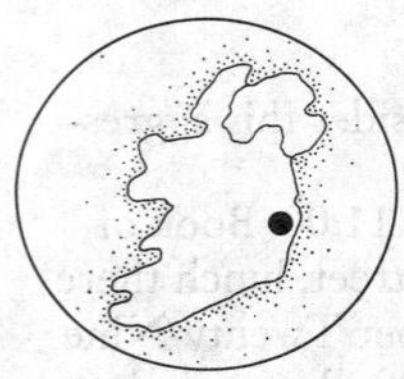

DUBLIN

With reminders of its stirring history and rich culture on every corner, Ireland's capital and largest city is a sightseer's delight. Dublin's fair city will have you humming "Cockles and mussels, alive, alive-O."

Founded as a Viking trading settlement in the ninth century, Dublin grew to be a center of wealth and commerce second only to London in the British Empire. Dublin, the seat of English rule in Ireland for 700 years, was the heart of a "civilized" Anglo-Irish area (eastern Ireland) known as "the Pale." Anything "beyond the Pale" was considered uncultured and almost barbaric . . . purely Irish.

The Golden Age of English Dublin was the 18th century. The British Empire was on a roll, and Dublin was right there with it. Largely rebuilt during this Georgian era, Dublin—even with its tattered edges—became an elegant and cultured capital.

Then nationalism and human rights got in the way. The ideas of the French Revolution inspired Irish intellectuals to buck British rule and, after the revolt of 1798, life in Dublin was never quite the same. But the 18th century left a lasting imprint on the city. Georgian (that's British for neoclassical) squares and boulevards gave the city an air of grandness. The National Museum, National Gallery, and many government buildings are in the Georgian section of town. Few buildings (notably Christ Church Cathedral and St. Patrick's Cathedral) survive from before this Georgian period.

In the 19th century, with the closing of the Irish Parliament, the famine, and the beginnings of the struggle for independence, Dublin was treated—and felt—more like a colony than a partner. The tension culminated in the Rising of 1916, independence, and the tragic civil war. With many of its elegant streets left in ruins, Dublin emerged as the capital of the only former colony in Europe.

While bullet-pocked buildings and dramatic statues keep memories of Ireland's recent struggle for independence alive, it's boom time now, and the city is looking to a bright future. Locals are enjoying the "Celtic Tiger" economy—the best in Europe—while visitors enjoy a big-town cultural scene wrapped in a small-town smile.

Planning Your Time

Dublin deserves three nights and two days. Consider this aggressive sightseeing plan:

Day 1: 10:15–Trinity College guided walk, 11:00–Book of Kells and Old Library, 12:00–Browse Grafton Street, lunch there or picnic on Merrion Square, 13:30–Visit Number Twenty-Nine Georgian House, 15:00–National Museum, 17:00–Return to hotel, rest, have dinner—eat well for less during "early-bird specials," 19:30–Evening walk (musical or literary), 22:00–Irish music in Temple Bar area.

Day 2: 10:00–Dublin Castle tour, 11:00–Historic town walk, 13:00–Lunch, 14:00–O'Connell Street walk, 16:00–Kilmainham Jail, 18:00–Guinness Brewery tour finishing with view of city, Evening–Catch a play, concert, or Comhaltas traditional music in Dun Laoghaire (pron. DUN leary).

Orientation (area code: 01)

Greater Dublin sprawls with over a million people—nearly a third of the country's population. But the center of touristic interest is a tight triangle between O'Connell Bridge, St. Stephen's Green, and Christ Church Cathedral. Within this triangle you'll find Trinity College (Book of Kells), Grafton Street (top pedestrian shopping zone), Temple Bar (trendy nightlife center), Dublin Castle, and the hub of most city tours and buses.

The River Liffey cuts the town in two. Focus on the southern half (where nearly all your sightseeing will take place). Dublin's main drag, O'Connell Street (near Abbey Theater and the outdoor produce market) runs north of the river to the central O'Connell Bridge, then continues as the main city axis—mostly as Grafton Street—to St. Stephen's Green. The only major sights outside your easy-to-walk triangle are the Kilmainham Jail and the Guinness Brewery (both west of the center).

Tourist Information

Dublin's main tourist information office (TI) is a big shop with little to offer other than promotional fliers and long lines (Mon–Sat 9:00–17:30, Sun July–Aug only 10:30–15:00, located in a former church on Suffolk Street, 1 block off Grafton Street,

Dublin

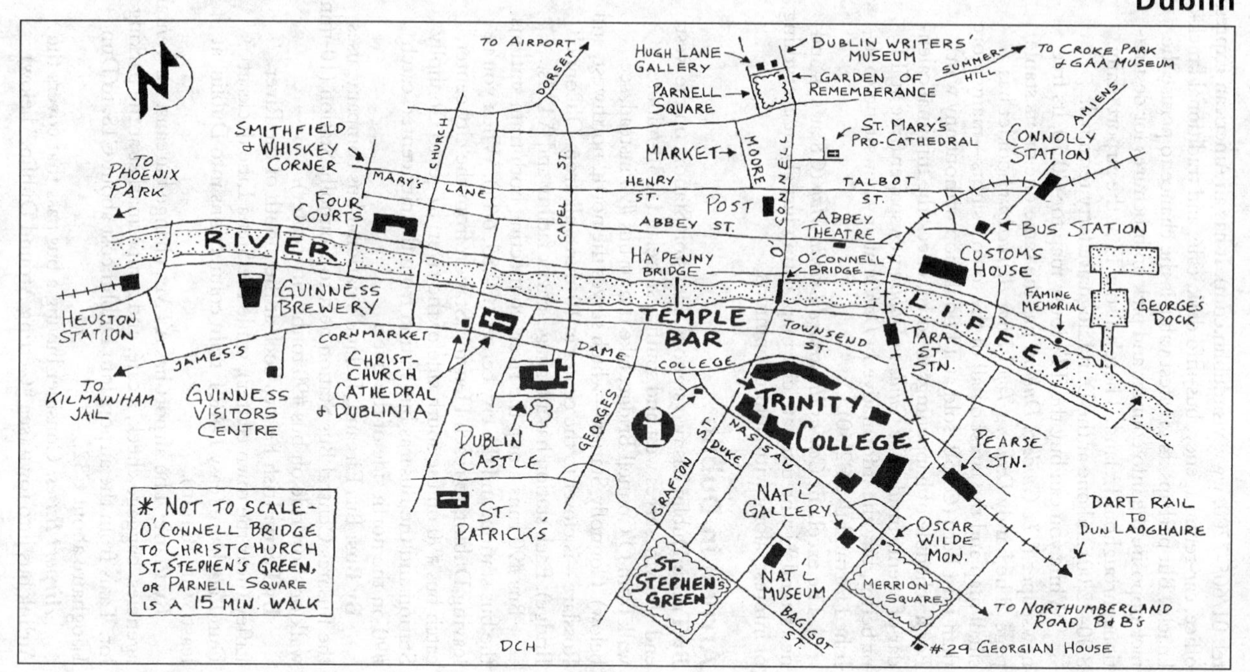
TO AIRPORT
DORSET
HUGH LANE GALLERY
DUBLIN WRITERS' MUSEUM
GARDEN OF REMEMBERANCE
PARNELL SQUARE
SUMMERHILL
TO CROKE PARK & GAA MUSEUM
AMIENS
SMITHFIELD & WHISKEY CORNER
CHURCH
MARY'S LANE
ST.
CAPEL
MARKET
MOORE
O'CONNELL
ST. MARY'S PRO-CATHEDRAL
CONNOLLY STATION
TO PHOENIX PARK
HENRY ST.
TALBOT ST.
FOUR COURTS
POST O
ABBEY ST.
ABBEY THEATRE
BUS STATION
RIVER
HA'PENNY BRIDGE
O'CONNELL BRIDGE
CUSTOMS HOUSE
LIFFEY
FAMINE MEMORIAL
GEORGE'S DOCK
HEUSTON STATION
GUINNESS BREWERY
TEMPLE BAR
TOWNSEND ST.
TARA ST. STN.
CORNMARKET
JAMES'S
DAME
COLLEGE
TO KILMAINHAM JAIL
GUINNESS VISITORS CENTRE
CHRIST-CHURCH CATHEDRAL & DUBLINIA
TRINITY COLLEGE
GEORGES
DUBLIN CASTLE
ST.
NASSAU
DUKE
GRAFTON
PEARSE STN.
* NOT TO SCALE - O'CONNELL BRIDGE TO CHRISTCHURCH ST. STEPHEN'S GREEN, OR PARNELL SQUARE IS A 15 MIN. WALK
ST. PATRICK'S
NAT'L GALLERY
OSCAR WILDE MON.
DART RAIL TO DUN LAOGHAIRE
ST. STEPHEN'S GREEN
NAT'L MUSEUM
MERRION SQUARE
BAGGOT ST.
TO NORTHUMBERLAND ROAD B&B's
#29 GEORGIAN HOUSE
DCH

tel. 01/605-7700, www.visitdublin.com). It has an American Express office, car-rental agency, bus-info desk, café, and traditional knick-knacks. But perhaps its greatest value is the chance to peruse the rack opposite the info counter and pick up brochures for destinations throughout Ireland. There's also a TI at the airport (daily 8:00–22:00) and one at the Dun Laoghaire ferry terminal.

While you can buy the TI's lousy map for €0.50, its free newspaper *(The Guide to Dublin)* has the same one on its staple page. The handy *Dublin's Top Visitor Attractions* booklet has a small map and the latest on all of the town's sights—many more than I list here (€3.50, sold at TI bookshop without any wait). For a schedule of happenings in town, check the minimal calendar of events inside *The Guide to Dublin* newspaper (free at TI), or better, buy the informative *In Dublin* at any newsstand (published fortnightly, €2.50).

The excellent *Collins Illustrated Dublin Map* (€8 at TIs and newsstands) is the ultimate city map, listing just about everything of interest, along with helpful opinions.

Arrival in Dublin

By Train: Dublin has two stations. Heuston Station, on the west end of town, serves west and southwest Ireland (a 30-minute walk from O'Connell Bridge; take taxi or bus #90 instead, see below). Connolly Station—which serves the north, northwest, and Rosslare—is closer to the center (a 10-min walk from O'Connell Bridge). Each station has a luggage-check facility and ATMs.

Bus #90 runs along the river, connecting both train stations, the bus station, and the city center (€0.85, 6/hr). When you're leaving Dublin, to reach Heuston Station from the city center, catch bus #90 on the south side of the river; to get to Connolly Station and the Busaras bus station from the city center, catch #90 on the north side of the river.

By Bus: Bus Eireann, Ireland's national bus company, uses the Busaras Central Bus Station next to Connolly Station (10-min walk or short ride on bus #90 to the city center).

By Ferry: Irish Ferries dock at the mouth of the River Liffey (near the town center), while the Stena Line docks at Dun Laoghaire (easy DART train connections into Dublin, at least 3/hr, 20 min).

By Plane: The airport has ATMs, change bureaus, car-rental agencies, baggage check, a café, and a supermarket at the parking lot. Taxis from the airport into Dublin cost about €18, to Dun Laoghaire about €32.

Airport Buses: Consider buying a bus pass that covers the Airlink bus into town (see "Getting Around Dublin," below), but read this first to see if Airlink is best for you. To get to the recommended accommodations in the **city center,** take Airlink bus #748 (not #747) and ask the driver which stop is closest to your hotel (€4.50, €2.50 with Aer Lingus boarding pass, pay driver, 6/hr, 40 min, connects airport with Heuston train station and Busaras bus station, near Connolly train station). For the **St. Stephen's Green** neighborhood, the Aircoach is your best bet (€5, 4/hr, runs 5:30–22:30; pay driver and confirm best stop for your hotel). If you're staying in **Dun Laoghaire,** take Airlink bus #746 direct to Dun Laoghaire.

City Bus: To get from the airport cheaply to downtown Dublin, take the city bus from the airport; buses marked #16A, #41A, #41B, and #41C go to Marlborough Street, a five-minute walk from O'Connell Bridge (€1.50, exact change required, 3/hr, 40 min).

Helpful Hints

Tourist Victim Support Service: This thoughtful service can be helpful if you run into any problems (Mon–Sat 10:00–18:00, Sun 12:00–18:00, tel. 01/478-5295).

U.S. Embassy: It's on 42 Elgin Road in the Ballsbridge neighborhood (Mon–Fri 8:30–12:00 for passport concerns, tel. 01/668-7122 or 01/668-8777, www.usembassy.ie).

Internet Access: There are Internet cafés on nearly every street. The one at the top of Dame Street is open 24 hours a day.

Laundry: Capricorn Launderette, a block southwest of Jury's Inn Christ Church on Patrick Street, is full-service only (Mon–Fri 7:30–20:00, Sat 9:00–18:00, Sun 10:00–16:00, tel. 01/473-1779). The All-American Launderette offers self- and full-service options (Mon–Sat 8:30–19:00, Sun 10:00–18:00, 40 South Great George's Street, tel. 01/677-2779).

Car Rental: For Dublin car-rental information, consider Avis (tel. 01/605-7502, www.avis.ie) or Hertz (tel. 01/660-2255, www.hertz.com).

Festivals: St. Patrick's Day is a five-day extravaganza in Dublin (www.stpatricksday.ie). June 16 is Bloomsday, dedicated to the Irish author James Joyce and featuring the Messenger Bike Rally. On rugby weekends (about 4 per year), hotels raise their prices and are packed. Book ahead during festival times and for any weekend.

Getting around Dublin

You'll do most of Dublin on foot. Big green buses are cheap and cover the city thoroughly. Most lines start at the four quays (pron. keys), or piers, nearest O'Connell Bridge. If you're away from the center, nearly any bus takes you back downtown. Tell the driver where you're going, and he'll ask for €0.75, €1.05, or €1.30, depending on the number of stops. Bring exact change or lose any excess.

Passes: The bus office at 59 Upper O'Connell Street has free "route network" maps and sells city-bus passes. The three-day Rambler costs €9 (covers Airlink airport bus but not DART trains) and the three-day Short Hop pass costs €13.50 (includes DART but not Airlink). Passes are also sold at each TI (bus info tel. 01/873-4222).

DART: Speedy commuter trains connect Dublin with Dun Laoghaire (ferry terminal and recommended B&Bs, at least 3/hr, 20 min, €1.50).

Taxi: Taxis are honest, plentiful, friendly, and good sources of information (under €6 for most downtown rides, €30 per hour for a guided joyride available from most any cab).

Tours of Dublin

While the physical treasures of Dublin are mediocre by European standards, the city has a fine story to tell and people with a natural knack for telling it. It's a good town for walking tours and the competition is fierce. Pamphlets touting creative walks are posted all over town. There are medieval walks, literary walks, 1916 Easter Rising walks, Georgian Dublin walks, and more. The evening walks are great ways to meet other travelers.

▲▲Historical Walking Tour—This is your best introductory walk. A group of hardworking history graduates—many of whom claim to have done more than just kiss the Blarney Stone—enliven Dublin's basic historic strip (Trinity College, Old Parliament House, Dublin Castle, and Christ Church Cathedral) with the story of their city, from its Viking origin to the present. Guides speak at length about the roots of Ireland's struggle with Britain. As you listen to your guide's story, you stand in front of buildings that aren't much to see but are lots to talk about (daily May–Sept at 11:00 and 15:00, Oct–April only Fri, Sat, and Sun at 12:00). From May to September, the same group offers more focused tours at noon (1916 Easter Rising "Terrible Beauty" walks on Mon and Fri; juicy slice-of-old-life Dublin "Sex & the City" walks on Sat, Sun, and Wed; and gritty "Architecture & Society" walks on Tue and Thu). All walks last two hours and cost €10 (but get the student discount with this book, depart from front gate of Trinity College, private walks also available, tel. 01/878-0227, www.historicalinsights.ie).

The 1916 Rebellion company offers, as you might guess, **1916 Rebellion Walks** (€10 but get student price with this book, 2 hrs, daily mid-April–Sept Mon–Sat at 11:30, Sun at

13:00, depart from International Bar at 23 Wicklow Street, tel. 01/676-2493, www.1916rising.com).

▲Dublin Literary Pub Crawl—Two actors take 30 or so tourists on a walk, stopping at four pubs. Half the time is spent enjoying their entertaining banter, which introduces the novice to the high *craic* (conversation) of Joyce, O'Casey, and Yeats. The two-hour tour is punctuated with 20-minute pub breaks (free time). While the beer lubricates the social fun, it dilutes the content of the evening (€10, April–Oct daily at 19:30, plus Sun at noon; Nov–March Thu–Sun only; can normally just show up but call ahead in July–Aug when it can fill up, meet upstairs in Duke Pub, off Grafton on Duke Street, tel. 01/670-5602, www.dublinpubcrawl.com).

▲▲Traditional Irish-Music Pub Crawl—This is similar to the Literary Pub Crawl but features music. You meet upstairs at 19:30 at Gogarty's Pub (Temple Bar area, corner of Fleet and Anglesea) and spend 40 minutes each in the upstairs rooms of three pubs listening to two musicians talk about, play, and sing traditional Irish music. While having only two musicians makes the music a bit thin (Irish music aficionados will tell you you're better off just finding a good session), the evening, though touristy, is not gimmicky. It's an education in traditional Irish music. The musicians demonstrate a few instruments and really enjoy introducing rookies to their art (€10, €1 discount with this book, beer extra, April–Oct nightly; Nov and Feb–March Fri–Sat only, allow 2.5 hrs, expect up to 50 tourists, tel. 01/478-0193).

▲Hop-on Hop-off Bus Tours—Two companies (Dublin City Tours and City Sightseeing/Guide Friday) offer hop-on hop-off bus tours of Dublin, doing virtually identical 90-minute circuits, allowing you to hop on and off at your choice of about 16 stops. Buses are mostly topless, with running live commentaries. They go to Guinness Brewery but not to Kilmainham Jail. Buy your ticket on board. Each company's map, free with ticket, details various discounts you'll get on Dublin's sights. Your ticket's valid for the day you purchase it—not for 24 hours (daily, 4/hr from 9:30–17:30, until 18:30 in summer, fewer buses Nov–March with shorter hours 9:30–15:30). **Dublin City Tour** runs the green-and-cream buses (€10, driver narrates, tel. 01/873-4222). **City Sightseeing/Guide Friday** costs a bit more but includes Phoenix Park and comes with a guide and a driver, rather than a driver who guides (€12, black-and-gold buses, tel. 01/676-5377).

▲Viking Splash Tours—If you'd like to ride in a WWII amphibious vehicle—driven by a Viking-costumed guide who is as liable to spout history as he is to growl—this is for you. The tour starts with a group roar from the Viking within us all. At first the guide talks as if he were a Viking ("When we came here in 841 . . ."), but soon the patriot emerges as he tags Irish history onto the sights you pass. Near the end of the 75-minute tour (punctuated by occasional group roars at passersby), you don a life jacket for a slow spin up and down a boring canal. Kids who expect a Viking splash may feel they've been trapped in a classroom, but historians will enjoy the talk more than the gimmick (€14, Feb–Nov Tue–Sun 10:00–17:00, sometimes later in summer, closed Mon, about hourly, depart from Bull Alley, beside St. Patrick's Cathedral; ticket office at 64–65 Patrick Street, on gray days boat is covered but still breezy—dress warmly, tel. 01/855-3000, www.vikingsplashtours.com).

Sights—Dublin's Trinity College

▲Trinity College—Founded in 1592 by Queen Elizabeth I to establish a Protestant way of thinking about God, Trinity has long been Ireland's most prestigious college. Originally the student body was limited to rich Protestant males. Women were admitted in 1903, and Catholics, though allowed entrance by the school much earlier, were given formal permission to study at Trinity in the 1970s. Today half of Trinity's 12,500 students are women, and 70 percent are culturally Catholic (although only about 20 percent of Irish youth are churchgoing).

▲▲Trinity College Tour—Inside the gate of Trinity, students organize and lead 30-minute tours of their campus. You'll get a rundown on the mostly Georgian architecture; a peek at student life, both in the early days and today; and enjoy the company of a witty Irish college kid who talks about the school (late May–Sept daily 10:15–15:30; late Feb and early May usually weekends only, weather permitting; look for small blue kiosk inside gate, the €9 tour fee includes the €7 fee to see the Book of Kells, where the tour leaves you).

▲▲▲Book of Kells in the Trinity Old Library—The only Trinity campus interior welcoming tourists—just follow the signs—is the Old Library, with its precious Book of Kells. The first-class *Turning Darkness into Light* exhibit puts the 680-page illuminated manuscript in its historical and cultural context and prepares you for the original book and other precious manuscripts in the treasury. The exhibit is a one-way affair leading to the actual treasury, which shows only four books under glass in one display case. Make a point to spend at least half an hour in the exhibit (before reaching the actual Book of Kells). The video clips showing the exacting care that went into the "monkuscripts" and the ancient art of bookbinding are especially interesting.

Written on vellum (baby calfskin) in the eighth or early ninth century—probably by Irish monks in Iona, Scotland—this

South Dublin

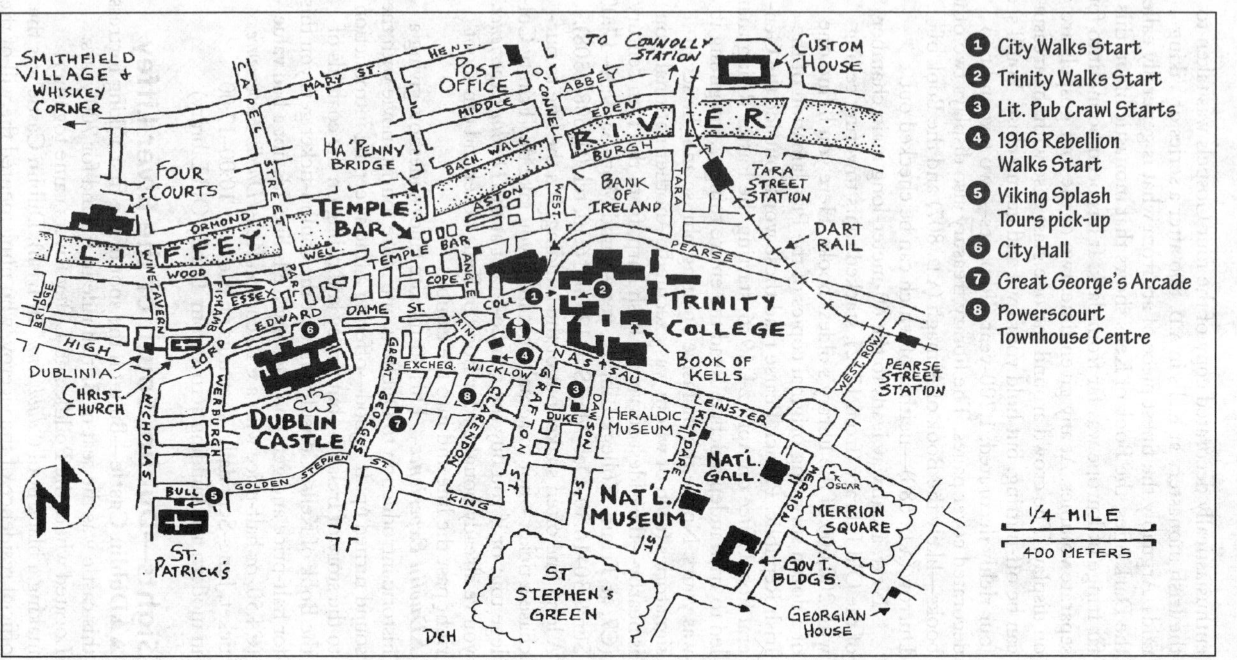

enthusiastically decorated copy of the four Gospels was taken to the Irish monastery at Kells in A.D. 806 after a series of Viking raids. Arguably the finest piece of art from what is generally called the Dark Ages, the Book of Kells shows that monastic life in this far fringe of Europe was far from dark. It has been bound into four separate volumes. At any given time, two of the four gospels are on display. The crowd around the one glass case with the treasures can be off-putting, but hold your own and get up close. You'll see four richly decorated, 1,200-year-old pages—two text and two decorated cover pages. The library treasury also displays two other books—likely the Book of Armagh (A.D. 807) and the Book of Durrow (A.D. 680)—neither of which can be checked out.

Next, a stairway leads to the 60-meter-long main chamber of the Old Library (from 1732), stacked to its towering ceiling with 200,000 of the library's oldest books. Here you'll find one of a dozen surviving original copies of the Proclamation of the Irish Republic. Patrick Pearse read these words outside the General Post Office on April 24, 1916, starting the Easter Rising that led to Irish independence. Read the entire thing . . . imagining it was yours. Notice the inclusive opening phrase and the seven signatories (each of whom was executed). Another national icon is nearby—the oldest surviving Irish harp, from the 15th century (€7, at Trinity College Library, year-round Mon–Sat 9:30–17:00, Sun 9:30–16:30, Oct–May Sun 12:00–16:30, tel. 01/608-2308). A long line often snakes out of the building. It's the line to purchase a ticket—not to actually get in. If you take the Trinity College tour or if you buy the combo-ticket at the *Dublin Experience*, you've already bought your Book of Kells ticket and can scoot right past the line and into the exhibit.

▲***Dublin Experience***—This 40-minute fancy slideshow giving a historic introduction to Dublin is one more tourist movie with the sound turned up. It's good—offering a fine sweeping introduction to the story of Ireland—but pricey and riding on the coattails of the Book of Kells. Considering that the combo-ticket gets you this for half-price and gets you past any Kells line, it's not a bad value (€4.50, or half-price with a €10 combo Kells/*Dublin Experience* ticket, June–Sept daily, showings on the hour 10:00–17:00, in modern arts building across from Trinity Old Library).

Sights—Dublin, South of the River Liffey

▲▲**Dublin Castle**—Built on the spot of the first Viking fortress, this castle was the seat of British rule in Ireland for 700 years. Located where the Poddle and Liffey Rivers came together, making a black pool ("*dubh linn*" in Irish), Dublin Castle was the official residence of the viceroy, who implemented the will of the

British royalty. In this stirring setting, in 1922, the Brits handed power over to Michael Collins and the Irish. Today it's used for fancy state and charity functions. The 45-minute tours offer a room-by-room walk through the lavish state apartments of this most English of Irish palaces (€4.25, 4/hr, Mon–Fri 10:00–17:00, Sat–Sun 14:00–17:00, tel. 01/677-7129). The tour finishes with a look at the foundations of the Norman tower and the best remaining chunk of the 13th-century town wall.

Dublin City Hall—The first neoclassical building in this very neoclassical city stands proudly overlooking Dame Street, in front of the gate to Dublin Castle. Built in 1779 as the Royal Exchange, it introduced the neoclassical style (then very popular on the continent) to Ireland. Step inside (it's free) to feel the prosperity and confidence of Dublin in her 18th-century glory days. In 1852 it became the city hall. Under the grand rotunda, a cycle of heroic paintings tell the city's history. Pay your respects to the 18-foot-tall statue of Daniel O'Connell (the great orator and "liberator" who won Catholic emancipation in 1829 from those vile Protestants over in London). The greeter sits like the Maytag repairman at the information desk, eager to give you more information. Downstairs is a simple *Story of the Capital* exhibition—storyboards and video clips of Dublin's history (€4, Mon–Sat 10:00–17:00, Sun 14:00–17:00).

Dublinia—This tries valiantly, but fails, to be a "bridge to Dublin's medieval past." The amateurish look at the medieval town starts with a walk through dim rooms of tableaus, followed by several rooms of medieval exhibits, a scale model of old Dublin, and an interesting room devoted to medieval fairs. Then, after piles of stairs, you get a tower-top view of Dublin's skyline of churches and breweries (€5.75, €7 includes Christ Church Cathedral, saving you €1.75; April–Sept daily 10:00–17:00, Oct–March daily 11:00–16:00, brass rubbing, coffee shop, across from Christ Church Cathedral, tel. 01/679-4611).

Christ Church Cathedral—The first church here, built of wood in about 1040 by King Sitric, dates back to Viking times. The present structure dates from a mix of periods: Norman and Gothic, but mostly Victorian neo-Gothic (1870s restoration work). The unusually large crypt under the cathedral—actually the oldest building in Dublin—contains stocks, statues, and the cathedral's silver (€3 donation to church, €3 extra for crypt silver exhibition, free brochure with self-guided tour, daily 10:00–17:00). Because of Dublin's British past, neither of its top two churches is Catholic. Christ Church Cathedral and the nearby St. Patrick's Cathedral are both Church of Ireland. In Catholic Ireland they feel hollow and are more famous than visit-worthy.

Evensong: At Christ Church, a 45-minute evensong service is sung regularly (less regularly during the summer) several times a week (Wed at 18:00—girls' choir, Thu at 18:00—adult choir, Sat at 17:00—adult choir, and Sun at 15:30—adult choir). The 13th-century St. Patrick's Cathedral, where Jonathan Swift (author of *Gulliver's Travels*) was dean in the 18th century, also offers evensong (Sun at 15:15, Mon–Fri at 17:30, but not Wed July–Aug).

▲▲▲**National Museum**—Showing off the treasures of Ireland from the Stone Age to modern times, this museum is itself a national treasure and wonderfully digestible under one dome. Ireland's Bronze Age gold fills the center. Up four steps, the prehistoric Ireland exhibit rings the gold. In a corner (behind a 2,000-year-old body), you'll find the treasury with the most famous pieces (brooches, chalices, and other examples of Celtic metalwork) and an 18-minute video (played on request), giving an overview of Irish art through the 13th century. The collection's superstar is the gold, enamel, and amber eighth-century Tara Brooch. Jumping way ahead (and to the opposite side of the hall), a special corridor features *The Road to Independence*, with guns, letters, and death masks recalling the fitful birth of the "Terrible Beauty" (1900–1921, with a focus on the 1916 Easter Rising).

The best Viking artifacts in town are upstairs with the medieval collection. If you'll be visiting Cong (in Connemara, near Galway), seek out the original Cross of Cong (free entry, Tue–Sat 10:00–17:00, Sun 14:00–17:00, closed Mon, good café, Kildare Street 2, between Trinity College and St. Stephen's Green). Greatest-hits tours are given several times a day (€1.50, 40 min, tel. 01/677-7444 in morning for schedule).

▲**National Gallery**—Along with a hall featuring the work of top Irish painters, this has Ireland's best collection of European masters. It's impressive—although not nearly as extensive as those in London or Paris (free, Mon–Sat 9:30–17:30, Thu until 20:30, Sun 12:00–17:30, guided tours on weekends, Merrion Square West, tel. 01/661-5133, www.nationalgallery.ie).

▲▲**Grafton Street**—Once filled with noisy traffic, today Grafton Street is Dublin's liveliest pedestrian shopping mall. A five-minute stroll past street musicians takes you from Trinity College up to St. Stephen's Green (and makes you wonder why American merchants are so terrified of a car-free street). Walking by a buxom statue of "sweet" Molly Malone (known by locals as "the tart with the cart"), you'll soon pass two venerable department stores: the Irish Brown Thomas and the English Marks & Spencer. An alley leads to the Powerscourt Townhouse Shopping Centre, which tastefully fills a converted Georgian mansion. The huge, glass-covered St. Stephen's Green Shopping Centre and the peaceful and green Green itself mark the top of Grafton Street.

▲**St. Stephen's Green**—This city park, originally a medieval commons, was enclosed in 1664 and gradually surrounded with fine Georgian buildings. Today it provides 22 acres of grassy refuge for Dubliners. On a sunny afternoon, it's a wonderful world apart from the big city.

▲▲**Number Twenty-Nine Georgian House**—The carefully restored house at Number 29 Lower Fitzwilliam Street gives an intimate glimpse of middle-class Georgian life—which seems pretty high-class. From the sidewalk, descend the stairs to the basement-level entrance (at the corner of Lower Fitzwilliam and Lower Mount Streets). Start with an interesting 12-minute video (you're welcome to bring in a cup of coffee from the café) before joining your guide, who takes you on a fascinating 35-minute walk through this 1790 Dublin home (€3.25, Tue–Sat 10:00–17:00, Sun 14:00–17:00, closed Mon and last half of Dec, tel. 01/702-6165, www.esb.ie).

▲**Merrion Square**—Laid out in 1762, the square is ringed by elegant Georgian houses decorated with fine doors—a Dublin trademark—with elegant knobs and knockers. The park, once the exclusive domain of the residents, is now a delightful public escape. More inviting than St. Stephen's Green, it's ideal for a picnic. If you want to know what "snogging" is, walk through the park on a sunny day. Oscar Wilde, lounging wittily on the corner nearest the town center and surrounded by his clever quotes, provides a fun photo op.

▲**Temple Bar**—This was a Georgian center of craftsmen and merchants. As it fell on hard times in the 19th century, the lower rents attracted students and artists, giving the neighborhood a bohemian flair. With recent government tax incentives and lots of development money, the Temple Bar district has become a thriving cultural (and beer-drinking) hotspot. Today this much-promoted center of trendy shops, cafés, theaters, galleries, pubs with live music, and restaurants feels like the heart of Dublin. Dublin's "Left Bank"—actually on the right bank—fills the cobbled streets between Dame Street and the river. ("Bar" means a walkway along the river.) The central **Meeting House Square** (just off Essex Street) hosts free street theater, a lively organic-produce market (Sat 9:30–15:00), and a book market (Sat 11:00–18:00). The square is surrounded by interesting cultural centers.

For a listing of events and galleries, visit the **Temple Bar Information Centre** (Eustace Street, tel. 01/671-5717, www.temple-bar.ie). Rather than follow particular pub or restaurant recommendations (mine are below, under "Eating"), venture down a few side lanes off the main drag to see what looks good.

The pedestrian-only **Ha' Penny Bridge,** named for the half-pence toll people used to pay to cross it, leads from Temple Bar over the River Liffey to the opposite bank and more sights.

Sights—Dublin, North of the River Liffey

▲▲O'Connell Bridge—This bridge spans the River Liffey, which has historically divided the wealthy, cultivated south side from the poorer, cruder north side. While there's plenty of culture north of the river, even today "the north" is considered rougher and less safe. (Currently, the big investment seems to be directed to this area which, in time, is expected to be another fresh and lively prosperity zone.)

From the bridge look upriver (west) as far upstream as you can see. The big concrete building houses the city planning commission. Maddening to locals, this eyesore is in charge of making sure new buildings in the city are built in good taste. It marks (and covers) the place where the Vikings established Dublin in the ninth century.

Across the river stands the Four Courts, today's Supreme Court building, bombed and burned in 1922 during the tragic civil war that followed Irish independence. The closest bridge upstream—the elegant iron Ha' Penny Bridge—leads left into the Temple Bar nightlife district. Just beyond that old-fashioned 19th-century bridge is Dublin's pedestrian Millennium Bridge, inaugurated in 2000. (Note that buses leave from O'Connell Bridge—specifically Aston Quay—for the Guinness Brewery and the Kilmainham Jail.)

Turn 180 degrees and look downstream to see the tall union headquarters—for now the tallest building in the Republic—and lots of cranes. Booming Dublin is developing downstream. The Irish (forever clever tax fiddlers) have subsidized and revitalized this formerly dreary quarter with great success. A short walk downstream along the north bank leads to a powerful series of modern statues memorializing the great famine of 1845–1849.

▲▲O'Connell Street Stroll—Dublin's grandest street leads from O'Connell Bridge through the heart of north Dublin. Since the 1740s, it has been a 45-yard-wide promenade. Ever since the first O'Connell Bridge connected it to the Trinity side of town in 1794, it's been Dublin's main drag. (But it was only named O'Connell after independence was won in 1922.) The street, though lined with fast-food and souvenir shops, echoes with history. Take the following stroll:

Statues line O'Connell Street, celebrating great figures in Ireland's fight for independence. At the base of the street stands **Daniel O'Connell** (1775–1847), known as "the Liberator,"

North Dublin

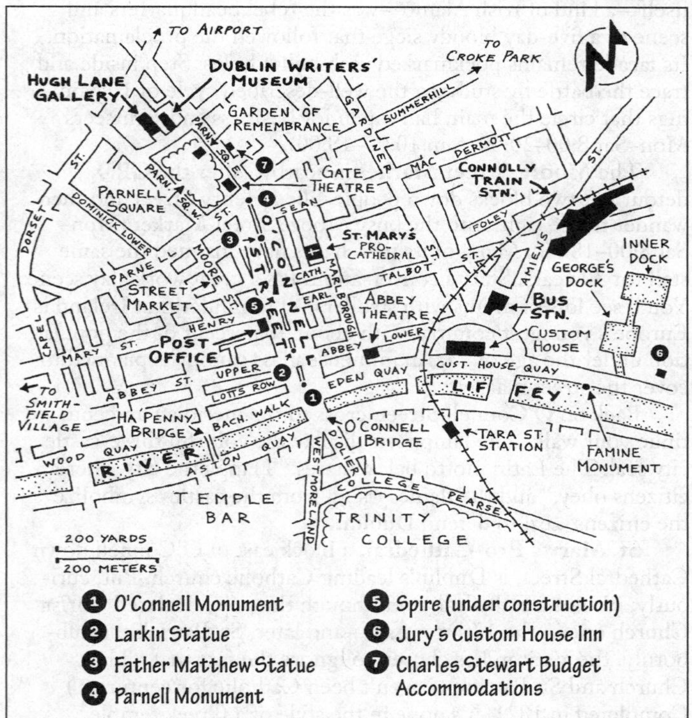

who founded the Catholic Association and was a strong voice for Irish Catholic rights in the British parliament.

Looking a block east down Abbey Street you can see the famous **Abbey Theatre**—rebuilt after a fire and now a nondescript modern building. It's still the much-loved home of the Irish National Theatre.

The statue of **James Larkin** honors the founder of the Irish Workers' Union. The one monument that didn't wave an Irish flag—a tall column crowned by a statue of the British hero of Trafalgar, Admiral Nelson—was blown up in 1966 . . . the IRA's contribution to the local celebration of the 50th anniversary of the Easter Rising. This vacant spot will be marked by the 120-yard-tall steel spike called the O'Connell Street Monument (planned for 2003).

The **General Post Office** is not just any P.O. It was from here that Patrick Pearse read the Proclamation of Irish Independence in 1916 and kicked off the Easter Rising. The GPO building itself—a kind of Irish Alamo—was the rebel headquarters and scene of a five-day bloody siege that followed the proclamation. Its facade remains pockmarked with bullet holes. Step inside and trace the battle by studying the well-described cycle of 10 paintings that circle the main hall (open for business and sightseers Mon–Sat 8:00–20:00, Sun 10:00–18:00).

The **Moore Street Market** is nearby. After the GPO, detour left two blocks down people-filled Henry Street and then wander to the right into the busy Moore Street Market (Mon–Sat 8:00–18:00). Many of its merchants have manned the same stall for 30 years. Start a conversation. It's a great workaday scene. You'll see lots of mums with strollers—a reminder that Ireland is Europe's youngest country, with about 40 percent of the population under the age of 25. An immense glass canopy is planned to cover the street market.

Back on O'Connell Street, cross to the meridian and continue your walk. The lampposts display the colorful three-castle city seal. The Latin motto below states, "Happy the city where citizens obey," and the flames rising from the castles symbolize the citizens' zeal to defend Dublin.

St. Mary's Pro-Cathedral, a block east of O'Connell down Cathedral Street, is Dublin's leading Catholic church. But, curiously, it's not a cathedral, even though the pope declared Christ Church one in the 12th century—and later, St. Patrick's. (Stubbornly, the Vatican has chosen to ignore the fact that Christ Church and St. Patrick's haven't been Catholic for centuries.) Completed in 1821, it's done in the style of a Greek temple.

Continuing up O'Connell Street, you'll find a statue of **Father Matthew,** a leader of the temperance movement of the 1830s who, some historians claim, was responsible for enough Irish peasants staying sober to enable Daniel O'Connell to organize them into a political force. (Perhaps understanding this dynamic, the USSR was careful to keep the price of vodka affordable.) The fancy Gresham Hotel is a good place for an elegant tea or beer.

Charles Stewart Parnell stands boldly at the top of O'Connell Street. The names of the four ancient provinces of Ireland and all 32 Irish counties (North *and* South, since this was erected before Independence) ring the statue, honoring the member of Parliament who nearly won Home Rule for Ireland in the late 1800s. (A sex scandal cost him the support of the Church, which let the air out of any chance for a free Ireland.)

Continue straight up Parnell Square East. At the Gate Theater (on the left), Orson Welles and James Mason got their acting starts.

The Garden of Remembrance (top of the square, on left) honors the victims of the 1916 Rising. The park was dedicated by Eamon de Valera in 1966 on the 50th anniversary of the uprising that ultimately led to Irish independence. The bottom of the cross-shaped pool is a mosaic of Celtic weapons, symbolic of how the early Irish would proclaim peace by throwing their weapons into the river. The Irish flag flies above the park: green for Catholics, orange for Protestants, and white for the hope that they can live together in peace. Across the street...

The **Dublin Writers' Museum** fills a splendidly restored Georgian mansion. No country so small has produced such a wealth of literature. As interesting to fans of Irish literature as it is boring to those who aren't, this three-room museum features the lives and works of Dublin's great writers (€4, Mon–Sat 10:00–17:00, Sun 11:00–17:00, June–Aug Mon–Fri until 18:00, helpful audioguide available, 18 Parnell Square North, tel. 01/872-2077). With hometown wits such as Swift, Yeats, Joyce, and Shaw, there is a checklist of residences and memorials to see. Those into James Joyce may want to hike 350 meters east to see the James Joyce Center at 35 North Great George Street (more Joyce memorabilia is in Dun Laoghaire's James Joyce Museum).

Hugh Lane Gallery (next door to the Dublin Writers' Museum) is a fine little gallery in a grand neoclassical building with a bite-size selection of Pre-Raphaelite, French Impressionist, and 19th- and 20th-century Irish paintings (Tue–Thu 9:30–18:00, Fri–Sat 9:30–17:00, Sun 11:00–17:00, closed Mon, tel. 01/874-1903). Sir Hugh went down on the *Lusitania* in 1915; due to an unclear will, his collection is shared by this gallery and the National Gallery in London.

Your walk is over. Here on the north end of town, you'll never be closer to the Gaelic Athletic Association Museum (described below). Otherwise, hop on your skateboard and return to the river.

Sights—Dublin's Smithfield Village

Huge investments may make Smithfield Village—until recently a run-down industrial area—the next Temple Bar. It's worth a look for "Cobblestores" (a redeveloped Duck Lane lined with fancy crafts and gift shops), the old Jameson distillery whiskey tour, and a chimney observatory with big Dublin views. The sights are clustered close together, two blocks north of the river behind the Four Courts—the Supreme Court building.

The Old Jameson Distillery—Whiskey fans enjoy visiting the old distillery. You get a 10-minute video, 20-minute tour, and a free shot in the pub. Unfortunately, the "distillery" feels fake and put together for tourism. In my opinion, the Midleton tour near

Charles Stewart Parnell (1846–1891)

Parnell, who led the Irish movement for Home Rule, did time in Kilmainham Jail. A Cambridge-educated Protestant and member of Parliament, he had a vision of a modern and free Irish Republic filled mostly with Catholics but not set up as a religious state. Momentum seemed to be on his side. With the British Prime Minister of the time, Gladstone, in favor of a similar form of Home Rule, it looked as if all of Ireland was ripe for independence. Then a sex scandal broke around Parnell and his mistress. The press, egged on by the powerful Catholic bishops (who didn't want a free but secular Irish state), battered away at the scandal until finally Parnell was driven from office. Sadly, after that, Ireland became mired in the Troubles of the 20th century: an awkward independence (1921) featuring a divided island, a bloody civil war, and sectarian violence ever since. It's said Parnell died of a broken heart. Before he did, this great Irish statesman requested to be buried outside of Ireland.

Cork (in the huge, original factory) is a better overall experience. If you do take the Jameson tour, be sure to volunteer energetically when the guide offers the chance to take the whiskey taste test at the end (€7, daily 9:30–18:00, last tour at 17:30, Bow Street, tel. 01/807-2355).

The Chimney—Built in 1895 for the distillery, the chimney is now an observatory. Ride the elevator 175 feet up for a Dublin panorama not quite as exciting as the view from the Guinness Brewery's Gravity Bar (overpriced at €6, Mon–Fri 9:30–17:30, Sat–Sun 11:00–17:30, tel. 01/817-3838).

Sights—Outer Dublin

The jail and the Guinness Brewery are the main sights outside of the old center. Combine them in one visit.

▲▲▲Kilmainham Gaol (Jail)—Opened in 1796 as the Dublin County Jail and a debtors' prison and considered a model in its day, it was used frequently as a political prison by the British. Many of those who fought for Irish independence were held or executed here, including leaders of the rebellions of 1798, 1803, 1848, 1867, and 1916. National heroes Robert Emmett and Charles Stewart Parnell each did time here. The last prisoner to be held here was Eamon de Valera (later president of Ireland). He was released on July 16, 1924, the day Kilmainham was finally shut down. The buildings, virtually in ruins, were restored in the 1960s. Today it's a shrine to the Nathan Hales of Ireland.

Start your visit with a guided tour (1 hr, 2/hr, includes 25 min in prison chapel for a rebellion-packed video, spend waiting time in museum). It's touching to tour the cells and places of execution while hearing tales of terrible colonialism and heroic patriotism alongside Irish schoolkids who know these names well. The museum is an excellent exhibit on Victorian prison life and Ireland's fight for independence. Don't miss the museum's dimly lit Last Words 1916 hall upstairs, displaying the stirring last letters patriots sent to loved ones hours before facing the firing squad (€4.75, April–Sept daily 9:30–18:00, Oct–March 9:30–17:00, last admission 1 hour before closing; €5 taxi, bus #51b, #78a, or #79 from Aston Quay or Guinness, tel. 01/453-5984). I'd taxi to the jail and then catch the bus from there to Guinness (leaving the prison, take three rights, crossing no streets, to the bus stop and hop bus #51b or #78a).

▲**Guinness Brewery**—A visit to the Guinness Brewery is, for many, a pilgrimage. Arthur Guinness began brewing the famous stout here in 1759. By 1868 it was the biggest brewery in the world. Today the sprawling brewery fills several city blocks. Around the world, Guinness brews more than 10 million pints a day. The home of Ireland's national beer welcomes visitors, for a price, with a sprawling new museum (but there are no tours of the actual working brewery). The museum fills the old fermentation plant, used from 1902 through 1988, vacated, and then opened in 2000 as a huge shrine-like place. Stepping into the middle of the ground floor, look up. A tall beer glass–shaped glass atrium—14 million pints big—leads past four floors of exhibitions and cafés to the skylight. Atop the building, the Gravity Bar provides visitors with a commanding 360-degree view of Dublin—with vistas all the way to the sea—and a free beer. The actual exhibit makes brewing seem more grandiose than it is and treats Arthur like the god of human happiness. Highlights are the cooperage (with old film clips showing the master wood-keg makers plying their now-extinct trade), a display of the brewery's clever ads, and the Gravity Bar, which really is spectacular (€13—including a €4 pint, daily 9:30–17:00, enter on Market Street, bus #78A from Aston Quay near O'Connell Bridge, or bus #123 from Dame Street and O'Connell Street, tel. 01/408-4800). Hop-on hop-off bus tours stop here.

▲**Gaelic Athletic Association Museum**—The GAA was founded in 1884 as an expression of an Irish cultural awakening. While created to foster the development of Gaelic sports—specifically Irish football and hurling (and to ban English sports such as cricket and rugby)—it played an important part in the fight for independence. This museum, at the newly expanded 97,000-seat Croke

Park Stadium, offers a high-tech, interactive introduction to Ireland's favorite games. Relive the greatest moments in hurling and Irish-football history. Then get involved. Pick up a stick and try hurling, kick a football, and test your speed and balance. A 15-minute film clarifies the connection between sports and Irish politics (€3.75, May–Sept daily 9:30–17:00; Oct–April Mon–Sat 10:00–17:00, Sun 12:00–17:00; on game Sundays the museum is open 12:00–17:00 to new stand ticket-holders only; under the new stand at Croke Park, from O'Connell Street walk 20 min or catch bus #3, #11, #11a, #16, #16a, #16c, or #123; tel. 01/855-8176).

Hurling or Irish Football at Croke Park—Actually seeing a match here, surrounded by incredibly spirited Irish fans, is a fun experience. Hurling is like airborne hockey with no injury time-outs, and Irish football is a rugged form of soccer. Matches are held on most Sunday afternoons outside of winter. Tickets (€15–35) are available at the stadium except during championships.

Greyhound Racing—For an interesting lowbrow look at another local pastime, consider going to the dog races and doing a little gambling (€7, generally Wed, Thu, and Sat at 20:00, Shelbourne Park, tel. 01/668-3502). Greyhounds race on the other days at Harold's Cross Racetrack (Mon, Tue, and Fri at 20:00, tel. 01/497-1081).

Shopping

Shops are open roughly Monday to Saturday from 9:00 to 18:00, and until 20:00 on Thursday. They have shorter hours on Sunday (if they're open at all). The best shopping area is Grafton, with its neighboring streets and arcades (such as the fun Great George's Arcade between Great George's and Drury Streets), and nearby shopping centers (Powerscourt and St. Stephen's Green).

For antiques, try Francis Street. For a street market, consider Mother Redcaps (all day Fri–Sun, bric-a-brac, antiques, crafts, Back Lane, Christ Church). For produce, noise, and color, visit Moore Street (Mon–Sat 8:00–18:00, near General Post Office). For raw fish, get a whiff of Michan Street (Tue–Sat 7:00–15:00, behind Four Courts building). Saturdays at Temple Bar's Meeting House Square, it's food in the morning (from 9:00) and books in the afternoon (until 18:00). Temple Bar is worth a browse any day for its art, jewelry, new-age paraphernalia, books, music, and gift shops.

Entertainment and Theater in Dublin

Ireland has produced some of the finest writers in both English and Irish, and Dublin houses some of Europe's finest theaters. While Handel's *Messiah* was first performed in Dublin (1742), these days

Dublin is famous for its rock bands (U2, Thin Lizzie, and Sinead O'Connor all got started here).

Abbey Theatre is Ireland's national theater, founded by W. B. Yeats in 1904 to preserve Irish culture during British rule (Lower Street, tel. 01/878-7222, www.abbeytheatre.ie). **Gate Theatre** does foreign plays as well as Irish classics (Cavendish Row, tel. 01/874-4045, www.gate-theatre.ie). **Point Theatre,** once a railway terminus, is now the country's top live-music venue (North Wall quay, tel. 01/836-3633, www.thepoint.ie). At the **National Concert Hall,** the National Symphony Orchestra performs most Friday evenings (Earlsfort Terrace, off St. Stephen's Green, tickets €11–18, tel. 01/475-1666, www.nch.ie). Street theater takes the stage in Temple Bar on summer evenings.

Pub Action: Folk music fills the pubs, and street entertainers are everywhere. For the latest on live theater, music, cultural happenings, restaurant reviews, pubs, and current museum hours, pick up a copy of the twice-monthly *In Dublin* (€2.50, any newsstand).

The Temple Bar area thrives with music—traditional, jazz, and pop. It really is *the* comfortable and fun place for tourists and locals (who come here to watch the tourists). **Gogarty's Pub** (corner of Fleet and Anglesea) has top-notch sessions upstairs nightly from 21:00. Use this as a kick-off for your Temple Bar evening fun.

A 10-minute hike up the river west of Temple Bar takes you to a twosome with a local and less-touristy ambience. **The Brazen Head,** famous as Dublin's oldest pub, is a hit for an early dinner and late live music, with smoky, atmospheric rooms and a courtyard made to order for balmy evenings (on Bridge Street, tel. 01/677-9549). **O'Shea's Merchant Pub,** just across the street, is encrusted in memories and filled with locals taking a break from the grind. They have live traditional music nightly (the front half is a restaurant, the magic is in the back half).

Irish Music in Nearby Dun Laoghaire

For an evening of pure Irish music, song, and dance, check out the **Comhaltas Ceoltoiri Eireann,** an association working to preserve this traditional slice of Irish culture. It got started when Elvis and company threatened to steal the musical heart of the new generation. Judging by the pop status of traditional Irish music these days, Comhaltas accomplished its mission. Their "Seisiun" evening is a stage show mixing traditional music, song, and dance (€10, July–Aug Mon–Thu at 21:00, followed by informal music session at 22:30). Fridays all year long they have a *ceilidh* (pron. KAY-lee) where everyone does set dances (€7 includes friendly pointers, 21:30–00:30). On Wednesdays, Fridays, and Saturdays at 21:30, there are informal sessions by the fireside. All musicians are welcome. Performances are held in Cuturlann na Eireann, near the Seapoint DART stop or a 20-minute walk from Dun Laoghaire, at 32 Belgrave Square, Monkstown (tel. 01/280-0295, www.comhaltas.com). Their bar is free and often filled with music.

Sleeping in Dublin

(€1 = about $1, country code: 353, area code: 01)

Sleep Code: **S** = Single, **D** = Double/Twin, **T** = Triple, **Q** = Quad, **b** = bathroom, **s** = shower only, **CC** = Credit Cards accepted, **no CC** = Credit Cards not accepted. Breakfast is included unless otherwise noted.

To help you easily sort through these listings, I've divided the rooms into three categories, based on the price for a standard double room with bath:

Higher Priced—Most rooms more than €130.

Moderately Priced—Most rooms €65–130.

Lower Priced—Most rooms €65 or less.

Dublin is popular and rooms can be tight. Book ahead for weekends any time of year, particularly in summer and during rugby weekends. Prices are often discounted on weeknights (Mon–Thu) and from November through February.

Big and practical places (both cheap and moderate) are most central at Christ Church on the edge of Temple Bar. For classy, older Dublin accommodations, you'll pay more and stay a bit farther out (east of St. Stephen's Green). For a small-town escape with the best budget values, take the convenient DART train (at least 3/hr, 20 min) to nearby Dun Laoghaire.

Sleeping near Christ Church

These places face Christ Church Cathedral, a great locale just a five-minute walk from the best evening scene at Temple Bar and 10 minutes from the sightseeing center (Trinity College and Grafton Street). Full Irish breakfasts, which usually cost about €9 at the hotels, are half the price at the many small cafés nearby (consider the Applewood café at 1b Werburgh Street, next to Burdoch's Fish & Chips). The cheap hostels in this neighborhood have some double rooms.

MODERATELY PRICED

Harding Hotel is a hardwood, 21st-century, Viking-style place with 53 institutional-yet-hotelesque rooms. The rooms are simpler than Jurys (below), but they're also more intimate (Sb-€60, Db/Tb-€89–96, tell them Rick sent you and get 10 percent off, breakfast-€6–9, CC, Internet access,

Dublin Hotels

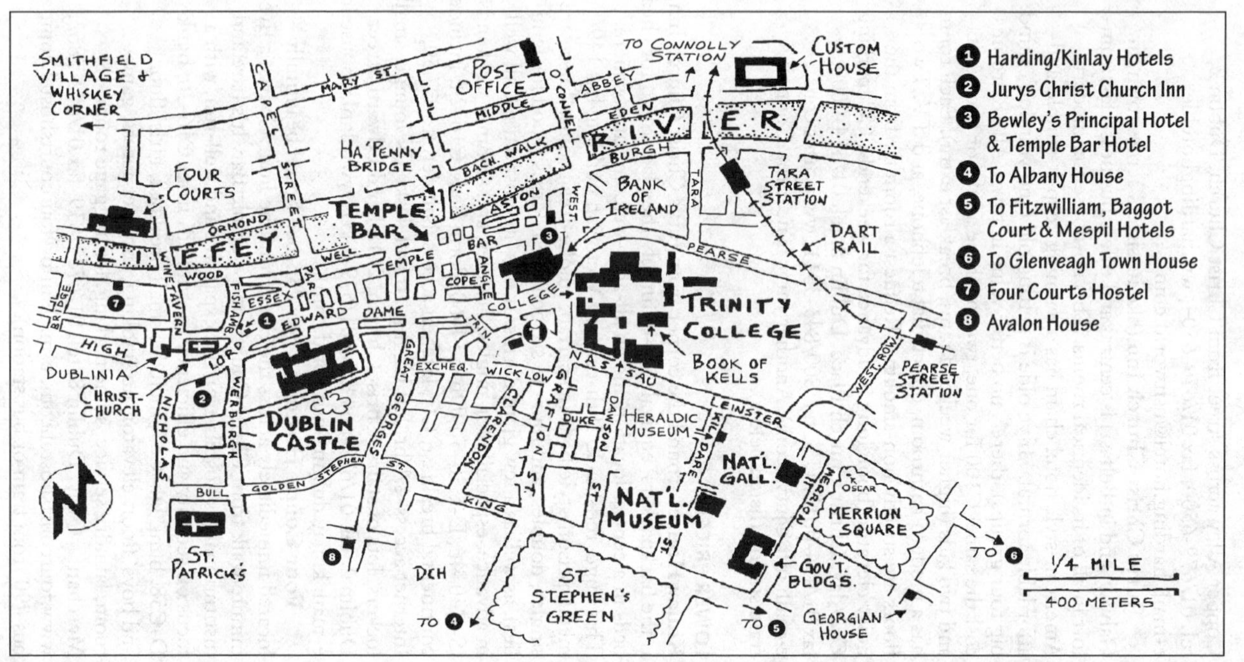

Copper Alley across street from Christ Church, Dublin 2, tel. 01/679-6500, fax 01/679-6504, ww.hardinghotel.ie, e-mail: harding.hotel@usitworld.com).

Jurys Christ Church Inn (like its sisters across town, in Galway, and in Belfast) is central and offers business-class comfort in all of its identical rooms. This no-nonsense, modern, American-style hotel chain has a winning keep-it-simple-and-affordable formula. If ye olde is getting old (and you don't mind big tour groups), there's no better value in town. All 182 rooms cost the same: €100 for one, two, or three adults or two adults and two kids (higher weekend rates, breakfast extra). Each room has a modern bathroom, direct-dial telephone, and TV. Two floors are strictly non-smoking. Request a room far from the noisy elevator (book long in advance for weekends, CC, parking €12/day, Christ Church Place, Dublin 8, tel. 01/454-0000, fax 01/454-0012, U.S. tel. 800/843-3311, www.jurys.com, e-mail: info@jurys.com). Another Jurys is near the Connolly train station (listed below).

LOWER PRICED

Kinlay House, around the corner from Jurys Christ Church Inn, is the backpackers' equivalent—definitely the place to go for cheap beds in a central location and an all-ages-welcome atmosphere. This huge, red-brick, 19th-century Victorian building has 149 metal, prison-style beds in spartan, smoke-free rooms. There are singles, doubles, and four- to six-bed coed dorms (good for families), as well as a few giant dorms. It fills up most days. Call well in advance, especially for singles, doubles, and summer weekends (S-€40–46, D-€50–56, Db-€54–60, dorm beds-€16–24, includes continental breakfast, CC, kitchen access, launderette-€7.50, Internet access-€4/hr, left luggage, travel desk, TV lounge, small lockers, lots of stairs, Christ Church, 2–12 Lord Edward Street, Dublin 2, tel. 01/679-6644, fax 01/679-7437, www.kinlayhouse.ie, e-mail: kinlay.dublin@usitworld.com).

Four Courts Hostel is a new 236-bed hostel beautifully located immediately across the river from the Four Courts, a five-minute walk from Christ Church and Temple Bar. It's bare and institutional (as hostels are), but expansive and well-run, with a focus on security and efficiency (dorm beds from €16–20, bunk D-€58, bunk Db-€65, includes small breakfast, girls' floor and boys' floor, elevator, no smoking, Internet access, game room, laundry service, some parking, left luggage room, 15 Merchant's Quay, Dublin 8, tel. 01/672-5839, fax 01/672-5862, www.fourcourtshostel.com, e-mail: info@fourcourtshostel.com, bus #90 from train or bus station).

Sleeping between Trinity College and Temple Bar

HIGHER PRICED

Bewley's Principal Hotel rents 70 decent rooms. For its size, it has an intimate feel, with character (Sb-€115, Db-€139, often mid-week deals, breakfast-€10, CC, non-smoking rooms, request a quiet room off the street, 19-20 Fleet Street, Dublin 2, tel. 01/670-8122, fax 01/670-8103, www.bewleysprincipalhotel.com).

Temple Bar Hotel is a 130-room business-class place, very centrally located midway between Trinity College and the Temple Bar action (Sb-€140, Db-€185, Tb-€250, often discounted, CC, smoke-free rooms, Fleet Street, Temple Bar, Dublin 2, tel. 01/ 677-3333, fax 01/677-3088, e-mail: templeb@iol.ie).

MODERATELY PRICED

Trinity College turns its 800 student-housing rooms on campus into no-frills, affordable accommodations in the city center each summer (mid-June–Sept, S-€47, Sb-€58, D-€94, Db-€116, CC, includes continental breakfast, cooked breakfast €2.50 extra, Trinity College, Dublin 2, tel. 01/608-1177, fax 01/671-1267, www2.tcd.ie/accom, e-mail: reservations@tcd.ie).

Sleeping near St. Stephen's Green

HIGHER PRICED

Albany House's 40 rooms come with classic furniture, high ceilings, Georgian elegance, and some street noise. Request the huge "superior" rooms, which are the same price (Sb-€90, Db-€140, €120 in slow times, Tb-€160, Una promises 10 percent off with this book in 2003, includes breakfast, CC, back rooms are quieter, smoke-free, just 1 block south of St. Stephen's Green at 84 Harcourt Street, Dublin 2, tel. 01/ 475-1092, fax 01/475-1093, http://indigo.ie/~albany, e-mail: albany@indigo.ie).

The Fitzwilliam has an inviting lounge and rents 13 decent rooms (Sb-€75, Db-€135, CC, 10 percent discount with cash, children under 16 sleep free, 41 Upper Fitzwilliam Street, Dublin 2, tel. 01/662-5155, fax 01/676-7488, e-mail: fitzwilliamguesthouse @eircom.net, Declan Carney).

Baggot Court Accommodations rents 11 similar rooms a block farther away and without a lounge (Sb-€90, Db-€150, Tb-€210, CC, entirely non-smoking, free parking, 92 Lower Baggot Street, Dublin 2, tel. 01/661-2819, fax 01/661-0253, e-mail: baggot@indigo.ie).

LOWER PRICED

Avalon House, near Grafton Street, rents 281 backpacker beds (S-€30, Sb-€33, D/twin-€56, Db/twin-€60, dorm beds-€15-20, includes continental breakfast, CC, elevator, Ireland bus tickets, Internet access, launderette across street, a few minutes off Grafton Street at 55 Aungier Street, Dublin 2, tel. 01/475-0001, fax 01/475-0303, www.avalon-house.ie).

Sleeping Away from the Center, East of St. Stephen's Green

HIGHER PRICED

Mespil Hotel is a huge, modern, business-class hotel renting 256 identical three-star rooms (each with a double and single bed, phone, TV, voice-mail, and modem hookup) at a good price with all the comforts. This is a cut above Jurys Inn, for a little more money (Sb, Db, or Tb-€135, breakfast-€12.50, CC, elevator, non-smoking floor, apartments for weeklong stays, 10-min walk southeast of St. Stephen's Green or bus #10, Mespil Road, Dublin 4, tel. 01/667-1222, fax 01/667-1244, www.leehotels.ie, e-mail: mespil@leehotels.ie).

MODERATELY PRICED

Glenveagh Town House rents 13 rooms—Victorian upstairs and modern downstairs—southeast of the city center, a 15-minute walk from Trinity College (Sb-€63–70, Db-€100–130, less in slow times, includes breakfast, CC, car park, 31 Northumberland Road, Dublin 4, tel. 01/668-4612, fax 01/668-4559, e-mail: glenveagh@eircom.net). Catch bus #5, #6, #7, #8, or #45, which lumber down Northumberland Road into downtown Dublin every 10 minutes.

Sleeping near Connolly Train Station

MODERATELY PRICED

Jurys Inn Custom House, on Custom House Quay, offers the same value as the Jurys at Christ Church. Bigger (with 234 rooms) and not quite as well-located (in a boring neighborhood, a 10-min riverside hike from O'Connell Bridge), this Jurys is more likely to have rooms available (Db-€100, CC, Dublin 1, tel. 01/607-5000, fax 01/829-0400, U.S. tel. 800/843-3311, www.jurys.com, e-mail: info@jurys.com).

Charles Stewart Budget Accommodations is a big, basic place offering lots of forgettable rooms, many long and narrow with head-to-toe twins, in a great location for a good price

(S-€32, Sb-€63, D-€76, Db-€89, Tb-€121, Qb-€140, CC, includes cooked breakfast, just beyond top of O'Connell Street at 5 Parnell Square, Dublin 1, tel. 01/878-0350, fax 01/878-1387, e-mail: cstuart@iol.ie).

Sleeping and Eating in nearby Dun Laoghaire

(€1 = about $1, country code: 353, area code: 01, mail: County Dublin)

Dun Laoghaire (pron. DUN leary) is seven miles south of Dublin. This beach resort, with the ferry terminal for Wales and easy connections to downtown Dublin, is a great small-town base for the big city.

While buses run between Dublin and Dun Laoghaire, the DART commuter train is much faster (6/hr in peak times, at least 3/hr otherwise, 20 min, runs Mon–Sat about 6:30–23:15, Sun from 9:00, €1.50 one-way, €2.75 round-trip, Eurail valid but uses day of flexipass; for a longer stay consider the €13.50 Short Hop 3-day bus and rail ticket covering DART and Dublin buses). If you're coming from Dublin, catch a DART train marked "Bray" and get off at the Sandy Cove or Dun Laoghaire stop, depending on which B&B you choose; if you're leaving Dun Laoghaire, catch a train marked "Howth" to get to Dublin—get off at the central Tara Street station.

The Dun Laoghaire harbor was strategic enough to merit a line of Martello Towers (built to defend against an expected Napoleonic invasion). By the mid-19th century, the huge breakwaters—reaching like two muscular arms into the Irish Sea—were completed, protecting a huge harbor. Ships sailed regularly from here to Wales (60 miles away), and the first train line in Ireland connected the terminal with Dublin. While still a busy transportation hub, today the nearly mile-long breakwaters are also popular with strollers, bikers, birders, and fishermen. Hike out to the lighthouse at the end of the interesting East Pier.

The **Dun Laoghaire TI** is in the ferry terminal (Mon–Sat 10:00–18:00 year-round, closed Sun). Comhaltas Ceoltoiri Eireann, an association that preserves Irish folk music, offers lively shows in Dun Laoghaire (see "Irish Music in nearby Dun Laoghaire," above). Taxi fare from Dun Laoghaire to central Dublin is about €13, to the airport about €32. With easy free parking and DART access into Dublin, this area is ideal for those with cars (which cost €19 a day to park in Dublin). The Washerette laundry is located in the village of Sandycove (Mon–Sat 8:30–18:00, self- and full-serve, 2 Glasthule, across from church). The Net House Café provides a fast Internet connection 24 hours a day (28 Upper George Street, €3/30 min).

Dun Laoghaire

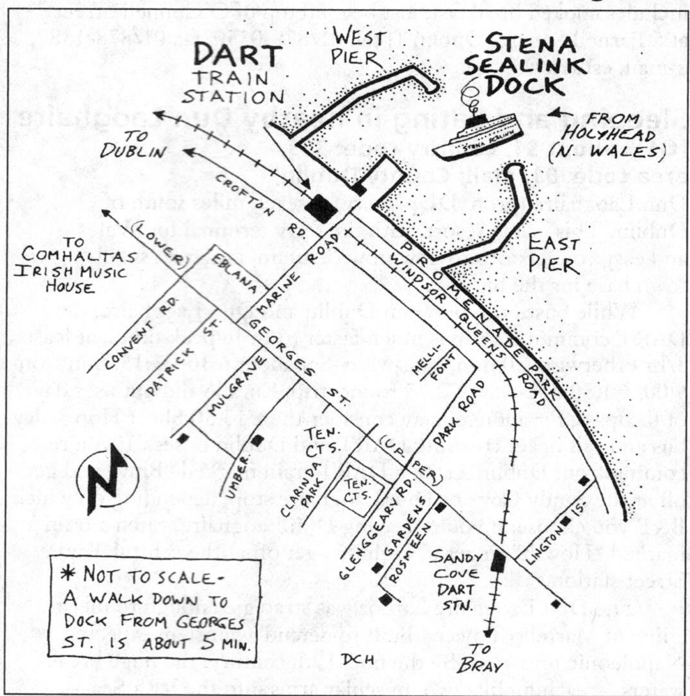

Sleeping near Sandycove DART Station

These listings are within several blocks of the Sandycove DART station and a seven-minute walk to the Dun Laoghaire DART station/ferry landing.

LOWER PRICED

Mrs. Kane's **Seaview B&B** is a modern house with three big, cheery rooms and a welcoming guests' lounge. While a few blocks farther out than the others, it's worth the walk for its bright and friendly feeling (Db-€65 through 2003 with this book, no CC, strictly smoke-free, just above Rosmeen Gardens at 2 Granite Hall, tel. & fax 01/280-9105, e-mail: seaviewbedandbreakfast@hotmail.com).

Windsor Lodge rents four fresh, cheery rooms on a quiet street a block off the harbor and a block from the DART station (Db-€60–64, family deals, no CC, non-smoking, 3 Islington Avenue, Sandycove, Dun Laoghaire, tel. & fax 01/284-6952, e-mail: winlodge@eircom.net, Mary O'Farrell).

Annesgrove B&B has four tidy rooms decorated in beige and brown (S-€40, D-€60, Db-€65, Tb-€90, includes breakfast, no CC, parking, close to park and beach, 28 Rosmeen Gardens, tel. 01/280-9801, Anne D'Alton). **Rosmeen House** is a similar grandfather-clock kind of place renting four smoke-free rooms (S-€40, Db-€65, no CC, 13 Rosmeen Gardens, tel. 01/280-7613, Joan Murphy).

Sleeping near Dun Laoghaire DART Station

Lynden B&B, with a classy 150-year-old interior hiding behind a somber front, rents four big rooms (S-€38, Sb-€43, D-€50, Db-€60, 10 percent discount with this book, no CC, past Mulgrave Street to 2 Mulgrave Terrace, tel. 01/280-6404, e-mail: lynden@iol.ie, Maria Gavin).

Innisfree B&B has a fine lounge and six big, bright, and comfy rooms (D-€48, Db-€52, 10 percent discount with this book, CC, from George Street hike up the plain but quiet Northumberland Avenue to #31, tel. 01/280-5598, fax 01/280-3093, e-mail: djsmyth@club1.ie, Brendan and Mary Smyth).

On the same street, you'll find two places renting four big, well-worn rooms each: **Mrs. Howard's B&B** (S-€34, Sb-€38, D-€52, Db-€58, no CC, TV lounge, 36 Northumberland Avenue, tel. 01/280-3262) and **Mrs. O'Sullivan's Duncree B&B** (D-€52, Db-€58, no CC, family room, no smoking, 16 Northumberland Ave, tel. 01/280-6118).

Eating in Dun Laoghaire

If you're staying in Dun Laoghaire, I'd definitely eat here and not in Dublin. Glasthule (called simply "the village" locally, just down the street from the Sandycove DART station) has a stunning array of fun, little, hardworking restaurants.

Bistro Vino is the rage lately, with cozy, candlelit, Mediterranean ambience and great food (€12–21 meals, daily 17:00–23:00, nightly €17 early-bird special 17:00–19:00, seafood, pasta, CC, arrive early or have a reservation, 56 Glasthule Road, tel. 01/280-6097).

Duzy's Café fills a classy but garishly painted modern-feeling old room above the Eagle House Pub with happy eaters and French-Irish cuisine. The menu is a joy and their €18.50 early-bird special—three courses with coffee on weeknights until 19:00—is a super value (€19–23 plates, nightly from 18:00, CC, 18 Glasthule Road, tel. 01/230-0210, run by John Dunne and Stephane Couzy).

The big **Eagle House** pub serves hearty €9 pub meals (until 21:00) in a wonderful but smoky atmosphere. This is a great local joint for a late drink. The nearby **Daniel's Restaurant**

and Wine Bar is less atmospheric but also good (€19 meals, closed Mon, 34 Glasthule Road, tel. 01/284-1027).

South Bank Restaurant, a jolly place filled with happy piano music, faces the water and serves fish and European cuisine (€19 main courses, nightly except Mon in winter, 1 Martello Terrace, directly down from Sandycove DART station, reservations smart, tel. 01/280-8788).

Walters Public House and Restaurant is a bright, modern place above a similar pub, offering good food to a dressy crowd (nightly 17:30–23:00, €13–21 meals, 68 Upper George's Street, tel. 01/280-7442).

George's Street, three blocks inland and Dun Laoghaire's main drag, has plenty of eateries and pubs, many with live music. A good bet for families is the kid-friendly **Bits and Pizza** (daily 12:00–24:00, off George's Street at 15 Patrick Street, tel. 01/284-2411).

Eating in Dublin

As Dublin does its boom-time jig, fine and creative eateries are popping up all over town. While you can get decent pub grub for €10 on just about any corner, consider saving pub grub for the countryside. And there's no pressing reason to eat Irish in cosmopolitan Dublin. Dublin's good restaurants are packed from 20:00 on, especially on weekends. Eating early (18:00–19:00) saves time and money (as many better places offer an early-bird special).

Eating Quick and Easy around Grafton Street

Cornucopia is a small, earth-mama-with-class, proudly vegetarian, self-serve place two blocks off Grafton. It's friendly and youthful, with hearty €8 lunches and €9.50 dinner specials (Mon–Sat 8:30–20:00, Sun 12:00–18:00, 19 Wicklow Street, tel. 01/677-7583).

O'Neill's offers dependable €9 carvery lunches in a labyrinth of a pub with a handy location across from the main TI (daily 12:00–15:30, Suffolk Street, tel. 01/679-3656).

Graham O'Sullivan Restaurant and Coffee Shop is a cheap, cheery cafeteria serving soup and sandwiches with a salad bar in unpretentious ambience (Mon–Fri 8:00–18:30, Sat 9:00–17:00, closed Sun, smoke-free upstairs, 12 Duke Street). Two pubs on the same street—**The Duke** and **Davy Burns**—serve pub lunches. (The nearby Cathach Rare Books shop at 10 Duke Street displays a rare edition of *Ulysses* among other treasures in its window).

Bewley's Café is an old-time local favorite offering light meals from €6 and full meals from €10. Sit on the ground floor among Harry Clarke windows and Art Deco lamps or upstairs in the bright atrium decorated by local art students (self-service daily 7:30–23:00, CC, 78 Grafton Street, tel. 01/635-5470).

Dublin Restaurants

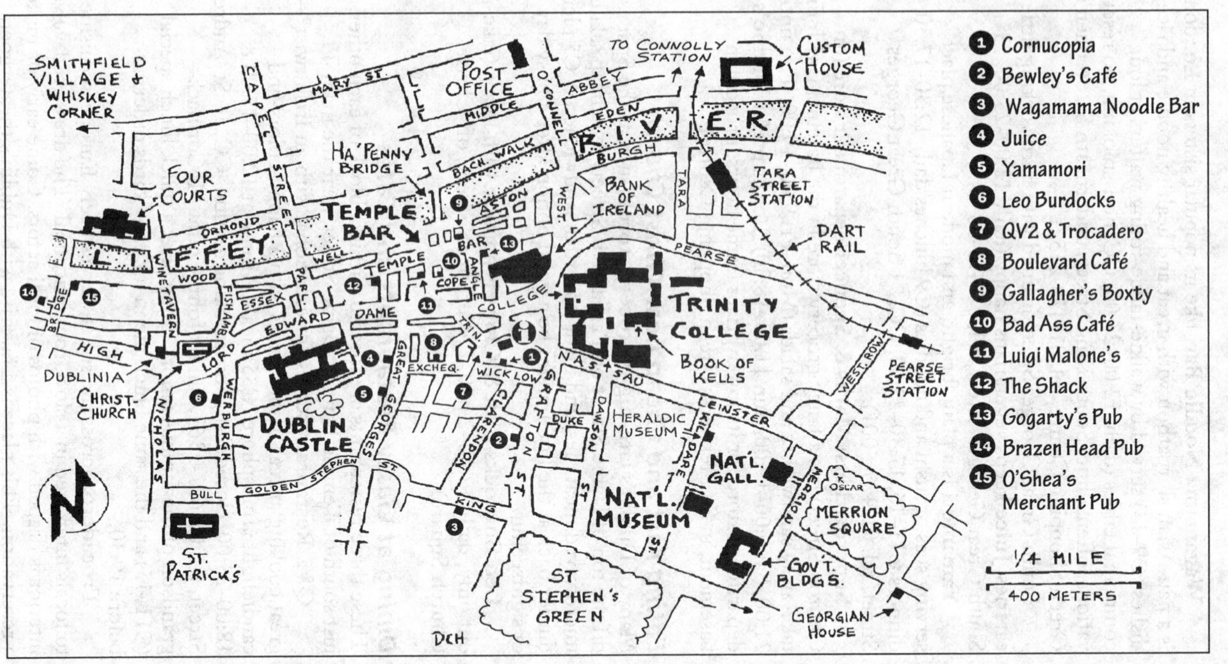

Wagamama Noodle Bar, like its popular sisters in London, is a pan-Asian slurpathon with great and healthy noodle and rice dishes (€9–13) served by walkie-talkie-toting waiters at long communal tables (daily 12:00–23:00, CC, non-smoking, no reservations, often a line, South King Street, underneath St. Stephen's Green Shopping Centre, tel. 01/478-2152).

South Great Georges Street is lined with hardworking little eateries. **Juice** keeps vegetarians happy (daily 12:00–23:00, 73 South Great Georges Street, tel. 01/475-7856).

Yamamori is a plain, bright, and modern Japanese place serving seas of sushi and noodles (€9 lunches daily 12:30–17:30, dinners €11–16, 17:30–23:00, CC, 71 South Great Georges Street, tel. 01/475-5001).

Supermarkets: Marks & Spencer department store (on Grafton Street) has a fancy grocery store in the basement with fine take-away sandwiches and salads (Mon–Fri 9:00–19:00, Thu until 21:00, Sat 9:00–19:00, Sun 11:00–18:30). Locals prefer **Dunne's** department store for its lower prices (same hours, grocery in basement, in St. Stephen's Green Shopping Centre).

Eating Fast and Cheap near Christ Church

Many of Dublin's **late-night grocery stores** (such as the Spar off the top of Dame Street on Parliament Street) sell cheap salads, microwaved meat pies, and made-to-order sandwiches. A €5 picnic dinner back at the hotel might be a good option after a busy day of sightseeing.

Leo Burdocks Fish & Chips is popular with locals (take-out only, daily 12:00–24:00, 2 Werburgh Street, off Christ Church Square).

Dining at Classy Restaurants and Cafés

These three restaurants are located within a block of each other, just south of Temple Bar and Dame Street, near the main TI.

QV2 Restaurant serves "international with an Irish twist"—great cooking at reasonable prices with a happy-colors-and-candlelight atmosphere (€35 meals, Mon–Sat 12:00–15:00 & 18:00–23:00, closed Sun, non-smoking section, CC, 14 St. Andrew Street, tel. 01/677-3363, run by John Count McCormack—grandson of the famous tenor). They offer a quick lunch special (€11–15) and the same lunch menu for early birds ordering before 19:30.

Trocadero, across the street, serves beefy European cuisine to locals interested in a slow, romantic meal. The dressy red-velvet interior is draped with photos of local actors. Come early or make a reservation. This place is a favorite with Dublin's theatergoers

(€26 meals, Mon–Sat 17:00–24:00, closed Sun, non-smoking section, CC, 3 St. Andrew Street, tel. 01/677-5545). The three-course early-bird special at €18 is a fine value (17:00–19:00, leave by 20:00).

Boulevard Café is a mod, local, likeable, trendy place serving Mediterranean cuisine, heavy on the Italian. They serve salads, pasta, and sandwiches for around €7, three-course lunch specials for €11.50 (Mon–Sat 12:00–16:00), and dinner plates for €13–15.50 (daily 17:30–24:00, CC, 27 Exchequer Street, smart to reserve for dinner, tel. 01/679-2131).

Eating at Temple Bar

Gallagher's Boxty House is touristy and traditional, a good, basic value with creaky floorboards and old Dublin ambience. Its specialty is boxties—the generally bland-tasting Irish potato pancake filled and rolled with various meats, veggies, and sauces. The "Gaelic Boxty" is liveliest (€13–15, also serves stews and corned beef, daily 12:00–23:30, non-smoking section, CC, 20 Temple Bar, tel. 01/677-2762). Popular Gallagher's takes same-day reservations only; to reserve for dinner, stop by between 12:00 and 15:00.

Bad Ass Café is a grunge diner serving cowboy/Mex/veggie/pizzas to old and new hippies. No need to dress up (€6.50 lunch and €16.50 3-course dinner deals, kids' specials, daily 11:30–24:00, CC, Crown Alley, just off Meeting House Square, tel. 01/671-2596).

Luigi Malone's, with its fun atmosphere and varied menu of pizza, ribs, pasta, sandwiches, and fajitas, is just the place to take your high school date (€10–20, daily 12:00–23:00, CC, corner of Cecila and Fownes Streets, tel. 01/679-2723).

The Shack, while a bit pricey and touristy, has a reputation for good quality and serves traditional Irish, chicken, seafood, and steak dishes (€15–26 entrées, CC, daily 11:00–23:00, across from Dublin Castle on Dame Street, tel. 01/670-9785). A second location is in the center of Temple Bar (24 East Essex Street, tel. 01/679-0043).

Transportation Connections—Dublin

By bus to: Belfast (7/day, 3 hrs), **Trim** (10/day, 1 hr), **Ennis** (11/day, 4.5 hrs), **Galway** (15/day, 3.5 hrs), **Limerick** (13/day, 3.5 hrs), **Tralee** (6/day, 6 hrs), **Dingle** (4/day, 8 hrs, €21.50, transfer at Tralee). Bus info: tel. 01/836-6111.

By train from Heuston Station to: Tralee (6/day, 4 hrs, talking timetable tel. 01/805-4266), **Ennis** (2/day, 4 hrs), **Galway** (5/day, 3 hrs, talking timetable tel. 01/805-4222).

By train from Connolly Station to: Rosslare (3/day, 3 hrs), **Portrush** (6/day, 5 hrs, €34 one-way, €47 round-trip, transfer in Belfast or Portadown), **Belfast** (8/day, 2 hrs, talking timetable tel. 01/836-3333). The **Dublin–Belfast train** connects the two Irish capitals in two hours at 90 mph on one continuous, welded rail (€29 one-way, €43 round-trip; round-trip the same day only €29 except Fri and Sun; from the border to Belfast one-way €18, €25 round-trip). Train info: tel. 01/836-6222. North Ireland train info: tel. 048/9089-9400.

Dublin Airport: The airport is well connected to the city center seven miles away (airport info: tel. 01/814-1111; also see "Arrival in Dublin," above). For list of airlines, see below.

Transportation Connections—Ireland and Britain

Dublin and London: The journey by boat plus train or bus takes 7–12 hours, all day, or all night (bus: 4/day, €25–42, British tel. 08705-143-219, www.eurolines.co.uk; train: 4/day, €61–118, Dublin train info: tel. 01/836-6222).

If you're going directly to London, flying is your best bet. Check **Ryanair** first (€82 round-trip, 90 min, Irish tel. 01/609-7878, www.ryanair.com). Other options include **British Airways** (Irish tel. 01/814-5201 or toll-free tel. in Ireland 1-800-626-747, in U.S. 800/247-9297, www.britishairways.com), **Aer Lingus** (tel. 01/886-8888, www.aerlingus.ie), and **bmi british midland** (Irish tel. 01/407-3036, U.S. tel. 800/788-0555, www.flybmi.com). To get the lowest fares, ask about round-trip ticket prices and book months in advance (though Ryanair offers deals nearly all of the time).

Dublin and Holyhead: Irish Ferries sails between Dublin and Holyhead in North Wales (dock is a mile east of O'Connell Bridge, 5/day: 2 slow, 3 fast; slow boats: 3.25 hrs, €30 one-way walk-on fare; fast boats: 1.75 hrs, €40; Dublin tel. 01/638-3333, Holyhead tel. 08705-329-129, www.irishferries.com).

Dublin and Liverpool: Norse Merchant Ferries sails most mornings (Tue–Sat) and every evening year-round from Dublin Harbor (8 hrs, €35–40 one-way by day, €40–45 one-way overnight, cabins €55–65 extra, car transport €120 for day crossing or €180 by night crossing, Dublin tel. 01/819-2999, British tel. 0870-800-4321, www.norsemerchant.com).

Dun Laoghaire and Holyhead: Stena Line sails between Dun Laoghaire (near Dublin) and Holyhead in North Wales (3/day, 2 hrs on HSS *Catamaran*, €36–42 one-way walk-on fare, €4 extra if paying with CC, reserve by phone—they book up long in advance on summer weekends, Dun Laoghaire tel. 01/204-7777, recorded info tel. 01/204-7799, can book online at www.stenaline.ie).

Ferry Connections—Ireland and France

Irish Ferries connect Ireland (Rosslare) with France (Cherbourg and Roscoff) every other day (less Jan–March). While Cherbourg has the quickest connection to Paris, your overall time between Ireland and Paris is about the same (20–25 hrs) regardless of which port is used on the day you sail. One-way fares vary from €60 to €120. Eurailers go half-price. In both directions, departures are generally between 16:00 and 20:00 and arrive late the next morning. While passengers can nearly always get on, reservations are wise in summer and easy by phone. If you anticipate a crowded departure, you can reserve a seat for €10. Doubles (or singles) start at €50. The easiest way to get a bed (except during summer) is from the information desk upon boarding. The cafeteria serves bad food at reasonable prices. Upon arrival in France, buses and taxis connect you to your Paris-bound train (Irish Ferries: Dublin tel. 01/661-0511, recorded info tel. 01/661-0715, Paris tel. 01 44 94 20 40, www.irishferries.com, e-mail: info@irishferries.com, European Ferry Guide: www.youra.com/ferry/intlferries.html).

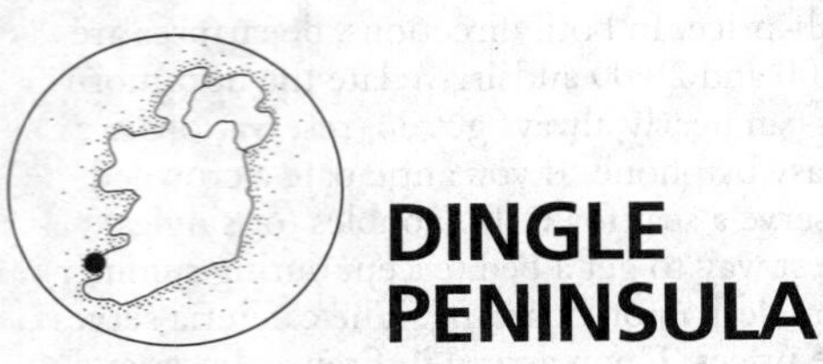

DINGLE PENINSULA

Dingle Peninsula, the westernmost tip of Ireland, offers just the right mix of far-and-away beauty, ancient archaeological wonders, and isolated walks or bike rides—all within convenient reach of its main town. Dingle town is just large enough to have all the necessary tourist services and a steady nocturnal beat of Irish folk music.

While the big tour buses clog the neighboring Ring of Kerry before heading east to slobber all over the Blarney Stone, Dingle—although crowded in summer—still feels like the fish and the farm really matter. Forty fishing boats sail from Dingle, tractor tracks dirty its main drag, and a faint whiff of peat fills its nighttime streets.

For 20 years, my Irish dreams have been set here on this sparse but lush peninsula where locals are fond of saying, "The next parish is Boston." There's a feeling of closeness to the land on Dingle. When I asked a local if he was born here, he thought for a second and said, "No, it was about six miles down the road." When I told him where I was from, a faraway smile filled his eyes, and he looked out to sea and sighed, "Ah, the shores of Americay." I asked his friend if he'd lived here all his life. He said, "Not yet."

Dingle feels so traditionally Irish because it's a Gaeltacht, a region where the government subsidizes the survival of the Irish language and culture. While English is always there, the signs, menus, and songs come in Gaelic. Children carry hurling sticks to class, and even the local preschool brags "ALL Gaelic."

Of the peninsula's 10,000 residents, 1,500 live in Dingle town. Its few streets, lined with ramshackle but gaily painted shops and pubs, run up from a rain-stung harbor always busy with fishing boats and yachts. Traditionally, the buildings were drab gray or whitewashed. Thirty years ago Ireland's "tidy town" competition prompted everyone to paint their buildings in playful pastels.

Dingle Peninsula Sights

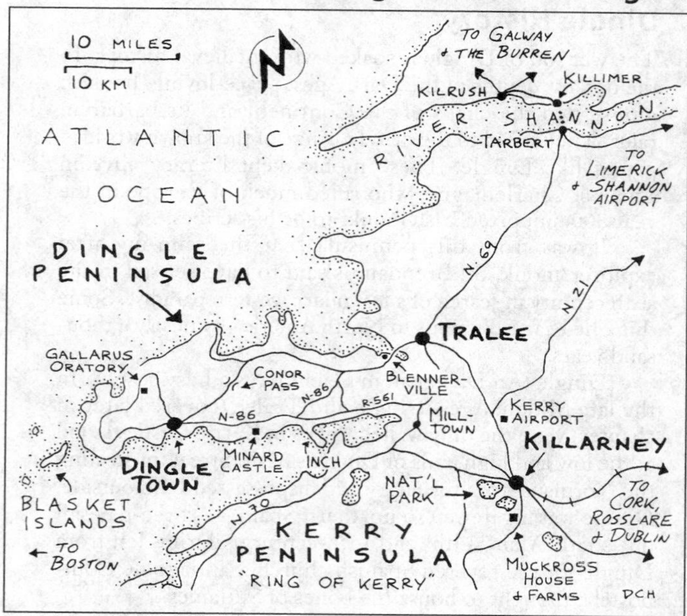

It's a peaceful town. The courthouse (1832) is open one hour a month. The judge does his best to wrap up business within a half hour. During the day you'll see teenagers—already working on ruddy beer-glow cheeks—roll kegs up the streets and into the pubs in preparation for another night of music and *craic* (fun conversation and atmosphere).

Planning Your Time

For the shortest visit, give Dingle two nights and a day. It takes 6–8 hours to get there from Dublin, Galway, or the boat dock in Rosslare. I like two nights because you feel more like a local on your second evening in the pubs. You'll need the better part of a day to explore the 30-mile loop around the peninsula by bike, car, or tour bus (see "Circular Tour" on page 764). To do any serious walking or relaxing, you'll need two or three days. It's not uncommon to find Americans slowing way, way down in Dingle town.

Orientation (area code: 066)

Dingle—extremely comfortable on foot—hangs on a medieval grid of streets between the harborfront (where the Tralee bus stops)

Dingle History

The wet sod of Dingle is soaked with medieval history. In the darkest depths of the Dark Ages, peace-loving, bookish monks fled the chaos of the Continent and its barbarian raids. They sailed to the drizzly fringe of the known world—places like Dingle. These monks kept literacy alive in Europe. Charlemagne, who ruled much of Europe in the year 800, imported Irish monks to be his scribes.

It was from this peninsula that the semi-mythical explorer/monk, St. Brendan, is said to have set sail in the sixth century in search of a legendary western paradise. Some think he beat Columbus to North America by nearly a thousand years.

Dingle (An Daingean in Gaelic) was a busy seaport in the late Middle Ages. Dingle and Tralee (covered later in chapter) were the only walled towns in Kerry. Castles stood at the low and high ends of Dingle's Main Street, protecting the Normans from the angry and dispossessed Irish outside. Dingle was a gateway to northern Spain—a three-day sail due south. Many 14th- and 15th-century pilgrims left from Dingle for the revered Spanish church, Santiago de Compostela, thought to house the bones of St. James.

In Dingle's medieval heyday, locals traded cowhides for wine. When Dingle's position as a trading center waned, the town faded in importance. In the 19th century it was a linen-weaving center. Until 1970 fishing dominated, and the only visitors were scholars and students of old Irish ways. In 1970 the movie *Ryan's Daughter* introduced the world to Dingle. The trickle of Dingle fans has grown to a flood as word of its musical, historical, gastronomical, and scenic charms—not to mention its friendly dolphin—has spread.

and Main Street (3 blocks inland). Nothing in town is more than a five-minute walk away. Street numbers are used only when more than one place is run by a family of the same name. Most locals know most locals, and people on the street are fine sources of information. Remember, locals love their soda bread, and tourism provides the butter. You'll find a warm and sincere welcome.

Tourist Information: The TI is a privately owned, for-profit business—little more than a glorified shop with a green staff who are disinclined to really know the town (July–Aug daily 9:00–19:00, June & Sept–Oct 9:30–17:30, Nov–May 10:00–17:00, closed Sun & Tue;

on Strand Street by the water, tel. 066/915-1188). For more knowledgeable help, drop by the Mountain Man shop (on Strand Street, see "Dingle Activities," below) or talk to your B&B host.

Helpful Hints

Before You Go: The local Web site (www.dingle-peninsula.ie) lists festivals and events. And www.celticwave.com is a good bet for music and arts listings. Look up old issues of *National Geographic* (April 1976 and Sept 1994).

Crowds: Crowds trample Dingle's charm throughout July and August. The absolute craziest are the Dingle Races (2nd weekend in Aug), Dingle Regatta (3rd weekend in Aug), and the Blessing of the Boats (end of Aug, beginning of Sept). The first Mondays in May, June, and August are bank holidays, giving Ireland's workers three-day weekends—and ample time to fill up Dingle. The town's metabolism (prices, schedules, activities) rises and falls with the tourist crowds—October through April is sleepy.

Banking: Two banks in town, both on Main Street, offer the same rates (Mon 10:00–17:00, Tue–Fri 10:00–16:00, closed Sat–Sun) and have cash machines. The TI happily changes cash and traveler's checks at mediocre rates. Expect to use cash (rather than credit cards) to pay for most peninsula activities.

Post Office: It's on Main Street near Benners Hotel (Mon–Fri 9:00–17:30, Sat 9:00–13:00, closed Sun).

Laundry: The launderette is full-service only—drop off a load before 10:00 and pick up late that afternoon (tiny load-€7, regular load-€10, Mon–Sat 9:00–17:30, closed Sun; Nov–April open only Mon, Wed, Fri 9:00–17:00, on Green Street down alley opposite church, tel. 066/915-1837).

Internet Access: Dingle Internet Café is on Main Street (€2.60/20 min, Apr–Sept Mon–Fri 10:00–19:00, Sat 10:00–18:00, Sun 13:00–18:00, shorter hours Oct–March, tel. 066/915-2478).

Bike Rental: Bike-rental shops abound. The best is Paddy's Bike Hire (€10/day or 24 hrs, €12 for better bikes, daily 9:00–19:00, helmets €1 extra, on Dykegate next to Grapevine Hostel, tel. 066/915-2311). Foxy John's (Main Street), Mountain Man (no helmets), and the Ballintaggert Hostel also rent bikes. If you're biking the peninsula, get a bike with skinny street tires, not slow and fat mountain-bike tires. Plan on leaving a credit card, driver's license, or passport as a security deposit.

Dingle Activities: The Mountain Man, a hiking shop run by a local guide, Mike Shea, is a clearinghouse for information, local tours, and excursions (July–Sept daily 9:00–21:00, Oct–June 9:00–18:00, just off harbor at Strand Street, tel. 066/915-2400, e-mail: irasc@eircom.net). Stop by for ideas on biking, hiking, horseback

The Voyage of St. Brendan

It has long been part of Irish lore that St. Brendan the Navigator (A.D. 484–577) and 12 followers sailed from the southwest of Ireland to the "Land of Promise" (what is now North America) in a currach—a wood-frame boat covered with ox hide and tar. According to a 10th-century monk who poetically wrote of the journey, St. Brendan and his crew encountered a paradise of birds, were attacked by a whale, and suffered the smoke of a smelly island in the north before finally reaching their Land of Promise.

The legend and its precisely described locations still fascinate modern readers. A British scholar of navigation, Tim Severin, re-created the entire journey from 1976 to 1977. He and his crew set out from Brendan Creek in County Kerry in a currach. The prevailing winds blew them to the Hebrides, the Faeroe Islands, Iceland, and finally to Newfoundland. While this didn't successfully prove that St. Brendan sailed to North America, it did prove that he could have.

St. Brendan fans have been heartened by an intriguing archaeological find in Connecticut. Called the "Gungywamp," the site includes a double circle of stones and a beehive-like chamber built in the same manner as the stone *clochans* huts on the Dingle Peninsula. The Gungywamp beehive chamber has been carbon-dated to approximately A.D. 600. Outside the chamber, a stone slab is inscribed with a cross that resembles the unique style of the Irish cross.

According to his 10th-century biographer, "St. Brendan sailed from the Land of Promise home to Ireland. And from that time on, Brendan acted as if he did not belong to this world at all. His mind and his joy were in the delight of heaven."

riding, climbing, peninsula tours, and trips to the Blaskets. They are the Dingle town contact for the Dunquin–Blasket Islands boats and shuttle-bus rides to the harbor (see "Blasket Islands," below).

Travel Agency: Maurice O'Connor at Galvin's Travel Agency can book train, long-distance bus, and plane tickets, and boat rides to France (Mon–Fri 9:30–18:00, Sat 9:30–17:00, closed Sun, John Street, tel. 066/915-1409).

Farmers Market: Every Saturday (10:00–14:00), local farmers fill the St. James churchyard (on Main Street) with their fresh produce and homemade marmalade.

Dingle Hotels and Services

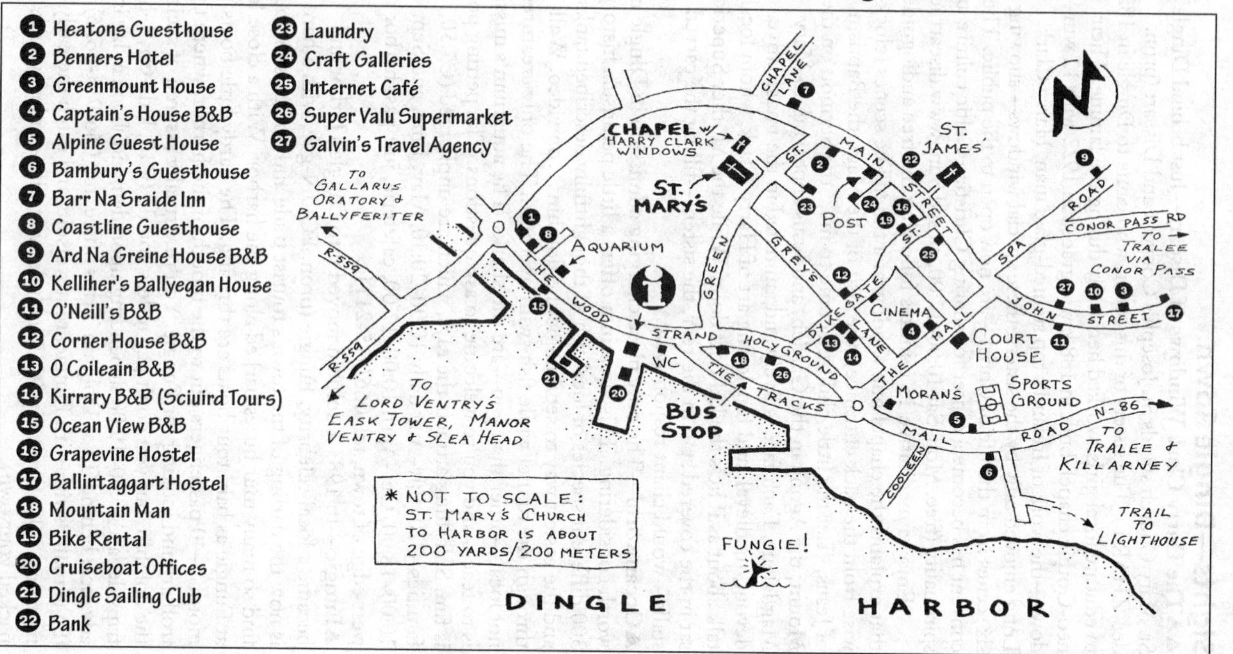
1 Heatons Guesthouse
2 Benners Hotel
3 Greenmount House
4 Captain's House B&B
5 Alpine Guest House
6 Bambury's Guesthouse
7 Barr Na Sraide Inn
8 Coastline Guesthouse
9 Ard Na Greine House B&B
10 Kelliher's Ballyegan House
11 O'Neill's B&B
12 Corner House B&B
13 O Coileain B&B
14 Kirrary B&B (Sciuird Tours)
15 Ocean View B&B
16 Grapevine Hostel
17 Ballintaggart Hostel
18 Mountain Man
19 Bike Rental
20 Cruiseboat Offices
21 Dingle Sailing Club
22 Bank
23 Laundry
24 Craft Galleries
25 Internet Café
26 Super Valu Supermarket
27 Galvin's Travel Agency
TO GALLARUS ORATORY & BALLYFERITER
R-559
TO LORD VENTRY'S EASK TOWER, MANOR VENTRY & SLEA HEAD
CHAPEL LANE
CHAPEL W/ HARRY CLARK WINDOWS
ST. MARY'S
AQUARIUM
THE WOOD
STRAND
WC
BUS STOP
GREEN
GREY'S
MAIN STREET
ST.
POST
ST. JAMES'
DYKE GATE LANE
CINEMA
THE MALL
HOLY GROUND
THE TRACKS
COURT HOUSE
SPA ROAD
CONOR PASS RD
TO TRALEE VIA CONOR PASS
JOHN STREET
MORAN'S
SPORTS GROUND
MAIL ROAD
N-86
TO TRALEE & KILLARNEY
COOLEEN
TRAIL TO LIGHTHOUSE
* NOT TO SCALE: ST. MARY'S CHURCH TO HARBOR IS ABOUT 200 YARDS/200 METERS
FUNGIE!
DINGLE HARBOR

Sights—Dingle Town

▲▲The Harry Clark Windows of Diseart—Just behind Dingle's St. Mary Church stands St. Joseph's Convent and Diseart (pron. dee-ZHART). The sisters of this order, who came to Dingle in 1829 to educate local girls, worked heroically during the famine. Their neo-Gothic chapel, built in 1884, was graced in 1922 with 12 windows—the work of Ireland's top stained-glass man, Harry Clark. Long enjoyed only by the sisters, these special windows—showing six scenes from the life of Christ—are now open to the public. The convent has become a center for sharing Christian Celtic culture and spirituality (free, Mon–Sat 10:00–17:00, closed Sun, www.diseart.ie).

Enjoy a meditative 15 minutes following the free audioguide that explains the chapel one window at a time. The scenes (clockwise from the back entrance): the visit of the Magi, the Baptism of Jesus, "Let the little children come to me," the Sermon on the Mount, the Agony in the Garden, and Jesus appearing to Mary Magdalene. Each face is lively and animated in the imaginative, devout, medieval, and fun-loving art of Harry Clark, whom locals talk about as if he's the kid next door. While the Mother Superior sat in the covered stall in the rear, the sisters—filling the carved stalls—would chant responsively.

▲Oceanworld—The only place charging admission in Dingle is worth considering. This aquarium offers a little peninsula history, 300 different species of local fish in thoughtfully described tanks, and the easiest way to see Fungie the dolphin . . . on video. Walk through the tunnel while fish swim overhead. The only creatures not local—other than you—are the sharks. The aquarium's mission is to teach, and you're welcome to ask questions. The petting pool is fun. Splashing attracts the rays, which are unplugged (€7.50, families-€20, July–Aug daily 10:00–20:30, May, June, and Sept 10:00–18:00, Oct–April 10:00–17:00, cafeteria, just past harbor on west edge of town, tel. 066/915-2111).

▲Fungie—In 1983 a dolphin moved into Dingle Harbor and became a local celebrity. Fungie (pron. FOON-gee, with a hard *g*) is now the darling of the town's tourist trade and one reason you'll find so many tour buses parked along the harbor. With a close look at Fungie as bait, tour boats are thriving. The hardy little boats motor 7–40 passengers out to the mouth of the harbor, where they troll around looking for Fungie. You're virtually assured of seeing the dolphin, but you don't pay unless you do (€10, kids-€5, 1-hour trips depart 10:00–19:00 depending upon demand, book a day in advance, behind TI at Dolphin Trips office, tel. 066/915-2626). To actually swim with Fungie, rent wetsuits and catch the early-morning 8:00–10:00 trip (€35 includes wetsuits—unless you've packed your own).

Dingle Area

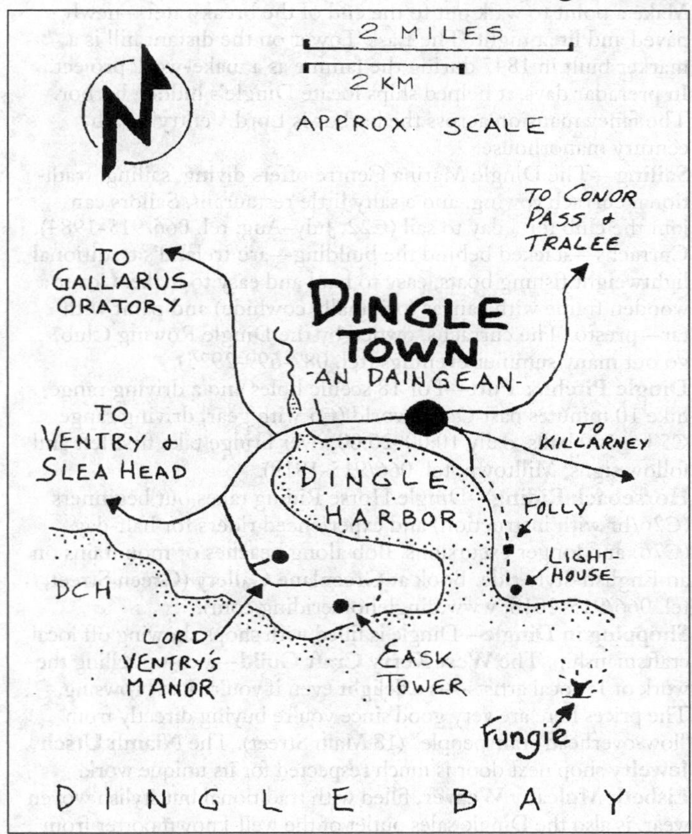

▲**Short Harbor Walk from Dingle**—For an easy stroll along the harbor out of town (and a chance to see Fungie, 90 min round-trip), head east from the roundabout past the Esso station. Just after Bambury's B&B, take a right, following signs to Skelligs Hotel. At the beach, climb the steps over the wall and follow the seashore path to the mouth of Dingle Harbor (marked by a tower—some 19th-century fat cat's folly). Ten minutes beyond that is a lighthouse. This is Fungie's neighborhood. If you see tourist boats out, you're likely to see the dolphin. The trail continues to a dramatic cliff.

The Harbor: The harbor was built on land reclaimed (with imported Dutch expertise) in 1992. The string of old stone shops facing the harbor was the loading station for the narrow-gauge railway that hauled the fish from Dingle to Tralee (1891–1953). Make a point to walk out to the end of the breakwater—newly paved and lit at night. The Eask Tower on the distant hill is a marker built in 1847 during the famine as a make-work project. In preradar days, it helped ships locate Dingle's hidden harbor. The fancy mansion across the harbor is Lord Ventry's 17th-century manorhouse.

Sailing—The Dingle Marina Centre offers diving, sailing, traditional currach rowing, and a salty little restaurant. Sailors can join the club for a day to sail (€22, July–Aug, tel. 066/915-1984). Currachs—stacked behind the building—are Ireland's traditional lightweight fishing boats, easy to haul and easy to make. Cover a wooden frame with canvas (originally cowhide) and paint with tar—presto. The currachs, owned by the Dingle Rowing Club, go out many summer evenings (tel. 087-699-2925).

Dingle Pitch & Putt—For 18 scenic holes and a driving range, hike 10 minutes past Oceanworld (€5 with gear, driving range €5 for 100 balls, daily 10:00–20:00, over bridge take first left and follow signs, Milltown, tel. 066/915-1819).

Horseback Riding—Dingle Horse Riding takes out beginners (€26/hr with instruction) and experienced riders for half-day (€76) and longer excursions. Bob along beaches or mountains on an English-style ride. Book at Greenlane Gallery (Green Street, tel. 066/915-2018, www.dinglehorseriding.com).

Shopping in Dingle—Dingle is filled with shops showing off local craftsmanship. The **West Kerry Craft Guild**—a co-op selling the work of 15 local artists—is a delight even if you're just browsing. The prices here are very good since you're buying directly from "low-overhead craftspeople" (18 Main Street). The **Niamh Utsch Jewelry** shop next door is much respected for its unique work. **Lisbeth Mulcahy Weaver,** filled with traditional but stylish woven wear, is also the Dingle sales outlet of the well-known potter from out on Slea Head (Green Street, tel. 066/915-1688).

Nightlife in Dingle Town

▲▲▲Folk Music in Dingle Pubs—Even if you're not into pubs, take a nap and then give these a whirl. Dingle is renowned among traditional musicians as a place to get work ("€40 a day, tax-free, plus drink"). The town has piles of pubs. There's music every night and rarely a cover charge. The scene is a decent mix of locals, Americans, and Germans. Music normally starts around 21:30, and the last call for drinks is "half eleven" (23:30), sometimes later on weekends. For a seat near the music, arrive early. If the place is chockablock, power in and find breathing room in the back. By midnight the door is usually closed and the chairs are stacked. For more information on traditional Irish music, check the fine local-music Web site, www.celticwave.com.

While two pubs, the Small Bridge Bar (An Droighead Beag) and O'Flaherty's, are the most famous for their good beer and folk music, make a point to wander the town and follow your ear. Smaller pubs may feel a bit foreboding to a tourist, but people—locals as well as travelers—are out for the *craic*. Irish culture is very accessible in the pubs; they're like highly interactive museums waiting to be explored. But if you sit at a table, you'll be left alone. Stand or sit at the bar and you'll be engulfed in conversation with new friends. Have a glass in an empty, no-name pub and chat up the publican. Pubs are smoky and hot (leave your coat home). The more offbeat pubs are more likely to erupt into leprechaun karaoke.

Pub crawl: The best pub crawl is along Strand Street to O'Flaherty's. Murphy's is lively, offering rock as well as ballads and traditional music. O'Flaherty's has a high ceiling and less smoke, and is dripping in old-time photos and town memorabilia—it's touristy but lots of fun, with nightly music in the summer.

Then head up Green Street. Dick Mack, across from the church, is nicknamed "the last pew." This is a tiny leather shop by day, expanding into a pub at night, with several rooms, a fine snug (private booth, originally designed to allow women to drink discreetly), reliably good beer, and a smoky and strangely fascinating ambience. Notice the Hollywood-type stars on the sidewalk recalling famous visitors. Established in 1899, the grandson of the original Dick Mack now runs the place. A painting in the window shows Dick Mack II with the local gang.

Green Street climbs to Main Street where two more Dick Mack–type places are filled with smoke and locals deep in conversation (but no music): Foxy John's (a hardware shop by day) and O Currain's (across the street, a small clothing shop by day).

A bit higher up Main Street is McCarthy's Pub, a smoke-stained relic. It's less touristy and has some fine traditional music sessions and occasional plays on its little stage. Wander downhill to the Small Bridge Bar at the bottom. With live music nightly, it's popular for good reason. While the tourists gather around the music, poke around the back, which leads to a nook actually closest to the musicians. Finally, head up Spa Road a few doors to An Conair—a.k.a. John Benny's, a clean, modern pub that offers good music and is often less crowded than the others. Farther up Spa Road, the big hotel has late-night dancing (see below).

Off-season: From October through April, the bands play on, though at fewer pubs: Small Bridge Bar (live music nightly), An Conair (Mon, Wed, Thu), McCarthy's (Fri, Sat), and Murphy's (Sat).

Music shops: Danlann Gallery sells musical instruments and woodcrafts (Mon–Fri 10:00–18:00, later in summer, "flexible" on weekends, CC, owner makes violins, Dykegate Street). Siopa an Phiobaire, exclusively a music shop, sells traditional wind instruments (Mon–Fri 10:00-17:00, closed Sat–Sun, CC, Craft Centre, on edge of town a few minutes' walk past Oceanworld, tel. 066/915-1778). Dingle Bodhrans sells homemade traditional goatskin drums and gives lessons (1-hour lesson-€25.50–51, rates are on "sliding scale," Mon–Sat 10:30–18:00, closed Sun, Green Street, enter red iron gate of small alley opposite church, tel. 087-245-7689, Andrea).
Folk concerts—Top local musicians offer a quality evening of live, acoustic, classic Irish music in the fine little St. James Church on Main Street (€10, Mon and Thu at 19:30, June–Aug only, see sign on church gate or drop by Murphy's Ice Cream for details).
Dancing—Some pubs host "set dancing" with live music (An Conair on Mon at 21:30, Small Bridge Bar on Thu). Hillgrove Hotel, up Spa Road a few hundred yards, is a modern hotel with traditional dances every Thursday at 23:00 and pop dancing other nights in summer. Locals say the Hillgrove "is a good time if you're pissed."
Theater—Dingle's great little theater is The Phoenix on Dykegate. Its film club (50–60 locals) meets here Tuesdays year-round at 20:30 for coffee and cookies, followed by a film at 21:00 (€6 for film, anyone is welcome). The leader runs it almost like a religion, with a sermon on the film before he rolls it. The regular film schedule for the week is posted on the door.

Sleeping in Dingle Town

(€1 = about $1, country code: 353, area code: 066, mail: Dingle, County Kerry)

Sleep Code: **S** = Single, **D** = Double/Twin, **T** = Triple, **Q** = Quad, **b** = bathroom, **s** = shower only, **CC** = Credit Cards accepted, **no CC** = Credit Cards not accepted. Prices vary with the season, with winter cheap and August tops.

To help you easily sort through these listings, I've divided the rooms into three categories, based on the price for a standard double room with bath:

Higher Priced—Most rooms more than €100.
Moderately Priced—Most rooms under €100.
Lower Priced—Most rooms €60 or less.

HIGHER PRICED

Heatons Guesthouse, big, peaceful, and American in its comforts, is on the water just west of town at the end of Dingle Bay—a five-minute walk past Oceanworld on The Wood. The 16 thoughtfully appointed rooms come with all the amenities (Db-€76–118, suite Db-€125–165, CC, creative breakfasts, parking, The Wood, tel. 066/915-2288, fax 066/915-2324, www.heatonsdingle.com, e-mail: heatons@iol.ie, Cameron and Nuala Heaton).

Benners Hotel was the only place in town a hundred years ago. It stands bewildered by the modern world on Main Street, with sprawling public spaces and 52 abundant, overpriced rooms—only its non-smoking rooms smell fresh (Db-€196 July–Aug, €154 May–June, €140 Sept–May, kids under 7-€19 extra, CC, tel. 066/915-1638, fax 066/915-1412, e-mail: benners@eircom.net).

MODERATELY PRICED

Greenmount House sits among chilly palm trees in the countryside at the top of town. A five-minute hike up from the town center, this guest house commands a fine view of the bay and mountains. John and Mary Curran run one of Ireland's best B&Bs, with five superb rooms (Db-€75–90—top price through the summer) and seven sprawling suites (Db-€100–130) in a modern building with lavish public areas and breakfast in a solarium (CC, reserve in advance, no children under 8, most rooms at ground level, parking, top of John Street, tel. 066/915-1414, fax 066/915-1974, e-mail: mary@greenmounthouse.com).

Captain's House B&B is a shipshape place in the town center, fit for an admiral, with eight classy rooms, peat-fire lounges, a stay-awhile garden, and a magnificent breakfast. Mary, whose mother ran a guest house before Dingle was discovered, loves her work and is very good at it (Sb-€50–55 Db-€80–100, great suite-€135, super breakfast in conservatory, CC, The Mall, tel. 066/915-1531, fax 066/915-1079, e-mail: captigh@eircom.net, Jim and Mary Milhench).

Alpine Guest House looks like a monopoly hotel, but that means comfortable and efficient. Its 13 spacious, bright, and fresh rooms come with wonderful sheep-and-harbor views, a cozy lounge, great breakfast, and friendly owners (Db-€55–84, Tb-€76–120, prices vary with room size and season, 10 percent discount with this book, CC, parking, Mail Road, tel. 066/915-1250, fax 066/915-1966, www.alpineguesthouse.com, e-mail: alpinedingle@eircom.net, Paul). If you're driving into town from Tralee, you'll see this a block uphill from the Dingle roundabout and Esso station.

Bambury's Guesthouse, big and modern with views of grazing sheep and the harbor, rents 12 airy, comfy rooms (Db-€70–100, prices depend on size and season, family deals, CC; coming in from Tralee it's on your left on Mail Road, 2 blocks before Esso station; tel. 066/915-1244, fax 066/915-1786, http://bamburysguesthouse.com/, e-mail: info@bamburysguesthouse.com).

Barr Na Sraide Inn, central and hotelesque, has 22 comfortable rooms (Db-€70–100, family deals, CC, self-service laundry, bar, parking, past McCarthy's pub, Upper Main Street, tel. 066/915-1331, fax 066/915-1446, e-mail: barrnasraide@eircom.net).

Coastline Guesthouse, on the water next to Heaton's Guesthouse (listed above), is a modern, sterile place with seven bright, spacious rooms (Sb-€60, Db-€82, Tb-€115, deals for 3-night stays, CC, non-smoking, parking, The Wood, tel. 066/915-2494, fax 066/915-2493, www.coastlinedingle.com, e-mail: coastlinedingle@eircom.net, Vivienne O'Shea).

Ard Na Greine House B&B is a charming, windblown, modern house on the edge of town. Mrs. Mary Houlihan rents four well-equipped, comfortable rooms (with fridges) to non-smokers only (Sb-€50, Db-€50–64, Tb-€76, CC, parking, 8-min walk up Spa Road, 3 doors beyond Hillgrove Hotel, tel. 066/915-1113).

Kelliher's Ballyegan House is a big, plain building with six fresh, comfortable rooms on the edge of town and great harbor views (Db-€62, Tb-€90, family deals, 10 percent off through 2003 with this book except in July & Aug, no CC, non-smoking, parking, TVs in rooms, Upper John Street, tel. 066/915-1702, Hannah and James Kelliher).

LOWER PRICED

O'Neill's B&B is a homey, friendly place with six decent rooms on a quiet street at the top of town (Db-€54 with this book through 2003, family deals, no CC, strictly non-smoking, parking, John Street, tel. 066/915-1639, Mary O'Neill).

Corner House B&B is my longtime Dingle home. It's a simple, traditional place with five large, uncluttered rooms run with a twinkle and a grandmotherly smile by Kathleen Farrell (S-€30, D-€60, T-€80, plenty of plumbing but it's down the hall, no CC, reserve with a phone call and reconfirm a day or 2 ahead, central as can be on Dykegate Street, tel. 066/915-1516). Mrs. Farrell, one of the original three B&B hostesses in a town now filled with them, is a great storyteller.

The following two B&Bs, which take up a quiet corner in the town center, are run by the same Collins—Coileain in Gaelic—family that does archaeological tours of the peninsula (below). Both offer pleasant rooms (O Coileain's are a bit bigger), bike rental (€8), identical prices (Db-€58–60), and a homey friendliness. **O Coileain B&B** is run by a young family—Rachel, Michael, and their two cute little girls (tel. 066/915-1937, e-mail: archeo@eircom.net). **Kirrary B&B,** just over the fence, is grandma's place, with a homey charm (tel. 066/915-1606, e-mail: collinskirrary@eircom.net, Eileen Collins).

Ocean View B&B rents three tidy rooms (2 with views) in a humble little waterfront row house overlooking the bay (S-€25, D-€42, CC, welcome treat on arrival, 5-min walk from center, 100 yards past Oceanworld at 133 The Wood, tel. 066/915-1659, e-mail: thewood@gofree.indigo.ie, Mrs. Brosnan).

***Hostels*: Grapevine Hostel** is a clean and friendly establishment, quietly yet very centrally located, with a cozy fireplace lounge and a fine members' kitchen. Each three- to eight-bed dorm has its own bathroom. Dorms are coed, but there's a girls' room established (29 beds, €12–14 each, laundry-€5, open all day, Dykegate Lane, tel. 066/915-1434, www.dinglehostel.com, e-mail: grapevine@dingleweb.com, run by Siobhan—pron: sheh-vahn).

Ballintaggart Hostel, a backpacker's complex, is housed in a stylish old manorhouse used by Protestants during the famine as a soup kitchen (for those hungry enough to renounce Catholicism). It comes complete with laundry service (€6.50), a classy study, a family room with a fireplace, and a resident ghost (130 beds, €12.50 in 10-bed dorms, €15 beds in Qb, Db-€45, no breakfast but there's a kitchen, a mile east of town on Tralee Road, tel. 066/915-1454, fax 066/915-2207, www.dingleaccommodation.com, e-mail: info@dingleaccommodation.com). Ask the Tralee bus to drop you here before arriving in Dingle. The hostel's shuttle bus does a nightly pub run in summer.

Eating in Dingle Town

For a rustic little village, Dingle is swimming in good food.

Budget tips: The Super Valu supermarket/department store, at the base of town, has everything and stays open late (Mon–Sat 8:00–21:00, Sun 8:00–19:00, until 22:00 in summer); consider a grand view picnic out on the end of the new pier walk. Smaller groceries are scattered throughout the town, such as Centra on Main Street (Mon–Sat 8:00–21:00, Sun 8:00–18:00).

Fancy restaurants serve early-bird specials from 18:00 to 19:00. Many "cheap and cheery" places close at 18:00, and pubs do good €10 dinners all over town. Most pubs stop serving food around 21:00 (to make room for their beer drinkers).

Adam's Bar and Restaurant is a tight, smoky place popular with locals for traditional food at great prices. Try their stew, corned beef and cabbage, or lemon-chicken sandwiches (May–Sept Mon–Sat €8 lunches 12:00–17:00, dinners 18:00–21:00, closed Sun, Upper Main Street).

The Old Smokehouse, your best moderate-value eating in town with fresh Dingle Bay fish and good vegetables, serves happy locals in a rustic woody setting (€16 plates, Tue–Sun 18:00–22:00, closed Mon, CC, tel. 066/915-1061).

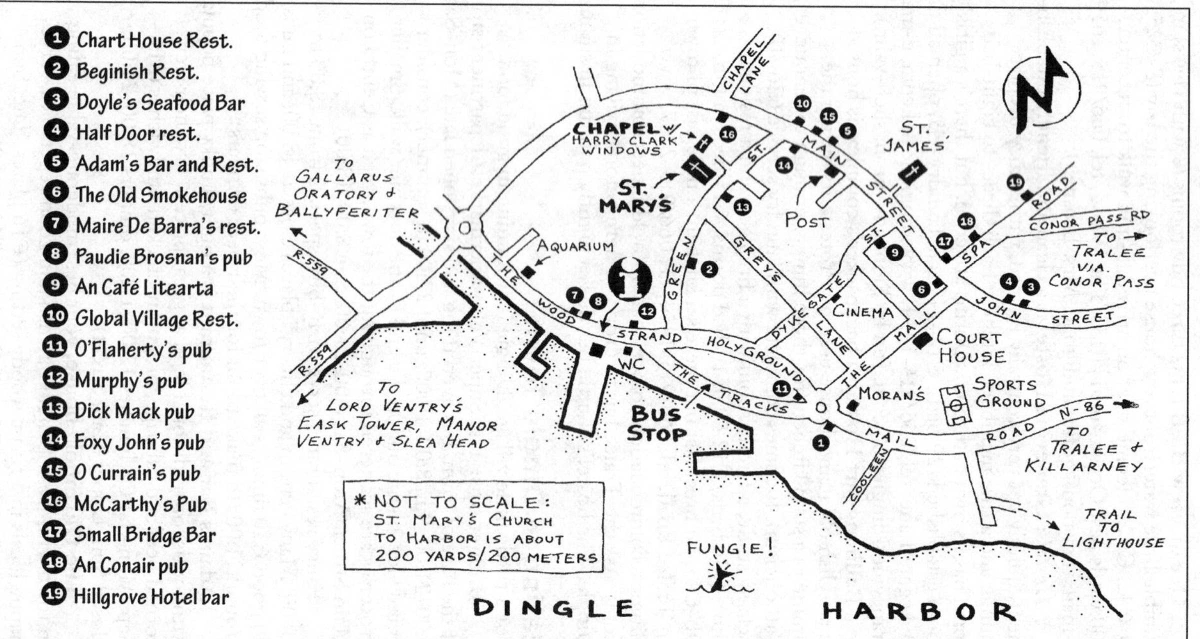
Dingle Restaurants
1 Chart House Rest.
2 Beginish Rest.
3 Doyle's Seafood Bar
4 Half Door rest.
5 Adam's Bar and Rest.
6 The Old Smokehouse
7 Maire De Barra's rest.
8 Paudie Brosnan's pub
9 An Café Litearta
10 Global Village Rest.
11 O'Flaherty's pub
12 Murphy's pub
13 Dick Mack pub
14 Foxy John's pub
15 O Currain's pub
16 McCarthy's Pub
17 Small Bridge Bar
18 An Conair pub
19 Hillgrove Hotel bar
TO GALLARUS ORATORY & BALLYFERITER
R-559
R-559
TO LORD VENTRY'S EASK TOWER, MANOR VENTRY & SLEA HEAD
CHAPEL W/ HARRY CLARK WINDOWS
CHAPEL LANE
ST. MARY'S
AQUARIUM
THE WOOD
STRAND
WC
BUS STOP
THE TRACKS
HOLYGROUND
GREEN
GREY'S
DYKE GATE
LANE
ST.
MAIN STREET
POST
ST. JAMES'
ST.
CINEMA
THE MALL
COURT HOUSE
MORAN'S
SPA
ROAD
CONOR PASS RD
TO TRALEE VIA CONOR PASS
JOHN STREET
SPORTS GROUND
MAIL ROAD
N-86
COOLEEN
TO TRALEE & KILLARNEY
TRAIL TO LIGHTHOUSE
* NOT TO SCALE: ST. MARY'S CHURCH TO HARBOR IS ABOUT 200 YARDS/200 METERS
FUNGIE!
DINGLE HARBOR

Maire De Barra's is a smoky pub serving the best €10 fresh-fish dinners in town, and traditional Irish fare as well (daily 12:30–21:30, music after 21:30, The Pier). **Paudie Brosnan's** pub, a few doors down, is also popular (and smoky).

An Café Litearta, a popular eatery hidden behind an inviting bookstore, serves tasty soup and sandwiches to a good-natured crowd of Gaelic-speaking smokers (daily 10:00–17:00, Dykegate Street).

The **Global Village Restaurant** is where Martin Bealin serves his favorite dishes, gleaned from his travels around the world. It's an eclectic, healthy, meat-eater's place popular with locals for its interesting cuisine (€18 dinners, good salads and great Thai curry, daily 18:00–22:00, CC, top of Main Street, tel. 066/915-2325).

Dingle's Four Fancy Restaurants

Chart House Restaurant serves contemporary cuisine with a menu dictated by what's fresh and seasonal. Settle back into the sharp, clean, lantern-lit harborside ambience (€26 dinners, CC, Wed–Mon 18:30–22:00, closed Tue, at roundabout at base of town, tel. 066/915-2255).

Beginish Restaurant, serving modern European fare with a fish forte in an elegant Georgian setting, is probably your best dressy splurge meal in town (€25 plates, €30 daily 3-course meal, dinner only, Tue–Sun 18:00–22:00, closed Mon, CC, you'll be glad you reserved ahead, Green Street, tel. 066/915-1321).

Two of Dingle's long-established top-notch restaurants—**Doyle's Seafood Bar** (more famous, with excellent seafood and service, tel. 066/915-1174) and **The Half Door** (heartier portions, tel. 066/915-1600)—are neighbors on John Street. They're in the guidebooks for good reason (and therefore filled with tourists), as they serve good food. Both take credit cards, have the same hours (Mon–Sat 18:00–22:00, closed Sun), offer an early-bird special (3-course meal-€30, 18:00–19:00), and take reservations (wise).

Transportation Connections—Dingle Town

The nearest train station is in Tralee.

By bus from Dingle to: Galway (4/day, 6.5 hrs), **Dublin** (3/day, 8 hrs), **Rosslare** (2/day, 9 hrs), **Tralee** (4/day, 75 min, €8); fewer departures on Sundays. Most bus trips out of Dingle require at least one or two (easy) transfers. Dingle has no bus station and only one bus stop, on the waterfront behind the Super Valu supermarket (bus info tel. 01/830-2222 or Tralee station at 066/712-3566). For more information, see "Transportation Connections—Tralee," page 776.

By car: Drivers choose two roads into town, the easy southern route or the much more dramatic, scenic, and treacherous Conor Pass (see "Transportation Connections—Tralee," page 776). It's 30 miles from Tralee either way.

Dingle Peninsula: Circular Tour by Bike or Car

A sight worth ▲▲▲, the Dingle Peninsula loop trip is about 30 miles long (go in clockwise direction). It's easy by car, or it's a demanding three hours by bike—if you don't stop.

While you can take the basic guided tour of the peninsula (see "Dingle Peninsula Tours," page 770), the route described in this section makes it unnecessary. A fancy map is also unnecessary with my instructions. I've keyed in mileage to help locate points of interest. If you're driving, as you leave Dingle, reset your odometer at Oceanworld. Even if you get off track or are biking, derive distances between points from my mileage key. To get the most out of your circle trip, read through this entire section before departing. Then go step by step (staying on R559 and following The Slea Head Drive signs). Roads are very congested in August.

The Dingle Peninsula is 10 miles wide and runs 40 miles from Tralee to Slea Head. The top of its mountainous spine is Mount Brandon—at 3,130 feet, the second-tallest mountain in Ireland. While only tiny villages lie west of Dingle Town, the peninsula is home to 500,000 sheep.

Leave Dingle Town west along the waterfront (0.0 miles at Oceanworld). There's an eight-foot tide here. The seaweed was used to make formerly worthless land arable. (Seaweed is a natural source of potash—organic farming before that was trendy.) Across the water, the fancy Milltown House B&B (with flags) was Robert Mitchum's home for a year during the filming of *Ryan's Daughter*. Look for the narrow mouth of this blind harbor (where Fungie frolics) and the Ring of Kerry beyond that. Dingle Bay is so hidden, ships needed the tower (1847) on the hill to find its mouth.

0.4 miles: At the roundabout, turn left over the bridge. The hardware-store building on the right was a corn-grinding mill in the 18th century.

0.8 miles: The Milestone B&B is named for the stone pillar (*gallaun* in Gaelic) in its front yard. This may have been a prehistoric grave or a boundary marker between two tribes. The stone goes down as far as it sticks up. The peninsula, literally an open-air museum, is dotted with more than 2,000 such monuments dating from the Neolithic Age (4,000 B.C.) through early Christian times. Another stone pillar stands in the field across the street in the direction of the yellow manorhouse of Lord Ventry (in the distance).

Dingle Peninsula Tour

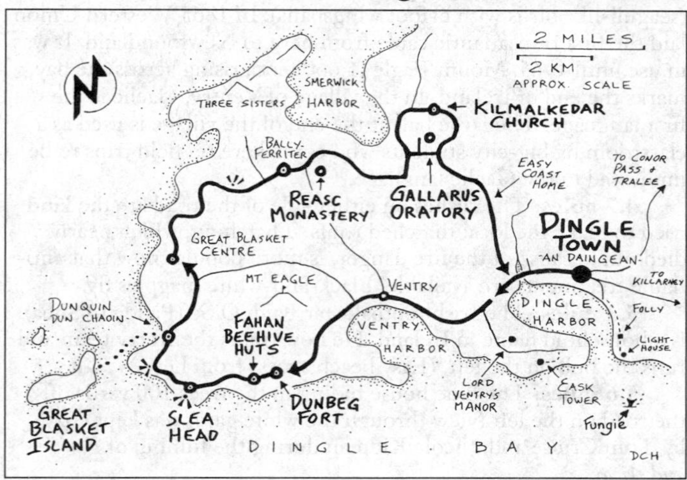

Lord Ventry, whose family came to Dingle as post–Cromwell War landlords in 1666, built this mansion about 1750. Today it houses an all-Gaelic boarding school for 140 high school–age girls.

As you drive past the Ventry estate, you'll pass palms, magnolias, fuschias, and exotic flora introduced to Dingle by Lord Ventry. The mild climate—it never snows—is produced by the Gulf Stream and is fine for subtropical plants. Consequently, fuschias—imported from Chile and spreading like weeds—line the roads all over the peninsula and redden the countryside from June to September. And over 100 inches of rain a year gives this area its "40 shades of green."

Ten yards past the Tobair Michael B&B (on left) a tiny white wall with a blue marker marks the St. Michael's Well. A Christianized Celtic holy well, it's still the site of a Mass on St. Martin's day. St. Martin was the Christian antidote to pagan holy places. Generally, when you see something dedicated to him, it sits upon something that pre-Christian people worshiped.

3 miles: Stay off the "soft margin" as you enjoy views of Ventry Bay, its four-mile-long beach (to your right as you face the water), and distant Skellig Michael, which you'll see all along this part of the route. Skellig Michael—jutting up like France's Mont St. Michel—contains the rocky remains of an eighth-century monastic settlement. Hermit monks lived here in obscure beehive huts—their main contact with the outside world being trading ships stopping between Spain and Scandinavia. Next to it is a smaller island, Little Skellig—a breeding ground for gannets (seagull-like birds with 6-foot wingspans). In 1865 Western Union laid the first transatlantic cable from here to Newfoundland. It was in use until 1965. Mount Eagle (1,660 feet), rising across the bay, marks the end of Ireland. In the village of Ventry, Gaelic is the first language. The large hall at the end of the village is used as a classroom by big-city students who come here on field trips to be immersed in the Gaelic language.

4.7 miles: The rushes on either side of the road are the kind used to make the local thatched roofs. Thatching, which nearly died out because of the fire danger, is more popular now that anti-flame treatments are available. Black-and-white magpies fly.

5.3 miles: The Irish football star Paidi O Se (Paddy O'Shea) is a household name in Ireland. He now trains the Kerry team and runs the pub on the left. (Easy beach access from here.)

5.6 miles: The blue house hiding in the trees 100 yards off the road on the left (view through the white gate) was kept cozy by Tom Cruise and Nicole Kidman during the filming of *Far and Away*.

6.6 miles: *Taisteaal go Mall* means "go slowly"; there's a peach-colored, two-room schoolhouse on the right (20 students, 2 teachers). On the left is the small Celtic and Prehistoric Museum, a strange private collection of prehistoric artifacts with no real connection to Dingle (overpriced at €5, daily 10:00–17:00).

6.9 miles: The circular mound on the right is a late–Stone Age ring fort. In 500 B.C. it was a petty Celtic chieftain's head quarters, a stone-and-earth stockade filled with little stone houses. These survived untouched through the centuries because of superstitious beliefs that they were "fairy forts." While this is unexcavated, recent digging has shown that people have lived on this peninsula since 4000 B.C.

7.3 miles: Look ahead up Mount Eagle at the patchwork of stone-fenced fields

7.7 miles: Dunbeg Fort, a series of defensive ramparts and ditches around a central *clochan*, though ready to fall into the sea, is open to tourists. There are no carvings to be seen, but the small *(beg)* fort *(dun)* is dramatic (€2, daily 9:30–20:00, descriptive handout). Forts like this are the most important relics left from Ireland's Iron Age (500 B.C. to A.D. 500). Since erosion will someday take this fort, it has been excavated. Alongside the road, the new stone-roofed house was built to blend in with the landscape and the region's ancient rock-slab architecture (A.D. 2000, tea inside, traditional currach in parking lot). Just 50 yards up the hill is a cottage abandoned by a family named Kavanaugh 150 years ago during the famine (€2, tel. 066/915-6241).

8.2 miles: A group of beehive huts, or *clochans*, is a short walk uphill (€2, daily 9:30–19:00, WC). These mysterious stone igloos, which cluster together within a circular wall, are a better sight than the similar group of beehive huts a mile down the road. Look over the water for more Skellig views.

Farther on, you'll ford a stream. There has never been a bridge here; this bit of road—nicknamed the "upside-down bridge"—was designed as a ford.

9.2 miles: Pull off to the left at this second group of beehive huts. Look downhill at the scant remains of the scant home that was burned as the movie equivalent of Lord Ventry tried to evict the tenants in *Far and Away*. Even without Hollywood, this is a bleak and godforsaken land. Look above at the patches of land slowly made into farmland by the inhabitants of this westernmost piece of Europe. Rocks were cleared and piled into fences. Sand and seaweed were laid on the clay, and in time it was good for grass. The created land, generally if at all tillable, was used for growing potatoes; otherwise it was only good for grazing. Much has fallen out of use now. Look behind at the Ring of Kerry in the distance and ahead at the Blasket Islands.

9.9 miles: At Slea Head, marked by a crucifix, a pullout, and great views of the Blasket Islands (described below), you turn the corner on this tour. On stormy days, the waves are "racing in like white horses."

10.4 miles: Pull into the little parking lot (at Dunchaoin sign) to view the Blaskets and Dunmore Head (the westernmost point in Europe) and to review the roadside map (which traces your route) posted in the parking lot. The scattered village of Dunquin has many ruined rock homes abandoned during the famine. Some are fixed up, as this is a popular place these days for summer homes. You can see more good examples of land reclamation, patch by patch, climbing up the hillside. Mount Eagle was the first bit of land Charles Lindberg saw after crossing the Atlantic on his way to Paris in 1927. Villagers here were as excited as he was—they had never seen anything so big in the air. Ahead, down a road on the left, a plaque celebrates the 30th anniversary of the filming of *Ryan's Daughter*.

11.9 miles: The Blasket Islanders had no church or cemetery on the island. This was their cemetery. The famous Blasket storyteller Peig Sayers (1873–1958) is buried in the center. At the next intersection, drive down the little lane that leads left (100 yards) to a small stone marker commemorating the 1588 shipwreck of the *Santa Maria de la Rosa* of the Spanish Armada. Below that is the often-tempestuous Dunquin Harbor, from which the Blasket ferry departs. Island farmers—who on a calm day could row across in

20 minutes—would dock here and hike 12 miles into Dingle to sell their produce. When transporting sheep, farmers would lash the sheep's pointy little hoofs together and place them carefully upside down in the currach—so they wouldn't puncture the frail little craft's canvas skin.

12 miles: Back on the main road, follow signs to the Great Blasket Centre.

13.5 miles: Leave the Slea Head Road left for the Great Blasket Centre (described below).

13.7 miles: Back at the turnoff, head left (sign to Louis Mulcahy Pottery).

14.5 miles: Passing land that was never reclaimed, think of the work it took to pick out the stones, pile them into fences, and bring up sand and seaweed to nourish the clay and make soil for growing potatoes. Look over the water to the island aptly named the "Sleeping Giant"—see his hand resting happily on his beer belly.

15.1 miles: The view is spectacular. Ahead, on the right, study the top fields, untouched since the planting of 1845, when the potatoes didn't grow, but rotted in the ground. The faint vertical ridges of the potato beds can still be seen—a reminder of the famine (easier to see a bit later). Before the famine, 50,000 people lived on this peninsula. After the famine, the population was so small that there was never again a need to farm so high up. Today only 10,000 live on the peninsula. Coast downhill. The distant hills are crowned by lookout forts built back when Britain expected Napoleon to invade.

18.3 miles: Ballyferriter (Baile an Fheirtearaigh), established by a Norman family in the 12th century, is the largest town on this side of Dingle. The pubs serve grub, and the old schoolhouse is a museum (€2, Easter–Sept daily 10:00–16:30, closed off-season). The early-Christian cross next to the schoolhouse looks real. Tap it... it's fiberglass—a prop from *Ryan's Daughter.*

19.1 miles: At the T-junction, signs direct you to Dingle ("An Daingean, 11 km") either way. Go left, via Gallarus (and still following Slea Head Way). Take a right over the bridge, still following signs to Gallarus.

19.5 miles: Just beyond the bridge and a few yards before the sign to Mainistir Riaise (Reasc Monastic enclosure), detour right up the lane. After 0.2 miles (the unsigned turnout on your right), you'll find the scant remains of the walled Reasc Monastery (dating from the 6th–12th centuries). The inner wall divided the community into sections for prayer and business (cottage industries helped support the monastery). In 1975 only the stone pillar was visible, as the entire site was buried. The layer of black felt marks where the original rocks stop and the excavators' reconstruction begins. The stone pillar is Celtic (c. 500 B.C.). When the Christians arrived in the fifth century, they didn't throw out the Celtic society. Instead, they carved a Maltese-type cross over the Celtic scrollwork. The square building was an oratory (church—you'll see an intact oratory at the next stop). The round buildings would have been *clochans*—those stone igloo-type dwellings. The monastery ran cottage industries with a double-duty kiln. Just outside the wall (opposite the oratory, past the duplex *clochan*, at the bottom end), find a stone hole with a passage facing the southwest wind. This was the kiln—fanned by the wind, it was used for cooking and drying grain. Locals would bring their grain to be dried and ground, and the monks would keep a tithe. With the arrival of the Normans in the 12th century, these small religious communities were replaced by relatively big-time state and church governments.

20 miles: Return to the main road, continue to the right.

21.1 miles: At the big hotel (Smerwick Harbor), turn left following the sign to Gallarus Oratory.

21.8 miles: At the big building (with camping sign), go right up a lane marked with a sign for the oratory. Another sign directs you to a small tourist center—with a shop, WC, and video theater. For €2 you get a 17-minute video overview of Dingle Peninsula's historic sights. (Bikers and hikers can avoid the entry fee by ignoring the visitors center sign and continuing up the lane 200 yards to a free entrance.)

The Gallarus Oratory, built about 1,300 years ago, is one of Ireland's best-preserved early-Christian churches. Shaped like an upturned boat, its finely fitted drystone walls are still waterproof. Notice the holes once used to secure covering at the door and the fine alternating stonework on the corners.

From the oratory the little lane leads directly up and over the hill, home to Dingle. To complete this tour, however, you should return to the main road and continue (following sign to An Mhuirioch).

22.9 miles: Turn right at the fork and immediately take a right (at the blue Shop sign) at the next fork. Pass a 19th-century church.

24.2 miles: The ruined Kilmalkedar church was the Norman center of worship for this end of the peninsula. It was built when England replaced the old monastic settlements in an attempt to centralize their rule. The 12th-century Irish Romanesque church is surrounded by a densely populated graveyard (which has risen noticeably above the surrounding fields over the centuries). In front of the church, you'll find the oldest medieval tombs, a stately early-Christian cross (substantially buried by the rising graveyard and therefore oddly proportioned), and a much older Ogham stone. This stone, which had already stood here 900 years when the church was built, is notched with the mysterious Morris code–type script the Celts used from the 3rd to 7th centuries. It marked a grave, indicating this was a pre-Christian holy spot. The hole was drilled through here centuries ago as a place where people would come to seal a deal—standing on the graves of their ancestors and in front of the house of God, they'd "swear to God" by touching fingers through this stone. You can still use this to renew your marriage vows (free, B.Y.O. spouse). The church fell into ruin during the Reformation. As Catholic worship went underground until the early 19th century, Kilmalkedar was never rebuilt.

24.6 miles: Continue uphill, overlooking the water. You'll pass another "fairy fort" (Ciher Dorgan) dating back to 1000 B.C. (free, go through the rusty "kissing gate").

25.5 miles: At the crest of the hill, enjoy a three-mile coast back into Dingle town (in the direction of the Eask Tower).

28.3 miles: *Tog Bog E* means "take it easy." At the T-junction, turn left. Then turn right at the roundabout.

29 miles: You're back into Dingle town. Well done.

Dingle Peninsula Tours

▲▲Sciuird Archaeology Tours—Sciuird (pron. SCREW-id) tours are offered by a father-son team with Dingle history—and a knack for sharing it—in their blood. Tim Collins (a retired Dingle police officer) and his son Michael give serious 2.5-hour minibus tours (€15, departing at 10:30 and 14:00, depending upon demand). Drop by the Kirrary B&B (Dykegate and Grey's Lane) or call 066/915-1606 to put your name on the list. Call early. Tours fill quickly in summer. Off-season (Oct–April) you may have to call back to see if the necessary five people signed up to make a bus go. While skipping the folk legends and the famous sights (such as Slea Head), your guide will drive down tiny farm roads (the Gaelic word for road literally means "cow path"), over hedges, and up ridges to hidden Celtic forts, mysterious stone tombs, and forgotten castles with sweeping seaside views. The running commentary gives an intimate peek into the history of Dingle. Sit as close to the driver as possible to get all the information. They do two completely different tours: west (Gallarus Oratory) and east (Minard Castle and a wedge tomb). I enjoyed both. Dress for the weather. In a literal gale with horizontal winds, Tim kept saying, "You'll survive it."

More Minibus Tours—Moran's Tour, which does a quickie minibus tour around the peninsula, offers meager narration and a short stop at the Gallarus Oratory (€15 to Slea Head, normally May–Sept at 10:00 and 14:00 from Dingle TI, 2.5 hrs; Moran's is at Esso station at roundabout, tel. 066/915-1155 or cellular 087-275-3333). There are always enough seats. But if no one shows up, consider a private Moran taxi trip around the peninsula (€45 for 3 people, cabby narrates 2.5-hour ride). The **Mountain Man** also runs three-hour minibus tours of the peninsula (€14/3 hrs, 3 tours daily June–Aug with demand, tel. 066/915-2400).

Eco-Cruises—Dingle Marine Eco Tours offers a two-hour birds-and-rocks boat tour of the peninsula. The guided tour sails either east toward Minard Castle or west toward the Blasket Islands (€25, April–Sept, departs 16:00, office around corner from TI, tel. 066/915-0768).

Blasket Islands

This rugged group of six islands off the tip of Dingle Peninsula seems particularly close to the soul of Ireland. The population of Great Blasket Island, home to as many as 160 people, dwindled until the government moved the last handful of residents to the mainland in 1953. Life here was hard. Each family had a cow, a few sheep, and a plot of potatoes. They cut their peat from the high ridge and harvested fish from the sea. There was no priest, pub, or doctor. These people formed the most traditional Irish community of the 20th century—the symbol of antique Gaelic culture.

Their special closeness to their island—combined with their knack for vivid storytelling—is inspirational. From this primitive but proud fishing/farming community came three writers of international repute whose Gaelic work—basically tales of life on Great Blasket—is translated into many languages. You'll find *Peig* (by Peig Sayers), *Twenty Years a-Growing* (Maurice O'Sullivan), and *The Islander* (Thomas O'Crohan) in shops everywhere.

In the summer there's a café and hostel (cellular 086-852-2321) on the island, but it's little more than a ghost town overrun with rabbits on a peaceful, grassy, three-mile-long poem. The Blasket ferry runs hourly, and in summer every half hour, depending on weather and demand (€20 round-trip, May–Oct). There may be a bus from Dingle town to Dunquin—leaving in the morning and picking up in the late afternoon—coordinated with the ferry schedule (€15 taxi service by Moran, tel. 066/915-1155; Dunquin ferry tel. 066/915-6422). Dunquin has a fine hostel (tel. 066/915-6121).

In summer, a fast boat called the *Peig Sayers* runs between Dingle town and the Blaskets. The ride (which may include a quick look at Fungie) traces the spectacular coastline all the way to Slea Head in a boat designed to slice expertly through the ocean chop. Because of the tricky landing at Great Blasket's primitive, tiny boat ramp, any substantial swell can make actually going ashore impossible (€35 round-trip, departing at 9:00, 11:00, 13:00, and 15:00, includes 40-min ride with free time to explore island, or €70 overnight trip includes dinner, a bed in the island's hostel, and breakfast; for info, call Mary at 066/915-1344).

▲▲**Great Blasket Centre**—This state-of-the-art Blasket and Gaelic heritage center gives visitors the best look possible at the language, literature, and way of life of the Blasket Islanders. See the fine 20-minute video (shows on the half hour), hear the sounds, read the poems, browse through old photos, and then gaze out the big windows at those rugged islands and imagine. Even if you never got past limericks, the poetry of these people—so pure and close to each other and nature—will have you dipping your pen into the cry of the birds (€3.20, Easter–Oct daily 10:00–18:00, until 19:00 July–Aug, cafeteria, on the mainland facing the islands, well-signposted, tel. 066/915-6444). Visit this center before visiting the islands.

Sights—East of Dingle Town

▲**Minard Castle**—Three miles southwest of Annascaul (off Lispole Road) is Minard Castle, the largest fortress on the peninsula. Built by the Norman Knights of Kerry in 1551, it was destroyed by Cromwell in about 1650.

Wander around the castle. With its corners undermined by Cromwellian explosives, it looks ready to split. Look up the garbage/toilet chute. As you enter the ruins, find the faint scallop in the doorway—the symbol of St. James. The castle had a connection to Santiago de Compostela in Spain. Medieval pilgrims would leave from here on a seafaring pilgrimage to northern Spain. Inside, after admiring the wall flowers, re-create the floor plan: ground floor for animals and storage; main floor with fireplace; thin living-quarters floor; and, on top, the defensive level.

The setting is dramatic, with the Ring of Kerry across the way and Storm Beach below. Storm Beach is notable for its sandstone boulders that fell from the nearby cliffs. Grinding against each other in the wave and tidal action, the boulders eroded into cigar-shaped rocks.

Next to the fortress, look for the "fairy fort," a Stone-Age fort from about 500 B.C.

▲**Puicin Wedge Tomb**—While pretty obscure, this is worth the trouble for its evocative setting. Above the hamlet of Lispole in Doonties, park your car and hike 10 minutes up a ridge. At the summit is a pile of rocks made into a little room with one of the finest views on the peninsula. Beyond the Ring of Kerry you may just make out the jagged Skellig Rock, noted for its eighth-century monastery.

Inch Strand—This four-mile sandy beach, shaped like a half moon, was made famous by *Ryan's Daughter*.

TRALEE

While Killarney is the tour-bus capital of county Kerry, Tralee is its true leading city. Except for the tourist complex around the TI and during a few festivals, Tralee feels like a bustling Irish town. A little outdoor market combusts on The Square (Thu–Sat).

Tralee's famous Rose of Tralee International Festival (usually mid-August), while a celebration of arts and music, climaxes with the election of the Rose of Tralee—the most beautiful woman at the festival. While the rose garden in the Castle Gardens surrounding the TI is in bloom from summer through October, Tralee's finest roses are going about their lives in the busy streets of this workaday town.

Orientation (area code: 066)

For the tourist, the heart of Tralee is Ashe Memorial Hall, housing the TI and Kerry the Kingdom, located near the rose garden and surrounded by the city park. Beyond the park is the Aqua Dome and steam railway that, if you were here 50 years ago, would chug-chug you to Dingle. Today it goes only to the touristy windmill.

Tourist Information: The TI is in Ashe Memorial Hall (July–Aug daily 9:00–19:00, Sept–June daily 9:00–17:00, tel. 066/712-1288).

Arrival in Tralee: From the train and bus station (both are located in the same building, with bike rental available), the Ashe Memorial Hall is a 10-minute walk through the center of town. Exit the station right, take a near-immediate left on Edward Street, then turn right on Castle Street and left on Denny. The Hall is at the end of Denny. Drivers should knock around the town center until they find a sign to the TI. Parking on the street requires a disk (€0.75/hr, sold at TI and newsstands—have them date it for you—or from machines on the street).

Sights—Tralee

▲▲Kerry the Kingdom—This is the place to learn about life in Kerry. The museum has three parts: Kerry slide show, museum, and medieval-town train ride. Get in the mood by relaxing for 15 minutes through the Enya-style, continuous slideshow of Kerry's spectacular scenery, then wander through 7,000 years of Kerry history in the museum (well described, no need for free headphones). The Irish say that when a particularly stupid guy moved from Cork to Kerry, he raised the IQ in both counties—but this museum is pretty well done. It starts with good background on the archaeological sites of Dingle and goes right up to a video showing highlights of the Kerry football team (a fun look at Irish football). The lame finale is a 12-minute, four-person train ride back in time to 1450 down a re-creation of Tralee's Main Street (€8, daily 9:30–17:30, closed Jan & Feb, €0.75 disk at TI for 1-hour parking, tel. 066/712-7777). Before leaving, garden enthusiasts will want to ramble through the rose garden in the adjacent park.

Blennerville Windmill—On the edge of Tralee, just off the Dingle road, spins a restored mill originally built in 1800. Its eight-minute video tells the story of the windmill, which ground grain to feed Britain as the country steamed into the Industrial Age (€4.50 gets you a 1-room emigration exhibit, the video, and a peek at the spartan interior of the working windmill, April–Oct daily 9:30-17:30, closed Nov–March, tel. 066/712-1064); heritage researchers can scan the famine-ship records database upstairs above the emigration exhibit.

A restored narrow-gauge steam railway runs hourly between Tralee's Ballyard Station and the windmill (€4.50 round-trip, save 10 percent if you buy windmill and steam railway tickets together, tel. 066/712-1064). In the 19th century, Blennerville was a major port for America-bound emigrants.

Siamsa Tire Theatre—The National Folk Theater of Ireland, Siamsa Tire (pron. shee-EM-sah TEE-rah), stages two-hour dance and theater performances based on Gaelic folk traditions. The songs are in Irish, but there's no dialogue (€16, April–Oct Mon–Sat at 20:30, next to Kingdom of Kerry building in park, tel. 066/712-3055, e-mail: siamsatire@eircom.net).

Swimming—The Aqua Dome is a modern-yet-fortified swim center—the largest indoor water world in Ireland—at the Dingle end of town, near the Ashe Memorial Hall. Families enjoy the huge slide, wave pool, and other wet amusements (€9, kids-€8, locker-€1, June–Aug daily 10:00–22:00, less off-season, tel. 066/712-8899 or 066/712-9150).

Music and Other Distractions—Tralee has several fine pubs within a few blocks of each other (on Castle Street and Rock Street) offering live traditional music most evenings. There's greyhound racing (Tue and Fri year-round plus Sat in summer, 20:00–22:15, 10 30-second races every 15 min, 10-min walk from station or town center, tel. 066/718-0008). Entry to the track costs €5—plus what you lose gambling (kids free). At just about any time of day, you can drop into a betting office to check out the local gambling scene.

Sleeping in Tralee
(€1 = about $1, country code: 353, area code: 066, mail: Tralee, County Kerry)

The first two places—a pleasant B&B and a fancy guest house—are located a 10-minute walk from the station up Oakpark Road (which turns into Oakpark Drive). A cab runs €4.

HIGHER PRICED

Meadowlands is a classy 58-room guest house with a bar serving great pub meals. If you want to splurge in Tralee, do it here (Db-€160–200, suites-€210, CC, Oakpark Road, leaving the station, walk up Oakpark Road, tel. 066/718-0444, fax 066/718-0964, e-mail: medlands@iol.ie).

LOWER PRICED

O'Shea's B&B, a simple, tidy, modern house, rents four comfy rooms (Sb-€35–40, Db-€56–60, Tb-€80, CC, non-smoking, 2 Oakpark Drive, nearly across street from Meadowlands—listed above, tel. 066/718-0123, fax 066/718-0188, e-mail: osheasofkerry@eircom.net, Mairead O'Shea).

Hostels: Cheap hostels abound in Tralee, some offering doubles as well as dorm beds. These two are central. The **Courthouse Lodge** is on 5 Church Street (€14 dorm beds, Db-€32, no CC, 5-min walk from station toward town center, take Ashe Street, tel. & fax 066/712-7199). **Finnegan's Hostel,** in a stately Georgian house from 1826, is a block from TI at 17 Denny Street (€16 beds in 3-bed dorm rooms, rustic cellar restaurant serving fine meals, CC, tel. 066/712-7610, e-mail: imptralee@indigo.ie).

A mile out of town—in different directions—you'll find the homey **Lisnagree Hostel** (€14 beds in shared quads, D-€32, no CC, a mile east of center just off N21, follow Boherboy to Ballinorig Road, tel. 066/712-7133) and the **Collis-Sandes House,** a run-down, neo-Gothic mansion in a peaceful forest with 100 cheap beds (€12 beds in 4- to 8-bed rooms, D-€39, Db-€44, includes sheets, breakfast-€2.50, CC, a mile north of station and town center; from the station head up Oakpark Drive, after about 8 blocks you'll see sign on left, tel. & fax 066/712-8658, www.colsands.com, e-mail: colsands@indigo.ie). They have a free shuttle service from the station—ring them upon arrival—and a Tralee pub run on summer evenings.

Eating in Tralee

The Cookery is good (€9 lunches Tue–Sat 12:30–17:30, €15–23 dinners Tue–Sat from 18:00, closed Sun–Mon, CC, a block off

The Square, 16 Abbey Street, tel. 066/712-8833), but it's cheaper to shop for a picnic at **Tesco,** the big grocery off The Square (Mon–Sat 8:30–20:00, Sun 10:00–18:00).

Transportation Connections—Tralee

Day trippers, beware: The station has lockers, but not enough.

By train to: Dublin (4/day, 3/day on Sun, 4 hrs, €47), **Rosslare** (1/day except Sun, 5 hrs, €21.50). Train info: tel. 066/712-3522.

By bus to: Dingle (6/day, less off-season and on Sun, 75 min, €8 one-way, €12 round-trip), **Galway** (8/day, 4 hrs), **Limerick** (8/day, 2 hrs), **Doolin/Cliffs of Moher** (2/day, 4 hrs), **Ennis** (9/day, 3 hrs, change in Limerick), **Rosslare** (3/day, 7 hrs, €21.50), **Shannon** (9/day, 2.5 hrs). Tralee's bus station is at the train station. Bus info: tel. 066/712-3566.

Car rental: Duggan's Garage Practical Car Hire rents Fiat Puntos (€100/48 hrs, includes everything but gas, must be 25 years old, CC, 2 blocks from train station on Ashe Street, tel. 066/ 712-1124, fax 066/712-7527).

Airports

Kerry Airport, a 45-minute drive from Dingle town, offers direct flights to **Dublin** and **London** (daily, €109 to London, €72 to Dublin; airport tel. 066/976-4644 or 066/976-4350, Ryanair tel. 01/609-7878, Aer Arann Express tel. 1-890-462-726, www.kerryairport.ie).

Shannon Airport, the major airport in Western Ireland, has direct flights to **Dublin** (2–3/day, 30 min) and **London** (6/day, 1 hr). Ryanair (www.ryanair.com) and Aer Lingus (www.aerlingus.ie) fly out of Shannon. Airport info: tel. 061/ 471-444. Shannon Airport TI: tel. 061/471-664 (daily 6:30–17:30, June–Sept until 19:00). Shannon Airport also has easy bus connections to **Limerick** (nearly hrly, 1 hr, can continue to Tralee—2 hrs, and Dingle—1.25 hrs more), **Ennis** (nearly hrly, 1 hr) and **Galway** (every 2 hrs, 2 hrs). Bus info: tel. 061/313-333.

Route Tips for Drivers

From Tralee to Dingle: Drivers choose between the narrow, but very exciting, Conor Pass road or the faster, easier, but still narrow N86 through Lougher and Anascaul. On a clear day Conor Pass comes with incredible views over Tralee Bay and Brandon Bay, the Blasket Islands, and the open Atlantic. Pull over at the summit viewpoint to look down on Dingle town and harbor. While in Kerry, listen to Radio Kerry FM 97. To practice your Gaelic, tune in to FM 94.4.

Between Tralee and Galway/Burren/Doolin: The Killimer–Tarbert ferry connection allows those heading north for the Cliffs of Moher (or south for Dingle) to avoid the 80-mile detour around the Shannon River. If you're going to Galway, the Limerick route is faster, but the ferry route is more scenic (1 trip/hr, 20 min, €13/carload, leaves on the half-hour going north and on the hour going south, until 21:00 April–Sept, until 19:00 Oct–March, no need to reserve, tel. 065/905-3124, www.shannonferries.com).

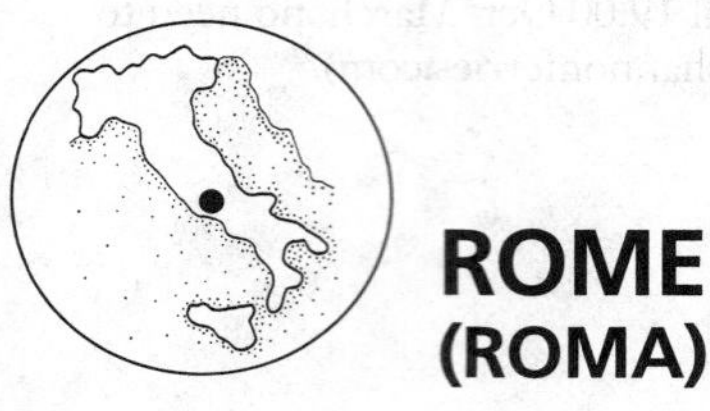

ROME
(ROMA)

Rome is magnificent and brutal at the same time. Your ears will ring, if you're careless you'll be run down or pickpocketed, and you'll be frustrated by the kind of chaos that only an Italian can understand. You may even come to believe Mussolini was a necessary evil.

But Rome is required, and if your hotel provides a comfortable refuge, if you pace yourself and accept (and even partake in) the siesta plan, if you're well-organized for sightseeing, and if you protect yourself and your valuables with extra caution and discretion, you'll do fine. You'll see the sights and leave satisfied.

Rome at its peak meant civilization itself. Everything was either civilized (part of the Roman Empire, Latin- or Greek-speaking) or barbarian. Today, Rome is Italy's political capital, the capital of Catholicism, and a splendid... "junk pile" is not quite the right term... of Western civilization. As you peel through its fascinating and jumbled layers, you'll find its buildings, cats, laundry, traffic, and 2.6 million people endlessly entertaining. And then, of course, there are the magnificent sights.

Tour St. Peter's, the greatest church on earth, and scale Michelangelo's 100-meter-tall (330-foot) dome, the world's largest. Learn something about eternity by touring the huge Vatican Museum. You'll find the story of Creation, bright as the day it was painted, in the recently restored Sistine Chapel. Do the "Caesar Shuffle" through ancient Rome's Forum and Colosseum. Savor Europe's most sumptuous building—the Borghese Gallery—and take an early evening "Dolce Vita Stroll" down the Via del Corso with Rome's beautiful people. Enjoy an after-dark walk from Trastevere to the Spanish Steps, lacing together Rome's Baroque and bubbly nightspots.

Rome Area

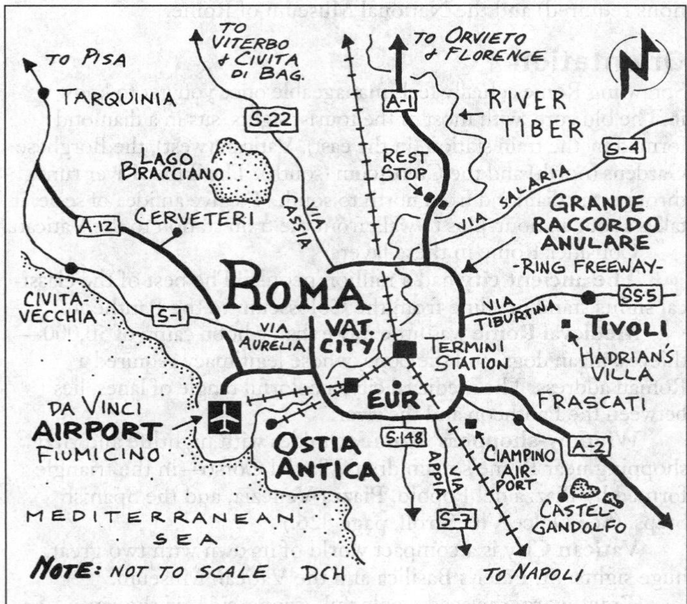

Planning Your Time

For most travelers, Rome is best done quickly. It's a great city, but it's exhausting. Time is normally short, and Italy is more charming elsewhere. To "do" Rome in a day, consider it as a side trip from Orvieto or Florence, and maybe before the night train to Venice. Crazy as that sounds, if all you have is a day, it's a great one.

Rome in a day: Vatican (2 hours in the museum and Sistine Chapel and 1 hour in St. Peter's), taxi over the river to the Pantheon (picnic on its steps), then hike over Capitol Hill, through the Forum, and to the Colosseum. Have dinner on Campo de' Fiori and dessert on Piazza Navona.

Rome in two to three days: Day one, do the "Caesar Shuffle" from the Colosseum and Forum over Capitol Hill to the Pantheon. After a siesta, join the locals strolling from Piazza del Popolo to the Spanish Steps (see my recommended "Dolce Vita Stroll," page 826). Have dinner near your hotel.

On the second day, see the Vatican City (St. Peter's, climb the dome, tour the Vatican Museum). Spend the evening walking from Trastevere to Campo de' Fiori—an atmospheric place for dinner—to the Trevi Fountain (see "Night Walk Across Rome," page 821). With a third day, add the Borghese Gallery (reservations required) and the National Museum of Rome.

Orientation

Sprawling Rome actually feels manageable once you get to know it. The old core, with most of the tourist sights, sits in a diamond formed by the train station (in the east), Vatican (west), the Borghese Gardens (north) and the Colosseum (south). The Tiber River runs through the diamond from north to south. To give an idea of scale, it takes about an hour-plus to walk from the train station to the Vatican.

Consider Rome in these layers:

The ancient city had a million people. The best of the classical sights stand in a line from the Colosseum to the Pantheon.

Medieval Rome was little more than a hobo camp of 50,000—thieves, mean dogs, and the pope, whose legitimacy required a Roman address. The medieval city, a colorful tangle of lanes, lies between the Pantheon and the river.

Window-shoppers' Rome twinkles with nightlife and ritzy shopping near Rome's main drag, Via del Corso—in the triangle formed by Piazza del Popolo, Piazza Venezia, and the Spanish Steps. (See Dolce Vita Stroll, page 826.)

Vatican City is a compact world of its own with two great, huge sights: St. Peter's Basilica and the Vatican Museum.

Trastevere, the seedy, colorful, wrong-side-of-the-river neighborhood/village, is Rome at its crustiest—and perhaps most "Roman."

Baroque Rome is an overleaf that embellishes great squares throughout the town with fountains and church facades.

Since no one is allowed to build taller than St. Peter's dome, the city has no modern skyline. And the Tiber River is ignored. After the last floods (1870), the banks were built up very high and Rome turned its back on its naughty, unnavigable river.

Tourist Information

While Rome has three main tourist information offices, the dozen or so TI kiosks scattered around the town at major tourist centers are handy and just as helpful. If all you need is a map, forget the TI and get one at your hotel.

The main TI, near Piazza della Repubblica's huge fountain, covers the city and the region. It's a five-minute walk out the front of the train station (Mon–Sat 9:00–19:00, next to car dealership, Via Parigi 5, free Internet access to Rome tourism sites, www.romaturismo.com, tel. 06-3606-4399). It's air-conditioned, less crowded, and more helpful than the station TI (see below), and it has seats and a study table.

Downtown Rome

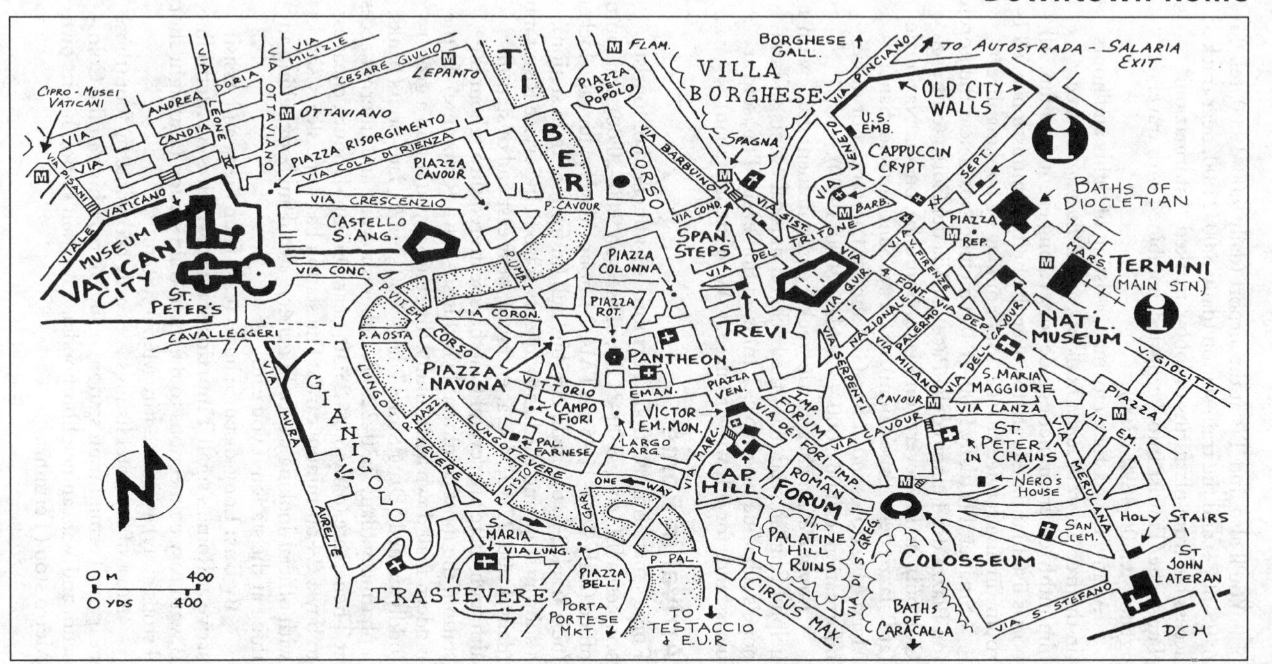

You'll also find TIs at the airport (daily 9:00–19:00, tel. 06-6595-6074) and the train station (daily 8:00–21:00, near track 3, accessible from platforms or lobby, marked "Informazioni Turistiche/Tourist Info," crowded, combined with travel agency, tel. 06-4890-6300).

At any TI, ask for a city map, a listing of sights and hours (in the free *Tesori di Roma* booklet), and *L'Evento*, the free bimonthly entertainment guide for evening events and fun. All hotels list an inflated rate to cover the hefty commission any TI room-finding service charges. Save money by booking direct.

Smaller TIs (daily 9:00–18:00) include kiosks near the Forum (on Piazza del Tempio della Pace), at Via del Corso (on Largo Goldoni), in Trastevere (on Piazza Sonnino), on Via Nazionale (at Palazzo delle Esposizioni), at Castel Sant' Angelo, Santa Maria Maggiore, and at San Giovanni in Laterano. For more information, call 06-3600-4399 (daily 9:00–19:00).

Roma c'è is a cheap little weekly entertainment guide with a helpful English section (at the back) on musical events and the pope's schedule for the week (new edition every Thu, sold at newsstands for €1, www.romace.it, Web site in Italian).

Arrival in Rome

Rome's main train station, **Termini**, is a minefield of tourist services: a TI (daily 8:00–21:00, off-season 9:00–20:00), train info office (daily 7:00–21:45), ATMs, 24-hour thievery, luggage lockers (near track 24), the main city-bus hub (in front of train station), a subway stop, and the handy, cheery Ciao Self-Service Ristorante (daily 11:00–22:30, WC at entrance, near east end of station; although there are several Ciao bars scattered throughout the station, the most comfortable is this sit-down Ristorante). In the modern mall downstairs, under the station, you'll find a grocery (oddly named "Drug Store," daily 7:00–24:00), late-hours banks, a pharmacy (daily 7:30–22:00), public showers, and Internet access at Thenetgate (daily 6:00–23:30, near Dunkin' Donuts, cheapest to buy a €4 60-minute card). The station has some sleazy sharks with official-looking cards. In general, avoid anybody selling anything at the station if you can.

By Bus: Long-distance buses (e.g., from Siena and Assisi) arrive at Rome's small **Tiburtina** station, which is on Metro line B, with easy connections to the main train station (a straight shot 4 stops away) and the entire Metro system.

Most of my hotel listings are easily accessible by foot (those near the Termini train station) or by Metro (those in the Colosseum and Vatican neighborhoods). The train station has its own Metro stop (Termini).

By Plane: If you arrive at the airport, catch a train (hrly, 30 min, €9) to Rome's train station or take (or share) a taxi to your hotel. For details, see "Transportation Connections," page 848.

Dealing with (and Avoiding) Problems

Theft Alert: With sweet-talking con artists meeting you at the station, well-dressed pickpockets on buses, and thieving gangs of children at the ancient sites, Rome is a gauntlet of rip-offs. There's no great physical risk, but green tourists will be scammed. Thieves strike when you're distracted. Don't trust kind strangers. Keep nothing important in your pockets. Assume you're being stalked. (Then relax and have fun.) Be most on guard while boarding and leaving buses and subways. Thieves crowd the door, then stop and turn while others crowd and push from behind. The sneakiest thieves are well-dressed businessmen (generally with something in their hands); lately, many are posing as tourists with Tevas, fanny packs, and cameras. Scams abound: Don't give your wallet to self-proclaimed "police" who stop you on the street, warn you about counterfeit (or drug) money, and ask to see your wallet.

If you know what to look out for, the gangs of children picking the pockets and handbags of naive tourists are not a threat but an interesting, albeit sad, spectacle. Gangs of city-stained children (sometimes as young as 8–10 years old), too young to be prosecuted but old enough to rip you off, troll through the tourist crowds around the Colosseum, Forum, Piazza Repubblica, and train and Metro stations. Watch them target tourists who are overloaded with bags or distracted with a video camera. The kids look like beggars and hold up newspapers or cardboard signs to confuse their victims. They scram like stray cats if you're onto them. A fast-fingered mother with a baby is often nearby. The terrace above the bus stop near the Colosseum Metro stop is a fine place to watch the action and maybe even pick up a few moves of your own.

Reporting Losses: To report lost or stolen passports and documents or to file an insurance claim, you must file a police report (at the train station with Polizia at track 1 or with Carabinieri at track 20, also at Piazza Venezia). To replace a passport, file the police report, then go to your embassy (see below). To report lost traveler's checks, call your bank (Visa—tel. 800-874-155, Thomas Cook/MasterCard—tel. 800-872-050, American Express—tel. 800-872-000), then file a police report. To report stolen or lost credit cards, call the company (Visa—tel. 800-877-232 or 800-819-014, MasterCard—tel. 800-870-866, American Express—tel. 800-874-333), then file a police report. All of these toll-free 800 numbers are Italian (dialed free in Italy), not American.

Embassies: United States (Mon–Fri 8:30–13:00 & 14:00–17:30, Via Vittorio Veneto 119/A, tel. 06-46741, www.usembassy.it) and Canada (Via Zara 30, tel. 06-445-981, www.canada.it).

Emergency Numbers: Police—tel. 113. Ambulance—tel. 118.

Hit and Run: Walk with extreme caution. Scooters don't need to stop at red lights, and even cars exercise what drivers call the "logical option" of not stopping if they see no oncoming traffic. As Vespa scooters become electric, they'll get quieter (hooray) but more dangerous for pedestrians. Follow locals like a shadow when you cross a street (or spend a good part of your visit stranded on curbs).

Staying/Getting Healthy: The siesta is a key to survival in summertime Rome. Lie down and contemplate the extraordinary power of gravity in the eternal city. I drink lots of cold, refreshing water from Rome's many drinking fountains (the Forum has 3). There's a pharmacy (marked by a green cross) in every neighborhood, including a handy one in the train station (daily 7:30–22:00, located downstairs, at west end), and a 24-hour pharmacy on Piazza dei Cinquecento 51 (next to train station on Via Cavour, tel. 06-488-0019). Embassies can recommend English-speaking doctors (see "Embassies," above). Consider MEDline, a 24-hour home medical service (tel. 06-808-0995, doctors speak English). Anyone is entitled to free emergency treatment at public hospitals. The hospital closest to the train station is Policlinico Umberto 1 (entrance for emergency treatment on Via Lancisi, translators available, Metro: Policlinico). The American Hospital, a private hospital on the outskirts, is used to helping Yankees (tel. 06-225-571).

Helpful Hints

Train Tickets and Reservations: Get train tickets and railpass-related reservations and supplements at travel agencies, rather than deal with the congested train station. The cost is either the same or there's a minimal charge. Your hotel can direct you to the nearest travel agency. Quo Vadis, near the Vatican, is helpful (Via della Conciliazione, 22-24, tel. 06-6880-4941, fax 06-6880-3191, e-mail: qv.viaggi@tiscalinet.it). American Express is near the Spanish Steps (Mon–Fri 9:00–17:30, Sat 9:00–12:30, no train tickets sold on Sat, closed Sun, Piazza di Spagna, 00187 Roma, tel. 06-67641).

Bookstore: Try American Bookstore (Via Torino 136, Metro: Repubblica, tel. 06-474-6877).

Internet Access: EasyEverything on Piazza Barberini (access from €0.50, open 24/7, 350 terminals, www.easyeverything.com).

Laundry: Your hotel can point you to the nearest launderette (usually open daily 8:00–22:00, about €6 to wash and dry a 15-pound load). The Bolle Blu chain comes with Internet access

(€4.25/hr, near train station at Via Milazzo 20, Via Palestro 59, and Via Principe Amedeo 116, tel. 06-446-5804).

Web Sites on Rome: www.romaturismo.com (music, exhibitions, events, in English), www.wantedinrome.com (job openings and real estate, but also festivals and exhibitions, in English), and www.vatican.va (the pope's Web site, in English).

Getting around Rome

Sightsee on foot, by city bus, or by taxi. I've grouped your sightseeing into walkable neighborhoods.

Public transportation is efficient, cheap, and part of your Roman experience. It starts running around 5:30 and stops around 23:30, sometimes earlier. After midnight, there are a few very crowded night buses, and taxis become more expensive and hard to get. Don't try to hail one—go to a taxi stand.

Buses and subways use the same ticket. You can buy tickets at newsstands, tobacco shops (*tabacchi*, marked by a black-and-white T sign), or at major Metro stations or bus stops, but not on board. Since many Metro stations have no human ticket-sellers and the machines are either broken or require exact change (helps to put in smallest-value coins first), it's easier to buy a few tickets above ground at newsstands or *tabacchi* (€0.80, good for 75 min—Metro ride and unlimited buses); all-day bus/Metro passes cost €3.25 (for more info, visit www.atac.roma.it). Fancy new tickets with bar codes eventually will replace the plain paper tickets. Until then, buses and the Metro have two different validation machines; if you've got a new ticket, use the one with the slot on top.

Buses (especially the touristic #64) and the subway are havens for thieves and pickpockets. Assume any commotion is a thief-created distraction.

By Metro: The Roman subway system (Metropolitana) is simple, with two clean, cheap, fast lines that intersect at Termini train station. While much of Rome is not served by its skimpy subway, these stops are helpful: Termini (train station, National Museum of Rome at Palazzo Massimo, recommended hotels), Repubblica (Baths of Diocletian/Octagonal Hall, main TI, recommended hotels), Barberini (Cappuccin Crypt, Trevi Fountain), Spagna (Spanish Steps, Villa Borghese, classy shopping area), Flaminio (Piazza del Popolo, start of recommended Dolce Vita Stroll down Via del Corso), Ottaviano (St. Peter's and Vatican City), Cipro-Musei Vaticani (Vatican Museum, recommended hotels), Colosseo (Colosseum, Roman Forum, recommended hotels), and E.U.R. (Mussolini's futuristic suburb).

By Bus: Bus routes are clearly listed at the stops. Ask the TI for a bus map. Punch your ticket in the orange stamping

Metropolitana: Rome's Subway

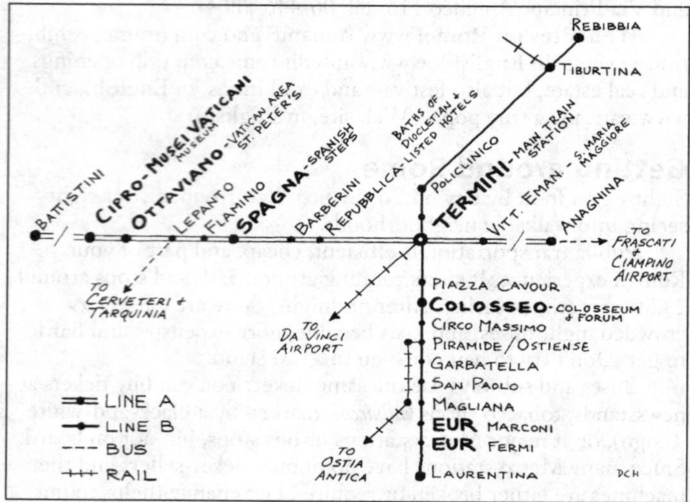

machine as you board (even if you've already stamped it for the Metro)—or you are cheating. Riding without a stamped ticket on the bus, while relatively safe, is stressful. Inspectors fine even innocent-looking tourists €52. If the validation machine won't work, you can write the date, time, and bus number on the ticket. Ideally, buy a bunch of tickets from a tobacco shop or newsstand first thing, so you can hop a bus without first having to search for a tobacco shop that's open.

Here are a few buses worth knowing about:

#64: Termini (train station), Piazza della Repubblica (sights), Via Nazionale (recommended hotels), Piazza Venezia (near Forum), Largo Argentina (near Pantheon), St. Peter's Basilica. Ride it for a city overview and to watch pickpockets in action (can get horribly crowded).

#40: This express route is especially helpful—it's the same route as #64, but with fewer stops, crowds, and pickpockets.

#8: This tram connects Largo Argentina with Trastevere (get off at Piazza Mastai).

#H: Express connecting Termini train station and Trastevere, with a few stops on Via Nazionale (for Trastevere, get off at Piazza Belli, just over bridge).

#492: Stazione Tiburtina, Piazza Barberini, Piazza Venezia, Piazza Cavour (Castel Sant' Angelo), Piazza Risorgimento (near Vatican Museum).

Daily Reminder

Sunday: These sights are closed: Vatican Museum (except for the last Sunday of the month, when it's free) and the Catacombs of San Sebastian. The Pantheon and E.U.R.'s Museum of Roman Civilization close early in the afternoon.
Monday: Many sights are closed: National Museum of Rome, Borghese Gallery, Capitol Hill Museum, Octagonal Hall and Museum of the Bath (both at Baths of Diocletian), Etruscan Museum, Castel Sant' Angelo, Trajan's Market, Protestant Cemetery, E.U.R.'s Museum of Roman Civilization, and Ostia Antica. All of the ancient sites and the Vatican Museum, among others, *are* open. The Baths of Caracalla close early in the afternoon.
Tuesday: All sights are open except for Nero's Golden House.
Wednesday: All sights are open except for the Catacombs of San Callisto.
Thursday: All sights are open except for the Cappuccin Crypt.
Friday/Saturday: All sights are open.

#714: Termini, Santa Maria Maggiore, San Giovanni in Laterano, Terme di Caracalla (Baths of Caracalla).

Rome has cute *electtrico* minibuses that wind through the narrow streets of old and interesting neighborhoods (daily except Sun). These are handy for sightseeing and fun for simply joyriding:

Electtrico #116: Through the medieval core of Rome from Campo de' Fiori to Piazza Barberini via the Pantheon.

Electtrico #117: San Giovanni in Laterano, Colosseo, Via dei Serpenti, Trevi Fountain, Piazza di Spagna, Piazza del Popolo.

"J" (for Jubilee) buses are bigger, come with a hostess, and provide more convenient access to some places farther out, such as St. Peter's (Cavalleggeri stop) and the Catacombs. Purchase tickets (€1) on the bus (info: tel. 800-076-287).

By Taxi: I use taxis in Rome more often than in other cities. They're relatively cheap and useful for efficient sightseeing in a big, hot city. Taxis start at about €2.75 (surcharges of €1 on Sun, €2.75 for night hours of 22:00–7:00, €1 surcharge for luggage, €7.25 extra for airport, tip about 10 percent by rounding up to the nearest euro). Sample fares: Train station to Vatican-€9; train station to Colosseum-€6; Colosseum to Trastevere-€7. Three or four companions with more money than time should taxi almost everywhere. It's tough to wave down a taxi in Rome. Find the nearest taxi stand. (Ask a local or in a shop, "*Dov'è una fermata dei tassi*?"

Some are listed on my maps.) Unmarked, unmetered taxis at train stations and the airport are usually a rip-off. Taxis listing their telephone number on the door have fair meters—use them. To save time and energy, have your hotel call a taxi; the meter starts when the call is received. (To call a cab on your own, dial 06-3570, 06-4994, or 06-88177.)

Tours of Rome

Scala Reale—Tom Rankin (an American architect in love with Rome and his Roman wife) runs Scala Reale, a company committed to sorting out the rich layers of Rome for small groups with a longer-than-average attention span. Their excellent walking tours vary in length from two to four hours and start at €16 per person. Try to book in advance, since their groups are limited to six and fill up fast. Their fascinating "Rome Orientation" walks lace together lesser-known sights from antiquity to the present (tel. 06-474-5673, 888/467-1986 in the U.S., www.scalareale.org, e-mail: info@scalareale.org).

If you're interested in week-long classes on Rome, look into the Institute for Roman Culture, an innovative, educational organization run by Tom Rankin and his colleague, archaeologist Darius Arya (see www.romanculture.org for prices, details, and booking).

Through Eternity—This company, which offers four walking tours led by native English speakers, gets mixed reviews from readers who like it or dislike it depending on the quality of their particular guide. The tours include St. Peter's and the Vatican Museum (€35, museum entry not included, 5.5 hrs, daily except Sun); the Colosseum and Roman Forum (€20, 2.5 hrs, daily); Rome at Twilight (€20, nightly); and a Wine Sampling Tour (€35, nightly, includes a glass at 4 or 5 wine bars and dinner). Call to get the schedule and to book in advance (max of 25 people, tel. 06-700-9336, cellular 347-336-5298, private tours possible, www.througheternity.com, e-mail: info@througheternity.com).

Rome Walks—Students working for this company give tours in fluent English. Sample tours include the Colosseum/Forum Walk (€33, includes Colosseum admission, 2.5 hrs); the Palatine Hill/Mouth of Truth Walk (€33, includes Palatine admission, 2 hrs); a Scandal Tour (€25, 2 hrs to dig up the dirt on Roman emperors, royalty, and popes); a Vatican City Walk (€45, includes admission to Vatican Museum, 4.5 hrs); and a Twilight Rome Evening Walk (€25, 2 hrs). Look online for the latest (www.romewalks.com) and book in advance by e-mail (info@romewalks.com) or phone (cellular 347-795-5175, private tours also available). You'll need to give your hotel name and phone number. Your guide will call or e-mail you to let you know the meeting place.

Tips on Sightseeing in Rome

Museums: Plan ahead. The marvelous Borghese Gallery and Nero's Golden House both require reservations. For the Borghese Gallery, it's safest to make reservations well in advance of your trip (for specifics, see page 804). You can wait until you're in Rome to call for a reservation time at Nero's Golden House, but it's wise to book ahead (see page 791).

A special **combo-ticket,** which costs €20, covers the National Museum of Rome, Colosseum, Palatine Hill, Baths of Caracalla, Crypt Balbi (medieval art), Museum of the Bath (Roman inscriptions), and Palazzo Altemps (so-so sculpture collection). The combo-ticket allows you to see seven sights for the price of three (purchase at participating sites, valid for 5 days). When you buy this, you can upgrade to a "Coupon Servizi" pass for an extra €5, giving you tours or audioguides at each site (normally €4 each). The big plus of this ticket is that you avoid the long lines at the Colosseum (if you purchase it at a participating site other than the Colosseum).

Get a current listing of **museum hours** from one of Rome's TIs: ask for the booklet *Tesori di Roma* (Treasures of Rome). Some museums may stay open later in summer (usually on Sat).

Churches: Churches tend to open early (around 7:00), close during lunch (roughly 12:00–15:00), and close late (around 19:00). Kamikaze tourists maximize their sightseeing hours by visiting churches before 9:00 and seeing the major sights that stay open during the siesta (St. Peter's, Colosseum, Roman Forum, Capitol Hill Museum, National Museum of Rome) while Romans are taking it cool and easy.

Many churches have "modest dress" requirements, which means no bare shoulders, miniskirts, or shorts—for men, women, or children. This dress code is only strictly enforced at St. Peter's. Elsewhere, you'll see many tourists in shorts touring many churches.

Miscellaneous tips: Carry a plastic water bottle that can be refilled at Rome's many public drinking spouts. Use museum and restaurant toilets when you can, because public restrooms are scarce.

Hop-on, Hop-off Bus Tour—The ATAC city bus tour offers your best budget orientation tour of Rome. In under two hours, you'll have 80 sights pointed out to you (by a live guide in English and maybe one other language). If you've got a little more time and money, you can get out at any of the nine stops and catch a later bus (though stops are poorly marked and the included map is useless). While the guide's spiel is limited to simple identification of the sights, this tour provides an efficient and economical orientation to Rome. The stops are: Piazza Barberini, Via Veneto, Villa Borghese, Piazza Cavour, St. Peter's Square, Corso Vittorio Emanuele (for Piazza Navona), Piazza Venezia, Colosseum, and Via Nazionale. I'd take the nonstop tour for €7.75; the hop-on-and-off tour is €13. Bus #110 departs every 30 minutes, at the top and bottom of the hour, from in front of the Termini train station (near platform C, buy tickets at info kiosk there—marked "i bus"—or buy on the bus and pay about 10 percent more, runs March–Sept 9:00–20:00, Oct–Feb 10:00–18:00, tel. 06-4695-2252).

Archeobus—This handy hop-on, hop-off bus runs hourly from the west side of Piazza Venezia way out the Appian Way. By far the easiest way to see the sights down this ancient Roman road, it includes a basic, uninspired two-hour (longer if there's traffic) tour in Italian and English in an air-conditioned minibus (buy €7.75 tickets at green kiosk on Piazza Venezia, valid 9:00–17:00, tel. 06-4695-4695).

Sights—From the Colosseum Area to Capitol Hill

Beware of gangs of young thieves, particularly between the Colosseum and the Forum; they're harmless if you know their tricks (see Theft Alert in "Helpful Hints," above).

▲St. Peter-in-Chains Church (San Pietro in Vincoli)—Built in the fifth century to house the chains that held St. Peter, this church is most famous for its Michelangelo statue. Check out the much-venerated chains under the high altar, then focus on Moses (free, Mon–Sat 7:00–12:30 & 15:30–19:00, Sun 7:30–12:30, a short walk uphill from the Colosseum, modest dress required).

Pope Julius II commissioned Michelangelo to build a massive tomb, with 48 huge statues, crowned by a grand statue of this egomaniacal pope. The pope had planned to have his tomb placed in the center of St. Peter's Basilica. When Julius died, the work had barely been started, and no one had the money or necessary commitment to Julius to finish the project. Michelangelo finished one statue—Moses—and left a few unfinished statues: Leah and Rachel flanking Moses in this church, the "prisoners" now in Florence's Accademia, and the "slaves" now in Paris' Louvre.

This powerful statue of Moses—mature Michelangelo—is worth studying. The artist worked on it in fits and starts for 30 years. Moses has received the Ten Commandments. As he holds the stone tablets, his eyes show a man determined to stop his tribe from worshiping the golden calf and idols . . . a man determined to win salvation for the people of Israel. Why the horns? Centuries ago, the Hebrew word for "rays" was mistranslated as "horns."

▲Nero's Golden House (Domus Aurea)—The barren remains of Emperor Nero's "Golden House" were reopened to the public in 1999. The original entrance to the house was all the way over at the Arch of Titus in the Forum. This massive house once sprawled across the valley (where the Colosseum now stands) and up the hill—the part you tour today. Larger even than Bill Gates' place, it was a pain to vacuum. A colossal, 33-meter-tall (100-foot) bronze statue of Nero towered over everything. The house incorporated an artificial lake (where the Colosseum was later built) and a forest stocked with game. It was decorated with the best multicolored marble and the finest frescoes. No expense was too great for Nero—his mistress soaked daily in the milk of 500 wild asses kept for her bathing pleasure.

Nero (ruled A.D. 54–68) was Rome's most notorious emperor. He killed his own mother, kicked his pregnant wife to death, crucified St. Peter, and—most galling to his subjects—was a bad actor. When Rome burned in A.D. 64, Nero was accused of torching it to clear land for an even bigger house. The Romans rebelled and Nero stabbed himself in the neck, crying, "What an artist dies in me!"

While only hints of the splendid, colorful frescoes survive, the towering vaults and the basic immensity of the place are impressive. As you wander through rooms that are now underground, look up at the holes in the ceiling. Imagine how much of old Rome still hides underground . . . and why the subway is limited to two lines.

Visits are allowed only with an escort (30 people, about every 30 min) and a reservation (€6.20, Wed–Mon 9:00–19:45, last entry at 18:40, closed Tue, tour lasts 50 min, audioguides-€2, but listen to the intro before entering or you'll be forever behind, 200 meters northeast of Colosseum, through a park gate, up a hill, and on the left). Guided tours in English are offered twice daily (€8.50); to reserve a place, call 06-3996-7700. If you just show up (particularly on a late afternoon on a weekday), you could luck out and get on a tour; if tours aren't booked up, the remaining seats are sold to drop-ins.

▲▲▲Colosseum—This 2,000-year-old building is *the* great example of Roman engineering. Using concrete, brick, and their trademark round arches, Romans constructed much larger buildings than the Greeks. But in deference to the higher Greek culture, they finished their no-nonsense megastructure by pasting all three orders of Greek columns (Doric, Ionic, and Corinthian) as exterior decorations. The Flavian Amphitheater's popular name, "Colosseum," comes from the colossal statue of Nero that once stood in front of it.

Romans were into "big." By putting two theaters together, they created a circular amphitheater. They could fill and empty its 50,000 numbered seats as quickly and efficiently as we do our superstadiums. Teams of sailors hoisted canvas awnings over the stadium to give fans shade. This was where ancient Romans, whose taste for violence was the equal of modern America's, enjoyed their Dirty Harry and *Terminator*. Gladiators, criminals, and wild animals fought to the death in every conceivable scenario. The floor of the Colosseum is missing, exposing underground passages. Animals were kept in cages here and then lifted up in elevators; they'd pop out from behind blinds into the arena. The gladiator didn't know where, when, or by what he'd be attacked.

Cost and Hours: €8 (exact change preferred, includes Palatine Hill visit within 24 hours, also covered by €20 combo-ticket, valid 7 days, daily 9:00–19:00, or one hour before sunset, Metro: Colosseo, tel. 06-3974-9907). Instead of waiting in line (sometimes an hour long) at the Colosseum to purchase a ticket, buy your Colosseum ticket at the Palatine Hill entrances nearby—inside the Forum entry (near Arch of Titus) and on Via di San Gregorio (facing Forum entry, with Colosseum at your back, go left on street). The €20 combo-ticket—covering the Colosseum, Palatine Hill, Baths of Caracalla, National Museum of Rome, Museum of the Bath, and more—also allows you to walk right into the Colosseum (if you've purchased it in advance at the Palatine Hill entrances or other participating sites; valid for 5 days; for details, see "Tips on Sightseeing in Rome," page 789). Or you can reserve a ticket in advance for an additional €1.50 fee (pick up at side window of Colosseum ticket office, call 06-3996-7700 to book, automated info in English).

Tours: You can rent an audioguide tour at the ticket office (€4 for 2 hours of use) or take a guided tour in English (€3.50, 60 min, offered several times daily, check at ticket office for schedule).

Nearby: Outside the entrance of the Colosseum, vendors sell handy little *Rome, Past and Present* books with plastic overlays to un-ruin the ruins (marked €11, offer €8). A WC is behind the Colosseum (facing ticket entrance, go right; WC is under stairway). The modern-day gladiators outside the Colosseum expect a fee if you snap a photo of them. A couple of fine eateries are close by; see page 845.

▲Arch of Constantine—This well-preserved arch, which stands between the Colosseum and the Forum, commemorates a military coup and, more importantly, the acceptance of Christianity in

The Forum Area

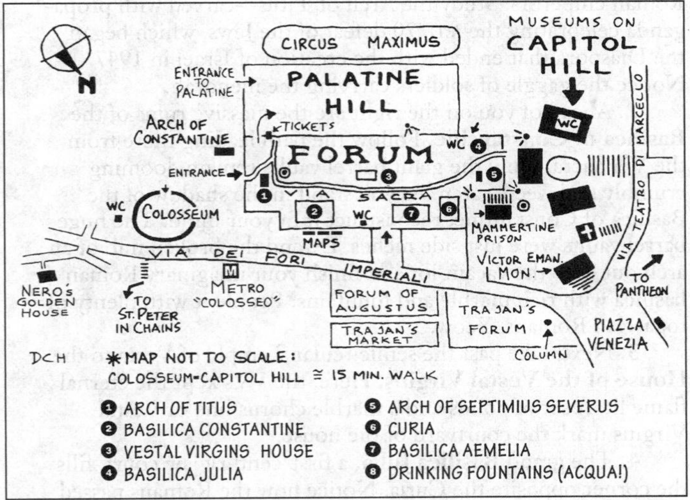

the Roman Empire. In A.D. 312, the ambitious Emperor Constantine (who had a vision he could win under the sign of the cross) defeated his rival, Maxentius. Constantine, who became sole emperor, legalized Christianity.

▲▲▲Roman Forum (Foro Romano)—This is ancient Rome's birthplace and civic center, and the common ground between Rome's famous seven hills (free admission to Forum, €8 for Palatine Hill, both keep the same hours: daily 9:00–19:00 or an hour before dark, Metro: Colosseo, tel. 06-3974-9907).

A €4 audioguide helps decipher the rubble (rent at gift shop at entrance on Via dei Fori Imperiali). Guided tours in English are offered once daily (€3.50); ask for information at the ticket booth at the Palatine Hill (near Arch of Titus). Sidewalk vendors sell cheap city guidebooks, such as the small red *Rome, Past and Present*, showing helpful before-and-after pictures (marked €11—offer €8).

With the help of the map in this section, follow this basic walk. Enter the Forum near the Arch of Constantine:

1. Start by the small **Arch of Titus** (opposite the drinking fountain) overlooking the remains of what was the political, social, and commercial center of the Roman Empire. The Via Sacra—the main street of ancient Rome—cuts through the Forum from here to Capitol Hill and the Arch of Septimius Severus on the opposite side. On the left, a ticket booth welcomes you to the

Palatine Hill (described below)—once filled with the palaces of Roman emperors. Study the Arch of Titus—carved with propaganda celebrating the A.D. 70 defeat of the Jews, which began the Diaspora that ended with the creation of Israel in 1947. Notice the gaggle of soldiers carrying the menorah.

2. Ahead of you on the right are the massive ruins of the **Basilica of Constantine.** Follow the path leading there from the Via Sacra. Only the giant barrel vaults remain, looming crumbly and weed-eaten. As you stand in the shadow of the Basilica of Constantine, reconstruct it in your mind. The huge barrel vaults were just side niches. Extend the broken nub of an arch out over the vacant lot and finish your imaginary Roman basilica with rich marble and fountains. People it with plenty of toga-clad Romans. Yeow.

3. Next, hike past the semicircular Temple of Vesta to the **House of the Vestal Virgins.** Here, the VVs kept the eternal flame lit. A set of ponds and a marble chorus line of Vestal Virgins mark the courtyard of the house.

4. The grand **Basilica Julia,** a first-century law court, fills the corner opposite the Curia. Notice how the Romans passed their time; ancient backgammon-type game boards are cut into the pavement.

5. The **Arch of Septimius Severus,** from about A.D. 200, celebrates that emperor's military victories. In front of it, a stone called Lapis Niger covers the legendary tomb of Romulus. To the left of the arch, the stone bulkhead is the Rostra, or speaker's platform. It's named for the ship's prows that used to decorate it as big shots hollered, "Friends, Romans, countrymen . . . ."

6. The plain, intact brick building near the Arch of Septimius Severus was the **Curia,** where the Roman senate sat. (Peek inside.) Roman buildings were basically brick and concrete, usually with a marble veneer, which in this case is long lost.

7. The **Basilica Aemilia** (second century B.C.) shows the floor plan of an ancient palace. This pre-Christian "basilica" design was later adopted by medieval churches. From here, a ramp leads up and out (past a WC and a fun headless statue to pose with).

▲Palatine Hill—The hill above the Forum contains scanty remains of the imperial palaces and the foundations of Rome, from Iron Age huts to the legendary house of Romulus (under corrugated tin roof in far corner). We get our word *palace* from this hill, where the emperors chose to live. The Palatine was once so filled with palaces that later emperors had to build out. (Looking up at it from the Forum, you see the substructure that supported these long-gone palaces.) The Palatine museum has sculptures and fresco fragments but is nothing special. From the pleasant garden, you'll get an overview of the Forum. On the far side, look down into an emperor's private stadium and then beyond at the dusty Circus Maximus, once a chariot course. Imagine the cheers, jeers, and furious betting. But considering how ruined the ruins are, the heat, the hill to climb, the €8 entry fee, and the relative difficulty in understanding what you're looking at, the Palatine Hill is a disappointment.

Cost and Hours: €8, includes Colosseum visit within 24 hours, also covered by €20 combo-ticket, daily 9:00–19:00, or one hour before sunset, Metro: Colosseo. The main entrance and ticket office—which also sells Colosseum tickets, enabling smart sightseers to avoid that long line—is near the Arch of Titus and the Colosseum. Another Palatine entrance is on Via di San Gregorio.

Tours: Audioguides cost €4. Guided tours in English are offered once daily (€3.50); ask for information at the ticket booth.

▲Mammertine Prison—The 2,500-year-old, cistern-like prison, which once held Saints Peter and Paul, is worth a look (donation requested, daily 9:00–12:30 & 14:30–18:30, at the foot of Capitol Hill, near Forum's Arch of Septimius Severus). When you step into the room, you'll hit a modern floor. Ignore that and look up at the hole in the ceiling, from which prisoners were lowered. Then take the stairs down to the level of the actual prison floor. As you descend, you'll walk past a supposedly miraculous image of Peter's face, created when a guard pushed him into the wall. Downstairs, you'll see the column to which Peter was chained. It's said that a miraculous fountain sprang up in this room so Peter could baptize other prisoners. The upside-down cross commemorates Peter's upside-down crucifixion.

Imagine humans, amid fat rats and rotting corpses, awaiting slow deaths. On the walls near the entry are lists of notable prisoners (Christian and non-Christian) and the ways they were executed: *strangolati*, *decapitato*, *morto di fame* (died of hunger)....

Sights—Capitol Hill Area

There are several ways to get to the top of Capitol Hill. If you're coming from the north (Piazza Venezia), take the grand stairs located to the right of the big, white Victor Emmanuel Monument (described below). Coming from the Forum, take either the steep staircase or the winding road, which converge at a great Forum overlook and a refreshing water fountain. Block the spout with your fingers; water spurts up for drinking. Romans, who call this *il nasone* (the nose), joke that a cheap Roman boy takes his date out for a drink at *il nasone*.

▲▲Capitol Hill (Campidoglio)—This hill was the religious and political center of ancient Rome. It's still the home of the city's government. Michelangelo's Renaissance square is bounded by two fine museums and the mayoral palace. Its centerpiece is a copy of the famous equestrian statue of Marcus Aurelius (the original is behind glass in the museum, a few steps away).

Michelangelo intended that people approach the square from the grand stairway off Piazza Venezia. From the top of the stairway, you see the new Renaissance face of Rome with its back to the Forum, facing the new city. Notice how Michelangelo gave the buildings the "giant order"—huge pilasters make the existing two-story buildings feel one-storied and more harmonious with the new square. Notice also how the statues atop these buildings welcome you, then draw you in. The terraces just downhill (past either side of the mayor's palace) offer fine views of the Forum.

▲▲Capitol Hill Museum—This museum encompasses two buildings (Palazzo dei Conservatori and Palazzo Nuovo), connected by an underground passage that leads to the vacant Tabularium and a panoramic overlook of the Forum (€8, Tue–Sun 9:00–20:00, last entry 19:00, closed Mon, Jan 1, May 1, and Dec 25, tel. 06-3996-7800).

For an orientation to the museum's two buildings, face the equestrian statue on Capitol Hill Square (with your back to the grand stairway). The Palazzo Nuovo is on your left and the Palazzo dei Conservatori is on your right (closer to the river). Ahead is the mayor's palace (Palazzo Senatorio); below it and out of sight are the Tabularium and underground passage.

You can buy your ticket at either building (but if you want to rent a €3.60 audioguide, go to Palazzo dei Conservatori).

The **Palazzo dei Conservatori** is one of the world's oldest museums, at 500 years old. Outside the entrance, notice the marriage announcements and, possibly, wedding-party photo ops. Inside the courtyard, have a look at giant chunks of a statue of Emperor Constantine; when intact, this imposing statue held court in the Basilica of Constantine in the Forum. The museum is worthwhile, with lavish rooms and several great statues. Tops is the original (500 B.C.) Etruscan *Capitoline Wolf* (the little statues of Romulus and Remus were added in the Renaissance). Don't miss the *Boy Extracting a Thorn* or the enchanting *Commodus as Hercules*. The second-floor painting gallery—except for two Caravaggios—is forgettable. The café upstairs, with a splendid patio with city views, is lovely at sunset.

Connect the two museums with the underground passage that leads to the **Tabularium**. Built in the first century A.D., this once held the archives of ancient Rome. The word *Tabularium* comes from tablet, on which the Romans wrote their laws. You won't see any tablets, but you will see a superb head-on view of the Forum from the windows.

The **Palazzo Nuovo** houses mostly portrait busts of forgotten emperors. But it has three must-see statues: the *Dying Gaul*, the *Capitoline Venus* (both on the first floor up), and the original gilded bronze equestrian statue of Marcus Aurelius (behind glass in museum courtyard). This greatest surviving equestrian statue of antiquity was the original centerpiece of the square. While most such pagan statues were destroyed by Dark Age Christians, Marcus was mistaken for Constantine (the first Christian emperor) and therefore spared.

From Capitol Hill to Piazza Venezia—Leaving Capitol Hill, descend the stairs leading to Piazza Venezia. At the bottom of the stairs, look left several blocks down the street to see a condominium actually built around surviving ancient pillars and arches of Teatro Marcello—perhaps the oldest inhabited building in Europe.

Still at the bottom of the stairs, look up the long stairway to your right (which pilgrims climb on their knees) for a good example of the earliest style of Christian church. While pilgrims find it worth the climb, sightseers can skip it. As you walk toward Piazza Venezia, look down into the ditch on your right and see how modern Rome is built on the forgotten frescoes and mangled mosaics of ancient Rome.

Piazza Venezia—This vast square is the focal point of modern Rome. The Via del Corso, which starts here, is the city's axis, surrounded by Rome's classiest shopping district. In the 1930s, Mussolini whipped up Italy's nationalistic fervor here from a balcony above the square (to your left with back to Victor Emmanuel Monument). Fascist masses filled the square screaming, "Four more years!" or something like that. Fifteen years later, they hung Mussolini from a meat hook in Milan.

Victor Emmanuel Monument—This oversized monument to an Italian king was part of Italy's rush to overcome the new country's strong regionalism and create a national identity after unification in 1870. It's now open to the public, offering a new view of the Eternal City (free, 242 steps to the top, long hours).

Romans think of the monument not as an altar of the fatherland but as "the wedding cake," "the typewriter," or "the dentures." It wouldn't be so bad if it weren't sitting on a priceless acre of ancient Rome and if they had chosen better marble (this is too in-your-face white and picks up the pollution horribly). Soldiers guard Italy's *Tomb of the Unknown Soldier* as the eternal flame flickers. At this level, stand with your back to the flame and see how Via del Corso bisects Rome.

▲Trajan's Column, Market, and Forum—This offers the grandest column and best example of "continuous narration" from antiquity. Over 2,500 figures scroll around the 40-meter-high (130-foot) column, telling of Trajan's victorious Dacian campaign (circa A.D. 103, in present-day Romania), from the assembling of the army at the bottom to the victory sacrifice at the top. The ashes of Trajan and his wife were held in the mausoleum at the base while the sun once glinted off a polished bronze statue of Trajan at the top. Today, St. Peter is on top. Study the propaganda that winds up the column like a scroll, trumpeting Trajan's wonderful military exploits. You can see this close up for free (always open and viewable, just off Piazza Venezia, across the street from the Victor Emmanuel Monument). Viewing balconies once stood on either side, but it seems likely Trajan fans came away only with a feeling that the greatness of their emperor and empire was beyond comprehension (for a rolled-out version of the column's story, visit the Museum of Roman Civilization at E.U.R., below). This column marked **Trajan's Forum**, which was built to handle the shopping needs of a wealthy city of over a million. Commercial, political, religious, and social activities all mixed in the forum.

For a fee, you can go inside **Trajan's Market** (boring) and part of Trajan's Forum; the entrance is uphill from the column on Via IV Novembre. The market was once filled with shops selling goods from all over the Roman Empire (€6.20, summer Tue–Sun 9:00–18:30, winter Tue–Sun 9:00–16:30, closed Mon, tel. 06-679-0048).

Sights—Pantheon Area

▲▲▲Pantheon—For the greatest look at the splendor of Rome, antiquity's best-preserved interior is a must (free, Mon–Sat 8:30–19:30, Sun and holidays 9:00–18:00, tel. 06-6830-0230). Because it became a church dedicated to the martyrs just after the fall of Rome, the barbarians left it alone, and the locals didn't use it as a quarry. The portico is called Rome's umbrella—a fun local gathering in a rainstorm. Walk past its one-piece granite columns (biggest in Italy, shipped from Egypt) and through the original bronze doors. Sit inside under the glorious skylight and enjoy classical architecture at its best.

The dome, 47 meters/142 feet high and wide, was Europe's biggest until the Renaissance. Michelangelo's dome at St. Peter's, while much higher, is one meter (about 3 feet) smaller. The brilliance of this dome's construction astounded architects through the ages. During the Renaissance, Brunelleschi was given permission to cut into the dome (see the little square hole above and to the right of the entrance) to analyze the material. The concrete dome gets thinner and lighter with height—the highest part is volcanic pumice.

This wonderfully harmonious architecture greatly inspired

Raphael and other artists of the Renaissance. Raphael, along with Italy's first two kings, chose to be buried here.

As you walk around the outside of the Pantheon, notice the "rise of Rome"—about five meters (15 feet) since it was built. Nearest WCs are at McDonald's and bars on the square. Great gelato is nearby (see page 843).

▲▲**Churches near the Pantheon**—The **Church of San Luigi dei Francesi** has a magnificent chapel painted by Caravaggio (free, Fri–Wed 7:30–12:30 & 15:30–19:00, Thu 7:30–12:30, sightseers should avoid Mass at 7:30 and 19:00, modest dress recommended).

The only Gothic church you'll see in Rome is **Santa Maria sopra Minerva**. On a little square behind the Pantheon to the east, past the Bernini statue of an elephant carrying an Egyptian obelisk, this Dominican church was built *sopra* (over) a pre-Christian temple of Minerva. Before stepping in, notice the high-water marks on the wall (right of door). Inside, you'll see that the lower parts of the frescoes were lost to floods. (After the last great flood, in 1870, Rome built the present embankments, finally breaking the spirit of the Tiber River.)

Rome was at its low ebb, almost a ghost town, through much of the Gothic period. Little was built during this time (and much of what was built was redone Baroque). This church is a refreshing exception.

St. Catherine's body lies under the altar (her head is in Siena). In the 1300s, she convinced the pope to return from France to Rome, thus saving Italy from untold chaos.

Left of the altar stands a little-known Michelangelo statue, *Christ Bearing the Cross*. Michelangelo gave Jesus an athlete's or warrior's body (a striking contrast to the more docile Christ of medieval art), but left the face to one of his pupils. Fra Angelico's simple tomb is farther to the left, on the way to the back door. Before leaving, head over to the right (south transept), pop in a coin for light, and enjoy a fine Filippo Lippi fresco showing scenes from the life of St. Thomas Aquinas.

Exit the church via its rear door (behind the Michelangelo statue), walk down Fra Angelico lane (spy any artisans at work), turn left, and walk to the next square. On your right, you'll find the **Chiesa di St. Ignazio** church, a riot of Baroque illusions. Study the fresco over the door and the ceiling in the back of the nave. Then stand on the yellow disk on the floor between the two stars. Look at the central (black) dome. Keeping your eyes on the dome, walk under and past it. Church building project runs out of money? Hire a painter to paint a fake, flat dome. (Both churches open early, take a siesta—Santa Maria

Pantheon Area

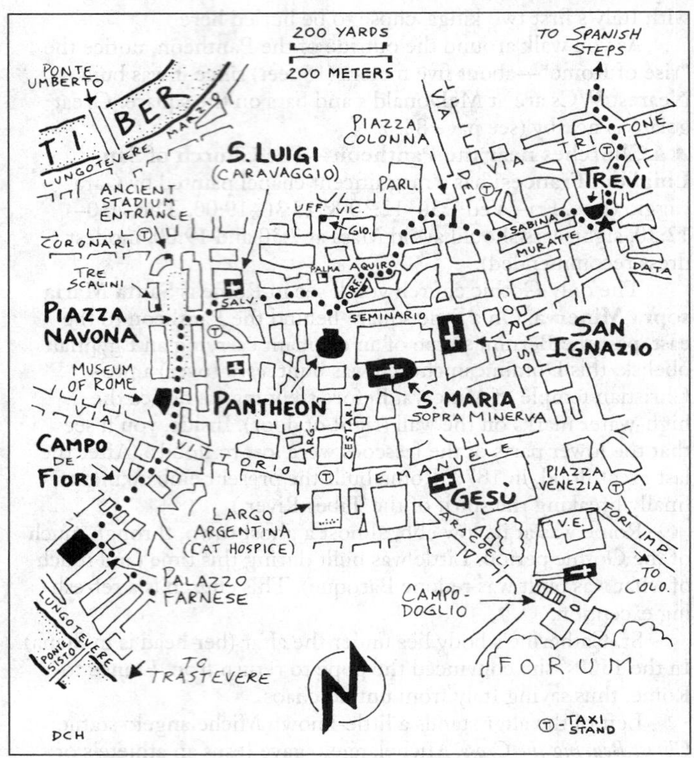

sopra Minerva closes at 12:00, St. Ignazio at 12:30, they reopen around 15:30, and close at 19:00. Modest dress is recommended.)

A few blocks away, back across Corso Vittorio Emmanuele, is the rich and Baroque **Gesu Church** (daily 7:00–12:00 & 15:00–20:00), headquarters of the Jesuits in Rome. The Jesuits powered the Church's Counter-Reformation. With Protestants teaching that all roads to heaven did not pass through Rome, the Baroque churches of the late 1500s were painted with spiritual road maps that said they did.

Walk out the Gesu Church and two blocks down Corso V. Emmanuele to the **Sacred Area** (Largo Argentina), an excavated square facing the boulevard, about four blocks south of the Pantheon. Stroll around this square and look into the excavated pit at some of the oldest ruins in Rome. Julius Caesar was assassinated near here. Today, it's a refuge for cats—some 250 of them are cared for by volunteers. You'll see them (and their refuge) at the far (west) side of the square.

▲Galleria Doria Pamphilj—This gallery, filling a palace on Piazza del Collegio Romano, offers a rare chance to wander through a noble family's lavish rooms with the prince who calls this downtown mansion home. Well, almost. Through an audioguide, the prince lovingly narrates his family's story, including how the Doria Pamphilj (pron. pahm-FEEL-yee) family's cozy relationship with the pope inspired the word nepotism. Highlights include paintings by Caravaggio, Titian, and Raphael, and portraits of Pope Innocent X by Velázquez (on canvas) and Bernini (in marble). The fancy rooms of the palace are interesting, with a mini-Versailles–like hall of mirrors and paintings stacked to the ceiling in the style typical of 18th-century galleries (€8, includes fine audioguide, Fri–Wed 10:00–17:00, closed Thu, from Piazza Venezia walk 2 blocks up Via del Corso and take a left, tel. 06-679-7323, www.doriapamphilj.it).

▲Trevi Fountain—This bubbly Baroque fountain of Neptune with his entourage, worth ▲ by day and ▲▲ by night, is a minor sight to art scholars but a major nighttime gathering spot for teens on the make and tourists tossing coins. (For more information, see "Self-Guided Walks in Rome," page 821.)

Sights—East Rome, near the Train Station

These sights are within a 10-minute walk of the train station. By Metro, use the Termini stop for the National Museum and the Piazza Repubblica stop for the rest.

▲▲▲National Museum of Rome in Palazzo Massimo—This museum houses the greatest collection of ancient Roman art anywhere, and includes busts of emperors and a Roman copy of the *Greek Discus Thrower*. The ground floor is a historic yearbook of marble statues from the second century B.C. to the second century A.D., with rare Greek originals.

The first floor is peopled by statues from the first through fourth centuries A.D. To see the second-floor collection of frescoes and mosaics that once decorated Roman villas, you must reserve an entry time for a free, 45-minute tour led by an Italian- (and sometimes English-) speaking guide; if interested, book the next available tour when you buy your ticket. Finally, descend into the basement to see fine gold jewelry, dice, an abacus, and vault doors leading into the best coin collection in Europe, with fancy magnifying glasses maneuvering you through cases of coins from ancient Rome to modern times.

Cost and Hours: €6, covered by €20 combo-ticket, Tue–Sun 9:00–19:45, closed Mon, open some summer Saturdays until

East Rome

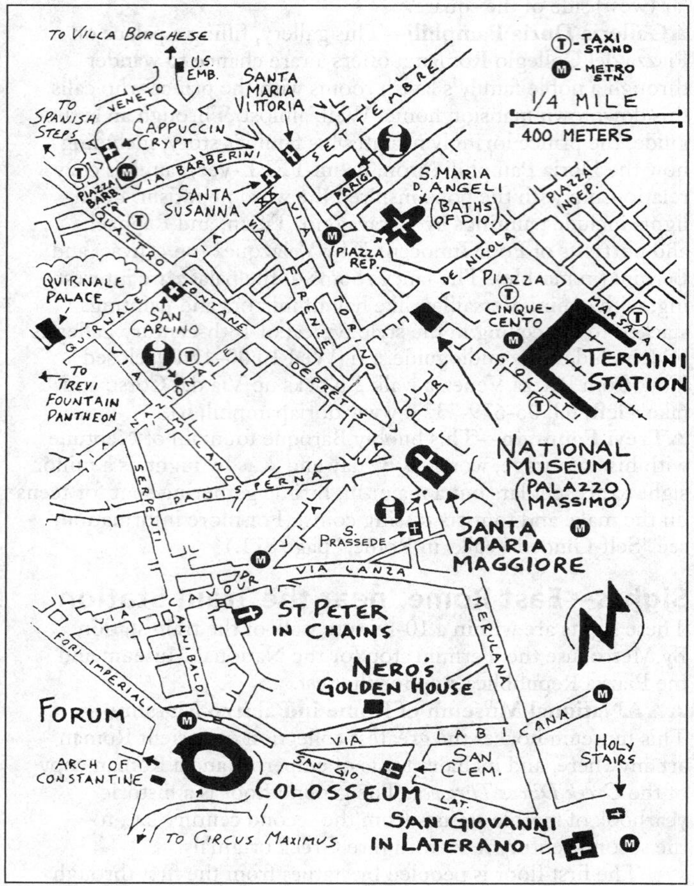

23:00, last entry 45 min before closing. An audioguide costs €4 (buy ticket first, then get audioguide at bookshop). The museum is about 100 meters (330 feet) from the Termini train station. As you leave the station, it's the sandstone-brick building on your left. Enter at the far end, at Largo di Villa Peretti (Metro: Termini, tel. 06-481-4144).

Baths of Diocletian—Around A.D. 300, Emperor Diocletian built the largest baths in Rome. This sprawling meeting place, with baths and schmoozing spaces to accommodate 3,000 bathers at a time, was a big deal in ancient Rome. While much of it is still closed, three sections are open: the Octagonal Hall, the Church of St. Mary of the Angels and Martyrs (both face Piazza della Repubblica), and the Museum of the Bath (across from the train station); see descriptions below.

▲▲Octagonal Hall—The Aula Ottagona, or Rotunda of Diocletian, was a private gymnasium in the Baths of Diocletian. Built around A.D. 300, these functioned until 537, when the barbarians cut Rome's aqueducts. The floor would have been seven meters (23 feet) lower (look down the window in the center of the room). The graceful iron grid supported the canopy of a 1928 planetarium. Today, the hall's a gallery, showing off fine bronze and marble statues—the kind that would have decorated the baths of imperial Rome. Most are Roman copies of Greek originals...gods, athletes, portrait busts. Two merit a close look: the *Defeated Boxer* (first century B.C., Greek and textbook Hellenistic) and the *Roman Aristocrat*. The aristocrat's face is older than the body. This bronze statue is typical of the day: Take a body modeled on Alexander the Great and pop on a portrait bust (free, Tue–Sat 9:00–14:00, Sun 9:00–13:00, closed Mon, borrow the English-description booklet, handy WC hidden in the back corner through an unmarked door).

▲Church of St. Mary of the Angels and Martyrs (Santa Maria degli Angeli e dei Martiri)—From Piazza della Repubblica, step through the Roman wall into what was the great central hall of the baths and is now a church (since the 16th century) designed by Michelangelo. When the church entrance was moved to Piazza Repubblica, the church was reoriented 90 degrees, turning the nave into long transepts and the transepts into a short nave. The 12 red granite columns still stand in their ancient positions. The classical floor was five meters (15 feet) lower. Project the walls down and imagine the soaring shape of the Roman vaults (free, Mon–Sat 7:00–18:30, Sun 8:00–19:30, closed to sightseers during Mass).

Museum of the Bath (Museo Nazionale Romano Terme di Diocleziano)—This museum, located on the grounds of the ancient Baths of Diocletian, has a misleading name. Rather than featuring the baths, it displays ancient Roman inscriptions on tons of tombs, steles, and tablets. Although well-displayed and described in English, the museum is difficult to appreciate quickly, and most travelers will find more history presented on a grander scale in the National Museum of Rome a block away (€5, covered by €20 combo-ticket, Tue–Sun 9:00–19:45, last entry 45 min before closing, closed Mon, Viale E. De Nicola 79, entrance faces Termini station, tel. 06-4782-6152).

▲Santa Maria della Vittoria—This church houses Bernini's statue of a swooning *St. Teresa in Ecstasy* (free, daily 7:00–13:00 &

15:00–19:00, on Largo Susanna, about 5 blocks northwest of train station, Metro: Repubblica). Once inside the church, you'll find St. Teresa to the left of the altar.

Teresa has just been stabbed with God's arrow of fire. Now the angel pulls it out and watches her reaction. Teresa swoons, her eyes roll up, her hand goes limp, she parts her lips . . . and moans. The smiling, Cupid-like angel understands just how she feels. Teresa, a 16th-century Spanish nun, later talked of the "sweetness" of "this intense pain," describing her oneness with God in ecstatic, even erotic, terms.

Bernini, the master of multimedia, pulls out all the stops to make this mystical vision real. Actual sunlight pours through the alabaster windows; bronze sunbeams shine on a marble angel holding a golden arrow. Teresa leans back on a cloud and her robe ripples from within, charged with her spiritual arousal. Bernini has created a little stage setting of heaven. And watching from the "theater boxes" on either side are members of the family that commissioned the work.

Santa Susanna—The home of the American Catholic Church in Rome, Santa Susanna holds Mass in English daily at 18:00 and Sunday at 9:00 and 10:30. Their excellent Web site in English, www.santasusanna.org, contains tips for travelers (Via XX Settembre 15, near recommended Via Firenze hotels, Metro: Repubblica, tel. 06-4201-4554).

Sights—North Rome: Villa Borghese and nearby Via Veneto

▲Villa Borghese—Rome's scruffy "Central Park" is great for people-watching (plenty of modern-day Romeos and Juliets). Take a row on the lake or visit the park's fine museums.

▲▲▲Borghese Gallery—This private museum, filling a cardinal's mansion in the park, offers one of Europe's most sumptuous art experiences. Because of the gallery's slick mandatory reservation system, you'll enjoy its collection of world-class Baroque sculpture—including Bernini's *David* and his excited statue of Apollo chasing Daphne, as well as paintings by Caravaggio, Raphael, Titian, and Rubens—with manageable crowds.

The essence of the collection is the connection of the Renaissance with the classical world. Notice the second-century Roman reliefs with Michelangelo-designed panels above either end of the portico as you enter. The villa was built in the early 17th century by the great art collector Cardinal Borghese, who wanted to prove that the glories of ancient Rome were matched by the Renaissance.

In the main entry hall, opposite the door, notice the thrilling relief of the horse falling (first century A.D., Greek). Pietro

Bernini, father of the famous Bernini, completed the scene by adding the rider.

Each room seems to feature a Baroque masterpiece. The best of all is in Room 3: Bernini's *Apollo Chasing Daphne*. It's the perfect Baroque subject—capturing a thrilling, action-filled moment. In the mythological story, Apollo races after Daphne. Just as he's about to reach her, she turns into a tree. As her toes turn to roots and branches spring from her fingers, Apollo is in for one rude surprise. Walk slowly around. It's more air than stone.

Cost and Hours: €8, Tue–Sun 9:00–19:30, sometimes on Sat. until 23:00 June–Sept, closed Mon. No photos are allowed.

Reservations: Reservations are mandatory and easy to get in English over the Internet (www.ticketeria.it) or by phone (tel. 06-32810; if you get an Italian recording, press 2 for English; office hours: Mon–Fri 9:00–19:00, Sat 9:00–13:00, office closed Sat in Aug). Every two hours, 360 people are allowed to enter the museum. Entry times are 9:00, 11:00, 13:00, 15:00, and 17:00 (plus 19:00 and 21:00 if open late on Sat, June–Sept). Reserve a *minimum* of several days in advance for a weekday visit, at least a week ahead for weekends. When you reserve, request a day and time (which you'll be given if available), and you'll get a claim number. While you'll be advised to come 30 minutes before your appointed time, you can arrive a few minutes beforehand. But don't be late, as no-show tickets are sold to standbys.

Visits are strictly limited to two hours. Concentrate on the first floor, but leave yourself 30 minutes for the paintings of the Pinacoteca upstairs; highlights are marked by the audioguide icons. The fine bookshop and cafeteria are best visited outside your two-hour entry window.

If you don't have a reservation, just show up (or call first and ask if there are openings; a late afternoon on a weekday is usually your best bet). Reservations are tightest at 11:00 and on weekends. No-shows are released a few minutes after the top of the hour. Generally, out of 360 reservations, a few will fail to show (but more than a few may be waiting to grab them).

Tours: Guided English tours are offered at 9:10 and 11:10 for €5; reserve with entry reservation (or consider the excellent audioguide tour for €4).

Location: The museum is in the Villa Borghese park. A taxi (tell the cabbie your destination: gah-leh-REE-ah bor-GAY-zay) can get you within 100 meters (330 feet) of the museum. Otherwise, Metro to Spagna and take a 15-minute walk through the park.

Etruscan Museum (Villa Giulia Museo Nazionale Etrusco)—The Etruscan civilization thrived in this part of Italy around 600

B.C., when Rome was an Etruscan town. The Etruscan civilization is fascinating, but the Villa Giulia Museum is extremely low-tech and in a state of disarray. I don't like it, and Etruscan fans will prefer the Vatican Museum's Etruscan section. Still, the Villa Giulia does have the famous "husband and wife sarcophagus" (a dead couple seeming to enjoy an everlasting banquet from atop their tomb; sixth century B.C. from Cerveteri), the *Apollo from Veio* statue (of textbook fame), and an impressive room filled with gold sheets of Etruscan printing and temple statuary from the Sanctuary of Pyrgi (€4.20, Tue–Sun 9:00–19:00, plus June–Sept Sat 21:00–23:45, closed Mon, closes earlier off-season, Piazzale di Villa Giulia 9, tel. 06-320-1951).

▲Cappuccin Crypt—If you want bones, this is the place. The crypt is below the church of Santa Maria della Immaculata Concezione on Via Veneto, just up from Piazza Barberini. The bones of more than 4,000 monks who died between 1528 and 1870 are in the basement, all artistically arranged for the delight—or disgust—of the always wide-eyed visitor. The soil in the crypt was brought from Jerusalem 400 years ago, and the monastic message on the wall explains that this is more than just a macabre exercise. Pick up a few of Rome's most interesting postcards (donation, Fri–Wed 9:00–12:00 & 15:00–18:00, closed Thu, Metro: Barberini, tel. 06-487-1185). A painting of St. Francis by Caravaggio is upstairs. Just up the street, you'll find the American Embassy, Federal Express, and fancy Via Veneto cafés filled with the poor and envious looking for the rich and famous.

Ara Pacis (Altar of Peace)—This will reopen in 2005, once restoration is complete. In 9 B.C., after victories in Gaul and Spain, Emperor Augustus celebrated the beginning of the Pax Romana by building this altar of peace. Peace is almost worshiped here. The north and south walls show a procession with realistic portraits of the imperial family in Greek Hellenistic style. It's a fine combination of Roman grandeur and Greek elegance. Even when the altar is not open, it can sometimes be seen through the windows (a long block west of Via del Corso on Via di Ara Pacis, on east bank of river near Ponte Cavour, nearest Metro: Spagna).

Sights—West Rome: Vatican City Area

▲▲▲St. Peter's Basilica—There is no doubt: This is the richest and most impressive church on earth. To call it vast is like calling God smart. Marks on the floor show where the next-largest churches would fit if they were put inside. The ornamental cherubs would dwarf a large man. Birds roost inside, and thousands of people wander about, heads craned heavenward, hardly noticing each other. Don't miss Michelangelo's *Pietà* (behind bulletproof

Vatican City Overview

glass) to the right of the entrance. Bernini's altar work and seven-story-tall bronze canopy *(baldacchino)* are brilliant.

For a quick self-guided walk through the basilica, follow these points (see map on page 809):

1. The atrium is larger than most churches. Notice the historic doors (the Holy Door, on the right, won't be opened until the next Jubilee Year, in 2025—see point 13 below).

2. The purple, circular porphyry stone marks the site of Charlemagne's coronation in A.D. 800 (in the first St. Peter's church that stood on this site). From here, get a sense of the immensity of the church, which can accommodate 95,000 worshipers standing on its six acres.

3. Michelangelo planned a Greek-cross floor plan rather than the Latin-cross standard in medieval churches. A Greek cross, symbolizing the perfection of God, and by association the goodness of man, was important to the humanist Michelangelo. But accommodating large crowds was important to the Church in the fancy Baroque age, which followed Michelangelo, so the original nave length was doubled. Stand halfway up the nave and imagine the stubbier design Michelangelo had in mind.

4. View the magnificent dome from the statue of St. Andrew. See the vision of heaven above the windows: Jesus, Mary, a ring of saints, rings of angels, and, on the very top, God the Father.

5. The main altar sits directly over St. Peter's tomb and under Bernini's 21-meter-tall (70-foot) bronze canopy.

6. The stairs lead down to the crypt to the foundation, chapels, and tombs of popes. (Do this last, since it leads you out of the church.)

7. The statue of St. Peter, with an irresistibly kissable toe, is one of the few pieces of art that predate this church. It adorned the first St. Peter's church.

8. St. Peter's throne and Bernini's starburst dove window is the site of a daily mass (Mon–Sat at 17:00, Sun at 17:45).

9. St. Peter was crucified here when this location was simply "the Vatican Hill." The obelisk now standing in the center of St. Peter's square marked the center of a Roman racecourse long before a church stood here.

10. For most, the treasury (in the sacristy) is not worth the admission.

11. The church is filled with mosaics, not paintings. Notice the mosaic version of Raphael's *Transfiguration*.

12. Blessed Sacrament Chapel.

13. Michelangelo sculpted his *Pietà* when he was 24 years old. A *pietà* is a work showing Mary with the dead body of Christ taken down from the cross. Michelangelo's mastery of the body is obvious in this powerfully beautiful masterpiece. Jesus is believably dead, and Mary, the eternally youthful "handmaiden" of the Lord, still accepts God's will . . . even if it means giving up her son.

The Holy Door (just to the right of the *Pietà*) was bricked shut at the end of the Jubilee Year 2000 and won't be opened until 2025. Every 25 years, the Church celebrates an especially festive year derived from the Old Testament idea of the Jubilee Year (originally every 50 years), which encourages new beginnings and the forgiveness of sins and debts. In the Jubilee Year 2000,

St. Peter's Basilica

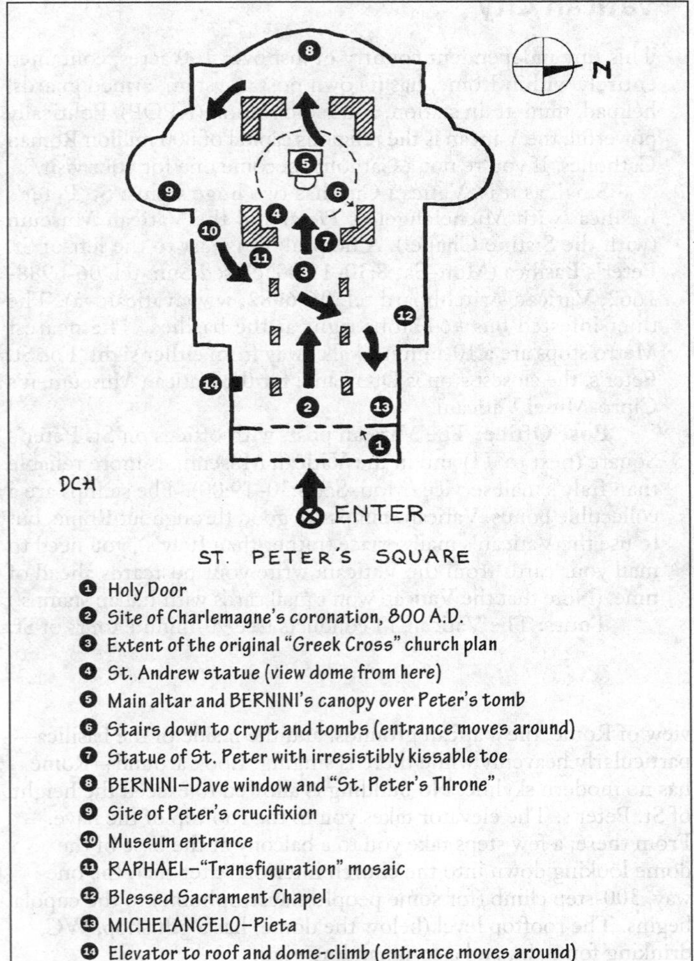

the pope tirelessly—and with significant success—promoted debt relief for the world's poorest countries.

14. An elevator leads to the roof and the stairway up the dome (€5, allow an hour to go up and down). The dome, Michelangelo's last work, is (you guessed it) the biggest anywhere. Taller than a football field is long, it's well worth the sweaty climb for a great

Vatican City

This tiny independent country of just over 100 acres, contained entirely within Rome, has its own postal system, armed guards, helipad, mini–train station, and radio station (KPOP). Politically powerful, the Vatican is the religious capital of 800 million Roman Catholics. If you're not a Catholic, become one for your visit.

Small as it is, Vatican City has two huge sights: St. Peter's Basilica (with Michelangelo's *Pietà*) and the Vatican Museum (with the Sistine Chapel). A helpful TI is just to the left of St. Peter's Basilica (Mon–Sat 8:30–19:00, closed Sun, tel. 06-6988-1662; Vatican switchboard tel. 06-6982, www.vatican.va). The thief-infested bus #64 stops right at the basilica. The nearest Metro stops are a 10-minute walk away from either sight: For St. Peter's, the closest stop is Ottaviano; for the Vatican Museum, it's Cipro-Musei Vaticani.

Post Office: The Vatican post, with offices on St. Peter's Square (next to TI) and in the Vatican Museum, is more reliable than Italy's mail service (Mon–Sat 8:30–19:00). The stamps are a collectible bonus. Vatican stamps are good throughout Rome, but to use the Vatican's mail service (rather than Italy's), you need to mail your cards from the Vatican; write your postcards ahead of time. (Note that the Vatican won't mail cards with Italian stamps.)

Tours: The Vatican TI conducts free 90-minute tours of St.

view of Rome, the Vatican grounds, and the inside of the basilica—particularly heavenly while there is singing. Look around—Rome has no modern skyline. No building is allowed to exceed the height of St. Peter's. The elevator takes you to the rooftop of the nave. From there, a few steps take you to a balcony at the base of the dome looking down into the church interior. After that, the one-way, 300-step climb (for some people claustrophobic) to the cupola begins. The rooftop level (below the dome) has a gift shop, WC, drinking fountain, and a commanding view.

Dress Code: The church strictly enforces its dress code: no shorts or bare shoulders (men and women); no miniskirts. You might be required to check any bags at a free cloakroom near the entry.

Hours of Church: Daily May–Sept 7:00–19:00, Oct–April 7:00–18:00. All are welcome to join in the hour-long Mass at the front altar (Mon–Sat at 8:30, 10:00, 11:00, 12:00, & 17:00; Sun and holidays 9:00, 10:30, 12:10, 13:00, 16:00, & 17:30). The church

Peter's (depart daily from TI at 14:15 also; Mon, Wed, and Fri at 15:00; confirm schedule at TI, tel. 06-6988-1662). Tours are the only way to see the Vatican Gardens; book at least a day in advance by calling 06-6988-4466 (€9, Mon–Sat 10:00–12:00, tours start at Vatican Museum tour desk and finish on St. Peter's Square). To tour the necropolis of St. Peter's and the saint's tomb, call the Excavations Office at 06-6988-5318 (€8, 2 hrs, office open Mon–Fri 9:00–17:00).

Seeing the Pope: Your best chances for a sighting are on Sunday and Wednesday. The pope usually gives a blessing at noon on Sunday from his apartment on St. Peter's Square (except Aug–Sept, when he speaks at his summer residence at Castel Gandolfo, 40 km/25 miles from Rome; train leaves Rome's Termini station at 8:35, returns after his talk). On Wednesday at 10:30, the pope blesses the crowds at St. Peter's from a balcony or canopied platform on the square (except in winter, when he speaks at 11:00 in the 7,000-seat Aula Paola VI Auditorium, next to St. Peter's Basilica). To find out the pope's schedule or to book a free spot for the Wednesday blessing (either for a seat on the square or in the auditorium), call 06-6988-4631. The weekly entertainment guide *Roma c'è* always has a "Seeing the Pope" section. If you don't want to see the pope, minimize crowd problems by avoiding these times.

is particularly moving at 7:00, while tourism is still sleeping. Volunteers who want you to understand and appreciate St. Peter's give free 90-minute tours (depart from TI daily at 14:15; also Mon, Wed, and Fri at 15:00; confirm schedule at TI, tel. 06-6988-1662); the tours are generally excellent but non-Christians can find them preachy. Seeing the *Pietà* is neat; understanding it is divine.

Cost and Hours of Dome: The view from the dome is worth the climb (€5 elevator plus 300-step climb, May–Sept daily 8:00–18:00, Oct–April daily 8:30–17:00).

▲▲▲Vatican Museum—The six kilometers (3.75 miles) of displays in this immense museum—from ancient statues to Christian frescoes to modern paintings—are topped by the Raphael Rooms and Michelangelo's glorious Sistine Chapel. (If you have a pair of binoculars, bring them.)

Even without the Sistine, this is one of Europe's top three or four houses of art. It can be exhausting, so plan your visit carefully, focusing on a few themes. Allow two hours for a quick visit, three or four for time to enjoy it. The museum has a nearly impossible-not-to-follow, one-way system (although, for the rushed visitor, the museum does clearly mark out four color-coded visits of different lengths—A is shortest, D longest). Tip: The Sistine Chapel has an exit (optional) that leads directly to St. Peter's Basilica, saving you the 10-minute walk back to the Vatican Museum exit; if you want to squirt out at the Sistine, see the Pinacoteca painting gallery first (described below) and don't get an audioguide (which needs to be returned at the entry/exit).

Start, as civilization did, in Egypt and Mesopotamia. Next, the Pio Clementino collection features **Greek and Roman statues**. Decorating its courtyard are some of the best Greek and Roman statues in captivity, including the *Laocoön* group (first century B.C., Hellenistic) and the *Apollo Belvedere* (a second-century Roman copy of a Greek original). The centerpiece of the next hall is the *Belvedere Torso* (just a 2,000-year-old torso, but one that had a great impact on the art of Michelangelo). Finishing off the classical statuary are two fine fourth-century porphyry sarcophagi; these royal purple tombs were made (though not used) for the Roman emperor Constantine's mother and daughter. They were Christians—and therefore outlaws—until Constantine made Christianity legal (A.D. 312). The tombs, crafted in Egypt at a time when a declining Rome was unable to do such fine work, have details that are fun to study.

After long halls of tapestries, old maps, broken penises, and fig leaves, you'll come to what most people are looking for: The Raphael Rooms (or *stanza*) and Michelangelo's Sistine Chapel.

These outstanding works are frescoes. A fresco (meaning "fresh" in Italian) is technically not a painting. The color is mixed into wet plaster, and, when the plaster dries, the painting is actually part of the wall. This is a durable but difficult medium, requiring speed and accuracy, as the work is built slowly, one patch at a time.

After fancy rooms illustrating the "Immaculate Conception of Mary" (a hard-to-sell, 19th-century Vatican doctrine) and the triumph of Constantine (with divine guidance, which led to his conversion to Christianity), you enter the first room completely done by **Raphael** and find the newly restored *School of Athens*. This is remarkable for its blatant pre-Christian classical orientation, especially since it originally wallpapered the apartments of Pope Julius II. Raphael honors the great pre-Christian thinkers—Aristotle, Plato, and company—who are portrayed as the leading artists of Raphael's day. The bearded figure of Plato is Leonardo da Vinci. Diogenes, history's first hippie, sprawls alone in bright blue on the stairs, while Michelangelo broods in the foreground—supposedly added late. Apparently, Raphael snuck a peek at the

Sistine Chapel and decided that his arch-competitor was so good he had to put their personal differences aside and include him in this tribute to the artists of his generation. Today's St. Peter's was under construction as Raphael was working. In the *School of Athens*, he gives us a sneak preview of the unfinished church.

Next (unless you detour through the refreshingly modern Catholic art section) is the brilliantly restored **Sistine Chapel**. The Sistine Chapel, the pope's personal chapel, is where, upon the death of the ruling pope, a new pope is elected. The College of Cardinals meets here and votes four times a day until a two-thirds-plus-one majority is reached and a new pope is elected.

The Sistine is famous for Michelangelo's pictorial culmination of the Renaissance, showing the story of Creation, with a powerful God weaving in and out of each scene through that busy first week. This is an optimistic and positive expression of the High Renaissance and a stirring example of the artistic and theological maturity of the 33-year-old Michelangelo, who spent four years on this work.

Later, after the Reformation wars had begun and after the Catholic army of Spain had sacked the Vatican, the reeling Church began to fight back. As part of its Counter-Reformation, a much older Michelangelo was commissioned to paint the *Last Judgment* (behind the altar). Brilliantly restored, the message is as clear as the day Michelangelo finished it: Christ is returning, some will go to hell and some to heaven, and some will be saved by the power of the rosary.

In the recent and controversial restoration project, no paint was added. Centuries of dust, soot (from candles used for lighting and Mass), and glue (added to make the art shine) were removed, revealing the bright original colors of Michelangelo. Photos are allowed (without a flash) elsewhere in the museum, but as part of the deal with the company who did the restoration, no photos are allowed in the Sistine Chapel.

For a shortcut, a small door at the rear of the Sistine Chapel allows groups and individuals (without an audioguide) to escape directly to St. Peter's Basilica. If you exit here, you're done with the museum. The Pinacoteca is the only important part left. Consider doing it at the start. Otherwise it's a 10-minute, heel-to-toe slalom through tourists from the Sistine Chapel to the entry/exit.

After this long march, you'll find the **Pinacoteca** (the Vatican's small but fine collection of paintings, with Raphael's *Transfiguration*, Leonardo's unfinished *St. Jerome*, and Caravaggio's *Deposition)*, a cafeteria (long lines, mediocre food), and the underrated early-Christian art section, before you exit via the souvenir shop.

Cost and Hours: €10, March–Oct Mon–Fri 8:45–15:45; Sat 8:45–13:45; Nov–Feb Mon–Sat 8:45–13:45, closed Sun except last Sun of the month (when it's free, crowded, and open 8:45–13:45). Last entry is about 90 minutes before the closing time (12:20 when museum closes at 13:45, 14:20 when museum closes at 15:45). The Sistine Chapel sometimes shuts down 30 minutes early.

The museum is generally hot and crowded. Saturday, the last Sunday of the month, and Monday are the worst; afternoons are best.

The museum is closed on many holidays (mainly religious ones) including—for 2003: Jan 1 and 6, Feb 11, March 19, Easter and Easter Monday (April 20 and 21), May 1 and 29, June 19, Aug 14 and 15, Nov 1, and Dec 8 and 25.

Modest dress (no short shorts or bare shoulders for men or women) is appropriate and often required. Museum tel. 06-6988-4947.

Tours: A tour in English is offered once daily at 11:00 (€16.50, 2 hrs, call 06-6988-4466 to reserve). You can rent a €5 audioguide (but if you do, you lose the option of taking the shortcut from the Sistine Chapel to St. Peter's, because the audioguide must be returned at the Vatican Museum entrance).

▲Castel Sant' Angelo—Built as a tomb for the emperor; used through the Middle Ages as a castle, prison, and place of last refuge for popes under attack; and today, a museum, this giant pile of ancient bricks is packed with history.

Ancient Rome allowed no tombs—not even the emperor's—within its walls. So Hadrian grabbed the most commanding position just outside the walls and across the river and built a towering tomb (circa A.D. 139) well within view of the city. His mausoleum was a huge cylinder (64 meters wide, 21 meters high; or 210 feet wide, 70 feet high) topped by a cypress grove and crowned by a huge statue of Hadrian himself riding a chariot. For nearly a hundred years, Roman emperors (from Hadrian to Caracalla in A.D. 217) were buried here.

In the year 590, the Archangel Michael appeared above the mausoleum to Pope Gregory the Great. Sheathing his sword, the angel signaled the end of a plague. The fortress that was Hadrian's mausoleum eventually became a fortified palace, renamed for the "holy angel."

Since Rome was repeatedly plundered by invaders, Castel Sant' Angelo was a handy place of last refuge for threatened popes. The elevated corridor connecting Castel Sant' Angelo with the Vatican was built in 1277. In anticipation of long sieges, rooms were decorated with papal splendor (you'll see paintings by Crivelli, Signorelli, and Mantegna). In the 16th century, during a sack of

Rome by troops of Charles V of Spain, the pope lived inside the castle for months with his entourage of hundreds (an unimaginable ordeal, considering the food service at the top-floor bar).

After you walk around the entire base of the castle, take the small staircase down to the original Roman floor. In the atrium, study the model of the castle in Roman times and imagine the niche in the wall filled with a towering "welcome to my tomb" statue of Hadrian. From here, a ramp leads to the right, spiraling 125 meters (410 feet). While some of the fine brickwork and bits of mosaic survive, the marble veneer is long gone (notice the holes in the wall which held it in place). At the end of the ramp, stairs climb to the room where the ashes of the emperors were kept. These stairs continue to the top, where you'll find the papal apartments. Don't miss the Sala del Tesoro (treasury), where the wealth of the Vatican was locked up in a huge chest. Do miss the 58 rooms of the military museum. The views from the top are great—pick out landmarks as you stroll around—and a restful coffee with a view of St. Peter's is worth the price.

Cost, Hours, Tours: €5, Tue–Sun 9:00–19:00, plus June–Sept Sat 21:00–23:45, closed Mon. You can take an English-language tour with an audioguide (€3.60) or live guide (€4.20, Tue–Fri at 15:00, Sat at 12:15 and 16:30, confirm times, tel. 06-3996-7600, Metro: Lepanto or bus #64, near Vatican City).

Ponte Sant' Angelo—The bridge leading to Castel Sant' Angelo was built by Hadrian for quick and regal access from downtown to his tomb. The three middle arches are actually Roman originals and a fine example of the empire's engineering expertise. The angels were designed by Bernini and finished by his students.

Sights—South Rome

If you visit Ostia Antica (see page 821), you can maximize sightseeing efficiency by visiting any of the sights in south Rome on your return.

▲St. Paul's Outside the Walls (Basilica San Paolo Fuori le Mura)—One of the greatest churches in Christendom, St. Paul's was originally built in 324, then destroyed by fire in the 1820s. Today, it's mammoth and pristine, rebuilt true to the ancient basilica plan. It feels sterile, but in a good way—like you're already in heaven. Along with St. Peter's Basilica, San Giovanni in Laterano, and Santa Maria Maggiore, this church is part of the Vatican rather than Italy. St. Paul is supposed to be buried under the altar (without his head, which San Giovanni in Laterano got). Alabaster windows light the vast interior, fifth-century mosaics decorate the triumphal arch leading to the altar, and mosaic portraits of all 264 popes, from St. Peter to John Paul II, ring the place—with blank spots ready for future popes. Find John Paul II (to right of the high altar: Jo Paulus II, no date) and John Paul I (to his right, with a reign of one month and three days). Wander the ornate yet peaceful cloister (closed 13:00–15:00). The courtyard leading up to the church is typical of early Christian churches; even the first St. Peter's had this kind of welcoming zone (free, daily 7:00–18:00, modest dress code enforced, Via Ostiense 186, Metro: San Paolo).

▲Montemartini Museum (Musei Capitolini Centrale Montemartini)—This museum houses a dreamy collection of 400 ancient statues, set evocatively in a classic 1932 electric power plant among generators and Metropolis-type cast-iron machinery. While the art is not as famous as the collections you'll see downtown, the effect is fun and memorable—and you'll encounter absolutely no tourists (€4.20, Tue–Sun 9:30–19:00, closed Mon, Via Ostiense 106, a short walk from Metro: Garbatella, tel. 06-574-8042).

Baths of Caracalla (Terme di Caracalla)—Today, it's just a shell—a huge shell—with all of its sculptures and most of its mosaics moved to museums. Inaugurated by Emperor Caracalla in A.D. 216, this massive complex could accommodate 1,600 visitors at a time. Today, you'll see a two-story, roofless brick building surrounded by a garden, bordered by ruined walls. The two large rooms at either end of the building were used for exercise. In between the exercise rooms was a pool flanked by two small, mosaic-floored dressing rooms. Niches in the walls once held statues. In its day, this was a remarkable place to hang out. For ancient Romans, the baths were a social experience.

The Baths of Caracalla functioned until Goths severed the aqueducts in the sixth century. In modern times, operas were performed here from 1938 to 1993. For the same reason concerts no longer take place in the Forum—to keep the ruins from becoming more ruined—the performances were discontinued (€5, covered by €20 combo-ticket, Mon 9:00–17:30, Tue–Sun 9:00–19:30, last entry 1 hour before closing, audioguide-€4, fine €8 guidebook—can read in shaded garden while sitting on a chunk of column, Metro: Circus Maximus, and a 5-min walk south along Via delle Terme di Caracalla, tel. 06-575-8628). Several of the baths' statues are now in Rome's Octagonal Hall; the immense *Toro Farnese* (a marble sculpture of a bull surrounded by people) snorts in Naples' Archaeological Museum.

Testaccio—Four fascinating but lesser sights cluster at the Piramide Metro stop between the Colosseum and E.U.R., in the gritty Testaccio neighborhood. (This is a quick and easy stop as you return from E.U.R., or when changing trains en route to Ostia Antica.)

Working-class since ancient times, Testaccio has recently gone trendy-bohemian, and visitors will wander through an awkward mix of yuppie and proletarian worlds, not noticing—but perhaps feeling—the "keep Testaccio for the Testaccians" graffiti.

Pyramid of Gaius Cestius: The Mark Antony/Cleopatra scandal (around the time of Christ) brought exotic Egyptian styles into vogue. A rich Roman magistrate, Gaius Cestius, had a pyramid built as his tomb. Made of brick covered in marble, it was completed in just 330 days (as stated in its Latin inscription) and fell far short of Egyptian pyramid standards. Later incorporated into the Aurelian Wall, it's now next to the Piramide Metro stop.

Porta Ostiense: This formidable gate (also next to Piramide Metro stop) is from the Aurelian Wall, begun in the third century under Emperor Aurelius. The wall, which encircled the city, was 20 kilometers (12 miles) long and eight meters (26 feet) high, with 14 main gates and 380 22-meter-tall (72-foot) towers. Most of what you'll see today is circa A.D. 400. The barbarians reconstructed this gate in the sixth century. (For more on the wall, visit the Museum of the Walls at Porta San Sebastian; see "Ancient Appian Way," below.)

Protestant Cemetery: The *Cimitero Acattolico per gli Stranieri al Testaccio* (cemetery for the burial of non-Catholic foreigners) is a Romantic tomb-filled park, running along the wall just beyond the pyramid. From the Piramide Metro stop, walk between the pyramid and the Roman gate on Via Persichetti, then go left on Caio Cestio to the gate of the cemetery. Ring the bell (donation box, April–Sept Tue–Sun 9:00–18:00, Oct–March 9:00–17:00, closed Mon).

Originally, none of the Protestant epitaphs were allowed to make any mention of heaven. Signs direct visitors to the graves of notable non-Catholics who have died in Rome since 1738. Many of the buried were diplomats. And many, such as poets Shelley and Keats, were from the Romantic Age; they came on the Grand Tour and—"captivated by the fatal charms of Rome," as Shelley wrote—never left. Head left toward the pyramid to find Keats' tomb, in the far corner. At the pyramid, look down on Matilde Talli's cat hospice (flier at the gate). Volunteers use donations to care for these "Guardians of the Departed" who "provide loyal companionship to these dead."

Monte Testaccio: Just behind the Protestant Cemetery (as you leave, turn left and continue 2 blocks down Caio Cestio) is a 35-meter-tall (115-foot) ancient trash mountain. It's made of broken *testae*—broken earthenware jars used to haul mostly wine 2,000 years ago, when this was a gritty port warehouse district. After 500 years of sloppy dock work, Rome's lowly eighth hill was built. Because the caves dug into the hill stay cool, trendy bars, clubs, and restaurants compete with gritty car-repair places for a spot. The neighborhood was once known for a huge slaughterhouse and a Gypsy camp that squatted inside an old military base.

Now it's home to the Villagio Globale, a site for concerts and techno-raves. For a youthful and lively night scene, adventurers might consider a trip out to Monte Testaccio (Metro: Piramide).

Ancient Appian Way *(Via Appia Antica)*

Since the fourth century B.C., this has been Rome's gateway to the East. The first section was perfectly straight. It was the largest, widest, fastest road ever, the wonder of its day, called the "Queen of Roads." Eventually, this most important of Roman roads stretched 700 kilometers (430 miles) to the port of Brindisi—where boats sailed for Greece and Egypt. Twenty-nine such roads fanned out from Rome. Just as Hitler built the autobahn system in anticipation of empire maintenance, the emperors realized the military and political value of a good road system. A central strip accommodated animal-powered vehicles, and elevated sidewalks served pedestrians. As it left Rome, the road was lined with tombs and funerary monuments. Imagine a funeral procession passing under the pines and cypress and past a long line of pyramids, private mini-temples, altars, and tombs.

Hollywood created the famous image of the Appian Way lined with Spartacus and his gang of defeated and crucified slave rebels. This image is only partially accurate. Spartacus was killed in battle.

Tourist's Appian Way: The road starts about three kilometers (less than 2 miles) south of the Colosseum at the massive San Sebastian Gate. The Museum of the Walls, located at the gate, offers an interesting look at Roman defense and a chance to scramble along a stretch of the ramparts (€2.60, Tue–Sun 9:00–19:00, closed Mon, tel. 06-7047-5284). A kilometer (0.6 mile) down the road are the two most historic and popular catacombs, those of San Callisto and San Sebastian (described below). Beyond that, the road becomes pristine and traffic-free, popular for biking and hiking.

To reach the Appian Way, take the Archeobus from Piazza Venezia (see page 790) or take the Metro to the Colli Albani stop, then catch bus #660 to Via Appia Antica—its last stop and the start of an interesting stretch of the ancient road. The segment between the third and 11th milestones is most interesting.

You can rent bikes at the Appian park office on weekends and holidays. To reach the office by bus (either Archeobus or city bus), get off at the park entrance—the Sede Parco Appia Antica stop (€2.50/hr, Via Appia Antica 42, tel. 06-512-6314, www.parcoappiaantica.org).

▲▲Catacombs—The catacombs are burial places for (mostly) Christians who died in ancient Roman times. By law, no one was allowed to be buried within the walls of Rome. While pagan Romans were into cremation, Christians preferred to be buried. But land was expensive and most Christians were poor. A few wealthy, landowning Christians allowed their land to be used as burial places.

The 40 or so known catacombs circle Rome about five kilometers (3 miles) from its center. From the first through the fifth centuries, Christians dug an estimated 600 kilometers (375 miles) of tomb-lined tunnels, with networks of galleries as many as five layers deep. The tufa—soft and easy to cut, though it becomes very hard when exposed to air—was perfect for the job. The Christians burrowed many layers deep for two reasons: to get more mileage out of the donated land, and to be near martyrs and saints already buried there. Bodies were wrapped in linen (like Christ's). Since they figured the Second Coming was imminent, there was no interest in embalming the body.

When Emperor Constantine legalized Christianity in 313, Christians had a new, interesting problem. There would be no more persecuted martyrs to bind them and inspire them. Thus the early martyrs and popes assumed more importance, and Christians began making pilgrimages to their burial places in the catacombs.

In the 800s, when barbarian invaders started ransacking the tombs, Christians moved the relics of saints and martyrs to the safety of churches in the city center. For a thousand years, the catacombs were forgotten. Around 1850, they were excavated and became part of the romantic Grand Tour of Europe.

Finding abandoned plates and utensils from ritual meals in the candlelit galleries led 18th- and 19th-century Romantics to guess that persecuted Christians hid out and lived in these catacombs. This Romantic legend grew. But catacombs were not used for hiding out. They are simply early Christian burial grounds. With a million people in Rome, the easiest way for the 10,000 or so early Christians to hide out was not to camp in the catacombs (which everyone, including the government, knew about), but to melt into the city.

The underground tunnels, while empty of bones, are rich in early Christian symbolism, which functioned as a secret language. The dove symbolized the soul. You'll see it quenching its thirst (worshiping), with an olive branch (at rest), or happily perched (in paradise). Peacocks, known for their "incorruptible flesh," symbolized immortality. The shepherd with a lamb on his shoulders was the "good shepherd," the first portrayal of Christ as a kindly leader of his flock. The fish was used because the first letters of these words—"Jesus Christ, Son of God, Savior"—spelled "fish" in Greek. And the anchor is a cross in disguise. A second-century bishop had written on his tomb: "All who understand these things, pray for me." You'll see pictures of people praying with their hands raised up—the custom at the time.

All catacomb tours are essentially the same. The **Catacombs of San Callisto** (a.k.a. Callixtus), the official cemetery for the Christians of Rome and burial place of third-century popes, is the most historic. Sixteen bishops (early popes) were buried here. Buy your €5 ticket and wait for your language to be called. They move lots of people quickly. If one group seems ridiculously large (over 50 people), wait for the next tour in English (Thu–Tue 8:30–12:00 & 14:30–17:30, closed Wed and Feb, closes at 17:00 in winter, Via Appia Antica 110, tel. 06-5130-1580). Dig this: The catacombs have a Web site (www.catacombe.roma.it) focusing mainly on San Callisto, featuring photos, site info, and a history.

The **Catacombs of San Sebastian** (Sebastiano) are 300 meters (985 feet) farther down the road (€5, Mon–Sat 8:30–12:00 & 14:30–17:30, closed Sun and Nov, closes at 17:00 in winter, Via Appia Antica 136, tel. 06-5130-1580).

E.U.R.

In the late 1930s, Italy's dictator, Benito Mussolini, planned an international exhibition to show off the wonders of his fascist society. But these wonders brought us World War II, and Il Duce's celebration never happened. The unfinished mega-project was completed in the 1950s and now houses government offices and big, obscure museums.

If Hitler and Mussolini won the war, our world might look like E.U.R. (pronounced "ay-oor"). Hike down E.U.R.'s wide, pedestrian-mean boulevards. Patriotic murals, aren't-you-proud-to-be-an-extreme-right-winger pillars, and stern squares decorate the soulless, planned grid and stark office blocks. Boulevards named for Astronomy, Electronics, Social Security, and Beethoven are more exhausting than inspirational. Today, E.U.R. is worth a trip for its Museum of Roman Civilization (described below).

The Metro skirts E.U.R. with three stops (10 min from the Colosseum). Use E.U.R. Magliana for the "Square Colosseum" and E.U.R. Fermi for the Museum of Roman Civilization (both described below). Consider walking 30 minutes from the palace to the museum through the center of E.U.R.

From the Magliana Metro stop, stairs lead uphill to the **Palace of the Civilization of Labor (Palazzo del Civilta del Lavoro)**, the essence of fascist architecture. With its giant, no-questions-asked, patriotic statues and its black-and-white simplicity, this is E.U.R.'s tallest building and landmark. It's understandably nicknamed the "Square Colosseum." Around the corner, Café Palombini is still decorated in a 1930s style and is now quite trendy with young Romans (daily 7:00–24:00, good gelato, pastries, and snacks, Piazzale Adenauer 12, tel. 06-591-1700).

▲Museum of Roman Civilization (Museo della Civilta Romana)—With 59 rooms filled with plaster casts and models illustrating the greatness of classical Rome, this vast and heavy museum gives a strangely lifeless, close-up look at Rome. Each room has a theme, from military tricks to musical instruments. One long hall is filled with casts of the reliefs of Trajan's Column. The highlight is the 1:250-scale model of Constantine's Rome—circa A.D. 300 (€4.20, Tue–Sat 9:00–18:45, Sun 9:00–13:30, closed Mon, Piazza G. Agnelli, from Metro: E.U.R. Fermi, walk 10 min up Via dell' Arte, you'll see its colonnade on the right, tel. 06-592-6041).

Sights—Near Rome

▲▲Ostia Antica—For an exciting day trip less than an hour from downtown Rome, pop down to the ancient Roman port of Ostia Antica. It's similar to Pompeii, but a lot closer and, in some ways, more interesting. Because Ostia was a working port town, it shows a more complete and gritty look at Roman life than does wealthy Pompeii. Wandering around today, you'll see the remains of the docks, warehouses, apartment flats, mansions, shopping arcades, and baths that served a once thriving port of 60,000 people. Later, Ostia became a ghost town, and it is now excavated. Start at the 2,000-year-old theater, buy a map, explore the town, and finish with its fine little museum (note that museum closes at 13:30).

Getting There: To get there, take the Metro's B Line to the Piramide stop (consider popping out to see the ancient Roman pyramid tomb, listed above in South Rome sights). From the Piramide stop, catch the Lido train to Ostia Antica (2/hr, use a Metro ticket). From the train station, cross the road via the blue sky bridge and walk straight down Via della Stazione di Ostia Antica, following signs to *Scavi di Ostia Antica*, about 400 meters (1,300 feet) to the gate.

Cost and Hours: €5, Tue–Sun 8:30–18:00 in summer, 9:00–16:00 in winter, closed Mon. Visit the museum in the morning before it closes (Tue–Sun 9:00–13:30, closed Mon, cafeteria in museum, tel. 06-5635-8099).

Tour: The well-done audioguide costs €5.

Self-Guided Walks in Rome

Night Walk Across Rome: Trastevere to the Spanish Steps

Rome can be grueling. But a fine way to enjoy this historian's rite of passage is an evening walk lacing together Rome's floodlit nightspots. Enjoying fine urban spaces, observing real-life theater vignettes, sitting so close to a Bernini fountain that traffic noises evaporate, watching water flicker its mirror on the marble, jostling with local teenagers to see all the gelato flavors, enjoying lovers straddling more than the bench, jaywalking past flak-proof vested *polizia*, marveling at the ramshackle elegance that softens this brutal city for those who were born here and can imagine living nowhere else—these are the flavors of Rome best tasted after dark. This walk is about three kilometers, or two miles, long (for a shortcut, skip Trastevere and start at Campo de' Fiori instead).

To get to Trastevere, the colorful neighborhood across *(tras)* the Tiber *(tevere)* River, you can take a taxi or ride the bus (from Vatican area—#23; or from Via Nazionale hotels—take the #40 express to Piazza Belli just over bridge, or catch #64, #70, #115, or #640 to Largo Argentina, then transfer to tram #8 and get off at Piazza Mastai). Consider having dinner in Trastevere (see "Eating," below).

Trastevere offers the best look at medieval-village Rome. The action all marches to the chime of the church bells. Go to Trastevere and wander. Wonder. Be a poet on Rome's Left Bank. This proud neighborhood was long an independent, working-class area. It's now becoming trendy, and high rents are driving out the source of so much color. Still, it's a great people scene, especially at night. Start your exploratory stroll at Piazza di Santa Maria in Trastevere. While today's fountain is 17th-century, there has been a fountain here since Roman times.

Santa Maria in Trastevere, one of Rome's oldest churches, was made a basilica in the fourth century, when Christianity was legalized (free, daily 7:30–13:00 & 15:00–19:00). It was the first church dedicated to the Virgin Mary. The portico (covered area just outside the door) is decorated with fascinating ancient fragments filled with early Christian symbolism. Most of what you see today dates from around the 12th century, but the granite columns come from an ancient Roman temple, and the ancient basilica floor plan (and ambience) survives. The 12th-century mosaics behind the altar are striking, and notable for their portrayal of Mary—the first showing her at the throne with Jesus in heaven. Look below the scenes from the life of Mary to see ahead-of-their-time paintings (by Cavallini, from 1300) that predate the Renaissance by 100 years.

Before leaving Trastevere, wander the backstreets. Then, from the church square (Piazza di Santa Maria), take Via del Moro to the river and cross on Ponte Sisto, a pedestrian bridge with a good view of St. Peter's dome. Continue straight ahead for one block. Take the first left, which leads down Via di Capo di Ferro through the scary and narrow darkness to Piazza Farnese, with its

Trastevere

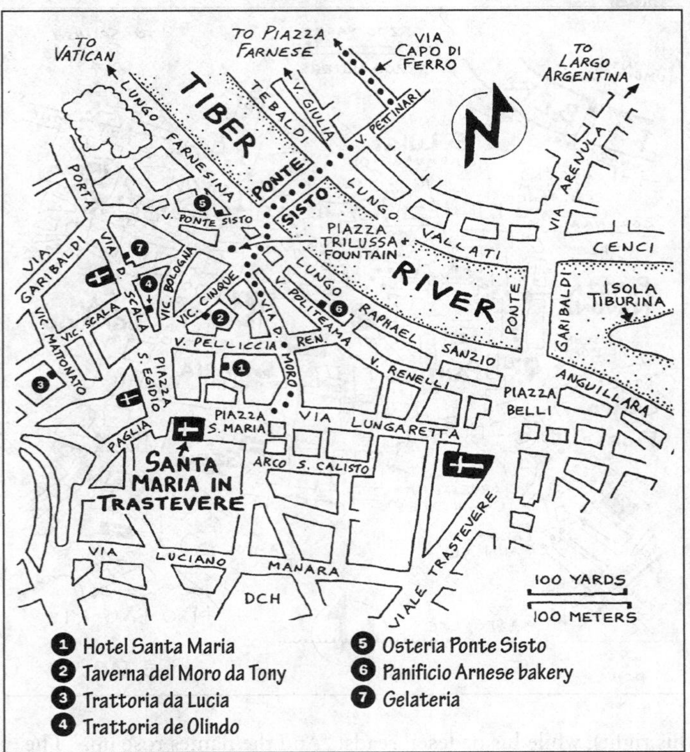

imposing Palazzo Farnese. Michelangelo contributed to the facade of this palace, now the French Embassy. The fountains on the square feature huge, one-piece granite hot tubs from the ancient Roman Baths of Caracalla.

One block from there (opposite the palace) is **Campo de' Fiori** (Field of Flowers), which is my favorite outdoor dining room after dark (see "Eating in Rome," page 839). The statue of Giordano Bruno, a heretic burned in 1600 for believing the world was round and not the center of the universe, marks the center of this great and colorful square. Bruno overlooks a busy produce market in the morning and strollers after dark. This neighborhood is still known for its free spirit. When the statue of Bruno was erected in 1889, local riots overcame Vatican protests against honoring a heretic. Bruno faces his executioner, the Vatican Chancellory (the big white building in the corner a bit to

From Campo de' Fiori to the Spanish Steps

his right), while his pedestal reads: "And the flames rose up." The square is lined with, and surrounded by, fun eateries. Bruno also faces La Carbonara restaurant, the only real restaurant on the square. The Forno, next door, is a popular place for hot and tasty take-out *pizza bianco* (plain but spicy pizza bread).

If Bruno did a hop, step, and jump forward, turned right, and marched 200 meters (650 feet), he'd cross the busy Corso Vittorio Emanuele and find **Piazza Navona**. Rome's most interesting night scene features street music, artists, fire-eaters, local Casanovas, ice cream, outdoor cafés (splurge-worthy if you've got time to sit and enjoy the human river of Italy), and fountains by Bernini, the father of Baroque art. The Tartufo "death by chocolate" ice cream (€3.50 to go, €7 at a table) made the Tre Scalini café (left of obelisk) world-famous among connoisseurs of ice cream and chocolate alike. This oblong piazza is molded around the long-gone Stadium of Domitian, an ancient chariot racetrack.

Leave Piazza Navona directly across from Tre Scalini café,

go (east) past rose peddlers and palm readers, jog left around the guarded building, and follow the brown sign to the **Pantheon** straight down Via del Salvatore (cheap pizza place on left just before the Pantheon, easy WC at McDonald's). Sit for a while and ponder under the Pantheon's floodlit, moonlit portico.

With your back to the Pantheon, head right, passing Bar Pantheon on your right. The Tazza d'Oro Casa del Caffè, one of Rome's top coffee shops, dates back to the days when this area was licensed to roast coffee beans. Look back at the fine view of the Pantheon from here.

With the coffee shop on your right, walk down Via degli Orfani to Piazza Capranica, with the big, plain, Florentine Renaissance-style Palazzo Capranica. Big shots, like the Capranica family, built stubby towers on their palaces—not for any military use . . . just to show off. Leave the piazza to the right of the palace, between the palace and the church. Via in Aquiro leads to a sixth-century B.C. Egyptian **obelisk** (taken as a trophy by Augustus after his victory in Egypt over Mark Antony and Cleopatra). Walk into the guarded square past the obelisk and face the huge parliament building. A short detour to the left (past Albergo National) brings you to some of Rome's most famous gelato. **Gelateria Caffè Pasticceria Giolitti** is cheap to go or elegant, pricey, and worthwhile for a sit among classy locals (open daily until very late, your choice: cone or *bicchierini*—cup, Via Uffici del Vicario 40). Gelato fans will want to visit the nearby **Gelateria della Palma**, also two blocks away, with better gelato (Via della Maddalena 20). Or head directly from the parliament into the next, even grander, square.

Piazza Colonna features a huge second-century column honoring Marcus Aurelius, the philosopher-emperor. The big, important-looking palace is the prime minister's residence. Cross Via del Corso, Rome's noisy main drag, and jog right (around the Y-shaped shopping gallery from 1928), heading down Via dei Sabini to the roar of the water, light, and people of the Trevi Fountain.

The **Trevi Fountain** is an example of how Rome took full advantage of water brought into the city by its great aqueducts. This watery Baroque avalanche was built in 1762 by Nicola Salvi, hired by a pope celebrating his reopening of the ancient aqueduct that powers it. Salvi used the palace behind the fountain as a backdrop for Neptune's "entrance" into the square. Neptune surfs through his watery kingdom while Triton blows his conch shell.

Romantics toss two coins over their shoulders, thinking it will give them a wish and assure their return to Rome. That may sound silly, but every year I go through this touristic ritual . . . and it actually seems to work.

Take some time to people-watch (whisper a few breathy *bellos* or *bellas*) before leaving. Facing the fountain, go past it on the right down Via delle Stamperia to Via del Triton. Cross the busy street and continue to the Spanish Steps (ask, "*Dov'è Piazza di Spagna?*"; pron. DOH-veh pee-AHT-zah dee SPAHN-yah), a few blocks and thousands of dollars of shopping opportunities away.

The **Piazza di Spagna** (rhymes with "lasagna"), with the very popular Spanish Steps, got its name 300 years ago, when this was the site of the Spanish Embassy. It's been the hangout of many Romantics over the years (Keats, Wagner, Openshaw, Goethe, and others). The Boat Fountain at the foot of the steps, which was done by Bernini's father, Pietro Bernini, is powered by an aqueduct. The piazza is a thriving night scene. Facing the steps, walk to your right about a block to tour one of the world's biggest and most lavish McDonald's. About a block on the other side of the steps is the Spagna Metro stop, which (usually until 23:30) will zip you home.

The Dolce Vita Stroll down Via del Corso

This is the city's chic and hip "cruise," from Piazza del Popolo (Metro: Flaminio) down a wonderfully traffic-free section of Via del Corso, and up Via Condotti to the Spanish Steps each evening around 18:00 (Sat and Sun are best). Strollers, shoppers, and flirts on the prowl fill this neighborhood of Rome's most fashionable stores (open after siesta 16:30–19:30). Throughout Italy, early evening is the time to stroll.

Start on **Piazza Popolo**. Historians: This area was once just inside medieval Rome's main entry. The delightfully car-free square is marked by an obelisk that was brought to Rome by Augustus after he conquered Egypt. (It once stood in the Circus Maximus.) The Baroque church of **Santa Maria del Popolo**—with Raphael's Chigi Chapel (pron. kee-gee, third chapel on left) and two Caravaggio paintings (side paintings in chapel left of altar)—is next to the gate in the old wall, on the far side of Piazza del Popolo, to the right as you face the gate (church open Mon–Sat 7:00–12:00 & 16:00–19:00, Sun 8:00–13:30 & 16:30–19:30).

From Piazza del Popolo, shop your way down **Via del Corso**. To rest your feet, join the locals sitting on the steps of various churches along the street.

At Via Pontefici, historians turn right and walk a block to see the massive, rotting, round brick **Mausoleum of Augustus**, topped with overgrown cypress trees. Beyond it, next to the river, is Augustus' Ara Pacis, or Altar of Peace (which should reopen in 2005).

From the mausoleum, return to Via del Corso and the 21st century, continuing straight until **Via Condotti**. Shoppers, take a left on Via Condotti to join the parade to the **Spanish Steps**.

The streets that parallel Via Condotti to the south (Borgogno and Frattini) are just as popular. You can catch a taxi home at the taxi stand a block south of the Spanish Steps (at Piazza Mignonelli, near American Express and McDonald's).

Historians: Ignore Via Condotti. Continue a kilometer (0.6 mile) down Via del Corso—straight since Roman times—to the Victor Emmanuel Monument. Climb Michelangelo's stairway to his glorious (especially when floodlit) square atop Capitol Hill. From the balconies at either side of the mayor's palace, catch the lovely views of the Forum as the horizon reddens and cats prowl the unclaimed rubble of ancient Rome.

Sleeping in Rome

(€1 = about $1, country code: 39)

Sleep Code: **S** = Single, **D** = Double/Twin, **T** = Triple, **Q** = Quad, **b** = bathroom, **s** = shower only, **CC** = Credit Cards accepted, **no CC** = Credit Cards not accepted, **SE** = Speaks English, **NSE** = No English. Breakfast is included in all but the cheapest places.

To help you sort easily through these listings, I've divided the rooms into three categories based on the price for a standard double room with bath:

Higher Priced—Most rooms more than €180.

Moderately Priced—Most rooms €180 or less.

Lower Priced—Most rooms €115 or less.

The absolute cheapest beds (dorms or some cramped doubles) in Rome are €18 in small, backpacker-filled hostels. A nicer hotel (around €130 with a bathroom and air-con) provides an oasis and refuge, making it easier to enjoy this intense and grinding city. If you're going door to door, prices are soft—so bargain. Built into a hotel's official price list is a kickback for a room-finding service or agency; if you're coming direct, they pay no kickback and may lower the price for you. Many hotels have high-season (mid-March–June, Sept–Oct) and low-season prices. If traveling outside of peak times, ask about a discount. Room rates are lowest in sweltering August. Easter, September, and Christmas are most crowded and expensive. On Easter weekend (April 18–20 in 2003), April 25, and May 1, the entire city gets booked up.

English works in all but the cheapest places. Traffic in Rome roars. My challenge: To find friendly places on quiet streets. With the recent arrival of double-paned windows and air-conditioning, night noise is not the problem it was. Even so, light sleepers should always ask for a *tranquillo* room. Many prices here are promised only to people who show this book and reserve directly, without using a room-finding service. And many places prefer hard cash.

Bed-and-breakfasts are booming in Rome, offering comfy

doubles in the old center for around €80. The Beehive hostel is a good contact for booking B&Bs in Rome (www.cross-pollinate.com, see "Sleeping in Hostels and Dorms," below).

Most hotels are eager to connect you with a shuttle service to the airport. It's reasonable and easy when you're leaving, but upon arrival, I think it's easiest to simply catch a cab or the shuttle train.

Almost no hotels have parking, but nearly all have a line on spots in a nearby garage (about €21/day).

Sleeping on Via Firenze (zip code: 00184)

I generally stay on Via Firenze because it's safe, handy, central, and relatively quiet. It's a 10-minute walk from the central train station and airport shuttle, and two blocks beyond Piazza della Repubblica and the TI. The Defense Ministry is nearby, so you've got heavily armed guards watching over you all night. Virtually all the city buses that rumble down Via Nazionale (#64, #70, #115, #640, and the #40 express) take you to Piazza Venezia (Forum) and Largo Argentina (Pantheon). From Largo Argentina, electric trolley #8 goes to Trastevere (first stop after crossing the river) and #64 (jammed with people and thieves) and the #40 express continue to St. Peter's. Farmacia Piram is the neighborhood 24-hour pharmacy (Via Nazionale 228, tel. 06-488-4437).

HIGHER PRICED

Residenza Cellini is a gorgeous new place with six rooms. It offers "ortho/anti-allergy beds" and four-star comforts and service (Db-€165, larger Db-€185, €30 discount in off-season—Aug plus mid-Nov–mid-March, these prices with this book and payment in cash through 2003, elevator, air-con, Via Modena 5, tel. 06-4782-5204, fax 06-4788-1806, www.residenzacellini.it, e-mail: residenzacellini@tin.it, SE).

MODERATELY PRICED

Hotel Oceania is a peaceful slice of air-conditioned heaven. This 16-room, manor house–type hotel is spacious and quiet, with spotless rooms, run by a pleasant father-and-son team (Sb-€105, Db-€135, Tb-€165, Qb-€192, these prices through 2003 with this book only, additional 25 percent off in Aug and winter, large roof terrace, TV room, CC, Via Firenze 38, 3rd floor, tel. 06-482-4696, fax 06-488-5586, www.hoteloceania.it, e-mail: hoceania@tin.it, son Stefano SE, dad Armando serves world-famous coffee).

Hotel Aberdeen, while a more formal place, offers the same great value, with minibars, phones, and showers in its 36 modern,

Hotels in East Rome

1. Hotel Oceania & Nardizzi
2. Hotel Aberdeen
3. Residence Adler & Residenza Cellini
4. Hotel Rex
5. Hotel Britannia
6. Hotel Sonya
7. Hotel Pensione Italia
8. Hotel Cortina
9. YWCA Casa per Studentesse
10. Suore di Santa Elisabetta
11. Hotel Montreal
12. Hotel Fenicia & Magic
13. Albergo Sileo
14. Hotel Duca d'Alba
15. Hotel Grifo
16. Pensione per Pelligrini
17. Hotel Paba
18. Hotel Lancelot
19. Casa Olmata Hostel
20. The Beehive Hostel
21. Gulliver's House Rome
22. Hotel Le Petit
23. Pharmacy

air-conditioned, and smoke-free rooms. It's warmly run by Annamaria, with support from her cousins Sabrina, Laura, and Cinzia (Sb-€102, Db-€139, Tb-€164, Qb-€190, prices through 2003 with this book only, €30 less per room in Aug and winter, CC, free Internet access, nearby parking-€21/day, Via Firenze 48, tel. 06-482-3920, fax 06-482-1092, check for deals online at www.travel.it/roma/aberdeen, e-mail: hotel.aberdeen@travel.it, SE).

Hotel Seiler is a last resort, with 33 sleepable rooms and too much chipped plaster (Sb-€83, Db-€119, Tb-€145, Qb-€165, these discounted prices good only with this book, CC, fans, elevator, Via Firenze 48, tel. 06-485-550, fax 06-488-0204, e-mail: acropoli@rdn.it, Silvio and Alessia SE).

LOWER PRICED

Residence Adler offers breakfast on a garden patio, wide halls, and eight quiet, elegant, and air-conditioned rooms in a great location. A good deal, it's run the old-fashioned way by a charming family (Db-€115, Tb-€150, Qb-€180, Quint/b-€195, prices through 2003 with this book only, CC, additional 5 percent off with cash, 15 percent off in Aug, Jan, and Feb; elevator, Via Modena 5, 2nd floor, tel. 06-484-466, fax 06-488-0940, www.hoteladler-roma.com, e-mail: info@hoteladler-roma.com, gracious Sr. Brando Massini NSE but tries).

Hotel Nardizzi Americana, with 18 simple, pleasant, air-conditioned rooms and a delightful rooftop terrace, is loosely run (Sb-€90, Db-€110, Tb-€135, Qb-€150, prices through 2003 with this book only, discounts for off-season and long stays, air-con, CC, additional 10 percent off with cash, elevator, Via Firenze 38, 4th floor, tel. 06-488-0368, fax 06-488-0035, SE).

Hotel Texas Seven Hills, a stark, institutional throwback to the 1960s, rents 18 dreary rooms (D-€83, Db-€93, often soft prices, CC, single-paned windows, Via Firenze 47, 1st elevator on the right to 3rd floor, tel. 06-481-4082, fax 06-481-4079, www.yellowpage.it/hoteltexas, e-mail: reserva@texas7hills.com, SE).

Sleeping between Via Nazionale and Basilica Santa Maria Maggiore (zip code: 00184 unless otherwise noted)

HIGHER PRICED

Hotel Britannia stands like a marble fruitcake, offering all the comforts in tight quarters. Lushly renovated with over-the-top classical motifs, its 33 air-conditioned rooms are small but comfortable with bright, modern bathrooms (Sb-€210, Db-€245, cheaper in Aug and off-season, CC, free parking, Via Napoli 64, tel. 06-488-3153, fax 06-488-2343, www.hotelbritannia.it, e-mail: info@hotelbritannia.it).

Hotel Rex is a business-class, modern fortress—a quiet, plain, and stately four-star place with 50 rooms and all the comforts (Sb-€206, Db-€258, Tb-€299, 25 percent less Aug and winter, CC, elevator, air-con, Via Torino 149, tel. 06-482-4828, fax 06-488-2743, e-mail: rex@hotelrex.net, SE).

MODERATELY PRICED

Hotel Le Petit has 11 colorful, cozy rooms with a modern flair (Sb-€80, Db-€135, Tb-€155, 20 percent off in low season, CC, air-con, Via Torino 122, tel. 06-4890-7085, fax 06-474-4645, www.hotel-le-petit.com, e-mail: lepetit@venere.it, SE).

Hotel Sonya is a small, family-run, but impersonal place with 23 comfortable, well-equipped rooms, a great location, and decent prices (Db-€119, Tb-€134, Qb-€155, Quint/b-€170, CC, air-con, elevator, facing the Opera at Via Viminale 58, tel. 06-481-9911, fax 06-488-5678, e-mail: hotelsonyaroma@katamail.com, Francesca SE).

Hotel Cortina rents 14 modern, air-conditioned rooms on a busy street. Ask for a quieter room on the courtyard or side street (Db-€140 in 2003 with this book, CC, Via Nazionale 18, tel. 06-481-9794, fax 06-481-9220, www.travel.it/roma/hotelcortina, e-mail: hotelcortina@pronet.it, John Carlo and Angelo SE).

LOWER PRICED

Hotel Pensione Italia, in a busy, interesting, and handy locale, is placed safely on a quiet street next to the Ministry of the Interior. Thoughtfully run by Andrea, Isabelle, and Alberico, it has 31 comfortable, airy, clean, and bright rooms (Sb-€75, Db-€100, Tb-€145, Qb-€165, air-con for €8 extra, prices through 2003 with this book and cash only, all rooms 20 percent off mid-July–Aug and winter, elevator, Via Venezia 18, just off Via Nazionale, tel. 06-482-8355, fax 06-474-5550, www.hotelitaliaroma.com, e-mail: hitalia@nettuno.it, SE). Most rooms have a fan. Their fine singles are all on the quiet courtyard and they have eight decent annex rooms across the street.

Hotel Montreal, run with care, is a bright, solid, business-class place on a big street a block southeast of Santa Maria Maggiore (Db-€115 but €90 in July–Aug, Tb-€140 but €120 in July–Aug, mention this book, CC, air-con, elevator, good security, 1 block from Metro: Vittorio, 3 blocks west of train station, Via Carlo Alberto 4, 00185 Roma, tel. 06-445-7797, fax 06-446-5522, www.hotelmontrealroma.com, e-mail: info@hotelmontrealroma.com, SE).

Clarin Hotel, a plain slumbermill with 21 rooms, is quiet, safe, and run-down (Db-€88, Tb-€109, Qb-€129, prices good with this book and cash, 3 percent extra with CC, Via Palermo 36, tel. 06-4782-5170, fax 06-4788-1393, e-mail: clarinhotel@hotmail.com, Renaldo, Franco, and Marco SE).

YWCA and Convents

YWCA Casa Per Studentesse accepts men and women. It's an institutional place, filled with white-uniformed maids, colorful Third-World travelers, and 75 single beds (€26 per person in 3- and 4-bed rooms, S-€31, Sb-€37, D-€62, Db-€74, includes breakfast except on Sun, elevator, Via C. Albo 4, tel. 06-488-0460, fax 06-487-1028). The YWCA faces a great little street market.

Suore di Santa Elisabetta is a heavenly Polish-run convent. While often booked long in advance and a challenge in communication, it's an incredible value (S-€31, Sb-€38, D-€51, Db-€66, Tb-€85, Qb-€103, CC, 23:00 curfew, elevator, fine view roof terrace, a block southwest of Basilica Santa Maria Maggiore at Via dell' Omata 9, tel. 06-488-8271, fax 06-488-4066, a little English spoken).

Pensione Per Pelligrini is another nun-run place with 39 big, simple rooms and lots of twin beds. There's a language barrier, but the price is right (S-€34, Sb-€41, D-€67, Db-€82, Tb-€93, breakfast-€4.25, closed Aug, peaceful garden, elevator, just off Piazza Vittorio Emmanuel II, Istituto Buon Salvatore, Via Leopardi 17, no sign, from station take bus #714, #649, or #360 or Metro: Vittorio, tel. 06-446-7147 or 06-446-7225, fax 06-446-1382, Sister Anna Maria SE).

Sleeping Cheap, Northeast of the Train Station (zip code: 00185)

The cheapest hotels in town are northeast of the station. Some travelers feel this area is weird and spooky after dark, but these hotels feel plenty safe. With your back to the train tracks, turn right and walk two blocks out of the station. The first two hotels are located in the same building.

LOWER PRICED

Hotel Fenicia rents 13 comfortable, well-equipped rooms at a fine price. The bigger rooms upstairs are quieter, but there's no elevator (Sb-€53, Db-€80, Tb-€103, bigger and fancier Db-€93, prices through 2003 with this book only, air-con-€10.50/day, breakfast-€5.25; they say they take CC but, according to readers, sometimes they don't; Via Milazzo 20, tel. & fax 06-490-342, www.hotelfenicia.it, e-mail: info@hotelfenicia.it, Georgio and Anna SE).

Hotel Magic has 10 clean, marbled rooms, high enough off the road to escape the traffic noise. It's family-run, though not with much warmth (Sb-€52, Db-€77, Tb-€103, Qb-€114, air-con-€10.50/ day, breakfast-€3.75, prices through 2003 with this book only, confirm rates, cheaper in Aug and winter, CC, thin walls, midnight curfew, Via Milazzo 20, 3rd floor, tel. & fax 06-495-9880, www .hotelmagicaroma.com, Carmela, Rosanna, and Caesarina NSE).

Albergo Sileo is a shiny-chandeliered, 10-room place. It has a contract to house train conductors who work the night shift, so most of the simple, pleasant rooms are rented from 19:00 to 9:00 only. If you can handle this, it's a great value. During the day, they store your luggage, and though you won't have access to a room, you're welcome to hang out in their lobby or bar (D-€39, Db-€47, Tb-€62, Db for 24 hours-€62—a steal, CC, elevator, Via Magenta 39, tel. & fax 06-445-0246, www.hotelsileo.com, friendly Alessandro and Maria Savioli NSE, daughter Anna SE).

Sleeping near the Colosseum (zip code: 00184)

These places are buried in a Roman world of exhaust-stained, medieval ambience. Take the subway one stop from the train station to the Cavour Metro stop. The *electtrico* bus line #117 (San Giovanni in Laterano, Colosseo, Trevi Fountain, Piazza di Spagna, and Piazza del Popolo) connects you with the sights.

HIGHER PRICED

Hotel Duca d'Alba, a tight and modern pastel/marble/ hardwood place, is more professional than homey (Sb-€134, Db-€201, much cheaper July–Aug and winter, extra bed-€21, CC, air-con, safes, phones, TV, elevator, Via Leonina 14, tel. 06-484-471, fax 06-488-4840, check Web site for deals, www.hotelducadalba.com, Angelo SE).

MODERATELY PRICED

Hotel Paba is a little six-room place, chocolate box–tidy and lovingly cared for by Alberta and Pasquale Castelli. While overlooking busy Via Cavour just two blocks from the Colosseum, it's quiet enough (Db-€124, extra bed-€21, show this book for 5 percent discount, CC, breakfast served in room, air-con, elevator, Via Cavour 266, tel. 06-4782-4902, fax 06-4788-1225, www.hotelpaba.com, e-mail: info@hotelpaba.com, SE).

Hotel Grifo has a homey, tangled floor plan with 20 dimly lit, modern rooms and a roof terrace. The double-paned windows almost keep out the Vespa noise (Db-€119, €109 July–Aug, CC, elevator, air-con, some rooms have terraces, 2 blocks off Via Cavour at Via del Boschetto 144, tel. 06-487-1395, fax 06-474-2323, e-mail: hotelgrifo@hotmail.com, Alessandro SE).

Hotel Lancelot, a favorite among United Nations workers, is big, with 60 rooms, a shady courtyard, rooftop terrace, bar, and restaurant. It's quiet, safe, well-run by Faris and Lubna Khan, and popular with returning guests (Sb-€93–108, Db-€144, Tb-€168, Qb-€183, add €10 for balcony, CC, air-con, elevator, parking-€11/day, behind Colosseum near San Clemente Church at Via Capo D'Africa 47, tel. 06-7045-0615, fax 06-7045-0640, www.lancelothotel.com, e-mail: info@lancelothotel.com, SE).

Sleeping near the Palatine (zip code: 00186)

LOWER PRICED

Hotel Casa Kolbe, located in a former monastery, rents out 63 monkish, spartan rooms with no fans or air-conditioning. With vast public spaces and a peaceful garden, it's popular with groups. But the location is great: it's on the river side of the Palatine ruins, on a quiet side street about a block from a little-used entrance to the Forum (Sb-€62, Db-€78, Tb-€98, Qb-€109, breakfast-€5.25, CC, elevator, garden, courtyard, not handy to public transit so taxi from the station, Via S. Teodoro 44, tel. 06-679-4974 or 06-679-8866, fax 06-6994-1550, Maurizio and Antonio SE).

Sleeping near Campo de' Fiori (zip code: 00186)

You pay a premium to stay in the old center, but each of these places is romantically set deep in the tangled backstreets near the idyllic Campo de' Fiori and, for many, that's worth the extra money.

MODERATELY PRICED

Casa di Santa Brigida overlooks the elegant Piazza Farnese. With soft-spoken sisters gliding down polished hallways, and pearly gates instead of doors, this lavish 23-room convent makes exhaust-stained Roman tourists feel like they've died and gone to heaven. If you're unsure of your destiny (and don't need a double bed), this is worth the splurge (Sb-€85, Db-€150, 3 percent extra with CC, great €16 dinners, roof garden, plush library, air-con, physical address: Monserrato 54, mailing address: Piazza Farnese 96, 00186 Roma, tel. 06-6889-2596, fax 06-6889-1573, www.brigidine.org/italia_roma, e-mail: hesselblad@tiscalinet.it, many of the sisters are from India and speak English). If you get no response to your fax or e-mail within three days, consider that a "no." Groups are very welcome here.

LOWER PRICED

Hotel Smeraldo, with 50 rooms, is well-run, clean, air-conditioned, and a great deal (Sb-€73, D-€73, Db-€114, Tb-€130, roof terrace, CC, Civolo dei Chiodaroli 9, midway between Campo de' Fiori and Largo Argentina, tel. 06-687-5929, fax 06-6880-5495, www.hotelsmeraldoroma.com, e-mail: albergosmeraldoroma@tin.it, SE).

Hotel Arenula, the only hotel in Rome's old Jewish quarter (or ghetto), is a fine place in the thick of old Rome, with 50 comfy rooms (Sb-€88, Db-€114, Tb-€134; €26 less in July, Aug, and winter; air-con-€10.50/day, no elevator, CC, just off Via Arenula at Via Santa Maria de' Calderari 47, tel. 06-687-9454, fax 06-689-6188, www.hotelarenula.com, e-mail: hotel.arenula@flashnet.it, SE).

Sleeping near the Pantheon (zip code: 00186)

These four places are buried in the pedestrian-friendly heart of ancient Rome, each within a four-minute walk of the Pantheon. You'll pay more here—but you'll save time and money by being exactly where you want to be for your early and late wandering.

HIGHER PRICED

Hotel Nazionale, a four-star landmark, is a 16th-century palace sharing a well-policed square with the national parliament. Its 90 rooms are served by lush public spaces, fancy bars, and a uniformed staff. It's a big hotel with a revolving front door, but it's a worthy splurge if you want security, comfort, and the heart of old Rome at your doorstep (Sb-€186, Db-€289, extra person-€62, suite-€439, less in Aug and winter, CC, air-con, elevator, Piazza Montecitorio 131, tel. 06-695-001, fax 06-678-6677, look online for discounts in summer and weekends, www.nazionaleroma.it, e-mail: hotel@nazionaleroma.it, SE).

MODERATELY PRICED

Hotel Due Torri hides out on a tiny, quiet street. It feels professional yet homey, with an accommodating staff, generous public spaces, and 26 comfortable-if-small rooms—four with balconies (Sb-€108, Db-€176, family apartment-€232 for 3 and €258 for 4, CC, air-con, Vicolo del Leonetto 23, a block off Via della Scrofa, tel. 06-6880-6956, fax 06-686-5442, www.hotelduetorriroma.com, e-mail: hotelduetorri@interfree.it, SE).

Residenza Zanardelli, a sumptuous little place with six classy and quiet rooms, is two blocks north of Piazza Navona (Db-€135, air-con-€10.50/day, no CC; on busy street but double-paned windows minimize noise; Via G. Zanardelli 7, tiny name next to doorbell, tel. 06-6821-1392 or 06-6880-9760, fax 06-6880-3802).

LOWER PRICED

Hotel Navona is a fine value, offering 41 basic rooms in an ancient building (with a perfect locale) a block off Piazza Navona. Top-floor

Hotels in the Heart of Rome

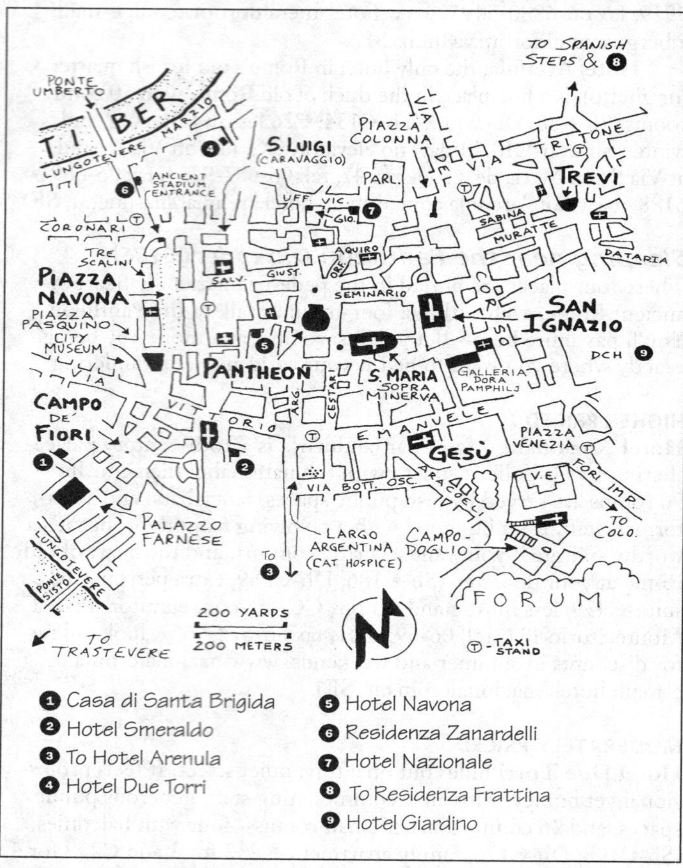

rooms come with wood-beamed character and more stairs (D-€100, Db-€110, air-con-€16/day, family rooms, no CC, Via dei Sediari 8, tel. 06-686-4203, fax 06-6880-3802, www.hotelnavona.com, e-mail: info@hotelnavona.com; run by a friendly Australian named Corry, his Italian wife Patricia, and her dad Pino, SE).

Sleeping near the Spanish Steps (zip code: 00187)

MODERATELY PRICED

Residenza Frattina is a pink palace in a posh locale. It has an old-fashioned feel and an unbeatable location on a main pedestrian shopping drag near Piazza di Spagna (Db-€180, Tb-€200, prices are soft, CC, air-con, Via Frattina 23, tel. & fax 06-679-5509, www.residenzafrattinacorso.com, e-mail: residenza.fratina@flashnet.it, SE).

Sleeping near Piazza Venezia (zip code: 00187)

MODERATELY PRICED

Hotel Giardino, run by Englishwoman Kate, offers pleasant rooms in a central location three blocks northeast of Piazza Venezia (Sb-€80, Db-€120, these discounted prices good with this book, CC but cash appreciated, double-paned windows, air-con-€7/night, Via XXIV Maggio 51, busy street off Piazza di Quirinale, tel. 06-679-4584, fax 06-679-5155, www.hotel-giardino-roma.com, e-mail: hotel_giardino@libero.it).

Sleeping in Trastevere (zip code: 00153)

To locate hotels, see the map on page 823.

MODERATELY PRICED

Hotel Santa Maria sits like a lazy hacienda in the midst of Trastevere. Surrounded by a medieval skyline, you'll feel as if you're on some romantic stage set. Its 18 small but well-equipped, air-conditioned rooms—former cells in a cloister—are all ground floor, circling a gravelly courtyard of orange trees and stay-awhile patio furniture. Because this is the only hotel in Trastevere, you'll pay about 25 percent more—but for poets, it's a deal (Db-€155, Tb-€191, Qb-€217, for this 20–25 percent discount it's cash only and a 3-night minimum, good with this book through 2003, smaller discounts also available with this book for shorter stays and credit cards and during off-season, a block north of Piazza Maria Trastevere at Vicolo del Piede 2, tel. 06-589-4626, fax 06-589-4815, www.htlsantamaria.com, e-mail: hotelsantamaria@libero.it, Stefano SE).

Sleeping "Three Stars" near the Vatican Museum (zip code: 00192)

To locate hotels, see the map on page 807.

HIGHER PRICED

Hotel Sant' Anna is pricey, but located on a charming-for-Rome pedestrian street that fills up with restaurant tables at dinnertime. Its 20 rooms are overly decorated with classical themes, though the furnishings are comfy (Sb-€145, Db-€190, Db-€145 July–Aug and winter, CC, air-con, elevator, courtyard, Borgo Pio 133, near intersection with Mascherino, a couple of blocks from entrance to St. Peter's, tel. 06-6880-1602, fax 06-6830-8717, www.travel.it/roma/santanna, Viscardo SE).

Hotel Bramante sits like a grand medieval lodge in the shadow of the fortified escape wall that runs from the Vatican to Castel San Angelo. The public spaces and the 16 rooms are generously sized, with rough wood beams and high ceilings (Sb-€142, Db-€210, Tb-€239, Qb-€250, 8 percent discount with this book, CC, air-con, no elevator, Vicolo delle Palline 24, tel. 06-6880-6426, fax 06-687-9881, www.hotelbramante.com, e-mail: bramante@excalhq.it, Maurizio and Loredana SE).

MODERATELY PRICED

Hotel Alimandi is a good value, run by the friendly and entrepreneurial Alimandi brothers—Paolo, Enrico, and Luigi—and the next generation, Marta and Germano. Their 35 rooms are air-conditioned, modern, and marbled in white (Sb-€90, Db-€150, Tb-€175, 5 percent discount with this book and cash, CC, closed Jan–mid Feb, elevator, grand buffet breakfast served in great roof garden, small gym, Internet access, pool table, piano lounge, free parking, down stairs directly in front of Vatican Museum, Via Tunisi 8, near Metro: Cipro-Musei Vaticani, reserve by phone, no reply to fax means they are full, tel. 06-3972-6300, toll-free in Italy tel. 800-122-121, fax 06-3972-3943, www.alimandi.org, e-mail: alimandi@tin.it, SE). They offer free airport pickup and drop-off, though you must reserve when you book your room and wait for a scheduled shuttle (every 2 hrs, see their Web site). Maria Alimandi rents out three rooms in her apartment, a 20-minute bus ride from the Vatican (Db-€83, see www.alimandi.org).

Hotel Spring House offers 51 attractive rooms—some with balconies or terraces (Db-€135, Tb-€155, Qb-€175, mention this book to get a 15 percent discount July–Aug and Jan–Feb, CC, Internet access, air-con, elevator, free loaner bikes, Metro: Cipro-Musei Vaticani, Via Mocenigo 7, 2 blocks from Vatican Museum, tel. 06-3972-0948, fax 06-3972-1047, www.hotelspringhouse.com, Stefano Gabbani SE).

Hotel Gerber is modern and air-conditioned, with 27 businesslike rooms, set in a quiet residential area (Sb-€100, Db-€130, Tb-€150, Qb-€170, 10 percent discount with this book in high season, 15 percent discount in low season, CC, Via degli Scipioni 241, a block from Metro: Lepanto, at intersection with Ezio, tel. 06-321-6485, fax 06-321-7048, www.hotelgerber.it, e-mail: info@hotelgerber.it, friendly pup Kira, Peter and Simonetta SE).

Hotel Emmaus offers 30 basic rooms on the south side of St. Peter's, just a communion-wafer's toss from the square (Sb-€105, Db-€150, Tb-€160, Qb-€180, CC, air-con, elevator,

Via delle Fornaci 23, tel. & fax 06-635-658, www.emmaushotel.it, e-mail: emmaus@flashnet.it, SE).

Sleeping in Hostels and Dorms (zip code: 00184)

For easy communication with young, friendly entrepreneurs, cheap dorm beds, and the very cheapest doubles in town—within a 10-minute hike of the train station—consider the following places:

Casa Olmata is a laid-back backpackers' place midway between the Termini train station and Colosseum (dorm beds €17–18, S-€35, bunk bed D-€44, one queen-size D-€55, lots of stairs, laundry service, free Internet access, video rentals, games, rooftop terrace with views, communal kitchen, dinners twice weekly, a block southwest of Basilica Santa Maria Maggiore, Via dell' Omata 36, 3rd floor, tel. 06-483-019, fax 06-474-2854, www.casaolmata.com, e-mail: casaolmata30@hotmail.com, Mirella and Marco).

The Beehive is especially good for older vagabonds. This tidy little place has dorms (€18 beds) and double rooms that are a great value (D-€60, Db-€80, T-€90, Tb-€120, Q-€120, Qb-€160, no CC). It's thoughtfully run by a friendly young American couple, Steve and Linda (no curfew or lock-out, 2 blocks south of Basilica Santa Maria Maggiore at Via Giovanni Lanza 99, tel. 06-474-0719, www.the-beehive.com). They hope to move to a new location by 2003; check their Web site to find their new address.

They also run a B&B booking service (fine private rooms in the old center, offering comparable quality for €65–95—about half the cost of a hotel, www.cross-pollinate.com).

Gulliver's House Rome is a fun little hostel in a safe and handy locale, run by helpful Simon and Sara. Its 24 beds in cramped quarters work fine for backpackers (€18 per bunk bed in 8-bed dorm, one D-€57, no CC, closed 12:00–16:00, 1:00 curfew, small kitchen, Via Palermo 36, tel. 06-481-7680, www.gulliversshouse.com, e-mail: info@gulliversshouse.com).

Eating in Rome

Romans spend their evenings eating rather than drinking, and the preferred activity is simply to enjoy a fine, slow meal, buried deep in the old city. Rome's a fun and cheap place to eat, with countless little eateries serving memorable €20 meals.

Although I've listed a number of restaurants, I recommend that you just head for a scenic area and explore. Piazza Navona, the Pantheon area, Campo de' Fiori, and Trastevere are neighborhoods packed with characteristic eateries. Sitting with tourists on a famous square enjoying the scene works fine. But for places more out of the way, consider my recommendations.

For Rome's best gelato, see "Eating near the Pantheon," below.

Eating in Trastevere

Colorful Trastevere is also now pretty touristy. Still, Romans join the tourists to eat on the rustic side of the Tiber River. Start at the central square (Piazza Santa Maria in Trastevere). Then choose: Eat with tourists enjoying the ambience of the famous square, or wander the backstreets in search of a mom-and-pop place with barely a menu. Consider the following places before making a choice (all are in the tangle of lanes between Ponte Sisto and the Piazza Santa Maria in Trastevere—see map on page 823):

At **Taverna del Moro da Tony**, Tony scrambles—with a great antipasti table—to keep his happy eaters (mostly tourists) well-fed and returning. Until we start telling him to "hold the mayo," his bruschetta will come buried in it (Tue–Sun 12:00–24:00, closed Mon, CC, off Via del Moro at Vicolo del Cinque 36, tel. 06-580-9165, SE).

For good home-cooking Roman-style, consider these two fun little places (within a block of each other): **Trattoria da Lucia** (closed Mon, indoor or outdoor seating, Vicolo del Mattonato 2, tel. 06-580-3601, NSE) and the homey **Trattoria de Olindo** (closed Sun, Vicolo della Scala 8, tel. 06-581-8835, NSE).

Osteria Ponte Sisto, a rough-and-tumble little place, specializes in traditional Roman cuisine with a menu that changes often. Since it's just outside of the tourist zone, it offers the best value and caters mostly to Romans. It's also easiest to find: As you approach Trastevere, crossing Ponte Sisto (pedestrian bridge), continue across the little square (Piazza Trilussa) and you'll find it on the right (daily 12:30–15:30 & 19:30–24:00, CC, Via Ponte Sisto 80, tel. 06-588-3411, SE).

The fine little **Gelateria alla Scala** (across from the church on Piazza della Scala) dishes up oh-wow pistachio (daily 12:30–24:00).

Eating on and near Campo de' Fiori

While it is touristy, Campo de' Fiori offers a classic and romantic square setting. And, since it is so close to the collective heart of Rome, it remains popular with locals. For greater atmosphere than food value, circle the square, considering each place. Bars and pizzerias seem to overwhelm the square. The **Taverna** and **Vineria** at numbers 16 and 15 offer good perches from which to people-watch and nurse a glass of wine. The only real restaurant is **La Carbonara**. While famous and atmospheric, it gets mixed reviews (closed Tue, Campo de' Fiori 23, CC, tel. 06-686-4783). Meals on small nearby streets are a better value, but lack that Campo de' Fiori magic.

Nearby, on the more elegant and peaceful Piazza Farnese, **Ostaria da Giovanni ar Galletto** has a dressier local crowd, great outdoor seating, and moderate prices. Giovanni and his son Angelo serve fine food, but sometimes they turn single diners away (closed

Sun, tucked in corner of Piazza Farnese at #102, CC, tel. 06-686-1714). Of all my listings, Giovanni offers perhaps the best al fresco dining experience.

Osteria Enoteca al Bric is a mod Italian/French bistro–type place run by a man who loves to cook and serves good wine. Wine-case lids decorate the wall like happy memories. With candlelit elegance and no tourists, it's perfect for the wine snob in the mood for pasta and fine cheese. Choose your bottle (or half bottle) from the huge selection lining the walls as you enter (open from 19:30, closed Mon, CC, 100 meters, or 330 feet, off Campo de' Fiori at Via del Pellegrino 51, tel. 06-687-9533).

Filetti de Baccala is a tradition for many Romans. Basically a fish bar with paper tablecloths and cheap prices, it has grease-stained, hurried waiters who serve old-time favorites—fried cod fillets, a strange bitter *puntarelle* salad, and delightful anchovies with butter—to nostalgic locals (Mon–Sat 17:30–23:00, closed Sun, a block east of Campo de' Fiori tumbling onto a tiny and atmospheric square, Largo dei Librari 88, no CC, tel. 06-686-4018).

Trattoria der Pallaro has no menu but plenty of return eaters. Paola Fazi—with a towel wrapped around her head, turban-style—and her family serve up a five-course festival of typically Roman food for €18, including wine, coffee, and a wonderful mandarin liqueur. Their slogan: "Here, you'll eat what we want to feed you." Make like Oliver Twist asking for more soup and get seconds on the mandarin liqueur (Tue–Sun 12:00–15:00 & 19:00–24:00, closed Mon, indoor/outdoor seating on quiet square, a block south of Corso Vittorio Emmanuele, down Largo del Chiavari to Largo del Pallaro 15, tel. 06-6880-1488).

Ristorante Grotte del Teatro di Pompeo, sitting atop an ancient theater, serves good food at fair prices (closed Mon, Via del Biscione 73, tel. 06-6880-3686). This is great if you want to dine on a characteristic street busy with strolling people.

Between Campo de' Fiori and Piazza Navona: For interesting bar munchies, try **Cul de Sac** on Piazza Pasquino (often crowded, daily 12:00–18:00 & 19:00–24:00, a block southwest of Piazza Navona). **L'Insalata Ricca**, next door, is a popular chain that specializes in hearty and healthy salads (daily 12:00–15:45 & 18:45–22:00, Piazza Pasquino 72, tel. 06-6830-7881). Another branch is nearby with more spacious outdoor seating (just off Corso Vittorio Emmanuele on Largo del Chiavari).

Eating near the Pantheon

You'll find a mix of cafeterias, groceries, restaurants, wine bars, and gelato shops.

Cafeterias: **Brek**, on Largo Argentina just south of the

Pantheon, is an appealing, self-service restaurant with a modern, efficient atmosphere and really cheap prices (daily 12:00–15:30 & 18:30–23:00, skip the sandwiches and pizza slices downstairs and go to the "free flow" cafeteria upstairs, northwest corner of square, Largo Argentina 1, tel. 06-6821-0353).

Il Delfino, also on Largo Argentina, is a tired but handy self-service cafeteria that serves throughout the day (daily 7:00–21:00, not cheap but fast). Across the side street, **Frullati di Frutta** sells refreshing fruity frappés.

Grocery: The ***alimentari*** on the Pantheon square will make you a sandwich for a temple-porch picnic. Sit at the base of a column in the shade and munch lunch.

Restaurants: **Osteria da Mario**, a great little mom-and-pop joint with a no-stress menu, serves delicious traditional favorites. You'll feel right at home with locals who know a good value. The pop (Mario), who passed away—you'll see his photo on the wall—would be happy with the way his wife and kids are carrying on (Mon–Sat 13:00–15:00 & 19:30–23:00, closed Sun, 2 blocks in front of Pantheon and to the left at Piazza delle Coppelle 51, tel. 06-6880-6349).

Ristorante Myosotis di Marsili, a dressy place with black-tie waiters and a coat check, is popular with local politicians and diners classy enough to look into the fish locker and make a knowledgeable choice. It has a traditional yet imaginative menu with a good wine list. Everything here is homemade (Mon–Sat 12:30–15:30 & 19:30–23:30, closed Sun, reservations smart, near Osteria da Mario, 2 blocks in front of Pantheon at Vicolo Della Vaccarella 3, tel. 06-686-5554).

Wine Bars: **Enoteca Spiriti**, a wine bar two blocks from the Pantheon, is run by Raffaele, son Matteo, and daughter Daria. They serve great wine ("*corposo*" means full-bodied) by the glass and light meals with integrity. Raffaele and I have designed a treat for travelers with this book: "A Taste of Italy for Two" includes two glasses of fine Amarone wine (or the equivalent in value), fresh bread, and a plate decorated with a tasty variety of Italian cheeses and meats for a total of €20. Choose: cool jazz interior or classic Roman sidewalk exterior (open at 12:30, very busy with local office workers at 13:30, dinner from 19:30, facing Pantheon walk around to the right and take 2 rights to Via S. Eustachio 5, no CC, no phone).

On Piazza de Pietra between the Pantheon and Via del Corso, classy **Osteria dell' Ingegno** (tel. 06-678-0662) and the simpler **Non Solo Bevi** offer hearty salads and good indoor/outdoor seating (daily 12:00–15:00, tel. 06-679-4519). Another Non Solo Bevi *enoteca* is several blocks north, tucked into a distant corner of the pedestrian square Piazza San Lorenzo. At this uncharacteristically

Restaurants in the Heart of Rome

1 Taverna, Vineria, & La Carbonara Rist.
2 Ostaria da Giovanni ar Galletto
3 Osteria Enoteca al Bric
4 Filetti de Baccala & Trattoria der Pallaro
5 Rist. Grotte del Teatro di Pompeo
6 Cul de Sac bar & L'Insalata Ricca Rist.
7 Brek Rist.
8 Il Delfino Rist. & Frullati di Frutta
9 Osteria da Mario Rist.
10 Rist. Myosotis di Marsili
11 Enoteca Spiriti
12 To Rist. alla Rampa, & Rist. Il Gabriello, Gusto
13 Rist. La Taverna degli Amici
14 Rist. Pizzeria Sacro e Profano
15 Trinity College
16 Giolitti Gelateria
17 Gelateria della Palma
18 Gelateria San Crispino
19 Non Solo Bevi (2 locations)

friendly place, Francesco and Lamberto (Beppo) serve fine wine and delightful toothpick munchies free with a glass. Their coffee *bomba* is memorable (Lucina 15, tel. 06-687-1683).

Gelato: Two of Rome's top ice-cream joints are a minute's walk in front of the Pantheon. The venerable **Giolitti's** is good, with cheap take-away prices and elegant Old World seating (just off Piazza Colonna and Piazza Monte Citorio at Via Uffici del Vicario 40, tel. 06-699-1243). But **Gelateria della Palma** is the new king of gelato—fresher, tastier, and with more options, including sugar-free and frozen-yogurt varieties (100 flavors, 2 blocks in front of Pantheon at Via della Maddalena 20, tel. 06-6880-6752).

Eating near the Spanish Steps

Ristorante alla Rampa is a classic old restaurant tucked away just around the corner from the touristy crush of the Spanish Steps. You'll get quality Roman cooking here, with great indoor/outdoor ambience, for a moderate price. They take no reservations, so arrive by 19:30 or be prepared to wait (closed Sun, 100 meters/330 feet east of Spanish Steps at Piazza Mignanelli 18, tel. 06-678-2621).

Ristorante Il Gabriello is inviting and small, offering a peaceful and local-feeling respite from all the top-end fashion shops in the area. Claudio serves while his brother cooks traditional Roman cuisine using fresh, organic products from their sister's farm (reasonable prices, dinner only, Mon–Sat 19:00–24:00, closed Sun, air-con, reservations smart, CC, Via Vittoria 51, 3 blocks from Spanish Steps, tel. 06-6994-0810).

Gusto is *the* trendy place in Rome today, with a restaurant, pizzeria, and wine bar. The only reason to eat here is to be surrounded by Rome's young and hip—which is not a bad thing (dinner from 19:45, reservations recommended, Piazza Augusto Imperatore 9, tel. 06-322-6273).

Eating near Piazza Venezia

Ristorante La Taverna degli Amici is a dressy yet friendly, candlelit place draped in ivy and tucked away on a sleepy square two blocks toward the Pantheon from the Victor Emmanuel Monument. This is a great and peaceful spot for a break before or after your Capitol Hill sightseeing. The waiters are friendly and the clientele is local and upscale (reserve for dinner to avoid the basement, Tue–Sun 12:30–15:00 & 19:30–24:00, closed Mon, CC, Piazza Margana 36, tel. 06-6920-0493).

For a woody English pub lunch break, **Trinity College** is a fine if smoky place serving creative salads and thriving with locals (just off Via del Corso, 3 blocks from Piazza Venezia at Via del Collegio Romano 6, tel. 06-678-6472).

Eating near the Trevi Fountain

Ristorante Pizzeria Sacro e Profano fills an old church with spicy south Italian (Calabrian) cuisine and some pricey exotic dishes. Run by friendly and helpful Pasquale and friends, this is just far enough away from the Trevi mobs. To avoid a shock when the bill comes, note that seafood is sold here by the *etto* (100-gram unit), not the portion, allow €25–45 per person depending on wine (a block off Via del Tritone at Via dei Maroniti 29, tel. 06-6791-836).

Romans in the know flock to **Gelateria San Crispino** for gelato made from ingredients such as basalmic vinegar, pear, and cinnamon. They only serve in cups because cones degrade the taste (Via della Panetteria 42, tel. 06-679-3924).

Eating between the Colosseum and St. Peter-in-Chains Church

You'll find good views but poor value in the restaurants directly behind the Colosseum. To get your money's worth, eat a block away from the Colosseum. There are two handy eateries at the top of Terme Di Tito, a block uphill from the Colosseum, near St. Peter-in-Chains church (of Michelangelo's Moses fame).

For a real restaurant meal, try **Ostaria da Nerone**. The Santis family serves traditional Roman cuisine in a homey indoor or outdoor setting (Mon–Sat 12:00–15:00 & 19:00–23:00, closed Sun, Via delle Terme di Tito 96, tel. 06-481-7952). Next door at **Caffè dello Studente**, Pina and Mauro serve typical "bar gastronomia" fare (pizza, toasted sandwiches, various drinks). Stand up at the crowded bar, take away, or enjoy the outdoor tables (Mon–Sat 7:30–21:30, closed Sun, tel. 06-488-3240).

Eating near Via Firenze and Via Nazionale Hotels

Snack Bar Gastronomia is a great local hole-in-the-wall for lunch or dinner (daily 7:00–24:00; fresh meat or veggie sandwiches, fresh squeezed juices, and Greek-style yogurt—yummy with fruit; ask the price first; Via Firenze 34). There's a classic, old-fashioned *alimentari* (grocery) across the street (7:00–19:30).

Popular for its top-quality Sicilian specialties, especially pastries and ice cream, **Pasticceria Dagnino** is frequented by people who work at my recommended hotels (daily 7:00–22:00, in Galleria Esedra off Via Torino, tel. 06-481-8660). Their *arancino*—a rice, cheese, and ham ball—is a greasy Sicilian favorite, and their cannoli is sweet. Direct the construction of your meal at the bar, pay for your trayful at the cashier, and climb upstairs, where you'll find the dancing Sicilian girls (free).

Hostaria Romana is a great place for traditional Roman cuisine. For an air-conditioned, classy local favorite, eat here

Restaurants in East Rome

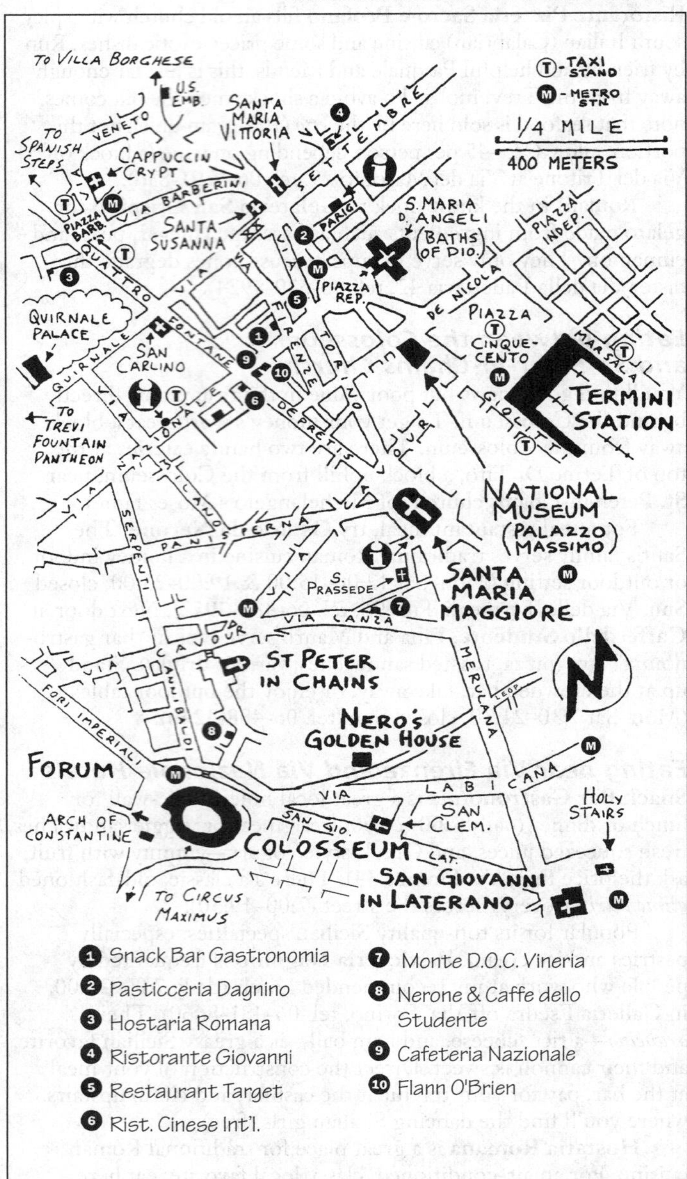

(closed Sun, midway between Trevi Fountain and Piazza Barberini, Via del Boccaccio 1, at intersection with Via Rasella, no reservations needed before 20:00, tel. 06-474-5284). Go ahead and visit the antipasto bar in person to assemble your plate. They're happy to serve an *antipasti misto della casa* and pasta dinner. Take a hard look at their *Specialita Romane* list.

Ristorante da Giovanni is a serviceable, hardworking place that's been feeding locals and tired travelers for 50 years (tired €12 *menu*, Mon–Sat 12:00–15:00 & 19:00–22:30, closed Sun and in Aug, CC, just off Via XX Settembre at Via Antonio Salandra 1, tel. 06-485-950).

Cafeteria Nazionale, with woody elegance, offers light lunches—including salads—at reasonable prices (Mon–Sat 7:00–20:00, closed Sun, CC, Via Nazionale 26-27, at intersection with Via Agostino de Pretis, tel. 06-4899-1716). The lunch buffet is a delight (€7.50, 12:30–15:00).

Ristorante Cinese Internazionale is your best neighborhood bet for Chinese (daily 12:00–15:00 & 18:00–23:00, inexpensive, no pasta, just off Via Nazionale behind Hotel Luxor at Via Agostino de Pretis 98, tel. 06-474-4064).

Restaurant Target is a soulless, modern, but handy place serving decent pizza and pasta near recommended hotels (open daily, indoor and outdoor seating, don't expect great service, Via Torino 33, tel. 06-474-0066).

The **McDonald's** restaurants on Piazza della Repubblica (free piazza seating outside), Piazza Barberini, and Via Firenze offer air-conditioned interiors and salad bars.

Flann O'Brien Irish Pub is an entertaining place for a light meal (of pasta or something *other* than pasta, served early or late when other places are closed), fine Irish beer, live sporting events on TV, and perhaps the most Italian crowd of all (daily 7:30–23:00, Via Nazionale 17, at intersection with Via Napoli, tel. 06-488-0418).

Eating near Santa Maria Maggiore

For a classy taste of Tuscany in a woody wine bar filled with local office workers, drop by **Monti D.O.C. Vineria Wine Bar** for lunch (chalkboard shows daily specials, daily 10:00–24:00, 2 blocks from basilica next to recommended Beehive hostel at Via Giovanni Lanza 93, tel. 06-487-2696).

Eating near the Vatican Museum and St. Peter's

Avoid the restaurant pushers handing out fliers near the Vatican: bad food, expensive menu tricks. Try any of these instead (see map on page 807).

Antonio's Hostaria dei Bastioni is tasty and friendly. It's conveniently located midway on your hike from St. Peter's to the Vatican Museum, with noisy streetside seating and a quiet interior (Mon–Sat 12:00–15:00 & 19:00–23:30, closed Sun, €5.25–6.25 pastas, €7.75 *secondi*, no cover charge, at corner of Vatican wall, Via Leone IV 29, CC, tel. 06-3972-3034). Antonio is your gracious host.

La Rustichella serves a sprawling antipasti buffet (€7.75 for a meal-sized plate). Arrive when they open at 19:30 to avoid a line and have the pristine buffet to yourself (Tue–Sun 12:30–15:00 & 19:30–23:00, closed Mon, near Metro: Cipro-Musei Vaticani, opposite church at end of Via Candia, Via Angelo Emo 1, CC, tel. 06-3972-0649). Consider the fun and fruity **Gelateria Millennium** next door.

Viale Giulio Cesare is lined with cheap **Pizza Rustica** shops and fun eateries, such as **Cipriani Self-Service Rosticcería** (Tue–Sun 10:00–22:00, closed Mon, pleasant outdoor seating, near Ottaviano subway stop, Viale Guilio Cesare 195). Restaurants such as **Tre Pupazzi**, which line the pedestrian-only Borgo Pio—a block from Piazza San Pietro—are worth a look.

Turn your nose loose in the wonderful **Via Andrea Doria** open-air market, three blocks north of the Vatican Museum (Mon–Sat roughly 7:00–13:30, until 16:30 Tue and Fri except summer, corner of Via Tunisi and Via Andrea Doria), or try the nearby **IN's supermarket** (Mon–Sat 8:30–13:30 & 16:00–20:00, closed Thu eve, a half block straight out from Via Tunisi entrance of open-air market, Via Francesco 18).

Transportation Connections—Rome

Termini is the central station (see "Arrival in Rome," on page 782; Metro: Termini). Tiburtina is the bus station (4 Metro stops away from train station; Metro: Tiburtina).

By train from Rome to: Venice (6/day, 5–8 hrs), **Florence** (12/day, 2 hrs, most stop at Orvieto en route), **Pisa** (8/day, 3–4 hrs), **Genova** (7/day, 6 hrs, overnight possible), **Milan** (12/day, 5 hrs, overnight possible), **Naples** (6/day, 2 hrs), **Brindisi** (2/day, 9 hrs), **Amsterdam** (2/day, 20 hrs), **Bern** (5/day, 10 hrs), **Frankfurt** (4/day, 14 hrs), **Munich** (5/day, 12 hrs), **Nice** (2/day, 10 hrs), **Paris** (5/day, 16 hrs), **Vienna** (3/day, 13–15 hrs). All-Italy train info: tel. 848-888-088 (automated, in Italian).

By bus to: Assisi (3/day, 3 hrs), **Siena** (7/day, 3 hrs).

Rome's Airports

Rome's two airports—Fiumicino (a.k.a. Leonardo da Vinci) and the small Ciampino—share the same Web site (www.adr.it).

Fiumicino Airport: Rome's major airport has a TI (Mon–Sat 8:00–19:00, closed Sun, tel. 06-6595-4471), ATMs, banks, luggage storage, shops, and bars.

A slick, direct **train** connects the airport and Rome's central Termini train station in 30 minutes. Trains run twice hourly in both directions from roughly 7:30 to 22:00. From the airport, trains depart at :07 and :37 past the hour. From the airport's arrival gate, follow signs to "Stazione/Railway Station." Buy your ticket from a machine or the Biglietteria office (€9, CC). Make sure the train you board is going to "Roma Termini," not "Roma Orte" or others.

Going from the Termini train station to the airport, trains depart at :21 and :51 past the hour, usually from tracks 25 or 26; to reach these tracks, take a 10-minute walk along track 24 to the end of the station (moving walkways are inside the building to the right on the lower level). Check the departure boards for "Fiumicino Aeroporto"—the local name for the airport—and confirm with an official or a local on the platform that the train is indeed going to the airport (€10.30, buy ticket from computerized yellow ticket machines, any *tabacchi* shop in station, or at the desk near entrance to track 26). Read your ticket: If it requires validation, stamp it in a yellow machine near the platform before boarding.

Your hotel can arrange a **taxi** to the airport at any hour for about €40. To get from the airport into town cheaply by taxi, try teaming up with any tourist also just arriving (most are heading for hotels near yours in the center). Splitting a taxi and hopping out once downtown at a taxi stand to take another to your hotel will save you about €15. Avoid unmarked, unmetered taxis.

For **airport information**, call 06-65951. To inquire about flights, call 06-6595-3640 (Alitalia: tel. 06-65643, British Air: toll-free tel. 848-812-266, Delta: toll-free tel. 800-864-114, KLM/Northwest: tel. 06-6501-1441, Lufthansa: tel. 06-6568-4004, SAS: tel. 06-6501-0771, United: tel. 0266-7481).

Ciampino Airport: Rome's smaller airport (tel. 06-794-941) handles budget and charter flights. To get to downtown Rome from the airport, take the LILA/Cotral bus (2/hr) to the Anagnina Metro stop, where you can connect by Metro to the stop nearest your hotel.

Driving in Rome

Greater Rome is circled by the Grande Raccordo Anulare. This ring road has spokes that lead you into the center. Entering from the north, leave the autostrada at the Settebagni exit. Following the ancient Via Salaria (and the black-and-white *Centro* signs), work your way doggedly into the Roman thick of things. This will take you along the Villa Borghese park and dump you right on Via Veneto (where there's an Avis office). Avoid rush hour and drive defensively: Roman cars stay in their lanes like rocks in an avalanche. Parking in Rome is dangerous. Park near a police station or get advice at your hotel. The Villa Borghese underground garage is handy (€18/day, Metro: Spagna).

Consider this: Your car is a worthless headache in Rome. Avoid a pile of stress and save money by parking at the huge, easy, and relatively safe lot behind the Orvieto station (follow P signs from autostrada) and catching the train to Rome (every 2 hrs, 75 min).

FLORENCE (FIRENZE)

Florence, the home of the Renaissance and birthplace of our modern world, is a "supermarket sweep," and the groceries are the best Renaissance art in Europe.

Get your bearings with a Renaissance walk. Florentine art goes beyond paintings and statues—there's food, fashion, and handicrafts. You can lick Italy's best gelato while enjoying some of Europe's best people-watching.

Planning Your Time

If you're in Europe for three weeks, Florence deserves a well-organized day. Make reservations in advance for the Uffizi Gallery (best Italian paintings anywhere) and Accademia (Michelangelo's *David*). For a day in Florence, see the Accademia, tour the Uffizi Gallery, visit the underrated Bargello (best statues), and do the Renaissance ramble (explained below).

Art-lovers will want to chisel out another day of their itinerary for the many other Florentine cultural treasures. Shoppers and ice cream–lovers may need to do the same.

Plan your sightseeing carefully. Some sights close Mondays and afternoons. While many spend several hours a day in lines, thoughtful travelers avoid this by making reservations or going late in the day. Places open at night are virtually empty.

Orientation

The Florence we're interested in lies mostly on the north bank of the Arno River. Everything is within a 20-minute walk of the train station, cathedral, or Ponte Vecchio (Old Bridge). The less impressive but more characteristic Oltrarno (south bank) area is just over the bridge. The huge, red-tiled dome of the cathedral

Florence Overview

(the Duomo) and its tall bell tower (Giotto's Tower) mark the center of historic Florence.

Tourist Information

There are three TIs in Florence: across from the train station, near Santa Croce, and on Via Cavour.

The TI across the square from the train station is most crowded—expect long lines (Mon–Sat 8:30–19:00, Sun 8:30–13:00; off-season Mon–Sat 8:30–17:30, Sun 8:30–13:00; with your back to tracks, exit the station—it's across the square in wall near corner of church, Piazza Stazione, tel. 055-212-245, www.firenze.turismo.toscana.it). Note: In the station, avoid the Hotel Reservations "Tourist Information" window (marked *Informazioni Turistiche Alberghiere*) near the McDonald's; it's not a real TI but a hotel reservation business.

The TI near Santa Croce Church is pleasant, helpful, and uncrowded (Mon–Sat 9:00–19:00, Sun 9:00–14:00, shorter hours off-season, Borgo Santa Croce 29 red, tel. 055-234-0444).

Another winner is the TI three blocks north of the Duomo (Mon–Sat 8:15–19:15, Sun 8:30–13:30, closed winter Sun, Via Cavour 1 red, tel. 055-290-832 or 055-290-833; Feltrinelli's bookstore across street, listed under "Helpful Hints," page 854).

At any TI, pick up a map, a current museum-hours listing (extremely important, since no guidebook—including this one—has ever been able to predict the hours of Florence's sights),

Daily Reminder

Sunday: Today, the Duomo's dome, Science Museum, and the Museum of Precious Stones are closed. These sights close early: the Duomo Museum (at 13:40), Baptistery's interior (at 14:00), and Dante's House (also at 14:00). A few sights are open only in the afternoon: Santa Croce Church (15:00–17:30) and the Brancacci Chapel and Santa Maria Novella (both 13:00–17:00).

The Museum of San Marco, which is open on the second and fourth Sunday of the month until 19:00, closes entirely—as does the Bargello—on the first, third, and fifth Sunday. The Medici Chapels and Modern Art Gallery (in Pitti Palace) close on the second and fourth Sunday.

Monday: The biggies are closed—Accademia (David) and Uffizi Gallery—as well as the Vasari Corridor and the Palatine Gallery/ Royal Apartments (in Pitti Palace).

The Medici Chapels and Modern Art Gallery (in Pitti Palace) close on the first, third, and fifth Monday of the month. The Museum of San Marco and Bargello close on the second and fourth Monday. The Orsanmichele Church and Boboli Gardens close on the first and last Monday.

Good bets: Duomo Museum, Giotto's Tower, Brancacci Chapel, Michelangelo's House, Dante's House, Science Museum, Palazzo Vecchio (maybe until 23:00 in summer), and churches.

Tuesday: All sights are open except for Dante's House, Michelangelo's House, and the Brancacci Chapel. The Science Museum closes early (13:00).

Wednesday: All sights are open except for the Medici Riccardi Palace.

Thursday: All sights are open. The Museum of Precious Stones stays open late (19:00), while these sights close early: Duomo (15:30) and Palazzo Vecchio (14:00).

Friday: All sights are open. The Church of Santa Maria Novella opens late (13:00–17:00) and Palazzo Vecchio closes late (maybe until 23:00 in summer).

Saturday: All sights are open, but the Science Museum closes early (13:00). These sights close early on the first Saturday of the month: Duomo (15:30) and the Duomo's dome (15:20). The Museum of San Marco stays open until 19:00. The Accademia, Uffizi, and Palatine Gallery/Royal Apartments may stay open until 22:00 in summer.

and any information on entertainment. The free, monthly *Florence Concierge Information* magazine lists museums, plus lots of information that I don't: concerts and events, markets, sporting events, church services, shopping ideas, bus and train connections, and an entire similar section on Siena. Get yours at the TI or from any expensive hotel (pick one up as if you're staying there).

Arrival in Florence

By Train: The station soaks up time and generates dazed and sweaty crowds. Try to get your tourist information and train tickets elsewhere. (You can get onward tickets and information at American Express—see "Helpful Hints," below.) With your back to the tracks, to your left are most of my recommended hotels; a 24-hour pharmacy (Farmacia Comunale, near McDonald's); city buses; and the entrance to the underground mall/passage that goes across the square to the church Santa Maria Novella (but because the tunnel, especially the surface point near the church, is frequented by pickpockets, stay above ground). Baggage check is near track 16.

By Car: From the autostrada (north or south), take the Certosa exit (follow signs to *Centro;* at Porta Romana, go to the left of the arch and down Via Francesco Petrarca). After driving and trying to park in Florence, you'll understand why Leonardo never invented the car. Cars flatten the charm of Florence. Don't drive in Florence, and don't risk parking illegally (fines up to €150). The city has plenty of lots. For a short stay, park underground at the train station (€2/hr). The Fortezza da Basso is clearly marked in the center (€18.50/24 hrs). The least expensive lots are Parcheggio Parterre (Firenze Parcheggi, €10.50/24 hrs, perhaps cheaper with hotel reservation) and Parcheggio Oltrarno (near Porta Romana—pass through gate and on left, €10.50 per day). For parking information, call 055-500-1994.

By Plane: Florence has its own airport and Pisa's is nearby. See "Transportation Connections," page 886, for details.

Helpful Hints

Theft Alert: Florence has particularly hardworking thief gangs. They specialize in tourists and hang out where you do: near the train station, the station's underpass (especially where the tunnel surfaces), and major sights. Also, be on guard at two squares frequented by drug pushers (Santa Maria Novella and Santo Spirito). American tourists—especially older ones—are considered easy targets.

Medical Help: For a doctor who speaks English, call 055-475-411 (reasonable hotel calls, cheaper if you go to the

Tips on Sightseeing in Florence

Make Reservations to Avoid Lines: Florence has a great reservation system for its top five sights—Uffizi, Accademia, Bargello, Medici Chapels, and the Pitti Palace. You can show up and wait in line, or make a quick and easy telephone booking.

Two sights come with long lines: the Accademia *(David)* and the Uffizi (two-hour lines on busy days). These lines are easily avoided by making a reservation. Frankly, it's stupid not to.

While you can generally make a reservation a day in advance (upon arrival in Florence), you'll have a wider selection of entry times by calling a few days ahead. You dial 055-294-883 (Mon–Fri 8:30–18:30, Sat 8:30–12:00, closed Sun), an English-speaking operator walks you through the process, and two minutes later, you say *grazie* with appointments (15-minute entry window) and six-digit confirmation numbers for each of the top museums and galleries.

If you haven't called ahead, you can make reservations for the top sights at the minor, less crowded sights (such as the Museum of San Marco or Museum of Precious Stones). Clerks at the ticket booths at these sleepy sights can reserve and sell tickets to the major sights—often for admissions the same day—allowing you to skip right past the dreary mob scene.

Hours of Sights Can Change Suddenly: Because of labor demands, hours of sights change without warning. Pick up the latest listing of museum hours at a TI, or you'll miss out on something you came to see. Don't delay; you never know when a place will close for a holiday, strike, or restoration.

More Tips: The biggies (Uffizi and Accademia) close on Monday. The *Concierge Information* magazine lists which sights are open afternoons, Sundays, and Mondays (best attractions open Mon: Museo dell' Opera del Duomo, Giotto's Tower, Brancacci Chapel, Michelangelo's Casa Buonarroti, Dante's House, Science Museum, Palazzo Vecchio, and churches).

Several museums are closed alternating Sundays and Mondays (e.g., closed first, third, and fifth Sun and second and fourth Mon of each month); use the calendar in the appendix to figure out which day they're closed during your trip. Churches usually close from 12:30 to 15:00 or 16:00. Some museums close at 14:00 and stop selling tickets 30 minutes before that.

I like the €2.60 "new map" of Florence that lists the sights (sold at newsstands). Local guidebooks are cheap and give you a map and decent commentary on the sights.

clinic at Via L. Magnifico 59). The TI has a list of English-speaking doctors. A 24-hour pharmacy is at the train station.

Addresses: Street addresses list businesses in red and residences in black or blue (color-coded on the actual street number and indicated by a letter following the number in printed addresses: n = black, r = red). *Pensioni* are usually black but can be either. The red and black numbers each appear in roughly consecutive order on streets, but bear no apparent connection with each other. I'm lazy and don't concern myself with the distinction (if one number's wrong, I look for the other) and find my way around fine.

American Express: American Express offers all the normal services, but is most helpful as an easy place to get your train tickets, reservations, supplements (all the same price as at the station), or even just information on train schedules (Mon–Fri 9:00–17:30, Sat money exchange only 9:00–12:30, CC, 3 short blocks north of Palazzo Vecchio on Via Dante Alighieri 22 red, tel. 055-50981).

Long-Distance Telephoning: Small newsstand kiosks sell PIN phone cards that give you cheap international rates (10 minutes/€1).

Books: Feltrinelli International, a fine bookstore that sells fiction and guidebooks in English, is a few blocks north of the Duomo and across the street from the TI on Via Cavour (Mon–Sat 9:00–19:30, closed Sun, Via Cavour 20 red, tel. 055-219-524). Edison Bookstore sells CDs and novels on the Renaissance (daily 9:00–24:00, facing Piazza della Repubblica, tel. 055-213-110). Paperback Exchange also sells fiction and guidebooks (cheaper but smaller selection, Mon–Fri 9:00–19:30, Sat 10:00–13:00 & 15:30–19:30, closed Sun, shorter hours in Aug, at corner of Via Fiesolana and Via dei Pilastri, 6 blocks east of Duomo, tel. 055-247-8154).

Laundry: The Wash & Dry Lavarapido chain offers long hours and efficient self-service launderettes at several locations (about €6.20 for wash and dry, daily 8:00–22:00, tel. 055-580-480). Close to recommended hotels: Via dei Servi 105 (and a rival Laundromat at Via Guelfa 22 red, off Via Cavour; both near *David);* Via del Sole 29 red and Via della Scala 52 red (between train station and river), and Via dei Serragli 87 red (across the river in Oltrarno neighborhood).

Getting around Florence

I organize my sightseeing geographically and do it all on foot. A €1 ticket gives you one hour on the buses, €1.80 gives you three hours, and €4 gets you 24 hours (tickets not sold on bus—except after 21:00, buy in *tabacchi* shops or newsstands, validate on bus).

The minimum cost for a taxi ride is €4, or, after 22:00, €5 (rides in the center of town should be charged as tariff #1). A taxi ride from the train station to Ponte Vecchio costs about €8. Taxi fares and supplements are clearly explained on signs in each cab.

Tours of Florence

Walking Tours of Florence—This company offers a variety of tours (up to 4/day Mon–Sat) featuring downtown Florence, Uffizi highlights, or the countryside, presented by informative, entertaining, native English-speaking guides. The "Original Florence" walk hits the main sights, but gets offbeat to weave a picture of Florentine life in medieval and Renaissance times. You can expect lots of talking, which is great if you like history. Tours, offered year-round regardless of weather, start at their office and are limited to a maximum of 22; extra guides are available if more people show up (€24 for 3-hr Original Florence walk, office open Mon–Sat 8:30–18:00, closed for lunch off-season, Piazza Santo Stefano 2 black, a short block north of Ponte Vecchio; go east on tiny Vicolo San Stefano, in Piazza Santo Stefano at #2; booking necessary for Uffizi tour, private tours available, tel. 055-264-5033, cellular 0329-613-2730, www.artviva.com). The owner of the company, Rosanne Magers, also offers private tours (tel. 055-264-5033, e-mail: walkingtours @artviva.com).

Florentia—These top-notch historical walking tours of Florence and Tuscany are led by local scholars. The tours, ranging from introductory city walks to in-depth visits of museums and lesser-known destinations, are geared for thoughtful and well-heeled travelers (semi-private tours start at €45 per person, max 8 per group; private tours start at€180 for half-day tour, reserve in advance, tel. 055-225-535, U.S. tel. 510/549-1707, www.florentia .org, e-mail: info@florentia.org).

Florence Art Lectures—These 90-minute talks on the Florentine Renaissance, designed for English-speaking tourists, are held in a classy 13th-century palazzo near the Santa Croce Church (€20, offered May–Sept only, Mon–Sat at 14:30, includes glass of wine, espresso, or cold drink, Piazza Santa Croce 21, tel. 055-245-354, www.florenceart.org). They also offer art lectures combined with a lunch or dinner, as well as museum tours and city walking tours at sunset.

Local Guide—Paola Migilorini offers museum tours, city walking tours, and Tuscan excursions by van (€100 for 2-hr walking tour or Uffizi tour, Via S. Gallo 120, tel. 055-472-448, cellular 347-657-2611, www.florencetour.com, e-mail: info@florencetour.com).

A Florentine Renaissance Walk

Even during the Dark Ages, people knew they were in a "middle time." It was especially obvious to the people of Italy—sitting on the rubble of Rome—that there was a brighter age before them. The long-awaited rebirth, or Renaissance, began in Florence for good reason. Wealthy because of its cloth industry, trade, and banking; powered by a fierce city-state pride (locals would pee into the Arno with gusto, knowing rival city-state Pisa was downstream); and fertile with more than its share of artistic genius (imagine guys like Michelangelo and Leonardo attending the same high school)—Florence was a natural home for this cultural explosion.

Take a walk through the core of Renaissance Florence by starting at the Accademia (home of Michelangelo's *David*) and cutting through the heart of the city to Ponte Vecchio on the Arno River. (A 13-page, self-guided tour of this walk is outlined in my museum guidebook, *Rick Steves' Mona Winks*, and in *Rick Steves' Florence;* otherwise, you'll find brief descriptions below.)

At the Accademia, you'll look into the eyes of Renaissance man—humanism at its confident peak. Then walk to the cathedral (Duomo) to see the dome that kicked off the architectural Renaissance. Step inside the baptistery to view a ceiling covered with preachy, flat, 2-D, medieval mosaic art. Then, to learn what happened when art met math, check out the realistic 3-D reliefs on the doors. The painter, Giotto, also designed the bell tower—an early example of a Renaissance genius excelling in many areas. Continue toward the river on Florence's great pedestrian mall, Via de' Calzaiuoli (or "Via Calz")—part of the original grid plan given to the city by the ancient Romans. Down a few blocks, compare medieval and Renaissance statues on the exterior of the Orsanmichele Church. Via Calz connects the cathedral with the central square (Piazza della Signoria), the city palace (Palazzo Vecchio), and the Uffizi Gallery, which contains the greatest collection of Italian Renaissance paintings in captivity. Finally, walk through the Uffizi courtyard—a statuary think tank of Renaissance greats—to the Arno River and Ponte Vecchio.

Sights—On a Renaissance Walk through Florence

▲▲▲Accademia (Galleria dell' Accademia)—This museum houses Michelangelo's *David* and powerful (unfinished) *Prisoners*. Eavesdrop as tour guides explain these masterpieces. More than with any other work of art, when you look into the eyes of *David*, you're looking into the eyes of Renaissance man. This was a radical break with the past. Hello, humanism. Man was now a confident individual, no longer a plaything of the supernatural.

And life was now more than just a preparation for what happened after you died.

The Renaissance was the merging of art, science, and humanism. In a humanist vein, *David* is looking at the crude giant of medieval darkness and thinking, "I can take this guy." (David was an apt mascot for a town surrounded by big bully city-states.) Back on a religious track, notice *David*'s large and overdeveloped right hand. This is symbolic of the hand of God that powered David to slay the giant...and enabled Florence to rise above its crude neighboring city-states.

Beyond the magic marble are two floors of interesting pre-Renaissance and Renaissance paintings, including a couple of lighter-than-air Botticellis.

Cost, Hours, Location: €6.50 (plus €1.55 reservation fee). Open Tue–Sun 8:15–18:50, until 22:00 on holidays and maybe on summer Sat, closed Mon (last entry 30 min before closing, Via Ricasoli 60, tel. 055-238-8609). No photos or videos are allowed. The museum is most crowded on Sun, Tue, and the first thing in the morning. It's easy to reserve ahead; see page 855 for details.

Nearby: Piazza Santissima Annunziata, behind the Accademia, features lovely Renaissance harmony. Brunelleschi's Hospital of the Innocents (Spedale degli Innocenti, not worth going inside), with terra-cotta medallions by Luca Della Robbia, was built in the 1420s and is considered the first Renaissance building. The 15th-century Santissima Annunziata church facing the same square is worth a peek.

▲▲Duomo—Florence's Gothic Santa Maria del Fiori cathedral has the third-longest nave in Christendom (free, Mon–Wed and Fri–Sat 10:00–17:00 except first Sat of month 10:00–15:30, Thu 10:00–15:30, Sun 13:30–16:45, tel. 055-230-2885).

The church's noisy neo-Gothic facade from the 1870s is covered with pink, green, and white Tuscan marble. Since nearly all of its great art is stored in the Museo dell' Opera del Duomo (behind the church), the best thing about the interior is the shade. The inside of the dome is decorated by one of the largest paintings of the Renaissance, a huge (and newly restored) *Last Judgment* by Vasari and Zucarri.

Think of the confidence of the age: The Duomo was built with a hole awaiting a dome in its roof. This was before the technology to span it with a dome was available. No matter. They knew that someone soon could handle the challenge...and the local architect Brunelleschi did. The cathedral's claim to artistic fame is Brunelleschi's magnificent dome—the first Renaissance dome and the model for domes to follow.

Florence Sights

▲Climbing the Cathedral's Dome—For a grand view into the cathedral from the base of the dome, a peek at some of the tools used in the dome's construction, a chance to see Brunelleschi's "dome-within-a-dome" construction, a glorious Florence view from the top, and the equivalent of 463 plunges on a StairMaster, climb the dome (€6, Mon–Sat 8:30–19:00 except first Sat of month 8:30–15:20, closed Sun; enter from outside church on south or river side, arrive by 8:30 to avoid a long wait in line). When planning St. Peter's in Rome, Michelangelo rhymed (not in English), "I can build its sister—bigger, but not more beautiful, than the dome of Florence."

▲**Giotto's Tower (Campanile)**—If you're not interested in experiencing dome-within-a-dome architecture, you'll likely feel that climbing Giotto's 82-meter-tall (270-foot) bell tower beats scaling the neighboring Duomo's dome because it's 50 fewer steps, faster, and offers the same view plus the dome (€6, daily 8:30–19:30, last entry 40 min before closing).

▲▲**Museo dell' Opera del Duomo**—The underrated cathedral museum, behind the church at #9, is great if you like sculpture. It has masterpieces by Donatello (a gruesome wood carving of Mary Magdalene clothed in her matted hair, and the *cantoria*, a delightful choir loft bursting with happy children) and by Luca Della Robbia (another choir loft, lined with the dreamy faces of musicians praising the Lord). Look for a late Michelangelo *pietà* (Nicodemus, on top, is a self-portrait), Brunelleschi's models for his dome, and the original restored panels of Ghiberti's doors to the baptistery. This is one of the few museums in Florence open on Monday (€6, Mon–Sat 9:00–19:30, Sun 9:00–13:40, closed on holidays, tel. 055-230-2885). If you find all this church art intriguing, look through the open doorway of the Duomo art studio, which has been making and restoring church art since the days of Brunelleschi (a block toward the river from the Duomo at 23a Via dello Studio).

▲**Baptistery**—Michelangelo said its bronze doors were fit to be the gates of Paradise. Check out the gleaming copies of Ghiberti's bronze doors facing the Duomo. Making a breakthrough in perspective, Ghiberti used mathematical laws to create the illusion of receding distance on a basically flat surface. The earlier, famous competition doors are around to the right (north); Ghiberti, who beat Brunelleschi, got the job of designing these doors.

A local document from A.D. 860 already refers to Florence's oldest building as "ancient." Inside, sit and savor the medieval mosaic ceiling, where it's Judgment Day and Jesus is giving the ultimate thumbs up and thumbs down. Compare that to the "new, improved" art of the Renaissance (€3, interior open Mon–Sat 12:00–19:00, Sun 8:30–14:00, bronze doors are on the outside so always "open"; original panels are in the Museo dell' Opera del Duomo).

▲**Orsanmichele**—This ninth-century loggia (a covered courtyard) was a market used for selling grain (stored upstairs). Later, it was closed in to make a church. Notice the grain spouts on the pillars inside. The glorious tabernacle by Orcagna (1359) takes you back.

Study the sculpture in the niches outside. You can see man stepping out of the literal and figurative shadow of the Church in the great Renaissance sculptor Donatello's *St. George*. Look into George's face; he's a sensitive new-age guy (SNAG). The predella (platform) at the base of this statue shows St. George slaying the dragon to protect the wispy, melodramatic maiden. This was groundbreaking Renaissance emotion and perspective (free, daily 9:00–12:00 & 16:00–18:00, closed first and last Mon of month, on Via Calzaiuoli, enter through the back door, may be closed due to staffing problems). The iron bars spanning the vaults were the Italian Gothic answer to the French Gothic external buttresses. Across the street is . . .

▲Museo Orsanmichele—For some peaceful time alone with the original statues that filled the niches of Orsanmichele, climb to the top of the church (entry behind church, across street). Be there at 9:00, 10:00, and 11:00 daily, when the door is open and art-lovers in the know climb four flights of stairs to this little-known museum containing statues by Ghiberti, Donatello, and others (info in Italian, but picture guides on wall help you match art with artists). Upstairs is a tower room with city views (free). A block away, you'll find the . . .

▲Mercato Nuovo—This market loggia is how Orsanmichele looked before it became a church. Originally a silk and straw market, Mercato Nuovo still functions as a rustic market today (at intersection of Via Calimala and Via Porta Rossa). Prices are soft.

Notice the circled *X* in the center, marking the spot where people hit after being hoisted up to the top and dropped as punishment for bankruptcy. You'll also find Porcellino (a statue of a wild boar, nicknamed "little pig"), which people rub and give coins to in order to ensure their return to Florence. Nearby is a wagon selling tripe (cow innards) sandwiches.

▲Palazzo Vecchio—This fortified palace, once the home of the Medici family, is a Florentine landmark. But if you're visiting only one palace interior in town, the Pitti Palace is better. The Palazzo Vecchio interior is wallpapered with mediocre magnificence, worthwhile only if you're a real Florentine art and history fan. The museum's most famous statues are Michelangelo's *Genius of Victory*, Donatello's static *Judith and Holofernes*, and Verrocchio's *Winged Cherub* (a copy tops the fountain in the free courtyard at entrance, original inside).

Scattered throughout the museum are a dozen computer terminals with information in English on the Medici family, Palazzo Vecchio, and the building's architecture and art, including an animated clip showing how Michelangelo's *David* was moved from the square to the Accademia (€5.70, Fri–Wed 9:00–19:00, Thu 9:00–14:00, in summer maybe open until 23:00 on Mon and Fri, ticket office closes 1 hour earlier, WC in second courtyard can be accessed without paying palace admission, tel. 055-276-8465).

Even if you don't go to the museum, do step into the free

courtyard (behind the fake *David*) just to feel the essence of the Medici. Until 1873, Michelangelo's *David* stood at the entrance, where the copy is today. While the huge statues in the square are important only as the whipping boys of art critics and rest stops for pigeons, the nearby Loggia dei Lanzi has several important statues. Look for Cellini's bronze statue of Perseus (with the head of Medusa). The plaque on the pavement in front of the fountain marks the spot where the monk Savonarola was burned in MCCCCXCVIII (for more on the monk, see "Museum of San Marco" listing, page 864).

▲▲▲Uffizi Gallery—The greatest collection of Italian paintings anywhere is a must, with plenty of works by Giotto, Leonardo, Raphael, Caravaggio, Rubens, Titian, and Michelangelo and a roomful of Botticellis, including his *Birth of Venus.* Make a reservation to avoid the long line (see below). Because only 780 visitors are allowed inside the building at any one time, there's generally a very long wait during the day. The good news: No Louvre-style mob scenes. The museum is nowhere near as big as it is great: Few tourists spend more than two hours inside. The paintings are displayed on one comfortable floor in chronological order, from the 13th through 17th centuries.

Essential stops are (in this order): Gothic altarpieces (narrative, pre-Realism, no real concern for believable depth) including Giotto's altarpiece, which progressed beyond "totem-pole angels"; Uccello's *Battle of San Romano,* an early study in perspective (with a few obvious flubs); Fra Filippo Lippi's cuddly Madonnas; the Botticelli room, filled with masterpieces, including a pantheon of classical fleshiness and the small *La Calumnia,* showing the glasnost of Renaissance free-thinking being clubbed back into the darker age of Savonarola; two minor works by Leonardo; the octagonal classical sculpture room with an early painting of Bob Hope and a copy of Praxiteles' *Venus de Medici*—considered the epitome of beauty in Elizabethan Europe; a view through the window of Ponte Vecchio—dreamy at sunset; Michelangelo's only surviving easel painting, the round *Holy Family;* Raphael's noble *Madonna of the Goldfinch;* Titian's voluptuous *Venus of Urbino;* and Duomo views from the café terrace at the end (WC near café).

Cost, Hours, Reservations: €8, plus €1.55 for recommended reservation, Tue–Sun 8:15–18:50, until 22:00 on holidays and maybe on summer Sat, closed Mon (last entry 45 min before closing; after entering take elevator or climb 4 long flights of stairs).

Avoid the two-hour peak season midday wait by making a telephone reservation. It's easy, slick, and costs only €1.55 (tel. 055-294-883, explained on page 193). At the Uffizi, walk briskly past the 200-meter-long (650-foot) line—pondering the IQ of this gang—to the special entrance for those with reservations (labeled in English "Entrance for Reservations Only"), give your number, pay (cash only), and scoot right in.

If you haven't called ahead, you may be able to book a ticket at Florence's lesser sights (such as the Museum of San Marco) or even at the Uffizi itself. At the Uffizi, ask the clerk (who stands at the entrance for people with reservations) if you can make a reservation in person. He may direct you to the ticket office, where you can secure a reservation for later in the day or the next day (depends on luck and availability). Also, Walking Tours of Florence does a guided tour of the museum Tuesday through Saturday which gets you inside without a wait (see "Tours of Florence," page 857).

Enjoy the Uffizi square, full of artists and souvenir stalls. The surrounding statues honor the earthshaking: artists, philosophers (Machiavelli), scientists (Galileo), writers (Dante), explorers (Amerigo Vespucci), and the great patron of so much Renaissance thinking, Lorenzo (the Magnificent) de' Medici.

▲**Ponte Vecchio**—Florence's most famous bridge is lined with shops that have traditionally sold gold and silver. A statue of Cellini, the master goldsmith of the Renaissance, stands in the center, ignored by the flood of tacky tourism. Notice the "prince's passageway" above. In less secure times, the city leaders had a fortified passageway connecting the Palace Vecchio and Uffizi with the mighty Pitti Palace, to which they could flee in times of attack. This passageway, called the Vasari Corridor, is open to the persistent by request only (€8, Tue–Sat at 9:30, closed Mon, tel. 055-265-4321).

Sights—Near the Accademia

▲▲**Museum of San Marco**—One block north of the Accademia on Piazza San Marco, this museum houses the greatest collection anywhere of medieval frescoes and paintings by the early Renaissance master Fra Angelico. You'll see why he thought of painting as a form of prayer, and couldn't paint a crucifix without shedding tears. Each of the monks' cells has a Fra Angelico fresco. Don't miss the cell of Savonarola, the charismatic monk who rode in from the Christian right, threw out the Medici, turned Florence into a theocracy, sponsored "bonfires of the vanities" (burning books, paintings, and so on), and was finally burned himself when Florence decided to change channels (€4, daily 8:15–13:50, Sat–Sun until 19:00, but closed first, third, and fifth Sun and second and fourth Mon of each month, tel. 055-238-8608). They can sell tickets (often with immediate reservation) to Uffizi and Accademia.

Museum of Precious Stones (Museo dell' Opificio delle Pietre Dure)—This unusual gem of a museum features mosaics of inlaid marble and semiprecious stones. You'll see remnants of the Medici workshop from 1588, including 500 different semi-precious stones, the tools used to cut and inlay them, and room after room of the sumptuous finished product. The fine loaner booklet describes it all in English (€2, Mon–Sat 8:15–14:00, Thu until 19:00, closed Sun, Via degli Alfani 78, around corner from Accademia). This ticket booth can also sell tickets with reservations (perhaps same-day) to the Uffizi and Accademia.

Sights—Heart of Florence

▲▲▲Bargello (Museo Nazionale)—This underrated sculpture museum is behind Palazzo Vecchio in a former prison that looks like a mini–Palazzo Vecchio. It has Donatello's painfully beautiful *David* (the very influential first male nude to have been sculpted in a thousand years), works by Michelangelo, and rooms of Medici treasures cruelly explained in Italian only—mention that English descriptions would be wonderful (€4, daily 8:15–13:50 but closed first, third, and fifth Sun and second and fourth Mon of each month, last entry 30 min before closing, Via del Proconsolo 4, tel. 055-238-8606).

Dante's House (Casa di Dante)—Dante's house consists of five rooms in an old building, with little of substance to show but lots of photos relating to his life and work. Although it's well-described in English, it's mainly of interest to literary buffs (€3, Mon and Wed–Sat 10:00–17:00, Sun 10:00–14:00, closed Tue, across the street and around the corner from Bargello, at Via S. Margherita 1).

▲Medici Chapels (Cappelli dei Medici)—This chapel, containing two Medici tombs, is drenched in lavish High Renaissance architecture and sculpture by Michelangelo (€6, daily 8:15–17:00 but closed the second and fourth Sun and the first, third, and fifth Mon of each month, tel. 055-238-8602). Behind San Lorenzo on Piazza Madonna is a lively market scene that I find just as interesting. Take a stroll through the huge, double-decker central market one block north.

▲Piazza della Repubblica--This large square, the belly-button of Florence, sits on the site of Florence's original Roman Forum. The lone column is the only remaining bit of Roman Florence except for the grid street plan. Look at the map to see the ghost of Rome: a rectangular fort with this square marking the intersection of the two main roads (Via Corso and Via Roma).

Today's piazza, framed by a triumphal arch, is really a nationalistic statement celebrating the unification of Italy. Florence, the capital of the country (1865–1870) until Rome was liberated, lacked a square worthy of this grand new country. So the neighborhood here was razed to open up a grand modern forum surrounded by grand circa-1890 buildings.

Medieval writers described Florence as so densely built up that when it rained, pedestrians didn't get wet. Torches were used to light the lanes in midday. The city was prickly with noble family towers (like San Gimignano) and had Romeo-and-Juliet-type family feuds. But with the rise of the Medicis (c. 1300), no noble family was allowed to have an architectural ego trip taller then their tower, and nearly all were taken down.

Science Museum (Museo di Storia della Scienza)—This is a fascinating collection of Renaissance and later clocks, telescopes, maps, and ingenious gadgets. One of the most talked-about bottles in Florence is the one here containing Galileo's finger. Loaner English guidebooklets are available. It's friendly, comfortably cool, never crowded, and just a block east of the Uffizi (€6.50, Mon and Wed–Fri 9:30–17:00, Tue and Sat 9:30–13:00, closed Sun, Piazza dei Giudici 1, tel. 055-239-8876).

Church of Santa Maria Novella—This 13th-century Dominican church, just south of the train station, is rich in art. Along with crucifixes by Giotto and Brunelleschi, there are fine examples of the early Renaissance mastery of perspective. The most famous is the *Holy Trinity* by Masaccio; it's opposite the entrance (€2.60, Mon–Thu and Sat 9:30–17:00, Fri and Sun 13:00–17:00).

A palatial **perfumery** is around the corner 100 meters (330 feet) down Via della Scala at #16 (free but shopping encouraged, Mon–Sat 9:30–19:30, closed Sun). Thick with the lingering aroma of centuries of spritzes, it started as the herb garden of the Santa Maria Novella monks. Well-known even today for its top-quality products, it is extremely Florentine. Pick up the history sheet at the desk and wander deep into the shop. From the back room, you can peek at the S. M. Novella cloister, with its dreamy frescoes, and imagine a time before Vespas and tourists.

Sights—Santa Croce and Nearby

▲▲Santa Croce Church—This 14th-century Franciscan church, decorated by centuries of precious art, holds the tombs of great Florentines (€3, Mon–Sat 9:30–17:30, Sun 15:00–17:30, in winter Mon–Sat 9:30–12:30 & 15:00–17:30, Sun 15:00–17:30, modest dress code enforced, tel. 055-244-619). The loud 19th-century Victorian Gothic facade faces a huge square ringed with tempting touristy shops and littered with tired tourists. Escape into the church.

Working counterclockwise from the entrance, you'll find the tomb of Michelangelo (with the allegorical figures of painting, architecture, and sculpture), a memorial to Dante (no body . . .

he was banished by his hometown over politics), the tomb of Machiavelli (the originator of hardball politics), a relief by Donatello of the Annunciation, and the tomb of the composer Rossini. To the right of the altar, step into the sacristy, where you'll find a bit of St. Francis' cowl and old sheets of music with the medieval and mobile C clef (two little blocks on either side of the line determined to be middle C). In the bookshop, notice the photos high on the wall of the devastating flood of 1966. Beyond that is a touristy—but mildly interesting—"leather school." The chapels lining the front of the church are richly frescoed. The Bardi Chapel (far left of altar) is a masterpiece by Giotto featuring scenes from the life of St. Francis. On your way out, you'll pass the tomb of Galileo (allowed in by the church long after his death).

The neighboring **Pazzi Chapel** by Brunelleschi is considered one of the finest pieces of Florentine Renaissance architecture (covered by €3 Santa Croce church admission, Thu–Tue 10:00–18:00, closed Wed, entrance outside church; facing facade, it's the door to the right).

▲Michelangelo's Home (Casa Buonarroti)—Fans enjoy Michelangelo's house, which has some of his early, much-less-monumental statues and sketches (€6.50, Wed–Mon 9:30–14:00, closed Tue, English descriptions, Via Ghibellina 70).

Sights—Florence, South of the Arno River

▲▲Pitti Palace—From the Uffizi, follow the elevated passageway (closed to non-Medicis) across the Ponte Vecchio bridge to the gargantuan Pitti Palace, which has five separate museums.

The **Palatine Gallery/Royal Apartments** features palatial room after chandeliered room, their walls sagging with paintings by the great masters. Its Raphael collection is the biggest anywhere (first floor, €6.50, Tue–Sun 8:30–18:50, maybe summer Sat until 22:00, closed Mon, buy tickets on right-hand side of courtyard).

The **Modern Art Gallery** features Romanticism, neoclassicism, and Impressionism by 19th- and 20th-century Tuscan painters (second floor, €5, daily 8:30–13:50 but closed second and fourth Sun and first, third, and fifth Mon).

The **Grand Ducal Treasures**, or Museo degli Argenti, is the Medici treasure chest entertaining fans of applied arts with jeweled crucifixes, exotic porcelain, gilded ostrich eggs, and so on (ground floor, €7.75, nearly the same hours as Modern Art Gallery).

The landscaped **Boboli Gardens** offer a shady refuge from the heat (€2, daily 9:00–18:30, June–Aug until 19:30, winter until 16:30, closed first and last Mon of month, behind palace).

▲Brancacci Chapel—For the best look at the early Renaissance master Masaccio, see his restored frescoes here (€3.10, Mon and

Wed–Sat 10:00–17:00, Sun 13:00–17:00, closed Tue, cross Ponte Vecchio and turn right a few blocks to Piazza del Carmine). Since only a few tourists are let in at a time, seeing the chapel often involves a wait. The neighborhoods around here are considered the last surviving bits of old Florence.

▲**Piazzale Michelangelo**—Across the river overlooking the city (look for the huge statue of *David*), this square is worth the 30-minute hike, drive, or bus ride (either #12 or #13 from the train station) for the view of Florence and the stunning dome of the Duomo. After dark, it's packed with local schoolkids, feeding their dates slices of watermelon. Just beyond it is the stark and beautiful, crowd-free Romanesque San Miniato Church.

Oltrarno Walk—If you never leave the touristy center, you don't really see Florence. There's more to the city than tourism. Ninety percent of its people live and work—mostly in small shops—where tourists rarely venture. This self-guided tour follows a perfectly straight line (you can't get lost). Cross the Ponte Vecchio and walk west on the road toward Pisa—it changes names, from Borgo San Jacopo and Via di Santo Spirito to Borgo Frediano, until you reach the city wall at Porta San Frediano. Along this route you can check out several of my favorite restaurants (described below). As you walk, consider these points:

After one block, at the fancy **Hotel Lungarno**, belly up to the Arno River viewpoint for a great look at Ponte Vecchio. Recall the story of Kesserling, the Nazi commander-in-chief of Italy who happened to be an art-lover. As the Nazis retreated in 1944, he was commanded to blow up all the bridges. Rather than destroy the venerable Ponte Vecchio, he disabled it by blowing up the surrounding neighborhood. Turn around and cross the street to see the ivy-covered nub of a medieval tower—ruined August 6, 1944.

Along this walk, you'll see plenty of artisans at work and inviting little **shops**. You're welcome to drop in but remember, it's rude not to say "*Buon giorno*" and "*Ciao*." "Can I take a look?" is "*Posso guardare?*" (pron. POH-soh gwahr-DAH-ray).

The streets are busy with *motorini* (Vespas and other motorbikes). While these are allowed in the city, nonresident cars are not (unless they are electric). Notice that parked cars have a *residente* permit on their dash. You'll see a police officer (likely a woman) later on the walk, keeping traffic out.

Look for little architectural details. Tiny shrines protect the corners of many blocks. Once upon a time, the iron spikes on the walls impaled huge candles, which provided a little light. Electricity changed all that, but notice there are no electric wires visible. They're under the streets.

This street is lined with apartment flats punctuated by the

occasional palazzo. The skyline and architecture are typical of the 13th to 16th centuries. Huge **palazzos** (recognized by their immense doors, lush courtyards, and grand stonework) were for big-shot merchants. Many have small wooden doors designed to look like stones (e.g., 3b on Borgo San Frediano). While originally for one family, these buildings are now subdivided, as evidenced by the huge banks of doorbells at the door.

The **Church of Santa Maria del Carmine**, with its famous Brancacci Chapel and Masaccio frescoes, is a short detour off Borgo San Frediano (described above).

A couple of blocks before Porta San Frediano (and its tower), look left up Piazza dei Nerli. The bold yellow schoolhouse was built during Mussolini's rule—grandly proclaiming the resurrection of the Italian empire.

Porta San Frediano (c. 1300), is part of Florence's medieval wall, which stretches grandly from here to the river. The tower was originally twice as high, built when gravity ruled warfare. During the Renaissance, when gunpowder dominated warfare, the tower—now just an easy target—was topped. In medieval times, a kilometer-wide strip outside the wall was cleared to deny attackers any cover. Notice the original doors, immense and studded with fat iron nails to withstand battering rams. Got a horse? Lash it to a ring.

Tour over. You passed several fun eateries, and the colorful Trattoria Sabatino is just outside the wall (all described in "Eating in Florence," page 880). *Ciao.*

Experiences—Florence

▲▲Gelato—Gelato is an edible art form. Italy's best ice cream is in Florence—one souvenir that can't break and won't clutter your luggage. But beware of scams at touristy joints on busy streets that turn a simple request of a cone into a €10 "tourist special."

The **Gelateria Carrozze** is very good (daily 11:00–24:00, closes at 21:00 in winter, on riverfront 30 meters, or 100 feet, from Ponte Vecchio toward the Uffizi, Via del Pesce 3). **Gelateria dei Neri** is another local favorite worth finding (2 blocks east of Palazzo Vecchio at Via Dei Neri 20 red, daily in summer 12:00–23:00, closed Wed in winter).

Vivoli's is the most famous (Tue–Sun 8:00–24:00, closed Mon, the last 3 weeks in Aug, and winter; opposite the Church of Santa Croce, go down Via Torta a block, turn right on Via Stinche; before ordering, try a free sample of their *riso* flavor—rice).

If you want an excuse to check out the little village-like neighborhood across the river from Santa Croce, enjoy a gelato at the tiny **no-name *gelateria*** at Via San Miniato 5 red (just before Porta San Miniato).

Shopping

Florence is a great shopping town. Busy street scenes and markets abound, especially near San Lorenzo, near Santa Croce, on Ponte Vecchio, and at Mercato Nuovo (a covered market square 3 blocks north of Ponte Vecchio, listed above in "Sights"). Leather (often better quality for less than the U.S. price), gold, silver, art prints, and tacky plaster mini-*David*s are most popular. Shops usually have promotional stalls in the market squares. Prices are soft in markets. Many visitors spend entire days shopping.

For ritzy Italian fashions, browse along Via de Tornabuoni, Via della Vigna Nuova, and Via Strozzi. Typical chain department stores are Coin (Mon–Sat 9:30–20:00, Sun 11:00–20:00, on Via Calzaiuoli, near Orsanmichele Church); Standa, a discount clothing/grocery chain (Mon–Sat 9:00–19:55, closed Sun, at intersection of Via Panzani and Via del Giglio, near train station) and La Rinascente (Piazza della Repubblica, Mon–Sat 9:00–21:00, Sun 10:30–20:00).

For shopping ideas, ads, and a list of markets, check out the *Florence Concierge Information* magazine described under "Tourist Information," above (free from TI and many hotels).

Side Trips to Fiesole and Siena

For a candid peek at **Fiesole**—a Florentine suburb—ride bus #7 (3/hr, departs from Piazza Adua at the northeast side of the station and also from Piazza San Marco) for about 25 minutes through neighborhood gardens, vineyards, orchards, and large villas to the last stop—Fiesole. This town is a popular excursion from Florence because of its small eateries and its good views of Florence. Catch the sunset from the terrace just below the La Reggia restaurant; from the Fiesole bus stop, face the bell tower and take the very steep Via San Francisco on your left. You'll find the view terrace near the top of the hill.

Connoisseurs of smaller towns (who won't be seeing Siena otherwise) should consider riding the bus to **Siena** (75 min by bus). This can be a day trip or an evening trip. Siena is magic after dark. Confirm when the last bus returns. For more information, see the Siena chapter.

Sleeping in Florence

(€1 = about $1, country code: 39)

Sleep Code: **S** = Single, **D** = Double/Twin, **T** = Triple, **Q** = Quad, **b** = bathroom, **s** = shower only, **CC** = Credit Cards accepted, **no CC** = Credit Cards not accepted, **SE** = Speaks English, **NSE** = No English. Unless otherwise noted, breakfast is included (but usually optional). English is generally spoken.

To help you sort easily through these listings, I've divided the rooms into three categories based on the price for a standard double room with bath:

Higher Priced—Most rooms more than €160.

Moderately Priced—Most rooms €160 or less.

Lower Priced—Most rooms €110 or less.

The accommodations scene varies wildly with the season. Spring and fall are very tight and expensive, while mid-July through August is wide open and discounted. November through February is also generally empty. With good information and a phone call ahead, you can find a stark, clean, and comfortable double with breakfast for about €65, with a private shower for €100 (less at the smaller places, such as the *soggiornos*). You get elegance for €140. Rooms with air-conditioning cost around €100—worth the extra money in the summer. Virtually all of the places are central, within minutes of the great sights. Few hotels escape Vespa noise at night.

Call direct to the hotel. Do not use the TI, which costs your host and jacks up the price. In slow times, budget travelers call around and find soft prices. Ask if you'll get a discount for paying in cash, for staying for three or more nights (or both), or for using this book. And ask if you can skip breakfast (the overpriced breakfasts are legally optional, though some hotels pretend otherwise).

Call ahead. I repeat, call ahead. Places will hold a room until early afternoon. If they say they're full, mention you're using this book.

Sleeping between the Station and Duomo (zip code: 50123)

HIGHER PRICED

Palazzo Castiglioni offers 16 grand rooms with all the conveniences in a peaceful, 19th-century palazzo package. Most rooms are spacious, several have frescoes, and all make a fine splurge (Db-€165, Db suite-€207, Tb-€207, air-con, elevator, Via del Giglio 8, tel. 055-214-886, fax 055-274-0521, e-mail: pal.cast@flashnet.it, Laura SE).

MODERATELY PRICED

Hotel Accademia is an elegant two-star hotel with marble stairs, parquet floors, attractive public areas, 22 pleasant rooms, and a floor plan that defies logic (Sb-€87, Db-€140, Tb-€170, these discounted prices are promised through 2003 only with this book, CC, air-con, TV, tiny courtyard, Via Faenza 7, tel. 055-293-451, fax 055-219-771, www.accademiahotel.net, e-mail: info@accademiahotel.net, SE).

Hotels in Florence

FORTEZZA DI BASSO
200 YARDS
200 METERS
TRAIN STATION
PIAZZA INDEPENDENZA
VIA S. ZANOBI
SAN MARCO
PIAZZA DELLA ANNUNZIATA
VIA 27 APRILE
MERCATO CENTRALE
VIA NAZIONALE
VIA GUELFA
ACC.
VIA ANTONIO
MARKET
FOUNDLING HOSPITAL
BUS STN.
VIA FAENZA
VIA CAVOUR
VIA RICASOLI
VIA DEI SERVI
VIA
VIA DELLA SCALA
VIA PANZANI
PIAZZA S.M. NOVELLA
VIA PALAZZUOLO
BANCHI
CERRETANI
DUOMO
VIA D. PERGOLA
VIA ORIUOLO
VIA SOLE
SPADA
VIA DE' FOSS
VIA TORNABUONI
STROZZI
PIAZZA REP.
VIA CALZAIOLI
CORSO
VIA PROCONSOLO
RIVER ARNO
CARRAIA
LUNGARNO
BARGELLO
PIAZZA SIGNORIA
S. TRIN.
CORSINI
PALAZZO VECCHIO
OLTRARNO
UFFIZI GALLERY
PONTE VECCHIO
DCH
1 HOTEL ACCADEMIA
2 HOTEL MORANDI ALLA CROCETTA
3 CASA RABATTI
4 SOGGIORNO PEZZATI
5 HOTEL ENZA
6 SOGGIORNO MAGLIANI
7 HOTEL LOGGIATO DEI SERVITI
8 DUE FONTANE HOTEL
9 OBLATE SISTERS OF THE ASSUMPTION
10 RESIDENZA DEI PUCCI
11 PALAZZO CASTIGLIONI & HOTEL ALDOBRANDINI
12 HOTEL BELLETTINI
13 HOTEL BASILEA
14 PENSIONE CENTRALE
15 HOTEL SOLE
16 SOGGIORNO BATTISTERO
17 HOTEL PENDINI
18 PENSIONE MAXIM
19 ALBERGO FIRENZE
20 HOTEL ELITE
21 TORRE GUELFA & ALESSANDRA HOTELS
22 PENSIONE BRETAGNA
23 FLORENCE WALKING TOURS

Residenza dei Pucci, a block north of the Duomo, has 12 tastefully decorated rooms—in soothing earth tones—with aristocratic furniture and tweed carpeting. It's fresh and bright (Sb-€130, Db-€145, Tb-€165, suite with grand Duomo view-€207 for 2 people, €233 for 4, claim a 10 percent discount through 2003 with this book and payment in cash, breakfast served in room, CC, Via dei Pucci 9, tel. 055-281-886, fax 055-264-314, http://residenzapucci.interfree.it, e-mail: residenzapucci@interfree.it, SE).

LOWER PRICED

Hotel Bellettini rents 34 bright, cool, well-cared-for rooms with inviting lounges and a touch of class. Its five rooms in an annex two blocks away are higher quality with all the comforts, but you need to come to the main hotel for breakfast (main building: S-€75, Sb-€95, D-€100, Db-€130, Tb-€170, Qb-€210; annex: Sb-€110, Db-€155, Tb-€209, CC, 5 percent discount with this book only if you claim it upon arrival, air-con, free Internet access, Via de' Conti 7, tel. 055-213-561, fax 055-283-551, www.firenze.net/hotelbellettini, e-mail: hotel.bellettini@dada.it, frisky Gina SE).

Hotel Aldobrandini, a good budget choice, has 15 decent, clean, affordable rooms, with the San Lorenzo market at its doorstep and the entrance to the Medici Chapel a few steps away (Ss-€42, Sb-€52, D-€67, Db-€83, CC, lots of night noise but has double-paned windows, fans, Piazza Madonna degli Aldobrandini 8, tel. 055-211-866, fax 055-267-6281, Ignazio SE).

Pensione Centrale, a traditional-feeling place with 18 spacious rooms, is indeed central, though run without warmth (D-€93, Db-€109, CC, quiet, some air-con rooms, often filled with American students, elevator, Via de' Conti 3, tel. 055-215-761, fax 055-215-216, www.pensionecentrale.it, e-mail: info@pensionecentrale.it). They sometimes send people to a nearby, noisier pension; confirm that your reservation is in fact for this place.

Sleeping near the Central Market (zip code: 50129)

MODERATELY PRICED

Hotel Basilea offers predictable three-star, air-conditioned comfort in its 38 modern rooms (Db-€110–160 depending on season, CC, elevator, terrace, free e-mail service, Via Guelfa 41, at intersection with Nazionale—a busy street, ask for rooms in the back, tel. 055-214-587, fax 055-268-350, www.florenceitaly.net, e-mail: basilea@dada.it).

LOWER PRICED

Casa Rabatti is the ultimate if you always wanted to be a part of a Florentine family. Its four simple, clean rooms are run with motherly warmth by Marcella and her husband, Celestino, who speak minimal English (D-€50, Db-€60, €25 per bed in shared quad or quint, prices good with this book, no breakfast, no CC, fans, no sign other than on doorbell, 5 blocks from station, Via San Zanobi 48 black, tel. 055-212-393, e-mail: casarabatti@inwind.it).

Soggiorno Pezzati Daniela is another little place with six homey rooms (Sb-€45, Db-€62, Tb-€86, cheaper off-season, no breakfast, no CC, all rooms have a fridge, air-con extra; marked only by small sign near door, Via San Zanobi 22, tel. 055-291-660, fax 055-287-145, www.soggiornopezzati.it, e-mail: 055291660@iol.it, Daniela SE). If you get an Italian recording when you call, hang on—your call is being transferred to a cell phone.

Soggiorno Magliani, central and humble with seven rooms, feels and smells like a great-grandmother's place. It's run with warmth by a friendly family duo, Vincenza and her English-speaking daughter, Cristina (S-€33, D-€43, cash only but secure reservation with CC, no breakfast, double-paned windows, near Via Guelfa at Via Reparata 1, tel. 055-287-378, e-mail: hotel-magliani@libero.it).

Sleeping East of the Duomo

The first two listings are near the Accademia, on Piazza S.S. Annunziata (zip code: 50122). The third is just off the square.

HIGHER PRICED

Hotel Loggiato dei Serviti, at the most prestigious address in Florence on the most Renaissance square in town, gives you Renaissance romance with hair dryers. Stone stairways lead you under open-beam ceilings through this 16th-century monastery's elegant public rooms. The 34 cells, with air-conditioning, TVs, minibars, and telephones, wouldn't be recognized by their original inhabitants. The hotel staff is both professional and friendly (Sb-€146, Db-€210, family suites from €263, book a month ahead during peak season, cheaper Aug and winter, CC, elevator, annex Piazza S.S. Annunziata 3, tel. 055-289-592, fax 055-289-595, www.loggiatodeiservitihotel.it, e-mail: info@loggiatodeiservitihotel.it, Simonetta, Francesca, and Andrea SE).

MODERATELY PRICED

Le Due Fontane Hotel faces the same great square but fills its old building with a smoky, 1970s, business-class ambience. Its 57 air-conditioned rooms are big and comfortable (Sb-€103, Db-€140, Tb-€196, these discounted prices are promised through 2003 but only if you claim them upon reserving, CC, elevator, Piazza S.S. Annunziata 14, tel. 055-210-185, fax 055-294-461, www.leduefontane.it, e-mail: leduefontane@dada.it, SE).

At **Hotel Morandi alla Crocetta**, a former convent, you're enveloped in a 16th-century cocoon. Located on a quiet street, with period furnishings, parquet floors, and wood-beamed ceilings, it draws you in (Sb-€100, Db-€160, breakfast-€11, CC, Via "Laura 50, a block off Piazza S.S. Annunziata, tel. 055-234-4747, fax 055-248-0954, www.hotelmorandi.it, e-mail: welcome @hotelmorandi.it, SE).

LOWER PRICED

The **Oblate Sisters of the Assumption** run a 20-room hotel in a Renaissance building with a dreamy garden and a quiet, institutional feel (S-€34, D-€62, Db-€67, elevator, no CC, Borgo Pinti 15, 50121 Firenze, tel. 055-248-0582, fax 055-234-6291, NSE).

Sleeping on or near Piazza Repubblica (zip code: 50123)

These are the most central of my accomodations recommendations, though given Florence's walkable core, nearly every hotel can be considered central.

MODERATELY PRICED

Hotel Pendini, a well-run three-star hotel with 42 old-time rooms (8 with views of the square), is popular and central, overlooking Piazza Repubblica (Sb-€86–110, Db-€110–150 depending on season, CC, elevator, fine lounge and breakfast room, air-con, Via Strozzi 2, reserve ASAP, tel. 055-211-170, fax 055-281-807, www.florenceitaly.net, e-mail: pendini @dada.it, SE).

Residenza Giotto has six bright, modern rooms and a terrace so close to the Duomo you can almost touch it (Sb-€120, Db-€130, Tb-€145, 10 percent discount with this book and payment in cash, breakfast in room, CC, Via Roma 6, 4th floor, tel. 055-214-593, fax 055-264-8568, www.residenzagiotto.it, e-mail: residenzagiotto@tin.it, SE).

Pensione Maxim, right on Via Calz, is a big, institutional-feeling place as close to the sights as possible. Its halls are narrow, but the 29 rooms are comfortable and well-maintained (Sb-€83, Db-€113, Tb-€148, Qb-€173, CC but pay first night in cash, Internet access, elevator, Via dei Calzaiuoli 11, tel. 055-217-474, fax 055-283-729, www.hotelmaximfirenze.it, e-mail: hotmaxim @tin.it, Paolo and Nicola Maioli SE).

LOWER PRICED

Soggiorno Battistero, next door to the baptistery, has seven simple, airy rooms, most with urban noise but also great views, overlooking the baptistery and square. You're in the heart of Florence (S-€73, Db-€95, Tb-€130, Qb-€140, these prices good with this book, 5 percent additional discount with cash, breakfast served in room, Internet access, CC, Piazza San Giovanni 1, 3rd floor, no elevator, tel. 055-295-143, fax 055-268-189, www.soggiornobattistero.it, e-mail: battistero@dada.it, lovingly run by Italian Luca and his American wife, Kelly).

Albergo Firenze, a big, efficient place, offers good, basic, and spacious rooms in a wonderfully central, reasonably quiet locale two blocks behind the Duomo (Sb-€67, Db-€88, Tb-€126, Qb-€156, cash only, must prepay first night with a bank draft or traveler's check, elevator, off Via del Corso at Piazza Donati 4, tel. 055-214-203, fax 055-212-370, SE).

Sleeping North of the Train Station (zip code: 50123)

MODERATELY PRICED

Hotel Beatrice, a three-star hotel popular with tour groups, is well-located if you've packed heavy—it's just a block north of the train and bus stations (Sb-€75–90, Db-€95–142, includes breakfast, CC, most rooms air-con, elevator, Via Fiume 11, tel. 055-216-790, fax 055-80-711, www.hotelbeatrice.it).

Sleeping South of the Train Station near Piazza Santa Maria Novella (zip code: 50123)

From the station (with your back to the tracks), cross the wide square to reach the Santa Maria Novella church and continue to the piazza in front of the church (avoid thief-ridden underground Galleria S. M. Novella tunnel leading from station under square to church). Piazza Santa Maria Novella, pleasant by day, gets a little sleazy after dark.

LOWER PRICED

Hotel Pensione Elite, run warmly by Maurizio and Nadia, is a fine value, with 10 comfortable rooms and a charm rare in this price range (Ss-€52, Sb-€72, Ds-€67, Db-€83, breakfast-€6, maybe CC, fans, at south end of square with back to church, go right to Via della Scala 12, 2nd floor, tel. & fax 055-215-395, SE).

Hotel Sole, a clean, cozy, family-run place with eight bright, modern rooms, is just off Santa Maria Novella toward the river (Sb-€47, Db-€78, Tb-€104, no breakfast, no CC, air-con, elevator, curfew at 1:00, Via del Sole 8, 3rd floor, tel. & fax 055-239-6094, friendly Anna NSE, but daughter SE).

Sleeping near Arno River and Ponte Vecchio (zip code: 50123)

HIGHER PRICED

Hotel Torre Guelfa is topped with a fun medieval tower with a panoramic rooftop terrace. Its 29 rooms vary wildly in size (small Db-from €145, standard Db-€170, Db junior suite-€220, 5 percent discount with cash). Room #15, with a private terrace—€210—is worth reserving several months in advance (CC, huge lobby, elevator, air-con, 2 blocks northwest of Ponte Vecchio, Borgo S.S. Apostoli 8, tel. 055-239-6338, fax 055-239-8577, www.hoteltorreguelfa.com, e-mail: torreguelfa@flashnet.it, Giancarlo, Carlo, and Sandro all SE).

MODERATELY PRICED

Hotel Pensione Alessandra is a 16th-century, peaceful place with 27 big, modern rooms (S-€82, Sb-€109, D-€119, Db-€150, T-€140, Tb-€181, Q-€155, Qb-€202, CC but 5 percent discount with cash, air-con, Internet access, Borgo S.S. Apostoli 17, tel. 055-283-438, fax 055-210-619, www.hotelalessandra.com, e-mail: info@hotelalessandra.com, SE).

LOWER PRICED

Pensione Bretagna is an Old World–ramshackle place run by helpful Antonio and Maura. Imagine eating breakfast under a painted, chandeliered ceiling overlooking the Arno River (S-€50, Sb-€59, small Db-€95, Db-€105, Tb-€129, Qb-€150, family deals, prices special with this book in 2003, CC, air-con, Internet access, just past Ponte San Trinita, Lungarno Corsini 6, tel. 055-289-618, fax 055-289-619, www.bretagna.it, e-mail: hotel@bretagna.it). They also run Soggiorno Althea, a cheaper place with nicer rooms, near Piazza San Spirito in the Oltrarno neighborhood (6 rooms, Db-€71, air-con, no breakfast, no reception desk, cellular 388-233-5341, www.florencealthea.it).

Sleeping in Oltrarno, South of the River (zip code: 50125)

Across the river in the Oltrarno area, between the Pitti Palace and Ponte Vecchio, you'll still find small traditional crafts shops, neighborly piazzas, and family eateries. The following places are a few minutes' walk from Ponte Vecchio.

Florence's Oltrarno Neighborhood

HIGHER PRICED

Hotel Lungarno is the place to stay if money is no object. This deluxe, four-star hotel with 70 rooms strains anything stressful or rough out of Italy, and gives you only service with a salute, physical elegance everywhere you look, and fine views over the Arno and Ponte Vecchio (Sb-€225, Db-€360, Db facing river-€460, fancier suites, great riverside public spaces, CC, 100 meters, or 330 feet, from Ponte Vecchio at Borgo San Jacopo 14, tel. 055-27261, fax 055-268-437, www.lungarnohotels.com, e-mail: bookings@lungarnohotels.com, SE).

MODERATELY PRICED

Hotel La Scaletta, an elegant, dark, cool place with 13 rooms, a labyrinthine floor plan, lots of Old World lounges, and a romantic and panoramic roof terrace, is run by Barbara, her son Manfredo, and daughters Bianca and Diana (S-€52, Sb-€95, D-€105, Db-€113–130, Tb-€115–150, Qb-€130–170, higher price is for quieter rooms in back, €5–10 discount if you pay cash, CC, air-con in 10 rooms and fans in others, elevator, bar with fine wine at good prices, Via Guicciardini 13 black, 150 meters, or 500 feet, south of Ponte Vecchio, tel. 055-283-028, fax 055-289-562, www.lascaletta.com, e-mail: info@lascaletta.com, SE). Secure your reservation with a personal check or traveler's check. Manfredo loves to cook. If he's cooking dinner, eat here. He serves a €10 "Taste of Tuscany" deal (plate of quality Tuscan meats and cheeses with bread and 2 glasses of robust Chianti)—ideal for a light lunch on the terrace.

Hotel Silla, a classic three-star hotel with 36 cheery, spacious, pastel, and modern rooms, is a fine value. It faces the river and overlooks a park opposite the Santa Croce Church (Sb-€120, Db-€170, Tb-€210, mention this book for a discount, CC, elevator, air-con, Via dei Renai 5, tel. 055-234-2888, fax 055-234-1437, www.hotelsilla.it, e-mail: hotelsilla@tin.it, Laura SE).

Pensione Sorelle Bandini is a ramshackle, 500-year-old palace on a perfectly Florentine square, with cavernous rooms, museum-warehouse interiors, a musty youthfulness, cats, a balcony lounge-loggia with a view, and an ambience that, for romantic bohemians, can be a highlight of Florence. Mimmo or Sr. Romeo will hold a room until 16:00 with a phone call (D-€103, Db-€125, T-€141, Tb-€171, includes breakfast—which during low times is optional, saving €9 per person—no CC, elevator, Piazza Santo Spirito 9, tel. 055-215-308, fax 055-282-761, SE).

LOWER PRICED

Soggiorno Pezzati Alessandra is a warm and friendly place renting five great rooms in the Oltrarno neighborhood (Sb-€45, Db-€62, Tb-€86, Qb-€108, cheaper off-season, no breakfast, no CC, all rooms have a fridge, air-con extra, Via Borgo San Frediano 6, tel. 055-290-424, fax 055-218-464, e-mail: alex170169@libero.it, Alessandra). If you get an Italian recording when you call, hang on—your call is being transferred to a cellular phone.

Istituto Gould is a Protestant Church–run place with 33 clean but drab rooms, twin beds, and modern facilities (S-€30, Sb-€35, D-€44, Db-€52, Tb-€63, €20 per person in quads, no breakfast, no CC, quieter rooms in back, Via dei Serragli 49, tel. 055-212-576, fax 055-280-274, e-mail: gould.reception

@dada.it). You must arrive when the office is open (Mon–Fri 9:00–13:00 & 15:00–19:00, Sat 9:00–13:00, no check-in Sun, SE).

Ostello Santa Monaca, a cheap hostel, is a few blocks south of Ponte Alla Carraia, one of the bridges over the Arno (€15.50 beds, 4- to 20-bed rooms, breakfast extra, CC, 1:00 curfew, Via Santa Monaca 6, tel. 055-268-338, fax 055-280-185).

Sleeping Away from the Center

MODERATELY PRICED

Hotel Ungherese is good for drivers. It's northeast of the city center (near Stadio, en route to Fiesole), with easy, free street parking and quick bus access (#11 and #17) into central Florence (Sb-€72, Db-€123, extra bed-€30, these discounted prices available with this book, pay cash to get additional 7 percent discount, rooms are 20 percent less off-season, includes breakfast, CC, air-con, Via G. B. Amici 8, tel. & fax 055-573-474, www.hotelungherese.it, e-mail: hotel.ungherese@dada.it, Giovanni, Francesca SE). It has great singles and a backyard garden terrace (ask for a room on the garden). They can recommend good eateries nearby.

LOWER PRICED

Villa Camerata, classy for an IYHF hostel, is on the outskirts of Florence (€14.50 per bed with breakfast, 4- to 12-bed rooms, must have IYHF card, no CC, ride bus #17 to Salviatino stop, Via Righi 2, tel. 055-601-451).

Eating in Florence

To save money and time for sights, you can keep lunches fast and simple, eating in one of the countless self-service places and pizzerias or just picnicking (try juice, yogurt, cheese, and a roll for €5). For good sit-down meals, consider the following. Remember, restaurants like to serve what's fresh. If you're into flavor, go for the seasonal best bets—featured in the *Piatti del Giorno* (special of the day) sections of the menus.

Eating in Oltrarno, South of the River

For a change of scene, eat across the river in Oltrarno (see map on page 878). Here are a few good places just over Ponte Vecchio.

At Piazza San Felicita: A block south of Ponte Vecchio is the unpretentious and happy Piazza San Felicita, with two good restaurants. The cozy and candlelit **Trattoria Bordino**, just up the street and actually built into the old town wall (c. 1170), serves tasty and beautifully presented Florentine cuisine "with international influence" (a little pricey, Mon–Sat 12:00–14:30 & 19:30–22:30, closed Sun, Via Stracciatella 9 red, tel. 055-213-048). Right on the square, the more touristy **Ristorante Bibo** serves "*cucina tipica Fiorentina*" with a pink-tablecloth-and-black-bowties dressiness and leafy, candlelit outdoor seating (good €15 3-course meal, CC, reserve for outdoor seating, Wed–Mon 12:00–14:30 & 19:00–22:30, closed Tue, Piazza San Felicita 6 red, tel. 055-239-8554).

On Via di Santo Spirito/Borgo San Jacopo: Several good and colorful restaurants line this multi-named street a block off the river in Oltrarno. I'd survey the scene (perhaps following the self-guided Oltrarno walk described on page 868) before making a choice.

At **Cammillo Trattoria,** while Cammillo is slurping spaghetti in heaven, his granddaughter Chiara carries on the tradition, mixing traditional Tuscan with "creative" modern cuisine. With a charcoal grill and a team of white-aproned waiters cranking out wonderful food in a fun, dressy-but-down-to-earth ambience, this place is a hit (full dinners about €36 plus wine, Thu–Tue 12:00–14:30 & 19:30–22:30, closed Wed, CC, Borgo San Jacopo 57 red, reservations smart, tel. 055-212-427).

Other inviting places along this street: **Osteria del Cinghiale Bianco** is popular but cramped (around €30 for dinner plus wine, Borgo San Jacopo 43 red, air-con, Thu–Tue 12:00–15:00 & 18:30–23:30, closed Wed, reservations wise, tel. 055-215-706). The more relaxed **Trattoria Angiolino** serves good, old-fashioned local cuisine (about €20 for dinner plus wine, Tue–Sun 12:00–14:30 & 19:30–22:30, closed Mon, Via di Santo Spirito 36 red, tel. 055-239-8976). **Trattoria Sabatino** is spacious and disturbingly cheap, with family character, red-checkered tablecloths, a simple menu, and the fewest tourists of all. A wonderful place to watch locals munch, it's just outside the Porta San Frediano (medieval gate), a 15-minute walk from Ponte Vecchio (Mon–Fri 12:00–14:30 & 19:20–22:00, closed Sat–Sun, Via Pisana 2 red, tel. 055-225-955, NSE). If you eat here, read my self-guided Oltrarno walk (on page 868) before hiking out to the gate.

At Piazza Santo Spirito: This classic Florentine square (lately a hangout for drug pushers, therefore a bit seedy-feeling and plagued by Vespa bag-snatchings) has two popular little restaurants offering good local cuisine every night of the week, indoor and on-the-square seating (reserve for on-the-square), moderate prices, and impersonal service: **Borgo Antico** (Piazza Santo Spirito 6 red, tel. 055-210-437) and **Osteria Santo Spirito** (pricier, more peaceful outdoor seating, Piazza Santo Spirito 16 red, tel. 055-238-2383).

Ricchi Caffè, next to Borgo Antico, has fine gelato and

Restaurants in Florence

FORTEZZA DI BASSO
200 YARDS
200 METERS
TRAIN STATION
MERCATO CENTRALE
PIAZZA INDEPENDENZA
SAN MARCO
PIAZZA DELLA ANNUNZIATA
ACC.
FOUNDLING HOSPITAL
MARKET
BUS STN.
VIA NAZIONALE
VIA S. ZANOBI
VIA 27 APRILE
VIA GUELFA
VIA ANTONIO
VIA FAENZA
VIA PANZANI
VIA CAVOUR
VIA RICASOLI
VIA DEI SERVI
VIA D. PERGOLA
VIA DELLA SCALA
VIA PALAZZUOLO
PIAZZA S.M. NOVELLA
BANCHI
CERRETANI
DUOMO
VIA ORIUOLO
SOLE
SPADA
VIA FOSSI
VIA TORNABUONI
STROZZI
PIAZZA REP.
VIA CALZAIOLI
CORSO
VIA PROCONSOLO
BARGELLO
PIAZZA SIGNORIA
PALAZZO VECCHIO
BORGO DEI GRECI
CARRAIA
LUNGARNO
CORSINI
S. TRIN.
RIVER ARNO
DCH
OLTRARNO
PONTE VECCHIO
UFFIZI GALLERY
1 OSTERIA BELLEDONNE
2 RIST. LA SPADA
3 TRATTORIA MARIONE
4 TRATTORIA SOSTANZA-TROIA
5 TRATTORIA IL CONTADINO
6 TRATTORIA DA GIORGIO
7 LA GROTTA DI LEO
8 MERCATO CENTRALE MARKET
9 TRATTORIA LA BURRASCA & OSTERIA LA CONGREGA
10 SELF-SERVICE REST. LEONARDO
11 RIST. IL CAVALLINO
12 OSTERIA VINI E VECCHI SAPORI
13 CANTINETTA DEI VERRAZZANO & RIST. PAOLI
14 I FRATELLINI WINE & SANDWICH SHOP
15 TRATTORIA ICCHE C'E C'E
16 PICNIC SPOT IF IT'S NOT TOO HOT

shaded outdoor tables. After noting the plain facade of the Brunelleschi church facing the square, step inside the café, and pick your favorite of the many ways it might be finished. **Café Cabiria,** next door, is a great local hangout with good light meals and a cozy, funky Florentine room in back.

Trattoria Casalinga is an inexpensive standby. Famous for its home cooking, it's now filled with tourists rather than locals. But it sends them away full, happy, and with euros left for gelato (Mon–Sat 12:00–14:30 & 19:00–21:45, closed Sun and all of Aug, CC, just off Piazza Santo Spirito, near the church at Via dei Michelozzi 9 red, after 20:00 reserve or wait, tel. 055-218-624).

Eating North of the River

Eating near Santa Maria Novella and the Train Station

Osteria Belledonne is a crowded and cheery bohemian hole-in-the-wall serving great food at good prices. I loved the meal but had to correct the bill—read it carefully. They take only a few reservations. Arrive early or wait (Mon–Fri 12:00–14:30 & 19:00–22:30, closed Sat–Sun, Via delle Belledonne 16 red, tel. 055-238-2609).

Ristorante La Spada, nearby, is another fine local favorite serving typical Tuscan cuisine with less atmosphere and more menu (€11 lunch special, about €20 for dinner plus wine, daily 12:00–15:00 & 19:00–22:30, air-con, near Via della Spada at Via del Moro 66 red, evening reservations smart, tel. 055-218-757).

Trattoria Marione serves good home-cooked-style meals to a local crowd in a happy, food-loving ambience (closed Sun, dinners run about €15 plus wine, pretty smoky, Via della Spada 27 red, tel. 055-214-756).

Trattoria Sostanza-Troia is a characteristic and well-established place with shared tables and a loyal local following. Whirling ceiling fans and walls strewn with old photos create a time-warp ambience. They offer two seatings, requiring reservations: one at 19:30 and one at 21:00 (dinners for about €15 plus wine, great steaks, lunch 12:00–14:00, closed Sat, Via del Porcellana 25 red, tel. 055-212-691).

Two smoky chow houses for local workers offer a €9, hearty, family-style, fixed-price menu with a bustling working-class/budget-Yankee-traveler atmosphere (Mon–Sat 12:00–14:30 & 18:15–21:30, closed Sun, 2 blocks south of train station): **Trattoria il Contadino** (Via Palazzuolo 69 red, tel. 055-238-2673) and **Trattoria da Giorgio** (across the street at Via Palazzuolo 100 red). Arrive early or wait. The touristy **La Grotta di Leo** (a block away) has a cheap, straightforward menu and edible food and pizza (daily 11:00–1:00, Via della Scala 41 red, tel. 055-219-265). Because these places are a block from the station, they are handy, but the street scene is shabby.

Eating near the Central and San Lorenzo Markets

For mountains of picnic produce or just a cheap sandwich and piles of people-watching, visit the huge Central Market—**Mercato Centrale** (Mon–Sat 7:00–14:00, closed Sun, a block north of the San Lorenzo street market).

Trattoria la Burrasca is a funky, family-run place ideal for Tuscan home cooking. It's small (10 tables) and inexpensive, with pasta for €4. Anna and Antonio Genzano have cooked and served here with passion since 1982. If Andy Capp were Italian, he'd eat here for special nights out. Everything but the desserts is homemade. And, if you want good wine for cheap prices, order it here (Fri–Wed 12:00–15:00 & 19:00–22:00, closed Thu, Via Panicale 6b, at the north corner of Central Market, tel. 055-215-827, NSE).

Osteria la Congrega brags that it's a Tuscan wine bar designed to help you lose track of time. In a fresh and romantic two-level setting, creative chef/owner Mahyar has designed a fun, easy menu featuring modern Tuscan cuisine, with top-notch local meat and produce. He offers fine vegetarian dishes. With just 10 uncrowded tables, the restaurant requires reservations for dinner (moderate with €13 dinner plates, CC, daily 12:00–15:00 & 19:00–23:00, Via Panicale 43 red, tel. 055-264-5027).

For a cheap lunch, try **Trattoria San Zanobi's** Pasta Break Lunch (most pastas around €5, Via San Zanobi 33 red, a couple blocks northeast of the Central Market, tel. 055-475-286).

Eating near the Accademia and Museum of San Marco

Gran Caffè San Marco, conveniently located on Piazza San Marco, offers reasonably priced pizzas, sandwiches, and desserts (no cover charge, self-service and restaurant, Piazza San Marco 11 red, across square from Museum of San Marco entrance, tel. 055-215-833).

Eating near the Cathedral (Duomo)

Self-Service Restaurant Leonardo is fast, cheap, air-conditioned, and very handy, just a block from the Duomo, southwest of the baptistery (€3 pastas, €4 main courses, Sun–Fri 11:45–14:45 & 18:45–21:45, closed Sat, upstairs at Via Pecori 5, tel. 055-284-446). Luciano (like Pavarotti) runs the place with enthusiasm.

Eating near Palazzo Vecchio

Piazza Signoria, the square facing the old city hall, is ringed by beautifully situated yet touristic eateries. Any will do for a reasonably priced pizza. Perhaps the best value is **Ristorante il Cavallino** (€10 fixed-price lunch menu, €16 fixed-price dinner menu, great outdoor seating in shadow of palace, tel. 055-215-818).

Osteria Vini e Vecchi Sapori is a colorful hole-in-the-wall serving traditional food, including plates of mixed *crostini* (€0.75 each—you choose), half a block north of Palazzo Vecchio (Tue–Sun 10:00–23:00, closed Mon, Via dei Magazzini 3 red, facing the bronze equestrian statue in Piazza della Signoria, go behind its tail into the corner and to your left, NSE).

Cantinetta dei Verrazzano is a long-established bakery/café/wine bar, serving delightful sandwich plates in an elegant old-time setting, and hot focaccia sandwiches to go. The *Specialita Verrazzano* is a fine plate of four little *crostini* (like mini-*bruschetta*) featuring different local breads, cheeses, and meats (€7). The *Tagliere di Focacce*, a sampler plate of mini–focaccia sandwiches, is also fun. Either of these dishes with a glass of Chianti makes a fine, light meal. Paolo describes things to make eating educational. As office workers pop in for a quick bite, it's traditional to share tables at lunchtime (Mon–Sat 12:30–21:00, closed Sun, just off Via Calzaiuoli on a side street across from Orsanmichele Church at Via dei Tavolini 18, tel. 055-268-590).

At **I Fratellini,** a colorful hole-in-the-wall place, the "little brothers" have served peasants rustic sandwiches and cheap glasses of Chianti wine since 1875. Join the local crowd, then sit on a nearby curb or windowsill to munch, placing your glass on the wall rack before you leave (€4 for sandwich and wine, 20 meters/65 feet in front of Orsanmichele Church on Via dei Cimatori).

Ristorante Paoli serves great local cuisine to piles of happy eaters under a richly frescoed Gothic vault. Because of its fame and central location, it's filled mostly with tourists, but for a dressy, traditional splurge meal, this is my choice (Wed–Mon 12:00–14:00 & 19:00–22:00, closed Tue, reserve for dinner, €20 tourist menu, à la carte is pricier, CC, midway between old square and cathedral at Via de Tavolini 12 red, tel. 055-216-215). Salads are flamboyantly cut and mixed from a trolley right at your table.

Trattoria Icche C'è C'è (dialect for "whatever is, is"; pron. EE-kay CHAY chay) is a small, family-style place where fun-loving Gino serves good traditional meals (moderate, not too touristy, closed Mon, midway between Bargello and river at Via Magalotti 11 red, tel. 055-216-589).

Osteria del Porcellino—a rare place that serves late—is delightful and a bit pricey, packed with a mix of locals and in-the-know tourists, and run with style and enthusiasm by friendly chef Enzo (daily 18:00–1:00, summer lunches, indoor/outdoor, CC, Via Val di Lamona 7 red, half a block behind Mercato Nuovo, reserve for dinner, tel. 055-264-148).

Trattoria Nella serves good, typical Tuscan cuisine—including the best gnocchi in town—at affordable prices. Arrive early or be disappointed (Mon–Sat 12:00–14:30 & 19:30–22:00, closed Sun, 3 blocks northwest of Ponte Vecchio, Via delle Terme 19 red, tel. 055-218-925).

Transportation Connections—Florence

By train to: Assisi (3/day, 2 hrs, more frequent with transfers, direction: Foligno), **Orvieto** (6/day, 2 hrs), **Pisa** (2/hr, 1 hr), **La Spezia** (for the Cinque Terre, 2/day direct, 2 hrs, or change in Pisa), **Venice** (7/day, 3 hrs), **Milan** (12/day, 3–5 hrs), **Rome** (hrly, 2.5 hrs), **Naples** (10/day, 4 hrs), **Brindisi** (3/day, 11 hrs with change in Bologna), **Frankfurt** (3/day, 12 hrs), **Paris** (1/day, 12 hrs overnight), **Vienna** (4/day, 9–10 hrs). Train info: tel. 848-888-088.

Buses: The SITA bus station, a block west of the Florence train station, is user-friendly (but remember, bus service drops dramatically on Sunday). Schedules are posted everywhere, with TV monitors indicating imminent departures. You'll find buses to: **San Gimignano** (hrly, 1.75 hrs), **Siena** (hrly, 75-min *corse rapide* fast buses, faster than the train, avoid the 2-hr *diretta* slow buses), and the **airport** (hrly, 15–30 min). Bus info: tel. 055-214-721 from 9:30 to 12:30; some schedules are in the *Florence Concierge Information* magazine.

Taxi to Siena: For around €100, you can arrange a ride directly from your Florence hotel to your Siena hotel. For a small group or for people with more money than time, this can be a good value.

Airports

The **Amerigo Vespucci Airport** (www.safnet.it), several kilometers northwest of Florence, has a TI, cash machines, car rental agencies, and easy connections by airport shuttle bus with Florence's bus station, a block west of the train station (€4, 2/hr, 15–30 min, from Florence runs 5:30–23:00, from airport 6:00–23:30). Airport info: 055-306-1300, flight info: 055-306-1700 (domestic), 055-306-1702 (international). Allow about €16 to €20 for a taxi.

International flights often land at Pisa's **Galileo Galilei Airport** (also has TI and car rental agencies, www.pisa-airport.com), an hour from Florence by train (runs hrly; if you're leaving Florence for this airport, catch the train at Florence's train station at platform #5). Flight info: 050-500-707.

PISA

Pisa was a regional superpower in its medieval heyday (11th, 12th, and 13th centuries), rivaling Florence and Genoa. Its Mediterranean empire, which included Corsica and Sardinia, helped make it a wealthy republic. But the Pisa fleet was beaten (in 1284, by Genoa) and its port silted up, leaving the city high and dry, with only its Field of Miracles and its university keeping it on the map.

Pisa's three important sights (the cathedral, the baptistery, and the bell tower) float regally on the best lawn in Italy. Even as the church was being built, the Piazza del Duomo was nicknamed the Campo dei Miracoli, or Field of Miracles, for the grandness of the undertaking. The style throughout is Pisa's very own "Pisan Romanesque," surrounded by Italy's tackiest ring of souvenir stands. This spectacle is tourism at its most crass. Wear gloves.

The Leaning Tower recently reopened after a decade of restoration and topple prevention. To ascend, you'll have to make a reservation when you buy your €15 ticket (for details, see "Sights," below).

Planning Your Time

Seeing the tower and the square and wandering through the church are 90 percent of the Pisan thrill. Pisa is a touristy quickie. By car, it's a headache. By train, it's a joy. Train travelers may need to change trains in Pisa, anyway. Hop on the bus and see the tower. If you want to climb it, go straight to the ticket booth to snare an appointment—usually for a couple of hours later (or check www.duomo.pisa.it before you go to see if you can book online). Sophisticated sightseers stop more for the Pisano carvings in the cathedral and baptistery than for a look at the tipsy tower. There's nothing wrong with Pisa, but I'd stop only to see the Field of Miracles and get out of town. By car, it's a 45-minute detour from the freeway.

Orientation

Tourist Information: One TI is at the train station (summer: Mon–Sat 9:00–19:00, Sun 9:30–15:30; winter: Mon–Sat 9:00–19:00 and possibly closed Sun; to your left as you exit station, tel. 050-42291) and another is near the Leaning Tower (Mon–Fri 9:00–18:00, Sat–Sun 10:30–16:30, outside the medieval wall, hidden behind souvenir stands in a nook of the wall, about 100 meters, or 330 feet, to the left of the gate before you enter the Field of Miracles, tel. 050-560-464). Another TI is at the airport (tel. 050-503-700). Beware of pickpockets in Pisa.

Pisa

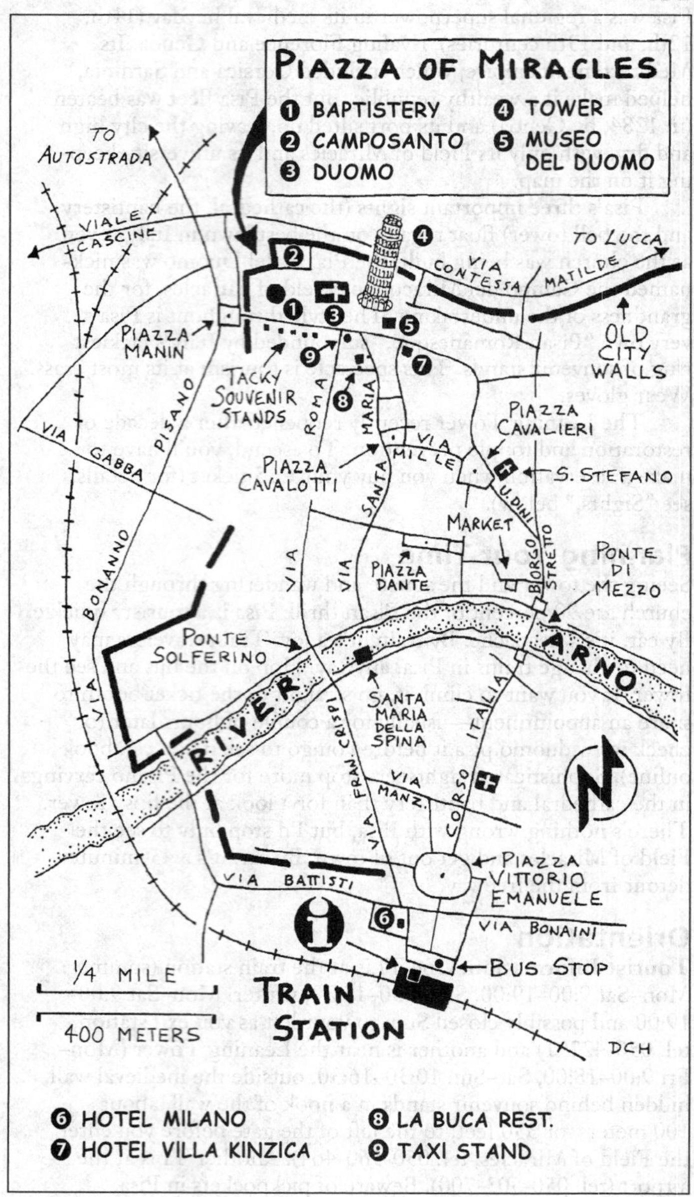
PIAZZA OF MIRACLES
1 BAPTISTERY
2 CAMPOSANTO
3 DUOMO
4 TOWER
5 MUSEO DEL DUOMO
TO AUTOSTRADA
VIALE CASCINE
TO LUCCA
VIA CONTESSA MATILDE
OLD CITY WALLS
PIAZZA MANIN
TACKY SOUVENIR STANDS
VIA ROMA
VIA SANTA MARIA
PIAZZA CAVALIERI
VIA MILLE
S. STEFANO
U. DINI
VIA GABBA
VIA PISANO
PIAZZA CAVALOTTI
MARKET
BORGO STRETTO
PONTE DI MEZZO
VIA BONANNO
PIAZZA DANTE
PONTE SOLFERINO
ARNO
RIVER
SANTA MARIA DELLA SPINA
VIA FRAN. CRISPI
CORSO ITALIA
VIA MANZ.
PIAZZA VITTORIO EMANUELE
VIA BATTISTI
VIA BONAINI
BUS STOP
1/4 MILE
400 METERS
TRAIN STATION
DCH
6 HOTEL MILANO
7 HOTEL VILLA KINZICA
8 LA BUCA REST.
9 TAXI STAND

Arrival in Pisa

By Train: To get to the Field of Miracles from the station, you can **walk** (25–30 min, get free map from TI at station, they'll mark the best route on your map), take a **taxi** (€8, at taxi stand at station or call 050-541-600), or catch a **bus**. The latest information on the bus route to the Field of Miracles is posted in the train information office in Pisa's station lobby (or ask at TI). It's likely bus #3 (3/hr) which leaves from in front of the station, across the street at the big hotel. Buy an €0.80 ticket from the *tabacchi*/magazine kiosk in the station's main hall or at any *tabacchi* shop (good for 1 hr, round-trip OK, 10-minute ride one-way to tower). Confirm the bus route number or risk taking a long tour of Pisa's suburbs. The correct bus will let you off at Piazza Manin, in front of the gate to the Field of Miracles. To return to the station, catch the bus from across the street where you got off (confirm the stop with a local or at the TI).

The train station no longer has a baggage check. If necessary, you could store your bag at the airport (€6/per piece per day); it's only a 5-minute ride on bus #3 (same bus route as to the Field of Miracles but catch bus going in opposite direction) and still make it to the tower on the same bus ticket.

By Car: To get to the Leaning Tower, follow signs to the Duomo or Campo dei Miracoli, located on the north edge of town. If you're coming from the Pisa Nord autostrada exit, you won't have to mess with the city center, but you will have to endure some terrible traffic. There's no option better than the €1-per-hour pay lot just outside the town wall a block from the tower.

By Plane: From Pisa's airport, take bus #3 into town (€0.80, 3/hr, 5 min) or a taxi (€6). Flight info: 050-500-707 (www.pisa-airport.com).

Prices

Pisa has a scheme to get you into its neglected secondary sights: the baptistery, cathedral museum (Museo dell' Opera del Duomo), Camposanto cemetery, and fresco museum (Museo delle Sinopie).

For any one monument, you'll pay €5; for two monuments, the cost is €6; for four monuments, it's €8.50; and for the works (including the cathedral), you'll pay €10.50. By comparison, the cathedral alone is a bargain (€2). You can buy any of these tickets at the usually crowded ticket office (behind tower and cathedral entrance), or more easily at the Camposanto cemetery, Museo dell' Opera del Duomo, or Museo delle Sinopie (near baptistery, almost suffocated by souvenir stands); note that you can buy a ticket just for, say, the cathedral at any of these points.

For marathon sightseers, there's a €13 Universalis ticket that covers all of the above sights, the Museo Nazionale di San Matteo, and many others, purchasable only at the Tower of Santa Maria, behind the baptistery.

No matter what ticket you get, you'll have to pay another €15 to climb the Leaning Tower. Tickets for the ascent are sold only at the crowded ticket office behind the tower and duomo.

Sights—Pisa

▲▲Leaning Tower—Started in the 12th century, this most famous example of Pisan Romanesque architecture was leaning even before its completion. Notice how the architect, for lack of a better solution, kinked up the top section. The 294 tilted steps to the top were closed for years, as engineers worked to keep the bell tower from toppling. The formerly clean and tidy area around the tower was turned into a construction zone, as engineers used steam pipes to dry out the subsoil and huge weights to stabilize (but not straighten out) the tower.

Now 30 people an hour can clamber to the top for €15 (Mon–Sat 8:00–17:20, Sun 9:00–17:00). To make the necessary reservation, go straight to the ticket office behind the tower. You choose a time slot (40 minutes) for your visit at the time of purchase; it will likely be a couple of hours before you're able to go up (you could see the rest of the monuments and grab lunch while waiting). There are plans to set up online booking; check www.duomo.pisa.it or call 050-560-547 for the latest.

Note that even though the ticket office sign says the visit is guided, that only means you'll be accompanied by a museum guard to make sure you don't stay up past your scheduled 40-minute appointment time. Not including the climb, you'll have about 25 minutes for vertigo on top.

▲▲Cathedral—The huge Pisan Romanesque church (known as the duomo), with its carved pulpit by Giovanni Pisano, is artistically more important than its more famous bell tower (€2, open daily, summer: Mon–Sat 10:00–20:00, Sun 13:00–19:40; spring and fall: Mon–Sat 10:00–17:40, Sun 13:00–17:40; winter: Mon–Sat 10:00–12:45 & 15:00–16:45, Sun 15:00–16:45). Shorts are OK as long as they're not short shorts. Big backpacks are not allowed, nor is storage provided (but ticket-taker might let you leave bag at entrance).

Baptistery—The baptistery, the biggest in Italy, is interesting for its great acoustics (open daily, summer: 8:00–19:40; spring and fall: 9:00–17:40; winter: 9:00–16:40; located in front of cathedral). If you ask nicely and leave a tip, the ticket-taker uses the place's echo power to sing haunting harmonies with himself. The pulpit, by Nicola Pisano (1260), inspired Renaissance art to follow, but the same artist's pulpit and carvings in Siena were just as impressive to me—in a more enjoyable atmosphere. Notice that even the baptistery leans nearly two meters (5 feet).

Other Sights at the Field of Miracles—For Pisan art, see the **Museo dell' Opera del Duomo**, displaying treasures of the cathedral, including sculptures (12th–14th century), paintings, silverware, and ancient Egyptian, Etruscan, and Roman artifacts (same hours as baptistery; housed behind tower, Piazza Arcivescovado 18).

Skip the **Camposanto** cemetery bordering the cathedral square, even if its "Holy Land dirt" does turn a body into a skeleton in a day (same hours as baptistery).

The **Museo delle Sinopie**, housed in a 13th-century hospital, features the sketchy frescoes that were preparatory work for the frescoes in the cemetery (same hours as baptistery, hidden behind souvenir stands, across street from baptistery entrance).

The much-advertised **Panoramic Walk on the Wall**, which includes just a small section of the medieval wall, isn't worth your time or €2.20 (March–Dec daily 10:00–18:00, entrance near baptistery, at Porta Leone).

More Sights—The **Museo Nazionale di San Matteo**, in a former convent, displays 12th- to 15th-century sculptures, illuminated manuscripts, and paintings by Martini, Ghirlandaio, Masaccio, and others (€4.20, Tue–Sat 8:30–19:00, Sun 9:30–13:30, closed Mon, on river near Piazza Mazzini at Lungarno Mediceo, tel. 050-541-865).

Walking between the station and Field of Miracles in the pedestrian zone from Via G. Oberdan to Piazza Vittorio Veneto shows you a student-filled, classy, Old World town with an Arno-scape much like its rival upstream. A little **fruit market** is pinched and squeezed into Piazza Vettovaglie (Mon–Sat 7:00–18:00, near river, between station and tower). A **street market** attracts shoppers Wednesday and Saturday mornings between Via del Brennero and Via Paparrelle (just outside of wall, about 6 blocks east of tower).

Sleeping and Eating in Pisa
(€1 = about $1, country code: 39, zip code: 56100)

Consider **Hotel Milano**, near the station, offering 10 spacious rooms with faded-but-clean bedspreads (D-€47, Db-€65, breakfast extra, CC, air-con, Via Mascagni 14, tel. 050-23162, fax 050-44237, e-mail: hotelmilano@csinfo.it). Or try the pricier **Hotel Villa Kinzica**, with 33 modern rooms within a block of the Field of Miracles—ask for a room with a view of the tower (Db-€104, CC, elevator, most rooms air-con, attached restaurant, Piazza Arcivescovado 2, tel. 050-560-419, fax 050-551-204).

Eating: For a quick lunch or dinner, the pizzeria/trattoria **La Buca**—just a block from the tower—has a good reputation among locals (Sat–Thu 12:00–15:30 & 19:00–23:00, closed Fri, CC, at Via Santa Maria and Via G. Tassi, tel. 050-560-660).

Bar Costa Gelateria has a good assortment of homemade gelati a block from the Museo dell' Opera del Duomo on Via Santa Maria 100 (daily 8:00–24:00, tel. 050-551-016).

For a cheap, fast, and tasty meal a few steps from the train station, try cheery **La Lupa Ghiotta Tavola Calda.** It's got everything you'd want from a *ristorante* at half the price, with fast-er service (you can build your own salad—5 ingredients for €4.50, Mon and Wed–Sat 12:00–15:30 & 19:00–24:00, Tue 12:00–15:30, Sun 19:00–24:00, Viale Bonaini 113, tel. 050-21018).

Transportation Connections—Pisa

By train to: Florence (hrly, 1 hr), **La Spezia** (hrly, 1 hr, gateway to Cinque Terre), **Siena** (change at Empoli: Pisa–Empoli, hrly, 30 min; Empoli–Siena, hrly, 1 hr). Even the fastest trains stop in Pisa, and you might be changing trains here whether you plan to stop or not. Train info: tel. 848-888-088.

By car: The drive between Pisa and Florence is that rare case where the non-autostrada highway (free, more direct, and at least as fast) is a better deal than the autostrada. When departing for Florence, San Gimignano, or Siena, follow the blue *superstrada* signs (green signs are for the autostrada) for the SS road (along the city wall east from the tower—away from the sea) for Florence (and later Siena). If departing for the Cinque Terre, catch the Genova-bound autostrada. The white stuff you'll see in the mountains as you approach La Spezia isn't snow—it's Carrara marble, Michelangelo's choice for his great art. From Pisa to La Spezia takes about an hour.

VENICE (VENEZIA)

Soak all day in this puddle of elegant decay. Venice is Europe's best-preserved big city. This car-free urban wonderland of a hundred islands—laced together by 400 bridges and 2,000 alleys—survives on the artificial respirator of tourism.

Born in a lagoon 1,500 years ago as a refuge from barbarians, Venice is overloaded with tourists and is slowly sinking (unrelated facts). In the Middle Ages, the Venetians, becoming Europe's clever middlemen for East-West trade, created a great trading empire. By smuggling in the bones of St. Mark (San Marco, A.D. 828), Venice gained religious importance as well. With the discovery of America and new trading routes to the Orient, Venetian power ebbed. But as Venice fell, her appetite for decadence grew. Through the 17th and 18th centuries, Venice partied on the wealth accumulated through earlier centuries as a trading power.

Today, Venice is home to about 65,000 people in its old city, down from a peak population of nearly 200,000. While there are about 500,000 in greater Venice (counting the mainland, not counting tourists), the old town has a small-town feel. Locals seem to know everyone. To see small-town Venice away from the touristic flak, escape the Rialto–San Marco tourist zone and savor the town early and late without the hordes of vacationers day-tripping in from cruise ships and nearby beach resorts. A 10-minute walk from the madness puts you in an idyllic Venice few tourists see.

Planning Your Time

Venice is worth at least a day on even the speediest tour. Hyper-efficient train travelers take the night train in and/or out. Sleep in the old center to experience Venice at its best: early and late. For a one-day visit, cruise the Grand Canal, do the major sights

Venice Overview

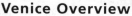

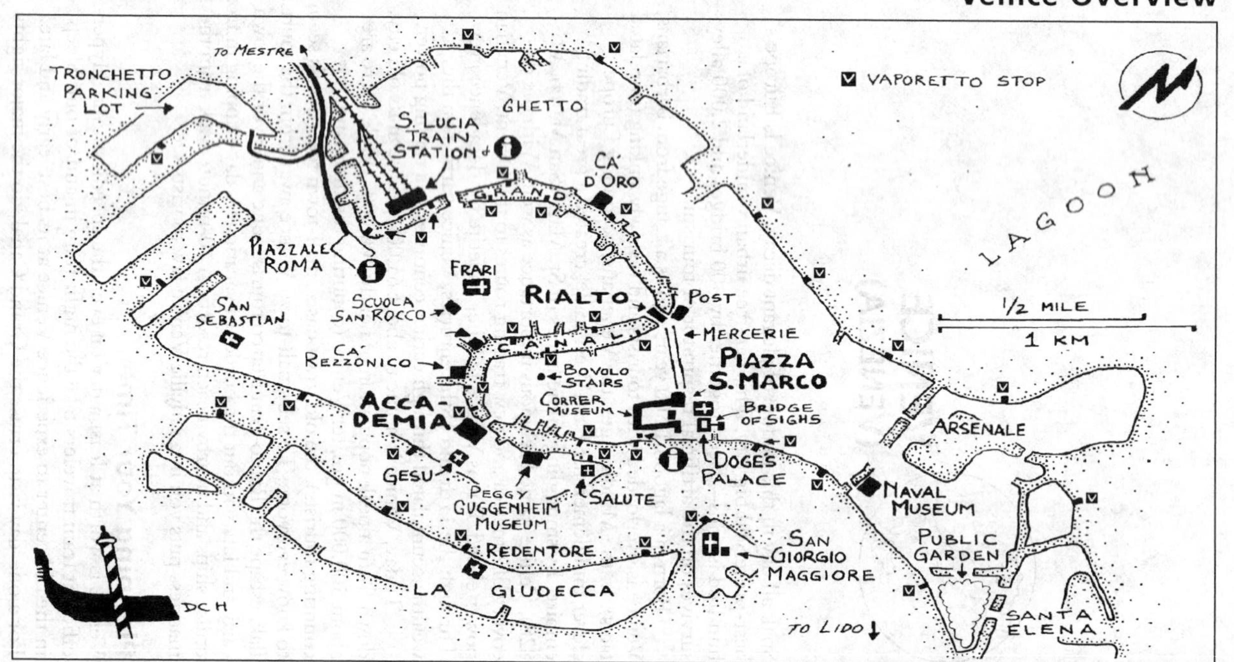

on St. Mark's Square (the square itself, Doge's Palace, and St. Mark's Basilica), see the Church of the Frari (Chiesa dei Frari) for art, and wander the backstreets on a pub crawl (see "Eating in Venice," page 933). Venice's greatest sight is the city itself. Make time to simply wander. While doable in a day, Venice is worth two. It's a medieval cookie jar, and nobody's looking.

Orientation

The island city of Venice is shaped like a fish. Its major thoroughfares are canals. The Grand Canal winds through the middle of the fish, starting at the mouth where all the people and food enter, passing under the Rialto Bridge, and ending at St. Mark's Square (San Marco). Park your 21st-century perspective at the mouth and let Venice swallow you whole.

Venice is a car-free kaleidoscope of people, bridges, and odorless canals. The city has no real streets, and addresses are hopelessly confusing. Each district has about 6,000 address numbers. Luckily, it's easy to find your way, since many street corners have a sign pointing you to the nearest major landmark, such as San Marco, Accademia, Rialto, and Ferrovia (the train station). To find your way, navigate by landmarks, not streets. Obedient visitors stick to the main thoroughfares as directed by these signs and miss the charm of backstreet Venice.

Tourist Information

There are TIs at the train station (daily 8:00–20:00, crowded and surly); at St. Mark's Square (Mon–Sat 9:45–15:15; with your back to St. Mark's, it's in far left corner of square); and near St. Mark's Square vaporetto boat stop on the lagoon (daily 9:00–18:00, sells vaporetto tickets, rents audioguides at €3.65/hr for self-guided walking tours). Smaller offices are at Tronchetto, Piazzale Roma, and the airport. For a quick question, save time by phoning 041-529-8711. Web sites on Venice: www.govenice.org (official TI site), www.veniceforvisitors.com, and www.meetingvenice.it.

At any TI, pick up a free city map and the free *Leo* bimonthly magazine, which comes with an insert, *Leo Bussola*, listing museum hours, exhibitions, and musical events (in Italian and English). Confirm your sightseeing plans. Ask for the fine brochures outlining three offbeat Venice walks. The free periodical entertainment guide *Un Ospite di Venezia* (a monthly listing of events, nightlife, museum hours, train and vaporetto schedules, emergency telephone numbers, and so on) is available at the TI or fancy hotel reception desks (www.aguestinvenice.com).

Maps: The €3.10 Venice map on sale at postcard racks has much more detail than the TI's free map, but the "Illustrated

Venice Map" by Magnetic North is by far the best (€6.20, listing nearly every shop, hotel, and restaurant). Also consider the little guidebook (sold alongside the postcards), which comes with a city map and explanations of the major sights.

Arrival in Venice

A three-kilometer-long (2-mile) causeway (with highway and train lines) connects Venice to the mainland. Mestre, Venice's sprawling mainland industrial base, has fewer crowds, cheaper hotels, and plenty of parking lots, but no charm. Don't stop here, unless you're parking your car in a lot. Trains regularly connect Mestre with Venice's Santa Lucia station (6/hr, 5 min). Don't leave your train at Venezia-Mestre—the next stop is Venezia Santa Lucia (end of the line for Venice).

By Train: Venice's **Santa Lucia train station** plops you right into the old town on the Grand Canal, an easy vaporetto ride or fascinating 40-minute walk to St. Mark's Square. Upon arrival, skip the station's crowded TI because the two TIs at St. Mark's Square are better, and it's not worth a long wait for a minimal map (buy a good one, such as Magnetic North's "Illustrated Venice Map" for €6.20, from a newsstand and skip the wait). Confirm your departure plan (stop by train info desk or just study the *partenze*—departure—posters on walls).

Consider storing unnecessary heavy bags, although lines for **baggage check** might be very long (platform 14, €2.60/12 hrs, €5.20/24 hrs, daily 5:00–24:00; there are no lockers).

Then walk straight out of the station to the canal. The dock for **vaporetto** #82 is on your left (for downtown Venice; most recommended hotels; and Grand Canal Tour—see page 904); the dock for #1, #51 and #52 is on your right (for some recommended hotels). Buy a €3.10 ticket (or €9.30 all-day pass) at the ticket window and hop on a boat for downtown (direction: Rialto or San Marco). Some boats only go as far as Rialto *(solo Rialto)*, so confirm with the conductor.

By Car: The freeway ends at Venice in a parking lot on the edge of the island. Follow the green lights directing you to a parking lot with space, probably Tronchetto (across the causeway and on the right), which has a huge, multistoried garage (€15.50/day, half price with discount coupon from your hotel, tel. 041-520-7555). From there, you'll find travel agencies masquerading as TIs and vaporetto docks for the boat connection (#82) to the town center. Don't let taxi boatmen con you out of the cheap €3.10 vaporetto ride. Parking in Mestre is easy and cheap (open-air lots €4.10/day, €5.20/day garage across from Mestre train station, easy shuttle-train connections to Venice's Santa Lucia Station—6/hr, 5 min).

By Plane: Venice's airport on the mainland, 10 kilometers (6 miles) north of the city, has a TI, cash machines, car-rental agencies, a few shops and eateries, and good connections by bus and speedboat to the city center. Airport info: tel. 041-260-611, flight info: tel. 041-260-9260.

Romantics can jet to St. Mark's Square by Alilaguna **speedboat** (easiest transportation to historical center, €9.80, 1/hr, 70 min, runs 6:15–24:00 from airport; 4:50–22:50 from St. Mark's Square, generally departing airport 10 min after the hour, www.alilaguna.com). A **water taxi** zips you directly to your hotel in 30 minutes for €80. **Buses** connect the airport and the Piazzale Roma vaporetto stop: Catch either the blue ATVO shuttle bus (€2.60, 2/hr, 20 min, 5:30–20:40 to airport, 8:30–24:00 from airport, www.atvo.it) or the cheaper orange ACTV bus #5 (€0.75, 1–3/hr, 20–40 min, 4:40–1:00).

Passes for Venice

To help control (and confuse?) its flood of visitors, Venice now offers cards and passes that cover some museums and/or transportation. For most visitors, the simple Museum Card (for the Doge's Palace and Correr Museum) or Museum Pass will do.

Note that none of these cards or passes cover some of Venice's important attractions—the sights within St. Mark's Basilica, the Campanile, Accademia, Peggy Guggenheim Museum, Scuola Grande di San Rocco, and the Frari Church.

Museum Card and Museum Pass: The main **Museum Card** covers the museums of St. Mark's Square: Doge's Palace, Correr Museum, and two museums accessed from within the Correr—the National Archaeological Museum and the Monumental Rooms of Marciana National Library (€9.50, called "*Museum Card per i Musei di Piazza San Marco*," valid for 3 months; purchase it at the Correr Museum—then use your card at the Doge's Palace to bypass the long line).

The pricier **Museum Pass** includes the St. Mark's Square museums listed above, plus Ca' Rezzonico (Museum of 18th-Century Venice), Mocenigo Palace museum (textiles and costumes), Casa Goldoni (home of the Italian playwright), and museums on the islands—Murano's Glass Museum and Burano's Lace Museum (€15.50, valid for 3 months).

Venice also (pointlessly) offers a couple of other Museum Cards: €8 for the museums of the 18th-century (called "*Museum Card per area del Settecento*"; the museums are Ca' Rezzonico, Casa Goldoni, and Palazzo Mocenigo) and €6 for the island museums (called "*Museum Card per i musei delle isole*," covering Murano's Glass Museum and Burano's Lace Museum).

Daily Reminder

Sunday: The Church of San Giorgio Maggiore (on island near St. Mark's Square) hosts a Gregorian Mass at 11:00. The Rialto market consists mainly of souvenir stalls today (fish and produce sections closed). These sights are open only in the afternoon: Frari Church (13:00–18:00, closed Sun in Aug) and St. Mark's Basilica (14:00–17:00). The Dalmatian School is closed in the afternoon. It's a bad day for a pub crawl, as most pubs are closed.
Monday: All sights are open except for the Rialto fish market, Dalmatian School, and Torcello Museum (on Torcello island). The Accademia and Ca' d'Oro (House of Gold) close early in the afternoon (14:00).
Tuesday: All sights are open except the Peggy Guggenheim Museum, Ca' Rezzonico (Museum of 18th-Century Venice), and the Lace Museum (on Burano island).
Wednesday: All sights are open except the Glass Museum (on Murano island).
Thursday/Friday: All sights are open.
Saturday: All sights are open (Peggy Guggenheim Museum until 22:00 April–Oct) except the Jewish Museum.

Are the Museum Cards and Passes worth it? If you want to see just the Doge's Palace, get the Museum Card (€9.50, includes Correr Museum). If you want to add Ca' Rezzonico (€6.70 entry), you'll save money by getting the Museum Pass. With a Museum Card or Pass (sold at participating museums), you'll breeze past any lines.

Venice Cards: Personally, I'd skip these, but here's the information. These cards cover Venice's public transportation, the few public toilets, and if you get the "orange" version, some sights.

The **Blue Venice Card** covers all your vaporetto and *traghetto* (gondola crossing of Grand Canal, normally €0.40) rides—plus entry to public toilets: 1 day-€11, 3 days-€23, 7 days-€41; cheaper for "Juniors" under 30. (If all you want is a vaporetto pass, you can get a 24-hour pass for €9.30 at any vaporetto dock; described under "Getting around Venice," page 901.)

The **Orange Venice Card**, which also includes transportation and toilets, gets you into the museums covered by the Museum Pass. It's like getting a Blue Venice Card and a Museum Pass for: 1 day-€26, 3 days-€43, and 7 days-€58; cheaper for "Juniors" under 30.

Hefty supplements—which vary depending on which Venice Card and how many days you get—cover transportation to and from Marco Polo Airport and parking at San Giuliano car park with transportation to the city center.

Venice only issues 30,000 cards a day. You must reserve your card at least 48 hours in advance by going online (www.venicecard.it) or calling 011-30-041-271-4747 from the United States or 899-909-090 within Italy. Pay for the card when you pick it up at one of many offices around Venice (see www.venicecard.it for details).

Note that you don't need a Venice Card of any color to enter the city. A Museum Card or Museum Pass makes the most sense for most travelers.

Helpful Hints

Venice is expensive for locals as well as tourists. The demand is huge, supply is limited, and running a business is costly. Things just cost more here; everything must be shipped in and hand-trucked to its destination. Perhaps the best way to enjoy Venice is to just succumb to its charms and blow a lot of money.

Get Lost: Accept the fact that Venice was a tourist town 400 years ago. It was, is, and always will be crowded. While 80 percent of Venice is, in fact, not touristy, 80 percent of the tourists never notice. Hit the backstreets.

Venice is the ideal town to explore on foot. Walk and walk to the far reaches of the town. Don't worry about getting lost. Get as lost as possible. Keep reminding yourself, "I'm on an island, and I can't get off." When it comes time to find your way, just follow the directional arrows on building corners or simply ask a local, "*Dov'è San Marco*?" ("Where is St. Mark's?") People in the tourist business (that's most Venetians) speak some English. If they don't, listen politely, watching where their hands point, say "*Grazie*," and head off in that direction. If you're lost, pop into a hotel and ask for its business card—it comes with a map and a prominent "you are here."

Take Breaks: Grab a cool place to sit down, relax, and recoup from sightseeing—meditate in a pew in an uncrowded church or buy a cappuccino and a fruit cup in a café.

Etiquette: Walk on the right and don't loiter on bridges. Picnicking is technically forbidden (keep a low profile). Dress modestly. Men should keep their shirts on.

Water: Venetians pride themselves on having pure, safe, and tasty tap water piped in from the foothills of the Alps; you can actually see the mountains from Venice bell towers on crisp, clear winter days.

Pigeon Poop: If bombed by a pigeon, resist the initial response to wipe it off immediately—it'll just smear into your hair. Wait until it dries and flake it off cleanly.

Services

Money: ATMs are plentiful and the easiest way to go. Bank rates vary. I like the Banca di Sicilia, a block toward St. Mark's Square from Campo San Bartolomeo. The American Express change desk is just off St. Mark's Square (see "Travel Agencies," below). Non-bank exchange bureaus, such as Exacto, will cost you $10 more than a bank for a $200 exchange. A 24-hour cash machine near the Rialto vaporetto stop exchanges U.S. dollars and other currencies at fair rates (when it's not out of order).

Travel Agencies: If you need to get train tickets, pay supplements, or make reservations, avoid the time-consuming trip to the crowded station by using a downtown travel agency.

Kele & Teo Viaggi e Turismo is good and handy (CC for train tickets only, Mon–Fri 8:30–19:00, Sat 9:00–19:00, Sat afternoon and Sun no train tickets available, at Ponte dei Bareteri on the Mercerie midway between Rialto and St. Mark's Square, tel. 041-520-8722, e-mail: incoming@keleteo.com).

American Express books flights, sells train tickets, and makes train reservations (travel agency: Mon–Fri 9:00–17:30, closed Sat–Sun; change desk: Mon–Sat 7:00–19:30, closed Sun; about 2 blocks off St. Mark's Square at 1471, en route to Accademia, tel. 041-520-0844).

Rip-offs, Theft, and Help: While pickpockets work the crowded main streets, docks, and vaporetti (wear your money belt and carry your day bag in front), the dark, late-night streets of Venice are safe. A service called Venezia No Problem tries to help tourists who've been mistreated by any Venetian business (toll-free tel. 800-355-920, for complaints only, not for information).

"Rolling Venice" Youth Discount Pass: This worthwhile €2.60 pass gives those under 30 discounts on sights and transportation, plus information on cheap eating and sleeping. In summer, they may have a kiosk in front of the train station (July–Sept daily 8:00–20:00). Their main office, near St. Mark's Square, is open year-round (Mon–Fri 9:00–14:00, closed Sat–Sun, from American Express head toward St. Mark's Square, first left, first left again through "Contarina" tunnel, follow white sign to Commune di Venezia and see the sign, Corte Contarina 1529, 3rd floor, tel. 041-274-7651).

Church Services: The **San Zulian Church** (the only church in Venice that you can actually walk around) offers a Mass in English at 9:30 on Sunday (May–Sept, 2 blocks toward Rialto off St. Mark's Square). Gregorians would enjoy the sung Gregorian Mass on Sunday at 11:00 and the rest of the week at 8:00 at **San Giorgio Maggiore Church** (on island of San Giorgio Maggiore, visible from Doge's Palace, catch vaporetto #82 from "San Marco

M.V.E." stop, located 200 meters/650 feet east of St. Mark's Square, at third bridge along waterfront). Call 041-522-7827 to confirm times.

Laundry: There is a self-service launderette (open daily) and two full-service laundries (both closed Sat–Sun).

The modern, cheap **Bea Vita** self-serve *lavanderia* is across the canal from the train station (daily 8:00–22:00, from station go over bridge, take first right, first left, first right).

At either of the following full-service laundries, you can get a nine-pound load washed and dried for €16—confirm price carefully. Drop it off in the morning and pick it up that afternoon. (Call to be sure they're open.) Don't expect to get your clothes back ironed, folded, or even entirely dry. **Lavanderia Gabriella** is near St. Mark's Square (Mon–Fri 8:00–19:00, closed Sat–Sun, 985 Rio Terra Colonne, from San Zulian Church go over Ponte dei Ferali, then take first right down Calle dei Armeni, tel. 041-522-1758). **Lavanderia S.S. Apostoli** is near the Rialto Bridge on the St. Mark's side (Mon–Fri 8:30–12:00 & 15:30–19:00, closed Sat–Sun, just off Campo S.S. Apostoli on Salizada del Pistor, tel. 041-522-6650).

Post Office: A large post office is off the far end of St. Mark's Square (on the side of square opposite St. Mark's Basilica, Mon–Sat 8:10–18:00, closed Sun, shorter hours off-season), and a branch is near the Rialto Bridge (on St. Mark's side, Mon–Fri 8:10–13:30, Sat 8:10–12:30, closed Sun).

Haircuts: I've been getting my hair cut at Coiffeur Benito for 15 years. Benito has been keeping local men and women trim for 25 years. He's an artist—actually a "hair sculptor"—and a cut here is a fun diversion from the tourist grind (€19.50 for women, €16.50 for men, Tue–Sat 8:30–13:30 & 15:30–19:30, closed Sun–Mon, behind San Zulian Church near St. Mark's Square, Calle S. Zulian Gia del Strazzanol 592A, tel. 041-528-6221).

Getting around Venice

By Vaporetto: The public transit system is a fleet of motorized bus-boats called vaporetti. They work like city buses except that they never get a flat, the stops are docks, and if you get off between stops, you may drown. For most, only two lines matter: #1 is the slow boat, taking 45 minutes to make every stop along the entire length of the Grand Canal; #82 is the fast boat that zips down the Grand Canal in 25 minutes, stopping mainly at Tronchetto (car park), Piazzale Roma (bus station), Ferrovia (train station), Rialto Bridge, San Tomá (Frari Church), the Accademia Bridge, and St. Mark's Square. Some #82 boats go only as far as Rialto—confirm with the conductor before boarding. Buy a €3.10 ticket, ideally before boarding (at the booth at the dock) or from a conductor on board (before you sit down or you risk being fined). Families of three or more pay €2.60 per person. A round-trip *(andata e ritorno)* costs €5.20 (good for 2 trips within a day on any line).

A 24-hour pass (€9.30, cheaper for families) pays for itself in three trips. The cheaper "Itinerary Ticket" covers only stops on the Grand Canal and Murano, Burano, and Torcello (€7.75, valid for 12 hours). Also consider the 72-hour (€18.10) and one-week (€31) passes. It's fun to be able to hop on and off spontaneously. Technically, luggage costs the same as dogs—€3.10—but I've never been charged. Riding free? There's a 1-in-10 chance a conductor will fine you €20.

For vaporetto fun, take the Grand Canal Tour (see page 904); avoid rush hour, when boats are packed heading to St. Mark's Square early in the day and packed heading to the train station late in the day. If you like joyriding on vaporetti, ride a boat around the city and out into the lagoon and back. Ask for the circular route—*circulare*, pronounced "cheer-koo-LAH-ray." It's usually the #51 or #52, leaving from the San Zaccaria vaporetto stop (near the Doge's Palace) and from all the stops along the perimeter of Venice.

By *Traghetto*: Only three bridges cross the Grand Canal, but *traghetti* (gondolas) shuttle locals and in-the-know tourists across the Grand Canal at several handy locations (see Downtown Venice map on page 903; routes also marked on pricier maps sold in Venice). Take advantage of these time-savers. They can also save money. For instance, while most tourists take the €3.10 vaporetto to connect St. Mark's with La Salute Church, a €0.40 *traghetto* does the job (free with Venice Blue or Orange Card). Most people stand while riding. *Traghetti* generally run from 6:00 until 20:00, sometimes until 23:00.

By Water Taxi: Venetian taxis, like speedboat limos, hang out at most busy points along the Grand Canal. Prices, which average €30 to €40 (about €75 to the airport), are a bit soft. Negotiate and settle before stepping in. For travelers with lots of luggage or for small groups, taxi rides can be a worthwhile and time-saving convenience—and extremely scenic to boot.

Walking Tours of Venice

Audioguide Tours—The TI at the lagoon (near St. Mark's Square) rents audioguides for self-guided walking tours of Venice (2 hrs-€5, 24 hrs-€10, just punch the number of what you'd like described—exteriors only).

Classic Venice Bars Tour—Debonair local guide Alessandro Schezzini is a connoisseur of Venetian *bacaros*—classic old bars serving traditional *cicchetti* (local munchies). He offers evening

Downtown Venice

1. HOTEL RIVA
2. LOCANDA PIAVE
3. LOCANDA CASA QUERINI
4. HOTEL CAMPIELLO
5. ALBERGO PAGANELLI
6. ALBERGO DONI
7. HOTEL FONTANA
8. ALBERGO CORONA
9. HOTEL ASTORIA
10. LOCANDA GAMBERO
11. HOTEL BEL SITO
12. ALLOGGI ALLA SCALA
13. LOCANDA STURION & HOTEL LOCANDA OVIDIUS
14. ALBERGO GUERRATO
15. HOTEL CANADA
16. HOTEL GIORGIONE
17. LOCANDA LA CORTE
18. FORESTERIA DELLA CHIESA VALDESE
19. TO HOTEL GEREMIA

tours that involve stopping and sampling a snack and a glass of wine at three of these. The fee (about €30 per person) includes wine, *cicchetti*, and a great insight into this local tradition (6–8 per group, tours don't depart without a minimum of 6 people, so call a couple of days ahead to arrange and he'll match up smaller parties to form a group, tel. & fax 041-534-5367, cellular 33-5530-9024, e-mail: venische@tiscalinet.it).

Venicescapes—Michael Broderick's private theme tours of Venice are intellectually demanding and beyond the attention span of most mortal tourists, but for the curious with stamina, he's enthralling. Michael's challenge: to help visitors gain a more solid understanding of Venice. For a description of all six of his itineraries, see www.venicescapes.org (book well in advance, 4–6-hr tour: €275 for 2, €50 per person after that, plus admissions and transportation, tel. 041-520-6361, e-mail: info@venicescapes.org).

American Express Tours—AmEx runs a couple of basic bilingual tours daily (€24, 2 hrs, depart from AmEx office, about 2 blocks off St. Mark's Square in direction of Accademia, 9:00 tour visits St. Mark's Square and the Doge's Palace, 15:00 tour goes to the Frari Church and includes a gondola ride, tel. 041-520-0844).

Local Guides—Alessandro Schezzini gets beyond the clichés and into offbeat Venice (€90, 2.5 hrs, listed above under "Classic Venice Bars Tour"). Elisabetta Morelli is a good, licensed guide who can also provide tours in museums (€130, 2 hrs, tel. 041-526-7816, cellular 328-753-5220, e-mail: bettamorelli@inwind.it).

Grand Canal Tour of Venice

For a ▲▲▲ joyride, introduce yourself to Venice by boat. Cruise the entire Canal Grande from Tronchetto (car park) or Ferrovia (train station) all the way to San Marco. You can ride boat #1 (slow and ideal, 45 min) or #82 (too fast, 25 min, be certain you're on a "San Marco via Rialto" boat because some boats don't go farther than Rialto). The cruise is interesting any time of day, but the least crowded at night, when vaporettos are nearly empty.

If you can't snag a front seat, lurk nearby and take one when it becomes available or find an outside seat in the stern. This ride has the best light and fewest crowds early or late. Twilight is magic. After dark, chandeliers light up the building interiors. While Venice is a barrage on the senses that hardly needs a narration, these notes give the cruise a little meaning and help orient you to this great city. Some city maps (on sale at postcard racks) have a handy Grand Canal map on the back.

Overview: Venice, built in a lagoon, sits on pilings driven nearly five meters (15 feet) into the clay (alder wood worked best). About 40 kilometers (25 miles) of **canals** drain the city, dumping like streams into the Grand Canal. Technically, there are three canals: Grand, Giudecca, and Cannaregio. The other 45 "canals" are referred to as *rio* (rivers), but the only natural river is this main street of Venice, about five meters (15 feet) deep. Because of the river's faster current, sediment never settled here.

Venice is a city of **palaces**. The most lavish were built fronting the Grand Canal. This cruise is the only way to really appreciate the front doors of this unique and historic chorus line of mansions dating from the days when Venice was the world's richest city. Strict laws prohibit any changes in these buildings, so while landowners gnash their teeth, we can enjoy Europe's best-preserved medieval city—slowly rotting. Many of the grand buildings are now vacant. Others harbor chandeliered elegance above mossy, empty ground floors. Ages ago, the city was nicknamed "Venice the Red" for the uniform, red brick, dust-colored stucco of its buildings. Today, you'll see a bit of the original red along with the modern colors.

Start at **Tronchetto** (the bus and parking lot) or the **train station**. I'll orient by the vaporetto stops.

Venice's main thoroughfare is busy with traffic. You'll see all kinds of **boats:** taxis, police boats, garbage boats, ambulances, and even brown-and-white UPS boats. Venice's sleek, black, graceful **gondolas** are a symbol of the city. While used gondolas cost around €10,000, new ones run up to €30,000 apiece. Today, with over 400 gondoliers joyriding around the churning vaporetti, there's a lot of congestion on the Grand Canal. Watch your vaporetto driver curse the (better-paid) gondoliers.

Ferrovia vaporetto stop: The Santa Lucia **train station**, one of the few modern buildings in town, was built in 1954. It's been the gateway into Venice since 1860, when the first station was built. "F.S." stands for "Ferrovie dello Stato," the Italian state railway system. The bridge at the station is the first of only three that cross the Canal Grande.

Riva di Biasio: Just past this vaporetto stop, look left down the broad Cannaregio Canal. The twin pink six-story buildings, known as the "skyscrapers," are a reminder of how densely populated the world's original **ghetto** was. Set aside as the local Jewish quarter in 1516, the area became extremely crowded. This urban island (behind the San Marcuola stop) developed into one of the most closely knit business and cultural quarters of all the Jewish communities in Italy. For more information, visit the Jewish Museum in this neighborhood (see "Sights," below).

San Stae: Opposite the San Stae stop, look for the faded frescoes (left bank, on lower story). Imagine the grand facades of the Grand Canal at its grandest.

Ca' d'Oro: The lacy Ca' d'Oro, or "House of Gold" (left bank, next to vaporetto stop) is considered the most elegant Venetian Gothic palace on the canal. Unfortunately, there's little to see inside (€3, Mon 8:15–14:00, Tue–Sun 8:15–19:15, free peek through hole in door of courtyard). "Ca" refers to "house." Because only the house of the doge (Venetian ruler) could be called a palace, all other palaces are technically "Ca."

Farther along, on the right, the outdoor **fish and produce market** bustles with people in the morning, but is quiet the rest of the day. Find the *traghetto* gondola ferrying shoppers—standing like Washington crossing the Delaware—back and forth.

The huge **post office**, with *servizio postale* boats moored at its blue posts, is on the left just before the Rialto Bridge. Above the post office, the golden angel of the Campanile (bell tower) faces the wind and marks St. Mark's Square, where this tour will end.

Rialto: A major landmark of Venice, the **Rialto Bridge** is lined with shops and tourists. The third bridge on this spot, it was built in 1592. Earlier Rialto Bridges could open to let in big ships. After 1592, much of the Grand Canal was closed to shipping and became a canal of palaces. With a span of 42 meters (140 feet) and foundations stretching 200 meters (660 feet) on either side, the Rialto was an impressive engineering feat in its day. Locals call the summit of this bridge the "icebox of Venice" for its cool breeze. Tourists call it a great place to kiss. *Rialto* means "high river bank." The restaurants with views of the bridge feature high prices and low quality.

Rialto, a separate town in the early days of Venice, has always been the commercial district, while San Marco was the religious and governmental center. Today, a street called the Mercerie connects the two, providing travelers with human traffic jams and a mesmerizing gauntlet of shopping temptations. The restaurants that line the canal feature great views, midrange prices, and low quality.

San Silvestro: We now enter a long stretch of important **merchants' palaces**, each with a proud and different facade. Since ships couldn't navigate beyond the Rialto Bridge (to reach the section of the Grand Canal you just came from), the biggest palaces—with the major shipping needs—lie ahead. Many feature the Roman palace design of twin towers flanking a huge set of central windows. These were showrooms designed to let in maximum sunlight.

Just after the San Silvestro stop, you'll see (on the right) the palace of a 15th-century **"captain general of the sea."** The Venetian equivalents of five-star admirals were honored with twin obelisks decorating their palaces. This palace flies three flags: Italy (green-white-orange), the European Union (blue with ring of stars), and Venice (the lion).

Sant' Angelo: Notice how many buildings have a foundation of waterproof white stone *(pietra d'Istria)*, upon which the bricks sit high and dry. Many canal-level floors are abandoned; the rising water level takes its toll. The posts—historically and gaily painted with the equivalent of family coats of arms—don't rot under water, but the wood at the water line does.

Look at how the rich marble facades are just a veneer covering no-nonsense brick buildings. Look up at the characteristic **funnel-shaped chimneys**. These forced embers through a loop-the-loop channel until they were dead—required in the days when stone palaces were surrounded by humble wooden buildings and a live spark could make a merchant's workforce homeless.

Take a deep whiff of Venice. What's all this nonsense about stinky canals? All I smell is my shirt. By the way, how's your captain? Smooth dockings? To get to know him, stand up in the bow and block his view.

San Tomá: After the San Tomá stop, look down the side canal (on the right, before the bridge) to see the traffic light, the fire station, and the fireboats ready to go.

We now prepare to round the hairpin turn and double back toward St. Mark's. The impressive **Ca' Foscari** (right side) dominates the bend in the canal. Its four stories get increasingly ornate as they rise from the water—from simple Gothic arches at water level, to Gothic with a point, to Venetian-Gothic arches topped with four-leaf clovers, to still more medallions and laciness that look almost Moorish. Wow.

Ca' Rezzonico: The grand, heavy, white Ca' Rezzonico, directly at the stop of the same name, houses the Museum of 18th-Century Venice. Across the canal is the cleaner and leaner Palazzo Grassi, which often showcases special exhibitions.

These days, when buildings are being renovated, huge murals with images of the building mask the ugly scaffolding. Corporations hide the scaffolding out of goodwill (and to get their name on the mural).

Accademia: The wooden Accademia Bridge crosses the Grand Canal and leads to the Accademia Gallery (right side), filled with the best Venetian paintings. The bridge was put up in 1932 as a temporary one. Locals liked it, so it stayed. Cruising under the bridge, you'll get a classic view of the domed La Salute Church ahead.

The low white building among greenery (on the right, between the bridge and the church) is the **Peggy Guggenheim Museum**. The American heiress "retired" here, sprucing up the palace that had been abandoned in mid-construction; the locals call it the *palazzo non finito*. Peggy willed the city her fine collection of modern art.

Just before the Salute stop (on the right), the house with the big windows and the red and wild Andy Warhol painting on the living-room wall (often behind white drapes) was lived in by rock singer Mick Jagger. In the 1970s, this was notorious as Venice's rock-and-roll-star **party house**.

Salute: A crown-shaped dome supported by scrolls stands atop **La Salute Church**. This Church of Saint Mary of Good Health was built to coax God into delivering the Venetians from the devastating plague of 1630 (which eventually killed about a third of the city's population). It's claimed that more than a million trees were piled together to build a foundation reaching below the mud to the solid clay.

Much of the surrounding countryside was deforested by Venice. Trees were exported and consumed locally to fuel the furnaces of Venice's booming glass industry, to build Europe's biggest merchant marine, and to prop up this city in the mud.

Across the canal (left side), several **fancy hotels** have painted facades that hint at the canal's former glory.

As the Grand Canal opens up into the lagoon, the last building on the right with the golden ball is the 16th-century **Customs House** (Dogana da Mar, not open to the public). Its two bronze Atlases hold a statue of Fortune riding the ball. Arriving ships stopped here to pay their tolls.

As you prepare to disembark at San Marco/Vallaresso, look from left to right out over the lagoon. On the left, a wide harbor-front walk leads past the town's most elegant hotels to the green area in the distance. This is the public garden, the largest of Venice's few parks, which hosts the Biennale art show (see page 918). Farther in the distance is the **Lido**, the island with Venice's beach. It's tempting, with sand and casinos, but its car traffic breaks into the medieval charm of Venice.

The dreamy white church that seems to float is the architect Palladio's **San Giorgio Maggiore**. It's just a vaporetto ride away (#82 from San Marco M.V.E. dock). Across the lagoon (to your right) is a residential island called **Giudecca**.

San Marco/Vallaresso: Get off at the San Marco/Vallaresso stop. Directly ahead is **Harry's Bar**. Hemingway drank here when it was a characteristic no-name *osteria* and the gondoliers' hangout. Today, of course, it's the overpriced hangout of well-dressed Americans who don't mind paying triple for their Bellinis (peach juice with *prosecco* wine) to make the scene. St. Mark's Square is just around the corner.

Sights—Venice, on St. Mark's Square

For information on Venice's Museum Card and Museum Pass, see page 897.

▲▲▲St. Mark's Square (Piazza San Marco)—Surrounded by splashy and historic buildings, Piazza San Marco is filled with music, lovers, pigeons, and tourists by day and is your private rendezvous with the Middle Ages late at night. Europe's greatest dance floor is the romantic place to be. St. Mark's Square is about the first place in Venice to flood (you might see stacked wooden benches; when the square floods, these are put end to end to make elevated sidewalks).

With your back to the church, survey one of Europe's great urban spaces, and the only square in Venice to merit the title "Piazza." Nearly two football fields long, it's surrounded by the offices of the republic. On the right are the "old offices" (16th-century Renaissance). On the left are the "new offices" (17th-century Baroque). Napoleon, after enclosing the square with the more simple and austere neoclassical wing across the far end, called this "the most beautiful drawing room in Europe."

The clock tower, a Renaissance tower built in 1496, marks the entry to the Mercerie, the main shopping drag, which connects St. Mark's Square with the Rialto. From the piazza, you can see the bronze men (Moors) swing their huge clappers at the top of each hour. In the 17th century, one of them knocked an unsuspecting worker off the top and to his death—probably the first-ever killing by a robot. Notice the world's first "digital" clock on the tower facing the square (with dramatic flips every 5 minutes).

For a slow and pricey evening thrill, invest €6.20 (plus €4 if the orchestra plays) in a beer or coffee at one of the elegant cafés with the dueling orchestras (see Caffè Florian, described below in "Nightlife in Venice.") If you're going to sit awhile and savor the scene, it's worth the splurge. If all you have is €1, buy a bag of pigeon seed and become popular in a flurry. To get everything airborne, toss your sweater in the air.

Venice's best TIs (and WCs) are nearby. One TI is on the square, the other on the lagoon. To find the TI on the square, stand with your back to the church and go to the far corner on your left; the office is tucked away in the arcade (daily 9:00–17:00; near this TI is a €0.50 WC open daily 8:00–21:00—it's a few steps beyond St. Mark's Square en route to the AmEx office and the Accademia; see *Albergo Diorno* sign marked on pavement). The other TI is on the lagoon (daily 9:00–18:00, walk toward the water by the Doge's Palace, go right; nearby WCs open daily 9:00–19:00).

▲▲St. Mark's Basilica—Since about A.D. 830, this basilica has housed the saint's bones. The mosaic above the door at the far

Floods and a Dying City

Venice floods about 60 times a year—normally in March and November—when the wind blowing up from Egypt and high barometric pressure on the lower Adriatic Sea are most likely to combine to push water up to this top end of the sea. (There is no real lunar tide in the Mediterranean.)

Floods start in St. Mark's Square. The entry of the church is nearly the lowest spot in town. (You might see stacked wooden benches; when the square floods, these are put end to end to make elevated sidewalks). The measuring devices at the base of the outside of the Campanile bell tower (near the exit, facing St. Mark's Square) show the current sea level *(livello marea)*. When the water level rises one meter (3 feet), a warning siren sounds. It repeats if a serious flood is imminent. Find the mark showing the high-water level from the terrible floods of 1966 (waist-level, on right).

In 1965, Venice's population was over 150,000. Since the flood of 1966, the population has been shrinking. Today the population is about 65,000 . . . and geriatric. Sad, yes, but imagine raising a family here: The fragile nature of the city means piles of regulations (no biking, and so on), and costs are high—even though the government is now subsidizing rents to keep people from moving out. You can easily get glass and tourist trinkets, but it's hard to find groceries. And floods and the humidity make house maintenance an expensive pain.

left of the church shows two guys carrying Mark's coffin into the church. Mark looks pretty grumpy after the long voyage from Egypt.

The church, built in Eastern style to underline Venice's connection with Byzantium (thus protecting it from the ambition of Charlemagne and his Holy Roman Empire), is decorated by booty from returning sea captains—a kind of architectural Venetian trophy chest.

To enter the church, modest dress is required even of kids (no shorts or bare shoulders). In peak season, there can be long lines of people waiting to get into the church. People who ignore the dress code hold up the line while they plead fruitlessly with—or put on extra clothes under the watchful eyes of—the dress code police.

The church has 4,000 square meters (43,000 square feet) of Byzantine mosaics, the best and oldest of which are in the atrium (turn right as you enter and stop under the last dome—this may be roped off, but dome is still visible). Facing the church, gape up (it's OK, no pigeons), and read clockwise the story of Adam and Eve that rings the bottom of the dome. Now, facing the piazza, look domeward for the story of Noah, the ark, and the flood (two by two, the wicked being drowned, Noah sending out the dove, a happy rainbow, and a sacrifice of thanks).

Step inside the church (stairs on right lead to bronze horses) and notice the marble floor richly decorated in mosaics. As in many Venetian buildings, because the best foundation pilings were made around the perimeter, the interior floor rolls. As you shuffle under the central dome, look up for the Ascension (free, Mon–Sat 9:30–17:00, Sun 14:00–17:00, no photos, tel. 041-522-5205). See the schedule board in the atrium, listing free English guided tours (schedules vary but April–Oct there can be up to 4/day). The church is particularly beautiful when lit (unpredictable schedule, maybe middays 11:00–12:00, Sat–Sun 14:00–17:00, plus 18:45 Mass on Sat). During peak times, the line can be very long. Free reservations may be available at www.alata.it—if the Web site is working (print out your time and present it when you enter, to the left of the general entry).

In the **Galleria and Museum** upstairs, you can see an up-close mosaic exhibition, a fine view of the church interior, a view of the square from the balcony with bronze horses, and (inside, in their own room) the newly restored original horses. These well-traveled horses, made during the days of Alexander the Great (4th century B.C.), were taken to Rome by Nero, to Constantinople/Istanbul by Constantine, to Venice by crusaders, to Paris by Napoleon, back "home" to Venice when Napoleon fell, and finally indoors and out of the acidic air (€1.60, daily 9:45–17:00, winter until 16:00, enter from atrium either before or after you tour church).

San Marco's **treasury** (with informative audioguide free for the asking) and **altarpiece** (€2.10 each, daily 9:45–17:10, 16:10 in winter) give you the best chance outside of Istanbul or Ravenna to see the glories of Byzantium. Venetian crusaders looted the Christian city of Constantinople and brought home piles of lavish loot (until the advent of TV evangelism, perhaps the lowest point in Christian history). Much of this plunder is stored in the treasury *(tesoro)* of San Marco. As you view these treasures, remember most were made in A.D. 500, while western Europe was still rutting in the mud. Beneath the high altar lies the body of St. Mark ("Marxus") and the Pala d'Oro, a golden altarpiece made with 80 Byzantine enamels (A.D. 1000–1300). Each shows a religious scene set in gold and precious stones. Both of these sights are interesting and historic, but neither is as much fun as two bags of pigeon seed.

Tips on Sightseeing in Venice

Crowd Control: Crowds can be a serious problem at the Accademia (to minimize crowds, go early or late); St. Mark's Basilica (consider reserving online at www.alata.it); Campanile bell tower (go late—it's open until 21:00 in the summer); and the Doge's Palace. For the Doge's Palace, you have three options for avoiding the ticket-sales line: Buy your Museum Card or Museum Pass at the Correr Museum (then step right up to the Doge's Palace turnstile, skipping the long line); visit the Doge's Palace at 17:00 (if it's April–Oct), when lines disappear; or book a "Secret Itineraries" tour (see page 913).

Hours: The Accademia is open earlier (daily at 8:15) and closes later (19:15 Tue–Sun) than most sights in Venice. Some sights close earlier off-season (e.g., Doge's Palace; Correr Museum; the Campanile; and St. Mark's Museum, Treasury, and Golden Altarpiece).

Churches: Modest dress is recommended at churches and required at St. Mark's Basilica—no bare shoulders, shorts, or short skirts. Some churches are closed to sightseers on Sunday morning (e.g., St. Mark's Basilica and Frari Church) and many are closed from roughly 12:00 to 15:00 Monday through Saturday (e.g., La Salute and San Giorgio Maggiore).

▲▲▲Doge's Palace (Palazzo Ducale)—The seat of the Venetian government and home of its ruling duke, or doge, this was the most powerful half-acre in Europe for 400 years.

The Doge's Palace was built to show off the power and wealth of the republic and remind all visitors that Venice was number one. In typical Venetian Gothic style, the bottom has pointy arches, and the top has an Eastern or Islamic flavor. Its columns sat on pedestals, but in the thousand years since they were erected, the palace has settled into the mud, and the bases have vanished.

Enjoy the newly restored facades from the courtyard. Notice a grand staircase (with nearly naked Moses and Paul Newman at the top). Even the most powerful visitors climbed this to meet the doge. This was the beginning of an architectural power trip. The doge, the elected-for-life duke or leader of this "dictatorship of the aristocracy," lived with his family on the first floor near the halls of power. From his living quarters (once lavish, now sparse), you'll follow the one-way route through the public rooms of the top floor, finishing with the Bridge of Sighs and the prison.

The place is wallpapered with masterpieces by Veronese and Tintoretto. Don't worry much about the great art. Enjoy the building.

In room 12, the Senate Room, the 200 senators met, debated, and passed laws. From the center of the ceiling, Tintoretto's *Triumph of Venice* shows the city in all her glory. Lady Venice, in heaven with the Greek gods, stands high above the lesser nations, who swirl respectfully at her feet with gifts.

The Armory—a dazzling display originally assembled to intimidate potential adversaries—shows remnants of the military might the empire employed to keep the East-West trade lines open (and the local economy booming). Squint out the window at the far end for a fine view of Palladio's San Giorgio Maggiore Church and the *lido* (cars, casinos, crowded beaches) in the distance.

The giant Hall of the Grand Council (55 meters/180 feet long, capacity 2,000) is where the entire nobility met to elect the senate and doge. Ringing the room are portraits of 76 doges (in chronological order). One, a doge who opposed the will of the Grand Council, is blacked out. Behind the doge's throne, you can't miss Tintoretto's monsterpiece, *Paradise*. At 160 square meters (1,700 square feet), this is the world's largest oil painting. Christ and Mary are surrounded by a heavenly host of 500 saints. Its message to electors who met here: Make wise decisions and you'll ultimately join that holy crowd.

Walking over the Bridge of Sighs, you'll enter the prisons. In the privacy of his own home, a doge could sentence, torture, and jail his opponents secretly. As you walk back over the bridge, squeeze your arm through the marble lattice window and wave to the gang of tourists gawking at you.

Cost: €9.50 for Museum Card that also covers the Correr Museum, or get a €15.50 Museum Pass covering several more museums; see page 897 for details. If the line is very long at the Doge's Palace, buy your Museum Card or Pass at the Correr Museum across the square. With that, you can go directly through the Doge's turnstile (you might have to push your way through the throngs).

Hours: April–Oct daily 9:00–19:00, Nov–March daily 9:00–17:00, last entry 90 min before closing.

Tours: Audioguides cost €5.50. For a live tour, consider the "Secret Itineraries Tour," which follows the doge's footsteps through rooms not included in the general admission price. Call 041-522-4951 at least two or three days in advance to confirm times and reserve a spot; they take only 25 people per tour (€12.50, at 10:00 and 11:30 in English, 1.25 hrs). The cost includes admission only to the Doge's Palace (and allows you to bypass the long line).

While the tour skips the main halls inside, it finishes inside the palace and you're welcome to visit the halls on your own.

▲▲Correr Museum (Museo Civico Correr)—The city history museum is now included (whether you like it or not) with the admission to the Doge's Palace. In the Napoleon Wing, you'll see fine neoclassical works by Canova. Then peruse armor, banners, and paintings re-creating festive days of the Venetian republic. The top floor lays out a good overview of Venetian art, including several paintings by the Bellini family. And just before the cafeteria is a room filled with traditional games. There are English descriptions and great Piazza San Marco views throughout (€9.50 Museum Card includes Doge's Palace, or €15.50 Museum Card includes more museums, see page 897 for details, April–Oct daily 9:00–19:00, Nov–March 9:00–17:00, last entry 90 min before closing, enter at far end of square directly opposite church, tel. 041-522-5625).

▲Campanile di San Marco—The lofty bell tower was once half as tall—a lighthouse marking the entry of the Grand Canal and part of the original fortress/palace which guarded its entry. Ride the elevator 92 meters (300 feet) to the top of the bell tower for the best view in Venice. This tower crumbled into a pile of bricks in 1902, a thousand years after it was built. For an ear-shattering experience, be on top when the bells ring (€6, June–Sept daily 9:00–21:00, Oct–May until 19:00). The golden angel at its top always faces into the wind. Beat the crowds and enjoy crisp air at 9:00.

More Sights—Venice

▲▲Accademia (Galleria dell' Accademia)—Venice's top art museum, packed with highlights of the Venetian Renaissance, features paintings by Bellini, Veronese, Tiepolo, Giorgione, Testosterone, and Canaletto. It's just over the wooden Accademia Bridge. Expect long lines in the late morning because they allow only 300 visitors in at a time; visit early or late to miss crowds (€6.20, Mon 8:15–14:00, Tue–Sun 8:15–19:15, shorter hours off-season, last entry 45 min before closing, no photos allowed, vaporetto stop: Accademia, tel. 041-522-2247). The dull audioguides (€3.60, €5.20 with 2 earphones, or €6 for a palm-pilot) don't let you fast-forward to works you want to hear about; you have to listen to the whole spiel for each room.

There's a decent pizzeria at the bridge (Pizzeria Accademia Foscarini; see "Eating in Venice," page 933), a public WC under it, and usually a classic shell game being played on top of it (study the system as partners in the crowd win big money). Nearby sights include the Peggy Guggenheim Museum and La Salute Church.

▲Peggy Guggenheim Museum—This popular collection of

far-out art offers one of Europe's best reviews of the art styles of the 20th century. Stroll through Cubism (Picasso, Braque), surrealism (Dalí, Ernst), futurism (Boccione, Carra), American abstract expressionism (Pollock), and a sprinkling of Klee, Calder, and Chagall (€6.50, April–Oct Wed–Mon 10:00–18:00, Sat until 22:00, closed Tue, audioguide-€4, guidebook-€18, free 15 minute tours given daily in English at 12:00 and 16:00, free baggage check, pricey café, photos allowed only in garden and terrace—a fine and relaxing perch overlooking Grand Canal, 5-minute walk from Accademia, tel. 041-240-5411). The place is run (cheaply) by American interns working on art history degrees.

▲▲Frari Church (Chiesa dei Frari)—My favorite art experience in Venice is seeing art *in situ*—the setting for which it was designed—and my favorite example is the Chiesa dei Frari. The Franciscan "church of the friars" and the art that decorates it are warmed by the spirit of St. Francis. It features the work of three great Renaissance masters: Donatello, Bellini, and Titian, each showing worshipers the glory of God in human terms.

In Donatello's wood carving of St. John the Baptist (just to the right of the high altar), the prophet of the desert—dressed in animal skins and almost anorexic from his diet of bugs 'n' honey—announces the coming of the Messiah. Donatello was a Florentine working at the dawn of the Renaissance.

Bellini's *Madonna and the Saints* painting (in the chapel farther to the right) came later, done by a Venetian in a more Venetian style—soft focus without Donatello's harsh realism. While Renaissance humanism demanded Madonnas and saints that were accessible and human, Bellini places them in a physical setting so beautiful it creates its own mood of serene holiness. The genius of Bellini, perhaps the greatest Venetian painter, is obvious in the pristine clarity, rich colors (notice Mary's clothing), believable depth, and reassuring calm of this three-paneled altarpiece. It's so good to see a painting in its natural setting.

Finally, glowing red and gold like a stained-glass window over the high altar, Titian's *Assumption* sets the tone of exuberant beauty found in the otherwise sparse church. Titian the Venetian—a student of Bellini—painted steadily for 60 years . . . you'll see a lot of his art. As stunned apostles look up past the swirl of arms and legs, the complex composition of this painting draws you right to the radiant face of the once dying, now triumphant Mary as she joins God in heaven.

Be comfortable discreetly freeloading off of passing tours. For many, these three pieces of art make a visit to the Accademia Gallery unnecessary (or they may whet your appetite for more). Before leaving, check out the neoclassical, pyramid-shaped tomb of

Canova and (opposite that) the grandiose tomb of Titian. Compare the carved marble Assumption behind Titian's tombstone portrait with the painted original above the high altar (€2.10, Mon–Sat 9:00–18:00, Sun 13:00–18:00, closed Sun in Aug, last entry 15 min before closing, no visits during services, audioguides €1.60/person, €2.60/double set, modest dress recommended, tel. 041-523-4864).

▲Scuola di San Rocco—Next to the Frari Church, another lavish building bursts with art, including some 50 Tintorettos. The best paintings are upstairs, especially the *Crucifixion* in the smaller room. View the neck-breaking splendor with one of the mirrors *(specchio)* available at the entrance (€5.20, includes free and informative audioguide, daily 9:00–17:00, or see a concert here and enjoy the art as an evening bonus—see "Nightlife in Venice," below). For *molto* Tiepolo (14 stations of the cross), drop by the nearby Church of San Polo.

▲Ca' Rezzonico, the Museum of 18th-Century Venice—This grand Grand Canal palazzo offers the best look in town at the life of Venice's rich and famous in the 1700s. Wandering among furnishings from that most decadent century, you'll see the art of Guardi, Canaletto, Longhi, and Tiepolo (€6.70, April–Oct Wed–Mon 10:00–18:00, Nov–March 10:00–17:00, closed Tue, last entry 60 min before closing, audioguide-€5.50, vaporetto: Ca' Rezzonico, tel. 041-520-4036).

Dalmatian School (Scuola Dalmata dei San Giorgio)—This school (which means "meeting place") is a reminder that Venice was Europe's most cosmopolitan place in its heyday. It was here that the Dalmatian community (people from the present-day region of Croatia) worshiped in their own way, held neighborhood meetings, and worked to preserve their culture. The chapel on the ground floor has the most exquisite Renaissance interior in Venice, with a cycle painted by Carpaccio ringing the room (€3, Tue–Sat 9:30–12:30 & 15:30–18:30, Sun 9:30–12:30, closed Mon, between St. Mark's Square and Arsenale, on Calle dei Furlani, 3 blocks southeast of Campo San Lorenzo, tel. 041-522-8828).

Jewish Ghetto—The word "ghetto," which comes from *getti* (the jets of the brass foundry once located here), was inherited by Venice's Jewish community when it was confined to the site of Venice's former copper foundries in 1516. Notice how this ghetto island, dominated by the Campo di Ghetto Nuovo square and connected with the rest of Venice by only three bridges, would be easy to isolate. While little survives from that time or the Jewish community, in its day the square was densely populated—lined with proto-skyscrapers seven to nine stories high. This original ghetto becomes most interesting after touring the Jewish Museum (€3, June–Sept Sun–Fri 10:00–19:30, Oct–May Sun–Fri 10:00–17:30, closed Sat, English guided tours for €8 leave hourly 10:30–16:30, later in summer, Campo di Ghetto Nuovo, tel. 041-715-359).

Santa Elena—For a pleasant peek into a completely untouristy, residential side of Venice, catch the boat from St. Mark's Square to the neighborhood of Santa Elena (at the fish's tail). This 100-year-old suburb lives as if there were no tourism. You'll find a kid-friendly park, a few lazy restaurants, and beautiful sunsets over San Marco.

Gondola Rides

A rip-off for some, this is a traditional must for romantics. Gondoliers charge about €62 for a 50-minute ride during the day; from 20:00 on, figure on €77 to €105 (for *musica*—singer and accordionist, it's an additional €88 during day, €98 after 20:00). You can divide the cost—and the romance—among up to six people. Glide through nighttime Venice with your head on someone else's shoulder. Follow the moon as it sails past otherwise unseen buildings. Silhouettes gaze down from bridges while window glitter spills onto the black water. You're anonymous in the city of masks as the rhythmic thrust of your striped-shirted gondolier turns old crows into songbirds. This is extremely relaxing (and I think worth the extra cost to experience at night). Since you might get a narration plus conversation with your gondolier, talk with several and choose one you like who speaks English well. Women, beware . . . while gondoliers can be extremely charming, local women say anyone who falls for one of these guys "has hams over her eyes."

For a glimpse at the most picturesque gondola workshop in Venice, visit the Accademia neighborhood. Walk down the Accademia side of the canal called Rio San Trovaso. As you approach Giudecca Canal, you'll see the beached gondolas on your right across the canal.

For cheap gondola thrills, stick to the €1.60 one-minute ferry ride on a Grand Canal *traghetto* or hang out on a bridge along the gondola route and wave at (or drop leftover pigeon seed on) romantics.

Festivals

Venice's most famous festival is **Carnevale** (Feb 21–March 4 in 2003). Carnevale, which means "farewell to meat," originated centuries ago as a wild two-month-long party leading up to the austerity of Lent. In Carnevale's heyday—the 1600s and 1700s—you could do pretty much anything with anybody from any social class if you were wearing a mask. These days, it's a tamer 10-day celebration, culminating in a huge dance lit with fireworks on St. Mark's Square. Sporting masks and costumes, Venetians from kids to businessmen join in the fun. Drawing the biggest crowds of the year, Carnevale has nearly been a victim of its success, driving away many locals (who skip out on the craziness to go ski in the Dolomites).

In 2003, the city hosts the **Venice Biennale International Art Exhibition**, a world-class contemporary art exhibition spread over the sprawling Castello Gardens and the Arsenale. Artists representing 65 nations from around the world offer the latest in contemporary art forms: video, computer art, performance art, and digital photography, along with painting and sculpture (€13, open daily generally March–Nov 10:00–18:00, Sat until 22:00; vaporetto stop: Giardini/Biennale; for details, see www.labiennale.org). This festival is held every other year.

Venetian festival days that fill the city's hotels with visitors and its canals with decked-out boats are **Feast of the Ascension Day** (mid-May), **Feast and Regatta of the Redeemer** (parade and fireworks, July 19 and 20, 2003), and the **Historical Regatta** (old-time boats and pageantry, Sept 1–7, 2003). Each November 21 is the **Feast of Our Lady of Good Health.** On this local day of "Thanksgiving," a bridge is built over the Grand Canal so the city can pile into the Salute Church and remember how it survived the gruesome plague of 1630. On this day, Venetians eat smoked lamb from Dalmatia (which was the cargo of the first ship let in when the plague lifted).

Venice is always busy with special musical and artistic events. The free monthly ***Un Ospite di Venezia*** lists all the latest—in English (free at TI or from fancy hotels).

Shopping

Shoppers like Carnevale masks, lace (a specialty of Burano, see below, but sold in Venice as well), empty books with handmade covers, and paintings—especially of Venice. If you're buying a substantial amount from nearly any shop, bargain. It's accepted and almost expected. Offer less and offer to pay cash; merchants are very conscious of the bite taken by credit-card companies.

Popular **Venetian glass** is available in many forms: vases, tea sets, decanters, glasses, jewelry, lamps, sculptures (such as solid-glass aquariums), and on and on. Shops will ship it home for you; snap a photo of it before it's packed up. For simple, easily packable souvenirs, consider glass-bead necklaces (sold cheap at vendors' stalls, expensive at shops).

If you're serious about glass, visit the small shops on Murano Island. Murano's glass-blowing demonstrations are fun; you'll usually see a vase and a "leetle 'orse" made from molten glass.

In Venice, glass-blowing demos are given by various companies around St. Mark's Square for tour groups. **Galleria San Marco,** a tour group staple, offers great demos just off Piazza San Marco every few minutes. They have agreed to let individual travelers flashing this book sneak in with tour groups to see the show (and sales pitch). And, if you buy anything, show this book and they'll take 20 percent off the price listed. (The gallery faces the square behind the orchestra nearest the church at #153, go through it, cross the alley, get in good with the guard, and climb the stairs with the next group, daily 9:30–12:00 & 14:00–17:00, manager Adriano Veronese, tel. 041-271-8650.)

Salizada San Samuele is a nontouristy street with several artsy shops. Livio de Marchi's wood sculpture shop is delightful even when it's closed. Check out the window displays for his latest creations: socks, folded shirts, teddy bears, "paper" sacks, all carved from wood (Mon–Fri 9:30–12:30 & 13:30–18:30, nearest major landmark is Accademia Bridge—on St. Mark's side, Salizada San Samuele 3157, vaporetto stop: San Samuele; if approaching by foot, follow signs to Palazzo Grassi, tel. 041-528-5694, www.liviodemarchi.com).

Venice Lagoon

The island of Venice sits in a lagoon—a calm section of the Adriatic protected from wind and waves by the neutral breakwater of the *lido.* Four interesting islands hide out in the lagoon.

San Giorgio Maggiore is the dreamy island you can see from the waterfront by St. Mark's Square. The impressive church, designed by Palladio, features art by Tintoretto and a bell tower with oh-wow views of Venice (free entry to church, daily 9:30–12:30 & 15:30–18:30, closed Sun to sightseers during Mass; Gregorian Mass sung on Sun at 11:00 and Mon–Sat at 8:00; €3 for bell tower lift, closes 30 min before church's closing time). To reach the island from St. Mark's Square, take the five-minute vaporetto ride on #82, departing from the "San Marco (M.V.E.)" stop, 200 meters (650 feet) east of St. Mark's Square, at the third bridge along the waterfront (Note: This is not the same vaporetto stop as "San Marco.")

The islands of **Murano, Burano,** and **Torcello** are reached easily, cheaply, and slowly by vaporetto. Pick up a free map of the islands from any TI. Depart from San Zaccaria dock nearest the Bridge of Sighs/Doge's Palace. Line #12 connects all three islands, or take #41 to Murano (get off at Murano Colonna), then #12 to the other islands. If you plan to visit even two of these islands, get a 24-hour €9.30 vaporetto pass or a 12-hour €7.75 "Itinerary Ticket" for convenience. Four-hour speedboat tours of these three lagoon destinations leave twice a day from the dock near the

Venice Lagoon

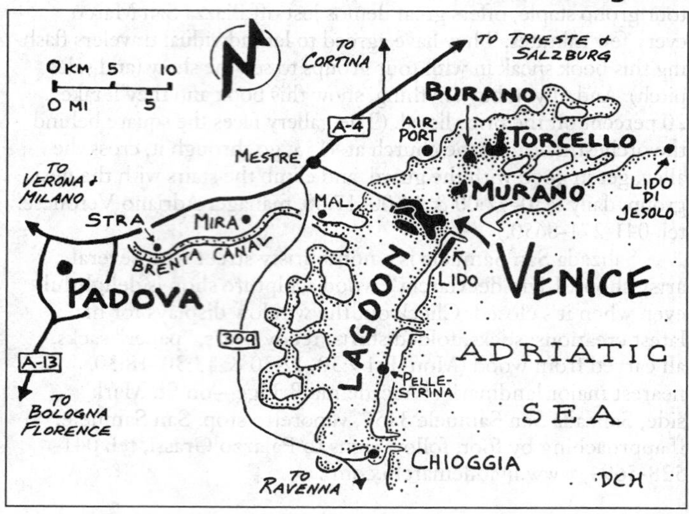

Doge's Palace—look for the signs and booth (€16, usually at 9:30 and 14:30; off-season 1/day at 14:30, tel. 041-523-8835 or 041-522-2159); the tours are speedy indeed, stopping for roughly 35 minutes at each island.

Murano, famous for its glass factories, has the Glass Museum, which displays the very best of 700 years of Venetian glassmaking and exhibits of ancient and modern glass art (Museo Vetrario, €4, covered by €15.50 Museum Pass, Thu–Tue 10:00–17:00, last entry 30 min before closing, closed Wed, tel. 041-739-586). You'll be tempted by salesmen offering free speedboat shuttles from Piazza San Marco to Murano. If you're interested in glass, it's handy. You must watch the show, but then you're free to buy or escape and see the rest of the island. Numerous glass factories *(fabbrica* or *fornace)* offer demonstrations all over the island—check one out, and then wander up Via Fondamenta Vetrai toward the Glass Museum. Get off the beaten path by taking the backstreets behind the Duomo on Calle di Conterie for a look at village Venezia. Head to the Faro vaporetto stop and take the #12 to either Burano or Torcello or the #41 back to San Zaccaria.

Burano, famous for its lace, is a sleepy island with a sleepy community—village Venice without the glitz. Lace fans enjoy the Lace Museum (Scuola di Merletti, €4.10, covered by €15.50 Museum Pass, Wed–Mon 10:00–17:00, closed Tue, tel. 041-730-034). The park next to Burano's only vaporetto dock is perfect for a waterfront picnic. While the main drag leading from the vaporetto stop into town is lined with shops and packed with tourists, simply wander to the far side of the island and the mood shifts. Explore to the right of the leaning tower for a peaceful yet intensely pastel, small-town lagoon world. Benches lining a little promenade at the water's edge make another tranquil picnic spot. As you head back to the dock, notice the marble tables on Campo Pescaria where the fish market used to be held. Hungry? Try the huge *bruschetta* at Bruschetteria al Vecio Pipa (daily 11:30–16:30, Fondamente San Mauro 397, tel. 041-730-045).

Torcello is dead except for its church, which claims to be the oldest in Venice (€5.20 for church, tower, and museum, daily 10:30–17:30 but museum closed Mon, tel. 041-730-761). It's impressive for its mosaics, but not worth a look on a short visit unless you really love mosaics and can't make it to Ravenna.

Nightlife in Venice

Venice is quiet at night, as tour groups are back in the cheaper hotels of Mestre on the mainland, and the masses of day-trippers return to their beach resorts. **Gondolas** can cost nearly double, but are doubly romantic and relaxing under the moon. Vaporettos are uncrowded, and it's a great time to cruise the Grand Canal on slow boat #1.

Take your pick of traditional Vivaldi **concerts** in churches throughout town. Vivaldi is as trendy here as Strauss in Vienna and Mozart in Salzburg. In fact, you'll find frilly young Vivaldis all over town hawking concert tickets. The TI has a list of this week's Baroque concerts (tickets from €18, shows start at 21:00 and generally last 90 min). If you see a concert at Scuola di San Rocco, you can enjoy the art (which you're likely to pay €5.20 for during the day) for free during the intermission. The general rule of thumb: musicians in wigs and tights offer better spectacle, musicians in black-and-white suits are better performers. Consider the venue carefully.

On St. Mark's Square, the dueling **café orchestras** entertain. Every night, enthusiastic musicians play the same songs, creating the same irresistible magic. Hang out for free behind the tables (which allows you to easily move on to the next orchestra when the musicians take a break) or spring for a seat and enjoy a fun and gorgeously set concert. If you sit awhile, it can be €10 well spent (€6 drink plus a one-time €4 fee for entertainment).

Caffè Florian, on St. Mark's Square, is the most famous Venetian café and one of the first places in Europe to serve coffee. It's been the place for a discreet rendezvous in Venice since 1720. Today, it's most famous for its outdoor seating and orchestra, but do walk through its 18th-century, richly decorated rooms, where Casanova, Lord Byron, Charles Dickens, and Woody Allen have all paid too much for a drink (reasonable prices at bar in back, tel. 041-520-5641).

You're not a tourist, you're a living part of a soft Venetian night . . . an alley cat with money. Streetlamp halos, live music, floodlit history, and a ceiling of stars make St. Mark's magic at midnight. In the misty light, the moon has a golden hue. Shine with the old lanterns on the gondola piers where the sloppy Grand Canal splashes at the Doge's Palace . . . reminiscing. Comfort the small statues of the four frightened tetrarchs (ancient Byzantine emperors) where the Doge's Palace hits the basilica. Cuddle history.

Sleeping in Venice
(€1 = about $1, country code: 39)

Sleep Code: **S** = Single, **D** = Double/Twin, **T** = Triple, **Q** = Quad, **b** = bathroom, **s** = shower only, **CC** = Credit Cards accepted, **no CC** = Credit Cards not accepted, **SE** = Speaks English, **NSE** = No English. Breakfast is included unless otherwise noted. Air-conditioning, when available, is usually only turned on in summer.

To help you sort easily through these listings, I've divided the rooms into three categories based on the price for a standard double room with bath:

Higher Priced—Most rooms more than €180.
Moderately Priced—Most rooms €180 or less.
Lower Priced—Most rooms €130 or less.

Reserve a room as soon as you know when you'll be in town. Book direct—not through any tourist agency. Most places take a credit card number for a deposit. If everything's full, don't despair. Call a day or two in advance and fill in a cancellation. If you arrive on an overnight train, your room may not be ready. Drop your bag at the hotel and dive right into Venice.

I've listed prices for peak season: April, May, June, September, and October. Prices can get soft in July, August, and winter. Hotels sometimes give discounts if you stay at least three nights and/or pay cash. If on a budget, ask for a cheaper room or a discount. Always ask.

Virtually all of these hotels are central. See the map on page 903 for hotel locations. I've listed rooms mainly in two neighborhoods: in the Rialto–San Marco action and in a quiet Dorsoduro area behind the Accademia Gallery. If a hotel has a Web site, check it. Hotel Web sites are particularly valuable for Venice, because they often come with a map that at least gives you the illusion you can easily find the place.

Sleeping between St. Mark's Square and Campo Santa Maria di Formosa (zip code: 30122 unless otherwise noted)

MODERATELY PRICED

Locanda Piave, with 27 fine rooms above a bright and classy lobby, is fresh, modern, and comfortable (Db-€139–155, Tb-€190, Qb-€210, family suites-€250 for 4, €280 for 5–6, prices good through 2003 with this book, CC but discount with cash, air-con; vaporetto #51 or #1 to San Zaccaria, to the left of Hotel Danieli is Calle de le Rasse—take it, turn left at end, turn right nearly immediately at square—S.S. Filippo e Giacomo—on Calle Rimpeto La Sacrestie, go over bridge, take second left, hotel is 2 short blocks ahead on Ruga Giuffa 4838/40, Castello, tel. 041-528-5174, fax 041-523-8512, www.elmoro.com/alpiave, e-mail: hotel.alpiave @iol.it, Mirella, Paolo, and Ilaria SE, faithful Molly NSE). They have a couple of apartments for €200 to €232 (for 3–4 people, includes breakfast and kitchenette, cheaper in Aug).

Locanda Casa Querini, run by Patty, is an air-conditioned, plush, 11-room place on a quiet square tucked away behind St. Mark's (Db-€130, this special price good only with this book and payment in cash; CC, 3-min walk from St. Mark's Square, exactly halfway between San Zaccaria vaporetto stop and Campo Santa Maria Formosa at Campo San Giovanni Novo 4388, Castello, 30100 Venezia, tel. 041-241-1294, fax 041-241-4231, e-mail: casaquerini@hotmail.com, Silvia SE).

LOWER PRICED

Hotel Riva, with gleaming marble hallways and bright modern rooms, is romantically situated on a canal along the gondola serenade route. You could actually dunk your breakfast rolls in the canal (but don't). Sandro may hold a corner *(angolo)* room if you ask, and there are also a few rooms overlooking the canal. Confirm prices and reconfirm reservations, as readers have had trouble with both (Sb-€78, 2 D with adjacent showers-€95, Db-€110, Tb-€157, Qb-€190, Ponte dell' Angelo, also spelled Anzolo, Castello 5310, 30122 Venezia, tel. 041-522-7034, fax 041-528-5551). To reach the hotel from St. Mark's Square, face St. Mark's Basilica, walk behind it on the left along Calle de la Canonica, take the first left (at blue "Pauly & C" mosaic in street), continue straight, go over the bridge, and angle right to the hotel.

Corte Campana has three comfy, quiet rooms just behind St. Mark's Square (Db-€70–130, Tb-€105–150, Qb-€140–200, buffet breakfast-€11; facing St. Mark's Basilica, take Calle Canonica—to the far left of the church—turn left on Calle dell'

Anzolo and another right on Calle del Remedio, follow signs to Hotel Remedio and enter little courtyard to your right, go up three flights of steps and ring bell at Calle del Remedio 4410, Castello, tel. 041-523-3603, cellular 389-272-6500, e-mail: cortecampana70@hotmail.com, enthusiastic Riccardo SE).

Sleeping on or near the Waterfront, East of St. Mark's Square (zip code: 30122)

These places, about one canal down from the Bridge of Sighs, on or just off the Riva degli Schiavoni waterfront promenade, rub drainpipes with Venice's most palatial five-star hotels. The first two, while a bit pricey because of their location, are professional and comfortable. Ride the vaporetto to San Zaccaria (#51 from train station, #82 from Tronchetto car park).

MODERATELY PRICED

Hotel Campiello, a lacy and bright little 16-room, air-conditioned place, was once part of a 19th-century convent. It's ideally located 50 meters (165 feet) off the waterfront (Sb-€119, Db-€119–180, CC, 8 percent discount with cash, 30 percent discount mid-Nov–Feb excluding Christmas and Carnevale; behind Hotel Savoia, up Calle del Vin off the waterfront street—Riva degli Schiavoni 4647, San Zaccaria, tel. 041-520-5764, fax 041-520-5798, www.hcampiello.it, e-mail: campiello@hcampiello.it, family-run for 4 generations, sisters Monica and Nicoletta).

Albergo Paganelli is right on the waterfront—on Riva degli Schiavoni—and has a few incredible view rooms (S-€90, Sb-€125, Db-€150–181, Db with view-€200, request *con vista* for view, CC, air-con, prices often soft, at San Zaccaria vaporetto stop, Riva degli Schiavoni 4182, Castello, tel. 041-522-4324, fax 041-523-9267, www.hotelpaganelli.com, e-mail: hotelpag@tin.it). With spacious rooms, carved and gilded headboards, chandeliers, and hair dryers, this elegant place is a good value. Seven of their 22 rooms are in a less interesting but equally comfortable *dipendenza* (annex), a block off the canal.

Hotel Fontana is a cozy, two-star, family-run place with 14 rooms and lots of stairs on a touristy square two bridges behind St. Mark's Square (Sb-€55–110, Db-€85–170, family rooms, fans, 10 percent discount with cash, quieter rooms on canal side, piazza views can be noisier, 2 rooms have terraces, see Web site for off-season deals, CC; vaporetto #51 to San Zaccaria, find Calle de le Rasse—to left of Hotel Danieli—take it, turn right at end, continue to first square, Campo San Provolo 4701, Castello, tel. 041-522-0579, fax 041-523-1040, www.hotelfontana.it, e-mail: htlcasa@gpnet.it).

LOWER PRICED

Albergo Doni is a dark, hardwood, clean, and quiet place with 12 dim-but-classy rooms run by a likable smart aleck named Gina (D-€80, Db-€107, T-€108, Tb-€142, ceiling fans, secure telephone reservations with CC but must pay in cash, Riva degli Schiavoni, Calle del Vin 4656, San Zaccaria N., tel. & fax 041-522-4267, e-mail: albergodoni@libero.it, Nicolo and Gina SE). Leave Riva degli Schiavoni on Calle del Vin and go 100 meters (330 feet) with a left jog.

Albergo Corona is a homey, confusing, Old World place with eight basic rooms, lots of stairs, and no breakfast (D-€63, vaporetto #1 to San Zaccaria dock, take Calle de le Rasse—to left of Hotel Danieli, turn left at end, take right at square—Campo S.S. Filippo e Giacomo—on Calle Rimpeto La Sacrestie, take first right, then next left on Calle Corona to #4464, tel. 041-522-9174).

Sleeping North of St. Mark's Square (zip code: 30124)

MODERATELY PRICED

Locanda Gambero, with 32 rooms, is a comfortable and very central three-star hotel run by Sandro (Sb-€77–140, Db-€115–180, Tb-€155–249, Internet in lobby, air-con, CC, 5 percent discount for payment in cash; from Rialto vaporetto #1 dock, go straight inland on Calle le Bembo, which becomes Calle dei Fabbri; or from St. Mark's Square go through Sotoportego dei Dai then down Calle dei Fabbri to #4687, at intersection with Calle del Gambero, tel. 041-522-4384, fax 041-520-0431, e-mail: hotelgambero@tin.it, Christian and Luciana run the day shift, cheery Giorgio the night shift, all SE). Gambero runs the pleasant, Art Deco–style La Bistrot on the corner, which serves old-time Venetian cuisine.

LOWER PRICED

Hotel Astoria has 24 simple rooms tucked away a few blocks off St. Mark's Square (D-€103, Db-€124, some suites available, €10 discount July–Aug if you pay cash, closed mid-Nov–mid-March, CC, 2 blocks from San Zulian Church at Calle Fiubera #951; from Rialto vaporetto #1 dock, go straight inland on Calle le Bembo, which becomes Calle dei Fabbri, turn left on Calle Fiubera, tel. 041-522-5381, fax 041-528-8981, www.hotelastoriavenezia.it, e-mail: info@hotelastoriavenezia.it, Alberto and Enrico SE).

Sleeping West of St. Mark's Square (zip code: 30124)

HIGHER PRICED

Hotel Bel Sito, friendly for a three-star hotel, has Old World character and a picturesque location—facing a church on a small square between St. Mark's Square and the Accademia. With solid wood furniture, its rooms feel elegant (Sb-€130, Db-€195, CC, air-con, elevator, some rooms with views; vaporetto #1 to Santa Maria del Giglio stop, take narrow alley to square, hotel at far end to your right, Santa Maria del Giglio 2517, San Marco, tel. 041-522-3365, fax 041-520-4083, e-mail: belsito@iol.it).

Sleeping Northwest of St. Mark's Square (zip code: 30124)

LOWER PRICED

Alloggi alla Scala, a seven-room place run by Signora Andreina della Fiorentina, is homey, central, and tucked away on a quiet square that features a famous spiral stairway called Scala Contarini del Bovolo (small Db-€77, big Db-€87, extra bed-€26, breakfast-€7.75, CC, 5 percent discount for payment in cash, tell her when you reserve if you'll be paying by credit card, sometimes overbooks and sends overflow to her sister's lesser accommodations, Campo Manin 4306, San Marco, tel. 041-521-0629, fax 041-522-6451, daughter Emma SE). To find the hotel from Campo Manin, follow signs to (on statue's left) "Scala Contarini del Bovolo" (€2.10, daily 10:00–17:30, views from top).

Sleeping near the Rialto Bridge (zip code: 30125 unless otherwise noted)

The first three hotels are on the west side of the Rialto Bridge (away from St. Mark's Square) and the last three are on the east side of the bridge (on St. Mark's side). Vaporetto #82 quickly connects the Rialto with both the train station and the Tronchetto car park.

On West Side of Rialto Bridge

HIGHER PRICED

Hotel Locanda Ovidius, with an elegant Grand Canal view terrace, a breakfast room with a wood-beam ceiling, and nine bright, comfortable rooms, is on the Grand Canal (Sb-€77–155, Db-€130–210, Db with view-€185–260, check Web site for special offers, CC, air-con, Calle del Sturion 677a, tel. 041-523-7970, fax 041-520-4101, www.hotelovidius.com, e-mail: info@hotelovidius.com).

Locanda Sturion, with air-conditioning and all the modern comforts, is pricey because it overlooks the Grand Canal (Db-€132–202, Tb-€195–265, family deals, canal-view rooms cost about €16 extra, CC, 69 steps to lobby, 100 meters, 330 feet, from Rialto Bridge, opposite vaporetto dock, Calle Sturion 679, San Polo, Rialto, tel. 041-523-6243, fax 041-522-8378, www.locandasturion.com, e-mail: info@locandasturion.com, SE). They require a personal check or traveler's check for a deposit.

LOWER PRICED

Albergo Guerrato, overlooking a handy and colorful produce market one minute from the Rialto action, is run by friendly, creative, and hardworking Roberto and Piero. Giorgio takes the night shift. Their 800-year-old building is Old World simple, airy, and wonderfully characteristic (D-€82, Db-€106, big top floor Db-€127, T-€103, Tb-€133, Qb-€153, prices promised through 2003 with this book in hand, cash only; €2 maps sold in their lobby; walk over the Rialto away from St. Mark's Square, go straight about 3 blocks, turn right on Calle drio la Scimia—not Scimia, the block before—and you'll see the hotel sign, Calle drio la Scimia 240a, 30125 San Polo, tel. 041-522-7131 or 041-528-5927, fax 041-241-1408, e-mail: hguerrat@tin.it, SE). My tour groups book this place for 50 nights each year. Sorry. If you fax without calling first, no reply within three days means they are booked up. (It's best to call first.) They rent family apartments in the old center (great for groups of 4–8) for around €55 per person.

On East Side of Rialto Bridge

HIGHER PRICED

Hotel Giorgione, a professional, four-star hotel in a 15th-century palace, has plush public spaces, pool tables, Internet access, a garden terrace, and 72 spacious rooms with all the comforts (Sb-€90–150, Db-€130–255, pricier superior rooms and suites available, extra bed-€60, 10 percent discount with Web reservations, CC, elevator, air-con, Campo S.S. Apostoli 4587, 30131 Venezia, tel. 041-522-5810, fax 041-523-9092, www.hotelgiorgione.com).

MODERATELY PRICED

Hotel Canada has 25 small, sleepable rooms (S-€87, Sb-€119, D-€129, Db-€153, Tb-€189, Qb-€236, CC, air-con-€7.75 extra per night; rooms on canal come with view and aroma; rooms facing church are noisier but fresh; Castello San Lio 5659, 30122 Venezia, tel. 041-522-9912, fax 041-523-5852, SE). This hotel is ideally located on a small, lively square, just off Campo San Lio between the Rialto and St. Mark's Square.

LOWER PRICED

Locanda Novo Venezia, a charming eight-room place in a 15th-century palazzo, run by industrious Claudio and Ivan, is just off a super square—Campo dei S.S. Apostoli, just north of the Rialto Bridge (Db-€130 with this book, family deals for up to 6 in a room, CC, air-con, Calle dei Preti 4529, Cannaregio, 30121 Venezia, tel. 041-241-1496, fax 041-241-5989, www.locandanovo.com, e-mail: info@locandanovo.com).

Sleeping near S.S. Giovanni e Paoli (zip code: 30122)

MODERATELY PRICED

Locanda la Corte, a three-star hotel, has 18 attractive, high-ceilinged, wood-beamed rooms—done in pastels—bordering a small, quiet courtyard (Sb-€104, standard Db-€175, superior Db-€185, suites available, CC, air-con; vaporetto #52 from train station to Fondamente Nove, exit boat to your left, follow waterfront, turn right after second bridge to get to S.S. Giovanni e Paolo square; facing Rosa Salva bar, take street to left—Calle Bressana, hotel is a short block away at bridge; Castello 6317, tel. 041-241-1300, fax 041-241-5982, www.locandalacorte.it).

Sleeping near the Accademia Bridge (zip code: 30123 unless otherwise noted)

When you step over the Accademia Bridge, the commotion of touristy Venice is replaced by a sleepy village. This quiet area, next to the best painting gallery in town, is a 10-minute walk from St. Mark's Square and a 15-minute walk from the Rialto. The fast vaporetto #82 connects Accademia Bridge with the train station (in about 15 min) and St. Mark's Square (5 min). The hotels are located near the south end of the Accademia Bridge (see map on page 930), except for the last listing (Fondazione Levi), at the north end of the bridge (St. Mark's side).

On South Side of Accademia Bridge

HIGHER PRICED

Hotel American is a small, cushy, three-star hotel on a lazy canal next to the delightful Campo San Vio (a tiny overlooked square facing the Grand Canal). At this Old World hotel with 30 rooms, you'll get better rates Sunday through Thursday (Sb-€105–171, Db-€155–

233, Db with view-€155–269, extra bed-€26–52, CC, air-con, free Internet access in lobby, 30 meters/100 feet off Campo San Vio and 200 meters/650 feet from Accademia Gallery; facing Accademia, go left, forced right, take 2nd left—following yellow sign to Guggenheim Museum, cross bridge, take immediate right to #628 Accademia, tel. 041-520-4733, fax 041-520-4048, check www.hotelamerican.com for deals, e-mail: reception@hotelamerican.com, Marco SE).

Hotel Belle Arti is a good bet if you want to be in the old center without the tourist hordes. With a grand entry and all the American hotel comforts, it's a big, 67-room, modern, three-star place sitting on a former schoolyard (Sb-€114–150, Db-€145–210, Tb-€186–255, the cheaper rates apply to July–Aug and winter, CC, plush public areas, air-con, elevator, 100 meters/330 feet behind Accademia Gallery; facing gallery, take left, then forced right, Via Dorsoduro 912, tel. 041-522-6230, fax 041-528-0043, www.hotelbellearti.com, e-mail: info@hotelbellearti.com, SE).

MODERATELY PRICED

Pensione Accademia fills the 17th-century Villa Maravege. While its 27 comfortable and air-conditioned rooms are nothing extraordinary, you'll feel aristocratic gliding through its grand public spaces and lounging in its breezy garden (Sb-€83–123, standard Db-€129–181, superior Db-€155–227, one big family-of-5 room with grand canal view, family deals, CC; facing Accademia Gallery, take first right, cross first bridge, go right, Dorsoduro 1058, tel. 041-523-7846, fax 041-523-9152, www.pensioneaccademia.it, e-mail: info@pensioneaccademia.it).

Hotel Galleria has 10 compact and velvety rooms, most with views of the Grand Canal. Some rooms are quite narrow; ask for a larger room (S-€66–90, D-€90–97, Db-€110–140, 2 big canal-view Db-€135, includes breakfast in room, CC, fans, near Accademia Gallery, and next to recommended Foscarini restaurant, 4 extra rooms available near Peggy Guggenheim Museum with varying prices—ask, Dorsoduro 878a, tel. 041-523-2489, tel. & fax 041-520-4172, www.hotelgalleria.it, e-mail: galleria@tin.it, SE).

Hotel Agli Alboretti is a cozy, family-run, 24-room place in a quiet neighborhood a block behind the Accademia Gallery. With red carpeting and wood-beamed ceilings, it feels elegant (Sb-€96, 2 small Db-€123, Db-€150, Tb-€180, Qb-€210, CC, air-con; 100 meters, or 330 feet, from the Accademia vaporetto stop on Rio Terra a Foscarini at Accademia 884; facing Accademia Gallery, go left, then forced right, tel. 041-523-0058, fax 041-521-0158, www.aglialboretti.com, e-mail: alborett@gpnet.it, SE).

Pensione La Calcina, the home of English writer John Ruskin in 1876, comes with all the three-star comforts in a

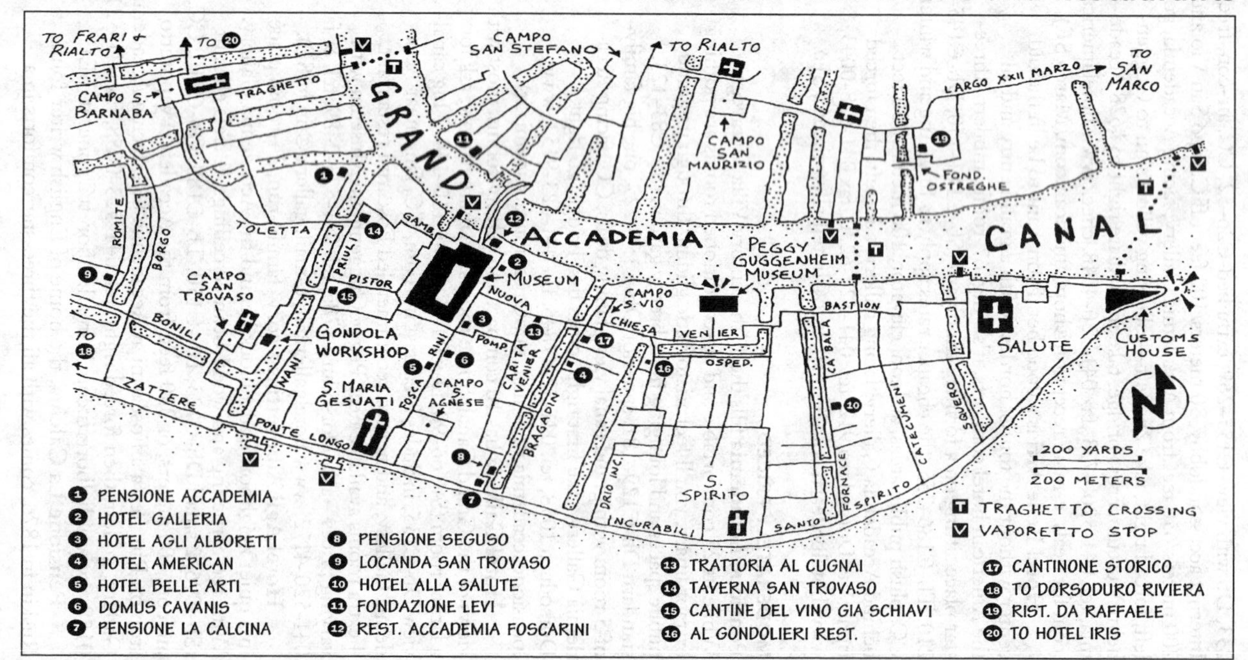
Accademia Area Hotels and Restaurants
TO FRARI & RIALTO
TO 20
CAMPO S. BARNABA
TRAGHETTO
GRAND
CANAL
CAMPO SAN STEFANO
TO RIALTO
CAMPO SAN MAURIZIO
LARGO XXII MARZO
TO SAN MARCO
FOND. OSTREGHE
TOLETTA
GAMB.
ACCADEMIA
MUSEUM
PEGGY GUGGENHEIM MUSEUM
ROMITE
BORGO
PRIULI
PISTOR
NUOVA
CAMPO SAN TROVASO
BONILI
TO 18
GONDOLA WORKSHOP
POMP.
RINI
CAMPO S. VIO
CHIESA
VENIER
OSPED.
BASTION
CA' BALA
SALUTE
CUSTOMS HOUSE
NANI
S. MARIA GESUATI
FOSCA
CAMPO S. AGNESE
CARITA
VENIER
BRAGADIN
ZATTERE
PONTE LONGO
DRIO INC.
INCURABILI
S. SPIRITO
SANTO
SPIRITO
FORNACE
CATECUMENI
SQUERO
200 YARDS
200 METERS
T TRAGHETTO CROSSING
V VAPORETTO STOP
1 PENSIONE ACCADEMIA
2 HOTEL GALLERIA
3 HOTEL AGLI ALBORETTI
4 HOTEL AMERICAN
5 HOTEL BELLE ARTI
6 DOMUS CAVANIS
7 PENSIONE LA CALCINA
8 PENSIONE SEGUSO
9 LOCANDA SAN TROVASO
10 HOTEL ALLA SALUTE
11 FONDAZIONE LEVI
12 REST. ACCADEMIA FOSCARINI
13 TRATTORIA AL CUGNAI
14 TAVERNA SAN TROVASO
15 CANTINE DEL VINO GIA SCHIAVI
16 AL GONDOLIERI REST.
17 CANTINONE STORICO
18 TO DORSODURO RIVIERA
19 RIST. DA RAFFAELE
20 TO HOTEL IRIS

professional yet intimate package. Its 29 rooms are squeaky clean, with good wood furniture, hardwood floors, and a peaceful canal-side setting facing Giudecca (S-€65–77, Sb-€97, Sb with view-€110, Db-€130–145, Db with view-€160–185, prices vary with room size and season, CC, air-con, rooftop terrace, killer sundeck on canal and canalside buffet-breakfast terrace, Dorsoduro 780, at south end of Rio di San Vio, tel. 041-520-6466, fax 041-522-7045, e-mail: la.calcina@libero.it). They also rent apartments nearby (max 2 people, €140–250, air-con and amenities). From the Tronchetto car park or station, catch vaporetto #51 or #82 to Zattere (at vaporetto stop, exit right and walk along canal to hotel).

Pensione Seguso, next door to Pensione La Calcina, is almost an Addams-Family-on-vacation time warp. Signora Seguso runs her place as her parents did, with the beds, freestanding closets, lamps, and drapes all feeling like your great-grandmother's. The upside is the commanding canalside setting. The downside is that dinner is required during high season (Db with dinner-€210 maximum price for 2 people, slow season Db-€140 without dinner, CC, elevator, Zattere 779, tel. 041-522-2340, fax 041-528-6096, e-mail: what's that?).

Hotel Alla Salute, a basic retreat buried deep in Dorsoduro, is ideal for those wanting a quiet Venice with three-star comforts (Db-€135, facing the canal Rio delle Fornace near La Salute church, tel. 041-523-5404, fax 041-522-2271, e-mail: hotel.salute.dacici@iol.it).

Locanda San Barnaba rents 13 pleasant rooms about 50 meters (165 feet) from the Ca' Rezzonico vaporetto stop (Sb-€70–110, Db-€120–160, superior Db-€130–170, junior suite-€160–210, includes breakfast, CC, air-con, private garden, Calle del Traghetto 2785-2786, tel. 041-241-1233, fax 041-241-3812, www.locanda-sanbarnaba.com, e-mail: info@locanda-sanbarnaba.com).

LOWER PRICED

Domus Cavanis, across the street from—and owned by—Hotel Belle Arti, is a big, practical, plain place with a garden, renting 30 quiet and simple rooms (Db-€103, extra bed-€50, includes breakfast at Hotel Belle Arti, elevator, TV, phones, reception closes at 23:00, Dorsoduro 895, tel. 041-522-7374, fax 041-522-8505, e-mail: info@hotelbellearti.com).

Locanda San Trovaso is sparkling new, with seven classy, spacious rooms—three with canal views—and a peaceful location on a small canal (Sb-€77–95, Db-€115–130, CC, small roof terrace, Dorsoduro 1351; take vaporetto #82 from Tronchetto or #51 from Piazzale Roma or train station, get off at Zattere, exit left, cross bridge, turn right at tiny Calle Trevisan, cross bridge, cross adjacent bridge, take immediate right, then first left, tel. 041-277-1146, fax 041-277-7190, www.locandasantrovaso.com, e-mail: s.trovaso@tin.it, Mark and his son Alessandro SE).

On North Side of Accademia Bridge

MODERATELY PRICED

Recently opened **Locanda Art Déco**, on a street filled with antique and art shops near St. Mark's Square and the Accademia, rents lovingly furnished rooms (Db-€67–165, Tb-€103–215 depending on room and season, CC, air-con, Calle delle Botteghe 2966, near Campo San Stefano, 30124 Venezia, tel. 041-277-0558, fax 041-270-2891, www.locandaartdeco.com, e-mail: info @locandaartdeco.com).

LOWER PRICED

Fondazione Levi, a guest house run by a foundation that promotes research on Venetian music, offers 21 quiet, institutional yet comfortable rooms (Sb-€57, Db-€93, Tb-€108, Qb-€127, twin beds only, elevator; 80 meters/260 feet from base of Accademia Bridge on St. Mark's side; from Accademia vaporetto stop, cross Accademia Bridge, take immediate left—cross bridge Ponte Giustinian and then go down Calle Giustinian directly to the Fondazione, buzz the "Foresteria" door to the right, San Vidal 2893, 30124 Venezia, tel. 041-786-711, fax 041-786-766, e-mail: foresterialevi@libero.it, SE).

Sleeping between Frari Church and the Grand Canal (zip code: 30125)

MODERATELY PRICED

Hotel Iris is a cozy respite, with 19 rooms off the beaten path (S-€70, Sb-€93, D-€99, Db-€135, includes breakfast, air-con, CC; from Campo dei Frari, head south to Campo San Tomá, then take right on Calle del Campanile to Rio della Frescada, hotel is on other side of Ristorante Giardinetto before first bridge to the right, San Polo 2910/A, tel. & fax 041-522-2882, www.irishotel.com).

Sleeping near the Train Station (zip code: 30121)

MODERATELY PRICED

Hotel San Geremia, a three-minute walk from the station, offers 20 rooms at decent prices near the Ferrovia vaporetto stop. Head left outside the station and follow Lista di Spagna to Campo San Geremia. With the bridge in front of you, the hotel is to your left at Campo San Geremia 290/A (Db-€110–145, the higher price is for weekends, CC, self-service laundry and Internet café nearby, tel. 041-716-245, fax 041-524-2342, e-mail: sangeremia@yahoo.it).

Cheap Dormitory Accommodations

Foresteria della Chiesa Valdese, warmly run by the Methodist church, offers dorms and doubles, halfway between St. Mark's Square and the Rialto Bridge. This run-down but charming old place has elegant ceiling paintings (dorm bed-€18, D-€52, Db-€67, family apartment-€103 for 5, must check in and out when office is open: 9:00–13:00 & 18:00–20:00, from Campo Santa Maria di Formosa, walk past Bar all' Orologio to end of Calle Lunga and cross bridge, Castello 5170, 30122 Venezia, tel. & fax 041-528-6797, fax 041-241-6328, e-mail: veneziaforesteria@chiesavaldese.org).

Venice's **youth hostel** on Giudecca Island is crowded and inexpensive (€16 beds with sheets and breakfast in 10- to 16-bed rooms, membership required, office open daily 7:00–9:30 & 13:30–23:00, catch vaporetto #82 from station to Zittele, tel. 041-523-8211). The budget cafeteria welcomes non-hostelers (nightly 17:00–23:30).

Eating in Venice

While touristy restaurants are the scourge of Venice, and most restaurateurs believe you can't survive in Venice without catering to tourists, there are plenty of places that are still popular with locals and respect the tourists who happen in. First trick: Walk away from triple-language menus. Second trick: Order the daily special. Third trick: Most seafood dishes are the local catch-of-the-day.

For romantic—and usually pricey—meals along the water, see "Eating with a Romantic Canalside Setting," below. For dessert, it's gelato (see end of this chapter).

Eating between Campo Santi Apostoli and Campo S.S. Giovanni e Paolo

For locations, see map on page 936.

Antiche Cantine Ardenghi de Lucia e Michael is a leap of local faith and an excellent splurge. Effervescent Michael and his wife, Lucia, proudly cook Venetian for a handful of people each night by reservation only. You must call first. You pay €50 per person and trust them to wine, dine, and serenade you with Venetian class. The evening can be quiet or raucous depending on who and how many are eating. While the menu is heavy on crustaceans, Michael promises to serve plenty of veggies and fruit as well. Find #6369. There's no sign, the door's locked, and the place looks closed. But knock, say the password *(La Repubblica Serenissima)*, and you'll be admitted. From Campo S.S. Giovanni e Paolo, pass the church-like hospital (notice the illusions painted on its facade), go over the bridge to the left, and take the first right on Calle della Testa to #6369 (you must reserve the day before, Tue–Sat 20:00–24:00, closed Sun–Mon, tel. 041-523-7691, cellular 389-523-7691).

The following two colorful *osterias* are good for *cicchetti* (munchies), wine-tasting, or a simple, rustic, sit-down meal surrounded by boisterous local ambience:

Osteria da Alberto has the best variety of *cicchetti* (18:15–19:30) and great sit-down meals from 19:30 to 23:00 (CC, closed Sun, midway between Campo Santi Apostoli and Campo S.S. Giovanni e Paolo, next to Ponte de la Panada on Calle Larga Giacinto Gallina, tel. 041-523-8153).

Osteria al Promessi Sposi does *cicchetti* with gusto and offers a little garden for sit-down meals (great cod and polenta). This fun place is proud to be Venetian (Thu–Tue 9:00–23:00, closed Wed, a block off Campo S.S. Apostoli and a block inland from Strada Nova at Calle dell' Oca, tel. 041-522-8609).

You'll find pubs opposite Campo St. Sofia across Strada Nova.

Eating in Dorsoduro, near the Accademia

For restaurant locations, see map on page 930.

Restaurant/Pizzeria Accademia Foscarini, next to the Accademia Bridge and Galleria, offers decent €5–7 pizzas in a great canalside setting (Wed–Mon 7:00–23:00 in summer, until 21:00 in winter, closed Tue, Dorsoduro 878C, tel. 041-522-7281).

Trattoria al Cugnai is an unpretentious place run by three gruff sisters serving decent food (Tue–Sun 12:00–15:00 & 19:00–21:30, closed Mon, midway between Accademia Gallery and Campo San Vio, tel. 041-528-9238). Enjoy a quiet sit on Campo San Vio (benches with Grand Canal view) for dessert.

Taverna San Trovaso is an understandably popular restaurant/pizzeria. Arrive early or wait (CC, Tue–Sun 12:00–14:50 & 19:00–21:50, closed Mon, air-con, 100 meters/330 feet from Accademia Gallery on San Trovaso canal; facing Accademia, take a right and then a forced left at canal). On the same canal, **Enoteca Cantine del Vino Gia Schiavi**—much-loved for its *cicchetti*—is a good place for a glass of wine and appetizers (Mon–Sat 8:00–14:30 & 15:30–20:00, closed Sun, S. Trovaso 992, tel. 041-523-0034). You're welcome to enjoy your wine and finger-food while sitting on the bridge.

Al Gondolieri is considered one of the best restaurants for meat—not fish—in Venice. Its sauces are heavy and prices are high, but carnivores love it (Wed–Mon 12:00–13:00 & 19:00–22:00, closed Tue and for lunch Jul–Aug, reservations smart, Dorsoduro 366 San Vio, behind Guggenheim Museum on west end of Rio delle Torreselle, tel. 041-528-6396).

Cantinone Storico, also in this neighborhood, is described below under "Eating with a Romantic Canalside Setting."

Eating near St. Mark's Square

Osteria da Carla, two blocks west of St. Mark's Square, is a fun and very local hole-in-the-wall where the food is good and the price is right. They have hearty tuna salads and a daily pasta special along with traditional antipasti, polenta, and decent wine by the glass. While you can eat outside, you don't want table #3 (Mon–Sat 8:00–22:00, closed Sun; from American Express head toward St. Mark's Square, first left down Frezzeria, first left again through "Contarina" tunnel, at Sotoportego e Corte Contarina, sign over door says "Pietro Panizzolo"—it's historic and can't be removed, tel. 041-523-7855, Carlo SE).

Eating on Campo S. Angelo

Ristorante Aqua Pazza (literally, "crazy water") provides good pizza in a wonderful setting on a square (check out the leaning tower over your shoulder) midway between the Rialto, Accademia, and St. Mark's. The owner is from Naples and he delights locals with Amalfi/Naples cuisine. That means perhaps the best—and most expensive—pizza in Venice (Tue–Sun 12:00–15:00 & 19:00–23:00, closed Mon, Campo S. Angelo 3809, tel. 041-277-0688).

Eating in Cannaregio

For great local cuisine, far beyond the crowds in a rustic setting, hike to **Osteria Al Bacco** (closed Mon, reservations recommended, Fondamenta Cappuccine, Cannaregio 3054, halfway between train station and northernmost tip of Venice, tel. 041-717-493).

Near the train station, consider **Brek**, a popular self-service cafeteria (at Lista di Spagna 124; with back to station, facing canal, go left on Rio Terra—it becomes Lista di Spagna in 2 short blocks, tel. 041-244-0158).

Eating with a Romantic Canalside Setting

Of course, if you want a canal view, it comes with lower quality or a higher price. But the memory is sometimes most important.

Restaurant al Vagon is popular with tourists because nearly everyone gets a seat right on the canal. The food and prices are

Venice Restaurants

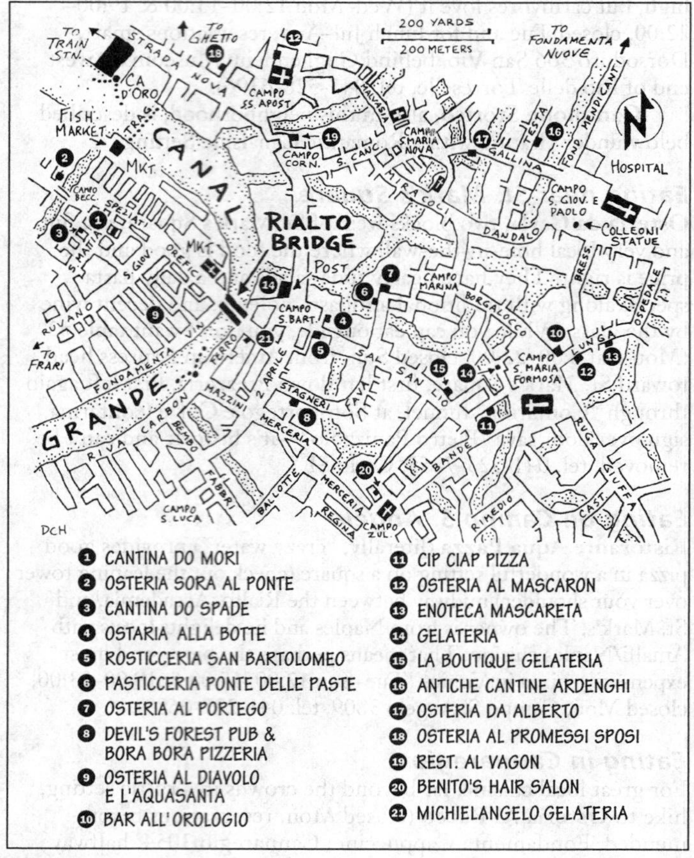

acceptable and the ambience glows (moderate prices, Wed–Mon 19:00–22:00, closed Tue, 3-min walk north of Rialto just before Campo S.S. Apostoli, overlooking canal called Rio dei Santi Apostoli, tel. 041-523-7558).

Ristorante da Raffaele is *the* place for classy food on a quiet canal. It's filled with top-end tourists and locals who want to pay well for the best seafood. The place was a haunt of the avant-garde a few generations ago. Today, it's on a main gondolier thoroughfare—in fact, many guests arrive or depart by gondola. Make a reservation if you want a canalside table (you do). While the multilingual menu is designed for the tourists, locals stick with the daily specials (expensive, CC, Fri–Wed 18:30–22:30, closed Thu, exactly halfway between Piazza San Marco and the Accademia Bridge at Ponte delle Ostreghe, tel. 041-523-2317). Before leaving, wander around inside to see the owner's fabulous old weapons collection.

Ristorante Cantinone Storico sits on a peaceful canal in Dorsoduro between the Accademia Bridge and the Peggy Guggenheim Museum. It's dressy, specializes in fish, has six or eight tables on the canal, and is worth the splurge (daily 12:30–14:30 & 19:30–21:30, reservations wise, on the canal Rio de S. Vio, tel. 041-523-9577).

The "Dorsoduro Riviera," the long promenade along the south side of the Dorsoduro (a 5-min walk south of Accademia Bridge), is lined with canalside restaurants away from the crush of touristic Venice. Places immediately south of the Accademia Bridge (near the Zattere vaporetto stop) are decent but more touristic. At the west end (near the S. Basilio vaporetto stop), try **Trattoria B. Basilio** and **Pizzeria Riviera** (a local fave for pizza); both come with local crowds and wet views.

For a Grand Canal view from the Rialto Bridge, consider **Al Buso**, at the northeast end of the Rialto Bridge. Of the several touristy restaurants that hug the canal near the Rialto, this is recommended by locals as offering the best value (daily 9:00–24:00, dine from 11:00–23:00, Ponte di Rialto 5338, tel. 041-528-9078).

The Stand-Up Progressive Venetian Pub-Crawl Dinner

My favorite Venetian dinner is a pub crawl. A *giro di ombra* (pub crawl) is a tradition unique to Venice—ideal in a city with no cars. (*Ombra* means shade, from the old days when a portable wine bar scooted with the shadow of the Campanile across St. Mark's Square.)

Venice's residential backstreets hide plenty of characteristic bars with countless trays of interesting toothpick munchies *(cicchetti)*. This is a great way to mingle and have fun with the Venetians. Real *cicchetti* (chi-KET-tee) pubs are getting rare in these fast-food days, but locals appreciate the ones that survive.

I've listed plenty of pubs in walking order for a quick or extended crawl below. If you've crawled enough, most of these bars make a fine one-stop, sit-down dinner.

Try fried mozzarella cheese, gorgonzola, calamari, artichoke hearts, and anything ugly on a toothpick. Meat and fish *(pesce;* PESH-shay) munchies can be expensive; veggies *(verdure)* are cheap, around €3 for a meal-sized plate. In many places, there's a set price per food item (e.g., €1). To get a plate of assorted appetizers for €5 (or more, depending on how hungry you are), ask for: "*Un piatto classico di cicchetti misti da €5.*"(Pron. oon pee-AH-toh KLAH-see-koh dee cheh-KET-tee MEE-stee da CHING-kway ay-OO-roh.) Bread sticks *(grissini)* are free for the asking.

Drink the house wines. A small glass of house red or white wine *(ombra rosso* or *ombra bianco)* or a small beer *(birrino)* costs about €1. A liter of house wine costs around €3.60. *Vin bon*, Venetian for fine wine, may run you from €1.60 to €2.60 per little glass. *Corposo* means full-bodied. A good last drink is *fragolino*, the local sweet wine—*bianco* or *rosso*. It often comes with a little cookie *(biscotti)* for dipping.

Bars don't stay open very late, and the *cicchetti* selection is best early, so start your evening by 18:00. Most bars are closed on Sunday. When just munching appetizers, you can stand around the bar or grab a table in the back—usually for the same price.

Cicchetteria *West of the Rialto Bridge*

Cantina do Mori, famous with locals (since 1462) and savvy travelers (since 1982), is a classy place for fine wine and *francobollo* (a spicy selection of 20 tiny sandwiches called "stamps"). Choose from the featured wines in the barrel on the bar. Order carefully or they'll rip you off. From Rialto Bridge, walk 200 meters (650 feet) down Ruga degli Orefici away from St. Mark's Square—then ask (Mon–Sat 17:00–20:30, closed Sun, stand-up only, arrive early before the *cicchetti* are gone, San Polo 429, tel. 041-522-5401).

A few steps from the Rialto fish market, you'll find Campo delle Beccarie and two little places serving traditional munchies. On this square, as you face the restaurant Vini da Pinto, **Ostaria Sora al Ponte** is to your right, just over the bridge (each item €0.75, assemble by pointing, Tue–Sun until 22:00, closed Mon, July and Aug closed Sun), and **Cantina do Spade** is in the alley directly behind Vini da Pinto (head around building to your left, take a right through archway; closed Sun).

Eating near the Rialto Bridge

Eating East of the Rialto Bridge, near Campo San Bartolomeo

Osteria "Alla Botte" Cicchetteria is an atmospheric place packed with a young, local, bohemian-jazz clientele. It's good for a *cicchetti* snack with wine at the bar (see the posted, enticing selection of wines by the glass) or for a light meal in the small, smoke-free room in the back (Fri–Tue 10:00–15:00 & 18:00–23:00, closed Wed–Thu and Sun afternoons, 2 short blocks off Campo San Bartolomeo in the corner behind the statue—down Calle de la Bissa, notice the "day after" photo showing a debris-covered Venice after the notorious 1989 Pink Floyd open-air concert, tel. 041-520-9775).

If the statue on the Campo San Bartolomeo walked backward 20 meters (60 feet), turned left, and went under a passageway, he'd hit **Rosticceria San Bartolomeo**. This cheap—if confusing—self-service restaurant has a likeably surly staff (good €5–6 pasta, great fried *mozzarella al prosciutto* for €1.40, delightful fruit salad, and €1 glasses of wine, prices listed on wall behind counter, no cover or service charge, daily 9:30–21:30, tel. 041-522-3569). Take out or grab a table.

From Rosticceria San Bartolomeo, continue over a bridge to Campo San Lio (a good landmark). Here, turn left, passing Hotel Canada and following Calle Carminati straight about 50 meters (165 feet) over another bridge. On the right is the pastry shop *(pasticceria)* and straight ahead is Osteria Al Portego (at #6015). Both are listed below:

Pasticceria Ponte delle Paste is a feminine and pastel *salon de tè*, popular for its pastries and aperitifs. Italians love taking 15-minute breaks to sip a *spritz* aperitif with friends after a long day's work, before heading home. Ask sprightly Monica for a *spritz al bitter* (white wine, *amaro*, and soda water, €1.30; or choose from the menu on the wall) and munch some of the free goodies on the bar around 18:00 (daily 7:00–20:30, Ponte delle Paste).

Osteria al Portego is a friendly, local-style bar serving great *cicchetti* and good meals (Mon–Fri 9:00–22:00, closed Sat–Sun, tel. 041-522-9038). The *cicchetti* here can make a great meal, but you should also consider sitting down for an actual dinner. They have a fine little menu.

The **Devil's Forest Pub**, an air-conditioned bit of England tucked away a block from the crowds, is—strangely—more Venetian these days than the *tipico* places. Locals come here for good English and Irish beer on tap, big salads (€6.70, lunch only), hot bar snacks, and an easygoing ambience (daily 8:00–24:00, meals 12:00–15:30, bar snacks all the time, closed Sun in Aug, no cover or service charge, fine prices, backgammon and chess boards available-€2.10, a block off Campo San Bartolomeo on Calle dei Stagneri, tel. 041-520-0623). Across the street, **Bora Bora Pizzeria** serves pizza and salads from an entertaining menu (Thu–Tue 12:00–15:00 & 19:15–22:30, closed Wed, CC, tel. 041-523-6583).

Eating West of the Rialto Bridge

Osteria al Diavolo e l'Aquasanta, three blocks west of the Rialto, serves good pasta and makes a handy lunch stop for sightseers (Wed–Mon 12:00–15:00 & 18:00–24:00, closed Mon eve and all day Tue, hiding on a quiet street just off Rua Vecchia S. Giovanni, on Calle della Madonna, tel. 041-277-0307).

La Rivetta Ristorante offers several Venetian specialties under €10 apiece. Scenically located on a canal, it's on the main drag between the Rialto Bridge and Campo San Polo (open daily, San Polo 1479, tel. 041-523-1481).

Eating on or near Campo Santa Maria di Formosa

Campo Santa Maria di Formosa is just plain atmospheric (as most squares with a Socialist Party office seem to be). For a balmy outdoor meal, you could split a pizza with wine on the square. **Bar all' Orologio** has a good setting and friendly service but mediocre "freezer" pizza (happy to split a pizza for pub-crawlers, Mon–Sat 6:00–23:00, closed Sun and in winter at 18:00). For a picnic pizza snack on the square, cross the bridge behind the canalside *gelateria* and grab a slice to go from **Cip Ciap Pizza** (Wed–Mon 9:00–21:00, closed Tue; facing *gelateria*, take bridge to the right; Calle del Mondo Novo). Pub-crawlers get a salad course at the fruit-and-vegetable stand next to the water fountain (Mon–Sat, closes about 19:30 and on Sun).

From Campo Santa Maria di Formosa, follow the yellow sign to "S.S. Giov e Paolo" down Calle Longa Santa Maria di Formosa, and head down the street to **Osteria al Mascaron**, a delightful little restaurant seemingly made to order for pirates gone good (#5225, Mon–Sat 11:30–15:00 & 19:00–23:30, closed Sun, reservations smart, tel. 041-522-5995). Their *antipasto della casa* (a €13 plate of mixed appetizers) is fun, and the *Pasta Scogliera* (€26, rockfish spaghetti for 2) makes a grand meal.

Enoteca Mascareta, a wine bar with much less focus on food, is 30 meters (100 feet) farther down the same street (#5183, Mon–Sat 18:00–24:00, closed Sun, tel. 041-523-0744).

The *gelateria* Zanzibar on the canal at Campo Santa Maria di Formosa is handy (open 7:00–24:00 in summer, 8:00–21:00 winter; for more, see "Gelato," below).

Cheap Meals

A key to cheap eating in Venice is **bar snacks,** especially stand-up mini-meals in out-of-the-way bars. Order by pointing. *Panini* (sandwiches) are sold fast and cheap at bars everywhere. Basic, reliable ham-and-cheese sandwiches (white bread, crusts trimmed) come toasted—simply ask for "toast"; these make a great supplement to Venice's skimpy hotel breakfasts.

For budget eating, I like small ***cicchetti*** **bars** (see "Pub-Crawl Dinner," above); for speed, value, and ambience, you can get a filling plate of local appetizers at nearly any of the bars.

Pizzerias are cheap and easy—try for a sidewalk table at a scenic location. If you want a fast-food pizza place, try **Spizzico** on Campo San Luca.

The **produce market** that sprawls for a few blocks just past the Rialto Bridge (best 8:00–13:00, closed Sun) is a great place to assemble a picnic. The adjacent fish market is wonderfully slimy. Side lanes in this area are speckled with fine little hole-in-the-wall munchie bars, bakeries, and cheese shops.

The **Mensa DLF**, the public transportation workers' cafeteria, is cheap and open to the public (daily 11:00–14:30 & 18:00–22:00). Leaving the train station, turn right on the Grand Canal, walk about 150 meters (500 feet) along the canal, up eight steps, and through the unmarked door.

Gelato

La Boutique del Gelato is one of the best *gelaterias* in Venice (daily 10:00–21:30, closed Dec–Jan, 2 blocks off Campo Santa Maria di Formosa on corner of Salizada San Lio and Calle Paradiso, next to Hotel Bruno, #5727—just look for the crowd).

For late-night gelato at Rialto, try **Michielangelo**, just off Campo San Bartolomeo, on the St. Mark's side of the Rialto Bridge on Salizada Pio X (daily 10:00–22:00). At St. Mark's Square, the **Al Todaro** *gelateria* opposite the Doge's Palace is open late (daily 8:00–24:00, 8:00–20:00 in winter, closed Mon in winter).

Transportation Connections—Venice

By train to: Padua (1/hr, 30 min), **Vicenza** (1/hr, 1 hr), **Verona** (1/hr, 90 min), **Ravenna** (1/hr, 3–4 hrs, transfer in Ferrara or Bologna), **Florence** (7/day, 3 hrs), **Dolomites** (8/day to Bolzano, about hourly, 4 hrs with 1 transfer; catch bus from Bolzano into mountains), **Milan** (1/hr, 3–4 hrs), **Monterosso/Cinque Terre** (2/day, 6 hrs, departs Venice at 10:00 and 15:00), **Rome** (7/day, 5 hrs, slower overnight), **Naples** (change in Rome, plus 2–3 hrs), **Brindisi** (3/day, 11 hrs, change in Bologna), **Bern** (3/day, change in Milan, 8 hrs), **Munich** (2/day, 8 hrs), **Paris** (4/day, 11 hrs), and **Vienna** (4/day, 9 hrs). Train and *couchette* reservations (about €18) are easily made at a downtown travel agency. Italy train info: 848-888-088 (automated, in Italian).

SIENA

Break out of the Venice–Florence–Rome syndrome and savor Italy's hill towns. Experience the texture of Tuscany, the slumber of Umbria, and the lazy towns of Lazio.

For starters, here's one of my favorites. Tuscany's Siena seems to be every Italy connoisseur's pet town. In my office, whenever Siena is mentioned, someone moans, "Siena? I luuuv Siena!" Nearby San Gimignano (see end of chapter) is the quintessential hill town, with Italy's best surviving medieval skyline.

Seven hundred years ago, Siena was a major military power in a class with Florence, Venice, and Genoa. With a population of 60,000, it was even bigger than Paris. In 1348, a disastrous plague weakened Siena. Then, in the 1550s, her bitter rival, Florence, really "salted" her, forever making Siena a nonthreatening backwater. Siena's loss became our sightseeing gain, as its political and economic irrelevance pickled it purely Gothic. Today, Siena's population is still 60,000, compared to Florence's 420,000.

Siena's thriving historic center, with red-brick lanes cascading every which way, offers Italy's best Gothic city experience. Most people do Siena, just 50 kilometers (30 miles) south of Florence, as a day trip, but it's best experienced at twilight. While Florence has the blockbuster museums, Siena has an easy-to-enjoy soul: Courtyards sport flower-decked wells, alleys dead-end at rooftop views, and the sky is a rich blue dome. Right off the bat, Siena becomes an old friend.

Pleasing those who dream of a Fiat-free Italy, pedestrians rule in the old center of Siena. Sit at a café on the red-bricked main square. Take time to savor the first European city to eliminate automobile traffic from its main square (1966) and then, just to be silly, wonder what would happen if they did it in your city.

Planning Your Time

On a quick trip, consider spending three nights in Siena (with a whole-day side trip into Florence and a day to relax and enjoy Siena). Whatever you do, enjoy a sleepy medieval evening in Siena. After an evening in Siena, you can see its major sights in half a day. San Gimignano is an overrun, pint-sized Siena. Don't rush Siena for San Gimignano (with less than 24 hours for Siena, skip San Gimignano). Note that San Gimignano, with good bus connections, also makes an easy day trip from Florence.

Orientation

Siena lounges atop a hill, stretching its three legs out from Il Campo. This main square, the historic meeting point of Siena's neighborhoods, is for pedestrians only. And most of those pedestrians are students from the local university. Everything I mention is within a 15-minute walk of the square. Navigate by landmarks, following the excellent system of street-corner signs. The typical visitor sticks to the San Domenico–Il Campo axis.

Siena is one big sight. Its essential individual sights come in two little clusters: the square (city hall, museum, tower) and the cathedral (baptistery, cathedral museum with its surprise viewpoint). Check these sights off and you're free to wander.

Tourist Information: Pick up a free town map from the main TI at #56 on Il Campo; look for the yellow Change sign—bad rates, good information (Mon–Sat 8:30–19:30, tel. 0577-280-551, www.siena.turismo.toscana.it). The little TI at San Domenico is for hotel promotion only and sells a Siena map for €0.60.

Museum Passes: Siena offers a variety of passes. If you're staying for two days or more, consider getting the €16 combo-ticket (called Siena Itinerari d'Arte) that covers eight sights, including Museo Civico, Santa Maria della Scala, Museo dell' Opera, baptistery, Piccolomini Library (in the cathedral), and more (valid for 7 days, sold at participating sites). This pass covers a wider range of sights than the other passes that cost and cover less (e.g., just religious sights or just city museums). In general, if you see two-thirds of the sights covered by a pass, you'll save money.

Arrival in Siena

By Train: The small train station has a bar and bus office. The baggage checkroom and lockers have been closed indefinitely.

The station is located on the outskirts of town. To get to the city center, take a taxi or a city bus. The **taxi stand** is to your far right as you exit the station; allow about €8 to your hotel (for taxis at station, call 0577-44504, for taxis at Piazza Matteotti in the center, call 0577-49222). For the **city bus**, buy a €0.75 ticket from the Bus Ticket Office in the station lobby (daily 6:15–19:30, ask for city map—it's free and just a bus route map, but helps get you started). You can also buy a bus ticket from the blue machine in the lobby (touch screen for English and select "urban" for type of ticket). Then cross the parking lot and the street to reach the sheltered bus stop. Catch any orange city bus to get into town (punch ticket in machine on bus to validate it). You'll end up at one of three stops—Piazza Gramsci/Lizza, Piazza Sale, or Stufa Secca—all within several blocks of each other (buses run about every 7 min, fewer on Sun; if you get off at Stufa Secca's tiny square, you're soon faced with two uphill roads—take the one to the right for one block to reach the main drag, Banchi di Sopra).

To get to Siena's train station from the center of Siena, catch the city bus at Piazza del Sale or Stufa Secca; note that bus stops are rarely marked with a "bus stop" sign, but instead with a posted schedule and sometimes with yellow lines painted on the pavement, showing a bus-sized rectangle and the word "bus." Confirm with the driver that the bus is going to the *stazione* (pron. stat-zee-OH-nay). Purchase your ticket in advance from a *tabacchi* shop.

By Bus: Some buses arrive in Siena at the train station (see "Arrival By Train," above), others at Piazza Gramsci (a few blocks from city center), and some stop at both. The main bus companies are Sena and Tran. You can store baggage underneath Piazza Gramsci in Sotopassaggio la Lizza (€2.75, daily 7:00–19:30, no overnight).

By Car: Drivers coming from the autostrada take the Porta San Marco exit and follow the *Centro*, then *Stadio*, signs (stadium, soccer ball). The soccer-ball signs take you to the stadium lot (Parcheggio Stadio, €1.50/hr, €12.50/day) at the huge, bare-brick San Domenico Church. The Fortezza lot nearby charges the same. Or park in the lot underneath the railway station. You can drive into the pedestrian zone (a pretty ballsy thing to do) only to drop bags at your hotel. You can park free in the lot below the Albergo Lea, in white-striped spots behind Hotel Villa Liberty, and behind the Fortezza. (The signs showing a street cleaner and a day of the week indicate which day the street is cleaned; that's a €105 tow-fee incentive to learn the days of the week in Italian.)

Helpful Hints

Local Guide: Roberto Bechi, a hardworking Sienese guide, specializes in off-the-beaten-path tours of Siena and the surrounding countryside. Married to an American (Patti) and having run restaurants in Siena and the United States, Roberto communicates well with Americans. His passions are Sienese culture, Tuscan history, and local cuisine. Book well in advance (full-day tours from €65–95 per person, half-day tours from €30–50 per person, tel. & fax 0577-704-789, www.toursbyroberto.com, e-mail: tourrob@tin.it; for U.S. contact, fax Greg Evans at 540/434-4532).

Internet Access: In this university town, there are lots of places to get plugged in. **Internet Point** is just off Piazza Matteotti, on Via Paradiso (across street from McDonald's) and **Internet Train** is near Il Campo, at Via di Città 121 (tel. 0577-226-366).

Markets: On Wednesday morning, the weekly market—consisting mainly of clothes—sprawls between the Fortress and Piazza Gramsci along Viale Cesare Maccabi and the adjacent Viale XXV Aprile. The produce market is held a block from Il Campo, behind the city hall (Mon–Sat mornings).

Laundry: Two modern, self-service places are Lavarapido Wash and Dry (daily 8:00–22:00, Via di Pantaneto 38, near Logge del Papa) and Onda Blu (daily 8:00–21:00, Via del Casato di Sotto 17, 50 meters, or 165 feet, from Il Campo).

Sights—Siena's Main Square

▲▲▲Il Campo—Siena's great central piazza is urban harmony at its best. Like a people-friendly stage set, its gently tilted floor fans out from the tower and city hall backdrop. It's the perfect invitation to loiter. Think of it as a trip to the beach without sand or water.

Il Campo was located at the historic junction of Siena's various competing districts, or *contrada,* on the old marketplace. The brick surface is divided into nine sections, representing the council of nine merchants and city bigwigs who ruled medieval Siena. At the square's high point, look for the *Fountain of Joy*, the two naked guys about to be tossed in, and the pigeons politely waiting their turn to gingerly tightrope down slippery spouts to slurp a drink. (You can see parts of the original fountain, of which this is a copy, in an interesting exhibit at Siena's Santa Maria della Scala museum, listed below.) At the square's low point is the city hall and tower. The chapel located at the base of the tower was built in 1348 as thanks to God for ending the Black Plague (after it killed more than a third of the population).

To say Siena and Florence have always been competitive is an understatement. In medieval times, a statue of Venus stood on Il Campo (where the *Fountain of Joy* is today). After the plague hit Siena, the monks blamed this pagan statue. The people cut it to pieces and buried it along the walls of Florence.

The market area behind the city hall, a wide-open expanse since the Middle Ages, originated as a farming area within the city walls to feed the city in times of siege. Now the morning produce

Siena Sights

market is held here Monday through Saturday. (The public WCs closest to Il Campo are each about a block away: at Via Beccheria—a few steps off Via de Città—and on Casato di Sotto; €0.60.)

▲Museo Civico—The Palazzo Publico (city hall), at the base of the tower, has a fine and manageable museum housing a good sample of Sienese art. In the following order, you'll see: the Sala Risorgimento, with dramatic scenes of Victor Emmanuel's unification of Italy (surrounded by statues that don't seem to care); the chapel, with impressive inlaid wood chairs in the choir; and the Sala del Mappamondo, with Simone Martini's *Maesta* (Enthroned Virgin) facing the faded *Guidoriccio da Fogliano* (a mercenary providing a more concrete form of protection). Next is the Sala della Pace—where the city's fat cats met. Looking down on the oligarchy during their meetings were two interesting frescoes showing the effects of good and bad government. Notice the whistle-while-you-work happiness of the utopian community ruled by the utopian government (in the better-preserved fresco) and the fate of a community ruled by politicians with more typical values (in a terrible state of repair). The message: Without justice, there can be no prosperity. The rural view out the window is essentially the view from the top of the big stairs—enjoy it from here (€6.50, combo-ticket with tower-€9.50, daily March–Oct 10:00–19:00, July–Sept until 23:00, Nov–Jan 10:00–16:00, last entry 45 min before closing; audioguide-€3.75 for 1 person, €5.25 for 2; tel. 0577-292-111).

▲City Tower (Torre del Mangia)—Siena gathers around its city hall, not its church. It was a proud republic; its "declaration of independence" is the tallest secular medieval tower in Italy. The 100-meter-tall (330-foot) Torre del Mangia was named after a hedonistic watchman who consumed his earnings like a glutton consumes food (his chewed-up statue is in the courtyard, to the left as you enter). Its 300 steps get pretty skinny at the top, but the reward is one of Italy's best views (€5.50, combo-ticket with Museo Civico-€9.50, daily 10:00–19:00, mid-July–mid-Sept until 23:00, Nov–March 10:00–16:00, closed in rain, sometimes long lines, limit of 30 tourists at a time, avoid midday crowd).

▲Pinacoteca (National Picture Gallery)—Siena was a power in Gothic art. But the average tourist, wrapped up in a love affair with the Renaissance, hardly notices. This museum takes you on a walk through Siena's art, chronologically from the 12th through the 15th centuries. For the casual sightseer, the Sienese art in the city hall and cathedral museums is adequate. But art fans enjoy this opportunity to trace the evolution of Siena's delicate and elegant art (€4.25, Sun–Mon 8:30–13:15, Tue–Sat 8:15–19:15, plus possibly 20:30–23:30 on Sat in summer, tel. 0577-281-161). From Il Campo, walk out Via di Città to Piazza di Postierla and go left on San Pietro.

Sights—Siena's Cathedral Area

▲▲▲Duomo—Siena's cathedral is as Baroque as Gothic gets. The striped facade is piled with statues and ornamentation, and the interior is decorated from top to bottom. The heads of 172 popes peer down from the ceiling, over the fine inlaid art on the floor. This is one busy interior. (Modest dress is required for entry.)

To orient yourself in this *panforte* of Italian churches, stand under the dome and think of the church floor as a big clock. You're the middle, and the altar is high noon: you'll find the *Slaughter of the Innocents* roped off on the floor at 10:00, Pisano's pulpit between two pillars at 11:00, Bernini's chapel at 3:00, two Michelangelo statues (next to doorway leading to a shop, snacks, and WC) at 7:00, the library at 8:00, and a Donatello statue at 9:00. Take some time with the floor mosaics in the front. Nicola Pisano's wonderful pulpit is crowded with delicate Gothic storytelling from 1268. To understand why Bernini is considered the greatest Baroque sculptor, step into his sumptuous *Cappella della Madonna del Voto.* This last work in the cathedral, from 1659, is enough to make a Lutheran light a candle. Move up to the altar and look back at the two Bernini statues: Mary Magdalene in a state of spiritual ecstasy, and St. Jerome playing the crucifix like a violinist lost in beautiful music.

The Piccolomini altar is most interesting for its two Michelangelo statues (the lower big ones). Paul, on the left, may be a self-portrait. Peter, on the right, resembles Michelangelo's more famous statue of Moses. Originally contracted to do 15 statues, Michelangelo left the project early (1504) to do his great *David* in Florence.

The Piccolomini Library—worth the €1.50 entry—is brilliantly frescoed with scenes glorifying the works of a pope from 500 years ago. It contains intricately decorated, illuminated music scores and a statue (a Roman copy of a Greek original) of the Three Graces (library open Sun 13:30–19:30, Tue–Sat same as church hours, below). Donatello's bronze statue of St. John the Baptist, in his famous rags, is in a chapel to the right of the library.

Hours: The church is open mid-March–Oct daily 7:30–19:30 but Sun 10:15–14:00 is reserved for worship only; Nov–mid-March Mon–Sat 7:30–17:00, Sun 14:30–17:30. In September, when much of the elaborate mosaic floor is uncovered, you'll pay a fee to enter the church (€2.75 for Pavimento Cattedrale).

Audioguides: There's a daunting number of audioguides. An audioguide for just the church costs €3.10; to add the library, it's €3.60; and to add the Cathedral Museum (Museo dell' Opera de Panorama), it's €5.25. For the church and museum only, it's €4.25. Two headphones are available at a price break.

▲Santa Maria della Scala—This renovated old hospital-turned-museum (opposite the duomo entrance) was used as a hospital as recently as the 1980s. Now it displays a lavishly frescoed hall, a worthwhile exhibit on Quercia's *Fountain of Joy* (downstairs), and a so-so archaeological museum (subterranean, in labyrinthine tunnels). The entire museum is a maze, with various exhibitions and paintings plugged in to fill the gaps.

The frescoes in the **Pellegrinaio Hall** show medieval Siena's innovative health care and social welfare system in action (c. 1442, wonderfully described in English). The hospital was functioning as early as the 11th century, nursing the sick and caring for abandoned children (see frescoes). The good work paid off, as bequests and donations poured in, creating the wealth that's evident in the chapels elsewhere on this floor. The Old Sacristy was built to house precious relics, including a Holy Nail thought to be from Jesus' cross.

Downstairs, the engaging exhibit on Jacopo della Quercia's early-15th-century ***Fountain of Joy*** doesn't need much English description, fortunately, because there isn't much. In the 19th century, the *Fountain of Joy* in Il Campo was deteriorating. It was dismantled, and plaster casts were made of the originals. Then replicas were made, restoring the pieces as if brand-new. The *Fountain of Joy* that stands in Il Campo today is a replica. In this exhibit, you'll see the plaster casts of the original, eroded panels paired with their restored twins. Statues originally stood on the edges of the fountain (see the statues and drawings). In general, the pieces at the beginning and end of the exhibit are original. If there's a piece in a dim room near the exit of the exhibit, it's likely an original chunk awaiting cleaning.

The **Archaeological Museum**, way downstairs, consists mainly of pottery fragments in cases lining tunnel after tunnel. It's like being lost in a wine cellar without the wine. Unless there's an exhibition, it's not worth the trip.

Cost and Hours: €5.25, daily 10:00–18:00, Fri–Sat in summer until 23:00, off-season 11:30–16:30, closed some Sundays. The chapel just inside the museum entrance door is free (as you enter the museum, it's to your left; English description inside chapel entry).

▲Baptistery—Siena is so hilly that there wasn't enough flat ground on which to build a big church. What to do? Build a big church and prop up the overhanging edge with the baptistery. This dark and quietly tucked-away cave of art is worth a look (and €2.50) for its cool tranquillity and the bronze panels and angels—by Ghiberti, Donatello, and others—adorning the pedestal of the baptismal font (daily mid-March–Sept 9:00–19:30, Oct 9:00–18:00, Nov–mid-March 10:00–13:00 & 14:30–17:00).

▲▲Cathedral Museum (Museo dell' Opera e Panorama)—Siena's most enjoyable museum, on the Campo side of the church (look for the yellow signs), was built to house the cathedral's art. The ground floor is filled with the cathedral's original Gothic sculpture by Giovanni Pisano (who spent 10 years in the late 1200s carving and orchestrating the decoration of the cathedral) and a fine Donatello *Madonna and Child.* Upstairs to the left awaits a private audience with Duccio's *Maesta (Enthroned Virgin)*. Pull up a chair and study one of the great pieces of medieval art. The flip side of the *Maesta* (displayed on the opposite wall), with 26 panels—the medieval equivalent of pages—shows scenes from the Passion of Christ. Climb onto the "Panorama dal Facciatone." From the first landing, take the skinnier second spiral for Siena's surprise view. Look back over the duomo and consider this: When rival republic Florence began its grand cathedral, proud Siena decided to build the biggest church in all Christendom. The existing cathedral would be used as a transept. You're atop what would have been the entry. The wall below you, connecting the duomo with the museum of the cathedral, was as far as Siena got before a plague killed the city's ability to finish the project. Were it completed, you'd be looking straight down the nave—white stones mark where columns would have stood (€5.50, worthwhile €2.60 40-minute audioguide, daily mid-March–Sept 9:00–19:30, Oct 9:00–18:00, Nov–mid-March 9:00–13:30, tel. 0577-283-048).

Sights—Siena's San Domenico Area

Church of San Domenico—This huge brick church is worth a quick look. The bland interior fits the austere philosophy of the Dominicans. Walk up the steps in the rear for a look at various paintings from the life of Saint Catherine, patron saint of Siena. Halfway up the church on the right, you'll see a metal bust of Saint Catherine, a small case containing her finger, and her actual head (free, daily March–Oct 7:00–13:00 & 14:30–18:30, Nov–Feb 9:00–13:00 & 15:00–18:00; WC for €0.60 at far end of parking lot—facing church entrance, it's to your right).

Sanctuary of Saint Catherine—Step into Catherine's cool and peaceful home. Siena remembers its favorite hometown girl, a simple, unschooled, but mystically devout girl who, in the mid-1300s, helped convince the pope to return from France to Rome. Pilgrims have come here since 1464. Since then, architects and artists have greatly embellished what was probably a humble home (her family worked as wool-dyers). Enter through the courtyard and walk to the far end. The chapel on your right was built over the spot where Saint Catherine received the stigmata while praying. The chapel on your left used to be the kitchen. Go down the stairs to the left of the chapel/kitchen to reach the saint's room. The saint's bare cell is behind see-through doors. Much of the art throughout the sanctuary depicts scenes from the saint's life (free, daily 9:30–18:00, winter 9:30–13:30 & 15:00–18:30, Via Tiratoio). It's a few downhill blocks toward the center from San Domenico (follow signs to the Santuario di Santa Caterina).

Nightlife—Join the evening *passeggiata* (peak strolling time is

19:00) along Via Banchi di Sopra with gelato in hand. **Nannini's** at Piazza Salimbeni has fine gelato (daily 11:00–24:00).

The **Enoteca Italiana** is a good wine bar in a cellar in the Fortezza/Fortress (Mon 12:00–20:00, Tue–Sat 12:00–1:00, closed Sun, sample glasses in 3 different price ranges: €1.55, €2.75, €5.25, bottles and snacks available, CC, cross bridge and enter fortress, go left down ramp, tel. 0577-288-497).

Shopping—Shops line Via Banchi di Sopra, the *passeggiata* route. For a department store, try Upim on Piazza Matteotti (Mon–Sat 9:30–19:50, closed Sun). The large, colorful scarves/flags, each depicting the symbol of one of Siena's 17 different neighborhoods (such as the wolf, the turtle, the snail, etc.), are easy-to-pack souvenirs, fun for decorating your home (€7.25 apiece for large size, sold at souvenir stands).

Siena's Palio

In the Palio, the feisty spirit of Siena's 17 *contrada* (neighborhoods) lives on. These neighborhoods celebrate, worship, and compete together. Each even has its own historical museum. *Contrada* pride is evident any time of year in the colorful neighborhood banners and parades. (If you hear distant drumming, run to it for some medieval action.) But *contrada* pride is most visible twice a year—on July 2 and August 16—when they have their world-famous horse race, the Palio di Siena. Ten of the 17 neighborhoods compete (chosen by lot), hurling themselves with medieval abandon into several days of trial races and traditional revelry. On the big day, jockeys and horses go into their *contrada*'s church to be blessed ("Go and win," says the priest). It's considered a sign of luck if a horse leaves droppings in the church.

On the evening of the big day, Il Campo is stuffed to the brim with locals and tourists, as the horses charge wildly around the square in this literally no-holds-barred race. A horse can win even if its rider has fallen off. Of course, the winning neighborhood is the scene of grand celebrations afterward. The grand prize: simply proving your *contrada* is numero uno. All over town, sketches and posters depict the Palio. This is not some folkloristic event. It's a real medieval moment. If you're packed onto the square with 15,000 people who each really want to win, you won't see much, but you'll feel it. While the actual Palio packs the city, you could side-trip in from Florence to see horse-race trials each of the three days before the big day (usually at 9:00 and around 19:30).

▲**Palio al Cinema**—This 20-minute film, *Siena, the Palio, and Its History*, helps re-create the craziness of the Palio. See it at the Cinema Moderno in Piazza Tolomei, two blocks from Il Campo (runs May–Sept only, €5.25, with this book pay €4.25, or €7.75

for 2; Mon–Sat 9:30–17:30, English showings generally hourly at :30 past the hour, schedule posted on door, closed Sun, air-con, tel. 0577-289-201). Call or drop by to confirm when the next English showing is scheduled—there are usually seven a day. At the ticket desk, you can buy the same show on video (discounted from €13 to €10.50 with this book, video must be labeled "NTSC American System" or it'll be a doorstop at your home).

Sleeping in Siena

(€1 = about $1, country code: 39, zip code: 53100)

Sleep Code: **S** = Single, **D** = Double/Twin, **T** = Triple, **Q** = Quad, **b** = bathroom, **s** = shower only, **CC** = Credit Cards accepted, **no CC** = Credit Cards not accepted, **SE** = Speaks English, **NSE** = No English. Breakfast is generally not included. Have breakfast on Il Campo or in a nearby bar.

To help you sort easily through these listings, I've divided the rooms into three categories based on the price for a standard double room with bath:

Higher Priced—Most rooms more than €110.

Moderately Priced—Most rooms €110 or less.

Lower Priced—Most rooms €80 or less.

Finding a room is tough during Easter or the Palio in early July and mid-August. Call ahead any time of year, as Siena's few budget places are listed in all the budget guidebooks. While day-tripping tour groups turn the town into a Gothic amusement park in midsummer, Siena is basically yours in the evenings and off-season.

Nearly all hotels listed lie between Il Campo and the Church of San Domenico (see map on page 954). About a third of the listings don't take credit cards, no matter how earnestly you ask. Cash machines are plentiful on the main streets.

Sleeping near Il Campo

HIGHER PRICED

These two places are a 10-minute walk from Il Campo.

Hotel Duomo is a classy place with 23 spacious rooms (Sb-€110, Db-€150, Tb-€175, Qb-€200, includes breakfast, CC, air-con, picnic-friendly roof terrace, free parking, follow Via di Città, which becomes Via Stalloreggi, to Via Stalloreggi 38, tel. 0577-289-088, fax 0577-43043, www.hotelduomo.it, e-mail: booking@hotelduomo.it, Stefania SE). If you arrive by train, take a taxi (€8); if you drive, go to Porta San Marco and follow the signs to the hotel, drop off your bags, and then park in nearby "Il Campo" lot.

Pensione Palazzo Ravizza, elegant and friendly, has an

aristocratic feel and a peaceful garden (Db-€148–255, suites available, includes breakfast and dinner, cheaper mid-Nov–Feb, CC, elevator, back rooms face open country, good restaurant, half pension required in summer, free parking, Via Pian dei Mantellini 34, tel. 0577-280-462, fax 0577-221-597, www.palazzoravizza.it, e-mail: bureau@palazzoravizza.it, SE).

LOWER PRICED

Each of these listings is forgettable but inexpensive, and just a horse wreck away from one of Italy's most wonderful civic spaces.

Piccolo Hotel Etruria, a good bet for a hotel with 19 decent rooms but not much soul, is just off the square (S-€39, Sb-€44, Db-€73, Tb-€91, Qb-€114, breakfast-€4.75, CC, with your back to the tower, leave Il Campo to the right at 2:00, Via Donzelle 1-3, curfew at 0:30, tel. 0577-288-088, fax 0577-288-461, e-mail: hetruria@tin.it, Fattorini family SE).

Albergo Tre Donzelle, with its 27 plain, institutional rooms next door to Piccolo Hotel Etruria, makes sense only if you think of Il Campo as your terrace (S-€34, D-€47, Db-€60, CC, Via Donzelle 5, tel. 0577-280-358, fax 0577-223-933, Signora—pron. seen-YOR-ah—Iannini SE).

Locanda Garibaldi is a modest, very Sienese restaurant/*albergo*. Gentle Marcello wears two hats, as he runs a fine, busy restaurant downstairs and seven pleasant rooms up a funky, artsy staircase (Db-€70, Tb-€89, family deals, no CC, takes reservations only a week in advance, half a block downhill off the square at Via Giovanni Dupre 18, tel. 0577-284-204, NSE).

Hotel Cannon d'Oro, a few blocks up Via Banchi di Sopra, is spacious and group-friendly (30 rooms, Sb-€66, Db-€82, Tb-€104, Qb-€122, these discounted prices promised through 2003 with this book, family deals, breakfast-€6, CC, Via Montanini 28, tel. 0577-44321, fax 0577-280-868, e-mail: cannondoro@libero.it, Maurizio and Debora SE).

Albergo La Perla, a last resort, is a funky, jumbled, 13-room place with a narrow maze of hallways, stark rooms, old bedspreads, miniscule bathrooms, and laissez-faire environment (Sb-€50, Db-€65, Tb-€90, no CC, a block off Piazza Independenza at Via della Terme 25, tel. 0577-47144). Attilio and his American wife, Deborah, take reservations only a day or two ahead. Ideally, call the morning you'll arrive.

Sleeping near San Domenico Church

These hotels are also within a 10-minute walk of Il Campo. Albergo Bernini and Alma Domus, which enjoy views of the old town and cathedral, are the best values in town.

Siena Hotels and Restaurants

TO HOSTEL
TO TRAIN STATION
FORTEZZA
VIALE FRANCHI
LA LIZZA
VIALE MACCARI
25 APR.
V. GARI
PIAZZA SALE
VIA STUFASECCA
PIAZZA GRAMSCI
BUSES TO FLORENCE -
100 YDS.
100 m
VIALE TOZZI
MONT.
ENOTECA ITALIA
P
STADIO
PIAZZA MATTEOTTI
POST
PIAZZA SALIMBENI
PIAZZA TOLOMEI
VIALE
VIALE DEI MILLE
VIA CURTATONE
PARADISIO
McD
VIA DI SAPIENZA
ROSSI
BANCHI DI SOPRA
TO PARKING & AUTOSTRADA
WC
CAMPOREGGIO
PITTORI
S. CAT.
S. ANT. GALLUZZA
TERME
TERMINI
MUSEO CIVICO
CITY HALL & TOWER
SAN DOMENICO
SANCT. S. CAT.
P. IND.
BANCHI DI SOTTO
ESTERINA FONT.
COSTONE
DIACCETO
WC
TO
BAPT.
VIA PELL.
IL CAMPO
PANT.
PORRIONE
SALICOTTO
DUOMO
PIAZZA DUOMO
CASTORO
VIA DI CITTA
WC
DI SOTTO
SANTA MARIA DELLA SCALA
CAPITANO
CAS.
MUSIC ACADEMY
PIAZZA MERCATO
CATHEDRAL MUSEUM
STALLOREGGI
S. PIETRO
PINACOTECA
-PICTURE GALL.-
TO 4 & 18
1 PICCOLO HOTEL ETRURIA
2 ALBERGO TRE DONZELLE
3 ALBERGO LA PERLA
4 TO HOTEL DUOMO
5 HOTEL CANNON D'ORO
6 LOCANDA GARIBALDI
7 ALBERGO BERNINI
8 ALMA DOMUS
9 HOTEL CHIUSARELLI
10 TO ALBERGO LEA & HOTEL LIBERTY
11 JOLLY HOTEL SIENA
12 PIZZERIA SPADAFORTE
13 RISTORANTE GALLO NERO
14 OSTERIA IL TAMBURINO
15 OSTERIA DA DIVO
16 IL VERROCHIO
17 CIAO CAFETERIA
18 TO PENSIONE PAL. RAVIZZA
19 TO HOTEL SANTA CATARINA & PALAZZO VALLI
20 SOTTOPASSAGGIO LA LIZZA
21 LAUNDROMATS

HIGHER PRICED

Hotel Villa Liberty has 18 big, bright, comfortable rooms (S-€75, Db-€130, includes breakfast, CC, only one room with twin beds; elevator, bar, air-con, TVs, courtyard, facing fortress at Viale V. Veneto 11, tel. 0577-44966, fax 0577-44770, www.villaliberty.it, e-mail: info@villaliberty.it, SE).

Jolly Hotel Siena, for people who want a four-star hotel, has 126 rooms that are clean but dated. Across the street from Piazza Gramsci, it's convenient if you're arriving by bus and you've got lots of luggage—and money (Sb-€124–160, Db-€170–233, includes breakfast, CC, non-smoking floor, Piazza La Lizza, tel. 0577-288-448, fax 0577-41272, e-mail: siena@jollyhotels.it).

MODERATELY PRICED

Albergo Bernini makes you part of a Sienese family in a modest, clean home with nine fine rooms. Friendly Nadia and Mauro welcome you to their spectacular view terrace for breakfast and picnic lunches and dinners. Outside of breakfast and checkout time, Mauro, an accomplished accordionist, might play a song for you if you ask (Sb-€77, D-€62, Db-€82, breakfast-€7, less in winter, no CC, midnight curfew, on the main San Domenico–Il Campo drag at Via Sapienza 15, tel. & fax 0577-289-047, www.albergobernini.com, e-mail: hbernin@tin.it, son Alessandro SE).

Hotel Chiusarelli, a proper hotel in a beautiful building with a handy location, comes with traffic noise at night—ask for a quieter room in the back (49 rooms, S-€57, Sb-€72, Db-€108, Tb-€146, includes big buffet breakfast, CC, suites available, air-con, pleasant garden terrace, across from San Domenico at Viale Curtatone 15, tel. 0577-280-562, fax 0577-271-177, www.chiusarelli.com, e-mail: info@chiusarelli.com, SE).

Albergo Lea is a sleepable place in a residential neighborhood a few blocks away from the center (past San Domenico) with 11 rooms and easy parking (S-€52, Db-€93, Tb-€120, cheaper in winter, includes breakfast, CC, rooftop terrace, Viale XXIV Maggio 10, tel. & fax 0577-283-207, SE).

LOWER PRICED

Alma Domus is ideal—unless nuns make you nervous, you need a double bed, or you plan on staying out past the 23:30 curfew (no mercy given). This quasi-hotel (not a convent) is run with firm but angelic smiles by sisters who offer clean and quiet rooms for a steal and save the best views for foreigners. Bright lamps, quaint balconies, fine views, grand public rooms, top security, and a friendly atmosphere make this a great value. The checkout time is strictly 10:00, but they will store your luggage in their secure courtyard (Db-€59, Tb-€72, Qb-€90, no CC, ask for view room—*con vista*, elevator, from San Domenico walk downhill with the church on your right toward the view, turn left down Via Camporegio, make a U-turn at the little chapel down the brick steps to Via Camporegio 37, tel. 0577-44177 and 0577-44487, fax 0577-47601, NSE).

Sleeping Farther from the Center

The first two listings are near Porta Romana.

HIGHER PRICED

Hotel Santa Caterina is a three-star, 18th-century place, best for drivers who need air-conditioning. Professionally run with real attention to quality, it has 22 comfortable rooms with a delightful garden (Sb-€98, small Db-€98, Db-€133, Tb-€179, mention this book to get these prices, includes buffet breakfast, elevator, CC; garden side is quieter but street side—with multipaned windows—isn't bad, fridge in room, parking-€12/day—request when you reserve, 100 meters, or 330 feet, outside Porta Romana at Via E.S. Piccolomini 7, tel. 0577-221-105, fax 0577-271-087, www.hscsiena.it, e-mail: info@hscsiena.it, SE). A city bus runs frequently (Mon–Sat 4/hr, Sun 2/hr) to the town center. A taxi to/from the station runs around €8.

Palazzo di Valli, with 11 spacious rooms and a garden, is 800 meters (0.5 mile) beyond Porta Romana (the Roman gate) and feels like it's in the country. Catch the city bus into town (Db-€140, Tb-€170, includes breakfast, CC, parking, Via E.S. Piccolomini, bus to center Mon–Sat 4/hr, Sun 2/hr; tel. 0577-226-102, fax 0577-222-255, Camarda family SE). From the autostrada, exit at Siena Sud in the direction of Porta Romana.

Frances' Lodge is a small farmhouse B&B 1.5 kilometers (1 mile) out of Siena. English-speaking Franca and Franco rent four modern rooms in a rustic yet elegant old place with a swimming pool, peaceful garden, eight acres of olive trees and vineyards, and great Siena views (Db-€150–180, Tb-€210,easy parking, near shuttle bus into town, Strada di Valdipugna 2, tel. 0577-281-061, fax 0577-222-224, www.franceslodge.it).

MODERATELY PRICED

Casa Laura has five clean, well-maintained rooms, some with brick-and-beam ceilings (Db-€83 with breakfast, €73 without, cheaper off-season or for 3 nights or more, CC, Via Roma 3, about a 10-min walk from Il Campo toward Porta Romana, closed Nov–March, tel. 0577-226-061, fax 0577-225-240, e-mail: labenci@tin.it, NSE).

LOWER PRICED

Siena's **Guidoriccio Youth Hostel** has 120 cheap beds, but, given the hassle of the bus ride and the charm of downtown Siena at night, I'd skip it (office open 15:00–1:00, €13 beds in doubles, triples, and dorms with sheets and breakfast, CC, bus #10 from train station or bus #15 from Piazza Gramsci, Via Fiorentina 89 in Stellino neighborhood, tel. 0577-52212, SE).

Eating in Siena

Sienese restaurants are reasonable by Florentine and Venetian standards. Even with higher prices, lousy service, and lower-quality food, consider eating on Il Campo—a classic European experience.

Pizzeria Spadaforte, at the edge of Il Campo, has a decent setting, mediocre pizza, and tables steeper than its prices (daily 12:00–16:00 & 19:30–22:30, CC, to far right of city tower as you face it, tel. 0577-281-123).

For authentic Sienese dining at a fair price, eat at **Locanda Garibaldi**, down Via Giovanni Dupre at #18, within a block of Il Campo (€15 *menu*, Sun–Fri opens at 12:00–14:00 for lunch and 19:00–21:00 for dinner, arrive early to get a table, closed Sat). Marcello does a nice little *piatto misto dolce* for €2.75, featuring several local desserts with sweet wine.

Osteria il Tamburino is friendly, small, and intimate and serves up tasty meals (Mon–Sat 12:00–14:30 & 19:00–20:30, closed Sun, CC, follow Via di Città off Il Campo, becomes Stalloreggi, Via Stalloreggi 11, tel. 0577-280-306).

Taverna San Giuseppe, a local favorite, offers traditional food with a creative flair. Reserve or arrive early (Mon–Sat 12:15–14:15 & 17:15–21:45, closed Sun, Via Giovanni Dupre 132, tel. 0577-42286).

Antica Osteria Da Divo is the place for a fine €40 meal. The kitchen is creative, the food is fresh and top-notch, and the ambience is candlelit. You'll get a basket of exotic fresh breads. They offer excellent seasonal dishes. The lamb goes baaa in your mouth. And the chef is understandably proud of his desserts (daily 12:00–14:30 & 19:00–22:00, CC, Via Franciosa 29, facing baptistery door, take the far right and walk one long curving block, reserve for summer eves, tel. 0577-286-054).

Trattoria La Tellina has patient waiters and great food, including homemade tiramisu. Arrive early to get a seat (Via dell Terme 52, between St. Catherine's House and Piazza Tolomei—where Palio film is shown, tel. 0577-283-133).

Osteria Nonna Gina wins praise from locals for its good

quality and prices (Tue–Sun 12:30–14:30 & 19:30–20:30, closed Mon, CC, Piano dei Mantellini 2, 10-min walk from Il Campo, near Hotel Duomo, tel. 0577-287-247).

Ristorante Gallo Nero is a friendly "grotto" for Tuscan cuisine. Popular with groups, this "black rooster" serves *ribollita* (hearty Tuscan bean soup) and offers a €23 "medieval *menu*," as well as several Tuscan *menus*, starting at €16 (daily 12:00–15:30 & 19:00–24:00, CC, 3 blocks down Via del Porrione from Il Campo at #65, tel. 0577-284-356).

Il Verrochio, a block away—tucked between a church and loggia—serves a decent €13 *menu* in a cozy, wood-beamed setting (daily 12:00–14:30 & 19:00–22:00, closed Wed in winter, CC, Logge del Papa 1, tel. 0577-284-062).

Le Campane, two blocks off Il Campo, is classy and a little pricey (daily 12:15–14:30 & 19:15–22:00, closed Mon in winter, CC, indoor/outdoor seating, a few steps off Via di Città at Via delle Campane 6, tel. 0577-284-035).

Osteria la Chiacchera, while touristy, is an atmospheric, tasty, and affordable hole-in-the-brick-wall (daily 11:00–24:00, CC, 2 rooms, below Pension Bernini at Costa di San Antonio 4, reservations wise, skip the *trippa*—tripe, tel. 0577-280-631).

Cheap Meals, Snacks, and Picnics

Snack with a view from a small balcony overlooking Il Campo. Survey these three places from Il Campo to see which has a free table. On Via di Città, you'll find **Gelateria Artigiana,** which has perhaps Siena's best ice cream, and **Barbero d'Oro,** which serves cappuccino and *panforte* (€1.75/100 grams/3.5 oz; balcony with 2 tables, closed Sun). **Bar Paninoteca** is on Vicolo di S. Paolo, on the stairs leading down to Il Campo (sandwiches, has a row of chairs on balcony, closed Mon).

At the bottom of Il Campo, a **Ciao** cafeteria offers easy self-service meals, no ambience, and no views. The crowded **Spizzico,** a pizza counter in the front half of Ciao, serves huge, inexpensive quarter pizzas; on sunny days, people take the pizza, trays and all, out on Il Campo for a picnic (daily 11:00–22:00, non-smoking section—*non fumatori*—in back, CC only in cafeteria, to left of city tower as you face it).

Budget eaters look for *pizza al taglio* shops, scattered throughout Siena, selling pizza by the slice. Picnickers enjoy the market held mornings (except Sun) behind Il Campo, on Piazza del Mercato. Of the grocery shops scattered throughout town, the biggest is called simply **Alimentari;** it's one block off Piazza Matteotti, toward Il Campo. Their pesto is the besto (Mon–Sat 8:00–19:30, Via Pianigiani 5, no sign).

Sienese Sweets

All over town, **Prodotti Tipici** shops sell Sienese specialties. Siena's claim to caloric fame is its *panforte*, a rich, chewy concoction of nuts, honey, and candied fruits that impresses even fruitcake-haters (although locals prefer a white macaroon-and-almond cookie called *ricciarelli*).

Transportation Connections—Siena

By train to: Florence (9/day, 1.75 hrs, last one at 21:00).

By bus to: Florence (2/hr, 1.25–2 hrs, by Tran bus), **San Gimignano** (6/day, 1.25 hrs, by Tran bus, more frequent with transfer in Poggibonsi), **Assisi** (2/day, 2 hrs, by Sena bus; the morning bus goes direct to Assisi, the afternoon bus might terminate at Santa Maria Angeli, from here catch a local bus to Assisi, 2/hr, 20 min), **Rome** (7/day, 3 hrs, by Sena bus, arrives at Rome's Tiburtina station), **Milan** (4/day, 14 hrs). Buses also connect Siena with Montepulciano, Montalcino, Chiusi, Pienza, and the San Galgano Monastery (see More Hill Towns in Orvieto chapter for information on these towns; get schedule in Siena). Schedules get sparse on Sunday.

Buses depart Siena from Piazza Gramsci, the train station, or both; confirm when you purchase your ticket. You can get tickets for Tran buses or Sena buses at the train station (Tran bus office: Mon–Sat 5:50–20:00; for Sena, buy tickets at *tabacchi* shop unless they've opened a separate office in the station), or easier and more central, under Piazza Gramsci at Sottopassaggio La Lizza (Tran bus office: daily 5:50–20:00, tel. 0577-204-225, toll-free tel. 800-373-760; Sena bus office: Mon–Sat 7:45–19:45, Sun 15:30–19:30, tel. 0577-283-203, www.senabus.it).

Sottopassaggio La Lizza, under Piazza Gramsci, has a cash machine (neither bus office accepts credit cards), luggage storage (€2.75/day, €1.50/half day, daily 7:00–19:30, no overnight storage), posted bus schedules, TV monitors (listing imminent departures), an elevator, and expensive WCs (€0.55). If you decide to depart Siena after the bus offices close, you can buy the ticket directly from the driver (and get charged a supplement).

On schedules, the fastest buses are marked *corse rapide*. Note that if a schedule lists your departure point as Via Tozzi or La Lizza, you catch the bus at Piazza Gramsci (Via Tozzi is the street that runs alongside Piazza Gramsci and La Lizza is the name of the bus station).

SAN GIMIGNANO

The epitome of a Tuscan hill town, with 14 medieval towers still standing (out of an original 72!), San Gimignano is a perfectly preserved tourist trap, so easy to visit and visually pleasing that it's a good stop. In the 13th century, back in the days of Romeo and Juliet, towns were run by feuding noble families. They'd periodically battle things out from the protection of their respective family towers. Pointy skylines were the norm in medieval Tuscany. But in San Gimignano, fabric was big business, and many of its towers were built simply to hang dyed fabric out to dry.

While the basic three-star sight here is the town of San Gimignano itself, there are a few worthwhile stops. From the town gate, shop straight up the traffic-free town's cobbled main drag to Piazza del Cisterna (with its 13th-century well). The town sights cluster around the adjoining Piazza del Duomo. Thursday is market day (8:00–13:00), but for local merchants, every day is a sales frenzy.

Tourist Information: The TI is in the old center on Piazza Duomo (daily March–Oct 9:00–13:00 & 15:00–19:00, Nov–Feb 9:00–13:00 & 14:00–18:00, changes money, tel. 0577-940-008, www.sangimignano.com, e-mail: prolocsg@tin.it). To see virtually all of the city's sights, consider a €10.50 combo-ticket (covers Collegiata, Torre Grossa, Museo Civico, archaeological museum, and more).

Sights—San Gimignano

Collegiata—This Romanesque church, with round windows and wide steps, is filled with fine Renaissance frescoes (€3.50, Mon–Fri 9:30–19:30, Sat 9:30–17:00, Sun 13:00–17:00).

Torre Grossa—The city's tallest tower can be scaled (€4.25, 60 meters/200 feet tall, March–Oct daily 9:30–19:20, Nov–Feb Sat–Thu 10:30–16:20, closed Fri), but the free *rocca* (castle), a short hike behind the church, offers a better view and a great picnic perch, especially at sunset.

Museo Civico—This museum, on Piazza Popolo, has a classy little painting collection with a 1422 altarpiece by Taddeo di Bartolo, honoring Saint Gimignano. You can see the saint with the town in his hands surrounded by events from his life (€3.75, €6.25 combo-ticket with Torre Grossa, same hours as Torre Grossa).

Sleeping and Eating in San Gimignano
(€1 = about $1, country code: 39, zip code: 53037)

Carla Rossi offers rooms and apartments—most with views—throughout the town (Db-from €60, most around €100, no CC, no breakfast, Via di Cellole 81, tel. & fax 0577-955-041, cellular 36-8352-3206, www.appartamentirossicarla.com, e-mail: cabusini@tin.it, SE). For a listing of private rooms, stop by or call **Associazione Strutture Extralberghiere** (Db-€52, no CC, no breakfast, Piazza della Cisterna, tel. 0577-943-190).

Eating: **Osteria del Carcere** has good food and prices (Via del Castello 13, no CC, just off Piazza della Cisterna, tel. 0577-941-905). Shops guarded by wild boar statues sell boar by the gram; carnivores buy some boar (*cinghiale*—pron. cheen-GAH-lay), cheese, bread, and wine and enjoy a picnic in the garden by the castle.

Transportation Connections—San Gimignano

To: Florence (hrly buses, 75 min, change in Poggibonsi; or catch the frequent 20-min shuttle bus to Poggibonsi and train to Florence), **Siena** (5/day, 1.25 hrs, or can change in Poggibonsi to catch train to Siena), **Volterra** (6/day, 2 hrs, change in Poggibonsi and Colle di Val d'Elsa). In San Gimignano, bus tickets are sold at the bar just inside the town gate. The town has no baggage-check service.

Drivers: You can't drive within the walled town of San Gimignano, but a car park awaits just a few steps outside.

ASSISI

Assisi is famous for its hometown boy, St. Francis, who made very good.

Around the year 1200, a simple friar from Assisi challenged the decadence of Church government and society in general with a powerful message of non-materialism, simplicity, and a "slow down and smell God's roses" lifestyle. Like Jesus, Francis taught by example. A huge monastic order grew out of his teachings, which were gradually embraced (some would say co-opted) by the Church. Clare, St. Francis' partner in poverty, founded the Order of the Poor Clares. Catholicism's purest example of simplicity is now glorified in beautiful churches. In 1939, Italy made Francis and Clare its patron saints.

Francis' message of love and sensitivity to the environment has a broad and timeless appeal. But any pilgrimage site will be commercialized, and the legacy of St. Francis is Assisi's basic industry. In summer, this Umbrian town bursts with flash-in-the-pan Francis fans and Franciscan knickknacks. Those able to see past the tacky friar mementos can actually have a "travel on purpose" experience.

Planning Your Time

Assisi is worth a day and a night. The town has a half day of sightseeing and another half day of wonder. The essential sight is the Basilica of St. Francis. For a good visit, take the Assisi Welcome Walk (below), ending at the basilica. Schedule time to linger on the main square. Hikers enjoy sunset at the castle.

Most visitors are day-trippers. While the town's a zoo by day, it's a delight at night. Assisi after dark is closer to a place Francis could call home.

Orientation

Crowned by a ruined castle at the top, Assisi spills downhill to its famous Basilica of St. Francis. The town is beautifully preserved and rich in history. The 1997 earthquake did more damage to the tourist industry than to the local buildings. Fortunately tourists are returning—whether art-lovers or pilgrims or both—drawn by Assisi's powerful sights.

Tourist Information: The TI is in the center of town on Piazza del Comune (Mon–Sat 9:00–14:00 & 15:30–18:30, Sun 9:00–13:00, tel. 075-812-534; visit www.umbria2000.it for info on Umbria, e-mail: info@iat.assisi.pg.it).

Also on (or just off) Piazza del Comune, you'll find the Roman temple of Minerva, a Romanesque tower, banks, a finely frescoed pharmacy, and an underground Roman Forum.

A combo-ticket *(biglietto cumulativo)* for €5.25 covers three sights—Rocca Maggiore (castle), Pinacoteca (paintings), and the Roman Forum; you'd need to see all three sights to save money (sold at participating sites).

Market day is Saturday on the Piazza Matteotti (which has a good parking garage). Your hotel may give you an Assisi Card, which offers discounts on parking and some restaurants.

Arrival in Assisi

By Train and Bus: City buses connect Assisi's train station with the old town of Assisi on the hilltop (€0.80, 2/hr, about 15–20 min), stopping at Piazza Unita d'Italia (near Basilica of St. Francis), then Largo Properzio (near Basilica of St. Clare), and finally Piazza Matteotti (top of old town). Going to the old town, buses usually leave from the train station at :16 and :46 past the hour. Going to the train station from the old town, buses usually run from Piazza Matteotti at :10 and :40 past the hour, and from Piazza Unita d'Italia at :17 and :47 past the hour. At Piazza Unita d'Italia, there are two bus stops *(fermata bus):* one sign reads *per f.s. S.M. Angeli* (take this bus to get to the train station), and the other reads *per P. Matteotti* (this bus goes to the top of the old town). Note that you can take this bus within Assisi to save a long walk uphill (e.g., visit basilica, walk down to bus stop, then catch bus up to the middle or top of town).

By Taxi: Taxis from the station to the old town run about €10. There are legitimate extra charges for luggage and night service, but beware: Many taxis rip off tourists by using tariff #2; the meter should be set on tariff #1 (€2.50 drop). You can check bags at the train station (€2.75, daily 7:00–19:30), but not in the old town. When departing the old town of Assisi, you'll find taxi stands at Piazza Unita d'Italia and the Basilica of St. Clare (or have your hotel call for you, tel. 075-812-600).

By Car: Drivers just coming in for the day should follow the signs to Piazza Matteotti's wonderful underground parking garage at the top of the town (which comes with bits of ancient Rome in the walls, €1/hr, or €11/day with Assisi Card—offered by many hotels; open 7:00–21:00, until 23:00 in summer).

Helpful Hints

Travel Agency: You can get train tickets and most bus tickets (but not for Siena) at Agenzia Viaggi Stoppini, between Piazza del Comune and the Basilica of St. Clare (Mon–Fri 9:00–12:30 & 15:30–19:00, Sat 9:00–12:30, closed Sun, Corso Mazzini 31, tel. 075-812-597). For Siena, you buy tickets on the bus (see "Transportation Connections," below).

Internet Access: Internet World has several computers and a non-smoking room (Thu–Tue 11:00–13:00 & 14:00–22:00, Wed 16:00–22:00, Via San Gabriele 25, a long block off Piazza del Comune, tel. 075-812-327).

Guide: Anne Robichaud, an American who has lived here since 1975, gives pricey though informative tours of the town and the countryside. Make it clear what you want (half day from €66 per person, full day from €99, cooking lessons, tel. 075-802-334, fax 075-813-698, www.annesitaly.com). Thanks to Anne for her help with the following self-guided walk.

Assisi Welcome Walk

There's much more to Assisi than St. Francis and what all the blitz tour groups see.

This walk, rated ▲▲, covers the town from Piazza Matteotti at the top, down to the Basilica of St. Francis at the bottom. To get to Piazza Matteotti, ride the bus from the train station (or from Piazza Unita d'Italia) to the last stop, or drive there (underground parking with Roman ruins).

The Roman Arena: Start 50 meters (165 feet) beyond Piazza Matteotti (at intersection at far end of parking lot, away from the city center—see map). A lane, named Via Anfiteatro Romano, leads to a cozy circular neighborhood built around a Roman arena. Assisi was an important Roman town. Circle the arena counterclockwise (the chain stretched across the road is to keep cars out, not you). Imagine how colorful the town laundry must have been in the last generation, when the women of Assisi gathered here to do their wash. Adjacent to the laundry is a small rectangular pool filled with water; above it are the coats of arms of the town's leading families. A few steps farther, hike up the stairs to the top of the hill for an aerial view of the oval arena. The Roman stones have long been absorbed into the medieval architecture. It was Roman tradition

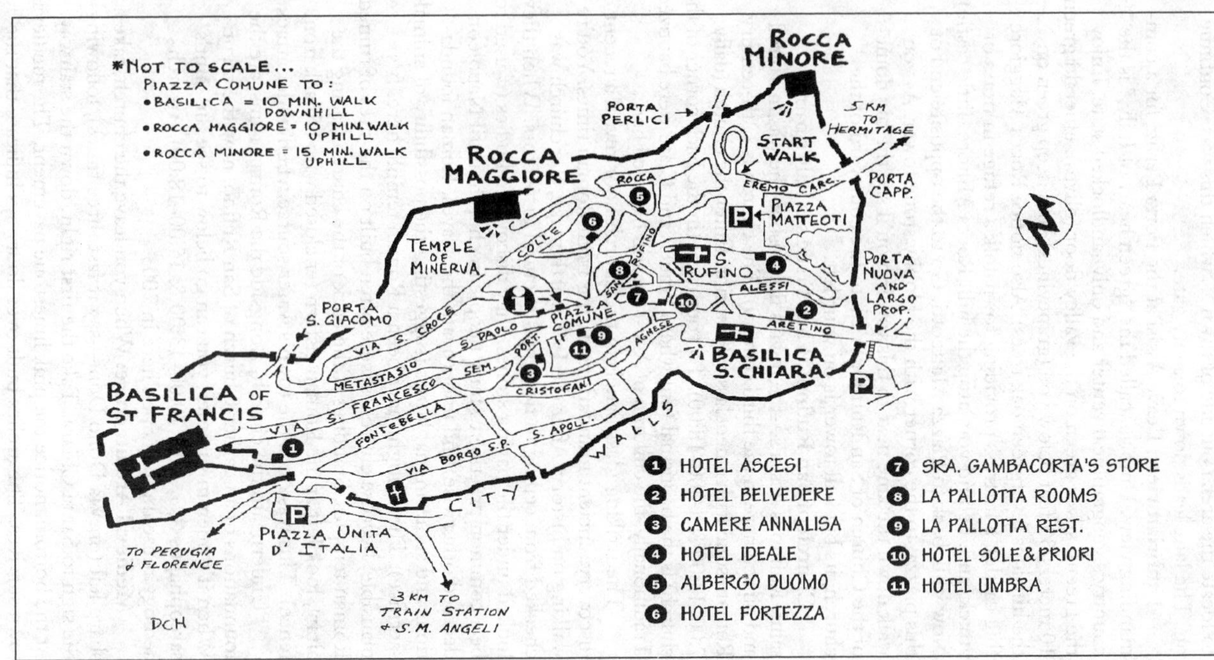
Assisi
*NOT TO SCALE...
PIAZZA COMUNE TO:
•BASILICA = 10 MIN. WALK DOWNHILL
•ROCCA MAGGIORE = 10 MIN. WALK UPHILL
•ROCCA MINORE = 15 MIN. WALK UPHILL
ROCCA MINORE
ROCCA MAGGIORE
PORTA PERLICI
5 KM TO HERMITAGE
START WALK
EREMO CARC.
PORTA CAPP.
ROCCA
PIAZZA MATTEOTI
COLLE
TEMPLE OF MINERVA
S. RUFINO
RUFINO
SAN
ALESSI
PORTA NUOVA AND LARGO PROP.
PORTA S. GIACOMO
PIAZZA COMUNE
ARETINO
VIA S. CROCE
S. PAOLO
PORT.
AGNESE
BASILICA S. CHIARA
METASTASIO
SEM.
CRISTOFANI
BASILICA OF ST FRANCIS
VIA S. FRANCESCO
FONTEBELLA
S. APOLL.
VIA BORGO S.P.
CITY WALLS
PIAZZA UNITA D' ITALIA
TO PERUGIA & FLORENCE
3 KM TO TRAIN STATION & S. M. ANGELI
DCH
1 HOTEL ASCESI
2 HOTEL BELVEDERE
3 CAMERE ANNALISA
4 HOTEL IDEALE
5 ALBERGO DUOMO
6 HOTEL FORTEZZA
7 SRA. GAMBACORTA'S STORE
8 LA PALLOTTA ROOMS
9 LA PALLOTTA REST.
10 HOTEL SOLE & PRIORI
11 HOTEL UMBRA

to locate the arena outside of town . . . which this was. Continue on. The lane leads down to a city gate.

Umbrian view: Leave Assisi at the Porta Perlici for a commanding view. Umbria, called the "green heart of Italy," is the country's geographical center and only landlocked state. Enjoy the greens: silver green on the valley floor (olives), emerald green 10 meters/33 feet below you (grapevines), and deep green on the hillsides (evergreen oak trees). Also notice Rocca Maggiore (big castle), a fortress providing townsfolk a refuge in times of attack, and, behind you, atop the hill, Rocca Minore (little castle). Now walk back to Piazza Matteotti. Go to the opposite end of this piazza, to the corner with the blobby stone tower. As you walk down the lane next to this tower, you'll see the big dome of the Church of San Rufino. Walk to the courtyard of the church; its big bell tower is on your left.

Church of San Rufino: While Francis is Italy's patron saint, Rufino is Assisi's—the town's first bishop (he was martyred and buried here in the third century). The church is 12th-century Romanesque with a neoclassical interior. Enter the church (daily 7:00–13:00 & 14:00–18:00). To your right (in the back corner of the church) is the baptismal font where Francis and Clare were baptized. Traditionally, the children of Assisi are still baptized here.

The striking glass panels in the church floor reveal a recent discovery: ancient foundations dating from Roman times. You're walking on history. After the 1997 earthquake, the church was checked from ceiling to floor by structural inspectors. When they looked under the paving stones, they discovered bodies (it used to be a common practice to bury people in church, until Napoleon decreed otherwise) and underneath the graves, Roman foundations and some animal bones (suggesting the possibility of animal sacrifice). There might have been a Roman temple here. It's plausible, because churches were often built on the sites of ruined Roman temples. Standing at the back of the church (facing the altar), look left at the Roman cistern (enclosed with a black iron fence). This was once the town's water source when under attack.

Underneath the church, alongside the Roman ruins, are the foundations of an earlier Church of San Rufino, now the crypt. When it's open in summer, you can go below to see the saint's sarcophagus (€3, daily 10:00–13:00 & 15:00–18:00). An archaeology museum may open here in 2003.

Medieval Architecture: When you leave the church, take a sharp left (on Via Dono Doni—say it fast three times), following the sign to Santa Chiara. Take the first right, down the stairway. At the bottom, notice the pink limestone pavement. The medieval town survives. The arches built over doorways indicate that the buildings date from the 12th through the 14th century. The vaults that turn lanes into tunnels are reminders of medieval urban expansion (mostly 15th century). While the population grew, people wanted to live protected within the walls, so Assisi became more dense. Medieval Assisi had five times the population density of today's Assisi. Notice the floating gardens. Assisi has a flowering balcony competition each June. When you arrive at a street, turn left, going slightly uphill for a block, then jog right, following the "S. Chiara" sign down to the Basilica of St. Clare.

Basilica of St. Clare (Santa Chiara): For a description of this stark, impressive church built to honor St. Clare, see "More Sights—Assisi," below.

Another Umbrian View: Belly up to the viewpoint in front of the basilica. On the left is the convent of St. Clare; below you, the olive grove of the Poor Clares since the 13th century; and, in the distance, a grand Umbrian view. Assisi overlooks the richest and biggest valley in otherwise hilly and mountainous Umbria. The municipality of Assisi has a population of 29,000, but only 1,000 people live in the old town. The lower town grew up with the coming of the railway in the 19th century. In the haze, the blue-domed church is St. Mary of the Angels (Santa Maria degli Angeli, see description below), the cradle of the Franciscan order, marking the place St. Francis lived and worked. This church, a popular pilgrimage sight today, is the first Los Angeles. Think about California. The Franciscans named L.A. (after this church), San Francisco, and even Santa Clara.

Arches and Artisans: From Via Santa Chiara, you can see two arches over the street. The arch at the back of the church dates from 1265. (Beyond it—out of view, the Porta Nuova, from 1316, marks the final expansion of Assisi.) Toward the city center (on Via Santa Chiara, the high road), an arch indicates the site of the Roman wall.

Forty meters (130 feet) before this arch, pop into the souvenir shop at #1b. The plaque over the door explains that the old printing press (a national monument now, just inside the door) was used to make fake documents for Jews escaping the Nazis in 1943 and 1944. The shop is run by a couple of artisans: The man makes frames out of medieval Assisi timbers; the woman makes the traditional Assisi, or Franciscan, cross-stitch.

Just past the gate and on your left is the La Pasteria natural products shop at Corso Mazzini 18b (across from entrance of Hotel Sole). Cooks love to peruse Umbrian wines, herbs, pâtés, and truffles, and sample an aromatic "fruit infusion." Ahead at Corso Mazzini 14d, the small shop (Poiesis) sells olive-wood carvings. Drop in. It's said that St. Francis made the first nativity scene to help teach the Christmas message. That's why you'll see so many of these in Assisi. Even today, nearby villages are enthusiastic about their "living" manger scenes. The Lisa Assisi shop (at Corso Mazzini 25b, across the street and to your right) has a delightful bargain basement with surviving bits of a 2,000-year-old mortarless Roman wall. Ahead of you, the columns of the Temple of Minerva mark the Piazza del Comune (described below). Sit at the fountain on the square for a few minutes of people-watching—don't you love Italy? Within 200 meters (650 feet) of this square, on either side, were the medieval walls. Imagine a commotion of 5,000 people confined within these walls. No wonder St. Francis needed an escape for some peace and quiet. I'll meet you over at the temple on the square.

Roman Temple/Christian Church: Assisi has always been a spiritual center. The Romans went to great lengths to make this Temple of Minerva a centerpiece of their city. Notice the columns cutting into the stairway. It was a tight fit here on the hilltop. The stairs probably went down triple the distance you see today. The church of Santa Maria sopra (over) Minerva was added in the ninth century. The bell tower is 13th century. Pop inside the temple/church (Mon–Sat 7:15–19:00, from 8:15 on Sun, closes at 17:00 in winter). Today's interior is 17th-century Baroque. Flanking the altar are the original Roman temple floor stones. You can even see the drains for the bloody sacrifices that took place here. Behind the statues of Peter and Paul, the original Roman embankment peeks through.

A few doors back toward the fountain, step into the 16th-century vaults from the old fish market. Notice the Italian flair for design. Even a smelly fish market was finely decorated. The art style is "grotesque"—literally, a painting in a grotto. This was painted in the early 1500s, a few years after Columbus brought turkeys back from the New World. The turkeys painted here may just be that bird's European debut. (Public WCs are a few steps off Piazza del Comune; near the fountain, go through Via dell' Arco dei Priori, then down the street on the left.)

Church of San Stefano: From the main square, hike past the temple up the high road, Via San Paolo. After 200 meters (650 feet), a sign directs you down a lane to San Stefano, which used to be outside the town walls in the days of St. Francis. Legend is that its bells miraculously rang on October 3, 1226, the day St. Francis died. Surrounded by cypress, fig, and walnut trees, it's a delightful bit of offbeat Assisi. Step inside. This is the typical rural Italian Romanesque church—no architect, just built by simple stonemasons who put together the most basic design. The lane zigzags down to Via San Francesco. Turn right and walk under the arch toward the Basilica of St. Francis.

Via San Francesco: This was the main drag leading from the town to the basilica holding the body of St. Francis. Francis was a big deal even in his own day. He died in 1226 and was made a saint in 1228—the same year the basilica's foundations were laid—and his body was moved in by 1230. Assisi was a big-time pilgrimage center, and this street was a booming place. Notice the fine medieval balcony just below the arch. A few meters farther down (on the left), cool yourself at the fountain. The hospice next door was built in 1237 to house pilgrims. Notice the three surviving faces of its fresco: Jesus, Francis, and Clare.

Basilica of St. Francis

A ▲▲▲ sight, the Basilica de San Francesco is one of the artistic and religious highlights of Europe. In 1226, St. Francis was buried (with the outcasts he had stood by) outside of his town on the "Hill of the Damned"—now called the "Hill of Paradise." The basilica is frescoed from top to bottom by the leading artists of the day: Cimabue, Giotto, Simone Martini, and Pietro Lorenzetti. A 13th-century historian wrote, "No more exquisite monument to the Lord has been built."

From a distance, you see the huge arcades "supporting" the basilica. These were 15th-century quarters for the monks. The arcades lining the square leading to the church housed medieval pilgrims.

There are three parts to the church: the upper basilica, the lower basilica, and the saint's tomb (below the lower basilica). Modest dress is required to enter the church—no sleeveless tops or shorts for men, women, or children (free entry, daily 6:30–19:00, relic chapel in lower basilica closes at 18:30, tel. 075-819-0084, www.sanfrancescoassisi.org, e-mail: assisisanfrancesco@krenet.it).

In the 1997 earthquake, the lower basilica—with walls nearly three meters (9 feet) thick—was undamaged. The upper basilica, with bigger windows and walls only one meter (3 feet) thick, was damaged. After restoration was completed, the entire church was reopened to visitors in late 1999.

Start at the lower entrance in the courtyard. Opposite the entry to the lower basilica is the information center Ask about their tours in English—or call or e-mail in advance. (Mon–Sat 9:00–12:00 & 14:00–17:00, Sun 14:00–17:00, tel. 075-819-0084, e-mail: assistours@aol.com; a WC is a half block away—from courtyard, look up the road at the squat brick building; walk alongside the right of it to find the WC). The info center sells an excellent guidebook, *The Basilica of Saint Francis—A Spiritual Pilgrimage* (€2.50, by Goulet, McInally, and Wood) which I used as a source for the following self-guided tour.

The Basilica of St. Francis, a theological work of genius, can be difficult for the 21st-century tourist/pilgrim to appreciate. Since the basilica is the reason most people visit Assisi, and the message of St. Francis has even the least devout blessing the town Vespas, I've designed a *Mona Winks*–type tour with the stress on the place's theology, rather than art history.

At the doorway of the lower basilica, look up and see St. Francis (in a small gold triangle), who greets you with a Latin inscription (arching over the doorway). Sounding a bit like John Wayne, he says the equivalent of "Slow down and be joyful, pilgrim. You've reached the Hill of Paradise, and this church will knock your spiritual socks off." Start with the tomb (turn left into the nave, midway down the nave to your right follow signs and go downstairs to the tomb). Grab a pew (for more light to read by, sit in back).

The message: Francis' message caused a stir. He traded a life of power and riches for one of obedience, poverty, and chastity. The Franciscan existence (Brother Sun, Sister Moon, and so on) is a space where God, man, and the natural world frolic harmoniously. Franciscan friars, known as the "Jugglers of God," were a joyful part of the community. In an Italy torn by fighting between towns and families, Francis promoted peace and the restoration of order. (He set an example by reconstructing a crumbled chapel.) While the Church was waging bloody Crusades, Francis pushed ecumenism and understanding. Even today the leaders of the world's great religions meet here for summits.

This rich building seems to contradict the teachings of the poor monk it honors, but it was built as an act of religious and civic pride to remember the hometown saint. It was also designed, and still functions, as a pilgrimage center and a splendid classroom.

The tomb: In medieval times, pilgrims came to Assisi because St. Francis was buried here. Holy relics were the "ruby slippers" of medieval Europe. They gave you power—got your prayers answered and helped you win wars—and ultimately helped you get back to your eternal Kansas. Assisi made no bones about promoting the saint's relics, but hid his tomb for obvious reasons of security. Not until 1818 was the tomb opened to the public. The saint's remains are above the altar in the stone box with the iron ties. His four closest friends are buried in the corners of the room. Opposite the altar, up four steps in between the entrance and exit, notice the small gold box behind the metal grill; this contains the remains of Francis' rich Roman patron, Jacopa dei Settesoli. Climb back to the lower nave.

The lower basilica is appropriately Franciscan, subdued and Romanesque. The nave was frescoed with parallel scenes from the lives of Christ and Francis—connected by a ceiling of stars.

Unfortunately, after the church was built and decorated, the popularity of the Franciscans meant side chapels needed to be built. Huge arches were cut out of some scenes, but others survive. In the fresco directly above the entry to the tomb, Christ is being taken down from the cross (just the bottom half of his body can be seen, to the left), and it looks like the story is over. Defeat. But in the opposite fresco (above the tomb's exit), we see Francis preaching to the birds, reminding the faithful that the message of the Gospel survives.

These stories directed the attention of the medieval pilgrim to the altar, where, through the sacraments, he met God. The church was thought of as a community of believers sailing toward God. The prayers coming out of the nave (*navis*, or ship) fill the triangular sections of the ceiling—called *vele*, or sails—with spiritual wind. With a priest for a navigator and the altar for a helm, faith propels the ship.

Stand behind the altar (toes to the bottom step) and look up. The three scenes in front of you are, to the right, "Obedience" (Francis wearing a yoke); to the left, "Chastity" (in a tower of purity held up by two angels); and straight ahead, "Poverty." Here Jesus blesses the marriage as Francis slips a ring on Lady Poverty. In the foreground two "self-sufficient" merchants (the new rich of a thriving North Italy) are throwing sticks and stones at the bride. But Poverty, in her patched wedding dress, is fertile and strong, and even those brambles blossom into a rosebush crown.

Putting your heels to the altar and bending back like a drum major, look up at Francis, who traded a life of earthly simplicity for glory in heaven. Now, turn to the right and march…

In the corner, steps lead down into the relic chapel. Circle the room clockwise. You'll see the silver chalice and plate Francis used for the bread and wine of the Eucharist (in small, dark, windowed case set into wall, marked *Calice con Patena*). Francis believed that his personal possessions should be simple, but the items used for worship should be made of the finest materials. In the corner display case is a small section of the haircloth worn by Francis as penitence. In the next corner are the tunic and slippers Francis wore during his last days. Next, find a prayer (in a fancy silver stand) that St. Francis wrote for Brother Leo, signed with his tau cross. Next is a papal document (1223) legitimizing the Franciscan order and assuring his followers that they were not risking a (deadly) heresy charge. Finally, see the tunic lovingly patched and stitched by followers of the five-foot, four-inch-tall St. Francis.

Return up the stairs to the lower basilica. You're in the transept. This church brought together the greatest Sienese (Martini and Lorenzetti) and Florentine (Cimabue and Giotto) artists of the day. Look around at the painted scenes. In 1300, this was radical art—believable homespun scenes, landscapes, trees, real people. Study the crucifix (by Giotto) with the eight sparrowlike angels. For the first time, holy people are expressing emotion: One angel turns her head sadly at the sight of Jesus, and another scratches her hands down her cheeks, drawing blood. Mary, previously in control, has fainted in despair. The Franciscans, with their goal of bringing God to the people, found a natural partner in Europe's first modern painter, Giotto.

To see the Renaissance leap, look at the painting to the right. This is by Cimabue—it's Gothic, without the 3-D architecture, natural backdrop, and slice-of-life reality of the Giotto work. Cimabue's St. Francis is considered by some to be the earliest existing portrait of the saint. To the left, at eye level, enjoy the Martini saints and their exquisite halos.

Francis' friend, "Sister Death," was really not all that terrible. In fact, Francis would like to introduce you to her now (above and to the right of the door leading into the relic chapel). Go ahead, block the light and meet her. I'll wait for you upstairs, in the courtyard, next to the fine bookstore. By the way, monks in robes are not my idea of easy-to-approach people, but the Franciscans are still God's jugglers (and most of them speak English).

From the courtyard, climb the stairs to the **upper basilica**. Built later than the lower, the upper basilica is brighter, Gothic (the first Gothic church in Italy, 1228), and nearly wallpapered by Giotto. This gallery of frescoes by Giotto and his assistants shows 28 scenes from the life of St. Francis.

Look for these scenes:

- **A common man spreads his cape before Francis** (immediately to right of altar, as you face altar) out of honor and recognition to a man who will do great things. Symbolized by the rose window, God looks over the 20-year-old Francis, a dandy imprisoned in his selfishness. A medieval pilgrim fluent in symbolism would understand this because the Temple of Minerva (which you saw today on Assisi's Piazza del Comune) was a prison at that time. The rose window, which never existed, is symbolic of God's eye.
- **Francis offers his cape to a needy stranger** (next panel). Prior to this act of kindness, Francis had been captured in battle, held as a prisoner of war, and then released.
- **Francis is visited by the Lord in a dream** (next panel) and told to leave the army and go home.
- **Francis relinquishes his possessions** (two panels down), giving his dad his clothes, his credit cards, and even his time-share condo on Capri. Naked Francis is covered by the bishop, symbolizing his transition from a man of the world to a man of the Church.

• **The pope has a vision** (next panel) of a simple man propping up his teetering Church. This led to the papal acceptance of the Franciscan reforms.

• **Christ appears to Francis** being carried by a seraph—a six-winged angel (other side of church, fourth panel from the door). For the strength of his faith, Francis is given the marks of his master, the "battle scars of love" . . . the stigmata. Throughout his life, Francis was interested in chivalry; now he's joined the spiritual knighthood.

• **Francis preaches to the birds** (to the right of the exit). Francis was more than a nature-lover. The birds, of different species, represent the diverse flock of humanity and nature, all created and loved by God and worthy of each other's love.

Before you leave, look at the ceiling above the altar and front entrance to see large tan patches; these careful repairs were made after the basilica was damaged in the 1997 earthquake. It's a blessing that so many of the frescoes remain.

Near the outside of the upper basilica are the Latin pax (peace) and the Franciscan tau cross in the grass. Tav ("tau" in Greek), the last letter in the Hebrew alphabet, is symbolic of faithfulness to the end. Francis signed his name with this simple character. Tav and pax. For more pax, take the high lane back to town, up to the castle, or into the countryside.

More Sights—Assisi

▲Basilica of Saint Clare (Basilica di Santa Chiara)—Dedicated to the founder of the order of the Poor Clares, this Umbrian Gothic church is simple, in keeping with the Poor Clares' dedication to a life of contemplation. The church was built in 1265, and the huge buttresses were added in the next century. The interior's fine frescoes were whitewashed in Baroque times. The Chapel of the Crucifix of San Damiano, on the right (actually an earlier church incorporated into this one), has the crucifix that supposedly spoke to St. Francis, leading to his conversion in 1206. Stairs lead from the nave down to the tomb of Saint Clare. Her tomb is at the far end. The walls depict scenes from Clare's life and death (1193–1253); the saint's robes are in a large case between the stairs. The attached cloistered community of the Poor Clares has flourished for 700 years (church open daily 6:30–12:00 & 14:00–18:00).

Roman Forum (Foro Romano)—For a look at Assisi's Roman roots, tour the Roman Forum, which is actually under Piazza del Comune. The floor plan is sparse, the odd bits and pieces obscure, but it's well-explained in English (a 10-page booklet is loaned to you when you enter) and you can actually walk on an ancient

Roman road. For an orientation, look at the poster for sale at the entry to get an idea of the original setting of forum and temple (€2 entry, or included in €5.25 combo-ticket, daily 10:00–13:00 & 15:00–18:00, closes at 17:00 in winter; from Piazza del Comune, go one-half block down Via San Francesco, it's on your right).

Pinacoteca—This small museum attractively displays its 13th- to 17th-century art (mainly frescoes), with general information in English in nearly every room. There's a Giotto Madonna (damaged) and a rare secular fresco (to right of Giotto), but it's mainly a peaceful walk through a pastel world, best for art-lovers (€2.20, included in €5.25 combo-ticket, daily 10:00–13:00 & 14:00–18:00, Via San Francesco 10, on main drag between Piazza del Comune and Basilica of St. Francis, tel. 075-812-033).

▲**Rocca Maggiore**—The "big castle" offers a good look at a 14th-century fortification and a fine view of Assisi and the Umbrian countryside (€2.20, included in €5.25 combo-ticket, daily 10:00–sunset, opens at 9:00 July–Aug). If you're counting euros, the view is just as good from outside the castle, and the interior is pretty bare. For a picnic with the same birdsong and views that inspired St. Francis, leave all the tourists and hike to the Rocca Minore (small castle) above Piazza Matteotti.

Santa Maria degli Angeli

This flat, modern part of Assisi has one major sight: The basilica that marks the spot where Francis lived, worked, and died.

▲▲**St. Mary of the Angels (Basilica di Santa Maria degli Angeli)**—This huge basilica, towering above the buildings below Assisi, was built around the tiny but historic Porziuncola Chapel (now directly under the dome). When the pope gave Francis his blessing, he was given this *porziuncola,* or "small portion"—a little land with a fixer-upper chapel—on which Francis and his followers established their order. As you enter, notice the sketch on the door showing the original little chapel with the monks' huts around it and Assisi before it had its huge basilica. Francis lived here after he founded the Franciscan Order in 1208, and this was where he consecrated St. Clare as the Bride of Christ. A chapel called Cappella del Transito marks the place where Francis died (behind and to the right of the Porziuncola Chapel). Follow signs to the Roseta (Rose Garden). Francis, fighting off a temptation that he never named, threw himself onto roses. As the story goes, the thorns immediately dropped off the roses. Ever since, thornless roses have grown here. Look through the window at the rose garden (to the right of the statue of Francis petting a sheep). The Rose Chapel (Cappella delle Rose) is built over the place where Francis lived. The bookshop has some books in English and the free *museo* has a few monastic cells interesting to pilgrims (museum open Mon–Sat 9:00–12:00 & 15:00–18:00, Sun 15:00–18:00).

Hours: The basilica is open May–Oct 7:00–18:30, Nov–April 7:00–12:00 & 14:00 until sunset. There's a little TI to your right as you face the church (supposedly open daily 9:00–12:00 & 15:00–18:00 but may be closed, tel. 075-80511). A WC is 40 meters (130 feet) to the right of the TI, behind the hedge.

Transportation Connections: To get to Basilica di Santa Maria degli Angeli from Assisi's train station, it's quicker to walk (exit station left, take first left at McDonald's, 5-minute walk) than to take the orange city bus' circuitous route (though with lots of luggage, you might prefer the bus). When you're leaving the basilica, you can catch the bus directly to the station and on to the old town of Assisi (as you leave church, stop is to your right, next to basilica). The orange city buses run twice hourly (buses to the old town depart the basilica at :10 and :40 after the hour; tickets cost €0.80 if you buy at *tabacchi* or newsstand, €1.10 if you buy from driver; 15–20 minute ride up to old town).

It's efficient to visit this basilica either on your way to the old town of Assisi or when you leave. You can easily walk to the basilica from the station (baggage check available, €2.75, access through shop). If you're heading to Siena next, visit the basilica right before you leave, because that's where you'll catch the bus to Siena (as you leave basilica, stop is to your right, across the street, buy ticket on bus); see "Transportation Connections—Assisi," below.

Sleeping in Assisi

(€1 = about $1, country code: 39, zip code: 06081)

Sleep Code: **S** = Single, **D** = Double/Twin, **T** = Triple, **Q** = Quad, **b** = bathroom, **s** = shower only, **CC** = Credit Cards accepted, **no CC** = Credit Cards not accepted, **SE** = Speaks English, **NSE** = No English.

To help you sort easily through these listings, I've divided the rooms into three categories based on the price for a standard double room with bath:

Higher Priced—Most rooms more than €90.

Moderately Priced—Most rooms €90 or less.

Lower Priced—Most rooms €55 or less.

The town accommodates large numbers of pilgrims on religious holidays. Finding a room at any other time should be easy. See the map on page 965 for hotel locations.

HIGHER PRICED

Hotel Umbra, the best splurge in the center, feels like a quiet villa in the middle of town (25 rooms, Sb-€77, Db-€92, Tb-€120, includes breakfast, CC, air-con, peaceful garden and view terrace, most rooms have views, good restaurant, dinner only, 100 meters, or 330 feet, below Piazza del Comune at Via degli Archi 6, tel. 075-812-240, fax 075-813-653, www.hotelumbra.it, e-mail: humbra@mail.caribusiness.it, family Laudenzi SE).

Hotel Dei Priori is a three-star, palatial place in the old center, with big, quiet, recently renovated rooms that have all the comforts (Db-€100–120, superior Db-€140–160, includes breakfast, CC, elevator, air-con, Corso Mazzini 15, tel. 075-812-237, fax 075-816-804, www.assisihotel.net, e-mail: info@assisihotel.net, SE).

MODERATELY PRICED

Hotel Ideale, on the top edge of town overlooking the valley, offers 12 bright, modern rooms, view balconies, peaceful garden, free parking, and a warm welcome (Sb-€47, Db-€78, includes big-for-Italy breakfast, CC, most rooms with views, Piazza Matteotti 1, tel. 075-813-570, fax 075-813-020, www.hotelideale.it, e-mail: info@hotelideale.it, sisters Lara and Ilaria SE). This hotel, at the top of the old town, is close to the bus stop (and parking lot) at Piazza Matteotti, easy to reach by public transportation.

Hotel Sole is well-located, with 40 spacious, comfortable rooms in a 15th-century building (Sb-€41, Db-€62, Tb-€81, breakfast-€6.25, CC, half its rooms are in a newer annex across the street, some rooms have views and balconies, elevator in annex, Corso Mazzini 35, 100 meters, or 330 feet, before Basilica of St. Clare, tel. 075-812-373, fax 075-813-706, e-mail: soleassisi@hotmail.com, SE).

Hotel Belvedere, which offers good views and 16 basic rooms, is run by Enrico and his American wife, Mary (Db-€76, breakfast-€5.25, elevator, 2 blocks past Basilica of St. Clare at Via Borgo Aretino 13, tel. 075-812-460, fax 075-816-812, e-mail: assisihotelbelvedere@hotmail.com, SE). Their attached restaurant is good, by request and reservation only.

LOWER PRICED

Hotel Ascesi has an inviting little lobby, nine pleasant rooms, and a tiny terrace, located within a block of the Basilica of St. Francis (Sb-€34, Db-€52, breakfast-€3.75, CC, air-con, Via Frate Elia 5, walk up from Piazza Unita d'Italia, take a left at Piazzetta Ruggero Bonghi, see sign on right, tel. & fax 075-812-420, e-mail: hotelascesi@libero.it). This hotel is near the bus stop and parking lot at the bottom of town (Piazza Unita d'Italia), handy if you're packing lots of luggage.

Hotel La Fortezza is a simple, modern, and quiet place with seven rooms (Db-€49, Tb-€67, Qb-€78, CC, a short block above Piazza del Comune at Vicolo della Fortezza 19b, tel. 075-812-993, fax 075-819-8035, www.lafortezzahotel.com, e-mail: lafortezza@lafortezzahotel.com, Lorenzo SE).

Albergo Il Duomo is tidy and *tranquillo*, with nine rooms on a stair-step lane one block up from San Rufino (S-€29, Sb-€31, D-€35, Db-€42, breakfast-€4.25, CC, Vicolo S. Lorenzo 2; from Church of San Rufino follow sign, then turn left on stair-stepped alley; tel. & fax 075-812-742, www.hotelsanrufino.it, e-mail: info@sanrufino.it, Carlo SE).

Camere Annalisa Martini is a cheery home swimming in vines and roses in the town's medieval core. Annalisa speaks English and enthusiastically accommodates her guests with a picnic garden, a washing machine (small load-€3), a refrigerator, and six homey rooms (S-€20, Sb-€23, D-€31, Db-€36, Tb-€47, Qb-€57, 3 rooms share 2 bathrooms, no breakfast, no CC, 1 block from Piazza del Comune, go downhill toward basilica, turn left on Via S. Gregorio to #6, tel. & fax 075-813-536).

La Pallotta, a recommended restaurant (see "Eating," below), offers seven clean, bright rooms (note that rooms and restaurant are in different locations). Rooms #12 and #18 have views (Db-€47, CC, view terrace, Via San Rufino 4, go up short flight of stairs outside building to reach entrance, a block off Piazza del Comune, tel. & fax 075-812-307, www.pallottaassisi.it, SE).

Signora Gambacorta rents several decent rooms and has a roof terrace on a quiet lane (Via Sermei 9) just above St. Chiara. There is no sign or reception desk, so you'll need to check in at her shop a half block east of Piazza del Comune at San Gabriele 17—look for the sign "Bottega di Gambacorta" (S-€20 Db-€40, Tb-€60, 2-night stays preferred, no breakfast but has kitchen, store open Mon–Wed and Fri–Sat 8:00–13:00 & 16:30–19:30, Thu 8:00–13:00, closed Sun—if you can't arrive when store is open, call when you arrive, tel. 075-812-454, fax 075-813-186, www.ilbongustaio.com/inglese/eerooms.htm, e-mail: geo@umbrars.com, a little English spoken). She also has two apartments for stays of at least four nights (3 rooms-€90/day, 5 rooms-€200/day, kitchen, no breakfast).

Hostel: Francis probably would have bunked with the peasants in Assisi's **Ostello della Pace** (€13 beds in 4- to 8-bed rooms, Qb-€15 apiece, includes breakfast, dinner-€8, CC, laundry, lockout 10:00–15:30, get off bus at Piazza Unita d'Italia, then take 10-min walk to Via di Valecchie 177, tel. & fax 075-816-767, Giuseppe SE).

Eating in Assisi

For a fine Assisian perch and good regional cooking, relax on a terrace overlooking Piazza del Comune at **Taverna dei Consoli** (€13 4-course *menu*, also à la carte, Thu–Tue 12:00–14:30 & 19:00–21:30, closed Wed and Jan, CC, tel. 075-812-516, friendly owner Moreno, who doesn't speak English, recommends the *bruschetta*, *stringozzi*—noodles, *agnello*—lamb, and *cinghiale*—boar). Moreno also runs **Locanda del Podestà** with the same high standards (12:00–15:30 & 19:00–22:00, 5-min walk uphill from basilica, San Giacomo 6C, tel. 075-813-034).

La Pallotta, a local favorite run by a friendly, hardworking family, offers regional specialties, such as *piccione* (pigeon), *coniglio* (rabbit), and more typical food (€14.50 *menu*, Wed–Mon 12:00–14:30 & 19:15–21:30, closed Tue, CC, also rents rooms—see listing above, a few steps off Piazza del Comune, through gate across from temple/church, Vicolo della Volta Pinta, tel. 075-812-649).

Osteria Piazzetta dell Erba is a fun, little, family-run place a block above Piazza del Comune, serving good, basic Umbrian specialties next to the Gambacorta grocery (Tue–Sun 12:00–14:00 & 19:00–21:45, closed Mon, CC, Via San Gabriele 156, tel. 075-815-352).

Pizzeria/Tavola Calda dal Carro is popular, affordable, and friendly (good pizzas and €12 *menu*, closed Wed, Vicolo di Nepis 2, leave Piazza del Comune on Via San Gabriele, then take first right—down a stepped lane, tel. 075-815-249).

Ristorante San Francesco is the place to splurge for dinner (Thu–Tue 12:00–14:30 & 19:30–22:00, closed Wed, CC, facing Basilica of St. Francis at Via San Francesco 52, tel. 075-812-329).

For a picnic of Umbrian treats, try **La Bottega dei Sapori** for its good prosciutto sandwiches and speciality items, including truffle paste. Friendly Fabrizio may give you a taste (9:00–20:00, Piazza del Comune 34, tel. 075-812-294).

Transportation Connections—Assisi

By train to: Rome (5/day, 1.75–2.5 hrs), **Florence** (5/day, 2–2.75 hrs, more with transfers at Terontola and Cortona), **Orvieto** (7/day, 2 hrs, transfer in Terontola), **Siena** (6/day, 3.25 hrs, transfers in Chiusi and Terontola; bus is more efficient). Train station: tel. 075-804-0272, train info: tel. 848-888-088.

By bus to: Rome (3/day, 3 hrs, departs Assisi's Piazza Unita d'Italia, arrives at Rome's Tiburtina station), **Siena** (1/day, 2 hrs, €8.25, pay driver, departs from Basilica di Santa Maria degli Angeli near Assisi train station; to get from station to basilica, exit station left, take first left at McDonald's; as you face basilica, bus stop is to your left across street). Don't take the bus to Florence (1/day, departs Piazza Unita d'Italia at 6:45 a.m., 2.75 hrs); the train is better.

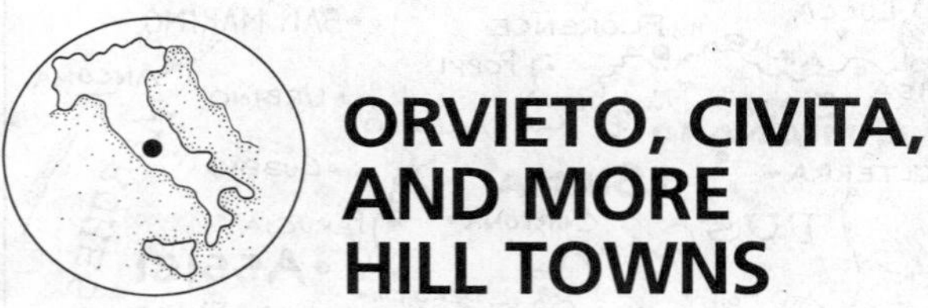

ORVIETO, CIVITA, AND MORE HILL TOWNS

Sun-dried tomatoes, homemade pasta, wispy cypress-lined driveways following desolate ridges to fortified 16th-century farmhouses, and dusty old-timers warming the same bench day after day while soccer balls buzz around them like innocuous flies... the sun-soaked hill towns of Tuscany and Umbria offer what to many is the quintessential Italian experience.

Tuscany and Umbria have replaced Provence as *the* trendy destination in Europe among Americans. If you really want to do the *Under the Tuscan Sun* thing correctly, you'll need to supplement this book with one specializing in the subtle delights of this area. You'll also need a readiness to encounter plenty of like-minded tourists—especially if you visit any hill town that is a household word among American travelers.

In this chapter, I cover the grand and classic town of Orvieto; my longtime favorite, the tiny, obscure, and (to be honest) dying hilltown of Civita; and a smattering of the most noteworthy towns of Umbria and Tuscany. If you have the time (or a car) and a hankering to see what all the fuss over this region is about, this material will give you the basics.

For a relaxing break from the intensity, traffic, and obligatory museums of big-city Italy, settle down in an *agriturismo*—a farmhouse that rents out rooms to travelers (usually for a minimum of a week in high season). These rural B&Bs—almost by definition in the middle of nowhere—provide a good home base from which to find the magic of Tuscany and Umbria. See the end of this chapter for information on *agriturismo* lodgings, some specific listings, and resources for finding out more.

Orvieto and Civita are doable by public transportation. The other hill towns mentioned in the chapter are easier to visit

Hill Towns

by car. This rugged and hilly region, with its meager public transportation and tortured little roads, seems bigger than it is. With a car and some motion-sickness pills, it's a delight.

Planning Your Time

Orvieto and Civita are worth a day and an overnight—ideally, an afternoon, night, and morning. Most people start with Orvieto, which is an easy train stop on the Florence–Rome line, then continue to Civita by bus.

Orvieto has a good half day of sightseeing. Spend the night in Orvieto if you want a variety of restaurants, or in Civita if you want peace. Civita is also worth a half day; a chunk of that time is spent hiking to and from the town from Bagnoregio (connected by bus with Orvieto, daily except Sun).

ORVIETO

Umbria's grand hill town, while no secret, is worth a quick look. The town sits majestically on a big chunk of tufa rock. Streets are lined with exhaust-stained buildings made from the volcanic stuff.

Hill Towns: Public Transportation

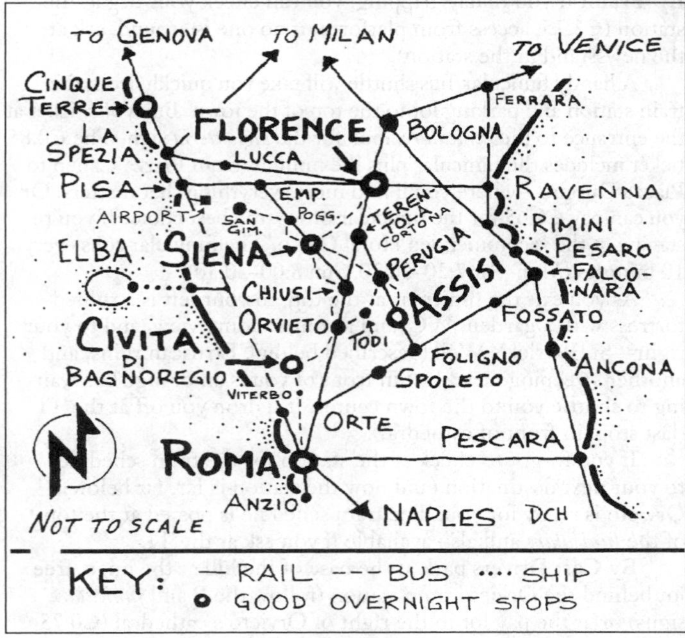

Orvieto—just off the freeway, with three popular claims to fame (cathedral, Classico wine, and ceramics)—is loaded with tourists by day and quiet by night. Drinking a shot of wine in a ceramic cup as you gaze up at the cathedral lets you experience Orvieto all at once.

Piazza Cahen is a key transportation hub at the entry to the hilltop town. As you exit the funicular, the town center is straight ahead.

Tourist Information: The TI is at Piazza Duomo 24 on the cathedral square (Mon–Fri 8:15–14:00 & 16:00–19:00, Sat 10:00–13:00 & 16:00–19:00, Sun 10:00–12:00 & 16:00–18:00, tel. 0763-341-772). Pick up the free city map and ask about train and bus schedules. The TI sells a €1.50 admission ticket for the Chapel of St. Brizio (within the cathedral). For a longer visit, consider buying the €10.50 Carta Unica combo-ticket, which covers entry to the chapel, Archaeological Museum (Museo Claudio Faina e Museo Civico), Underground Orvieto Tours, and Torre del Moro (tower), plus your public transportation (bus and funicular) for one day or five hours of parking (at *parcheggio* Campo della Fiera).

Market Days: Drop by Piazza del Popolo with your cloth shopping bag on Tuesday and Saturday mornings.

Arrival in Orvieto

By Train: If you're day-tripping, you can check your bag at the station (€2.75, access from platform; if no one is around, ask at the newsstand in the station).

A handy funicular/bus shuttle will take you quickly from the train station and parking lot to the top of the town. Buy your ticket at the entrance to the *funiculare;* look for the *biglietteria* sign. The €0.85 ticket includes the funicular plus the minibus from Piazza Cahen to Piazza Duomo—where you'll find most everything that matters. Or you can pay €0.65 for the funicular only—the best choice if you're staying at the recommended Hotel Corso. The funicular runs every 10 minutes (Mon–Sat 7:20–20:30, Sun 8:00–20:30).

As you exit the funicular at the top, to your left is a ruined fortress with a garden, WC, and a commanding view, and to your right—St. Patrick's Well (described below), Etruscan ruins, and another sweeping view. Just in front of you is an orange bus waiting to shuttle you to the town center. It'll drop you off at the TI (last stop, in front of cathedral).

If you forgot to check at the station for the train schedule to your next destination (and now the station is far, far below), Orvieto is ready for you. The train schedule is posted at the top of the *funiculare* and also available if you ask at the TI.

By Car: Drivers park at the base of the hill at the huge, free lot behind the Orvieto train station (follow the P and *funiculare* signs) or at the pay lot to the right of Orvieto's cathedral (€0.75 for first hour, €0.60/hr thereafter).

Sights—Orvieto's Piazza Duomo

▲▲Duomo—The cathedral has Italy's most striking facade (from 1330), thanks to architect Lorenzo Maitani and many others. Grab a gelato (to the left of the church) and study this fascinating, gleaming mass of mosaics and sculpture.

At the base of the cathedral, the broad marble pillars carved with biblical scenes tell the story of the world from left to right. The pillar on the far left shows the Creation (see the snake and Eve), next is the Tree of Jesse, next the New Testament (look for Mary and a manger, etc.), and on the far right—the Last Judgment (with hell, of course, at the bottom). Each pillar is topped by a bronze symbol of one of the evangelists: angel (Matthew), lion (Mark), eagle (John), and bull (Luke). The bronze doors are modern, by the Sicilian sculptor Emilio Greco. (A museum devoted to Greco's work is to the right of the church; it's labeled simply *Museo.*) In the mosaic below the rose window, Mary is transported to heaven. In the uppermost mosaic, Mary is crowned.

Why such an impressive church in a little tufa town? Because

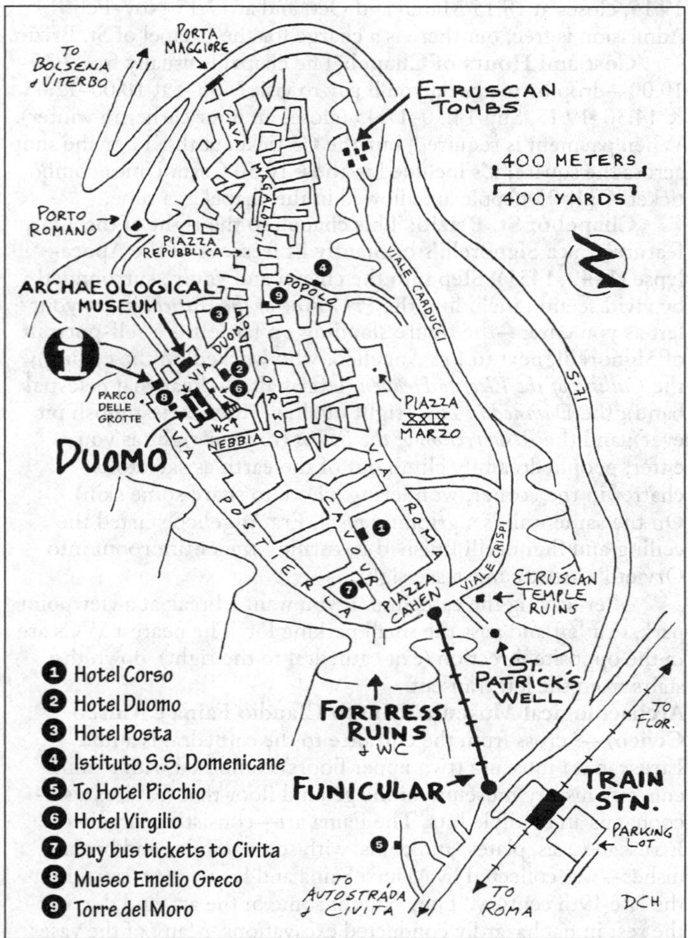

of a blood-stained cloth. In the 1260s, a Bohemian priest—who doubted that the bread used in Communion was really the body of Christ—came to Rome on a pilgrimage. On his return journey, he worshiped in Bolsena, near Orvieto. During Mass, the bread bled, staining a linen cloth. The cloth was brought to the pope, who was visiting Orvieto at the time. Such a miraculous relic required a magnificent church. You can see the actual cloth from the Miracle of Bolsena displayed in the chapel to the left of the altar.

Hours of Cathedral: April–Sept daily 7:30–12:45 & 14:30–19:15; closes at 18:15 March and Oct, and at 17:15 Nov–Feb. Admission is free, but there is a charge for the Chapel of St. Brizio.

Cost and Hours of Chapel: The chapel is usually free 7:30–10:00—drop by to check; you'll pay to visit Mon–Sat 10:00–12:45 & 14:30–19:15, Sun 14:30–17:45 (closes an hour earlier in winter). When payment is required, buy the €3 ticket at the TI or the shop across the square; it's included in the €10.50 Carta Unica combo-ticket. Only 25 people are allowed in the chapel at a time.

Chapel of St. Brizio: This chapel, to the right of the altar, features Luca Signorelli's brilliantly lit frescoes of the Apocalypse (1449–1451). Step into the chapel and you're surrounded by vivid scenes, including the *Preaching of the Antichrist* (to your left as you enter—the figure standing on far left is a self-portrait of Signorelli, next to Fra Angelico, who worked on the ceiling); the *Calling of the Elect to Heaven* (left of altar—hear that celestial band); the *Damned in Hell* (right of altar—the scariest mosh pit ever); and the *Resurrection of the Bodies* (to your right as you enter; people dreamily climb out of the earth as skeletons chatter in the corner, wondering where to snare some skin). On the same wall is a gripping *pietà*. Fra Angelico started the ceiling and Signorelli finished it, turning the entire room into Orvieto's artistic must-see sight.

After leaving the cathedral, if you want a break at a viewpoint park, exit left and pass the small parking lot. The nearest WCs are in the opposite direction (exit cathedral to the right), down the stairs from the left transept.

Archaeological Museum (Museo Claudio Faina e Museo Civico)—Across from the entrance to the cathedral is a fine Etruscan art museum (two upper floors) combined with a miniscule city history museum on the ground floor that features a sarcophagus and temple bits. The Faina art—consisting largely of Etruscan vases, plates, and coins, with some jewelry and bronze dishes—was collected by Mauro Faina and his nephew starting in the late 19th century. They bought some of the art, and dug up the rest in haphazardly conducted excavations. Many of the vases came from the Etruscan necropolis (Crocifisso del Tufo) just outside Orvieto. The English placards in most rooms offer some information, especially on the Faina family (€4.25, included in €10.50 Carta Unica combo-ticket, April–Sept Tue–Sun 9:30–18:00, Oct–March 10:00–17:00, closed Mon, audioguide, WC after ticket desk and on top floor, tel. 0763-341-511). Look out the windows at the duomo's glittering facade.

▲Museo Emilo Greco—This museum displays the work of Emilio Greco (1913–1995), the Sicilian artist who designed the doors of Orvieto's cathedral. His sketches and bronze statues show his absorption with gently twisting and turning nudes. In the back left corner of the museum, look for the sketchy outlines of women—simply beautiful. The artful installation of his work in this palazzo, with walkways and even a spiral staircase up to the ceiling, allows you to view his sculptures from different directions (€2.50, €4.50 includes St. Patrick's Well, April–Sept daily 10:30–13:00 & 14:00–18:30, closes 1 hour earlier Oct–March, no English but not essential, next to duomo, marked *Museo*, tel. 0763-344-605).

Underground Orvieto Tours (Parco delle Grotte)—Guides weave a good archaeological history into an hour-long look at about 100 meters (330 feet) of caves (€5.50, included in €10.50 Carta Unica combo-ticket, English tours daily at 12:15 and 17:15, confirm times by calling 0763-344-891 or checking with TI). Orvieto is honeycombed with Etruscan and medieval caves. You'll see the remains of an old olive press, two impressive 40-meter-deep (130-foot) Etruscan well shafts, and the remains of a primitive cement quarry; but, if you want underground Orvieto, this is the place to get it.

More Sights—Orvieto

Torre del Moro—For yet another viewpoint, this distinctive square tower comes with 250 steps and an elevator. The elevator goes only partway up, leaving you with a mere 173 steps to scurry up (€2.75, included in €10.50 Carta Unica combo-ticket, April–Oct daily 10:00–19:00, May–Aug until 20:00, Nov–March 10:30–13:00 & 14:30–17:00, terrace on top, at intersection of Corso Cavour and Via Duomo).

St. Patrick's Well (Posso de S. Patrizio)—Engineers are impressed by this deep well—53 meters (175 feet) deep and 13 meters (45 feet) wide—designed in the 16th century with a double-helix pattern. The two spiral stairways allow an efficient one-way traffic flow; intriguing now, but critical then. Imagine if donkeys and people, balancing jugs of water, had to go up and down the same stairway. At the bottom is a bridge that people could walk on to scoop up water.

The well was built because a pope got nervous. After Rome was sacked in 1527 by renegade troops of the Holy Roman Empire, the pope fled to Orvieto. He feared that even this little town (with no water source on top) would be besieged. He commissioned a well, which was started in 1527 and finished 10 years later. It was a huge project. Even today, when a local is faced with a difficult task, people say, "It's like digging St. Patrick's Well." The unusual name came from the well's supposed resemblance to the Irish saint's cave. It's not worth climbing up and down a total of 495 steps; a quick look is painless but pricey (€3.50, €4.50

includes Museo Emilio Greco, April–Sept daily 10:00–18:45, Oct–March closes an hour earlier; the well is to your right as you exit *funiculare)*. Bring a sweater if you descend to the chilly depths.

View Walks—For short, pleasant walks, climb the medieval wall (access at western end of town, between Piazza S. Gionvenale and Via Garibaldi) or stroll the promenade park on the northern edge of town (along Viale Carducci, which becomes Gonfaloniera).

Sights near Orvieto

Wine-Tasting—Orvieto Classico wine is justly famous. For a short tour of a local winery with Etruscan cellars, visit Tenuta Le Velette, where English-speaking Corrado and Cecilia Bottai will welcome you—if you've called ahead to set up an appointment (€8 for tour and tasting, Mon–Fri 8:30–12:00 & 14:00–17:00, Sat 8:30–12:00, closed Sun, tel. 0763-29144, fax 0763-29114). From their sign (5 min past Orvieto at top of switchbacks just before Canale, on Bagnoregio road), cruise down a long, tree-lined drive, then park at the striped gate (must call ahead; no drop-ins).

Sleeping in Orvieto

(€1 = about $1, country code: 39, zip code: 05018)

Sleep Code: **S** = Single, **D** = Double/Twin, **T** = Triple, **Q** = Quad, **b** = bathroom, **s** = shower only, **CC** = Credit Cards accepted, **no CC** = Credit Cards not accepted, **SE** = Speaks English, **NSE** = No English.

To help you sort easily through these listings, I've divided the rooms into three categories based on the price for a standard double room with bath:

Higher Priced—Most rooms more than €90.
Moderately Priced—Most rooms €90 or less.
Lower Priced—Most rooms €55 or less.

All of the recommended hotels are in the old town (see page 983) except Hotel Picchio, which is near the station.

HIGHER PRICED

Hotel Duomo, centrally located, is super-duper modern, with splashy art and 17 sleek rooms named after artists who worked on the duomo (Sb-€63, Db-€93, Db suite-€114, Tb-€114, includes breakfast, CC, elevator, air-con, double-paned windows keep out noise, a block from duomo, behind *gelateria* at Via di Maurizio 7, tel. 0763-341-887, fax 0763-394-973, www.argoweb.it/hotel_duomo, e-mail: hotelduomo@tiscalinet.it, SE).

MODERATELY PRICED

Hotel Corso is friendly and clean, with 18 comfy, modern rooms, some with balconies and views (Sb-€59, Db-€81, 10 percent discount with this book, buffet breakfast-€6.50, CC, air-con, elevator, garage, on main street up from funicular toward duomo at Via Cavour 339, tel. & fax 0763-342-020, www.argoweb.it/hotel_corso, e-mail: hotelcorso@libero.it, SE).

Hotel Virgilio has modern but faded and overpriced rooms shoehorned into an old building, ideally located on the main square facing the cathedral (Sb-€62, Db-€85, breakfast-€6, send personal or traveler's check for first night's deposit, CC, elevator, noisy church bells every 15 min, Piazza Duomo 5, tel. 0763-341-882, fax 0763-343-797, www.hotelvirgilio.com, e-mail: info@hotel.virgilio.com, SE). They also have a cheaper *dependencia*—a double and quad in a one-star hotel a few doors away (Db-€57, Qb-€103).

Hotel Posta is a five-minute walk from the cathedral into the medieval core. It's a big, old, formerly elegant but well-cared-for-in-its-decline building with a breezy garden, a grand old lobby, and 20 spacious, clean, plain rooms with vintage rickety furniture and good mattresses (S-€31, Sb-€36, D-€43, Db-€56, breakfast-€6, no CC, Via Luca Signorelli 18, tel. & fax 0763-341-909, NSE).

LOWER PRICED

The sisters of the **Istituto SS Domenicane** rent 15 spotless twin rooms in their heavenly convent with a peaceful terrace (Sb-€41, Db-€52, 2-night minimum, breakfast-€5.25, no CC, elevator, parking, just off Piazza del Popolo at Via del Popolo 1, tel. & fax 0763-342-910, www.argoweb.it/istituto_sansalvatore/istituto.it.html, NSE).

Hotel Picchio, with 19 newly remodeled rooms, is a wood-and-marble place, more comfortable but with less character than others in the area. It's in the lower, plain part of town, 300 meters (985 feet) from the train station (Sb-€36, Db-€48, Tb-€59, ask for the Rick Steves 5 percent discount; some rooms with air-con, fridge, and phone; Via G. Salvatori 17, 05019 Orvieto Scalo, tel. & fax 0763-301-144, e-mail: dan_test@libero.it, family-run by Marco and Picchio, SE). A trail leads from here up to the old town.

Franco Sala, who runs the Antico Forno restaurant and a B&B in Civita, also rents a centrally located **one-bedroom apartment** in Orvieto (€100 up to 4 people, 2-night minimum, kitchen, tel. 0761-760-016).

Eating in Orvieto

Near the duomo, consider **Pergola**—its affordable menu is popular with locals (Thu–Tue 12:30–14:30 & 19:30–22:00, closed Wed, Via dei Magoni 9, tel. 0763-343-065). **La Palomba** is also a good bet

(Thu–Tue 12:30–14:15 & 19:30–22:00, closed Wed, Via Cipriano Manente, just off Piazza della Repubblica, tel. 0763-343-395).

For a bit of a splurge, try **Antico Bucchero** for its classy candlelit ambience and fine food (Thu–Tue 12:30–15:00 & 19:00–24:00, closed Wed, CC, indoor/outdoor seating, Via de Cartori 4, a half block south of Corso Cavour, between Torre del Moro and Piazza della Repubblica, tel. 0763-341-725).

Osteria San Patrizio, near the funicular, is good (12:00–15:00 & 19:00–22:30, closed Sun eve and Mon, Corso Cavour 312, tel. 0763-341-245).

For dessert, try the deservedly popular *gelateria* **Pasqualetti** (daily 12:30–1:00, until 20:30 Nov–March, Piazza Duomo 14, next to left transept of church; another branch is at Corso Cavour 56).

Enoteca Tozzi, to the left of the duomo, serves up rustic *panini* sandwiches—try the roast suckling pig (*porchetta*, pron. por-KET-tah) if it's available (9:00–21:00, until 18:00 in winter, Piazza Duomo 13, tel. 0763-344-393).

Transportation Connections—Orvieto

By train to: Rome (19/day, 75 min, consider leaving your car at the large car park behind Orvieto station), **Florence** (14/day, 2.25 hrs), **Siena** (8/day, 2–3 hrs, change in Chiusi; all Florence-bound trains stop in Chiusi). The train station's Buffet della Stazione is surprisingly good if you need a quick focaccia sandwich or pizza picnic for the train ride.

By bus to Bagnoregio (near Civita): It's a 70-minute, €1.50 bus ride. Departures in 2002 from Orvieto's Piazza Cahen on the blue Cotral bus, daily except Sunday: 6:20, 9:10, 12:40, 13:55, 15:45, 17:40, and 18:20 (buses stop at Orvieto's train station 5 min later). During the school year (roughly Sept–June), there are additional departures at 7:20 and 7:50. Buy your ticket at the *tabacchi* stop on Corso Cavour (also confirm the schedule) a block up from the *funiculare*. To find the bus stop, face the *funiculare;* the stop is at the far left end of Piazza Cahen where the blue buses are parked (no schedule posted; confirm departure and return times with driver). Once you're in Bagnoregio, you'll find the Bagnoregio–Orvieto bus schedule posted at the bus stop.

CIVITA DI BAGNOREGIO

Perched on a pinnacle in a grand canyon, the traffic-free village of Civita is Italy's ultimate hill town. Curl your toes around its Etruscan roots.

Civita is terminally ill. Only 15 residents remain as, bit by bit, the town is being purchased by rich big-city Italians who come here to escape. Apart from its permanent (and aging) residents

Orvieto and Civita Area

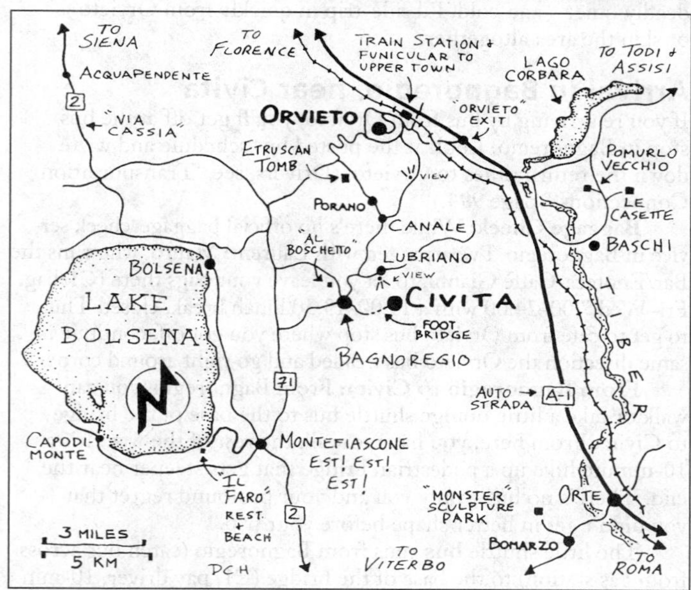

and those who have weekend homes here, there is a group of Americans—introduced to the town through a small University of Washington architecture program—who have bought into the rare magic of Civita. When the program is in session, 15 students live with residents and study Italian culture and architecture.

Civita is connected to the world and the town of Bagnoregio by a long pedestrian bridge—and a Web site (www.civitadibagnoregio.it). While Bagnoregio lacks the pinnacle-town romance of Civita, it's actually a healthy, vibrant community (unlike Civita, the suburb it calls "the dead city"). In Bagnoregio, get a haircut, sip a coffee on the square, and walk down to the old laundry (ask, "*Dov'è la lavanderia vecchia?*"). A Grand Spesa supermarket is 300 meters (985 feet) from the bus stop (Mon–Sat 8:30–13:00 & 17:00–20:00, closed Sun; take main drag from town gate—away from Civita, angle right at pyramid monument). A lively market fills the bus parking lot each Monday.

From Bagnoregio, yellow signs direct you along its long, skinny spine to its older neighbor, Civita. Enjoy the view as you walk up the bridge to Civita. Be prepared for the little old ladies of Civita, who can be aggressive at getting money out of visitors—tourists are their only source of support. Off-season, Civita,

Bagnoregio, and Al Boschetto (see "Sleeping," below) are all deadly quiet—and cold. I'd side-trip in quickly from Orvieto or skip the area altogether.

Arrival in Bagnoregio, near Civita

If you're arriving by bus from Orvieto, you'll get off at the bus stop in Bagnoregio. Look at the posted bus schedule and write down the return times to Orvieto. (Drivers, see "Transportation Connections," page 994.)

Baggage Check: While there's no official baggage-check service in Bagnoregio, I've arranged with Laurenti Mauro, who runs the Bar/Enoteca/Caffè Gianfu, to let you leave your bags there (€1/bag, Fri–Wed 7:00–24:00 with a 13:00–13:30 lunch break, closed Thu; to get to café from Orvieto bus stop where you got off, continue in same direction the Orvieto bus headed and go right around corner).

From Bagnoregio to Civita: From Bagnoregio, you can walk or take a little orange shuttle bus to the base of the bridge to Civita. From here, you have to walk the rest of the way. It's a 10-minute hike up a pedestrian bridge that gets steeper near the end. There's no bus—only you and your profound regret that you didn't get in better shape before your trip.

The little shuttle **bus** runs from Bagnoregio (catch bus across from gas station) to the base of the bridge (€1, pay driver, 10-min ride, first bus at 7:39, last at 18:20, 1–2/hr except during 13:00–15:30 siesta). If you'll want to return to Bagnoregio by bus, check the schedule posted near the bridge (at edge of car park, where bus let you off) before you head up to Civita.

To **walk** from Bagnoregio to the base of Civita's bridge (about 20 min, fairly level), take the road going uphill (overlooking the big parking lot), then take the first right and an immediate left onto the main drag, Via Roma. Follow this straight out to the belvedere for a superb viewpoint. From the viewpoint, backtrack a few steps, and take the stairs down to the road leading to the bridge.

Civita Orientation Walk

Civita was once connected to Bagnoregio. The saddle between the separate towns eroded away. Photographs around town show the old donkey path, the original bridge. It was bombed in World War II and replaced in 1965 with the new **bridge** you're climbing today. The town's hearty old folks hang on the bridge's hand railing when fierce winter weather rolls through.

Entering the town, you'll pass through a cut in the rock (made by Etruscans 2,500 years ago) and under a 12th-century Romanesque **arch**. This was the main Etruscan road leading to the Tiber Valley and Rome.

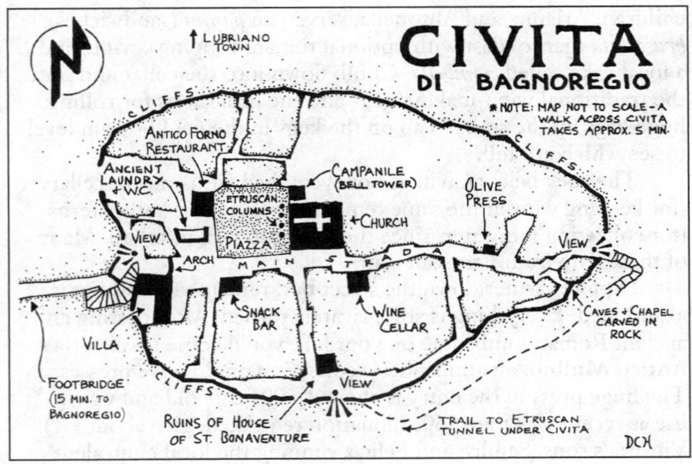

Inside the town gate, on your left is the old **laundry** (in front of the WC). On your right, a fancy wooden door and windows (above the door) lead to thin air. This was the facade of a Renaissance palace—one of five that once graced Civita. It fell into the valley riding a chunk of the ever-eroding rock pinnacle. Today, the door leads to a remaining chunk of the palace—complete with Civita's first hot tub—owned by the "Marchesa," a countess who married into Italy's biggest industrialist family.

Peek into the museum next door if it's open (Wed and Sat–Sun 10:00–13:00, marked *Benvenuti a Civita*) and check out the **viewpoint** a few steps away. Nearby is the site of the long-gone home of Civita's one famous son, Saint Bonaventure, known as the "second founder of the Franciscans."

Now wander to the **town square** in front of the church, where you'll find Civita's only public phone, bar, and restaurant—and a wild donkey race on the first Sunday of June and the second Sunday of September. The church marks the spot where an Etruscan temple, and then a Roman temple, once stood. The pillars that stand like giants' bar stools are ancient—Roman or Etruscan.

Go into the **church**. You'll see frescoes and statues from "the school of Giotto" and "the school of Donatello," a portrait of the patron saint of your teeth (notice the scary-looking pincers), and an altar dedicated to Marlon Brando (or St. Ildebrando).

The basic grid street plan of the ancient town survives. Just around the corner from the church, on the main street, is Rossana and Antonio's cool and friendly **wine cellar** (their sign reads: *bruschette con prodotti locali*). Pull up a stump and let them or their children, Arianna and Antonella, serve you *panini* (sandwiches), *bruschetta* (garlic toast with optional tomato topping), wine, and a local cake called *ciambella*. Climb down into the cellar and note the traditional wine-making gear and the provisions for rolling huge kegs up the stairs. Tap on the kegs in the cool bottom level to see which are full.

The rock below Civita is honeycombed with ancient cellars (for keeping wine at the same temperature all year) and cisterns (for collecting rainwater, since there was no well in town). Many of these date from Etruscan times.

Explore farther down the street but, remember, nothing is abandoned. Everything is still privately owned. After passing an ancient Roman tombstone on your left, you'll come to Vittoria's **Antico Mulino**, an atmospheric collection of old olive presses. The huge press in the entry is about 1,500 years old and was in use as recently as the 1960s (donation requested, give about €1). Vittoria's sons, Sandro and Felice, running the local equivalent of a lemonade stand, toast delicious *bruschetta* on weekends and holidays (roughly 11:00–19:00). Choose your topping (chopped tomato is super) and get a glass of wine for a fun, affordable snack.

Farther down the way and to your left, Maria (for a donation of about €1) will show you through her **garden** with a grand view (Maria's Giardino) and share historical misinformation (she says Civita and Lubriano were once connected). Maria's husband, Peppone, used to carry goods on a donkey back and forth on the path between the old town and Bagnoregio.

At the end of town, the main drag winds downhill past small **Etruscan caves** to your right. The first two were used as stables until last year. The third cave is an unusual chapel, cut deep into the rock, with a barred door—this is the **Chapel of the Incarcerated** (Cappella del Carcere). In Etruscan times, the chapel may have originally been a tomb, and in medieval times, it was used as a jail. When Civita's few residents have a religious procession, they come here, in honor of the Madonna of the Incarcerated.

After the chapel, the paving-stone path peters out into a dirt trail leading down and around to the right to a **tunnel**. Dating from the Etruscan era, the tunnel may have served as a shortcut to the river below. It was widened in the 1930s so farmers could get between their scattered fields more easily, and now the residents use it as a shortcut in fall to collect chestnuts from the trees that cover the hillside. Backtrack to the town square.

Evenings on the town square are a bite of Italy. The same people sit on the same church steps under the same moon, night after night, year after year. I love my cool, late evenings in Civita. If you visit in the morning, have cappuccino and rolls at the small café on the town square.

Whenever you visit, stop halfway up the donkey path and listen to the sounds of rural Italy. Reach out and touch one of the monopoly houses. If you know how to turn the volume up on the crickets, do so.

Sleeping in Civita and Bagnoregio

(€1 = about $1, country code: 39, zip code: 01022)

When you leave the tourist crush, life as a traveler in Italy becomes easy, and prices tumble. Finding a room is easy in small-town Italy. Drivers who would like to experience rural Italy should check the ***Agriturismo*** section at the end of this chapter for farmhouse B&Bs near Orvieto.

In Civita

Civita B&B, run by Franco Sala, who also owns the Antico Forno restaurant, has three comfortable rooms overlooking Civita's main square. Call a minimum of one day in advance to reserve (D-€57, Db-€67, €13 more for optional half pension, CC, Piazza del Duomo Vecchio, 01022 Civita di Bagnoregio, tel. 0761-760-016, cellular 34-7611-5426, www.civitadibagnoregio.it, e-mail: fsala@pelagus.it). Drivers should request a parking pass when they call.

For information about a fully furnished and equipped two-bedroom **Civita apartment** with a terrace and cliffside garden ($800/week, 1-week minimum Sat to Sat, personal checks OK), call Carol Watts in Kansas (785/539-0815, evenings or weekends, http://homepage.mac.com/cmwatts/civita.html, e-mail: cmwatts@mac.com).

In Bagnoregio

Hotel Fidanza, in Bagnoregio near the bus stop, is tired but decent and the only hotel in town. Of its 25 rooms, #206 and #207 have views of Civita (Sb-€52, Db-€62, breakfast-€5.50, no CC, attached restaurant, Via Fidanza 25, Bagnoregio/Viterbo, tel. & fax 0761-793-444).

Just outside Bagnoregio is **Al Boschetto.** The Catarcia family speaks no English, so have an English-speaking Italian call for you (Sb-€34, D-€44, Db-€49, breakfast-€3, CC, Strada Monterado, Bagnoregio/Viterbo, tel. 0761-792-369). Most of the 25 rooms, while very basic, have private showers. The Catarcia family (Angelino, his wife Perina, sons Gianfranco and Domenico, daughter-in-law Giuseppina, and the grandchildren) offers a candid look at rural Italian life. Meals are uneven in quality, and the men are often tipsy (which can pose a problem for women). If the men invite you down deep into the gooey, fragrant bowels of the cantina, be warned: The theme song is "*Trinka Trinka Trinka,*" and there are no rules unless the female participants set them. The Orvieto bus drops you at the town gate (no bus on Sun). The hotel is a 15-minute walk out of town past the old arch (follow *Viterbo* signs); turn left at the pyramid monument and right at the first fork (follow *Montefiascone* sign). Civita is a pleasant 45-minute walk (back through Bagnoregio) from Al Boschetto.

Eating in and near Civita

In Civita, try **Trattoria Antico Forno**, which serves up pasta at affordable prices (daily for lunch at 12:00 and sporadically for dinner at 19:00, on main square, also rents rooms—see above, tel. 0761-760-016). At **Da Peppone**, the small café/bar on the square, you can get simple treats (daily 9:30–12:30 & 14:00–19:00, closed 17:00 and Mon or Tue in winter).

Hostaria del Ponte offers light, creative cuisine at the parking lot at the base of the bridge to Civita (Tue–Sat 12:30–16:00 & 19:30–24:00, Sun 12:30–16:00, closed Mon, great view terrace, tel. 0761-793-565).

In Bagnoregio, check out **Ristorante Nello il Fumatore** (Sat–Thu 12:00–15:00 & 19:00–22:00, closed Fri, on Piazza Fidanza). At **Al Boschetto,** you'll get country cooking, such as bunny (just outside Bagnoregio; see "Sleeping," above).

Transportation Connections—Bagnoregio

To Orvieto: Public buses (7/day, 70 min) connect Bagnoregio to the rest of the world via Orvieto. Departures in 2002 from Bagnoregio, daily except Sunday: 5:30, 6:50, 9:50, 10:10, 13:00, 14:25, and 17:20. During the school year (roughly Sept–June), buses also run at 6:35, 13:35, and 16:40 (for info on Orvieto, see "Connections—Orvieto," above).

Driving from Orvieto to Bagnoregio: Orvieto overlooks the autostrada (and has its own exit). The shortest way to Civita from the freeway exit is to turn left (below Orvieto) and follow the signs to Lubriano and Bagnoregio.

The more winding and scenic route takes 20 minutes longer: From the freeway, pass under hill-capping Orvieto (on your right, signs to Lago di Bolsena, on Viale I Maggio), then take the first left (direction: Bagnoregio), winding up past great Orvieto views through Canale, and through farms and fields of giant shredded wheat to Bagnoregio.

Either way, just before Bagnoregio, follow the signs left to Lubriano and pull into the first little square by the church on your right for a breathtaking view of Civita. Then return to the Bagnoregio road. Drive through Bagnoregio (following yellow Civita signs) and park at the base of the steep pedestrian bridge leading up to the traffic-free, 2,500-year-old, canyon-swamped pinnacle town of Civita di Bagnoregio.

MORE HILL TOWNS

If you haven't gotten your fill of hill towns, here are more to check out. There are three main regions in central Italy, listed here in order of touristic popularity and accessibility: Tuscany, Umbria, and Le Marche.

Tuscany is our image of village Italy, with its manicured hills, rustic farms, and towns clinging to nearly every hill. Yet many who visit Tuscany, famous as the cradle of the Renaissance, never get out of the crowds of Florence. You'll find manageable train and bus connections throughout most of the region, but a car is fun.

Landlocked **Umbria**, the "Green Heart of Italy," is known for Assisi, famous worldwide as the hometown of St. Francis. Yet a short distance away from Assisi's touristic bustle, you'll find plenty of pleasant towns with more of the peace that Francis was seeking.

Le Marche is much less discovered. Its landscape is more wild and less manicured. The town of Urbino is the region's highlight. To unlock Le Marche's charms, a car is essential.

TUSCANY

▲▲Cortona—Cortona clings by its fingernails to the top of a mountain, dangling above views of the Tuscan and Umbrian landscape below. Frances Mayes' books, such as *Under the Tuscan Sun,* have placed this town in the touristic limelight, just as Peter Mayle's books popularized (and populated) the Luberon region in France. But even before Mayes ever published a book, Cortona was considered one of the classic Tuscan hill towns.

Unlike many hill towns, Cortona is worth visiting for its art alone. The Museo Diocesano has a small but interesting collection, including powerful works by native son Signorelli and two wonderful luminous Fra Angelicos. The Museo dell'Accademia Etrusca, housed in a former palace, has an eclectic collection of paintings, Etruscan artifacts and jewelry, and Egyptian mummies.

Cortona lies above the Terontola station (8 km, or 5 miles, away) on the Florence–Perugia line. Frequent buses connect the station with Piazza Garibaldi and the sights. The **TI** is at Via Nazionale 42 (tel. 0575-630-352). There are lots of cafés for lunch, or assemble a picnic and dine alfresco. Cortona's San

Marco hostel, housed in a remodeled 13th-century palace, is one of Italy's best (Via Maffei 57, tel. 0575-601-392). Drivers will find *agriturismo* listings for farmhouse B&Bs at the end of this chapter.

▲Chiusi—This small hill town (rated ▲▲ for Etruscan fans), which was once one of the most important Etruscan cities, is now a key train junction on the Florence–Rome line. The region's trains (to Siena, Orvieto, and Assisi) go through or change at this hub.

Highlights include the Archaeological Museum and the Etruscan tombs located just outside of town near Lago di Chiusi (€4, Mon–Sat 9:00–19:30, Sun 9:00–13:00, Via Porsenna 7, tel. 0578-20177). One of the tombs is multichambered, with several sarcophagi; while another, the Tomba della Scimmia (Tomb of the Monkey) has some well-preserved frescoes. Visiting the tombs requires a guide, arranged through the TI or the Archaeological Museum (5 people allowed to view at a time).

Troglodyte alert! The Cathedral Museum on the main square has an underground labyrinth of Etruscan tunnels (dark, so bring a flashlight). The mandatory guided tour ends in a large Roman cistern from which you can climb the church bell tower for an expansive view of the countryside (museum-€2, labyrinth-€3, combo-ticket-€4, daily 9:30–12:45 & 16:00–19:00, tours 11:00–16:00).

The **TI** is on the main square (daily in summer 9:00–12:30 & 15:30–19:00, otherwise mornings only, tel. 0578-227-667). Trains connect Chiusi with Rome, Florence, Siena, and more. Buses link the station (3 km, or less than 2 miles, away) with the town center.

▲▲Montepulciano—Long and skinny, Montepulciano stretches out lazily across a ridge. Due to its time under Medici rule, Montepulciano has an interesting mix of Renaissance buildings. To explore this Tuscan gem on a downhill stroll, take the shuttle bus from Piazza San Agnese up to Piazza Grande (and the TI, tel. 0578-717-484).

At Piazza Grande, the Palazzo Comunale (a mini-version of Florence's Palazzo Vecchio) looms across from Palazzo Contucci. Here you'll find an *enoteca* (wine bar) where you can sample the famous Vino Nobile di Montepulciano. From Piazza Grande, take Viale Sangallo downhill. The road snakes its way past shops, palaces, and *enotecas* through the old Porta al Prato gate back to Piazza San Agnese. Just outside the city walls is the Church of San Biagio, a Renaissance masterpiece by Sangallo.

Buses take you from Montepulciano's train station on the Florence–Rome line to the parking lot below Piazza San Agnese at the bottom of town. From here, it's a 25-minute walk up to Piazza Grande (or a quick bus ride). Buses connect Montepulciano with Siena as well.

▲Montalcino—Famous for its Brunello di Montalcino red wines, this hill town (rated ▲▲▲ for wine-lovers), once part of Siena's empire, is worth a visit for its *enoteca*, housed inside the 14th-century *fortezza* at the edge of town (tel. 0577-849-211, www.enotecalafortezza.it). After sampling a glass of the local *vino*, wander down into the heart of town at Piazza Garibaldi. The TI is on this square (tel. 0577-849-331). Besides the *fortezza* and the Brunello, Montalcino's main sight is the Museo Civico on Via Ricasoli, where you'll find art from the late Gothic/early Renaissance period. For an atmospheric café, try Antica Fiaschetteria on Piazza del Popolo. Non–wine-lovers may find Montalcino a bit too focused on *vino*, but one sip of Brunello makes even wine skeptics believe that Bacchus was on to something. Note that the Rosso di Montalcino wine is also good at half the price. Those with sweet tooths will enjoy munching Ossi di Morta ("bones of the dead"), a crunchy cookie with almonds.

Buses connect Montalcino with Siena.

▲Pienza—In the 1400s, local pope Pius II of the Piccolomini family decided to remodel his hometown in the current Renaissance style. Propelled by papal clout, the town of Corsignano was transformed into a jewel of Renaissance architecture and renamed Pienza. The focal point is the Piazza Pio II, with the Duomo and Palazzo Piccolomini. The TI is in Palazzo Pubblico (tel. 0578-749-071).

Buses connect Pienza with Siena and Montepulciano.

▲▲Crete Senese Drive—Sometimes it seems that all of Tuscany is one big scenic route, but my favorite drive is this one between Montepulciano and Montalcino on the S-146 road. This area is known as the Crete Senese ("Crests of Siena"), a series of undulating hills that provides postcard views at every turn. You'll see an endless parade of classic Tuscan scenes, with rolling hills topped with medieval towns, olive groves, rustic stone farmhouses, rows of vineyards, and a skyline punctuated with cypress trees.

San Galgano Monastery—Of southern Tuscany's several evocative monasteries, San Galgano is the best. Way off the beaten track, this sight is for drivers only. San Galgano was a 12th-century saint who renounced his past as a knight by miraculously burying his sword up to its hilt into a stone. After his death, a large monastery complex grew up. Today, all you'll see is the roofless, ruined abbey and, on a nearby hill, the Chapel of San Galgano with its fascinating dome and sword in the stone. The adjacent gift shop sells a little bit of everything from wine to postcards to herbs. Other more accessible Tuscan monasteries worth visiting include San Antimo (10 km, or 6 miles, south of Montalcino) and Monte Oliveto Maggiore (25 km, or 15 miles, south of Siena).

One bus a day from Siena stops at San Galgano. Buses

link Montalcino with San Antimo, and Siena with Monte Oliveto Maggiore.

▲**U.S. Cemetery**—Whatever one's feelings about war, the sight of endless rows of white marble crosses and Stars of David never fails to be moving. This particular cemetery is the final resting place of more than 4,000 Americans who died in the liberation of Italy during World War II. Their memory lives on in two Italian cemeteries, one in Nettuno near Rome and this one just south of Tavernuzze, 12 kilometers (7 miles) south of Florence. Climb the hill past the perfectly manicured grassy lawn, lined with grave markers, to the memorial, where maps and history of the Italian campaign detail the Allied advance (daily mid-April–Sept 8:00–18:00, Oct–mid-April 8:00–17:00, WC, just off Via Cassia road that parallels the *superstrada* between Florence and Siena, 3 km, or 1.9 miles, south of Florence Certosa exit on A-1 autostrada). Buses from Florence stop just outside the cemetery.

UMBRIA

▲**Gubbio**—This handsome town climbs Monte Ingino in northeast Umbria. Tuesday is market day, when Piazza 40 Martiri (named for 40 locals shot by the Nazis) bustles. Nearby, the ruins of the Roman amphitheater are perfect for a picnic. Head up Via della Repubblica to reach the main square with the imposing Palazzo dei Consoli. Farther up, Via San Gerolamo leads to the funky lift that will carry you up the hill in two-person "baskets" for a stunning view from the top, where the basilica of St. Ubaldo is worth a look.

Buses run to Perugia, Rome, and Florence. The TI is at Piazza Odersi (tel. 075-922-0693).

▲**Deruta**—Pottery-lovers the world over start to salivate when the name Deruta is mentioned. Colorful Deruta pottery, considered to be Italy's best, features designs popular since Renaissance times. The high-quality local clay attracted artisans centuries ago, and today artists still practice their craft. Deruta is actually two towns: the upper hill town and the lower strip. The upper town, full of small shops run by local artisans, warrants a wander; prices and quality are higher up here. Ceramic fans drop by the Museo Regionale della Ceramica (closed Tue), in the upper town, next to the TI on the main square. Below, a commercial strip parallel to the *superstrada* is lined with larger commercial outlets and factories. Many offer demonstrations of their time-honored craft. Prices are about one-third cheaper than in the United States, and most will ship your purchases home with a guarantee of safe delivery.

Buses connect Deruta with Perugia.

▲**Bevagna**—This sleeper of a town south of Assisi has Roman ruins, interesting churches, and more. Locals offer their guiding services for free (usually Italian-speaking only) and are excited to show visitors their town. Get a map at the **TI** on Piazza Silvestri (tel. 0742-361-667) and wander. Highlights are the Roman mosaics, remains of the arena that now houses a paper-making shop, the Romanesque church of San Silvestro, and a gem of a 19th-century theater. Bevagna has all the elements of a hill town except one—a hill. A couple of hours is plenty to see the main sights. For an overnight, consider the fancy Hotel Palazzo Brunamonti (Db-€110, Corso Matteotti 79, tel. 0742-361-932, fax 0742-361-948, www.brunamonti.com, e-mail: hotel@brunamonti.com). Buses connect Bevagna with Foligno.

Montefalco—Famous for its Sagrantino wine and its site (Montefalco means Falcon's Mountain), this village is dubbed the "Balcony of Umbria" for its expansive views. Intact medieval walls surround the town. The Museo Civico San Francesco displays frescoes by Gozzoli (Fra Angelico's pupil) of the life of St. Francis. There is no TI, but the people at the museum can answer questions.

A few buses a day run to Bevagna.

▲Spello—Umbrian hill town aficionados always include Spello on their list. Just 10 kilometers (6 miles) south of Assisi, this town is much less touristy than its neighbor to the north. Spello will give your legs a workout. Via Consolare goes up, up, up to the top of town. Views from the terrace of the restaurant Il Trombone will have you singing a tune. The **TI** is on Piazza Matteotti 3 (tel. 0742-301-009).

Spello is on the Perugia–Assisi–Foligno train line. Buses run to Assisi.

LE MARCHE

▲▲Urbino—Urbino is famous for being the hometown of the artist Raphael and architect Bramante, yet the town owes much of its fame to the Duke of Montefeltro. This mercenary general turned Urbino into an important Renaissance center, attracting artists such as Piero della Francesca, Uccello, and Raphael's papa, Giovanni Santi.

The Ducal Palace, with more than 300 rooms, is the main course of a visit to Urbino. Highlights include great paintings such as Raphael's *La Muta*, the remarkable *intarsio* (inlaid wood) walls of the duke's study, the vast cellars, and the Renaissance courtyard (€4.20, Sun–Mon 9:00–14:00, Tue–Sat 9:00–19:00). Note that during busy periods, you need to reserve a ticket for the palace in person. For information on how to reserve, call the **TI** (Piazza Duca Federico 35, across from palace, tel. 0722-2613) or the booking office in the palace (tel. 0722-329-057).

Stop by the Oratory of St. John to see its remarkable frescoed interior. Nearby, the Church of San Giuseppe has a dreamy stucco ceiling, with angels peering down through whipped-cream clouds at the huge nativity diorama below. In the adjacent church, a Baroque trompe l'oeil ceiling is worth a look. Fans visit the Casa di Raffaello, but the artist's famous works are in Florence and Rome. For a fabulous view, climb up to the Giardini Pubblici park, where a grassy hillside provides a panorama of Urbino and the hills of Le Marche.

A couple of good restaurants are Taverna degli Artisti (great pizzas, Via Bramante) and Il Coppiere (Via Santa Margherita), where your entire meal, including the post-dinner grappa, can involve truffles, if you like. The *enoteca* on Via Raphael merits a stop, but the action in town is at the bustling Piazza della Repubblica, with an endless parade of students and locals.

Urbino is well off the beaten tourist path. Frequent buses connect Pesaro (on the Ravenna–Pescara train line) with Urbino, terminating at the Borgo Mercatale parking lot below the town, where an elevator lifts you up to the base of the slender towers of the Ducal Palace (or walk 5 min steeply up Via Mazzini to Piazza della Repubblica).

Agriturismo

Agriturismo (or agricultural tourism) began in the 1960s to encourage farmers to remain on their land, produce food, and offer accommodation to tourists. These rural Italian B&Bs are ideal for couples or families traveling by car.

Some properties are simple and rustic, while others are downright luxurious, offering amenities such as swimming pools and stables. The quality of the rooms varies, but they are usually simple, clean, and comfortable. Most serve tasty homegrown food. And most require a minimum-night stay, usually a week. July and August are especially busy. Off-season shorter stays are possible.

Be aware that agricultural tourism is organized "*alla Italiana*," which means, among other things, a lack of a single governing body. You'll find a listing of several *agriturismo* farms below. For more options, go to www.agriturist.it, which lists over 1,700 farms throughout Italy. If you'd prefer to use an agency, consider Farm Holidays in Tuscany. They book rooms and apartments at 300 farms in Tuscany, Umbria, and elsewhere in Italy (Mon–Fri 9:00–13:00 & 15:00–18:00, Via Manin 20, 58100 Grosseto, tel. 0564-417-418, www.it-farmholidays.it, Andrea Mazzanti SE). Book several months in advance for high season (May–Sept). Generally, a 25 percent deposit is required (lost if you cancel), and the balance is due one month before arrival.

For more information on *agriturismo*, visit www.initaly.com, www.italyfarmholidays.com, www.agriturismoitaly.it, www.rent-villas.com, www.italianvillas.com, and www.tuscanyumbria.com.

Agriturismo Listings

Near Orvieto

Agriturismo Le Casette, outside the village of Baschi, is outstanding, with rooms in several restored stone farmhouses clustered around a grassy lawn and a swimming pool with a fabulous view of the green Umbrian landscape (Db-€70, includes breakfast; for a room, breakfast, and a home-cooked dinner, pay €50–60 per person per day; minimum 1-week stays preferred July–Aug, CC, 12 km, or 7 miles, southeast of Orvieto, tel. 0744-957-645, fax 0744-950-500, www.pomurlovecchio-lecasette.it, e-mail: pomurlovecchio@tiscalinet.it, run by charming Minghelli family, Daniela speaks "a leetle" English). The same family also owns **Pomurlo Vecchio**, a 12th-century tower house with three rooms a few kilometers away (same prices, tel. 0744-950-190, fax 0744-950-500).

Agriturismo Sant' Angelo rents four apartments in an old stone farmhouse on a hillside near Monte Rufeno Natural Park Reserve, about 20 kilometers (12 miles) northwest of Orvieto. Each apartment has a living room and kitchen and sleeps up to four (2-night stay required). The entire villa also can be rented (apartment for 2 people/2 nights-€310–620 depending on season, weekly-€620–1,033, villa-€2,376–4,132, no CC, pool, horseback riding, mountain bikes, S.S. Cassia Nord Km 136.300, tel. 0763-734-738 or 0763-730-150, cellular 338-366-5475, www.agriturismosantangelo.it, e-mail: info@agriturismosantangelo.it, SE).

Agriturismo Pomonte Umbria, a short drive from Civita and Orvieto, offers home-cooked meals, lovely vistas, and seven comfortable rooms in a newly built guest house (€26 per person, includes breakfast, €42-half pension, €52-full pension, CC, Loc. Canino di Orvieto 1, Corbara, 12 km, or 7 miles, east of Orvieto, tel. 076-330-4041, fax 076-330-4080, www.orvienet.it/agriturismo.pomonte, e-mail: info@pomonte.it, SE).

Near Assisi

Podere La Fornace is a renovated farmhouse in the tiny village of Tordibetto, just a few kilometers outside Assisi. The four apartments (with 1–3 bedrooms) have full kitchens and a living room that can sleep an extra person. Local wine, olive oil, and pasta are available on-site; if you stay for a week, they'll include your breakfast ingredients (apartment-€75–240 depending on size and season, 3-night minimum, games for children, swimming pool, bikes, Via Ombrosa 3, tel. 075-801-9537, cellular 338-990-2903, fax 075-801-9630, www.lafornace.com, e-mail: info@lafornace.com, SE).

In Montalcino

La Crociona, a farm and working vineyard in Montalcino (45 min south of Siena), rents seven fully equipped apartments. Fiorella Vannoni and Roberto & Barbara Nannetti offer wine-tasting and cooking classes (Db-€67–105, Qb-€93–155, lower weekly rates, CC, pool, La Croce, Montalcino, tel. 0577-847-133, tel. & fax 0577-848-007, www.lacrociona.com, e-mail: lacrociona@tin.it, SE).

Near Urbino

At **Locanda della Valle Nuova,** a 185-acre organic farm near Urbino, they raise cattle, pigs, and poultry; grow grapes for their wine; and harvest wheat for their homemade bread and pasta. The six rooms—named by color—are tranquil and cozy (Db-€90 includes buffet breakfast, Db-€125 also includes 5-course evening meal, no CC, 3-night minimum, reserve 1 day in advance, swimming pool, horseback riding, La Cappella 14, Sagrata di Fermingnano, tel. & fax 0722-330-303, www.vallenuova.it, e-mail: gsavini@supereva.it, SE).

Near Cortona

Casa San Martino, in the village of Lisciano Niccone (midway between Cortona and Perugia), is a 250-year-old farmhouse run as a B&B by American Italophile Lois Martin. Using this comfortable hilltop countryside as a home base, those with a car can tour Assisi, Orvieto, and Civita. While Lois reserves the summer (June–Aug) for one-week stays, she'll take guests staying a minimum of three nights for the rest of the year (Db-€160, 10 percent discount for my readers—mention this book when you reserve, includes breakfast, views, pool, washer/dryer, house rental available, Casa San Martino 19, Lisciano Niccone, 20 km, or 12 miles, east of Cortona, tel. 075-844-288, fax 075-844-422). Lois' neighbors, Ernestine and Gisbert Schwanke, run the charming **La Villetta di San Martino B&B** (Db-€110 includes hearty country breakfast, minimum2-night stay, kitchen, sitting room, fireplace, San Martino 36, tel. & fax 075-844-309, e-mail: erni@netemedia.net, SE).

Country House Montali is perched on a hilltop (roughly between Cortona and Chiusi), within an hour's drive of Orvieto and Assisi. The architect owners have restored an old farmhouse and built three single-story houses for guests. Olive trees and trails surround the property, which overlooks nearby Lake Trasimeno. The owners offer vegetarian meals and cooking courses designed to prove that healthy food can be tasty (10 rooms, €67.15–77.50 per person half pension, swimming pool, Via Montali 23, Tavernelle di Panicale, 40 km, or 25 miles, south of Cortona, tel. 075-835-0680, www.montalionline.com, e-mail: montali@montalionline.com, SE).

Near Siena

Agriturismo Le Trappoline, on I Sodi Farm in Chianti about a 20-minute drive east of Siena, is a recently renovated farmhouse with panoramic vistas and ample grounds for country walks. Guests stay in one of four apartments with one or two bedrooms and fully equipped kitchens (€39–80 per bedroom depending on season, must rent entire apartment, 1-week stays usually required, 2-night stays okay off-season, large pool, Località Monti Gaiole, tel. 0577-747-012, www.agrisodi.com, e-mail: info@agrisodi.com, Danilo and Gabriella Casini, some English spoken).

Family-friendly **Agriturismo Il Molinello**, in the clay hills about 30 minutes southeast of Siena, rents four apartments carved out of a medieval mill (€28–60 per bedroom, must rent entire apartment, 1-week stays usually required, off-season discounts, pets and short stays welcome off-season, organic vegetables and fruit, wine tastings, children's toys, large swimming pool, mountain bike rentals, Località Molinello, tel. 0577-704-791, cellular 335-692-5720, fax 0577-705-605, www.molinello.com, e-mail: info@molinello.com, Alessandro and Elisa Draghi SE).

Parri Nada Farmhouse is tucked away in the vineyards in the hills of Chianti about a 20-minute drive northeast of Siena. Luca and Elena Masti rent two rooms in their quaint, comfortable farmhouse (D-€70, 1-night rentals okay, pool and private yard, Località Santa Chiara 4, tel. & fax 0577-359-072, cellular 380-321-4681, www.farm-house.it, e-mail: info@farm-house.it).

Poste Regie, a B&B in Ancaiano, about 20 minutes west of Siena, rents three double rooms in a restored Tuscan villa on a country road (D-€65, includes breakfast, Via della Montagnola 68, cellular 349-475-4995, fax 0577-45387, www.posteregie.com, e-mail: reservations@posteregie.com, Beatrice Marzolla).

THE CINQUE TERRE

The Cinque Terre (pron. CHINK-weh TAY-reh), a remote chunk of the Italian Riviera, is the traffic-free, lowbrow, underappreciated alternative to the French Riviera. There's not a museum in sight. Just sun, sea, sand (well, pebbles), wine, and pure unadulterated Italy. Enjoy the villages, swimming, hiking, and evening romance of one of God's great gifts to tourism. For a home base, choose among five villages, each of which fills a ravine with a lazy hive of human activity—calloused locals, sunburned travelers, and no Vespas. Vernazza is my favorite home base. While the Cinque Terre is now well-discovered (www.cinqueterre.it), I've never seen happier, more relaxed tourists.

The chunk of coast was first described in medieval times as "the five lands." Tiny communities grew up in the protective shadows of the castles (in feudal times, the land was the property of the castles), ready to run inside at the first hint of a Turkish "Saracen" pirate raid. Many locals were kidnapped and ransomed or sold into slavery somewhere far to the east. As the threat of pirates faded, the villages grew, with economies based on fish and grapes. Until the advent of tourism in this generation, the towns were remote. Even today, traditions survive, and each of the five villages comes with a distinct dialect and proud heritage. The region has just become a national park, and its natural and cultural wonders will be carefully preserved.

Now that the Cinque Terre is a national park, you need to pay a park entrance fee. You have two options: buying a Hiking Pass or a Cinque Terre Card. The Hiking Pass costs €3 (kids under 4 free; comes with map) and is valid for one day. The pricier Cinque Terre Card covers the park entrance fee and your transportation on the local trains (from Levanto to La Spezia, including all Cinque

Terre towns) plus the shuttle buses that run about twice an hour within each Cinque Terre town (€5.20/1 day, €12.40/3 days, €19.60/week, kids 4–12 half-price, under 4 free; includes map, brochure, and train schedule). A new pass for €13 covers hiking and local trains, shuttle buses, and boats for one day. Passes, valid until midnight of the day they expire, are sold at train stations and some trailheads. Validate your pass (unless it's a Hiking Pass) at a train station by punching it into the yellow machine.

Over the next decade, Italy has quiet plans for the Cinque Terre. For the sake of tranquillity, a new train line will be built inland for the noisy fast trains, leaving the Cinque Terre tracks for just the pokey milk-run trains.

Sadly, a few ugly, noisy Americans are giving tourism a bad name here. Even hip young locals are put off by loud, drunken tourists. They say (and I agree) that the Cinque Terre is a special place.

It deserves a special dignity. Party in Viareggio or Portofino, but be mellow in the Cinque Terre. Talk softly. Help keep it clean. In spite of the tourist crowds, it's still a real community, and we are guests.

Planning Your Time

The ideal minimum stay is two nights and a completely uninterrupted day. The Cinque Terre is served by the milk-run train from Genoa and La Spezia. Speed demons arrive in the morning, check their bags in La Spezia, take the five-hour hike through all five towns, laze away the afternoon on the beach or rock of their choice, and zoom away on the overnight train to somewhere back in the real world. But be warned: The Cinque Terre has a strange way of messing up your momentum.

The towns are each just a few minutes apart by hourly train or boat. There's no checklist of sights or experiences; just a hike, the towns themselves, and your fondest vacation desires. Study this chapter in advance and piece together your best day, mixing hiking, swimming, trains, and a boat ride. For the best light and coolest temperatures, start your hike early.

Market days perk up the towns from 8:00 to 13:00 on Tuesday in Vernazza, Wednesday in Levanto, Thursday in Monterosso, and Friday in La Spezia.

Getting around the Cinque Terre

By Train: At La Spezia, the gateway to the Cinque Terre, you'll transfer to the milk-run Cinque Terre train. There might be a TI at the station in summer. If not, skip the 20-minute hike to La Spezia's main TI at Via Mazzini near the waterfront (daily in summer 9:00–13:00 & 15:00–18:00; winter Mon–Sat 9:00–13:00 & 14:00–17:00, Sun 9:00–13:00, tel. 0187-718-997).

At the station, buy your €1.20 train ticket or Cinque Terre Card, and take the half-hour train ride into the Cinque Terre town of your choice. Once in the Cinque Terre, you'll get around the villages more cheaply by train but more scenically by boat.

Cinque Terre Train Schedule: Since the train is the Cinque Terre lifeline, many shops and restaurants post the current schedule. Try to get a photocopied schedule—it'll come in handy (comes with Cinque Terre Card).

Trains leave La Spezia for the Cinque Terre villages (last year's schedule, only daily trains listed—there are others that run only weekdays or only Sundays as well) at 7:12, 8:17, 10:08, 11:24, 12:29, 13:20, 14:29, 15:08, 16:18, 18:26, 19:26, 20:26, 21:14, 22:28, and 0:35.

Trains leave Monterosso al Mare for La Spezia (departing

Vernazza about 4 minutes later, last year's schedule) at 6:30, 8:09, 9:08, 10:12, 12:16, 13:14, 14:16, 15:08, 16:16, 17:12, 17:31, 18:22, 18:42, 19:22, 20:12, 22:29, 23:23, and 0:19.

Do not rely on these train times. Check the current posted schedule and then count on half the trains being 15 minutes or so late (unless you're late, in which case they are right on time).

To orient yourself, remember that directions are "*per* (to) Genoa" or "*per* La Spezia." Note that many trains leaving La Spezia skip them all or stop only in Monterosso. The five towns are just minutes apart by train. Know your stop. After leaving the town before your destination, go to the door to slip out before mobs pack in. Since the stations are small and the trains are long, you might get off the train deep in a tunnel, and you might need to flip open the handle of the door yourself.

The train stations should be staffed at all five Cinque Terre towns. Stations sell train tickets; the Cinque Terre Card, which covers the park entrance fee plus train and bus travel on the Cinque Terre (€5.20/1 day, €12.40/3 days, and €19.60/week); and maybe the Hiking Pass (€3 for park entrance fee).

The Cinque Terre Card, which includes the national park entry fee, is convenient, but if you're on a tight budget, you can save a bit of money by buying a one-day Hiking Pass (€3) and paying separately for your train travel.

It's cheap to buy individual train tickets to travel between the towns. Since a one-town hop costs the same as a five-town hop (€1.20) and every ticket is good for six hours with stopovers, save money and explore the region in one direction on one ticket. Stamp the ticket at the station machine before you board.

If you have a Eurailpass, don't spend one of your valuable flexi-days on the cheap Cinque Terre.

By Boat: From Easter to late October (through Nov if weather is good), a daily boat service connects Monterosso, Vernazza, Manarola, Riomaggiore, and Portovenere (on Sun, a boat makes an afternoon run to Portofino). Boats provide a scenic way to get from town to town and survey what you just hiked. It's also the only efficient way to visit the nearby resort of Portovenere; the alternative is a tedious train/bus connection via La Spezia. In peaceful weather, the boats are more reliable than the trains. Boats go about hourly, from 10:30 until 18:00 from Monterosso and from 9:00 until 17:10 from Portovenere (about €3 per single hop or €11.50 for an all-day pass to the Cinque Terre towns, buy tickets at little stands at each town's harbor, tel. 0187-777-727). A more frequent boat service connects Monterosso and Vernazza (about hourly to Monterosso, less frequently to Vernazza, tel. 0187-817-452). Schedules are posted at docks, harbor bars, and hotels.

Events on the Cinque Terre

mid-May	Monterosso: Lemon Festival
June 22	Monterosso: Corpus Domini (procession on carpet of flowers)
June 24	Riomaggiore and Monterosso: Festival in honor of St. John the Baptist
June 29	Corniglia: Festival of St. Peter and St. Paul
July 20	Vernazza: Festival for patron saint, St. Margaret
Aug 10	Manarola: Festival for patron saint, St. Lawrence
Aug 15	All towns: Ascension of Mary
Sept 8	Monterosso: Maria Nascente, or "Rising Mary" (fair with handicrafts)

By Foot: A scenic trail runs along the coast, connecting each of the five Cinque Terre towns (see "Hiking," page 1013). Sometimes severe rains can wash out trails, especially in winter. Ask around if the trails are open.

VERNAZZA

With the closest thing to a natural harbor—overseen by a ruined castle and an old church—and only the occasional noisy slurping up of the train by the mountain to remind you of the modern world, Vernazza is my Cinque Terre home.

The action is at the harbor, where you'll find a kids' beach, plenty of sunning rocks, outdoor restaurants, a bar hanging on the edge of the castle (great for evening drinks), and a tailgate-party street market every Tuesday morning. In the summer, the beach becomes a soccer field, where teams fielded by local bars and restaurants provide late-night entertainment. In the dark, locals fish off the promontory, using glowing bobs that shine in the waves.

The town's 500 residents, proud of their Vernazzan heritage, brag that "Vernazza is locally owned. Portofino has sold out." Fearing the change it would bring, keep-Vernazza-small proponents stopped the construction of a major road into the town and region. Families are tight and go back centuries; several generations stay together. Leisure time is devoted to the *passeggiata*—strolling lazily together up and down the main street. Sit on a bench and study the passersby. Then explore the characteristic alleys, called *carugi.* In October, the cantinas are draped with drying grapes. In the winter, the population shrinks as many people move to more comfortable big-city apartments.

A steep five-minute hike in either direction from Vernazza gives you a classic village photo op (for the best light, head toward Corniglia in the morning, toward Monterosso in the evening). Franco's Bar, with a panoramic terrace, is at the tower on the trail toward Corniglia.

Vernazza has ATMs and two banks (in center and top of town). A shuttle bus (free with Cinque Terre Card, otherwise €1.50) runs twice an hour from the top of the main street to the parking lot.

You can buy train tickets, Hiking Passes, and Cinque Terre Cards at the Vernazza train station/TI—staffed by helpful trio Eliano, Diego, and Francesco (daily in summer 8:00–22:00, in winter 8:00–20:00, tel. 0187-812-533, a little English spoken). You can also store luggage here (€0.50/hr). Accommodations are listed near the end of this chapter.

Internet Access and Laundry: The slick Internet Point, run by Alberto and Isabella, is in the village center (daily 9:30–20:00, tel. 0187-812-949). The Blue Marlin bar (run by Carmen and Massimo, 6:45–24:00, open daily in Aug, otherwise closed Thu) also offers Internet access plus a self-service laundry (€4.60 wash, €4.60 dry, English instructions, buy tokens at Blue Marlin bar—note hours above, laundry open daily 8:00–22:00, Via Roma 49, tel. 0187-821-149, 30 meters, or 100 feet, below train station).

Sights—Vernazza

▲▲Vernazza Top-Down Orientation Walk—Walk uphill until you hit the parking lot—with a bank, a post office, and a barrier that keeps all but service vehicles out. Vernazza's shuttle buses run locals back and forth up into the hills from this point (€1.50–2.50, free with Cinque Terre Card). The tidy new square is called Fontana Vecchia, after a long-gone fountain. Older locals remember the river filled with townswomen doing their washing. Begin your saunter downhill to the harbor.

Just before the Pension Sorriso sign, you'll see the ambulance barn (big brown wood doors) on your right. A group of volunteers is always on call for a dash to the hospital, 30 minutes away in La Spezia. Opposite that is a big empty lot next to Pension Sorriso. Like many landowners, the owner of the Sorriso had plans to expand, but the government said no. The old character of these towns is carefully protected.

Across from Pension Sorriso is the honorary clubhouse for the ANPI (members of the local WWII resistance). Only five ANPI old-timers survive. Cynics consider them less than heroes. After 1943, Hitler called up Italian boys over 15. Rather than die

Vernazza

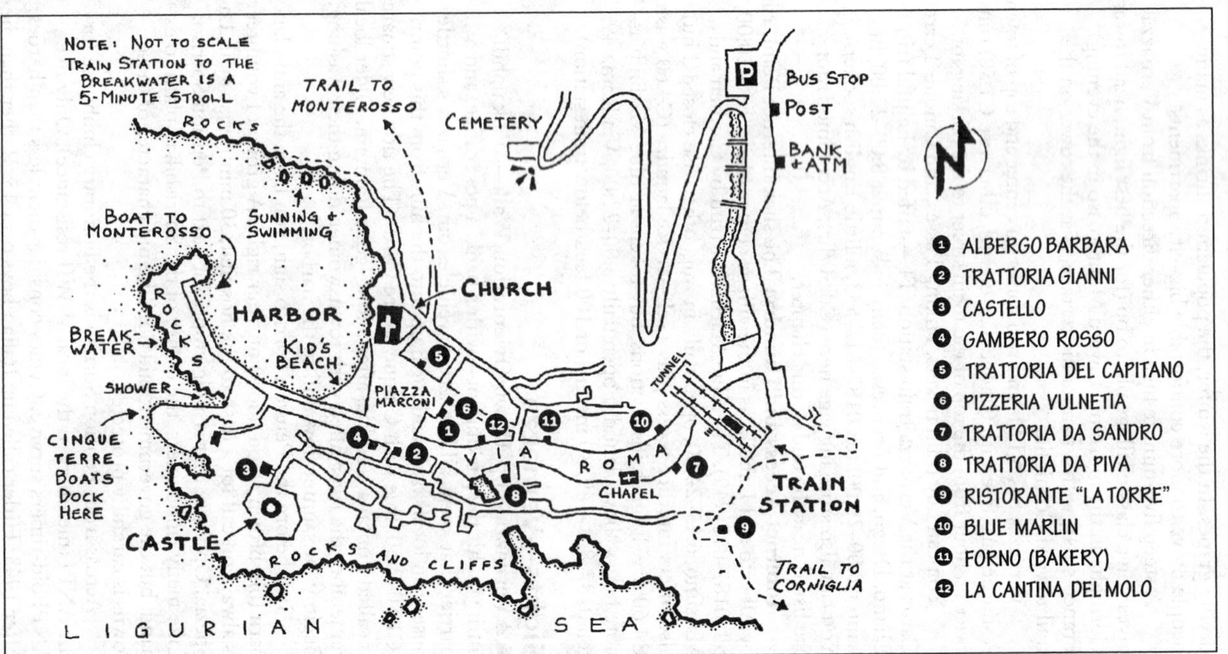

NOTE: NOT TO SCALE
TRAIN STATION TO THE BREAKWATER IS A 5-MINUTE STROLL
TRAIL TO MONTEROSSO
CEMETERY
P
BUS STOP
POST
BANK + ATM
ROCKS
SUNNING + SWIMMING
BOAT TO MONTEROSSO
CHURCH
HARBOR
ROCKS
BREAK-WATER
KID'S BEACH
SHOWER
PIAZZA MARCONI
TUNNEL
CINQUE TERRE BOATS DOCK HERE
VIA ROMA
CHAPEL
TRAIN STATION
CASTLE
ROCKS AND CLIFFS
TRAIL TO CORNIGLIA
LIGURIAN SEA
1 ALBERGO BARBARA
2 TRATTORIA GIANNI
3 CASTELLO
4 GAMBERO ROSSO
5 TRATTORIA DEL CAPITANO
6 PIZZERIA VULNETIA
7 TRATTORIA DA SANDRO
8 TRATTORIA DA PIVA
9 RISTORANTE "LA TORRE"
10 BLUE MARLIN
11 FORNO (BAKERY)
12 LA CANTINA DEL MOLO

on the front for Hitler, they escaped to the hills. Only to remain free did they become "resistance fighters."

A few steps farther along, you'll see a monument (marble plaque in wall to your left) to those killed in World War II. Not a family was spared. Study this: Soldiers "*morti in combattimento*" fought for Mussolini, some were deported to *Germania*, and "partisans" were killed later fighting against Mussolini.

The tiny monorail *trenino* (as you're facing plaque, look up on the wall on your right) is parked quietly here except in September and October, when it's busy helping locals bring down the grapes. The path to Corniglia leaves from here (it runs above plaque, starting at your left). Behind you is a tiny square playground, decorated with three millstones, which no longer grind local olives into oil. From here, Vernazza's tiny river goes underground.

In the tunnel under the railway tracks, you'll see a door marked "Croce Verde Vernazza" (Green Cross). Posted on the other side of the tunnel is the "P.A. Croce Verde Vernazza" (in a small green display case), the list of volunteers ready for ambulance duty each day of the month.

The train tracks are above you. The second set of tracks (nearer the harbor) was recently renovated to lessen the disruptive noise; locals say it made no difference.

Follow the road downhill. Until the 1950s, Vernazza's river ran open through the center of town from here to the *gelateria*.

Wandering through this main business center, you'll pass many locals doing their *vasca* (laps) past the entrepreneurial Blue Marlin bar (about the only nightspot in town) and the tiny Chapel of Santa Marta (the small stone building with iron grillwork over the window, across from Il Baretto), where Mass is celebrated only on special Sundays. Next you'll see a grocery, *gelateria*, bakery, pharmacy, another grocery, and another *gelateria*.

On the left, in front of the second *gelateria*, an arch leads to what was a beach where the river used to flow out of town. Continue on down to the harbor square and breakwater. Vernazza, with the only natural harbor of the Cinque Terre, was established as the sole place boats could pick up the fine local wine. (The town is named for a kind of wine.) Peek into the tiny street behind the Vulnetia restaurant with the commotion of arches. Vernazza's most characteristic side streets, called *carugi*, lead up from here. The trail (above the church toward Monterosso) leads to the classic view of Vernazza (best photos just before sunset).

▲▲▲The Burned-Out Sightseer's Visual Tour of Vernazza—Sit at the end of the harbor breakwater (perhaps with a glass of local white wine or something more interesting from Bar Capitano—borrow the glass, they don't mind), face the town, and see . . .

The harbor: In a moderate storm, you'd be soaked, as waves routinely crash over the *molo* (breakwater, built in 1972). The train line (to your left), constructed 130 years ago to tie a newly united Italy together, linked Turin and Genoa with Rome. A second line (hidden in a tunnel at this point) was built in the 1960s. The yellow building alongside the tracks was Vernazza's first train station. You can see the four bricked-up alcoves where people once waited for trains. Vernazza's fishing fleet is down to three small fishing boats (with the net spools); the town's restaurants buy up everything they catch. Vernazzans are more likely to own a boat than a car. In the '70s, tiny Vernazza had one of the top water polo teams in Italy, and the harbor was their "pool." Later, when a real pool was required, Vernazza dropped out of the league.

The castle: On the far right, the castle, which is now a grassy park with great views, still guards the town (€1, daily 10:00–18:30, from harbor, take stairs by Trattoria Gianni and follow signs to Castello restaurant, tower is a few steps beyond, see the photo and painting gallery rooms). It's called *Belforte,* or "loud screams," for the warnings it made back in pirating days. The highest umbrellas mark the recommended Castello restaurant (see "Eating," page 310). The squat tower on the water is great for a glass of wine (follow the rope to the Belforte Bar, open Wed–Mon 8:00–24:00, closed Tue, tel. 0187-812-222; inside the submarine-strength door, a photo of a major storm shows the entire tower under a wave).

The town: Vernazza has two halves. *Sciuiu,* on the left (literally, "flowery"), is the sunny side, and *luvegu,* on the right (literally, "dank"), is the shady side. The houses below the castle were connected by an interior arcade—ideal for fleeing attacks. The pastel colors are regulated by a commissioner of good taste in the community government. The square before you is locally famous for some of the region's finest restaurants. The big, red, central house, the 12th-century site where Genoan warships were built, used to be a kind of guardhouse.

Above the town: The small, round tower above the guardhouse, another part of the city fortifications, reminds us of Vernazza's importance in the Middle Ages, when it was a key ally of Genoa (whose archenemies were the other maritime republics of Pisa, Amalfi, and Venice). Franco's Bar, just behind the tower, welcomes hikers finishing, starting, or simply contemplating the Corniglia–Vernazza hike, with great town views (8:00–22:00). Vineyards fill the mountainside beyond the town. Notice the many terraces. Someone calculated that the vineyard terraces of the Cinque Terre have the same amount of stonework as the Great Wall of China. Wine production is down nowadays, as the younger residents choose less physical work. But locals still work their plots and proudly serve their family wines. A single steel train line winds up the gully behind the tower. This is for the vintner's *trenino*, the tiny service train.

The church, school, and city hall: Vernazza's Ligurian Gothic church, built with black stones quarried from Punta Mesco (the distant point behind you), dates from 1318. The gray-and-red house above and to the left of the spire is the local elementary school (which about 25 children attend). High school is in the "big city," La Spezia. The red building to the right of (and below) the schoolhouse is the former monastery and present city hall. Vernazza and Corniglia function as one community. Through most of the 1990s, the local government was communist. In 1999, they elected a coalition of many parties working to rise above ideologies and simply make Vernazza a better place. Finally, on the top of the hill, with the best view of all, is the town cemetery, where most locals plan to end up.

Cinque Terre Hiking and Swimming

▲▲▲Hiking—All five towns are connected by good trails. Experience the area's best by hiking from one end to the other. The entire 11-kilometer (7-mile) hike can be done in about four hours, but allow five for dawdling. While you can detour to dramatic hill-top sanctuaries (one trail leads from Vernazza's cemetery uphill), I'd keep it simple by following the easy red-and-white-marked low trails between the villages. Good hiking maps (about €5, sold everywhere, not necessary for this described walk) cover the expanded version of this hike, from Portovenere through all five Cinque Terre towns to Levanto, and more serious hikes in the high country. Get local advice to make sure trails are open, particularly in spring.

Since I still get the names of the Cinque Terre towns mixed up, I think of the towns by number: Riomaggiore (town #1), Manarola (#2), Corniglia (#3), Vernazza (#4), and resorty Monterosso (#5).

Riomaggiore–Manarola (20 min): Facing the front of the train station in Riomaggiore (town #1), go up the stairs to the right, following signs for the Via dell' Amore. The film-gobbling promenade—wide enough for baby strollers—leads down the coast to Manarola. While there's no beach here, stairs lead down to sunbathing rocks.

Manarola–Corniglia (45 min): The walk from Manarola (#2) to Corniglia (#3) is a little longer and a little more rugged than that from #1 to #2.

Ask locally about the more difficult nine-kilometer (6-mile) inland hike to Volastra (shuttle buses run hourly to Volastra from Manarola, €2.50). This tiny village, perched between Manarola and Corniglia, hosts the Five-Terre wine co-op; stop by the Cantina Sociale. If you take this high road between Manarola and Corniglia, allow two hours; in return, you'll get sweeping views and a closer look at the vineyards.

Corniglia–Vernazza (90 min): The hike from Corniglia (#3) to Vernazza (#4)—the wildest and greenest of the coast—is most rewarding. From the Corniglia station and beach, zigzag up to the town (taking the steeper corkscrew stairs, the longer road, or the shuttle bus). Ten minutes past Corniglia toward Vernazza, you'll see the nude Guvano beach far below (see below). The trail leads past a bar and picnic tables, through lots of fragrant and flowery vegetation, and scenically into Vernazza.

Vernazza–Monterosso (90 min): The trail from Vernazza (#4) to Monterosso (#5) is a scenic up-and-down-a-lot trek. Trails are rough (and some readers report "very dangerous") but easy to follow. Camping at the picnic tables midway is frowned upon. The views just out of Vernazza are spectacular.

Short Hiking Tour—For a guided tour, consider spending a day with a hardworking and likable American student, Sean Risatti, who liked the Cinque Terre so much he moved in (€40, almost daily April–Oct, departing Monterosso at 10:00 or Vernazza at 10:45, book at cinqueterretrek@hotmail.com or at either Internet point in Monterosso: The Net or Fishnet Internet Lounge). The day—which is a great way to meet other travelers—includes a hike from Vernazza to Manarola, lots of information, special glimpses of the area, and a dinner that evening.

▲Swimming—Wear your walking shoes and pack your swim gear. Several of the beaches have showers (no shampoo, please) that may work better than your hotel's. Underwater sightseeing is full of fish—goggles are sold in local shops. Sea urchins can be a problem if you walk on the rocks; consider using Aquasocks or fins.

Here's a beach review:

Riomaggiore: The beach is rocky, but clean and peaceful. It's a two-minute walk from the harbor: face the harbor, then take the path to your left. At the La Conchiglia bar, go down the stairs to the right of the bar. Follow the path to the beach.

Manarola: Manarola has no sand, but the best deepwater swimming of all. The first "beach," with a shower, ladder, and wonderful rocks (with daredevil high-divers), is my favorite. The second has tougher access and no shower, but feels more remote and pristine (follow paved path around point).

Corniglia: This hilltop town has a rocky man-made beach below its station. It's clean and uncrowded, and the beach bar has showers, drinks, and snacks.

The nude Guvano (GOO-vah-noh) beach (between Corniglia

and Vernazza) made headlines in Italy in the 1970s, as clothed locals in a makeshift armada of dinghies and fishing boats retook their town beach. But big-city nudists still work on all-around tans in this remote setting. From the Corniglia train station, follow the road north, go over the tracks, then zigzag below the tracks, following signs to the tunnel in the cliff (walk past the *proprieta privata* sign). When you buzz the intercom, the hydraulic *Get Smart*–type door is opened from the other end. After a 15-minute hike through a cool, moist, and dimly lit unused old train tunnel, you'll emerge at the Guvano beach—and get charged €5 (€4 with this guidebook). The beach has drinking water, but no WC. A steep (free) trail leads from the beach up to the Corniglia–Vernazza trail. The crowd is Italian counterculture: pierced nipples, tattooed punks, hippie drummers in dreads, and nude exhibitionist men. The ratio of men to women is about three to two. About half the people on the pebbly beach keep their swimsuits on.

Vernazza: The village has a children's sandy cove, sunning rocks, and showers by the breakwater. There's a ladder on the breakwater for deepwater access. The tiny *acque pendente* (waterfall) cove which locals call their *laguna blu*, between Vernazza and Monterosso, is accessible only by small hired boat.

Monterosso: The town's beaches, immediately in front of the train station, are easily the Cinque Terre's best and most crowded. It's a sandy resort with everything rentable . . . lounge chairs, umbrellas, paddleboats, and usually even beach access. Beaches are free only where you see no umbrellas.

Cinque Terre Towns

Note: Readers of this book fill Vernazza. For this reason, you might prefer to stay in one of these towns with fewer Americans. See "Sleeping," below, for accommodations for each town.

▲▲Riomaggiore (town #1)—The most substantial non-resort town of the group, Riomaggiore is a disappointment from the train station. But walk through the tunnel next to the train tracks (or ride the elevator through the hillside to the top of town), and you land in a fascinating tangle of pastel homes leaning on each other as if someone stole their crutches. There's homemade gelato at the Bar Central on main street, and, if Ivo is there, you'll feel right at home. When Ivo closes, the gang goes down to the harborside with a guitar.

Riomaggiore's **TI** is inside the train station (Mon–Fri 7:00–20:00 in winter, until 22:00 in summer, tel. 0187-920-633). The shuttle bus takes locals and tourists up and down Riomaggiore's steep main street (free with Cinque Terre Card, 2/hr, just flag it down).

Introductory Walk: Here's an easy loop trip through Riomaggiore that maximizes views and minimizes walking uphill.

Riomaggiore

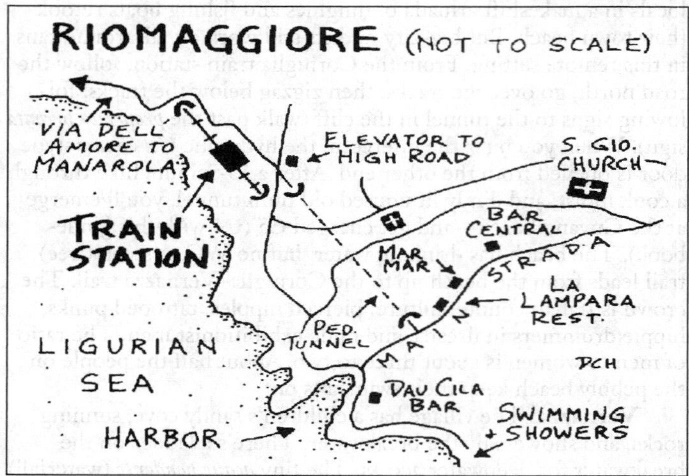

Start at the train station (if you arrive by boat, take the tunnel alongside the tracks to get to the station). From the station, take the elevator up to the top of town (€0.55, free with Cinque Terre Card, entrance at railway tunnel). At the top, go right, following the walkway—with spectacular sea views—around the cliff. Ignore the steps marked *Marina Seacoast* (harbor). Instead, continue along the path; it's a five-minute, fairly level walk to the church. Continue past the church and then take a right down the stairs to Via Columbo, Riomaggiore's main street. Stroll down Via Columbo. Just past the WC, you'll see flower boxes on the street, sometimes blocking it; these slide back electrically to let the shuttle bus get past. On your way down the hill, you'll pass colorful, small shops, including a bakery, a couple of grocery shops, and a self-service laundry (daily 7:30–19:30, next door to Edi Rooms). When Via Columbo dead-ends, on your left you'll find the stairs down to the harbor, boat dock, and a 200-meter (650-foot) trail to the beach *(spiaggia)*. To your right is the tunnel, running alongside the tracks, which takes you directly to the station. Either take a train or hop a boat (from the harbor) to your next destination.

For hikes from Riomaggiore, consider the cliff-hanging trail that leads from the beach to a hilltop botanical garden (free with Cinque Terre Card) and old WWII bunkers. Another climbs scenically to the Madonna di Montenero sanctuary high above the town.

Riomaggiore also has a diving center (scuba, snorkeling, boats, Via San Giacomo, tel. 0187-920-014).

Manarola

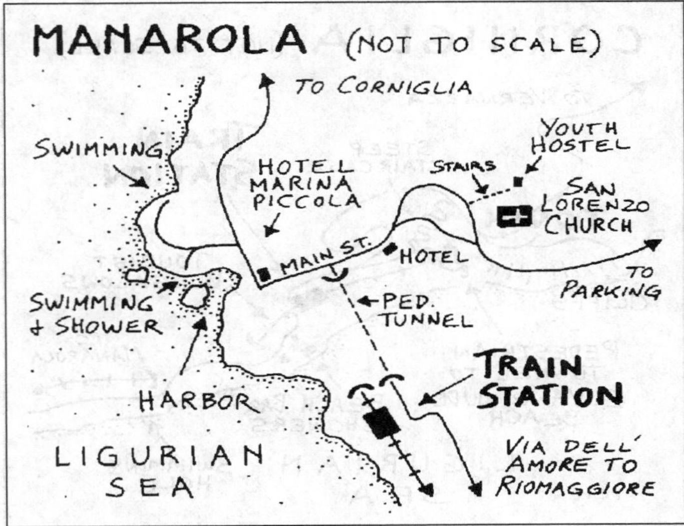

▲Manarola (town #2)—Like town #1, #2 is attached to its station by a 200-meter-long (650-foot) tunnel. Manarola is tiny and picturesque, a tumble of buildings bunny-hopping down its ravine to the fun-loving harbor. Notice how the I-beam crane launches the boats. Facing the harbor, look at the hillside to your right, dotted with a bar in the middle. It's Punta Bonfiglio, an entertaining park/game area/bar with the best view playground on the coast. The gate farther up the hillside is the entrance to the cemetery. From here you can get poster-perfect views of Manarola (2-min walk from the harbor on path to Corniglia).

Within Manarola, the shuttle bus takes people between main street and the parking lot (free with Cinque Terre Card, 2/hr, just flag it down). In the middle of town, across from the railway tunnel, you'll see Bar Aristide, which sometimes shows outdoor movies on weekends in August by hanging a screen over part of the tunnel entrance (closed Mon, Via Discovolo 290, tel. 0187-920-000). At the top of the town, you'll find great views, the church, and a cluster of accommodations, including a super hostel (see "Sleeping," page 1028).

The simple, wooden, religious scenes that you'll likely see on the hillside are the work of local resident Mario Andreoli. Before his father died, Mario promised him he'd replace the old cross on the family's vineyard. Mario's been adding figures ever

Corniglia

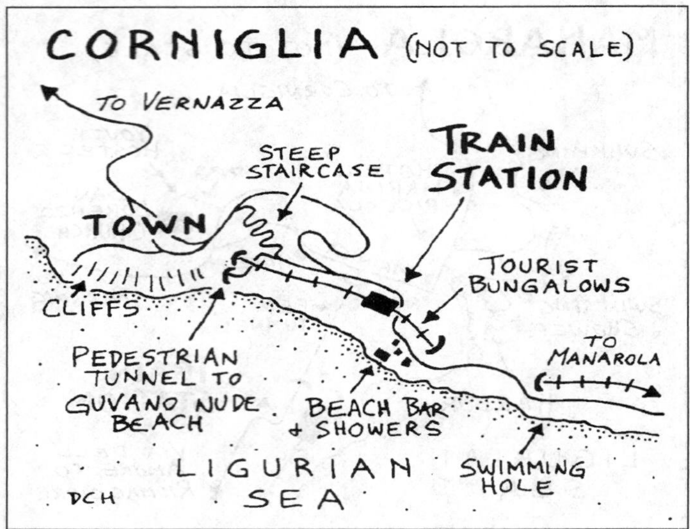

since. After recovering from a rare illness, he redoubled his efforts. The scenes, which do change occasionally (a sheep here, an apostle there), are sometimes left up year-round. On religious holidays, everything's lit up: the Nativity, the Last Supper, the Crucifixion, the Resurrection, and more.

▲▲Corniglia (town #3)—From the station, a footpath zigzags up nearly 400 stairs to the only town of the five not on water. Take the bus (€1.50, free with Cinque Terre Card, 2/hr). Originally settled by a Roman farmer who named it for his mother, Cornelia (how Corniglia is pronounced), the town and its ancient residents produced a wine so famous that vases found at Pompeii touted its virtues. Today, wine is still its lifeblood. Follow the pungent smell of ripe grapes into an alley cellar and get a local to let you dip a straw into a keg. Remote and less visited, Corniglia has fewer tourists, cooler temperatures, a windy belvedere (on its promontory), a few restaurants, and plenty of private rooms for rent (ask at any bar or shop). Past the train station (toward Manarola) you'll find Corniglia's beach. The well-hung Guvano beach is in the opposite direction (toward Vernazza).

▲▲▲Vernazza (town #4)—See beginning of chapter.

▲▲Monterosso al Mare (town #5)—This is a resort with cars, hotels, rentable beach umbrellas, crowds, and a thriving nightlife. The town is split into the old and new, connected by a tunnel.

Monterosso

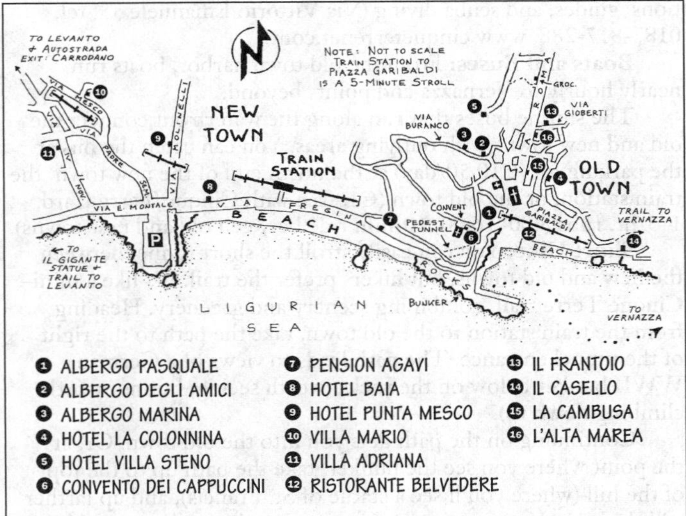

The train station is in the new town, along with the Cinque Terre park office (*Parco Nazionale delle Cinque Terre*, daily 8:00–22:00, shorter hours in winter, in the station, tel. 0187-817-059, e-mail: parconazionale5terre@libero.it); the **TI** (daily Mon–Sat 10:00–12:45 & 14:15–19:00, Sun 10:00–12:45, closed Nov–Easter, exit station and go left a few doors, tel. 0187-817-506); several recommended accommodations; and a statue—*Il Gigante*. This 14-meter-tall (46-foot) statue, which once held a trident, looks as if it were hewn from the rocky cliff, but it's made of reinforced concrete, and dates from the beginning of the 20th century.

Along the waterfront, in the new part of town or the breakwater of the old town, look for all the towns of the Cinque Terre strung out along the coast.

Monterosso's old town contains Old World charm, small crooked streets, and plenty of Internet access.

Internet Access: Kate's Fishnet Internet Lounge—a welcoming, well-run center for local information—has several computers and digital camera photo services (daily in summer 10:00–20:00 & 21:30–24:00, in winter Mon 10:00–13:00, Tue–Sun 10:00–13:00 & 16:00–20:00, Via Roma 17, can book accommodations, tel. 0187-817-373, www.fishnet.it). A few steps farther into the alley is The Net, offering 10 high-speed computers, classical music if Renato's on duty, and a free cuppa joe to patrons. Renato and Enzo happily provide information on the Cinque Terre and book accommodations, guides, and scuba diving (Via Vittorio Emanuele 55, tel. 0187-817-288, www.cinqueterrenet.com).

Boats and Buses: From the old town harbor, boats run nearly hourly to Vernazza and points beyond.

The shuttle buses that run along the waterfront connect the old and new towns with outlying areas. You can catch the bus at the parking lot (€10.50/day) at the north end of the new town, the train station, or the old town (€1, free with Cinque Terre Card, 1–3/hr, runs 8:00–16:00, 10-min ride between old and new towns).

Short Hike: You can easily stroll the short tunnel between the new and old towns, but hikers prefer the trail. It's like a mini–Cinque Terre trail, combining scenery and greenery. Heading from the train station to the old town, take the path to the right of the tunnel entrance. The path leads to views of a German WWII bunker below on the rocks (worth seeing, but not worth climbing down to).

Continuing on the path gets you into the old town. Or, at the point where you see the bunker, take the path up to the top of the hill (where you'll see a statue of St. Francis), and up farther still through the woods to reach a gate (marked *Convento e Chiesa Cappuccini)* leading to a church with a Van Dyck painting of the Crucifixion (accommodations next to church, see "Sleeping," below). You're a world away from the resort town below.

A trail to the right of the church leads up to the cemetery; appreciate its flowers, photos, and your beating heart. Backtrack to the St. Francis statue, and take the trail down into the old town. (Reversing this, if you're going from the old town to the new, take the trail to the right of the tunnel entrance; go right on Zii di Frati to see the church, or continue straight to get to the new town). Allow a total of 30 minutes if you include the church and cemetery.

Nightlife: Young travelers and night owls gather at Fast Bar on Via Roma in the old town to mix travel tales and beer (sandwiches and snacks served until midnight, closes 1:30). For nightlife with a sea view, wander up to Il Casello by the *bocce* courts on the road toward Vernazza; its outdoor tables are sandwiched between the old town beaches (Wed–Mon 11:30–2:00, closed Tue, tel. 0187-818-330). Many of the little bars and *enotecas* (wine bars) in the old town stay open late during the summer months—wander the backstreets until you find your favorite.

Cinque Terre Cuisine 101

A few menu tips: *Accuighe* (pron. ah-CHOO-gay) are anchovies, a local specialty—always served the day they're caught. If you've always hated anchovies (the harsh, cured-in-salt American kind), try them fresh here. *Tegame alla Vernazza* is the most typical main course in Vernazza: anchovies, potatoes, tomatoes, white wine, oil, and herbs. *Pansotti* is ravioli with ricotta and spinach, often served with a hazelnut or walnut sauce . . . delightful and filling. While antipasto is cheese and salami in Tuscany, here you'll get *antipasti di mare*, a plate of mixed fruits of the sea and a fine way to start a meal. For many, splitting this and a pasta dish is plenty. Try the fun local dessert: *torte della nonna* (grandmother's cake), with a glass of *sciacchetrà* for dunking (see "Wine," below).

▲▲Pesto—This is the birthplace of pesto. Basil, which loves the temperate Ligurian climate, is mixed with cheese (half *Parmigiano* cow cheese and half pecorino sheep cheese), garlic, olive oil, and pine nuts, and then poured over pasta. Try it on spaghetti, *trenette*, or *trofie* (made of flour with a bit of potato, designed specifically for pesto). Many also like pesto lasagna. If you become addicted, small jars of pesto are sold in the local grocery stores (you can take it home or spread it on focaccia here).

▲▲Wine—The *vino delle Cinque Terre*, respected throughout Italy, flows cheap and easy throughout the region. It is white—great with the local seafood. D.O.C. is the mark of top quality. Red wine is better elsewhere. For a sweet dessert wine, the local *sciacchetrà* wine is worth the splurge (€2.60 per glass, often served with a cookie). While 10 kilos of grapes yield seven liters of local wine, *sciacchetrà* is made from near-raisins, and 10 kilos of grapes make only 1.5 liters of *sciacchetrà*. The word means "push and pull" . . . push in lots of grapes, pull out the best wine. If your room is up a lot of steps, be warned: *Sciacchetrà* is 18 percent alcohol, while regular wine is only 11 percent. In the cool, calm evening, sit on the Vernazza breakwater with a glass of wine and watch the phosphorescence in the waves.

Sleeping and Eating on the Cinque Terre
(€1 = about $1, country code: 39)

Sleep Code: **S** = Single, **D** = Double/Twin, **T** = Triple, **Q** = Quad, **b** = bathroom, **s** = shower only, **CC** = Credit Cards accepted, **no CC** = Credit Cards not accepted, **SE** = Speaks English, **NSE** = No English. Breakfast is included only in real hotels.

To help you sort easily through these listings, I've divided the rooms into three categories based on the price for a standard double room with bath:

Higher Priced—Most rooms more than €100.
Moderately Priced—Most rooms €100 or less.
Lower Priced—Most rooms €50 or less.

If you're trying to avoid my readers, stay away from Vernazza. Monterosso is a good choice for the younger crowd (more nightlife) and rich, sun-worshiping softies (who prefer firm reservations for hotels with private bathrooms). Wine-lovers and mountain goats like Corniglia. Sophisticated Italians and Germans choose Manarola. Travelers who show up without reservations enjoy Riomaggiore for its easy room-booking services.

While the Cinque Terre is too rugged for the mobs that ravage the Spanish and French coasts, it's popular with Italians, Germans, and Americans in the know. Hotels charge the most and are packed on Easter, in August, and on summer Fridays and Saturdays. August weekends are worst. But €60 doubles abound throughout the year. Outside of August weekends, you can land a comfortable €65 double room in a private home on any day by just arriving in town (ideally by noon) and asking around at bars and restaurants, or simply by approaching locals on the street. This seems scary, but it's true.

For the best value, visit three private rooms and snare the best. Going direct cuts out a middleman and softens prices. Plan on paying cash. Private rooms are generally bigger and more comfortable than those offered by the pensions and they offer the same privacy as a hotel room.

If you want the security of a reservation, make it long in advance for a hotel (small places generally don't take reservations made weeks ahead). If you don't get a reply to your faxed request for a room, assume the place is fully booked.

Sleeping in Vernazza (zip code: 19018)

Vernazza, the essence of the Cinque Terre, is my favorite. There are two recommended pensions and piles of private rooms for rent.

To reserve ahead, call, fax, or e-mail. As a last resort, write: address letters to 19018 Vernazza, Cinque Terre, La Spezia. If you arrive without a reservation, you can call these places from the pay phone at the bottom of the stairs at the train station. Or drop by the nearest shop or bar; most locals know someone who rents rooms.

Anywhere you stay here will require some climbing. Night noises can be a problem if you're near the station.

A new parking lot (€1/hour or €8/day) and a hardworking shuttle service make driving to Vernazza a reasonable option for drivers with nerves of steel. The little shuttle bus runs twice an hour (generally with helpful, English-speaking Beppe behind the wheel).

Usually, when a price range is listed, the lower price is charged during winter (roughly Nov–March) and the higher price the rest of the year. The first two are pensions (see map on page 1010 for location), the rest are private rooms.

MODERATELY PRICED

Trattoria Gianni rents 23 small rooms just under the castle. The funky ones are artfully decorated à la shipwreck and are up lots of tight, winding, spiral stairs, and most have tiny balconies and grand views. The new, comfy rooms lack views but have modern bathrooms and a super-scenic, cliff-hanger private garden. Marisa, who rarely smiles at anyone (not just you), requires a two-night minimum and check-in before 16:00 (S-€35, D-€58, sinks and bathrooms down the hall; Db-€70, Tb-€86, CC but 10 percent discount for cash, Piazza Marconi 5, closed Jan–Feb, tel. & fax 0187-812-228, tel. 0187-821-003, e-mail: info@giannifranzi.it, a little English spoken). Pick up your keys at Trattoria Gianni's restaurant/reception on the harbor square and hike up dozens of stairs to #41 (funky, *con vista mare*) or #47 (new, *nuovo*) at the top. (Note: My tour company books this place 50 nights of the season.) Telephone three days in advance and leave your first name and time of arrival.

LOWER PRICED

Albergo Barbara, on the harbor square, is run by kindly Giuseppe and his Swiss wife, Patricia. Their nine clean, modern rooms share three public showers and WCs (S-€36–€47 depending on season, D without view-€43, D with small view-€45, D with big view-€55, bunky family Q-€67, 2-night stay preferred, call before 17:00 on the day of arrival or lose your room, loads of stairs, fans, closed Dec–Jan, Piazza Marconi 30, call to reserve instead of fax, tel. & fax 0187-812-398, cellular 338-793-3261, SE). The two big doubles on the main floor come with grand harbor views and are the best value (top-floor doubles have small windows and small views). The office is on the top floor of the big, red, vacant-looking building facing the harbor.

Private Rooms (Affitta Camere)

These are the best values in Vernazza. The town is honeycombed year-round with pleasant, rentable private rooms and apartments with kitchens (cheap for families). They are usually reluctant to reserve rooms far in advance. It's easiest to call a day or two ahead or simply show up in the morning and look around. The rooms cost about €45–60 for a double, depending on the view, season, and plumbing. Some have killer views, most have lots of stairs and cost the same as a small dark place on a back lane over the train tracks. Little or no English is spoken at these places. Any main-street business has a line on rooms for rent.

MODERATELY PRICED

Franca Maria rents two sharp, comfortable rooms overlooking the harbor square (Db-€42–72, Qb-€83–105 depending on season, the 2 side-by-side doubles can turn into a quad, Piazza Marconi 30, tel. 0187-812-002, fax 0187-812-956, son Giovanni's e-mail: metalgearsolid@inwind.it—he has rooms to rent as well). It's just a few steps up from the harbor—a rarity in vertical Vernazza.

Martina Callo rents four fine, lofty rooms overlooking the square, up plenty of steps near the church tower (Db-€50–60, Qb-€93–103; room #1-Qb with harbor view, room #2-Qb huge family room with no view, room #3-Db with grand view terrace, room #4-roomy Db with no view; heating in winter; ring bell at Piazza Marconi 26, tel. & fax 0187-812-365, e-mail: roomartina@supereva.it).

Affitta Camere da Anna-Maria offers five pleasant rooms up spiral staircases (Db-€65–67 with view or terrace—the terrace room is best, Via Carattino 64, turn left at pharmacy, climb Via Carattino to #64, tel. 0187-821-082).

Tonino Basso rents four super, clean, modern rooms—each with its own computer for free Internet access—near the post office, in the only building in Vernazza that has an elevator. Rooms come with a private bath but no views (Sb-€60, Db-€70, Tb-€100, Qb-€110, CC, tel. 0187-821-264, cellular 335-269-436, fax 0187-821-260, e-mail: toninobasso@libero.it; when you arrive, call cellular number from train station—phones at bottom of stairs—and Tonino will meet you; or the Gambero Rosso restaurant at harbor can find him—but then you'll have to backtrack to get to his rooms).

Giuseppina's Villa, a cozy apartment with a low-ceilinged loft, has one window, no view, and a kitchen. The woman at the grocery store nearest the harbor (with *Salumi e Formaggi* on the awning) can check if it's available (€25 per person, Via S. Giovanni Battista 7, only a short climb from harbor, tel. 0187-812-026). Giuseppina also rents a double room up the street (no view, but has a garden, terrace, and kitchen) and her sister owns **Villa Antonia**, two newly remodeled rooms with a shared bath on the main drag (Db-€75, tel. 0187-812-343).

Nicolina rents four decent rooms: a large one with a view, two overlooking Vernazza's main drag, and one without any view. Inquire at Pizzeria Vulnetia on the harbor square or reserve in advance by phone (Db-€55-65, Qb with terrace and view-€127, Piazza Marconi 29, tel. & fax 0187-821-193, Frederica).

Armanda rents a one-room apartment without a view near the Castello (€62, Piazza Marconi 15, tel. 0187-812-218, cellular 347-306-4760).

Moggia Manuela rents rooms at the top of town near the old fountain (Db-€62, Qb-€110, cheaper Nov–mid-April, Via Gavino 22, tel. 0187-812-397, cellular 333-416-374).

Giuliano Basso rents three fine rooms that share a view

balcony (Db-€65, CC, open year-round, above train station, direction: Corniglia, take a right before Sorriso's, then take left fork, 5-min walk to harbor, cellular 333-341-4792, www.cdh.it/giuliano, e-mail: giuliano@cdh.it).

Annamaria Galleno rents a double room with bath, without a view (€52–60, tel. 0187-821-133).

Rosa Vitali rents two apartments, one for three people (has terrace), the other (for 4 people) has windows overlooking the main street (€70–110 a night, tel. 0187-821-181, cellular 340-267-5009).

LOWER PRICED

Egi Rooms, run by friendly Egidio Verduschi, offers rooms right in the center of the main drag. The common area includes a partial kitchen (no stove but fridge and sink), comfy living room, and shared bath (€25–40 per person depending on season, Via Visconti 9, call a day ahead to reserve, cellular 380-258-1712, e-mail: egidioverduschi@libero.it).

Eating in Vernazza

If you enjoy Italian cuisine, Vernazza's restaurants are worth the splurge. All take pride in their cooking and have similar prices. Wander around at about 20:00 and compare the ambience.

The **Castello**, run by gracious and English-speaking Monica, her husband Massimo, kind Mario, and the rest of her family, serves great food with great views, just under the castle (Thu–Tue 12:00–15:00 for lunch, 15:00–19:00 for drinks and snacks, 19:00–22:00 for dinner, closed Wed and Nov–April, tel. 0187-812-296).

Four fine places fill the harborfront with happy eaters: **Gambero Rosso**, considered Vernazza's best restaurant, feels classy and costs only a few euros more than the others (Tue–Sun 12:00–15:00 & 19:00–22:00, closed Mon and Nov–March, CC, Piazza Marconi 7, tel. 0187-812-265). **Trattoria del Capitano** might serve the best food for the money (Thu–Tue 12:00–15:00 & 19:00–22:30, closed Wed except in Aug, closed Dec–Jan, CC, tel. 0187-812-201, Paolo SE). **Trattoria Gianni** is also good, especially for seafood (daily 12:30–15:00 & 19:00–22:00 in July–Aug, otherwise closed Wed). **Ristorante Pizzeria Vulnetia** serves regional specialties and the best harborside pizza (Tue–Sun 12:00–16:00 & 18:30–23:00, closed Mon, Piazza Marconi 29, tel. 0187-821-193).

Trattoria da Sandro, on the main drag, mixes Genovese and Ligurian cuisine with friendly service, and can be a peaceful alternative to the harborside scene (Wed–Mon 12:00–15:00 & 19:00–22:00, closed Tue, CC, just below train station, Via Roma 60, tel. 0187-812-223, Gabriella SE). The more offbeat and intimate

Trattoria da Piva may come with late-night guitar strumming (Tue–Sun 12:00–14:30 & 19:00–22:00, closed Mon, Via Carattino 6, around corner from pharmacy, tel. 0187-812-194).

For basic grub, a grand view, and perfect peace, hike to Franco's **Ristorante "La Torre"** for a dinner at sunset (Wed–Mon 20:00–21:30, sometimes closed Tue, on trail toward Corniglia, tel. 0187-821-082).

The main street is creatively determining tourists' needs and filling them. The **Blue Marlin** bar offers a good selection of sandwiches, salads, and *bruschetta*. Try the **Forno** bakery for good focaccia and veggie tarts, and the several bars for sandwiches and pizza by the slice. Grocery stores make inexpensive sandwiches to order (Mon–Sat 8:00–13:00 & 17:00–19:30, Sun 7:30–13:00). The town's two *gelaterias* are good. **La Cantina del Molo**, the wine shop, will uncork the bottle you buy and supply cups to go (daily 10:30–20:00, until 22:00 in summer, owner makes 5 of the wines, tasting possible). Most harborside bars will let you take your glass on a breakwater stroll.

Breakfast: Locals take breakfast about as seriously as flossing. A cappuccino and a pastry or a piece of focaccia does it. The two harborfront bars offer the most ambience (you can walk out with the cup, grab a view picnic bench, and return the cup when you're done). The bakery opens early, offering freshly made focaccia. The Blue Marlin serves a special €6.20 breakfast: ham and cheese focaccia, an assortment of fresh local pastries, juice, and cappuccino (Fri–Wed 6:45–24:00, closed Thu; open daily in Aug; just below station, tel. 0187-821-149).

Sleeping in Riomaggiore (zip code: 19017)

Riomaggiore has organized its private room scene better than its neighbors. Several agencies within a few meters of each other on the main drag (with regular office hours, English-speaking staff, and e-mail addresses) manage a corral of local rooms for rent. Expect lots of stairs. The town's shuttle bus service makes getting in and out of town from the parking lot easier.

Room-Finding Services

MODERATELY PRICED

Edi's Rooms rents five fine rooms and 12 apartments—half have views (Db-€52–80, Qb-€104 depending on view, season, and number of people, CC, office open 8:00–20:00 in summer, otherwise 9:00–13:00 & 15:00–19:00, Via Colombo 111, tel. & fax 0187-920-325, tel. 0187-760-842, e-mail: edi-vesigna@iol.it).

Mar Mar Rooms, run by Mario Franceschetti, has 12 pleasant rooms, 10 apartments and a mini-hostel (dorm bed-€21, Db apartments-€55–100, seaview rooms maybe €60–80, bunky family deals, can request kitchen and balcony, CC, Internet access and small self-service laundry in office, 30 meters, or 100 feet, above train tracks on main drag next to Lampara restaurant, Via Malborghetto 4, tel. & fax 0187-920-932, e-mail: marmar@5terre.com). The same people run the recommended Albergo Caribana (below) using the same e-mail address; specify what you're interested in when you write. Mar Mar also rents kayaks (double kayaks €8/hr, cheaper by the half day).

Luciano and Roberto Fazioli loosely run five apartments, nine rooms, and a basic 11-bed mini-hostel (dorm bed-€15.50–21, D-€50–70, Db-€50–83, apartments-€21–70 per person, open at whim—making it difficult to check in and out, Via Colombo 94, tel. 0187-920-904, e-mail: robertofazioli@libero.it).

Private Rooms and Hotels

HIGHER PRICED

For a real hotel, consider **Villa Argentina**. It's on the top ridge of town (15-min walk uphill from "downtown"), with 15 crisply clean, modern rooms, fine balconies (for 9 rooms), and sea views. While this is a good choice for drivers, the little bus that shuttles people (and their luggage) between the top and bottom of town makes this hotel a possibility for train travelers (Db-€120, includes breakfast, no CC, Via de Gasperi 37, go through tunnel from station, wait for bus or walk 15 min uphill, then take a left at parking booth, tel. 0187-920-213, fax 0187-920-213, e-mail: villaargentina@libero.it).

MODERATELY PRICED

Michielini Anna rents four clean, attractive apartments in the center with kitchens and no views (€52/2 people, €93/3 people, €104/4 people mid-April–Sept, less during low season, CC to reserve but please pay cash, cheaper for longer stays, 2 nights preferred June–Sept, across from Bar Central at Colombo 143, ring bell to open door; to call friendly Daniela who speaks good English, call 0187-920-950 or cellular 328-131-1032; for solo-Italiano-speaking mother, try tel. & fax 0187-920-411; e-mail: anna.michielini@tin.it, another e-mail: michielinis@yahoo.it).

Albergo Caribana has six modern rooms with views and shared terraces. At the edge of town, it's a five-minute walk to the center. The easy parking makes this especially appealing to drivers (Db-€64–85, depending on season, includes breakfast, Via Sanctuario 114, tel. 0187-920-773, tel. & fax 0187-920-932, e-mail: marmar@5terre.com). The same people run Mar Mar Rooms, a room-finding service (see above), using the same e-mail address; specify what you want when you write.

Eating in Riomaggiore

Ristorante La Lampara serves a *frutti di mare* pizza, *trenete al pesto*, and the aromatic *spaghetti al cartoccio*—spaghetti with mixed seafood cooked in foil (€13 tourist *menu*, Wed–Mon 12:00–15:30 & 18:00–24:00, closed Tue, CC, on Via Colombo just above tracks, tel. 0187-920-120). Groceries and delis (such as Da Simone) on Via Colombo sell food to go, including pizza slices; have your picnic at the harbor.

Bar Central, run by friendly Ivo and Alberto, is a good stop for breakfast, cheeseburgers, Internet access, and live music (sometimes in summer). Ivo lived in San Francisco, fills his bar with only the best San Franciscan rock, speaks great English, and can even help you find a room. During the day, Bar Central is a shaded place to relax with other travelers. At night, it offers the only action in town (daily 7:30–1:00, closed Mon in winter only, Via Colombo 144, tel. 0187-920-208, e-mail: barcentr@tin.it). And there's prizewinning gelato next door.

While the late-night fun is at Ivo's Bar Central, take a walk down to the harborside **Dau Cila** bar (10:30–0:30, closed Tue) for jazz, nets, and mellow *limoncino*—a drink of lemon juice, sugar, and pure alcohol (a.k.a. *limoncello* elsewhere in Italy).

Sleeping in Manarola
(zip code: 19010)

Manarola has plenty of private rooms. Ask in bars and restaurants. Otherwise, you'll find a modern three-star place halfway up the main drag, a cluster of great values around the church at the peaceful top of town (a 5-min hike above the train tracks), and a salty place on the harbor. The town's handy shuttle bus service makes getting to and from your car easier.

MODERATELY PRICED

Up the hill, the utterly normal **Albergo ca' d'Andrean** is quiet, comfortable, modern, and very hotelesque, with 10 big, sunny rooms and a cool garden oasis complete with lemon trees (Sb-€60, Db-€80, breakfast-€6, closed Nov, Via A. Discovolo 101, tel. 0187-920-040, fax 0187-920-452, www.cadandrean.it, e-mail: cadandrean@libero.it, Simone SE).

Affitta Camere de Baranin rents eight newly renovated, airy, refreshing rooms (Db-€53–73, Db with view and breakfast-€85, CC to reserve but please pay cash, Internet access; climb stairway against wall beyond church square—with your back to the church, stairway is at 7:00, follow sign to Trattoria dal Billy, Via Rollandi 29, tel. & fax 0187-920-595, www.baranin.com, Sara and Silvia SE).

La Torretta has four compact apartments with kitchens, five doubles, and one quad, all attractively designed by the young, English-speaking architect/manager Gabriele Baldini (student Db-€26–36, Db-€52–72, Db apartment-€57–77, Qb-€83–124, prices vary with season, reserve with CC, cancellation fee, views, big garden; with your back to church, it's at 10:00—look left across the square toward the sea, Piazza della Chiesa, Vico Volto 14, tel. & fax 0187-920-327, also rents a Tuscan villa, see www.cinqueterre .net/torretta, e-mail: torretta@cdh.it).

Marina Piccola has 10 bright, modern rooms on the water, so they figure a warm welcome is unnecessary (Db-€80 for 1-day stays, otherwise half pension required at €72 per person, CC, Via allo Scalo 16, tel. 0187-920-103, fax 0187-920-966, www .hotelmarinapiccola.com).

LOWER PRICED

Casa Capellini rents four fine rooms; one has a view balcony, another a 360-degree terrace (D-€42, €36 for 2 or more nights; Db-€47, €42 for 2 or more nights; the *alta camera* on the top, with a kitchen, private terrace, and knockout view-€57, €52 for 2 or more nights; 2 doors down the hill from the church, with your back to the church, it's at 2:00, Via Ettore Cozzani 12, tel. 0187-920-823 or 0187-736-765, e-mail: casa.capellini@tin.it, NSE).

Ostello 5-Terre, Manarola's modern and well-run hostel, stands like a Monopoly hotel behind the church square. It's smart to reserve at least two weeks in advance in high season (one week in off-season). You book with your credit card number; if you cancel with less than three days' notice, you'll be charged for one night. This is not a party hostel; quiet is greatly appreciated (May–Sept: beds-€19, Qb-€76, new Db rooms planned for 2003; off-season: beds-€16, Qb-€64, closed early Jan–mid-Feb, CC, 48 beds in 4- to 6-bed rooms, not coed except for couples and families, office closed 13:00–17:00, rooms closed 10:00–17:00, curfew–1:00, off-season: office and rooms closed until 16:00 and curfew at 24:00, open to anyone of any age, laundry, safes, phone cards, Internet access, book exchange, elevator, optional €3.50 breakfast and €4.50–6 dinner, great roof terrace and sunset views, Via B. Riccobaldi 21, tel. 0187-920-215, fax 0187-920-218, www.cinqueterre.net/ostello, e-mail: ostello@cdh.it). They rent bikes, kayaks, and snorkeling gear.

Sleeping in Corniglia (zip code: 19010)

Perched high above the sea on a hilltop, Corniglia has plenty of private rooms (generally Db-€52). To get to the town from the station, catch the shuttle bus or take a 15-minute uphill hike.

If you hike, choose between a long road or lots of stairs. At the top of the stairs, turn left to reach the town (if you've taken the road, just stay on the road). The main drag is Via Fieschi, stretching to the tip of the promontory and its viewpoint park.

MODERATELY PRICED

For this first listing, take the road (rather than the stairs) up from the station. **Domenico Spora** has eight apartments scattered throughout town, all with views, terraces, and private bath (Db-€65, Qb-€110, Via Villa 19, tel. 0187-812-293, NSE). Her place is about three-fourths of the way up the hill from the station.

For the rest of the listings, if you've taken the stairs up from the station, turn left at the top of the stairs and walk up Via Fieschi.

At the main square, you'll see **La Lanterna** bar, which rents 10 sleepable rooms in town, some with a view (D-€50, Db-€60, also has 6 new rooms in Comeneco a 30-min walk away—better for drivers, tel. 0187-812-291, Via Fieschi 72, www.5terre.com).

Louisa Cristiana rents a great apartment with three doubles and a big comfy living room/kitchen with a view terrace on the tiny soccer court near the end of Via Fieschi at the top of the town (Db-€52, grand apartment for 2 people-€103, for 4 people-€114, for 6 people-€130, cheaper in winter, Via Fieschi 215, call English-speaking daughter Cristiana at tel. 0187-812-236—she works at Bar Matteo on Via Fieschi, below main square; also tel. & fax 0187-812-345; daughter rents small apartment for €57).

Villa Cecio, more like a hotel, has eight rooms on the outskirts of town (Db-€75, views, on main road 200 meters, or 650 feet, toward Vernazza, tel. 0187-812-038).

LOWER PRICED

Pelligrini, on a quiet side street, offers three comfortable rooms (one with a balcony) that share two baths and a terrace (D-€42; going up Via Fieschi, take a left at Via Solferino, then go right, left, and left to find #34; tel. 0187-812-184 or 0187-821-176).

Villa Sandra has five good doubles (D-€47—2 have terraces, Db-€52) and an apartment (Db-€62–68; Via Fieschi 212, tel. & fax 0187-812-384, www.cinqueterre-laposada.com, e-mail: la_posada@libero.it).

Sleeping in Monterosso (zip code: 19016)

Monterosso al Mare, the most beach-resorty of the five Cinque Terre towns, offers maximum comfort and ease. There are plenty of hotels and rentable beach umbrellas, shops, and cars. The TI (Pro Loco) can give you a list of €30-per-person doubles (pricier for a single) in a private home (Mon–Sat 10:00–12:45 & 14:15–19:00, Sun 10:00–12:45; exiting station, TI is to your left; tel. 0187-817-506) or check with either of the Internet cafés in town.

Monterosso is 30 minutes off the freeway (exit: Carrodano). Parking is easy in the huge, beachfront guarded lot (€10.50/day).

Recommended hotels are listed for the old town and the new town (connected by a tunnel), with a convent-run place in between. To locate hotels, see the map on page 308. My favorite is the Hotel Villa Steno in the old town. To get to the old town from the station, exit left, walk along the waterfront, and go through the tunnel.

Sleeping in the Old Town

HIGHER PRICED

The lovingly managed **Hotel Villa Steno** features great view balconies, private gardens off some rooms, air-conditioning, and the friendly help of English-speaking Matteo. Of his 16 rooms, 12 have view balconies (Sb-€85, Db-€130, Tb-€150, Qb-€170, includes hearty buffet breakfast, CC, €10 discount per room per night if you pay cash and show this book, Internet access, self-service laundry—guests only, 10-min hike from train station to the top of old town at Via Roma 109, tel. 0187-817-028 or 0187-818-336, fax 0187-817-354, www.pasini.com, e-mail: steno@pasini.com). Readers get a free Cinque Terre info packet and a glass of the local sweet wine, *sciacchetrà*, when they check in—ask. The Steno has a tiny parking lot (free, but call to reserve a spot).

Albergo Pasquale is a modern, comfortable place, run by the same family who owns Hotel Villa Steno (see listing above). It's just a few steps from the beach, boat dock, tunnel entrance (to new town), and train tracks. The air-conditioning minimizes any train noise (Sb-€85, Db-€130, Tb-€150, Qb-€170, includes breakfast, CC, €10 discount per room per night if you pay cash and show this book, readers get a free glass of the local sweet wine—*sciacchetrà*—at check-in, same-day laundry service, Via Fegina 4, tel. 0187-817-550 or 0187-817-477, fax 0187-817-056, e-mail: pasquale@pasini.com, Felicita and Marco SE).

The next two places, next door to each other on a quiet street, both require half pension during peak season: the fancy **Albergo degli Amici** (40 modern rooms, Db-€90–124, breakfast extra, Db with half pension-€150—required July–Aug, CC, no views from rooms, peaceful above-it-all view garden with "sun beds"—lawn chairs with movable sun shades, Via Buranco 36, tel. 0187-817-544, fax 0187-817-424, www.cinqueterre.it/hotel_amici) and the less fancy **Albergo Marina** (23 decent rooms, Db with required half pension-€97–126, CC, elevator, air-con, garden

with lemon trees, next door at Via Buranco 40, tel. & fax 0187-817-242 or 0187-817-613, www.hotelmarinacinqueterre.it).
To get to the Amici and Marina from the old town harbor, go to the left of the arcaded building with the bell tower and turn left after a block; for the next listing go to the right of the arcaded building up Via Roma.

MODERATELY PRICED

Hotel La Colonnina, a comfy, modern place on a sleepy side street, takes reservations in advance only for three-night stays. For a shorter stay, just call a day or two ahead to see if they have space (Db-€95, no breakfast, elevator, garden, rooftop terrace, Via Zuecca 6, tel. 0187-817-439). In the old town by the train tracks, look for the playground and the square with a statue of Garibaldi; Via Zuecca is directly behind him (the hotel is one block up, to the right).

Sleeping between the Old and New Towns

MODERATELY PRICED

The religious **Convento dei Cappuccini** rents 15 spartan rooms on the hill above the tunnel connecting the old and new parts of town. The terrace, overlooking the garden and a long stretch of coastline, has a tremendous panoramic view. It's a steep hike on foot, or take a taxi (€8) to the cemetery 200 meters/650 feet) away—go around or walk through cemetery to reach the convent. Its door is to the left of the church (S-€34, D-€68, Db-€78, all twins, includes breakfast, dinner extra and optional, reserve ahead, must send a deposit of 30 percent—personal check OK, 19016 Monterosso, tel. 0187-817-531, e-mail: monterosso.convento @libero.it, truly NSE, but e-mail in English is OK). To hike to the convent from the station (15 min), follow the recommended walk listed in Cinque Terre Towns/Monterosso, above.

Sleeping in the New Town

Turn right leaving the station for the following listings.

HIGHER PRICED

The central, waterfront **Hotel Baia** has appealing, high-ceilinged rooms, but the staff is rude (Db-€100–140, includes breakfast, CC, slow elevator, balconies, request view—same price, Via Fegina 88, tel. 0187-817-512, fax 0187-818-322).

Hotel Punta Mesco has 17 new, modern rooms (Db-€104, CC, discount with cash, no views, free parking, exit right from station, take first right, Via Molinelli 35, tel. 0187-817-495, www .hotelpuntamesco.it).

Villa Adriana, run by brusque Austrian nuns, has 55 decent, clean rooms divided between a 19th-century villa and an adjacent, modern annex. With a strict 23:00 curfew, a lofty setting (up off the street with a tropical garden as its front yard), and a religious, institutional atmosphere, it's peaceful (Sb-€65, Db-€130, half pension required June–mid-Sept: Sb-€75, Db-€140, CC, double and twins available, some views, attached chapel, elevator, parking, exit right from station, walk along waterfront, turn right at Via IV Novembre, 300 meters, or 985 feet, off beach, Via IV Novembre 23, reception at back of building, tel. 0187-818-109, fax 0187-818-128, SE).

MODERATELY PRICED

Villa Mario, good for backpackers, has three basic rooms with a view terrace and a squawky bird (Db-€62–72, exit right from station, take second right, walk 5 min uphill, Via Padre Semeria 28, tel. & fax 0187-818-030).

Turn left out of the station for **Pension Agavi**, which has 10 bright, airy rooms (Sb-€47, Db-€85, refrigerators, Fegina 30, tel. 0187-817-171, cellular 336-258-467, fax 0187-818-264, www.paginegialle.it/hotelagavi, e-mail: hotel.agavi@libero.it, spunky Hillary SE).

Eating in Monterosso's Old Town

Ristorante Belvedere is a good bet for good value. Their *Amphora di Pesce*—mixed seafood stew (€42/2 people minimum)—is inspiring (Wed–Mon 12:00–14:30 & 19:00–22:00, closed Tue, CC, right on the harbor, across from Albergo Pasquale, tel. 0187-817-033).

La Cambusa serves up traditional Ligurian cuisine to hungry locals and tourists alike (Tue–Sun 12:00–14:30 & 18:45–22:30, closed Mon except July–Aug, Via Garibaldi 10, tel. 0187-817-690).

Lots of shops and bakeries sell pizza and focaccia for an easy picnic at the beach. **L'Alta Marea** offers a specialty fish ravioli, the catch of the day, and huge crocks of fresh, steamed mussels (Thu–Tue 12:00–15:00 & 18:30–22:30, closed Wed, Via Roma 54, tel. 0187-817-170). **Il Frantoio** makes tasty pizza to go (Wed–Fri 9:00–14:00 & 16:00–20:00, closed Thu, Via Gioberti 1, just off Via Roma, tel. 0187-818-333). For a quick salad or sandwich near the beach, try **Il Casello,** next to the *bocce* court on the trail to Vernazza (Wed–Mon 11:30–2:00, closed Tue, tel. 0187-818-330).

Transportation Connections—Cinque Terre

The five towns of the Cinque Terre are on a milk-run train line described earlier in this chapter. Hourly trains connect each town with the others, La Spezia, and Genoa. While a few of the milk-run trains go to more distant points (Milan or Pisa), it's faster to change in La Spezia or Monterosso to a bigger train. Train info: Monterosso tel. 0187-817-458 or 848-888-088 (automated in Italian).

From La Spezia by train to: Rome (10/day, 4 hrs), **Pisa** (hrly, 1 hr, direction: Livorno, Rome, Salerno, Naples, etc.), **Florence** (hrly, 2.5 hrs, change at Pisa), **Milan** (hrly, 3 hrs direct or 4 hrs with change in Genoa), **Venice** (2 direct 6-hr trains/day).

From Monterosso by train to: Venice (2/day, 6 hrs), **Milan** (3/day, 3 hrs), **Genova** (9/day, 1.25 hrs), **Turin** (5/day, 3.25 hrs), **Pisa** (3/day, 1.5 hrs), **Sestri Levante** (hrly, 15 min, most trains to Genova stop here), **La Spezia** (nearly hrly, 20 min), **Levanto** (nearly hrly, 6 min).

Tips for Drivers

All of the Cinque Terre towns except Corniglia have a parking lot and a shuttle bus to get you into town. Monterosso's guarded beachfront lot fills only on August weekends (€10.50/day).

To drive to Monterosso or Vernazza, exit the autostrada at Uscita Carrodano west of La Spezia (note that the drive down to Vernazza is scenic, narrow, and treacherous). To drive to Riomaggiore, leave the freeway at La Spezia.

You can park your car near the train stations in La Spezia or Levanto (the first town past Monterosso). Confirm that parking is OK and leave nothing inside to steal. In La Spezia, the garage near the station can store your car for about €13 per day.

NEAR THE CINQUE TERRE

La Spezia, a gateway to the Cinque Terre, is simply a place to stay if you can't find a room in the Cinque Terre (20–30 min away by train). Carrara is a quickie for marble-lovers who are driving between Pisa and La Spezia. The picturesque village of Portovenere, near La Spezia, has scenic boat connections with Cinque Terre towns. Levanto has a long beach and a scenic trail to Monterosso (2.5-hour hike, or easier, 6 min by train). Sestri Levante, on a narrow peninsula flanked by two beaches, is for sunseekers (15 min by train from Cinque Terre). Santa Margherita Ligure (75 min by train from the Cinque Terre) is more of a real town, with actual sights, beaches, and easy connections with Portofino by trail, bus, or boat.

LA SPEZIA

When all else fails, you can stay in a noisy, bigger town such as La Spezia. While just a quick train ride away from the fanciful Five Terre, La Spezia feels like work-a-day Italy.

Cinque Terre Area

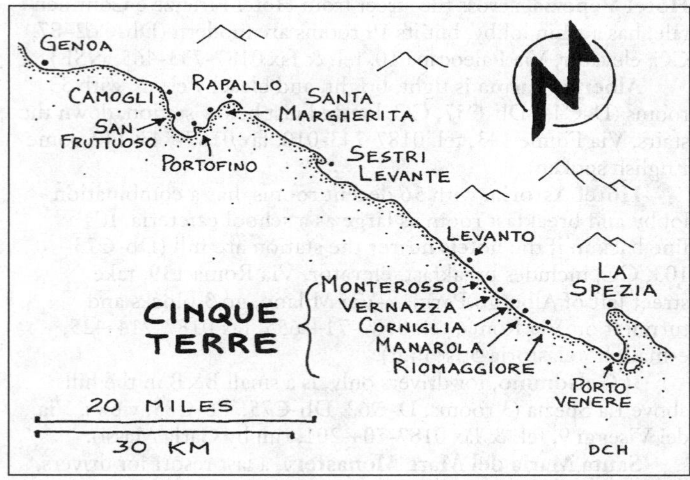

The TI is a 20-minute walk from the station, near the waterfront (Mon–Sat 9:00–13:00 & 15:00–18:00, Sun 9:00–13:00, Viale Mazzini 45, tel. 0187-770-900). There's usually a kiosk branch at the station in summer. If not, skip it.

Sights are slim. On Friday mornings, a huge open-air market sprawls along Via Garibaldi (about 6 blocks from station). The pedestrian zone on Via del Prione to the gardens along the harbor makes a pleasant stroll. The **Museo Amedeo Lia** displays Italian paintings from the 13th to 18th centuries (€6.20, Tue–Sun 10:00–18:00, closed Mon, last entry 30 min before closing, no photos allowed, 10-min walk from station at Via Prione 234, tel. 0187-731-100, www.castagna.it/mal).

Sleeping in La Spezia

(€1 = about $1, country code: 39)

The first four hotels are within a five-minute walk from the station. The last two are for drivers only. Only the first has air-conditioning.

HIGHER PRICED

The grand, old, but newly restored **Hotel Firenze e Continentale** has 68 rooms with all the classy comforts (Sb-€69–80, Db-€115, maybe €93 in slow time, includes buffet breakfast, CC, air-con, double-paned windows, some non-smoking rooms, elevator, parking-€13/day, Via Paleocapa 7, tel. 0187-713-200, fax 0187-714-930, www.hotelfirenzecontinentale.it, SE).

MODERATELY PRICED

Hotel Venezia, across the street from Hotel Firenze e Continentale, has a plain lobby, but its 19 rooms are modern (Db-€62–87, CC, elevator, Via Paleocapa 10, tel. & fax 0187-733-465, NSE).

Albergo Parma is tight, bright, and bleachy clean, with 33 rooms (D-€44, Db-€57, CC, located just below station, down the stairs, Via Fiume 143, tel. 0187-743-010, fax 0187-743-240, some English spoken).

Hotel Astoria, with 56 decent rooms, has a combination lobby and breakfast room as large as a school cafeteria. It's a fine backup if the hotels nearer the station are full (Db-€73–103, CC, includes breakfast, elevator, Via Roma 139, take street left of Albergo Parma—Via Milano, go 3 blocks and turn left on Via Roma, tel. 0187-714-655, fax 0187-714-425, e-mail: hotelastoria@tiscali.it).

Il Gelsomino, for drivers only, is a small B&B in the hills above La Spezia (3 rooms, D-€62, Db-€75, Tb-€85, views, Via dei Viseggi 9, tel. & fax 0187-704-201, run by Carla Massi).

Santa Maria del Mare Monastery, a last resort for drivers, rents 100 comfortable rooms high above La Spezia in a scenic but institutional setting (Db-€78, Castellazzo Stra, tel. 0187-700-365 or 0187-711-332, e-mail: mare@tamnet.it).

CARRARA

Perhaps the world's most famous marble quarries are just east of La Spezia in Carrara. Michelangelo himself traveled to these valleys to pick out the marble that he would work into his masterpieces. The towns of the region are dominated by marble. The quarries higher up are vast digs that dwarf their hardworking trucks and machinery. The Carrara museum allows visitors to trace the story of marble-cutting here from pre-Roman times until today. For a guided visit, Sara Paolini is excellent (€78/half-day tour, tel. 0585-632-617, cellular 347-888-3833, e-mail: casara00@hotmail.com). She is accustomed to meeting and joining drivers at the Carrara freeway exit.

PORTOVENERE

While the gritty port of La Spezia offers little in the way of redeeming touristic value, the nearby resort of Portovenere is enchanting. This Cinque Terre–esque village clings to a rocky promontory jutting into the sea, protecting the harbor from the crashing waves. On the harbor, next to colorful bobbing boats, a row of restaurants—perfect for alfresco dining—feature local specialities such as *trenette* pasta with pesto and spaghetti *frutti di mare*.

Local boats take you on excursions to nearby islands or over to Lerici, the town across the bay. Lord Byron swam to Lerici (not recommended). Hardy hikers enjoy the two-hour (or more) hike to Riomaggiore, the nearest Cinque Terre town.

Portovenere is an easy day trip from the Cinque Terre by boat (Easter–late Oct, nearly hrly 10:00–18:00), or take the bus from La Spezia (25 min). In peak season, buses shuttle drivers from the parking lot just outside Portovenere to the harborside square.

Sleeping: If you forgot your yacht, try **Albergo Il Genio**, in the building where the main street hits the piazza (Db-€62–83, Piazza Bastreri 8, tel. 0187-790-611). If your *vita* is feeling *dolce*, consider **Grand Hotel Portovenere** (from €108 for viewless double off-season to €375 for view suite in summer with half pension, tel. 0187-792-610, fax 0187-790-661, e-mail: ghp@village.it).

LEVANTO

Graced with a long, sandy beach, Levanto is packed in summer. The rest of the year, it's just a small, sleepy town, with less colorful charm and fewer tourists than the Cinque Terre towns. Levanto has a new section (gridded-street plan) and a twisty old town (bisected by a modern street), plus a few pedestrian streets, a castle (not open), and a scenic, no-wimps-allowed hike to Monterosso (1.5 hrs).

For an energetic day trip, hike from Monterosso to Levanto, play in the surf (or collapse on the beach), take a look at the town, and catch the boat or the train back home.

From the Levanto train station to the TI, it's a 10-minute walk (head down the stairs in front of the station, cross the bridge, then follow Corso Roma to Piazza Mazzini). Drivers can park free at the train station (there's also a free lot north of TI, but it's near a pay lot—confirm you're in the free one). At the TI, pick up a map (Mon–Sat 9:00–13:00 & 15:00–18:00, Sun 9:00–13:00, longer hours in summer, shorter in winter, tel. 0187-808-125).

The beach is just two blocks away from the TI. During the summer, half the beach is free *(libero)*, the other half is broken up into private sections that require an admission fee. Off-season, roughly October through May, when the sea is free, you can stroll the entire beach. Facing the harbor, the boat dock is to your far left and the diving center is at your far right (you can rent boats in summer at either place).

The old town, several blocks from the TI and beach, clusters around Piazza del Popolo. Until 10 years ago, the town market *(mercato)* was held at the 13th-century loggia in the square. Explore the backstreets. To get to the trailhead to Monterosso: From Piazza del Popolo, head uphill to the striped church, Chiesa di S. Andrea (with your back to the loggia, go straight ahead—across the square and up Via Don Emanuele Toso to the church). From the church courtyard, follow the sign to the *castello* (castle), go around the castle, and turn left. You'll see the sign for Punta Mesco, the rugged tip of the peninsula. From here you can hike up (1.5 hrs to Monterosso), or—if you have second thoughts—hike down, taking the stairs to the beach. You'll end up near the dock, where you can catch the boat for the Cinque Terre towns.

For picnic supplies, try Levanto's modern, covered *mercato* (Mon–Sat 9:00–13:00, closed Sun, fish and produce market, between train station and TI; the street it's on—only a decade old—hasn't yet been officially named). On Wednesday morning, an open-air market fills the street in front of the *mercato*.

To get to the Cinque Terre, take the train (nearly hrly, 6 min to Monterosso) or the boat (2/day, stops at every Cinque Terre town except Corniglia, Easter–Oct).

Sleeping in Levanto

(€1 = about $1, country code: 39, zip code: 19015)

In the popular beach town, a number of hotels require you to take half pension (lunch or dinner) in summer. A self-service **laundry** is at Piazza Staglieno 38 (daily 8:30–23:00).

MODERATELY PRICED

Ristorante la Loggia has eight pleasant rooms perched above the old loggia on Piazza del Popolo (Db-€47–62, includes breakfast, half pension not required, air-con, request balcony, quieter rooms in back, apartment available, attached restaurant, Piazza del Popolo 7, tel. & fax 0187-808-107, www.locandalaloggia.it).

Albergo Primavera has 17 comfortable rooms—10 with terraces but no views—just a half block from the beach (Db-€98, Db with half pension required June–Aug-€134, buffet breakfast, closed Nov–Jan, CC, Via Cairoli 5, a block from TI, tel. 0187-808-023, fax 0187-801-588, e-mail: info@primaverahotel.com, friendly staff speaks a little English).

Hotel Europa, also a block from the TI, is a good bet, with 22 decent, well-maintained rooms (Db-€88, Db with half pension required April–Aug-€164, CC, roof terrace, elevator, Via Dante Alighieri 41, tel. 0187-808-126, fax 0187-808-594, e-mail: albeurop@tin.it).

LOWER PRICED

Hostel: The **Ostello Ospitalia del Mare** offers 67 beds, bright rooms, Internet access, and a terrace in a well-built building in the old town (beds-€19–28 in 2-, 4-, 6-, and 8-bed rooms with private bath, includes breakfast and sheets, CC, anyone welcome, not coed except for couples and families, no curfew, office hours daily 8:00–13:00 & 14:30–23:00, Via San Nicolo 1, tel. 0187-802-562, fax 0187-803-696, www.ospitaliadelmare.it, SE).

Eating in Levanto

Totano Blu offers Ligurian specialties and pizzas at reasonable prices in the old town (Fri–Wed 12:00–14:00 & 19:00–22:00, Thu 19:00–22:00, Via Molinelli 10/12, tel. 0187-808-714). **Osteria Tumelin** is a bit spendier, but has great fresh seafood and ambience (Fri–Wed 12:00–14:30 & 19:00–22:30, closed Thu, Via D. Grillo, across street from loggia, tel. 0187-808-379).

Antico Caffe' Roma, a favorite among locals for affordable seafood and pasta, has alfresco dining in the back (Wed–Mon 12:00–15:00 & 19:00–22:00, closed Tue, Piazza Staglieno 10, tel. 0187-808-514).

Focaccerie, *rosticcerie*, and delis with take-out pasta abound on Via D. Alighieri. **Polleria** sells roasted chicken and potatoes to go (Tue–Sun 8:00–12:30 & 16:00–20:00, closed Mon, Via Cairoli 3). **Focacceria il Falcone** has a great selection of focaccia with different toppings (Tue–Sun 9:30–20:00, closed Mon, Via Cairoli 19). Piazza C. Colombo, with its benches and sea view, makes an excellent picnic site. For a shadier setting, lay out your spread on a bench near Piazza Staglieno.

For dessert, sample **Il Penguino Gelateria** on Piazza Staglieno 38 (Thu–Tue 8:00–late, closed Wed) or **Il Porticciolo Gelateria** at the end of Via Cairoli in Piazzeta Marina (closed Mon).

SESTRI LEVANTE

This peninsular town is squeezed as skinny as a hot dog between its two beaches. The pedestrian-friendly Corso Columbo, which runs down the middle of the peninsula, is lined with shops selling take-away pizza, pastries, and beach paraphernalia. The rocky, forested bluff at the end of the peninsula is inaccessible to the public (it's the huge backyard of the fancy Hotel Castelli). Market day is Saturday at Piazza Aldo Moro (8:00–13:00).

The best, quick visit from the station (luggage storage-€2.60—if the office is closed, ask at the newsstand) starts with a five-minute walk to the TI to get a map (May–Sept Mon–Sat 9:30–12:30 & 15:30–18:30, Sun 9:30–12:30 & 16:30–19:30, Oct–April closes at 17:30 and on Sun; go straight out of station on Via Roma, turn left at fountain in park, TI at next square—Piazza S. Antonio 10, tel. 0185-457-011). Roads fan out from Piazza S. Antonio like spokes. From the TI, you're one "spoke" away from Corso Columbo (to the left of Bermuda Bar) that runs up the peninsula. Stroll this street until nearly the end (about 5 min). Just before you get to the large white church at the end, turn off for either beach (the free public beach, Baia del Silencio, is on your left). Or head uphill behind the church to the Hotel Castelli for a drink at their view café (so-so view, reasonably priced drinks, café is at end of parking lot to your right). On the way up the hill you'll pass the evocative arches of a ruined chapel, bombed during World War II, and left as a memorial.

Most people are here for the sun. The beaches are named after the bays *(baias)* they border. The bigger beach, Baia delle Favole, is divided up much of the year (May–Sept) into sections that you pay to enter. The fees, which can soar up to €24 in August, generally include chairs, umbrellas, and fewer crowds. There are several small free sections: at the ends and in the middle (look for *libere* signs). The town's other beach, Baia del Silencio, is narrow, virtually all free, and packed, providing a good chance to see Italian families at play. There isn't much more to do than unroll a beach towel and join in.

You're in good company. Hans Christian Andersen enjoyed his visit here in the mid-1800s, writing, "What a fabulous evening I spent in Sestri Levante!" One of the bays—Baia delle Favole—is named in his honor (*favole* means fairy tale). The last week of May is a street festival, culminating in a ceremony for locals who write the best fairy tales (4 prizes for 4 age groups, from pre-kindergarten to adult). The "Oscar" awards are little mermaids. The small mermaid curled on the edge of the fountain (behind the TI) is another nod to the beloved Danish storyteller.

Even Hans found Sestri Levante easy to reach by train, just 15 minutes away from Monterosso (hourly connections with Monterosso, nearly hourly with other Cinque Terre towns).

Sleeping and Eating in Sestri Levante

(€1 = about $1, country code: 39, zip code: 16039)

HIGHER PRICED

Hotel Due Mari has three stars, 49 fine rooms, and a rooftop terrace with a super view of both beaches. Ideally, reserve well in advance (Db-€95–130 depending on view, Db with half pension required July–Aug-€136–172, CC, some air-con, elevator, garden, swimming pool with heated seawater, take Corso Columbo to the end, hotel is behind church, free parking first day—then €8/day, Vico del Coro 18, tel. 0185-42695, fax 0185-42698, www.duemarihotel.it, e-mail: hotelduemari@inwind.it, SE).

Hotel Helvetia, overlooking Baia del Silencio, is another good three-star bet, with 24 bright rooms, a large view terrace, and a peaceful atmosphere (Db-€114–160 depending on view/balcony, includes breakfast, CC, air-con, elevator, parking-€10/day, from Corso Columbo turn left on Palestro and angle left at square, Via Cappuccini 43, tel. 0185-41175, fax 0185-457-216, www.rainbownet.it/helvetia, SE).

MODERATELY PRICED

Hotel Elisabetta, less central and cheaper, has 38 comfortable rooms on a busy street at the end of Baia delle Favole, a block from the beach (Db-€70–80 depending on season, half pension available but not required, CC, ask for quieter room in back, Via Novara 7, walk straight out of station, then turn right at park, 12-min walk, tel. 0185-41128, fax 0185-487-206, e-mail: albergoelisabetta@libero.it, NSE).

Hotel dei Fiori has 15 basic rooms across Piazza S. Antonio from the TI office (Db-€55–68, includes breakfast, CC, double-paned windows, request a *tranquillo* room in back, Via Nazionale 12, tel. & fax 0185-41147, NSE).

Eating in Sestri Levante

At **L'Osteria Mattana**, where everyone shares long tables, you can mix with locals while enjoying traditional cuisine (Tue–Sun 19:30–22:30, also Fri–Sun 12:30–14:30, closed Mon, Via XXV Aprile 26, take Corso Columbo from TI, turns into XXV Aprile, restaurant on right, tel. 0185-457-633). **Polpo Mario** is classier but affordable, with a good people-watching location on the main drag (Tue–Sun 12:00–14:30 & 19:30–22:30, closed Mon, Via XXV Aprile 163, tel. 0185-480-203). **Ristorante Previna** has good seafood and pizzas at fair prices (closed Wed, Piazza della Repubblica 23, tel. 0185-482-397).

SANTA MARGHERITA LIGURE

If you need the movie star's Riviera, park your yacht at Portofino. Or you can settle down in the nearby and more personable Santa Margherita Ligure (15 min by bus from Portofino and 75 min by train from the Cinque Terre). While Portofino's velour allure is tarnished by snobby residents and a nonstop traffic jam in peak season, Santa Margherita tumbles easily downhill from its train station. The town has a fun resort character and a breezy promenade.

On a quick day trip, walk the beach promenade, see the small old town, and catch the bus (or boat) to Portofino to see what all the fuss is about. With more time, Santa Margherita makes a fine overnight stop.

Tourist Information: Pick up a map at the TI (daily 9:00–12:30 & 15:00–19:30, in winter Mon–Sat 9:00–12:30 & 14:30–17:30, closed Sun, Via XXV Aprile 2b, tel. 0185-287-485, www.apttigullio.liguria.it).

Arrival by Train: To get to the city center from the station, take the stairs marked *Mare* (Sea) down to the harbor. The harborfront promenade is as wide as the skimpy beach. (The real beaches, which are pebbly, are a 10-min walk farther on, past the port.)

To get to the pedestrian-friendly old town and the TI, take a right at Piazza Veneto (with the roundabout, flags, and park) onto Largo Antonio Giusti. For the TI, angle left on Via XXV Aprile. For the old town (a block off Piazza Veneto), head toward the TI, but turn left on Via Torino, which opens almost immediately onto Piazza Caprera, a square with a church and fruit vendors (Mon–Sat morn) in the midst of pedestrian streets.

Day-trippers: If the train station still doesn't store luggage, you might be able to check it at Hotel Terminus, next to the station (€5/day).

Internet Access: Internet Point gives readers with this book a free additional 30 minutes (€5.20/30 min, daily 9:00–21:00, Via Guinchetto 39, off Piazza Mazzini, tel. 0185-293-092, run by owners of recommended Hotel Fasce). **Papiluc's Bar** offers Internet access until 2:00 (see "Eating in Santa Margherita Ligure," page 1045).

Sights—Santa Margherita Ligure

Villa Durazzo—If you need a sight more than a beach or hike, wander through this 17th-century villa. It's the distinctive (garish?), green-shuttered, rust-colored building atop the hill, a couple of blocks inland from Piazza Martiri della Libertà. The building has changed aristocratic hands several times, and, in the early 20th century, even served as a grand hotel. It was sold to the city in 1973. The interior has some period furniture, several grand pianos, chandeliers, and paintings strewn with cupids on the walls and ceilings. Even with the furniture, it's a bit stark. You can tour it on your own with an English info sheet, or, if you call ahead—even on the same day—you might snare a tour in English (€5.20, or €6.20 with tour, summer Tue–Sun 9:00–17:00, winter Tue–Sun 9:30–16:00, closed Mon, WC in adjacent building, tel. 0185-205-449).

The **garden** surrounding the villa is laced with dirt trails and stone-mosaic paths. The greenery, unkempt and evocative at the base of the hill, is tamed on top, with manicured hedges, statuary, and a wide mosaic terrace offering a view of the sea and marina. Bring a picnic and find a bench (free, daily 9:00–19:00 in summer, until 17:00 in winter).

Castle—The small castle overlooking the harbor, just off Piazza Martiri della Libertà, is open if there's an exhibit; check with the TI. If the castle is closed, walk uphill just past the castle to the church for the view from its terrace.

Markets—Around 16:00 on weekdays, fishing boats dock at the fish market to unload their catch, which is then sold to waiting customers. The market—Mercato del Pesce—is the rust-colored building with arches and columns on Via Marconi, on the harbor, just past the castle. The **open-air market**, a commotion of clothes and produce, is held every Friday morning on Corso Matteotti (between the castle and harbor).

Side-Trip to Portofino

Santa Margherita Ligure, with its aristocratic architecture, hints of old money, whereas Portofino, with its sleek shops, reeks of the new. Fortunately, a few pizzerias, bars, and grocery shops are mixed in with Portofino's jewelry shops, art galleries, and clothing boutiques, making the town bearable. The *piccolo* harbor, classic Italian architecture, and wooded peninsula can even turn Portofino into an appealing package, if you look past the glitzy wrapping.

Portofino's **TI** is downhill from the bus stop, on your right (daily in summer 10:30–13:30 & 14:00–19:30, in winter Tue–Sun 10:30–13:30 & 14:30–17:30, closed Mon, Via Roma 35, tel. 0185-269-024). Pick up a free town map and a rudimentary hiking map. Trails are signed well enough.

For hikers, the best thing about Portofino is leaving it. Options include the well-trodden path that leads out to the lighthouse at the point (20 min, nonstop views; the medieval castle en route may still be under restoration in 2003); the pedestrian promenade to Paraggi (20 min, parallels main road, ends at ritzy beach where it's easy to catch the bus back to Santa Margherita Ligure); the trail to Santa Margherita Ligure (1 hr); and the trail to San Fruttuoso Abbey (2.5 hrs, steep at beginning and end).

The 11th-century **San Fruttuoso Abbey,** accessible only by foot or boat (from Portofino or Santa Margherita) isn't the main attraction. The intriguing draw is a statue of Christ of the Abyss (Cristo degli Abissi), 18 meters (60 feet) underwater. Boats run from the abbey to the Christ, where you can look down to see him, his arms outstretched, reaching upward.

Getting to Portofino from Santa Margherita: Portofino is an easy day trip by bus, boat, or foot.

Catch **bus** #82 from Santa Margherita's train station or at bus stops along the harbor (€1, 2–3/hr, 15 min, buy tickets at bar at station, at bus kiosk at Piazza Veneto—open daily 7:10–19:40, or at any shop that displays a *Biglietti Bus* sign).

The **boat** makes the trip with more class and without the traffic jams (€3.60 one-way, €6 round-trip, hrly in summer, 2/day in spring and fall, 2/day only on Sun in winter, dock is off Piazza Martiri della Libertà, a 2-min walk from Piazza Veneto, call to confirm or pick up schedule from TI, tel. 0185-284-670, www.traghettiportofino.it); the boats run between Rapallo and the San Fruttuoso Abbey, stopping in between at Santa Margherita Ligure and Portofino.

Hikers call the one-hour **Santa Margherita–Portofino hike** one of the best on the Riviera (5 km, or 3 miles, start at Via Maragliano, several blocks past the castle).

Sleeping in Santa Margherita Ligure
(€1 = about $1, country code: 39, zip code: 16038)

HIGHER PRICED

For a room with a view, try **Hotel Laurin.** All of its 43 rooms face the sea, most have terraces, and there's a heated pool and sundeck on the third floor (Sb-€75–105, Db-€119–155 depending on season, air-con, double-paned windows, elevator, Lungomare G. Marconi 3, past the castle, about a 15-min walk from station, CC, tel. 0185-289-971, fax 0185-285-709, www.laurinhotel.it, e-mail: info@laurinhotel.it).

Hotel Jolanda is two blocks east of the TI and 100 meters (330 feet) from the sea (Db-€122, superior Db-€130, CC, Via Luisito Costa 6, tel. 0185-287-512 or 0185-287-513, fax 0185-284-763, www.hoteljolanda.it, e-mail: desk@hoteljolanda.it).

MODERATELY PRICED

Hotel Fasce is a hardworking place with 18 bright rooms and a happy clientele (Sb-€77, Db-€92, Tb-€118, Qb-€138, includes breakfast, happy hour welcome drink, CC, free round-trip train tickets to Cinque Terre for 3-night stays, parking-€16/day, free bikes, English newspapers, roof garden, laundry service-€16, a 10-min walk from the station at Via Bozzo 3, taxi from station costs about €10, tel. 0185-286-435, fax 0185-283-580, www.hotelfasce.it, run enthusiastically by Jane Fasce—an Englishwoman—and her husband, Aristide).

Hotel Fiorina, with 55 airy rooms decorated in a light-and-dark color scheme, is on a busy square with quieter rooms in the back. It's family-run with pride and care (Db-€89 with breakfast, Db-€74 without breakfast, half pension possible, CC, fans in every room, sun terrace—no view, Piazza Mazzini 26, 2 blocks inland from pedestrian Piazza Caprera, tel. 0185-287-517, fax 0185-281-855, www.paginegialle.it/hfiorina, e-mail: fiorinasml@libero.it, SE).

At **Hotel Nuova Riviera**, a stately old villa, the Sabini family offers 12 non-smoking rooms (Db-€90, Tb-€116, Qb-€145, discount of €5 per day if you pay cash, includes breakfast, CC, mother Angela cooks dinner—optional, fans in every room, some balconies, Internet access, free parking—first-come, first-served, peaceful garden, 10-min walk from station; walking or driving, follow signs to hospital, on Piazza Mazzini see hotel signs, Via Belvedere 10, tel. & fax 0185-287-403, www.nuovariviera.com, e-mail: info@nuovariviera.com, pleasant daughter Cristina and temperamental son Giancarlo SE). Their annex is cheaper (3 nights preferred, D-€62, T-€88, Q-€104, 4 rooms share 2 bathrooms, includes breakfast, cash only). Note that if you cancel your reservations, you'll be billed for one night. They also rent a nearby apartment by the week (for 2 people-€530, for 4-€830, deposit required, cellular 329-982-2689, e-mail: info@villinomatilde.com).

By the Train Station

These three hotels, close to the train station, all come with train noise.

HIGHER PRICED

Nuovo Hotel Garden is tucked away down a side street. From its 31 comfortable rooms to its restaurant, the hotel is high-quality (Db-€58–114 depending on season, CC, terrace, bar, double-paned windows on train side, Via Zara 13, a block from train station—instead of taking the stairs down to harbor, face stairs and go right, tel. 0185-285-398, fax 0185-290-439, www.nuovohotelgarden.com, SE).

MODERATELY PRICED

Hotel Conte Verde, next door to Nuovo Hotel Garden, rents 33 rooms (some newly remodeled) of varying quality and price. Ask if a room with a big terrace is available (Sb-€50–99, D-€52–78, Db-€70–155, price depends on season and size, includes breakfast, exercise room and hydromassage, CC, garden, 6 free bikes, big public areas, parking-€11/day—call ahead to reserve, Via Zara 1, tel. 0185-287-139, fax 0185-284-211, e-mail: info@hotelconteverde.com, SE).

Hotel Terminus, with 24 rooms right at the station, works hard to keep its customers satisfied (Db-€87, includes huge breakfast, CC, terrace, good meals, some view rooms, triple-paned windows, ask for room away from tracks, tel. 0185-286-121, fax 0185-282-546, Angelo SE).

Eating in Santa Margherita Ligure

Ristorante il Faro, which serves good seafood and more, is atmospheric, with rows of wine bottles lining its wainscoted walls (€25 and €30 *menus,* à la carte options, lunch from 12:20, dinner from 19:20, closed Tue, 2 blocks inland from port, Via Maragliano 24a, tel. 0185-286-867).

Ristorante "A' Lampara," on the same street, is the locals' favorite for affordable Genovese cuisine. Try their specialty fish ravioli—*ravioli di pesce* (Fri–Wed 12:00–14:00 & 19:30–22:00, closed Thu, Via Maragliano 33, tel. 0185-288-926).

Ristorante il Nostromo, cheaper and more central, offers a €17 menu plus à la carte options (closed Tue, Via dell' Arco 6, a block off Piazza Veneto, take Via Gramsi and turn inland on Via dell' Arco, tel. 0185-281-390). **Papiluc's Bar**, a rare Internet café that's actually a café, is on the same street, a few doors down (Fri–Wed 6:30–2:00, closed Thu, Via dell' Arco 20, tel. 0185-282-580). **Dal Baffo,** nearby, is a good pizzeria (Wed–Mon 12:00–15:00 & 18:30–1:00, closed Tue, Corso Matteotti 56, tel. 0185-288-987).

Da Pezzi is a cheap and cheerful greasy spoon packed with locals munching *farinata* (thin focaccia made from chickpeas) at the bar and enjoying pesto and fresh fish in the dining room (Sun–Fri 11:45–14:00 & 18:00–21:00, closed Sat, on Via Cavour, no reservations accepted).

The Doro Centry **supermarket** is just off Piazza Mazzini (Mon–Sat 8:30–12:30 & 15:30–19:30, Sun 8:30–12:30, Dogali 34, across from Hotel Fiorina).

Transportation Connections—Santa Margherita Ligure

By train to: Sestri Levante (hrly, 30 min), **Monterosso** (hrly, 1 hr), **La Spezia** (hrly, 1.5 hrs), **Pisa** (3/day, 2.25 hrs, more with transfer in La Spezia), **Genoa** (hrly, 45–60 min), **Milan** (4/day, 2 hrs, more with transfer in Genoa), **Ventimiglia** (2/day, 3.5 hrs, to French border, change in Genoa), **Venice** (2/day, 5.25 hrs). For **Florence**, you'll transfer in La Spezia or Pisa or both (allow 3.5–4 hrs).

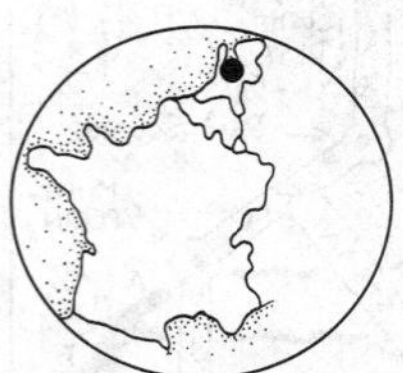

AMSTERDAM

Amsterdam is a progressive way of life housed in Europe's most 17th-century city. Physically, it's built upon millions of pilings. But more than that, it's built on good living, cozy cafés, great art, street-corner jazz, stately history, and a spirit of live-and-let-live. It has more than 700,000 people and about as many bikes. It also has more canals than Venice and about as many tourists.

During its Golden Age in the 1600s, Amsterdam was the world's richest city, an international sea-trading port, and the cradle of capitalism. Wealthy, democratic burghers built a planned city of canals lined with trees and townhouses topped with fancy gables. Immigrants, Jews, outcasts, and political rebels were drawn here by its tolerant atmosphere, while painters like young Rem-brandt captured that atmosphere on canvas. But all this history is only the beginning.

Approach the city not as a historian but as an ethnologist observing a strange culture. Stroll through any neighborhood, and see things that are commonplace here but rarely found elsewhere. Carillons chime quaintly in neighborhoods selling sex, as young professionals smoke pot with impunity next to old ladies in bonnets selling flowers. Observe the neighborhood's "social control," where a man feels safe in his home knowing he's being watched by the hookers next door.

The Dutch people are unique. They may be the world's most handsome people—tall, healthy, and with good posture—and the most open, honest, and refreshingly blunt. As connoisseurs of world culture, they appreciate Rembrandt paintings, Indonesian food, and the latest French film—but with an unsnooty, blue-jeans attitude.

Be warned: Amsterdam, a bold experiment in freedom, may box your Puritan ears. Take it all in, then pause to watch the sunset—at 10:00 p.m.—and see the Golden Age reflected in a quiet canal.

Planning Your Time

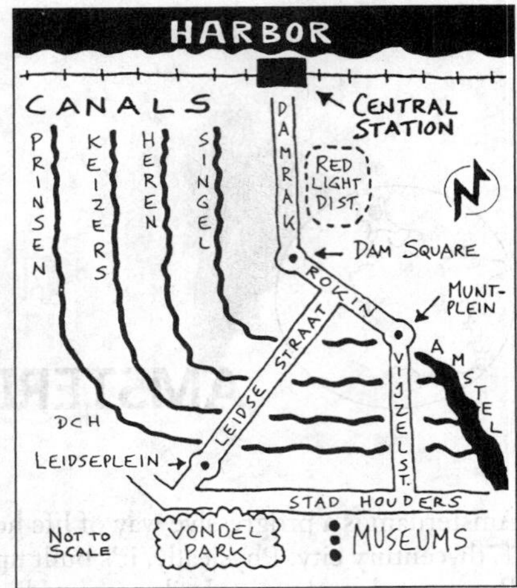

Amsterdam is worth a full day of sightseeing on even the busiest itinerary. While the city has a couple of must-see museums, its best sight is its own breezy ambience. The city's a joy on foot. It's a cheerier and faster joy by bike. Here are the essential stops for a day in Amsterdam:

In the morning, see the city's two great art museums: the Van Gogh and the Rijksmuseum (cafeteria lunch). Walk from the museums to the Singel flower market, then take a relaxing hour-long, round-trip canal cruise from the dock at Spui (see "Tours of Amsterdam," below). After the cruise, stroll through the peaceful Begijnhof courtyard and tour the nearby Amsterdam History Museum. Visiting the Anne Frank House after 18:00 (it's open until 21:00) will save you an hour in line. Have a memorable dinner: Try Dutch pancakes or a *rijsttafel*, an Indonesian smorgasbord.

On a balmy evening, Amsterdam has a Greek-island ambience. Stroll through the Jordaan neighborhood for the idyllic side of town or wander down Leidsestraat to Leidseplein for the roaring café and people scene. For a late-night spetacle, tour the Red Light District.

With extra time: With two days in Holland, I'd side-trip by bike, bus, or train to an open-air folk museum and visit Edam or Haarlem. With a third day, I'd do the other great Amsterdam museums. With four days, I'd do the "historic triangle" of Enkhuizen, Hoorn, and Medemblik, or visit The Hague.

Orientation (area code: 020)

Amsterdam's central train station, on the north edge of the city, is your starting point (TI, bike rental, and trams fanning out to all points). Damrak is the main street axis, connecting the station with Dam Square (people watching and hangout center) and its Royal Palace. From this spine, the city spreads out like a fan, with 90 islands, hundreds of bridges, and a series of concentric canals (named "Prince's," "Gentleman's," and "King's") laid out in the 17th century, Holland's Golden Age. Amsterdam's major sights are within walking distance of Dam Square.

To the east of Damrak is the old part of the city (today's Red Light District), and the west is the new part with the Anne Frank House and the Jordaan neighborhood. Museums and Leidseplein nightlife cluster at the south edge of the city center.

Tourist Information

There are four VVV offices ("VVV" is Dutch for TI—tourist information office): inside the train station (Mon–Sat 8:00–20:00, Sun 9:00–17:00), in front of the train station (daily 9:00–17:00), on Leidsestraat (less crowded, daily 9:00–19:00), and at the airport.

Avoid the crowded, inefficient VVV offices if you can. For €0.60 a minute, you can save yourself a trip by calling the tourist information toll line at 0900-400-4040 (Mon–Fri 9:00–17:00). If you're staying in nearby Haarlem, use the helpful, friendly, and rarely crowded Haarlem TI (see Haarlem chapter) to answer most of your Amsterdam questions and provide you with the brochures. Consider buying a city map (€2), *Day by Day* entertainment calendar (€1.50), and any of the €1 walking-tour brochures (*Discovery Tour through the Center*, *The Former Jewish Quarter*, *Walks through Jordaan*).

At Amsterdam's Centraal Station, GWK Change has hotel reservations windows with clerks that sell phone cards (local and international) and cheaper city maps (€1.60) and can answer basic tourist questions with shorter lines (one office is at track 4/5, the other is in west tunnel at the right end of station as you leave platform, tel. 020/627-2731).

Don't use the TI (or GWK) to book a room; you'll pay €5 per person and your host loses 13 percent—meaning you'll likely pay a higher rate. The phone system is easy, everyone speaks English, and the listings in this book are a better value than the potluck booking you'd get from the TI.

Helpful Hints

Theft Alert: Tourists are considered green and rich, and the city has more than its share of hungry thieves—especially on trams and at the many hostels. Wear your money belt.

Street Smarts: A *plein* is a square, *kerk* means church, *gracht* means canal, and most canals are lined by streets with the same name. When walking around town, be aware of silent transportation—trams and bicycles. (Don't walk on tram tracks or pink bicycle paths.)

Shop Hours: Many shops close all day Sunday and Monday morning.

Maps: The free and cheap tourist maps can be confusing. Consider paying a bit more (€2) for a top-notch map. I like the "Carto Studio Centrumkaart Amsterdam" or, better yet, the "Amsterdam: Go where the locals go" map by Amsterdam Anything.

Telephones: Calling the United States from a phone booth is now very cheap—you'll get about five minutes for a euro. Handy telephone cards (€5 or €10) are sold at TIs, the GVB public-transit office (in front of train station), tobacco shops, post offices, and train stations.

Happy Birthday: On the Queen's Birthday on April 30, Amsterdam turns into a gigantic garage sale/street market. Book your hotel room ahead if you'll be staying in Amsterdam (or Haarlem) on this holiday.

Internet Access: It's easy at cafés all over town. Two huge easyEverything Internet cafés offer hundreds of terminals with fast and cheap access 24/7 (€1/40 min, Damrak 33, a block in front of train station, and at Reguliersbreestraat 22, between Mint Tower and Rembrandtplein). "Coffeeshops" (which sell marijuana) also offer Internet access, letting you surf the Net with a special bravado.

Useful Phone Numbers and Web Sites

Amsterdam's "911" Emergency Telephone Number: 112
Schiphol Airport: toll tel. 0900-7244-7465
Taxi: 020/677-7777
Entertainment (AUB Ticket Office): toll tel. 0900-0191
Tourist Information: toll tel. 0900-400-4040
Tourist Information Online: www.amsterdam.nl (City of Amsterdam), www.holland.com (Netherlands Board of Tourism).

Arrival in Amsterdam

By Train: Amsterdam swings, and the hinge that connects it to the world is its perfectly central Centraal Station. Walk out the door, and you're in the heart of the city. You'll nearly trip over trams ready to take you anywhere your feet won't. Straight ahead is Damrak street, leading to Dam Square. With your back to the entrance of the station, the TI and GVB public-transit offices are just ahead and to your left. And on your right is a vast, multistoried bike garage.

By Plane: From Schiphol Airport, take the direct train to Amsterdam (6/hr, 20 min, €3). A taxi from Schiphol to Amsterdam's Centraal Station costs €35. The KLM Hotel Bus departs from lane A7 in front of the airport (2 routes—ask the attendant which is best for you, 3/hr, 20 min, €10). The bus stops directly in front of the Westerkerk church (near the Anne Frank House and many recommended hotels).

If you're staying in Haarlem, take a direct express bus to Haarlem (4/hr, 40 min, €3.50, #300 from lane B2 in front of the airport).

Getting around Amsterdam

The helpful GVB transit-information office is in front of the train station and next to the TI. Its free multilingual *Public Transport Amsterdam Tourist Guide* includes a transit map and explains ticket options and tram connections to all the sights.

By Bus, Tram, and Métro: Trams #2 and #5 travel the north-south axis from Centraal Station to Dam Square to Leidseplein to Museumplein. Tram #14 goes east-west (Westerkerk-Dam Square-Muntplein-Waterlooplein-Plantage). If you get lost in Amsterdam, 10 of the city's 17 trams take you back to the central train station.

The Métro (underground train) is used mostly for commuting to the suburbs, but it does connect Centraal Station with some sights east of Damrak (Nieuwemarkt-Waterlooplein-Weesplein).

Individual **tickets** cost €1.50 and give you an hour on the buses, trams, and Métro system (pay as you board on trams and buses; for the Métro, buy tickets from machines).

Strip cards are cheaper than individual tickets. Any downtown bus or tram ride costs two strips (good for 1 hour of transfers). A card with 15 strips costs €6 at the GVB public-transit office, machines at the train station, post offices, airport, or tobacco shops throughout the country; shorter strip tickets (2, 3, and 8 strips) are also sold on some buses and trams. Strip cards are good on buses all over the Netherlands (e.g., 6 strips for Haarlem to the airport), and you can share them with your partner.

A €5.50 **Day Card** gives you unlimited transportation on the buses and Métro for a day in Amsterdam; you'll almost break even if you take three trips (valid until 6:00 the following morning; buy as you board or at the GVB public-transit office, which also sells a better-value 2-day version for €8.50; sometimes costs €0.50 more if you buy it on board).

The **Amsterdam Pass** offers unlimited use of the tram, bus, and Métro as well as free or discounted admissions to many city sights and boat rides (€26/1 day, €36/2 days, €46/3 days, sold at GVB public-transit office and TIs). If you'll be using the tram a lot and seeing lots of museums, this pass can save you about a third on your transportation and sightseeing. (It doesn't include the Anne Frank House).

By Foot: The longest walk a tourist would take is 45 minutes

Amsterdam

from the station to the Rijksmuseum. Watch out for silent but potentially painful bikes, trams, and crotch-high curb posts.

By Bike: Everyone—bank managers, students, pizza delivery boys, and police—uses this mode of transport. It's *the* smart way to travel, where 40 percent of all traffic rolls on two wheels. You'll get around town by bike literally faster than you can by taxi. On my last visit, I rented a bike for five days, parked it outside my hotel, enjoyed wonderful mobility, and felt pretty smart. I highly encourage this for anyone who wants to get maximum fun per hour in Amsterdam. One-speed bikes, with "brrringing" bells and two locks (use them both; bike thieves are bold and brazen here), rent for about €8 per day (cheaper for longer periods) at any number of places. Hotels can send you to the nearest spot.

MacBike is the bike rental powerhouse with a huge and efficient outlet at Centraal Station (daily 9:00–17:45, €4/2 hrs, €7/day, €9/24 hrs, €11.50/2 days, more for 3 gears, at west end of station just before Ibis Hotel, tel. 020/625-3845, can reserve online, www.macbike.nl). MacBike gives out a free basic "Great Waterland Bicycle Tour" brochure (3 hr, 20 km) and sells several booklets outlining bike tours in and around Amsterdam for €1. For those staying near the Anne Frank House, Frederic Rent a Bike is also good (€10/24 hours, cheaper longer, daily 9:00–17:30, Brouwersgracht 78, tel. 020/624-5509).

No one wears helmets. For safety, use arm signals, stay in the obvious and omnipresent bike lanes, yield to traffic on the right, and fear tram tracks. Try to cross tram tracks at a perpendicular angle to avoid catching your tire in the rut. You must walk your bike through pedestrian zones. Lock your bike to something unmovable or lose it. Warning: Police are ticketing bikers as drivers. Obey traffic signals.

By Boat: While the city is great on foot or bike, another option is the "Museum Boat," with an all-day ticket that shuttles tourists from sight to sight. Tickets cost €13.50 (with sight discounts worth about €2.25). The sales booths in front of the Centraal Station (and the boats) offer handy free brochures with museum times and admission prices. The narrated ride takes 90 minutes if you don't get off (every 30 min in summer, every 45 min off-season, 7 stops, live quadrilingual guide, departures 9:30–17:00, discounted after 13:00 to €11.50, tel. 020/530-1090). A similar "Canal Bus" is nearby. If you're looking for a floating nonstop tour, the regular canal tour boats (without the stops) give more information, cover more ground, and cost less (see "Tours of Amsterdam," below).

By Taxi: Amsterdam's taxis are expensive (€2.50 drop and €1.50 for each kilometer). You can wave them down, find a rare taxi stand, or call one (tel. 020/677-7777) for a pick-up. Given the fine tram system, taxis are rarely a good value.

By Car: Forget it—frustrating one-ways, terrible parking, and meter maids with a passion for "booting" cars wrongly parked.

Tours of Amsterdam

▲▲Canal-Boat Tours—These long, low, tourist-laden boats leave continually from several docks around the town for a relaxing, if uninspiring, one-hour quadrilingual introduction to the city (€6.50, 2/hr, more frequent in summer). One very central company is at the corner of Spui and Rokin streets, about five minutes from Dam Square (daily 10:00–22:00, tel. 020/623-3810). No fishing allowed, but bring your camera. Some prefer to cruise at night, when the bridges are illuminated.

Adam's Apple Tours—This walking tour offers a 90-minute English-only look at the historic roots of Amsterdam. You'll have a small group and a caring guide starting at Centraal Station, ending at the Dam Square (€12, 10:00, 13:00, and 15:00 most days May–Sept, call 020/616-7867 to check times and book, www.adamsapple.nl).

Bike Tours—The Yellow Bike Tour company offers a three-hour long city tour (€17, at 9:30 and 13:00) and a six-hour tour of the countryside (€23, April–Nov daily at 11:00, 35 km, Nieuwezijds Kolk 29, 3 blocks from Centraal Station, tel. 020/620-6940).

Wetlands Safari, Nature Canoe Tours near Amsterdam—If you'd like to get some exercise and a dose of the *polder* country and village life, consider this tour. Majel Tromp, a young villager who speaks great English, takes groups limited to 15 people. The program: Meet at the VVV tourist office outside the Centraal Station at 9:30, catch a bus, stop for coffee, take a canoe trip with several stops, tour a village by canoe, munch a rural canalside picnic lunch (included), then canoe and bus back into the big city by 14:30 (€30, 10 percent off with this book, May–mid-Sept Mon–Fri, reservations required, tel. 020/686-3445 or cellular 06-5355-2669, www.wetlandssafari.nl).

Private Guide—Ab Walet is a likeable, hardworking, and knowledgeable local guide who enjoys personalizing tours for Americans interested in knowing his city better. He specializes in history and architecture and exudes a passion for Amsterdam (€70/half-day, €120/day, tel. 020/671-2588, cellular 06-2069-7882, e-mail: abwalet@yahoo.com).

Do-It-Yourself Bike Tour of Amsterdam—A day enjoying the bridges, bike lanes, and sleepy off-the-beaten-path canals on your own one-speed is an essential Amsterdam experience. The real joys of Europe's best-preserved 17th-century city are the countless intimate glimpses it offers: the laid-back locals sunning on their porches under elegant gables, rusted bikes that look as if they've been lashed to the same lamppost since the 1960s, wasted hedonists planted on canalside benches, and happy sailors permanently moored but still manning the deck.

For a good day, rent a bike at Centraal Station (see "By Bike" under "Getting Around," above). Head west down Haarlemmerstraat, working your wide-eyed way down the Prinsengracht canal (drop into Café 't Papeneiland at Prinsengracht 2), and detouring through the gentrified small streets of the Jordaan neighborhood before popping out at Westerkerk under the tallest spire in the city.

Pedal out to the lush and peaceful Vondelpark, and then cut back through the center of town (Leidseplein to the Mint Tower, down Rokin street to the Dam Square). From there, cruise the Red Light District by following Oudezijds Voorburgwal past the Oude Kerk (Old Church) to Zeedijk street, and return to the train station.

From Centraal Station, you can escape into the countryside by hopping on the free ferry behind the station. In five minutes, Amsterdam will be gone, and you'll be rolling through your very own Dutch painting (get free "Great Waterland Bicycle Tour" brochure from MacBike rental shop, on west side of train station).

Sights—Southwest Amsterdam

▲▲▲Rijksmuseum—Built to house the nation's greatest art, the Rijksmuseum packs several thousand paintings into 200 rooms. To survive, focus on the Dutch masters: Rembrandt, Hals, Vermeer, and Steen.

The Rijksmuseum will close for a massive renovation from the fall of 2003 until 2007. During this time, its masterpieces will be on display in the Philips Wing (south wing—the part of the huge building nearest the Van Gogh Museum).

If you visit before autumn, follow the museum's chronological layout to see painting evolve from narrative religious art, to religious art, to the Golden Age, when secular art dominated. With no local church or royalty to commission big canvases in the post-1648 Protestant Dutch republic, artists had to find different patrons. They specialized in portraits of the wealthy city class (Hals), pretty still lifes (Claesz), and nonpreachy slice-of-life art (Steen). The museum has four quietly wonderful Vermeers. And, of course, a thoughtful brown soup of Rembrandt, including *Night Watch*. Works by Rembrandt show his excellence as a portraitist for hire (*De Staalmeesters*) and offer some powerful psychological studies, such as *St. Peter's Denial*—with a betrayed Jesus in the murky background (€8, free if under 18, helpful audioguide-€3.50, daily 10:00–17:00, great bookshop, decent cafeteria, tram #2 or #5 from train station, Stadhouderskade 42, tel. 020/674-7000, www.rijksmuseum.nl).

▲▲▲Van Gogh Museum—Near the Rijksmuseum, this remarkable museum showcases 200 paintings by the troubled artist whose art seemed to mirror his life. In 2003, the museum celebrates the artist's 150th birthday with new exhibitions (included with admission), starting with the artists who influenced van Gogh (mid-Feb–mid-June), then concentrating on the artists Vincent influenced (July–mid-Oct). Exhibitions are held in the striking new wing adjacent to the museum (€7.25, €2 if under 18, daily

Museumplein

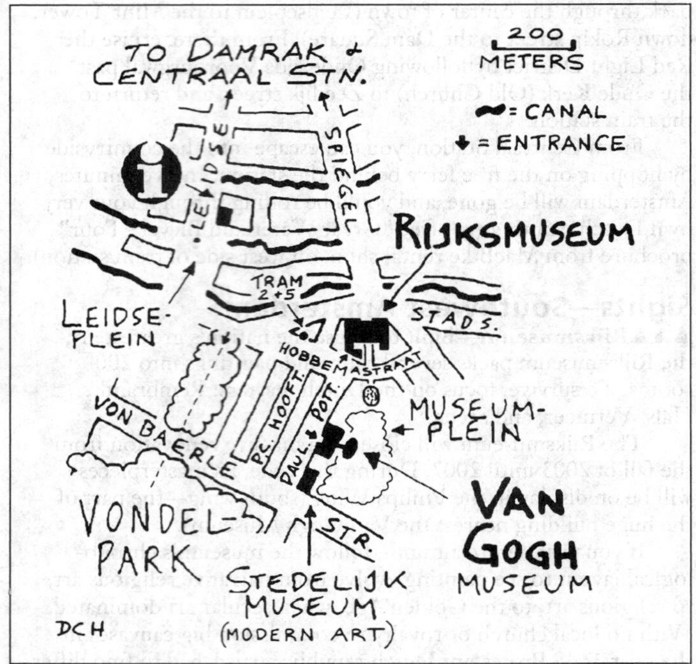

10:00–18:00, good audioguide-€3, Paulus Potterstraat 7, tel. 020/ 570-5200, www.vangoghmuseum.nl).

Stedelijk Modern Art Museum—Next to the Van Gogh Museum, this place is fun, far-out, and refreshing—and unfortunately, closed until 2005. It has mostly post-1945 art but also a sometimes-outstanding collection of Monet, van Gogh, Cézanne, Picasso, and Chagall, and a lot of special exhibitions.

▲**Museumplein**—Bordered by the Rijks, Van Gogh, and Stedelijk museums and the Concertgebouw (classical music hall), this square is interesting even to art haters. Amsterdam's best acoustics are found underneath the Rijksmuseum, where street musicians perform everything from chamber music to Mongolian throat singing. Mimes, human statues, and crafts booths dot the square. Coster Diamonds offers tours showing stone cutting and polishing. Skateboarders careen across a concrete "tube," while locals enjoy a park bench or a coffee at the Cobra café.

▲**Heineken Brewery**—The leading Dutch beer is no longer brewed here, but this old brewery now welcomes visitors to a slick and entertaining beer-appreciation experience. It's really the most enjoyable beer tour I've encountered in Europe. You'll learn as much as you want, marvel at the huge vats and towering ceilings, see videos, and go on rides. "What's it like to be a Heineken bottle and be filled with one of the best beers in the world? Try it for yourself." An important section recognizes a budding problem of our age, vital to people as well as beer — this planet's scarcity of clean water. With globalization, corporations are well on the way to owning the world's water supplies (€7.50 for self-guided hour-long tour and 3 beers or soft drinks, must be over age 18, Tue–Sun 10:00–18:00, last entry 17:00, closed Mon, tram #16, #24, or #25 to Stadhouderskade 78, an easy walk from the Rijksmuseum, tel. 020/523-9666).

▲Leidseplein—Brimming with cafés, this people-watching mecca is an impromptu stage for street artists, accordionists, jugglers, and unicyclists. Sunny afternoons are liveliest. The Boom Chicago theater (see "Nightlife in Amsterdam," below) fronts this square. Stroll nearby Lange Leidsedwarsstraat (1 block north) for a taste-bud tour of ethnic eateries from Greek to Indonesian.

▲▲Vondelpark—This huge and lively city park is popular with the Dutch—families with little kids, romantic couples, strolling seniors, and hippies sharing blankets and beers. It's a popular venue for free summer concerts. On a sunny afternoon, it's a hedonistic scene that seems to say "Parents . . . relax."

Amsterdam Film Museum—It's not a "museum" but a theater. In three 80-seat theaters, it shows several films a day, from small foreign productions to 70-mm classics drawn from its massive archive (€6.25, always in the original language, often English subtitles, Vondelstraat 69, tel. 020/589-1400, www.filmmuseum.nl).

Houseboat Museum Amsterdam—Small sail-powered cargo ships became uneconomical with the advent of modern cargo boats in the 1930s. Almost worthless, they found a new use—as houseboats lining the canals of Amsterdam. Today, 2,500 such boats—with their cargo holds turned into elegantly cozy living rooms—are called home by locals. For a peek into this world, visit this tiny museum. Captain Vincent enjoys showing visitors around the museum, which feels so lived in because it was until 1997 (€2.50, March–Oct Wed–Sun 11:00–17:00, closed Mon–Tue, Nov–Feb Fri–Sun 11:00–17:00, closed Mon–Thu, Prinsengracht opposite #296 facing Elandsgracht, tel. 020/427-0750).

Sights—Central Amsterdam, near Dam Square

▲▲Anne Frank House—A pilgrimage for many, this house offers a fascinating look at the hideaway of young Anne during the Nazi occupation of the Netherlands during World War II. Pick up the

English pamphlet at the door. Recently expanded, the exhibit now offers more thorough coverage of the Frank family, the diary, the stories of others who hid, and the Holocaust. In summer, skip the hour-long daytime lines by arriving after 18:00 (last entry is 20:30). Visit after dinner (€6.50, April–Aug daily 9:00–21:00, Sept–March daily 9:00–19:00, Prinsengracht 263, near Westerkerk church, tel. 020/556-7100, www.annefrank.nl).

For an interesting glimpse of Holland under the Nazis, rent the powerful movie *Soldier of Orange* before you leave home.

Westerkerk Church—Near the Anne Frank House, this landmark church (generally open April–Sept 11:00–15:00) has a barren interior, Rembrandt buried somewhere under the pews, and Amsterdam's tallest steeple. The tower is open by tour only. The mandatory €3 guided tour (in English and Dutch) tells of the church and its carillon, and gets you up to the view (45 min, departures on the hour, April–Sept Mon–Sat 10:00–17:00, last trip at 17:00, closed Sun and in winter, tel. 020/689-2565).

Royal Palace (Koninklijk Paleis)—The palace, right on Dam Square, was built as a lavish city hall for Amsterdam, when the country was a proud new Dutch Republic and Amsterdam was awash in profit from trade. When constructed (around 1660), this building was one of Europe's finest. Today it's the official (but not actual) residence of the Queen and has a sumptuous interior (while it pretends that it's open to the public, this is rare and for the near future it's closed because of an asbestos problem, tel. 020/624-8698).

▲Begijnhof—Stepping into this tiny, idyllic courtyard in the city center, you escape into the charm of old Amsterdam. Notice house #34, a 500-year-old wooden structure (rare since repeated fires taught city fathers a trick called brick). Peek into the "hidden" Catholic church, dating from the time when post-Reformation Dutch Catholics couldn't worship in public. It's opposite the English Reformed church, where the Pilgrims worshiped while waiting for their voyage to the New World (marked by a plaque near the door). Be considerate of the people who live around the courtyard (free, daily 10:00–17:00, on Begijnensteeg lane, just off Kalverstraat between #130 and #132, pick up flier at office near entrance, open weekdays 10:00–16:00).

▲Amsterdam History Museum—Follow the city's growth from fishing village to world trader to hippie haven. This creative and hardworking museum features Rembrandt's paintings, fine English descriptions, and a carillon loft. The loft comes with push-button recordings of the town bell tower's greatest hits and a self-serve carillon "keyboard" to ring a few bells yourself (€6.50, Mon–Fri 10:00–17:00, Sat–Sun 11:00–17:00, good-value

Central Amsterdam

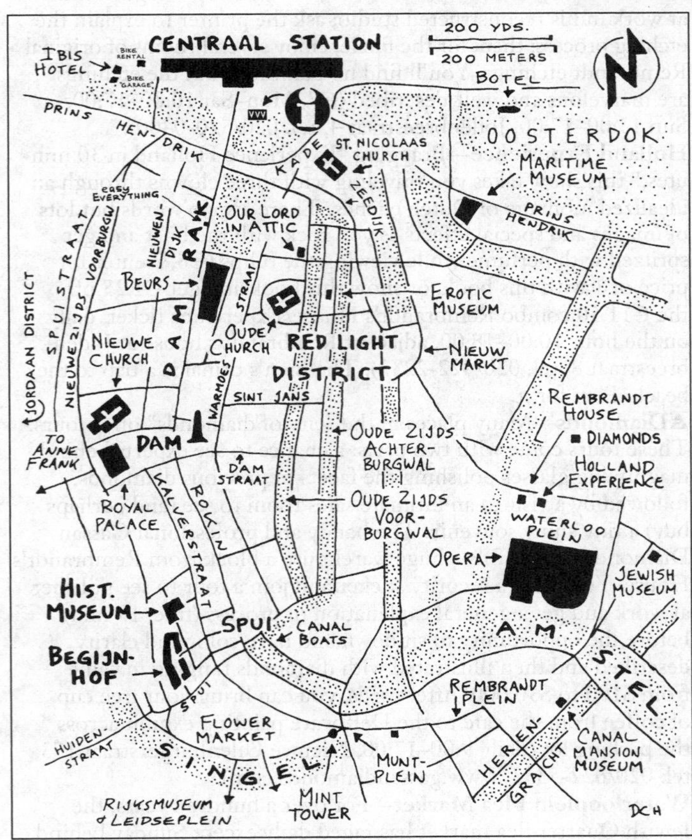

restaurant, next to Begijnhof, Kalverstraat 92, tel. 020/523-1822). Its free pedestrian corridor—lined with old-time group portraits—is a powerful teaser.

Sights—Southeast Amsterdam

To reach these sights from the train station, take tram #9, #14, or #20. All of these sights except the last two (Tropenmuseum and Maritime Museum) are close to each other and could easily be connected into an interesting walk.

▲Rembrandt's House—Tour the place this way: See the 10-minute introductory video (Dutch and English showings alternate); tour Rembrandt's reconstructed house (filled with exactly what his bankruptcy inventory of 1656 said he owned); imagine him at work in his reconstructed studio; ask the printer to explain the etching process; then, for the finale, enjoy several rooms of original Rembrandt etchings. You'll find no paintings, but the etchings are marvelous and well-described (€7, Mon–Sat 10:00–17:00, Sun 13:00–17:00, Jodenbreestraat 4, tel. 020/520-0400).

Holland Experience—Bragging "Experience Holland in 30 minutes," this show takes you traveling with three clowns through an idealized montage of Dutch clichés. There are no words but lots of images and special effects as you rock with the boat and get spritzed with perfume while viewing the tulips (€8, 2 enter for price of 1 with this book, or show this book and get €1.25 off the €11.50 combo Rembrandt's House/Experience ticket, daily on the hour 10:00–18:00, adjacent Rembrandt's house at Jodenbreestraat 8, tel. 020/422-2233). The men's urinal is a trip to the beach. Plan for it.

▲Diamonds—Many places in the "city of diamonds" offer tours. These tours come with two parts: a chance to see experts behind magnifying glasses polishing the facets of precious diamonds, followed by a visit to an intimate sales room to see (and perhaps buy) a tiny shiny souvenir. The handy and professional Gassan Diamonds facility fills a huge warehouse a block from Rembrandt's House. You'll get a security sticker and join a tour to see polisher at work and get a general explanation of process (free, 15 min) before the opportunity to sit down and have color and clarity described and then illustrated with diamonds ranging in value from $100 to $30,000. Afterwards, you can bring your free cup of coffee from the café to the Delftware painting exhibit across the parking lot (daily 9:00–17:00, Nieuwe Uilenburgerstraat 173, tel. 020/622-5333, www.gassandiamonds.com).

Waterlooplein Flea Market—For over a hundred years, the Jewish Quarter flea market has raged daily except Sunday behind the Rembrandt House. The long narrow park is filled with stalls selling cheap clothes, hippie stuff, old records, tourist knickknacks, and garage sale junk.

▲Jewish History Museum—Four historic synagogues have been joined by steel and glass to make one modern complex telling the story of the Jews in Amsterdam through the centuries (€5, daily 11:00–17:00, good kosher café, Jonas Daniel Meijerplein 2, tel. 020/626-9945).

De Hortus Botanical Garden—This is a unique oasis of tranquility within the city (no cell phones allowed because "our collection of plants is a precious community, treat it with respect"). One of the oldest botanical gardens in the world, it dates from 1638, when medicinal herbs were grown here. Today, among its

Waterlooplein

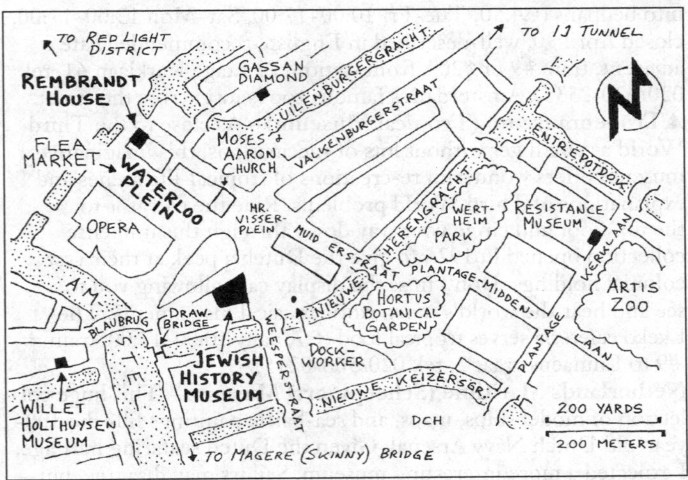

6,000 different kinds of plants—most of which were collected by the Dutch East India Company in the 17th and 18th centuries—you'll find medicinal herbs, several greenhouses (one with a fluttery butterfly house—a hit with kids), cacti, and a tropical palm house. Much of it is thoughtfully described in English: "A Dutch merchant snuck a coffee plant out of Ethiopia, which ended up in this garden in 1706. This first coffee plant in Europe was the literal granddaddy of the coffee cultures of Brazil—long the world's biggest coffee producer." (€5, Mon–Fri 9:00–17:00, Sat–Sun 11:00–17:00, Plantage Middenlaan 2A, tel. 020/625-8411.)

▲**Dutch Theatre (Hollandsche Schouwburg)**—This is a moving memorial. Once a lively theater in the Jewish neighborhood, this was used as an assembly hall for local Jews destined for Nazi concentration camps. On the wall, 6,700 family names pay tribute to the 104,000 Jews deported and killed by the Nazis. Upstairs is a small history exhibit on Jews here during World War II. The ruined theater offers little to actually see but plenty to think about—notice the hopeful messages visiting school groups attach to the wooden tulips (free, daily 11:00–16:00, Plantage Middenlaan 24, tel. 020/626-9945).

▲▲**Dutch Resistance Museum (Verzetsmuseum)**—This is an impressive look at how the Dutch resisted their Nazi occupiers from 1940 to 1945. You'll see propaganda movie clips, study forged ID cards under a magnifying glass, and read of ingenious, clever, and courageous efforts to hide local Jews from the

Germans. And at the end of the war, Nazi helmets were turned into bedpans (€4.50, Tue–Fri 10:00–17:00, Sat–Mon 12:00–17:00, closed April 30, well-described in English, recommended café adjacent, tram #9 or #20A from station, Plantage Kerklaan 61, tel. 020/620-2535). Amsterdam's famous zoo is just across the street.

▲Tropenmuseum (Tropical Museum)—As close to the Third World as you'll get without lots of vaccinations, this imaginative museum offers wonderful re-creations of tropical-life scenes and explanations of Third World problems. Ride the elevator to the top floor and circle your way down through this immense collection opened in 1926 to give the Dutch a peek at their vast colonial holdings. Don't miss the display case allowing you to see and hear the world's most exotic musical instruments. The Ekeko cafeteria serves tropical food (€7, daily 10:00–17:00, tram #9 to Linnaeusstraat 2, tel. 020/568-8215).

Netherlands Maritime (Scheepvaart) Museum—This huge collection of model ships, maps, and sea-battle paintings fills the 300-year-old Dutch Navy Arsenal. Given the Dutch seafaring heritage, I expected a more interesting museum. Sailors may disagree, but—even with its recreation of an 18th-century Dutch East India Company ship manned with characters in old costumes—I found the place pretty lifeless (€6.75, daily 10:00–17:00, closed Mon off-season, English explanations, don't waste your time with 30-min movie, bus #22 or #32 to Kattenburgerplein 1, tel. 020/523-2222).

Sights—Rembrandtplein and Neighborhood

▲Herengracht Canal Mansion (Willet Holthuysen Museum)—This 1687 patrician house offers a fine look at old Amsterdam's wealthy, with a good 15-minute English introductory film and a 17th-century garden in back (€4.50, Mon–Fri 10:00–17:00, Sat–Sun 11:00–17:00, tram #4 or #9 to Herengracht 605, 1 block southeast of Rembrandtplein, tel. 020/523-1870).

Tuschinsky Theater—This movie palace from the 1920s still glitters inside and out. Still a working theater, it's a delightful old place to see first-run movies (a half-block from Rembrandtplein down Reguliersbreestraat). The exterior is an interesting hybrid of styles, forcing the round peg of Art Nouveau into the square hole of Art Deco. The stone-and-tile facade features stripped-down, functional Art Deco squares and rectangles, but is ornamented with Art Nouveau elements—Tiffany lamp-style windows, garlands, curvy iron lamps, Egyptian pharaohs, and exotic gold lettering over the door. Inside, the sumptuous decor features red carpets, nymphs on the walls, and semi-abstract designs. Grab a seat in the lobby and watch the ceiling morph (Reguliersbreestraat 26–28).

Sights—Red Light District

▲▲Our Lord in the Attic (Amstelkring)—Near the train station in the Red Light District, you'll find a fascinating hidden Catholic church (from 1663) filling the attic of a 17th-century merchants' house. When hard-line Protestants took power in 1578, Catholics were forbidden to worship openly, so worshippers gathered secretly to say Mass in homes and offices. In 1663, a wealthy merchant built Our Lord in the Attic, one of a handful of such places in Amsterdam serving as a secret parish church until Catholics were allowed in 1795 to once again worship in public. This unique church, embedded within a townhouse in the middle of the Red Light District, comes with a little bonus: a rare glimpse inside a historic Amsterdam home (€4.50, Mon–Sat 10:00–17:00, Sun 13:00–17:00, Oudezijds Voorburgwal 40, tel. 020/624-6604).

▲▲Red Light District—Europe's most touristed ladies of the night shiver and shimmy as they have since 1700 in 450 display-case windows between the Oudezijds Achterburgwal and Oudezijds Voorburgwal, surrounding the Oude Kerk (Old Church). Drunks and druggies make the streets uncomfortable late at night, but it's a fascinating walk at any other time after noon.

The neighborhood, one of Amsterdam's oldest, has had prostitutes since 1200. Prostitution is entirely legal here, and prostitutes are generally entrepreneurs, renting a space and running their own businesses. Popular prostitutes net around €300 a day (S&F, €25–50) and fill out tax returns.

The **Prostitution Information Center**, open to the public, offers a small booklet that answers most of the questions tourists have about the Red Light District (free, Tue, Wed, Fri, and Sat 11:30–19:30, facing Oude Kerk church at Enge Kerksteeg 3).

Sex Museums—Amsterdam has two sex museums: one in the Red Light District and one a block in front of the train station on Damrak. While visiting one can be called sightseeing, visiting both is hard to explain. Here's a comparison:

The Erotic Museum in the Red Light District is less offensive, with its five floors relying heavily on badly dressed dummies of prostitutes posed in various acts. It also has a lot of uninspired paintings, videos, phone sex, old photos, and sculptures (€5, daily 11:00–24:00, along the canal at Oudezijds Achterburgwal 54, tel. 020/624-7303).

The Damrak sex museum goes deeper, telling the story of pornography from Roman times through 1960. Every sexual deviation is uncovered in various displays, and the nude and

Red Light District

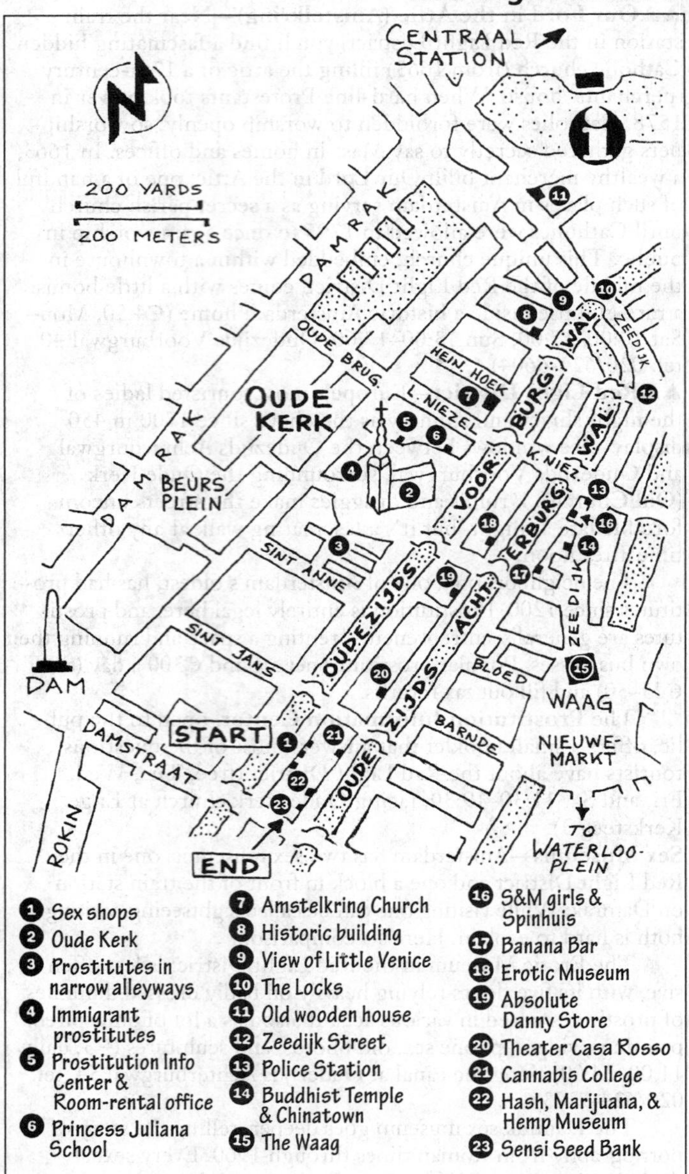

CENTRAAL STATION
200 YARDS
200 METERS
DAMRAK
OUDE BRUG
OUDE KERK
HEIN. HOEK
L. NIEZEL
BURG
WAL
ZEEDIJK
K. NIEZ
VOOR
BEURS PLEIN
SINT ANNE
ERBURG
OUDEZIJDS
ACHT.
SINT JANS
DAM
BLOED
WAAG
BARNDE
START
NIEUWE-MARKT
DAMSTRAAT
OUDE
ZIJDS
ROKIN
END
TO WATERLOO-PLEIN
1 Sex shops
2 Oude Kerk
3 Prostitutes in narrow alleyways
4 Immigrant prostitutes
5 Prostitution Info Center & Room-rental office
6 Princess Juliana School
7 Amstelkring Church
8 Historic building
9 View of Little Venice
10 The Locks
11 Old wooden house
12 Zeedijk Street
13 Police Station
14 Buddhist Temple & Chinatown
15 The Waag
16 S&M girls & Spinhuis
17 Banana Bar
18 Erotic Museum
19 Absolute Danny Store
20 Theater Casa Rosso
21 Cannabis College
22 Hash, Marijuana, & Hemp Museum
23 Sensi Seed Bank

pornographic art is a cut above that of the other sex museum. Also interesting are the early French pornographic photos and memorabilia from Europe, India, and Asia. You'll find a Marilyn Monroe tribute and some S&M displays, too (€5, daily 10:00–23:30, Damrak 18, a block in front of station).

▲**Marijuana and Hemp Museum**—This is a collection of dope facts, history, science, and memorabilia (€6, daily 11:00–22:00, Oudezijds Achterburgwal 148, tel. 020/623-5961). While small, it has a shocker finale: the high-tech grow room in which dozens of varieties of marijuana are cultivated in optimal hydroponic (among other) environments. Some plants stand five feet tall and shine under the intense grow lamps. The view is actually through glass walls into the neighboring Sensi Seed Bank Grow Shop, which sells carefully cultivated seeds and all the gear needed to grow them. It's an interesting neighborhood.

The **Cannabis College Foundation**, "dedicated to ending the global war against the cannabis plant through public education," is next door at #124 (free, daily 11:00–19:00, tel. 020/423-4420, www.cannabiscollege.com).

Shopping

Amsterdam brings out the browser even in those who were not born to shop. Ten general markets, open six days a week, keep folks who brake for garage sales pulling U-ies. Shopping highlights include Waterlooplein (the flea market); the huge Albert Cuyp street market; various flower markets (such as the Singel Canal market near mint tower/*Munttoren*, daily except Sun); diamond dealers (free cutting and polishing demos on Potterstraat behind Rijksmuseum; on Dam Square; and at Gassan Diamonds near Rembrandt's House—see "Sights—Southeast Amsterdam," above); and Kalverstraat, Amsterdam's soul-less but teeming pedestrian/shopping street (parallel to Damrak).

For something a little different, stroll **The Nine Little Streets** (De Negen Straatjes), home to 190 diverse shops mixing festive, creative, nostalgic, practical, and artistic items. The cross streets make a tic-tac-toe with a couple of canals just west of Kalverstraat. (Look for the zone where Hartenstraat, Wolvenstraat, and Huidenstraat cross Keizersgracht and Herrengracht canals.)

To experience a Dutch shopping mall, drop by the **Magna Plaza Shopping Center.** This former main post office in a grand 19th-century building has been transformed into a stylish mall with 40 boutiques. You'll find fashion, luxury goods, and gift shops galore. It's just behind the Royal Palace a block off Dam Square.

Nightlife in Amsterdam

On summer evenings, people flock to the main squares for drinks at outdoor tables. Leidseplein is the glitziest, surrounded by theaters, restaurants, and nightclubs. The slightly quieter Rembrandtplein (with adjoining Thorbeckeplein) is the center of gay discos. Spui features a full city block of bars. And Nieuwemarkt, on the east edge of the Red Light District, is a bit rough, but is probably the most local.

Boom Chicago (in English) and *Uitkrant* (in easy-to-decipher Dutch) are two free publications (available at TIs and many bars) that list festivals and performances of theater, film, dance, cabaret, and live rock, pop, jazz, and classical music. The **AUB ticket office** at Stadsschouwburg Theater (Leidseplein 26, tel. 0900-0191) is the best one-stop-shopping box office for theater, classical music, and major rock shows.

Music—You'll find classical music at the Concertgebouw (at the far south end of Museumplein, tel. 020/675-4411) and at the former Beurs (on Damrak, tel. 020/627-0466), and opera and dance at the new opera house on Waterlooplein (tel. 020/551-8100). In the summer, Vondelpark hosts open-air concerts.

Two rock music (and hip-hop) clubs near Leidseplein—Melkweg (Lijnbaansgracht 234a, tel. 020/531-8181, www.melkweg.nl) and Paradiso (Weteringschans 6, tel. 020/626-4521, www.paradiso.nl)—present big-name acts that you might recognize if you're younger than I am.

Jazz has a long tradition at the Bimhuis nightclub, east of the Red Light District (concerts Thu–Sat, Oude Schans 73–77, box office tel. 020/623-1361, www.bimhuis.nl).

Comedy—Boom Chicago, an R-rated comedy theater act, was started 10 years ago by a group of Americans on a graduation tour. They have been entertaining tourists and locals alike ever since. The show is a series of rude, clever, and high-powered skits offering a raucous look at Dutch culture and local tourism (€16, nightly at 20:15, dinner seating early in the 270-seat Leidseplein Theater, Leidseplein 12, tel. 020/423-0101, www.boomchicago.nl). They do two shows: *Best of Boom* (a collection of their greatest hits over the years) and a new show for locals and return customers. Meals are optional and a good value.

Movies—Catch modern movies in the 1920s setting of the classic Tuschinski Theater (between Muntplein and Rembrandtplein; see "Sights—Rembrandtplein," above). It's not unusual for movies at cinemas to be sold out—consider buying tickets during the day.

Also consider the Amsterdam Film Museum,which shows several films a day, varying from obscure to classic (€6.25, always in original language, often English subtitles, Vondelstraat 69, near Vondelpark, tel. 020/589-1400, www.filmmuseum.nl).

Sleeping in Amsterdam

(€1 = about $1, country code: 31, area code: 020)

Sleep Code: **S** = Single, **D** = Double/Twin, **T** = Triple, **Q** = Quad, **b** = bathroom, **s** = shower only, **CC** = Credit Cards accepted, **no CC** = Credit Cards not accepted. Nearly everyone speaks English in the Netherlands, and prices include breakfast unless noted.

To help you easily sort through these listings, I've divided the rooms into three categories based on the price for a standard double room with bath:

Higher Priced—Most rooms €140 or more.

Moderately Priced—Most rooms less than €140.

Lower Priced—Most rooms less than €80.

Greeting a new day by descending your steep stairs and stepping into a leafy canalside scene—graceful bridges, historic gables, and bikes clattering on cobbles—is a fun part of experiencing Amsterdam. Amsterdam is a tough city for budget accommodations and any room under €140 will have its rough edges. Still, you can sleep well and safely in a great location for €80 per double.

Amsterdam is jammed during convention periods, the Queen's Birthday (April 30), and on summer weekends. Many hotels will not take weekend bookings for people staying less than three nights.

Parking in Amsterdam is even worse than driving. You'll pay €32 a day to park safely in a garage—and then hike to your hotel.

While I prefer sleeping in cozy Haarlem (see next chapter), those into more urban charms will find that, with the exception of the times noted above, Amsterdam has plenty of beds.

Sleeping near the Train Station

HIGHER PRICED

Ibis Amsterdam Hotel is a modern and efficient 187-room place towering over the station and a multi-story bicycle garage. It offers a central location, comfort, and good value without a hint of charm (Db-€149, family-€176, skip breakfast and save €12 per person, CC, book long in advance, air-con, smoke-free rooms on request, Stationsplein 49, tel. 020/638-9999, fax 020/620-0156, www.ibishotel.com).

MODERATELY PRICED

Amstel Botel, the city's only remaining "boat hotel," is a shipshape, bright, and clean floating hotel with 175 rooms (Sb/Db-€81, Tb-€90, worth the extra €5 per room for canal view, breakfast-€8, CC, elevator, €25/day parking pass, 400 meters from train station, on your left as you leave station, you'll see

Amsterdam Hotels

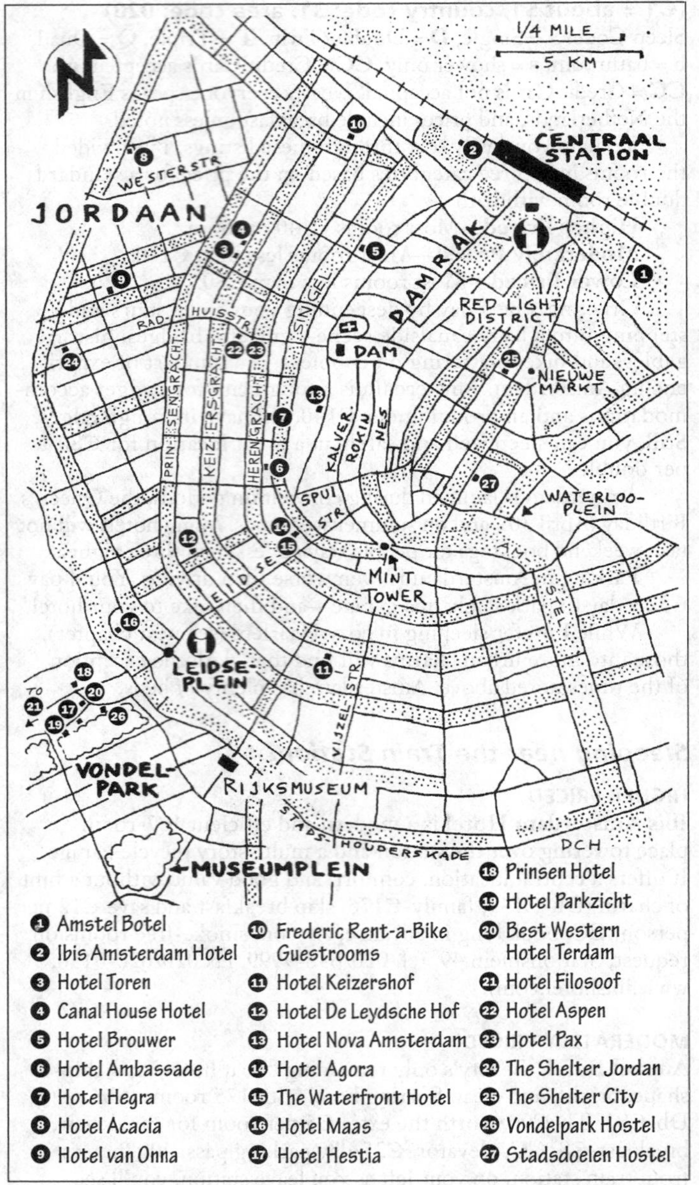

the sign and the big white boat on Oosterdokskade, tel. 020/626-4247, fax 020/639-1952, www.amstelbotel.com).

Sleeping between Dam Square and the Anne Frank House

HIGHER PRICED

Hotel Toren is a chandeliered historic mansion in a pleasant, quiet canalside setting in downtown Amsterdam. This splurge, run by Eric and Petra Toren, is classy yet friendly and two blocks northeast of the Anne Frank House. The least expensive four-star in town—it's a great value (Sb-€100–120, Db-€125–160, deluxe canalside Db-€215, Tb-€160–185, "bridal suites" for €205–230, prices vary with season, 10 percent discount for cash with this book, breakfast buffet-€12, CC, air-con, Keizersgracht 164, tel. 020/622-6352, fax 020/626-9705, www.toren.nl). Bernarda, who runs the bar, is a great source of local advice.

Canal House Hotel, a few doors down, offers a rich 17th-century atmosphere. Above generous and elegant public spaces, tangled antique-filled halls lead to 26 spacious, tastefully appointed rooms. Evenings come with candlelight and soft music (Db-€150, big Db-€190, CC, elevator, Keizersgracht 148, tel. 020/622-5182, fax 020/624-1317, www.canalhouse.nl, e-mail: info@canalhouse.nl).

Hotel Ambassade—lacing together 60 rooms in eight houses—is an amazingly elegant and fresh place sitting aristocratically but daintily on the Heren canal. Its public rooms are palatial, with a library and plush antique furnishings. This is a rare family-run hotel of this size (Sb-€158, Db-€188, Db suite-€260, Tb-€310, extra bed-€30, breakfast-€14—and actually worth it, CC, elevator, free Internet access, Herengracht 341, tel. 020/555-0222, www.ambassade-hotel.nl, e-mail: info@ambassade-hotel.nl).

Sleeping between Dam Square and the Anne Frank House

MODERATELY PRICED

Hotel Brouwer, a woody and homey old-time place situated peacefully but centrally on the Singel canal, rents eight plain rooms up lots of very steep stairs (Sb-€45, Db-€85, located between train station and Dam Square, near Lijnbaanssteeg at Singel 83, tel. 020/624-6358, fax 020/520-6264, www.hotelbrouwer.nl, e-mail: akita@hotelbrouwer.nl).

Hotel Hegra is a rare find—it's simple, inexpensive, comfy, sedate, and cat-friendly with 11 rooms, run by Robert de Vries. The place is well-worn but feels safe (D-€60, Ds-€75, Db-€85, includes breakfast, CC, Herengracht 269, tel. 020/623-7877, fax 020/623-8159). The lack of a Web site is in keeping with the character of Robert's management.

Sleeping in the Jordaan

MODERATELY PRICED

Hotel Acacia's 20 good rooms fill a funky cheese-wedge-shaped building on a canal and a great work-a-day square buried deep in the Jordaan (Sb-€65, Db-€80, Tb-€100, Qb-€120, Quint/b-€130, 5 percent extra to pay with CC, 3-night minimum for advance reservations, some larger studios, parking, bus #18 from station, Lindengracht 251, tel. 020/622-1460, fax 020/638-0748, www.hotelacacia.nl, e-mail: acacia.nl@wxs.nl, Gerard). The Acacia also rents four fine rooms or apartments in two **Acacia Houseboats** moored adjacent to the hotel. This is your best opportunity for that old-time houseboat Amsterdam experience in a quintessential Amsterdam neighborhood (Db-€95-110, Tb-€115, Qb-€130, see Web site for details).

Hotel van Onna is a smoke-free, professional-feeling place renting 41 simple, industrial-strength rooms. The beds are a bit springy—but the price is unbeatable and the location makes you want to crack out your easel (Sb-€40, Db-€80, Tb-€120, no CC, reserve only by phone, Bloemgracht 102, tel. 020/626-5801, www.netcentrum.com/onna/, Luiz).

***Near the Jordaan*: Frederic Rent A Bike Guestrooms**, with a bike rental shop as the reception, is a collection of private rooms on a gorgeous canal just outside the Jordaan, a five-minute walk from the train station. Frederic has amassed about 100 beds ranging from dumpy €60 doubles to spacious and elegant €160 apartments. Some places are great for families and groups of up to six. He also rents houseboat apartments. All are displayed in living color on his Web site (bike shop open daily 9:00–18:00, cash only, Brouwersgracht 78, tel. 020/624-5509, www.frederic.nl).

Sleeping in the Spui and Leidseplein Neighborhoods

The area around Amsterdam's rip-roaring nightlife center (Leidseplein) is colorful, comfortable, and convenient. These canalside places are within a five-minute walk of Leidseplein but in generally quiet and characteristic settings.

HIGHER PRICED

Hotel Nova Amsterdam, a bright, spacious place offering professional service and reliability, rents 60 stark yellow and beechwood rooms in a great locale (Sb-€100, Db-€140, Tb-€170, Qb-€200, CC, elevator, midway between Dam Square and Spui at Nieuwezijds Voorburgwal 276, tel. 020/623-0066, fax 020/627-2026, e-mail: novahotel@wxs.nl).

Hotel Maas is a big, quiet, and stiffly hotelesque place. While on a busy street rather than a canal, it's a handy option (S-€80, Sb-€105, one D-€95, Db-€145, suite-€205, prices vary with view and room size, extra person-€20, hearty breakfast, CC, elevator, tram #1, #2, or #5 from station; Leidsekade 91, tel. 020/623-3868, fax 020/622-2613, www.hotelmaas.nl).

MODERATELY PRICED

Hotel Keizershof is wonderfully Dutch, with six bright, airy rooms in a 17th-century canal house. A steep spiral staircase leads to rooms named after old-time Hollywood stars. The enthusiastic hospitality of the De Vries family gives this place a friendly, almost small-town charm (S-€45, D-€65, Ds-€75, Db-€90, 3-night minimum, fine family-style breakfast around a big table, use CC to secure room but pay in cash for these prices, strictly non-smoking, tram #16, #24, or #25 from train station; Keizersgracht 618, where Keizers canal crosses Spiegelstraat, tel. 020/622-2855, fax 020/624-8412, www.vdwp.nl/keizershof).

Two well-located places offering mediocre values are side by side overlooking the Singel canal where it hits Koningsplein: **Hotel Agora** (16 rooms, Db-€110, view Db-€125, CC, Singel 462, tel. 020/627-2200, fax 020/627-2202, www.hotelagora.nl), and **The Waterfront Hotel,** which feels cozier with lots of steep stairs and rustic yet nice rooms (10 rooms, Db-€105, view Db-€125, Singel 458, tel. & fax 020/421-6621, www.waterfront.demon.nl).

LOWER PRICED

Hotel De Leydsche Hof, canalside with simple, quiet rooms, is open only from Easter through mid-September. Its peaceful demeanor almost allows you to overlook the flimsy cots and old carpets (Ds-€60, Ts-€90, Qs-€110, no breakfast, no CC, 10-min walk from Leidseplein, Leidsegracht 14, near where Keizersgracht hits Leidsegracht, tel. 020/623-2148, run by friendly Mr. Piller).

Sleeping near Vondelpark

These options cluster around Vondelpark in a safe neighborhood that lacks the canal flavor but is only a short walk from the action. The first four places are in a pleasant nook between the rollicking Leidseplein and the breezy Vondelpark. They are easily connected with the train station via trams #1, #2, or #5. The last place has more personality but is farther away.

HIGHER PRICED

Best Western Hotel Terdam is an 89-room American-style hotel well situated on a quiet street just across the bridge from bustling Leidseplein (Db-€130–170 depending on season and air-con, breakfast likely not included but often used as a bargaining chip, CC, elevator, Tesselschadestraat 23, tel. 020/612-6876, fax 020/683-8313, www.ams.nl).

MODERATELY PRICED

Hotel Hestia, on a safe and sane street, feels very professional with 18 clean, bright and generally spacious rooms (Sb-€80, very small Db-€95, Db-€105–130, Tb-€160, Qb-€190, CC, elevator, Roemer Visscherstr 7, tel. 020/618-0801, fax 020/685-1382, www.hestia.demon.nl).

Prinsen Hotel, with 45 nicely appointed but generally cramped rooms, is family-run with a peaceful garden and a safe, professional feel (small Db on weekdays-€116, small Db on weekends-€128, bigger Db-€138, CC, elevator, Vondelstraat 36, tel. 020/616-2323, fax 020/616-6112, www.prinsenhotel.nl).

Hotel Parkzicht, an old-fashioned place with extremely steep stairs, rents 13 big, plain rooms on a quiet street bordering Vondelpark (S-€39, Sb-€49, Db-€77–90, Tb-€110–120, Qb-€120–130, CC, closed Nov-March, Roemer Visscherstraat 33, tel. 020/618-1954, fax 020/618-0897, e-mail: hotel@parkzicht.nl).

Hotel Filosoof greets you with Aristotle and Plato in the foyer and classical music in its generous lobby. Its 38 rooms are decorated with themes; the Egyptian room has a frieze of hieroglyphics. Philosophers' sayings hang on the walls, and thoughtful travelers wander down the halls or sit in the garden, rooted deep in discussion. The rooms are small, but the hotel is endearing (Db-€111–122, Tb-€150–170, CC, elevator, 3-min walk from tram #1 line, get off at Jan Peter Heierstraat, Anna Vondelstraat 6, tel. 020/683-3013, fax 020/685-3750, www.hotelfilosoof.nl).

Lower Priced Backpacker Hotels and Hostels

Cheap hotels line the convenient but noisy main drag between the town hall and the Anne Frank House. Expect a long, steep, and depressing stairway, noisy front rooms, and quieter rooms in the back.

Hotel Aspen, a good value for a budget hotel, is tidy, stark, and well-maintained (8 rooms, S-€32, D-€41, Db-€64, Tb-€75, Qb-€87, no breakfast, CC, Raadhuisstraat 31, tel. 020/626-6714, fax 020/620-0866, e-mail: info@hotelaspen.nl, run by Esam and Hanne). A few doors away, **Hotel Pax** has large, plain, but airy backpacker-type rooms (S-€25–34, D-€37–57, Db-€55–85, T-€50–68, Q-€55–77, no breakfast, prices vary with size and season, CC, 2 showers and 2 toilets for 8 rooms, Raadhuisstraat 37, tel. 020/624-9735, run by two young brothers: Philip and Peter).

The Shelter Jordan is a scruffy, friendly, Christian-run, 100-bed place in a great neighborhood. While most of Amsterdam's hostels are pretty wild, this place is drug-free and alcohol-free with boys on one floor and girls on another. These are Amsterdam's best budget beds, in 14- to 20-bed dorms (€16, includes sheets and breakfast, maximum age 35, CC, Internet access, non-smoking, 02:00 curfew, near Anne Frank House, Bloemstraat 179, tel. 020/624-4717, www.shelter.nl, e-mail: jordan@shelter.nl). The Shelter serves hot meals, runs a snack bar, offers lockers, leads nightly Bible studies, and closes the dorms from 10:30 to 13:00. Its sister hostel, **The Shelter City**, in the Red Light District, is similar but definitely not preaching to the choir (€16, includes breakfast and sheets, CC, maximum age 35, curfew, Barndesteeg 21, tel. 020/625-3230, fax 020/623-2282, www.shelter.nl, e-mail: city@shelter.nl).

The city's two official hostels are **Vondelpark**, Amsterdam's top hostel (€18–24 with breakfast, D-€66, nonmembers pay €2.25 extra, no CC, lots of school groups, 4–20 beds per dorm, right on the park at Zandpad 5, tel. 020/589-8996, fax 020/589-8955, www.njhc.org/vondelpark) and **Stadsdoelen** (€17 with breakfast, nonmembers pay €2.25 extra, no CC, just past Dam Square, Kloveniersburgwal 97, tel. 020/624-6832, fax 020/639-1035, www.njhc.org, e-mail: stadsdoelen@njhc.org). While generally booked long in advance, a few beds open up each day at 11:00.

Eating in Amsterdam

Traditional Dutch food is basic and hearty, with lots of bread, cheese, soups, and fish. Lunch and dinner are served at American times (roughly 12:00–14:00 and 18:00–21:00).

Dutch taste treats include cheese, pancakes (*pannenkoeken*), Dutch gin (*jenever*), light pilsner beer, and "syrup waffles" (*stroopwafel*).

Experiences you owe your tongue in Holland: trying a raw herring (outdoor herring stands are all over), lingering over coffee in a "brown café," sipping an old *jenever* with a new friend, and consuming an Indonesian feast—a *rijsttafel*.

Budget Tips: Get a sandwich to go, and grab a park bench on a canal. Sandwiches (*broodjes*) of fresh bread and delicious cheese are cheap at snack bars, delis, and *broodje* restaurants.

Ethnic fast-food stands abound, offering a variety of meats wrapped in pita bread. Easy to buy at grocery stores, yogurt in the Netherlands (and throughout northern Europe) is delicious and drinkable right out of its plastic container. A central supermarket is **Albert Heijn**, at the corner of Koningsplein and Singel Canal near the flower market (Mon–Sat 10:00–20:00, Sun 12:00–18:00).

Restaurants

Of Amsterdam's thousand-plus restaurants, no one knows which are best. I'd pick an area and wander. The rowdy food ghetto thrives around Leidseplein. Wander along Leidsedwarsstraat—restaurant row. The area aroun d Spui canal and that end of Spuistraat is also trendy and a bit less rowdy. For fewer crowds and more charm, find something in the Jordaan district. The best advice: your hotelier's. Most keep a reliable eating list for their neighborhood and know which places keep their travelers happy.

Here are some handy places to consider:

Eating near Spui in the Center

The first four places all cluster along the colorful, student-filled Grimburgwal lane near the intersection of Spui and Rokin (midway between Dam Square and the Mint Tower).

The city university's **Atrium** is a great budget cafeteria (€4.50 meals, Mon–Fri 11:00–15:00 & 17:00–19:30, closed Sat–Sun, from Spui, walk west down Landebrug Steeg past the canalside Café 't Gasthuys 3 blocks to Oudezijds Achterburgwal 237, go through arched doorway on the right, tel. 020/525-3999).

Café 't Gasthuys, one of Amsterdam's many "brown cafés" (named for their smoke-stained walls), serves light meals and good sandwiches and offers indoor or peaceful canalside seating (daily 12:00–24:00, Grimburgwal 7, tel. 020/624-8230).

Pannenkoekenhuis Upstairs is a tiny and characteristic perch up some extremely steep stairs where Arno Jakobs cooks and serves delicious €7 pancakes to four tables (daily from noon, Grimburgwal 2, tel. 020/626-5603).

Restaurant Kapitein Zeppos—named for a Belgian TV star from the '60s—serves French/Dutch food in a relatively big and festive setting. The light lunch specials—soups and sandwiches—cost €5 to €10. Dinners go for around €20 (daily 11:00–15:30 & 17:30–23:00, just off Grimburgwal at Gebed Zonder End 3, tel. 020/624-2057).

De Jaren Café ("The Years") is a stark and trendy place for soup, salads, sandwiches, or just coffee over a newspaper. On a sunny day, its canalside patio is popular with yuppies

Amsterdam Restaurants

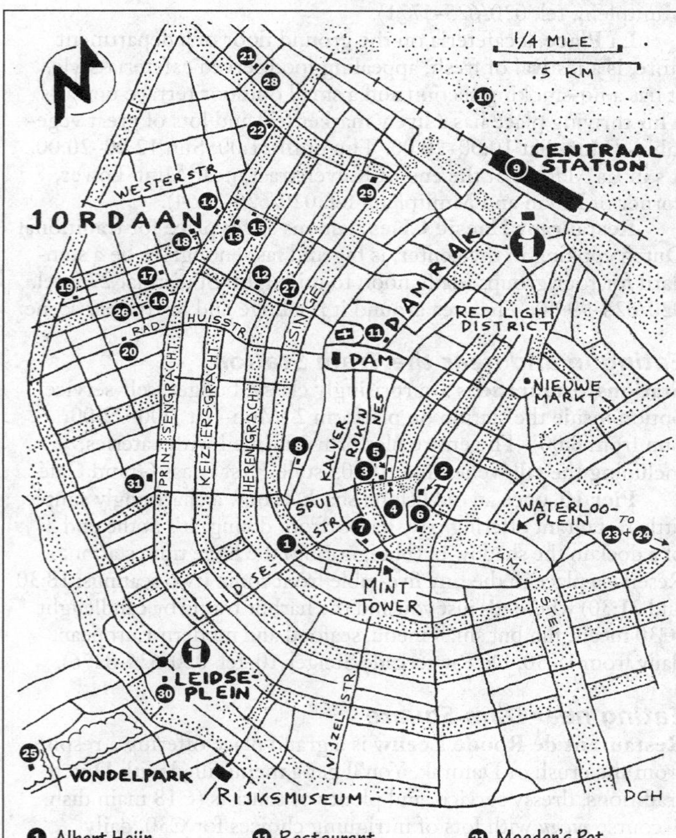

1. Albert Heijn Supermarket
2. Atrium Cafeteria
3. Café 't Gasthuys
4. Pannenkoekenhuis Upstairs
5. Restaurant Kapitein Zeppos
6. De Jaren Café
7. La Place
8. Restaurant Haesje Claes
9. Stationsrestauratie
10. Pier 10
11. Restaurant de Roode Leeuw
12. Restaurant de Luwte
13. Pancake Bakery
14. De Bolhoed
15. Dimitri's
16. De Groene Lantaarn
17. Café Restaurant de Reiger
18. Café 't Smalle
19. Restaurant Vliegende Schotel
20. Long Pura Restaurant
21. Moeder's Pot
22. Café 't Papeneiland
23. To Rest. Plancius
24. To Taman Sari Restaurant
25. Café Vertigo

Coffeeshops:

26. Paradox
27. The Grey Area
28. Coffee Shop Relax
29. Siberia Coffeeshop
30. The Bulldog
31. La Tertulia

(daily 10:00–24:00, Nieuwe Doelenstraat 20–22, just up from Muntplein, tel. 020/625-5771).

La Place, a cafeteria on the ground floor of a department store, is a festival of fresh, appealing food served cafeteria-style. It has a no-smoking section and a small outdoor terrace upstairs. This thriving place has a lively market feel and lots of great vegetables (Mon–Sat 10:00–20:00, Thu until 21:00, Sun 12:00–20:00, it's in La Marche at the end of Kalverstraat, near Mint Tower, corner of Rokin and Muntplein, tel. 020/620-2364).

Restaurant Haesje Claes, famous as *the* place for traditional Dutch cooking in the center, is big and fast enough to be a standard for tour groups (daily noon to midnight, Spuistraat 275, tel. 020/624-9998). The area around it is a huge and festive bar scene.

Eating in and near the Train Station

Stationsrestauratie is a surprisingly classy, budget, self-service option inside the station on platform 2 (Mon–Sat 7:00–22:00, Sun from 8:00). The entire platform 2 is lined with eateries, including the tall, venerable, 1920s-style First Class Grand Café.

Pier 10, once an old fishing shack, is now a charmingly simple little restaurant offering cozy harborfront dining. It's at the end of a dock in the shadow of (but ignoring) the huge train station. Reserve a place in the tiny five-table front room (two seatings: 18:30 and 21:30) where it's just you and the harbor traffic by candlelight (€30 meals, fun but small menu, seafood and modern European, daily from 18:30, De Ruyterkade Steiger 10, tel. 020/624-8276).

Eating near Dam Square

Restaurant de Roode Leeuw is a grand place offering a respite from the crush of Damrak. You'll get a menu filled with Dutch traditions, dressy service, and plenty of tourists (€18 main dish, 3-course *menu* with lots of intriguing choices for €30, daily 12:00–22:00, Damrak 93–94, tel. 020/555-0666).

Eating near the Anne Frank House and in the Jordaan District

Except for the last two places, these are all within a few scenic blocks of Anne Frank's house, providing handy lunches and atmospheric dinners in Amsterdam's most characteristic neighborhood.

Restaurant de Luwte is painfully romantic on a picturesque street overlooking a canal, with lots of candles, a muted but fresh mod interior, and French Mediterranean cuisine (€18 main courses, €35 for a full meal, big dinner salads for €15, daily 18:00–22:00, CC, Leliegracht 26, tel. 020/625-8548).

The **Pancake Bakery** serves good pancakes in a nothing-special family atmosphere. Their menu features a fun selection of ethnic theme pancakes—including Indonesian for those who want two experiences in one (€8.25 pancakes, splitting OK, daily 12:00–21:30, Prinsengracht 191, tel. 020/625-1333).

De Bolhoed, across the canal, serves serious vegetarian and vegan food with an ambience Buddha would dig (€13 meals, daily 12:00–22:00, Prinsengracht 60, tel. 020/626-1803).

Dimitri's is a nondescript little place serving creative salads with a few outdoor tables on a street filled with bikes and cobbles (€9 main-course salads, breakfasts too, daily 8:00–22:00, Prinsenstraat 3, tel. 020/627-9393).

De Groene Lantaarn ("The Green Lantern") is fun for fondue. The menu offers fish, meat, and cheese (Dutch ...not Swiss) with salad and fruit for €17 to €22 (Thu–Sun from 18:00, closed Mon–Wed, a few blocks into the Jordaan at Bloemgracht 47, tel. 020/620-2088).

Café Restaurant de Reiger must offer the best cooking of any *eetcafé* in the Jordaan. They are famous for their fresh ingredients and delightful bistro ambience. While they have an English menu, ask for a translation of the daily specials (€15) on the chalkboard. The café, which is crowded late and on weekends, takes no reservations but you're welcome to have a drink at the bar while you wait (daily 11:00–15:30 & 18:00–22:30, glass of house wine for €2.50, veggie options, non-smoking section, Niewe Leliestraat 34, tel. 020/624-7426).

Café 't Smalle is extremely charming with three zones where you can enjoy a light lunch or a drink: canalside, inside around the bar, and up some steep stairs in a quaint little loft. While open daily until midnight, they serve food only at lunch from 12:00 to 17:00 (plenty of interesting wines by the glass posted, at Egelantiersgracht 12 where that canal hits Prinsengracht, tel. 020/623-9617).

Restaurant Vliegende Schotel is a folksy, unvarnished little Jordaan eatery decorated with children's crayon art with a cheap and fun meatless menu featuring fish and vegetarian fare. Nothing trendy about this place—just locals who like food and don't want to cook (daily 17:00–23:00, non-smoking section, wine by the glass, Nieuwe Leliestraat 162, tel. 020/625-2041).

Long Pura is a good place for authentic Indonesian. While pricey, filled with tourists, and on a noisy street, it's conveniently located, friendly, and proudly serves reliably delicious rice-table extravaganzas in a tastefully Indonesian setting (€31 for *rijsttafel*, €37 with appetizer and dessert, daily 18:00–23:00, Rozengracht 46, tel. 020/623-8950).

Moeder's Pot, a six-table neighborhood eatery with great character and charm, is gruff with the smell of fried food and cigarettes. Hearty main courses come with fried potatoes and vegetables, applesauce, and salad. The place is not central but puts you in a charming little neighborhood at the seaside edge of the Jordaan (€7–15, Mon–Sat 11:00–22:00, closed Sun, Vinkenstraat 119, no phone).

Café 't Papeneiland is a classic "brown café." With Delft tiles, an evocative old stove, and a stay-awhile perch overlooking a canal with welcoming benches, it's been the neighborhood hangout since the 17th century (overlooking northwest end of Prinsengracht at #2, tel. 020/624-1989). While the café serves light meals, most come here to nurse a drink and chat.

Eating near the Botanical Garden and Dutch Resistance Museum

Restaurant Plancius, adjacent to the Dutch Resistance Museum, is a mod, handy spot for lunch. With good indoor and outdoor seating, it's popular with the broadcasters from the nearby local TV studios (creative breakfasts and light lunches €5–8, daily 9:00–24:00, Plantage Kerklaan 61a, tel. 020/330-9469).

Taman Sari Restaurant is the local choice for Indonesian, serving hearty quality €9 dinners and *rijsttafel* dinners for €14 to €18 (daily 17:00–23:00, 32 Plantage Kerklaan, tel. 020/623-7130).

Eating near Vondelpark

Café Vertigo offers a fun selection of excellent soups and sandwiches. Grab an outdoor table and watch the world spin by (daily 11:00–24:00, beneath Film Museum, Vondelpark 3, tel. 020/612-3021).

Drugs and Coffeeshops

Amsterdam, Europe's counterculture mecca, thinks "victimless crime" is a contradiction in terms. Heroin and cocaine are strictly illegal in the Netherlands, and the police stringently enforce laws prohibiting their sale and use. But, while hard drugs are definitely out, marijuana causes about as much excitement as a bottle of beer.

Throughout the Netherlands, you'll see "coffeeshops"—pubs selling marijuana. The minimum age for purchase is 18 years. Coffeeshops can sell up to five grams of marijuana per person per day. Locals buy marijuana by asking, "Can I see the cannabis menu?" The menu looks like the inventory of a drug bust. Display cases show various joints or baggies for sale. The Dutch put a little tobacco into their pre-rolled joints. To avoid the tobacco, you either need to get cigarette papers with your baggie (dispensed free like toothpicks) or borrow a bong. Baggies usually cost €5—smaller contents mean better quality.

Most of downtown Amsterdam's countless coffeeshops feel grungy and foreboding to anyone over thirty. The neighborhood places (and those in small towns throughout the countryside) are much more inviting to people without piercings, tattoos, and favorite techno artists. I've listed a few places with a more pub-like ambience for Americans wanting to go local but within reason.

Paradox is the most *gezellig* (cozy) coffeeshop I found—a mellow, graceful place. The manager, Ludo, is patient with descriptions and is happy to walk you through all your options. This is a rare coffeeshop that serves light meals. The juice is fresh, the music is easy, and the neighborhood is charming. Colorful murals with bright blue skies are all over the walls, creating a fresh and open feeling (loaner bongs, games, no CC, daily 10:00–20:00, 2 blocks from Anne Frank House at 1e Bloemdwarsstraat 2, tel. 020/623-5639).

The Grey Area coffeeshop is a cool, welcoming, and smoky hole-in-the-wall appreciated among local aficionados as a seven-time winner of Amsterdam's Cannabis Cup award. Judging by the proud autographed photos on the wall, many of America's most famous tokers have smoked here. You're welcome to just nurse a bottomless cup of coffee (open Tue–Sun high noon to 20:00, closed Mon, between Dam Square and Anne Frank House at Oude Leliestraat 2, tel. 020/420-4301, www.greyarea.nl, run by two friendly Americans, Steven and John).

Coffee Shop Relax is simply the neighborhood pub serving a different drug. It's relaxed with a helpful staff and homey atmosphere with plants, couches, and bar seating. The great straightforward menu chalked onto the board behind the bar details what they have to offer (daily 10:00–24:00, a bit out of the way, but a pleasant Jordaan walk to Binnen Orangestraat 9).

Siberia Coffeeshop is central but feels cozy with a friendly canalside ambience (daily 11:00–23:00, Internet access, helpful staff, fun English "menu" that explains the personalities of each item, a variety of €4 bags, Brouwersgracht 11).

La Tertulia is a sweet little mother-daughter-run place with pastel décor, a fishpond, and a cheery terrarium ambience (Tue–Sat 11:00–19:00, closed Sun–Mon, games, sandwiches, Prinsengracht 312, www.coffeeshopamsterdam.com).

The Bulldog is the high-profile, leading touristy chain of coffeeshops. They are young but welcoming with reliable selections. They are pretty comfortable for green tourists wanting to just hang out for a while. The flagship branch, in a former police station right on Leidseplein is very handy, offering fun outdoor seating to watch the world skateboard by (daily 9:00–24:00, Leidseplein 17, tel. 020/625-6278, www.bulldog.nl).

Transportation Connections—Amsterdam

Amsterdam's train-information center requires a long wait. Save lots of time by getting train tickets and information in a small-town station, at the airport upon arrival, or from a travel agency. For phone information, dial 0900-9292 for local trains or 0900-9296 for international trains (€0.50/min, daily 7:00–24:00, wait through recording and hold . . . hold . . . hold . . .).

By train to: Schiphol Airport (6/hr, 20 min, €3), **Haarlem** (6/hr, 15 min, €5.50 same-day return), **The Hague** (2/hr, 50 min), **Rotterdam** (4/hr, 1 hr), **Bruges** (hrly, 3.5–4.25 hrs, 1–3 transfers; transfers are timed closely—be alert and check with conductor), **Brussels** (2/hr, 3 hrs, €30), **Ostende** (hrly, 4 hrs, change in Antwerp), **London** (2/day, 8 hrs, train to Hoek van Holland, then ferry across Channel, then train from Harwich to London; or 8/day, 6.5 hrs, with transfer to Eurostar Chunnel train in Brussels, Eurostar discounted with railpass, www.eurostar.com), **Copenhagen** (5/day, 10 hrs, transfer in Osnabrück and Hamburg; or 3-hr train to Duisberg and transfer to 11-hr night train), **Frankfurt** (8/day, 5–6 hrs, transfer in Köln or Duisburg), **Munich** (7/day, 9 hrs, transfer in Mannheim, Hanover, or Köln, one 11-hr direct night train), **Bonn** (10/day, 3 hrs, some direct but most transfer in Köln), **Bern** (5/day, 9 hrs, one direct but most transfer in Basel, Köln, or Brussels), **Paris** (5/day, 5 hrs, required fast train from Brussels with €11 supplement). If you don't have a railpass, the cheapest way to get to Paris is by bus (Euroline buses make the 8-hour trip five times daily, about €39 or €60 round-trip compared to €100 second-class by train; bus station in Amsterdam at Julianaplein 5, Amstel Station, 5 stops by Metro from Centraal Station, tel. 020/560-8788, www.eurolines.com).

Amsterdam's Schiphol Airport

The airport, like most of Holland, is English-speaking, user-friendly, and below sea level. Its banks offer fair rates (24 hrs daily, in arrival area).

Schiphol (pron. SKIP-pol) Airport has easy connections with **Amsterdam** by train (6/hr, 20 min, €3) and by KLM Hotel Bus (3/hr, 20 min, €10, leaves from lane A7 in front of the airport, 2 routes—ask attendant which comes closest to your hotel, one bus stops at Westerkerk church near Anne Frank House and many recommended hotels). Allow about €35 for a taxi to Amsterdam.

Schipol also has good connections with **Haarlem** by train (2/hr, 40 min, transfer at Amsterdam-Sloterdijk, €4.55) and by bus #300 (4/hr, 40 min, departs from lane B2 in front of the airport, €3.50). Figure on about €32 to Haarlem by taxi.

The airport also has a train station of its own. You can validate your Eurailpass and hit the rails immediately or, to stretch your train pass, buy an inexpensive ticket into Amsterdam today and start the pass later.

Schiphol flight information (tel. 0900-72447465, €0.10/min) can give you flight times and your airline's Amsterdam number for reconfirmation before going home (€0.45/min to climb through its phone tree). To reach the airlines, dial: KLM at 020/649-9123 or 020/4747747, NW is same as KLM, Martainair at 020/601-1222, SAS at 0900-746-63727, American Airlines at 06/022-7844, British Air at 023/554-7555, and EasyJet at 023/568-4880.

If you have time to kill at Schiphol, check out the Dutch Masters. The Rijksmuseum loans a dozen or so of its masterpieces from the Golden Age to the "Rijksmuseum Schiphol," a free little art gallery behind the passport check between pier E and F.

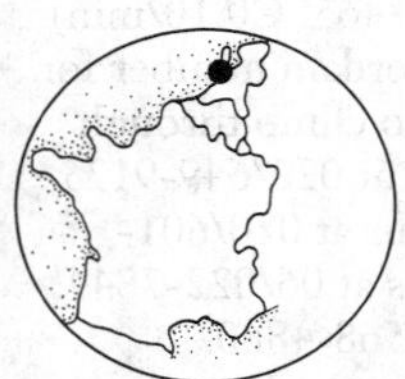

HAARLEM

Cute, cozy, and handy to the airport, Haarlem is a fine home base, giving you small-town, overnight warmth with easy access (15 min by train) to wild and crazy Amsterdam.

Bustling Haarlem gave America's Harlem its name back when New York was "New Amsterdam," a Dutch colony. For centuries, Haarlem has been a market town, buzzing with shoppers heading home with fresh bouquets, nowadays by bike.

Enjoy the market on Monday (clothing) or Saturday (general), when the square bustles like a Brueghel painting with cheese, fish, flowers, and families. Make yourself at home; buy some flowers to brighten your hotel room.

Orientation (area code: 023)

Tourist Information: Haarlem's TI (VVV), at the train station, is friendlier, more helpful, and less crowded than Amsterdam's. Ask your Amsterdam questions here (Mon–Fri 9:30–17:30, Sat 10:00–14:00, closed Sun, tel. 0900-616-1600, €0.50/min, helpful parking brochure). Their €1 *Holiday Magazine* is not necessary, but it's free if you buy the fine €2 town map. The little computer terminal prints out free maps 24/7 on the curb outside the TI.

Arrival in Haarlem: As you walk out of the train station (which has lockers), the TI is on your right and the bus station is across the street. Two parallel streets flank the train station (Kruisweg and Jansweg). Head up either street, and you'll reach the town square and church within 10 minutes. If you need help, ask a local person to point you toward the "*Grote Markt*" (Main Square).

Parking is expensive on the streets and €1 an hour in several central garages. Two main garages let you park overnight for €1 (at the train station and near Die Raeckse Hotel).

Helpful Hints

Bike Rental: You can rent bikes at the train station (€6/day, €45 deposit and passport number, Mon–Sat 6:00–24:00, Sun 7:30–24:00).

Changing Money: The handy GWK change office at the train station offers fair exchange rates (Mon–Fri 8:00–20:00, Sat 9:00–18:00, Sun 10:00–18:00).

Internet Access: Try Internet Café Amadeus (in the Hotel Amadeus overlooking Market Square, €1/15 min) or nearly any coffeeshop, if you don't mind marijuana smoke.

Laundromat: My Beautiful Launderette is handy, self-service, and cheap (€5 wash and dry, daily 8:30–20:30, bring lots of change, near Vroom Dreesman department store at Boter Markt 20).

Festival: On April 26, 2003, an all-day Flower Parade of floats wafts through eight towns, including Haarlem.

Local Guide: Consider Walter Schelfhout (€75/2-hr walk, tel. 023/535-5715).

Sights—Haarlem

▲▲Market Square (Grote Markt)—Haarlem's market square, where 10 streets converge, is the town's delightful centerpiece... as it has been for 700 years. To enjoy a coffee or beer here while simmering in Dutch good living is a quintessential European experience. In recent studies, the Dutch were found to be the most content people in Europe and the people of Haarlem were found to be the most content in the Netherlands.

Observe. Sit and gaze at the church, appreciating the same scene Dutch artists captured in oil paintings that now hang in museums.

Just a few years ago, trolleys ran through the square and cars were parked everywhere. But today it's a people zone, with market stalls filling the square on Mondays and Saturdays and café tables on other days.

This is a great place to build a picnic with Haarlem finger foods—raw herring, local cheese (Gouda and Edam), a *frikandel* (little corn-dog sausage), French fries with mayonnaise, *stroopwafels* (waffles with syrup), and *poffertjes* (little sugar doughnuts).

▲Great Church (Grote Kerk)—This 15th-century Gothic church (now Protestant) is worth a look, if only for its Oz-like organ (30 meters/100 feet high, its 5,000 pipes impressed both Handel and Mozart). One of the best-known landmarks in the Netherlands, the Great Church is visible from miles around, rising above the flat plain that surrounds it.

The church was built over a 150-year period (c. 1390-1540) in the late Gothic style of red and gray brick, topped with a lead-covered wood roof and a stacked tower with a golden crown and a rooster weathervane.

Haarlem

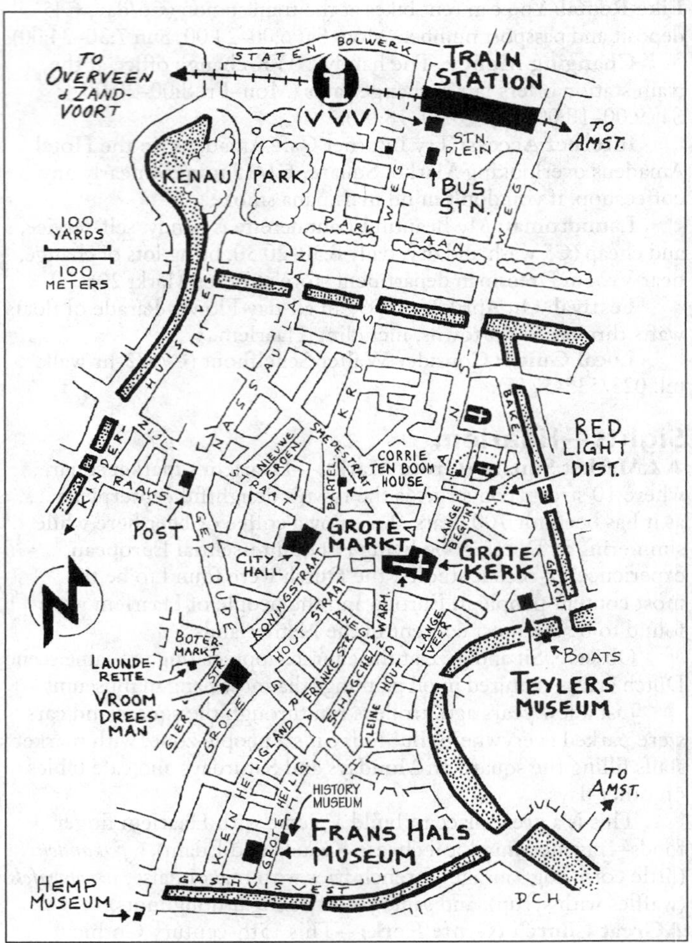

To enter, find the small *Entrée* sign behind the church at Oude Groenmarkt 23 (€1.50, Mon–Sat 10:00–16:00, closed Sun to tourists, tel. 023/532-4399). Consider attending a concert to hear Holland's greatest pipe organ (regular free concerts Tue at 20:15 mid-May–mid-Oct, additional concerts Thu at 15:00 July–Aug, confirm schedule at TI or at www.bavo.nl).

▲▲**Frans Hals Museum**—Haarlem is the hometown of Frans Hals (c. 1582-1666), and this refreshing museum, once an almshouse for old men back in 1610, displays many of his greatest paintings. Hals was an articulate visual spokesman for his generation—the generation of the Golden Age. Stand eye-to-eye with life-size, lifelike portraits of Haarlem's citizens—brewers, preachers, workers, bureaucrats, and housewives—and see the people who built the Golden Age, then watched it start to fade. A new wing, opening in 2003, ties this Dutch slice-of-life art to . . . slices of Dutch life. Various Golden Age paintings will be paired with exhibits explaining more about daily life during the 17th century.

Along with Frans Hals work, the museum features Peter Brueghel the Younger's painting *Proverbs* illustrating 72 old Dutch proverbs. To peek into old Dutch ways, identify some with the help of the English-language key (€5.40, Tue–Sat 11:00–17:00, Sun 12:00–17:00, closed Mon, Groot Heiligland 62, tel. 023/511-5775, www.franshalsmuseum.nl).

History Museum—This small museum, across the street from the Frans Hals Museum, offers a glimpse of old Haarlem. Request the English version of the 10-minute video. Study the large-scale model of Haarlem in 1822 while its fortifications were still intact, and enjoy the new "time machine" computer and video display that shows you various aspects of life in Haarlem at different points in history (€1, Tue–Sat 12:00–17:00, Sun 13:00–17:00, closed Mon, Groot Heiligland 47, tel. 020/542-2427). The adjacent architecture museum (free) may be of interest to architects.

Corrie Ten Boom House—Haarlem is home to Corrie Ten Boom, popularized by *The Hiding Place*, an inspirational book and movie about the Ten Boom family's experience protecting Jews from Nazis.

The clock shop was the Ten Boom family business. The elderly father and his two daughters—Corrie and Betsy, both in their fifties—lived above the store. In Corrie's bedroom, on the top floor at the back, the family built a second, secret room—the hiding place, where they could hide up to seven Jews at a time. Devoutly religious, the family had a long tradition of tolerance, having for generations hosted prayer meetings here in their home for both Jews and Christians.

In February 1944, the Gestapo—tipped off that the family was harboring Jews—burst into the Ten Boom house. Finding a suspiciously high number of ration coupons, the Nazis arrested the family (but failed to find the six Jews in the hiding place, who later escaped). Corrie's father and sister died while in prison, but Corrie survived the Ravensbruck concentration camp to tell her story in her memoir.

The Ten Boom House is open for 60-minute English

Marijuana in Haarlem

Haarlem is a laid-back place to observe the Dutch approach to recreational marijuana. The town is dotted with 16 casual coffeeshops where pot is casually sold and smoked by easy-going, non-criminal types.

If you don't like the smell of pot, avoid places sporting Rastafarian yellow, red, and green colors, wildly painted walls, and plants in the windows.

If you want an introduction to the whole scene, stop in at the friendly **Global Hemp Museum**, the hub of Haarlem's coffeeshop action. Actually more of a hemp-products store, Global Hemp does run a humble museum upstairs (shop free, museum €2.50, Internet access-€1.50/30 min, Mon–Sat 11:00–20:00, summer Sun 12:00–20:00, Houtplein 16a, tel. 023/534-9939).

Willie Wortel Sativa Coffeeshop, next door to the Global Hemp Museum, is one of the best established coffeeshops (daily 9:00–24:00, in front of train station at Kruisweg 46). The display-case "menu" explains what's on sale (€2.50 joints, €5 baggies, space cakes, no alcohol, only soft drinks, mellow music).

'T Theehuis, which feels more like a mini-hippie teahouse, is Haarlem's first coffeeshop with 50 different varieties on its menu and a friendly staff (daily 13:00–22:00, a block off Market Square at Smedestraat 25).

High Times offers smokers 16 varieties of joints in racks behind the bar (neatly prepacked in trademarked "Joint Packs," €2–3.50, daily 12:00–23:00, Internet access, Lange Veerstraat 47). Across the street, Crack is the wild and leathery place to go for loud music, pool, and darts (Lange Veerstraat 32).

tours; the tours are sometimes mixed with preaching (donation accepted, April–Oct Tue–Sat 10:00–16:00, Nov–March Tue–Sat 11:00–15:00, closed Mon, 50 meters north of Market Square at Barteljorisstraat 19, the clock-shop people get all wound up if you go inside—wait at the door, where tour times are posted, tel. 023/531-0823).

▲**Teylers Museum**—Famous as the oldest museum in Holland, Teylers is interesting mainly as a look at a 200-year-old museum—fossils, minerals, and primitive electronic gadgetry. New exhibition halls (with rotating exhibits) have freshened up the place.

Stop by if you enjoy mixing, say, Renaissance sketches with pickled extinct fish (€4.50, Tue–Sat 10:00–17:00, Sun 12:00–17:00, Spaarne 16, tel. 023/531-9010).

Canal Cruise—Making a scenic loop through and around Haarlem, these little trips by Woltheus Cruises are more relaxing than informative (€6.50, Tue–Sun 10:00–17:00, closed Mon, 70 min, 5/day, across canal from Teylers Museum at Spaarne 11a, tel. 023/535-7723).

Red Lights—Wander through a little red light district as precious as a Barbie doll—and legal since the 1980s (2 blocks northeast of Market Square, off Lange Begijnestraat, no senior or student discounts). Don't miss the mall marked by the red neon sign reading *t'Steegje*. The nearby *t'Poortje* (office park) costs €6.

Nightlife in Haarlem

Haarlem's evening scene is great. The bars around the Grote Kerk and Lange Veerstraat are colorful and lively. You'll find plenty of music. The best show in town: the café scene on Market Square. In good weather, café tables tumble happily out of the bars.

For trendy local crowds, sip a drink at **Studio Café** (daily 12:00–24:00, on Market Square, next to Hotel Carillon, tel. 023/531-0033). Tourists gawk at the old-fashioned belt-driven ceiling fans in **Café 1900** across from the Corrie Ten Boom House (daily 9:00–00:30, live music Sun night except in July, Barteljoris Straat 10, tel. 023/531-8283).

Sleeping in Haarlem

(€1 = about $1, country code: 31, area code: 023)

Sleep Code: **S** = Single, **D** = Double/Twin, **T** = Triple, **Q** = Quad, **b** = bathroom, **s** = shower only, **CC** = Credit Cards accepted, **no CC** = Credit Cards not accepted.

To help you easily sort through these listings, I've divided the rooms into three categories based on the price for a standard double room with bath:

Higher Priced—Most rooms €100 or more.
Moderately Priced—Most rooms less than €100.
Lower Priced—Most rooms less than €65.

The helpful Haarlem TI, just outside the train station, can nearly always find you a €20 bed in a private home (for a €4.50-per-person fee plus a cut of your host's money). Avoid this if you can; it's cheaper to reserve direct. Nearly every Dutch person you'll encounter speaks English.

Haarlem is most crowded in April and May (especially Easter weekend) and in July and August.

The listed prices include breakfast (unless otherwise noted) and usually include the €1.70-per-person-per-day tourist tax. To avoid this town's louder-than-normal street noises, forgo views for a room in the back. Hotels and the TI have a useful parking brochure.

Sleeping in the Center

HIGHER PRICED

Hotel Lion D'Or is a classy 34-room business hotel with all the professional comforts and a handy location. Don't expect a warm welcome (Sb-€115–125, Db-€145–165, extra bed-€10, CC, elevator, some non-smoking rooms, across the street from train station at Kruisweg 34, tel. 023/532-1750, fax 023/532-9543, www.goldentulip.nl/hotels/gtliondor).

MODERATELY PRICED

Hotel Amadeus, on Market Square, has 15 small, bright, and basic rooms. Some have views of the square. This characteristic hotel, ideally located above an early 20th-century dinner café, is relatively quiet. Its lush old lounge/breakfast room, on the second floor, overlooks the square, and Mike and Inez take good care of their guests (Sb-€52.50, Db-€73.50, Tb-€90, Qb-€100, includes tax, 2-night stay and cash get you a 5 percent discount, 12-min walk from train station, CC, steep climb to lounge, then an elevator, Grote Markt 10, tel. 023/532-4530, fax 023/532-2328, www.amadeus-hotel.com). The hotel also runs a five-terminal Internet café.

Hotel Carillon also overlooks the town square but comes with a little more traffic and bell-tower noise. Many of the 22 well-worn rooms are small, and the stairs are ste-e-e-p. The front rooms come with great town-square views and street noise (tiny loft singles-€30, Db-€72, Tb-€94, Qb-€102, includes tax, 12-min walk from train station, CC, no elevator, Grote Markt 27, tel. 023/531-0591, fax 023/531-4909, www.hotelcarillon.com, e-mail: info@hotelcarillon.com).

Hotel Joops (pron. yopes, rhymes with ropes) rents 30 hotel rooms within a block of the hotel—which is just behind the cathedral (hotel Db-€65–85, Tb-€95) and also administers a corral of 80 other rooms, scattered in buildings within a block of the church. The 80 rooms are a mixed bunch, ranging from cheap, well-worn, depressing rooms (avoid these if you can afford it; S-€30, D-€55, T-€75) to modern new suites with kitchenettes (Db-€70–90) for about the same price as the hotel rooms (breakfast-€9.50 extra, credit cards OK, 5 percent discount for cash, Oude Groenmarkt 20, Internet access, minimal service, tel. 023/532-2008, fax 023/532-9549, www.dutchhotels.nl/joops.hotel, e-mail: joops@easynet.nl).

Die Raeckse Hotel—family-run and friendly—is not as central as the others, with less character and more traffic noise, but its 21 rooms are decent and comfortable (Sb-€55, Db-€70–80 depending upon the size, Tb-€93, Qb-€105, extra bed-€20, CC, Raaks 1, tel. 023/532-6629, fax 023/531-7937, www.die-raeckse.nl, e-mail: dieraeckse@zonnet.nl). A big cheap garage is across the street.

LOWER PRICED

Bed and Breakfast House de Kiefte, your get-into-a-local-home budget option, epitomizes the goodness of B&Bs. Marjet (mar-yet) and Hans, a frank, interesting Dutch couple who speak English fluently, rent four bright, cheery, non-smoking rooms (includes breakfast and travel advice) in their quiet, 1892 home (Ds-€50, T-€70, Qs-€90, Quint/s-€105, cash only, minimum 2 nights, all rooms with very steep stairs, family loft sleeps up to 5, kids over 4 welcome, Coornhertstraat 3, tel. 023/532-2980, cellular 06-5474-5272). It's a 15-minute walk or €7 taxi ride from the train station and a five-minute walk from the center. From Grote Markt (Market Square), walk to the right of City Hall straight out Zijlstraat and over the bridge and take a left on the fourth street.

Sleeping near Haarlem

MODERATELY PRICED

Hotel Haarlem Zuid—with 300 rooms and very American—is sterile but a good value for those interested only in sleeping and eating. It sits in an industrial zone, a 20-minute walk from the center on the road to the airport (Db-€80, breakfast-€12, CC, elevator, free parking, laundry service, fitness center, inexpensive hotel restaurant, Toekanweg 2, tel. 023/536-7500, fax 023/536-7980, www.hotelhaarlemzuid.nl, e-mail: haarlemzuid@valk.com). Buses #70, #71, and #72 connect the hotel with the train station and Market Square every 10 minutes. Bus #80 makes runs to the beach or Amsterdam. Fast airport bus #300 stops at the hotel.

LOWER PRICED

Pension Koning, a 15-minute walk north of the train station or a quick hop on bus #71, has five simple rooms in a row house in a residential area (S-€23, D-€46, T-€69, 2-night minimum, includes breakfast, no CC, Kleverlaan 179, tel. 023/526-1456).

Hostel Haarlem, completely renovated and with all the youth-hostel comforts, charges €18 to €21 for beds in eight-bed dorms (€2.50 extra for nonmembers, includes sheets and breakfast,

Haarlem Hotels and Restaurants

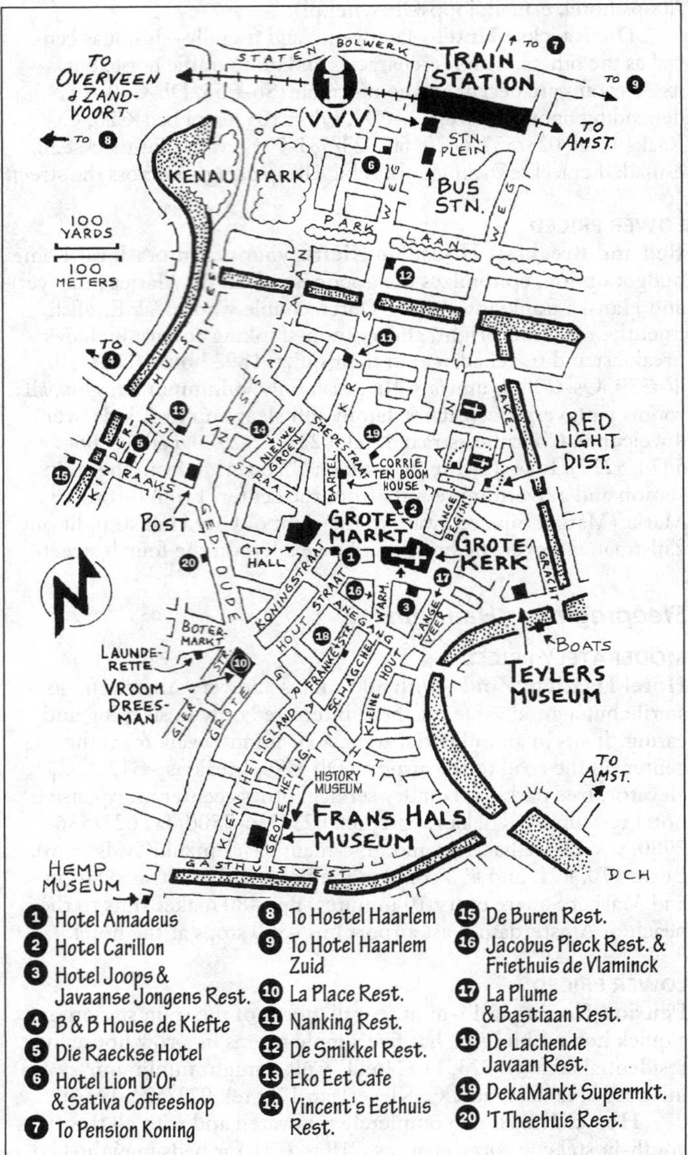

TO OVERVEEN & ZANDVOORT
TO 8
STATEN BOLWERK
TRAIN STATION
TO 7
TO 9
TO AMST.
(VVV)
STN. PLEIN
BUS STN.
KENAU PARK
100 YARDS
100 METERS
PARK LAAN
TO 4
RED LIGHT DIST.
CORRIE TEN BOOM HOUSE
GROTE MARKT
CITY HALL
GROTE KERK
POST
BOATS
TEYLERS MUSEUM
LAUNDERETTE
VROOM DREESMAN
BOTER-MARKT
TO AMST.
HISTORY MUSEUM
FRANS HALS MUSEUM
HEMP MUSEUM
GASTHUIS VEST
DCH
1 Hotel Amadeus
2 Hotel Carillon
3 Hotel Joops & Javaanse Jongens Rest.
4 B & B House de Kiefte
5 Die Raeckse Hotel
6 Hotel Lion D'Or & Sativa Coffeeshop
7 To Pension Koning
8 To Hostel Haarlem
9 To Hotel Haarlem Zuid
10 La Place Rest.
11 Nanking Rest.
12 De Smikkel Rest.
13 Eko Eet Cafe
14 Vincent's Eethuis Rest.
15 De Buren Rest.
16 Jacobus Pieck Rest. & Friethuis de Vlaminck
17 La Plume & Bastiaan Rest.
18 De Lachende Javaan Rest.
19 DekaMarkt Supermkt.
20 'T Theehuis Rest.

CC, daily 7:30–24:00, Jan Gijzenpad 3, 3 km from Haarlem station—take bus #2 from platform A1, or a 5-min walk from Santpoort Zuid train station, tel. 023/537-3793, fax 023/537-1176, www.njhc.org/haarlem, e-mail: haarlem@njhc.org).

Eating in Haarlem

Eating between Market Square (Grote Markt) and the Train Station

Pancakes for dinner? **Pannekoekhuis "De Smikkel"** serves a selection of over 50 dinner (meat, cheese, etc.) and dessert pancakes. The pancakes (€8 each) are filling. With the €1.25-per-person cover charge, splitting is OK (daily 12:00–21:00, Sun from 16:00, closed Mon in winter, 2 blocks in front of station, Kruisweg 57, tel. 023/532-0631).

Nanking Chinese-Indonesian Restaurant serves Chinese and an inexpensive Indonesian *rijsttafel* (daily 16:00–22:00, Kruisstraat 16, a few blocks off Grote Markt, tel. 023/532-0706).

Enjoy a sandwich or coffee surrounded by trains and 1908 architecture in the classy **Brasserie Haarlem Station Restaurant** (daily 7:30–20:00, snacks only, between tracks #3 and #6 at the station).

Eating on or near Zijlstraat

Eko Eet Café is great for a cheery, tasty vegetarian meal (€9.50 *menu*, daily 17:30–21:30, Zijlstraat 39, tel. 023/532-6568).

Vincent's Eethuis serves the best cheap, basic Dutch food in town. This former St. Vincent's soup kitchen now feeds more gainfully employed locals than poor (€6, free seconds on veggies, friendly staff, Mon–Fri 12:00–14:00 & 17:00–19:30, closed Sat–Sun, Nieuwe Groenmarkt 22).

The cheery **De Buren** offers handlebar-mustache fun, serving happy locals traditional Dutch food such as *draadjesvlees* (beef stew with applesauce) and *oma's kippetje* (grandmother's chicken). Gerard and Marjo love their work. Enjoy their entertaining and creative menu, made especially for you (€11–16 dinners, "you choose the sauce," Wed–Sun 17:00–22:00, closed Mon–Tue, back garden terrace, outside the tourist area at Brouwersvaart 146, follow Raaks Straat west across the canal from Die Raeckse Hotel, tel. 023/534-3364).

Eating between the Market Square and Frans Hals Museum

Jacobus Pieck Eetlokaal is popular with locals for its fine-value "global cuisine" (€9.50 plate of the day, Mon 10:00–17:00,

Tue–Sat 10:00–22:00, closed Sun, Warmoesstraat 18, behind church, tel. 023/532-6144).

Friethuis de Vlaminck is the place for a (€1.35) cone of old-fashioned French fries (Warmoesstraat 3, Tue–Sat until 18:00, closed Sun–Mon, behind church).

La Plume steak house is noisy with a happy, local, and carnivorous crowd (€12–18 meals, daily from 17:30, CC, Lange Veerstraat 1, tel. 023/531-3202).

Bastiaan serves good Mediterranean cuisine in a classy atmosphere (€16 dinners, Tue–Sat from 18:00, closed Sun–Mon, CC, Lange Veerstraat 8, tel. 023/532-6006).

De Lachende Javaan ("The Laughing Javanese") serves the best Indonesian food in town. Their €17 *rijsttafel* is great (light eaters can split this extravaganza—€3.85 for extra plate, Tue–Sun from 17:00, closed Mon, CC, Frankestraat 25, tel. 023/532-8792).

Javaanse Jongens, a new place serving Indonesian in a fresh, woody, almost-bistro ambience, offers anyone with this book a free *tembuka* appetizer plate with their meal (€19 splittable *rijsttafel*, daily 17:00–22:00, CC, Oude Groenmarkt 8, tel. 023/531-1200).

La Place serves a healthy budget lunch with Haarlem's best view. Sit on the top floor or roof garden of the Vroom Dreesman department store (Mon 11:00–17:30, Tue–Sat 9:30–17:30, Thu until 20:30, closed Sun, on the corner of Grote Houtstraat and Gedempte Oude Gracht, tel. 023/515-8700).

Picnic shoppers head to the **DekaMarkt supermarket** (Mon 11:00–20:00, Tue–Sat 8:30–20:00, Thu until 21:00, closed Sun, Gedemple Oude Gracht 54, between Vroom Dreesman department store and post office).

Transportation Connections—Haarlem

By train to: Amsterdam (6/hr, 15 min, €3.20 one-way, €5.50 same-day return, ticket not valid on "Lovers Train," a misnamed private train that runs hrly), **Delft** (2/hr, 40 min), **Hoorn** (4/hr, 1 hr), **The Hague** (4/hr, 35 min), and **Alkmaar** (2/hr, 30 min).

To **Schiphol Airport:** by **taxi** (about €32), by **train** (2/hr, 40 min, transfer at Amsterdam-Sloterdijk, €4.55); by **bus** (6/hr, 45 min, bus #300 leaves from Haarlem's Vroom Dreesman department store and from Haarlem's train station in the "Zuidtangent" lane, €3.50).

NETHERLANDS DAY TRIPS

The Netherlands are tiny. The sights listed below are an easy day trip by bus or train from Amsterdam or Haarlem. Match your interest with the village's specialty: flower auctions, folk museums, cheese, Delft porcelain, beaches, or modern art.

Netherlands Day Trips

DELFT

Peaceful as a Vermeer painting (he was born here) and lovely as its porcelain, Delft is a typically Dutch town with a special soul. Enjoy it best by simply wandering around, watching people, munching local syrup waffles, or daydreaming from the canal bridges.

Tourist Information: The TI is a tourist's dream, offering a good €2 brochure on Delft (includes excellent map and a self-guide "Historical Walk through Delft"); guided walks (May–Aug Wed and Fri 14:00 and 15:30); and a number of €1.80 brochures describing self-guided walking tours (Mon–Sat 9:00–17:30, April–Sept also Sun 11:00–15:00, tel. 015/213-0100 fax 015/215-8695, www.vvvdelft.nl).

Market Days: Multiple all-day markets are held on Thursdays (general on Market Square, flower on Hippolytusbuurt Square) and on Saturdays (general on Brabantse Turfmarkt and Burgwal, flea market at Hippolytusbuurt Square, and sometimes an art market at Heilige Geestkerkhof).

Sights—Delft

Royal Dutch Delftware Manufactory—The blue earthenware made at Delft's Koninklijke Porceleyne Fles is famous worldwide and the biggest tourist attraction in town. The Dutch East India Company, headquartered here, had imported many exotic goods, including Chinese porcelain. The Chinese designs became trendy and were copied by many of the local potters. Three centuries later their descendants are still going strong, and you can see them at work in this factory. Catch an English-language tour (prices vary depending on tour, April–Oct 10:00, 11:00, 14:00, and 15:00) or take a self-guided tour at any time: watch the short video, follow the small tile arrows, and feel free to stop and chat with any of the artisans (€2.50 entry, April–Oct 9:00–17:00, Nov–March daily 9:30–17:00, Rotterdamsweg 196, from train station catch tram #1 or bus #63, #121, or #129 and get off at TU Aula bus stop, 5-min walk from tram or bus stop, tel. 015/251-2030).

Sleeping in Delft

(€1 = about $1, country code: 31, area code: 015)

Herberg De Emauspoort, a picture-perfect family-run hotel, is relaxed, friendly, and ideally located around the family's 80-year-old bakery. Rooms overlook the canalside or peek into the courtyard. Romantics can stay in one of their gipsy caravans ("Pipo de Clown" or "Mammaloe"). Borrow bikes for free or rent a canoe for the day (16 rooms, Db-€96, Tb-€115, Qb-€140, CC, near main square at Vrouwenregt 9–11, tel. 015/219-0219, fax 015/214-8251, www.emauspoort.nl, e-mail: emauspoort@emauspoort.nl).

Hotel Leeuwenbrug, a former warehouse, has 36 cozy rooms, an Old World atmosphere, and a helpful and friendly staff (Sb-€72–105, Db-€87–120, prices varies seasonally, ask for off-season pricing, includes breakfast, CC, Koornmarkt 16, tel. 015/214-7741, fax 015/215-9759, www.leeuwenbrug.nl, e-mail: sales@leeuwenbrug.nl).

'T Raedthuys, located in the heart of Delft on the main square, has 11 tired, basic rooms (S-€38, D-€48, Db-€65, Q-€90, Qb-€100, ask for off-season discount, CC, enter through restaurant, Markt 38–40, tel. 015/212-5115, fax 015/213-6069, www.raedthuys-delft.com).

Transportation Connections—Delft

To: Amsterdam (2 trains/hr, 40 min), **The Hague** (you can take the train but the tram is easier: catch tram #1—Scheveningen to The Hague's city center, purchase tickets at TI).

EDAM

For the ultimate in cuteness and peace, make tiny Edam your home. It's sweet but palatable and 30 minutes by bus from Amsterdam (2/hr).

While Edam is known today for cheese, it was once an industrious shipyard and port. But having a canal to the sea caused such severe flooding in town—cracking walls and spilling into homes—that a frustrated resident even built a floating cellar (now in the Edam Museum). To stop the flooding, the harbor was closed off with locked gates (you'll see the gates in Dam Square next to TI). The harbor silted up, forcing the decline of the shipbuilding trade.

For a fun peek into a 400-year-old home, tour the small, quirky Edam Museum. Learn about the town's trade history upstairs and about Fris Pottery on the top floor (€2, Tue–Sat 10:00–16:30, Sun 13:30–16:30, closed in winter, on Dam Square, tel. 0299/372-644).

Edam's Wednesday market is held year-round, but it's best in July and early August, when the focus is on cheese, and you—along with piles of other tourists—can meet the cheese traders, local farmers, and even the cheese queen.

Tourist Information: The TI, often staffed by volunteers, is on Dam Square. Pick up the "Edam Holland" free brochure and consider the €2 "A Stroll Through Edam" self-guided walking tour (April–Sept Mon–Sat 10:00–17:00, closed Sun, Oct–March Mon–Sat 10:00–15:00, closed Sun, WC, ATM just outside, tel. 0299/315-125, www.vvv-edam.nl, e-mail: info@vvv-edam.nl).

Sleeping and Eating in Edam

(€1 = about $1, country code: 31, area code: 0299)

Sleep Code: **S** = Single, **D** = Double/Twin, **T** = Triple, **Q** = Quad, **b** = bathroom, **s** = shower only, **CC** = Credit Cards accepted, **no CC** = Credit Cards not accepted.

Hotel De Fortuna—an eccentric canalside mix of flowers, a cat of leisure, a pet turtle, and duck noises—offers steep stairs and low-ceilinged rooms in several ancient buildings in the old center of Edam (Db-€85–98, includes breakfast, CC, garden patio, attached restaurant, Spuistraat 3, tel. 0299/371-671, fax 0299/371-469, www.fortuna-edam.nl, e-mail: fortuna@fortuna-edam.nl).

Damhotel, centrally located on a canal around corner from TI, has attractive, comfortable rooms with a plush feel (Sb-€55, Db-€90, Tb-€125, Qb-€170, includes breakfast, CC, attached restaurant, Keizersgracht 1, tel. 0299/371-766, fax 0299/374-031, www.damhotel.nl).

***Eating*: Tai Wah** offers take-out Chinese/Indonesian (eat in De Fortuna garden) and indoor seating (Mon and Wed–Sat

16:00–21:00, Sun 13:00–21:00, closed Tue, Lingerzijde 62, tel. 0299/371-088). Picnickers stock up at the Toppers grocery (to the left of the Edam Museum).

Transportation Connections—Edam

From Amsterdam, take direct bus #114 (30 min) or bus #110 for a scenic route through the town of Volendam (45 min).

ARNHEM

Arnhem, an hour southeast of Amsterdam, has two fine sights: the Arnhem Open-Air Dutch Folk Museum and the Kröller-Müller Museum, featuring modern art in a huge park.

Arnhem's **TI** is the train station (Mon 11:00–17:30, Tue–Thu 9:00–17:30, Fri 10:00–16:00, closed Sat–Sun, tel. 026/442-6767).

▲▲Kröller-Müller Museum and Hoge Veluwe National Park—Near Arnhem, Hoge Veluwe National Park is the Netherlands' largest (13,000 acres) and is famous for its Kröller-Müller Museum. This huge, striking modern-art collection, including 55 paintings by van Gogh, is set deep in the forest. The park has hundreds of white bikes you're free to use to make your explorations more fun. At the Bekoezerscentrum (visitors' center), you'll find maps, WCs, a cafeteria-style restaurant, and a playground for children. While riding through the vast green woods, make a point to get off your bike to climb an inland sand dune (€5 to enter park, €5 more for museum, museum open Tue–Sun 10:00–17:00, closed Mon, easy parking, tel. 031/859-1041).

To reach the museum from Amsterdam, take the train to Ede-Wageningen, where bus #110 goes directly into the Hoge Veluwe National Park. Ask the driver where to get off for the visitors' center or the art museum.

To get to the park from the Arnhem train station, catch the bus to Otterlo, then switch to bus #110, which will take you into the park (1/hr). At this time there is no direct connection between Arnhem and the Kröller-Muller Museum. Consider a taxi (have the visitors' center call for you).

▲▲Arnhem Open-Air Dutch Folk Museum—Arnhem has the Netherlands' first and biggest folk museum. You'll enjoy a huge park of windmills, old farmhouses (gathered from throughout the Netherlands and reassembled here), traditional crafts in action, and a pleasant education-by-immersion in Dutch culture.

Visit the Entrance Pavilion for a free map or the English guidebook (€4). See the multimedia exhibit, HollandRama. Ask about special events and activities (especially for kids) as you enter (€11, Easter–Oct daily 10:00–17:00, tel. 026/357-6111, www.openluchtmuseum.nl).

Hit the highlights: any farmhouse, the drawbridge, little village (with bakery and old-time toys in the main square), the laundry, paper mill (usually a demo in progress), and the Freia Steam-Dairy Factory (where you can sample free cheese). The park has several good budget restaurants. The rustic Pancake House serves hearty (splittable) Dutch flapjacks and the De Kasteelboerderji Café-Restaurant (with a traditional €8 *dagmenu*, or plate of the day) is a friendly place that can feed 300 visitors at once.

To reach the open-air museum (*openluchtmuseum*) from the Arnhem train station, take bus #3 (direction: Alteveer) or the faster #13 (4/hr, 15 min, runs July–Aug only).

Transportation Connections—Arnhem

Trains connect Arnhem with **Amsterdam** (2/hr, 70 min, likely transfer in Utrecht).

By car from Amsterdam, take A2 south to Utrecht, then A12 east to Arnhem. Just before Arnhem, take the Arnhem Nord exit *Openluchtmuseum* (exit #26) and follow signs to the nearby museum. (If driving from Haarlem, skirt Amsterdam to the south on E9, then follow signs to Utrecht).

More Sights—Netherlands

Zaanse Schans Open-Air Museum—This 17th-century Dutch village turned open-air folk museum puts Dutch culture—from cheese making to wooden-shoe carving—on a lazy Susan.

Located in the town of Zaandijk, this is your easiest one-stop look at traditional Dutch culture. At the visitors' center, pick up the free brochure/map and ask about the day's scheduled events (bike rentals, lockers, WC, tel. 075/616-8228). The park hosts the Netherlands' best collection of windmills. Take an inspiring climb to the top of a whirring windmill; gather a group and ask for a tour. Visit the bakery, take a boat tour, sample cheese, and see a wooden shoe being made.

Zaanse Schans' museum, with a multimedia presentation and included audioguide, explains Holland's industrial past and present (€4.50, closed Mon though park open daily). The Pannenkoeken Restaurant offers delicious and traditional sweet and/or savory pancakes (€4–7, cash only, closes at 18:00).

Cost and Hours: The entrance to the grounds is free, but you must pay a euro or more to go in the windmills and other sights in the park (daily 8:30–17:30, until 17:00 in winter, parking €3.40/hr, tel. 075/616-8218, www.zaanseschans.nl). Zaanse Schans is your typical big-bus tour stop. To avoid the masses, visit early or late.

Getting There: The park is 15 minutes by train north of Amsterdam. Take the Alkmaar-bound train to Station

Koog-Zaandijk and then walk, following the teal signs—past a fragrant chocolate factory—for 10 minutes.

If driving from Amsterdam, take the A8 (direction: Zaanstad/ Purmeend), turn off at Purmerend A7, then follow signs to Zaanse Schans.

▲▲**Enkhuizen's Zuiderzee Museum**—This lively, open-air folk museum in the salty old town of Enkhuizen has a "Living on Urk" village (patterned after an old Dutch fishing town), populated by people who do a convincing job of role-playing no-nonsense 1905 Dutch villagers. No one said "Have a nice day" back then. You can eat herring hot out of the old smoker and see barrels and rope made. Children enjoy playing at the dress-up chest, trying out old-time games, and making sailing ships out of old wooden shoes (€9, early April–late Oct daily 10:00–17:00, July–Aug free tours at 13:30, private guide for €40, tel. 0228/351-111, www.zuiderzeemuseum.nl). Take the train from Amsterdam direct to Enkhuizen. To get to the museum from the station, catch a shuttle boat (4/hr) or take a pleasant 15-minute walk.

▲▲**Aalsmeer Flower Auction**—Get a bird's-eye view of the huge Dutch flower industry. Wander on elevated walkways (through what's claimed to be the biggest commercial building on earth) over literally trainloads of freshly-cut flowers. About half of all the flowers exported from Holland are auctioned off here in four huge auditoriums. Stop at one of the "listening posts" for on-the-spot information (€4, Mon–Fri 7:30–11:00, closed Sat–Sun, the auction wilts after 9:30 and on Thu, gift shop, cafeteria; bus #172 from Amsterdam's station, 2/hr, 60 min; from Haarlem take bus #140 and transfer to bus #172 or #77 in Aalsmeer, 2/hr, 60 min; tel. 0297/392-185). Aalsmeer is close to the airport and a handy last fling before catching a late morning weekday flight out.

▲▲▲**Keukenhof**—This is the greatest bulb-flower garden on earth. Each spring six million flowers, enjoying the sandy soil of the Dutch dunes and *polderland*, conspire to make even a total garden hater enjoy them. This 100-acre park is packed with tour groups daily (€11.50, open March 21–May 28 in 2003, daily 8:00–19:30, last tickets sold at 18:00, tel. 0252/465-555, www.keukenhof.nl).

To get to Keukenhof from Amsterdam, take the train to Leiden, then catch bus #54 to the garden (allow 75 min total). From Haarlem, catch bus #50 or #51 to Lisse, then bus #54 to Keukenhof (allow 45 min total). Go late in the day for the best light and the fewest groups.

Note that Holland's 2003 Flower Parade will be held on April 26. This all-day parade, featuring floats decorated with blossoms instead of crepe paper, runs through eight towns, including Lisse and Haarlem.

Zandvoort—For a quick and easy look at the windy coastline in a shell-lover's Shangri-La, visit the beach resort of Zandvoort, a breezy 45-minute bike ride or an eight-minute car or train ride west of Haarlem (from Haarlem, follow road signs to Bloemendaal). South of the main beach, bathers work on all-over tans.

▲Hoorn—This is an elegant, quiet, and typical 17th-century Dutch town north of Amsterdam which entertains tourists with a steam-engine museum, bakery, and castle. The Hoorn TI rents bikes and has a good walking tour brochure (tel. 072/511-4284).

Historic Triangle—Any TI offers a flier describing the "Historic Triangle," an all-day excursion from Amsterdam that connects the towns of Hoorn, Medemblik, and Enkhuizen by steam train and boat.

First, to get from Amsterdam to Hoorn by train, allow an hour and €15 round-trip. Then hop on the steam train from Hoorn to Medemblik (60 min), followed by a boat ride to Enkhuizen (60 min). This "Triangle" route runs twice a day in July and August. Off-season, it's usually offered twice a day on weekends and once daily on weekdays except Monday—but confirm at a TI (€18, tel. 0229/214-862).

▲Alkmaar—Holland's cheese capital is especially fun (and touristy) during its weekly cheese market (Fridays April–Aug 10:00–12:30, TI tel. 072/511-4284).

▲▲The Hague (Den Haag)—Locals say the money is made in Rotterdam, divided in The Hague, and spent in Amsterdam. The Hague is the Netherlands' seat of government and the home of several engaging museums. The Hague's TI is at the train station (Mon–Sat 9:00–17:30, later in summer, Sun 10:00–17:00, tel. 06-3403-505, €0.45/min).

The **Mauritshuis'** delightful, easy-to-tour art collection stars Vermeer and Rembrandt (€7, Tue–Sat 10:00–17:00, Sun 11:00–17:00, Korte Vijverberg 8, tel. 070/302-3456). Across the pond, the **Torture Museum** (Gevangenpoort) shows the medieval mind at its worst (€3.75, Tue–Fri 11:00–17:00, Sat–Sun 12:00–17:00, closed Mon, required tours on the hour, last one at 16:00, ask ticket taker if film and talk will be in English before you commit, tel. 070/346-0861).

For a look at the 19th century's attempt at virtual reality, tour **Panorama Mesdag**, a 360-degree painting of nearby Scheveningen in the 1880s with a 3-D sandy-beach foreground (€4, Mon–Sat 10:00–17:00, Sun 12:00–17:00, Zeestraat 65, tel. 070/310-6665). The nearby **Peace Palace**, a gift from Andrew Carnegie, houses the International Court of Justice (€3.40, Mon–Fri, guided tours only at 10:00, 11:00, 14:00, or 15:00, closes without warning—call ahead or check at TI, tram #7 or #8 from station, tel. 070/302-4137).

Scheveningen, the Dutch Coney Island, has a newly renovated pier and is liveliest on sunny summer afternoons (from the Hague train station, take tram #1, #8, or #9 to Gevers Deynootplein/Kurhaus and walk via Palace Promenade to the Boulevard).

Madurodam, a mini-Holland amusement park, is a kid-pleaser (€10, kids 4–11-€7, Sept–mid-March daily 9:00–18:00, mid-March–June until 20:00, July–Aug until 22:00, George Maduroplein 1, tram #1 or #9 from Hague train station, tel. 070/355-3900, www.madurodam.nl).

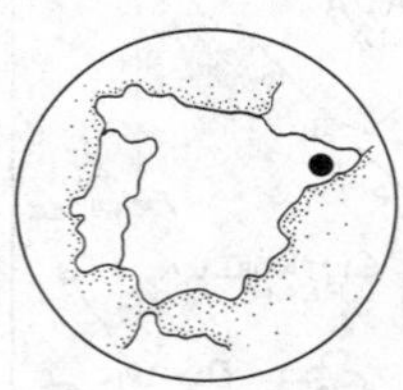

BARCELONA

Barcelona is Spain's second city and the capital of the proud and distinct region of Catalunya. With Franco's fascism now history, Catalan flags wave once again. Language and culture are on a roll in Spain's most cosmopolitan and European corner.

Barcelona bubbles with life in its narrow Gothic Quarter alleys, along the grand boulevards, and throughout the chic, grid-planned new town. While Barcelona had an illustrious past as a Roman colony, Visigothic capital, 14th-century maritime power, and—in more modern times—a top Mediterranean trading and manufacturing center, it's most enjoyable to throw out the history books and just drift through the city. If you're in the mood to surrender to a city's charms, let it be in Barcelona.

Planning Your Time

Sandwich Barcelona between flights or overnight train rides. There's little of earth-shaking importance within eight hours by train. It's as easy to fly into Barcelona as into Madrid, Lisbon, or Paris for most travelers from the United States. Those renting a car can cleverly start here, fly to Madrid, see Madrid and Toledo, and pick up the car as they leave Madrid.

On the shortest visit, Barcelona is worth one night, one day, and an overnight train or evening flight out. The Ramblas is two different streets by day and by night. Stroll it from top to bottom at night and again the next morning, grabbing breakfast on a stool in a market café. Wander the Gothic Quarter, see the cathedral, and have lunch in Eixample (pron. eye-SHAM-plah). The top two sights in town, Gaudí's Sacred Family Church and the Picasso Museum, are usually open until 20:00. The illuminated fountains (on Montjuïc) are a good finale for your day.

Barcelona

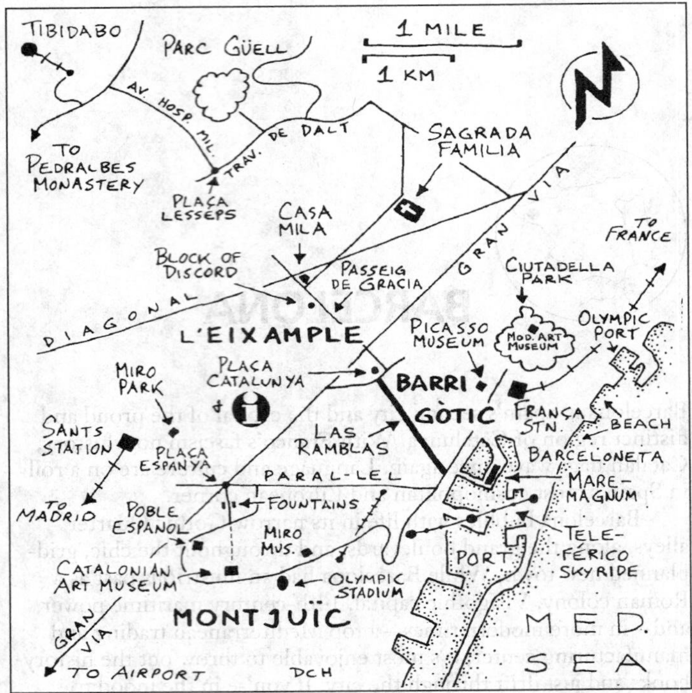

Of course, Barcelona in a day is insane. To better appreciate the city's ample charm, spread your visit over two or three days.

Orientation

Orient yourself by locating these essentials on the map: Barri Gòtic/Ramblas (old town), Eixample (fashionable modern town), Montjuïc (hill covered with sights and parks), and Sants Station (train to Madrid). The soul of Barcelona is in its compact core—the Barri Gòtic (Gothic Quarter) and the Ramblas (main boulevard). This is your strolling, shopping, and people-watching nucleus. The city's sights are widely scattered, but with a map and a willingness to figure out the sleek subway system (or a few euros for taxis), all is manageable.

Tourist Information

There are four useful **TIs** in Barcelona: at the **airport** (an office in both terminal A and terminal B, daily 9:00–21:00, tel. 934-784-704);

at the **Sants train station** (daily 8:00–20:00, near track 6); and **Plaça de Catalunya** (daily 9:00–21:00, on main square near recommended hotels, look for red sign; has room-finding service). The TI at Plaça de Catalunya offers walking tours in English of the Gothic Quarter (€7, 2 hrs, Sat–Sun at 10:00, meet at TI, call to reserve, toll call tel. 906-301-282—€0.40/minute, www.barcelonaturisme.com) and also has a half-price ticket booth—"Tiquet 3"—where you can drop by in the early evening (3 hours before showtime) to see what tickets are available. The all-Catalunya TI office is at **Passeig de Gràcia** 107 (Mon–Sat 10:00–19:00, Sun 10:00–13:00, tel. 932-384-000).

At any TI, pick up the free small map or the large city map (€1.20), the brochure on public transport, and the free quarterly *See Barcelona* guide with practical information on museum hours, restaurants, transportation, history, festivals, and so on.

Throughout the summer, you'll see young red-jacketed tourist info helpers on the streets in the touristed areas of town.

Arrival in Barcelona

By Train: Although many international trains use the França Station, all domestic (and some international) trains use Sants Station. Both França and Sants have baggage lockers and subway stations: França's station is Barceloneta (2 blocks away), and Sants' is Sants Estacio (under the station). Sants Station has a good TI, a world of handy shops and eateries, and a classy, quiet Sala Euromed lounge for travelers with first-class reservations (TV, free drinks, study tables, and coffee bar). Subway or taxi to your hotel. Most trains to/from France stop at the subway station Passeig de Gràcia, just a short walk from the center (Plaça de Catalunya, TI, hotels).

By Plane: Barcelona's **El Prat de Llobregat Airport,** 12 kilometers southwest of town, is connected cheaply and quickly by **Aerobus** (immediately in front of arrivals lobby, 4/hr until 24:00, 20 min to Plaça de Catalunya, buy €3.30 ticket from driver) or by RENFE **train** (walk through the overpass from airport to station, 2/hr at :13 and :43 after the hour, 20 min to Sants Station and Plaça de Catalunya, €2.20). A **taxi** to or from the airport costs under €18. The airport has a post office, pharmacy, left luggage, and ATMs (avoid the gimmicky machines before the baggage carrousels, use the bank-affiliated ATMs at the far-left end of arrival hall as you face the street). Airport info: tel. 932-983-467 or 932-983-465.

Getting around Barcelona

By Subway: Barcelona's Metro, among Europe's best, connects just about every place you'll visit. It has five color-coded lines. Rides cost €1. The T-10 Card for €5.60 gives you 10 tickets good for all local bus and Metro lines as well as the separate FGC line and RENFE train lines. Pick up the TI's guide to public transport. One-, two-, and three-day passes are available (for €4.20, €7.60, and €10.80).

By Hop-on Hop-off Bus: The handy Tourist Bus (*Bus Turistic*) offers two multistop circuits in colorful double-decker buses (red route covers north Barcelona—most Gaudí sights; blue route covers south—Gothic Quarter, Montjuïc) with multilingual guides (27 stops, 2 hours per route, April–Dec 9:00–21:30, buses run every 8–20 min, most frequent in summer, buy tickets on bus). Ask for a brochure (which has a good city map) at the TI or at a pick-up point. One-day (€14) and two-day (€18) tickets include about 20 percent discounts on the city's major sights—which will likely reimburse you for half the tour cost over the course of your visit.

By Taxi: Barcelona is one of Europe's best taxi towns. Taxis are plentiful and honest (€1.20 drop charge, €0.80/km, extras posted in window). Save time by hopping a cab (Ramblas to Sants Station—€4, luggage—€0.80/piece).

Helpful Hints

Theft Alert: You're more likely to be pickpocketed here—especially on the Ramblas—than about anywhere else in Europe. Most of the crime is nonviolent, but muggings do occur. Be on guard. Leave valuables in your hotel, and wear a money belt.

Here are a few common street scams, easy to avoid if you recognize them. Most common is the too-friendly local who tries to engage you in conversation by asking for the time, whether you speak English, and so on. If you suspect the person is more interested in your money than your time, ignore him and move on. A common street gambling scam is the pea-and-carrot game, a variation on the shell game. The people winning are all ringers and you can be sure that you'll lose if you play. Also beware of groups of women aggressively selling carnations, people offering to clean off a stain from your shirt, and people picking things up in front of you on escalators. If you stop for any commotion or show on the Ramblas, put your hands in your pockets before someone else does. Assume any scuffle is simply a distraction by a team of thieves.

U.S. Consulate: Passeig Reina Elisenda 23 (tel. 932-802-227).

Emergency Phone Numbers: Police—092, Emergency—061, directory assistance—010.

24-hour Pharmacy: Near the Boqueria Market at #98 on the Ramblas.

American Express: AmEx offices are at Passeig de Gràcia 101 (with all the travel agency services, Mon–Fri 9:30–18:00, Sat 10:00–12:00, Metro: Diagonal, tel. 934-152-371) and at La

Ramblas 74, opposite the Liceu Metro station (banking services only, daily 9:00–24:00, tel. 933-011-166).

Local Guides: The Barcelona Guide Bureau is a co-op with plenty of excellent local guides who give personalized four-hour tours for €150 (Via Laietana 54, tel. 932-682-422 or 933-107-778, www.bgb.es; Joanna Wilhelm is good). Barcelona Guided Tours leads daily walking tours (departing from Plaça Catalunya, Mon–Fri, 10:30 for the Gothic Quarter, 13:00 for Modernism, €13, tel. 653-622-763 for details).

Internet Access: When **easyEverything** arrived, prices for Internet access fell all over town. Europe's favorite Internet access—with piles of computers, drinks, and munchies—is open 24/7 and offers zippy access (€1/30 min) at two central locations: one is half a block west of Plaça de Catalunya on Ronda Universitat and another near the seedy bottom of the Ramblas at #31. The rival **BBiGG** is at Calle Comtal 9, near Plaça de Catalunya (daily 9:00–02:00, 300 terminals, tel. 933-014-020).

Cheap Rental Cars: Consider Easycar.com for its great rates (tel. 902-182-028,www.easycar.com).

Introductory Walk: From Plaça de Catalunya down the Ramblas

A ▲▲▲ sight, Barcelona's central square and main drag exert a powerful pull as many visitors spend a major part of their time here doing laps on the Ramblas. Here's a top-to-bottom orientation walk:

Plaça de Catalunya—This vast central square, littered with statues of Catalan heroes, divides old and new Barcelona and is the hub for the Metro, bus, airport shuttle, and both hop-on and hop-off buses (red northern route leaves from El Corte Inglés, blue southern route from west side of Plaça). The grass around its fountain is the best public place in town for serious necking. Overlooking the square, the huge **El Corte Inglés** department store offers everything from bonsai trees to a travel agency, plus one-hour photo developing, haircuts, and cheap souvenirs (Mon–Sat 10:00–22:00, closed Sun, pick up an English directory flier, supermarket in basement, 9th-floor terrace cafeteria/restaurant with great city view—take elevator from entrance nearest the TI, tel. 933-063-800).

Four great boulevards start from Plaça de Catalunya: the Ramblas, the fashionable Passeig de Gràcia, the cozier but still fashionable Rambla Catalunya, and the stubby, shop-filled, pedestrian-only Portal de L'Angel. Homesick Americans can even find a Hard Rock Café. Locals traditionally start or end a downtown rendezvous at the venerable Café Zurich.

"You're not in Spain, You're in Catalunya!"

This is a popular pro-nationalist refrain you might see on T-shirts or stickers around town. Catalunya is *not* the land of bullfighting and flamenco that many visitors envision when they think of Spain (best to wait until you're in Madrid or Sevilla for those).

The region of Catalunya—with Barcelona as its capital—has its own language, history, and culture, and the people have a proud independent spirit. Historically, Catalunya has often been at odds with the central Spanish government in Madrid. The Catalan language and culture have been repressed or outlawed at various times in Spanish history, most recently during the Franco era. Three of Barcelona's monuments are reminders of that suppression: The Parc de la Ciutadella was originally a much-despised military citadel, constructed in the 18th century to keep locals in line. The Castle of Montjuïc, built for similar reasons, has been the site of numerous political executions, including hundreds during the Franco era. The Sacred Heart Church atop Tibidabo, completed under Franco, was meant to atone for the sins of Barcelonans during the Spanish Civil War—the main sin being opposition to Franco. Although rivalry between Barcelona and Madrid has calmed down in recent times, it rages any time the two cities' football clubs meet.

To see real Catalan culture, look for the *sardana* dance (described in "Sights") or an exhibition of castellers. These teams of human-castle builders come together for festivals throughout the year to build towers that can reach over 15 meters (50 feet)

Cross the street from the café to reach . . .

Ramblas Walk Stop #1: The top of the Ramblas—Begin your ramble 20 meters down at the ornate fountain (near #129).

More than a Champs-Élysées, this grand boulevard takes you from rich at the top to rough at the port in a 1.5-kilometer, 20-minute walk. You'll raft the river of Barcelonan life past a grand opera house, elegant cafés, retread prostitutes, pickpockets, power-dressing con men, artists, street mimes, an outdoor bird market, great shopping, and people looking to charge more for a shoeshine than you paid for the shoes.

Grab a bench and watch the scene. Open up your map and read some history into it: You're about to walk right across medieval Barcelona from Plaça de Catalunya to the harbor. Notice how the higgledy-piggledy street plan of the medieval town was high, topped off by the bravest member of the team—a child! The Gràcia festival in August and the Mercè fesitival in September are good times to catch the castellers.

The Catalan language is irrevocably tied to the history and spirit of the people here. Since the end of the Franco era in the mid-1970s, the language has made a huge resurgence. Now most school-age children learn Catalan first and Spanish second. Although Spanish is understood here (and the basic survival words are the same), Barcelona speaks Catalan. Here are the essential Catalan phrases:

Hello	*Hola*	(OH-lah)
Please	*Si us plau*	(see oos plow)
Thank you	*Gracies*	(GRAH-see-es)
Goodbye	*Adeu*	(ah-DAY-oo)
Exit	*Sortida*	(sor-TEE-dah)
Long live Catalunya!	*Visca Catalunya!*	(BEE-skah . . .)

Most place-names in this chapter are listed in Catalan. Here is a pronunciation guide:

Barcelona	bar-sah-LOH-nah
Plaça de Catalunya	PLAS-sah duh cat-ah-LOON-yah
Eixample	eye-SHAM-plah
Passeig de Gràcia	PAH-sage duh grass-EE-ah
Catedral	CAH-tah-dral
Barri Gòtic	BAH-rrree GAH-teek
Montjuïc	MOHN-jew-eek

contained within the old town walls—now gone but traced by a series of roads named Ronda (meaning "to go around"). Find the Roman town, occupying about 10 percent of what became the medieval town—with tighter roads yet around the cathedral. The sprawling modern grid plan beyond the Ronda roads is from the 19th century. Breaks in this urban waffle show where a little town was consumed by the growing city. The popular Passeig de Gràcia boulevard was literally the road to Gràcia (once a town, now a characteristic Barcelona neighborhood).

Rambla means "stream" in Arabic. The Ramblas used to be a drainage ditch along the medieval wall that once defined what's now called the Gothic Quarter. "Las Ramblas" is plural, a succession of five separately named segments, but address numbers treat it as a single long street.

From Plaça de Catalunya down the Ramblas

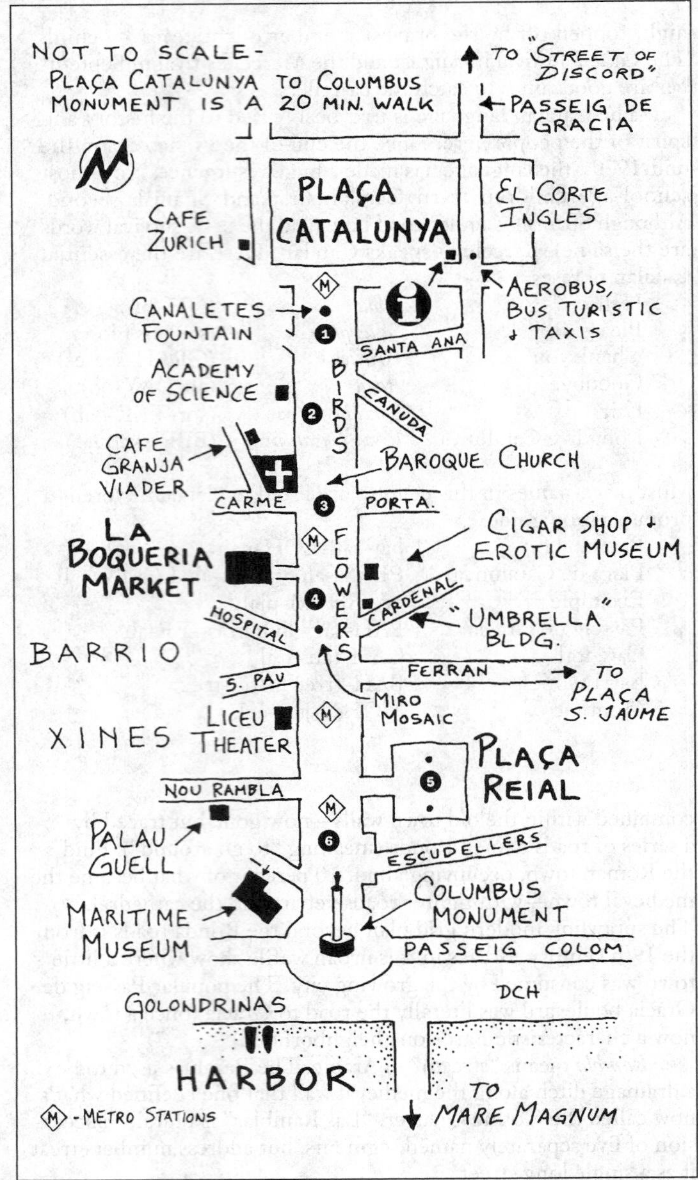
NOT TO SCALE-
PLAÇA CATALUNYA TO COLUMBUS MONUMENT IS A 20 MIN. WALK
TO "STREET OF DISCORD"
PASSEIG DE GRACIA
PLAÇA CATALUNYA
EL CORTE INGLES
CAFE ZURICH
AEROBUS, BUS TURISTIC + TAXIS
CANALETES FOUNTAIN
1
SANTA ANA
ACADEMY OF SCIENCE
BIRDS
CANUDA
2
CAFE GRANJA VIADER
BAROQUE CHURCH
CARME
PORTA.
3
LA BOQUERIA MARKET
FLOWERS
CIGAR SHOP + EROTIC MUSEUM
4
CARDENAL
HOSPITAL
"UMBRELLA" BLDG.
BARRIO
FERRAN
TO PLAÇA S. JAUME
S. PAU
MIRO MOSAIC
LICEU THEATER
XINES
PLAÇA REIAL
5
NOU RAMBLA
6
PALAU GUELL
ESCUDELLERS
MARITIME MUSEUM
COLUMBUS MONUMENT
PASSEIG COLOM
DCH
GOLONDRINAS
HARBOR
TO MARE MAGNUM
M -METRO STATIONS

You're at Rambla Canaletes, named for the fountain. The black-and-gold Fountain of Canaletes is the beginning point for celebrations and demonstrations. Legend says that one drink from the fountain ensures that you'll return to Barcelona one day. All along the Ramblas you'll see newspaper stands (open 24 hours, selling phone cards) and ONCE booths (selling lottery tickets that support Spain's organization of the blind, a powerful advocate for the needs of disabled people).

Got some change? As you wander downhill, drop coins into the cans of the human statues (the money often kicks them into entertaining gear). Warning: Wherever people stop to gawk, pickpockets are at work.

Walk 100 meters downhill to #115 and…

Ramblas Walk Stop #2: Rambla of the Little Birds— Traditionally, kids bring their parents here to buy pets, especially on Sundays. Apartment-dwellers find birds, turtles, and fish easier to handle than dogs and cats. Balconies with flowers are generally living spaces, those with air-conditioning are generally offices. The Academy of Science's clock (at #115) marks official Barcelona time—synchronize. The Champion supermarket (at #113) has cheap groceries and a handy deli with cooked food to go. A newly-discovered Roman necropolis is in a park across the street, 50 meters behind the big modern Citadines Hotel (go through the passageway at #122). Local apartment-dwellers blew the whistle on contractors who hoped they could finish their building before anyone noticed the antiquities they had unearthed. Imagine the tomb-lined road leading into the Roman city of Barcino 2,000 years ago.

Another 100 meters ahead takes you to Carrer del Carme (at #2), and…

Ramblas Walk Stop #3: Baroque Church—The big plain church lining the boulevard is Baroque, unusual in Barcelona. While Barcelona's Gothic age was rich (with buildings to prove it), the Baroque age hardly left a mark (the city's importance dropped when New World discoveries shifted lucrative trade to ports on the Atlantic). The Bagues jewelry shop across Carrer del Carme from the church is known for its Art Nouveau jewelry (exactingly duplicated from the c. 1898 molds of Masriera, displayed in the window; buzz to get inside). At the shop's side entrance, step on the old-fashioned scales (free, in kilos) and head down the lane opposite (behind the church, 30 meters) to a place expert in making you heavier. Café Granja Viader (follow the narrow lane behind the church; see "Eating," below) has specialized in baked and dairy delights since 1870.

Stroll through the Ramblas of Flowers to the subway stop marked by the red M (near #100), and…

Ramblas Walk Stop #4: La Boqueria—This lively produce

market is an explosion of chicken legs, bags of live snails, stiff fish, delicious oranges, and sleeping dogs (#91, Mon–Sat 8:00–20:00, best mornings after 9:00, closed Sun). The Conserves shop sells 25 kinds of olives (straight in, near back on right, 100-gram minimum, €0.20–0.40). Full legs of ham (*jamón serrano*) abound; *Paleta Iberica de Bellota* are best and cost about €120 each. Beware: *Huevos de toro* are bull testicles—surprisingly inexpensive . . . and oh so good. Drop by a cafe for an *espresso con leche* or breakfast (*tortilla española*—potato omelet). For lunch and dinner options, consider La Gardunya, located at the back of the market (see "Eating," below).

The Museum of Erotica is your standard European sex museum—neat if you like nudes and a chance to hear phone sex in four languages (€7.20, daily June–Sept 10:00–24:00, shorter hours Oct–May, across from market at #96).

At #100, Gimeno sells cigars (appreciate the dying art of cigar boxes). Go ahead . . . buy a Cuban cigar (singles from €1). Tobacco shops sell stamps.

Farther down the Ramblas at #83, the Art Nouveau Escriba Café—an ornate world of pastries, little sandwiches, and fine coffee—still looks like it did on opening day in 1906 (daily 8:30–21:00, indoor/outdoor seating, tel. 933-016-027).

Fifty meters farther, find the much-trod-upon anchor mosaic (a reminder of the city's attachment to the sea) created by noted abstract artist Joan Miró that marks the midpoint of the Ramblas. (The towering statue of Columbus in the distance marks the end of this hike.) From here, walk down to the Liceu Opera House (reopened after a 1994 fire, tickets on sale Mon–Fri 14:00–20:30, tel. 902-332-211; 30-minute €5 tours in English daily at 10:00, reserve in advance, tel. 934-859-914). From the Opera House, cross the Ramblas to Café de l'Opera for a beverage (#74, tel. 933-177-585). This bustling café, with modernist decor and a historic atmosphere, boasts it's been open since 1929, even during the Spanish Civil War. Continue to #46; turn left down an arcaded lane to a square filled with palm trees . . .

Ramblas Walk Stop #5: Plaça Reial—This elegant neoclassical square comes complete with old-fashioned taverns, modern bars with patio seating, a Sunday coin and stamp market (10:00–14:00), Gaudí's first public works (the two colorful helmeted lampposts), and characters who don't need the palm trees to be shady. Herbolari Ferran is a fine and aromatic shop of herbs, with fun souvenirs such as top-quality saffron, or *safra* (Mon–Sat 9:30–14:00 & 16:30–20:00, closed Sun, downstairs at Plaça Reial 18). The small streets stretching toward the water from the square are intriguing but less safe.

Back across the Ramblas, **Palau Güell** offers an enjoyable look at a Gaudí interior (€3 for 75-min English/Spanish tour, usually open Mon–Sat 10:00–19:00, Carrer Nou de la Rambla 3–5, tel. 933-173-974). If you'll see Casa Milà, skip the climb to this rooftop.

Farther downhill, on the right-hand side, is . . .

Ramblas Walk Stop #6: Chinatown—This is the world's only Chinatown with nothing even remotely Chinese in or near it. Named for the prejudiced notion that Chinese immigrants go hand in hand with poverty, prostitution, and drug dealing, the actual inhabitants are poor Spanish, Arab, and Gypsy people. At night the Barri Xines features prostitutes, many of them transvestites, who cater to sailors wandering up from the port. A nighttime visit gets you a street-corner massage—look out. Better yet—stay out.

The Rambla of the Sea—The bottom of the Ramblas is marked by the Columbus Monument. And just beyond that, **La Rambla de Mar** ("Rambla of the Sea") is a modern extension of the boulevard into the harbor. A popular wooden pedestrian bridge—with waves like the sea—leads to Maremagnum, a soulless Spanish mall with a cinema, huge aquarium, restaurants (see recommended Tapas Maremagnum), and piles of people. Late at night it's a rollicking youth hangout. It's a worthwhile stroll.

Ramblas Sights at the Harbor

Columbus Monument (Monument a Colóm)—Marking the point where the Ramblas hits the harbor, this 60-meter-tall (197-foot) monument built for an 1888 exposition offers an elevator-assisted view from its top (€2, June–Sept daily 9:00–20:30, Oct–March Mon–Fri 10:00–13:30 & 15:30–18:30, Sat–Sun 10:00–18:30, April–May until 19:30, the harbor cable car offers a better—if less handy—view). It's interesting that Barcelona would so honor the man whose discoveries ultimately led to its downfall as a great trading power. It was here in Barcelona that Ferdinand and Isabel welcomed Columbus home after his first trip to America.

Maritime Museum (Museo Maritim)—Housed in the old royal shipyards, this museum covers the salty history of ships and navigation from the 13th to the 20th century, showing off the Catalan role in the development of maritime technology (for example, the first submarine is claimed to be Catalan). With fleets of seemingly unimportant replicas of old boats explained in Catalan and Spanish, landlubbers may find it dull—but the free audioguide livens it up for sailors (€5.40, daily 10:00–19:00, closed Mon off-season). For just €0.60 more, visit the old-fashioned sailing ship *Santa Eulàlia*, docked in the harbor across the street.

Golondrinas—Little tourist boats at the foot of the Columbus Monument offer 30-minute harbor tours (€3.20, daily 11:00–20:00). A glass-bottom catamaran makes longer tours up the coast (€8 for

75 min, 4/day, daily 11:30–18:30.) For a picnic place, consider one of these rides or the harbor steps.

Sights—Gothic Quarter (Barri Gòtic)

The Barri Gòtic is a bustling world of shops, bars, and nightlife packed between hard-to-be-thrilled-about 14th- and 15th-century buildings. The area around the port is seedy. But the area around the cathedral is a tangled yet inviting grab bag of undiscovered courtyards, grand squares, schoolyards, Art Nouveau storefronts, baby flea markets (Thursdays), musty junk shops, classy antique shops (Carrer de la Palla), street musicians strumming Catalan folk songs, and balconies with domestic jungles behind wrought-iron bars. Go on a cultural scavenger hunt. Write a poem.

▲Cathedral—As you stand in the square facing the cathedral, you're facing what was Roman Barcelona. To your right, letters spell out BARCINO—the city's Roman name. The three towers on the building to the right are mostly Roman.

The colossal **cathedral,** started in about 1300, took 600 years to complete. Rather than stretching toward heaven, it makes a point of being simply massive (similar to the Gothic churches of Italy). The west front, though built according to the original plan, is only 100 years old (note the fancy, undulating rose window). The cathedral welcomes visitors daily (8:00–13:30 & 16:30–19:30; cloisters: daily 9:00–13:00 & 17:00–19:00; tel. 933-151-554).

The spacious interior—characteristic of Catalan Gothic—was supported by buttresses. These provided walls for 28 richly ornamented chapels. While the main part of the church is fairly plain, the chapels, sponsored by local guilds, show great wealth. Located in the community's most high-profile space, they provided a kind of advertising to illiterate worshipers. Find the logos and symbols of the various trades represented. The Indians Columbus brought to town were supposedly baptized in the first chapel on the left.

The **chapels** ring a finely carved 15th-century choir (*coro*). Pay €1 for a close-up look (with the lights on) at the ornately carved stalls and the emblems representing the various knights of the Golden Fleece who once sat here. The chairs were folded up, giving VIPs stools to lean on during the standing parts of the Mass. Each was creatively carved and—since you couldn't sit on sacred things—the artists were free to enjoy some secular fun here. Study the upper tier of carvings.

The **high altar** sits upon the tomb of Barcelona's patron saint, Eulàlia. She was a 13-year-old local girl tortured 13 times by Romans for her faith and finally crucified on an X-shaped cross. Her X symbol is carved on the pews. Climb down the stairs for a close look at her exquisite marble sarcophagus.

Barcelona's Gothic Quarter Sights

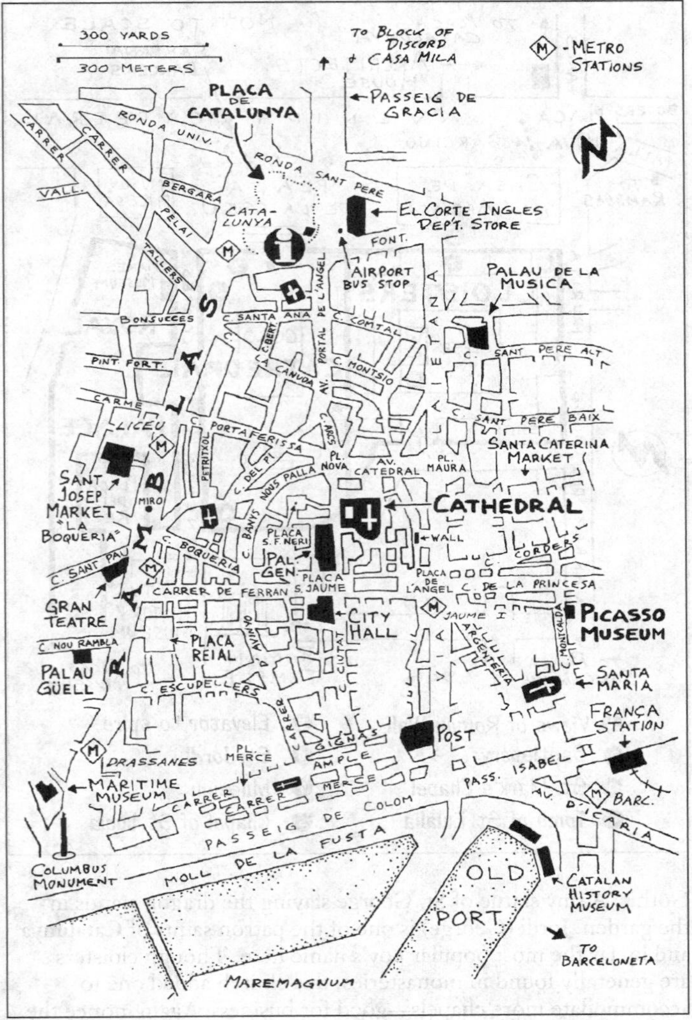

Ride the **elevator** to the roof and climb a tight spiral staircase up the spire for a commanding view (€1.40, Mon–Fri 10:30–12:30 & 16:30–18:00, closed Sat–Sun, start from chapel left of high altar).

Enter the **cloister** (through arch, right of high altar). From there, look back at the arch, an impressive mix of Romanesque and

Barcelona's Cathedral

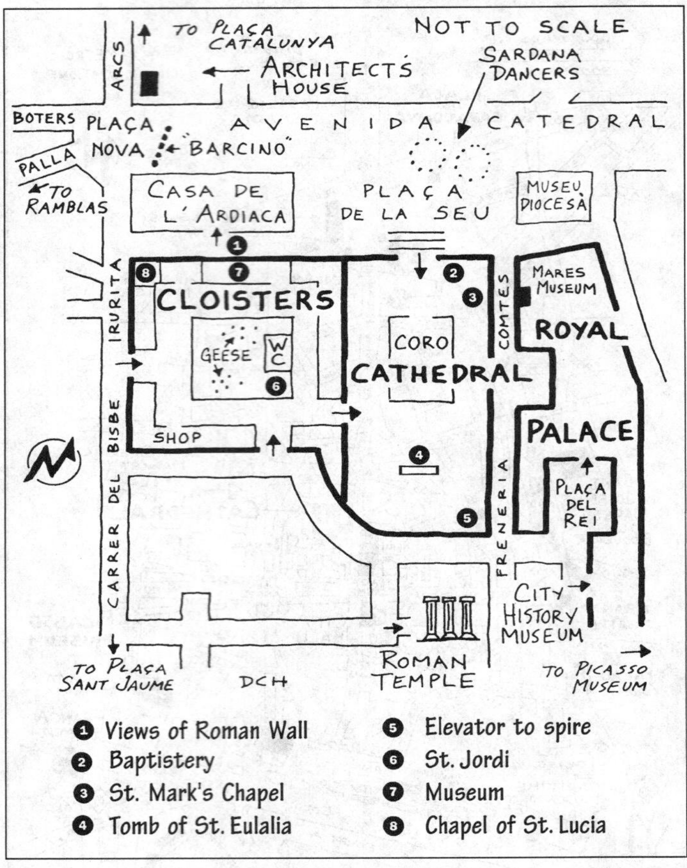

Gothic. A tiny statue of St. George slaying the dragon stands in the garden. Jordi (George) is one of the patron saints of Catalunya and by far the most popular boy's name here. Though cloisters are generally found in monasteries, this church added one to accommodate more chapels—good for business. Again, notice the symbols of the trades or guilds. Even the pavement is filled with symbols—similar to Americans getting their name on a brick for helping to pay for something.

Long ago the resident geese—there are always 13 in memory of Eulàlia—functioned as an alarm system. Any commotion would get them honking, alerting the monk in charge.

From St. Jordi, circle to the right (past a WC hidden on the left). The skippable little €0.60 **museum** (far corner) is one plush room with a dozen old religious paintings. In the corner the dark, barrel-vaulted Romanesque Chapel of Santa Lucia was a small church predating the cathedral and built into the cloister. The candles outside were left by people hoping for good eyesight (Santa Lucia's specialty). Farther along, the Chapel of Santa Rita (her forte: impossible causes) usually has the most candles. Complete the circle and exit at the door just before the place you entered.

Walk uphill, following the church. From the end of the apse turn right 50 meters up Carrer del Paradis to the **Roman Temple** (Temple Roma d' August). In the corner a sign above a millstone in the pavement marks "Mont Tabor, 16.9 meters." Step into the courtyard for a peek at a surviving corner of the imposing temple which once stood here on the city's highest hill, keeping a protective watch over Barcino (free, daily 10:00–14:00 & 16:00–20:00).

Plaça del Rei—The Royal Palace sat on King's Square (a block from the cathedral) until Catalunya became part of Spain in the 15th century. Then it was the headquarters of the local Inquisition. Columbus came here to show King Ferdinand souvenirs from what he thought was India.

▲City History Museum—For a walk through the history of the city, take an elevator down 20 meters (and 2,000 years) to stroll the streets of Roman Barcelona. You'll see sewers, models of domestic life, and bits of an early Christian church. Then a new exhibit in the 11th-century count's palace shows you Barcelona through the Middle Ages (€3.50 includes museum, presentation, and visits to Pedralbes Monastery and Verdaguer House Museum, see museum pamphlet for details; June–Sept Tue–Sat 10:00–20:00, Sun 10:00–14:00, closed Mon; Oct–May Tue–Sat 10:00–14:00 & 16:00–20:00, Sun 10:00–14:00, closed Mon, Plaça del Rei, tel. 933-151-111).

Frederic Mares Museum—This classy collection combines medieval religious art with a quirky bundle of more modern artifacts—old pipes, pinups, toys, and so on (Tue–Sat 10:00–15:00, Sun 10:00–14:00, closed Mon, Carrer del Comtes, off Plaça de la Seu, next to cathedral, tel. 933-105-800).

▲*Sardana* Dances—The patriotic *sardana* dances are held at the cathedral (most Sun at 12:00) and at Plaça de Sant Jaume (often on Sun at 18:00 in spring and summer, 18:30 in fall and winter). Locals of all ages seem to spontaneously appear. They gather in circles after putting their things in the center—symbolic of community and sharing (and the ever-present risk of theft). Holding hands, they raise their arms as they hop and sway gracefully to the band. The band *(cobla)* consists of a long flute, tenor and soprano oboes, strange-looking brass instruments, and a tiny bongolike drum *(tambori)*. The rest of Spain mocks this lazy circle dance, but, considering what it takes for a culture to survive within another culture's country, it is a stirring display of local pride and patriotism.

Shoe Museum (Museu del Calçat)—Shoe-lovers enjoy this two-room shoe museum (with a we-try-harder attendant) on the delightful Plaça Sant Felip Neri (€1.20, Tue–Sun 11:00–14:00, closed Mon, 1 block beyond outside door of cathedral cloister, behind Plaça de G. Bachs, tel. 933-014-533). The huge shoe at the entry is designed to fit the foot of the Columbus Monument at the bottom of the Ramblas.

Plaça de Sant Jaume—On this stately central square (pron. jau-mah) of the Gothic Quarter, two of the top governmental buildings in Catalunya face each other: The Barcelona city hall (Ajuntament, free Sun 10:00–13:30) and the seat of the autonomous government of Catalunya (Palau de la Generalitat). *Sardana* dances take place here many Sundays (see "*Sardana* Dances," above).

▲▲▲Picasso Museum—This is the best collection of Picasso's (1881–1973) work in Spain, and—since he spent his formative years (age 14–21) in Barcelona—the best collection of his early works anywhere. It's scattered through two Gothic palaces, six blocks from the cathedral.

Picasso's personal secretary amassed a huge collection of his work and bequeathed it to the city. Picasso, happy to have a fine museum showing off his work in the city of his youth, added to the collection throughout his life. (Sadly, since Picasso vowed never to set foot in a fascist, Franco-ruled Spain and he died 2 years before Franco, the artist never saw the museum.)

This is a great chance to see Picasso's earliest, more realistic art; to appreciate his genius; and to better understand his later, more challenging art (€5, free on first Sun of month, Tue–Sat 10:00–20:00, Sun 10:00–15:00, closed Mon, free and required bag check, Montcada 15–19, Metro: Jaume, tel. 933-196-310). If there's a line at the ticket window, use the second ticket booth (down the street at #21). The ground floor offers a handy array of services (bookshop, WC, bag check, and cafeteria). For a good lunch, see "Eating near the Picasso Museum" on page 1138.

While the rooms are constantly rearranged, the collection is always presented chronologically. With the help of thoughtful English descriptions for each stage, it's easy to follow the evolution of Picasso's work. You'll see his art evolve in these twelve stages:

Stage 1—Boy wonder, age 12–14, 1895–1897: Pablo's earliest art is realistic and serious. A budding genius emerges at age 12 as Pablo moves to Barcelona and gets serious about art.

Even this young, his portraits of grizzled peasants show great psychological insight and flawless technique. You'll see portraits of Pablo's first teacher, his father *(Padre del Artista)*. Displays show his art-school work. Every time Pablo starts breaking rules, he's sent back to the standard classic style. The assignment: Sketch nude models to capture human anatomy accurately. Three self-portraits (1896) show the self-awareness of a thoughtful genius blossoming. When Pablo was 13, his father quit painting to nurture his young prodigy. Look closely at the portrait of his mother *(Retrato de la Madre del Artista)*. Pablo, then age 15, is working on the fine details and gradients of white in her blouse and the expression in her cameo-like face. Notice the signature. Spaniards keep both parents' surnames: Pablo Ruiz Picasso. Pablo was closer to his mom than his dad. Eventually he kept just his mom's name.

Stage 2—Málaga, exploration of nature: During a short trip to Málaga, Picasso dabbles in Impressionism (unknown in Spain at the time).

Stage 3—Sponge, influenced by local painters: As a 15-year-old, Pablo dutifully enters art-school competitions. His first big painting—while forced to show a religious subject *(First Communion)*—is more an excuse to paint his family. Notice his sister Lola's exquisitely painted veil. This painting was heavily influenced by local painters.

Science and Charity—which won second prize at a fine-arts exhibition—got Picasso the chance to study in Madrid. Now Picasso conveys real feeling. The doctor (Pablo's father) represents science. The nun represents charity and religion. But nothing can help as the woman is clearly dead (notice her face and lifeless hand). Pablo painted a little perspective trick: Walk back and forth across the room to see the bed stretch and shrink. Four small studies for this painting, hanging in the back of the room, show how this was an exploratory work. The frontier: light.

Picasso travels to Madrid for further study. Finding the stuffy fine-arts school in Madrid stifling, Pablo hangs out in the Prado Gallery and learns by copying the masters. Notice his nearly perfect copy of Felipe IV by Valázquez.

Stage 4—Independence: Having absorbed the wisdom of the ages, in 1898, Pablo visits Horta, a rural Catalan village, and finds his artistic independence.

Stage 5—Sadness, 1899–1900: Pablo's good friend dies, he's poor, and without love. He returns to Barcelona. It's 1900 and Art Nouveau is the rage. Upsetting his dad, Pablo quits art school and falls in with the avant-garde crowd. These bohemians congregate daily at Els Quarte Gats, or The Four Cats (slang for "a few crazy people"—see page 1136). Further establishing his artistic freedom, he paints portraits—no longer of his family... but of his new friends. Still a teenager, Pablo puts on his first one-man show.

Stage 6—Paris, 1900–1901: Nineteen-year-old Picasso arrives in Paris, a city bursting with life, light, and love. Dropping the surname Ruiz, Pablo establishes his commercial brand name: "Picasso." Here the explorer Picasso goes Bohemian, befriending poets, prostitutes, and artists. He paints Impressionist landscapes like Monet, posters like Toulouse-Lautrec, still-lifes like Cezanne, and bright-colored Fauvist works like Matisse. (La Espera—with her bold outline and strong gaze—pops out from the Impressionistic background.) It was Cezanne's technique of "building" a figure with "cubes" of paint that inspired Picasso to soon invent Cubism.

Stage 7—Blue Period, 1901–1904: The bleak weather and poverty Picasso experiences in Paris leads to his Blue Period. He cranks out piles of blue art just to stay housed and fed. With blue—the coldest color—backgrounds and depressing subjects, this period was revolutionary in art history. Now the artist is painting not what he sees but what he feels. The touching portrait of a mother and child, *Desamparados* (*Despair*, 1903), captures the period well. Painting misfits and street people, Picasso, like Velázquez and Toulouse-Lautrec, sees "the beauty in ugliness." Back home in Barcelona, Picasso paints his hometown at night from rooftops *(Terrats de Barcelona)*. Still blue, here we see proto-Cubism... five years before the first real Cubist painting.

Stage 8—Rose: The woman in pink *(Retrato de la Sra. Canals)*, painted with classic Spanish melancholy, finally lifts Picasso out of his funk, moves him out of the blue and into a happier Rose Period (of which this museum has only one painting).

Stage 9—Cubism, 1907–1920: Pablo's invention in Paris of the shocking Cubist style is well known—at least I hope so, since this museum has no true Cubist paintings. In the age of the camera, the Cubist gives just the basics (a man with a bowl of fruit) and lets you finish it.

Stage 10—Eclectic, 1920–1950: Picasso is a painter of many styles. We see a little post-Impressionistic Pointillism in a portrait that looks like a classical statue. After a trip to Rome, he paints beefy women, inspired by the three-dimensional sturdiness of ancient statues. The expressionist horse symbolizes to Spaniards the innocent victim. In bullfights, the horse—clad with blinders and pummeled by the bull—has nothing to do with the fight. To take the symbolism in a deeper, more human direction, to Picasso the horse was feminine and the bull masculine. Picasso would mix all these styles and symbols—including this image of the horse—in his masterpiece *Guernica* (in Madrid) to show the horror and chaos of modern war.

Stage 11—Picasso and Velázquez, 1957: Notice the print of Velázquez's *Las Meninas* (in Madrid's Prado) that introduces this section. Picasso, who had great respect for Velázquez, painted over 50 interpretations of the painting many consider the greatest painting by anyone ever. These two Spanish geniuses were artistic equals. Picasso seems to enjoy a relationship with Velázquez. Like artistic soul mates, they spar and tease. He dissects Velázquez, and then injects playful uses of light, color, and perspective to horse around with the earlier masterpiece. In the big black-and-white canvas, the king and queen (reflected in the mirror in the back of the room) are hardly seen while the self-portrait of the painter towers above everyone. The two women of the court on the right look like they're in a tomb—but they're wearing party shoes. In these rooms, see the fun Picasso had playing paddleball with Velázquez's masterpiece—filtering Velázquez's realism through the kaleidoscope of Cubism.

Stage 12—Windows, 1957: All his life, Picasso said, "Paintings are like windows open to the world." Here we see the French Riviera—with simple black outlines and Crayola colors, he paints sun-splashed nature and the joys of the beach. He died with brush in hand, still growing. To the end—through his art—he continued exploring and loving life. As a child, Picasso was forced to paint as an adult. Now, as an old man (with little kids of his own and an also-childish artist Chagall for a friend), he paints like a child.

Textile and Garment Museum (Museu Textil i de la Indumentaria)—If fabrics from the 12th to 20th centuries leave you cold, have a *café con leche* on the museum's beautiful patio (€3.50, Tue–Sat 10:00–18:00, Sun 10:00–15:00, closed Mon, free entrance to patio—an inviting courtyard with a WC and coffeshop, which is outside museum but within the walls, 30 meters from Picasso Museum at Montcada 12–14).

▲▲Catalan Concert Hall (Palau de la Música Catalana)—This concert hall, finished in 1908, features *the* best modernist interior in town. Inviting arches lead you into the 2,000-seat hall. A kaleidoscopic skylight features a choir singing around the sun while playful carvings and mosaics celebrate music and Catalan culture. Admission is by tour only and starts with a relaxing 20-minute video (€5, 1 hr, in English, daily on the hour 10:00–15:00, maybe later, tel. 932-967-200). Ask about concerts (300 per year, inexpensive tickets, www.palaumusica.org).

Sights—Eixample

Uptown Barcelona is a unique variation on the common grid-plan city. Barcelona snipped off the building corners to create light and spacious eight-sided squares at every intersection. Wide sidewalks, hardy shade trees, chic shops, and plenty of Art Nouveau fun make the Eixample a refreshing break from the old town. For the best Eixample example, ramble Rambla Catalunya (unrelated to the more famous Ramblas) and pass through Passeig de Gràcia (described below, Metro: Passeig de Gràcia for Block of Discord or Diagonal for Casa Milà).

The 19th century was a boom time for Barcelona. By 1850 the city was busting out of its medieval walls. A new town was planned to follow a gridlike layout. The intersection of three major thoroughfares—Gran Vía, Diagonal, and Meridiana—would shift the city's focus uptown.

The Eixample, or "Expansion," was a progressive plan in which everything was made accessible to everyone. Each 20-block-square district would have its own hospital and large park, each 10-block-square area would have its own market and general services, and each five-block-square grid would house its own schools and day-care centers. The hollow space found inside each "block" of apartments would form a neighborhood park.

While much of that vision never quite panned out, the Eixample was an urban success. Rich and artsy big shots bought plots along the grid. The richest landowners built as close to the center as possible. For this reason, the best buildings are near the Passeig de Gràcia. While adhering to the height, width, and depth limitations, they built as they pleased—often in the trendy new modernist style.

Sights—Gaudí's Art and Architecture

Barcelona is an architectural scrapbook of the galloping gables and organic curves of hometown boy Antonio Gaudí. A devoted Catalan and Catholic, he immersed himself in each project, often living on-site. He called Parc Güell, La Pedrera, and the Sagrada Familia all home.

▲▲▲Sagrada Familia (Holy Family) Church—Gaudí's most famous and persistent work is this unfinished landmark. He worked on the church from 1883 to 1926. Since then, construction has moved forward in fits and starts. Even today, the half-finished church is not expected to be completed for another 50 years. One reason it's taking so long is that the temple is funded exclusively by private donations and entry fees. Your admission helps pay for the ongoing construction (€6, daily April–Oct 9:00–20:00, Nov–March 9:00–18:00; €3 extra for tours in English: 4/day April–Oct, usually 2/day Nov–March; Metro: Sagrada Familia, tel. 932-073-031, www.sagradafamilia.org).

When the church is finished, a dozen 100-meter spires (representing the apostles) will stand in groups of four and mark the three entry facades of the building. The center tower (honoring Jesus), will reach 170 meters up (560 feet) and be flanked by 125-meter-tall towers (400 feet) of Mary and the four evangelists. A unique exterior ambulatory will circle the building like a cloister turned inside out.

1. Passion Facade (on the side where you enter): This shows Gaudí's spiritual drive. Inspired by Gaudí's vision, it's full of symbolism from the Bible (find the stylized alpha and omega over the door; Jesus, hanging on the cross, has an open book for hair; the grid of numbers all add up to 33—Jesus' age at the time of his death). The distinct face of the man on the lower left is a memorial to Gaudí.

Judge for yourself how the recently completed and controversial Passion facade by Josep Maria Subirachs fits with Gaudí's original formulation. Now look high above: The colorful ceramic caps of the columns symbolize the mitres (formal hats) of bishops. This is only a side entrance. The nine-story apartment flat to the right will be torn down to accommodate the grand front entry of this church.

Now walk down to your right to the...

2. Museum (in church basement): The museum displays physical models used for the church's construction. As you wander, you'll see how the church's design is a fusion of nature, architecture, and religion. The columns seem light, with branches springing forth and capitals that look like palm trees. The U-shaped choir hovers above the nave, tethered halfway up the columns. Find the hanging model showing how Gaudí used gravity to calculate the perfect parabolas incorporated into the church design (the mirror above this model shows how the right-side-up church is derived from this).

Gaudí lived on the site for more than a decade and is buried in the crypt. When he died in 1926, only the stubs of four spires stood above the building site. A window allows you to look down into the neo-Gothic 19th-century crypt (which is how the church began) to see the tomb of Gaudí. There's a move afoot to make Gaudí a saint. Perhaps some day, this tomb will be a place of pilgrimage. Gaudí was certainly driven to greatness by his passion for God. When undertaking a lengthy project, he said, "My client [meaning God] is not in a hurry." You'll peek into a busy workshop where the slow and steady building pace is maintained.

Outside, just after leaving the building, you'll encounter the...

3. Nativity Facade: This really shows Gaudí's vision. It was the only real decorative part of the church finished in his lifetime, and shows scenes from the birth and childhood of Jesus along with angels playing musical instruments.

Finally you walk through the actual...

4. Construction Zone: With the cranking cranes, rusty forests of rebar, and scaffolding requiring a powerful faith, the Sagrada Familia Church offers a fun look at a living, growing,

Gaudí & Modernist Sights

bigger-than-life building. Take the lift on the Passion side (€1.20) or the stairs on the Nativity side (free but often miserably congested) up to the dizzy lookout bridging two spires. You'll get a great view of the city and a gargoyle's-eye perspective of the loopy church. If there's any building on earth I'd like to see, it's the Sagrada Familia . . . finished.

▲Palau Güell—This is a good chance to enjoy a Gaudí interior (see "Introductory Walk—Ramblas," above). Curvy.

▲▲Casa Milà (La Pedrera)—This Gaudí exterior laughs down on the crowds filling Passeig de Gràcia. Casa Milà, also called La Pedrera (the Quarry), has a much-photographed roller coaster of melting-ice-cream eaves. This is Barcelona's quintessential modernist building.

Visits come in three parts: apartment, attic, and rooftop. Buy the €6 ticket to see all three. Starting with the apartment, an elevator whisks you to the *Life in Barcelona 1905–1929* exhibit

Modernisme

The Renaixensa (Catalan cultural revival) gave birth to Modernisme (Catalan Art Nouveau) at the end of the 19th century. Barcelona is its capital. Its Eixample neighborhood shimmers with the colorful, leafy, flowing, blooming shapes of Modernisme in doorways, entrances, facades, and ceilings.

Meaning "a taste for what is modern," this free-flowing organic style lasted from 1888 to 1906. Breaking with tradition, artists experimented with glass, tile, iron, and brick. Decoration became structural. It comes with three influences: nature, exotic (such as Chinese), and a fanciful Gothic twist to celebrate Catalan's medieval glory days. Modernisme was a way of life as Barcelona burst into the 20th century.

Antoni Gaudí is Barcelona's most famous modernist artist. From four generations of metalworkers, a lineage of which he was quite proud, he incorporated ironwork into his architecture and came up with novel approaches to architectural structure and space.

Two more modernist architects famous for their unique style are Lluís Domènech i Muntaner and Josep Puig i Cadafalch. You'll see their work on the Block of Discord.

(well-described in English). Then you walk through a sumptuously furnished Art Nouveau apartment. Upstairs in the attic, wander under brick arches—enjoying a multimedia exhibit of models, photos, and videos of Gaudí's works. From there a stairway leads to the fanciful rooftop where chimneys play volleyball with the clouds. From here, you can see Gaudí's other principal works, the Sagrada Familia, Casa Batllo, and Parc Güell (daily 10:00–20:00; free tours in English Mon–Fri at 17:30, Sat–Sun and holidays at 11:00; Passeig de Gràcia 92, Metro: Diagonal, tel. 934-845-995). At ground level of Casa Milà, poke into the dreamily painted original entrance courtyard (free). The first floor hosts free art exhibits. During the summer, a concert series called "Pedrera by Night" features live music—jazz, flamenco, tango—a glass of champagne, and the chance to see the rooftop illuminated (€9, July–Sept Fri–Sat at 22:00, tel. 934-845-900).

▲**The Block of Discord**—Four blocks from Casa Milà you can survey a noisy block of competing late-19th-century facades. Several of Barcelona's top modernist mansions line Passeig de Gràcia (Metro: Passeig de Gràcia). Because the structures look as though they are trying to outdo each other in creative twists, locals nicknamed the block between Consell de Cent and Arago, the "Block of Discord." First (at #43) and most famous is Gaudí's Casa Batlló, with skull-like balconies and a tile roof that suggests a cresting dragon's back (Gaudí based the work on the popular St. Jordi-slays-the-dragon legend). By the way, if you're tempted to snap your photos from the middle of the street, be careful—Gaudí died under a streetcar.

Next door, at Casa Amatller (#41), check out architect Puig i Cadafalch's creative mix of Moorish, Gothic, and iron grillwork. This is the only place in town to purchase Modernist Route combo-tickets. For €3.60, you get a 50 percent discount to 10 of the most important modernist sights in Barcelona (valid for 1 month). Even if you only see Sagrada Familia and Casa Milà, you'll save money with this ticket.

On the corner (at #35) is Casa Lleo Morera, by Lluís Domènech i Muntaner, who did the Catalana Concert Hall (you'll see similarities). The perfume shop halfway down the street has a free and interesting little perfume museum in the back. The Hostal de Rita restaurant, just around the corner on Carrer Arago, serves a fine three-course lunch for a great price at 13:00 (see "Eating," below).

▲**Park Güell**—Gaudí fans enjoy the artist's magic in this colorful park (free, daily 9:00–20:00) and small Gaudí Museum (€2.50, daily 10:00–20:00, closes off-season at 18:00, red Tourist Bus or bus #24 from Plaça de Catalunya; €6 by taxi). Gaudí intended this garden to be a 60-residence housing project—a kind of gated community—rather than a park. As a high-income housing development, it flopped. As a park, it's a delight offering another peek into the eccentric genius of Gaudí. From the bus stop, you'll hike uphill three blocks to the main (lower) entry to the park. (Taxis take you right there.) Notice the mosaic medallions that say "park" in English, reminding folks that this is modeled on an English garden.

Imagine living here 100 years ago, when this gated community was filled with Barcelona's wealthy. Stepping past fancy gate houses (which now house a good bookshop and an audiovisual intro), you walk by Gaudí's wrought-iron gas lamps (1900–1914)—his dad was a blacksmith and he always enjoyed this medium. Climb the grand stairway past the ceramic dragon fountain. At the top drop by the Hall of 100 Columns, a produce market for the neighborhood's 60 mansions. The fun columns—each different, made from concrete and rebar, topped with colorful ceramic and studded with broken bottles and bric-a-brac—add to the market's vitality. After shopping, continue up. Look left down the playful "pathway of columns" that support a long arcade. Gaudí drew his inspiration from nature, and this arcade is like a surfer's perfect tube. From here, continue up to the terrace. Sit on a colorful bench—designed to fit your body ergonomically—and enjoy one of Barcelona's best views. Look for the Sagrada Familia church in the distance.

When considering the failure of Park Güell, consider also that it was an idea just a hundred years ahead of its time. Back then high-society ladies didn't want to live so far from the cultural action. Today, the surrounding neighborhoods are some of the wealthiest in town and a gated community here would be a big hit.

Sights—Barcelona's Montjuïc

The Montjuïc (Mount of the Jews), overlooking Barcelona's hazy port, has always been a show-off. Ages ago it had the impressive fortress. In 1929 it hosted an international fair, from which most of today's sights originated. And in 1992 the Summer Olympics directed the world's attention to this pincushion of attractions.

There are many ways to reach Montjuïc: on the blue Tourist Bus route (see "Getting around Barcelona," above);by bus #50 from the corner of Gran Vía and Passeig de Gràcia (€1, every 10 min); take the Metro to Parallel and catch the funicular (€1.70 one-way, €2.50 round-trip, Mon–Sat 10:45–20:00, closed Sun); or by taxi (about €7). The first three options leave you at the *teleférico* (cable car), which you can take to the Castle of Montjuïc (€3.20 one-way, €4.50 round-trip, daily 11:00–21:00, less off-season, tel. 934-430-859). Alternatively, from the same spot, you can walk uphill 20 minutes through the pleasant park. Only a taxi gets you doorstep delivery. From the port, the fastest and most scenic way to Montjuïc is via the 1929 Transbordador Aereo (at tower in port, ride elevator up to catch dangling gondola, €7.20 round-trip, 4/hr, daily 10:30–19:00, tel. 934-430-859).

Castle of Montjuïc—The castle offers great city views and a military museum (€1.20, Tue–Sun 9:30–20:00, closed Mon). The seemingly endless museum houses a dull collection of guns, swords, and toy soldiers. An interesting section on the Spanish-American War covers Spain's valiant fight against American aggression (from its perspective). Unfortunately, there are no English descriptions. Those interested in Jewish history will find a fascinating collection of ninth-century Jewish tombstones. The castle itself has a fascist past. It was built in the 18th century by the central Spanish government to keep an eye on Barcelona and stifle citizen revolt. When Franco was in power, the castle was the site of hundreds of political assassinations.

▲Fountains (Font Magica)—Music, colored lights, and huge amounts of water make an artistic and coordinated splash on summer nights (Fri–Sun, 20-min shows start on the half-hour, 21:30–24:00, in summer Thu eve, too, from Metro: Plaça Espanya, walk toward towering National Palace).

Spanish Village (Poble Espanyol)—This tacky five-acre model village uses fake traditional architecture from all over Spain as a shell to contain gift shops. Craftspeople do their clichéd thing only in the morning (not worth your time or €6). After hours it's a popular local nightspot.

▲▲Catalan Art Museum (Museo Nacional d'Art de Catalunya)—Often called "the Prado of Romanesque art," this is a rare, world-class collection of Romanesque art taken mostly from remote Catalan village churches in the Pyrenees (saved from unscrupulous art dealers—many American).

The Romanesque wing features frescoes, painted wooden altar fronts, and ornate statuary. This classic Romanesque art—with flat 2-D scenes, each saint holding his symbol, and Jesus (easy to identify by the cross in his halo)—is impressively displayed on replicas of the original church ceilings.

In the Gothic wing, fresco murals give way to vivid 14th-century paintings of Bible stories on wood. A roomful of paintings by the Catalan master Jaume Huguet (1412–1492) deserves a close look.

Before you leave, ice-skate under the huge dome over to the air-conditioned cafeteria. This was the prime ceremony room and dance hall for the 1929 International Exposition (museum €5, Tue–Sat 10:00–19:00, Thu until 21:00, Sun 10:00–14:30, closed Mon, tel. 936-220-375). The museum is in the massive National Palace building above the fountains, near Plaça Espanya (Metro: Plaça Espanya, then hike up or ride the bus; the blue Tourist Bus and bus #50 stop close by).

▲Fundació Joan Miró—For something more up-to-date, this museum—showcasing the modern-art talents of yet another Catalan artist—has the best collection of Joan Miró art anywhere. You'll also see works by other modern Spanish artists (such as Alexander Calder's *Mercury Fountain*). If you don't like abstract art, you'll leave scratching your head, but those who love this place are not faking it... they understand the genius of Miró and the fun of abstract art.

As you wander, consider this: Miró believed that everything in the cosmos is linked—colors, sky, stars, love, time, music, dogs, men, women, dirt, and the void. He mixed these things creatively, as a poet uses words. It's as liberating for the visual artist to be abstract as it is for the poet: Both can use metaphors rather than being confined to concrete explanations. Miró would listen to music and paint. It's interactive, free interpretation. He said, "For me, simplicity is freedom."

To enjoy Miró's art: 1) meditate on it, 2) read the title (for example, *The Smile of a Tear*), 3) meditate on it again. There's no correct answer, it's pure poetry. Devotees of Miró say they fly with him and don't even need drugs. Take advantage of the wonderful audioguide, included with admission (€7.20, July–Sept Tue–Sat 10:00–20:00, Thu until 21:30, Sun 10:00–14:30, closed Mon, Oct–June closes at 19:00 Tue–Sat).

More Sights—Barcelona

▲Monastery of Pedralbes—Long a museum showing off the monastery's six centuries of history (with a peaceful cloister and cells set up for worship, giving a peek into the everyday life of the cloistered nuns), the monastery now also houses an exquisite Thyssen-Bornemisza collection of paintings. The small, two-room collection features medieval art (with a pristine Fra Angelico altarpiece), along with German (Cranach), Italian Renaissance (Titian), Baroque (Valázquez, Rubens), and Late Venetian Baroque (Canaletto, Guardi) works. Unfortunately, it's far from the center (€3, Tue–Sun 10:00–14:00, closed Mon, buses: #22, #63, #64, #75, tel. 932-801-434).

Tibidabo—Tibidabo comes from the Latin for "to thee I shall give," the words the devil used when he was tempting Christ. It's still an enticing offer: At the top of Barcelona's highest peak, you're offered the city's oldest fun-fair, the neo-Gothic Sacred Heart Church, and—if the weather and air quality are good—a near-limitless view of the city and the Mediterranean.

Getting there is part of the fun: Start by taking the FGC line—similar to but separate from the Metro, also covered by the T-10 ticket—from the Plaça de Catalunya station (under Café Zurich) to the Tibidabo stop. The red Tourist Bus stops here, too. Then take Barcelona's only remaining tram—the Tramvia Blau—from Plaça John F. Kennedy to Plaça Dr. Andreu (€2.40, 2–4/hr). From there, take the cable car to the top (€2.40, tel. 906-427-017).

Citadel Park (Parc de la Ciutadella)—Barcelona's biggest, greenest park, originally the site of a much-hated military citadel, was transformed in 1888 for a World's Fair (Universal Exhibition). The stately Triumphal Arch at the top of the park was built as the main entrance. Inside you'll find wide pathways, plenty of trees and grass, the zoo, the Geology and Zoology Museums, and the Modern Art Museum (see below). In Barcelona, which suffers from a lack of real green space, this park is a haven. Enjoy the ornamental fountain that the young Antonio Gaudí helped design, and consider a jaunt in a rowboat on the lake in the center of the park (€1.20/person for 30 min). Check out the tropical Umbracle greenhouse and the Hivernacle winter garden, which has a pleasant café-bar (daily 8:00–20:00, Metro: Arc de Triomf, east of França train station).

Modern Art Museum (Museu d'Art Modern)—This manageable museum in Citadel Park exhibits Catalan sculpture, painting, glass, and furniture by Gaudí, Casas, Llimona, and more (€3, Tue–Sat 10:00–19:00, Thu until 21:00, Sun 10:00–14:30, closed Mon).

Barcelona's Beach—Take the trek through the charming Barceloneta neighborhood to the tip of this man-made peninsula. The beaches begin here and stretch for four kilometers up the coast to the Olympic Port and beyond. Everything you see here—palm trees, cement walkways, and tons of sand—was installed in the mid-1980s in an effort to shape up the city for the 1992 Olympic Games. The beaches are fine for sunbathing (beach chair rental €3/day), but the water quality is questionable for swimming. Take a lazy stroll down the seafront promenade to the Olympic Port, where you'll find bars, restaurants, and, at night, dance clubs.

Nightlife in Barcelona

Refer to the *See Barcelona* guide (free from TI) and find out the latest at a TI. Sights open daily until 20:00 include the Picasso Musuem, Casa Milà, and Gaudí's Sagrada Famila and Parc Güell. On Thursday, the Modern Art Museum and Catalan Art Museum stay open until 21:00 and the Joan Miró museum until 21:30. On Montjuïc, the fountains on Plaça Espanya make a splash on weekend evenings (Fri–Sun, plus Thu in summer).

For music, consider a performance at Casa Milà ("Pedrera by Night" summer concert series), the Liceu Opera House, or the Catalan Concert Hall (all listed above). Two decent music clubs are La Boite (477 Diagonal, near El Corte Inglés) and Jamboree (on Plaça Reial).

Sleeping in Barcelona

(€1 = about $1, country code: 34)

Sleep Code: S = Single, **D** = Double/Twin, **T** = Triple, **Q** = Quad, **b** = bathroom, **s** = shower only, **CC** = Credit Cards accepted, **no CC** = Credit Cards not accepted, **SE** = Speaks English, **NSE** = No English.

To help you easily sort through these listings, I've divided the rooms into three categories, based on the price for a standard double room with bath (during high season):

Higher Priced—Most rooms more than €150.

Moderately Priced—Most rooms €150 or less.

Lower Priced—Most rooms €100 or less.

Book ahead. If necessary, the TI at Plaça de Catalunya has

a room-finding service. Barcelona is Spain's most expensive city. Still, it has reasonable rooms. Cheap places are more crowded in summer; fancier business-class places fill up in winter and offer discounts on weekends and in summer. Prices listed do not include the 7 percent tax or breakfast (ranging from simple €3 spreads to €13.25 buffets) unless otherwise noted. While many recommended places are on pedestrian streets, night noise is a problem almost everywhere (especially in cheap places, which have single-pane windows). For a quiet night, ask for "*tranquilo*" rather than "*con vista*."

Sleeping in Eixample

For an uptown, boulevardian neighborhood, sleep in Eixample, a 10-minute walk from the Ramblas action.

MODERATELY PRICED

Hotel Gran Vía, filling a palatial mansion built in the 1870s, offers Botticelli and chandeliers in the public rooms; a sprawling, peaceful sun garden; and 54 spacious, comfy, air-conditioned rooms. While borderline ramshackle, it's charming and an excellent value (Sb-€70, Db-€105, Tb-€130, prices valid through 2003 but only by reserving direct with this book, CC, Internet access, elevator, quiet, Gran Vía de les Corts Catalanes 642, 08007 Barcelona, tel. 933-181-900, fax 933-189-997, e-mail: hgranvia@nnhotels.es, Juan Gomez SE).

Hotel Continental Palacete is a new place filling a 100-year-old chandeliered mansion. With flowery wallpaper and cheap but fancy furniture under ornately gilded stucco, it's gaudy in the city of Gaudí. But it's friendly, clean, quiet, and well located and the beds are good. Owner Señora Vallet (whose son, José, runs the recommended Hotel Continental—see "Hotels with Personality on or near the Ramblas," below) has a creative vision for this 19-room hotel (Sb-€95-150, Db-€120-150, Tb-€150-180, includes breakfast, CC, air-con, 2 blocks north of Plaça de Catalunya at corner of Carrer Diputacio, Rambla de Catalunya 30, tel. 934-457-657, fax 934-450-050, www.hotelcontinental.com, e-mail: palacete@hotelcontinental.com).

LOWER PRICED

Hotel Residencia Neutral, with a classic Eixample address and 28 very basic rooms, is a family-run time warp (tiny Sb-€27, Ds-€41, Db-€47, extra bed-€9, €4 breakfast in pleasant breakfast room, CC, elevator, no air-con, thin walls and some street noise, elegantly located 2 blocks north of Gran Vía at Rambla Catalunya 42, 08007 Barcelona, tel. 934-876-390, fax 934-876-848, owner Ramon SE). Its sister hotel, **Hotel Universal,** lacks the friendly feel and is stark but well located (Db-€55, Sb-€42, no breakfast, Arago 281, tel. 934-879-762).

Sleeping in Business-Class Comfort near Plaça de Catalunya and the Top of the Ramblas

These nine places have sliding glass doors leading to plush reception areas, air-conditioning, and newly renovated modern rooms. Most are on big streets within two blocks of Barcelona's exuberant central square (zip code: 08002 unless otherwise noted). Being business hotels, they have hard-to-pin-down prices fluctuating wildly with the demand.

HIGHER PRICED

Hotel Catalonia Albinoni, the best located of all these places, elegantly fills a renovated old palace with wide halls, hardwood floors, and 74 modern rooms with all the comforts. It overlooks a thriving pedestrian boulevard. Front rooms have views; balcony rooms on the back are quiet and come with sun terraces (Db-€166, extra bed-€18, CC, family rooms, air-con, elevator, a block down from Plaça de Catalunya at Portal de l'Angel 17, tel. 933-184-141, fax 933-012-631, e-mail: albinoni@hoteles-catalonia.es).

Hotel Duques de Bergara boasts four stars. It has splashy public spaces, slick marble and hardwood floors, 150 comfortable rooms, and a garden courtyard with a pool a world away from the big-city noise (Sb-€144, Db-€180, Tb-€204, CC, air-con, elevator, a half-block off Plaça de Catalunya at Bergara 11, tel. 933-015-151, fax 933-173-442, www.hoteles-catalonia.es, e-mail: duques@hoteles-catalonia.es).

Hotel Occidental Reding, on a quiet street a five-minute walk west of the Ramblas and Plaça de Catalunya action, rents 44 modern business-class rooms (Db-€110 in low season, €160 in high, extra bed-€42, CC, air-con, elevator, near Metro: University at Gravina 5, 08001 Barcelona, tel. 934-121-097, fax 932-683-482, e-mail: reding@occidental-hoteles.com).

Hotel Barcelona is another big, American-style hotel with 72 bright, prefab, comfy rooms (Sb-€143, Db-€170, Db with terrace-€215, CC, air-con, elevator, a block from Plaça de Catalunya at Caspe 1–13, tel. 933-025-858, fax 933-018-674, e-mail: hotelbarcelona@husa.es).

Hotel Duc de la Victoria, with 150 rooms, is a new, professional-yet-friendly business-class hotel, buried in the Gothic Quarter but only three blocks off the Ramblas (Sb/Db-€160 Mon–Thu and €125 Fri–Sun, summer rate Db-€100, superior rooms—bigger and on a corner with windows on 2 sides—are worth €15 extra, air-con, elevator, CC, groups get weekend rate,

Barcelona's Gothic Quarter Hotels

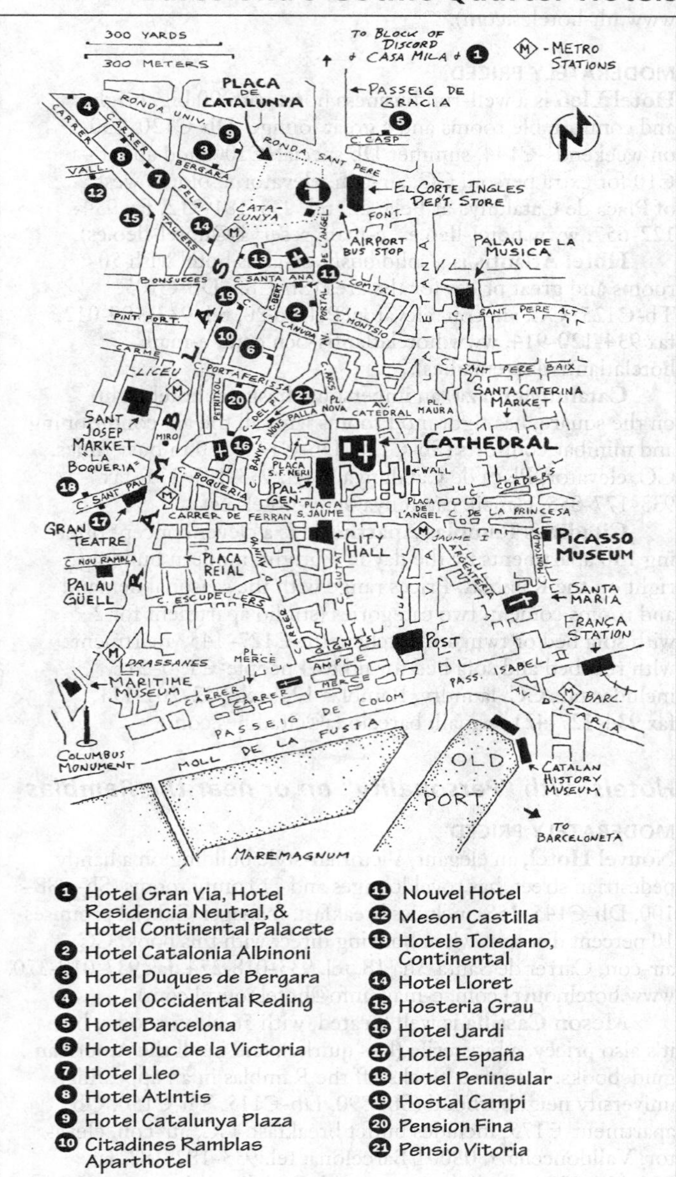

Duc de la Victoria 15, tel. 932-703-410, fax 934-127-747, www.nh-hoteles.com).

MODERATELY PRICED

Hotel Lleo is a well-run business hotel with 90 big, bright, and comfortable rooms and a great lounge (Db-€120–130, on weekends-€144, summer Db special-€100, add about €10 for extra person, CC, air-con, elevator, 2 blocks west of Plaça de Catalunya at Pelai 22, tel. 933-181-312, fax 934-122-657, www.hotel-lleo.es, e-mail: reservas@hotel-lleo.es).

Hotel Atlantis is a solid business-class hotel with 50 rooms and great prices for the area (Sb-€85, Db-€105, Tb-€125, CC, air-con, elevator, Pelayo 20, tel. 933-189-012, fax 934-120-914, www.hotelatlantis-bcn.com, e-mail: hotelatlantis@retemail.es).

Catalunya Plaza, an impersonal business hotel right on the square, has tight mod rooms with all the air-conditioning and minibar comforts (Sb-€120, Db-€144–210 in busy times, CC, elevator, Plaça de Catalunya 7, tel. 933-177-171, fax 933-177-855, e-mail: catalunya@city-hotels.es).

Citadines Ramblas Aparthotel is a clever concept offering 130 apartments by the day in a bright, modern building right on the Ramblas. Prices range with the seasonal demand and rooms come in two categories (studio apartment for 2 with sofa bed or twin and kitchenette-€127–145, apartment with real bed and sofa bed for up to 4 people-€190–216, includes tax, CC, laundry, Ramblas 122, tel. 932-701-111, fax 934-127-421, e-mail: barcelona@citadines.com).

Hotels with "Personality" on or near the Ramblas

MODERATELY PRICED

Nouvel Hotel, an elegant, Victorian-style building on a handy pedestrian street, has royal lounges and 71 comfy rooms (Sb-€88–100, Db-€145–158, includes breakfast, manager Gabriel promises 10 percent discount when booking direct with this book, CC, air-con, Carrer de Santa Ana 18, tel. 933-018-274, fax 933-018-370, www.hotelnouvel.com, e-mail: info@hotelnouvel.com).

Meson Castilla is well located, with 56 clean rooms, but it's also pricey, a bit sterile (less quirky), and in all the American guidebooks. It's three blocks off the Ramblas in an appealing university neighborhood (Sb-€90, Db-€115, Tb-€150, Qb apartment-€175, includes buffet breakfast, CC, air-con, elevator, Valldoncella 5, 08001 Barcelona, tel. 933-182-182, fax 934-124-020, e-mail: hmesoncastilla@teleline.es).

LOWER PRICED

Hotels Toledano, Residencia Capitol, Continental, and Lloret overlook the Ramblas (at the top, very near Plaça de Catalunya) and offer classic tiny view-balcony opportunities if you don't mind the noise. The last three (Jardi, España, and Peninsular) are a few blocks away from the boulevard at about its midpoint. These places are generally family-run with ad-lib furnishings, more character, and much lower prices.

Hotel Toledano, overlooking the Ramblas, is suitable for backpackers and popular with dust-bunnies. Small, folksy, and borderline dumpy, it's warmly run by Albert Sanz, his father Juan, Juanma, and trusty Daniel on the nightshift (Sb-€29, Db-€50, Tb-€63, Qb-€71, CC, front rooms have Ramblas-view terraces, back rooms have air-con and no noise—request your choice when you call; Rambla de Canaletas 138, tel. 933-010-872, fax 934-123-142, www.hoteltoledano.com, e-mail: reservas@hoteltoledano.com). The Sanz family also runs **Hostal Residencia Capitol** one floor above—quiet, plain, cheaper, and also appropriate for backpackers (S-€22, D-€34, Ds-€39, Q-€51, 5-bed room-€58).

Hotel Continental has comfortable rooms, double-thick mattresses, and wildly clashing carpets and wallpaper. To celebrate 100 years in the family, José includes a free breakfast and an all-day complimentary coffee bar. Choose a Ramblas-view balcony or quiet back room (Db with double bed-€70, with twin-€80, with balcony-€94, extra bed-€12, includes tax, special family room, CC, fans in rooms, elevator, Internet access, Ramblas 138, tel. 933-012-570, fax 933-027-360, www.hotelcontinental.com, e-mail: ramblas@hotelcontinental.com).

Hotel Lloret is a big, dark, Old World place on the Ramblas with plain, neon-lit rooms. A dark, dusty elevator cage fills the stairwell like Darth Vader—but on a hot day, you're glad it's there (Sb-€46, Db-€70, Tb-€84, extra bed-€6, choose a noisy Ramblas balcony or *tranquilo* in the back, CC, air-con in summer, Rambla de Canaletas 125, tel. 933-173-366, fax 933-019-283).

Hosteria Grau is a homey, almost alpine place, family-run with 27 clean and woody rooms just far enough off the Ramblas (S-€27, D-€45, Ds-€47, Db-€53, family suites with 2 bedrooms-€112, €6 extra charged July–Sept, CC, fans, 200 meters up Calle Tallers from Ramblas at Ramelleres 27, 08001 Barcelona, tel. 933-018-135, fax 933-176-825, www.intercom.es/grau, e-mail: hgrau@lix.intercom.es, Monica SE).

Hotel Jardi is a clean and newly remodeled place on a breezy little square in the Gothic Quarter. Tight little balcony rooms overlooking the peaceful leafy square are most expensive

(Db-€75 with square view, €70 on interior, extra bed-€10, CC, air-con, elevator, halfway between Ramblas and cathedral on Plaça Sant Josep Oriol #1, tel. 933-015-900, fax 933-425-733, e-mail: hoteljardi@retemail.es). Rooms with balconies enjoy an almost Parisian ambience and minimal noise.

Hotel España is a big, creaky circa 1900 place with lavish public spaces still sweet with Art Nouveau decor. While it's 100 meters off the Ramblas on a borderline seedy street, it feels safe (75 rooms, Sb-€46, Db-€88, Tb-€120, includes tax and breakfast, air-con, elevator, near Metro: Liceu at Sant Pau 9, tel. 933-181-758, fax 933-171-134, www.hotelespanya.com, e-mail: hotelespanya@hotelespanya.com).

Hotel Peninsular, farther down that same street, is thoughtfully run and a unique value in the old center. A former monastery, the 80 still basic and thinly furnished rooms—once monks' cells—gather prayerfully around a peaceful courtyard (S-€22, Sb-€45, D-€45, Db-€65, Tb-€80, prices include tax and breakfast and are the same year-round, CC, air-con, elevator, Carrer Sant Pau, tel. 933-023-138, fax 934-123-699, Alex and Augustin SE).

Humble Cheaper Places Buried in Gothic Quarter

Hostal Campi—big, quiet, and ramshackle—is a few doors off the top of the Ramblas. The streets can be noisy, so request a quiet room in the back (24 rooms, D-€38, Db-€46, T-€50, no CC, Canuda 4, tel. & fax 93-301-3-545, e-mail: hcampi@terra.es, friendly Sonia and Margarita SE). **Pension Fina** offers more cheap sleeps (25 rooms, S-€30, D-€45, Db-€50, no CC, Portaferrissa 11, tel. & fax 933-179-787). **Pensio Vitoria** has loose tile floors and 12 basic rooms, each with a tiny balcony. It's more dumpy than homey, but consider the price (D-€26, Db-€34, T-€30, Tb-€36, cheaper off-season, CC, a block off daydreamy Plaça dei Pi at Carrer la Palla 8, tel. & fax 933-020-834, Andres SE).

Eating in Barcelona

Barcelona, the capital of Catalan cuisine, offers a tremendous variety of colorful places to eat. Many restaurants close in August (or July), when the owners vacation.

Eating Simply yet Memorably near the Ramblas and in the Gothic Quarter

Taverna Basca Irati serves 40 kinds of hot and cold Basque *pintxos* for €1 each. These are open-faced sandwiches—like Basque sushi but on bread. Muscle in through the hungry local crowd. Get an empty plate from the waiter, then help yourself.

It's a Basque honor system: You'll be charged by the number of toothpicks left on your plate when you're done. Wash it down with a €1 glass of Rioja (full-bodied red wine), Txakoli (spritely Basque white wine), or *sidra* (apple wine) poured from on high to add oxygen and bring out the flavor (daily 12:00–24:00, a block off the Ramblas, behind arcade at Carrer Cardenal Casanyes 17, near Metro: Liceu, tel. 933-023-084).

Juicy Jones, next door, is a tutti-frutti vegetarian place with garish colors, a hip veggie menu (served downstairs), and a stunning array of fresh-squeezed juices served at the bar (lunch and dinner menu-€7, daily 10:00–24:30, Carrer Cardenal Casanyes 7). Pop in for a quick "juice of the day."

Restaurant Elisabets is a happy little neighborhood eatery popular with locals for its "home-cooked" three-course €7 lunch special. Stop by for lunch, survey what those around you are enjoying, and order what looks best (Mon–Sat 13:00–16:00, closed Sun, tapas only in the evening, 2 blocks west of Ramblas on far corner of Plaça Bonsucces at Carrer Elisabets 2, tel. 933-175-826).

Café Granja Viader is a quaint time warp, family-run since 1870. This feminine place—specializing in baked and dairy delights, toasted sandwiches, and light meals—is ideal for a traditional breakfast (note the "Esmorzars" specials posted). Try a glass of *orxata* (horchata—almond milk, summer only), *llet mallorquina* (Majorca-style milk with cinnamon, lemon, and sugar), or *suis* (literally, "Switzerland"—hot chocolate with a snowcap of whipped cream). Described on the Ramblas walk above, it's a block off the boulevard behind El Carme church (Mon 17:00–20:45, Tue–Sat 9:00–13:45 & 17:00–20:45, closed Sun, Xucla 4, tel. 933-183-486).

La Gardunya, located at the back of La Boqueria market, offers tasty meat and seafood meals made with fresh ingredients bought directly from the market (€9 lunch menus include wine and bread, €11.50 dinner menus don't include wine, Mon–Sat 13:00–16:00 & 20:00–24:00, closed Sun, Carrer Jerusalem 18, tel. 933-024-323).

Tired tourists consider **La Poma** for a good pizza, pasta, salads in a bright modern setting at the top of the Ramblas with comfortable views of all the street action (daily 9:00–24:00, Ramblas 117).

Homesick tourists flock to **The Bagel Shop,** which offers fresh bagels and brownies (Mon–Sat 9:30–21:30, Sun 11:00–16:00, Carrer Canuda 25, tel. 933-024-161).

Shoestring tourists buy **groceries** at El Corte Inglés (Mon–Sat 10:00–22:00, closed Sun, supermarket in basement, Plaça de Catalunya) and Champion Supermarket (Mon–Sat 9:00–22:00, closed Sun, Ramblas 113).

Dining in the Gothic Quarter

A chain of five bright, modern restaurants with high-quality traditional cuisine in classy bistro settings with great prices has stormed Barcelona. Because of their three-course (with wine) €7 lunches and €13 dinners, all are crowded with locals and tourists in the know. They take no reservations and are marked by long lines at the door. Arrive 15 minutes before opening or be prepared to wait. The first three are within a block of the Plaça Reial, the fourth is near the Catalan Concert Hall, and the fifth (Hostal de Rita) is described in the Eixample section below: **La Fonda** (daily 13:00–15:30 & 20:30–23:30, a block from Plaça Reial at Escudellers 10, tel. 933-017-515); **Les Quinze Nits** (on La Plaça Reial at #6—you'll see the line, tel. 933-173-075); **La Crema Canela** (feels cozier than the others in this chain, daily 13:30–15:45 & 20:00–24:00, Ptge. Madoz 6, 30 meters north of Plaça Reial, tel. 933-182-744); and **La Dolca Herminia** (2 blocks toward Ramblas from Catalan Concert Hall at Magdalenes 27, tel. 933-170-676).

Els Quatre Gats, Picasso's hangout (and the place he first showed off his paintings), still has a bohemian feel in spite of its tourist crowds. Before the place was founded in 1897, the idea of a café for artists was mocked as a place where only *quatre gats*—"four cats," meaning crazies—would go (€27 meals, Mon–Sat 8:30–24:00, Sun 17:00–24:00, live piano Mon–Sat from 21:00, Sun from 20:00, CC, Montsio 3, tel. 933-024-140).

El Pintor Restaurante serves perhaps the best €30 dinner in town. Under medieval arches and rough brick with candles and friendly service you'll enjoy Catalan and Mediterranean cuisine (daily 13:30–16:30 & 20:0024:00, from Plaça de Sant Jaume walk north on Carrer Sant Honorat to #7, reserve for eve, tel. 933-014-065).

Restaurante Agut, buried deep in the Gothic Quarter four blocks off the harbor, is a fine place with an enticing menu (in English) for local-style food in a local-style setting. It's almost dressy with white table cloths and candles (Tue–Sat 13:30–16:00 & 21:00–24:00, closed Sun, Mon, and Aug, Carrer Gignas 16, reservations smart for dinner, tel. 933-151-709).

Eating Out at Sea—Maremagnum

Tapasbar Maremagnum is a big, rollicking sports-bar kind of tapas restaurant, great for large groups. It's a fun way to end your Ramblas walk, a 10-minute stroll past the Columbus Monument straight out the dock, with breezy harbor views and good local food with emphasis on the sea (daily 11:00–24:00, Moll d'Espanya, tel. 932-258-180, www.tapasbar.es).

Barcelona's Gothic Quarter Restaurants

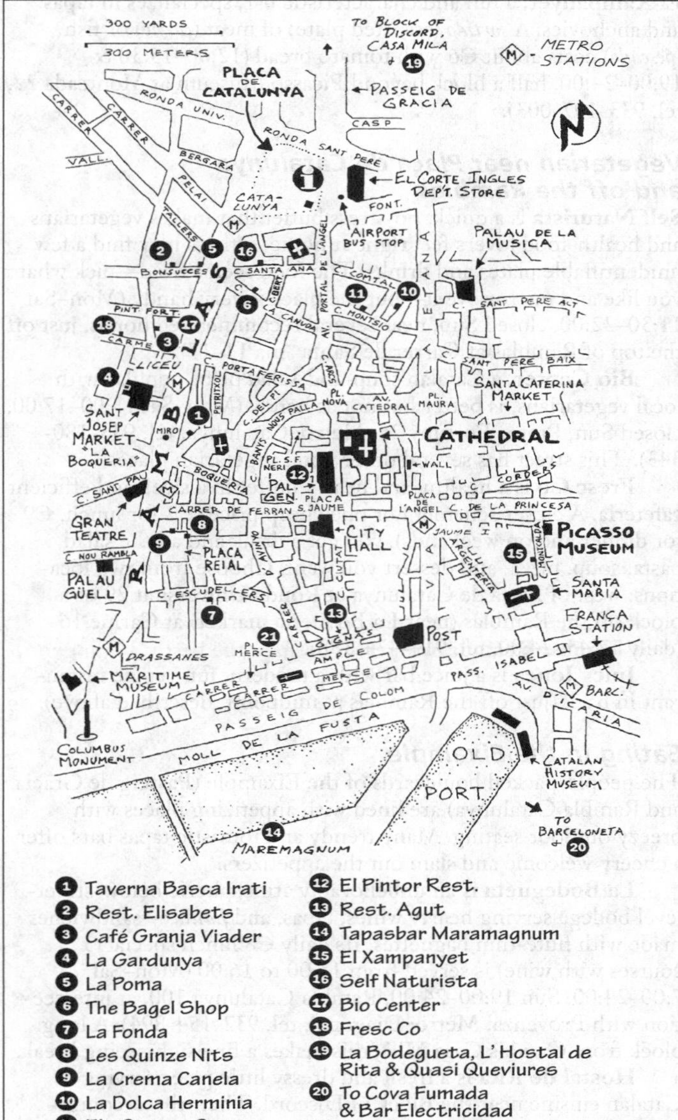

Eating Near the Picasso Museum

El Xampanyet, a fun and characteristic bar, specializes in tapas and anchovies. A *sortido* (assorted plate) of meat (*carne*) or fish (*pescado*) costs about €6 with tomato bread (12:00–15:30 & 19:00–24:00, half a block beyond Picasso Museum at Montcada 22, tel. 933-197-003).

Vegetarian near Plaça de Catalunya and off the Ramblas

Self Naturista is a quick, no-stress buffet that makes vegetarians and health-food lovers feel right at home. Others may find a few unidentifiable plates and drinks. The food seems tired—pick what you like and microwave it—but the place is very handy (Mon–Sat 11:30–22:00, closed Sun, near several recommended hotels, just off the top of Ramblas at Carrer de Santa Ana 11–17).

Bio Center, a Catalan soup-and-salad place popular with local vegetarians, is better but not as handy (Mon–Sat 13:00–17:00, closed Sun, Pintor Fortuny 25, Metro: Catalunya, tel. 933-180-343). This street has several other good vegetarian places.

Fresc Co is a healthy and hearty buffet in a sleek and efficient cafeteria. A clever scheme: For one cheap price (€7 for lunch, €9 for dinner and on weekends), you get a drink and all the salad, pasta, soup, pizza, and dessert you want. Choose from two locations: west of Plaça de Catalunya at Ronda Universitat 29 or a block off the Ramblas (near La Boqueria market) at Carme 16 (daily 12:45–24:00, tel. 914-474-388).

Juicy Jones is a juice bar with a modern, fun veggie restaurant in back (just off the Ramblas at midpoint, described above).

Eating in the Eixample

The people-packed boulevards of the Eixample (Passeig de Gràcia and Rambla Catalunya) are lined with appetizing places with breezy outdoor seating. Many trendy and touristic tapas bars offer a cheery welcome and slam out the appetizers.

La Bodegueta is an unbelievably atmospheric below-street-level bodega serving hearty wines, tapas, and *flautas*—sandwiches made with flute-thin baguettes. Its daily €8 lunch special (3 courses with wine) is served from 13:00 to 16:00 (Mon–Sat 7:00–24:00, Sun 19:00–24:00, Rambla Catalunya 100, at intersection with Provenza, Metro: Diagonal, tel. 932-154-894). A long block from Gaudí's Casa Milà, this makes a fine sightseeing break.

Hostal de Rita is a fresh and dressy little place serving Catalan cuisine near the Block of Discord. Their three-course-with-wine lunch (€6.60, Mon–Fri at 13:00) and dinner (€12, daily from 20:30) specials are a great value (a block from the Passeig de

Gracia Metro stop, near corner of Carrer de Pau Claris and Carrer Arago at Arago 279, tel. 934-872-376). Like its four sister restaurants described above, its prices attract long lines, so arrive just before the doors open or wait.

Quasi Queviures serves upscale tapas, sandwiches, and the whole nine yards—classic food served fast from a fun menu with modern decor and a sports-bar ambience. For €10, you can try three tiny dishes and a glass of wine (daily 7:00–24:00, between Gran Via and Via Diputacio at Passeig de Gràcia 24, tel. 933-174-512).

Sandwich Shops

Bright, clean, and inexpensive sandwich shops are proudly holding the cultural line against the fast-food invasion hamburgerizing the rest of Europe. You'll find great sandwiches at **Pans & Company** and **Bocatta,** two chains with outlets all over town. Catalan sandwiches are made to order with crunchy French bread. Rather than butter, locals prefer *pa amb tomaquet* (pron. pah ahm too-MAH-kaht), a mix of crushed tomato and olive oil. Study the instructive multilingual menu fliers to understand your options.

Eating near the Harbor in Barceloneta

Barceloneta is a charming beach suburb of the big city. A grid plan of long, narrow, laundry-strewn streets surrounds the central Plaça Poeta Boscan. For an entertaining evening, wander around the perimeter of this slice-of-life square. Plenty of bakeries, pastry shops, and tapas bars ring a colorful covered produce market. Drop by the two places listed here or find your own restaurant (an unpleasant 15-min walk, Metro: Barceloneta, or taxi). During the day a lively produce market fills one end of the square. At night kids play soccer and ping-pong.

Cova Fumada is the neighborhood eatery. Josep Maria and his family serve famously fresh fish (Mon–Fri 17:30–20:30, closed Sat–Sun and Aug, Carrer del Baluarte 56, on corner at Carrer Sant Carles, tel. 932-214-061). Their *sardinas a la plancha* (grilled sardines, €3) are fresh and tasty. *Bombas* (potato croquets with pork, €1) are the house specialty. It's macho to have it *picante* (spicy with chili sauce); gentler taste buds prefer it *alioli,* with garlic cream. Catalan *bruschetta* is *pan tostado* (toast with oil and garlic, €1). Wash it down with *vino tinto* (house red wine, €0.60).

At **Bar Electricidad,** Lozano is the neighborhood source for cheap wine. Drop in. It's €1.10 per liter; the empty plastic water bottles are for takeaway. Try a €0.70 glass of Torroja Tinto, the best local red; Priorato Dulce, a wonderfully sweet red; or the homemade candy-in-heaven Vermouth (Mon–Sat 8:00–13:00

& 15:00–19:00, closed Sun, across square from Cova Fumada, Plaça del Poeta Bosca 61, tel. 932-215-017, NSE).

The Olympic Port, a swank marina district, is lined with harborside restaurants and people enjoying what locals claim is the freshest fish in town (a short taxi ride past Barceloneta from the center).

Tapas on Carrer Merce in the Gothic Quarter

While tapas aren't as popular in Catalunya as they are in the rest of Spain, Barcelona boasts great *tascas*—colorful local tapas bars. Get small plates (for maximum sampling) by asking for "*tapas,*" not "*raciónes.*" Glasses of *vino tinto* go for about €0.50.

While trendy uptown places are safer, better lit, and come with English menus and less grease, these places will stain your journal.

From the bottom of the Ramblas (near the Columbus Monument), hike east along Carrer Clave. Then follow the small street that runs along the right side of the church (Carrer Merce), stopping at the *tascas* that look fun. For restaurant dining in the area, Restaurante Agut (described above) comes with tablecloths and polite service. But for a montage of edible memories, wander Carrer Merce west to east considering these places and stopping wherever looks most inviting:

La Jarra is known for its tender *jamón canario con patatas* (baked ham with salty potatoes). Across the street, **La Pulperia** serves up fried fish. A block down the street, at **Tasca del Molinero** you can sauté your chorizo *al diablo* (sausage from hell). It's great with the regional specialty, *pan con tomate.* Across the street, **La Plata** keeps things wonderfully simple, serving extremely cheap plates of sardines, little salads, and small glasses of keg wine. **Tasca el Corral** serves mountain favorites from northern Spain such as *queso de cabrales* (very moldy cheese) and chorizo (spicy sausage) with *sidra* (apple wine sold by the €4 bottle). **Sidreria Tasca La Socarrena** (at #21), being a *sidreria,* is the only place that serves hard cider by the glass. At the end of Carrer Merce, **Bar Vendimia** serves up tasty clams and mussels (hearty *raciónes* for €3 a plate—they don't do smaller portions so order sparingly). Their *pulpo* (octopus) is more expensive and the house specialty. Carrer Ample and Carrer Gignas, the streets paralleling Carrer Merce inland, have more refined barhopping possibilities.

Transportation Connections—Barcelona

By train to: Lisboa (1/day, 17 hrs with change in Madrid, €107), **Madrid** (7/day, 7–9 hrs, €31–41), **Paris** (3/day, 11–15 hrs, €72–102, night train, reservation required), **Sevilla** (3/day, 11 hrs,

€38), **Granada** (2/day, 12 hrs, €46), **Málaga** (2/day, 14 hrs, €39), **Nice** (1/day, 12 hrs, €58, change in Cerbère), **Avignon** (5/day, 6–9 hrs, €38). Train info: tel. 902-240-202.

By bus to: Madrid (12/day, 8 hrs, half the price of a train ticket, departs from station Barcelona Nord at Metro: Marina).

By plane: To avoid 10-hour train trips, check the reasonable flights from Barcelona to Sevilla or Madrid. Iberia Air (tel. 902-400-500) and Air Europa (tel. 902-401-501 or 932-983-907) offer $80 flights to Madrid. Airport info: tel. 932-983-467.

NEAR BARCELONA: FIGUERES, CADAQUES, SITGES, AND MONTSERRAT

Four fine sights are day-trip temptations from Barcelona. For the ultimate in Surrealism and a classy but sleepy port-town getaway, consider a day or two in Cadaques with a stop at the Dalí Museum in Figueres. Figueres is an hour from Cadaques and two hours from Barcelona. For the consummate day at the beach, head 45 minutes south to the charming and gay-friendly resort town, Sitges. Pilgrims with hiking boots head an hour into the mountains for the most sacred spot in Catalunya—Montserrat.

FIGUERES

▲▲▲Dalí Museum—This is the essential Dalí sight. Inaugurated in 1974, the museum is a work of art in itself. Dalí personally conceptualized, designed, decorated, and painted it, intending to showcase his life's work. Highlights include the epic Palace of the Wind ceiling, the larger-than-life Mae West room (complete with fireplaces for nostrils), fun mechanical interactive art (Dalí was into action; bring lots of coins), and the famous squint-to-see Abraham Lincoln. Other major and fantastic works include the tiny *Spectre du Sex-Appeal*, *Soft Self Portrait*, and the red-shoe riddle of *Zapato y Vaso de Leche*. The only real historical context provided is on the easy-to-miss and unlabeled earphone info boxes in the Mae West room. While not in English, it's plenty entertaining (€9, daily July–Sept 9:00–19:45, Oct–June 10:30–17:45, last entry 45 min before closing, free bag check has your bag waiting for you at the exit, tel. 972-677-500). Dalí, who was born in Figueres in 1905, is buried in the museum. From the train station, follow Museu Dalí signs to the museum.

Connections: Figueres is an easy day trip from Barcelona or a stopover (trains from France stop in Figueres; lockers at station). Trains from Barcelona depart Sants Station or the RENFE station at Metro: Passeig de Gràcia (hrly, 2 hrs, €15 round-trip).

CADAQUES

Since the late 1800s, Cadaques has served as a haven for intellectuals and artists alike. Salvador Dalí, raised in nearby Figueres, brought international fame to this sleepy Catalan port in the 1920s. He and his wife, Gala, set up home and studio at the adjacent Port Lligat. Cadaques inspired Surrealists such as Eluard, Magritte, Duchamp, Man Ray, Buñuel, and García Lorca. Even Picasso was drawn to this enchanting coastal *cala* (cove), and he painted some of his Cubist works here.

In spite of its fame, Cadaques is laid-back and feels off the beaten path. If you want a peaceful beach-town escape near Barcelona, there's no better place. From the moment you descend into the town, taking in whitewashed buildings and deep blue waters, you'll be struck by the port's tranquility and beauty. Have a glass of *vino tinto* or *cremat* (a traditional brandy-and-coffee drink served flambé-style) at one of the seaside cafés and savor the lapping waves, brilliant sun, and gentle breeze.

The **Casa Museu Salvador Dalí,** once Dalí's home, gives fans a chance to explore his labyrinthine compound (€8, Tue–Sun 10:30–21:00, closes spring and fall at 18:00, closed Mon and winter, 30-min walk over hill from Cadaques to Port Lligat, limited visits, call to reserve a time, tel. 972-251-015).

The **TI** is at Carrer Cotxe 2 (Mon–Sat 9:00–14:00 & 16:00–21:00, Sun 10:00–13:00, shorter hours and closed Sun off-season, tel. 972-258-315).

Sleeping and Eating: These affordable options are conveniently located in the main square, around the corner from the TI and across from the beach—**Hostal Marina** (D-€27, Ds-€33, Db-€48, breakfast-€3, CC, Riera 3, tel. & fax 972-258-199) and **Hostal Cristina** (24 rooms, D-€36, Ds-€42, Db-€48, CC, La Riera, tel. & fax 972-258-138, David and Rebecca SE). **Hotel Llane Petit,** many of whose 37 spacious rooms have view balconies, is on the harbor, a 10-minute walk south of the city center (Db-€65–100, CC, air-con, elevator, Dr. Bartomeus 37, tel. 972-251-020, fax 972-258-778, http://interhotel.com/spain/es/hoteles/2645.html,SE).

For a fine dinner, try **Casa Anita,** down a narrow street from La Residencia. Sitting with others around a big table, you'll enjoy house specialties such as *calamars a la plancha* (grilled squid) and homemade *helado* (ice cream). Muscatel from a glass *porron* finishes off the tasty meal (Juan and family, tel. 972-258-471).

Connections: Cadaques is reached by Sarfa buses from Figueres (3/day, 50 min, €3) or from Barcelona (5/day, 2.5 hrs, €10.50, 2/day off-season, tel. 932-656-508).

Sights near Barcelona

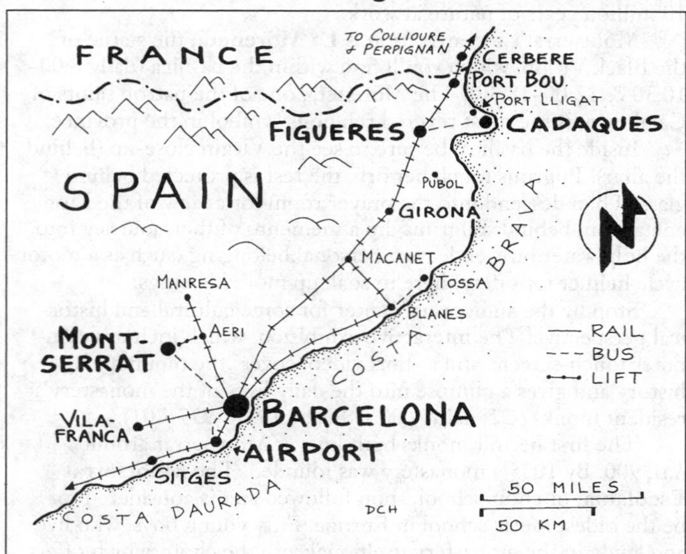

SITGES

Sitges is one of Catalunya's most popular resort towns and a world-renowned vacation destination among the gay community. Despite its jet-set status, the old town has managed to retain its charm. Nine beaches extend about 1.5 kilometers southward from town. Stroll down the seaside promenade, which stretches from the town to the end of the beaches. About halfway down, the crowds thin out, and the beaches become more intimate and cove-like. Along the way, restaurants and *chiringuitos* (beach-front bars) serve tapas, paella, and drinks. Take time to explore the old town's streets and shops. On the waterfront, you'll see the 17th-century Sant Bartomeu i Santa Tecla Church. It's a quick hike up for a view of town, sea, and beaches.

Connections: Southbound trains depart Barcelona from Sants Station and from the RENFE station at Plaça de Catalunya (hrly, €4.20 round-trip).

MONTSERRAT

Montserrat, with its unique rock formations and mountain monastery, is a popular day trip from Barcelona (50 km away). This has been Catalunya's most important pilgrimage site for a thousand years. Hymns ascribe this "serrated mountain" to little angels who carved the rocks with golden saws. Geologists blame 10 million years of nature at work.

Montserrat's top attraction is **La Moreneta,** the statue of the Black Virgin, which you'll find within the basilica (daily 8:00–10:30 & 12:00–18:30). The Moreneta, one of the patron saints of Catalunya, is the most revered religious symbol in the province.

Inside the basilica, be sure to see the Virgin close-up (behind the altar). Pilgrims touch her orb; the rest is protected behind glass. Then descend into the prayer room for a view of the Moreneta from behind. Pilgrims dip a memento of their journey into the holy water or even leave a personal belonging (such as a motorcycle helmet for safety) here to soak up more blessings.

Stop by the audiovisual center for some cultural and historical perspective. The interactive exhibition, which includes computer touch-screens and a short video, covers the mountain's history and gives a glimpse into the daily lives of the monastery's resident monks (€2, daily 9:00–18:00, tel. 938-777-701).

The first hermit monks built huts at Montserrat around A.D. 900. By 1025 a monastery was founded. The **Montserrat Escolania,** or choir school, soon followed and is considered to be the oldest music school in Europe. Fifty young boys, who live and study in the monastery itself, make up the choir, which offers performances (Mon–Sat at 13:00 & 18:45, Sun at 12:00, choir on vacation in July). Note: Catch the early show. If you attend the evening performance, you'll miss the last funicular down the mountain.

The **Museu de Montserrat** offers prehistoric tools, religious art, ancient artifacts, and a few paintings by masters such as El Greco, Caravaggio, Monet, Picasso, and Dalí (€4.50, July–Sept daily 9:30–19:00, Oct–June Mon–Fri 10:00–18:00, Sat–Sun 9:30–18:30).

The Moreneta was originally located in the **Santa Cova** (holy cave), a 40-minute hike down from the monastery. The path is lined with statues depicting scenes from the life of Christ. While the original Black Virgin statue is now in the basilica, a replica sits in the cave. A three-minute funicular ride cuts 20 minutes off the hike (€1.60 one-way, €2.50 round-trip).

The **Sant Joan funicular** (see below) continues another 250 meters above the monastery (€3.80 one-way, €6.10 round-trip). At the top of the funicular, a 20-minute walk takes you to the Sant Joan chapel and the starting point of numerous hikes, described in the TI's "Six Itineraries from the Monastery" brochure.

Sleeping: You can sleep in the old **monks' cloister**—now equipped with hotel and apartment facilities—far more comfortably than did its original inhabitants (D-€77, fine restaurant attached, tel. 938-777-701).

Connections: Ferrocarriles Catalanes trains leave hourly for Montserrat from Barcelona's Plaça Espanya (€12 round-trip, cash only, Eurailpass not valid, tel. 932-051-515). The Trans-Montserrat ticket includes the train trip, cable-car ride, and unlimited funicular rides (€20). The TotMontserrat ticket includes all of this, plus the museum and a self-serve lunch (€34). If you plan to do it all, you'll save a little money (roughly €1.80) with either ticket (buy at Plaça Espanya or TI). If you don't plan on taking either funicular, it's cheaper to buy just the train ticket (includes cable car).

To get from Barcelona to Montserrat, enter the Plaça Espanya Metro station next to the Plaza Hotel. Follow signs to the "FF de la Generalitat" underground station, then look for train line R5 (direction Manresa, departures at :36 past each hour, 45 min). Get off at the Aeri de Montserrat stop at the base of the mountain, where the cable car awaits (the round-trip from Barcelona includes cable-car ride, 4/hr). To be efficient, note that departures at :15 past the hour make the trains leaving at :36 past the hour. The last efficient departure is at 18:15. The last cable-car departs the monastery at 18:45 (17:45 off-season), entailing a 45-minute wait for the train.

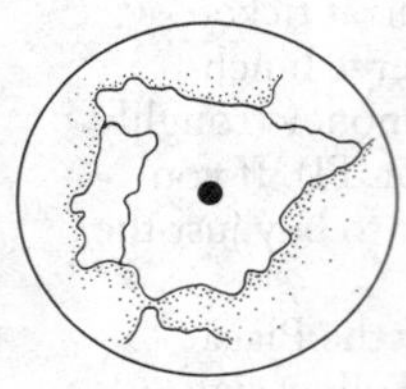

MADRID

Today's Madrid is upbeat and vibrant, still enjoying a post-Franco renaissance. You'll feel it. Even the living-statue beggars have a twinkle in their eyes.

Madrid is the hub of Spain. This modern capital—Europe's highest, at more than 615 meters (2,000 feet)—has a population of more than four million and is young by European standards. Only 400 years ago, King Philip II decided to move the capital of his empire from Toledo to Madrid. One hundred years ago Madrid had only 400,000 people, so 90 percent of the city is modern sprawl surrounding an intact, easy-to-navigate historic core.

Dive headlong into the grandeur and intimate charm of Madrid. The lavish Royal Palace, with its gilded rooms and frescoed ceilings, rivals Versailles. The Prado has Europe's top collection of paintings. The city's huge Retiro Park invites you for a shady siesta and a hopscotch through a mosaic of lovers, families, skateboarders, pets walking their masters, and expert bench-sitters. Save time for Madrid's elegant shops and people-friendly pedestrian zones.

The city is working hard—installing posts to keep cars off sidewalks, restoring old buildings, and making the streets safer after dark—to make Madrid more livable . . . and fun to visit.

On Sundays, cheer for the bull at a bullfight or bargain like mad at a mega–flea market. Lively Madrid has enough street-singing, barhopping, and people-watching vitality to give any visitor a boost of youth.

Planning Your Time

Madrid's top two sights, the Prado and the palace, are each worth a half day. On a Sunday (Easter–Oct), consider allotting extra time for a bullfight. Ideally, give Madrid two days and spend them this way:

Day 1: Breakfast of *churros* (see "Eating," below) before a brisk, good-morning-Madrid walk for 20 minutes from Puerta del Sol to the Prado; spend the rest of the morning at the Prado; afternoon siesta in Retiro Park or modern art at Centro Reina Sofia *(Guernica)* and/or Thyssen-Bornemisza Museum; dinner at 20:00, with tapas around Plaza Santa Ana (see "Tapas: The Madrid Pub-Crawl Dinner" on page 1178).

Day 2: Follow this book's "Puerta del Sol to Royal Palace Walk"; tour the Royal Palace, lunch near Plaza Mayor; afternoon free for other sights or shopping. Be out at the magic hour—before sunset—when beautifully lit people fill Madrid.

Note that Sunday is Market day (El Rastro flea market, stamp and coin market on Plaza Mayor) and that the Prado and the Thyssen-Bornemisza Museum close on Monday. For a good day-trip possibility from Madrid, see the next chapter ("Toledo").

Orientation

The historic center is enjoyably covered on foot. No major sight is more than a 20-minute walk or a €3.50 taxi ride from Puerta del Sol, Madrid's central square. Divide your time between the city's top three attractions: the Royal Palace, the Prado, and its barhopping, contemporary scene.

The Puerta del Sol marks the center of Madrid. The Royal Palace to the west and the Prado Museum and Retiro Park to the east frame Madrid's historic center. Southwest of Puerta del Sol is a 17th-century district with the slow-down-and-smell-the-cobbles Plaza Mayor and memories of pre-industrial Spain. North of Puerta del Sol runs Gran Vía, and between the two are lively pedestrian shopping streets. Gran Vía, bubbling with expensive shops and cinemas, leads to the modern Plaza de España. North of Gran Vía is the gritty Malasaña quarter, with its colorful small houses, shoemakers' shops, sleazy-looking hombres, milk vendors, bars, and hip night scene.

Tourist Information

Madrid has five TIs: **Plaza Mayor** at #3 (Mon–Sat 10:00–20:00, Sun 10:00–15:00, tel. 915-881-636); **near the Prado Museum** (Mon–Sat 9:00–19:00, Sun 9:00–15:00, Duque de Medinaceli 2, behind Palace Hotel, tel. 914-294-951); **Chamartin** train station (Mon–Sat 8:00–20:00, Sun 9:00–15:00, tel. 913-159-976); **Atocha** train station (daily 9:00–21:00); and at the **airport** (daily 8:00–20:00, tel. 913-058-656). The general tourist information number is 915-881-636 (www.munimadrid.es). During the summer, small

Madrid

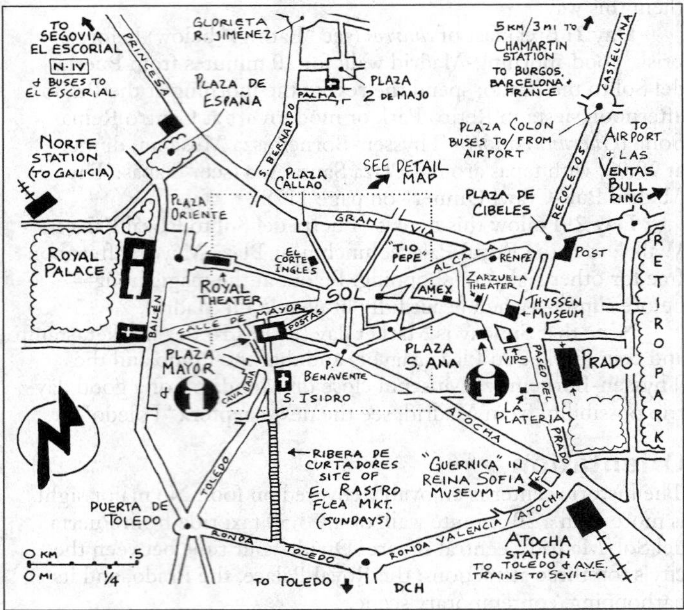

temporary stands with yellow umbrellas pop up at touristed places such as Puerta del Sol, and their yellow-shirted student guides are happy to help out lost tourists. Confirm your sightseeing plans and pick up a city map and the *Enjoy Madrid* publication. The free bus map has the most detailed map of the center. The TI has the latest on bullfights and zarzuela (the local light opera).

For entertainment listings, the TI's free *En Madrid/What's On* is not as good as the easy-to-decipher Spanish-language weekly entertainment guide *Guía del Ocio* (€1, sold at newsstands), which lists events, restaurants, and movies ("v.o." means a movie is in its original language rather than dubbed).

If you're heading to other destinations in Spain, ask any Madrid TI for free maps and brochures (ideally in English). Since many small-town TIs keep erratic hours and run out of these pamphlets, get what you can here. You can get schedules for buses and some trains, avoiding unnecessary trips to the various stations. The TI's free and amazingly informative *Mapa de Comunicaciones España* lists all the Turismos and highway SOS numbers with a road map of Spain. (If they're out, ask for the route map sponsored by the Paradores Hotel chain.)

Arrival in Madrid

By Train: Madrid's two train stations, Atocha and Chamartin, are both on subway lines with easy access to downtown Madrid. Each station has all the services. Chamartin handles most international trains. Atocha generally covers southern Spain including the AVE trains to Sevilla. Both stations offer long-distance trains *(largo recorrido)* as well as smaller, local trains (*regionales* and *cercanias*) to nearby destinations. To travel between Chamartin and Atocha, don't bother with the subway (which involves a transfer)—the *cercanias* trains are faster (6/hr, 12 min, €1.20, free with railpass—show it at ticket window in the middle of the turnstiles, departing from Atocha's track 2 and generally Chamartin's track 2 or 3—but check the Salidas Immediatas board for the next departure).

Chamartin: The TI is opposite track 19. The impressively large *Centro de Viajes/Travel Center* customer-service office is in the middle of the building. You can use the Club Intercity lounge if you have a first-class railpass and first-class seat or sleeper reservations. The *cercanias* platforms cluster around track 5. The station's Metro stop is Chamartin. (If you arrive by Metro at Chamartin, follow signs to *Información* to get to the lobby rather than signs to *Vias*, which send you directly to the platforms.)

Atocha: Atocha is split into two halves, connected by a corridor of shops. On one side are the slick AVE trains, some Talgo trains, and a botanical garden (in the towering old-station building, complete with birds, places to sit, and a cafeteria). On the other side of the station you'll find the local *cercanias*, *regionales*, some Talgos, and the Metro stop named Atocha RENFE. (Note that the stop named simply "Atocha" is a different Metro stop in Madrid—not at the train station.) Each side of the station has separate schedules; this can be confusing if you're in the wrong side of the building. The tiny TI handles tourist info only—not train info (Mon–Sat 9:00–21:00, Sun 9:00–13:00, 50 meters straight ahead of the Metro's turnstiles, ground floor). For train info, try the customer-service office called *Atención al Cliente* (daily 7:00–23:00); although there's one office for each half of the building, the office on the AVE side (just off the botanical garden) is more likely to speak English.

Atocha's Club AVE is a lounge reserved solely for AVE business or first-class ticket-holders or Eurailers with a reservation (likely closed in 2003 for renovation, daily 6:30–22:30, upstairs on AVE side of station, free drinks, newspapers, showers, and info service).

To buy tickets at Atocha for the local *cercanias* trains (for example, to Toledo), go to the middle of the *cercanias* side and get your ticket from ticket windows in the small rectangular offices (marked *Venta de Billetes sin reserva*). You can buy AVE and other long-distance train tickets in the bigger ticket offices in either half of the building; the airier *Taquillas* office on the AVE side (next to *Atención al Cliente* off the botanical garden) is more pleasant. Since station ticket offices can get really crowded, it's often quicker to buy your ticket at an English-speaking travel agency (such as in El Corte Inglés) or at the downtown RENFE office, which offers train information, reservations, tickets, and minimal English (Mon–Fri 9:30–20:00, closed Sat–Sun, CC, go in person, 2 blocks north of the Prado at Calle Alcala 44, tel. 902-240-202, www.renfe.es). For more details, see "Transportation Connections" at the end of the chapter.

By Bus: Madrid's three key bus stations, all connected by Metro, are Larrea (for Segovia, Metro: Príncipe Pío), Estación Sur Autobuses (for Toledo, Àvila, and Granada, on top Metro: Méndez Alvaro, tel. 914-684-200), and Estación Intercambiador (for El Escorial, in Metro: Moncloa). For details, see "Transportation Connections" at the end of this chapter.

By Plane: For information on Madrid's Barajas Airport, see "Transportation Connections" at the end of this chapter.

Getting around Madrid

By Subway: Madrid's subway is simple, speedy, and cheap (€1/ride, runs 6:00–1:30). The €5, 10-ride Metrobus ticket can be shared by several travelers and works on both the Metro and buses (sold at kiosks, tobacco shops, and in Metro). The city's broad streets can be hot and exhausting. A subway trip of even a stop or two saves time and energy. Most stations offer free maps (*navegamadrid*; www.metromadrid.es). Navigate by subway stops (shown on city maps). To transfer, follow signs to the next subway line (numbered and color-coded). End stops are used to indicate directions. Insert your ticket in the turnstile, then retrieve it as you pass through. Green *Salida* signs point to the exit. Using neighborhood maps and street signs to exit smartly can save lots of walking.

By Bus: City buses, while not as easy as the Metro, can be useful (bus maps at TI or info booth on Puerta del Sol, €0.90 tickets sold on bus, or €5 for a 10-ride Metrobus—see "By Subway," above; buses run 6:00–24:00).

By Taxi: Madrid's 15,000 taxis are easy to hail and reasonable (€1.40 drop, €0.70 per km; €4 supplement for airport, train/bus stations, bags, Sunday, and night service). Threesomes travel as cheaply by taxi as by subway. A ride from the Royal Palace to the Prado costs about €3.50.

Helpful Hints

Theft Alert: Be wary of pickpockets, anywhere, anytime, but particularly on Puerta del Sol (main square), the subway, and crowded streets. Assume a fight or any commotion is a scam to distract people about to become victims of a pickpocket. Wear your money belt. The small streets north of Gran Vía are particularly dangerous, even before nightfall. Muggings occur, but are rare. Victims of a theft can call 902-102-112 for help (English spoken).

Embassies: The U.S. Embassy is at Serrano 75 (tel. 915-872-200); the Canadian Embassy is at Nuñez de Balboa 35 (tel. 914-233-250).

Travel Agencies and Free Maps: The grand department store, El Corte Inglés, has two travel agencies (on first and seventh floors, Mon–Sat 10:00–22:00, just off Puerta del Sol) and gives out free Madrid maps (at the information desk, immediately inside the door, just off Puerta del Sol at intersection of Preciados and Tetuan; has post office and supermarket in basement). El Corte Inglés is taking over the entire intersection; the main store is the tallest building, with the biggest sign.

American Express: The AmEx office at Plaza Cortes 2 sells train and plane tickets, and even accepts Visa and MasterCard (Mon–Fri 9:00–19:30, Sat 10:00–14:00, closed Sun, 2 blocks from Metro: Banco de España, opposite Palace Hotel, tel. 913-225-445).

Books: For books in English, try **Fnac Callao** (Calle Preciados 8, tel. 915-956-190), **Casa del Libro** (English on ground floor in back, Gran Vía 29, tel. 915-212-219), and **El Cortes Inglés** (guidebooks and some fiction, in its Libreria branch kitty-corner from main store, see listing within "Travel Agencies," above).

Laundromat: The self-service Lavamatique is the most central, just west of the Prado (Mon–Sat 9:00–20:00, closed Sun, Cervantes 1).

Internet Access: The popular **easyEverything** offers 250 fast, cheap terminals 24/7 at Calle de la Montera (a block above Puerta del Sol and a block below piles of tattoo shops and prostitutes). **NavegaWeb,** centrally located at Gran Vía 30, is also good (daily 9:00–24:00). **BBiGG** is at Calle Alcalá 21 (daily 9:00–02:00, 300 terminals, near Puerta del Sol, tel. 916-647-700). **Zahara's** Internet café is at the corner of Gran Vía and Mesoneros (Mon–Fri 9:00–24:00, Sat–Sun 9:00–24:00).

Tours of Madrid

Madrid Vision Hop-On Hop-Off Bus Tours—Madrid Vision offers three different hop-on hop-off circuits of the city (historic, modern, and monuments). Buy a ticket (€10/1 day, €13/2 days) and you can hop from sight to sight as you like, listening to a recorded commentary along the way. Each route has about 15 stops and takes about 75 minutes, with buses departing every 10 or 15 minutes. The three routes intersect at the south side of Puerta del Sol (at #5, daily 10:00–19:00, until 21:00 in summer, tel. 917-791-888).

Walking Tours—British expatriate Stephen Drake-Jones gives entertaining, informative walks of historic old Madrid almost nightly (along with more specialized walks, such as Hemingway, Civil War, and Bloody Madrid). A historian with a passion for the memory of Wellington (the man who stopped Napoleon), Stephen is the founder and chairman of the Wellington Society. For €25 you become a member of the society for one year and get a free two-hour tour that includes stops at two bars for local drinks and tapas. Eccentric Stephen takes you back in time to sort out Madrid's Hapsburg and Bourbon history. Chairman Stephen likes his wine. If that's a problem, skip the tour. Tours start at the statue on Puerta del Sol (maximum 10 people, tel. 609-143-203 to confirm tour and reserve a spot, www.wellsoc.org, e-mail: chairman@wellsoc.org). Members of the Wellington Society can take advantage of Stephen's help line (if you're in a Spanish jam, call him to translate and intervene) and assistance by e-mail (for questions on Spain, your itinerary, and so on). Stephen also does private tours and day trips to great spots in the countryside for small groups (about €350 per group per day, explained on his Web site).

Typical Big Bus City Sightseeing Tours—Juliatours offers standard, inexpensive guided bus tours departing from Gran Vía 68 (tel. 915-599-605). Consider these tours: a three-hour city tour (€19, daily at 9:45 and 15:00); Madrid by Night (€12, a 2-hour floodlit overview, nightly at 20:30); Valley of the Fallen and El Escorial (€42, makes the day trip easy, covering both sights adequately with commentary en route, Tue–Sun at 8:45 and 15:00); and a marathon tour of El Escorial, Valley of the Fallen, and Toledo (€85, Tue–Sun at 8:30). If you want to pick up a rental car in Toledo, you could take this tour, stowing your luggage under the bus, then leave the tour at Toledo.

Introductory Walk: From Madrid's Puerta del Sol to the Royal Palace

Connect the sights with the following walking tour. Allow an hour for this one-kilometer (half-mile) walk, not including your palace visit.

▲▲Puerta del Sol—Named for a long-gone medieval gate with the sun carved onto it, Puerta del Sol is ground zero for Madrid. It's a hub for the Metro, buses, and pickpockets.

Stand by the statue of King Charles III and survey the square. Because of his enlightened urban policies, Charles III (who ruled until 1788) is affectionately called the "best mayor of Madrid." He decorated the city squares with fine fountains, got those meddlesome Jesuits out of city government, established the public school system, made the Retiro a public park rather than a royal retreat, and generally cleaned up Madrid.

Look behind the king. The statue of the bear pawing the strawberry bush and the madrono trees in the big planter boxes are symbols of the city. Bears used to live in the royal hunting grounds outside Madrid. And the madrono trees produce a berry that makes the traditional *madroño* liqueur.

The king faces a red-and-white building with a bell tower. This was Madrid's first post office, established by Charles III in the 1760s. Today it's the governor's office, though it's notorious for having been Franco's police headquarters. An amazing number of those detained and interrogated by the Franco police "tried to escape" by flying out the windows to their deaths. Notice the hats of the civil guardsmen at the entry. It's said the hats have square backsides so the men can lean against the wall while enjoying a cigarette.

Crowds fill the square on New Year's Eve as the rest of Madrid watches the action on TV. As Spain's "Big Ben" atop the governor's office chimes 12 times, Madrileños eat one grape for each ring to bring good luck through the coming year.

Cross Calle Mayor. Look at the curb directly in front of the entrance of the governor's office. The scuffed-up marker is "kilometer zero," marking the center of Spain. To the right of the entrance, the plaque on the wall marks the spot where the war against Napoleon started. Napoleon wanted his brother to be king of Spain. Trying to finagle this, Napoleon brought nearly the entire Spanish royal family to France for negotiations. An anxious crowd gathered outside this building awaiting word of the fate of their royal family. This was just after the French Revolution, and there was a general nervousness between France and Spain. When locals heard that Napoleon had appointed his brother as the new king of Spain, they gathered angrily in the streets. The French guard simply massacred the mob. Goya, who worked just up the street, observed the event and captured the tragedy in his paintings *2nd of May, 1808* and *3rd of May, 1808*, now in the Prado.

Walking from Puerta del Sol to Plaza Mayor: On the corner of Calle Mayor and Puerta del Sol, across from McDonald's, is the busy *confiteria* Salon la Mallorquina (daily 9:00–21:00). Cross Calle Mayor to go inside. The shop is famous for its sweet Napolitana cream-filled pastry (€1) and savory, beef-filled *agujas* pastries (€1.50)—if you can't finish yours, the beggar at the front door would love to. See the racks with goodies hot out of the oven. Look back toward the entrance and notice the tile above the door

Heart of Madrid

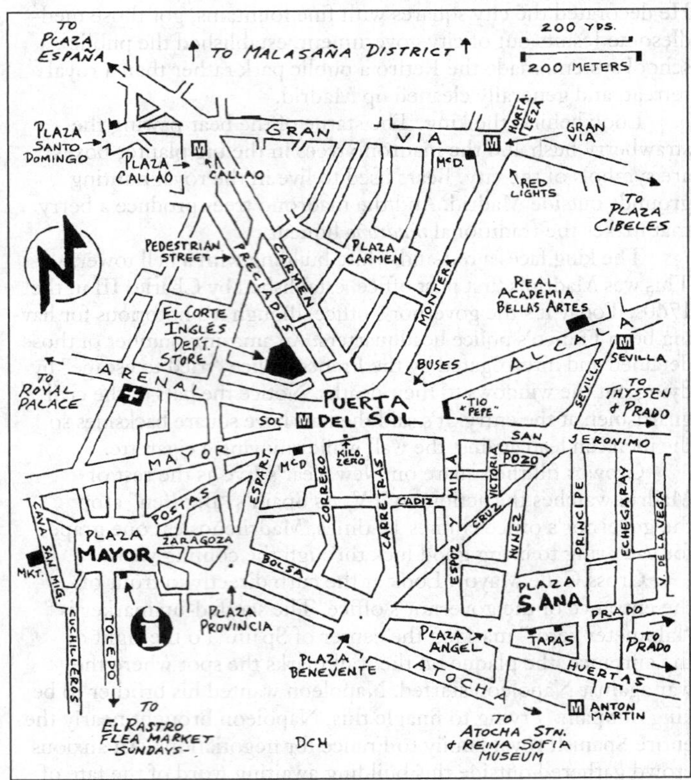

with the 18th-century view of the Puerta del Sol. Compare this with today's view out the door. This was before the square was widened, when a church stood where the Tío Pepe sign stands today. The French used this church to detain local patriots awaiting execution. (The venerable Tío Pepe sign, advertising a famous sherry for over 100 years, was Madrid's first billboard.)

Cross busy Calle Mayor (again), round McDonald's, and veer left up the pedestrian alley called Calle de Postas. The street sign shows the post coach heading for that famous first post office. Medieval street signs included pictures so the illiterate could "read" them. Fifty meters up the street, at Calle San Cristobal, drop into Pans & Company, a popular sandwich chain. Pick up their translated flier illustrating that Spain is a country of four languages: Catalan (spoken in and around Barcelona), Euskara

(Basque), Galego (a Gaelic language spoken in northwest Spain—Galicia), and Castilian (what we call Spanish). From here, hike up Calle San Cristobal. Within two blocks, you'll pass the local feminist bookshop (Libreria Mujeres) and reach a small square. At the square notice the big, brick 17th-century Ministry of Foreign Affairs building (with the pointed spire)—originally a jail for rich prisoners who could afford the cushy cells. Turn right and walk down Calle de Zaragoza under the arcade into . . .

Plaza Mayor—This square, built in 1619, is a vast, cobbled, traffic-free chunk of 17th-century Spain. Each side of the square is uniform, as if a grand palace were turned inside out. The statue is of Philip III, who ordered the square's construction. Upon this stage, much Spanish history was played out: bullfights, fires, royal pageantry, and events of the gruesome Inquisition. Reliefs serving as seatbacks under the lampposts tell the story. During the Inquisition, many were tried here. The guilty were paraded around the square (bleachers were built for bigger audiences, the wealthy rented balconies) with billboards listing their many sins. They were then burned. The fortunate were slowly strangled as they held a crucifix, hearing the reassuring words of a priest as this life was squeezed out of them.

The square is painted a democratic shade of burgundy—the result of a citywide vote. Since Franco's death in 1975, there's been a passion for voting here. Three different colors were painted as samples on the walls of this square, and the city voted for its favorite.

A stamp-and-coin market bustles here on Sundays from 10:00 to 14:00, and on any day it's a colorful and affordable place to enjoy a cup of coffee. Throughout Spain, lesser *plazas mayores* provide peaceful pools in the river of Spanish life. The TI is at #3, on the south side of the square. The building decorated with painted figures, on the north side of the square, is the Casa de la Panaderia, which used to house the Bakers' Guild (interior closed to public).

The Torre del Oro Bar Andalu is a good place for a drink to finish off your Plaza Mayor visit (northwest corner of square, to the left of the Bakers' Guild, daily 8:00–15:00 & 18:00–24:00). This bar is a temple to bullfighting. Warning: They push expensive tapas on tourists. A *caña* (small beer) shouldn't cost more than €1.50. The bar's ambience is "Andalu" (Andalusian). Look under the stuffed head of Barbero the bull. At eye level you'll see a *puntilla*, the knife used to put a bull out of its misery at the arena. This was the knife used to kill Barbero.

Notice the breath-taking action caught in the bar's many photographs. At the end of the bar in a glass case is the "suit of lights" the great El Cordobes wore in his ill-fated 1967 fight.

From Plaza Mayor to the Royal Palace

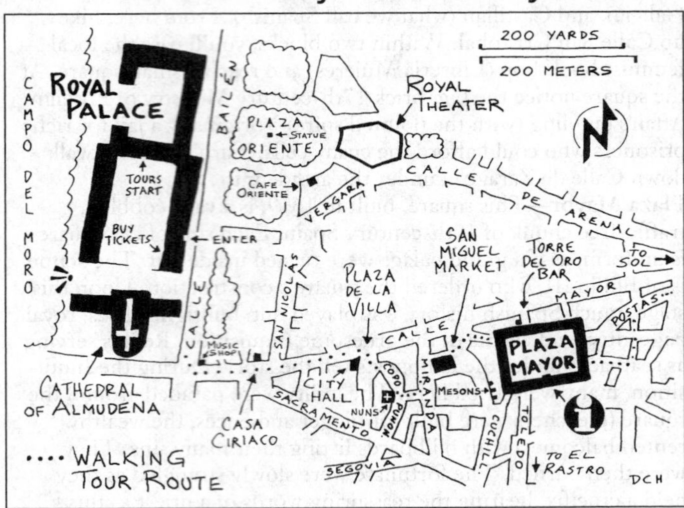

With Franco in attendance, El Cordobes went on and on, long after he could have ended the fight, until finally the bull gored him. El Cordobes survived; the bull didn't. Find Franco with El Cordobes at the far end, to the left of Segador the bull. Under the bull is a photo of El Cordobes' illegitimate son, El Cordobes, kissing a bull. Disowned by El Cordobes and using his dad's famous name after a court battle, El Cordobes is one of this generation's top fighters.

Walking from Plaza Mayor to the Royal Palace: Leave Plaza Mayor on Calle Cuidad Rodrigo (far right corner from where you entered the square, and to your right as you exit Torre del Oro). You'll pass a series of fine turn-of-the-20th-century storefronts and shops such as the recommended Casa Rua, famous for its cheap *bocadillos de calamares*—fried squid-ring sandwiches.

From the archway you'll see the covered Mercado de San Miguel (green iron posts, on left). Before you enter the market, look left down the street Cava de San Miguel. If you like sangria and singing, come back around 22:00 and visit one of the *mesones* (such as Guitarra, Tortilla, or Boqueron) that line the street. These cavelike bars stretch way back and get packed with locals who—emboldened by sangria, the setting, and Spain—might suddenly just start singing. It's a lowbrow, electric keyboard, karaoke-type ambience, best on Friday and Saturday nights.

Wander through the newly renovated produce market and

consider buying some fruit (Mon–Fri 9:00–14:30 & 17:15–20:15, Sat 9:00–14:30, closed Sun). Leave the market on the opposite (downhill) side and follow the pedestrian lane left. At the first corner, turn right, and cross the small plaza to the modern brick convent. The door on the right says *venta de dulces;* to buy inexpensive sweets from the cloistered nuns, buzz the *monjas* button, then wait patiently for the sister to respond over the intercom. Say "*dulces*" (pron. DOOL-thays) and she'll let you in (Mon–Sat 9:30–13:00 & 16:00–18:30, closed Sun). When the lock buzzes, push open the door and follow the sign to *torno,* the lazy Susan that lets the sisters sell their baked goods without being seen (smallest quantities: half, or *medio,* kilo). Of the many choices (all good), consider *pastas de almendra* (crumbly) or *mantecados de yema* (moist and eggy).

Follow Calle del Codo (where those in need of bits of armor shopped—see the street sign) uphill around the convent to Plaza de la Villa, the city-hall square. Ahead, four flags—of city, state, nation, and Europe—grace the city hall. The statue in the garden is of Don Bazan—mastermind of the Christian victory over the Muslims at the naval battle of Lepanto in 1571. This pivotal battle, fought off the coast of Greece, ended the Muslim threat to Christian Europe. The mayor's office is behind the don.

From here, busy Calle Mayor leads downhill a couple more blocks to the Royal Palace. Halfway down (on the left) there's a tiny square opposite the recommended Casa Ciriaco restaurant (#84). The statue memorializes the 1906 anarchist bombing that killed 23 people as the royal couple paraded by on their wedding day. While the crowd was throwing flowers, an anarchist threw a bouquet lashed to a bomb from a balcony of #84 (the building was a hotel at the time). Photos of the event hang just inside the door of the restaurant.

Continue down Calle Mayor. Within a couple of blocks you'll come to a busy street, Calle de Bailen. (The Garrido-Bailen music store is *the* place to stock up on castanets, unusual flutes, and Galician bagpipes.) Across the busy street is the **Cathedral of Almudena,** Madrid's new cathedral. Built between 1883 and 1993, its exterior is a contemporary mix and its interior is neo-Gothic with a colorful ceiling, glittering 5,000-pipe organ, and the 13th-century coffin (empty, painted leather on wood, in a chapel behind the altar) of Madrid's patron saint, Isidoro. Next to the cathedral is the . . .

▲▲Royal Palace (Palacio Real)—Europe's third-greatest palace (after Versailles and Vienna's Schönbrunn) with arguably the most lavish interior, is packed with tourists and royal antiques. After a fortress burned down on this site, King Phillip V commissioned this huge 18th-century palace as a replacement. Phillip V was very

French (born in Versailles). He ruled Spain for 40 years and never learned to speak Spanish. He ordered this palace built to be his own Versailles. It's big—over 2,000 rooms with tons of lavish tapestries, a king's ransom of chandeliers, priceless porcelain, and bronze decor covered in gold leaf. While the royal family lives in a mansion a few kilometers away, the place still functions as a royal palace and is used for formal state receptions and tourist daydreams.

A simple one-floor, 24-room, one-way circuit is open to the public. You can wander on your own or join an English tour (get time of next tour and decide as you buy your ticket; tours depart about every 20 min). The tour guides, like the museum guidebook, show a passion for meaningless data. Your ticket includes the armory and the pharmacy, both on the courtyard and worth a quick look (€6 without a tour, €7 with a tour, April–Sept Mon–Sat 9:00–19:00, Sun 9:00–16:00; Oct–March Mon–Sat 9:30–18:00, Sun 9:00–15:00, last tickets sold an hour before closing, palace can close without warning if needed for a royal function; note the beer-stein urinals—the rage in Madrid—in the WC just past the ticket booth; Metro: Opera, tel. 915-597-404 or 914-548-800). The €2 audioguides cover only marginally more of interest than what I describe below (and would never mention beer-stein urinals). The palace is most crowded on Wednesdays, when it's free for locals.

If you tour on your own, here are a few details beyond what you'll find on the little English descriptions posted in each room:

The Palace Lobby: In the old days, horse-drawn carriages would drop you off here. Today, a sign divides the visitors waiting for a tour and those going in alone.

The Grand Stairs: Fancy carpets are rolled down (notice the little metal bar-holding hooks) for formal occasions. At the top of the first landing, the blue and red coat of arms is of the current—and popular—constitutional monarch, Juan Carlos. While Franco chose him to be the next dictator, J.C. knew Spain was ripe for democracy. Rather than become "Juan the Brief" (as some were nicknaming him), he turned real power over to the parliament. You'll see his (figure) head on the back of the Spanish euro coin. At the top of the stairs (before entering first room, right of door) is a white marble bust of J.C.'s great-great-g-g-g-great-grandfather Phillip V. The grandson of France's King Louis XIV, he began the Bourbon dynasty in Spain in 1700. That dynasty survives today with Juan Carlos.

Guard Room: The guards hung out here. Notice the clocks. Charles IV, a great collector, amassed over 700—all in working order and displayed throughout the palace.

Hall of Columns: Originally a ballroom, today this room is used for formal ceremonies. (For example, this is the place where Spain formally joined the European Union in 1985—see plaque on far wall.) The tapestries (like most you'll see in the palace) are 17th-century Belgian.

Throne Room: Red velvet walls, lions, and frescoes of Spanish scenes symbolize the monarchy in this rococo riot. The chandeliers are the best in the house. The thrones are only from 1977. This is where ambassadors give their credentials to the king, who receives them relatively informally . . . standing rather than seated in the throne. Two rooms later you'll find . . .

Charles IV Antechamber: The four paintings are of King Charles IV (looking a bit like a dim-witted George Washington) and his wife (who wore the pants in the palace)—all originals by Goya. Velázquez's masterpiece *Las Meninas* originally hung here. The ceiling fresco, the last great work by Tiepolo, celebrates the vast Spanish empire—upon which the sun also never set. Find the American Indian (hint: follow the rainbow to the macho, red-caped conquistador). The clock, showing Cronus, god of time, in marble, bronze, and wood, sits on a music box. The gilded decor you see throughout the palace is bronze with gold leaf.

Gasparini Room: This room, its painted stucco ceiling and inlaid Spanish marble floor restored in 1992, was the royal dressing room. The Asian influence was trendy at the time. Dressing, for a divine monarch, was a public affair. The court bigwigs would assemble here as the king, standing on a platform—notice the height of the mirrors—would pull on his leotards. In the next room, the silk wallpaper is new; notice the J.C.S. initials of King Juan Carlos and Queen Sofia. Passing through the silk room, you reach the . . .

Charles III Salon: This salon, decorated in 19th-century neoclassical style, is dominated by a chandelier in the shape of the fleur-de-lis (symbol of the Bourbon family). The thick walls separating each room hide service corridors for servants who scurried about generally unseen.

Porcelain Room: The 300 separate plates that line this room were disassembled for safety during the Civil War. (Find the little screws in the greenery that hide the seams.) The Yellow Room leads to the . . .

Gala Dining Room: Five or six times a year the king entertains up to 150 guests at this bowling lane–size table—which can be extended to the length of the room. Find the two royal chairs. (Hint: With the modesty necessary for 21st-century monarchs, they are just a tad higher than the rest.) The parquet floor was the preferred dancing surface when balls were held in this fabulous room. The table in the next room would be lined with an exorbitantly caloric dessert buffet.

Cinema Room: In the early 20th century the royal family enjoyed "Sunday afternoons at the movies" here. Today it stores glass cases filled with the silver tableware used for fancy dining functions.

Stradivarius Room: The queen likes classical music. When you perform for her, do it with these precious 300-year-old violins. About 300 Antonius Stradivarius–made instruments survive. This is the only matching quartet: two violins, a viola, and a cello. The next room was the children's room—with kid-sized musical instruments.

Royal Chapel: The Royal Chapel is used only for funerals. The royal coffin sits here before making the sad trip to El Escorial to join the rest of Spain's past royalty.

Billiards and Smoking Rooms: The billiards room and the smoking room were for men only. The porcelain and silk of the smoking room imitates a Chinese opium den which, in its day, was furnished only with pillows.

Queen's Boudoir: The next room was for the ladies, decorated just after Pompeii was excavated and therefore in fanciful ancient-Roman style. You'll exit down the same grand stairway you climbed 24 rooms ago.

Across the courtyard is a fine park view and the **armory** displaying the armor and swords of El Cid, Ferdinand, Charles V, and Phillip II. Near the exit is a cafeteria and a bookstore, which has a variety of books on Spanish history.

As you leave the palace, walk around the corner to the left along the palace exterior to the grand yet people-friendly Plaza de Oriente. Throughout Europe, energetic governments are turning formerly car-congested wastelands into public spaces like this. Madrid's latest mayor is nicknamed "the mole" for all the digging he's doing. Where's all the traffic? Under your feet.

To return to Puerta del Sol: With your back to the palace, face the equestrian statue of Philip IV and (behind the statue) the Royal Theater (*Teatro Real*, neoclassical, rebuilt in 1997, open for visits Tue–Fri at 13:00, Sat–Sun at 11:30, closed Mon, tel. 915-160-660). Walk behind the Royal Theater (on the right, passing Café de Oriente—a favorite with theater-goers) to another square where you'll find the Opera Metro stop and Calle Arenal which leads back to Puerta del Sol.

Sights—Madrid's Museum Neighborhood

Three great museums are in east Madrid. From the Prado to the Thyssen-Bornemisza Museum is a five-minute walk; Prado to Centro Reina Sofia is a 10-minute walk.

Museum Pass: If you plan to visit all three museums, you'll save 25 percent by buying the Paseo del Arte combo-ticket (€7.75, sold at each museum). Note that the Prado and Centro Reina Sofia museums are free on Saturday afternoon and Sunday (and anytime for those under 18 and over 65); the Prado and Thyssen-Bornemisza are closed Monday; and the Reina Sofia is closed Tuesday.

▲▲▲**Prado Museum**—The Prado holds my favorite collection of paintings anywhere. With more than 3,000 canvases, including entire rooms of masterpieces by Velázquez, Goya, El Greco, and Bosch, it's overwhelming. Pick up the English floor plan as you enter. Take a tour or buy a guidebook (or bring along the Prado chapter from *Rick Steves' Mona Winks*—available without maps and photos for free at www.ricksteves.com/prado). Focus on the Flemish and northern (Bosch, Dürer, Rubens), the Italian (Fra Angelico, Raphael, Titian), and the Spanish art (El Greco, Velázquez, Goya).

Follow Goya through his stages, from cheery *(The Parasol)* to political (*2nd of May, 1808* and *3rd of May, 1808*) to dark ("Negras de Goya": e.g., *Saturn Devouring His Children*). In each stage, Goya asserted his independence from artistic conventions. Even the standard court portraits from his "first" stage reflect his politically liberal viewpoint, subtly showing the vanity and stupidity of his royal patrons by the looks in their goony eyes. His political stage, with paintings such as the *3rd of May, 1808*, depicting a massacre of Spaniards by Napoleon's troops, makes him one of the first artists with a social conscience. Finally, in his gloomy "dark stage," Goya probed the inner world of fears and nightmares, anticipating our modern-day preoccupation with dreams. Also, seek out Bosch's *The Garden of Earthly Delights*—a three-paneled altarpiece showing creation, the "transparency of earthly pleasures," and the resulting hell. Bosch's self-portrait looks out from hell (with the birds leading naked people around the brim of his hat), surrounded by people suffering eternal punishments appropriate to their primary earthly excesses.

The art is constantly rearranged by the Prado's management, so even the Prado's own maps and guidebooks are out of date. Regardless of the latest location, most art is grouped by painter, and better guards can point you in the right direction if you say, "*¿Dónde está . . . ?*" and the painter's name as Españoled as you can (e.g., Titian is "Ticiano" and Bosch is "El Bosco"). The Murillo entrance—at the end closest to the Atocha train station—often has shorter lines. Lunchtime, from 14:00 to 16:00, is least crowded (€3; free on Sat afternoon after 14:30, all day Sun, and to anyone under 18 and over 65; covered by €7.75 Paseo del Arte combo-ticket; Tue–Sat 9:00–19:00, Sun 9:00–14:00, closed Mon, last

Madrid's Museum Neighborhood

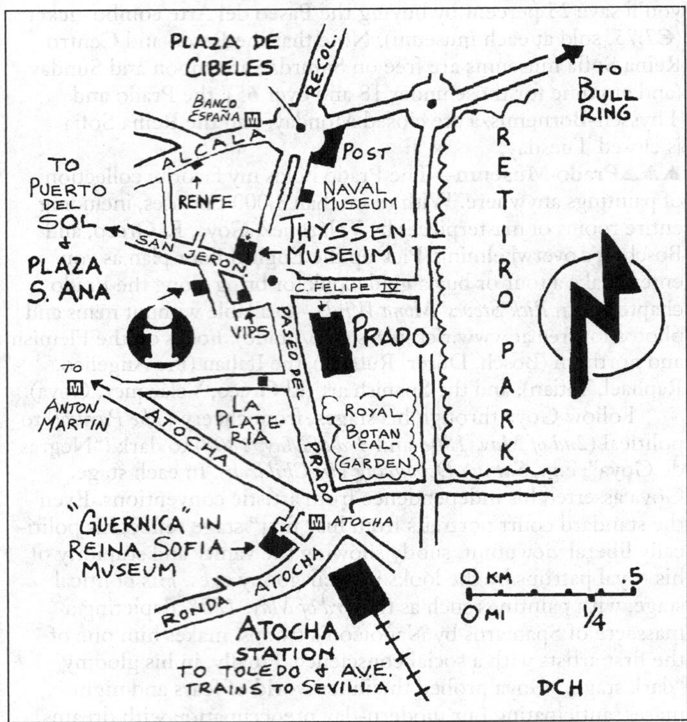

entry 30 min before closing; free, mandatory baggage check after your things are scanned just like at the airport; no water bottles inside; photos allowed but no flash; cafeteria at Murillo end; Paseo de Prado, Metro: Banco de España or Atocha—each a 15-min walk from the museum, tel. 913-302-800, http://museoprado.mcu.es). Cabs picking you up at the Prado are likely to overcharge. Insist on the fare meter.

While you're in the neighborhood, consider a visit to the Charles III Botanical Garden (listed under "Sights Near the Prado," below).

▲▲Thyssen-Bornemisza Museum—Locals call this stunning museum simply the Thyssen (pron. tee-sun). It displays the impressive collection that Baron Thyssen (a wealthy German married to a former Miss Spain) sold to Spain for $350 million. It's basically minor works by major artists and major works by minor artists (major works by major artists are in the Prado).

But art lovers appreciate how the good baron's art complements the Prado's collection by filling in where the Prado is weak (Impressionism). For a delightful walk through art history, ride the elevator to the top floor and do the rooms in numerical order from Primitive Italian (room 1) to Surrealism and Pop Art (room 48). It's kitty-corner from the Prado at Paseo del Prado 8 in Palacio de Villahermosa (€5, or €7 to add current exhibition; covered by €7.75 Paseo del Arte combo-ticket, children under 12 enter free, Tue–Sun 10:00–19:00, closed Mon, ticket office closes at 18:30, audioguide-€3, free baggage check, café, shop, no photos, Metro: Banco de España or Atocha, tel. 914-203-944, www.museothyssen.org). If you're tired, hail a cab at the gate and zip straight to the Centro Reina Sofia.

▲▲Centro Reina Sofia—In this exceptional modern-art museum, ride the fancy glass elevator to the second floor and follow the room numbers for art from 1900 to 1950. The fourth floor continues the collection from 1950 to 1980. The museum is most famous for Picasso's *Guernica* (room 6), an epic painting showing the horror of modern war. Guernica, a village in northern Spain, was the target of the world's first saturation-bombing raid, approved by Franco and carried out by Hitler. Notice the two rooms of studies for *Guernica,* filled with iron-nail tears and screaming mouths. *Guernica* was exiled to America until Franco's death, and now it reigns as Spain's national piece of art.

The museum also houses an easy-to-enjoy collection by other modern artists, including more of Picasso (3 rooms divide his art into pre–civil war, *Guernica,* and post–civil war) and a mind-bending room of Dalís (room 10). Enjoy a break in the shady courtyard before leaving (€3, free Sat afternoon after 14:30 and all day Sun, always free to those under 18 and over 65; covered by €7.75 Paseo del Arte combo-ticket; hardworking audioguide-€2.50, Mon and Wed–Sat 10:00–21:00, Sun 10:00–14:30, closed Tue, good brochure, no photos, no tours in English, free baggage check, Santa Isabel 52, Metro: Atocha, across from Atocha train station, look for exterior glass elevators, tel. 914-675-062, http://museoreinasofia.mcu.es).

Sights Near the Prado

▲Retiro Park—Siesta in this 350-acre green and breezy escape from the city. At midday on Saturday and Sunday, the area around the lake becomes a street carnival, with jugglers, puppeteers, and lots of local color. These peaceful gardens offer great picnicking and people-watching. From the Retiro Metro stop, walk to the big lake (El Estanque), where you can cheaply rent a rowboat. Past the lake, a grand boulevard of statues leads to the Prado.

Charles III's Botanical Garden (Real Jardín Botánico)—After your Prado visit, you can take a lush and fragrant break in this sculpted park, wandering among trees from around the world. The flier in English explains that this is actually more than a park—it's a museum of plants (€1.50, daily 10:00–20:00, until 18:00 in winter, entry opposite Prado's Murillo entry, Plaza de Murillo 2).

Naval Museum—This tells the story of Spain's navy from the Armada to today (free, Tue–Sun 10:00–14:00, closed Mon, a block north of the Prado across boulevard from Thyssen-Bornemisza Museum).

More Sights—Madrid

Chapel San Antonio de la Florida—Goya's tomb stares up at a splendid cupola filled with his own frescoes. On June 13, local ladies line up here to ask St. Anthony for a boyfriend, while outside a festival rages, with street musicians, food, and fun (€2, Tue–Fri 10:00–14:00 & 16:00–20:00, Sat–Sun 10:00–14:00, closed Mon, July and Aug only 10:00–14:00, Glorieta de San Antonio de la Florida, Metro: Príncipe Pío, tel. 915-420-722). This chapel is near the bus station with service to Segovia. If you're day-tripping to Segovia, it's easy to stop by before or after your trip.

Next door to the chapel is Restaurante Casa Mingo, popular for its cheap chicken, chorizo, and *cabrales* cheese served with cider. Ask the waiter to pour the cider for you. For dessert, try the *tarta de Santiago* almond cake (daily 11:00–24:00, Paseo de la Florida 34, tel. 915-477-918).

Royal Tapestry Factory (Real Fabrica de Tapices)—Have a look at the traditional making of tapestries (€2, some English tours, Mon–Fri 10:00–14:00, closed Sat–Sun and Aug, Calle Fuenterrabia 2, Metro: Menendez Pelayo, take Gutenberg exit, tel. 914-340-550, call before visiting as it has been closed for restoration). You can actually order a tailor-made tapestry (starting at $10,000).

Moncloa Tower (Faro de Moncloa)—This tower's elevator zips you up 92 meters (300 feet) to the best skyscraper view in town (€1.20, Tue–Fri 10:00–14:00 & 17:00–19:00, Sat–Sun 10:30–17:30, closed Mon, Metro: Moncloa, tel. 915-448-104). If you're going to El Escorial by bus, this is a convenient sight near the bus station.

Teleferico—For city views, ride this cable car from downtown over Madrid's sprawling city park to Casa de Campo (€2.60 one-way, €3.60 round-trip, daily from 11:00, fall and winter from 12:00, departs from Paseo del Pintor Rosales, Metro: Arguelles, tel. 915-417-450, www.teleferico.com). Do an immediate round-trip to skip Casa de Campo's strange mix of rental rowboats, prostitutes, a zoo, addicts, and an amusement park.

Shopping

Shoppers focus on the colorful pedestrian area between Gran Vía and Puerta del Sol. The giant Spanish department store El Corte Inglés is a block off Puerta del Sol and a handy place to pick up just about anything you need (Mon–Sat 10:00–21:30, closed Sun, free maps at info desk, supermarket in basement).

▲**El Rastro**—Europe's biggest flea market, held on Sundays and holidays, is a field day for shoppers, people-watchers, and thieves (9:00–15:00, best before 12:00). Thousands of stalls titillate more than a million browsers with mostly new junk. If you brake for garage sales, you'll pull a U-turn for El Rastro. Start at the Plaza Mayor and head south or take the subway to Tirso de Molina. Hang on to your wallet. Munch on a *pepito* (meat-filled pastry). Europe's biggest stamp market thrives simultaneously on Plaza Mayor.

Nightlife

▲▲▲**Bullfight**—Madrid's Plaza de Toros hosts Spain's top bullfights on Sundays and holidays from March through mid-October and nearly every day during the San Isidro festival (May through mid-June—generally sold out long in advance). Fights start between 17:00 and 19:00 (early in spring and fall, late in summer). Tickets range from €3.50 to €100. There are no bad seats at the Plaza de Toros; paying more gets you in the shade and/or closer to the gore. (The action often intentionally occurs in the shade to reward the expensive-ticket holders.) To be close to the bullring, choose areas 8, 9, and 10; for shade 1, 2, 9, 10; for shade/sun: 3, 8; for the sun and cheapest seats: 4, 5, 6, 7. (Note that fights advertised as "Gran Novillada con Picadores" feature younger bulls and rookie matadors.)

Hotels and booking offices are convenient but they add 20 percent and don't sell the cheap seats. Telephone both offices before you buy (Plaza Carmen 3—daily 9:30–13:30 & 16:00–19:00, tel. 915-312-732 and Calle Victoria 3—daily 10:00–14:00 & 17:00–19:00, tel. 915-211-213). To save money, stand in the bullring ticket line. About a thousand tickets are held back to be sold on the five days leading up to a fight, including the day of the fight. The bullring is at Calle Alcala 237 (Metro: Ventas, tel. 913-562-200, www.las-ventas.com).

Madrid's **bullfighting museum** is not as good as Sevilla's or Ronda's (Museo Taurino, at the back of bullring, free, Tue–Fri & Sun 9:30–14:30, closed Sat–Mon and early on fight days, tel. 917-251-857).

▲▲Zarzuela—For a delightful look at Spanish light opera that even English speakers can enjoy, try zarzuela. Guitar-strumming Napoleons in red capes; buxom women with masks, fans, and castanets; Spanish-speaking pharaohs; melodramatic spotlights; and aficionados clapping and singing along from the cheap seats where the acoustics are best—this is zarzuela ...the people's opera. Originating in Madrid, zarzuela is known for its satiric humor and surprisingly good music. The season, which runs from January through June, features a mix of zarzuela and traditional opera. The rest of the year is devoted to ballet. You can buy tickets at Theater Zarzuela (€8–28, box office open 12:00–18:00 for advance tickets or until showtime for that day, Jove-llanos 4, near the Prado, Metro: Banco de España, tel. 915-245-400, http://teatrodelazarzuela.mcu.es). The TI's monthly guide has a special zarzuela listing.

▲Flamenco—Madrid has two easy and affordable options for taking in a flamenco performance.

Taberna Casa Patas attracts big-name flamenco artists. At this intimate (30-table) and smoky venue you'll pay €25 (for cover and first drink) and 90 minutes later you'll know why this place is called, literally, "the house of legs." Since this is for locals as well as tour groups, the flamenco is contemporary and may be jazzier than your notion—it depends on who's performing (Mon–Thu at 22:00, Fri–Sat at 21:00 and 24:00, closed Sun, reservations are smart, Canizares 10, tel. 914-298-471 or 913-690-496, www.casapatas.com). Its restaurant is a logical place for dinner (Mon–Sat from 20:00) before the show or, since this place is three blocks south of the recommended Plaza Santa Ana tapas bars, this could be your post-tapas-crawl entertainment.

Las Carboneras is more downscale—an easygoing, folksy little place a few steps from Plaza Mayor with a nightly 60-minute flamenco show (€15 includes a stool in the back and a drink, €32 gets you a table up front with dinner and unlimited cheap drinks, Mon–Thu at 22:30, Fri–Sat at 23:00, closed Sun, earlier shows possible if a group books in advance, reservations possible but generally not necessary, Plaza del Conde de Miranda 1, tel. 915-428-677).

Regardless of what your hotel receptionist may want to sell you, other flamenco places like Arco de Cuchilleros (Calle de los Cuchilleros 7), Café de Chinitas (Calle Torija 7, just off Plaza Mayor), and Torres Bermejas (off Gran Vía) are filled with tourists and pushy waiters.

Mesones—Just west of Plaza Mayor, the lane called Cava de San Miguel is lined with *mesones*, long, skinny cave-like bars famous for drinking and singing late into the night. Toss lowbrow locals, Spanish karaoke, electric keyboards, crass tourists, cheap sangria, and greasy calamari in a late-night blender and turn it on. Probably lively only on Friday and Saturday, but you're welcome to pop in to several and see what you can find.

Sleeping in Madrid

(€1 = about $1, country code: 34)

Sleep Code: **S** = Single, **D** = Double/Twin, **T** = Triple, **Q** = Quad, **b** = bathroom, **s** = shower only, **CC** = Credit Cards accepted, **no CC** = Credit Cards not accepted, **SE** = Speaks English, **NSE** = No English. Breakfast is not included unless noted. In Madrid, the 7 percent IVA tax is sometimes included in the price.

To help you easily sort through these listings, I've divided the rooms into three categories, based on the price for a standard double room with bath during high season:

Higher Priced—Most rooms €100 or more.
Moderately Priced—Most less than €100.
Lower Priced—Most rooms less than €60.

Madrid has plenty of centrally located budget hotels and *pensiónes.* You'll have no trouble finding a sleepable double for $30, a good double for $60, and a modern air-conditioned double with all the comforts for $100. Prices are the same throughout the year, and it's almost always easy to find a place. Anticipate full hotels May 15 to May 25 (the festival of Madrid's patron Saint Isidro) and the last week in September (conventions). All of the accommodations I've listed are within a few minutes' walk of Puerta del Sol.

Sleeping in the Pedestrian Zone between Puerta del Sol and Gran Vía

(zip code: 28013)

Predictable and away from the seediness, these are good values for those wanting to spend a little more. Their formal prices may be inflated, and some offer weekend and summer discounts whenever it's slow. Use Metro: Sol for all but Hotel Opera (Metro: Opera). See map on page 1169 for location.

HIGHER PRICED

Hotel Arosa charges the same for all of its 134 rooms, whether they're sleekly remodeled Art Deco or just aging gracefully. Ask for a remodeled room with a terrace (Sb-€108, Db-€168, Tb-€224, 20 percent cheaper July–Aug, tax not included, breakfast-€12, CC, air-con, memorably tiny triangular elevator, Calle Salud 21, a block off Plaza del Carmen, tel. 915-321-600, fax 915-313-127, e-mail: arosa@hotelarosa.com).

The huge **Hotel Liabeny** is a business-class hotel with

222 plush, spacious rooms and all the comforts (Sb-€105, Db-€140, Tb-€162, 25 percent cheaper July–Aug, tax not included, breakfast-€12, CC, air-con, if one room is smoky ask for another, off Plaza Carmen at Salud 3, tel. 915-319-000, fax 915-327-421, www.liabeny.com, e-mail: liabeny@apunte.es).

Hotel Opera, a serious, modern hotel with 79 classy rooms, is located just off Plaza Isabel II, a four-block walk from Puerta del Sol toward the Royal Palace (Sb-€75, Db-€105, Db with big view terrace-€114, Tb-€137, tax not included, buffet breakfast-€8, CC, air-con, elevator, ask for a higher floor—there are 8—to avoid street noise; consider their "singing dinners" offered nightly at 22:00—average price €42—reservations wise, Cuesta de Santo Domingo 2, Metro: Opera, tel. 915-412-800, fax 915-416-923, www.hotelopera.com, e-mail: reservas@hotelopera.com). Hotel Opera's cafeteria is understandably popular.

Hotel Santo Domingo has artsy paintings, an inviting lounge, and 120 rooms, each decorated differently (Sb-€120, Db-€178, tax not included, pricier superior rooms are not necessary, CC, air-con, elevator, smoke-free floor, facing Metro: Santo Domingo, Plaza de Santo Domingo 13, tel. 915-479-800, fax 915-475-995, www.hotelsantodomingo.com). Prices drop €30—and breakfast is included—on weekends (Fri–Sun) and July–Aug.

MODERATELY PRICED

Hotel Europa has red-carpet charm: a royal salon, plush halls with happy muzak, polished wood floors, an attentive staff, and 80 squeaky-clean rooms with balconies overlooking the pedestrian zone or an inner courtyard (Sb-€52, Db-€65, Tb-€93, Qb-€110, Quint/b-€125, tax not included, breakfast-€5, easy phone reservations with credit card, CC, fans, elevator, fine lounge on 2nd floor, Calle del Carmen 4, tel. 915-212-900, fax 915-214-696, www.hoteleuropa.net, e-mail: info@hoteleuropa.net, Antonio and Fernando Garaban and their helpful and jovial staff, Javi and Jim, SE). The convenient Europa cafeteria/restaurant next door is a great scene, fun for breakfast, and a fine value any time of day.

Hotel Regente is a big and traditional place with 145 tastefully decorated but comfortable air-conditioned rooms, a great location, and a great value (Sb-€52, Db-€78, Tb-€90, tax not included, breakfast-€4.50, CC, midway between Puerta del Sol and Plaza del Callao at Mesonero Romanos 9, tel. 915-212-941, fax 915-323-014, e-mail: info@hotelregente.com).

Euromadrid Hotel—like a cross between a Motel 6 and an old hospital—rents 43 white rooms in a modern but well-worn shell (big Sb-€56, Db-€78, tight Tb-€88, includes buffet breakfast but not tax, CC, air-con, discounted rate for

Madrid's Center Hotels & Restaurants

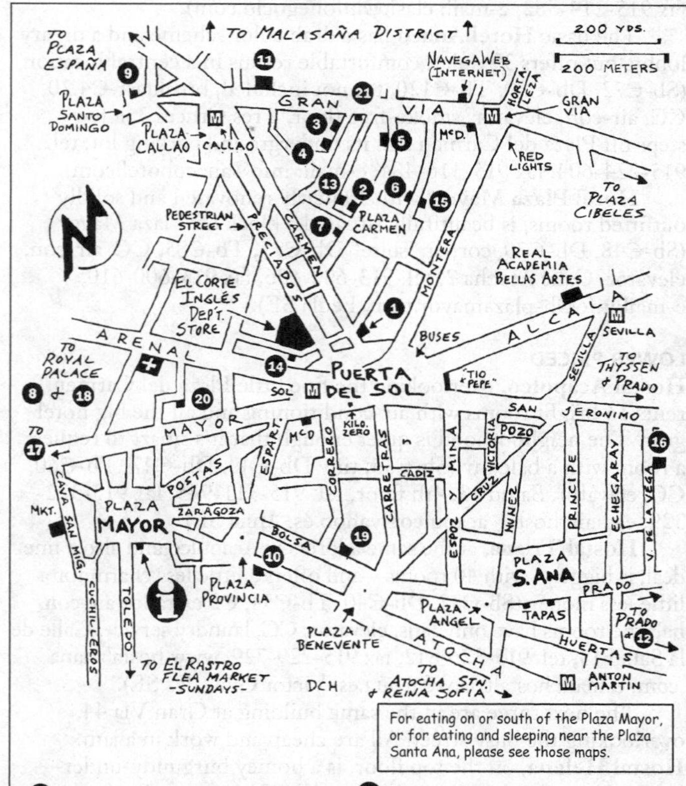

1. Hotel Europa & Cafeteria
2. Hostal Acapulco & Hostal Triana
3. Hotel Regente
4. Hotel Santo Domingo
5. Hotel Arosa
6. Hotel Anaco
7. Hotel Liabeny
8. To Hotel Opera
9. Euromadrid Hotel
10. Hotel Plaza Mayor
11. Hotels at Gran Via #44
12. Hotel Green Lope de Vega, La Plateria Bar Museo, & VIPS/Starbucks
13. Rest. Puerto Rico
14. Casa Labra Taberna Rest.
15. Artemisia II
16. Artemisia I
17. To Casa Ciriaco
18. To La Bola Taberna & Café Ricordi
19. Bar Majaderitos
20. Chocolatería San Ginés
21. Zahara Internet Café

parking-€12/day, Mesonero Romanos 7, tel. 915-217-200, fax 915-214-582, e-mail: clasit@infonegocio.com).

The basic **Hotel Anaco** has a drab color scheme and a dreary lobby, but offers 39 quiet, comfortable rooms in a central location (Sb-€72, Db-€89, Tb-€120, tax not included, breakfast-€4.20, CC, air-con, elevator, smoke-free floor, Tres Cruces 3, a few steps off Plaza del Carmen and its underground parking lot, tel. 915-224-604, fax 915-316-484, e-mail: info@anacohotel.com).

Hotel Plaza Mayor, with 30 newly renovated and solidly outfitted rooms, is beautifully situated a block off Plaza Mayor (Sb-€48, Db-€70, corner "suite" Db-€75, Tb-€85, CC, air-con, elevator, Calle Atocha 2, tel. 913-600-606, fax 913-600-610, e-mail:info@h-plazamayor.com, Fedla SE).

LOWER PRICED

Hostal Acapulco, overlooking the fine little Plaza del Carmen, rents 16 bright rooms with air-conditioning and all the big hotel gear. The neighborhood is quiet enough that it's smart to request a room with a balcony (Sb-€35, tiny Db-€42, Db-€47, Tb-€60, CC, elevator, Salud 13, 4th floor, tel. 915-311-945, fax 915-322-329, e-mail: hostal_acapulco@yahoo.es, Anna SE).

Hostal Triana, at the same address as Acapulco and also a fine deal, is bigger—with 40 rooms—and offers a little less charm for a little less money (Sb-€32, Db-€40, Tb-€54, €2 extra for air-con, half the rooms have only fans, elevator, CC, laundry service, Calle de la Salud 13, tel. 915-326-812, fax 915-229-729, www.hostaltriana.com, e-mail: hostaltriana@nauta.es, Victor Gonzalez SE).

The next three are in the same building at Gran Vía 44, overlooking the busy street. All are cheap and work in a jam. **Hostal Helena,** on the top floor, is a homey burgundy-under-heavy-drapes kind of place renting eight fine rooms. Enjoy the great little roof garden (S-€30, Ds-€42, Db-€54, Tb-€54, CC, elevator, Gran Vía 44, tel. 915-411-529, NSE). The next two are well-worn with stark rooms and traffic noise: **Hostal Residencia Valencia** (Sb-€32, Ds-€44, Db-€47, Tb-€62, includes tax, CC, 5th floor, tel. 915-221-115, fax 915-221-113, e-mail: hostalvalencia@wanadoo.es, Antonio SE) and **Hostal Residencia Continental** (Sb-€29, Db-€42, includes tax, CC, 3rd floor, tel. 915-214-640, fax 915-214-649, www.hostalcontinental.com, e-mail: continental@mundivia.es, Andres SE).

Sleeping on or near Plaza Santa Ana (zip code: 28012 unless otherwise noted)

The Plaza Santa Ana area has small, cheap places mixed in with fancy hotels. While the neighborhood is noisy at night, it has a rough but charming ambience, with colorful bars and a central location (3 min from Puerta del Sol's Tío Pepe sign; walk down Calle San Jerónimo and turn right on Príncipe; Metro: Sol). To locate hotels, see map on the next page.

HIGHER PRICED

Suite Prado, two blocks toward the Prado from Plaza Santa Ana, is a good value, offering 18 sprawling, elegant, air-conditioned suites with a modern yet homey feel (suites are all the same size charging €120 for single, €150 double, and €172 triple occupancy, sitting rooms, refrigerators, kitchens, extra kid free, breakfast at café next door-€3.60, CC, elevator, Manuel Fernandez y Gonzalez 10, at intersection with Venture de la Vega, 28014 Madrid, tel. 914-202-318, fax 914-200-559, www.suiteprado.com, e-mail: hotel@suiteprado.com, Anna SE).

LOWER PRICED

Residencia Hostal Lisboa, across the street from Suite Prado (above), is also a good value (25 rooms, Sb-€45, Db-€53, Tb-€70, CC, air-con, elevator, Ventura de la Vega 17, tel. 914-294-676, fax 914-299-894, www.hostallisboa.com, e-mail: hostallisboa@inves.es, SE).

Hostal R. Veracruz II, between Plaza Santa Ana and Puerta del Sol, rents 22 decent, quiet rooms (Sb-€36, Db-€49, Tb-€63, no breakfast, CC, elevator, air-con, Victoria 1, 3rd floor, tel. 915-227-635, fax 915-226-749, NSE).

Because of the following two places, I list no Madrid youth hostels. At these cheap hotels, fluent Spanish is spoken, bathrooms are down the hall, and there's no heat during winter. For supercheap beds in a dingy time warp, consider **Hostal Lucense** (13 rooms, S-€15–18, D-€18–21, Db-€30–36, T-€27, €1.20 per shower, no CC, Nuñez de Arce 15, tel. 915-224-888, run by Sr. and Sra. Muñoz, both interesting characters, Sr. SE) and **Casa Huéspedes Poza** (14 rooms, same prices, street noise, and owners—but Sr. does the cleaning, at Nuñez de Arce 9, tel. 915-224-871).

Sleeping Near the Prado (zip code: 28014)

HIGHER PRICED

Hotel Green Lope de Vega is your best business-class hotel value near the Prado. A four-star place opened in 2000, it's a "cultural themed" hotel inspired by the 18th-century writer Lope de Vega. It feels cozy and friendly for a formal business-class hotel (60 rooms, Sb-€125, Db-€155, Tb-€198, 1 child

sleeps free, prices about 20 percent lower on weekends and during most of the summer, CC, air-con, elevator, easy parking, Calle Lope de Vega 49, tel. 913-600-011, fax 914-292-391, www.green-hoteles.com, e-mail: lopedevega@green-hoteles.com, SE).

LOWER PRICED

Two fine budget places are at Cervantes 34 (Metro: Anton Martin). **Hostal Gonzalo**—with 15 spotless, comfortable rooms, well run by friendly and helpful Javier—is deservedly in all the guidebooks.

Reserve in advance (Sb-€36, Db-€44, Tb-€56, CC, elevator, 3rd floor, tel. 914-292-714, fax 914-202-007). Downstairs, the nearly as polished **Hostal Cervantes,** also with 15 rooms, is also good (Sb-€36, Db-€45, Tb-€57, CC, 2nd floor, tel. 914-298-365, fax 914-292-745, www.hostal-cervantes.com, SE).

Eating in Madrid

In Spain, only Barcelona rivals Madrid for taste-bud thrills. You have three dining choices: an atmospheric sit-down meal in a well-chosen restaurant, an unmemorable basic sit-down meal, or a stand-up meal of tapas in a bar or (more likely) in several bars. Many restaurants are closed in August (especially through the last half).

Eating Cheaply North of Puerta del Sol

Restaurante Puerto Rico has good meals, great prices, and few tourists (Mon–Sat 13:00–16:30 & 20:30–24:00, closed Sun, Chinchilla 2, between Puerta del Sol and Gran Vía, tel. 915-322-040).

Hotel Europa Cafeteria is a fun, high-energy scene with a mile-long bar, traditionally clad waiters, great people-watching, local cuisine, and super prices (daily 7:30–24:00, next to Hotel Europa, 50 meters off Puerta del Sol at Calle del Carmen 4, tel. 915-212-900).

Corte Inglés' seventh-floor cafeteria is popular with locals (Mon–Sat 10:00–11:30 & 13:00–16:15 & 17:30–20:00, closed Sun, has nonsmoking section, just off Puerta del Sol at intersection of Preciados and Tetuan).

Casa Labra Taberna Restaurante is famous among locals as the place where the Spanish Socialist party was founded in 1879 . . . and where you can get great cod. Packed with locals, it's a wonderful scene with three distinct sections: the stand-up bar (cheapest, 2 different lines for munchies and drinks), a peaceful little sit-down area in back (a little more expensive but still cheap; good €4 salads), and a fancy little restaurant (€15 lunches). Their tasty little €1 *bacalao* (cod) dishes put it on the map (daily 11:00–15:30 & 18:00–23:00, a block off Puerta del Sol at Calle Tetuan 12, tel. 915-310-081).

***Vegetarian*: Artemisia II** is a hit with vegetarians who like good, healthy food in a smoke-free room (great €9 three-course lunch menu, daily 13:30–16:00 & 21:00–24:00, CC, 2 blocks north of Puerta del Sol at Tres Cruces 4, a few steps off Plaza Carmen, tel. 915-218-721). **Artemisia I** is like its sister (same hours, 4 blocks east of Puerta del Sol at Ventura de la Vega 4 off San Jerónimo, tel. 914-295-092).

Eating on or near Plaza Mayor

Many Americans are drawn to Hemingway's favorite, **Sobrino del Botín** (daily 13:00–16:00 & 20:00–24:00, CC, Cuchilleros 17, a block downhill from Plaza Mayor, tel. 913-664-217). It's touristy, pricey (€24–30 average), and the last place he'd go now, but still, people love it and the food is excellent. If phoning to make a reservation, choose between the downstairs (for dark, medieval-cellar ambience) or upstairs (for a still-traditional but airier and lighter elegance). While this restaurant boasts it's the oldest in the world (dating from 1725), a nearby restaurant brags, "Hemingway never ate here."

Restaurante los Galayos is less touristy and plenty *típico* with good local cuisine (daily 8:00–24:00, lunch specials, lunch from 13:00, dinner anytime, arrive early or make a reservation, 30 meters off Plaza Mayor at Botoneras 5, tel. 913-663-028). For many, dinner right on the square at a sidewalk café is worth the premium (consider Cerveceria Pulpito, southwest corner of the square at #10).

La Torre del Oro Bar Andalu on Plaza Mayor has soul. Die-hard bullfight aficionados hate the gimmicky Bull Bar listed under "Tapas," below. Here the walls are lined with grisly bullfight photos from annual photo competitions. Read the gory description above in the Introductory Walk. Have a drink but be careful not to let the aggressive staff bully you into high-priced tapas you don't want (daily 8:00–15:00 & 18:00–24:00, closed Jan, Plaza Mayor 26, tel. 913-665-016).

Plaza Mayor is famous for its *bocadillos de calamares.* For a cheap and tasty squid-ring sandwich, line up at **Casa Rua** at Plaza Mayor's northwest corner, a few steps up Calle Ciudad Rodrigo (daily 9:00–23:00). Hanging up behind the bar is a photo/ad of Plaza Mayor from the 1950s, when the square contained a park.

Eating on Calle Cava Baja, South of Plaza Mayor

Few tourists frequent this traditional neighborhood—Barrio de los Austrias, named for the Hapsburgs. It's three minutes south of Plaza Mayor, or a 10-minute walk from Puerta del Sol. The street, Cava Baja, is lined with a diverse array of restaurants and tapas bars and clogged with locals out in search of a special meal. For a good authentic Madrileño dinner experience, take time to survey the many places along this street between the first and last listings described below and choose your favorite. A key wine-drinking phrase is *mucho cuerpo* (full-bodied).

Posada de la Villa serves Castilian cuisine in a 17th-century posada. Peek into the big oven to see what's cooking (€30 meals, Mon–Sat 13:00–16:00 & 20:00–24:00, closed Sun and Aug, Calle Cava Baja 9, tel. 913-661-860).

El Schotis is less expensive and specializes in bull stew and fish dishes. Named after a popular local dance, the restaurant retains the traditional character of old Madrid (daily 12:00–17:00 & 20:00–24:00, Calle Cava Baja 11, tel. 913-653-230).

Julian de Tolosa, a classy, elegantly simple place popular with locals who know good food, offers a small, quality menu of Basque cuisine from T-bone steak to red *tolosa* (Toulouse) beans (Mon–Sat 13:30–16:00 & 21:00–24:00, Sun 13:30–16:00, Calle Cava Baja 18, tel. 913-658-210).

Taberna los Lucio has good tapas, salads, egg dishes, and wine (Wed–Mon 13:00–16:00 & 20:30–24:00, closed Tue, Calle Cava Baja 30, tel. 913-662-984).

For a splurge, dine with power-dressing locals at **Casa Lucio.** While the king and queen of Spain eat here, it's more stuffy than expensive (daily 13:00–17:00 & 21:00–24:00, Calle Cava Baja 35, unless you're the king or queen, reserve several days in advance, tel. 913-653-252).

Taberna Tempranillo, ideal for hungry wine-lovers, offers tapas and 250 kinds of wine. Use their fascinating English menu to assemble your dream meal. Arrive by 20:00 or wait (daily 13:00–15:30 & 20:00–24:00, closed Aug, Cava Baja 38, tel. 913-641-532).

Eating near Calle Cava Baja

El Madroño is a fun tapas bar that preserves chunks of old Madrid. A tile copy of Velázquez' famous *Drinkers* grins from its facade. Inside, look above the stairs for photos of 1902 Madrid. Study the coats of arms of Madrid through the centuries as you try a *vermut* on tap and a €2 sandwich (Tue–Sun 10:00–24:00, closed Mon, Plaza Puerta Cerrada 7, tel. 913-645-629).

Taberna los Austrias, two blocks away, serves tapas, salads, and light meals on wood-barrel tables (daily 12:00–16:00 & 20:00–24:00, Calle Nuncio 17).

Next door is **Taberna de los 100 Vinos** (Tavern of 100 Wines), a classy wine bar serving top-end tapas and fine wine by the glass—see the chalk board (Tue–Sat 13:00–16:00 & 20:00–24:00, closed Sun–Mon, Calle Nuncio 17).

Eating near the Royal Palace

Casa Ciriaco is popular with locals who appreciate good traditional cooking (€25 meals, Thu–Tue 13:30–16:00 & 20:30–24:00, closed Wed and Aug, halfway between Puerta del Sol and the Royal Palace at Calle Mayor 84, tel. 915-480-620). It was from this building in 1906 that an anarchist bombed the royal couple on their wedding day (for details, see "Introductory Walk," page 1152). A photo of the carnage is inside the front door.

Eating South of Plaza Mayor

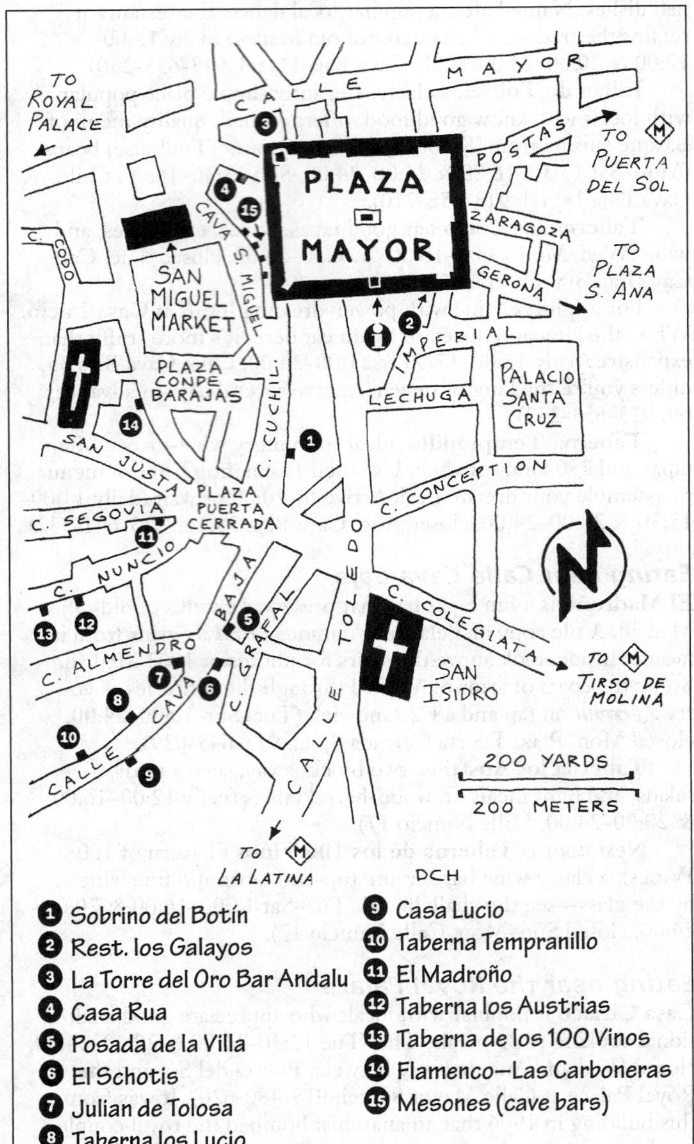
TO ROYAL PALACE
CALLE MAYOR
POSTAS
TO PUERTA DEL SOL
PLAZA MAYOR
ZARAGOZA
TO PLAZA S. ANA
GERONA
C. CODO
CAVA S. MIGUEL
SAN MIGUEL MARKET
IMPERIAL
PALACIO SANTA CRUZ
PLAZA CONDE BARAJAS
LECHUGA
C. CUCHIL.
SAN JUSTA
PLAZA PUERTA CERRADA
C. CONCEPCION
C. SEGOVIA
C. NUNCIO
BAJA
C. GRAFAL
C. TOLEDO
C. COLEGIATA
TO TIRSO DE MOLINA
C. ALMENDRO
CAVA
SAN ISIDRO
CALLE
CALLE
200 YARDS
200 METERS
TO LA LATINA
DCH
1 Sobrino del Botín
2 Rest. los Galayos
3 La Torre del Oro Bar Andalu
4 Casa Rua
5 Posada de la Villa
6 El Schotis
7 Julian de Tolosa
8 Taberna los Lucio
9 Casa Lucio
10 Taberna Tempranillo
11 El Madroño
12 Taberna los Austrias
13 Taberna de los 100 Vinos
14 Flamenco—Las Carboneras
15 Mesones (cave bars)

La Bola Taberna specializes in *cocido Madrileño*—Madrid stew. This is a touristy but tastefully elegant and friendly place stewing various meats, carrots, and garbanzo beans in earthen jugs. The €15 stew, which consists of two courses (first you enjoy the broth as a soup) is big enough to split (weekdays 13:00–16:00 & 20:30–23:00, often closed Sat–Sun, no CC, midway between the Royal Palace and Gran Vía at Calle Bola 5, tel. 915-476-930).

Café Ricordi, just a block from the Royal Theater, is a delightfully romantic little spot, perfect for theater-goers. You can enjoy tiny sandwiches with a glass of wine, coffee, and an elegant sweet, or a full meal in this café/bar/restaurant (daily 11:00–24:00, Calle Arrieta 5, tel. 915-479-200).

Eating near the Prado

Each of the big-three art museums has a decent cafeteria. Or choose from these three places, all within a block of the Prado:

La Plateria Bar Museo is a hardworking little café/wine bar with a good menu for tapas, light meals, and hearty salads (listed as *raciones* and *1/2 raciones* on the chalk board). Its tables spill onto the leafy little Plaza de Platarias de Matinez (daily 8:00–24:00, directly across busy boulevard Paseo del Prado from Atocha end of Prado, tel. 914-291-722).

Taberna de Dolores, a winning formula since 1908, is a commotion of locals enjoying €2 *canapes* (open-face sandwiches), tasty *almejas* (clams) and *cañas* (small beers) at the bar or at a few tables in the back (daily 13:00–24:00, Plaza de Jesus 4, tel. 914-292-243).

VIPS is where good-looking, young tour guides eat cheap and filling salads. This bright, popular chain restaurant is engulfed in a big bookstore (daily 9:00–24:00, across Paseo del Prado boulevard from northern end of Prado in Galeria del Prado under Palace Hotel facing Plaza Canovas). Spain's first Starbucks opened in April 2001, just next door.

Fast Food and Picnics

Fast Food: For an easy, light, cheap meal, try **Rodilla**—a popular sandwich chain with a shop on the northeast corner of Puerta del Sol at #13 (Mon–Fri 9:30–23:00, opens on Sat at 10:00, Sun at 11:00). **Pans & Company,** with shops throughout Madrid and Spain, offers healthy, tasty sandwiches and chef's salads (daily 9:00–24:00, on Puerta del Sol, Plaza Callão, Gran Vía 30, and many more).

Picnics: The department store **El Corte Inglés** has a well-stocked **deli** downstairs (Mon–Sat 10:00–22:00, closed Sun). A perfect place to assemble a cheap picnic is downtown Madrid's neighborhood market, **Mercado de San Miguel.** How about breakfast surrounded by early-morning shoppers in the market's café? (Mon–Fri 9:00–14:30 & 17:15–20:15, Sat 9:00–14:30, closed Sun; to reach the market from Plaza Mayor, face the colorfully painted building and exit from the upper left-hand corner.) The **Museo del Jamón** (Museum of Ham) sells cheap picnics to go (see tapas pub-crawl dinner below).

Churros con Chocolate

If you like danish and coffee in American greasy-spoon joints, you must try the Spanish equivalent: Greasy *churros* (or the thicker *porras)* dipped in pudding-like hot chocolate. **Bar Majaderitos** is a good bet (daily 7:00–22:30, Sun from 9:00, best in morning, 2 blocks off Tío Pepe end of Puerta del Sol, south on Espoz y Mina, turn right on Calle de Cadiz). Their tasty grilled cheese (with ham and/or egg) sandwich rounds out your breakfast. With luck, the *churros* machine in the back will be cooking. Notice the expressive WC signs.

The classy **Chocolatería San Ginés** is much loved by locals for its *churros* and chocolate (Tue–Sun 19:00–7:00, closed Mon). While empty before midnight, it's packed with the disco crowd in the wee hours; the popular Joy disco is next door. Dunk your *churros* into the pudding-like hot chocolate, as locals have done here for over 100 years (from Puerta del Sol, take Calle Arenal 2 blocks west, turn left on book-lined Pasadizo de San Ginés, you'll see the café—it's at #5, tel. 933-656-546).

Tapas: The Madrid Pub-Crawl Dinner

For maximum fun, people, and atmosphere, go mobile and do the "tapa tango," a local tradition of going from one bar to the next, munching, drinking, and socializing. Tapas are the toothpick appetizers, salads, and deep-fried foods served in most bars. Madrid is Spain's tapa capital—tapas just don't get any better. Grab a toothpick and stab something strange, but establish the prices first, especially if you're on a tight budget or at a possible tourist trap. Some items are very pricey, and most bars push larger *raciones* rather than smaller tapas. The real action begins late (around 20:00). But for beginners, an earlier start, with less commotion, can be easier. The litter on the floor is normal; that's where people traditionally toss their trash and shells. Don't worry about paying until you're ready to go. Then ask for *la cuenta* (the bill).

Prowl the area between Puerta del Sol and Plaza Santa Ana. There's no ideal route, but the little streets (in this book's map) between Puerta del Sol, San Jerónimo, and Plaza Santa Ana hold tasty surprises. Nearby, the street Jesus de Medinaceli is also lined with popular tapas bars. Below is a five-stop tapa crawl. These places are good, but don't be blind to making discoveries on your own.

1. From Puerta del Sol, walk east a block down Carrera de San Jerónimo to the corner of Victoria Street. Across from the Museo del Jamón, you'll find **La Taurina Cervecería,** a bullfighters' Planet Hollywood (daily 8:00–24:00). Wander among trophies and historic photographs. Each stuffed bull's head is named, along with its farm, awards, and who killed him. Among the many gory photos study the first post: It's Che Guevara, Orson Welles, and Salvador Dalí all enjoying a good fight. Around the corner, the Babe Ruth of bullfighters, El Cordobes, lies wounded in bed. The photo below shows him in action. Kick off your pub crawl with a drink here. Inspired, I went for the *rabo de toro* (bull-tail stew, €10.50)—and regretted it. If a fight's on, the place will be packed with aficionados gathered around the TV. Across the street at San Jerónimo 5 is the...

2. Museo del Jamón (Museum of Ham), tastefully decorated—unless you're a pig (or vegetarian). This frenetic, cheap, stand-up bar is an assembly line of fast and simple *bocadillos* and *raciones*. Options are shown in photographs with prices. For a small sandwich, ask for a *chiquito* (€0.60, unadvertised). The best ham is the pricey *jamón Iberico*—from pigs who led stress-free lives in acorn-strewn valleys. Just point and eat (daily 9:00–24:00, sit-down restaurant upstairs). Next, forage halfway up Calle Victoria to the tiny...

3. La Casa del Abuelo, for seafood-lovers who savor sizzling plates of tasty little *gambas* (shrimp) and *langostinos* (prawns). Try *gambas a la plancha* (grilled shrimp, €4), *gambas al ajillo* (pron. ahh-hheee-yoh, shrimp version of escargot, cooked in oil and garlic and ideal for bread dipping—€5.50), and a €1.20 glass of red wine (daily 11:30–15:30 & 18:30–23:30, Calle Victoria 12). Continue uphill and around the corner to...

4. Casa Toni, for refreshing bowls of gazpacho—the cold tomato-and-garlic soup (€1.50, available all year but only popular when temperatures soar). Their specialty is *berenjena*, deep-fried slices of eggplant (€3.60) and *champiñones*—sauteed mushrooms (daily 11:30–16:00 & 18:00–23:30, closed July, Calle Cruz 14). Now it's...

5. Your choice. Madrid is the New York City of Spain for cuisine—you can find anything. This is your chance to try colorful specialties from regions you won't be visiting. For instance, across from the shrimp place (stop #3), **Oreja de Oro** (Golden Ear) is named for what it sells—sautéed pig's ears (*oreja*—€2.50). While the pig's ears are a Madrid specialty, the place is Galician and people come here for *pulpo* (octopus), *pimientos de padron* (green peppers . . . some sweet and a few hot surprises), and the distinctive *ribeiro* (pron. ree-BAY-roh) wine, served Galician-style, in characteristic little ceramic bowls (to disguise its lack of clarity). On the next street over, **Sidreria La Creacion** is Asturian (the mountainous north of Spain), serving Asturian munchies and cider, traditionally poured high through the air to be oxygenated; notice the goofy wall pumps over buckets for that purpose (Nunez de Arce 14). The neighborhood is thriving with people and taste treats. Explore. **La Ria,** at Pasaje Matheu 5, is famous for its mussels (€3, *con limon* or *picante,* slurp the meat, scoop the juice with the shell, and toss the shells on the floor as you smack your lips).

If you're hungry for more, and want a more trendy, up-to-date tapas scene, head for Plaza Santa Ana. The south side of the square is lined with lively bars offering good tapas, drinks, and a classic setting right on the square. Consider **Cerveceria de Santa Ana** (tasty tapas with two zones: rowdy beer-hall and classier sit-down) and **La Moderna** (wine, paté, and cheese plates).

If you're picking up speed and looking for a place filled with old tiles and young people, power into **Bar Viva Madrid** (Calle Manuel Fernandez y Gonzalez, tel. 914-293-640). The same street has other late-night bars filled with music.

For a more gentle late-night slice of Madrid, hike over to **Bar el Oso y el Madroño,** where the proprietor serves patrons and happily cranks his 19th-century mechanical organ (commotion and new friends at the bar, tables in back, closed Mon and Aug, Calle la Bolsa 4, 2 blocks south of Puerta del Sol, tel. 915-227-796).

Transportation Connections—Madrid

By train to: Toledo (9/day, 1 hr, from Madrid's Atocha station—the *cercanias* [pron. theyr-kah-NEE-ahz] section, not the AVE section; if day-tripping there's a direct Madrid–Toledo express at 8:34 and a Toledo–Madrid express at 18:56), **Segovia** (9/day, 2 hrs, both Chamartin and Atocha stations), **Ávila** (8/day, 90 min, from Chamartin and Atocha), **Salamanca** (5/day, 2.5 hrs, from Chamartin), **Barcelona** (7/day, 8 hrs, mostly from Chamartin, 2 overnight), **Granada** (2/day, 6–9 hrs), **Sevilla** (18/day, 2.5 hrs by AVE, 3.5 hrs by Talgo, from Atocha), **Córdoba** (17 AVE trains/day, 2 hrs, from Atocha), **Málaga** (6/day, 4 hrs, from Atocha), **Lisbon** (1/day departing at 20:45, 10 hrs, pricey over-night Hotel Train from Chamartin), **Paris** (4/day, 12–16 hrs, 1 direct overnight—an expensive Hotel Train, from Chamartin).

Spain's AVE (pron. AH-vay) bullet train opens up some good itinerary options. Pick up the brochure at the station. Prices vary with times and class. The basic Madrid–Sevilla second-class fare is €63 (€12 less on the almost-as-fast Talgo). AVE is heavily discounted for Eurail passholders (the Madrid–Sevilla second-class trip costs Eurailers about €9). So far AVE only covers Madrid–Córdoba–Sevilla, but in 2004 it will extend to Barcelona. Consider this exciting day trip to Sevilla from Madrid: 7:00 depart Madrid, 8:45–12:40 in Córdoba, 13:30–21:00 in Sevilla, 23:30 back in Madrid. Reserve each AVE segment (tel. 902-240-202 for Atocha AVE info). General train info: tel. 902-240-202.

Drivers Note: Avoid driving in Madrid. Rent your car when you depart. It's cheapest to make car-rental arrangements before you leave home. In Madrid, consider Easycar.com (great rates, tel. 902-182-028, www.easycar.com), **Europcar** (central reservations tel. 902-105-030, San Leonardo 8 office tel. 915-418-892, Chamartin station tel. 913-231-721, airport tel. 913-937-235), **Hertz** (central reservations tel. 902-402-405, Gran Vía 88 tel. 915-425-803, Chamartin station tel. 917-330-400, airport tel. 913-937-228), **Avis** (Gran Vía 60 tel. 915-472-048, airport tel. 913-937-222), **Alamo** (central reservations tel. 902-100-515), and **Budget** (central reservations tel. 901-201-212, www.budget.es). Ask about free delivery to your hotel. At the airport, most rental cars are returned at Terminal 1.

Madrid's Barajas Airport

Sixteen kilometers east of downtown, Madrid's modern airport has three terminals. You'll likely land at Terminal 1, which has a helpful English-speaking TI (marked "Oficina de Información Turistica," Mon–Fri 8:00–20:00, Sat 9:00–13:00, closed Sun, tel. 913-058-656); an ATM (part of the BBVA bank) far busier than the lonely American Express window; a 24-hour exchange office (plus shorter-hour exchange offices); a flight info office (marked simply "Information" in airport lobby, open 24 hrs/day, tel. 902-353-570); a post-office window; a pharmacy; lots of phones (buy a phone card from the machine near the phones); a few scattered Internet terminals (small fee); eateries; a RENFE office (where you can get train info and buy train tickets; daily 8:00–21:00, tel. 913-058-544); and on-the-spot car-rental agencies (see above). The three terminals are connected by long indoor walkways; it's about an eight-minute walk between terminals (the Metro is in Terminal 2).

Iberia is Spain's airline, connecting many cities in Spain as well as international destinations (Velázquez 130, phone answered 24 hrs/day, tel. 902-400-500, www.iberia.com).

Getting between the Airport and Downtown: By public transport, consider an affordable, efficient **airport bus/taxi**

combination. Take the airport bus (#89, usually blue) from the airport to Madrid's Plaza Colón (€2.40, 4/hr, 20–30 min, leaves Madrid 4:30–24:00, leaves airport 5:15–2:00; stops at both Terminals 1 and 2; at the airport the bus stop is outside Terminal 1's arrivals door—cross the street filled with taxis to reach stop marked Bus on median strip; at Plaza Colón the stop is usually underground, though may be above ground at Calle Serrano). Then, to reach your hotel from Plaza Colón, catch a taxi (insist on meter, ride to hotel should be far less than €6, to avoid supplement charge for rides from a bus station, it's a little cheaper to go upstairs and flag down a taxi). Or from Plaza Colón, take the subway (from the underground bus stop, walk up the stairs and face the blue "URBIS" sign high on a building—the subway stop, M. Serrano, is 50 meters to your right; it takes two transfers to reach Puerta del Sol). At the airport, remember it's bus #89 you want; ignore bus #101, a holdover from the time when the airport didn't have a Metro stop (it runs to the Canillejas Metro stop on Madrid's outskirts).

You can take the **Metro** all the way between the airport and downtown. The airport's futuristic Aeropuerto Metro stop in Terminal 2 provides a cheap but time-consuming way into town (€1, or get a shareable 10-pack for €4.50; takes 45 min with 2 transfers; at airport, access Metro at check-in level; from Terminal 1 arrivals level, stand with your back to baggage claim, then go to your far right, up the stairs, and follow red-and-blue Metro diamond signs to Metro station, 8-minute walk; to get to Puerta del Sol from the airport, transfer at Mar de Cristal to brown line #4 direction Arguelles, then transfer at Goya to red line #3 direction Cuatro Caminos).

For a **taxi** to or from the airport, allow €20 (€4 airport supplement is legal). Cabbies routinely try to get €30—a rip-off. Insist on the meter.

TOLEDO

An hour south of Madrid, Toledo teems with tourists, souvenirs, and great art by day, delicious roast suckling pig, echoes of El Greco, and medieval magic by night. Incredibly well preserved and full of cultural wonder, the entire city has been declared a national monument.

Spain's historic capital is 2,000 years of tangled history—Roman, Visigothic, Moorish, and Christian—crowded onto a high, rocky perch protected on three sides by the Tajo (Tagus) River. It's so well preserved that the Spanish government has forbidden any modern exteriors. The rich mix of Jewish, Moorish, and Christian heritages makes it one of Europe's art capitals.

Perched strategically in the center of Iberia, Toledo was for centuries a Roman transportation hub with a thriving Jewish population. The city was a Visigothic capital back in 554 and—after a period of Moorish rule—Spain's political capital until 1561, when it reached its natural limits of growth as defined by the Tajo River Gorge. During its Golden Age, Toledo was famous for intellectual tolerance—a city for the humanities, where God was known by many names. When the king moved to more spacious Madrid, Toledo was mothballed, only to be rediscovered by 19th-century Romantic travelers who wrote of it as a mystical place.

Today Toledo thrives as a provincial capital and a busy tourist attraction. It remains the historic, artistic, and spiritual center of Spain. In spite of tremendous tourist crowds, Toledo sits enthroned on its history, much as it was when Europe's most powerful king and El Greco called it home.

Planning Your Time

To properly see Toledo's museums (great El Greco), cathedral (best in Spain), and medieval atmosphere (best after dark), you'll

Toledo

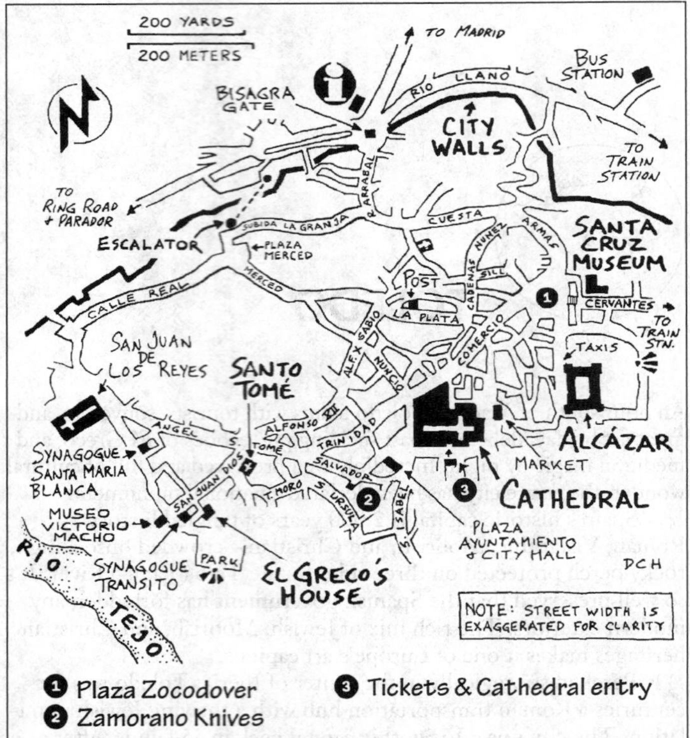

need two nights and a day. Plan carefully for lunch closings and note that a few sights are closed Monday.

Toledo is just 60 minutes away from Madrid by bus (2/hr), train (10/day), or taxi (about €65 one-way from Puerta del Sol—negotiate ride without a meter). A car is useless in Toledo. Ideally, see the town outside of car-rental time (pick up or drop your car here—Hertz is at train station, tel. 925-253-890, Avis is on Calle Armac below main square, tel. 925-214-535).

Orientation

Lassoed into a tight tangle of streets by the sharp bend of the Tajo River (called the Tejo where it hits the Atlantic, in Lisbon), Toledo has Spain's most confusing medieval street plan. But it's a small town of 65,000, the major sights are well signposted, and most locals will politely point you in the right direction.

El Greco's Art

Born on Crete and trained in Venice, Domenikos Theotocopoulos (tongue-tied friends just called him "The Greek") came to Spain to get a job decorating El Escorial. He failed there but succeeded in Toledo, where he spent the last 37 years of his life. He mixed all three regional influences into his palette. From his Greek homeland, he absorbed the solemn, abstract style of icons. In Venice he learned the bold use of color and dramatic style of the later Renaissance. These styles were then fused in the fires of fanatic Spanish-Catholic devotion.

Not bound by the realism so important to his 16th-century contemporaries, El Greco painted dramatic visions of striking colors and figures—bodies unnatural and elongated as though stretched between heaven and earth. He painted souls, not faces. His work is on display at nearly every sight in Toledo. Thoroughly modern in his disregard of realism, he didn't impress the austere Spanish king. But his art seems as fresh as contemporary art today.

If driving into town, enjoy a scenic big-picture orientation by following the Ronda de Toledo signs on a big circular drive around the city. The best time for this is the magic hour before sunset when the top viewpoints are busy with tired old folks and frisky young lovers.

Look at the map and take a mental orientation-walk past Toledo's main sights. Starting in the central Plaza Zocódover, go southwest along the Calle Comercio. After passing the cathedral on your left, follow the signs to Santo Tomé and the cluster of other sights. The visitor's city lies basically along one small but central street—and most tourists never stray from this axis. Make a point to get lost. It's a small town, bounded on three sides by the river. When it's time to get somewhere, I pull out the map or ask, "*¿Dónde está Plaza Zocódover?*"

Tourist Information

Toledo has two TIs. The one that covers Toledo as well as the region is in a small, free-standing brick building just outside the Bisagra Gate (the last surviving gate of the 10th-century fortifications), where those arriving by train or bus enter the old town (Mon–Fri 9:00–18:00, Sat 9:00–19:00, Sun 9:00–15:00, longer hours in summer, tel. 925-220-843). The second TI is in front of the cathedral on Plaza Ayuntamiento (Mon 10:30–14:30, Tue–Sun 10:30–14:30 & 16:30–19:00, tel. 925-254-030). Consider the readable local guidebook, *Toledo, Its Art and Its History* (small version for €6, sold all over town). It explains all of the sights (which generally provide no on-site information) and gives you a photo to point at and say, "*¿Dónde está . . . ?*"

Arrival in Toledo

"Arriving" in Toledo means getting uphill to Plaza Zocódover. From the **train station,** that's a 20-minute hike, €3 taxi ride, or easy bus ride (#5 or #6, €0.80, pay on bus, confirm by asking, "*¿Para Plaza Zocódover?*"). You can stow extra baggage in the station's lockers (buy tokens at ticket booth). Consider buying a city map at the kiosk; it's better than the free one at the TI. If you're walking, turn right as you leave the station, cross the bridge, pass the bus station, go straight through the roundabout, and continue uphill to the TI and Bisagra Gate.

If you arrive by **bus,** go upstairs to the station lobby. You'll find lockers and a small bus-information office near the lockers and opposite the cafeteria. Confirm your departure time (probably every half hour on the hour to Madrid). When you buy your return ticket to Madrid—which you can put off until just minutes before you leave—specify you'd like a *directo* bus; the *ruta* trip takes longer (60 min vs. 75). From the bus station, Plaza Zocódover is a 15-minute walk (see directions from train station, above), €2.50 taxi ride, or short bus ride (catch #5 downstairs, underneath the lobby, €0.80, pay driver).

A new series of escalators runs near the Bisagra Gate, giving you a free ride up, up, up into town (daily 8:00–22:00). You'll end up near the synagogues and far from Plaza Zocódover (but this doesn't matter). It's great for drivers, who can park free in the streets near the base of the escalator or for a fee (€12/day) in the parking lot across from it. Toledo is no fun to drive in. If you don't park near the escalator, drive into town and park in the Garage Alcázar (opposite the Alcázar in the old town—€1.20/hr, €12/day).

Sights—Toledo

▲▲▲**Cathedral**—Holy Toledo! Spain's leading Catholic city has a magnificent cathedral. Shoehorned into the old center, its exterior is hard to appreciate. But the interior is so lofty, rich, and vast that it'll have you wandering around like a Pez dispenser stuck open, whispering "Wow."

Cost and Hours: While the basic cathedral is free, seeing the great art—located in four separate places within the cathedral

Toledo Cathedral

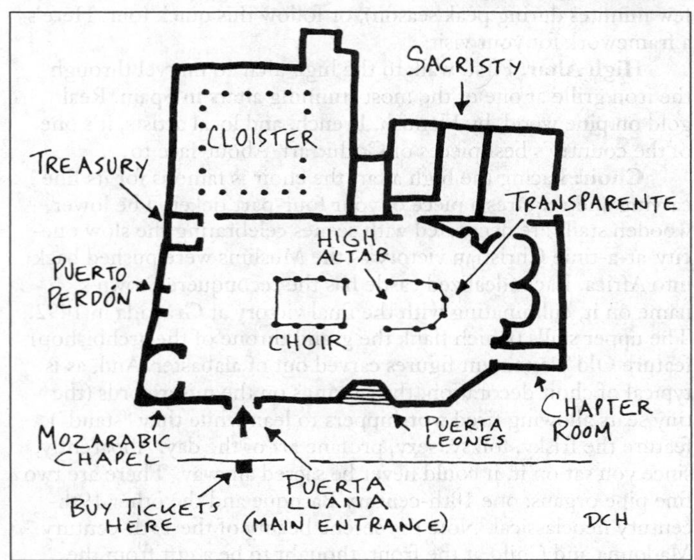

(the choir, chapter house, sacristy, and treasury)—requires a €4.80 ticket sold in the Tienda la Catedral shop opposite the church entrance (shop open Mon–Sat 10:30–18:30, Sun 14:00–18:00; also rents audioguides for €3). The strict dress-code sign covers even your attitude: no shorts, no tank tops... and no slouching.

The cathedral itself is free and open to the public daily (10:30–12:00 & 16:00–18:00, no WC in cathedral or cathedral shop). The four sights inside are open 10:30–18:00. Even though the cathedral closes from 12:00 to 16:00, if you have a ticket you can get in and tour the cathedral as well, with fewer crowds. (Note that the cloister is closed to everyone 13:00–15:30.)

Self-Guided Tour: Holy redwood forest, Batman! Wander among the pillars. Sit under one and imagine a time when the light bulbs were candles and the tourists were pilgrims—before the No Photo signs, when every window provided spiritual as well as physical light. The cathedral is primarily Gothic, but since it took over 200 years to build (1226–1495), you'll see a mix of styles—Gothic, Renaissance, and Baroque. Enjoy the elaborate wrought-iron work, lavish wood carvings, window after colorful window of 500-year-old stained glass, and a sacristy with a collection of paintings that would put any museum on the map.

This confusing collage of great Spanish art deserves a close look. Hire a private guide, freeload on a tour (they come by every few minutes during peak season), or follow this quick tour. Here's a framework for your visit:

High Altar: First, walk to the high altar to marvel through the iron grille at one of the most stunning altars in Spain. Real gold on pine wood, by Flemish, French, and local artists, it's one of the country's best pieces of Gothic art. About-face to...

Choir: Facing the high altar, the choir is famous for its fine carving and requires a piece of your four-part ticket. The lower wooden stalls are decorated with scenes celebrating the slow one-city-at-a-time Christian victory as the Muslims were pushed back into Africa. Each idealized castle has the reconquered town's name on it, culminating with the final victory at Granada in 1492. The upper stalls (which flank the grand throne of the archbishop) feature Old Testament figures carved out of alabaster. And, as is typical of choir decoration, the carvings on the misericords (the tiny seats allowing tired worshippers to lean while they "stand") feature the frisky, folksy, sexy, profane art of the day. Apparently, since you sat on it, it could never be sacred anyway. There are two fine pipe organs: one 18th-century Baroque and the other 19th-century neoclassical. Note the serene beauty of the 13th-century Madonna and Child at the front, thought to be a gift from the French king to Spain.

The iron grille of the choir is notable for the dedication of the man who built it. Domingo de Cespedes, a Toledo ironworker, accepted the commission to build the grille for 6,000 ducats. The project, which took from 1541 to 1548, was far more costly than he anticipated. The medieval Church didn't accept cost overruns, so to finish it, he sold everything he owned and went into debt. He died a poor—but honorable—man.

Chapter House: Face the altar and go around it to your right to the chapter house *(sala capitular)*. Its lavish ceiling celebrates Italian Renaissance humanism with a ground-breaking fresco. You're surrounded by interesting Bible-storytelling frescoes and a pictorial review of 1,900 years of Toledo archbishops. Though the upper row of portraits were not painted from life, the lower portraits were, and therefore are of more historic and artistic interest. Imagine sitting down to church business surrounded by all this tradition and theology. As you leave, notice the iron-pumping cupids carved into the pear tree panels lining the walls.

The ***transparente***, behind the high altar, is a unique feature of the cathedral. In the 1700s a hole was cut into the ceiling to let a sunbeam brighten the Mass. Melding this big hole into the Gothic church presented a challenge that resulted in a Baroque masterpiece. Gape up at this riot of angels doing flip-flops, babies breathing thin air, bottoms of feet, and gilded sunbursts. Study the altar, which looks chaotic but is actually thoughtfully structured: the good news of salvation springs from baby Jesus, up past the angel (who knows how to hold a big fish correctly), to the Last Supper high above, and beyond into the light-filled dome. I like it, as did, I guess, the long-dead cardinal whose faded red hat hangs from the edge of the hole. (A perk that only cardinals enjoy is choosing the place in the cathedral where their hat will hang until it rots.)

Sacristy: The cathedral's sacristy has 20 El Grecos as well as masterpieces by Goya, Titian, Rubens, Velázquez, Caravaggio, and Bellini. First, notice the fine perspective work on the 18th-century ceiling (frescoed by Lucca Giordano from Naples). Then walk to the end of the room for the most important painting in the collection. El Greco's first masterpiece, from 1579, *The Spoliation* (a.k.a. *The Denuding of Christ*) hangs above the marble altar. This was one of El Greco's first Toledo commissions after arriving from Venice. Notice the parallel contrasts: Jesus' delicate hand before a flaming red tunic and Jesus' noble face among the sinister mob. On the right is a rare religious painting by Goya, the *Betrayal of Christ*, which shows Judas preparing to kiss Jesus, identifying him to the Roman soldiers. Enjoy the many other El Grecos. Find the small but lifelike 17th-century carving of St. Francis by Pedro de Mena (to your right as you entered the door).

Treasury: The *tesoro* has plenty to see. The highlight is the three-meter-high, 430-pound monstrance—the tower designed to hold the Holy Communion bread (the Host) during the festival of Corpus Christi (body of Christ) as it parades through the city. Built in 1517 by a man named Arfe, it's made of 5,000 individual pieces held together by 12,500 screws. There are diamonds, emeralds, rubies, and 400 pounds of gold-plated silver. The inner part is 35 pounds of solid gold. Yeow. The base is a later addition from the Baroque period. Traditionally, it's thought that much of this gold and silver arrived in Columbus' first load home. To the right of the monstrance find the fancy sword of Franco. To the right of that is a gift from St. Louis, the king of France—a 700-year-old Bible printed and beautifully illustrated by French monks. (It's actually a copy, and the precious original is stored elsewhere.) Imagine the exquisite experience for medieval eyes of reading this, with its lavish illustrations. The finely painted small crucifix on the opposite side—by the great Gothic Florentine painter Fra Angelico—depicts Jesus alive on the back and dead on the front. This was a gift from Mussolini to Franco. Hmmm. There's even a gift in this room from Toledo's sister city, Toledo, Ohio.

If you're at the cathedral between 9:00 and 9:15, you can peek into the otherwise-locked **Mozarabic Chapel** *(Capilla Mozarabe).*

The Visigothic Mass, the oldest surviving Christian ritual in Western Europe, starts at 9:15 (9:45 on Sun). You're welcome to partake in this stirring example of peaceful coexistence of faiths—but once the door closes, you're a Visigoth for 30 minutes.

▲▲Santa Cruz Museum—For years, this museum has been in a confused state of renovation—not really open, not really closed. During renovation, the museum's cloister and a room full of its best art will be open and free. If the core of the building is filled with a temporary exhibit, you can generally wander in for a free look. The building's Plateresque facade is worth seeing anytime.

This great Renaissance building was an orphanage and hospital, built from money left by the humanist and diplomat Cardinal Mendoza when he died in 1495. The cardinal, confirmed as Chancellor of Castile by Queen Isabel, was so influential he was called "the third king." The building is in the form of a Greek cross under a Moorish dome. After renovation, the arms of the building—formerly wards—will be filled with 16th-century art, tapestries, furniture, armor, and documents. It'll be a stately, classical, music-filled setting with a cruel lack of English information (Mon–Sat 10:00–18:30, Sun 10:00–14:00, just off Plaza Zocódover, go through arch, Cervantes 3).

The collection includes 15 El Grecos. The highlight: the impressive *Assumption of Mary*—a spiritual poem on canvas (notice old Toledo on the bottom). Painted one year before El Greco's death in 1614, this is considered the culmination of his artistic development.

Find the lavish but faded Astrolabe Tapestry (c. 1480, Belgian) which shows a new world view at the dawn of the Renaissance and the age of discovery: God oversees all, as Atlas spins the Cosmos containing the circular Earth, and the wisdom gang (far right) heralds the new age.

An enormous blue banner hangs like a long, skinny tooth opposite the entry. This flew from the flagship of Don Juan of Austria and recalls the pivotal naval victory over the Muslims at the Battle of Lepanto in 1571 off the coast of Greece. Lepanto was a key victory in the centuries-long struggle of Christian Europe against the Muslim threat.

▲Alcázar—This huge former imperial residence—built on the site of Roman, Visigothic, and Moorish fortresses—dominates the Toledo skyline. The Alcázar became a kind of right-wing Alamo during Spain's civil war when a force of Franco's Nationalists (and hundreds of hostages) were besieged for two months. Finally, after many fierce but futile Republican attacks, Franco sent in an army that took Toledo and freed the Alcázar. The place was rebuilt and glorified under Franco. Today it's an army museum with civil war exhibits giving you an interesting—and right-wing—look at the horrors of Spain's recent past (€1.20, Tue–Sun 9:30–14:30, closed Mon).

▲Tourist Train—For great city views, hop on the cheesy Tren Imperial Tourist Tram. Crass as it feels, you get a 50-minute putt-putt through Toledo and around the Tajo River Gorge. It's a great way to get a general city overview and for non-drivers to enjoy views of the city from across the Tajo Gorge (€3.60, buy ticket from driver, daily from 11:00, leaves Plaza Zocódover on the hour, tape-recorded English/Spanish commentary, no photo stops but it goes slow; for the best views of Toledo across the gorge, sit on right side, not behind driver; tel. 925-142-274).

Sights—Southwest Toledo

▲Santo Tomé—A simple chapel holds El Greco's most-loved painting. *The Burial of the Count of Orgaz* couples heaven and earth in a way only The Greek could. It feels so right to see a painting left in situ where the artist put it 400 years ago. Take this slow. Stay a while—let it perform. The year is 1323. You're at the burial of the good count. After a pious and generous life, he left his estate to the Church. Saints Augustine and Steven have even come down for the burial—to usher the good count directly to heaven. "Such is the reward for those who serve God and his saints."

More than 250 years later, in 1586, a priest hired El Greco to make a painting of the burial to hang over the count's tomb. The painting has two halves divided by a serene line of noble faces. The physical world ends with the line of nobles. Above them a spiritual wind blows, as colors change and shapes stretch. Notice the angel, robe caught up in that wind, "birthing" the soul of the count through the neck of a celestial womb into Heaven—the soul abandoning the physical body to join Christ the Judge. Mary and John the Baptist both intervene on behalf of the arriving soul. This is Counter-Reformation propaganda—notice Jesus pointing to St. Peter who controls the keys to the pearly gates. Each face is a detailed portrait. El Greco himself (eyeballing you, 7th figure in from the left) is the only one not involved in the burial. The boy in the foreground—pointing to the two saints as if to say, "One's from the first century, the other's from the fourth... it's a miracle!"—is El Greco's son (€1.20, daily 10:00–18:45, until 17:45 off-season, free audioguide, tel. 925-256-098).

Museo El Greco and "El Greco's House"—Along with a replica of a house like El Greco's, you'll see about 20 El Greco paintings, including his masterful *View of Toledo* and portraits of the Apostles (€2, free Sat afternoon from 14:30 and all day Sun; Tue–Sat 10:00–14:00 & 16:00–17:45, Sun 10:00–13:45, closed Mon,

Samuel Levi 3). While many call this El Greco's House, it's actually a traditionally furnished Renaissance "monument house" built near where he likely lived.

Sinagoga del Transito (Museo Sefardi)—Built in 1366, this is the best surviving slice of Toledo's Jewish past (but it's likely closed through 2003 for renovation). The museum displays Jewish artifacts, including costumes, menorahs, and books, regrettably without a word of English description (€2.50, free Sat afternoon from 14:30 and all day Sun; Tue–Sat 10:00–14:00 & 16:00–17:45, Sun 10:00–13:45, closed Mon, near Museo El Greco, with same price and hours, on Calle de los Reyes Católicos).

Sinagoga de Santa Maria Blanca—This synagogue-turned-church with Moorish arches is an eclectic but harmonious gem and a vivid reminder of the three cultures that shared this city (€1.20, daily 10:00–14:00 & 15:30–19:00, closes off-season at 18:00, no photos allowed, Calle de los Reyes Católicos 2–4).

Museo Victorio Macho—After *mucho* El Greco, try Macho. Overlooking the gorge, this small, attractive museum—once the home and workshop of the early-20th-century sculptor Victorio Macho—offers several rooms of his bold work interspersed with view terraces. The highlight is *La Madre*, Macho's life-size sculpture of an older woman sitting in a chair. But the big draw for many is the air-conditioned theater featuring a fast-moving nine-minute video sweep through Toledo's history (for more information, you can request the 29-minute long version, €3, half price for young and old, Mon–Sat 10:00–19:00, Sun 10:00–15:00, request video showing in English, Plaza de Victorio Macho 2, between the two *sinagogas* listed above, tel. 925-284-225.)

The **river gorge view** from the Museo Vitorio Macho terrace (or free terraces nearby) shows well how the River Tajo served as a formidable moat protecting the city. Imagine trying to attack from this side. The 14th-century bridge on the right and the remains of a bridge on the left connected the town with the region's *cigarrales*—mansions of wealthy families with orchards of figs and apricots that dot the hillside even today.

San Juan de los Reyes Monasterio—St. John of the Monarchs is a grand, generally Flemish-style monastery, church, and cloisters—thought-provoking because the Catholic Monarchs (Isabel and Ferdinand) planned to be buried here. But after the Moors were expelled in 1492 from Granada, their royal bodies were planted there to show Spain's commitment to maintaining a Moor-free peninsula. Today the courtyard is a delightful spot where happy critters carved into the columns seem to chirp with the birds in the trees (€1.20, daily 10:00–13:45 & 15:30–18:45, San Juan de los Reyes 2, tel. 925-223-802).

And for Dessert: *Mazapan*

Toledo's famous almond-fruity-sweet *mazapan* is sold all over town. Locals say the best is made by **Santo Tomé** (several outlets, including a handy one on Plaza Zocódover, daily 9:00–22:22). Browse their tempting window displays. They sell *mazapan* goodies individually (2 for about €1, *sin relleno* is for purists, *de piñon* has pine nuts, *imperiales* is with almonds, others have fruit fillings) or in small mixed boxes. Their *Toledanas* is a crumbly cookie favorite with a subtle thread of pumpkin filling.

For a sweet and romantic evening moment, pick up a few pastries and head down to the cathedral. Sit on the Plaza del Ayuntamiento's benches (or stretch out on the stone wall to the right of the TI). The fountain is on your right, Spain's best-looking city hall is behind you, and her top cathedral, built back when Toledo was Spain's capital, shines brightly against the black night sky before you.

Shopping

Toledo probably sells as many souvenirs as any city in Spain. This is the place to buy medieval-looking swords, armor, maces, three-legged stools, and other nouveau antiques. It's also Spain's damascene center, where, for centuries, craftspeople have inlaid black steel with gold, silver, and copper wire.

At the workshop of English-speaking **Mariano Zamorano,** you can see swords and knives being made. Judging by what's left of Mariano's hand, his knives are among the sharpest (Mon–Sat 9:00–14:00 & 16:00–19:00, closed Sat afternoon and Sun, Calle Ciudad 19, near cathedral and Plaza Ayuntamiento, tel. 925-222-634, www.marianozamorano.com).

El Martes, Toledo's colorful outdoor flea market, bustles on Paseo de Marchen (near TI at Bisagra Gate) on Tuesdays from 9:00 to 14:00.

Sleeping in Toledo

(€1 = about $1, country code: 34)

Sleep Code: **S** = Single, **D** = Double/Twin, **T** = Triple, **Q** = Quad, **b** = bathroom, **s** = shower only, **CC** = Credit Cards accepted, **no CC** = Credit Cards not accepted, **SE** = Speaks English, **NSE** = No English. Breakfast and the 7 percent IVA tax are not included unless noted. Toledo's zip code is 45001, unless otherwise noted.

To help you easily sort through these listings, I've divided the rooms into three categories, based on the price for a standard double room with bath during high season:

Higher Priced—Most rooms €90 or more.
Moderately Priced—Most less than €90.
Lower Priced—Most rooms less than €60.

Madrid day-trippers darken the sunlit cobbles, but few stay to see Toledo's medieval moonrise. Spend the night. Spring and fall are high season; November through March and July and August are low. (See hotel maps on pages 1195 and 1197.)

Sleeping near Plaza Zocódover

MODERATELY PRICED

Hotel Las Conchas, a new three-star hotel, gleams with marble and sheer pride. It's so sleek and slick it almost feels more like a hospital than a hotel. Its 35 rooms are plenty comfortable (Sb-€49, Db-€65, Db with terrace-€75, breakfast-€4.50, includes tax, 5 percent discount with this book, CC, air-con, near the Alcazar at Juan Labrador 8, tel. 925-210-760, fax 925-224-271, www.lasconchas.com, e-mail: lasconchas@ctv.es, Sole SE).

LOWER PRICED

Hotel Imperio is well run, offering 21 basic air-con rooms with marginal beds in a handy old-town location (Sb-€28, Db-€40, Tb-€54, includes tax, 5 percent discount with this book, CC, elevator, cheery café, from Calle Comercio at #38 go a block uphill to Calle Cadenas 5, tel. 925-227-650, fax 925-253-183, www.terra.es/personal/himperio, e-mail: himperio@teleline.es, friendly Pablo SE).

Hostal Centro rents 23 modern, clean, and comfy rooms just around the corner (Sb-€30, Db-€42, Tb-€60, no CC, roof garden, 50 meters off Plaza Zocódover, first right off Calle Comercio at Calle Nueva 13, tel. 925-257-091, fax 925-257-848, e-mail: hcentro4@aolavant.com, SE).

The quiet, modern **Hostal Nuevo Labrador,** with 12 clean, shiny, and spacious rooms, is another good value (Sb-€27, Db-€40, Tb-€52, Qb-€60, includes tax, no breakfast, CC, elevator, Juan Labrador 10, 45001 Toledo, tel. 925-222-620, fax 925-229-399, NSE).

Hotel Maravilla, wonderfully central and convenient, has gloomy, claustrophobic halls and 17 simple rooms (Sb-€25, Db-€40, Tb-€54, Qb-€65, includes tax, CC, back rooms are quieter, air-con, a block behind Plaza Zocódover at Plaza de Barrio Rey 7, tel. 925-228-317, fax 925-228-155, e-mail: hostalmaravilla@infonegocio.com, Felisa Maria SE).

Sleeping near the Bisagra Gate

HIGHER PRICED

Hostal del Cardenal, a 17th-century cardinal's palace built into Toledo's wall, is quiet and elegant with a cool garden and

Central Toledo

1 Plaza Zocódover
2 Hotel Sol
3 Hostal & Rest. del Cardenal
4 Hotel Santa Isabel
5 La Posada de Manolo
6 Hotel Pintor El Greco
7 To Hostal Gavilánes II, Hostal Madrid & Hotel Maria Cristina
8 To Youth Hostel San Servando
9 To Parador Conde de Orgaz & Hotel La Almazara
10 Los Cuarto Tiempos Rest.
11 Casa Aurelio I
12 Casa Aurelio II & III on Sinagoga Street & Pizzeria Pastucci
13 Rest. Lopez de Toledo
14 Rest. La Perdiz
15 Rest. Meson Palacios
16 Bar Cerveceria Gambrinus
17 Taverna de Amboades
18 Mercado Municipal

a stuffy restaurant. This poor man's parador, at the dusty old gate of Toledo, is closest to the station but below all the old-town action—however, the new escalator takes the sweat out of getting into town (Sb-€56, Db-€90, Tb-€117, 20 percent cheaper mid-Dec through mid-March, breakfast-€6.50, CC, air-con, nearby parking-€12/day, *serioso* staff, enter through town wall 100 meters below Puerta Bisagra, Paseo de Recaredo 24, 45004 Toledo, tel. 925-224-900, fax 925-222-991, www.cardenal.asernet.es, e-mail: cardenal@asernet.es).

LOWER PRICED

Hotel Sol, with 25 plain, modern, and clean rooms, is a great value on a quiet street halfway between the Bisagra Gate and Plaza Zocódover (Sb-€33, Db-€46, Tb-€58, includes tax, breakfast-€3.50, 10 percent discount with this book, CC, air-con, parking-€7/day 50 meters down lane off busy main drag at Hotel Real, Azacanes 8, 45003 Toledo, tel. 925-213-650, fax 925-216-159, www.fedeto.es/hotel-sol, José Carlos SE). Their "Hostal Sol" annex across the street is just as comfortable and a bit cheaper. A handy Laundromat is next door.

Sleeping beyond the Cathedral, Deep in Toledo

HIGHER PRICED

Hotel Pintor El Greco, at the far end of the old town, has 33 plush and modern-feeling rooms with all the comforts, yet it's in a historic 17th-century building. A block from Santo Tomé in a Jewish Quarter garden, it's very quiet (Sb-€80, Db-€104, plus tax, includes breakfast, CC, air-con, elevator, Alamillos del Transito 13, tel. 925-285-191, fax 925-215-819, www.hotelpintorelgreco.com).

MODERATELY PRICED

La Posada de Manolo rents 14 thoughtfully furnished rooms across from the downhill corner of the cathedral. Manolo Junior recently opened "The House of Manolo" according to his father's vision of a comfortable place with each of its three floors themed a little differently—Moorish, Jewish, and Christian (Sb-€36, Db-€66, big Db-€72, includes breakfast, 10 percent discount when booked directly with this book, CC, air-con, no elevator, nice view terrace, Calle Sixto Ramon Parro 8, tel. 925-282-250, fax 925-282-251, www.laposadademanolo.com, e-mail: laposadademanolo@wanadoo.es).

Toledo Plaza Zocódover

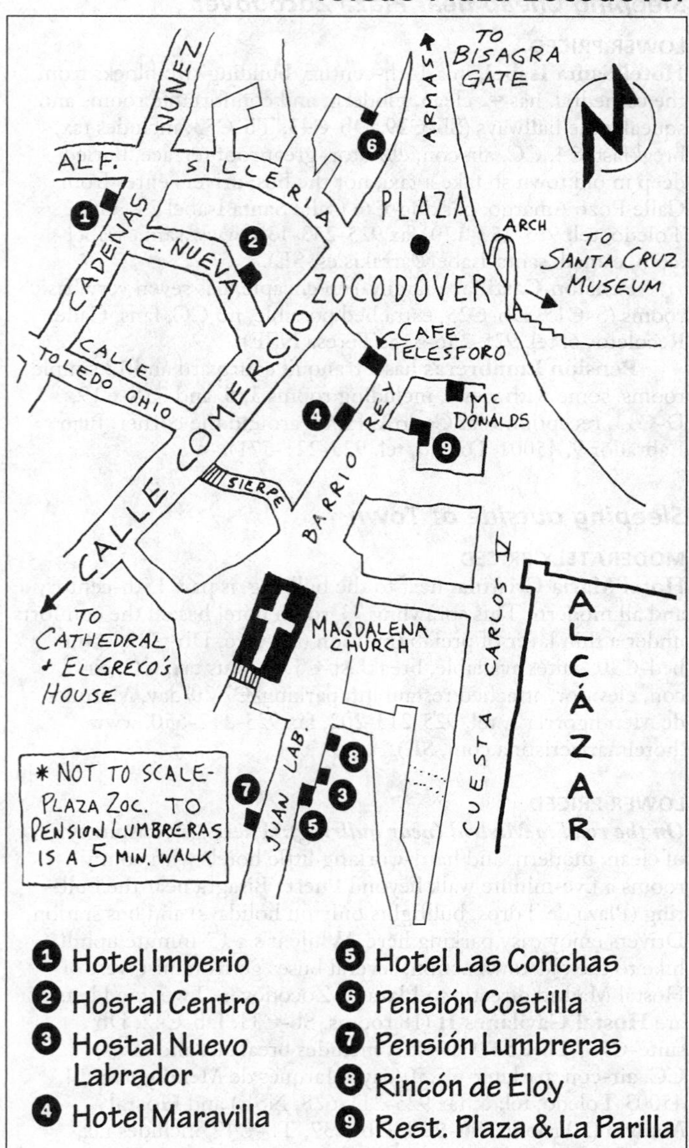

1 Hotel Imperio
2 Hostal Centro
3 Hostal Nuevo Labrador
4 Hotel Maravilla
5 Hotel Las Conchas
6 Pensión Costilla
7 Pensión Lumbreras
8 Rincón de Eloy
9 Rest. Plaza & La Parilla

Sleeping Cheap near Plaza Zocódover

LOWER PRICED

Hotel Santa Isabel, in a 15th-century building two blocks from the cathedral, has 42 clean, modern, and comfortable rooms and squeaky tile hallways (Sb-€29, Db-€43, Tb-€53, includes tax, breakfast-€4, CC, air-con, elevator, great roof terrace, buried deep in old town so take a taxi, not the bus; drivers enter from Calle Pozo Amargo, parking-€6; Calle Santa Isabel 24, 45002 Toledo, tel. 925-253-120, fax 925-253-136, www.santa-isabel.com, e-mail: santa-isabel@arrakis.es, SE).

Pensión Castilla, a family-run cheapie, has seven very basic rooms (S-€15, Db-€25, extra bed possible, no CC, fans, Calle Recoletos 6, tel. 925-256-318, Teresa NSE).

Pensión Lumbreras has a tranquil courtyard and 12 simple rooms, some with views, including rooms 3, 6, and 7 (S-€19, D-€33, reception is at Carlo V Hotel around the corner, Juan Labrador 9, 45001 Toledo, tel. 925-221-571).

Sleeping outside of Town

MODERATELY PRICED

Hotel Maria Cristina, next to the bullring, is part 15th-century and all modern. This sprawling 73-room hotel has all the comforts under a thin layer of prefab tradition (Sb-€56, Db-€89, extra bed-€30, suites available, breakfast-€5.50, plus tax, CC, air-con, elevator, attached restaurant, parking-€7.20/day, Marques de Mendigorria 1, tel. 925-213-202, fax 925-212-650, www.hotelmariacristina.com, SE).

LOWER PRICED

On the road to Madrid (near bullring): There's a conspiracy of clean, modern, and hard-working little hotels with comfy rooms a five-minute walk beyond Puerta Bisagra near the bullring (Plaza de Toros, bullfights only on holidays) and bus station. Drivers enjoy easy parking here. While it's a 15-minute uphill hike to the old-town action, several buses go from just west of Hostal Madrid directly to Plaza de Zocódover. Two good bets are **Hostal Gavilánes II** (18 rooms, Sb-€33, Db-€42, Db suite-€77, Tb-€56, Qb-€67, includes breakfast and taxes, CC, air-con, parking-€5.50/day, Marqués de Mendigorría 14, 45003 Toledo, tel. & fax 925-211-628, NSE) and **Hostal Madrid** (20 rooms, Sb-€29, Db-€37, Tb-€49, includes tax, breakfast-€2.40, CC, air-con, parking-€6.50/day, Calle Marqués de Mendigorría 7, 45003 Toledo, tel. 925-221-114, fax 925-228-113, NSE). This *hostal* rents nine lesser rooms in an annex across the street.

***Hostel*:** The **Albergue Juvenil San Servando** youth hostel is lavish but cheap, with small rooms for two, three, or four people; a swimming pool; views; and good management (106 beds, €8.50 per bed if under age 26, €11 if age 26 or older, hostel membership required, no CC, in San Servando castle 10-min walk from train station, 15-min hike from town center, over Puente Viejo outside town, tel. 925-224-554, reservations tel. 925-267-729, NSE).

Sleeping outside of Town with the Grand Toledo View

HIGHER PRICED

Toledo's **Parador Nacional Conde de Orgaz** is one of Spain's best-known inns, enjoying the same Toledo view El Greco made famous from across the Tajo Gorge (76 rooms, Sb-€60, Db-€114, Db with view-€129, Tb with view-€174, breakfast-€8.50, CC, 3 windy kilometers from town at Cerro del Emperador, 45002 Toledo, tel. 925-221-850, fax 925-225-166, www.parador.es, e-mail: toledo@parador.es, SE).

LOWER PRICED

Hotel Residencia La Almazara was the summer residence of a 16th-century archbishop of Toledo. Fond of its classic Toledo view, El Greco hung out here for inspiration. A lumbering old place with cushy public rooms, 28 simple bedrooms, and a sprawling garden, it's truly in the country but just three kilometers out of Toledo (Sb-€26, Db-€37, Db with view-€42, Tb-€48, 10 rooms have view, fans, CC, Ctra. de Piedrabuena 47, follow the signs from the circular Ronda de Toledo road, P.O. Box 6, Toledo 45080, tel. 925-223-866, fax 925-250-562, www.hotelalmazara.com, e-mail: hotelalmazara@ribernet.es).

Eating in Toledo

Dining in Traditional Elegance

A day full of El Greco and the romance of Toledo after dark puts me in the mood for partridge *(perdiz)*, roast suckling pig *(cochinillo asado)*, or baby lamb *(cordero)* similarly roasted after a few weeks of mother's milk. After dinner find a *mazapan* place (such as Santo Tomé) for dessert.

Los Cuatro Tiempos Restaurante offers gamey local specials in a tasteful and elegant setting with good service

(€25 dinners, daily 13:30–16:00 & 20:30–23:00, at downhill corner of cathedral at Sixto Ramon Parro 5, tel. 925-223-782).

Toledo's three **Casa Aurelio** restaurants all offer traditional cooking (game, roast suckling pig, traditional soup), a classy atmosphere, and good-value €30 meals (13:00–16:30 & 20:00–23:30, all closed Sun, each closed either Mon, Tue, or Wed, CC, air-con). All are within three blocks of the cathedral: Plaza Ayuntamiento 4 is festive (tel. 925-227-716), Sinagoga 6 is most *típico* (tel. 925-222-097), and Sinagoga 1 is new and dressiest (popular with Toledo's political class, tel. 925-221-392).

Restaurante Cason Lopez de Toledo, a fancy restaurant located in an old noble palace, specializes in Castilian food, particularly venison and partridge. Its character unfolds upstairs (€18 meals, Mon–Sat 13:30–16:00 & 20:30–23:30, closed Sun, Calle Silleria 3, near Plaza Zocódover, tel. 925-254-774).

Hostal del Cardenal Restaurante, a classic hotel restaurant near the Bisagra Gate at the bottom of town, is understandably popular with tourists for its decent traditional dishes (daily 13:00–16:00 & 20:30–23:30, Puerto de Recaredo 24, tel. 925-224-900).

For a splurge near the Santa Tomé sights, consider the classy **La Perdiz,** which offers partridge (as the restaurant's name suggests), venison, suckling pig, fish, and more (Tue–Sat 12:00–23:00, closes Sun about 16:00, closed Mon and first half of Aug, Calle de los Reyes Católicos 7, tel. 925-214-658).

Eating Simply but Well

Restaurante-Meson Palacios serves good food at cheap prices (Mon–Sat from 13:00 and from 19:30, closed Sun, on Alfonso X, near Plaza de San Vicente).

Rincón de Eloy is bright, modern, and a cool refuge for lunch on a hot day (€9 menu, Mon–Sat 13:00–16:00 & 20:00–22:30, closed Sun, air-con, Juan Labrador 16, near Alcázar, tel. 925-229-399).

Bar Cerveceria Gambrinus is a good tapas bar (*chapatas* are little sandwiches, *tablitas* are "little plates") with restaurant seating in its leafy courtyard or in back (daily 9:00–24:00, near Santa Tomé at Santa Tomé 10, tel. 925-214-440).

Restaurants Plaza and **La Parrilla** share a tiny square behind Plaza Zocódover (facing the Casa Telesforo on Plaza Zocódover, go left down alley 30 meters to Plaza de Barrio Rey). The bars and cafés on Plaza Zocódover are reasonable, seasoned with some fine people-watching.

At **Taverna de Amboades,** a humble but earnest wine-and-tapas bar near the Bisagra Gate, expert Miguel Angel enjoys explaining the differences among Spanish wines. To try some really good wines with quality local cheese and meat, drop by and let Miguel impress you (2 quality wines and a plate of cheese and meat for €7, Tue–Sat 19:30–24:00, also Thu–Sun 12:30–16:00, closed Mon, Alfonso VI 5, cellular 678-483-749).

Pizzeria Pastucci is the local favorite for pizza (Tue–Sun 12:00–16:00 & 19:00–24:00, closed Mon, near cathedral at Calle de la Sinagoga 10).

Picnics are best assembled at the **Mercado Municipal** on Plaza Mayor (on the Alcázar side of cathedral, open Mon–Sat until 14:00, closed Sun). This is a fun market to prowl, even if you don't need food. If you feel like munching a paper plate–size Communion wafer, one of the stalls sells crispy bags of *obleas*—a great gift for your favorite pastor.

Transportation Connections—Toledo

Far more buses than trains connect Toledo with Madrid.

To Madrid: by bus (2/hr, 60–75 min, *directo* is faster than *ruta*, Madrid's Estación sur Autobuses, Metro: Méndez Alvaro, Continental bus company, tel. 925-223-641), **by train** (9/day, 50–75 min, Madrid's Atocha station), **by car** (65 kilometers, 1 hr). Toledo bus info: tel. 925-215-850; train info: tel. 902-240-202.

Route Tips for Drivers

Arriving in Toledo by car: View the city from many angles along the Circumvalación road across the Tajo Gorge. Stop at the street-side viewpoint or drive to Parador Conde de Orgaz just south of town for the view (from the balcony) that El Greco made famous in his portrait of Toledo.

As people have for centuries, you may enter Toledo via the Bisagra Gate. Or, to take advantage of the new escalator (opposite recommended Hostal del Cardenal, explained above), park across the street at the pay lot or free on the streets beyond. Those driving into town can park across the street from the Alcázar (€1.20/hr, €12/day).

Toledo to Madrid (65 km, 1 hr): It's a speedy *autovía* north, past one last bullboard to Madrid (on N-401). The highways converge into M30, which circles Madrid. Follow it to the left ("Nor" or "Oeste") and take the Plaza de España exit to get back to Gran Vía. If you're airport-bound, keep heading into Madrid until you see the airplane symbol (N-II). Turn in your rental car at terminal T-1.

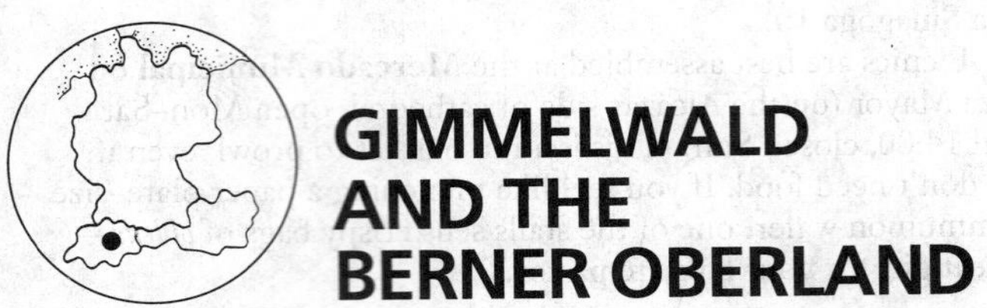

GIMMELWALD AND THE BERNER OBERLAND

Frolic and hike high above the stress and clouds of the real world. Take a vacation from your busy vacation. Recharge your touristic batteries up here in the Alps, where distant avalanches, cowbells, the fluff of a down comforter, and the crunchy footsteps of happy hikers are the dominant sounds. If the weather's good (and your budget's healthy), ride a gondola from the traffic-free village of Gimmelwald to a hearty breakfast at Schilthorn's 3,000-meter (10,000-foot) revolving Piz Gloria restaurant. Linger among alpine whitecaps before riding, hiking, or parasailing down 1,500 meters (5,000 feet) to Mürren and home to Gimmelwald.

Your gateway to the rugged Berner Oberland is the grand old resort town of Interlaken. Near Interlaken is Switzerland's open-air folk museum, Ballenberg, where you can climb through traditional houses from every corner of this diverse country.

Ah, but the weather's fine and the Alps beckon. Head deep into the heart of the Alps and ride the gondola to the stop just this side of heaven—Gimmelwald.

Planning Your Time

Rather than tackle a checklist of famous Swiss mountains and resorts, choose one region to savor—the Berner Oberland. Interlaken is the administrative headquarters and a fine transportation hub. Use it for business (banking, post office, laundry, shopping) and as a springboard for alpine thrills. With decent weather, explore the two areas (south of Interlaken) that tower above either side of the Lauterbrunnen Valley: Kleine Scheidegg/Jungfrau and Mürren/Schilthorn. Ideally, home-base three nights in the village of Gimmelwald and spend a day on each side of the valley. On a speedy train trip, you can overnight into and out of Interlaken.

For the fastest look, consider a night in Gimmelwald, breakfast at the Schilthorn, an afternoon doing the Männlichen-to-Wengen hike, and an evening or night train out. What? A nature-lover not spending the night high in the Alps? Alpus interruptus.

Getting around the Berner Oberland

For more than 100 years, this has been the target of nature-worshiping pilgrims. And Swiss engineers and visionaries have made the most exciting alpine perches accessible by lift or train. Part of the fun (and most of the expense) here is riding the many lifts. Generally, scenic trains and lifts are not covered on train passes, but a Eurailpass or Eurail Selectpass give you a 25 percent discount on even the highest lifts (without the loss of a flexi-day). Ask about discounts for early morning and late afternoon trips, youths, seniors, families, groups, and those staying awhile. The Junior Card for families pays for itself in the first hour of trains and lifts: children under 16 travel free with parents (20 SF/1 child, 40 SF/2 or more children; available at Swiss train stations). Get a list of discounts and the free fare and time schedule at any Swiss train station. Study the "Alpine Lifts in the Berner Oberland" chart in this chapter. Lifts generally go at least twice hourly, from about 7:00 until about 20:00 (sneak preview: www.jungfrau.ch). Drivers can park at the gondola station in Stechelberg (1 SF/2 hrs, 5 SF/day) for the lift to Gimmelwald, Mürren, and the Schilthorn, or at the train station in Lauterbrunnen (2 SF/2 hrs, 9 SF/day) for trains to Wengen and Kleine Scheidegg.

INTERLAKEN

When the 19th-century Romantics redefined mountains as something more than cold and troublesome obstacles, Interlaken became the original alpine resort. Ever since, tourists have flocked to the Alps because they're there. Interlaken's glory days are long gone, its elegant old hotels eclipsed by the new, more jet-setty alpine resorts. Today, its shops are filled with chocolate bars, Swiss Army knives, and sunburned backpackers.

Orientation

Efficient Interlaken is a good administrative and shopping center. Take care of business, give the town a quick look, and view the live TV coverage of the Jungfrau and Schilthorn weather in the window of the Schilthornbahn office on the main street (at Höheweg 2, also on TV in most hotel lobbies). Then head for the hills. Stay in Interlaken only if you suffer from alptitude sickness (see "Sleeping in Interlaken" at the end of this chapter).

Interlaken

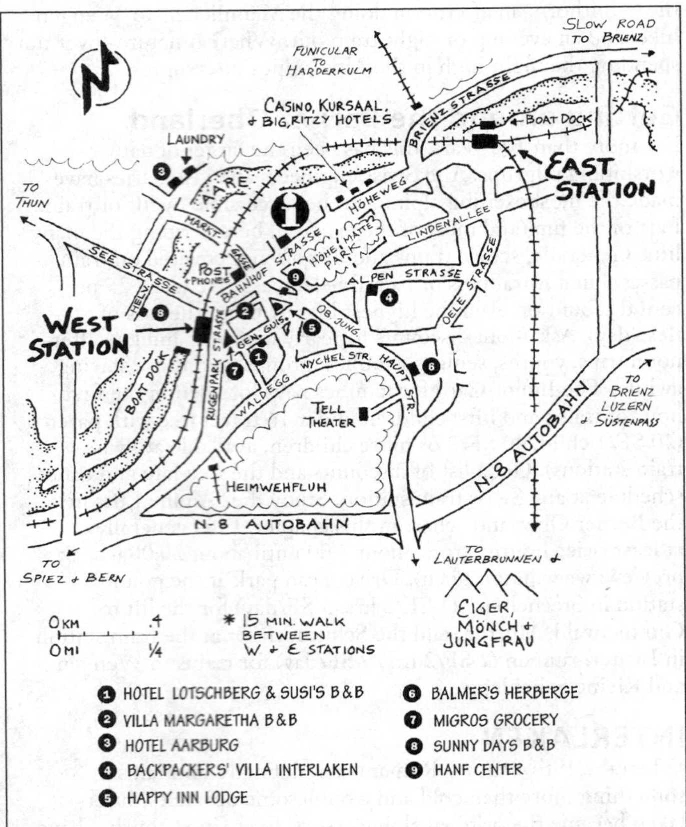

Tourist Information: The TI has good information for the region, advice on alpine lift discounts, and a room-finding service (July–Sept Mon–Fri 8:00–18:30, Sat 8:00–17:00, Sun 10:00–12:00 & 16:00–18:00; Oct–June Mon–Fri 8:00–12:00 & 13:30–18:00, Sat 9:00–12:00, closed Sun, tel. 033-826-5300, www.interlakentourism.ch; attached to Hotel Metropole on the main street between the West and East stations, a 10-min walk from either). While the Interlaken/Jungfrau region map costs 2 SF, good mini-versions are included in the many free transportation and hiking brochures. Pick up a Bern map if that's your next destination.

Arrival in Interlaken: Interlaken has two train stations: East *(Ost)* and West. Most major trains stop at the Interlaken-West station. This station's helpful and friendly train information desk answers tourists' questions as well (travel center for in-depth rail questions, Mon–Fri 8:00–18:00, Sat–Sun 8:00–12:00 & 14:00–18:00, Nov–March also closed Mon–Fri 12:00–14:00, ticket windows-daily 6:00–20:45, tel. 033-826-4750). There's a fair exchange booth next to the ticket windows. Ask at the station about discount passes, special fares, railpass discounts, and schedules for the scenic mountain trains.

It's a pleasant 20-minute walk between the West and East stations, or an easy, frequent train connection (2/hr, 3.20 SF). From the Interlaken-East station, private trains take you deep into the mountainous Jungfrau region (see "Transportation Connections" at the end of this chapter).

Helpful Hints

Telephone: Phone booths cluster outside the post office near the West station. For efficiency, buy a phone card from a newsstand. (Gimmelwald's only public phone—at the gondola station—takes only cards, not coins.)

Laundry: Friendly Helen Schmocker's *Wäscherei* (laundry) has a change machine, soap, English instructions, and a pleasant riverside locale (open daily 7:00–22:00 for self-service; for full service: Mon–Fri 8:00–12:00 & 13:30–18:00, Sat 8:00–12:00 & 13:30–16:00, drop off in the morning and pick up that afternoon, tel. 033-822-1566; exit left from West station and follow the main street to the post office, turn left and take Marktgasse over 2 bridges to Beatenbergstrasse).

Warning: On Sundays and holidays, small-town Switzerland is quiet. Hotels are open, and lifts and trains run, but many restaurants and most stores are closed. If this concerns you, call the Interlaken TI to see if a holiday falls during your visit.

Stores: A brand new **Migros supermarket** is across the street from Interlaken-West train station (Mon–Thu 8:00–18:30, Fri 8:00–21:00, Sat 7:30–16:00, closed Sun). The **Co-op Pronto** mini-market has longer hours (daily 6:00–22:00, across from TI). There's lots of buzz surrounding Interlaken's **Hanf Center**, a small shop selling a wide selection of products made from hemp, including clothes, paper, noodles, and beer (Mon 13:30–18:30, Tue–Fri 10:00–12:00 & 13:30–18:30, Sat 10:00–16:00, closed Sun, Jungfraustrasse 47, near end of Höhematte Park closest to West station, tel. 033-823-1552).

Sights—Interlaken

Boat Trips—*Interlaken* means "between the lakes"—Thun and Brienz, to be exact. You can explore these lakes on a lazy boat trip (8/day mid-June–mid-Sept, fewer off-season, free with Eurail/Eurail Selectpass but uses a flexi-day, schedules at TI). The boats on **Lake Thun** (4 hrs, 40 SF round-trip) stop at the **St. Beatus Höhlen Caves** (16 SF, April–mid-Oct daily 10:30–17:00, closed mid-Oct–March, 30-min boat ride from Interlaken, tel. 033-841-1643, www.beatushoehlen.ch) and two visit-worthy towns: Spiez (1 hr from Interlaken) and Thun (1.75 hrs). The boats on **Lake Brienz** (3 hrs, 32 SF round-trip) stop at the super-cute and quiet village of Iseltwald (45 min away) and at Brienz (1.25 hrs away, near Ballenberg Open-Air Folk Museum).

Adventure Trips—For the adventurer with money and little concern for personal safety, several companies offer high-adrenaline trips such as rafting, canyoning (rappelling down watery gorges), bungee jumping, and paragliding. Most adventure trips cost from 90 to 180 SF. Interlaken companies include: Alpin Raft (tel. 033-823-4100, www.alpinraft.ch), Alpin Center (at Wilderswil station and across from Balmer's youth hostel, tel. 033-823-5523, www.alpincenter.ch), Swiss Adventures (tel. 033-773-7373, www.swissadventures.ch), and Outdoor Interlaken (tel. 033-826-7719, www.outdoor-interlaken.ch).

Recent fatal accidents have understandably hurt the adventure-sport business in the Berner Oberland. In July 1999, 21 tourists died canyoning on the Saxetenbach River, 16 kilometers (10 miles) from Interlaken; they were battered and drowned by a flash flood filled with debris. In May 2000, an American died bungee jumping from the Stechelberg–Mürren gondola (the operator used a 180-meter rope for a 100-meter jump). Also in 2000, a landslide killed several hikers. Enjoying nature up close comes with risks. Adventure sports increase those risks dramatically. Use good judgment.

GIMMELWALD

Saved from developers by its "avalanche zone" classification, Gimmelwald was (before tourism) one of the poorest places in Switzerland. Its traditional economy was stuck in the hay, and its farmers, unable to make it in their disadvantaged trade, survived only by Swiss government subsidies (and working the ski lifts in the winter). For some travelers, there's little to see in the village. Others enjoy a fascinating day sitting on a bench and learning why they say, "If heaven isn't what it's cracked up to be, send me back to Gimmelwald." Gimmelwald is my home base in the Berner Oberland (see "Sleeping in Gimmelwald," below).

Take a walk through the town. This place is for real. Most of the 130 residents have the same last name: von Allmen. They are tough and proud. Raising hay in this rugged terrain is labor intensive. One family harvests enough to feed only 15 or 20 cows. But

Gimmelwald

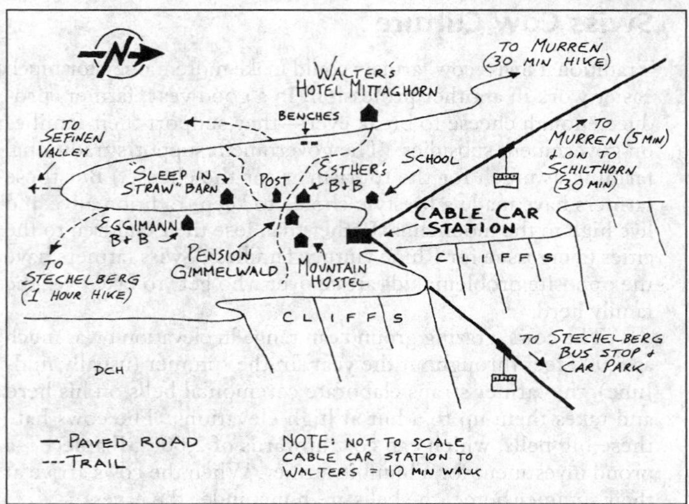

they'd have it no other way, and, unlike the absentee-landlord town of Mürren, Gimmelwald is locally owned. (When word got out that urban planners wished to develop Gimmelwald into a town of 1,000, locals pulled some strings to secure the town's bogus avalanche-zone building code.)

The huge sheer cliff face that dominates your mountain views from Gimmelwald (and Mürren) is the Schwarzmönch (Black Monk). The three peaks above (or behind) it are, left to right, the Eiger, Mönch, and Jungfrau.

Do not confuse obscure Gimmelwald with touristy and commercialized Grindelwald, just over the Kleine Scheidegg ridge.

A Walk through Gimmelwald

Gimmelwald, while tiny with one zigzag street, gives a fine look at a traditional mountain Swiss community. Here's a quick walking tour:

Gondola Station: When the lift came in the 1960s, this village's back end became Gimmelwald's front door. This was, and still is, a farm village. Stepping off the gondola, you see a sweet little hut. Set on stilts to keep out mice, the hut was used for storing cheese (the rocks on the rooftop keep the shingles on through wild winter winds). Notice the yellow alpine "street sign" showing where you are, the altitude (1,363 meters/4,470 feet), and how many hours ("Std.") and minutes it takes to walk to nearby points.

Swiss Cow Culture

Traditional Swiss cow farmers could make more money for much easier work in another profession. In a good year, farmers produce enough cheese to break even—they support their families on government subsidies. (The government supports traditional farming as much for the tourism as for the cheese.) But these farmers have made a lifestyle choice to keep tradition alive and live high in the mountains. Rather than lose their children to the cities (a big issue for Rhine vintner families), Swiss farmers have the opposite problem: kids argue over who gets to take over the family herd.

The cows' grazing ground can range in elevation by as much as 5,000 feet throughout the year. In the summer (usually mid-June), the farmer straps elaborate ceremonial bells on his herd and takes them up to a hut at high elevations. The cows hate these big bells, which can cost upwards of 2,000 SF apiece—a proud investment for a humble farmer. When the cows arrive at their summer home, the bells are hung under the eaves.

These high-elevation summer stables are called alps. Try to find some on a Berner Oberland tourist map (e.g., Wengernalp, Grütschalp, Schiltalp). The cows stay at the alps for about 100 days. The farmers hire a team of cheese makers to work at each alp—mostly hippies, students, and city slickers eager to spend three summer months high in the mountains. Each morning, the

Behind the cheese hut stands the village schoolhouse. In Catholic-Swiss towns, the biggest building is the church. In Protestant towns, it's the school. Gimmelwald's biggest building is the school (2 teachers, 17 students, and a room that doubles as a chapel when the Protestant pastor makes his monthly visit). Don't let Gimmelwald's low-tech look fool you: in this school, each kid has his or her own Web site. In the opposite direction, just beyond the little playground, is Gimmelwald's Mountain Hostel.

Walk up the lane 50 meters (165 feet), past the shower in the phone booth, to Gimmelwald's . . .

"Times Square": From this tiny intersection, we'll follow the town's main street (away from gondola station, where most yellow arrows are pointing). Most of the buildings used to house two families and are divided vertically right down the middle. The writing on the post office building is a folksy blessing: "Summer brings green, winter brings snow. The sun greets the day, the stars greet hired hands get up at 5:00 to milk the cows, take them to pasture, and make the cheese—milking the cows again when they come home in the evening.

Every alp also has a resident herd of pigs. Cheese-making leftovers (*Molke*, or whey) can damage the ecosystem if thrown out—but pigs love the stuff. Cheese makers claim that bathing in whey improves the complexion—but maybe that's just the altitude talking.

Meanwhile, the farmers—glad to be free of their bovine responsibilities—turn their attention to making hay. The average farmer has a few huts at various altitudes, each surrounded by small hay fields. The farmer follows the seasons up into the mountains, making hay and storing it above the huts. In the fall, the cows come down from the alps and spend the winter moving from hut to hut, eating the hay the farmer spent the summer preparing for them.

Throughout the year, you'll see farmers moving their herd to various elevations. If snow is in the way, farmers sometimes use tourist gondolas to move their cows. Every two months or so, Gimmelwald farmers bring together cows that aren't doing so well and herd them into the gondola to meet the butcher in the valley below.

the night. This house will keep you warm. May God give us his blessings." The date indicates when it was built or rebuilt (1911).

"Main Street": Walk up the road. Notice the announcement board: one side for tourist news, the other for local news. Cross the street and peek into the big new barn, dated 1995. This is part of the "Sleep in Straw" association, which rents out barn spots to travelers when the cows are in the high country. To the left of the door is a cow scratcher. Swiss cows have legal rights (e.g., in the winter, they must be taken out for exercise at least 3 times a week). This big barn is built in a modern style. Traditionally, barns were small (like those on the hillside high above) and closer to the hay. But with trucks and paved roads, hay can be moved easier and farther, and farms need more cows to be viable. Still, even a well-run big farm hopes just to break even. The industry survives only with government subsidies (see "Swiss Cow Culture," above). Go just beyond the next barn and look to your right.

Water Fountain/Trough: This is the site of the town's historic water supply. Local kids love to bathe in this when the cows aren't drinking from it. From here, detour left down a lane about 50 meters (165 feet), along a wooden fence and past pea-patch gardens) to the next trough and the oldest building in town, "Husmättli," from 1658. Study the log-cabin construction. Many are built without nails.

Back on the paved road, continue uphill. Gimmelwald has a strict building code. For instance, shutters can only be natural, green, or white. Notice the cute cheese hut on the right (with stones on the shingles and alpine cheese for sale). It's full of strong cheese—up to three years old. On the left (at B&B sign) is the home of Olle and Maria (the village school teachers). Gimmelwald heats with wood, and, since the wood needs to age a couple of years to burn well, it's stacked everywhere. Fifty meters (165 feet) farther along is the...

Alpenrose: At the old schoolhouse, big ceremonial cowbells hang under its uphill eave. These swing from the necks of cows during the alpine procession from the town to the high Alps (mid-June) and back down (around Sept 20). At the end of town, notice the dramatic Sefinen Valley. The road switches back at the...

Gimmelwald Fire Station: Check out the notices up above on the fire station building. Every Swiss male does a year in the military, then a few days a year in the reserves until about age 40. The 2003 Swiss Army calendar tells the reserves when and where to go. The *Schiessübungen* poster details the shooting exercises required this year. In keeping with the William Tell heritage, each Swiss man does shooting practice annually for the military (or spends 3 days in jail).

High Road: Follow the high road to Hotel Mittaghorn. The resort of Mürren hangs high above in the distance. And high on the left, notice the hay field with terraces. These are from WWII days, when Switzerland, wanting self-sufficiency, required all farmers to grow potatoes. From Hotel Mittaghorn, you can return to Gimmelwald's "Times Square" via the stepped path.

Gimmelwald After Dark—Evening fun in Gimmelwald is found at the hostel (offering a pool table, Internet access, lots of young Alp-aholics, and a good chance to share information on the surrounding mountains) or at Pension Gimmelwald's terrace restaurant next door. Walter's bar (in Hotel Mittaghorn) is a local farmers' hang-out. When they've made their hay, they come here to play. Although they look like what some people would call hicks, they speak some English and can be fun to get to know. Sit outside (benches just down the lane from Walter's) and watch the sun tuck the mountaintops into bed as the moon rises over the Jungfrau. If this isn't your idea of nightlife, stay in Interlaken.

Lauterbrunnen Valley: West Side Story

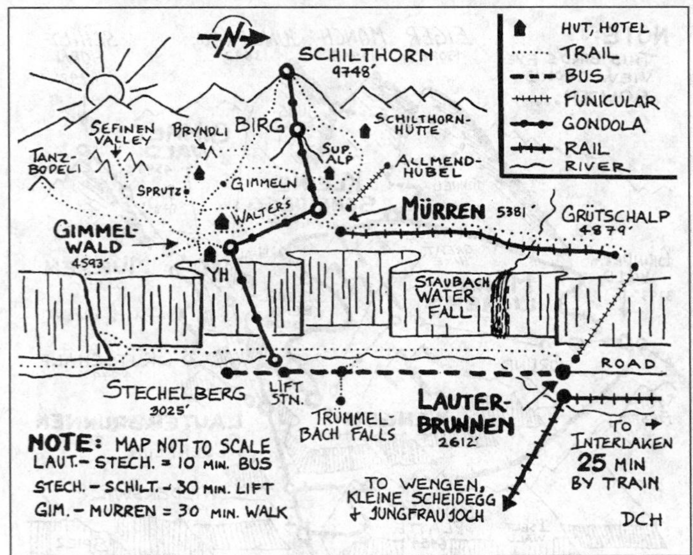

Alpine Excursions

There are days of possible hikes from Gimmelwald. Many are a fun combination of trails, mountain trains, and gondola rides. Don't mind the fences (although wires can be solar-powered electric); a hiker has the right-of-way in Switzerland. However, as late as June, snow can curtail your hiking plans (the Männlichen lift doesn't even open until the first week in June). Before setting out on any hike, get advice from a knowledgeable local to confirm that it is safe, accessible, and doable before dark. Clouds can roll in anytime, but skies are usually clearest in the morning. That means you need rain gear *and* sunscreen, regardless of the current weather. Don't forget a big water bottle and some munchies. Refer to maps (within this chapter) as you read about the following hikes.

▲▲▲The Schilthorn: Hikes, Lifts, and a 3,000-Meter (10,000-Foot) Breakfast—The Schilthornbahn carries skiers, hikers, and sightseers effortlessly to the 3,000-meter (10,000-foot) summit of the Schilthorn, where the Piz Gloria station (of James Bond movie fame) awaits, with a revolving restaurant, shop, and panorama terrace. Linger on top. Piz Gloria has a free "touristorama" film room showing a multiscreen slide show and explosive highlights from the James Bond thriller that featured the Schilthorn *(On Her Majesty's Secret Service)*.

Berner Oberland

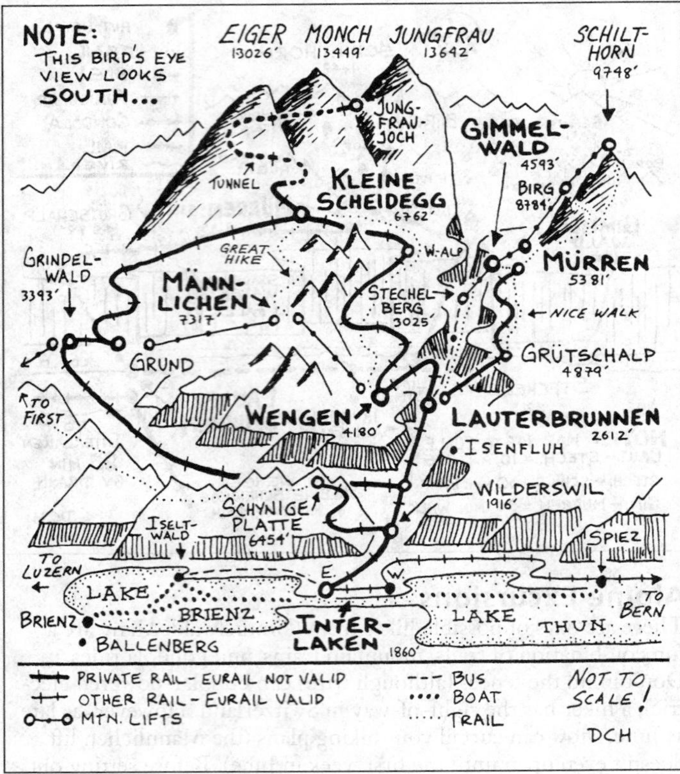

Watch hang gliders set up, psych up, and take off, flying 30 minutes with the birds to distant Interlaken. Walk along the ridge out back. This is a great place for a photo of the "mountain-climber you." For another cheap thrill, ask the gondola attendant to crank down the window (easiest on the Mürren–Birg section). Then stick your head out the window . . . and you're hang gliding.

The early-bird and afternoon-special **gondola tickets** (58 SF round-trip, before 9:00 or after 15:30) take you from Gimmelwald to the Schilthorn and back at a discount (normal rate-77 SF, or 91 SF from the Stechelberg car park to the Schilthorn; parking-1 SF/2 hrs, 5 SF/day). These same discounted fares are available all day long in the shoulder season (roughly May and Oct). Ask the Schilthorn station for a gondola souvenir decal (Schilthornbahn, in Stechelberg, tel. 033-856-2141). For breakfast at 3,000 meters,

Alpine Lifts in the Berner Oberland

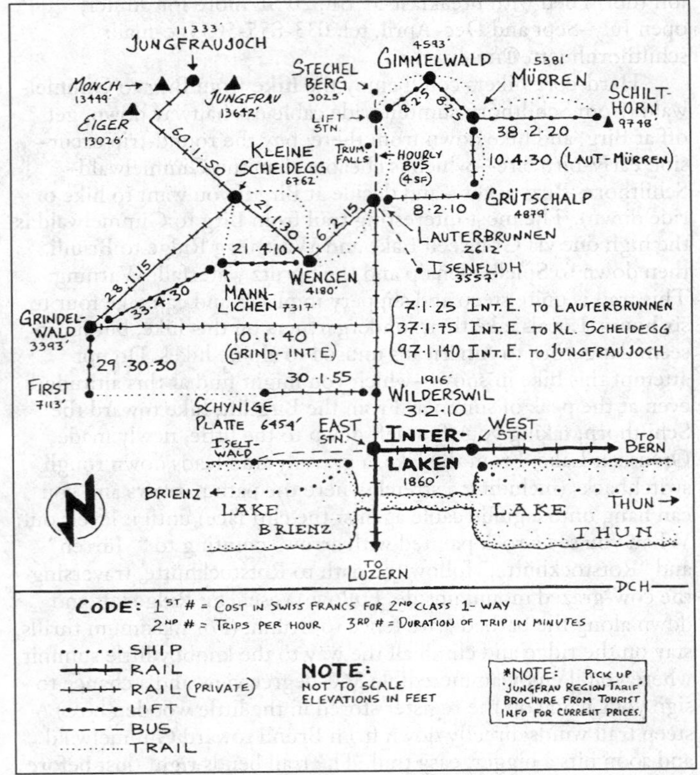

there's no à la carte, only a 15-SF and a 22.50-SF meal. If you're going for breakfast before 9:00, consider an early-bird-plus-breakfast combo-ticket to save a few francs (70.60 SF round-trip from Gimmelwald, 81.60 SF from Stechelberg). Ask for more hot drinks if necessary. If you're not revolving, ask them to turn it on.

Lifts go twice hourly, and the ride (including 2 transfers) to the Schilthorn takes 30 minutes. Watch the altitude meter in the gondola. (The Gimmelwald–Schilthorn hike is free if you don't mind a 1,500-meter/5,000-foot altitude gain.) You can ride up to the Schilthorn and hike down, but it's tough (weather can change; wear good shoes). Youth hostelers scream down the ice fields on plastic-bag sleds from the Schilthorn mountaintop. (English-speaking doctor in Lauterbrunnen.)

Just below Birg is **Schilthornhütte**. Drop in for soup, cocoa, or a coffee schnapps. You can spend the night in the hut's crude loft (dorm bed with breakfast-35 SF, 20 SF more for dinner, open July–Sept and Dec–April, tel. 033-855-5053, e-mail: schilthornhuette@muerren.ch).

Hard-core hikers could enjoy the **hike** from Birg to Gimmelwald (from Schilthorn summit, ride cable car halfway down, get off at Birg, and hike down from there; buy the round-trip excursion early-bird fare—which is cheaper than the Gimmelwald–Schilthorn–Birg ticket—and decide at Birg if you want to hike or ride down). The most interesting trail from Birg to Gimmelwald is the high one via Grauseeli Lake and Wasenegg Ridge to Brünli, then down to Spielbodenalp and the Sprutz waterfall. Warning: This trail is quite steep and slippery in places and can take four to six hours. Locals take their kindergartners on this hike, but it can seem dangerous to Americans unused to alpine hikes. Do not attempt this hike in snow—which you might find at this altitude even at the peak of summer. From the Birg lift, hike toward the Schilthorn, taking your first left down to the little, newly made Grauseeli Lake. From the lake, a gravelly trail leads down rough switchbacks (including a stretch where the path narrows and you can hang onto a guide cable against the cliff face) until it levels out. When you see a rock painted with arrows pointing to "Mürren" and "Rotstockhütte," follow the path to Rotstockhütte, traversing the cow-grazed mountainside. Follow Wasenegg Ridge left and down along the barbed-wire fence to Brünli. (For maximum thrills, stay on the ridge and climb all the way to the knobby little summit, where you'll enjoy an incredible 360-degree view and a chance to sign your name on the register stored in the little wooden box.) A steep trail winds directly down from Brünli toward Gimmelwald and soon hits a bigger, easy trail. The trail bends right (just before the popular restaurant/mountain hut at Spielbodenalp), leading to Sprutz. Walk under the Sprutz waterfall, then follow a steep, wooded trail that will deposit you in a meadow of flowers at the top side of Gimmelwald.

▲▲North Face Trail from Mürren—For a pleasant two-hour hike (6 km/4 miles, 1,946 meters–1,638 meters), ride the Allmendhubel funicular up from Mürren (cheaper than Schilthorn, good restaurant at top). From there, follow the well-promoted and well-described route circling around to Mürren (or cut off near the end down to Gimmelwald). You'll enjoy great views, flowery meadows, mountain huts, and a dozen information boards along the way describing the climbing history of the great peaks around you.

▲▲▲The Männlichen–Kleine Scheidegg Hike—This is my favorite easy alpine hike. It's entertaining all the way, with glorious Jungfrau, Eiger, and Mönch views. That's the Young Maiden being protected from the Ogre by the Monk. (Note that trails may be snowbound into June; ask about conditions at the lift stations or local TI. If the Männlichen lift is closed, take the train straight from Lauterbrunnen to Kleine Scheidegg.)

If the weather's good, descend from Gimmelwald bright and early to Stechelberg. From here, get to the Lauterbrunnen train station by post bus (3.80 SF, bus is synchronized to depart with the arrival of each lift) or by car (parking at the large multistoried pay lot behind the Lauterbrunnen station-2 SF/2 hrs, 9 SF/day). At Lauterbrunnen, buy a train ticket to Männlichen (26.80 SF one-way). Sit on the right side of the train for great waterfall views on your way up to Wengen. In Wengen, walk across town (buy a picnic, but don't waste time here if it's sunny) and catch the Männlichen lift (departing every 15 min, beginning the first week of June) to the top of the ridge high above you.

From the Wengen–Männlichen lift station, turn left and hike uphill 20 minutes north to the little peak (Männlichen Gipfel) for that king- or queen-of-the-mountain feeling. Then take an easy hour's walk—facing spectacular alpine panorama views—to Kleine Scheidegg for a picnic or restaurant lunch. To start the hike, leave the Wengen–Männlichen lift station to the right. Walk past the second Männlichen lift station (this one leads to Grindelwald, the touristy town in the valley to your left). Ahead of you in the distance, left to right, are the north faces of the Eiger, Mönch, and Jungfrau; in the foreground is the Tschuggen peak, and behind it, the Lauberhorn. This hike will take you around the left (east) side of this ridge. Simply follow the signs for Kleine (Kl.) Scheidegg, and you'll be there in about an hour—a little more for gawkers, picnickers, and photographers. You might have to tiptoe through streams of melted snow—or some small snow banks, even well into the summer—but the path is well-marked, well-maintained, and mostly level all the way to Kleine Scheidegg.

About 35 minutes into the hike, you'll reach a bunch of benches and a shelter with spectacular, unobstructed views of all three peaks—the perfect picnic spot. Fifteen minutes later on the left, you'll see the first sign of civilization: Restaurant Grindelwaldblick, offering a handy terrace lunch stop with tasty, hearty, and reasonable food (daily, closed Dec and May, see "Sleeping and Eating in Kleine Scheidegg," below). After 10 more minutes, you'll be at the Kleine Scheidegg train station, with plenty of other lunch options (including Bahnhof Buffet, see "Sleeping and Eating in Kleine Scheidegg," below).

From Kleine Scheidegg, you can catch the train to "the top of Europe" (see "Jungfraujoch," below). Or head downhill, riding the train or hiking (30 gorgeous min to Wengernalp station;

90 more steep min from there into the town of Wengen). The alpine views might be accompanied by the valley-filling mellow sound of Alp horns and distant avalanches.

If the weather turns bad or you run out of steam, catch the train early at the little Wengernalp station along the way. After Wengernalp, the trail to Wengen is steep and, while not dangerous, requires a good set of knees. Wengen is a good shopping town. (For accommodations, see "Sleeping in Wengen," below.) The boring final descent from Wengen to Lauterbrunnen is knee-killer steep—catch the train.

▲▲▲Jungfraujoch—The literal high point of any trip to the Swiss Alps is a train ride through the Eiger to the Jungfraujoch. At 3,400 meters (11,333 feet), it's Europe's highest train station. The ride from Kleine Scheidegg takes about an hour, including two five-minute stops at stations actually halfway up the notorious North Face of the Eiger. You have time to look out windows and marvel at how people could climb the Eiger and how the Swiss built this train more than a hundred years ago. Once you reach the top, study the Jungfraujoch chart to see your options (many of them are weather dependent). There's a restaurant, history exhibit, ice palace (a cavern with a gallery of ice statues), and a continuous 20-minute video. A tunnel leads outside, where you can ski (30 SF for gear and lift ticket), sled (free loaner discs with deposit), ride in a dog sled (6 SF, mornings only), or hike 45 minutes across the ice to Mönchsjochhütte (a mountain hut with a small restaurant). An elevator leads to the Sphinx observatory for the highest viewing point from which you can see Aletsch Glacier—Europe's longest at nearly 18 kilometers (11 miles)—stretch to the south. The first trip of the day to Jungfraujoch is discounted; ask for a Good Morning Ticket and return from the top by noon (Nov–April you can get Good Morning rates for first or second train and stay after noon, train runs all year, round-trip fares to Jungfraujoch: from Kleine Scheidegg-normally 99 SF, 62 SF for first trip of day—about 8:02; from Lauterbrunnen-145.60 SF, 108.60 SF for first trip—about 7:08, confirm times and prices, discounts for Eurail/Eurail Selectpass and Swiss railpass holders, get leaflet on lifts at a local TI or call 033-828-7233, www.jungfrau.ch). For a trilingual weather forecast, call 033-828-7931; if it's cloudy—skip the trip.

▲▲Hike from Schynige Platte to First—The best day I've had hiking in the Berner Oberland was when I made the demanding six-hour ridge walk high above Lake Brienz on one side, with all that Jungfrau beauty on the other. Start at Wilderswil train station (just above Interlaken) and catch the little train up to Schynige Platte (2,000 meters/6,560 feet). Walk through the flower display garden and into the wild alpine yonder. The high point is Faulhorn

(2,680 meters/8,790 feet, with its famous mountaintop hotel). Hike to a small gondola called "First" (2,168 meters), then descend to Grindelwald and catch a train back to your starting point, Wilderswil. Or, if you have a regional train pass or no car but endless money, return to Gimmelwald via Lauterbrunnen from Grindelwald over Kleine Scheidegg. For an abbreviated ridge walk, consider the Panoramaweg, a short loop from Schynige Platte to Daub Peak.

▲Mountain Biking—Mountain biking is popular and accepted (as long as you stay on the clearly marked mountain-bike paths). A popular ride is the round-trip "Mürren Loop" that runs from Mürren to Gimmelwald, down the Sefinen Valley to Stechelberg, Lauterbrunnen (by funicular, bike costs same as person-7.80 SF), Grütschalp, and back to Mürren. You can rent bikes in Mürren (Stäger Sport, 25 SF/4 hrs, 35 SF/day, daily 9:00–17:00, closed May and Nov, across from TI/Sportzentrum, tel. 033-855-2355, www.staegersport.ch) or in Lauterbrunnen (Imboden Bike, 25 SF/4 hrs, 35 SF/day, 10 SF extra for full suspension, daily 8:30–18:30, closed Nov, tel. 033-855-2114).

You can also bike the Lauterbrunnen Valley from Lauterbrunnen to Interlaken. It's a gentle downhill ride via a peaceful bike path over the river from the road. Rent a bike at Lauterbrunnen (see above), bike to Interlaken, and return to Lauterbrunnen by train (to take bike on train, pay 3.30 SF extra from East station or 4.60 SF extra from West station). Or rent a bike at either Interlaken station, take the train to Lauterbrunnen, and ride back.

▲More Hikes near Gimmelwald—For a not-too-tough, three-hour walk (but there's a scary 20-minute stretch) with great Jungfrau views and some mountain farm action, ride the funicular from Mürren to Allmendhubel (1,934 meters/6,344 feet) and walk to Marchegg, Saustal, and Grütschalp (a drop of about 500 meters), where you can catch the panorama train back to Mürren. An easier version is the lower Bergweg from Allmendhubel to Grütschalp via Winteregg. For an easy family stroll with grand views, walk from Mürren just above the train tracks to either Winteregg (40 min, restaurant, playground, train station) or Grütschalp (60 min, train station), then catch the panorama train back to Mürren. An easy, go-as-far-as-you-like trail from Gimmelwald is up the Sefinen Valley. Or you can wind from Gimmelwald down to Stechelberg (60 min).

You can get specifics at the Mürren TI. For a description of six diverse hikes on the west side of Lauterbrunnen, pick up the fine and free *Mürren–Schilthorn Hikes* brochure. This 3-D map of the Mürren mountainside makes a useful and attractive souvenir. For the other side of the valley, get the *Wandern*

Jungfraubahnen brochure, also with a handy 3-D map of hiking trails (both brochures free at stations, hotels, and TIs).

Rainy-Day Options

When it rains here, locals joke that they're washing the mountains. If clouds roll in, don't despair. They can roll out just as quickly, and there are plenty of good bad-weather options.

▲▲Cloudy-Day Lauterbrunnen Valley Walk—There are easy trails and pleasant walks along the floor of the Lauterbrunnen Valley. For a smell-the-cows-and-flowers lowland walk—ideal for a cloudy day, weary body, or tight budget—follow the riverside trail from Stechelberg's Schilthornbahn station for five kilometers (3 miles) to Lauterbrunnen's Staubbach Falls, near the town church (you can reverse the route, but it's a gradual uphill to Stechelberg). Detour to Trümmelbach Falls (below) en route. There's a fine, paved, car-free, riverside path all the way.

If you're staying in Gimmelwald: Take the lift down to Stechelberg (5 min), then walk to Lauterbrunnen, detouring to Trümmelbach Falls shortly after Stechelberg (15 min to falls, another 45 min to Lauterbrunnen). To return to Gimmelwald from Lauterbrunnen, take the funicular up to Grütschalp (10 min), then either walk (90 min to Gimmelwald) or take the panorama train (15 min) to Mürren. From Mürren it's a downhill walk (30 min) to Gimmelwald. (This loop trip can be reversed.)

▲Trümmelbach Falls—If all the waterfalls have you intrigued, sneak a behind-the-scenes look at the valley's most powerful one, Trümmelbach Falls (10 SF, July–Aug daily 8:30–18:00, Easter–June and Sept–mid-Nov daily 9:00–17:00, closed mid-Nov–Easter, on Lauterbrunnen–Stechelberg road, take postal bus from Lauterbrunnen TI or Stechelberg gondola station, tel. 033-855-3232). You'll ride an elevator up through the mountain and climb through several caves (which some find claustrophobic) to see the melt from the Eiger, Mönch, and Jungfrau grinding like God's band saw through the mountain at the rate of up to 20,000 liters a second (5,200 gallons; nearly double the beer consumption at Oktoberfest). The upper area is the best; if your legs ache, skip the lower ones and ride down.

Lauterbrunnen Folk Museum—The Heimatmuseum in Lauterbrunnen shows off the local folk culture (free if you're staying in the region, 2 SF if you're staying in Interlaken, 3 SF otherwise, mid-June–mid-Oct Tue, Thu, and Sat–Sun 14:00–17:30, closed off-season, just over bridge and below church at the far end of town, tel. 033-855-1388).

Mürren Activities—This low-key alpine resort town offers a variety of rainy-day activities, from its shops to its slick Sportzentrum (sports center) with pools, steam baths, squash, and a fitness center (for details, see "Sleeping in Mürren," below). On Wednesday nights at 20:30 from June through August, Mürren's Sportzentrum hosts a lively free cultural night with alpenhorns, folk music, and local wine.

Interlaken Boat Trips—Consider taking a boat trip from Interlaken (see "Sights—Interlaken," above).

▲▲Swiss Open-Air Folk Museum at Ballenberg—Across Lake Brienz from Interlaken, the Swiss Open-Air Museum of Vernacular Architecture, Country Life, and Crafts in the Bernese Oberland is a rich collection of traditional and historic farmhouses from every region of the country. Each house is carefully furnished, and many feature traditional craftspeople at work. The sprawling 50-acre park, laid out roughly as a huge Swiss map, is a natural preserve providing a wonderful setting for this culture-on-a-lazy-Susan look at Switzerland.

The Thurgau house (#621) has an interesting wattle-and-daub (half-timbered construction) display, and house #331 has a fun bread museum. Visit the new chocolate shop. Use the 2-SF map/guide. The more expensive picture book is a better souvenir than guide (16-SF entry, half price after 16:00, houses open May–Oct daily 10:00–17:00, park stays open later, craft demonstration schedules are listed just inside the entry, tel. 033-952-1030, www.ballenberg.ch).

A reasonable outdoor cafeteria is inside the west entrance, and fresh bread, sausage, mountain cheese, and other goodies are on sale in several houses. Picnic tables and grills with free firewood are scattered throughout the park.

The little wooden village of Brienzwiler (near the east entrance) is a museum in itself, with a lovely little church.

To get from Interlaken to Ballenberg: Take the train from Interlaken to Brienz (hrly, 30 min, 7.20 SF one-way from West station). From Brienz, catch a bus to Ballenberg (10 min, 3 SF one-way) or hike (45 min, slightly uphill). If you have the time, consider coming back by boat (Brienz boat dock next to train station, one-way to Interlaken-16 SF). Trains also run occasionally from Interlaken to Brienzwiler, a 20-min uphill walk to the museum (every 2 hrs, 30 min, 9.20 SF one-way from West station). A "RailAway" combo-ticket, available at either Interlaken station, includes transportation to and from Ballenberg and your admission (32 SF from West, 30.40 SF from East, add 9.20 SF to return by boat instead).

Mystery Park—This new theme park in Wilderswil (just south of Interlaken) promises to explore intriguing mysteries from the past to the future, from building Stonehenge and the pyramids to the challenge of maintaining a space station on Mars. Planners ran out of money in the middle of construction and, at press time, were still trying to scare up new investors. Locals joke that the real mystery is whether and when the park will open (for info, ask at Interlaken TI, call 033-827-5757, or see www.mysterypark.ch).

Sleeping and Eating in the Berner Oberland (1.50 SF = about $1, country code: 41)

Sleep Code: **S** = Single, **D** = Double/Twin, **T** = Triple, **Q** = Quad, **b** = bathroom, **s** = shower only, **CC** = Credit Cards accepted, **no CC** = Credit Cards not accepted, **SE** = Speaks English, **NSE** = No English.

To help you sort easily through these listings, I've divided the rooms into three categories based on the price for a standard double room with bath:

Higher Priced—Most rooms more than 150 SF.

Moderately Priced—Most rooms 150 SF or less.

Lower Priced—Most rooms 90 SF or less.

Unless otherwise noted, breakfast is included and credit cards are not accepted. Many hotels, restaurants, and shops, especially in Mürren, are closed between Easter and late May.

Sleeping and Eating in Gimmelwald (1,350 meters/4,500 feet, country code: 41, zip code: 3826)

To inhale the Alps and really hold it in, sleep high in Gimmelwald. Poor but pleasantly stuck in the past, the village has a creaky hotel, happy hostel, decent pension, a couple of B&Bs, and even a Web site (www.gimmelwald.ch). The only bad news is that the lift costs 7.40 SF each way to get there.

MODERATELY PRICED

Maria and Olle Eggimann rent two rooms—Gimmelwald's most comfortable—in their alpine-sleek chalet. Eighteen-year town residents, Maria and Olle, who job-share the village's only teaching position and raise three kids of their own, offer visitors a rare inside peek at this community (D-110 SF, Db with kitchenette-180 SF for 2 or 3 people, optional breakfast-18 SF, no CC, last check-in 19:30, 3-night minimum for advance reservations; from gondola continue straight for 200 meters/ 650 feet along the town's only road, B&B on left, CH-3826 Gimmelwald, tel. 033-855-3575, e-mail: oeggimann@bluewin.ch, SE fluently).

LOWER PRICED

Hotel Mittaghorn, the treasure of Gimmelwald, is run by Walter Mittler, a perfect Swiss gentleman. Walter's hotel is a classic, creaky, alpine-style place with memorable beds, ancient down comforters (short and fat; wear socks and drape the blanket over your feet), and a million-dollar view of the Jungfrau Alps. The loft has a dozen real beds, several sinks, down comforters, and a fire ladder out the back window. The hotel has one shower for 10 rooms (1 SF/5 min). Walter is careful not to let his place get too hectic or big, and he enjoys sensitive Back Door travelers. He runs the hotel with a little help from Rosemarie from the village.

To some, Hotel Mittaghorn is a fire waiting to happen, with a kitchen that would never pass code, lumpy beds, teeny towels, and minimal plumbing, run by an eccentric old grouch. These people enjoy Mürren, Interlaken, or Wengen, and that's where they should sleep. Be warned, you'll see more of my readers than locals here, but it's a fun crowd—an extended family (D-70–80 SF, T-100 SF, Q-125 SF, loft beds-25 SF, 6-SF surcharge per person for 1-night stays except in loft, all with breakfast, no CC, closed Nov–March, CH-3826 Gimmelwald, tel. 033-855-1658, www.ricksteves.com/mittaghorn). Reserve by telephone only, then reconfirm by phone the day before your arrival. Walter usually offers his guests a simple 15-SF dinner. Hotel Mittaghorn is at the top of Gimmelwald, a five-minute climb up the steps from the village intersection.

Mountain Hostel is a beehive of activity, as clean as its guests, cheap, and friendly. Phone ahead, or to secure one of its 50 dorm beds the same day, call after 9:30 and leave your name. The hostel has low ceilings, a self-service kitchen, a mini-grocery, a free pool table, and healthy plumbing. It's mostly a college-age crowd; families and older travelers will probably feel more comfortable elsewhere. Petra Brunner has lined the porch with flowers. This relaxed hostel survives with the help of its guests. Read the signs (please clean the kitchen), respect Petra's rules, and leave it tidier than you found it. The place is one of those rare spots where a congenial atmosphere spontaneously combusts, and spaghetti becomes communal as it cooks (20 SF per bed in 6- to 15-bed rooms, sheets included, showers-1 SF, no breakfast, hostel membership not required, no CC, Internet access-12 SF/hour, laundry-5 SF/load, 20 meters, or 65 feet, from lift station, tel. & fax 033-855-1704, www.mountainhostel.com, e-mail: mountainhostel@tcnet.ch).

Pension Restaurant Gimmelwald, next door, offers 13 basic rooms under low, creaky ceilings (D-110 SF, Db-130 SF, T-150 SF, Q-180 SF, 5 SF per person surcharge for 1-night stays).

It also has sheetless backpacker beds (25–35 SF in small dorm rooms) and a similar camaraderie. The pension has a scenic terrace overlooking the Jungfrau and the hostel, and is the village's only restaurant, offering good meals (closed late Oct–Christmas and mid-April–mid-May, CC, non-smoking rooms but restaurant can get smoky, 50 meters/165 feet from gondola station; reserve by phone, plus obligatory reconfirmation by phone 2–3 days before arrival; tel. 033-855-1730, fax 033-855-1925, e-mail: pensiongimmelwald@tcnet.ch, Liesi and Mäni).

Esther's Guesthouse, overlooking the main intersection of the village, is like an upscale mini-hostel with five clean, basic, and comfortable rooms sharing two bathrooms and a great kitchen (S-40 SF, D-80–95 SF, T-100–120 SF, Q-150 SF, no CC, 2-night stays preferred, make your own breakfast or pay 12 SF and Esther will make it for you, no smoking, tel. 033-855-5488, fax 033-855-5492, www.esthersguesthouse.ch, e-mail: evallmen@bluewin.ch, some English spoken).

Schlaf im Stroh ("Sleep in Straw") offers exactly that, in an actual barn. After the cows head for higher ground in the summer, the friendly von Allmen family hoses out their barn and fills it with straw and budget travelers. Blankets are free, but bring your own sheet, sleep sack, or sleeping bag. No beds, no bunks, no mattresses, no kidding (22 SF, 10 SF for kids up to 10, thereafter kids pay their age plus 1 SF, no CC, includes breakfast and a modern bathroom, showers-2 SF, open mid-June–mid-Oct, depending on grass and snow levels, almost never full; from lift, continue straight through intersection, barn marked "1995" on right, run by Esther with same contact info as above).

Eating in Gimmelwald

Pension Gimmelwald, the only restaurant in town, serves a hearty breakfast buffet for 13.50 SF, fine lunches, and good dinners (10–20 SF), featuring cheese fondue, a fine *Rösti*, local organic produce, homemade pies, and spherical brownies (daily 7:30–23:00). The hostel has a decent members' kitchen, but serves no food. Hotel Mittaghorn serves dinner only to its guests (15 SF); follow dinner with a Heidi Cocoa (cocoa *mit* peppermint schnapps) or a Virgin Heidi. Consider packing in a picnic meal from the larger towns. If you need a few groceries and want to skip the hike to Mürren, you can buy the essentials—noodles, spaghetti sauce, and candy bars—at the Mountain Hostel's reception desk.

The local farmers sell their produce. Esther (at the main intersection of the village) sells cheese, sausage, bread, and Gimmelwald's best yogurt—but only until the cows go up in June.

Sleeping in Mürren (1,650 meters/5,500 feet, country code: 41, zip code: 3825)

Mürren—pleasant as an alpine resort can be—is traffic-free and filled with bakeries, cafés, souvenirs, old-timers with walking sticks, GE employees enjoying incentive trips, and Japanese tourists making movies of each other with a Fujichrome backdrop. Its chalets are prefab-rustic. Sitting on a ledge 600 meters (2,000 feet) above the Lauterbrunnen Valley, surrounded by a fortissimo chorus of mountains, the town has all the comforts of home (for a price) without the pretentiousness of more famous resorts. With help from a gondola, train, and funicular, hiking options are endless from Mürren. Mürren has an ATM (by the Co-op grocery), and there are lockers at both the train and gondola stations (located a 10-min walk apart, on opposite ends of town).

Mürren's **TI** can help you find a room, give hiking advice, and change money (July–Sept Mon–Fri 9:00–12:00 & 13:00–18:30, Thu until 20:30, Sat 13:00–18:30, Sun 13:00–17:30, less off-season, above the village, follow signs to Sportzentrum, tel. 033-856-8686, www.wengen-muerren.ch). The slick **Sportzentrum** (Sports Center) that houses the TI offers a world of indoor activities (13 SF to use pool and whirlpool; 8 SF for Gimmelwald, Lauterbrunnen, and Interlaken hotel guests; free for guests at most Mürren hotels—ask your hotelier for a voucher, pool open Mon–Fri 13:00–18:30, Thu until 20:30, closed Sun, May, and Nov–mid-Dec).

You can rent **mountain bikes** and hiking boots at Stäger Sport (bikes-25 SF/4 hrs, 35 SF/day, boots-12 SF/day, daily 9:00–17:00, closed May and Nov, across from TI/Sportzentrum, tel. 033-855-2355, www.staegersport.ch). You can use the **Internet** at Eiger Guesthouse (12 SF/hr, daily 8:00–23:00, tel. 033-856-5460, across from train station). Top Apartments will do your **laundry** by request (25 SF per load, unreliable hours: Mon–Sat 9:00–11:00 & 15:00–17:00, closed Sun, behind and across from Hotel Bellevue, look for blue triangle, call first to drop off in morning, tel. 033-855-3706). They also have a few cheap rooms (35 SF/person first night, 25 SF/person each additional night).

Prices for accommodations are often higher during the ski season. Many hotels and restaurants close in spring, roughly from Easter to late May, and any time between late September and mid-December.

HIGHER PRICED

Hotel Alpina is a simple, modern place with 24 comfortable rooms and a concrete feeling—a good thing, given its cliff-edge position

Mürren

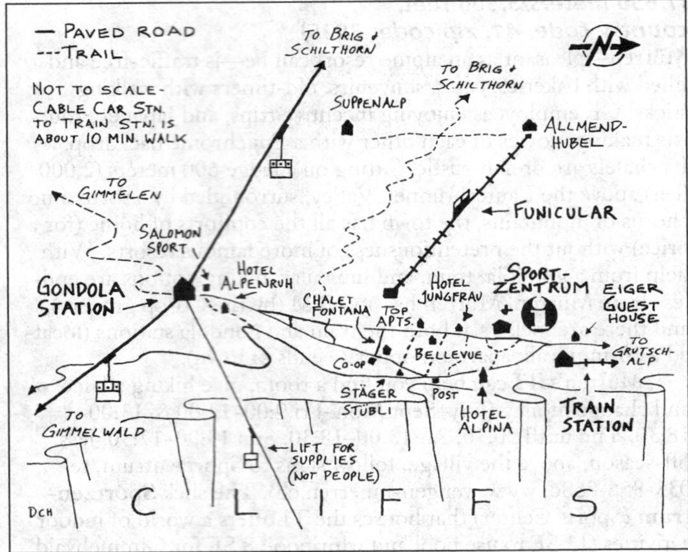

(Sb-75–95 SF, Db-140–170 SF, Tb-180–210 SF, Qb-210–240 SF with awesome Jungfrau views and balconies, 4–5 person apartments-220–280 SF, CC, exit left from station, walk 2 min downhill, tel. 033-855-1361, fax 033-855-1049, www.muerren.ch /alpina, e-mail: alpina@muerren.ch, Taugwalder family).

Hotel Bellevue has a homey lounge, great view terrace, hunter-themed "Jägerstübli" restaurant, and 17 good rooms at fair rates, most with balconies and views. The more expensive rooms are newly renovated and larger (Sb-95–125 SF, Db-150–210 SF, CC, Internet access, tel. 033-855-1401, fax 033-855-1490, www.muerren.ch/bellevue, e-mail: bellevue-crystal@bluewin.ch, run by friendly and hardworking Ruth and Othmar Suter).

Hotel Jungfrau offers 29 modern and comfortable rooms (Sb-95–110 SF, Db-190–210 SF with view, Sb-90–110 SF, Db-170–200 SF without, without breakfast-10 SF less per person, CC, elevator, near TI/Sportzentrum, tel. 033-855-4545, fax 033-855-4549, www.hoteljungfrau.ch, e-mail: mail@hoteljungfrau.ch).

Hotel Blumental has 16 older but nicely furnished rooms and a fun, woodsy game/TV lounge (Sb-75–80 SF, Db-150–170 SF, CC, non-smoking rooms but smoky lobby, tel. 033-855-1826, fax 033-855-3686, www.muerren.ch/blumental, e-mail: blumental@muerren.ch, von Allmen family).

Hotel Alpenruh is yuppie-rustic and overpriced, but it's the only hotel in Mürren open year-round. The 26 comfortable rooms come with views and some balconies (Sb-105–120 SF, Db-180–210 SF, Tb-225–270 SF, prices vary with season, CC, elevator, attached restaurant, free sauna, tanning bed-10 SF/20 min, free vouchers for breakfast atop Schilthorn, atop Allmendhubel, or at hotel, 10 meters from gondola station, tel. 033-856-8800, fax 033-856-8888, www.muerren.ch/alpenruh, e-mail: alpenruh@schilthorn.ch).

MODERATELY PRICED

Eiger Guesthouse offers 14 good budget rooms. This is a friendly, creaky, easygoing home away from home (S-60–65 SF, Sb-80–85 SF, D-100–110 SF, Db-130–140 SF, 39–45-SF beds in 2- and 4-bunk rooms, with sheets and breakfast, CC, Internet access, closed Nov and for one month after Easter, across from train station, tel. 033-856-5460, fax 033-856-5461, www.muerren.ch/eigerguesthouse, e-mail: eigerguesthouse@muerren.ch, well-run by Scotsman Alan and Swiss Véronique). The restaurant serves good, reasonably priced dinners. Its pool room—with public Internet access—is a popular local hangout.

Haus Mönch, a basic, blocky lodge run by Hotel Jungfrau, offers 20 woodsy, well-worn but fine rooms, plus good Jungfrau views (Db-130–144 SF, Tb-180 SF, without breakfast-10 SF less per person, CC, near TI and Sportzentrum, tel. 033-855-4545, fax 033-855-4549, www.hoteljungfrau.ch, e-mail: mail@hoteljungfrau.ch).

LOWER PRICED

Chalet Fontana, run by charming Englishwoman Denise Fussell, is a rare budget option in Mürren, with simple, crispy-clean, and comfortable rooms (35–45 SF per person in small doubles or triples with breakfast, 5 SF cheaper without breakfast, 1 apartment with kitchenette-50 SF per person, third and fourth person-10 SF each, no CC, closed Nov–April, across street from Stägerstübli restaurant in town center, tel. 033-855-2686, cellular 078-642-3485, e-mail: chaletfontana@muerren.ch). If no one's home, check at the Ed Abegglen shop next door (tel. 033-855-1245, off-season only).

Eating in Mürren

For a rare bit of ruggedness, eat at the **Stägerstübli** (15–30-SF lunches and dinners, daily 11:30–22:00). **Kandahar Snack Bar** has fun, creative, and inexpensive light meals; a good selection of coffees, teas, and pastries; and impressive views (take-out available, run by lively Canadian Lesley, daily 8:30–19:00, at the

Sportzentrum). The **Edelweiss** self-serve restaurant is reasonable and wins the best-view award (daily 9:00–18:00, next to Hotel Alpina). The recommended **Eiger Guesthouse** and **Hotel Bellevue** also have good restaurants (see "Sleeping in Mürren," above). For picnic fixings, shop at **Co-op** (Mon–Fri 8:00–12:00 & 13:45–18:30, Sat until 16:00, closed Sun).

Sleeping in Wengen (1,260 meters/4,200 feet, country code: 41, zip code: 3823)

Wengen, a bigger, fancier Mürren on the other side of the valley, has plenty of grand hotels, many shops, tennis courts, mini-golf, and terrific views. Minor celebrities (such as Graham Greene) come here to disappear. This traffic-free resort is an easy train ride above Lauterbrunnen and halfway up to Kleine Scheidegg and Männlichen, and offers more activities for those needing distraction from the scenery. Hiking is better from Mürren and Gimmelwald. The **TI** is one block from the station; go up to the main drag, turn left, and look ahead on the left (June–Sept and Dec–mid-April daily 9:00–18:00; mid-April–May and Oct–Nov Mon–Fri 9:00–18:00, closed Sat–Sun; tel. 033-855-1414, www.wengen-muerren.ch).

HIGHER PRICED

Hotel Berghaus, in a quiet area a five-minute walk from the main street, offers 19 rooms above a fine restaurant specializing in fish (Sb-82–117 SF, Db-164–234 SF, CC, elevator, call on phone at station hotel board for free pick-up, go up street aross from Bernerhof, bear right then left at fork, 200 meters/650 feet more past church on the left, tel. 033-855-2151, fax 033-855-3820, www.wengen.com/hotel/berghaus, e-mail: berghaus @wengen.com, Fontana family).

MODERATELY PRICED

Two bright, cheery, family-friendly places are five minutes from the station on the other side of the tracks: leave the station toward Co-op store, turn right and go under rail bridge, bear right (paved path) at the fork, follow the road down and around.

Bären Hotel, run by friendly Thérèse and Willy Brunner, offers 14 tidy rooms with perky bright-orange bathrooms (Sb-60–90 SF, Db-120–160 SF, Tb-180–210 SF, CC, family rooms, tel. 033-855-1419, fax 033-855-1525, www.wengen.com/hotel /baeren, e-mail: baeren@wengen.com).

Familienhotel Edelweiss has 25 bright rooms, lots of fun public spaces, a Christian emphasis, and a jittery Chihuahua named Speedy (Sb-65–75 SF, Db-130–150 SF, CC, non-smoking, each room has balcony or TV, great family rooms, elevator, TV lounge, game room, meeting room, kids' playroom, tel. 033-855-2388, fax 033-855-4288, www.vch.ch/edelweiss, e-mail: edelweiss@vch.ch, Bärtschi family).

Follow the tracks uphill three minutes to **Hotel Eden**—with 18 spotless, homey rooms—warmly run by Kerstin Bucher. Call first; she may retire in 2003 (S-75 SF, D-150 SF, Db-164 SF, CC, rooms without baths have balcony views, tel. 033-855-1634, fax 033-855-3950).

LOWER PRICED

Clare and Andy's Chalet (Trogihalten) offers three rustic, low-ceilinged rooms below the station (1-room studio: Sb-47 SF, Db-78 SF; 2-room suite: Sb/Db-94 SF, Tb-123 SF, Qb-164 SF; 4-room flat: Tb-141 SF, Qb-168 SF, about 37 SF extra for each additional person, breakfast-12 SF, dinner by request-28 SF, 4-night minimum preferred, prices higher for shorter stays, no CC, all rooms with balconies, leave station to the left and follow paved path next to Bernerhof downhill, soon after path becomes gravel look ahead and to the right, tel. & fax 033-855-1712, http://home.sunrise.ch/aregez, e-mail: regez.chalet.wengen@spectraweb.ch, Clare's English, Andy's Swiss).

Sleeping and Eating in Kleine Scheidegg (2,029 meters/6,762 feet, country code: 41, zip code: 3801)

Both of these places also serve meals.

Sleep face to face with the Eiger at Kleine Scheidegg's moderately priced **Bahnhof Buffet** (dorm bed-63 SF, D-150 SF, prices include breakfast and dinner, CC, tel. 033-828-7828, fax 033-828-7830, www.bahnhof-scheidegg.ch) or at the lower-priced **Restaurant Grindelwaldblick** (35 SF for bed in 12-bed room, no CC, no sheets, closed Nov and May, tel. 033-855-1374, fax 033-855-4205, www.grindelwaldblick.ch). Confirm price and availability before ascending.

Sleeping near the Stechelberg Lift (840 meters/2,800 feet, country code: 41, zip code: 3824)

Stechelberg is a hamlet at the end of the valley.

MODERATELY PRICED

Hotel Stechelberg, at road's end, is surrounded by waterfalls and vertical rock, with 20 comfortable, spacious, and quiet rooms and a lovely garden terrace (D-78–98 SF, Db-120–146 SF, T-138 SF,

Tb-186 SF, Q-168 SF, Qb-228 SF, CC, post bus stops here, tel. 033-855-2921, fax 033-855-4438, www.stechelberg.ch).

LOWER PRICED

Nelli Beer, renting three rooms in a quiet, scenic, and folksy setting, is your best Stechelberg option (S-35 SF, D-60 SF, 2-night minimum, no CC, over river behind Stechelberg post office at big *Zimmer* sign, get off post bus at post office, tel. 033-855-3930, some English spoken).

Naturfreundehaus Alpenhof is a rugged alpine lodge for hikers (46 beds, 4–8 per coed room, 19 SF per bed, no CC, breakfast-8 SF, dinner-15 SF, no sheets, tel. 033-855-1202).

Sleeping in Lauterbrunnen (780 meters/2,600 feet, country code: 41, zip code: 3822)

Lauterbrunnen—with a train station, funicular, bank, shops, and many hotels—is the valley's commercial center. This is the jumping-off point for Jungfrau and Schilthorn adventures. It's idyllic, in spite of the busy road and big buildings. Stop by the friendly **TI** to check the weather forecast and to buy any regional train or lift tickets you need (June–Aug Mon–Fri 8:00–19:00, Sat–Sun 10:00–16:00; Sept–Oct Mon–Fri 8:00–12:30 & 13:30–17:00, Sat–Sun 10:00–16:00; Nov–May Mon–Fri 8:00–12:30 & 13:30–17:00, closed Sat–Sun, 1 block up from station, tel. 033-856-8568, www.wengen-muerren.ch). You can rent **mountain bikes** at Imboden Bike on the main street (25 SF/4 hrs, 35 SF/day, 10 SF extra for full suspension, daily 8:30–18:30, closed Nov, tel. 033-855-2114). The Valley Hostel on the main street also runs an **Internet café** (15 SF/hr) and a small **launderette** (10 SF/load, don't open dryer door until machine is finished or you'll have to pay another 5 SF to start it again; both daily 8:00–22:00, less Nov–April, tel. 033-855-2008).

MODERATELY PRICED

Hotel Staubbach, a big Old World place—one of the first hotels in the valley (1890)—is being lovingly restored by hard-working American Craig and his Swiss wife, Corinne. Its 30 plain, comfortable rooms are family-friendly, there's a kids' play area, and the parking is free. Many rooms have great views. They keep their prices down by providing room-cleaning only after every third night (S-55 SF, Ss-60 SF, Sb-100 SF, D-80 SF, Db-110 SF, figure 40 SF per person in family rooms sleeping up to 6, 10 SF extra per room for 1-night stays, includes buffet breakfast, CC, elevator, 4 blocks up from station on the left, tel. 033-855-5454, fax 033-855-5484, www.staubbach.ch, e-mail: hotel@staubbach.ch).

LOWER PRICED

Valley Hostel is practical, friendly, and comfortable, offering inexpensive beds for quieter travelers of all ages, with a pleasant garden and the welcoming Abegglen family: Martha, Alfred, Stefan, and Fränzi (D with bunk beds-52 SF, twin D-60 SF, beds in larger family-friendly rooms-22 SF each, no breakfast but kitchen is available, no CC, most rooms have balconies, cheese fondue on request for guests 18:00–20:00-16 SF per person, non-smoking, Internet access, laundry, 2 blocks up from train station, tel. & fax 033-855-2008, www.valleyhostel.ch, e-mail: info@valleyhostel.ch).

Chalet im Rohr, a creaky, old, woody place, has oodles of character and 26-SF beds in big one- to four-bed rooms (2 SF discount after second night, no breakfast, common kitchen-0.50 SF per person, no CC, closed for 3 weeks after Easter, below church on main drag, tel. & fax 033-855-2182).

Matratzenlager Stocki is rustic and humble, with the cheapest beds in town (14 SF with sheets in easygoing little 30-bed coed dorm with kitchen, no CC, closed Nov–Dec; across river from station, go below station to parking and take last right before garage, walk on path and then turn left over bridge, walk up and to the right 200 meters/650 feet; tel. 033-855-1754).

Two campgrounds just south of town provide 15- to 35-SF beds (in dorms and 2-, 4-, and 6-bed bungalows, no sheets, kitchen facilities, no CC, big English-speaking tour groups): **Mountain Holiday Park-Camping Jungfrau**, romantically situated beyond Staubbach Falls, is huge and well-organized by Hans (tel. 033-856-2010, fax 033-856-2020, www.camping-jungfrau.ch). It also has fancier cabins (22 SF per person). **Schützenbach Retreat**, on the left just past Lauterbrunnen toward Stechelberg, is simpler (tel. 033-855-1268, www.schutzenbach-retreat.ch).

Sleeping in Obersteinberg (1,800 meters/5,900 feet, country code: 41, zip code: 3824)

Here's a wild idea: **Mountain Hotel Obersteinberg** is a working alpine farm with cheese, cows, a mule shuttling up food once a day, and an American (Vickie) who fell in love with a mountain man. It's a 2.5-hour hike from either Stechelberg or Gimmelwald. They rent 12 primitive rooms and a bunch of loft beds. There's no shower, no hot water, and only meager solar-panel electricity. Candles light up the night, and you can take a hot-water bottle to bed if necessary (S-81 SF, D-162 SF, includes linen, sheetless dorm beds-64 SF, these prices include breakfast and dinner, without meals S-37 SF, D-73 SF, dorm beds-20 SF, closed Oct–May, tel. 033-855-2033). The place is filled with locals and Germans on weekends, but is all yours on weekdays. Why not hike there from Gimmelwald and leave the Alps a day later?

Sleeping in Isenfluh
(1,068 meters/3,560 feet, country code: 41, zip code: 3807)

In the tiny hamlet of Isenfluh, which is even smaller than Gimmelwald and offers better views, **Pension Waldrand** offers a restaurant and four reasonable rooms (Db-120–140 SF, Tb-150 SF, includes breakfast, CC, hourly bus from Lauterbrunnen, tel. 033-855-1227, fax 033-855-1392, www.waldrand.com).

Sleeping in Interlaken
(country code: 41, zip code: 3800)

I'd head for Gimmelwald or at least Lauterbrunnen (20 min by train or car). Interlaken is not the Alps. But if you must stay, see the map on page 1204.

HIGHER PRICED

Hotel Lotschberg, with a sun terrace and 21 wonderful rooms, is run by English-speaking Susi and Fritz and is the best real hotel value in town. Happy to dispense information, these gregarious folks pride themselves on a personal touch that sets them apart from other hotels. Fritz also organizes guided adventures (Sb-92–110 SF, Db-129–155 SF, big Db-162–190 SF, extra bed-25 SF, family deals, cheaper prices are for Nov–May, CC, non-smoking, elevator, Internet access-10 SF/hr, laundry service-9 SF/load, bike rental, discounted parasailing if you "Fly with Fritz"; 3-min walk from station, exit right from West station, take a left before big Migros store, then take first right and then first left to General Guisanstrasse 31, tel. 033-822-2545, fax 033-822-2579, www.lotschberg.ch, e-mail: hotel@lotschberg.ch).

MODERATELY PRICED

Sunny Days B&B, run by British Dave and Swiss Brigit, has nine colorful, cheery rooms ideal for families (Sb-98–102 SF, Db-110–148 SF, extra adult in room-45 SF, each additional child under 16-38 SF, discounts for longer stays Nov–March, CC, great breakfast, Internet access-16 SF/hr, laundry service-18 SF/load; exit left out of West station and take first bridge to your left, after crossing bridges turn left on peaceful Helvetiastrasse and go 3 blocks to #29; tel. 033-822-8343, fax 033-823-8343, www.sunnydays.ch, e-mail: mail@sunnydays.ch).

Guest House Susi's B&B is Hotel Lotschberg's no-frills, cash-only annex, run by Fritz and Susi (same contact info as Hotel

Lotschberg, above), offering nicely furnished, cozy rooms (Sb-72–90 SF, Db-98–125 SF, apartments with kitchenettes for 2 people-100 SF; for 4–5 people-175 SF, cheaper prices Nov–May, no CC).

Hotel Aarburg offers 13 plain, peaceful rooms in a beautifully located but run-down old building a 10-minute walk from the West station (Sb-80 SF, Db-130 SF, CC, next to launderette at Beatenbergstrasse 1, tel. 033-822-2615, fax 033-822-6397, e-mail: hotel-aarburg@tcnet.ch).

LOWER PRICED

Villa Margaretha, run by perky, English-speaking Frau Kunz-Joerin, offers the best cheap beds in town. It's a big Victorian house with a garden on a quiet residential street. Keep your room tidy and you'll have a friend for life (D-86 SF, T-129 SF, Q-172 SF, 3 rooms share a big bathroom, 2-night minimum, apartment-156–162 SF with a 1-week minimum stay, closed Oct–April, no CC, no breakfast served but dishes and kitchenette available, lots of rules to abide by; walk up small street directly in front of the West station's parking lot entrance, go 3 blocks and look to your right for Aarmühlestrasse 13, tel. 033-822-1813).

Backpackers' Villa Interlaken is a creative guest house run by a Methodist church group. It's fun, youthful, and great for families, without the frat-party ambience of Balmer's (below). Rooms are comfortable and half come with Jungfrau-view balconies (D-88 SF, T-120 SF, Q-144 SF, dorm beds in 5- to 7-bed rooms with lockers and sheets-32 SF per person, 5 SF more per person for rooms with toilets and Jungfrau-view balconies, CC, includes breakfast, kitchen, garden, movies, small game room, Internet access-10 SF/hr, laundry-10 SF/load, bike rental, no curfew, open all day, check-in 16:00–22:00, 10-min walk from either station, across grassy field from TI, Alpenstrasse 16, tel. 033-826-7171, fax 033-826-7172, www.villa.ch, e-mail: backpackers@villa.ch).

For many, **Balmer's Herberge** is backpacker heaven. This Interlaken institution comes with movies, table tennis, a launderette (8 SF/load), bar, restaurant, swapping library, Internet access (20 SF/hr), tiny grocery, bike rental, currency exchange, excursions, a shuttle-bus service (which meets every arriving train), and a friendly, hardworking staff. This little Nebraska is home for those who miss their fraternity. It can be a mob scene, especially on summer weekends (dorm beds-24 SF, S-40 SF; D, T, or Q-28–34 SF per person, includes sheets and breakfast, CC, non-smoking, open year-round, easy Internet reservations recommended 5 days in advance, Hauptstrasse 23, in Matten, 15-min walk from either Interlaken station, tel. 033-822-1961, fax 033-823-3261, www.balmers.com, e-mail: balmers@tcnet.ch).

Happy Inn Lodge has 16 cheap rooms above a lively, noisy restaurant a five-minute walk from the West station (S-30–40 SF, D-60–80 SF, bunk in 4–8 bed dorms-22 SF, breakfast-8 SF, CC, Rosenstrasse 17, tel. 033-822-3225, fax 033-822-3268, www.happy-inn.com).

Transportation Connections—Interlaken

If you plan to arrive at the Zurich Airport and want to head straight for Interlaken and the Alps, see "Zurich Airport," below. Train info: toll tel. 0900-300-3004.

From Interlaken by train to: Spiez (2/hr, 20 min), **Brienz** (hrly, 30 min), **Bern** (hrly, 50 min), **Zurich** and **Zurich Airport** (hrly, 2.25 hrs, most direct but some with transfer in Bern). While there are a few long trains from Interlaken, you'll generally connect from Bern.

By train from Bern to: Lausanne (hrly, 70 min), **Zurich** (hrly, 70 min), **Appenzell** (hrly, 4.25, transfers in Zurich and Gossau or Bern and Gossau, or 5 hrs, change in Luzern and Herisau), **Salzburg** (4/day, 8 hrs, transfers include Zurich), **Munich** (7/day, 5.5–6.5 hrs, transfers in Zurich or Mannheim), **Frankfurt** (hrly, 4.5 hrs, some direct, some transfer in Basel or Mannheim), **Paris** (4/day, 4.5 hrs).

Interlaken to Gimmelwald: Take the train from the Interlaken East *(Ost)* Station to Lauterbrunnen. From here, you have two options.

1) The faster, easier way—best in bad weather or at the end of a long day with lots of luggage—is to ride the post bus from Lauterbrunnen station (3.80 SF, hourly bus departure coordinated with arrival of train, stop: Schilthornbahn) to Stechelberg and the base of the Schilthornbahn gondola station (tel. 033-856-2141), where the gondola will whisk you in five thrilling minutes up to Gimmelwald.

2) The more scenic route is to catch the funicular to Mürren (across the street from the train station). Ride up to Grütschalp, where a special scenic train *(Panorama Fahrt)* will roll you along the cliff into Mürren (total trip from Lauterbrunnen to Mürren: 30 min). From there, either walk a paved 30 minutes downhill to Gimmelwald, or walk 10 minutes across Mürren to catch the gondola (costs 7.40 SF and once in Gimmelwald, you'll have a 2- to 5-min uphill hike to reach accommodations).

By **car**, it's a 30-minute drive from Interlaken to Stechelberg. The pay parking lot (1 SF/2 hrs, 5 SF/day) at the Stechelberg gondola station is safe. Gimmelwald is the first stop above Stechelberg on the Schilthorn gondola (7.40 SF, 2/hr at :25 and :55, get off at first stop). Note that for a week in early May and from mid-November through early December, the Schilthornbahn is closed for servicing. You can drive to Lauterbrunnen and to Stechelberg, but not to Gimmelwald (park in Stechelberg, and take the gondola) or to Mürren, Wengen, or Kleine Scheidegg (park in Lauterbrunnen and take the train).

Zurich Airport

Smooth, compact, and user-friendly, the Zurich Airport is a major transportation hub and an eye-opening introduction to Swiss efficiency. Swiss airlines use the A concourse, and most others use the B concourse; both funnel to the same immigration line. To find a Suisse Bank exchange office (daily 6:00–22:00), upscale chocolate and watch stores, and Internet access, bypass the immigration line and go to the back wall behind the big staircase. Eateries and ATMs are plentiful before and after immigration. The train station underneath the airport (with a mini-mall, a post office, and a tidy grocery) can whisk you about anywhere you'd want to go in Europe, including downtown Zurich (5.40 SF, 10 min, leaves every 10 min—much cheaper than the 50-SF taxi ride). For flight information, call the automated toll number: 0900-300-313 (press 2 for English).

If you have to catch an early morning flight, don't spend a fortune to stay near the airport (Hilton, Db starting at 250 SF, tel. 018-285-050). Sleep near the train station downtown. Check into your hotel, stroll through the Lindenhof for some nice city views, then head for Bürkliplatz to catch an evening Limmatschiff boat ride on Lake Zurich (5.40 SF, free with Eurail/Eurail Selectpass and Swiss railpass, 2/hr, daily 11:00–19:00, later mid-Jun–Sept; fun 90-min ride on lake, then up the Limmat River and back to the Landesmusem across from the station). Zip to the airport in the morning on the frequent and fast train (see above). **Hotel Leoneck**, a 10-minute uphill walk from the station, offers 70 modern yet kitschy bovine-themed rooms at a good price. The hotel—and the good attached "Crazy Cow" restaurant (daily 6:00–24:00)—somehow manage to make Swiss cows seem cool; enjoy the moo-velous mural in your bedroom (Sb-100–140 SF, Db-150–185 SF, Tb-185–240 SF, Qb-240–290 SF, CC, non-smoking rooms, elevator, Internet access-20 SF/hr, Leonhardstrasse 1, tel. 012-542-222, fax 012-542-200, www.leoneck.ch, e-mail: info@leoneck.ch).

Transportation Connections—Zurich Airport

By train to: Interlaken (hrly, 2.5 hrs), **Bern** (2/hr, 1.5 hrs), **Murten** (hrly, 2.75 hrs, change in Fribourg, Switzerland), **Lausanne** (2/hr, 2.75 hrs), **Munich** (4/day, 4.25 hrs), **Appenzell** (2/hr, 2 hrs with transfer in St. Gallen or 1.5 hrs with transfer in Gossau).

APPENDIX

Let's Talk Telephones

To make international calls, you need to break the codes: the international access codes and country codes (see below). For information on making local, long-distance, and international calls, see "Telephones" in this book's introduction.

International Access Codes

When dialing direct, first dial the international access code (011 if you're calling from the U.S.A. or Canada; 00 if you're calling from Europe). Virtually all European countries use "00" as their international access code; the only exceptions are Finland (990) and Lithuania (810).

Country Codes

After you've dialed the international access code, dial the code of the country you're calling.

Austria—43
Belgium—32
Britain—44
Canada—1
Czech Rep.—420
Denmark—45
Estonia—372
Finland—358
France—33
Germany—49
Gibraltar—350
Greece—30
Ireland—353
Italy—39
Morocco—212
Netherlands—31
Norway—47
Portugal—351
Spain—34
Sweden—46
Switzerland—41
U.S.A.—1

European National Tourist Offices in the United States

Austrian Tourist Office: Box 1142, New York, NY 10108-1142, tel. 212/944-6880, fax 212/730-4568, www.austria-tourism.com, e-mail: info@oewnyc.com. Ask for their "Vacation Kit" with map. Fine hikes and city information.

Belgian National Tourist Office: 780 Third Ave. #1501, New York, NY 10017, tel. 212/758-8130, fax 212/355-7675, www.visitbelgium.com, e-mail: info@visitbelgium.com. Hotel and city guides; brochures for ABC lovers—antiques, beer, and chocolates; map of Brussels; and a list of Jewish sights.

British Tourist Authority: 551 Fifth Ave., 7th floor, New York, NY 10176, tel. 800/462-2748, fax 212/986-1188, www.travelbritain.org, e-mail: travelinfo@bta.org.uk. Request the

European Calling Chart

Just smile and dial, using this key: AC = Area Code, LN = Local Number.

European Country	Calling long distance within...	Calling from the U.S.A./ Canada to...	Calling from another European country to...
Austria	AC (Area Code) + LN (Local Number)	011 + 43 + AC (without the initial zero) + LN	00 + 43 + AC (without the initial zero) + LN
Belgium	LN	011 + 32 + LN (without initial zero)	00 + 32 + LN (without initial zero)
Britain	AC + LN	011 + 44 + AC (without initial zero) + LN	00 + 44 + AC . (without initial zero) + LN
Czech Republic	LN	011 + 420 + LN	00 + 420 + LN
Denmark	LN	011 + 45 + LN	00 + 45 + LN
Estonia	LN	011 + 372 + LN	00 + 372 + LN
Finland	AC + LN	011 + 358 + AC (without initial zero) + LN	00 + 358 + AC (without initial zero) + LN
France	LN	011 + 33 + LN (without initial zero)	00 + 33 + LN (without initial zero)
Germany	AC + LN	011 + 49 + AC (without initial zero) + LN	00 + 49 + AC (without initial zero) + LN
Gibraltar	LN	011 + 350 + LN	00 + 350 + LN From Spain: 9567 + LN
Greece	LN	011 + 30 + LN	00 + 30 + LN

European Country	Calling long distance within…	Calling from the U.S.A./ Canada to…	Calling from another European country to…
Ireland	AC + LN	011 + 353 + AC (without initial zero) + LN	00 + 353 + AC (without initial zero) + LN
Italy	LN	011 + 39 + LN	00 + 39 + LN
Morocco	LN	011 + 212 + LN (without initial zero)	00 + 212 + LN (without initial zero)
Netherlands	AC + LN	011 + 31 + AC (without initial zero) + LN	00 + 31 + AC (without initial zero) + LN
Norway	LN	011 + 47 + LN	00 + 47 + LN
Portugal	LN	011 + 351 + LN	00 + 351 + LN
Spain	LN	011 + 34 + LN	00 + 34 + LN
Sweden	AC + LN	011 + 46 + AC (without initial zero) + LN	00 + 46 + AC (without initial zero) + LN
Switzerland	LN	011 + 41 + LN (without initial zero)	00 + 41 + LN (without initial zero)
Turkey	AC (if no initial zero is included, add one) + LN	011 + 90 + AC (without initial zero) + LN	00 + 90 + AC (without initial zero) + LN

- The instructions above apply whether you're calling a fixed phone or cell phone.
- The international access codes (the first numbers you dial when making an international call) are 011 if you're calling from the U.S.A./Canada, or 00 if you're calling from virtually anywhere in Europe. Finland and Lithuania are the only exceptions. If calling from either of these countries, replace the 00 with 990 in Finland and 810 in Lithuania.
- To call the U.S.A. or Canada from Europe, dial 00 (unless you're calling from Finland or Lithuania), then 1 (the country code for the U.S.A. and Canada), then the area code and number. In short, 00 + 1 + AC + LN = Hi, mom!

Britain Vacation Planner. Free maps of London and Britain. Regional information, garden tour map, and urban cultural activities brochure.

Czech Tourist Authority: 1109 Madison Ave., New York, NY 10028, tel. 212/288-0830, fax 212/288-0971, www.czechcenter.com, e-mail: travelczech@pop.net. To get a weighty information package (1–2 lbs, no advertising), send a check for $4 to cover postage and specify places of interest. Basic information and map are free.

Denmark (see Scandinavia)

French Government Tourist Office: For questions and brochures (on regions, barging, and the wine country), call 410/286-8310. Ask for the Discovery Guide. Materials delivered in 4 to 6 weeks are free; there's a $4 shipping fee for information delivered in 5 to 10 days. Their Web site is www.franceguide.com, and their offices are . . .

In New York: 444 Madison Ave., 16th floor, New York, NY 10022, fax 212/838-7855, e-mail: info@francetourism.com.

In Illinois: 676 N. Michigan Ave. #3360, Chicago, IL 60611-2819, fax 312/337-6339, e-mail: fgto@mcs.net.

In California: 9454 Wilshire Blvd. #715, Beverly Hills, CA 90212, fax 310/276-2835, e-mail: fgto@gte.net.

German National Tourist Office: 122 E. 42nd Street, 52nd floor, New York, NY 10168, tel. 212/661-7200, fax 212/661-7174, www.visits-to-germany.com, e-mail: gntony@aol.com. Maps, Rhine schedules, castles, biking, and city and regional information.

Irish Tourist Board: 345 Park Ave., 17th floor, New York, NY 10154, tel. 800/223-6470 or 212/418-0800, fax 212/371-9052, www.irelandvacations.com. Useful "Ireland Magazine," Ireland map, events calendar, golfing, outdoor activities, and historic sights. The Irish Tourist Board now also provides information to travelers who wish to visit Northern Ireland. Learn more about sightseeing opportunities and ask about a vacation planner packet, maps, walking routes, and horseback riding.

Italian Government Tourist Board: Check www.italiantourism .com and contact the nearest office . . .

In New York: 630 Fifth Ave. #1565, New York, NY 10111, brochure hotline tel. 212/245-4822, tel. 212/245-5618, fax 212/ 586-9249, e-mail: enitny@italiantourism.com.

In Illinois: 500 N. Michigan Ave. #2240, Chicago, IL 60611, brochure hotline tel. 312/644-0990, tel. 312/644-0996, fax 312/ 644-3019, e-mail: enitch@italiantourism.com.

In California: 12400 Wilshire Blvd. #550, Los Angeles, CA 90025, brochure hotline tel. 310/820-0098, tel. 310/820-1898, fax 310/820-6357, e-mail: enitla@earthlink.net.

Netherlands Board of Tourism: 355 Lexington Ave., 19th floor,

New York, NY 10017, tel. 888/GO-HOLLAND, fax 212/370-9507, www.goholland.com, e-mail: info@goholland.com. Great country map, events calendar, and seasonal brochures; $5 donation requested for mailing (pay on receipt).

Scandinavian Tourism: P.O. Box 4649, Grand Central Station, New York, NY 10163, tel. 212/885-9700, fax 212/885-9710, www.goscandinavia.com, e-mail: info@goscandinavia.com. Good general booklets on all the Scandinavian countries. Ask for specific country info and city maps.

Tourist Office of Spain: Check their Web sites (www.okspain.org and www.tourspain.es) and contact their nearest office . . .

In New York: 666 Fifth Ave., 35th floor, New York, NY 10103, tel. 212/265-8822, fax 212/265-8864, e-mail: oetny@tourspain.es.

In Illinois: 845 N. Michigan Ave. #915E, Chicago, IL 60611, tel. 312/642-1992, fax 312/642-9817, e-mail: chicago@tourspain.es.

In Florida: 1221 Brickell Ave. #1850, Miami, FL 33131, tel. 305/358- 1992, fax 305/358-8223, e-mail: oetmiami@tourspain.es.

In California: 8383 Wilshire Blvd. #956, Beverly Hills, CA 90211, tel. 323/658-7188, fax 323/658-1061, e-mail: losangeles@tourspain.es.

Switzerland Tourism: For questions and brochures call 877/794-8037. Comprehensive "Welcome to the Best of Switzerland" brochure, great maps, and hiking material. Or contact 608 Fifth Ave., New York, NY 10020, fax 212/262-6116, www.myswitzerland.com, e-mail: info.usa@switzerland.com.

U.S. Embassies and Consulates

Austria: U.S. Embassy, Marriott Building 4th floor, Gartenbaupromenade 2, Vienna, tel. 01/31339, www.usembassy-vienna.at/consulate

Belgium: U.S. Embassy, Regentlaan 27 Boulevard du Regent, Brussels, tel. 02/508-2111, **www.usembassy.be**

Britain: U.S. Embassy, 55 Upper Brook Street, London, tel. 020/7499-9000, www.usembassy.org.uk (also see Scotland, below)

Czech Republic: U.S. Embassy, Trziste 15, Prague, tel. 257-530-663, www.usembassy.cz

Denmark: U.S. Embassy, Dag Hammarskjolds Alle 24, Copenhagen, tel. 35 55 31 44, www.usembassy.dk

France: U.S. Embassy, 2 avenue Gabriel, Mo: Concorde, Paris, tel. 01 43 12 22 22, www.amb-usa.fr

Germany: U.S. Embassy, Clayallee 170, Berlin, tel. 030/832-9233, www.usembassy.de

Ireland: U.S. Embassy, 42 Elgin Road, Dublin, tel. 01/668-7122 or 01/668-8777, www.usembassy.ie

2003

JANUARY

S	M	T	W	T	F	S
			1	2	3	4
5	6	7	8	9	10	11
12	13	14	15	16	17	18
19	20	21	22	23	24	25
26	27	28	29	30	31	

FEBRUARY

S	M	T	W	T	F	S
						1
2	3	4	5	6	7	8
9	10	11	12	13	14	15
16	17	18	19	20	21	22
23	24	25	26	27	28	

MARCH

S	M	T	W	T	F	S
						1
2	3	4	5	6	7	8
9	10	11	12	13	14	15
16	17	18	19	20	21	22
23/30	24/31	25	26	27	28	29

APRIL

S	M	T	W	T	F	S
		1	2	3	4	5
6	7	8	9	10	11	12
13	14	15	16	17	18	19
20	21	22	23	24	25	26
27	28	29	30			

MAY

S	M	T	W	T	F	S
				1	2	3
4	5	6	7	8	9	10
11	12	13	14	15	16	17
18	19	20	21	22	23	24
25	26	27	28	29	30	31

JUNE

S	M	T	W	T	F	S
1	2	3	4	5	6	7
8	9	10	11	12	13	14
15	16	17	18	19	20	21
22	23	24	25	26	27	28
29	30					

JULY

S	M	T	W	T	F	S
		1	2	3	4	5
6	7	8	9	10	11	12
13	14	15	16	17	18	19
20	21	22	23	24	25	26
27	28	29	30	31		

AUGUST

S	M	T	W	T	F	S
					1	2
3	4	5	6	7	8	9
10	11	12	13	14	15	16
17	18	19	20	21	22	23
24/31	25	26	27	28	29	30

SEPTEMBER

S	M	T	W	T	F	S
	1	2	3	4	5	6
7	8	9	10	11	12	13
14	15	16	17	18	19	20
21	22	23	24	25	26	27
28	29	30				

OCTOBER

S	M	T	W	T	F	S
			1	2	3	4
5	6	7	8	9	10	11
12	13	14	15	16	17	18
19	20	21	22	23	24	25
26	27	28	29	30	31	

NOVEMBER

S	M	T	W	T	F	S
						1
2	3	4	5	6	7	8
9	10	11	12	13	14	15
16	17	18	19	20	21	22
23/30	24	25	26	27	28	29

DECEMBER

S	M	T	W	T	F	S
	1	2	3	4	5	6
7	8	9	10	11	12	13
14	15	16	17	18	19	20
21	22	23	24	25	26	27
28	29	30	31			

Italy: American Embassy at Via Veneto 119, Rome, tel. 06-46741, www.usembassy.it; U.S. Consulate General at Lungarno Vespucci 38, Florence, tel. 055-239-8276, www.usembassy.it/florence

The Netherlands: U.S. Embassy at Lange Voorhout 102, The Hague, tel. 070/310-9209, www.usemb.nl; U.S. Consulate at Museumplein 19, Amsterdam (for passport concerns), tel. 020/575-5309, www.usemb.nl/consul.htm

Scotland: U.S. Consulate General, 3 Regent Terrace, Edinburgh, tel. 0131/556-8315, www.usembassy.org.uk/scotland

Spain: U.S. Embassy, Serrano 75, Madrid, tel. 915-872-240 or 915-872-200, www.embusa.es/cons/services.html

Switzerland: U.S. Embassy, Jubilaeumsstrasse 95, Bern, tel. 031-357-7234, www.us-embassy.ch/

VAT Rates and Minimum Purchases Required to Qualify for Refunds

Country	VAT Rate*	Minimum Purchase in Local Currency	Minimum Purchase in US Dollars
Austria	16.7%	€75	$75
Belgium	17%	€125	$125
Czech Republic	5-22%	1001 kč	$30
Denmark	20%	301 kr	$40
France	16.4%	€175	$175
Germany	13.8%	€25	$25
Great Britain	15%	£30	$45
Ireland	16.7%	—	$0
Italy	16.7%	€155	$155
Netherlands	15%	€137	$137
Spain	13.8%	€90	$90
Switzerland	7%	400 SF	$270

**VAT Rate indicates the percentage of the total purchase price that is VAT.*

Source: Global Refund Tax-Free Shopping

Please note: Figures are subject to change. For more information, visit europeforvisitors.com/europe/articles/taxfree_shopping.htm, www.traveltax.msu.edu/vat/vat.htm, www.globalrefund.com, and www.cashback.it.

Climate

Here is a list of average temperatures (first line—average daily low; second line—average daily high; third line—days of no rain). This can be helpful in planning your itinerary, but I have never found European weather to be particularly predictable, and these charts ignore humidity.

J	F	M	A	M	J	J	A	S	O	N	D
AUSTRIA • Vienna											
25°	28°	30°	42°	50°	56°	60°	59°	53°	44°	37°	30°
34°	38°	47°	58°	67°	73°	76°	75°	68°	56°	45°	37°
16	17	18	17	18	16	18	18	20	18	16	16
BELGIUM • Brussels											
30°	32°	36°	41°	46°	52°	54°	54°	51°	45°	38°	32°
40°	44°	51°	58°	65°	72°	73°	72°	69°	60°	48°	42°
10	11	14	12	15	15	14	13	17	14	10	12

	J	F	M	A	M	J	J	A	S	O	N	D
CZECH REPUBLIC • Prague												
	23°	24°	30°	38°	46°	52°	55°	55°	49°	41°	33°	27°
	31°	34°	44°	54°	64°	70°	73°	72°	65°	53°	42°	34°
	18	17	21	19	18	18	18	19	20	18	18	18
DENMARK • Copenhagen												
	29°	28°	31°	37°	45°	51°	56°	56°	51°	44°	38°	33°
	37°	37°	42°	51°	60°	66°	70°	69°	64°	55°	46°	41°
	14	15	19	18	20	18	17	16	14	14	11	12
FRANCE • Paris												
	34°	34°	39°	43°	49°	55°	58°	58°	53°	46°	40°	36°
	43°	45°	54°	60°	68°	73°	76°	75°	70°	60°	50°	44°
	14	14	19	17	19	18	19	18	17	18	15	15
GERMANY • Berlin												
	23°	23°	30°	38°	45°	51°	55°	54°	48°	40°	33°	26°
	35°	38°	48°	56°	64°	70°	74°	73°	67°	56°	44°	36°
	15	12	18	15	16	13	15	15	17	18	15	16
GREAT BRITAIN • London												
	36°	36°	38°	42°	47°	53°	56°	56°	52°	46°	42°	38°
	43°	44°	50°	56°	62°	69°	71°	71°	65°	58°	50°	45°
	16	15	20	18	19	19	19	20	17	18	15	16
IRELAND • Dublin												
	34°	35°	37°	39°	43°	48°	52°	51°	48°	43°	39°	37°
	46°	47°	51°	55°	60°	65°	67°	67°	63°	57°	51°	47°
	18	18	21	19	21	19	18	19	18	20	18	17
ITALY • Rome												
	40°	42°	45°	50°	56°	63°	67°	67°	62°	55°	49°	44°
	52°	55°	59°	66°	74°	82°	87°	86°	79°	71°	61°	55°
	13	19	23	24	26	26	30	29	25	23	19	21
NETHERLANDS • Amsterdam												
	31°	31°	34°	40°	46°	51°	55°	55°	50°	44°	38°	33°
	40°	42°	49°	56°	64°	70°	72°	71°	67°	57°	48°	42°
	9	9	15	14	17	16	14	13	11	11	9	10
SPAIN • Madrid												
	35°	36°	41°	45°	50°	58°	63°	63°	57°	49°	42°	36°
	47°	52°	59°	65°	70°	80°	87°	85°	77°	65°	55°	48°
	23	21	21	21	21	25	29	28	24	23	21	21

	J	F	M	A	M	J	J	A	S	O	N	D
SWITZERLAND • Geneva												
	29°	30°	36°	42°	49°	55°	58°	58°	53°	44°	37°	31°
	38°	42°	51°	59°	66°	73°	77°	76°	69°	58°	47°	40°
	20	19	22	21	20	19	22	20	20	21	19	21

Numbers and Stumblers

- Europeans write a few of their numbers differently than we do. 1 = 1, 4 = 4, 7 = 7. Learn the difference or miss your train.
- In Europe, dates appear as day/month/year, so Christmas is 25/12/03.
- Commas are decimal points and decimals commas. A dollar and a half is $1,50, and there are 5.280 feet in a mile.
- When pointing, use your whole hand, palm down.
- When counting with fingers, start with your thumb. If you hold up your first finger to request one item, you'll probably get two.
- What Americans call the second floor of a building is the first floor in Europe.
- Europeans keep the left "lane" open for passing on escalators and moving sidewalks. Keep to the right.

Metric Conversion (approximate)

1 inch = 25 millimeters
1 foot = 0.3 meter
1 yard = 0.9 meter
1 mile = 1.6 kilometers
1 centimeter = 0.4 inch
1 meter = 39.4 inches
1 kilometer = .62 mile

32 degrees F = 0 degrees C
82 degrees F = about 28 degrees C
1 ounce = 28 grams
1 kilogram = 2.2 pounds
1 quart = 0.95 liter
1 square yard = 0.8 square meter
1 acre = 0.4 hectare

Faxing Your Hotel Reservation

Use this handy form for your fax or find it online at www.ricksteves.com/reservation. Photocopy and fax away.

One-Page Fax

To: ______________________ @ ______________________
hotel *fax*

From: ______________________ @ ______________________
name *fax*

Today's date: ____ /____ /____
day *month* *year*

Dear Hotel ______________________,

Please make this reservation for me:

Name: ______________________

Total # of people: ____ # of rooms: ____ # of nights: ____

Arriving: ____ /____ /____ My time of arrival (24-hr clock): ____
day *month* *year*

(I will telephone if I will be late)

Departing: ____ /____ /____
day *month* *year*

Room(s): Single___ Double___ Twin___ Triple___ Quad___

With: Toilet___ Shower___ Bath___ Sink only___

Special needs: View___ Quiet___ Cheapest___ Ground Floor___

Credit card: Visa___ MasterCard___ American Express___

Card #: ______________________

Expiration date: ______________________

Name on card: ______________________

You may charge me for the first night as a deposit. Please fax, e-mail, or mail me confirmation of my reservation, along with the type of room reserved, the price, and whether the price includes breakfast. Please also inform me of your cancellation policy. Thank you.

____
Signature

____
Name

____
Address

____
City *State* *Zip Code* *Country*

____
E-mail Address

Road Scholar Feedback for BEST OF EUROPE 2003

We're all in the same travelers' school of hard knocks. Your feedback helps us improve this guidebook for future travelers. Please fill this out (or use the online version at www.ricksteves.com/feedback), attach more info or any tips/favorite discoveries if you like, and send it to us. As thanks for your help, we'll send you our quarterly travel newsletter free for one year. Thanks! ***Rick***

Of the recommended accommodations/restaurants used, which was:

Best ____________________

Why? ____________________

Worst ____________________

Why? ____________________

Of the sights/experiences/destinations recommended by this book, which was:

Most overrated ____________________

Why? ____________________

Most underrated ____________________

Why? ____________________

Best ways to improve this book:

____

____

I'd like a free newsletter subscription:

____ Yes ____ No ____ Already on list

____
Name

____
Address

____
City, State, Zip

____
E-mail Address

Please send to: ETBD, Box 2009, Edmonds, WA 98020

INDEX OF SIGHTS

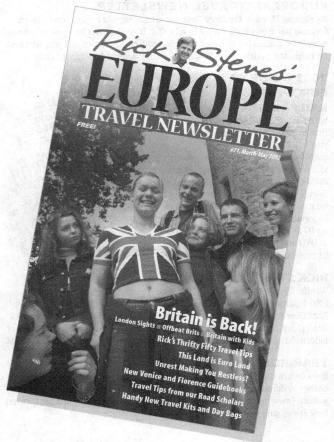